THEOLOGICAL WORDBOOK OF THE OLD TESTAMENT

Volume 1

R. Laird Harris, *Editor*

Gleason L. Archer, Jr., *Associate Editor*

Bruce K. Waltke, *Associate Editor*

MOODY PRESS
CHICAGO

Theological wordbook of the Old Testament

Includes bibliographies and index.
1. Bible. O.T.—Dictionaries—Hebrew. 2. Bible. O.T.—Theology—Dictionaries. I. Harris, Robert Laird. II. Archer, Gleason Leonard, 1916– . III. Waltke, Bruce K.
BS440.T49 221.4′4′0321 80-28047
ISBN 0-8024-8631-2 (set)

Printed in the United States of America

INTRODUCTION

The value of books for theological word study of the Old and New Testaments has long been recognized. W. E. Vine's word studies are well-known in the New Testament field. The major work, *Theological Dictionary of the New Testament,* is now being matched by an extensive *Theological Dictionary of the Old Testament,* which will run into many volumes.

Theological Wordbook of the Old Testament follows in this tradition, but approaches the matter from a practical and less exhaustive viewpoint than the major studies. The busy pastor or earnest Christian worker who has neither the time nor background for detailed technical study should yet have a tool for the study of the significant theological words of the Hebrew Bible. The editors and Moody Press are of the conviction that essential to the right understanding of the theological terms of the Old Testament is a belief in the Bible's truth. Spiritual things are "spiritually discerned" (I Cor 2:14). Therefore, about thirteen years ago, they enlisted the help of some forty evangelical scholars who would write essay definitions of the important theological terms in the Old Testament that would be helpful to their brothers in the work of interpreting Scripture.

Word study does not lead to a total understanding of the Old Testament text—or any text. Words must always be taken in context. They have an area of meaning, thus *'āmar* may sometimes mean "speak," sometimes "command." Thus, it overlaps with *dābar* on the one hand and *ṣāwâ* on the other. Also, the etymologies of words are not always determinative of meanings. In English we use words every day that are of pagan origin but no longer bear any such connotation. We derive the names of our months from Roman deities and our weekdays from the Norse mythologies, but we believe in neither. The Hebrews also did not invent their language. It was used in Canaan before the Conquest. Therefore, some Hebrew words may be of Canaanite origin, which is not to suggest that the Hebrews used them with the original Canaanite connotation. Biblical usage is therefore the best criterion of the meaning of a word, and to that end our authors have depended heavily on their concordances. But usage is often limited, and all the evidence available was evaluated, we think judiciously. There will be differences of opinion among our readers as to some of the conclusions here presented. Such differences will arise in part from different viewpoints brought to bear on the subject. Obviously these studies are neither complete nor final, but the editors and authors believe that the definitions given can be well defended. We hope that the work may result in the edification of the church of Christ through the assistance it may give to her ministers and His servants.

Often it was not easy to decide which words would be defined, and of those, which ones would receive lengthy discussion. In many cases, the decisions made could be questioned. Partly because of this and partly because of the convenience of having all the Old Testament words at least touched upon in one reference book, it was decided to include also the vocables not chosen for essay treatment and give them one-line definitions—usually following the lead of the long-time standard, *Hebrew and English Lexicon of the Old Testament,* by Francis Brown, S. R. Driver, and C. A. Briggs.

It was decided not to include the Old Testament names, except for a few of special theological import, like Abraham, Jerusalem, Jordan, and so on. For the principles of name formation in the Hebrew world, one may consult the work of Dr. Allan A. MacRae, "The Semitic Names in the Nuzi Tablets," in *Nuzi Personal Names,* ed. I. J. Gelb, University of Chicago, 1943.

The bibliographies following many of the articles were supplied largely by the contributors, but the editors also attempted to supplement their material. Dr. Tom Finch, a recent graduate of Dallas Theological Seminary, combed leading theological journals of the past thirty years, especially those in English, for articles bearing on the meaning of the words under discussion.

The editors then checked those articles as to their applicability. Other sources have often been noted, such as the *Theological Dictionary of the New Testament* (which has an index of Hebrew words discussed) and the *Theologisches Handbuch zum Alten Testament*. The *Theological Dictionary of the Old Testament* was not largely available.

The listing is arranged according to the consonants of the Hebrew alphabet (see "Suggestions for Use" for details). The Wordbook collects related words and defines nouns, adjectives, and so on, together with the root from which they are derived. Grouping together related words has the advantage of convenience and economy. It perhaps has a disadvantage of overemphasizing etymology above usage. It has a further disadvantage in that nouns with prefixes appear out of their alphabetical order. To obviate this problem, any word whose spelling differs from that of its root is listed in the proper alphabetical sequence with a numerical cross reference to the root. (Again, for details see "Suggestions for Use.")

In Hebrew, as is well known, most of the roots are verbs, and they are built on a tri-consonantal pattern. With only twenty-two consonants, a system of tri-consonantal roots is somewhat limited. The Hebrew vocabulary was far less than the rich English vocabulary of around 750,000 words. And the biblical vocabulary is only a percentage—an unknown percentage—of the words in use in the living language. Even so, some combinations of letters form one, two, or even more roots using the same consonants. These roots are marked as I, II, III, and so forth. Actually, the various authorities sometimes differ as to whether one root has two somewhat divergent meanings or whether two separate roots are involved. In such cases, the writers usually discuss the question.

The value of the Wordbook is largely due to the faithful work of the forty-six contributors who agreed to study the words assigned them and compress their study into the allowed format. Their articles are signed.

The contributors were asked to study their words from the viewpoint of biblical usage, etymological background, comparison with cognate languages, translations in the ancient versions, synonyms, antonyms, and theological significance. Also, they were to consider the use of their words in passages of special difficulty. Naturally, not all of those items were applicable to every word. And the writers felt the pressure of fitting their study into the narrow limitations of a two-volume book of this nature. Many things they would have liked to include could not be worked in.

It should be explained that although the contributors held the same high view of the truthfulness of the Bible and the reliability of its text, they were of different denominational and exegetical traditions. The editors in general have allowed the writers to speak for themselves. Some variations in treatment may therefore be expected. For instance, some use the name "Yahweh" for Israel's God, some the word "Lord," some "Jehovah." (This matter is discussed under the possible root of the name, *hāyâ*.) In a number of cases where a writer gave only one opinion on a particular question, the editors for the sake of completeness mentioned a different view. In cases of significance, these additions were submitted to the contributors and approved. In less significant cases, the editors themselves added such additional material, believing that it did not violate the integrity of the author. If in any such case, time and circumstances prevented conference and the authors' views have not been fairly represented, the editors can only express sincere regret and hope that no harm has been done. In some cases when helpful additional material, perhaps speculative, or other views were available, the editors have added bracketed material with their own initials.

All the articles were read by the editor. Also, the two associate editors each read about half of the articles. So all were double-checked. Final responsibility for what may be amiss rests with the editor.

The work has taken much longer than expected. Selecting authors and encouraging them to meet deadlines was a long process. A number of the authors, as well as the editors, were heavily involved in the translation of the *New International Version* and gave it priority. But the contributors were careful and faithful, and the material in time became voluminous. We are indebted to Chrisona Peterson (now Mrs. Julian Schmidt), our copy editor, for her very extensive work in editing, styling, alphabetizing, cutting, pasting (ad infinitum), and proofreading. Dr. Tom Finch has already been mentioned in connection with his work on the bibliographies. Two students at Covenant Seminary, Jeffrey Weir and Ken Wolf, worked on the Index of Correspondence, between the numbers of the Wordbook and those of Strong's Concordance, found at the back of the book. Moody Press and its representatives, first David E. Douglass, then William G. Crider, were most helpful and supportive at every turn. Finally, hearty thanks are due to the Xerox machine and the process of computer tape printing, which greatly assists in producing a book of complicated typography and considerable extent like this one.

With gratitude to the Lord for the completion of this work, we pray for His blessing upon it (Psalm 90:17).

R. Laird Harris
Gleason J. Archer, Jr.
Bruce K. Waltke

CONTRIBUTORS

Entries are made in order of authors' last names.

R.L.A. ALDEN, Robert, L., Ph.D., Professor of Old Testament, Conservative Baptist Theological Seminary, Denver, Colorado

R.H.A. ALEXANDER, Ralph H., Th.D., Professor of Old Testament Language and Exegesis, Western Conservative Baptist Seminary, Portland, Oregon

R.B.A. ALLEN, Ronald B., Th.D., Professor of Old Testament Language and Exegesis, Western Conservative Baptist Seminary, Portland, Oregon

G.L.A. ARCHER, Gleason L., Ph.D., Professor of Old Testament and Semitic Languages, Trinity Evangelical Divinity School, Deerfield, Illinois

H.J.A. AUSTEL, Hermann J., Ph.D., Dean, North West Baptist Seminary, Tacoma, Washington

A.B. BOWLING, Andrew, Ph.D., Associate Professor of Bible and Religion, John Brown University, Siloam Springs, Arkansas

G.L.C. CARR, G. Lloyd, Ph.D., Associate Professor of Bible and Theological Studies, Gordon College, Wenham, Massachusetts

G.G.C. COHEN, Gary G., Th.D., President, Clearwater Christian College, Clearwater, Florida

W.B.C. COKER, William B., Ph.D., Associate Professor of Bible, Asbury College, Wilmore, Kentucky

L.J.C. COPPES, Leonard J., Th.D., Pastor, Harrisville, Pennsylvania

R.D.C. CULVER, Robert D., Th.D., Professor of Old Testament and Hebrew, Winnipeg Theological Seminary, Otterburne, Manitoba, Canada

C.L.F. FEINBERG, Charles L., Th.D., Ph.D., Former Dean and Professor Emeritus of Semitics and Old Testament, Talbot Theological Seminary, La Mirada, California

M.C.F. FISHER, Milton C., Ph.D., President and Professor of Old Testament, Reformed Episcopal Seminary, Upper Darby, Pennsylvania

P.R.G. GILCHRIST, Paul R., Ph.D., Professor of Biblical Studies, Covenant College, Lookout Mountain, Tennessee

L.G. GOLDBERG, Louis, Th.D., Professor of Theology and Jewish Studies, Moody Bible Institute, Chicago, Illinois

V.P.H. HAMILTON, Victor P., Ph.D., Chairman of Division of Philosophy and Religion, Asbury College, Wilmore, Kentucky

R.L.H. HARRIS, R. Laird, Ph.D., Professor of Old Testament, Covenant Theological Seminary, St. Louis, Missouri

J.E.H. HARTLEY, John E., Ph.D., Chairperson, Division of Philosophy and Religion, Azusa Pacific College, Azusa, California

C.D.I. ISBELL, Charles D., Ph.D., Former Associate Professor of Old Testament, Nazarene Theological Seminary, Kansas City, Missouri

W.C.K. KAISER, Walter C., Ph.D., Dean and Chairman of the Old Testament and Semitic Languages, Trinity Evangelical Divinity School, Deerfield, Illinois

E.S.K. KALLAND, Earl S., Th.D., D.D., Professor Emeritus of Old Testament and Former Dean of Conservative Baptist Seminary, Denver, Colorado

J.P.L. LEWIS, Jack P., Ph.D., Professor of Bible, Harding Graduate School of Religion, Memphis, Tennessee

G.H.L. LIVINGSTON, G. Herbert, Ph.D., Professor of Old Testament, Asbury Theological Seminary, Wilmore, Kentucky

T.E.M. MCCOMISKEY, Thomas E., Ph.D., Professor of Old Testament and Semitic Languages, Trinity Evangelical Divinity School, Deerfield, Illinois

A.A.M. MACRAE, Allan A., Ph.D., President and Professor of Old Testament, Biblical School of Theology, Hatfield, Pennsylvania

E.A.M. MARTENS, Elmer A., Ph.D., President and Professor of Old Testament, Biblical Seminary, Fresno, California

J.N.O. OSWALT, John N., Ph.D., Associate Professor of Biblical Languages and Literature, Asbury Theological Seminary, Wilmore, Kentucky

R.D.P. PATTERSON, R. D., Ph.D., Professor of Old Testament, Grand Rapids Baptist Seminary, Grand Rapids, Michigan

J.B.P. PAYNE, J. Barton, Ph.D., Late Professor of Old Testament, Covenant Theological Seminary, St. Louis, Missouri

C.R. ROGERS, Cleon, Th.D., Director, Freie Theologische Akademie, Seeheim, West Germany

J.B.S. SCOTT, Jack, B., Ph.D., Former Professor of Old Testament, Reformed Theological Seminary, Jackson, Mississippi

C.S. SCHULTZ, Carl, Ph.D., Professor of Old Testament, Houghton College, Houghton, New York

E.B.S. SMICK, Elmer B., Ph.D., Professor of Old Testament, Gordon-Conwell Theological Seminary, South Hamilton, Massachusetts

CONTRIBUTORS

J.E.S. SMITH, James E., Th.D., Academic Dean and Professor of Old Testament, Central Florida Bible College, Orlando, Florida

H.G.S. STIGERS, Harold G., Ph.D., Former Professor, Author, and Lecturer, Glendale, Missouri

G.V.G. VAN GRONINGEN, Gerard, Ph.D., President, Trinity Christian College, Palos Heights, Illinois

B.K.W. WALTKE, Bruce K., Th.D., Ph.D., Professor of Old Testament, Regents College, Vancouver, British Columbia, Canada

C.P.W. WEBER, Carl Philip, Ph.D., Teacher, Letcher High School, Whitesburg, Kentucky

W.W. WHITE, William, Ph.D., Specialist in Biblical Languages, Warrington, Pennsylvania

M.R.W. WILSON, Marvin R., Ph.D., Professor of Biblical Studies, Gordon College, Wenham, Massachusetts

D.J.W. WISEMAN, Donald J., D. Lit., Professor of Assyriology, School of Oriental and African Studies, London, England

L.W. WALKER, Larry, Ph.D., Professor of Old Testament and Hebrew, Mid-America Baptist Seminary, Memphis, Tennessee

H.W. WOLF, Herbert, Ph.D., Associate Professor of Old Testament, Wheaton College, Wheaton, Illinois

L.J.W. WOOD, Leon J., Ph.D., Late Professor of Old Testament, Grand Rapids Bible Seminary, Grand Rapids, Michigan

E.Y. YAMAUCHI, Edwin, Ph.D., Professor and Director of Graduate Studies, History Department, Miami University, Oxford, Ohio

R.F.Y. YOUNGBLOOD, Ronald F., Ph.D., Associate Dean of Graduate School and Professor of Old Testament, Wheaton College, Wheaton, Illinois

SUGGESTIONS FOR USE

The Wordbook is essentially a Hebrew lexicon and can be used like any other Hebrew lexicon. However, it has certain special features which are designed to facilitate its use, especially for those less at home in the Hebrew language. It is primarily intended to be a ready tool for the pastor and the serious student, who want to study carefully and understand more fully the sacred text.

Transliteration of the Hebrew Letters

One feature of the Wordbook is its use of transliteration of the Hebrew into English letters. This is not only in line with the practice in Ugaritic and Akkadian studies, but will doubtless be of assistance to the non-specialist to whom the Hebrew characters are unfamiliar. The system of transliteration used does not claim to be final or scientific; it is practical. Actually, there is not full agreement on early Hebrew pronunciation, the length and quality of its vowels, etc. But this system aims to give an English equivalent for every consonant; its vowel notation, too, gives a one-to-one equivalence which will allow the Hebrew to be fully reproduced from any transliterated form.

As is well known, only the consonants were written in early Hebrew and, in general, the consonants are of more importance in carrying the meaning of a Hebrew word while the vowels are more significant in marking the form. There are twenty-two consonants (twenty-three if Sin and Shin are distinguished) and most of these have a parallel in the English alphabet. The Hebrew letters Zayin, Lamed, Mem, Nun, Samekh, Qoph, Resh and Shin are easily represented as the English letters z, l, m, n, s, q, r, and sh. See the transliteration table.

There are six Hebrew consonants whose pronunciation may be "hard" or "soft." These are the so-called Beghadh-Kephath letters, b, g, d, k, p, t: the Hebrew letters Beth, Gimel, Daleth, Kaph, Pe and Taw. When written with a hardening dot in the middle, these letters are pronounced like their English equivalents. If there is a vowel sound before them (and if they are not doubled) they are pronounced differently, but mean exactly the same thing (i.e. they differ phonetically, but not phonemically). Technically speaking, these six letters are stops, but they receive a fricative pronunciation, i.e. the point of articulation is not entirely closed, if a vowel sound precedes them. This variant pronunciation may be represented approximately as b/v, g/gh, d/th (as *th* in "that"), k/kh, p/f, and t/th (as *th* in "thin"). Some systems of transliteration represent this variation of these six stops. But since it makes no difference at all in the meaning of the words, it has been judged better to represent all these letters always by their sound as stops—the "hard" pronunciation. So Beth is always b; Gimel, g; Daleth, d; Kaph, k; Pe, p; and Taw, t. (In some systems of transliteration the soft pronunciation is represented thus: bh, gh, dh, kh, ph, th; in others it is ḇ, g̱, ḏ, ḵ, p̱, and ṯ.)

Two consonants are called emphatics. Their ancient pronunciation is difficult to determine accurately, but the Teth is some kind of a "t" and the Tsadhe some kind of an "s." They are represented as ṣ and ṭ respectively. (In some systems of transliteration the Tsadhe is written "ts".)

Three more consonants have no equivalent in English. They are guttural sounds made in the larynx. They are usually represented thus: 'Aleph by an apostrophe ('), and ʿAyin by a reverse apostrophe (ʿ), and Heth by a ḥ. There is another kind of "h" used in Ugaritic, Arabic and Akkadian, not in Hebrew, which is made with the tongue not quite against the roof of the mouth (technically a voiceless palatal fricative). This is represented, when it occurs, by ḫ.

SUGGESTIONS FOR USE

A second "s" apparently was pronounced exactly like Samekh, "s," though it looks like Shin (having a dot over the left upper corner instead of the right). To distinguish this letter Sin from the Samekh we use an acute accent over the Sin, thus: ś.

The remaining three consonants He, Waw, and Yodh are sometimes pronounced and sometimes silent, being used in conjunction with vowels. When they are pronounced, their pronunciation is like that of their English equivalents, He, h; Waw, w; and Yodh, y. In some systems of transliteration the Waw is called Vav and pronounced "v" because of past German influence on Hebrew studies. If, however, these letters are used as vowels, the long vowel resulting is always (and only then) marked with a circumflex accent ˆ. Examples will be given below.

All double consonants (those marked in Hebrew by a doubling dot in the middle of the letter) are simply written twice in the transliteration.

The consonantal transliterations may be listed as follows:

ʾAleph	א	
Beth	ב or בּ	b
Gimel	ג or גּ	g
Daleth	ד or דּ	d
He (pronounced *hay*)	ה or הּ (final consonantal הּ)	h
Waw	ו	w
Zayin	ז	z
Heth (or Ḥet)	ח	ḥ
Teth	ט	ṭ
Yodh (or Yod)	י	y
Kaph	כ כּ or ךְ	k
Lamedh	ל	l
Mem	מ or ם	m
Nun (pronounced *noon*)	נ or ן	n
Samekh	ס	s
Ayin	ע	ʿ
Pe (pronounced *pay*)	פ פּ or ףּ	p
Tsadhe	צ or ץ	ṣ
Qoph (English q, but not qu)	ק	q
Resh	ר	r
Sin (pronounced *seen*)	שׂ	ś
Shin (pronounced *sheen*)	שׁ	sh
Taw	ת or תּ	t

There are thirteen full vowels in Hebrew and four half-vowels. Another sign, which marks the end of a syllable (the silent shewa) has no sound and is not marked in the present system. The transliterations of these vowels and also their pronunciation following the letter "m" are as follows:

Pathah	ַ	a	מַ	ma as in man
Qameṣ	ָ	ā	מָ	mā as in ma
Final Qameṣ with vocalic He	ָה	â	מָה	mâ as in ma
Hiriq	ִ	i	מִ	mi as in pin
Hiriq with Yodh	ִי	î	מִי	mî as ee in seen
Seghol	ֶ	e	מֶ	me as in met
Sere	ֵ	ē	מֵ	mē as ay in may
Sere with Yodh	ֵי	ê	מֵי	mê as ay in may

Qameṣ-Hatuph (in closed syllable)	ָ	o	מָ	mo as au in naught
Holem	ֹ	ō	מֹ	mō as in mole
Holem with Waw	וֹ	ô	מוֹ	mô in mole
Qibbuṣ (short in closed syllable)	ֻ	ū	מֻ	mū oo in nook
Shureq (always with Waw)	וּ	û	מוּ	mû as oo in fool

Various other combinations of vowels and silent consonants are self-explanatory:

Qameṣ with final consonantal He	ָהּ	āh	מָהּ	māh
Qameṣ with final vocalic 'Aleph	ָא	ā'	מָא	mā'
Sere with final vocalic He	ֵה	ēh	מֵה	mēh
Seghol with final vocalic He	ֶה	eh	מֶה	meh

The half-vowels are all pronounced virtually alike—like "o" in Democrat:

Shewa	ְ	^{e}	מְ	m^e
Hateph-pathah	ֲ	ă	מֲ	mă
Hateph-seghol	ֱ	ĕ	מֱ	mĕ
Hateph-qames	ֳ	ŏ	מֳ	mŏ

A few examples of transliterated words are: דָּבַר *dābar,* דֹּבֵר *dōbēr,* דֹּבְרָה *dōb^{e}ra,* דָּבוּר *dābûr,* מְדַבֵּר *m^{e}dabbēr,* אֲדֻבַּר *'ădūbbar.*

For those less familiar with the use of Hebrew in transcription, a little attention to the above tables will make the visualization of the equivalent Hebrew letters easy. For those less familiar with the Hebrew characters, the use of transcription will make the word studies fully usable.

It may here be added that the transliteration is the same for Aramaic and similar for Arabic, Ugaritic, and Akkadian. In Ugaritic and Arabic there are a few extra consonants: Ha, ḫ for another kind of palatal "h" already mentioned; Ghain, ğ or ǵ for another kind of ʿAyin; ḏ and ḍ for other kinds of "d"; ẓ for another emphatic sibilant; and š often used for "sh." The system found in L.H. Gray, *Introduction to Semitic Comparative Linguistics* (Columbia Univ., 1934) is followed.

The asterisk preceding a verbal root indicates that although this root is quoted in the Qal form, it only appears in the derived stems, Piel, Hiphil, etc.

The dagger before a word indicates that this word is specifically treated in the discussions of meaning below.

Finding Words in the Lexicon

In the standard Hebrew lexicon, Brown, Driver and Briggs (BDB) printed in 1905, the words are arranged under the roots from which they are derived. Thus for *mizbēaḥ* "altar," one must look under the verb *zābaḥ* "to sacrifice." In the more recent lexicons, like Koehler and Baumgartner, the words are arranged alphabetically. So the word *mizbēaḥ* is found under "m." In the Theological Wordbook of the Old Testament, the advantages of both of these systems appear. The words, indeed, are arranged under the roots; the verbal root and the derived words are discussed together. But all the derivatives are also listed in their proper alphabetical position with a convenient numerical cross reference to lead the user to the root verb where, if it is theologically important, a discussion of the meaning of the root verb and all its derivatives will be found.

SUGGESTIONS FOR USE

An effort has been made to list alphabetically all the derivatives whose consonants differ from those of the verbal root even if their proper alphabetical position is close to the root itself. The exception to this practice is the treatment of feminine forms of masculine nouns, which end in "â." These are given as derivatives in their proper place under their root verb, but they are not usually cross referenced if there is a corresponding masculine form. Thus, מָגוֹר (*māgôr*) from גּוּר (gûr), no. 332, will be found under מ "m" and will have a cross reference, no. 332a under *gûr* no. 332. But the feminine form מְגוֹרָה (*m*ᵉ*gôrâ*) does not have a cross reference. It will be found by looking for מָגוֹר (*māgôr*) no. 332a which refers to the root no. 332 under which both the masculine and feminine nouns appear. Nouns with consonants identical to the verb are not cross referenced.

In the alphabetical arrangement, the vowels are completely disregarded, except that the vowel letters He, Waw, and Yodh are treated as consonants. For instance, מִדָּה is followed by מָדוּ then מַדּוּחַ then מָדוֹן מַדּוּעַ מְדוּרָה מְדִינָה and מַדְמֵנָה

Note that in the transcription, the letters with circumflex always include the Hebrew vowel letters, He ה, Waw ו, or Yodh י and these letters are considered in the alphabetization; but the vowels without vowel letters are not considered. The doubling of letters also is not considered in the alphabetic arrangement. Of course, the order of the Hebrew alphabet as given above in the transliteration chart is the one followed.

In Hebrew there is considerable freedom in writing the Holem with Waw (full writing) or without Waw (defective writing). The same applies to the Hiriq with or without the Yodh. In most cases, both forms are given and are alphabetized accordingly in two different places. Sometimes, however, if the variant spelling is quite minor it may have been overlooked. So if, for instance, חוֹר *ḥôr* is not found under Heth, Waw and Yodh, it would be advisable to look under חֹר *ḥōr* where it does appear. Remember always that to find a word in the Hebrew alphabetization that has been transcribed into English, it is necessary to consider only the consonants, but this includes the vowel letters which are indicated by the circumflex. Thus, *m*ᵉ*gôrâ*, mentioned above, would be alphabetized under Mem "m," Gimel "g," Waw "w," Resh "r," and He "h."

In cases where there is a difference in the Hebrew text between the written consonants (the Kethib) and the vowels attached (the Qere), both forms are not always noted, but an effort has been made to list one or the other reading.

All of the biblical Hebrew vocables are included in the Wordbook. Those judged for one reason or another to be of theological significance are given essay-type definitions. The rest, on which there is no special disagreement or theological question, are given one-line definitions, usually following BDB. Proper names of people or places are not included except in cases like Abraham, Jerusalem, Jordan where there is special theological interest. It is not, perhaps, necessary to apologize for the brevity of the definitions. Scholars who wish to do extensive research on individual words will want to look elsewhere, and the bibliographies usually appended should give some assistance. But the Wordbook is already large enough to fulfill its purpose—to help the serious Bible student and pastor in his work of interpreting the Word of God. Valuable material for further study of Hebrew words may be found in Kittel's *Theological Dictionary of the New Testament* and Colin Brown's *New International Dictionary of New Testament Theology*. Both of these works have indexes to the Hebrew words treated at various places.

In order to make the material in the Wordbook more accessible, there is a numerical index at the back which correlates the numbers of the Hebrew words as given in *Strong's Exhaustive Concordance of the Bible* with the numbers of the roots and derivatives as given in the Wordbook. If a word is being studied in any verse of the Old Testament, that word can easily be found in Strong and its Hebrew number noted. Then one may enter the index at the back of the Wordbook and find the number used in the Wordbook listing and easily turn to it. For further details, consult the heading of the Index. The Strong numbers of names are normally omitted, but the

Strong entries marked "Chaldee" (i.e. Aramaic) are listed. They all are found in the Aramaic section in the back of the Wordbook.

In a work of this nature perfection is unattainable. The comparison with Strong even brought to light misprints remaining after years of use and many reprintings. But an effort has been made to proofread the Wordbook carefully. As errors and omissions are brought to our attention they will be corrected in future printings.

ABBREVIATIONS

General Abbreviations

adj.	adjective
adv.	adverb
Akk.	Akkadian
Aram.	Aramaic
BA	Biblical Aramaic
c.	*circa* (about)
cf.	*confer* (compare)
chap.	chapter
fem.	feminine
Gr.	Greek
Heb.	Hebrew
impf.	imperfect
impv.	imperative
inf.	infinitive
inf.abs.	infinitive absolute
inf. const.	infinitive construct
MS, MSS	manuscript (s)
masc.	masculine
op.cit.	*opus citandum* (previously cited)
part.	participle
pf.	perfect
pl.	plural
q.v.	*quod vide* (which see)
sing.	singular
Ug.	Ugaritic
v., vv.	verse (s)

Books of the Bible

Old Testament

Gen
Ex
Lev
Num
Deut
Josh
Jud
Ruth
I Sam
II Sam
I Kgs
II Kgs
I Chr
II Chr
Ezr
Neh
Est
Job
Ps
Prov
Eccl
Song
Isa
Jer
Lam
Ezk
Dan
Hos
Joel
Amos
Ob
Jon
Mic
Nah
Hab
Zeph
Hag
Zech
Mal

New Testament

Mt
Mk
Lk
Jn
Acts
Rom
I Cor
II Cor
Gal
Eph
Phil
Col
I Thess
II Thess
I Tim
II Tim
Tit
Phm
Heb
Jas
I Pet
II Pet
I Jn
II Jn
III Jn
Jude
Rev

Books and Journals

AB	Anchor Bible (cited by author and book)
AI	Roland deVaux, *Ancient Israel: Its Life and Institutions*, trans. 1961
AisWUS	J. Aistleitner, *Wörterbuch der ugaritischen Sprache*, 4th ed., 1974
ANET	*Ancient Near Eastern Texts*, ed. J. Pritchard, 3d rev. ed. 1969
AOOT	K. Kitchen, *Ancient Orient and the Old Testament*, 1966
ASV	American Standard Version of the Bible
AV	Authorized (King James) Version of the Bible
BA	*Biblical Archaeologist*
BASOR	*Bulletin of the American Schools of Oriental Research*

ABBREVIATIONS

BDB — Brown, Driver, Briggs, *A Hebrew-English Lexicon of the Old Testament,* 1905
BETS — *Bulletin of the Evangelical Theological Society* (later the Journal)
Bib — *Biblica*
BL — H. Bauer and H. Leander, *Historische Grammatik der hebräischen Sprache des A. T.,* 1922
BS — *Bibliotheca Sacra*
BWANT — *Beiträge zum Wissenschaft vom Alten und Neuen Testament*
CAD — *The Assyrian Dictionary* of the Oriental Institute of the Univ. of Chicago, 1956ff.
CBQ — *Catholic Biblical Quarterly*
DBT — *Dictionary of Biblical Theology,* ed. X. L. duFour, 1967
DSS — Dead Sea Scrolls
DTOT — A. B. Davidson, *Theology of the Old Testament,* 1904
EQ — *Evangelical Quarterly*
ETOT — W. Eichrodt, *Theology of the Old Testament,* I, II, trans. 1965
Exp — *The Expositor*
ExpT — *The Expository Times*
FSAC — W. Albright, *From the Stone Age to Christianity,* rev. ed. 1957
GB — W. Gesenius, F. Buhl, *Hebräisches und aramäisches Handwörterbuch,* 17th ed. 1915
GKC — W. Gesenius, E. Kautzsch, A. Cowley, *Hebrew Grammar,* 2d English ed., 1910
HCHL — W. Holladay, *Concise Hebrew and Aramaic Lexicon of the Old Testament,* 1971
HDB — *Hastings Dictionary of the Bible,* 1911
HIOT — R. K. Harrison, *Introduction to the Old Testament,* 1969
HUCA — *Hebrew Union College Annual*
IB — *Interpreter's Bible*
ICC — *International Critical Commentary* (cited by author and book)
IDB — *Interpreter's Dictionary of the Bible,* ed. G. Buttrick, 1962
IEJ — *Israel Exploration Journal*
ISBE — *International Standard Bible Encyclopedia,* ed. J. Orr, 1929
JAOS — *Journal of the American Oriental Society*
JBL — *Journal of the Society of Biblical Literature and Exegesis*
JBR — *Journal of Bible and Religion*
JETS — *Journal of the Evangelical Theological Society* (formerly Bulletin)
JNES — *Journal of Near Eastern Studies*
JQR — *Jewish Quarterly Review*
JSS — *Journal of Semitic Studies*
JTOT — E. Jacob, *Theology of the Old Testament,* 1958
KAI — H. Donner and W. Rollig, *Kanaanäische u. aramäische Inschriften,* I, II, III 1964–66
KB — L. Koehler and W. Baumgartner, *Lexicon in Veteris Testamenti Libros,* 2d ed., Eng.-Ger., 1958
KD — K. Keil and F. Delitzsch, *Commentary on the Old Testament*
KJV — King James Version of the Bible
LAP — J. Finegan, *Light from the Ancient Past,* rev. ed., 1959
Lis — G. Lisowsky, *Koncordanz zum hebräischen Alten Testament,* 2d ed., 1958
LXX — The Septuagint Version of the Old Testament in Greek
Moscati — S. Moscati, *An Introduction to the Comparative Grammar of the Semitic Languages,* 1964
MT — The Masoretic Text of the Hebrew Bible
NASB — New American Standard Version of the Bible
NBC — *New Bible Commentary,* 2d ed., ed. F. Davidson, A. Stibbs, E. Kevan, 1954
NBD — *New Bible Dictionary,* ed. J. Douglas, 1962
NEB — New English Bible
NIV — New International Version of the Bible
NTS — *New Testament Studies*
Or — *Orientalia*
OTOT — G. Oehler, *Theology of the Old Testament,* rev. trans. G. E. Day, 1883, repr. Zondervan
OTS — *Old Testament Studies*
PEQ — *Palestine Exploration Quarterly*
PTOT — J. B. Payne, *Theology of the Older Testament,* 1962
PTR — *Princeton Theological Review*
RB — *Revue Biblique*
RSP — L. Fisher, *Ras Shamra Parallels,* I, II, 1972–75
RSV — Revised Standard Version of the Bible
RTWB — A. Richardson, *Theological Word Book of the Bible,* 1950
SJT — *Scottish Journal of Theology*
SOT — R. Girdlestone, *Synonyms of the Old Testament, their Bearing on Christian Doctrine,* 1897, repr. Eerdmans
SOTI — G. Archer, *Survey of Old Testament Introduction,* 2d ed., 1974
TDOT — H. Botterweck and H. Ringren, *Theological Dictionary of the O. T.,* I–III, 1974ff.
THAT — E. Jenni u. C. Westermann, *Theologisches Handbuch zum Alten Testament*

ThT	*Theology Today*
TOT	*Theology of the Old Testament* (author specified for different titles)
TS	*Theological Studies*
UT	C. H. Gordon, *Ugaritic Textbook,* 1965 (Grammar cited by chapter and section; texts cited by chap (16) and no. of line. Glossary cited by chap (19) and no. of word)
Vos,BT	G. Vos, *Biblical Theology,* 1948
vRTOT	G. von Rad, *Theology of the Old Testament,* Eng. ed. I, II, 1962–65
vS.AkkH	W. vonSoden, *Akkadisches Handwörterbuch*
VT	*Vetus Testamentum* (Supplements, Supp VT)
Vulg	The Vulgate version of the Bible in Latin
WBC	*Wycliffe Bible Commentary,* ed. C. Pfeiffer and E. Harrison, 1962
WBE	*Wycliffe Bible Encyclopedia,* ed. C. Pfeiffer, H. Vos, J. Rea, 1975
WJT	*Westminster Theological Journal*
YBIs	E. J. Young, *The Book of Isaiah,* vols. I, II, III, 1965–72.
YGC	W. Albright, *Yahweh and the Gods of Canaan,* 1968
ZAW	*Zeitschrift für alttestamentliche Wissenschaft*
Zor	F. Zorrell and L. Semkowski, *Lexicon hebraicum et aramaicum V. T.,* 1940ff.
ZPEB	*Pictorial Encyclopedia of the Bible,* ed. M. Tenney, Zondervan, I–V, 1975

א

א

אָב (*'āb*). See no. 4a.
אֵב (*'ēb*). See no. 1a.
אֹב (*'ōb*). See no. 37a.

1 אבב (*'bb*). **Assumed root of the following.**
  1a אֵב (*'ēb*) ***freshness, fresh green.***
  1b †אָבִיב (*'ābîb*) ***barley.***

'ābîb. ***Barley.*** This noun refers to barley that is already ripe, but still soft, the grains of which are eaten either rubbed or roasted (KB). The ASV and RSV agree (but see Lev 2:14). The seventh plague brought ruinous hail upon Egypt's barley crop at least two weeks before it was fully ripened and ready for harvest (Ex 9:31). Abib was also the early name (later, Nisan) of the first month of the Jewish calendar (the month of Passover). In that month the barley came to ear, but the usual time of harvest was the second month (Iyyar). According to Lev 2:14 the grain offering was to consist of the firstfruits of *'ābîb*. This root occurs ten times.

Bibliography: Smick, E. B., "Calendar," in WBE.

L.J.C.

2 אָבַד (*'ābad*) ***perish, be destroyed;*** Piel and Hiphil ***destroy.***

Derivatives

  2a אֹבֵד (*'ōbēd*) ***destruction*** (Num 24:20, 24 only).
  2b אֲבֵדָה (*'ăbēdâ*) ***lost thing*** (e.g. Deut 22:3; Ex 22:8).
  2c אַבְדָן (*'abdān*) ***destruction*** (Est 8:6; 9:5).
  2d †אֲבַדּוֹן (*'ăbaddôn*) ***destruction, ruin, Abaddon.***

The verb *'ābad* is a common word for to die, or, in the case of things, reputation, etc., to pass away. (The cognates in Akkadian, Arabic, and Ugaritic express similar ideas.) In the Piel and Hiphil it is used transitively in the sense of kill or break down (houses, idols, kingdoms). Egypt was destroyed (Ex 10:7; KJV, NASB; "ruined," RSV, NIV) though Pharaoh would not admit it. Joshua warned that if Israel sinned they would soon perish from the land (Josh 23:16). Jonah's gourd came up in a night and perished in a night (Jon 4:10). The foolish and senseless people perish (Ps 49:10 [H 11]). The man without understanding will perish like the beasts (Ps 49:20 [H 21]).

Probably the main theological question about this root is whether it refers merely to physical death or also to eternal punishment. It is not an easy question. Obviously the word usually refers to some great loss, in most cases death. Esther's famous self-dedication, "If I perish, I perish" (4:16), had her self sacrificing death in view—only that.

The verses that may look beyond the grave to further affliction for the wicked may be listed: Ps 49:10 [H 11]; cf. vv. 12, 20 [H 13, 21]); 73:27 (cf. vv. 18, 19); 83:17 [H 18]; Prov 10:28; 11:7 (cf. 24:20); and Ezk 28:16. These verses, like many others, can be interpreted to refer only to death of the body. But they are in a context of consideration of the hereafter. One's conclusion will doubtless be influenced by general considerations. If the OT "has no belief in any life beyond the grave worthy of the name," as N. Snaith says (DIOT, p. 89), then these verses will not be pressed to speak of eternal destruction of the wicked. But if immortality is found repeatedly in Ps, Prov, etc. as M. Dahood argues, then they may (See *Psalms*, III, in AB, pp. xli–lii and Smick, E. B., in Bibliography).

Psalms 49 and 73 are frequently cited as referring to a future life. Psalm 49:15 [H 16] uses the significant phrase "he will take me," the verb used for Elijah's translation to heaven and also used in Ps 73:24, "take me to glory." It is not far-fetched therefore to think that terms like "perish," (*'ābad* or *dāmâ* II q.v.), or "their tombs their houses forever" or "decay in the grave" (NIV) or "death will feed on them" may well refer to everlasting destruction. Psalm 83:17 [H 18] is perhaps not as clear as the others, but the emphasis on the total overthrow of the wicked is impressive. Ezekiel 28:16, if it refers as many think to Satan who inspired the prince of Tyre, does not bear on the punishment of the wicked, but on Satan himself. He who once walked in the holy mountain of God, in the midst of the stones of fire will be disgraced (*ḥālal*) and destroyed (*'ābad*) and in the process removed from (*min*) the mountain of God and the stones of fire. It sounds like eternal punishment.

'ăbaddôn. Destruction, Abaddon. This word is transliterated in Rev 9:11 and used as the Hebrew name of the devil, called in Greek Apollyon. This usage is not identical with the OT usage, but is an interesting commentary on it. The word is used six times in the OT. Twice it is in parallel with *sh^e'ôl* (q.v.), (Prov 15:11; 27:20) and once with *qeber* "grave" (Ps 88:11 [H 12]). The sixth time (Job 31:12) the word stands alone. It is obvious that the word refers to the destruction of the grave, but the contexts are not clear enough to prove that it refers to eternal destruction. The passages in Job and Prov are poetic personifications and do not clearly refer to sinners more than to the righteous. Psalm 88 refers to the troubles of the Psalmist and though it is highly poetic, can hardly be referred to a place of torment. On such matters other passages must also be consulted (e.g. Job 27:13–23; Isa 66:22–24).

Bibliography: Heidel, A., "Death and the Afterlife," in *The Gilgamesh Epic,* 2d ed., Univ. of Chicago, 1949, pp. 137–223. Harris, R. L., *Man—God's Eternal Creation,* Moody, 1971, pp. 162–177. Smick, E. B., "The Bearing of New Philological Data on the Subjects of Resurrection and Immortality in the OT," WTJ 21:1, pp. 12–21.

R.L.H.

3 אָבָה ('ābâ) ***I, accede to a wish, accept (a reproach), want to, be willing, consent to*** (ASV and RSV similar except in cases where secondary implications predominate).

Derivatives

3a †אֶבְיוֹן ('ebyôn) ***needy person.***
3b אֲבִיּוֹנָה ('ăbîyônâ) ***caperberry.***
3c אֵבֶה ('ēbeh) ***reed, papyrus.***
3d אֲבוֹי ('ăbôy) ***oh!*** (eytmology dubious.)

The primary meaning of this root is "the willingness (inclination) to do something under obligation or upon request." It is to be distinguished from *nādab* which implies volunteering, *rāṣôn* denoting a willing pleasurable to the doer, *ḥāpaṣ* implying a compliance suiting what is fitting, or a favorable disposition, and *yā'al* indicating an exertion of one's will to do something. Also, compare *'āwâ, yā'ab,* and *tā'ab.* Our root occurs 112 times. The verbal form occurs only in the Qal and all but twice with a negative particle (Isa 1:19; Job 39:9). Because in some cognate languages the root means "to be unwilling," G. J. Botterweck concludes that "the primary emphasis here is not on the intention as a psychological factor in the inner man (cf. *'āwâ,* usually with *nepesh* as subject!) but on the main behavioral patterns and actions in which the intention is manifested" (TDOT, I, p. 24). But possibly the cognates are only showing a polarity of meaning.

The basic meaning of the verb is set forth in those two cases where it is used positively (perhaps originally only with negative signification, B. Johnson, TDOT, I, pp. 24–26). Job 39:9 speaks of a wild ass whose natural inclination is to refuse man's service. In Isa 1:19, Israel is urged to show a positive intention toward God and not to "refuse" (*mā'an*) and "rebel" (*mārâ*), Isa 1:20. Here, as often elsewhere, *'ābâ* occurs with *shāma'.* Botterweck contrasts the two: "The difference seems to be that *'ābâ* denotes the first beginnings of a positive reaction, whereas *shāma'* indicates complete obedience" (TDOT, I, p. 25).

The idea of exercising the will is expressed when one is asked to acquiesce to another's request (e.g. in II Sam 13:25, David is not willing to go with Absalom). Another dimension is added in cases where the will is exercised against God's law or command (Ex 10:27; II Sam 13:14). Finally, the refusal to comply may carry overtones of perversity as when Israel will not hearken to God (Isa 30:9) in spite of his warning in Lev 26:21. The refusal of the people is summed up in the words, "but you would not" (Deut 1:26; Isa 30:15; cf. Mt 23:37).

This word is also used of God's unwillingness to destroy his people owing to his love for prominent men of faith (e.g. Moses, David, Deut 10:10; II Kgs 8:19; 13:23), and of his unwillingness to pardon them when his love and patience are repeatedly spurned (II Kgs 24:4).

Most interesting is Deut 2:30. Sihon will not let Israel pass. The scripture enigmatically explains that this unhampered exercise of his will is due to God's having hardened his heart in order to deliver him into Israel's hand.

'ebyôn. ***One in the state of wanting, a needy or poor person.*** The etymology is uncertain. ASV and RSV translate similarly. *'ebyôn* emphasizes "need" and thus is to be distinguished from *'onî* "afflicted," *dal* "poor," and *rāsh* "weak" (the Qal participle of *rîsh* "destitute"). This noun has a questionable connection with Ugaritic *'byn(t).* Some scholars say *'ebyôn* is of Egyptian derivation (Paul Humbert, *Revue de l'Histoire des Religions,* 32. 1, pp. 1–6), and others of general Semitic derivation (G. J. Botterweck, "*'ebyôn,*" in *TDOT,* I, pp. 27–41).

The *'ebyôn* is poor in a material sense. He may have lost his ancestral land (Ex 23:11). It may be that he has reverted to borrowing (Deut 15:7, 9, 11). He may be the recipient of special gifts on Purim (Est 9:22). He may be without clothing (Job 31:19) or lacking food (Ps 132:15). Certainly, used in this sense of material want the "poor" is one who has fallen on hard times (Job 30:25).

This noun is used socially of those needing protection. In the Mosaic legislation God provides protection for the needy among his people by commanding that they be treated fairly and that payment of loans should be forgiven them in the year of release (Deut 15:1–4). God commands his people to loan liberally to the needy (Deut 15:7, 9, 11) in spite of the release. And if a brother sells himself into slavery to pay his debts, he is to serve as a hired man only until the year of jubilee when he would go out free and return to the property of his fathers (Lev 25:39–41). Finally, God himself helps the righteous needy when there is no other helper (I Sam 2:8; Job 5:15; Ps 132:15; note the description of their plight in Job 24:2–14).

This social sense is found throughout the OT. In Prov the needy are those oppressed by the wicked (30:14). The king is to minister justice for them (31:9), and the good woman sees to their need (31:20). In the prophets (Jer, Ezk, Amos) the needy are those who are oppressed (contrary to Mosaic legislation) by the wicked (Amos 4:1) or who receive just treatment from the godly (Jer 22:16). Amos especially has a major concern for their rights. Cf. further Amos 2:6; 5:12; 8:4, 6). King Josiah is praised because "he judged the cause of the poor and needy" (II Kgs 22:16).

Isaiah refers to the needy as the firstborn (favored ones) of God. He tells us that God is their stronghold (Isa 25:4). The psalms (where thirty-three of the sixty occurrences appear) usually use the word in the sense of the righteous whose destitution is caused by enemies and who see their help in God alone. Hence, David can describe himself as needy (Ps 9:18 [H 19]; 86:1). The needy are the godly who walk uprightly (Ps 37:14). God's true spiritual people are the needy (Ps 72:4) who are oppressed by the wicked (Ps 12:5 [H 6]) within Israel and whose stronghold is God himself (Ps 109:31). Consequently, they cry to God for help (Ps 12:5 [H 6]; 70:5 [H 6]), and he delivers them (Ps 40:17 [H 18]).

Psalm 72:12 represents the Messiah as the fulfiller of God's promise to help the needy (cf. Isa 29:19).

Bibliography: Fensham, F. Charles, "Widow, Orphan, and Poor in Ancient Near Eastern Legal and Wisdom Literature," JNES 21: 129–39. Honeyman, A. M., "Some Developments of the Semitic Root 'by," JAOS 64: 81–82. Lambdin, Thomas O., "Egyptian Loan Words in the Old Testament," JAOS 73: 145–55. Patterson, Richard D., "The Widow, the Orphan, and the Poor in the Old Testament and the Extra-Biblical Literature," BS 130: 223–34. Richardson, TWB, p. 168. Van der Ploeg, J., "Les Pauvres d'Israel et leur Piéte," OTS 7: 237–42. Ward, William A., "Comparative Studies in Egyptian and Ugaritic," JNES 20: 31–40. TDOT, I, pp. 24–41. THAT, I, pp. 20–24.

L.J.C.

4 אבה (*'bh*) **II. Assumed root of the following.**

4a †אָב (*'āb*) ***father, forefather.*** ASV, RSV similar, except that *bêt 'āb* "father's house," may be rendered "family."

4b אַבְרָהָם (*'abrāhām*) ***Abraham,*** "father of a multitude."

'āb. ***Father, forefather.*** This primitive noun apparently is derived from such baby sounds as *abab* (cf. "Papa," in TDNT, V, p. 960), rather than from the verbal root *'bh,* Assyrian, *abû* "decide" (suggesting that the father is the "decider," BDB, p. 3). It designates primarily "begetter," though by extension, ancestor, and metaphorically, an originator, chief, or associate in some degree.

The noun *'āb* occurs 1191 times in the Hebrew OT, plus nine times in the Aramaic (the form *'ābî,* Job 34:36, KJV "my desire," is probably a verb, "I desire," from *bāyâ,* KB, cf. ASV, "would that"). Most instances refer to a literal father (from Gen 2:24, even before the fact of paternity, 4:1, down to Mal 1:6); but *'āb* may designate any man who occupies a position or receives recognition similar to that of a father: the "father" of a servant is his master (II Kgs 2:12); "a father to the poor" (Job 29:16) is their protector; "a father to the inhabitants of Jerusalem" (Isa 22:21) is their governor; and "a father to Pharaoh" (Gen 45:8) is his advisor. The title "Father" is thus used for one in authority (II Kgs 2:12), whether prophet (II Kgs 6:21), priest (Jud 18:19), or king (I Sam 24:11 [H 12]), or even—as a personification—the grave, "Thou art my father" (Job 17:14).

In other passages *'āb* refers to a grandfather (Gen 28:13; 32:9 [H 10]) or more remote ancestor (Gen 10:21; I Kgs 15:11; cf. Ex 10:6, "fathers' fathers"), especially if founding a tribal unit, e.g. Abraham as the father of the Hebrews (Deut 26:5; Isa 51:2; Jn 8:39), although Jacob is probably their "first forefather [who] sinned" (Isa 43:27; cf. v. 28 and cf. McKenzie, J., *Second Isaiah,* in AB, p. 59). If a clan congregated in one area, its ancestor could then be called, for example, the father of Tekoa or of Hebron (I Chr 2:24, 42). From this it was but a step to father as the founder of a group or guild, e.g. "the father of all who play the lyre and pipe" (Gen 4:21).

So Yahweh became the Father of Israel his son (Isa 63:16) when he formed the nation (Isa 64:8 [H 7]; Deut 32:18). Yet his fatherhood concerns primarily that covenantal, saving relationship, in which he loved Israel (Hos 11:1; Jer 31:20), "bought" them by redemption from Egypt (Deut 32:6), and continued to remember his "firstborn son" (Ex 4:22; Jer 31:9) with providential direction and fatherly care (Jer 31:9–10). He shows particular paternal concern for the fatherless (Ps 68:5 [H 6]), the poor, and the afflicted (cf. Prov 22:22–23).

Apostates could even "say to [an idol made from] a tree, 'You are my father' " (Jer 2:27). Occasionally the entire creation is related to God's fatherhood: his challenge to Job, "Has the rain a father?" (Job 38:28), suggests that, while man is not its "begetter," God is (vv. 4–5, 25–27; cf. the Ugaritic El's position as literal "father of mankind"). Yet just as in the NT, the OT (apart from the figurative "children" in Jer 3:19) never speaks of a universal fatherhood of God toward men (cf. G. B. Stevens's concession, *The Theology of the NT,* p. 70; cf. p. 68). Malachi's question, "Have we not all one father? hath not one God created us?" (2:10), is directed to those who inherit "the covenant of our fathers."

In a special sense David, Yahweh's anointed king over Israel and mediator of the Davidic covenant (Ps 89: 3, 28), appealed to God as his Father (v. 26 [H 27]); and the Lord replied, "I will make him my firstborn, the highest of the kings of the earth" (v. 27 [H 28]). But just as the next verse speaks of David's "seed . . . to endure forever," so the words, "I will be his Father, and he will be my son" (II Sam 7:14), refer to David (v. 12), and Solomon (v. 13*a*; I Chr 22:10*a*); but also they look beyond to the eternal Messiah (v. 13*b*) and speak of the unique fatherhood of Yahweh to his Son Jesus Christ (Heb 1:5). Similarly in Ps 2:7 (and I Chr 22:10*b*) the author David (Acts 4:25) sees beyond himself to God's future anointed one (Heb *Messiah,* Ps 2:2), the begotten Son of God. Christ would then, in turn, become an "eternal father" to his people (Isa 9:6, E. J. Young, *New International Commentary, Isaiah, I,* pp. 338–39).

But while Yahweh is to be "like a father . . . toward them that fear him" (Ps 103:13), i.e. toward the group of his "adopted [redeemed] sons," is he father also to the individual believer, as in the NT (Rom 8:15; Gal 4:6)? Jeremiah 3:4 says, "My Father, thou art the guide of my youth"; but this may well be the personified nation speaking (cf. H. Schultz' assertion of "nothing higher till the NT," *OT Theology,* II, p. 138). Yet individualization does appear in Ps 27:10, "When my father and mother forsake me, then the Lord will take me up" (cf. David's personal faith, I Sam 30:6; Ps 23), or in Prov 3:12, "Whom the Lord loves he reproves, even as a father the son in whom he delights." The infrequency of the divine name "Father" in the OT may have been due to its abuse in Canaanitish fertility cults (O. Baab, *The Theology of the OT,* p. 123, citing Jer 2:27; TDNT, V, p. 968).

Among the OT's proper nouns that employ the element *’āb,* the most famous is Abraham, though at his call he bore the shorter name, Abram (*’abrām,* Gen 11:26—12:1), literally, "Father [God] (is) lofty." But when Yahweh established his covenant with Abram (17:1–2), he said, "Your name will be Abraham (*’abrāhām*), for I will make you the father of a multitude, (*’ab-hămôn*) of nations" (v. 5). Some propose that the root *rāham* is no more than a variant of *rûm* "to be lofty" (E. A. Speiser, in AB, *Genesis,* pp. 124, 127). But in light of the known Arabic noun *ruhāmun,* "multitude" (KB, p. 8), the change in meaning which the verse itself teaches should be upheld. It thereby shifts the application of *’āb* from God to Abraham, who hereafter becomes "father" of the faithful, both in respect to his subjective attitude (of faith, Gal 3:7; Rom 4:16) and his objective inheritance (of righteousness, Gal 3:29; Rom 4:11, 13).

Bibliography: Anderson, K. T., "Der Gott meines Vaters," *Studia Theologia* 16: 178–88. Albright, W. F., "Abraham the Hebrew: A New Archaeological Interpretation," BASOR 163: 36–54. ________, "The Names *Shaddai* and Abram," JBL 54: 173–204. Cross, Frank Moore, "Yahweh and the God of the Patriarchs," HTR 55: 226–59. Eitan, I., "Two Onomatological Studies," JAOS 49: 30–33. Gibson, J. C. L., "Light from Mari on the Patriarchs," JSS 7: 44–62. LaGrange, M. J., "La Paternite de Dieu dans l'AT," RB 5: 481–99. Lehman, Manfred R., "Abraham's Purchase of Machpelah and Hittite Law," BASOR 129: 15–18. Payne, J. B., *Theology of the Older Testament,* Zondervan, 1962, pp. 304–307; 425–26. Pope, Marvin H., *El in the Ugaritic Texts,* Supp VT 3: 1–116, esp. p. 47f. Richardson, TWB, pp. 12, 76. Stöger, A., "Father," *Sacramentum Verbi,* I, 1970, pp. 260–65. Williams, James G., "The Prophetic 'Father'," JBL 85: 344–48. Wright, G. E., "The Terminology of Old Testament Religion and its Significance," JNES 1: 404–14. Young, E. J., "The God of the Fathers," WTJ 3: 24–40, TDNT, V, pp. 929–82. TDOT, I, pp. 1–18, 52–58. THAT, I, pp. 1–16.

J.B.P.

אֲבוֹי (*’ăbôy*). See no. 3d.

אֵבוּס (*’ēbûs*). See no. 10a.

אֲבַטִּחִים (*’ăbaṭṭiḥîm*). See no. 234a.

אָבִיב (*’ābîb*). See no. 1a.

אֶבְיוֹן (*’ebyôn*). See no. 3a.

אֲבִיּוֹנָה (*’ăbîyônâ*). See no. 3b.

אָבִיר (*’ābîr*), אַבִּיר (*’abbîr*). See nos. 13c,d.

5 *אָבַךְ (*’ābak*) ***turn.*** Occurs only in the Hithpael (Isa 9:17; Jud 7:3).

6 אָבַל (*’ābal*) ***I, mourn, lament.*** (ASV and RSV translate similarly, but more uniformly "mourn," while RSV occasionally reads "grieve.")

Derivatives

6a †אֵבֶל (*’ēbel*) ***mourning.***
6b אָבֵל (*’ābēl*) ***I, mourning, mourner;*** cf. Ugaritic.

'ābal describes mourning rites for the dead, though often, in its thirty-nine occurrences, it is used figuratively, "The land mourneth" (Isa 24:4). Some propose a separate meaning, "to dry up," when *'ābal* parallels *yābēsh* (Jer 12:4; 23:10; Amos 1:2; KB, p. 6): but "mourning" is contextually preferable (Jer 12:11).

Biblical mourning for the dead (expressed by *'ābal, sāpad,* etc.) involved emotion, usually expressed audibly (Jer 22:18; 48:36) and visibly (Gen 37:34; Ps 35:14; Mic 1:8), especially for the decease of important leaders (II Chr 35:24–25; Ezk 31:15). Professional mourning women could be hired (Jer 9:17; Eccl 12:5), or the emotion could be merely simulated (II Sam 14:2, *'ābal,* Hithpael, "feign oneself a mourner"; Mt 11:17). Yet the OT forbad such pagan exhibitions as tearing one's hair or flesh for the dead (Lev 19:28; 21:5; but see Jer 16:6; 41:5); for the OT gave an underlying assurance of immortality (Ps 73:24; Job 19:25–27; Prov 15:24) and held out the prospect of bodily resurrection (Ps 16:9–11; Isa 26:19; Dan 12:2).

'ēbel. ***Mourning.*** "Mourning" might last seven days (Gen 50:10; I Sam 31:13; cf. II Sam 11:27) or even seventy (Gen 50:3–4; thirty in Num 20:29; Deut 34:8). From the first incident arose the place-name Abel-mizraim: *'ābēl* the mourning, *miṣrayim,* of Egypt (Gen 50:11).

Bibliography: DeWard, Eileen F., "Mourning Customs in 1,2 Samuel," JJS 23: 1–27, 145–66. Tur-Sinai, N. H., "The Ark of God at Beit Shemesh (1 Sam. VI) and Peres 'Uzza (2 Sam. VI; 1 Chron XIII)," VT 1: 275–86. IDB, III, pp. 452–54. TDOT, I, pp. 44–47. THAT, I, pp. 27–30.

J.B.P.

7 **אבל** (*'bl*) **II. Assumed root of the following.**

7a †אָבֵל (*'ābēl*) ***II, stream, brook*** (KB, p. 6; cf. II Chr 16:4, *'ābēl māyim,* literally, stream of water), was once derived from an assumed root, *'ābal* II "grow green" (?), suggesting "meadow"(?) (BDB, p. 5), but is now associated with an Aramaic type of participial form of *yābal* (q.v.) "to bring" (W. F. Albright, BASOR 89:15); cf. Isa 30:25, *yiblê māyim,* literally, "ditches of water"). *'ābēl* occurs solely in four Jordanian or Transjordanian place-names: Abel-beth-maacah (II Sam 20:14–15, 18; I Kgs 15:20 = Abel-maim, II Chr 16:4), Abel-shittim (Num 33:49), Abel-keramim (Jud 11:33, which KJV translates "plain of the vineyards"), and Abel-meholah (7:22). (But see Jer 12:4; Amos 1:2; Jer 12:11, NIV.) *'ābēl,* found in I Sam 6:18 should be read, with some MSS, *'eben* "stone" (cf. vv. 14–15), as found in Genesis 50:11. See *'ābēl* I.

J.B.P.

8 אֲבָל (*'ăbāl*) ***surely.*** Adverb. Cf. *bal,* no. 246d, which also may have asseverative force.

9 אֶבֶן (*'eben*) ***stone.***

Derivative

9a אֹבֶן (*'ōben*) ***wheel, disk.***

'eben. ***Stone.*** The meaning of *'eben* is almost singularly "stone," and in the cognate Semitic languages both meaning and usage are the same. Stones are common in the middle east, and the word occurs more than 275 times in the Hebrew and Aramaic of the Bible. In all but a few places, which are cited below, the meaning is simply "stone."

In its first occurrence, *'eben* refers to precious stones (Gen 2:12). The usual meaning of *'eben hashshōham* is "onyx stone," although "cornelians" (NEB), lapis lazuli (Torah and NAB), and others appear here and the half dozen other places where these two words come together. Our English word "sapphire" reflects the Hebrew *sappîr.* This occurs with *'eben* in Ezk 1:26 and 10:1. An indication that the stone is valuable is the word *millu'îm,* which basically means "full." But the derived meaning is "consecrated." Notice this combination in Ex 25:7, where it means a jewelry "setting," and elsewhere. Sometimes *y^eqārâ* meaning "precious" or "costly" modifies it (II Sam 12:30 et al.). In I Chr 29:2, which includes several of the above combinations, the modifiers *pûk* and *riqmâ,* translated in the KJV as "glistening" and "of diverse colours," appear. Others have "antimony" and "colored" (RSV), "coloured" and "striped" (JB), "carnelian" and "mosaic" (NAB). In Prov 17:8 is found the expression *'eben ḥēn,* which is literally "stone of grace" and is usually rendered "precious" or the like. Isaiah 54:12 has two additional word combinations, *'eben 'eqdāḥ* and *'eben ḥēpeṣ*: "carbuncles" and "pleasant stones" (KJV), "garnet" and "jewels" (NEB), "crystal" and "precious stones" (JB). Ezekiel (28:14, 16) speaks of the "fire stone." From the context (especially v. 13 with its *'eben y^eqārâ*), this easily translated expression probably refers to a stone which sparkles. Even today diamonds are frequently described as fiery.

A second major category is "stone" used in the natural state. Genesis 11:3 is the first usage of the word as building material. Jacob used a stone pillow (Gen 28:11) and Moses sat on a stone (Ex 17:12). Stones were used to cover wells (Gen 29:2–3) and seal caves (Josh 10:18). Stones also served as pillars or cairns (Gen 31:45–46). Naturally, stones were used for throwing (Lev 20:2) and slinging (Jud 20:16).

The word "stone" is used as a title for God

(Gen 49:24, cf. *ṣûr* "rock"), and for the Messiah (Isa 28:16).

Stones were made into tablets for writing, as for the Ten Commandments (Ex 34:1), or into bowls (Ex 7:19). From stone the images of false deities were carved (Deut 28:36). The phrase "hewn stone" (*'eben gāzît*, Ex 20:25) refers to stones which were dressed or squared off.

The word *'eben* is used to denote the characteristics it possesses. Exodus 15:5 refers to its weight and 15:16 to its motionlessness. Elsewhere its commonness is noted (I Kgs 10:27). Job refers to its strength (6:12) and firmness (41:24 [H 16]). Akin to this last reference is Ezekiel's allusion to a "stony heart" (11:19).

Stones were used for weights (Lev 19:36), although the denominations or counterparts are imperfectly known to us. Note the "royal stone" of II Sam 14:26 (KJV "king's weight").

The word refers to "hailstones" (e.g. Josh 10:11), and to "limestones" (Isa 27:9; KJV "chalkstones").

The word "stone" appears in place names. The best known (mostly from the hymn "Come, Thou Fount") is "Eben-ezer" (Heb *'eben hā'ēzer*, I Sam 7:12). There is also the "stone of Bohan" (Josh 15:6, JB, translated "stone of Bohan" in KJV and "Eben-Bohan" in NAB), and the "stone of Zoheleth" (I Kgs 1:9, KJV; translated "Serpent's Stone" in RSV, "Slippery Stone" in the Berkley Version, and "Sliding Stone" in JB). The word *azel* (I Sam 20:19) connected with "stone" may be a preposition or adjective, not a proper name.

Note that if an altar was built with stones, they were to be undressed stones, doubtless to make impossible the engraving of idolatrous representations on them (Ex 20:25; Deut 27:5).

Bibliography: Diringer, David, "The Early Hebrew Weights Found at Lachish," PEQ 74: 82–103. Emerton, J. A., "The Meaning of אַבְנֵי קֹדֶשׁ in Lamentations 4:1," ZAW 79: 233–36. Harris, J. S., "The Stones of the High Priest's Breastplate," *Annual of Leeds University* 5: 40–62. LeBas, Edwin E., "Zechariah's Climax to the Career of the Corner-stone," PEQ 1950: 102–22. Seitz, Oscar J. F., "'What Do These Stones Mean?'" JBL 79: 247–54. Sellers, Ovid R., "Sling Stones of Biblical Times," BA 2: 41–44. Tiegman, Edward F., "The Stone Hewn from the Mountain," CBQ 18: 364–79. TDOT, I, pp. 48–51.

R.L.A.

אַבְנֵט (*'abnēṭ*). See no. 256a.

10 אָבַס (*'ābas*) ***feed, fatten.*** Occurs only in Prov 15:17; I Kgs 5:3.

Derivatives

10a אֵבוּס (*'ēbûs*) ***crib.***
10b מַאֲבוּס (*ma'ăbûs*) ***granary.*** Occurs only in Jer 50:26.

אֲבַעְבֻּעֹת (*'ăba'bū'ōt*). See no. 217a.

11 אבק (*'bq*) I. **Assumed root of the following.**
11a אָבָק (*'ābāq*) ***dust.***
11b אֲבָקָה (*'ăbāqâ*) ***powder.*** Occurs only in Song 3:6 in the phrase *'abqat rôkēl* "powders of merchant," i.e. scent powders.

12 *אָבַק (*'ābaq*) ***II, wrestle.*** Occurs only in the Niphal (Gen 32:25–26).

13 אבר (*'br*). **Assumed root of the following.**
13a †אֵבֶר (*ēber*), אֶבְרָה (*'ebrâ*) ***pinions.***
13b אָבַר (*'ābar*) ***to fly.***
13c †אָבִיר (*'ābîr*) ***strong.***
13d †אַבִּיר (*'abbîr*) ***mighty.***

'ēber, 'ebrâ. ***Feather or wing.*** These nouns are probably derived from the same root. A denominative verb, *'ābar* "to soar" or "to flutter," appears only in Job 39:26.

The adjective *'abbîr* "mighty," "strong," or "brave," is also probably derived from this root.

'ābîr. ***Mighty, the Mighty One of.*** This word occurs only in poetical passages. The first is Jacob's blessing on his son Joseph (Gen 49:24). The third stich of that verse, which contains this word, has the expression "the hands of the Mighty One," which is paralleled in the preceding line by the expression "hands were made strong." The following stich has "the stone of Israel" to parallel "the Mighty One of Jacob." The word "stone" is *'eben* which sounds something like *'ābîr* "Mighty One" and emphasizes his strength further.

The two appearances of the word *'ābîr* in Ps 132 (vv. 2, 5) are paralleled by the divine name YHWH. The same is true of its three appearances in Isaiah (1:24; 49:26; 60:16). Notice the distribution of the term throughout this book, often trisected by critics.

The name *'ābîr* used as a substitute for deity may be compared with *paḥad* the "Fear" of Isaac (q.v., Gen 31:42, 53). This word "Fear" is also taken by some as a surrogate for deity used especially in patriarchal times. It is possible to be translated "Kinsman." (Albright, FSAC, p. 248; Dahood, in AB, *Psalms*, I, p. 81.)

It is undeniable that *'ābîr* relates to the Akkadian *abāru* "be strong." Not so certain is the connection with the Ugaritic *'br* "bull" or "humped buffalo." However, as in Hebrew, it may be an element in a divine name in Ugaritic. The Ugaritic form *ibrd* may mean "the Mighty One of Hadd."

'abbîr. ***Horse, stallion, bull, Apis, chief, mighty, strong, valiant, stout(hearted), stubborn.*** See *'ābîr* for derivations and cognates in other Semitic languages and to that list add a New Egyptian cognate which definitely means "stallion" from the hieroglyph.

The word is used to denote strength or leadership in a man (I Sam 21:8; Job 24:22; 34:20; Jer 46:15; Lam 1:15), hardness of heart (Ps 76:5 [H 6]; Isa 46:12), angels (Ps 78:25), bulls (Ps 22:12 [H 13]; 50:13; 68:30; Isa 34:7; Jer 50:11), and horses (Jud 5:22; Jer 8:16; 47:3). Some in these last two groups may be interchanged. Isaiah 10:13 can be read as "strong man," "bull," or "Apis," the name of the sacred Egyptian bull (so RSV).

Bibliography: Alt, A., "The God of the Fathers" in *Essays on OT History and Religion*, tr. R. A. Wilson, Blackwell, 1966, pp. 25 ff. TDOT, I, pp. 42–43. THAT, I, pp. 25–26.

R.L.A.

אַבְרָהָם (*'abrāhām*). See no. 4b.

14 אַבְרֵךְ (*'abrēk*). ***Meaning dubious*** (Speiser, *Genesis* in AB, translates "attention!").

15 אגד (*'gd*). **Assumed root of the following.**
15a אֲגֻדָּה (*'ăguddâ*) ***band.***

16 אֱגוֹז (*'ĕgôz*) ***nuts*** (only in Song 6:11).

אֲגוֹרָה (*'ăgôrâ*). See no. 23a.

17 אגל (*'gl*). **Assumed root of the following.**
17a אֶגֶל (*'ēgel*) ***drop*** (only in Job 38:28).

18 אגם (*'gm*). **Assumed root of the following.**
18a אֲגַם (*'ăgam*) ***troubled pool.***
18b אָגֵם (*'āgēm*) ***sad*** (only in Isa 19:10).

19 אַגְמֹן (*'agmōn*), אַגְמוֹן (*'agmôn*) ***rush, bulrush.***

20 אגן (*'gn*). **Assumed root of the following.**
20a †אַגָּן (*'aggān*) ***bowl.*** ASV and RSV translate somewhat differently.

An *'aggān* is probably a large deep two-handled, ring-based bowl. This word occurs three times.

In Ex 24:6 Moses holds the blood of victims in *'aggānôt*. He dips a bunch of hyssop into the blood in order to sprinkle the people. In Isa 22:24 *'aggānôt* are common household vessels which can be hung on nails. The word appears in Assyrian *agan(n)u* "bowl" and Ugaritic (A. H. Honeyman, "The Pottery Vessels of the Old Testament," *Palestine Exploration Fund*, 1939, pp. 78–79).

R.L.A.

21 אגף (*'gp*). **Assumed root of the following.**
21a אֲגַף (*'ăgap*) ***band, army*** (occurs only in Ezk (12:14; 17:21; 38:6, 9, 22; 39:4).

22 אָגַר (*'āgar*) ***I, gather*** (food, Prov. 6:8; Deut 28:39; Prov 10:5).

23 אגר (*'gr*) **II. Assumed root of the following.**
23a אֲגוֹרָה (*'ăgôrâ*) ***payment*** (I Sam 2:36).
23b †אִגֶּרֶת (*'iggeret*) ***letter.***

'iggeret. ***Letter.*** ASV, RSV translate the same. This word means "letter" (royal and general). It may be a loan word from Akkadian *egirtu/igirtu* which parallels the Hebrew word in usage and refers to legal documents such as deeds (perhaps related to Persian *angira, angara* [R. Köbert, *Orientalia* 14: 478–79]). Hence, *'iggeret* may be a letter written on a clay tablet. Biblical Aramaic attests *'iggerâ* "letter." In Esther *'iggeret* is used synonymously with *sēper*, the usual Hebrew word for "letter" (cf. Est 9:20, 26). Another synonym is the Persian loan word *nishtᵉwan*. *'iggeret* occurs ten times in later passages containing historical connections with Babylonia or Assyria.

The *'iggeret* could be open or closed (Neh 6:5). If we are right in equating *'iggeret* with Akkadian *egirtu/igirtu*, then it refers to the ancient practice of writing the full text on a clay tablet and covering the tablet with an envelope of clay upon which a summary of the contents was written. Finally, it was properly sealed.

Bibliography: CAD 4, 45 "egirtu."

L. J. C.

אֲגַרְטָל (*'ăgarṭāl*). See no. 380a.

אֶגְרֹף (*'egrōp*). See no. 385a.

אֵד (*'ēd*). See no. 38d.

24 *אָדַב (*'ādab*) ***grieve.*** Occurs only in the Hiphil (I Sam 2:33).

אֱדוֹם (*'ĕdôm*). See no. 26e.
אֲדוֹמִי (*'ădômî*). See no. 26f.
אָדוֹן (*'ādôn*). See no. 27b.
אַדִּיר (*'addîr*). See no. 28b.

25 אדם (*'dm*) **I. Assumed root of the following.**
25a †אָדָם (*'ādām*) ***man, mankind, Adam.***
25b †אֲדָמָה (*'ădāmâ*) ***ground, land.***

'ādām. ***Man, mankind;*** **also** ***human (adj.), someone (indef.); Adam (the first man).*** The ASV and RSV translate the same with notable exceptions. In Job 31:33 the RSV obscures the reference to Adam. Although the etymology of *'ādām* cannot be explained with certainty (cf. TDOT, I, p. 78), the word probably relates to the original ruddiness of man's complexion (cf. F. Maas, *'ādām* TDOT, I, pp. 78–79). This word for man has to do with man as being in God's image, the crown of creation. It should be distinguished from *'îsh* (man as opposite of woman, or as man distinguished in his manliness), *'ĕnôsh* (man as weak and vulnerable), *geber* (man as mighty and noble), and *mᵉ tîm*. Ugaritic *'adm* normally means "people," and is parallel to *l'im*, or is used in the appellation *'ab 'adm*, "father of mankind." *'ādām* occurs exclusively in the singular absolute, 562 times.

'ādām also refers to generic man as the image of God and the crown of creation or is a personal name. Hence in Gen 1–3 it is the word usually used for man. (In later passages of Scripture it is difficult to distinguish in meaning from *'îsh*.) Here, man is distinct from the rest of creation in that: he was created by special and solemn divine counsel (Gen 1:26); his creation was an immediate act of God; he was created after the divine type; he was created with two distinct elements (Gen 2:7); he was placed in an exalted position (Gen 1:28); he was intended for a still higher (in the sense of a permanent and fulfilled) position. Hence, man (as *'ādām*) was the crown of creation. Genesis 1 sets forth *'ādām* as the goal and vice-regent of creation, while Gen 2 shows how the creation was formed as the scene of man's activity, i.e. it was formed around *'ādām*. In the first three chapters of Gen there is a wordplay on man, mankind, and the first man "Adam." *'ādām* connotes man in the image of God as to: soul or spirit (indicating man's essential simplicity, spirituality, invisibility, immortality), physical powers or faculties (the intellect and will with their functions), intellectual and moral integrity (true knowledge, righteousness, and holiness), body (as a fit organ of the soul sharing its immortality, and as the means through which man exercises his dominion), and dominion over the lower creation.

The image of God in man has been much discussed. Engnell, Wildberger, and von Rad refer it to man's dominion over the non-human world. Humbert and Koehler contend that it indicates man's external form, which seems inappropriate in view of the repeated assertion of God's spirituality. Brunner, Kierkegaard, and Berkhouwer think it refers to man's exceptional relationship with God. F. Horst declares that man is a creature who "hears the word of God, speaks to God in prayer and obeys him in service" (TDOT, I, p. 85). In contrast to these somewhat neo-orthodox approaches the image of God in the narrow sense refers to man as a rational-moral creature (cf. Deut 4:10–12). Significantly God's first words to man are both a command and a prohibition (Gen 2:16–17); man alone is responsible for his decision, man alone determines his destiny by volitional choice, and only man is judged as righteous or sinful by God's law. An older biblical theology holds that the "divine likeness is rather to be referred to the whole dignity of man in virtue of which human nature is sharply distinguished from that of the beasts; man as a free being is set over nature, and designed to hold communion with God, and to be his representative on earth" (G. F. Oehler, *Old Testament Theology*). Payne remarks that "the terms 'image' and 'likeness'... are used interchangeably.... The image thus connotes 'freedom' and 'blessedness', as it reflects within man the cosmic, ethical and beneficent sovereignty of the Testator himself.... The divine image thus implies all the various aspects of God's reflected glory and honor.... It may be defined, in summary, as the totality of man's higher powers that distinguish him from brute creation" (*PTOT*, p. 227). The apocryphal book of Ecclesiastes says of the creation of man: he "made them according to his image, and put the fear of man upon all flesh, and gave him dominion over beasts and fowls. Counsel and a tongue, and eyes, ears, and a heart, gave he them to understand. Withal he filled them with the knowledge of understanding, and showed them good and evil... and they shall praise his holy name, that they may search out his marvellous works" (Eccles 17:3–9).

Even after the fall *'ādām* is used of man! The image of God is still the central distinction. Hence, murder is an attack on the image of God (Gen 9:6). However, the fall lowered man's position before God (Gen 6:5–6; 8:21), ruptured his communion with God, and brought the curse of death on him so that he did not fulfill his intended exaltation. That part of the divine image consisting of true knowledge, righteousness, and holiness was destroyed. Only in and by Christ, the new Adam (Rom 5:12–21), can the original divine promise be realized.

'ădāmâ. ***Ground, land, earth.*** The ASV and RSV reflect the difficulties in deciding which of the English words to use in translation. Originally this word signified the red arable soil. From this it came to denote any cultivated, plantable ground and/or landed property. At times it approaches the meaning "home country" (see especially Jon

4:2), but probably not in a political sense (however, Isa 14:2; 19:17, and especially Ezekiel's almost exclusive "land of Israel," et al.). One should compare and distinguish *'ereṣ* "earth, land," and *'āpār,* "dry earth, dust." Also, contrast *ḥelqâ* "portion, field," *yabbāshâ* "dry land, dry ground," and *śādeh* "field, land, open country." *'ădāmâ* occurs 224 times.

The Bible makes much of the relationship between man (*'ādām*) and the ground (*'ădāmâ*). That this might be vivid in the mind of the reader we will transliterate the words in the following discussion. Initially, God made *'ādām* out of the *'ădāmâ* to till the *'ădāmâ* (Gen 3:23, to bring forth life?). The *'ădāmâ* was God's possession and under his care (Gen 2:6). Thus, the first *'ādām* (the man, Adam) and his family were to act as God's servants by obeying him in maintaining the divinely created and intended relationships vertically and horizontally. As long as this condition was sustained God caused the *'ădāmâ* to give its fruitfulness (blessing) to *'ādām.*

Then came sin. The unit *'ādām* (Adam and Eve; see also Rom 5:12) violated the created structure. The *'ădāmâ,* henceforth, brought forth thorns and thistles rather than freely giving fruit (Gen 3:17). Since *'ādām* had disrupted the paradisiacal life-producing state, he was driven off the paradisiacal *'ădāmâ* and sentenced to return to the *'ădāmâ* (Gen 3:19). He was driven to it rather than it being given to him. He was togo down rather than up. His life moved in and toward death rather than in and toward life. However, the gracious Creator did not completely destroy *'ādām.* He promised to bring forth from *'ādām* a lifegiver (Gen 3:15). As a token of that promise the Creator caused the *'ădāmâ* to give of its fruit (blessing) to *'ādām* (note the curse on Cain, Gen 4:12, 14, whereby the *'ădāmâ* was *no longer* to give its strength to him). Because of disobedience *'ādām* received a curse from the *'ădāmâ* rather than life. Thus, we see that *'ādām*/*'ădāmâ* are deeply involved in the pattern creation-fall-redemption.

This pattern is repeated throughout the OT. After the flood God said he would never again curse the *'ădāmâ* because of *'ādām* (Gen 8:21). He made a new covenant (creation) with Noah (Gen 9:1–17) who became the father of *'ādām* (since only Noah and his immediate family were in the ark, Gen 7:7). Noah became a tiller of the *'ădāmâ* (Gen 9:20), and God blessed his efforts. However, Noah sinned. In Abraham the promise (redemption) given by God through Noah to Shem emerges in the form of Paradise regained, i.e. the promised land (*'ădāmâ,* Gen 28:14–15).

In the Mosaic legislation God gives the *'ădāmâ* or takes it away according to the obedience of his people (Lev 20:24). Its fruitfulness depends upon their obedience (Deut 11:17). Solomon repeats this creation-fall-redemption pattern around *'ādām*/*'ădāmâ* (I Kgs 8:34, 40). This cycle governs the history of Israel (I Kgs 13:34; 14:15; II Kgs 21:8; 25:21). Nehemiah recognizes the same theological pattern (Neh 10:37 [H 38]).

In the eschaton God will change the inner constitution of *'ādām* (fully restore the divine image) so as to eliminate the possibility of a fall and assure eternal possession of the *'ădāmâ* which yields its fruit freely (Ezk 36:25–30; cf. Jer 31:33–34; II Cor 5:17; Heb 8:8–12)—the return to the garden of Eden (Ezk 36:35).

Bibliography: Asselin, David Tobin, "The Notion of Dominion in Genesis 1–3," CBQ 16:277–94. Bloom, Alfred, "Human Rights in Israel's Thought," Interp 8: 422–32. DeFraine, J., "Individue et Societe dans la Religion de l'Ancien Testament," Bib 33: 324–55, 445–75. Koehler, Ludwig, *Hebrew Man,* Abingdon, 1957. May, Herbert G., "Individual Responsibility and Retribution," HUCA 32: 107–20. Oehler, G. F., *Old Testament Theology,* Funk & Wagnall, 1883, pp. 146–47. Payne, J. Barton, *Theology of the Older Testament,* pp. 221–31. Porter, J. R., "The Legal Aspects of the Concept of 'Corporate Personality' in the Old Testament," VT 15: 361–80. Richardson, TWB, pp. 14–15. Thomas, D. W., ed., *Archaeology and Old Testament Study,* Oxford: Clarendon, 1967. Wright, J. Stafford, *Man in the Process of Time,* Eerdmans, 1956. TDOT, I, pp. 75–87, 88–98. THAT, I, pp. 41–56, 57–59.

L. J.C.

26 אדם (*'dm*) **II. Assumed root of the following.**

26a †אָדֹם (*'ādōm*), אָדֵם (*'ādēm*) ***be red.***
26b אָדֹם (*'ādōm*) ***red.***
26c אֹדֶם (*'ōdem*) ***carnelian.***
26d אֱדֹם (*'ĕdōm*) ***name of condiment.***
26e †אֱדוֹם (*'ĕdôm*) ***Edom.***
26f †אֲדוֹמִי (*'ădômî*) ***Edomite.***
26g אֲדַמְדָּם (*'ădamiddām*) ***be reddish.***
26h אַדְמוֹנִי (*'admônî*) ***red, ruddy.***

'ādōm, 'ādēm. ***To be red.*** The RSV and ASV translate the same.

Ugaritic *'adm* is the rouging done by the nobility after bathing. Also note Old Akkadian *'adāmu* "dark red," as of a garment, Akkadian *adamātu* "dark red soil" and *adamu* "red blood," and Aramaic *'ādam,* as of blood. The biblical stative describes the color of skin (like coral, Lam 4:7), war shields (parallel to scarlet, Nah 2:3 [H 4]), fermented wine (Prov 23:31), sin (Isa 1:18), and tabernacle curtains (Ex 25:5). The verbal form occurs ten times.

'ĕdôm. ***Edom, Edomite.*** This name was given to Esau, who desired red pottage more than his birthright (Gen 25:30; 36:1). He is described as having been "ruddy," *'adderet,* at birth (Gen 25:25). His descendants were identified by either of his names (Edom, Gen 36:9, or Esau, Jer 49:8, 10) or by Seir, the mountain where he settled (cf. II Chr 20:22–23). The Edomites assimilated some of the peoples settled in the land when they arrived (Deut 2:22, *ḥōrî,* q.v.). In the Bible the area assumed the name of its Edomite inhabitants. This word occurs ninety-eight times.

The history of Edom is an outworking of God's statements. In Gen 27:27–29, 39–40 Isaac prophetically blesses Jacob and Esau. The latter is to live in a desolate place (cf. N. Glueck, "Transjordan," in D. W. Thomas, ed., *Archaeology and Old Testament Study,* pp. 429–53), to live by the sword, and to serve his brother. Subsequently, he is to shake and cast off Jacob's yoke. Esau's immediate reaction was hostility.

Israel was not to force their way through Edom to the promised land (Num 20:14), and neither were they to despise their brother (Deut 23:7–8). When God did lead them through or past the borders of the land he strictly protected the rights of the Edomites to whom he had given the area (Deut 1:4–5). But the Edomites acted in a very "unbrotherlike" fashion, gathering themselves to repulse Israel. When Balaam the prophet was summoned by Balak, Balaam reiterated "Jacob's" supremacy, stating their future subjugation and possession of Edom (Num 24:18). The history of Israel attests repeated subjugations of and rebellions by Edom. So bitter was the Edomite hostility toward "Jacob" that they rejoiced when their brother was destroyed and led captive by the Babylonians (Ps 137:7). They gleefully joined in the fray (Amos 1:6, 9, 11), doing violence to Israel. They scornfully appropriated Jacob's land for themselves (Ezk 36:5). The prophets reaffirmed God's order. Edom was to be punished at the hands of the Babylonians and subjugated by Israel (Isa 11:14; Jer 27:3–6, Ob 1:1–21).

Such was and would be the pattern of Edom's history, that the Lord may be magnified beyond the border of Israel (Mal 1:5). What a clear illustration of divine election, "Jacob I loved and Esau I hated" (Rom 9:13).

'ădômî. ***Edomite.*** This adjective is the gentilic of *'ĕdôm.* It occurs eleven times.

Bibliography: Woudstra, M. H., "Edom and Israel in Ezekiel," *Calvin Theological Journal* 3: 21–35.

L.J.C.

אֲדַמְדָּם (*'ădamiddām*). See no. 26g.
אַדְמוֹנִי (*'admônî*). See no. 26h.

27 אדן (*'dn*). **Assumed root of the following.**
27a †אֶדֶן (*'eden*) ***pedestal.***
27b †אָדוֹן (*'ādôn*) ***lord.***

'eden. ***Pedestal, base, or socket.*** The ASV and RSV translate the same except in Song 5:15 (ASV "pillars," RSV "bases") and Job 38:6 (ASV "bases" RSV "foundation"). The *'eden* was a base into which pegs were inserted in order to hold planks and pillars upright. The word occurs fifty-four times and all but twice in Mosaic legislation regarding the tabernacle. The word emphasizes solidity, coming from a root meaning "be strong."

These bases were to be made of various metals depending on their location in the tabernacle. God's concern over such detail regarding worship is a principle that can hardly be ignored. In the OT, the ritual and the equipment connected with worship was no light thing. Every detail was prescribed by God and those who desired to please him were obligated to obey. It is not true, however, that attention to external detail at the expense of the appropriate inner spiritual disposition pleased God (see also *ʿānâ* "afflict, oppress, humble," Deut 6–11).

Job employs our word to describe the creating activity of God (38:6). It is paralleled with "cornerstone." Hence, comparing himself to a builder, God infers that he is the one who established the earth's footings, laid creation's cornerstone, and saw to the securing of the creation.

'ādôn. ***Lord, Lord, LORD, master, owner.*** No doubt exists about the meaning of this word. The Ugaritic *'adn* means "lord" or "father" and the Akkadian *adannu* carries a similar meaning, "mighty."

In the simple unsuffixed form or when pointed *'ădōnî* or *'ădōna(y),* for the first common singular suffix or with other pronominal suffixes, *'ādôn* usually refers to men. Sarah used it in reference to her husband (Gen 18:12), Abraham used it in addressing the angelic visitors (Gen 19:2). Abraham's servant repeatedly called his master by it in Gen 24. The pharaoh of Egypt was called by this title (Gen 40:1), as well as Joseph his "vizier" (Gen 42:10). Ruth used it of Boaz before they were married (2:13). Hannah addressed Eli the priest by this term (I Sam 1:15). Saul's servants called him by the title as well (I Sam 16:16). Likewise, officers less than the king, such as Joab, had this appellation (II Sam 11:9). In I Kgs 16:24 there is the unique reading "Shemer, 'owner' of the hill, Samaria." The prophet Elijah bore the title "lord" (I Kgs 18:7).

However, there are numerous passages, particularly in Psalms, where these forms, which are the only ones to apply to men, refer to God. Exodus 34:23 combines "the Lord, YHWH, the God of Israel" (*hā'ādōn yhwh 'ĕlōhê yisrā'ēl*).

Deuteronomy 10:17 uses both the singular and plural in the construction "Lord of lords" (*'ădōnê hā'ădōnîm;* cf. Ps 136:3). In Ps 8:1 [H 2] God has the title "YHWH our Lord" (*yhwh 'ădōnênû*). The Messiah bears this title in Ps 110:1.

Several personal names include the element *'ădōnî:* Adoni-bezek (Jud 1:5); Adonizedek (Jtsh 10:1); Adonijah (three men, I Kgs 1:8; II Chr 17:8; Neh 10:17); Adonikam (Ezr 2:13); and Adoniram (I Kgs 4:6).

When *'ādôn* appears in the special plural form, with a first common singular pronominal suffix (*'ădōnā*[*y*]), it always refers to God. It appears in this form more than three hundred times, mostly in Psalms, Lamentations, and the latter prophets. Just as *'ĕlōhîm* (God) is plural in Hebrew, so this word might also be called an intensive plural or plural of majesty. Only rarely is the suffix translated (cf. Gen 18:3; Isa 21:8; Ps 16:2).

To avoid the risk of taking God's name (YHWH) in vain, devout Jews began to substitute the word *'ădōnā(y)* for the proper name itself. Although the Masoretes left the four original consonants in the text, they added the vowels *ĕ* (in place of *ă* for other reasons) and *ā* to remind the reader to pronounce *'ădōnā(y)* regardless of the consonants. This feature occurs more than six thousand times in the Hebrew Bible. Most translations use all capital letters to make the title "LORD." Exceptions are the ASV and New World Translation which use "Jehovah," Amplified which uses "Lord," and JB which uses "Yahweh." What those cautious Jews did was similar to our custom of saying "that is" when we see the abbreviation "i.e." in the text. Later the Jews substituted other words such as "the name," "the blessed," or "heaven" (cf. Mk 14:61–62).

In those places where *'ădōnā(y) yhwh* occurs the latter word is pointed with the vowels from *'ĕlōhîm,* and the English renderings such as "Lord GOD" arose (e.g. Amos 7:1).

Bibliography: Zimmerman, Frank, "'El and Adonai," VT 12: 190–95. Richardson, TWB, p. 130. TDNT, III, pp. 1058–86. TDOT, I, pp. 59–72. THAT, I, pp. 31–37.

R.L.A.

28 *אָדַר (*'ādar*) ***to be majestic*** (occurs twice in the Niphal and once in the Hiphil).

Derivatives

28a אֶדֶר (*'eder*) ***glory, magnificence; mantle, cloak.***

28b †אַדִּיר (*'addîr*) ***majestic.***

28c †אַדֶּרֶת (*'adderet*) ***glory, cloak.***

Basically, this root connotes that which is superior to something else, and, therefore, that which is majestic. Because of the infrequent verbal usage in Hebrew and its occurrence in predominantly poetic passages, *'ādar* may be a North Canaanite loanword. Phoenician attests *'ādar* as a verb ("to be mighty"), in the Piel, "to make great," an adjective ("great, mighty"), and a noun ("noble, upper class"). In Ugaritic *'dr* means upper class or mighty. As an adjective it refers to the material from which Aqhat's bow is made (2 Aqht 6:20–23.) The noun *'eder* should be differentiated from *ḥōrîm* "nobles," and *śārîm* "princes." As an adjective *'addîr* should be compared to words like *'āmîṣ, gā'ôn, 'ayil* et al. The root occurs forty-six times.

This root is frequently used in reference to God. Moses sings that God showed that he was mighty in holiness by delivering the people from Egypt (Ex 15:10). Here the idea of superior power is set forth (cf. v. 6). His demonstrated power over Egypt made his majesty known and feared by the Philistines (I Sam 4:8). Although the sin of the Israelities caused sporadic defeats, God's eternal sovereignty subsequently overcame those kings who claimed temporary superiority (Ps 136:18). God's name is acclaimed as glorious over all in power and majesty (Ps 8:1 [H 2]). His exclusive lordship (power) over oceanic waves (Ps 93:4) and mountains (Ps 76:4 [H 5]) is rightly expressed by *'ādar.*

Not only is God exalted, but he sovereignly exalts other things, e.g. his law (Isa 42:21) whose majesty God will vindicate. God raised up Israel and clothed her with majesty. Ezekiel uses the figures of a vine and tree to describe how God cuts off and exalts Israel at will (Ezk 17:8, 23; cf. Zech 11:3).

'addîr. ***Mighty, majestic (adj.); noble, principal, stately.*** When used substantively, *'addîr* parallels "mighty ones" (Jud 5:13), "rulers" (Jer 30:21), and is sandwiched between "captains" and "governors" (II Chr 23:20) as the leaders of postexilic Israel. In the difficult verse Ps 16:3 it seems to refer to the saints. In the eschaton the Messiah is described as the one who will be over Israel (Jer 30:21) as the *'addîr.* This is to be none other than Jehovah himself (Isa 33:21).

'adderet. ***Mantle, cloak, majesty (noun); noble, majestic (adj.).*** The noun and adjective are used interchangeably (Ezk 17:8, 23; Zech 11:3). The noun "mantle" is at first surprising, but it refers to a costly robe (Josh 7:21) or prophets' mantle, etc. (II Kgs 2:8).

Bibliography: Ahlstrom, G., "'OR," VT 17: 1–2.

L.J.C.

28.1 אַדַרְכּוֹן (*'ădarkôn*) ***daric.*** This Persian loan word is probably to be distinguished from *dark^{e}mōnîm* "drachma," no. 453c. (So KB.)

29 אָהֵב (*'āhēb*) ***love, like, be in love, lovely.***

Derivatives

29a †אַהַב (*'ahab*) ***love.***
29b †אֹהַב (*'ōhab*) ***love.***
29c †אַהֲבָה (*'ahăbâ*) ***love.***

There is little variation in the basic meaning of this verb. The intensity of the meaning ranges from God's infinite affection for his people to the carnal appetites of a lazy glutton.

The verb appears in all moods of the Qal stem plus Niphal participle and Piel participle. The sixteen Piels are not intensive, but usually refer to illicit "lovers." The prophets Jeremiah (22:20, 22; 30:14), Ezekiel (16:36; 23:5, et al.), and Hosea (2:5–13) use the word to speak of Israel's adulterous relations. Zechariah has the word in the presumably messianic passage, "I was wounded in the house of my *friends*" (13:6).

'āhēb frequently describes love between human beings. The love of father for son is exemplified by Abraham and Isaac (Gen 22:2) and Israel and Joseph (Gen 37:3). A slave might "love" his master and wish to identure himself to him for the rest of his life (Ex 21:8). This is the word used in the rule "*love* your neighbor as yourself" (Lev 19:18). "Love" of the stranger is also incumbent on the faithful (Deut 10:19). Samson had apparently told Delilah that he "loved" her (Jud 14:16; 16:15). Ruth "loved" Naomi her mother-in-law (4:15), Elkanah "loved" his wife Hannah (I Sam 1:5), and Rebekah "loved" her son Jacob (Gen 25:28). Hiram's "love" for David illustrates international friendship or irenic politics between the two (I Kgs 5:1). Notice that nowhere is the love of children toward parents mentioned. Rather, they are to honor, revere, and obey.

People may love things concrete or abstract. Isaac "loved" savory meat (Gen 27:4); others are said to "love" oil (Prov 21:17), silver (Eccl 5:9), and gifts (Isa 1:23). The Psalmist "loved" God's commandments (Ps 119:47), law (v. 97), testimonies (v. 119), and precepts (v. 159). Men can "love" evil (Ps 52:3 [H 5]), or death (Prov 8:36), vanity (Ps 4:2 [H 3]), cursing (Ps 109:17), or a false oath (Zech 8:17). Or they can "love" good (Amos 5:15), truth and peace (Zech 8:19), salvation (Ps 40:16 [H 17]), and wisdom (Prov 29:3).

God has commanded man to "love" him (Deut 6:5), and the Psalms contain testimonies of obedience to that commandment (116:1; 145:20). Conversely, God "loves" men, especially his people Israel (Deut 4:37; Isa 43:4; Mal 1:2). The Lord also "loves" other things, such as the gates of Zion (Ps 87:2), righteousness and judgment (Ps 33:5), and the holy temple (Mal 2:11). In a few places the verb introduces an infinitive. Jeremiah (14:10) accused the people of loving to wander, while Isaiah charged them with loving to sleep (56:10). The verb itself is sometimes an infinitive, as in Josh 22:5 and Isa 56:6. At least once it is a gerund, "a time to *love*" (Eccl 3:8).

The participles often translate as "friend." From II Chr 20:7 comes the notion that Abraham is the "friend" of God. As noted above, the English word "lover," translating the Piel participle, often carries a derogatory connotation implying prostitution (Hos 2:7; 9:12; Ezk 16:33, 36–37; Jer 22:20, 22; 30:14; Lam 1:19; Zech 13:6, etc.).

'ahab. ***Love, lovely, lovers.*** (KJV and most others.) Berkeley translates "love-gifts" in Hos 8:9 and JB renders "fair" in Prov 5:19. This word occurs only in these two passages and is plural in both. The passage in Prov carries a good connotation, "lovely doe," but in Hosea the connotation is negative, "hired lovers."

'ōhab. ***Love.*** The JB translates "delight" in Prov 7:18.

This word means the object of love in Hos 9:10, where it is parallel to "shame" and "Baal." There it may be parsed as an infinitive construct. In Prov 7:18, its only other occurrence, *'ōhab* also has an illicit overtone.

'ahăbâ. ***Love.*** Typical of abstractions in Hebrew this noun is feminine. Like the cognates which share the same root letters, the meaning is "love."

The noun *'ahăbâ* describes the love of husband toward wife, as that of Jacob for Rachel (Gen 29:20). God's "love" for his people is designated by the same word (Deut 7:8; II Chr 2:11; et al.). Jonathan's affection for David is also *'ahăbâ* (I Sam 18:3; 20:17; cf. II Sam 1:26).

'ahăbâ occurs frequently in the wisdom literature and a few times in the latter prophets. Proverbs uses the word in its most abstract form: "love covers all sins" (10:12), "better a dinner where love is" (15:17; cf. Eccl 9:1, 6). Naturally, the word is used in the Song of Solomon. It is the term for "love" in several familiar verses. "His banner over me is love" (2:4). "I am sick of love" (2:5; 5:8). "Love is strong as death" (8:6). "Many waters cannot quench love" (8:7).

Famous passages in the prophets use this word as well. "I have loved you with an everlasting love" (Jer 31:3). "I drew them . . . with bands of love" (Hos 11:4). "And what does the LORD require of you but to do justice and to love mercy" (Mic 6:8), lit. "the love of mercy" (*'ahăbat ḥesed*).

Bibliography: Audet, Jean-Paul, "Love and Marriage in the Old Testament," *Scripture* 10: 65–83. McCarthy, Dennis J., "Notes on the Love of God in Deuteronomy and the Father-Son Relationship Between Yahweh and Israel," CBQ 27: 144–47. McKay, J. W., "Man's Love for God in

Deuteronomy and the Father/Teacher-Son/Pupil Relationship," VT 22: 426–35. Moran, William L., "The Ancient Near Eastern Background of the Love of God in Deuteronomy," Interp 19: 399–411. Torrance. T. F., "The Doctrine of Grace in the Old Testament," SJT 1: 55–65. TDNT, I, pp. 21–35; IX, pp. 124–27, 154–59. TDOT, I, pp. 99–117. THAT, I, pp. 60–72.

R.L.A.

30 אֲהָהּ (*'ăhāh*) ***alas, ah*** in most translations, but also ***"oh"*** (JB, Joel 1:15), ***"O"*** (NEB, Jer 4:10), and ***"oh no"*** (NAB, Ezk 4:14).

This interjection is common to both Hebrew and English; the translation "ah" is practically a transliteration (though the Oxford English Dictionary does not suggest a Hebrew derivation of "ah." Its origin is obscure). In most places it is used with "Lord GOD" (Josh 7:7; Jud 6:22; Jer 1:6; 4:10; 14:13; 32:17; Ezk 4:14; 9:8; 11:13; other occurrences are Jud 11:35; II Kgs 3:10; 6:5, 15; Joel 1:15).

Bibliography: THAT, I, p. 73.

R.L.A.

31 אֱהִי (*'ĕhî*) ***where*** (Hos 13:10, 14).

32 אָהַל (*'āhal*) ***I, to pitch a tent.*** Denominative verb.

Parent Noun

32a †אֹהֶל (*'ōhel*) ***tent, dwelling.***

Derivatives

32b †אָהֳלָה (*'ohŏlâ*) ***Oholah.***
32c †אָהֳלִיבָה (*'ohlŏlîbâ*) ***Oholibah.***

This verb occurs in the Qal (Gen 13:12, 18) and Piel (Isa 13:20).

'ōhel. ***Dwelling, home, tabernacle, tent*** (ASV and RSV similar).

'ōhel, a masculine noun, occurs 340 times and is used for the animal skin or goat's hair (Song 1:5) dwelling of nomadic people (Gen 4:20; 13:5; 18:16; 25:27; etc.), shepherds (Jer 6:3), women (Gen 31:33; Jud 4:17; cf. Isa 54:2), warriors (I Sam 17:54; Jer 37:10; etc.), and cattle (II Chr 14:14). It is also used for the bridal tent (II Sam 16:22).

The word *'ōhel* continued to be used for a habitation or home (I Kgs 8:66; 12:16; Ps 91:10; Jud 19:9), including David's palace (Isa 16:5) long after the Israelites had adopted more permanent dwellings. *'ōhel* is figuratively used for the people of Edom (Ps 83:7), Qedar (Ps 120:5; Song 1:5), Judah (Jer 30:18), Cushan (Hab 3:7), and others. The "tent of the daughter of Zion" (Lam 2:4) is a figure for Jerusalem.

The tabernacle was essentially a tent, composed of two layers of cloth and two layers of skins stretched over a wooden framework (Ex 26:7, 14–15). It is designated "tent of meeting" (*'ōhel mô'ēd,* Ex 33:7–11, etc.), as well as "tent of testimony" (*'ōhel 'ēdût,* Num 9:15; 17:22–23, etc.)

'ohŏlâ, 'ohŏlîbâ. ***Oholah, Oholibah.*** Ezekiel uses these nouns as symbolic names for Samaria and Jerusalem: Oholah ("her tent") and Oholibah ("my tent is in her," Ezk 23:4, etc.). The names Oholiab (tent of the father, Ex 31:6) and Oholibamah (tent of the high place, Gen 36:2, 41) are from this noun.

Bibliography: Ben-Mordecai, C. A., "The Tent of Meeting (Ex 33, 7–11)," JQR 30: 399–401. Clifford, R. J., "The Tent of El and the Israelite Tent of Meeting," CBQ 33: 221–27. Guillebaud, M.L.G., "The Tent over the Tabernacle," EQ 31: 90–96. Haran, Menahem, "The Nature of the 'Ohel mo'edh in Pentateuchal Sources," JSS 5: 50–65. Morgenstern, Julian, "The Ark, the Ephod, and the Tent," HUCA 17: 153–265; 18: 1–52. ———, "The Tent of Meeting," JAOS 38: 125–39. TDOT, I, pp. 118–29.

J.P.L.

33 *אָהַל (*'āhal*) ***II, to be clear, shine.*** Occurs once (in the Hiphil), in Job 25:5.

34 אהל (*'hl*) **III. Assumed root of the following.**
34a אָהָל (*'āhāl*) ***aloes.***

אָהֳלִיבָה (*'ohŏlîbâ*). See no. 32c.

35 אַהֲרוֹן (*'ahărôn*) ***Aaron.*** The older brother of Moses. A Levite and the first high priest.

The Bible records that Aaron was the son of Amram (I Chr 6:3). Aaron was the spokesman for Moses, who had complained to God that he was slow of speech (Ex 4:10–14).

Aaron married Elisheba the daughter of Amminadab the sister of Nahshon (Ex 6:23) and they had four sons: Nadab, Abihu, Eleazar, and Ithamar. The first two "offered strange fire" and died near the tabernacle (Lev 10:1–2; Num 3:4). The other two served as priests under Aaron until he died, and then Eleazar became the high priest (Num 20:26).

With Hur, Aaron held up Moses' arms, bearing the rod of God, during the battle with Amalek (Ex 17:12).

According to Ex 30, Aaron's duties included burning sweet incense daily (v. 7), lighting the lamps nightly (v. 8), and making atonement yearly (v. 10). Leviticus 16 outlines more responsibilities. He was to bring certain sacrifices for the atonement when he entered the holy place (v.

3). He wore the holy linen coat, linen underwear, a linen sash, and a linen mitre (v. 4). The actual procedures are described in the verses which follow in Lev 16.

It was Aaron who was culpable in the golden calf incident (Ex 32:35). One hears a note of insincerity in his protest, "I cast it (i.e. the people's gold) into the fire, and out came this calf" (Ex 32:24).

Aaron survived most of the wilderness journey and died at the age of 123 (Num 33:39). Moses and Eleazar witnessed his decease on Mount Hor (Num 20:25–29).

His name occurs only a few times in the historical books, once in the prophets (Mic 6:4), and only eight times in the Psalms. The best known is Ps 133:1–2 (cf. Ex 30:25, 30):

Behold, how good and how pleasant it is
For brethren to dwell together in unity!
It is like the precious oil upon the head,
That ran down upon the beard,
Even Aaron's beard;
That came down upon the skirt of his garments.

It was, of course, the oil not the beard that ran down to the skirt of his garments (cf. the NIV).

In the NT, Luke (1:5) makes a note of Elizabeth's descent from Aaron. Stephen refers to his outstanding sin of idolatry in the sermon recorded in Acts 7:40. And, naturally, references to Aaron appear in Hebrews (5:4; 7:11; 9:4). In this epistle, which stresses the superiority of Christ to various other divine institutions and OT personages (angels, Moses, the priesthood), Christ is superior to Aaron. Jesus, the Son of God, is called the great high priest (4:14) who though personally without sin, is touched with the feelings of our infirmities (4:15). As the argument develops, the apostle asserts that Christ is of the lineage of Melchizedek, a pre-Levitical priest-king (Heb 7:11). Through chapter 9 of the Epistle to the Hebrews its author underscores the superiority of Christ's work and continual ministry, "But Christ having come a high priest of the good things to come, through the greater and more perfect tabernacle, not made with hands, that is to say, not of this creation, nor yet through the blood of goats and calves, but through his own blood, entered in once for all into the holy place, having obtained eternal redemption" (vv. 11–12).

R.L.A.

36 או (*'ô*) ***or, whether, not the least, if, otherwise, also, and, then.***

The Ugaritic cognate is *'u* and the Akkadian is *'ū*.

This conjunction occurs almost three hundred times in the Hebrew Bible. Three-fourths of these are in the books of Moses and particularly in the legislation. Usually it introduces an alternative situation or an exception to a general principle. In Lev 13:47–49 *'ô* is used ten times.

R.L.A.

אַו (*'aw*). See no. 40a.

37 אוב (*'wb*). **Assumed root of the following.**
37a †אוֹב (*'ôb*) ***one that hath a familiar spirit*** (KJV and ASV).

Modern versions have a variety of terms including medium, ghost, spirit, spirit of the dead, necromancer, and wizard. In Job 32:19 the word means wineskin or bottle (NEB "bellows").

Hoffner lists the following cognates: Sumerian *ab(.làl)*, Hittite *a-a-bi*, Ugaritic *'eb*, and Assyrian *abu* (see bibliography).

The pair *'ôb* and *yidd^e'ônî* (q.v.) often appear together (Lev 19:31; 20:6, 27; Deut 18:11; I Sam 28:3, 9; II Kgs 21:6; 23:24; II Chr 33:6; Isa 8:19; 19:3). Since the former, which is feminine, refers to women who practice this variety of sorcery, and the other, which is masculine, refers to such men. The word *yidd^e'ônî* is derived from the root "to know" (*yāda'*).

God's people were commanded to stay away from these occultists (Lev 19:31). In fact, the punishment for turning to such "mediums" was death by stoning (Lev 20:27). Naturally, *'ôb* is included in the complete list of similar abominations in Deut 18:10–11. All of these occupations deal with the occult. Man has desired, from time immemorial, to know the future. In those days some occultists read cloud formations, others examined livers (Ezk 21:21 [H 26]), while still others consulted ghosts.

The word *'ôb* apparently refers to those who consulted ghosts, because I Sam 28 describes one in action. The famous "witch" of En-dor is an *'ôb*. Although Saul had outlawed "witches" and "wizards," he nevertheless consulted her. Disguising himself, he had the "medium" bring up Samuel from the dead. She was successful, and although he complained of being disturbed, he announced to Saul the bad news that God was displeased and that Saul and his sons would die the next day.

One explanation of this phenomenon is that God responded to the weakness of men and accommodated himself to what he himself had forbidden. It may have been that the woman was a bona fide and successful *'ôb* and that her other successes were not hoaxes. Apparently this diabolical device was a real threat to the faith of God's people. On the other hand, the interview may have come by way of a waking vision, sent by God but without involving any actual transportation of Samuel from the dead, even though his appearance in this vision conveyed an authentic message from God. Note, the woman was herself surprised.

Isaiah discredits these "necromancers" and implies by his choice of words that the sounds of spirits so raised are nothing more than ventriloquism: "The mediums and the wizards who chirp and mutter" (8:19). Isaiah makes two more analogies to the sounds made by an *'ôb:* "From low in the dust your words shall come . . . your speech shall whisper out of the dust" (29:4).

There is apparently no connection between the kind of black magic implied by the word *'ôb* and Elihu's use of it in Job 32:19. The near-universal judgment that *'ôb* means "wineskin" in this verse indicates that any relationship between the words is very tenuous. They may simply be chance homonyms.

One of the stops during the wilderness wanderings was Oboth (*'ôbôt*) which looks like a plural of *'ôb* (Num 21:10–11; 33:43–44). Yet it might be translated as "place of waterskins" or the like, which sounds more suitable for the name of a place than "sorcerers."

Other terms for diviners and divination are: *'ittî, 'ānan, 'ashshap, ḥarṭōm, yidd^{e}'ōnî, kāshap, naḥash, qāsam.*

Bibliography: Gaster, M., "Divination (Jewish)," in *Encyclopedia of Religion and Ethics,* IV, Scribners, 1955. Hoffner, Harry, Jr., "Second Millennium Antecedents to the Hebrew 'ob," JBL 86: 385–401. Lust, J., "On Wizards and Prophets," Supp VT 26: 133–42. Montague, Summers, *The History of Witchcraft,* University Books, 1956. Rabin, Chaim, "Hittite Words in Hebrew," Or 32: 113–39. TDOT, I, pp. 130–33.

R.L.A.

אוּבָל (*'ûbal*). See no. 835g.

38 אוד (*'wd*). **Assumed root of the following.**
38a אוּד (*'ûd*) ***brand, firebrand*** Amos 4:11; Zech 3:2; Isa 7:4).
38b †אוֹדָה (*'ôdâ*) ***cause.***
38c †אֵיד (*'êd*) ***distress, calamity.***
38d †אֵד (*'ēd*) ***mist.***

'ôdâ. ***Because, cause, concerning, sake, about, of, that, on account of.*** This feminine noun occurs only in the plural (*'ôdōt* or *'ōdôt*) and is always preceded by the preposition *'al* meaning "for" (except in II Sam 13:16 where most assume the *'al* is an orthographic irregularity). Otherwise the word appears in Gen 21:11, 25; 26:32; Ex 18:8; Num 12:1; 13:24: Josh 14:6; Jud 6:7; and Jer 3:8.

'êd. ***Calamity, destruction, ruin, disaster, distress, vengeance, trouble, misfortune, doom, terror, downfall, peril.*** Apart from one reference in Ezk 35:5), all twenty-two occurrences of *'êd* appear in poetical sections. Its use in Deut 32:35 is part of the Song of Moses, and II Sam 22:19 is identical to Ps 18:18 [H 19].

The expression "day of calamity" constitutes one-third of the references. It is parallel to "doom" (*'ătîdôt*) in Deut 32:35, "day of wrath" (*'ăbārôt*) in Job 21:30, and "the time of their punishment" (*p^{e}qūddātām*) in Jer 46:21. Note that Ezk 35:5 has "the time of their calamity" parallel to "the time of their final punishment" (*'ăwôn qēṣ*). In Ob the expression "day of their calamity" appears three times in one verse (13).

In Job 31:23, 30:12, and Ps 18:18 (parallel to II Sam 22:19), the righteous sufferer is in view. Otherwise the wicked person or nation deserves "destruction." Proverbs 1:26–27 and 6:15 illustrate the former while Jer 48:16 and 49:32 picture the latter.

This word is to be distinguished from the Sumerian loan word *'ēd* (אֵד), meaning "mist" or "flood" (see below).

'ēd. ***Mist*** (KJV, ASV, RSV,) ***vapor*** (Berkley Version) ***flood*** (JB, NEB) ***stream*** (NAB). These are the various translations of Gen 2:6. Most versions translate "mist" in Job 36:27.

Based on these two biblical contexts and the Akkadian and Sumerian cognates, *edû* and A.DÉ.A respectively, the meanings other than "mist" and "vapor" have been suggested. Earlier translators did not have access to the ancient cuneiform languages which help to determine the meaning of these difficult words. The LXX translators guessed at πηγή (spring) in Genesis and νεφέλη (cloud) in Job. The Akkadian *edû* refers to the annual inundation of Babylon by the Euphrates as well as to irrigation. If Eden was watered by floods and irrigation rather than rain, it may have been located in an area like southern Mesopotamia where it does not rain. Such a location would suggest that the paradisiacal situation was not worldwide but peculiar to Eden's immediate environs.

The Job passage is rich with meteorological details. However, "mist" is not demanded there; one of the several options such as "stream" would well fit.

Bibliography: Harris, R. Laird, "The Mist, the Canopy, and the Rivers of Eden," JETS 11: 177–79. Saebo, Wayne, "Die hebräischer Nomina 'ed und 'ed," *Studia Theologia* 24: 130–41. THAT, I, pp. 122–24. Speiser, E. A., " 'ED in the story of Creation" *Oriental and Biblical Studies, Collected Writings,* Univ of Phila. Press, 1967, pp. 23–34.

R.L.A.

39 אוה ('wh) I. **Assumed root of the following.**
39a אִי ('î) *I, coast, region.*

40 אָוָה ('āwâ) *II, desire, long, lust, covet, wait longingly, wish, sigh, crave, want, be greedy, prefer.*

Derivatives

40a †אַו ('aw) *desire.*
40b †אַוָּה ('awwâ) *desire.*
40c מַאֲוַי (ma'ăway) *desire.*
40d †תַּאֲוָה (ta'ăwâ) *desire.*

Often the subject of this verb is *nepesh* meaning variously "self," "soul," "appetite" (e.g. Deut 12:20; 14:26; I Sam 2:16; I Kgs 11:37; Job 23:13; Isa 26:9). Sometimes the object is "meat" (Deut 12:20), "fruit" (Mic 7:1), or delicate food (Prov 23:3, 6). The object may be "evil" itself (Prov 21:10) or a "kingdom" (II Sam 3:21; I Kgs 11:37). Occasionally the object is unspecific. According to Num 11:4 the people "lusted a lust" or "felt a gluttonous craving" (JPS). Other examples are Prov 21:26 and Eccl 6:2.

The last of the Ten Commandments in the form given in Deut uses this word: "Do not 'covet' your neighbor's house" (Deut 5:21b). In the phrase "do not 'covet' your neighbor's wife" (Deut 5:21*a*), the Hebrew verb is *ḥmd. ḥmd* is the only verb in the Ex parallel.

Of the twenty-seven occurrences of the word only four are in the prophets. Perhaps the best known is Amos 5:18, "Woe to you that 'desire' the day of the LORD."

Numbers 34:10 uses this verb (or another verb spelled identically) in a unique way. There it means "point out" (KJV), and many modern translations render "draw a line for" a border. Possibly this is derived from *tāwâ* (q.v.) meaning in the Hiphil "make a sign."

'aw. ***Desire.*** Proverbs 31:4 has the only occurrence of *'aw*. It may be a shortened masculine form of the feminine noun *'awwâ* (q.v.) also meaning "desire." Because it appears in construct it is pointed *'ēw* (in the Qere text).

'awwâ. ***Desire, lust, will.*** This feminine noun appears in Deut 12:15, 20–21; 18:6; I Sam 23:20; Jer 2:24; Hos 10:10. Note that *'awwâ* occurs in construct with *nepesh* (soul/mind) in all passages except the last one.

ta'ăwâ. ***Desire, pleasant, lust, greed, dainty, desirable.*** Like the other nouns built from the root *'wh* (*'aw* and *'awwâ*), this noun has the meaning of "desire" extending to both good and bad objects.

In Num 11:34–35 and 33:16–17, this feminine noun forms part of the name of the station in the wilderness, *qibrôt-hatta'ăwâ* ("Graves of Greed"). In Gen 49:26 it means "boundary," but that is probably a different word built instead on a root *tā'â* "to designate" or it may be a noun from *'āwâ* II "a mark," therefore "a boundary."

R.L.A.

41 *אָוָה ('āwâ) *III, sign, mark, describe with a mark.* Occurs only in the Hithpael (Num 34:10).

Derivative

41a †אוֹת ('ôt) *sign, mark, token, ensign, standard, miracle, miraculous sign, proof, warning.*

'ôt. This is the general word for "sign," and it covers the entire range of the English term and the Greek word *sēmeion*. On the pedestrian end of the scale it includes what amounts to a "signboard" or "standard" (Num 2:2). It also includes such important concepts as the rainbow "sign" to Noah (Gen 9:12–13, 17).

1. *'ôt* first occurs in Gen 1:14, where it refers to the luminaries serving as "signs" to distinguish the seasons. In Jer 10:2 it has a similar meaning.

2. According to Gen 4:15, the Lord set a "mark" on Cain. The meaning of this word is uncertain.

3. A third use of the word is illustrated by Gen 9:12–13, 17, according to which the rainbow is a "sign" of the covenant. Circumcision is the "sign" in Gen 17:11. Also, the Sabbath is to be a "sign," according to Ex 31:13, 17 and Ezk 20:12. It is this use of "sign" that is meant when Christians refer to the ordinances as outward "signs" of inward grace.

4. Most of the eighty occurrences of *'ôt* refer to "miraculous signs." All the plagues on the Egyptians are called "signs." In these contexts the complementary word *môpēt* (q.v.) meaning "wonders" often occurs (Ex 7:3; Deut 4:34; 6:22; 7:19; 26:8; Neh 9:10; Isa 20:3; et al.). This word *'ôt* is used in Isaiah's famous prophecy to Ahaz (7:11, 14). The shadow's advance on the palace steps was a "sign" for the ailing king Hezekiah (II Kgs 20:9; Isa 38:7). Likewise God showed Gideon a "sign" by igniting the offered food (Jud 6:17).

5. The word *'ôt* sometimes means "token." For example, Aaron's rod was to be a "warning to the rebellious" (Num 17:25 NAB and Heb, v. 10 in other English versions). In the same category are the stones in the Jordan (Josh 4:6), the hammered plates on the altar (Num 16:38 [H 17:3]), and the witness pillar in Egypt (Isa 19:20).

6. A dreamer or a prophet, true or false, could produce "signs" according to Deut 13:1ff. The fulfillment of Jeremiah's threat of punishment was a true "sign" (Jer 44:29), while Isaiah speaks of "signs" of liars (44:25).

Naturally, these categories are artificial and overlap. The simple facts that one Hebrew word covers them all is proof of that. The word "sign" either signifies the unusual event itself or in someway points to that unusual event. Or it may point backward to a historical event such as the stones in the Jordan (Josh 4:6), or even forward to such a promise as a thornless future world (Isa 55:13).

Bibliography: Knight, Harold, "The Old Testament Conception of Miracle," SJT 5: 355–61. Pritchard, James B., "Motifs of Old Testament Miracles," *Crozer Quarterly* 27: 97–109. Richardson, TWB, p. 152. Robinson, H. W., "The Nature-Miracles of the Old Testament," JTS 45: 1–12. TDNT, VII, pp. 209–29. THAT, I, pp. 91–94.

R.L.A.

42 אוֹי (*'ôy*). ***Woe! Alas! Oh!***

This onomatopoetic interjection occurs twenty-two times in the OT. Often the preposition "to" with a first person pronoun ("me" or "us") follows to indicate despair. Isaiah 6:5 is an example: "Woe to me because I am undone!" With the second or third person pronoun it indicates threat or denunciation. Numbers 21:29 illustrates this: "Woe to you, Moab!"

Possibly the slang expression Oy! in English is a transliteration of this Hebrew word coming into English through Yiddish.

Bibliography: Wanke, Gunther, "אוי und הוי," ZAW 78: 215–18.

43 אוה (*'wh*) **IV. Assumed root of the following.**
43a אִי (*'î*) ***II, jackal.***
43b אַיָּה (*'ayyâ*) ***hawk, falcon, kite.***

אֱוִיל (*'ĕwîl*), אֱוִילִי (*'ĕwîlî*). See no. 44a,b.

44 אול (*'wl*) **I. Assumed root of the following.**
44a †אֱוִיל (*'ĕwîl*) ***foolish.***
44b †אֱוִלִי (*'ĕwilî*) ***foolish*** (Zech 11:15).
44c †אִוֶּלֶת (*'iwwelet*) ***folly, foolishness, foolish.*** (ASV, RSV similar.)

'ĕwîl. ***Fool, foolish, foolish man,*** although the word is rendered "***fool***" in twenty of twenty-six usages (ASV same, RSV similar).

Some derive *'ĕwîl* from *yā'al* "be foolish," while another possibility is from an Arabic word meaning "be thick," and therefore "thick-brained" or "stupid."

The NIV renders "fool" in Prov 1:7 with a footnote: "The Hebrew words rendered *fool* in Proverbs, and often elsewhere in the OT denote one who is morally deficient." Such a person is lacking in sense and is generally corrupt. If one can posit a gradation in the words for fool, *'ĕwîl* would be one step below *k^e sîl* and only one step above *nābāl* (q.v.). An even stronger word in Prov is *lēṣ*, often translated "scoffer." The *'ĕwîl* is not only a *k^e sîl* because of his choices, but he is also insolent.

The *'ĕwîl* identifies himself as soon as he opens his mouth. He would be wise to conceal his folly by keeping quiet (Prov 17:28). When he starts talking without thinking, ruin is at hand (Prov 10:14). While a wise man avoids strife, the fool quarrels at any time (Prov 20:3). He cannot restrain himself and will "display his annoyance at once," whereas a wise man overlooks an insult (Prov 12:16 NIV). A fool has no balance in his relations with others. The wisdom instructor indicates that while stones and sand are most burdensome, a fool's anger is even more intolerable.

As indicated, *'ĕwîl* primarily refers to moral perversion or insolence, to what is sinful rather than to mental stupidity. This kind of a fool despises wisdom and is impatient with discipline. He who does not fear God is a fool and will be unable to grasp wisdom or benefit from godly discipline (Prov 1:7). While the wise accept godly instruction, the boastful or babbling fool who rejects it will fall down by the predicaments he makes for himself (Prov 10:8). Because a fool feels that his own way is without error, he does not seek or listen to counsel as the wise one does. The fool is overbearing in his attitude since he has all the answers (Prov 12:15). A fool despises his father's instructions, in contrast to the one who shows good sense in regarding reproof (Prov 15:5). This kind of fool is also licentious, taking sinful enjoyment with a wayward woman (Prov 7:22).

This moral perversion is seen in the statement, "Fools mock at guilt" (Prov 14:9). The word for guilt can also mean the trespass offering (Lev 5). Thus the fool scorns and despises restitution for the injuries and sins he commits (NIV, "mock at making amends for sin"). He flouts his responsibility to the community as a responsible person. On a contrary note the upright (or wise) have a good reputation and are well liked.

Even if a fool were pounded with a pestle in a mortar along with the grain, no desirable results would follow (Prov 27:22).

A deplorable situation was seen in the northern kingdom, when Hosea was called an *'ĕwîl* by the general populace (Hos 9:7). The people had forgotten the law of God (Hos 4:6) and they considered the precepts of the law a strange thing (8:12). In their perversity they regarded the teaching of the prophet as being contrary to their world view. Actually, through their twisted judgment, they gave themselves away as fools. The adjectival use of foolish follows the same idea of the noun's moral insolence. The tragedy is that this condition will never lead the foolish to know the Lord (Jer 4:22).

'iwwelet. ***Folly, foolishness,*** each twelve times, is associated with a *k^esîl* and overlaps in meaning. Thus, a fool displays his folly, i.e., his *'iwwelet* (Prov 13:16). The folly (*'iwwelet*) of fools is deceit (Prov 14:8). One is regarded a fool because of his folly (*'iwwelet*), since folly seems a special product of fools (*k^esilîm*).

But the aspect of moral insolence is prominent. A quick-tempered man acts foolishly and is likely to do things he might later regret (Prov 14:17). Likewise one who is quick-tempered makes his folly prominent to attract the attention of others (Prov 14:29). A foolish man perverts his own way. His kind of way is his own fault, not God's (Prov 19:3). Discipline is important to children because foolishness is part of a child's nature. A remedy for correction is the rod of discipline in order to drive the foolishness from him (Prov 22:15). One must keep in mind that this discipline is important to curb moral insolence that might lead in turn to rebellion against God. Proverbs emphasizes the necessity for discipline (13:24; 23:13–14; 29:15). But it is to be tempered with compassion and concern (1:8–9). The folly of a quick-tempered person is contrasted with the great understanding (*t^ebûnâ,* q. v.) of one slow to anger (Prov 14:29). Similarly, the senseless find joy in folly, while by contrast the one who walks straight is a man of understanding.

'ĕwilî. ***Foolish.*** Used only once in the sense of an overseer in Zech 11:15, describing the foolish shepherd who had no concern for the people to whom he was to minister.

Bibliography: Donald, Trevor, "The Semantic Field of 'Folly' in Proverbs, Job, Psalms, and Ecclesiastes," VT 13: 285–92. Greenstone, Julius, *Proverbs,* Jewish Publication Society, 1950. Harris, R. Laird, "Proverbs," in WBC. Kidner, Derek, *Proverbs,* Inter-Varsity, 1964, pp. 39–41. Walker, W. L., "Folly," in ISBE, II, pp. 1124–25. TDOT, I, pp. 137–39. THAT, I, pp. 77–78.

L.G.

45 אול (*'wl*) **II. Assumed root of the following.**
45a אוּל (*'ûl*) ***I, body, belly*** (Ps 73:4).
45b אוּל (*'ûl*) ***II, leading man, noble*** (II Kgs 24:15).
45c †אוּלָם (*'ûlām*) ***I, porch.***
45d †אַיִל (*'ayil*) ***I, ram.***
45e †אַיִל (*'ayil*) ***II, door post, jambs, pilaster.***
45f †אַיִל (*'ayil*) ***III, leader.***
45g †אַיִל (*'ayil*) ***IV, terebinth.***
45h †אֵלָה (*'ēlâ*) ***terebinth.***
45i †אֵלוֹן (*'ēlôn*) ***terebinth.***
45j †אֵילָם (*'êlām*) ***portico.***
45k אַיָּל (*'ayyāl*) ***stag, deer.***
45l †אַיָּלָה (*'ayyālâ*) ***doe.***

'ûlām. ***Porch, hall.*** (ASV uses "porch"; RSV has "porch, hall," or "vestibule.") Sometimes equated with *'êlām.* I occurs mainly in I Kgs and Ezk as part of a temple or palace. Apparently it was an enclosed porch or entrance hall, since it could have windows (Ezk 41:26) and is compared to a palace (I Kgs 7:8).

The question of the porch is bound up with the reconstruction of the temple, which is uncertain. The older view was that the temple had two rooms like the tabernacle, a main hall and the holy of holies. There was also a porch out front. The view favored by many today is that it was a three-room temple like Syrian temples that have been found. W. F. Albright held that the two pillars out front were free standing and totally outside the structure (*Archaeology and the Religion of Israel,* Johns Hopkins Press, 1946, pp. 143–48). More recent study would suggest that the front of the building was really a half-porch or vestibule with an open front. The two side walls may have had windows (though Ezk 41:26 may refer to windows in the front wall of the high main hall that rose above the porch). In any case, the front of the vestibule would have been open with the roof supported by the side walls and the two great pillars in front. This arrangement would have given a very imposing entrance similar to the palaces at Megiddo and elsewhere (D. Ussishkin, "King Solomon's Palaces," BA 36:85–98).

The height of the porch was surely not 120 (cubits) (II Chr 3:4, KJV) but 20 cubits (some LXX MSS). Probably the consonants for cubit *'mh* became reversed and were read as one hundred *m'h.*

A "porch" or "hall" figures prominently in connection with Solomon's temple, his palace complex, and the temple of Ezk 40–48. It is never used in connection with any other building. According to I Kgs 6:3, the hall in front of Solomon's temple was twenty cubits wide and ten cubits deep. Its width equaled that of the temple proper. This entrance hall added a third section to the holy place and holy of holies of the tabernacle. In the front of this "porch" or "vestibule" were set up the two pillars, Jachin and Boaz (I Kgs 7:21). The excavators of Arad think that they have found a porch area in the sanctuary at that site. The altar of burnt offering was built in front of the porch (II Chr 8:12), and this juxtaposition of porch and altar is noted elsewhere also (II Chr 15:8; cf. Matt 23:55). In Ezk 8:16 wicked men are seen at the entrance to the temple, "between the porch and the altar," worshiping the sun with their backs to God. Joel 2:17 describes godly priests weeping and praying "between the porch and the altar."

The "porch" of Solomon's palace complex is not well understood. The "hall of pillars" is associated with the "house of the forest of Lebanon" (I Kgs 7:2, 6). This hall of pillars, a colonnade structure, measured fifty cubits by thirty, and may have functioned as an entrance hall to the larger "forest of Lebanon" building. Another porch or portico stood in front of the hall of pillars (v. 6). The same word is used of the "hall of the throne," also called the "hall of judgment" (v. 7). The exact relationship of this hall to the other "halls" or "porches" of v. 6 is problematical. It may have been directly adjacent to the royal residence itself. Verse 8 indicates that Solomon built for Pharaoh's daughter a house modelled after the "hall of the throne."

The largest number of references to "porch" occur in Ezekiel 40–46 in connection with the hard-visualize temple described by the prophet. Several times the phrase "the porch of the gate" occurs (40:7–8, 15, 39; 44:3). These porches were porticos of the gates between the city and the outer court and the similar gates between the outer court and the inner. These gates are so described that we can compare them to the typical Solomonic gateways unearthed in Megiddo, Hazor, and Gezer. The "prince" was to enter and leave the temple by way of this "porch of the gate" (44:3; 46:2, 8). There were two tables on each side of this porch where the burnt offering, sin offering, and guilt offering were to be slaughtered (40:39). Probably the porch was also the place where the prince ate bread before the Lord (44:3).

In 40:48–49 the dimensions of "the porch of the temple" are given as twenty cubits in length and eleven in width. These measurements are almost identical to those of the porch of Solomon's temple. To reach the porch, a staircase flanked by pillars was provided (v. 49).

While many of the details regarding Ezekiel's "porch" remain obscure, it is clear that greater prominence is attached to this area and that, unlike Solomon's temple, distinct activities are associated with it.

Bibliography: Vincent, L. H., *Jerusalem de l'Ancien Testament,* II, Paris: J. Gabalda, 1956, p. 428. IDB, II, pp. 513–14, 657. See John B. Taylor, *Ezekiel* (Tyndale), for a sketch of Ezekiel's temple. Note especially the possible positions of the pillars in front of the structure or within the entrance to the "porch." The latter position is favored by the Solomonic palaces at Megiddo.

The plan of the gateways to the courts is better shown in W. Zimmerli *Biblische Kommentar zum A.T.*, II, pp. 1006, 1040.

'ayil ***I. Ram, male sheep.*** Like the word for "porch" (*'ûlām*), "ram" is probably derived from *'ûl* "to be first, in front of," pointing to the ram as the leader of the flock. It is mentioned prominently in the Bible. The ram was valued for its wool (II Kgs 3:4) and its tasty meat (Gen 31:38). Jacob presented rams along with other animals as a gift to Esau (Gen 32:15). The ratio of ten female lambs to one ram is typical in raising animals; the males are used for meat and the females kept for the next generation. It is noteworthy that most animals sacrificed were males. The sacrificial laws too were given in a way that was not impractical. Rams or their wool were included in the tribute payments which the Moabite king Mesha made to Ahab (II Kgs 3:4) and which the Arabians gave to Jehoshaphat (II Chr 17:11). Areas noted for their rams were Bashan and Nebaioth, which is probably Nabatea, in spite of the linguistic problem of the *t* and *ṭ*. Ram skins dyed red were an important covering for the tabernacle (Ex 25:5).

Rams were frequently offered as sacrifices. When God instituted his covenant with Abram, a ram was one of the animals slain (Gen 15:9). On Mount Moriah the ram caught in the bush became the substitute for the beloved Isaac (Gen 22:13). The "ram of ordination" was sacrificed at the consecration of Aaron and his sons to the priesthood (Ex 29:1, 22). When the altar of the tabernacle was dedicated, rams were among the offerings presented (Num 7:15, 21, etc.). Ezekiel visualizes a ram as a burnt offering at the dedication of a new altar (Ezk 43:23, 25).

Rams were offered as regular sacrifices throughout the year. Only a ram was to be used for a guilt offering (Lev 5:15f.; 19:21–22), called a "ram of atonement" (Num 5:8). Often rams were among the burnt offerings, linked with bulls and lambs. The order is usually given as bulls, rams, and lambs (Num 28:11; I Chr 29:21). Rams for burnt offerings were accompanied with grain offerings and liquid offerings, the amounts of which were less than those used for bulls but greater than those for lambs. They were offered at the new moon festival (Num 28:11–14), Passover (Num 28:19–20), Pentecost (Lev 23:18), and the Day of Atonement (Lev 16:3, 5). Rams were also slain as peace offerings (Lev 9:4f.). One ram for a peace offering was prescribed to fulfill a nazirite vow (Num 6:14, 17, 19).

Rams are mentioned in several passages that condemn the multiplication of sacrifices designed to please God automatically (I Sam 15:22; Isa 1:11; Mic 6:7). These familiar verses while demonstrating the importance of rams as sacrificial animals, indicate the importance of the worshiper's heart attitude.

In Dan 8, the ram symbolizes the kings of Media and Persia. In Ezk 34:17 "rams" are paired with male goats as symbols of the rich and powerful in Israel. These tyrants use their horns to oppress the weak of the flock (v. 21). The implication is that God will conduct a sacrifice and will destroy these fat and strong ones.

'ayil ***II. Projecting pillar, pilaster.*** *'ayil* occurs once in I Kgs 6:31 and twenty-one times in Ezk 40–41. According to I Kgs these "pillars" or "posts" were five-sided and were located at the entrance to the inner sanctuary of the temple. As depicted in Ezk, they feature palm tree ornaments (40:31) and are associated with the gates of the temple area and with the porch of the temple. Examples from the monarchy are described and pictured in Albright, *Archaeology of Palestine,* Pelican, 1961, pp. 125–26.

'ayil ***III. Mighty, leader.*** Some authorities consider *'ayil* III to be a separate word from *'ayil* I, ram (BDB), while others treat it as part of it (KB). There are only five possible usages of this word. The first, in Ex 15:15 (KJV, "mighty men"), compares the leaders of Moab with the chiefs of Edom. The plural form in each term shows that the reference is not restricted to the king.

In Ezk, where "ram" is used symbolically (see *'ayil* I, there are three instances of metaphorical usage. Ezekiel 17:13 refers to the "mighty of the land," the leaders and skilled workmen deported from Israel by Nebuchadnezzar. A parallel passage is II Kgs 24:15, which also contains the word *'êlê* as the preferred reading (Qere), though the the consonants in *'ûlê* (Kethib) may preserve the original root *'ûl* (see *'ayil* I). These "leading men" were exiled along with King Jehoiachin, his family, and officials.

The singular form occurs in Ezk 31:11, referring to the "despot of the nations," the king of Babylon who destroyed Assyria's power. There is some disagreement about Ezk 32:21. Many manuscripts have *'êlê* instead of *'ēlê*. If the former is correct, the expression refers to the once "mighty leaders" who have gone down to Sheol.

'ayil ***IV. Terebinth, oak.*** Probably from *'ul* "to be in front, prominent" (see *'ayil* I). The "oak of Paran" (El-paran) of Gen 14:6 may have been an important landmark because of its size (cf. the "oak of Moreh" in Gen 12:6). Some scholars believe that *'ayil* refers to a large tree, not a specific species. The terebinth grows to a thirty foot maximum.

The word is closely related to *'ēlâ,* another designation for the terebinth tree. In Isa 1:29–30 the two words seem almost interchangeable. Modern translations alternate between "oak" and "terebinth."

Of its five occurrences, the most important are in Isaiah. According to Isa 1:29, Zion will be ashamed of the oaks and gardens it has desired. This passage is clarified by Isa 57:5, which refers to "burning with lust among the oaks." According to Hos 4:13–14, the shade provided by large trees made them desirable as "high places," i.e. cultic shrines.

Another metaphorical usage (Isa 61:3) calls the faithful in Zion "oaks of righteousness," firmly planted by the Lord to withstand evil.

A possible reference to *'ayil* occurs in Ezk 31:14, where tall, proud trees, representing Assyria and Egypt, are felled by the Lord.

'ēlâ. ***Terebinth*** (usually the same in ASV, RSV). The exact identification of this tree is disputed. Most versions translate the word by the term "oak." The tree is infrequently mentioned in Scripture, being found in six distinct historical situations: where Jacob hid idols (Gen 35:4); where an angel met Gideon (Jud 6:11, 19); a valley where David fought Goliath (I Sam 17:2, 19); where Absalom caught his hair (II Sam 18:9); where the unnamed prophet rested (I Kgs 13:14); and where Saul's bones were buried (I Chr 10:12). It is used as a symbol of judgment (Isa 1:30; 6:13) and under its limbs Israel committed idolatry (Ezk 6:13; Hos 4:13).

'ēlôn. ***Terebinth, oak.*** (ASV and RSV usually translate "oak" with a marginal note "terebinth." The KJV erroneously translates as "plain.")

It is generally conceded to be the same as *'ēlâ.* The tree figures often in Abraham's travels (Gen 12:6; 13:18; 14:13; 18:1). A noted one is mentioned near Ebal and Gerizim (Deut 11:30). The RSV translates the term on one occasion "divining oak" (Jud 9:37), while ASV follows KJV in translating "the oak of Meonenim." Apparently certain such trees became so famous as landmarks that they were generally recognized by all as suitable for specifying rendezvous.

'ēlām. ***Porch, portico (*** KJV ***"arches").*** Closely related are *'ûlām* and *'ayil,* II. *'ēlām* occurs some sixteen times, only in Ezk 40:16–36 and always in the plural. These "porches," or "vestibules" or "colonnades" are associated with the guard rooms and side pillars of the gates of the temple (vv. 16, 21, 29, 33, 36). They were apparently side enclosures along the entire length of the gateway, or enlarged areas at the end of the gate. See the bibliography for suggested plans of these gateways.

'ayyālâ. ***Doe, hind.*** This noun is the feminine of *'ayyāl* "stag, deer." It is known in Ugaritic also (*'ylt*). All of its eleven occurrences are in poetic passages. Three times reference is made to the doe giving birth. In Ps 29:9 a thunderstorm called "the voice of the Lord" makes the doe go into labor (cf. Job 39:1). An alternative view as old as R. Lowth (1815) is cited by Dahood though rejected by him (in AB, *Psalms I,* p. 179). It reads *'ayyālōt* "does" as *'ēlōt* or *'êlōt* "oaks" and translates the line "makes the oaks bend." It is not only difficult to have the reading that the storm makes the does bear prematurely, but also the parallel line speaks of the storm stripping the forests—which would favor the reading "oaks" (so the NIV). During a severe drought, the doe gives birth only to abandon her young (Jer 14:5). This is apparently unusual owing to the affectionate nature of the doe (Prov 5:19).

Another trio of verses refers to the doe as a surefooted animal, able to make its way on high, dangerous terrain. The Psalmist rejoices that God has made his feet like a doe's feet in preparation for battle (18:33 [H 34] = II Sam 22:34). Habakkuk uses the same imagery to exult in the security God gives (3:19). When Jacob blesses Naphtali, he predicts that the tribe will be "a doe let loose" (Gen 49:21), roaming free and secure. Naphtali's part in the victory over Sisera may be in view (Jud 4:6; 5:18).

Twice in the Song of Solomon (2:7; 3:5) the daughters of Jerusalem are adjured "by the gazelles or by the does of the field." This is probably a word play on taking an oath using "LORD of hosts" and "god." "Gazelles" is identical to "hosts" (*ṣ*^{e}*bā'ôt*) and "does" (*'aylôt*) is very close to *'ĕlōhîm*.

The phrase "to the doe of the morning" introducing Ps 22 probably refers to the melody to be used.

Bibliography: Howie, Carl Gordon, "The East Gate of Ezekiel's Temple Enclosure and the Solomonic Gateway of Megiddo," BASOR 117: 13–19, esp. p. 16.

H.W.

46 אוּלַי (*'ûlay*) ***perhaps, suppose.***

This adverb is often associated with personal or national crises. Sarah expressed hope that Hagar would produce a child for her (Gen 16:2), and Balak hoped to curse Israel through Balaam (Num 22:6, 11). Jacob feared that Isaac would discover his deceit (Gen 27:12), and Job wondered if perhaps his children had cursed God (1:5). *'ûlay* also expresses mockery (Isa 47:12; I Kgs 18:27).

H.W.

אוּלָם (*'ûlām*) I. See no. 45c.

47 אוּלָם (*'ûlām*) ***II, but, however, nevertheless.***

This strong adversative is found ten times in Job, where Satan argues that God should test Job (1:11; 2:5) and where Job and his friends voice deep differences (5:8; 11:5; 13:3). God's sovereign will can be expressed through this term (Gen 48:19; Ex 9:16). Contrasts between past and present are emphasized (Gen 28:19; I Kgs 20:23).

H.W.

48 און (*'wn*) **I. Assumed root of the following.**
48a †אָוֶן (*'āwen*) ***trouble.***
48b †תְּאֻנִים (*t*^{e}*'ūnîm*) ***toil.***

'āwen. ***Trouble, sorrow, idolatry, wickedness, iniquity, emptiness.*** (RSV and NEB prefer "***evil***," and "***mischief***" over KJV's favorite, "***iniquity***.") The primary meaning of the word seems to have two facets: a stress on trouble which moves on to wickedness, and an emphasis on emptiness which moves on to idolatry. The word is used eighty-five times. A noun from an identical root *'wn* II is pronounced *'ôn* and means "vigor, wealth" (q.v.).

The root does not occur in verbal forms; normally it functions as a masculine noun, sometimes as an adjective.

One of the basic meanings of *'āwen* is "trouble" which is clearly shown in Gen 35:18. Just before she died, Rachel named her newborn son, Ben-oni, (son of sorrow). In Deut 26:14 and Hos 9:4 *'āwen* designates mourning in association with death. *'āwen* is sometimes in proximity to *'āmal* "toil, labor" (q.v.). In Job 5:6; Ps 90:10; and Hab 1:3, *'āwen* is parallel to *'āmāl* and emphasizes physical trouble. In Isa 10:1, Ps 7:14 [H 15] (cf. Job 4:8) *'āmāl* is the result of *'āwen* in the sense that sin brings trouble. The relationship between *'āwen* and *'āmal* is shown further by the tendency of the latter to drift to the connotation of deceitful words as in Ps 140:10. Also, both words occur with other words for deceit in Job 15:35; Ps 10:7; 36:3–4; 55:11; and Isa 59:4. Observe in Job 36:21 that *'āwen* is contrasted with another word for affliction *'ōnî* and both here and in Job 34:36 *'āwen* would seem to point to deceptive planning or speaking which leads to sorrow or rebellion.

In this sense of deception, *'āwen* is tied to thoughts and words in Prov 17:4; Isa 32:6; Ezk 11:2; Hos 12:12 and possibly Hos 6:8 (see LXX). From this base *'āwen* becomes a label for idolatry in Isa 66:3 and the phrase "Beth-aven," probably a name of shame for Bethel (Hos 5:8; 10:5, 8; cf. Amos 1:5; Ezk 30:17). Also the word describes idols in Isa 41:29, and seems to denote non-existence in Amos 5:5.

This trend of meaning in *'āwen* is reinforced by its proximity to standard Hebrew words for deception, fraud, and falseness in Prov 6:12, 18; 19:28; 22:8; Isa 29:20; Zech 10:2. It may be that this strand of meaning comes from a possible early kinship to *'āyin,* which means "nothing."

In by far the greater numbers of instances, the versions prefer to translate *'āwen* as "evil," "iniquity," or "wicked." But an interesting term occurs about twenty times in Job, Ps, and Prov; it is workers of iniquity (*'āwen*) and may designate men skilled in magic or idolatrous ritual.

Generally, biblical theologians have given little

attention to *'āwen* as a contributor to an understanding of sin. Since the word stresses the planning and expression of deception and points to the painful aftermath of sin, it should be noted more.

tᵉ'ūnîm. ***Toil.*** This masculine noun occurs in the plural, possibly to intensify the force of the word occurring only in Ezk 24:12. Translators have been unable to agree on its precise meaning, so we have "lies" (KJV), "in vain" (RSV), and "corrosion" (NEB).

Bibliography: Gelin, Albert, *Sin in the Bible,* Desclee, 1964. Guillaume, A., "The Root *'wn* in Hebrew," JTS 34: 62–64. Porubcan, Stefan, *Sin in the Old Testament,* Rome: Herder, 1963. Quell, G., *Sin,* London: Adam and Charles Black, 1951. Smith, C. R., *The Bible Doctrine of Sin,* London: Epworth, 1953. TDOT, I, pp. 140–46. THAT, I, pp. 81–83.

G.H.L.

49 און (*'wn*) **II. Assumed root of the following.**

49a †און (*'ôn*) ***vigor, wealth.***

This root occurs as a noun only twelve times. In Gen 49:3; Deut 21:17; Job 40:16; Ps 78:51; 105:36, the word designates reproductive power as evidenced in the firstborn son. In Isa 40:26–27 the creative power of God is highlighted. Physical strength and/or wealth is denoted in Job 18:12; 20:10; Hos 12:9.

G.H.L.

50 אוֹפִיר (*'ôpîr*) ***Ophir.***

This proper name refers to the eleventh son of Joktan (Gen 10:29) and to a region famous for its gold. The name is mentioned with "Sheba" and "Havilah" in Gen 10:28–29 and I Chr 1:22–23. Since those two designations are place names, some authorities feel that the person "Ophir" must be connected with the place. Others disavow any relationship between the two.

Ophir is first mentioned in connection with David, who had amassed three thousand talents of gold from Ophir for the construction of Solomon's temple (I Chr 29:4). Solomon joined with Hiram of Tyre to send ships from Ezion-geber to Ophir in quest of the same gold (I Kgs 9:28). These ships also brought a large number of almug trees and precious stones (I Kgs 10:11), and quantities of silver, ivory, apes, and baboons (peacocks? I Kgs 10:22). Actually, v. 22 does not mention Ophir, but the ships of Tarshish were most likely the large vessels that traveled to Ophir every three years (cf. II Chr 9:21). In I Kgs 22:49 King Jehoshaphat built "ships of Tarshish" to journey to Ophir in search of gold, but this venture in the century after Solomon came to grief before the ships could leave Ezion-geber. Some scholars believe that "Tarshish" normally means boats used for carrying ore or metals.

A reference to the gold of Ophir has been found on a preexilic sherd uncovered at Tell Qasileh. The inscription reads, "Gold of Ophir for Bethhoron, thirty shekels" (B. Maisler, "Two Hebrew Ostraca from Tell Qasile," JNES 10:265–67). This find indicates that at least one king after Jehoshaphat was successful in procuring additional Ophir gold.

The value of the gold of Ophir is implied in poetic passages. In Isa 13:12 it is compared to "pure gold" (cf. Job 28:15–16). In Ps 45:9 [H 10] the queen is depicted as clothed in gold from Ophir. In Job 22:24 the word "Ophir" is understood to mean "the gold of Ophir."

The site of Ophir has not been conclusively identified. Several theories have been formulated, taking into account the products identified with Ophir and the three-year length of the journey. Most likely the three years refers to one entire year and parts of two others. Perhaps the best case can be made for locating Ophir in the Somali Republic, a country on the horn of Africa, once called Punt. The products obtained in Ophir are known in Africa, and the Hebrew words for the two kinds of monkeys (apes and baboons?) are related to Egyptian words (*qf* and *ky*).

A different theory would place Ophir in India, where the commodities in question were also available, particularly if "almug" wood is sandalwood. Some identify Ophir with Supara, sixty miles north of Bombay. Trade between India and the Persian Gulf is attested from the second millennium B.C. Once Jerome translated Ophir as "India" (Job 28:16), reflecting a strong tradition in his day.

A third alternative is the southwestern coast of Arabia. The close relationship between Ophir and Sheba and Havilah in Gen 10:29 supports this identification. Maᶜafir in Yemen has been suggested as a site for Ophir. This theory does not preclude the possibility that some of the commodities were originally brought to Ophir from India.

Bibliography: Albright, William F., *Archaeology and the Religion of Israel,* Johns Hopkins, 1953, pp. 133–35, 212.

H.W.

51 אוּץ (*'ûṣ*) ***to hurry, urge, be pressed*** (with the same meaning in Arabic).

This verb is used four times in Prov to discourage haste to get rich (28:20) and hasty words or actions (29:20; 19:2; 21:5). In the famous Josh 10:13 the sun was in no hurry to set.

One's territory can be too "confining" (Josh

17:15), and persons can be "urged" into action (Ex 5:13; Gen 19:15).

H.W.

אוֹצָר (*'ôṣār*). See no. 154a.

52 אוֹר (*'ôr*) ***to be or become light, shine;*** in the Hiphil stem, ***to give light, cause to shine.*** Corresponds to Ugaritic *'r* "to be bright; to illumine," and Akkadian *urru* "day."

It occurs infrequently in the Qal and Niphal but some forty-five times in the Hiphil. It refers to the shining of the sun, but its metaphorical usages are more common.

Derivatives

52a †אוֹר (*'ôr*) ***light.***
52b †אוֹרָה (*'ôrâ*) ***I, light.***
52c אוֹרָה (*'ôrâ*) ***II, herb*** (only in II Kgs 4:39).
52d אוּר (*'ûr*) ***flame.***
52e †אוּרִים (*'ûrîm*) ***Urim.***
52f †מָאוֹר (*mā'ôr*) ***luminary.***
52g מְאוּרָה (*m^e'ûrâ*) ***(light) hole.***

The concept of light in Scripture is important, dealing with personal and impersonal forces on both literal and metaphorical levels. Light is closely related to life and happiness, which may account for the frequent comparisons between God and light. Since the ancient world often worshiped the sun, God's role as creator of light is stressed. Eventually, he will make the sun unnecessary (Isa 60:19–20).

Light is frequently used as an indicator of time, separating day from night (Gen 1:5). The emphasis is on the shining of the sun in the early morning (Gen 44:3; Jud 16:2), so that "light" can sometimes be translated "dawn" (Neh 8:3). A distinction may be drawn between "daybreak" and the "daylight" that follows (Jud 19:26) the rising of the sun (Isa 60:1–3). Amos (8:9) mentions a judgment of darkness that will strike Israel "in broad daylight."

Light is of course associated with light-bearing bodies, but it is distinct from them, as seen in its creation apart from the luminaries (Gen 1:3). The sun and the moon are the "greater light" and the "lesser light" (Gen 1:16; Ps 136:7), and the stars are closely associated as "stars of light" (Ps 148:3). "Every passage that speaks of the shining (*'ôr* in the Hiphil) or the light (*'ôr*) of the sun (Gen 1:14–16; Isa 30:20; 60:19; Jer 31:35; Ezk 32:8; Ps 136:7–9) also refers to the light of the moon and sometimes also of the stars" (TDOT, I, p. 151). These heavenly luminaries are an integral part of the wonder of the cosmos as founded by the Creator and serve as a clock to regulate the seasons (Gen 1:14; Ps 104:19; Jer 31:35f.). The OT avoids isolating the sun as "the light" lest the Hebrews succumb to the tendency to worship it (cf. Job 31:26–27). Another of God's lights was the pillar of fire that illumined the night for the Israelites during the wilderness wanderings (Ex 13:21; Ps 105:39). This was probably more awesome than lightning, which also displayed the glory of God (Ps 77:18 [H 19]; 97:4; Job 36:32).

Manmade lights included the sacred lampstand in the tabernacle (Num 4:9, 16; 8:2) which cast its light in the holy place. Lamps burning olive oil were highly valued for use in people's homes (Prov 13:9).

'ôr is used metaphorically when a person's face or the eyes are viewed as light-bearing objects. Sometimes literal eyesight is intended (Ps 38:10 [H 11], probably also the difficult I Sam 14:27), but more often the "light of the face" refers to a cheerful face expressing good will (Job 29:24). The favor of a king is seen in his face (Prov 16:15), and "the light of God's face" indicates divine approval (Ps 44:3 [H 4]; 89:15 [H 16]).

In the famous priestly blessing of Num 6:25, the Hiphil stem of the verb is used in a similar context: "The Lord make his face to shine upon you, and be gracious to you." This time-honored expression occurs five times in the Psalms, invoking God's saving and restoring presence on behalf of his servants (Ps 31:16 [H 17]; 67:1; [H 2]; 80:3, 7, 19 [H 80:4, 8, 20]; 119:135). In Dan 9:17 the great statesman implores the Lord of mercy to let his face shine upon his sanctuary and reverse the desolate conditions in Jerusalem. The expression finds a parallel in Ugaritic, "the countenace of the sun shines upon me," meaning "I enjoy the favor of the king."

Light can also symbolize general "life" or "prosperity." "To see the light" is "to be born" (Job 3:16), and the "light of life" is a poetic reference to being alive (Job 33:30; Ps 56:13 [H 14]).

Some, however, contend that this compound should be rendered "the land of the living" because this is the meaning of the word in Phoenician. It makes excellent sense in such passages as Job 33:30. The word "land" is found in Ps 116:9, a close parallel to Ps 56:13 [H 14]. Dahood (*Psalms, I, II* in AB) suggests the meaning "land of eternal life."

In Ps 36:9 [H 10] "light" is parallel to "the fountain of life." In line with this usage Dahood argues that "to see light" is often really to see the light of God's face in immortality (Ps 36:9 [H 10]; and contra Ps 49:19 [H 20]). This is the expression in Isa 53:11 when the LXX and DSS texts speak in this vein of immortality for the suffering servant (cf. Ps 17:15).

Job 22:28 describes prosperity as light shining on one's ways, and a few chapters later "good" is compared with "light" (30:26). Unfortunately,

Job has encountered "evil" and "darkness," a set of contrasts in line with Amos's portrayal of the day of the Lord as one of darkness and not light (5:18). A day without light speaks of trouble and calamity.

Prosperity and life are closely linked with joy, so it is appropriate to find "happiness" as a meaning for "light." The two concepts are parallel in Ps 97:11. In Est 8:16 (using *'ôrâ*) "light" is one of several words describing the relief and joy felt by the Jews in Persia when the decree to destroy them had been rescinded. Proverbs 15:30 speaks of the light of the eyes that makes the heart happy.

Another prominent metaphorical usage relates light to instruction. When a man finds wisdom, his face lights up (Eccl 8:1). The teaching of one's parents (Prov 6:23) as well as the word of God are a lamp to one's feet, a light to one's path (Ps 119:105, 130). In Psalm 19, which compares the written Scriptures to nature and to the sun in particular, the commandments of the Lord are said to enlighten the eyes (v. 8 [H 9]). Most likely the challenge to Israel "to walk in the light of the Lord" denotes adherence to the laws and teachings of God (Isa 2:3, 5; cf. 51:4). In a word, whereas darkness is associated with death (Job 3:5; 10:21; Ps 88:6; 91:6), failure and suffering (Jer 28:12; Amos 5:18, 20; Lam 3:2), folly (Job 37:19; 38:2; Eccl 2:13), and sin (Job 24:16; Ps 74:20; Prov 2:13; Jer 49:9), light is associated with life (Mal 3:20 [H 4:2]), salvation and prosperity (Job 29:3; Isa 58:8; Ps 36:10 [H 9]), wisdom (Ps 19:9 [H 8]; 119:105, 130; Prov 6:23; Dan 5:11), justice (Isa 42:1–3, 6; 49:6; 51:4f.; Mic 7:8).

The ultimate development is to compare God himself with light. The Lord is my light and my salvation (Ps 27:1), though a flaming fire to purge out wickedness (Isa 10:17). Isaiah describes the Messiah as a great light shining in a land of deep darkness (9:2 [H 1]). He will be "a light to the nations" so that God's salvation may reach the ends of the earth (42:6; 49:6).

Though the OT is careful not to identify God and the sun, the shining glory of God is described in terms of the sun (Ezk 43:2). He is the resplendent one (Ps 76:4 [H 5]) with healing in his wings, or rays (Mal 4:2 [H 3:20]). In the future age of bliss the glory of the Lord will rise upon us (Isa 60:1–3) and he, not the sun, will be an everlasting light (Isa 60:19–20).

'ûrîm. *Urim.* This word occurs seven times in the OT, only in the plural. A presumed singular *'ûr* "light" (ASV "flame," Isa 50:11), whence "fire" (Isa 31:9; 44:16). *'ûrîm* meant also east, region of light (Isa 24:15 NIV, NASB marg.). In all but two cases the Urim appear with the Thummim. Both were placed in the high priest's "breastplate of judgment" (Ex 28:30; Lev 8:8; see *ḥōshen*) and were involved in obtaining oracular judgments from God (Num 27:21).

Although *'ûrîm* probably derives from *'ôr* "be light" (q.v.), Ugaritic *'r* (so BDB, p. 22), other possibilities include *'ārar* "curse," and *'ārâ* "pluck off" (KB, p. 23). Only in postexilic times do Urim and Thummim occur without the article or its equivalent, indicating that despite KJV capitalization, these were originally common nouns, meaning "lights and perfections" (see *tāmam*), as the LXX and later Greek *phōtismoi kai teleotētes,* or, more freely, *dēlōsis kai alētheia* "illumination and truth."

The Urim and Thummim appear in Scripture without explanatory identification, except that they were to be put "in the breastplate . . . and be upon Aaron's heart" (Ex 28:30), which may suggest that these are none other than descriptive terms for the twelve precious stones of the immediately preceding context, inscribed with the names of the tribes of Israel (vv. 17–21), and set in the breastplate of judgment upon Aaron's heart (v. 29). But cf. Lev 8:8 which seems to say they are additional to the twelve. Josephus assigns oracular characteristics to the twelve stones, claiming they would shine when Israel was to be victorious in battle (*Antiquities,* 3. 8.9). Talmudic tradition suggests that the Shekinah would illumine letters in the tribal names to spell out revelations, (*Yoma,* 73,a–b; although five of the twenty-two Hebrew letters do not appear in these twelve names). Actually, the combining of "dreams, Urim, and prophets" (I Sam 28:6) indicates that, even as the first and last terms denote revelations to the mind of the petitioner through a prophetic intermediary, so Urim denotes a correspondingly personal revelation, through the mind of that priestly intermediary who wore the shining stones of the breastpiece in Israel's sanctuary (cf. Moses' association of Urim and Thummim with the tribe of Levi, Deut 33:8, and David's seeking divine guidance through the man who wore the priestly surplice (*'ēpôd,* q.v.) I Sam 23:9–12; 30:7–8, to which, in turn, the breastplate was attached (Ex 28:25–28).

Negative critics presume that the *'ûrîm* were images, magical dice, or divining disks, flipped like coins, giving a "yes" answer should the light (*'ûr*) side come up (cf. IDB, IV, p. 739 and the RSV emendation of I Sam 14:41). But *tōm* does not mean "dark." And the priestly oracles were not limited to yes-or-no answers (Jud 18:5–6; II Sam 5:19) but provided detailed explanations (Jud 1:1; I Sam 10:22; II Sam 5:23). Scripture condemns pagan, mechanical divination (Hos 4:12). Mention of official oracles ceases after the time of David (replaced by prophets?), and the breastpiece with its Urim seems to have perished in the exile (cf. Ezr 2:63; cf. Josephus's claim of a Maccabean destruction, *Antiquities,* 3.8, 9).

mā'ôr. ***Light, luminary.*** This masculine noun is a close synonym of *'ôr,* but occurs only twenty times. It is used of the lampstand in the tabernacle several times (Ex 35:14; Lev 24:2; Num 4:9, 16).

'ôrâ ***I. Light, joy.*** This feminine form of *'ôr* occurs only three times in the OT (Ps 139:12; Isa 26:19; Est 8:16).

Bibliography: Lindblom, J., "Lot-Casting in the Old Testament," VT 12: 164–78. Mangan, Edward A., "The Urim and Thummim," CBQ 1:133–38. May, H. G., "Ephod and Ariel," AJSL 56:44–69. Richardson, TWB, p. 129. Robertson, Edward, "The 'Urim and Thummim; What Were They?" VT 14: 67–74. TDNT, IX, pp. 316–27. TDOT, I, pp. 147–66. THAT, I, pp. 84–90.

H.W.

אוֹת (*'ôt*). See no. 41a.

53 *אוּת (*'ût*) ***consent, agree*** (Niphal only).

אוּרִים (*'ûrîm*). See no. 52e.

54 אָז (*'āz*) ***then.***

Derivative

54a †מֵאָז (*mē'āz*) ***in time past, long since, since.***

This adverb appears 130 times. It is related to Ugaritic *idk* "then." Its use in Hebrew is emphatic, occurring in many important contexts and often in poetic passages. As a temporal adverb, it can refer to both the past and present. After the great victory over Egypt at the Red Sea, "then Moses sang this song to the LORD" (Ex 15:1; cf. Num 21:17). "Then" introduces Joshua's request for the sun to stand still (Josh 10:12). When the temple was dedicated "then Solomon assembled all Israel (I Kgs 8:1).

'āz also occurs in future contexts, specifying the time when the eyes of the blind will be opened (Isa 35:5) or when the return from captivity will bring ecstasy (Isa 60:5). After Abraham's servant had sought a wife among his relatives, "then" he would be free from his oath (Gen 24:41; Ex 12:44).

The victory songs of Ex 15 and Jud 5 use *'āz* emphatically. When news about Israel's triumph was heard, "then the chiefs of Edom were dismayed" (Ex 15:15). In Jud 5:8, 11, 13 it is used to describe the sequence of the battle with the Canaanites.

"Then" can also express strict logical sequence. If Israel keeps the Sabbath, "then" they will find delight in the Lord (Isa 58:14). Apart from meditating in the law, David claims, "I would have perished" (Ps 119:92; cf. II Kgs 13:19).

mē'āz. ***Since.*** Derived from *min 'āz* "from then," as in Jer 44:18. It occurs eighteen times, seven times as a preposition or conjunction (Ruth 2:7; Gen 39:5). In the absolute it is used of the recent past (II Sam 15:34) or the more remote past. In Isa, a cluster of verses prove that God has "long since" predicted the future (44:8; 45:21; 48:3, 5, 7, 8). God's throne was established "from of old" (Ps 93:2), which looks beyond creation (Prov 8:22).

H.W.

55 אֵזוֹב (*'ēzôb*) ***hyssop.*** (ASV and RSV similar.)

This word occurs ten times, primarily in the Pentateuch. The English meaning is derived from the Greek ὕσσωπος, which is only an attempt to transliterate the Hebrew. Hyssop is a small plant that grows on walls (I Kgs 4:33 [H 5:13]), probably to be identified with marjoram of the mint family. It was used to apply blood and water in purification ceremonies.

The importance of hyssop stems from the Exodus. God told Moses to have each Israelite family slay a lamb, dip a bunch of hyssop in the blood in the basin and then smear some of the blood on the sides and top of the doorframe (Ex 12:22). When the Angel of the Lord passed by and saw the blood, he spared the firstborn son in that home. Thus, the hyssop functioned as a brush to apply the blood.

In Lev 14:4–6 hyssop is used in a purification ceremony for a man cured of leprosy. The hyssop, along with a live bird, cedar wood and scarlet yarn, was dipped in the blood of a bird killed over running water. The man being cleansed was then sprinkled seven times with this mixture of blood and water. The same procedure applied to a house which had a "leprous" outbreak (likely mildew, see *ṣāra'at*). It too was to be sprinkled seven times with the same mixture (Lev 14:49–52).

Similar was the procedure for persons or objects contaminated by contact with a corpse. Special ashes for purification were prepared by burning the body of a sacrificed red heifer and throwing on top of it cedar wood, hyssop, and scarlet yarn (Num 19:6). Whenever anyone or anything had been near a dead body, running water was added to the purification ashes, and hyssop was used to sprinkle the contaminated person and objects on the third and seventh days of their ritual uncleanness (Num 19:17–19). Any unclean person who failed to comply with these regulations was to be cut off from Israel.

In the Mishnah (H. Danby, Oxford, 1933) there are seventeen pages of rules for preparing and sprinkling this water (pp. 697–714). Needless to say, some of the rules give minutiae even to the ridiculous. The spiritual character, however, is lacking. These rules represent the ideas of the Pharisees of Jesus' day.

The combination of cedar, hyssop, and scarlet found in Lev and Num is intriguing. Cedar and hyssop seem to represent the most magnificent tree and most insignificant bush respectively (I Kgs 4:33 [H 5:13]). Cedar is a symbol of strength, splendor, and longevity and it may emphasize the importance of these rites.

In Heb 9:19 there is reference to Moses taking the blood of calves, water, scarlet wool, and hyssop in order to sprinkle the scroll of the covenant and all the people as he established the Sinai covenant, though the scarlet and the hyssop are not expressly mentioned in Ex 24:6–8.

When David in repentance cried out to God, "Purify me with hyssop, and I shall be clean" (Ps 51:7 [H 9]), he referred to the laws of Num 19. He knew that if he were not cleansed, he would be cut off from his people.

Perhaps the mention of the hyssop plant given to Christ on the cross (Jn 19:29) refers symbolically to the infinite purification that was accomplished through his death.

Bibliography: Harrison, R. K., "The Biblical Problem of Hyssop," EQ 26: 218–24. Shewell-Cooper, W. E., "Flora" ZPEB, II, p. 570.

H.W.

אֵזוֹר (*'ēzôr*). See no. 59a.
אַזְכָּרָה (*'azkārâ*). See no. 551d.

56 אָזַל (*'āzal*) ***to go away, about.***

This verb is used of a buyer who brags about his purchase after he goes his way (Prov 20:14). Israel also shifts its position, moving from one ally to another (Jer 2:36).

Three times the sense is "to be exhausted." Water "evaporates" (Job 14:11), Israel's strength was depleted (Deut 32:36), and Saul's bread was gone (I Sam 9:7).

Combined with *'ēz* "goat" it makes the word *'ăzā'zēl* "Azazel," "the goat of going out" or "Scapegoat" of Lev 16.

H.W.

57 *אָזַן (*'āzan*) ***I, listen, give ear.***

This verb is used only in the Hiphil stem, indicating it is denominative.

Parent Noun

57a †אֹזֶן (*'ōzen*) ***ear.***

Derivative

57b אָזֵן (*'āzēn*) ***implements, tools.***

'āzan occurs primarily in poetic books as a parallel to the verbs *shāma'* "to hear," and *hiqshîb* "to pay attention." Even where it is used in basically non-poetic books, it occurs in poetic passages, such as the songs of Lamech (Gen 4:23), of Moses (Deut 32:1) and of Deborah (Jud 5:3). The vast majority of its forty-two occurrences are in imperatival forms.

'ōzen. ***Ear, hearing.*** This noun occurs almost two hundred times and is applied most often to man, though it is used of a dog's ears (Prov 26:17) and of a sheep's ear, partially rescued from a lion (Amos 3:12). Anthropomorphically, God is said to possess "ears" or "hearing."

The ear can perhaps best be studied under three headings: as an organ of hearing, as a part of the body subject to symbolic actions, and as a sign of responsiveness and understanding. These usages are frequently interrelated.

The ear as the physical organ of hearing has been implanted by God (Ps 94:9), who himself can hear. The Psalmist uses a teleological argument for the nature of God from the human ear: "He who planted the ear, does he not hear?" (Ps 94:9). In contrast, the manmade ears of idols hear nothing at all (Ps 115:6; 135:17). When the physical organ is mentioned, frequently "hearing" is a good translation for "ears." "To speak in the ears" of someone is "to speak in his hearing" (Gen 44:18).

Since the ear represents hearing and obedience, it is involved in important symbolic actions. If a slave chose to serve his master permanently, his ear was pierced with an awl (Ex 21:6: Deut 15:17; cf. Ps 40:6 [H 7]). By this legal act, the slave was bound to obedience for his entire life. At the ordination of Aaron and his sons to the priesthood, some blood from the sacrificial ram was placed on the lobes of their right ears, thumbs, and big toes (Lev 8:23–24; Ex 29:20). Similar was the case of a person cleansed from leprosy. Blood as well as olive oil was applied to his right ear, thumb, and big toe on the eighth day of his purification ceremonies (Lev 14:14, 17).

Earrings were apparently given by the groom to the bride at a marriage (Ezk 16:12) (The "earring" for Rebekah [Gen 24:22 KJV] was a nose ring), but they are associated with idolatry in Gen 35:4. The Israelites tore off their gold earrings so that Aaron could make a golden calf (Ex 32:2–3). As a sign of complete rejection, the ears and nose were mutilated by the rampaging enemy (Ezk 23:25).

Most references to the ear or hearing involve a response from the hearer. To hear, or to incline the ear, means to pay close attention, e.g. to the words of the wise (Prov 22:17). How often God pleads with wayward Israel to listen and heed his warnings in view of impending judgment (Hos 5:1; Jer 13:15). Even heaven and earth are called to listen as witnesses of the covenant promises of Israel (Deut 32:1; Isa 1:2). Predictions of national disasters are said to make the ears ring or tingle, so shocking is the message (I Sam 3:11; II Kgs 21:12; Jer 19:3).

Twice, the term "hardness" or "heaviness" is applied to the ears of Israel. They have stopped their ears from hearing the word of God through the prophets (Zech 7:11–12), for God had brought on them judicial deafness (Isa 6:10; cf. II Chr 24:19; Neh 9:30). Like the idols, the nation had ears but could not hear (Jer 5:21). Once the people's ears are called "uncircumcised," closed to the words of their covenant God (Jer 6:10).

Hearing and understanding are closely linked on occasion (Job 13:1), and "ears" can almost mean "mind" (Job 33:15). Horst noted. "The ears are regarded as the instrument by which speech and orders are noted, not the brain, as with us. Hence the ear is the seat of 'insight' " (TDNT, V, p. 546). Proverbs 23:13 condemns refusal to hear the cry of the poor and thus remain ignorant of their plight. But the man who turns a deaf ear to talk of murder is commended (Isa 33:15). The importance of the organ to one's spiritual life is stated by Job: "Does not the ear test words, as the palate tastes food (Job 12:11).

Many references relate to God's ability to hear and take action. The arrogance of Assyria came to his ears and resulted in its destruction (Isa 37:29). Most passages deal with God's response to prayer. The Psalmist frequently pleads with God to hear his cry for help (Ps 80:1 [H 2]; 54:2 [H 4]) and save him from the enemy. At the dedication of the temple, Solomon asked that God's ears would ever be attentive to the prayers of his people (II Chr 6:40). Daniel turned toward that temple to ask God to incline his ear and do something about the ruins of Jerusalem (Dan 9:18). When prayer is not answered, it is not because God has become hard of hearing (Isa 59:1). The sin of Israel cut them off from his saving response (Deut 1:45).

"To uncover the ear" (*gālâ 'ōzen*) is "to disclose important information," such as a plot against the king (I Sam 22:8, 17). In a legal context, it means "to bring a matter to one's attention" (Ruth 4:4). When God is the subject, "uncover the ear" means "to reveal" truth to his servants (I Sam 9:15; II Sam 7:27).

Bibliography: Richardson, TWB, p. 104. TDNT, V, pp. 546–51. THAT, I, pp. 95–97.

H.W.

58 *אָזַן (*'āzan*) ***II, weigh, test, prove.*** Only in the Piel (Eccl 12:9).

58a †מאזן (*m'zn*) ***balances, scales.***

Always occurring in the dual, *mō'zenayim* indicates a pair of scales. Scales were used to weigh silver at a purchase (Jer 32:10). Accurate scales were God's delight (Lev 19:36; Prov 11:1), and the prophets condemned cheating merchants (Amos 8:5; Mic 6:11).

Job wanted his case weighed by God (Job 31:6). God is able to weigh the hills on balances (Isa 40:12), and he regards nations as the dust on scales (Isa 40:15).

The balances of antiquity were a simple bar suspended at the middle with pans on each end. For a picture of an Egyptian balance, see L. M. Petersen, "Balance" in ZPEB.

The weights were called *'ăbānîm* (q.v.) stones, being usually made of stone shaped and ground. The chief opportunity for cheating lay in the weights used.

H.W.

אָזֵק (*'ăzēq*). See no. 577b.

59 אָזַר (*'āzar*) ***to gird, clothe.*** (ASV, RSV translate similarly.)

Derivative

59a †אֵזוֹר (*'ēzôr*) ***waistband.***

This verb usually occurs in the Qal or Piel, once in the Niphal and three times in the Hithpael, primarily in the poetic books. Often military preparation is in view.

'ēzôr. ***Waistband, belt.*** Of its fourteen occurrences, eight are in Jer 13:1–11. Elijah wears a leather belt around his hairy garment (II Kgs 1:8), but Jeremiah dons a tight-fitting linen waistband (13:1, 11). He left it to rot by the Euphrates as a symbol of the corrupt nature of Israel (Jer 13:10–11).

The "belt" or "waistband" characterized soldiers' dress. The Assyrians did not wear a loose belt as they swept south (Isa 5:27; Ezk 23:15). God is the one who prepares or girds the Psalmist with strength for battle (Ps 18:32 [H 33], 39 [H 40] = II Sam 22:40). God girded Cyrus, perhaps equipping him with armor (Isa 45:5). The weak are armed with strength, but the arrogant are shattered (I Sam 2:4). God challenges the nations to gird themselves for battle, but they face certain defeat (Isa 8:9).

Sometimes the military significance is replaced by a more general "prepare for action." God commands Job to gird up his loins like a man and meet God's arguments (Job 38:3; 40:7). And Jeremiah is given the same order in preparation for a controversial ministry (Jer 1:17).

When God turned David's mourning into dancing, he clothed (girded) him with gladness (Ps 30:11 [H 12]). A similar metaphor characterizes the Messiah, who wears righteousness and truth around his waist (Isa 11:5).

In Ps 65:6 [H 7] God as Creator is said to be "girded with might." The King of the universe is "clothed with majesty," "girded with strength" (Ps 93:1).

Bibliography: Wright, G. E., "Israelite Daily Life," BA 18: 50–79.

H.W.

אֶזְרוֹעַ (*'ezrôa'*). See no. 583b.
אֶזְרָח (*'ezrāḥ*). See no. 580b.

60 אָח (*'āḥ*) ***I, alas!***
אָח (*'āḥ*) II, III. See no. 66a, 62a.
אֹחַ (*'ōaḥ*). See no. 65a.

61 אֶחָד (*'eḥad*) ***one, same, single, first, each, once,*** fem. *'aḥat* (אַחַת).

This word occurs 960 times as a noun, adjective, or adverb, as a cardinal or ordinal number, often used in a distributive sense. It is closely identified with *yāḥad* "to be united" and with *rō'sh* "first, head," especially in connection with the "first day" of the month (Gen 8:13). It stresses unity while recognizing diversity within that oneness.

'eḥad can refer to a certain individual (Jud 13:2) or a single blessing (Gen 27:38). Solomon *alone* was chosen by the Lord (I Chr 29:1). The notion of uniqueness is also found in II Sam 7:23 and Ezk 33:24 (for this verse with reference to God, see below). The phrase "in a single day" can refer to the suddenness of judgment (Isa 10:17; 47:9) or blessing (Isa 66:8).

Adverbially, *'eḥad* means "once" or "one time" (II Kgs 6:10). God solemnly swore to David "one time" that his descendants and throne would last forever (Ps 89:35 [H 36]). In Hag 2:6 the Lord warned that he would shake heaven and earth "once more in a little while." Yet this prediction of the overthrow of nations probably included a near as well as a far fulfilment (cf. Heb 12:26). The expression "in one day" denotes the swiftness of the Lord's acts (Isa 9:14 [H 13]; Zech 3:9).

Sometimes the phrase "as one man" can mean "all at once" (Num 14:15), but when Gideon was told he would defeat Midian "as one man" it probably meant "as easily as a single man" (Jud 6:16). The phrase can also refer to a nation aroused to take united action against gross injustice (Jud 20:8; I Sam 11:7). Zephaniah's mention of people serving God "with one shoulder" (3:9) likely means "shoulder to shoulder," solidly united. Likewise in Ex 24:3 "with one voice" expresses that all Israel was involved in entering into the Covenant with Yahweh.

The concept of unity is related to the tabernacle, whose curtains are fastened together to form one unit (Ex 26:6, 11; 36:13). Adam and Eve are described as "one flesh" (Gen 2:24), which includes more than sexual unity. In Gen 34:16 the men of Shechem suggest intermarriage with Jacob's children in order to become "one people."

Later, Ezekiel predicted that the fragmented nation of Israel would someday be reunited, as he symbolically joined two sticks (37:17). Once again Judah and Ephraim would be one nation with one king (37:22). Abraham was viewed as "the one" from whom all the people descended (Isa 51:2; Mal 2:15), the one father of the nation.

Diversity within unity is also seen from the fact that *'eḥad* has a plural form, *'ăḥādîm*. It is translated "a few days" in Gen 27:44; 29:20, and Dan 11:20. In Gen 11:1 the plural modifies "words": "the whole earth used the same language and the same words." Apparently it refers to the same vocabulary, the same set of words spoken by everyone at the tower of Babel. The first "same" in Gen 11:1 is singular, analogous to "the same law" of the Passover applying to native-born and foreigner (Ex 12:49; cf. Num 15:16), or to the "one law" of sure death for approaching the Persian king without invitation (Est 4:11).

In the famous Shema of Deut 6:4, "Hear, O Israel . . . the LORD is one," the question of diversity within unity has theological implications. Some scholars have felt that, though "one" is singular, the usage of the word allows for the doctrine of the Trinity. While it is true that this doctrine is foreshadowed in the OT, the verse concentrates on the fact that there is one God and that Israel owes its exclusive loyalty to him (Deut 5:9; 6:5). The NT also is strictly monotheistic while at the same time teaching diversity within the unity (Jas 2:19; 1 Cor 8:5–6).

[The lexical and syntactical difficulties of Deut 6:4 can be seen in the many translations offered for it in the NIV. The option "the LORD is our God, the LORD alone" has in its favor both the broad context of the book and the immediate context. Deuteronomy 6:4 serves as an introduction to motivate Israel to keep the command "to love (the LORD)" (v. 5). The notion that the LORD is Israel's only God suits this command admirably (cf. Song 6:8f). Moreover, these two notions, the LORD's unique relation to Israel and Israel's obligation to love him, are central to the concern of Moses' addresses in the book (cf. Deut 5:9f.; 7:9; 10:14ff., 20f., 13:6; 30:20; 32:12). Finally Zechariah employs the text with this meaning and applies it universally with reference to the eschaton: "The LORD will be king over all the earth; in that day the LORD will be (the only) one, and His name (the only) one" (14:9 NASB).

In Job 31:15 and Mal 2:10 the word is used to denote that one and the same God created all men. The reference to the one Shepherd in Eccl 12:11 probably indicates that God is the only source of wisdom. B.K.W.]

Bibliography: Knight, A. F., "The Lord is One," Exp T 79: 8–10. TDOT, I, pp. 193–200. THAT, I, pp. 104–106.

H.W.

62 אחה (*'ḥh*). **Assumed root of the following.**
62a †אָח (*'āḥ*) ***II, brother.***
62b אַחֲוָה (*'aḥăwâ*) ***brotherhood.***
62c †אָחוֹת (*'āḥôt*) ***sister.***

'āḥ. ***Brother, relative, fellow countryman, friend.*** From a root common to all Semitic languages, *'āḥ* occurs 630 times in the OT. Owing to its wide range of meanings and the practice of polygamy, it is sometimes necessary to describe a full brother as the son of one's mother (Deut 13:6 [H 7]; Ps 50:20; Jud 8:19). The relationship between full brothers was extremely close, so the admonition to kill a brother who has become an idolater is severe indeed (Deut 13:6 [H 7]). Every man is expected to be his brother's keeper (Gen 4:9). The OT is replete with stories about half-brothers, those with different mothers. Abraham was Sarah's half-brother (Gen 20:5, 12), and his sons Ishmael and Isaac were born to Hagar and Sarah. The rivalry between Joseph and his half-brothers turned into hatred (Gen 37:2–5), and Absalom's hatred for Amnon resulted in murder (II Sam 13:29). Even full brothers like Cain and Abel, or Jacob and Esau had similar experiences. The Levites, however, properly put loyalty to God above family solidarity when they killed their own sons and brothers guilty of idolatry (32:29).

More remote descendants from a common father are called brothers. Thus "brother" occurs together with "children of Israel" (Deut 24:7). "Brother" is used more widely of Abraham's nephew Lot (Gen 13:8) and Laban's nephew Jacob (Gen 29:15). Members of the same tribe are also called "brothers," fellow-Levites (Num 16:10) or Simeonites (Num 25:6). The "relatives" of Samson among whom he should have selected a wife probably refer to his own tribe of Dan (Jud 14:3).

The meaning also includes all the children of Israel generally, as the parallelism with "brothers" shows (Lev 25:46; Deut 3:18). This is doubtless the background of the NT usage of "brothers" as fellow believers. Moses' fellow countrymen slaving in Egypt were called "his brothers" (Ex 2:11; 4:18). All were descended from Abraham and Jacob. Israel's prophets (Deut 18:15) and kings (Deut 17:15) must be "brothers" and not foreigners. Israelites were not to take advantage of the financial distress of other Israelites (Lev 25:35; Neh 5:8), who were to be considered as "friends" ("neighbors," *rēa'*) or "brothers" (Deut 15:2). The word is used as a parallel or synonym with "neighbor" (Lev 19:17; Jer 9:4 [H 3]). In Prov there is reference to a friend who is better than a brother (18:24; 27:10). When David eulogized Jonathan, he called him a "brother" in this deep sense (II Sam 1:26).

Sometimes various nations claimed "brother" status. Israel referred to Edom as "my brother" (Num 20:14), partly because Esau and Isaac were sons of Abraham. Several times Edom is condemned for mistreating brother Israel (Amos 1:11; Ob 10, 12). Hiram, king of Tyre, called Solomon "my brother" (I Kgs 9:13), but it is also Tyre which is judged for ignoring a "treaty of friendship" (literally, "brotherhood," Amos 1:9).

"Brother" is also used by Jacob to address strangers politely (Gen 29:4). The old man of Gibeah calls his perverted neighbors "brothers" (Jud 19:23), when Job's term would have been more appropriate: "I have become a brother to jackals" (30:29). In the Mari tablets and west semitic inscriptions, the word is used to address persons of equal rank and to refer to professional colleagues as well as kinsmen.

Some authorities have attributed the importance of brothers to a fratriarchal framework. Rule of brothers is known in the near east, and Laban's behavior toward his sister Rebekah may be an example of fratriarchy. Even though their father was still living (Gen 24:50), it was Laban who played the leading role.

Speiser likens the claims of Abraham and Isaac that their wives were "sisters" to a similar custom in Nuzi where a high-born wife was adopted to be also a sister. This gave her higher status and helps to explain the actions of these patriarchs. Unfortunately, the custom was not recognized in Egypt and Gerar. It was evidently derived from an old fratriarchate. For details see E. A. Speiser *Oriental and Biblical Studies* (Univ. of Pennsylvania, 1967, pp. 62–82).

The responsibilities of brothers are also known through the institution of Levirate marriage. If a man died without having a son, his brother was obligated to marry the widow and name her firstborn son after his brother to "build up his brother's house" (Deut 25:5–10; Gen 38:7–9). It was a serious sin, however, to have sexual relations with a brother's wife while he was still alive (Lev 18:16; 20:21). The oldest son was given a double portion of the inheritance (Deut 21:17). A priest was permitted to defile himself for the death of a sister or brother (Lev 21:2). Apart from these, no other laws involving brothers are mentioned in OT legal materials.

'āḥôt. ***Sister, relative, beloved.*** Derived from the same root as "brother" and with the same semantic range, it occurs only 114 times. Again, the distinction between full sister and half-sister is not clear (Gen 20:5). Usually to indicate the latter the father is said to be the same (Ezk 22:11).

"Sister" can also be used in the sense of "close relative" (Gen 24:60), a woman of the same nationality (Num 25:18), or a close friend (Prov 7:4). The meaning "beloved" or "darling" is clear in Song 4:9–12 and 5:1–2, where "sister" occurs parallel to "bride" four times. This may stem from an earlier custom, according to which it was permissable to marry one's sister (Gen 20:5f.). In Hurrian society it was also the practice for husbands in the upper classes to adopt their wives as "sisters" to form the strongest marriage bond. This fratriarchal feature may explain the frequent wife-sister motif of Genesis (see *'āḥ* "brother").

In Lev 18:9, 11 sexual relations with a sister or half-sister are forbidden. Amnon's rape of his half-sister Tamar, Absalom's full sister, must be understood in this light (II Sam 13:1f.). Since "sister" is used in the expression "one to another" (Ex 26:3), some scholars interpret Lev 18:18 as a condemnation of polygamy. Context strongly argues against this, however.

Israel and Judah are called "sisters" in Jer 3:7, and Jerusalem is castigated as a sister of Samaria and Sodom (Ezk 16:46).

Bibliography: Gordon, C. H., "Fratriarchy in the Old Testament," JBL 54: 223–31. Neufeld, Edward, "The Prohibition against Loans at Interest in Ancient Hebrew Laws," HUCA 26: 355–412. Riemann, Paul A., "Am I My Brother's Keeper?" Interp 24: 482–91. Speiser, E. A., "The Wife-Sister Motif in the Patriarchal Narratives," in *Oriental and Biblical Studies,* University of Pennsylvania, 1967, pp. 62–82. TDOT, I, pp. 188–92. THAT, I, pp. 98–103. For a different view, cf. Kitchen, K. A., *The Bible in its World,* Paternoster, 1977, p. 70.

H.W.

63 אָחוּ (*'āḥû*) ***reeds, rushes.***

אַחֲוָה (*'aḥăwâ*). See no. 62b.
אָחוֹת (*'āḥôt*). See no. 62c.

64 אָחַז (*'āḥaz*) ***to take hold of, seize, grasp.***

Derivative

64a †אֲחֻזָּה (*'ăḥūzzâ*) ***possession.***

Most of the verb's sixty-eight occurrences are in the Qal stem, but several Niphal forms are found. Its uses are rather evenly divided between the literal and metaphorical, both positive and negative.

The basic idea of the root is "to take hold of." Jacob "took hold" of Esau's heel (Gen 25:26); Samson "took hold" of the city gate (Jud 16:3); Ruth "held" the cloak as Boaz poured six measures of barley into it (Ruth 3:15). The curtains of Xerxes's palace were held by cords of linen on silver rings (Est 1:6). Men could "hold" or "wear" swords (Song 3:8).

Pertaining to architecture, it is used of the floors of the side rooms that were "attached" to the temple by cedar beams (I Kgs 6:10), or of the footstool attached to the throne (II Chr 9:18, the only Hophal usage). Once it is applied to "bolting" the city gates (Neh 7:3).

Sometimes "to take hold of" has the violent connotation of "seize" or "catch." The Israelites caught Adoni-bezek (Jud 1:6) and Jephthah caught and killed the men of Ephraim unable to pronounce "Shibboleth" (Jud 12:6; II Sam 2:21). A ram is caught in a thicket (Gen 22:13) and a fish in a net (Eccl 9:12). Job says that God has "grasped me by the neck and shaken me to pieces" (16:12).

"To take" can also refer to selection, as the men taken by lot (I Chr 24:6) or the two percent of the plunder taken as the Levites' share (Num 31:30, 47).

Metaphorically, the righteous man is said to "hold to his way" (Job 17:9). One can "grasp" an idea or "take hold" of folly (Eccl 7:18; 2:3). God in his grace will "take hold of my right hand" as a sign of his guidance and favor (Ps 73:23; cf. Isa 45:1, *ḥāzaq*). Psalm 139:10 speaks of God's right hand leading and "laying hold" of the Psalmist. In Deut 32:41 the Lord sharpens his sword "to take hold of justice."

A common idiom is to be seized by pain, sorrow or fear, often as a woman in childbirth. Anguish grips the enemies of Israel (Ex 15:14–15), but Israel herself suffers labor pains as she faces exile (Jer 13:21). King Saul was seized by the agony of death on the battlefield (II Sam 1:9), and the nations of the world endure pain and anguish as the day of the Lord approaches (Isa 13:8–9).

In the Niphal stem the verb usually means "to acquire property," thus overlapping with the noun *'aḥūzzâ* "possession." Sometimes both noun and verb occur in the same verse (Josh 22:9, 19). The Niphal may arrive at this meaning through its reflexive use, "to take for oneself."

The property in view is almost always land. Hamor invited Jacob and his sons to "acquire property" in Shechem and Canaan (Gen 34:10). Later, Joseph gave his father and brothers possession of the best land of Egypt (Gen 47:11, 27), but only as a temporary residence.

'ăḥūzzâ. ***Possession, property.*** (KJV and ASV consistently use "possession" but RSV occasionally renders "property.") The majority of its sixty-six uses pertain to the possession of land (the verb is so used only in the Niphal). The word is also used in conjunction with "inheritance" (*naḥălâ*).

Normally the property under discussion was located in the land of Canaan. All of that land had been promised to Abraham as "an everlasting possession" (Gen 17:8), a promise repeated to Jacob (Gen 48:4). Five times in Genesis, Abraham's purchase of the Cave of Machpelah is mentioned (23:4, 9, 20; 49:30; 50:13). By gaining possession of this burial site for Sarah, Abraham made the down payment on the eventual full possession of the land. Canaan is called "the land of the LORD's possession" in Josh 22:19, to distinguish it from Transjordan where the tribes of Reuben, Gad, and Manasseh chose to settle (22:9).

Within Canaan each family had its individual property, considered its inheritance. Even if it had to be leased to others, or was consecrated to the Lord, the land always reverted to the original owner in the year of Jubilee (Lev 25:10, 13, 28; 27:24). The daughters of Zelophehad were successful in their bid to acquire property as an inheritance, since they had no brothers (Num 27:7).

The Levites received no land as a possession, but they did have cities and their surrounding fields (Lev 25:33). The *Lord* was the possession of the Levites; he was their inheritance and share (Ezk 44:28; Num 18:20).

It was the Lord who promised to the Messiah, son of David, that the ends of the earth would be his possession (Ps 2:8).

Once, in Lev 25:45–46, persons are called property. Israelites were allowed to keep resident aliens as their permanent possession.

Bibliography: Yaron, R., "A Document of Redemption from Ugarit," VT 10: 83–90. THAT, I, pp. 107–109.

H.W.

65 אחח ('ḥḥ) **I. Assumed root of the following.**
65a אֹחַ ('ōaḥ) ***jackal.*** Occurs only in Isa 13:21.

66 אחח ('ḥḥ) **II. Possible root of the following.**
66a אָח ('āḥ) ***III, firepot, brazier.***

67 אחל ('ḥl). **Assumed root of the following.**
67a אַחְלָה ('aḥlâ) ***ah that!***
67b †אַחְלָמָה ('aḥlāmâ) ***amethyst, jasper.***

'aḥlāmâ. ***Amethyst.*** Found only in Ex 28:19 and 39:12, refers to a stone in the third row on the breastpiece of judgment worn by the high priest. "Amethyst" is a transliteration of the Septuagint word. The identification is not certain. Amethyst is a purple stone, perhaps corundum. KB favors a red or brown jasper.

68 אָחַר ('āḥar) ***tarry, delay, defer.*** The RSV is similar, NIV "remain," "lose no time." The NIV uses "delay" usually in place of "tarry."

Derivatives

68a †אַחֵר ('aḥēr) ***another.***
68b אַחַר ('aḥar) ***after, behind (of place); after, afterwards (of time);*** used as an adverb, "afterwards" and also as a conjunction with *'ăshēr* "after that." Often used in the plural form *'aḥărê* especially with suffixes. A very common word.
68c אַחֲרַי ('aḥăray) ***afterwards; only in Prov 28:23.***
68d †אָחוֹר ('āḥôr) ***back part, the rear, mostly in adverbial phrases, "backward."***
68e אֲחֹרַנִּית ('ăḥōranît) ***backwards.***
68f אַחֲרוֹן (aḥărôn) ***hindermost, west, behind (of place), latter, last, coming after (of time);*** the feminine *'aḥărônâ* is used adverbially.
68g †אַחֲרִית ('aḥărît) ***after part, end (of place), latter part, future (of time).***

The verb *'āḥar* is only used seventeen times mainly in the Piel and is not as significant as its derivatives. It refers to situations of staying behind, delaying, waiting (but not waiting in hope like *yāḥal* or *qāwâ*).

'aḥēr. ***Another.*** This word is often used in normal situations, "another place," "other seven years," etc. Of remark is only the frequent phrase in the plural "other gods." It is used in the first commandment (Ex 20:3), in the warnings of Deut 13:2 [H 3] ff., of the prophets' rebukes (Jer 7:6 ff.). It appears sixty-three times according to BDB. Only in Ps 16:4 and Isa 42:8 is it used absolutely. In the difficult verse Ps 16:4, we may perhaps take the word "sorrows" (*'ass^{e}bôtām*) of the first stich from the root *'āṣab* II (as does the Targum) and read "their idols." This would make a better balance for "other [gods]" in the parallel.

'āḥôr. ***Back part, backwards.*** This derivative is less used than others (forty-one times). The common meaning is just "backward." Enemies are turned backward. It is used ethically in Jer 7:24, "they went backward and not forward." Ezekiel's scroll was written within and without (i.e. on the back).

Theologically, the only instance that calls for discussion is Ex 33:23, "thou shalt see my back, but my face shall not be seen" (KJV, most versions the same). But in no other place is the word used for the back of a person's anatomy. This is *gab* or *gaw* or *'ōrep*. The word *'āḥôr* means "back" in the sense of direction. Joab saw the battle before and behind him (II Chr 13:14). Ezekiel saw the apostate twenty-five leaders facing the east with their backs toward the temple, i.e. it was behind them (Ezk 8:16). Is it not therefore probable that in the theophany of Ex 33:23 the emphasis is not on an extreme anthropomorphism saying that Moses could see God's back but not his face? Rather, it was meant that Moses could see the glory and afterglow behind the Lord as he passed by, but his very presence could not be seen. Of course the anthropomorphism is possible and not even objectionable, but a semi-physical distinction between face and back is apparently not the strict meaning of the words.

'aḥărît. ***After part, latter part, future.*** Used sixty-one times, this word is also not as common as some other derivatives, but has theological import. As is clear from other derivatives, the general meaning of the root is after, later, behind, following. H. W. Wolff has likened the Hebrew conception of time to the view a man has when he is rowing a boat. He sees where he has been and backs into the future (lecture notes). It is true that *qedem* means "before" as well as "ancient times." So the root *'āḥar* refers to what is "behind" as well as to "future things." It might be observed that this is not necessarily due to the psychology of the Hebrews, for the usage was doubtless established in Canaanite before the Hebrews arrived. But *'aḥărît* does refer to the future.

There are two theological questions at issue. First, does *'aḥărît hayyāmîm* (the end of the days) refer to the general future, or more specifically to the last days, the final segment of time? The writer has argued elsewhere that it usually refers just to the general future ("The Last Days in the Bible and Qumran," in *Jesus of Nazareth, Savior and Lord,* ed. C. F. H. Henry, Eerdmans, 1966, pp. 74–79). The second question is, does *'aḥărît* alone sometimes refer to the future life?

As to the first point, the expression *'aḥărît hayyāmîm* is used fourteen times (Gen 49:1; Num 24:14; Deut 4:30; 31:29; Isa 2:2 = Mic 4:1; Jer 23:20; 30:24; 48:47; 49:39; Ezk 38:16; Dan 2:28 [Aram.] and 10:14; Hos 3:5). The KJV translates the Gen, Isa and Mic references with "last days," the rest with "latter days." The RSV uses "latter days" except for Gen and Deut 31:29 where it has "days to come." The NASB uses "latter days" seven times, "last days" six times and "days to come" in Gen and Num. The NIV uses "later days" in Deut 4:30; "last days" in Isa, Mic and Hos, "the future" in Dan 10:14 and "days to come" in the other passages.

It can be seen that none of these translations use the phrase as an invariable technical term for the final segment of time. The interpretation depends on the context. It is possible to use this phrase both for the eschaton and for the general future because obviously all eschatology is future, but not all future is eschatology. It does seem clear that Isa 2:2ff. (=Mic 4:1 ff.) refers to the eschaton ("last days" KJV, NASB, NIV), but that the reviving of Moab and Edom are simply prophesied for some future day (Jer 48:47; 49:39; cf. the Ammonites, 44:6). The above-cited article suggests that the corresponding NT phrase also often refers to the general future, not to the final segment of time. This brings into question the idea that the NT church thought of itself as living in the "last days." The "perilous times" spoken of in I Tim 4:1 may just be a serious warning for the indefinite future (cf. Mt 24:6).

On the second question, does *'aḥărît* alone ever refer to the future life, M. Dahood has claimed that it sometimes clearly does (*Proverbs and Northwest Semitic Philology,* Pontifical Biblical Institute, 1963, pp. 48–49, 51). There are several interrelated verses in Prov using our word. Proverbs 24:14 (parallel to 23:18) says there is an *'aḥărît* (NIV "future hope") for the righteous. His hope (*tiqwâ*) will not be cut off. Proverbs 11:7 says that when a wicked man dies, his hope (*tiqwâ*) perishes. For the righteous, Prov 12:28 promises life and immortality (*'al mawet,* "no death", Dahood, *op. cit.* p. 28). But the evil man has no future hope (*'aḥărît*) and the lamp of the wicked will be snuffed out (Prov 24:20, NIV). Dahood holds that Prov 20:20 refers to the afterlife: his lamp will be snuffed out in the sleep of darkness (i.e. death). There is thus an interlocking of the words *'aḥărît* in the sense of a blessed future after death, *tiqwâ* "hope" beyond death, and for the righteous *'al mawet* "no death." Dahood points out that the same collocation (except for *tiqwâ*) occurs in Ugaritic, II Aqhat VI 11. 26–36 which H. L. Ginsberg translates, "Ask for life O Aqhat, the Youth, ask for life (*ḥym*) and I'll give it thee, for deathlessness (*bl mt* = Heb. *'al mawet*), and I'll bestow it on thee. I'll make thee count years with Baal.... But Aqhat, the Youth answers.... Further life (*'uhryt* = Heb. *'aḥărît*)—how can mortal attain it? How can mortal man attain life enduring?" Certainly the collocation of verses in Prov along with the similar usage of the key words in Ugaritic seems to warrant Dahood's conclusion that the "affirmation of a future life... seems inescapable."

Bibliography: THAT, I, pp. 110–17.

R.L.H.

69 אֲחַשְׁדַּרְפְּנִים (*'ăḥashdarpᵉnîm*) ***satraps.***

70 אֲחַשְׁתְּרָן (*'ăḥashtᵉrān*) ***royal.*** Occurs only in Est 8:10–14.

אַט (*'aṭ*). See no. 72b.

71 אטד (*'ṭd*). **Assumed root of the following.**
71a אָטָד (*'āṭād*) ***bramble, buckthorn.***

אֵטוּן (*'ēṭûn*). See no. 73b.

72 אטט (*'ṭṭ*). **Assumed root of the following.**
72a †אִטִּי (*'iṭṭî*) ***charmer*** (KJV, ASV, NAB); sorcerer (RSV, amplified); magician (Berkeley); wizard (JB); oraclemonger (NEB).
72b אַט (*'aṭ*) ***gentleness,*** as adv., ***softly.***

'iṭṭî. ***Charmer.*** This word, describing some variety of occultist, appears only in Isa 19:3 where it is plural (*'iṭṭîm*). Because of the context, a list including idols, mediums, and wizards, its meaning can be easily guessed. Furthermore, the adverb *'aṭ* is formed of the same radicals meaning "slowly," "softly," "gently," or "secretly" (cf. Gen 33:14; II Sam 18:5; I Kgs 21:27; Job 15:11; Isa 8:6). There is an Arabic cognate which means "to emit a moaning or creaking sound." Isaiah 8:19 and 29:4 indicate that these various kinds of witches and wizards made low, chirping or muttering sounds. Although *'iṭṭî* does not appear in either passage, the general representation of necromancy in the Bible furnishes a satisfactory background to the understanding of *'iṭṭî* along these lines.

The Hebrew words *lā'aṭ, la'ṭ,* and *lāṭ* may also shed light. The first is a verb probably derived as a by-form from *lûṭ* that occurs as a term for "cover" or "cover over" in II Sam 19:5. The second is perhaps an adverb appearing in Jud 4:21 only and meaning "softly" or "secretly." The KJV translates the third *lāṭ* as "with enchantments" in Ex 7:22; 8:3, 14, and as "softly," "secretly," and "privily" in Ruth 3:7; I Sam 18:22 and 24:5, respectively.

R.L.A.

אִטִּי (*'iṭṭî*). See no. 72a.

73 אָטַם (*'āṭam*) ***shut, shut up.***

Derivative

73b אֵטוּן (*'ēṭûn*) ***thread, yarn.*** Occurs only in Prov 7:16.

74 אָטַר (*'āṭar*) ***shut up, close.*** Occurs only in Ps 69:16.

Derivative

74a אִטֵּר (*'iṭṭēr*) ***shut, bound.*** This adjective occurs only in Jud 3:15; 20:16.

75 אַי (*'ay*) ***where.***

Derivatives

75a אַיֵּה (*'ayyēh*) ***where?***
75b †אֵיךְ (*'êk*) ***how?***
75c †אֵיכָה (*'êkâ*) ***how? where?***
75d †אֵיכוֹ (*'êkô*) ***where?***
75e †אֵיכָכָה (*'êkākâ*) ***how?***
75f †אַיִן (*'ayin*) ***where?***
75g †אָן (*'ān*) ***where?***
75h †אֵיפֹה (*'êpōh*) ***where?***

The interrogative adverb *'ay* is related to the Ugaritic *'y*. Most of its thirty occurrences are in rhetorical questions. It combines with other adverbs to form *'êk* "how"; *'êkâ* "how, where"; *'êkākâ* "how"; *'êpōh* "where." The word *'ayyēh* is probably a lengthened form of *'ay*. The meaning and usage are almost identical. Parallel passages interchange *'ay* and *'ayyēh* (Isa 36:19 = II Kgs 19:13).

The interrogative adverb is sometimes used in requesting information (Gen 18:9; 22:7; I Sam 9:18), but more often no answer is expected. This is particularly true of poetic passages. If God is on your side, where is the fury of the oppressor (Isa 51:13) or, in Job 14:10, after man expires, where is he?

Frequently "where" is used by men questioning the existence and power of God. Individuals (Mic 7:10) as well as nations ask, "Where is your God?" (Ps 79:10; 115:2), or where is the word of God (Jer 17:15) or the God of justice? (Mal 2:17). Gideon, doubting, asked what happened to the miracles he had heard about (Jud 6:13). The same earnest longing characterizes the plea for God's action in Isa 63:11.

The Lord employed sarcasm to ask Judah where were her gods, when that idol-loving nation met distress (Deut 32:37; Jer 2:28). *'ay,* strengthened by the enclitic *zeh,* is used as the Lord asks where there is a house that could possibly contain him (Isa 66:1).

The strengthened interrogative also occurs in Est 7:5. The king asked where the queen's tormentor might be found. Rhetorical questions with *zeh* are illustrated by II Chr 18:23 and Job 38:19.

Combined with *mizzeh, 'ay* (or *'ê*) means "where have you come from?" This construction is used by human beings (I Sam 30:13), angels (Gen 16:8), and even by God in addressing Satan (Job 2:2).

'êk. ***How.*** This interrogative pronoun is used in simple questions, e.g. Jehoiakim's official asks Baruch, "How did you write these words?" (Jer 36:17). But usually it is used in rhetorical questions to indicate reproach ("how dare you say I love you," Jud 16:15), despair ("how the mighty have fallen," I Sam 1:19), amazement ("how the oppressor has ceased," Isa 14:4), horror ("how they are destroyed in a moment," Ps 73:19), or desire ("how I would set you among my sons," Jer 3:19).

'êkâ. ***How, where.*** A more emphatic form of *'êk,* applied to reasoning (Jer 8:8), mocking (Ps 73:11), and exclamations (Jer 48:17). Laments in particular are stressed (Isa 1:21; Lam 1:1; 2:1; 4:1–2). The meaning "where" is also attested (II Kgs 6:13; Song 1:7).

'êkô. ***Where.*** Found only in II Kgs 6:13, where the written text has *'êkoh.* This is probably another example of *'êkâ* "where."

'êkākâ. ***How.*** Formed *'ê* plus *kākâ,* "thus," it occurs twice in Song 5:3 in the sense of "must I."

In Est 8:6 the queen wonders how she can bear to see the destruction of the Jews.

'ayin. *Where.* Probably derived from *'ay*. This adverb is always combined with *min* in *mē'ayin*. It is a synonym of *'ê mizzeh* (see under *'āy*). Often travelers were asked, "Where have you come from?" (Gen 29:4; Jud 19:17), as God asked Satan in Job 1:7. It occurs in rhetorical questions expressing frustration (Num 11:13; II Kgs 6:27) or distress (Jer 30:7). According to Ps 121:1–2, one's help comes from the Lord. In this famous verse, the original KJV read, "I will lift up mine eyes unto the hilles: from whence commeth my helpe." The "from whence" was interpreted by some as a relative pronoun, indicating that the help was thought of as coming *via* the hills. But it seems more likely that the Hebrew is a question, and the answer is in v. 2—that is, in the Lord himself.

'ayin may be contrasted to the form *'ān*, which is not combined with *min*.

'ān. *Where.* Contracted from *'ayin*, it often occurs with the locative with verbs of motion to ask, "where to" in questions directed to man (Gen 32:17 [H 18]) or God (II Sam 2:1). The compound *'ad 'ānâ* "how long," is used by God, complaining about Israel's prolonged lack of faith or obedience (Ex 16:28; Num 14:11). Men also ask God how long it will be before he responds (Hab 1:2; Ps 13:1–2 [H 2–3]).

'êpô. *Where, what kind.* Infrequently used (nine times), it is compared with *'ay* or *'ayyê*. Once it means "what kind of men" (Jud 8:18). It is a combination of *'ay* (q.v.) and *pōh* (q.v.).

Bibliography: Muir, J., "The Significance of אין in Genesis 5,24 and Psalm 39,13," Exp T 50: 476–77. THAT, I, pp. 125–26.

H.W.

76 אִי (*'î*) ***III, alas!*** Occurs only in Eccl 4:10; 10:16.

77 אִי (*'î*) ***IV, not.*** This adverb is used only once (Job 22:30). It is probably to be identified in the name *'î kābôd* "No Glory."

אִי (*'î*) **I, II.** See nos. 39a, 43a.

78 אָיַב (*'āyab*) ***to be an enemy.*** (ASV, RSV translate similarly).

Derivatives

78a †אֵיבָה (*'êbâ*) ***enmity, hatred.***
78b †אִיּוֹב (*'îyôb*) ***Job.***

The basic meaning of the verb is "to be hostile to," "to be or treat as an enemy." This meaning is evident in the only non-participial occurrence of the word, Ex 23:22, where God becomes an enemy to Israel's enemies. In every other instance the word is used in the participial form *'ōyēb* meaning "enemy."

The Ugaritic cognate *'b* conveys the concept of hostility, as used in parallelism with *šn'* "hate" in UT 16: Text 51.7.35,36.

While the word usually refers simply to the enemies of a nation or an individual, theological implications are inherent in a number of contexts. The defeated enemy was a mark of God's blessing on Israel (Lev 26:7–8; Deut 6:19). But when Israel forsook God she could expect to be defeated at the hands of her enemies (Lev 26:17, 25, 32 etc.; Num 14:42; Deut 1:42; II Kgs 21:14).

Israel's victory over her enemies was conditioned upon obedience, e.g. observing God's commandments (Lev 26:3; cf. v. 7) and repenting (I Kgs 8:33; II Chr 6:24).

The defeat of David's enemies was a mark of God's favor on him (II Sam 7:9; 22:18, 41).

The destruction of Israel's enemies was seen as a result of God's intervention and thus became evidence of God's sovereignty (Josh 23:1; Jud 8:34; I Kgs 8:46).

Even God has enemies, but they will experience certain retribution (Isa 66:6; Ps 37:20; 68:1 [H 2]).

The word occurs in several contexts in an ethical sense. One should not rejoice over the fall of an enemy (Prov 24:17). Even one's enemies will be at peace with him when his ways please the Lord (Prov 16:7).

'êbâ. *Enmity, hatred.* The meaning of this word, as shown by the root *'āyab*, is "hostility" or "hatred." In most of its occurrences it connotes the hatred in which a hostile act is perpetrated whether in a legal context (Num 35:21–22) or a context describing the hostile acts of Israel's enemies (Ezk 25:15; 35:5).

'îyôb. *Job.* The etymology of the name Job is uncertain. Some have understood the name to be a derivative of *'āyab* "to be hostile," the participial form of which is the common word for "enemy." This supposed derivation would have the literary significance of depicting Job's adamant attitude in the face of his trials as he refused to accept the suffering imposed on him. If seen as a passive form of *'āyab* the name would connote the concept of "the object of hostility" (BDB) depicting Job as one who suffered at the hand of God. There is little linguistic evidence for these views however.

Another suggestion is that the name derives from the Arabic *'wb* "turn" and connotes the concept of repentance (BDB).

The name has been attested in various forms in several West Semitic texts as a common proper name (KB in loc.) which may mean either "no father" or "where is (my) father?" It is quite possible that the name bears no literary significance and is rather to be seen as the name of an ancient personage whose conduct in trial made him a worthy example of the godly man's attitude toward suffering.

Job is cited along with Noah and Daniel in Ezk 14:14,20 as an ancient worthy who was an example of righteousness.

Bibliography: Baab, O. J., "The Book of Job," Interp S: 329–43. Hawthorne, R. R., "Jobine Theology," BS 101: 64–75, 173–86, 290–303, 417–33; 102: 37–54. Pope, Marvin, *Job* in AB, pp. 6–7. TDNT, II, pp. 811–13. TDOT, I, pp. 212–18. THAT, I, pp. 118–21.

T.E.M.

אֵיד (*'êd*). See no. 38c.

אַיָּה (*'ayyâ*). See no. 43b.

אַיֵּה (*ayyēh*). See no. 75a.

אִיּוֹב (*'îyôb*). See no. 78b.

אֵיךְ (*'êk*), אֵיכָה (*'êkâ*). See no. 75.

79 אֱיָל (*'ĕyāl*) ***strength*** (ASV "help").

The connotation of help is supported by the Syriac from which this word is probably borrowed. The root *'ul* apparently occurs in Ugaritic, however, in parallelism with *'zm* (UT 19: no. 164) "strength." In Ps 88:4 [H 5], the word occurs in a couplet in which the writer describes himself as reckoned among the dead, a concept which seems to support the connotation "strength" in the expression "no strength" of line two.

79a אֱיָלוּת (*'ĕyālût*) ***strength.*** (ASV "succor"; RSV "help.")

The basic meaning of this word seems to be "strength" (see *'ĕyāl*. This feminine abstract use of the word occurs as a surrogate for God in Ps 22:20 (its only occurrence), where it is used in parallelism with the tetragrammeton. According to KB it is merely a feminine form of *'ĕyāl* above. For related words native to Hebrew see 'ûl.

T.E.M.

אַיִל (*'ayil*). See no. 45d,e,f,g.

אַיָּל (*'ayyāl*), אַיָּלָה (*'ayyālâ*). See no. 45k,l.

אֱיָלוּת (*'ĕyālût*). See no. 79a.

אֵילָם (*'êlām*). See no. 45j.

80 אים (*'ym*). **Assumed root of the following.**

80a †אָיֹם (*'āyōm*) ***terrible.***

80b †אֵימָה (*'êmâ*) ***dread.***

'āyōm. ***Terrible*** (RSV "dread"). In its occurrences (Song 6:4, 10; Hab 1:7), the word connotes the awesome dread inspired by a mighty army. It is used metaphorically in Song 6:4, 10.

'êmâ. ***Dread, fear, horror, idol, terrible, terror.*** (RSV similar except that it translates as "dread wrath" in Prov 20:2.)

In all of its occurrences the word *'êmâ* connotes the concept of "fear." It occurs only once in a metaphorical sense in Jer 50:38 where it means "idol"; evidently in the sense of that which is to be feared.

Bibliography: TDOT, I, pp. 219–21.

T.E.M.

81 אַיִן (*'ayin*) ***else, except, to be gone, incurable, neither, never, no, nowhere, none, nor, nor any, nor anything, not, nothing, to nought, past, unsearchable, well nigh, without.*** (ASV and RSV are similar.)

This word is basically a negative substantive used most frequently in the construct form (*'ên*). The word therefore has no single meaning and the exact translation must be determined in each context. The negative concept is always present wherever the word is used. It is characteristically used to negate a noun or noun clause, cf. GKC par. 152 d and i–o.

As indicated above, the word is used in numerous negative expressions. Some basic usages of this negative root in the OT are noted below.

The word may express the idea of absence as in Gen 2:5, the lack of men to till. Related to this concept is the expression of non-existence (I Sam 10:14) or of that which is gone, has disappeared (I Kgs 20:40). We see this same idea in Eccl 3:14 where it expresses nothingness. Akin also is the usage in Isa 44:12, where the concept is that of fading out or failing, in reference to a man's strength. Finally, absence is seen as primary in the negative time concept of Ezk 28:19, "no more," "never more."

A second basic usage of this negative root is in the idea of alternatives. In Gen 30:1, the concept is that of either/or. In Gen 44:26 it is expressed as a condition (unless/except). Still in Gen (Gen 45:6), the negative alternative is expressed (neither/nor).

The third usage we shall note is that of impossibility. This is expressed in a variety of ways. The grain of Joseph, impossible to number, is so rendered (Gen 41:49). Limits which cannot be exceeded are similarly expressed (II Chr 20:25). Perhaps the most frequent use of the root to express impossibility is in negative compound concepts such as incurable (II Chr 21:18), unsearchable (Job 5:9), and infinite (Nah 3:9).

At times the root expresses the simple negative "not" as in Jud 14:3. It can also convey the concept "almost" as it does in Ps 73:2. In this latter usage it is close in function to the parallel word *kīm'at* also meaning "almost," "nearly."

Frequently the negative root is joined to inseparable pronouns forming in one word both the subject and the negative as in Ps 59:13 [H 14], "they shall not be" (cf. Ps 73:5; Gen 5:24; Ex 5:10). Sometimes the simple negative root accompanies the independent pronoun as in Neh 4:17.

Other Semitic languages have similar words to convey this negative concept, although for the most part they are not cognates of our Hebrew word. Among Semitic cognates used in a similar way are the Moabite *'n,* the Assyrian *iânu,* and particularly the Ugaritic *'yn* (UT, 19: no. 99).

J.B.S.

אַיִן (*'ayin*). See no. 75f.

82 אֵיפָה (*'êpâ*) ***ephah.*** (ASV, RSV generally the same, but RSV sometimes supplies the word for clarification.)

It is a dry measure, frequently mentioned in the OT, estimated to be equivalent to from three-eighths to two-thirds of a bushel.

There were ten ephahs in a homer (which is thought to be a donkey load) and ten omers in one ephah. The seah was probably one-third of an ephah. The ephah was the same as the liquid measure, the bath.

There is much uncertainty in the size of the bath and ephah. Estimates vary from about twenty-two liters (twenty dry quarts) to about forty-five liters (forty-one dry quarts) with the former favored by most. Jar handles have been found stamped *btmlk* "bath of the royal standard." Unfortunately, no such jar has been found with enough pieces to reconstruct the jar and measure the capacity. Until that occurs, things are uncertain.

Moses had Aaron save one-tenth of an ephah of manna as a memorial (Ex 16:36). For a sin offering, one-tenth of an ephah of fine flour was required (Lev 5:11) and also for the offering on the day of Aaron's anointing (Lev 6:20 [H 13]; cf. Num 5:15; 28:5). In Ezk this is increased to one-sixth ephah for some offerings (Ezk 45:13; 46:14). Also, a cereal offering of one ephah was to accompany each bull or ram offered according to Ezk 45:24; 46:5, 11.

On one occasion a yield of an ephah for each homer planted indicated extremely hard times (Isa 5:10)—the yield being one tenth of the seed planted!

The ephah is used to measure such dry substances as flour, barley, and parched grain (Jud 6:19; Ruth 2:17; I Sam 17:17). Regarding the measurement of such grains, stern warnings were given. Different volumes of measure for the ephah were not allowed (Deut 25:14; Amos 8:5; Mic 6:10), rather, one just ephah was required (Lev 19:36; Deut 25:15; Ezk 45:10).

The ephah in Zech 5:6–10 is obviously figurative and much larger than the normal measuring container.

Bibliography: AI, pp. 199–203. Ap-Thomas, D. R., "The Ephah of Meal in Judges 6, 19," JTS 41: 175–77. Huey, F. B., "Weights and Measures," in ZPEB. Segre, Angelo, "A Documentary Analysis of Ancient Palestinian Units of Measure," JBL 64: 357–75.

J.B.S.

אֵיפֹה (*'êpōh*). See no. 75h.
אֵיפוֹא (*'êpô'*). See no. 144.

83 איש (*'ysh*). **Assumed root of the following.**
83a †אִישׁ (*'îsh*) ***man, mankind, champion, great man, husband, person, whatsoever, whosoever.*** (ASV, RSV similar.)

The word *'îsh* connotes primarily the concept of man as an individual and thus differs in that regard from the more general concepts inherent in the words *'ĕnôsh* and *'ādām* ("mankind").

Two possible roots have been suggested for the word, *'nsh* and *'ysh('wsh)*. If from the latter, the word *'îsh* may be related to the Akkadian *ishānu* meaning "strong."

The word is used variously in the OT. Most commonly it denotes any individual male. Less frequently it has the more specific connotation of "male," emphasizing the male sex, as distinct from the female sex (Ex 35:29; Lev 13:29; II Chr 15:13) or man in his sexual role ("to know a man," Gen 19:8, etc.). Characteristically this is *zākār*.

It is used in many technical expressions such as "man of the earth" (Gen 9:20) meaning "farmer," "man of the field," connoting a hunter (Gen 25:27) and "man of God," referring to a prophet (Deut 33:1, etc.).

Frequently the word functions as an individualizing element connoting the concept "each" as in "each person" (Gen 10:5). It also functions in a broadly inclusive sense meaning "whoever" (Lev 15:5).

One of the most common usages of *'îsh* is in the sense of "husband." The word begins to achieve significance in this sense first in Gen 2:23–24 where the origin of woman is described. While the derivation of *'ishshâ* from *'ish* suggested by this passage is difficult philologically (there may be no more than a word play), there is no question that the words "This... is bone of my bones... She shall be called woman because she was taken out of man" (v. 23), communicate a close and intimate relationship that Adam could not find apart from one who shared his own station and nature; indeed, his own life. It reflects God's desire to provide man with a companion who would be his intellectual and physical counterpart. The permanency intended in the relationship is expressed in the assertion that man should leave his parents and cleave to his wife.

A husband could divorce his wife under certain conditions (Deut 24:1–4) but divorce was not encouraged (Mal 2:16; Jer 3:1).

The relationship of husband to wife is used as a metaphor of God's relationship to his people. This relationship is the basis of assurance for the people of God in the book of Hosea where the marriage relationship forms a central motif (see Hos 2:16).

Man possesses great individual worth in the OT, for anyone who murders a man is himself to be put to death (Lev 24:17). God observes the ways of men (Job 34:21; Prov 5:21) and the invitation of wisdom goes out to all men (Prov 8:4) demonstrating God's concern for the individual.

As with *'ĕnôsh* a distinction obtains between God and man. Balaam observed that God was not man that he should lie (Num 23:19).

Bibliography: Hallevy, Raphael, "Man of God," JNES 17: 237–44. Hoffner, H. A., "Symbols for Masculinity and Femininity," JBL 85: 326–34. May, Herbert G., "Individual Responsibility and Retribution," HUCA 32: 107–20. TDOT, I, pp. 222–35. THAT, I, pp. 130–37.

T.E.M.

אִיתוֹן (*'îtôn*). See no. 188a.

84 אַךְ (*'ak*) ***surely*** (affirmative emphasis), ***but*** (restrictive emphasis), also as a particle of emphasis, not translated. (Great variety exists in actual translation due to the nature of this particle. Context and judgment of the translator will determine the word selected or whether to translate at all.)

This particle primarily conveys emphasis and often is not translated. When it is translated, the sense is either an emphatic affirmative (Gen 26:9; 29:14; Ex 31:13; Ex 31:13; Jer 19:19; Lam 2:16 etc.) or an emphatic restrictive (Gen 7:23; 9:4; 18:32; Ex 12:16; Lev 11:4; Num 22:20; Josh 22:19; I Sam 8:9, etc.).

At times either sense fits in the context, and translators differ in how they read it.

Many times no translation is preferable to either of the above alternatives. Only emphasis is intended, i.e. "Jacob was just gone out" (Gen 27:30); "the first day" (Ex 12:15); "on the tenth day" (Lev 23:27); "if the young men have kept themselves from women" (I Sam 21:4 [H 5]); "do not fret to do evil" (Ps 37:8).

Bibliography: Snaith, N. H., "The Meaning of Hebrew אַךְ," VT 14: 221–25.

J.B.S.

אַכְזָב (*'akzāb*). See no. 970b.
אַכְזָר (*'akzār*), אַכְזָרִי (*akzārî*). See nos. 971a,b.
אַכְזְרִיּוּת (*'akzeriyût*). See no. 971c.
אֲכִילָה (*'ăkîlâ*). See no. 85c.

85 אָכַל (*'akal*) ***eat, consume, devour, burn up, feed.*** (ASV and RSV are generally the same. One notable exception is found in Ps 27:2 where RSV has "slander" instead of "eat my flesh" in accordance with an Akkadian and Aramaic idiom, "to eat a piece of me" meaning "to slander me.")

Derivatives

85a †אֹכֶל (*'ōkel*) ***food.***
85b †אָכְלָה (*'oklâ*) ***food, fuel, meat, eating,*** describing often the act of consuming.
85c †אֲכִילָה (*ăkîlâ*) ***an eating, a meal, meat.***
85d †מַאֲכָל (*ma'ăkāl*) ***food, fruit, meat.***
85e †מַאֲכֶלֶת (*ma'ăkelet*) ***knife.***
85f מַאֲכֹלֶת (*ma'ăkōlet*) ***fuel.***
85g מַכֹּלֶת (*makkōlet*) ***food stuff, food.***

This same root occurs in Arabic, Assyrian and Aramaic as well as Ugaritic (UT 19: no. 104). Generally the meaning is the same but in the Aramaic as noted above, there is the idiomatic use with *qeraṣ* "to eat a piece of" meaning "to slander" (Dan 3:8).

The primary meaning of this root is "to consume." The object consumed depends on the subject. Predominantly, the subject is man or some animal and therefore the object consumed is some kind of food. If the subject is fire or some other non-animal consumer, then the object may be wood or other consumable material. Figuratively, droughts, famines, and pestilences are said to consume, meaning that they overcome. From this is also derived the usage of oppressors consuming their victims.

The basic meaning of "to consume" is used in at least six different ways. First, it occurs frequently in the context of hardship, whether deserved or not. Drought, fire, war, and other plagues devour the innocent as well as the guilty (Gen 31:40; Num 21:28; Jer 2:30; Joel 1:4; II Sam 18:8). Greedy oppressors, foreign nations as well as sinners in Israel, devour the innocent (Ps 14:4; Ps 79:7). Sometimes the devourer is an insect or an animal (I Kgs 21:23; Isa 51:8). Hardship is also associated with being forced to eat, actually or symbolically, what is unpleasant (Isa 36:12; Gen 3:14; Hos 10:13; Ps 127:2). This leads to the cause and effect relationship expressed in Ezk 18:2.

A second context for the root is in worship or devotion. Certain foods are either eaten (II Chr 30:18; Ex 23:15) or refused (Dan 1:12; 10:3) in devotion to the Lord. Sinners likewise eat before pagan gods (Ps 106:28; Ezk 18:11). The unbeliever is forbidden to eat in worship of the true God (Ex 12:48).

A third contextual use of the root, eating well, indicates prosperity (Joel 2:26; Gen 45:18; II Kgs 18:31; Prov 24:13; Deut 8:3) or the lack of prosperity when eating does not satisfy (Mic 6:14). Closely related to this is the circumstance of eating what others earned as a symbol of victory (Isa 61:6) but others eating of it symbolizes defeat (Isa 65:22).

A group of lesser contexts must also be noted. The root can denote being zealously involved or simply being consumed (Ps 69:9 [H 10]; Gen 31:15). Eating can also be indicative simply of reward for work done (Prov 27:18; Amos 7:12). One indication of the arrival of the blessed hope of believers is the time when no flesh, only vegetation, will be consumed (Isa 11:7), indicative of the state of blessedness before the fall of Adam into sin.

'ōkel. ***Food, meat, prey.*** This noun is a basic word for food. It first occurs in Gen 14:11 referring to the spoils of war. The primary use of the term is in the Joseph account (Gen 41–47). It seems throughout to refer to food seen as a necessity of life, vital. It is used particularly of that which the Lord provides. We see this in three stages: first, that provided for men and beasts in Eden before the fall (Gen 1:29–30); second, that provided for Noah and his family during the flood (Gen 6:21); and third, that provided after the flood to all men (Gen 9:3). God is the provider (Ex 16:15; Lev 11:39). Sometimes, in judgment, men become the food of fire (Ezk 15:4, 6; 21:32 [H 37]) and of wild beasts (Ezk 34:5, 8).

'oklâ. ***Food, fuel, meat, eating, often describing the act of consuming.*** This term is more general, anything which the Lord has determined to be edible.

'ăkilâ. ***An eating, a meal, meat.*** Occurs but once (I Kgs 19:8) and perhaps refers to some unique nourishment in that it sustains Elijah forty days.

ma'ăkāl. ***Food, fruit, meat.*** This term is also quite general in meaning but is used frequently of more dainty foods or delicacies (Gen 2:9; 3:6; 40:17; I Kgs 10:5; Job 33:20, etc.). These three derivatives have specialized and quite limited use.

ma'ăkelet. ***Knife.*** This word is used to denote the knife by which Abraham intended to sacrifice Isaac (Gen 22:6, 10) and the knife used by the Levite to dismember his concubine (Jud 19:29). It also describes the teeth of devourers of the poor slicing them in greed. *ma'ăkōlet* (two times) is found only in Isa 9 and means "fuel," occurring once in a passage of hope and once in a passage describing oppression (9:5 [H 4]; 9:19 [H 18]). *makkōlet* (once) apparently refers to a ration of food.

Bibliography: TDOT, I, pp. 236–41. THAT, I, pp. 138–41.

J.B.S.

86 אָכֵן (*'ākēn*) ***surely, truly, indeed.*** (In ASV and RSV generally the same although not always translated.)

The word occurs in four basic contexts expressing a note of surprise or exasperation: fear (Gen 28:16; Ex 2:14; Isa 40:7; Jer 3:23; 4:10; 8:8), warning (Job 32:8; Ps 82:7; Jer 3:20; Zeph 3:7), self-confidence (I Sam 15:32), and faith in God (Ps 31:22 [H 23]; 66:19; Isa 45:15; 49:4; 53:4; Jer 3:23). Among the Semitic languages it appears to be unique to Hebrew.

Bibliography: Goldbaum. Fredric J., "Two Hebrew Quasi-Adverbs: לכן and אכן," JNES 23: 132–35.

J.B.S.

87 אָכַף (*'ākap*) ***press, urge.*** Occurs only in Prov 16:26.

Derivative

87a אֶכֶף (*'ekep*) ***pressure.*** Occurs only in Job 33:7.

88 אכר (*'kr*). **Assumed root of the following.**

88a אִכָּר (*'ikkār*) ***plowman, husbandman.***

89 אַל (*'āl*) **I. Possible element of the following.**

89a אֶלְגָּבִישׁ (*'ĕlgābîsh*) ***hail.*** Occurs only in Ezk 13:11, 13; 38:22.

89b אַלְגּוּמִּים (*'algûmîm*) ***a tree*** (KJV "algum") from Lebanon.

89c אַלְמֻגִּים (*'almūggîm*) ***a tree*** (KJV "almug") from Lebanon. Occurs only in I Kgs 10:11–12.

89d אַלְקוּם (*'alqûm*) ***band of soldiers*** (Prov 30:31).

90 אַל (*'al*) ***II, not, no, nor, neither*** (this adverb of negation is usually reflected in ASV and RSV in the same general way, although the choice of negatives used varies).

This particle expresses the negative as either a wish (Gen 13:8; Jud 19:23) or a preference (Prov 17:12), thus indicating its more reserved intent than the very adamant *lō'*. Consistent with this concept, whenever it is used with a verb, the verb is in the jussive (which often is indistinguishable from the imperfect). Cf. GKC 109, c-e.

It can be also used in a command (II Kgs 9:15) but never with an imperative. The negative command is usually *lō'* with the indicative as in the Ten Commandments.

Finally, inasmuch as it expresses preference, it often occurs in prayers to God (Dan 9:19; Ps 31:1 [H 2]; 71:1), where it introduces a plea—"let me never. . . ."

Bibliography: Bright, John, "The Apodictic Prohibition: Some Observations," JBL 92: 184–204.

J.B.S.

אֵל (*'el*). See no. 93a.

91 אֶל (*'el*) ***unto, into, beside, against, in reference to.*** (ASV, RSV are generally the same but varying in the specific English preposition used due to differing interpretations.)

The preposition expresses primarily motion toward someone or something. As such, it occurs in a wide variety of contexts expressing motion, attitude, direction, or location.

Physical motion "toward" is the primary concept expressed by this preposition with numerous examples (e.g. Gen 1:9; 14:7). The motion sometimes carries "into" that which is approached, as in Gen 6:18 "into the ark."

Closely akin is the concept of mental motion as seen in God's grief "into" his heart (Gen 6:6).

We see also its use to express motion toward, in the sense of "in reference to," a kind of unseen gesture (Gen 20:2) where Abraham speaks "in reference to" his wife, not "to" her (cf. also I Sam 3:21, "in reference to" the ark being taken).

At times the sense of motion is lost altogether and the description of a state or condition prevails, e.g. Gen 24:11, "by a well"; or II Sam 14:30, "by mine" rather than "unto mine." For this reason, apparently, the preposition came to be interchangeable with *'al* at times, e.g. Gen 22:12, "upon the lad"; Josh 5:14, "upon his face." This interchange of *'al* and *'el* may have occurred in the living language but may partly be due to scribal changes. It was assisted by the circumstance that Aram has no *'el* and uses *'al* (from *'ālal* "go in") in the sense of Hebrew *'el*; cf. BDB, p. 41.

Finally, the preposition can also mean "against," although motion toward is evident, as in Gen 4:8, where Cain "rose up against Abel." Here *'el* no doubt retains something of the original sense of both physical and mental motion toward.

J.B.S.

אֶלְגָּבִישׁ (*'elgābîsh*). See no. 89a.
אַלְגֻּמִּים (*'algūmmîm*). See no. 89b.

92 אֵלֶּה (*'ēlleh*) ***these*** (the same in most translations).

This demonstrative pronoun serves as the plural of *zeh*. When it stands alone, without an accompanying noun or pronoun, it has the sense of "these things" (Deut 18:12).

It is generally in apposition with a substantive, with or without a suffix (Ex 10:1). It may also stand in the predicate position as an adjective, in which case the verb "to be" is understood (Gen 2:4, "These *are* the generations").

It takes the article only after substantives which are themselves determined by the article.

The pronoun occurs similarly in the cognate form in Arabic, Ethiopic, Syriac, and Aramaic.

J.B.S.

93 אלה (*'lh*). **Assumed root of the following.**
93a †אֵל (*'ēl*) ***god, God.***
93b †אֱלוֹהַּ (*'ĕlōah*) ***god, God.***
93c †אֱלֹהִים (*'ĕlōhîm*) ***gods, God.***

'lh is the assumed root of *'ēl, 'ĕlōah,* and *'ĕlōhîm,* which mean "god" or "God." The Ugaritic term for "god" or the "chief god" is *'il,* plural *'ilm,* occasionally plural *'ilhm* (cf. UT 19: no. 163). The Phoenician term is *'l* "El"; the plural is *'lm* which seems to be construed sometimes as a singular (cf. Z. Harris, *Grammar of the Phoenician Language,* Jewish Publication Society, 1936, p. 77). The Aramaic is *'ĕlāh,* plural *'ĕlāhîn.* The Akkadian form is *ilu.*

The view that the three Hebrew terms come from one root is much disputed and a final verdict is lacking. Some hold that the two are distinct, deriving *'ēl* from the root *'wl* (strong). Others see *'ĕlōhîm* derived from the root *'lh,* together with *'ĕlōah,* that root meaning "fear." Still others hold that both *'ēl* and *'ĕlōhîm* come from *'ĕlōah.*

More probable is the view that *'ĕlōhîm* comes from *'ĕlōah* as a unique development of the Hebrew Scriptures and represents chiefly the plurality of persons in the Trinity of the godhead (see *'ĕlōhîm*).

'ĕlōah is also a basic Hebrew term for the God of Israel, but is used less frequently (see *'ĕlōah* and *'ēl,* a separate though perhaps related generic term for God).

'ēl. ***God, god, mighty one, strength.*** In the common use of the word to denote either the generic name "god" or "the God" of Israel, the ASV and RSV are usually alike. However, in some specialized uses of the term they differ from KJV and from one another, e.g. ASV and RSV treat Jud 9:46 as a proper noun "El-Berith" while KJV translates "god"; Ps 29:1, RSV translates "heavenly beings" while ASV has "sons of the mighty"; Ps 50:1, ASV and RSV have "mighty one," KJV "mighty God;" Ps 80:10 [H 11], ASV renders "cedars of God," RSV has "mighty cedars" and KJV simply "goodly cedars": Ps 82:1, ASV says "congregation of God" but RSV translates "Divine counsel"; Ps 89:6 [H 7]) ASV and KJV "sons of the mighty" but RSV "Heavenly beings"; Isa 57:5, KJV has "idols" but ASV, RSV read as another Hebrew word, "oaks"; and finally, Ezk 32:21, KJV and ASV "strong among the mighty" while RSV renders it simply "mighty chiefs."

The primary meanings of this root as used in Scripture are "god" (pagan or false gods), "God" (the true God of Israel) and less frequently, "the mighty" (referring to men or angels). By far the predominant usage is for the true God and it is to this usage that we will give major attention.

The name "El" is a very ancient Semitic term. It is also the most widely distributed name among Semitic-speaking peoples for the deity, occurring in some form in every Semitic language except Ethiopic. Pope, in his study of "El" in the Ugaritic, notes that it is the most frequently occurring name for the deity in proper names throughout the ancient Semitic world (Marvin Pope, *El in the Ugaritic Texts,* p. 1).

We must agree with Pope that etymologically the bottom of the barrel has been scraped with little success (Pope, *El in the Ugaritic Texts,* p. 19). Most frequently mentioned suggestions for an original meaning are "power" or "fear" but these are widely challenged and much disputed. [It may be noted that even if the origin of the word in Canaanite or proto-Semitic is from a root meaning power, this by no means indicates the connotation in Hebrew religious usage. Our word "deity" comes from a root known in Sanskrit to mean "sky" but we do not worship a sky-god. R.L.H.]

The question of the relationship between the biblical use of *'ēl* and the Semitic concepts of El has received much attention particularly since the discovery of the Ugaritic texts, which have apparently established the fact that the term El was used in reference to a personal god and not merely as a generic term in the ancient Semitic world.

Space will not allow us to develop the various points of view on this matter. The article by Frank M. Cross, published in 1975, in the first volume of the *Theological Dictionary of the Old Testament,* gives much attention to this. Certainly we do not have to accept the view that assumes an ancient polytheism in Israel which was gradually refined so that various gods such as El, Shaddai, and Elyon were finally merged into Hebrew monotheism under the heading of Elohim or Yahweh. The bibliography following this article suggests further reading for those who would like to pursue this matter.

A. B. Davidson has observed the pronounced tendency in Scripture to accompany *'ēl* with epithets. Indeed, as we study the word as used in Scripture, we must conclude that it is almost always qualified by words or descriptions which further define the word. This leads A. B. Davidson to conclude that these qualifications both elevate the concept of El in Scripture and distinguish the term as used biblically from others who might be so named (A. B. Davidson, *Theology of the Old Testament,* p. 61).

A study of the various accompanying descriptions of El where the name occurs in Scripture leads to the rather solid conclusion that, from the beginning of the use of this term in Scripture, it was intended to distinguish the true El (God) from all false uses of that name found in other semitic cultures.

We note first the use of El in terms denoting God's greatness or superiority over all other gods: *ha'ēl haggādôl* "the great El" (Jer 32:18; Ps 77:13 [H 14]; 95:3); *hā'ēl 'ōsēh pele'* "El doing wonders" (Ps 77:14 [H 15]); *'ēl 'ēlîm* "El of els" ("God of gods," Dan 11:36); *'ēl 'ĕlōhê hārûḥôt lᵉkol-bāśār* "El, the God of the spirits of all flesh" (Num 16:22; 27:16).

Next, consider epithets relating to El's position: *'ēl hashshāmāyim* "El of heaven" (Ps 136:26); *'ēl mimā'al* "El that is above" (Job 31:28); *'ēl 'elyôn* "El most high" (Gen 14:18–19,20,22; Ps 78:35).

Again, as a precaution against overfamiliarity with God because of the use of a common Semitic term, God is described as *'ēl mistatēr* "El who hides himself" (i.e. known only by self-revelation, Isa 45:15). Yet God does see us at all times as Abraham affirmed, *'ēl rŏ'î* "El who sees me" (Gen 16:13).

Most specially El is accompanied in Scripture by those epithets which describe him as the Savior God of Israel. As such he is called *hā'ēl hanne'ĕmān* "Faithful El" (Deut 7:9); *hā'ēl haqqādôsh* "Holy El" (Isa 5:16); *'ēl 'ĕmet* "El of truth" (Ps 31:5 [H 6]; Deut 32:4); *'ēl shadday* "Almighty El" (Gen 17:1; 28:3; 35:11; 48:3; Ex 6:3; Ezk 10:5); *'ēl gibbôr* "El the heroic" (Isa 9:6 [H 5]; 10:21); *'ēl dē'ôt* "El of knowledge" (I Sam 2:3); *'ēl hakkābôd* "El of glory" (Ps 29:3); *'ēl 'ôlām* "El of eternity" (Gen 21:33); *'ēl-ṣaddîq* "Righteous El" (Isa 45:21); and *'ēl qannā'* "Jealous El" (Ex 20:5; Deut 4:24; 5:9; 6:15; Josh 24:19; Nah 1:2).

In contradistinction from all false "els" (gods), he is declared to be *'ēl ḥay* the "Living El" (Josh 3:10; I Sam 17:26, 36; II Kgs 19:4, 16; Ps 42:2 [H 3]; 84:2 [H 3]; Isa 37:4; Jer 10:10, 23:36; Dan 6:20, 26 [H 21,27]; Hos 1:10 [H 2:1]). In accord with strict biblical monotheism he is therefore *'ēl 'eḥād*, the one El (Mal 2:10). And in the passage most quoted elsewhere in the Old Testament El is described in terms of those attributes by which God desired to be known by his people (Ex 34:5–7; cf. Deut 4:31; II Chr 30:9; Neh 9:17, 31; Ps 103:8; Joel 2:13, etc.).

The very personal relationship between the El of Scripture and his believers is seen in the following epithets: *hā'ēl bêt-'ēl* "the El of Bethel" (Gen 31:13; 35:7); *'ēl sal'î* "El my rock" (Ps 42:9

[H 10]); *'ēl y^eshû'ātî* "El my Savior" (Isa 12:2); *'ēl ḥayyāy* "El of my life" (Ps 42:8 [H 9]); *'ēl gōmēr 'ālāy* "El the performer on me" (Ps 57:3); "the El of..." (Gen 49:25, etc.); *'ēlî* "My El" (Ps 89:26 [H 27]; 102:24 [H 25]; 118:28); *hā'ēl mā'ûzzî* "El my fortress" (II Sam 22:33); *hā'ēl ham'az^erēnî ḥāyil* "El the girder of me with strength" (Ps 18:32 [H 33]); *hā'ēl hannōtēn n^eqāmôt lî* "the El giving me vengeance" (Ps 18:47 [H 48]; II Sam 22:48).

Thus, in an evangelistic sense, he is described in such epithets as *'ēl m^ehōllekâ* "El who begat you" (Deut 32:18); *'ēl môshî'ām* "El their Savior" (Ps 106: 21); *'ēl môṣî'ô mimmiṣraim* "El his (their) bringer from Egypt" (Num 24:8; 23:22); *'ēl y^eshūrûn* "El of Jeshurun" (Deut 33:26); and *'ēl 'ĕlōhê yiśrā'el* "El the God of Israel" (Gen 33:20).

Frequently therefore we find the term "El" combined with or associated with the personal name for Israel's God, Yahweh (Josh 22:22; Ps 85:8 [H 9]; 118:27; Isa 42:5, etc.) which testifies that he is indeed *'ēl nōśē'* El who forgives (Ps 99:8) and consequently *hā'ēl y^eshû'ātēnû* "El of our salvation" (Ps 68:19–20 [H 20–21]).

Whether or not the name El can be identified etymologically with the concept of fear, it is clearly often associated with this idea in biblical epithets. He is called *hā'ēl haggādôl w^e hannôrā'* "El, great and terrible" (Neh 1:5; 4:14; 9:32; Deut 7:21; 10:17; Dan 9:4) or simply, *'ēl na'ărāṣ* "Terrible El" (Ps 89:7 [H 8]). He is also described as *'ēl g^emūlôt* "El of recompenses" (Jer 51:56) or more severely *'ēl nōqēm* "El the revenger" (Ps 99:8; Nah 1:2), and sometimes simply *'ēl n^eqām* "El of vengeance" (Ps 94:1). Being indignant is a continuous characteristic of El in Scripture (Ps 7:11 [H 12]).

Only in Job do we find extensive use of El without epithets. There the term is treated by Job and his friends as the common term for the true God and its use there, unlike other parts of Scripture, far outnumbers the occurrence of Elohim (q.v.).

'ĕlōah. *God, god* (ASV, RSV similar). The exact relationship between this name for God in Scripture and *'ēl* or *'elōhîm* is disputed and far from settled. It occurs in some of the oldest OT poetry (Deut 32:15, 17) and very frequently (forty-one times) in the debates between Job (an ancient believer) and his friends. It appears therefore to be an ancient term for God which was later dropped for the most part until the time of the exile and after, when there was great concern for a return to the more ancient foundations. It is not frequently used outside Job. It occurs once in Isa, once in Prov, twice in Hab, four times in the Ps, and then in the postexilic books: II Chr, Neh, and Dan, a total of five times.

Marvin H. Pope in his Book, *El in the Ugaritic Texts,* has noted that *'ĕlōah* never has the article although it is once determined by the suffix (Hab 1:11) and found once in the construct (Ps 114:7). He further points out that it never occurs in combination with another divine name.

We shall first look at the usage outside Job. Three times it occurs in parallel to "rock" as a descriptive term for God (Deut 32:15; Ps 18:31 [H 32]; Isa 44:8). Once it is found in a context in which God is described as a shield to those who take refuge in him (Prov 30:5). Three times it is used in a context of terror for sinners (Ps 50:22; 114:7; 139:19).

This would suggest that the term conveyed to God's people comfort and assurance while conveying fear to their enemies. The concepts of strength and might conveyed by the term are further seen in the three successive verses of Daniel's vision about the great anti-god (Dan 11:37–39). Here the anti-god's god (*'ĕlōah*) seems to be "strength" itself. In Hab 1:11 the term is used similarly.

In Hab 3:3, the prophet speaks of *'ĕlōah* coming from Teman. In Job, Teman is associated with one of Job's three friends, Eliphaz (Job 4:1). Interestingly, the term *'ĕloah,* used for God, is predominantly used in Job by Job and Eliphaz in their debating. Only in one context does Zophar use the term (11:5–7). Bildad never does. Of course Elihu uses it, perhaps in imitation of the former speakers (six times in chapters 33–37). God himself, in speaking to Job, uses the term twice: once in a context of his providence and once in parallel to "the Almighty" (see our discussion on the concept of might associated with the name).

This term for God was usually clearly used for Israel's God, the true God. This is evident from the fact that the Levites in the postexilic period used the term in quoting the descriptive revelation of God given in Ex 34:6–7, where the original revelation to Moses had used El and Yahweh (Neh 9:17).

The Hebrew word is quite similar to the Aramaic *'ĕlah,* the usual name for God in Biblical Aramaic. It has been suggested that the term has come, via Aramaic, from two elements: El and Ah (a shortened form of Ahyeh, Ex 3:14, "I shall be," the designation of Yahweh in the first person; Feigin, Samuel I., "The Origin of Elôh, 'God', in Hebrew," *JNES* 3: 259). This suggests the possibility that originally two separate gods were involved and later combined. Such a suggestion does not seem likely inasmuch as the term is in Scripture almost always used as a designation of the true God.

It is probably akin to the term El. It was in use quite early, then, after a period of neglect among God's people, the term was revived to a limited use perhaps through the contacts with Aramaic, where a similar term was in constant use.

'ĕlōhîm. ***God, gods, judges, angels.*** (Generally, agreement is found in ASV and RSV, however in some passages where the meaning is not clear they differ from KJV: Ex 31:6, where RSV has "God" but KJV "the judges"; similarly in Ex 22:28 [H 27] where RSV has "God" but KJV "the gods" or as a margin "judges.") This word, which is generally viewed as the plural of *'ĕlōah,* is found far more frequently in Scripture than either *'ēl* or *'ĕlōah* for the true God. The plural ending is usually described as a plural of majesty and not intended as a true plural when used of God. This is seen in the fact that the noun *'ĕlōhîm* is consistently used with singular verb forms and with adjectives and pronouns in the singular.

Albright has suggested that the use of this majestic plural comes from the tendency in the ancient near east toward a universalism: "We find in Canaanite an increasing tendency to employ the plural Ashtorôt 'Astartes', and Anatôt 'Anaths', in the clear sense of totality of manifestations of a deity'" (William F. Albright, *From the Stone Age to Christianity,* 2d ed., p. 213). But a better reason can be seen in Scripture itself where, in the very first chapter of Gen, the necessity of a term conveying both the unity of the one God and yet allowing for a plurality of persons is found (Gen 1:2, 26). This is further borne out by the fact that the form *'ĕlōhîm* occurs only in Hebrew and in no other Semitic language, not even in Biblical Aramaic (Gustav F. Oehler, *Theology of the Old Testament,* p. 88).

The term occurs in the general sense of deity some 2570 times in Scripture. Yet as Pope has indicated, it is difficult to detect any discrepancy in use between the forms *'ēl, 'ĕlōah,* and *'ĕlōhîm* in Scripture (Marvin H. Pope, *El in the Ugaritic Texts,* p. 10).

When indicating the true God, *'ĕlōhîm* functions as the subject of all divine activity revealed to man and as the object of all true reverence and fear from men. Often *'ĕlōhîm* is accompanied by the personal name of God, Yahweh (Gen 2:4–5; Ex 34:23; Ps 68:18 [H 19], etc.).

While the individual occurrences of the term *'ĕlōhîm* for God are far too numerous to treat here, some significant appositives and descriptive phrases or clauses associated with the name are given below. These descriptive words attached to the noun *'ĕlōhîm* really serve as titles and indicate the various titles by which God's people came to know him. The term *'ĕlōhîm* is the favorite term in titles. They are usually attached by means of the construct, the relative clause or by participial phrases rendered as titles.

The first category of titles pertains to his work of creation: Isa 45:18, "God, Former of the Earth"; Jon 1:9 "God of Heaven Who Made the Sea and the Dry Land."

A second category of titles expresses God's sovereignty: Isa 54:5, "God of All the Earth"; I Kgs 20:28, "God of the Hills"; Jer 32:27, "God of All Flesh." The God of All the Kingdoms of the Earth" (cf. Isa 37:16); God of Heaven (Neh 2:4, 20); "Yahweh God of the Heaven" (Gen 24:7; II Chr 36:23); God in the Heaven (II Chr 20:6); "The Lord God of the Heaven and God of the Earth" (Gen 24:3; see Deut 4:39; Josh 2:11); and finally "God of gods and Lord of Lords, the Great, the Mighty, and the Terrible Who Does Not Regard Favorites and Does Not Take Bribes" (Deut 10:17). All of these titles may be subsumed under the rather brief "God Most High" (Ps 57:2 [H 3]).

As sovereign God, *'ĕlōhîm* is often described as Judge: simply "God Judge" (Ps 50:6; 75:7 [H 8]) or "GodJudge in the Earth" (Ps 58:11 [H 12]).

Another category of titles focuses around God's majesty or glory. Among these we find "God of Eternity" (Isa 40:28); "God of Justice" (Isa 30:18); "God of Certainty" (Isa 65:16); "Living God" (Jer 10:10); and "This Holy God" (I Sam 6:20).

By far the most frequent category of titles are those pertaining to the Savior God. Here we include numerous constructs in which God is linked to individuals whom he has called: "Their God" (Gen 17:8); "The God of Abraham" (Gen 26:24); "The God of Abraham . . . and the God of Isaac" (Gen 28:13); "The God of Abraham, the God of Isaac, and the God of Jacob" (Ex 3:6), etc. (More than one hundred such titles are found in the Old Testament.) Sometimes to these titles is added the personal name, "Yahweh" (Gen 24:12).

Similarly, we find titles linking God by the construct grammatical form to Israel as a whole or to some part of it: "God of the Armies of Israel" (I Sam 17:45) or "God of Jerusalem" (II Chr 32:19).

All of these represent God as savior of his people as does the simple "God of Salvation" (I Chr 16:35; Ps 18:46 [H 47], etc.; cf. Ps 88:1 [H 2]).

Some titles reflect God's actions on behalf of his people in the past: "The Living God, Speaker from the Midst of the Fire" (Deut 5:23 [H 26]; cf. I Kgs 18:24); "God, the Bringer of Prisoners into Prosperity" (Ps 68:7); "God . . . the Bringer out to you Water from the Flinty Rock" (Deut 8:15); "Your God Who Separated You from the Peoples" (Lev 20:24).

And finally, we find titles expressing the intimacy of God with his people: "The God of Nearness" (Jer 23:23); "Your God in Whom you Trust" (II Kgs 19:10); "God Your Chastener" (Deut 8:5); The God Feeding Me My Life Long Until Now" (Gen 48:15); "God of My Righteousness" (Ps 4:1 [H 2]); "God of My Mercy (Ps 59:17 [H 18]); "God of My Strength" (Ps 43:2) and "Our God Being Merciful" (Ps 116:5).

In reference to one particularly difficult passage from the point of view of interpretation, which therefore bears on the translation, Cyrus Gordon has said, "It is my contention that here (Ex 22:8–9 [H 7, 8]) *'ĕlōhîm* does not mean God as the LXX translates, nor judges, which is the interpretation of Peshitto and Targum Onkelos, followed by Rashi and Ibn Ezra, by several English versions and by the Lexicon" (Cyrus H. Gordon, "*'ĕlōhîm* in its reputed meaning of rulers, judges," JBL 54: 140, 149). He goes on to demonstrate to his own satisfaction that from our knowledge of the Nuzi tablets we can conclude that "gods" is the better translation and that the passage refers to the "oaths of the gods" which he calls a well attested ancient oriental court procedure. He therefore sees this text as a heathen survival in the Mosaic legislation, one that was obliterated in the later Deuteronomic and priestly recensions.

This is unacceptable from the point of view of Scripture's attestation to being God's Word and its clear doctrine of the existence of only one God. The question of whether "God" or "judges" is to be used here is difficult. If "God" is correct, we understand by the passage that every man is ultimately answerable to God and stands or falls before God no matter what judgment men may make.

Bibliography: Albright, W. F., "The Names Shaddai and Abram," JBL 54: 175–92. ______, *From the Stone Age to Christianity,* Johns Hopkins, 1957. ______, *Archaeology and the Religion of Israel,* Johns Hopkins, 1942. Bailey, Lloyd R., "Israelite El Šadday and Amorite Bel Sade," JBL 87: 434–38. Cross, Frank Moore, "Yahweh and the God of the Patriarchs," HTR 55: 226–59. ______, "El and Yahweh," JSS 1: 25–37. ______, " 'My God' in the Old Testament," EQ 19: 7–20. Davidson, A. B., *The Theology of the Old Testament,* Edinburgh: T & T Clark. Della Vida. G. Levi, "El Elyon in Genesis 14: 18–20," JBL 63:1–9. Drafkorn, Ann E., "Ilani/Elohim," JBL 76: 216–24. Eerdmans, B. D., *The Religion of Israel,* Leiden, Universtaire pers Leiden, 1947. Feigin, Samuel J., "The Origin of 'Eloh, 'God,' in Hebrew," JNES 3: 259. Gordon, Cyrus H., "Elohim in its Repeated Meaning of Rulers, Judges," JBL 54: 140–44. Jacob, Edmond, *The Theology of the Old Testament,* Harper Brothers, 1955. Keil, Karl F., *Manual of Historico-Critical Introduction to the Canonical Scriptures of the Old Testament,* I, Eerdmans, 1952. Kelso, James A., "The Antiquity of the Divine Title," JBL 20: 50–55. Kohler, Ludwig, *Old Testament Theology,* Westminster, 1957. Kuhn, H. B., "God, Names of," in APEB. May, H. G., "El Shaddai," JBL 60: 114–45. ______, "The Patriarchal Ideal of God," JBL 60: 113–28. Miller, Patrick D., "El the Warrior," HTR 411–31. Pope, Marvin H., *El in the Ugaritic Texts,* Brill, 1955. Richardson, TWB, p. 89. Segal, M. H., "El, Elohim, and YHWH in the Bible," JQR 46: 89–115. Thomas, D. Winton, "A Consideration of Some Unusual Ways of Expressing the Superlative in Hebrew," VT 3: 209–24. Van Allman, J. J., *A Companion to the Bible,* Oxford, 1958. Weingreen, J., "The Construct-Genitive in Hebrew Syntax," VT 4: 50–59. Wilson, Robert Dick, "The Names of God in the Old Testament," PTR 18: 460–92.

J.B.S.

94 אָלָה (*'ālâ*) ***II, to swear, make a solemn oath.*** (RSV is generally better in translation than ASV, i.e. "laid an oath on" preferable to "adjured," I Sam 14:24). The term is used in expressing solemn oaths between men and between God and man.

Derivatives

94a †אָלָה (*'ālâ*) ***an oath, solemn statement, promise, curse*** (for broken oath), occurring more frequently than the verb.

94b †תַּאֲלָה (*ta'ălâ*) ***curse*** (punishment for broken oath), only once, Lam 3:65.

'ālâ. ***Oath.*** In its most basic form we see the noun used in the sense of a solemn promise between men (Gen 24:41; 26:28). For that reason it is also applied to solemn statements of testimony given in court (Lev 5:1; Prov 29:24) and before God (Num 5:21ff.; Jud 17:2; I Kgs 8:31; I Sam 14:24; Neh 10:29 [H 30]; Ezk 16:59; 17:13ff.).

From this we can see how it was used to express the very solemn covenant between God and his people (Deut 29:12 [H 11]) and more particularly, the warnings of judgment attached to that covenant should the people prove to be faithless (Deut 29: 14–21 [H 13–20]). It is used in this latter sense also in Isa 24:6; Jer 23:10; 29:18; 42:18; 44:12 and Dan 9:11.

ta'ălâ. ***Curse.*** (The same in ASV, RSV.) This noun occurs only once in Lam 3:65. It applies to the enemies of God's people and is described as dullness of heart.

Bibliography: Blank, Sheldon H., "The Curse, Blasphemy, the Spell, and the Oath," HUCA 23: 73–95. Brichto, Herbert C., *The Problem of "Curse" in the Hebrew Bible,* JBL Monograph Series, vol. XIII, Society of Biblical Literature and Exegesis, 1963. Lehman, Manfred R., "Biblical Oaths," ZAW 81: 74–92. Price, J. M., "The Oath in Court Procedure in Early Babylonia and the Old Testament," JAOS 49: 22–29. Scharbert, Josef, " 'Fluchen' und 'Segen' im

Alten Testament," Bib 39: 1–26. Tucker, G. M., "Covenant Forms and Contract Forms," VT 15: 487–503. TDNT, V, pp. 459–61. TDOT, I, pp. 261–66.

J.B.S.

95 אָלָה (*'ālâ*) ***III, wail.*** Only in Jon 1:8.
95a †אַלְיָה (*'alyâ*) ***fat tail*** (of sheep). (The same in ASV, RSV.)

This portion of the sheep was mentioned as a distinct part of the offering in the heave offering (Ex 29:22), in the peace offering (Lev 3:9; 9:19), in the guilt offering (Lev 7:3) and in the offering of consecration on the occasion of the ordination of Aaron and his sons to the priestly office. The fat tailed sheep are still the common ones in Palestine.

J.B.S.

אַלָּה (*'allâ*). See no. 100a.
אֵלָה (*'ēlâ*). See no. 45h.

96 אִלּוּ (*'illû*) ***if, though.*** Only in Eccl 6:6, Est 7:4.

97 אֱלוּל (*'ĕlûl*) ***Elul,*** the sixth month. Occurs only in Neh 6:15. For other month names see no. 613b.

אֵלוֹן (*'ēlôn*). See no. 45i.
אַלּוֹן (*'allôn*). See no. 100b.
אַלּוּף (*'allûp*). See no. 109b.

98 *אָלַח (*'ālaḥ*) ***be corrupt morally.*** Occurs only in the Niphal.

אַלְיָה (*'alyâ*). See no. 95a.

99 אלל (*'ll*) **I. Assumed root of the following.**
99a †אֱלִיל (*'ĕlîl*) ***something worthless*** (particularly as an object of worship), ***gods, idols.*** (Generally the same in the ASV and RSV.)

This term comes perhaps from a root meaning "to be weak, deficient." It is used primarily in Scripture to describe vain objects of worship, i.e. the gods of this world, whether literal idols made with hands, riches, or deceitful men.

In Lev 19:4, its first appearance, the word is parallel to "molten gods" (cf. 26:1). It is also applied to any works of one's hands as an object of worship (Isa 2:8; Hab 2:18).

In Isaiah's day, Jerusalem and Samaria were described as kingdoms of idols, i.e. a people who worshipped vain things (Isa 10:10–11). Such idols were classed along with divination and lies (Jer 14:14). They were clearly good for nothing (Isa 2:20; 31:7).

They even included people in whom men trusted but who were deceitful and of no value (Job 13:4; Isa 19:3; Zech 11:17).

In Scripture they are contrasted to the true God, the Lord, the Creator (Ps 96:5) and before him they tremble (Isa 19:1), are put to shame (Ps 97:7), and are destroyed (Isa 2:18).

Bibliography: TDOT, I, pp. 285–86. THAT, I, pp. 167–68.

J.B.S.

100 אלל (*'ll*) **II. Assumed root of the following.**
100a †אַלָּה (*'allâ*) ***oak.***
100b †אַלּוֹן (*'allôn*) ***oak.***

'allâ. ***Oak.*** This word is apparently from the root *'ll* and occurs only once in Josh 24:26. The meaning of the passage is uncertain. It refers to an oak *in* the sanctuary of the Lord under which Joshua set up a stone for a witness against Israel, after the people affirmed obedience to God's covenant. The ASV gets rid of the difficulty by translating the preposition as "by" rather than "in." The RSV is more literal.

'allôn. ***Oak*** (same in ASV and RSV). The term refers to one of the great trees of the forest (Isa 44:14). Three times in particular it is associated with Bashan where it symbolized pride (Isa 2:13; possibly Ezk 27:6) and very thick forests (Zech 11:2). Elsewhere it is also used to symbolize strength (Amos 2:9).

In Isa 6:13, the stump of the oak is likened to the remnant of Israel which survives after it is cut down.

Once, the oak is referred to as a place of pagan worship (Hos 4:13). It was also the tree where Deborah, Rebekah's maid, was buried (Gen 35:8).

J.B.S.

101 אַלְלַי (*'allay*) ***alas! woe!*** Occurs only in Mic 7:1; Job 10:15.

102 *אָלַם (*'ālam*) ***bind, be made dumb*** (Niphal).

Derivatives

102a אֲלֻמָּה (*'ălūmmâ*) ***sheaf.***
102b אֵלֶם (*'ēlem*) ***silence.***
102c אִלֵּם (*'illēm*) ***dumb.***

אַלְמֻגִּים (*'almūggîm*). See no. 89c.

103 אַלְמָן (*'almān*) ***widowed, forsaken, forsaken as a widow*** (the same in ASV, RSV).

The adjective occurs once in Jer 51:5 in the sense of Israel abandoned by God, as a widow, by her husband who had died.

J.B.S.

104 אַלְמֹן (*'almōn*) ***widowhood.*** (The same in ASV, RSV.)

This noun is used to describe the state of Babylon after God's judgment, in its one use, Isa 47:9.

J.B.S.

105 אַלְמָנָה (*'almānâ*) ***widow.*** (ASV and RSV the same.) The word has only one basic meaning, "widow."

The primary meaning, "widow," is seen throughout its usage in Scripture. The word first occurs in Gen 38:11 in the account of Judah's dealings with his daughterın-law, called a widow after her husband's death.

The several contexts in which we see the term used in Scripture will help us to see its significance in God's Word. First, we note God's care and concern for widows. God hears their cry (Ex 22:21–22) and he executes justice on their behalf (Deut 10:18). Therefore God deals with them out of exceptional pity, as defenseless. He is their judge in a special way (Ps 65:5 [H 6]), treating them with the same tenderness he shows to the orphans (Ps 146:9). He also protects their inheritance (Prov 15:25). When others are judged, a special call to faith is issued to them (Jer 49:11). To the end of the OT period, God expresses his concern for widows (Mal 3:5).

But being widows, they were restricted in some relationships while not in others. They could not marry priests (Lev 21:14; Ezk 44:22) unless widows of priests. However, widows who were daughters of priests could return to their father's home and eat again of the holy food of the priests (Lev 22:13). Also being widows did not exempt them from vows made (Num 30:9 [H 10]). All of this indicates that they were a unique category in Israel according to God's legislation and due special regard from the people.

The existence of widows was not indicative of good times and the presence of many widows in the land indicated God's displeasure with the people and punishment of them (Ex 22:24 [H 23]; Jer 15:8). Indeed, on two occasions, cities under God's judgment are called widows: Isa 47:8 (Babylon); Lam 1:1 (Jerusalem).

Because of God's concern for the widows, the people were frequently commanded to protect and provide for them, being careful to execute justice on their behalf. The people were blessed when they had regard for widows (Deut 14:29). Leaders were responsible to defend them and to see that justice was done (Isa 1:17, 23).

The reason for this concern is obvious. Widows were often elderly, often without much income, and easy prey for the unscrupulous. In a similar social situation the NT church is commanded to care for those who are "widows indeed," i.e. widows in need (I Tim 5:3–11).

Even in the time of Job the way one treated widows was indicative of his moral character. Job was accused of mistreating widows by Eliphaz who supposed that his troubles came from such evil conduct (Job 22:9). Job vehemently denied having mistreated them and claimed to have done them good (Job 29:13; cf. 31:16).

Thus oppression of widows became a frequent example of wickedness among men and nations (Ps 94:6; Isa 10:2, etc.).

The cognate root is found in Assyrian and Ugaritic (UT 19: no. 126) both for "widow" and "widowhood."

106 אַלְמָנוּת (*'almānût*) ***widowhood*** (same in ASV, RSV).

Twice the term is applied to the garments of Tamar, widow of Judah's sons (Gen 38:14, 19). It applies to a state of living for the concubines of David, defiled by Absalom (II Sam 20:3); and also to Israel figuratively (Isa 54:4).

Bibliography: Fensham, F. Charles, "Widow, Orphan, and Poor in Ancient Near Eastern Legal and Wisdom Literature," JNES 21: 129–39. Patterson, Richard, "The Widow, the Orphan, and the Poor in the Old Testament and the Extra-Biblical Literature," BS 130: 223–34. TDNT, IX, pp. 444–48. TDOT I, pp. 287–91. THAT, I, pp. 169–72.

J.B.S.

107 אַלְמֹנִי (*'almōnî*) ***someone, a certain one.***

108 אָלַף (*'ālap*) ***I, learn (Qal); teach (Piel).*** (ASV, RSV translate the same.)

Derivatives

108a אֶלֶף (*'elep*) ***cattle, oxen.***
108b †אַלּוּף (*'allûp*) ***docile.***

'alap is rare, occuring only four times (three in Job). In two contexts (Prov 22:25; Job 15:5) the teacher is evil. In the other two, Elihu uses the term, once describing himself as teacher, once putting words into the mouth of others (Job 33:33; 35:11). If his words are without knowledge (Job 38:2), then perhaps this word scripturally has only bad connotations and does not express teaching or learning that is valid.

'allûp ***I. Docile*** (adjective); ***friend*** (noun). (RSV and ASV differ considerably in some places where RSV translates "friend" while ASV prefers "guide" [Jer 3:4]). The primary sense is that of one who is always in company with another, i.e. a guide or companion or friend. As such, the companion is not expected to betray (Ps 55:13 [H 14]); he ought not to be forsaken (Prov 2:17); and it is tragic when such friends are divided (Prov 16:28; 17:9). However, times come when one cannot trust them (Mic 7:5).

J.B.S.

109 *אָלַף (*'ālap*) ***II, producing thousands*** (occurs only in the Hiphil, Ps 144:13). Denominative verb.

Parent Noun

109a †אֶלֶף (*'elep*) ***thousand*** (same in ASV, RSV).

Derivatives

109b †אַלּוּף (*'allûp*) ***chief.***

The verb, derived from the noun, is used only once (Ps 144:13), in a prayer asking God's blessings so that the sheep will produce thousands.

'elep. ***Thousand.*** This numeral, a feminine noun, usually precedes the noun it accompanies. When the accompanying noun precedes, it is plural. If other numbers are joined to *'elep* they usually precede it. The basic meaning is one thousand but it is often to be taken as a figurative term.

This numeral is usually employed in tabulations, censuses, and other enumerations in the basic sense of the figure 1000 (Gen 20:16; 24:60; Ex 12:37; Num 1:21ff.).

There are, however, several specialized usages. One is in the basic sense of the largest basic division of leadership in political oversight or military leadership (Ex 18:21; Num 1:16; 31:4; Deut 1:15; I Chr 13:1; 27:1; Amos 5:3).

From this usage another which developed was the application of the term as representative of the extreme, i.e. Eccl 6:6, an extreme number of years. This in turn is related to the practice of making the numeral representative of the opposite extreme of that which is quite small or few in number (Deut 32:30; Josh 23:10; Job 9:3; Isa 30:17). At times the concept seems simply to represent that which is excessive (Mic 6:7; Song 8:12).

A notable use of the term is in connection with God. In such contexts the basic idea seems to be "indefinite" or "innumerable," e.g. God's mercy is to be shown to thousands (Ex 20:6; 34:7; Deut 5:10; Jer 32:18). This mercy is also to reach to a thousand generations (Deut 7:9), as is his command (Ps 105:8). The cattle on a thousand hills belong to God (Ps 50:10). A thousand years are but as a day in his sight (Ps 90:4).

These examples show that God uses the term in reference to himself figuratively, an indefinite or innumerable amount. This same practice is seen in the NT, e.g. II Pet 3:8–10 and probably also in Rev 20:2, 5.

The root occurs in several Semitic languages besides Hebrew, e.g. Aramaic, Arabic, and Ugaritic (UT, 19: no. 133) with the same basic meaning of one thousand.

[It is occasionally alleged that since *'elep* means a company of a thousand men it could mean any military unit, even of reduced strength. From there it came to mean a family unit or clan, even a small one. But this means that the 1000's of the mustering of the soldiers in Num 1 and 26 is reduced to a small figure in accord with the desire of the commentator. The wilderness wandering and its miraculous supply is also reduced to naturalistic proportions. But it should be remembered that the conquest of Transjordan and of Palestine was not accomplished by a handful of men. Also such juggling must alter the text of the Numbers passages which by the addition of their totals clearly speak of 1000's of soldiers. R.L.H.]

'allûp. ***Chief, ruler of a thousand.*** (Generally the same in ASV, RSV but in Zech 9:7; 12:5–6, RSV has "clan.") The word occurs exclusively to describe a rank in the families or clans of Edom (Gen 36:15ff; Ex 15:15; I Chr 1:51ff.). This usage probably also lies back of the Matt reading in 2:6 where "princes" of Judah reflects a pointing *'allup* in Mic 5:2 [H 1].

Bibliography: Davis, John J., "Biblical Numerics," *Grace Journal* 5:30–4. ———, "The Rhetorical Use of Numbers in the Old Testament," *Grace Journal* 8: 40–48. Wenham, J. W., "Large Numbers in the Old Testament," *Tyndale Bulletin* 18:19–53. Wolf, C., "Terminology of Israel's Tribal Organization," JBL 65: 45–49. TDNT, IX, pp. 467–69.

J.B.S.

110 *אָלַץ (*'ālaṣ*) ***urge.*** Occurs only once, in Jud 16:16 (Piel).

111 אִם (*'im*) ***if, not, whether, when, since.*** (ASV, RSV vary considerably inasmuch as the context and interpretation of the text determine the exact translation of this particle.)

The basic meaning is "if" and this meaning can be seen in most of its occurrences. In the hundreds of passages where the word occurs, several basic types of contexts can be seen.

First, it occurs most often in conditional clauses, e.g. Gen 4:7; Jud 13:16; I Sam 20:14, etc.

Next we find many occurrences of *'im* in oath contexts in which, in reality, a larger context is assumed. In the larger, assumed context is an oath, only rarely stated in full (II Kgs 9:26; cf. Job 1:11).

Sometimes the oath involves a negative as in II Sam 19:14. David is here promising to make Amasa his new commander in place of Joab. He calls on the Lord to judge him severely (the judgment is never spelled out, perhaps because it is so awful as to be unspeakable) *if* Amasa is not to be David's commander.

Other examples of the full oath are found in I Kgs 20:10 (used by Ben-Hadad), II Kgs 6:31 (also Ben-Hadad). This suggests that the oath was in broader use than Israel alone, among the Semites at any rate.

From this fuller form of the oath, we see the practice frequently of abbreviating the oath, omitting "the Lord do so to me and more also." Thus in Gen 14:23, "If I shall take a thread or a sandal-thong or if I shall take from anything which is yours" or in other words "I will not take." Other examples of this abbreviated form, even at times apparently God swearing by him self, are as follows: Num 14:30 (God declaring that none except Caleb and Joshua will come in "______ if you will come in" = "you will not come in"; I Sam 17:55, "______ if I know" = "I do not know," etc.

The peculiar result of this idiom is that in such contexts *'im* has negative force; *'im lō'* is positive. This Hebrew idiom, coming through the LXX, is rightly interpreted in Heb 3:11, 18 (KJV), but missed in 4:3, 5 (KJV).

A third context in which *'im* occurs is that of alternatives. Frequently this idea is conveyed by a double use of *'im,* e.g. Ex 19:13, "*if* beast *if* man..." = "whether a beast or a man"; I Chr 21:12, "*if* three years... and *if* three months... and *if* three days..." = "whether... or... or...".

In some contexts *'im* seems to have the force of "when" as in Gen 38:9. Even here however, the meaning "if" is seen in the sense of a continuing condition: "whenever he came in... he would spill..." or "if he came in...", this is what he did. Here we see the waw joined to the verb as waw consecutive, making it in effect an imperfect.

We also find several cases of the use of *'im* in the sense of "since." In Job 14:5, for example, "since his days are numbered: may also be "*if* his days..." and in Job 22:20, "since our enemies are cut off" may equally read "surely our enemies..." (ASV, RSV) or even "*if* our enemies...". In Jer 23:38, we can read either "*if* you say" or "since you say."

Often we find *'im* used as an interrogative particle. In Gen 38:17, for example, we can read Tamar's response to Judah "will you give..." or "*if* you will give..." When the structure is accompanied by the sign of the interrogative as in Josh 5:13, then there is no uncertainty. Actually it is quite usual to have an interrogative *he* carried on by *'im* (cf. disjunctive and double questions, GKC par. 150, g. h).

Bibliography: Daube, David. "Direct and Indirect Causation in Biblical Law," VT 11: 246–69. Eitan, I., "Three 'im Particles in Hebrew," JAOS 54: 295. Lehman, Manfred R., "Biblical Oaths," ZAW 81: 74–92. Van Leeuwen, C. "Die Partikel אִם," OTS 18: 15–48.

J.B.S.

אֵם (*'ēm*). See no. 115a.

112 אָמָה (*'āmâ*) ***maid-servant, female slave.*** (ASV and RSV generally the same but RSV prefers "female slave" in the Pentateuchal regulatory passages regarding slaves, while ASV prefers "servant" or "maid.")

The term is applied both to literal slaves and to those who figuratively call themselves by this term as an expression of humility and submission.

The first occurrence of the term is in reference to Abimelech's female servants (Gen 20:17). We see too that the patriarchs had such servants: Hagar (Sarah), Bilhah (Rachel), etc. Even returning Israelites after the Exile counted these servants among their possessions (Ezr 2:65). They were also found in Egypt (Ex 2:5) and in Nineveh (Nah 2:7 [H 8]).

God, in giving the Law to Israel, provided for servants, male and female. They had rights (Ex 21:7, 20, 26, etc.). God was clearly concerned for their wellbeing and physical as well as spiritual needs (Ex 20:10; Lev 25:6). They were to worship with their master's family in spiritual fellowship (Deut 12:12, 18). But they were a possession.

A distinction was made between foreign slaves and Hebrew servants. The latter had more rights and freedoms (cf. Lev 25:44 and Deut 15:12–18). But clearly, God expected his children to show kindness and consideration for the needs of these female slaves (Job 19:15; 31:13).

Several uses of the term in a figurative sense are also found in Scripture. A wife or prospective wife often referred to herself or was referred to in this way in respect to her man, e.g. Ruth to Boaz (Ruth 3:9); Abigail to David (I Sam 25:14); Bathsheba to David (I Kgs 1:17).

Sometimes a woman so referred to herself in conversation, as Hannah to Eli (I Sam 1:16—cf. II Sam 6:22; 14:15; I Kgs 3:20).

Finally, in the highest sense, devout women addressed the Lord, calling themselves God's servants in a fashion much as Paul did in the NT: so Hannah (I Sam 1:11). This same attitude is seen in the Psalmist who referred to his mother as God's maidservant when addressing the Lord (Ps 86:16; 116:16; which, however, is taken by Dahood as from *'emet* and rendered your true son. "Psalms" AB *in loc.,* so also M. Mansoor JBL 76; p. 145 on the basis of a DSS text).

The cognate root is found in several Semitic languages, including Ugaritic (UT, 19: no. 147).

Bibliography: Fensham, G. Charles, "The Son of a Handmaid in Northwest Semitic," VT 19: 312–22. Rupprecht, A., "Christianity and the Slavery Question," JETS 6: 64–68.

J.B.S.

אַמָּה (*'ammâ*). See no. 115.
אֻמָּה (*'ūmmâ*). See no. 115e.

113 אָמוֹן (*'amôn*) ***I, Amon,*** an Egyptian God. (In Nah 3:8, RSV has "Thebes" and further translates "Nile" for "canal." ASV is more literal having "No-amon." In Jer 46:25, RSV translates "Amon of Thebes" while ASV has "Amon of No." These are the only two occurrences of the name.)

The term "Amon" refers to an Egyptian deity and therefore also to the city of that deity, i.e. "the city of Amon." Since one Egyptian term for "city" is "no" it is transliterated in ASV to "No-Amon," while RSV simply identifies it by the common opinion that the city was the famous Thebes.

As Thebes became prominent in Egypt, the god of the city became more generally acknowledged and finally identified with the great Egyptian god, Re or Ra, i.e. Amon Re.

In Scripture the city of this god is mentioned twice. In Jer 46:25, the city is mentioned as an object of God's wrath, sure to fall to Nebuchadnezzar because it symbolized the pride of Egypt. In Nah 3:8, it becomes an example by its fall of the sureness of the fall of all world cities, particularly of Nineveh.

J.B.S.

אָמוֹן (*'āmôn*). See no. 116l.
אֱמוּנָה (*'ĕmûnâ*). See no. 116e.
אָמוֹץ (*āmôṣ*). See no. 117c.
אַמִּיץ (*'ammîṣ*). See no. 117d.
אָמִיר (*'āmîr*). See no. 118d.

114 *אָמַל (*'āmal*) ***to languish, be exhausted.*** (Generally the same in ASV, RSV.)

Derivatives

114a †אֲמֵלָל (*'ămēlāl*) ***feeble.***
114b †אֻמְלַל (*'ūmlal*) ***feeble.***

The verb occurs primarily in the Pulal conjugation, describing a state of exhaustion or extremity. It is used to express the state into which the objects of God's punishment and discipline come: the proud mother who boasts over her barren rival (I Sam 2:5); Moab (Isa 16:8); Egypt (Isa 19:8); the whole world (Isa 24:4).

Words associated with it are "wither," "mourn," and "lament" (Isa 24:4; 33:9; Jer 14:2).

Most particularly, it describes the state of Israel and its people after the punishment of God has fallen (Isa 33:9; Jer 14:2), so also, Jerusalem after the fall (Lam 2:8). Clearly, God's objective in such discipline was to bring his people to their knees as a warning and to humble them (Hos 4:3; Joel 1:10, 12).

As an adjective, the term was therefore used by Israel's enemies as a term of derision (Neh 4:2 [H 3:34]) and by the truly humbled believer as an expression of his contrition and recognition of the need of God's help (Ps 6:2 [H 3]).

'ūmlal. ***Weak, feeble.*** (ASV, "withered away." RSV "languishing.") The adjective is used once as an expression of the Psalmist's contrite heart before God (Ps 6:2 [H 3]).

'ămēlāl. ***Feeble.*** (The same in ASV, RSV.) It occurs once, an adjective describing the Jews, used by their enemies (Neh 4:2 [H 3:34]).

J.B.S.

115 אמם (*'mm*). **Assumed root of the following.**
115a †אֵם (*'ēm*) ***mother.***
115b אַמָּה (*'ammâ*) ***I, mother city.***
115c †אַמָּה (*'ammâ*) ***II, cubit.***
115d אַמָּה (*'ammâ*) ***III,*** *only in Isa 6:4. Meaning doubtful.*
115e אֻמָּה (*'ūmmâ*) ***tribe, people.***

'ēm. ***Mother, point of departure*** (once). (ASV and RSV generally the same.)

The word always (except once) means "mother." In most occurrences it refers literally to the female parent. It is used at times in a figurative sense.

'ēm refers to Eve, figuratively as mother of all living beings (though she was also the literal mother, Gen 3:20); to Deborah as a mother in Israel (Jud 5:7); to a city as mother to its inhabitants (Isa 50:1; Ezk 16:44; Hos 2:2 [H 4]); and even to a worm as mother of Job (Job 17:14).

On some occasions the term is applied to nonhuman mothers: Ex 34:26; Deut 22:6.

In studying the contexts and senses in which the word is used we note several of particular interest, first, texts which relate to the duties of the mother. She is to be a source of comfort (Isa 66:13), a teacher (Prov 31:1), and a discipliner (Zech 13:3).

We note also what her children owe her. These obligations may be defined as positive duties and negative duties. On the positive side, her children owe her obedience (Gen 28:7), blessings (Prov 30:11), honor (Ex 20:12), fear (i.e. respect, Lev 19:3), and mourning when she has died (Ps 35:14). On the negative side, her children must not strike her (Ex 21:15), rob her (Prov 28:24), chase her away (Prov 19:26), bring her to shame (Prov 29:15; so Lev 18:7), set light by her (i.e. ridicule her, Deut 27:16), nor forsake her law

(Prov 1:8). This shows clearly the high standing of motherhood in a redeemed society.

Yet, the mother's role in her adult son's life was clearly subordinate to that of his wife (Gen 2:24). His duties to his mother could not supplant or take precedence over his duties to his wife.

A pagan mother could indeed love her son, and presumably the pagan son could feel a sense of duty to his mother (Jud 5:28).

The sense of guilt expressed by Job and the Psalmist (Job 31:18; Ps 51:5 [H 7]) does not indicate any particular blemish on their mothers but expresses the doctrine we call original sin.

The occurrence of the word in Ezk 21:21 [H 26] is unique and evidently means "the parting (fork) of the road" in the sense of the origin (mother) of the road.

The cognate root is found in most Semitic languages with the same basic meaning as the Hebrew: Phoenician, Arabic, Ethiopic, Aramaic, and Ugaritic (UT 19: no. 155).

'ammâ. ***Cubit,*** a linear measurement. (The same in ASV and RSV except where used in a figurative sense, see Isa 6:4; Jer 51:13).

The term is basically used to describe a linear measurement used at least from the time of Noah. It is used throughout Scripture into the postexilic period.

The measurement is estimated to be approximately 17½ inches or the average distance from the elbow to the tip of the middle finger. This is somewhat confirmed by information in the Siloam Inscription stating that the tunnel (which measures 1749 feet) was 1200 cubits long. This would make the cubit then used (in Hezekiah's day) approximately 17½ inches.

The cubit was used in building the ark of Noah (Gen 6), the tabernacle and its furnishing (Ex 25ff.), the temple of Solomon (I Kgs 6:ff.), and the temple seen by Ezekiel (Ezk 40ff.). It also measured the distance between the ark of the covenant and the people as they went into the promised land (Josh 3:4).

Goliath was over six cubits tall (I Sam 17:4), and Haman's gallows was fifty cubits high (Est 5:14). A portion of the wall of Jerusalem repaired in Nehemiah's day was 1000 cubits long.

At times it is used figuratively as in Isa 6:4, where the measure stands for the foundation of the threshhold of the temple in Isaiah's vision. Again in Jer 51:13, the term applies to the extent of covetousness or evil gain.

From its wide occurrence in other Semitic languages evidently this term was generally used as a standard measure throughout the ancient near east, but it varies somewhat from place to place and from time to time.

Bibliography: AI, pp. 196–99. Harrison, R. K., "The Matriarchate and the Hebrew Legal Succession," EQ 29: 29–34. Huey, F. B., "Weights and Measures," in ZPEB.

J.B.S.

116 אָמַן (*'āman*) ***to confirm, support, uphold (Qal); to be established, be faithful (Niphal); to be certain, i.e. to believe in (Hiphil).*** (ASV, RSV usually the same. One notable exception is Gen 15:6 where RSV has "believed," while ASV has "believed in.")

Derivatives

116a †אֹמֶן (*'ōmen*) ***faithfulness.***
116b †אָמֵן (*'āmēn*) ***verily, truly, amen.***
116c אָמָּן (*'ommān*) ***steady-handed one, artist.***
116d †אֵמוּן (*'ēmūn*) ***faithful, trusting.***
116e †אֱמוּנָה (*'ĕmûnâ*) ***firmness, fidelity, steadiness.***
116f †אָמְנָה (*'omnâ*) ***I, bringing up, nourishment.***
116g †אָמְנָה (*'omnâ*) ***II, verily, truly.***
116h †אֲמָנָה (*'ămānâ*) ***faith, support, sure, certain.***
116i †אֻמְנָם (*'ūmnām*) ***verily, indeed.***
116j אָמְנָם (*'omnām*) ***verily, truly.***
116k †אֱמֶת (*'ĕmet*) ***firmness, truth.***
116l †אָמוֹן (*'āmôn*) ***II, artificer, architect.***

This very important concept in biblical doctrine gives clear evidence of the biblical meaning of "faith" in contradistinction to the many popular concepts of the term. At the heart of the meaning of the root is the idea of certainty. And this is borne out by the NT definition of faith found in Heb 11:1.

The basic root idea is firmness or certainty. In the Qal it expresses the basic concept of support and is used in the sense of the strong arms of the parent supporting the helpless infant. The constancy involved in the verbal idea is further seen in that it occurs in the Qal only as a participle (expressing continuance). The idea of support is also seen in II Kgs 18:16, where it refers to pillars of support.

In the Hiphil (causative), it basically means "to cause to be certain, sure" or "to be certain about," "to be assured." In this sense the word in the Hiphil conjugation is the biblical word for "to believe" and shows that biblical faith is an assurance, a certainty, in contrast with modern concepts of faith as something possible, hopefully true, but not certain.

Following from this we find the word in the passive Qal participle used with a passive meaning "one who is established" or "one who is confirmed," i.e. "faithful one" (II Sam 20:19; Ps 12:1 [H 2]; 31:23 [H 24]).

In the Niphal conjugation the meaning is "to be established" (II Sam 7:16; I Chr 17:23; II Chr 6:17; Isa 7:9). The Niphal participle means "to be faithful, sure, dependable" and describes believers (Num 12:7; I Sam 2:35; Neh 9:8). This form is also used to describe that upon which all certainty rests: God himself (Deut 7:9), and his covenant (Ps 89:28 [H 29]).

One interesting illustration of the relationship between "belief" and "being established" is seen in Isa 7:9. Ahaz is told that unless he believes (Hiphil) he will not be established (Niphal), i.e. without faith he has no stability.

The various derivatives reflect the same concept of certainty and dependability. The derivative *'āmēn* "verily" is carried over into the New Testament in the word *amēn* which is our English word "amen." Jesus used the word frequently (Mt 5:18, 26, etc.) to stress the certainty of a matter. The Hebrew and Greek forms come at the end of prayers and hymns of praise (Ps 41:13 [H 14]); 106:48; II Tim 4:18; Rev 22:20, etc.). This indicates that the term so used in our prayers ought to express certainty and assurance in the Lord to whom we pray.

'ōmen. ***Faithfulness, truth*** (ASV, "truth"; RSV as an adjective, "true"). The noun is used once to describe God's counsel (Isa 25:1).

'āmēn. ***Verily, truly, amen.*** (Generally, the same in ASV, RSV.) The word expresses a certain affirmation in response to what has been said. It is used after the pronouncement of solemn curses (Num 5:22; Deut 27:15ff.; Neh 5:13; Jer 11:5) and after prayers and hymns of praise (I Chr 16:36; Neh 8:6; Ps 41:13 [H 14], etc.). Twice the term is used to describe the Lord (Isa 65:16), and once simply to approve the words of a man (I Kgs 1:36). Finally, Jeremiah uses the term once sarcastically in response to the false prophets (Jer 28:6).

'ēmûn. ***Trusting, faithfulness.*** (Basically the same in ASV, RSV.) The term is applied to nations as a measure of their righteousness and acceptability to God (Deut 32:20; Isa 26:2). It also applies to individuals who are contrasted to the bad (Prov 13:17) and the false (Prov 14:5). One to whom the term applies is rare indeed (Prov 20:6).

'ĕmûnâ. ***Firmness, faithfulness, fidelity.*** (ASV, RSV generally the same. Both give a marginal note in Hab 2:4 where they translate "faith" instead of "faithfulness" in accord with Paul's use of the verse in Rom 1:17; Gal 3:11.)

There are at least ten distinct categories in which this noun is used in Scripture. In its first occurrence in Scripture it expresses the sense of steady, firm hands, a very basic idea (Ex 17:12). From this mundane sense, Scripture moves almost entirely to a use of the word in connection with God or those related to God.

Basically, the term applies to God himself (Deut 32:4) to express his total dependability. It is frequently listed among the attributes of God (I Sam 26:23; Ps 36:5 [H 6]; Ps 40:10 [H 11]; Lam 3:23). It describes his works (Ps 33:4); and his words (Ps 119:86; 143:1).

'ĕmûnâ is also used to refer to those whose lives God establishes. He expects to see faithfulness in them (Prov 12:22; II Chr 19:9). Indeed, such faithfulness or a life of faith is characteristic of those justified in God's sight (Hab 2:4). God's word of truth establishes man's way of truth or faithfulness (Ps 119:30).

From this we can also see the concept of a duty being entrusted to a believer which becomes his trust (faithful responsibility, I Chr 9:22; II Chr 31:15, etc.) or office.

'omnâ ***I. Brought up, nurtured, sustained.*** (Same in ASV, RSV.) This noun speaks of Esther's having been sustained (strengthened and guided) by Mordecai as a child (Est 2:20).

'omnâ ***II. Truly, verily, actually.*** (The same in ASV, RSV.) In the two contexts in which this adverb occurs, the speaker is perhaps seeking to excuse his wrong, therefore "actually" may be the best translation (Gen 20:12; Josh 7:20).

'ămānâ. ***Settled provision, support.*** (ASV, RSV same.) This noun is used in connection with a firm commitment on the part of the people of Jerusalem in Nehemiah's day (Neh 9:38 [H 10:1]) and also applies to a fixed provision for the singers of that day (Neh 11:23).

'umnām. ***Indeed, really.*** (Same in ASV, RSV.) This word is always found in interrogative sentences and always suggests doubt on the part of the asker: Sarah's doubt of bearing a child (Gen 18:13); Balaam's doubt of Balak's power to promote him (Num 22:37); Solomon's doubt of God's dwelling only on earth (I Kgs 8:27; II Chr 6:18); the Psalmist's doubt that pagan gods judge righteously (Ps 58:1 [H 2]).

'ĕmet. ***Truth, faithfulness, verity.*** (ASV and RSV usually the same.) This word carries underlying sense of certainty, dependability.

We find it used in several categories of contexts, all of which relate to God directly or indirectly.

First, it is frequently applied to God as a characteristic of his nature. In Gen 24:27, for example, it describes God who leads Abraham's servant to the right wife for Isaac. In Ex 34:6, it is given as one of the verbal descriptions of God which constitute God's goodness. Other examples are Ps 25:5; 31:5 [H 6]; Jer 4:2; 10:10.

It is a term fittingly applied to God's words (Ps 119:142, 151, 160; Dan 10:21).

As a characteristic of God revealed to men, it therefore becomes the means by which men know and serve God as their savior (Josh 24:14; I Kgs 2:4; Ps 26:3; 86:11; Ps 91:4; Isa 38:3), and then, as a characteristic to be found in those who have indeed come to God (Ex 18:21; Neh 7:2; Ps 15:2; Zech 8:16).

Because it is an attribute of God which is manifest in man's salvation and life of service as God's child, the word is often coupled with another attribute of God related to our salvation, "mercy" or "love" (*ḥesed,* Gen 24:27; Ps 61:7 [H 8]; 85:10 [H 11]; 115:1; Prov 14:22; 16:6; 20:28).

And because these attributes of God's truth and mercy lead to God's peace toward sinful men, saved by God's grace, the word is also often coupled with peace (Isa 39:8; Jer 33:6).

As we study its various contexts, it becomes manifestly clear that there is no truth in the biblical sense, i.e. valid truth, outside God. All truth comes from God and is truth because it is related to God.

'āmôn ***II. Master-workman?, people?*** (There is considerable uncertainty about this word and its use and whether it is to be read as *'āmôn* or a variant of *hāmôn* "people." Therefore translations differ.) The word occurs only twice. In Prov 8:30, the meaning seems to be that of an artificer (one true in hand and skill). In Jer 52:15, it may mean simply "people" or perhaps "the skilled ones" (who remained in Jerusalem).

Bibliography: Bright, John, "Faith and Destiny," Interp 5: 3–26. Napier, B. D., "On Creation—Faith in the Old Testament," Interp 16:21–42. Perry, Edmund, "The Meaning of 'emuna in the Old Testament," JBR 21: 252–56. Ramsdell, Edward T., The Old Testament Understanding of Truth," JR 31: 264–73. Richardson, TWB, pp. 75, 269. TDNT, I, pp. 232–38; 335–36; VI, pp. 183–91; 194–202. TDOT, I, pp. 292–322. THAT, I, pp. 177–99.

J.B.S.

117 אָמֵץ (*'āmēṣ*) ***be stout, strong, alert, bold, be solid, hard.*** (KJV, ASV, and RSV translate similarly.)

Derivatives

117a †אֹמֶץ (*'ōmeṣ*) ***strength.***
117b †אַמְצָה (*'amṣâ*) ***strength.***
117c †אָמוֹץ (*'āmôṣ*) ***strong*** or ***piebald*** from.
117d †אַמִּיץ (*'ammîṣ*) ***strong.***
117e †מַאֲמָצָה (*ma'ămāṣâ*) ***power, strength.***

This verb is found forty-one times in the OT. Ugaritic attests a parallel to the term.

In the Piel stem the verb can be rendered "make firm," "strengthen," "secure," "harden" (one's mind). The Hiphil stem manifests the force of "exhibit strength," "feel strong." In the Hithpael stem the translation is "strengthen oneself," "persist in," "prove superior to," "make oneself alert." The first occurrence of the verb is in Gen 25:23 in the Qal stem. The Lord revealed to Rebekah, before her sons were born, that they would be progenitors of two nations, and that one would be stronger than the other. David sang a song of deliverance for the mercy which the Lord granted in delivering him from Saul, an enemy stronger than he (II Sam 22:18 with its parallel in Ps 18:17 [H 18]). David expressed a similar sentiment in his prayer in the cave (Psa 142:6 [H 7]). In the days of Jeroboam's revolt against the Davidic dynasty, the Lord defeated the northern kingdom and its forces at the hand of Abijah, and the Judean army "prevailed" despite a well laid ambush (II Chr 13:18).

As a parallel to the more usual verb *ḥāzaq,* the word is employed repeatedly in God's charge to Joshua to be strong for the arduous tasks he assumed at the death of Moses (Josh 1:6, 7, 9, 18). Moses spoke similar words of encouragement to his understudy (Deut 31:7, 23). He charged the people in like manner (Deut 31:6).

The Piel stem conveys the concept of making one's heart obstinate or hard against the right as in the case of Sihon, king of Heshbon (Deut 2:30). The hardening of Pharaoh's heart before the Exodus is described by two synonymous verbs. Amos employs the same stem in his warning to Israel that, when the Lord commences his visitation in wrath upon them, the strong will not be able to rely on their strength any more than the agile will be able to escape by flight (Amos 2:14).

In a remarkable poetic description of wisdom, the sacred writer indicates that Wisdom was present when God confirmed (made firm) the skies above (Prov 8:28). Joash's repairs on the temple were successful because of the devotion of the laborers who strengthened the structure (II Chr 24:13). *'āmēṣ* is used in the Piel stem in connection various subjects, including the physical strength of the virtuous woman for her numerous household tasks (Prov 31:17), power for the warrior to carry on his military duties (Nah 2:1 [H 2]), and the strengthening of Rehoboam's royal power at the defection of the northern tribes (II Chr 11:17). Isaiah's classic satire on idolatry speaks of how the idolator secures for himself the tree of his choice (Isa 44:14).

The Hithpael serves to designate the strength of the conspirators against Rehoboam (II Chr 13:7), and the determination of Ruth to follow Naomi (1:18).

The Hiphil expresses strength of faith and hope (Psa 27:14; 31:25).

'ōmeṣ. ***Strength.*** This noun is found only once, in Job 17:9, where it refers to the righteous growing stronger.

'amṣâ. ***Strength.*** The only OT reference to this word is Zech 12:5, expressing the reliance of Judean chiliarchs on the inhabitants of Jerusalem.

'āmōṣ. This adjective occurs only in the plural and only in Zech 6:3, 7 where it indicates horses harnessed to chariots. KJV renders "bay," RSV "dappled gray." The word is used to describe the fourth pair of horses in a series. The first three are given colors and it seems incongruous to call the last pair "strong." KB defines as "piebald" from a root *'āmēs* II witnessed to in Arabic.

'ammîs (spelled defectively *'ammiṣ*) ***Strong.*** The first occurrence refers to Absalom's well-laid conspiracy (II Sam 15:12). Job speaks of God's power (9:4, 19). Isaiah speaks of God who is strong to chasten Israel (28:2), and shows his might in creation (40:26). Amos uses the term of one who survives God's judgment (2:16).

ma'ămāṣ. ***Power, strength.*** This noun appears only once, in Job 36:19, in construct plural in Elihu's question to Job.

Bibliography: TDOT, I, pp. 323–27. THAT, I, pp. 209–10.

C.L.F.

118 אָמַר (*'āmar*) ***say, speak, say to oneself (think), intend, command, promise.*** (KJV, ASV, and RSV reveal similar renderings.)

Derivatives

118a אֹמֶר (*'ōmer*) ***speech, word.***
118b †אִמְרָה (*'imrâ*) ***utterance, speech.***
118c אֶמְרָה (*'emrâ*) ***utterance, speech.***
118d אָמִיר (*'āmîr*) ***top, summit of tree.***
118e מַאֲמַר (*ma'ămar*) ***word, command.***

The Niphal stem may be translated "it is said" and "be called." The Hiphil means "induce to say." The Hithpael conveys the force of "act proudly." The verb appears in the OT almost five thousand times. This common verb, as with its parallels in other languages, has a wide variety of meanings.

This verb shares with four others (pe-aleph verbs) the peculiarity of the quiescence of the initial consonant in a long *o,* revealing the loss of the consonantal value of the aleph.

The commonest usage of the verb is in direct conversation, whether the subject is God (Gen 1:3), the serpent in the garden of Eden (3:1), Adam, terrified, trying to hide from God (3:10), Balaam's ass in his attempt to divert the stubborn prophet (Num 22:28), the war horse eager for battle (Job 39:25), the sea disavowing Wisdom's abode in it (Job 28:22), the trees of the forest in search of a king (Jud 9:8). It is readily seen that the verb is pressed into service in literal contexts, personifications, allegories, and strict narratives. A variety of nouns, clauses, adverbs, prepositional phrases are employed after the verb. Even when synonymous verbs are used (*dibbēr, ṣāwâ, 'ānâ, shāba', nādar,* among others), the verb *'āmar* can be used in the infinitive form with the preposition, i.e. *lē'mōr* to introduce the command, oath, response etc.

A usage often confused and incorrectly interpreted on the basis of a study of the English versions alone, is "say in the heart" (Deut 8:17; Ps 14:1). The meaning is "think," a subvocal speaking.

Although there are only a few examples of the use, the verb sometimes means "promise." Such is the force of the verb in a passage pointing to God's promise to David for a perpetual dynasty (II Kgs 8:19), the promise to Israel to possess the land of promise (Neh 9:15), or Haman's promise to Ahasuerus to pay the king for the opportunity to destroy all the Jews of his realm (Est 4:7).

Although the Hebrew language has a well attested and frequently used verb for "command" (*ṣāwâ* q.v.), *'āmar* also serves for this meaning. This usage is found in God's command to Joshua (Josh 11:9), Hezekiah's command concerning the offerings after the cleansing of the temple (II Chr 29:24), and Ahasuerus's command by letters to reverse the edict to slaughter the Jews by hanging Haman and his sons (Est 9:25).

As in modern languages, the Niphal is employed to mean that which "is said" by way of a current saying (Gen 10:9; 22:14; Jer 16:14).

An interesting usage, though not a frequent one, is that of "avow," "induce to say." In his closing addresses, Moses reminded Israel that they had vowed through him to have God as their own (Deut 26:17–18).

The use of the verb as "act proudly" is found in Ps 94:4 (the Hithpael). In Isa 61:6 the sense appears to be "boast" in a good connotation.

The derivation of *'āmar* is said by Wagner (TDOT, I, p. 328) to be no longer disputed. The root occurs in all the Semitic languages with either the meaning "be visible," "make visible," "see" (Akkadian, Ethiopic, Ugaritic) or "say," "command" (Hebrew, Aramaic, Arabic). It seems probable that the meaning "to see" or "make visible" is the original meaning. The semantic development to "make plain" then "say" is natural.

Of the more than five thousand uses of the root, the majority hardly need comment. They are close to the equivalent English word, "say." Indeed, the infinitive with *l* becomes often just a mark of direct discourse somewhat like the quotation marks of English.

However the word "say" gathers various connotations from the contexts in which it is used and some of these are of theological interest. It is a question, however, how many of these special meanings are inherent in the word *'āmar* and how many are due to the context.

For instance, *'āmar* sometimes means "to

command." These are cases where the word is spoken by God or some competent human authority. God commanded (*'āmar*) Abram to go (Gen 12:1). The Lord had spoken (*'āmar*) to Joshua and Joshua executed that word as a command (*ṣāwâ*) (Josh 11:9). But in the case of the Ten Commandments the synonym *dābar* is used to introduce them. At their end the Lord said (*'āmar*) to Moses, "Thus you shall say (*'āmar*) to the Israelites." Thus the differences between *'āmar* and *dābar* need not be overemphasized.

The word *'āmar* is used repeatedly by God to introduce revelation. One would suppose that this usage emphasizes that God's revelation is a spoken, transmissable, propositional, definite matter. The "word" does not make it a revelation. God gives the revelation to persons as one person imparts knowledge to another—by spoken word. The word *dābar* is used in such a context also, "God spoke (dābar) unto Noah" (Gen 8:15). The formula is frequent in Lev, "The Lord spoke (*dābar*) unto Moses saying (*lē'mōr*), speak (*dābar*) unto the children of Israel" (Lev 12:1–2).

God's word is creative. Genesis 1 has the phrase "God said" (*'āmar*) some ten times. Half of these times it is "God said, let there be" and then it happened. At other times it says "God said, let there be" and then God proceeded to create. This creative word of God is signalized in Ps 33:9, "He spoke (*'āmar*) and it was done; he commanded and it stood fast." The parallel word, "he commanded" (*ṣāwâ*), and the situation in Gen 1 may give us a word of warning against thinking that the "creative word does what it says" (TDOT, I, p. 336), as if the word had a power independent of God. Rather, it is God the Creator who does what he will. This will of God is expressed in words of command and they are effective because he makes them so.

[The word of God was given to prophets from Moses to Malachi and they spoke and wrote these words to the people. Especially the prophets of the monarchy cite the word with the formula, "Thus saith (*'amar*) the Lord." Since the work of H. W. Wolff and C. Westermann (*Basic Forms of Prophetic Speech,* trans. by H. C. White, Westminster, 1967) and others, this has been taken as a messenger formula similar to that in secular use when a messenger bearing a letter speaks the letter in the name of his sender. The emphasis is on the source of the prophets' messages. The message is not an invention of the prophet. This formula occurs over 130 times in Jeremiah alone. The formula indeed lays emphasis on God, the revelator. It must be remembered, however, that the commission to Jeremiah is given once at the beginning of the book. The whole book, and not just the pieces introduced by the formula were the words of God through Jeremiah to his rebellious contemporaries. Note the lack of a formula, yet the claim to revelation in the matter of the writing of the scroll, "All the words that I have spoken (*dābar*) unto thee against Israel . . . from the day I spoke (*dābar*) unto thee . . . unto this day" (Jer 36:2). There is no magic in the vocable *'āmar.* The power is in God the speaker. R.L.H.]

'ōmer. ***Speech, word, thing, something.*** (KJV and ASV render in Job 22:28, ***thing;*** RSV, ***matter.***)

A word of wide connotations (cf. *dābār*) is variously translated in different contexts. Thus, the term under consideration has been rendered utterance, saying, discourse, matter, promise, plan, purpose, decree, command, and appointment. It is found six times in the OT. The references (Job 22:28; Ps 19:2–3 [H 3–4]; 68:11 [H 12]; 77:8 [H 9]; Hab 3:9) appear only in poetic passages and the lofty language of prophecy (poetry). (It should be stated here that *'ēmer* is used forty-nine times; some lexicons list the citations of both words together.) The parallels to the word are commandment, words, voice, meditation, prayer, and law (instruction). Unquestionably, the term most often employed for "word" is *dābār,* which is used of God 394 times with the force of commandment, prophecy, admonition, or encouragement. In Job 22:28 Eliphaz advises Job to find his delight and trust in God, so that if he decides on a "matter," it may be realized for him. The Psalmist in Ps 19:2–3 [H 3–4] refers to the "speech" of natural creation. The use in Ps 68:11 [H 12] possibly relates to the command of God pictured at the head of his army with the command relayed by heralds (fem of office) throughout the ranks. The force in Ps 77:8 [H 9] is to the "promise" of God to the righteous. The reference in the admittedly difficult Hab 3:9 seems to point to the "oaths" (that is, the promises) made to the tribes of Israel.

'imrâ. ***Word, utterance, speech, saying.*** (KJV and ASV similar, "word"; RSV, "promise.")

There are thirty-six uses of the word, mostly in poetry (nineteen references in Ps 119; seven in other psalms) in the singular collective. Because the concept is a prominent one, it is natural that synonyms will be employed to avoid repetition.

Bibliography: Heinsch, P., *Das Wort im Alten Testament und im Alten Orient,* 1922. Jacobs, E., *Old Testament Theology,* 1955, pp. 127–35. May, E., "The Logos in the Old Testament," CBQ 8: 393–98. Mowinckel, "The Spirit and the Word in the Pre-exilic Prophets," JBL 53: 199. Richardson, TWB, p. 232. Ringgren, H., *Word and Wisdom,* 1947. Rundgren, F., "Hebräisch basar 'Golderz' und 'amar 'Sagen', Zwei Entomologien," Or 32:178–83. TDNT, IV, pp. 91–100. TDOT, I, pp. 328–47. THAT, I, pp. 216–19. TWNT, IV, pp. 69ff.

C.L.F.

119 אֱמֹרִי (*'ĕmōrî*) ***Amorites*** (collective). (KJV, ASV, RSV similar, rendering Amorite[s].)

The name occurs eighty-seven times in the OT It was employed of Palestinian settlers in general. They are designated in place of the Canaanites as the people whom Israel was to destroy (Gen 15:16; II Kgs 21:11). Older settlers of Judah were called Amorites (Josh 10:5–6). Amorites were located on the west shore of the Dead Sea (Gen 14:7), at Hebron (Gen 14:13), Shechem (Gen 48:22), Gilead, Bashan (Deut 3:10), and Hermon (Deut 3:8; 4:48).

The Amorites lived in the mountains, as did the Hittites and Jebusites (Num 13:29), their name perhaps signifying mountain dwellers.

In Abraham's time the Amurru were the prominent people of western Asia. In the third millennium B.C. the Amorite kingdom spread over the greater part of Mesopotamia and Syria-Palestine, the latter being designated as the "land of the Amorites." Thus the name belongs to the early Babylonian period of Near Eastern history. An Amorite dynasty ruled in northern Babylonia with Babylon as their capital, to which Hammurabi belonged. Amorite kingdoms lasted to the time of Israel's conquest of Canaan, a fact attested by the Amarna Tablets and Hittite records. After the defeat of Sihon, an Amorite king, their kingdom disappeared.

Bibliography: Clay, Albert F., *The Empire of the Amorites,* Yale Oriental Series, Researches, 6, Yale University, 1919, p. 192. Gibson, J. C. L., "Light from Mari on the Patriarchs," JSS 7: 44–62. ______, "Observations on Some Important Ethnic Terms in the Pentateuch," JNES 20: 217–38. Lewy, Julius, "Amurritica," HUCA 32:31–74. Tur-Sinai, H., "The Amorite and the Amurru of the Inscriptions," JQR 39: 249–58. Van Seters, John, "The Terms 'Amorite' and 'Hittite' in the Old Testament," VT 22: 64–81. Livrani, M., "The Amorites," in *Peoples of OT Times,* ed. K. A. Kitchen, Clarendon Press, 1973.

C.L.F.

120 אֶמֶשׁ (*'emesh*) ***yesterday.***

אֱמֶת (*'emet*). See no. 116k.

121 אֹן (*'ōn*), אוֹן (*'ôn*) ***On.*** (KJV, ASV, RSV render similarly.)

The name appears only three times in the OT: Gen 41:45, 50 and 46:20. It was a city in Lower Egypt where lived Potiphera, the priest of On and father-in-law of Joseph. The Egyptian name was An, Ant, and Annu; later the city was named Heliopolis, "sun-city." It was known for the worship of the sun god Ra. The name occurs in Ex 1:11 in the LXX. Designated now by Tell Hisn and Matariyeh, On was from ancient times the important center of Egyptian sun worship. It has been suggested that Aven (the same Hebrew consonants as the fully written On) in Ezk 30:17 is the same as the On of Genesis (NIV Heliopolis). There were two Ons in Egypt, one in Upper Egypt and the other in Lower Egypt. The biblical On is the latter. It was about ten miles northeast of modern Cairo. The history of On is clothed in obscurity. In the era of the Pyramid Texts it boasted a great sanctuary. There was a temple of the sun to Ra and Atum. It is thought that Bethshemesh ("house of the sun") is a pseudonym for On in Jer 43:13. Figuring in Egyptian history in the uprising against the Assyrian Ashurbanipal, On has been deserted since 525 B.C.

C.L.F.

אָן (*'ān*). See no. 75g.

122 אָנָּא (*'ānnā'*) ***ah now! I beseech you.***

123 אנב (*'nb*). **Assumed root of the following.**
123a אַרְנֶבֶת (*'arnebet*) ***hare.***

124 אָנָה (*'ānâ*) ***I, mourn.***

Derivatives

124a אֲנִיָּה (*'ănîyâ*) ***mourning.*** This noun occurs only in Isa 29:2; Lam 2:5.
124b תַּאֲנִיָּה (*ta'ănîyâ*) ***mourning.*** Occurs only in Isa 29:2; Lam 3:5.

125 אנה (*'nh*) **II. Assumed root of the following.**
125a †אֳנִי (*'ŏnî*) ***ships, fleet.***
125b †אֳנִיָּה (*'ŏnîyâ*) ***ship.***

In I Kgs 10:11, KJV and ASV translate "navy"; RSV "fleet." The noun *ŏnîyâ* appears thirty-one times. It is the common word for ship (Jon 1:3). It is already attested in the Tell el-Amarna texts. The singular of this noun, a feminine noun, designates a single ship. The plural of this noun and the short collective form (*'ŏnî* "fleet") occur often. The phrase *'anshê 'ŏnniyôt* "seamen" denotes those who manned them (I Kgs 9:27). Because the Israelites had no good harbors on the Mediterranean in the north and because the hostile Philistines controlled the coastal area toward the south, the sea was not an area of traffic for the Hebrews. However, during the illustrious reign of Solomon, the nation enjoyed maritime activity, not so much on the Mediterranean, but the Gulf of Aqabah. Israel's acquaintance with seagoing vessels dates from their contact with the Phoenicians.

Bibliography: Barnett, R. D., "Early Shipping in the Near East," *Antiquity* 32:220–30.

Sasson, Jack M., "Canaanite Maritime Involvement in the Second Millenium B.C.," JAOS 86:126–38.

C.L.F.

126 *אָנָה (*’ānâ*) ***III, be opportune, meet.***

The verb occurs only four times, three times in the Piel or Pual meaning "cause to meet," i.e. "deliver" or in the passive "be caused to meet," i.e. "happen." In the Hithpael it develops into "seek a quarrel."

Derivatives

126a תַּאֲנָה (*ta’ănâ*) ***occasion, time of estrous*** (of a donkey Jer 2:24).

126b תֹּאֲנָה (*tō’ănâ*) ***opportunity*** (for a quarrel), Jud 14:4.

אֱנוֹשׁ (*’ĕnôsh*). See no. 136a.

127 *אָנַח (*ānaḥ*) ***sigh, groan, gasp.***

Derivative

127a †אֲנָחָה (*’ănāḥâ*) ***sighing, groaning.***

’ānaḥ occurs twelve times, only in the Niphal and mostly in poetic passages.

The term occurs in Ugaritic. This verb is not the most frequently used in the OT for the act of mourning. *sāpad* and *’ābal* refer more to public acts of mourning and wailing as at a funeral. *bākâ* refers to weeping in any sorrow as does *’ānaḥ*. So important was the duty of funerary mourning that its omission was a serious misfortune (I Kgs 14:13 *sāpad*). Those who were immediately involved in the mourning were the members of the deceased's family (Gen 50:10 *sāpad*). Apart from funerals, public mourning was connected with repentance (Ex 33:4 *’ābal*; Joel 1:13 *sāpad*; 2:12–13 *mispēd*). In pagan practices borrowed by Israel from her idolatrous neighbors lacerations and mutilations accompanied mourning (cf. the prophets of Baal on Mt. Carmel). Of the verb's twelve citations, four appear in Lam (1:4, 8, 11, 21) and four occur in Ezk (9:4; 21:11 (*bis*), 12). The remainder are in Ex 2:23; Prov 29:2; Isa 24:7; and Joel 1:18. The instances in Lam all relate to the destruction of Jerusalem in 587/86 B.C. Ezekiel's references point to exercise of heart on the part of those who sighed over Israel's desperate spiritual condition.

’ănāḥâ. ***Sighing, sigh, groaning.*** (KJV, ASV, RSV similar, "sighing.") This noun refers to groaning in either physical or mental distress. It occurs eleven times in the OT, only in the poetic (six times in Ps and Job) and prophetic books (three in Isa, one in Jer, and one in Lam).

C.L.F.

128 אֲנַחְנוּ (*’ănaḥnû*) ***we.*** (KJV, ASV, RSV are similar, "we.")

The term occurs 188 times, fewer than would be expected (see the short form *naḥnû*). As with other Hebrew pronouns, its use is often for emphasis (also in oblique cases) "just we." The first person plural pronominal suffix appears frequently. Ugaritic lacks an independent full form. It may be posited that the protosemitic form lacked the initial aleph and that this longer form with aleph developed in analogy to the singular *’ănî* and *’ānōkî*.

128a נַחְנוּ (*naḥnû*) ***we,*** reading discernible as a short form of *’ănaḥnû*. (KJV, ASV, and RSV render uniformly, "we.")

Ugaritic offers no parallel to this form, although it has a suffix related to it. The word appears only six times (Gen 42:11; Ex 16:7–8; Num 32:32; II Sam 17:12; and Lam 3:42). This short form of the pronoun may be the original.

C.L.F.

אֳנִי (*’ŏnî*). See no. 125a,b.

אֳנִיָּה (*’ănîyâ*). See no. 124a.

129 אֲנִי (*’ănî*) ***I.*** (KJV, ASV, and RSV are similar.)

It is not surprising that the important first person singular pronoun occurs hundreds of times in the OT. Its presence is attested in Ugaritic, although the word was formerly thought to be a characteristic of the late "P" document. The longer pronoun *’ānōkî* is also used in Ugaritic. In its independent form the pronoun is found as the subject in noun clauses. Because it is the pronoun of the speaker, it requires no further indication of gender. Since a participle manifests no elements of the finite verb, the personal pronoun is essential to indicate the subject of the clause. When the pronoun is added to the finite verb, it lends emphasis, as in II Sam 12:28, "Lest I myself capture the city." Though in later Hebrew the emphasis is not so clearly demarcated, in earlier Hebrew, in prose at least, the stress is unmistakable. Three areas of emphasis with the independent pronoun may be pointed out. 1. It is found after a verb with the pronominal suffix of the first person as in Gen 27:34 where Esau pleads, "Bless me, even me also." 2. It occurs after a noun with the first person pronominal suffix as in II Sam 18:33 [H 19:1]: "Would I had died (lit., would my death, even mine)." 3. It appears after a preposition with the pronominal suffix in I Sam 25:24, "Upon me, even me."

Bibliography: THAT, I, pp. 216–19.

C.L.F.

129.1 אֲנָךְ (*’ănāk*) ***plummet.*** Perhaps a loan word.

130 אָנֹכִי (*'ānōkî*) ***I.*** (KJV, ASV, and RSV render alike.)

This form of the first person singular pronoun occurs more than two hundred times in the OT, but less often than the shorter form. It is found in Assyrian and Ugaritic and other Semitic languages, but is lacking in Aramaic, Arabic, and Ethiopic. It has been suggested that the longer and shorter forms of the pronoun had parallel growths, the longer adding a demonstrative element (like Heb *kōh* "here"). In certain instances both pronouns are used interchangeably. In other cases they manifest a definite choice on two counts, either because of the demands of the rhythm or because of the apparent preference of writers of the exilic period for the shorter form. When the pronoun is added to a verb for emphasis, the short form is almost always used (Deut 12:30; Jer 17:18). In the rhetorical style of Deuteronomy the longer form is employed. Particular phrases are found now with one pronoun, and now with the other. It is always the short form in the phrase, "as I live" (Num 14:21). The longer form is regularly employed with a predicate (II Sam 1:8). In exilic OT books the usage of the short form far outstrips the long: Ezekiel employs the former 138 times and the latter once (36:28).

C.L.F.

131 *אָנַן (*'ānan*) ***complain, murmur.*** Occurs only in the Hithpoel (Lam 3:39; Num 11:1).

132 אָנַס (*'ānas*) ***compel, constrain.*** Only in Est 1:8.

133 אָנֵף (*'ānēp*) ***to be angry, to be displeased.*** (ASV, RSV similar.)

Derivatives

133a †אַף (*'ap*) ***I, nostril, face, anger.*** The double pe in the plural shows its derivation from *'ānēp*.

133b אֲנָפָה (*'ănāpâ*) ***an unclean bird*** (Lev 11:19; Deut 14:18). Its derivation is uncertain.

'ānēp is used to express the Lord's attitude of anger toward the covenant people when they have sinned, e.g. Moses (Deut 1:37), Aaron (Deut 9:20), the people (Deut 9:8). Men acknowledge God's prerogative, but plead that he not continue to be angry.

'ap. ***Nostril, face, anger.*** The term *'ap* in Hebrew refers first of all to a part of the body, specifically the nose, nostril, (snout of pigs, Prov 11:22) and also face (II Sam 25:23) or countenance (cf. UT 19: no. 264, an opening of the body, or possibly the body itself, e.g., nose, nipple). It is considered a vital part of the body. God made man a living being by breathing into his nose/nostrils (Gen 2:7). The nose, although referred to as the organ for smelling (Deut 33:10) or a place for ornaments (Isa 3:21) or for hooks by which to lead captives (II Kgs 19:28), is also spoken of as an organ necessary if a man's or animal's life is to continue (Isa 2:22).

By the act of breathing, emotions can be expressed. Perhaps it was observed that the nose dilates in anger. God is said to be "*'erek 'appayim*" (lit. "long of anger," i.e. long before getting angry) in such passages as Ex 34:6; Num 14:18; Ps 86:15; Neh 9:17. The thought is that God takes a long, deep breath as he holds his anger in abeyance. A ruler is said to be persuaded by a display of forbearance, patience, i.e. "the long of breath" (Prov 25:15).

The main use of *'ap* is to refer to the anger of men and of God. This anger is expressed in the appearance of the nostrils. *'ap* gives specific emphasis to the emotional aspect of anger and wrath, whereas its synonyms and terms related to them give particular expression to other aspects.

The anger of God is particularly related to the sin of his people, which pains and deeply displeases him (II Kgs 13:3). Sin offends and wounds his love. The emotional response to this is divine anger. This anger, though fierce (Jer 25:37) is not sinful, evil, or the source of capricious attitudes or deeds. However, it is expressed in chastisement (Ps 6:1 [H 2]; Isa 12:1) and punishment (II Sam 6:7; Jer 44:6).

Man's anger can be legitimate (II Sam 12:5). But the OT Scriptures warn that anger can be outrageous (Prov 27:4) and stirs up strife (Prov 29:22). In contrast, it is said that the man slow to anger appeases strife (Prov 15:18) and a wise man turns from it (Prov 29:8).

Bibliography: Erlandsson, S., "The Wrath of Yhwh," *Tyndale Bulletin* 23:111–16. Hanson, R. P. C., "The Wrath of God," Exp T 58: 216–18. McKenzie, John L., "Vengeance is Mine," *Scripture* 12: 33–39. Morris, L. L., "The Wrath of God," Exp T 63: 142–45. TDNT, V, pp. 392–418. TDOT, I, pp. 348–60. THAT, I, pp. 220–24.

G.V.G.

134 אָנַק (*ānaq*) ***cry, groan.***

Derivatives

134a אֲנָקָה (*'ănāqâ*) ***I, crying, groaning.***

134b אֲנָקָה (*'ănāqâ*) ***II, ferret or shrew-mouse.***

135 אָנַשׁ (*'ānash*) ***I, desperate, incurable, desperately wicked, woeful, very sick.*** (RSV similar except that it translates as "disaster" in Jer 17:16.)

The basic meaning of the word is "to be sick" (II Sam 12:15) but most frequently it is used to describe a wound or pain which is incurable as attested by the contexts of Jer 15:18; 30:12. It is used metaphorically in Isa 17:11; Jer 17:16. In Jer 17:9 it describes the desperate spiritual state of the heart in terms of illness.

136 אנשׁ (*'nsh*) **II. Assumed root of the following.**

136a †אֱנוֹשׁ (*'ĕnôsh*) ***man, mortal man, person.*** (ASV, RSV similar).

The basic meaning of *'ĕnôsh* is "man" in the sense of "mankind." The word can refer to an individual only in the most general sense (e.g. "blessed is the man who does this [Isa 56:2]) and thus lacks the specificity of *'îsh*. It is used mainly in the poetic material.

The verbal root of *'ĕnôsh* is uncertain. If it is a derivation of *'ānash* "to be weak, sick," the basic emphasis would be on man's weakness or mortality, a connotation permitted by some contexts, particularly those that emphasize man's insignificance (e.g., Ps 8:4 [H 5]; Job 7:17). The word may be derived from a different root *'ns* unattested in Hebrew but found in Arabic and Ugaritic. It has the connotation of friendliness or sociality in Arabic and the similar concept of companionability in Ugaritic. If derived from this root the basic emphasis of *'ĕnôsh* would be on man as a social being.

While it is true that the word frequently emphasizes man's frailty and humanness, these concepts may derive from the theological framework in which the ancient Hebrews viewed mankind and not necessarily from an inherent root meaning. The word frequently has a general sense and its usage in parallelism with other general terms for man such as *'ādām* (Ps 73:5), *b^{e}nê'ādām* (Ps 144:3), and its use in association with "land of the living" (Job 28:13) would seem to argue for derivation from the unattested *'nsh*. The stress would then be on man as he comprises the human race.

The basic meaning "mankind" is evident in such passages as Job 28:13; 36:24 [H 25]; Ps 90:3; Isa 13:12 and in Deut 32:26; Job 7:1; Isa 24:6 where it is used of man as the one who inhabits the earth.

A major theological concept underlying the use of this word is the fundamental distinction between God and man. Elihu sets forth this concept in his affirmation that God is greater than man (Job 33:12). The Psalmist calls on God to exercise his might so that man may recognize his insignificance before him (Ps 9:19–20 [H 20–21]). This fundamental difference is the basis of the affirmation in Ps 10:17–18 that "man who is of the earth" will no more strike terror. Man's sphere is earth, not heaven. He is mortal, not divine, and so cannot prevail against God. The distinction is also evident in man's mortality (Ps 90:3) and God's immortality (vv. 2, 4). God's nature as opposed to man's is set forth in such questions as, "Do you see as man sees?" (Job 10:4) and, "Are your years the years of a man?" (Job 10:5).

Man's insignificance in view of the vastness of the universe is set forth in the question, "What is man?" (Ps 8:4). His lot on earth is difficult (Job 7:1; 14:19), but he does enjoy God's providences (Ps 104:15; cf. v. 14).

The word *'ĕnôsh* reminds man of his transience and of his lowly position before the Almighty.

Messiah is described as being like the son of man (*'ĕnôsh* Dan 7:13) a term which describes his close relationship to the human race. (Note in the Daniel passage that there might be a studied contrast to the four preceding symbols of Kingdoms which are beasts.

Bibliography: TDOT, I, pp. 345–47.

T.E.M.

137 אנשׁ (*'nsh*) **III. Assumed root of the following.**

137a †אִשָּׁה (*'ishshâ*) ***woman, wife, female, each, every.*** (ASV and RSV similar.)

The word *'ishshâ* is the most common word for "woman" and "wife" in the OT.

The origin of woman is explained in Gen 2:23, 24. She is depicted as the physical counterpart of man, deserving of his unswerving loyalty. It is in this context (vv. 24–25) that the word is first used in the sense of "mate" or "wife."

The Bible holds woman in the highest regard and sets forth "graciousness" (Prov 11:16) and "worth" (Ruth 3:11) as womanly ideals. However, beauty without discretion is condemned (Prov 11:22).

Women held positions of prestige in the OT. The wise woman of Tekoa, Deborah, and Esther are only a few of the many women of influence in OT history.

There are, however, warnings against the adulterous woman and the harlot. Congress with them will lead to certain punishment (Prov 6:24–29) and even spiritual death (Prov 2:16–19).

The expression "born of a woman" *y^{e}lûd 'ishshâ* uses *'ishshâ* in a collective sense connoting man's mortality with its inherent frailties (Job 14:1; 15:14; 25:4).

Women were forbidden to wear men's clothing (Deut 22:5). See Hoffner (bibliog). They were permitted to be taken as booty in the conquest of a city (Deut 21:10–11).

The word *'ishshâ* occurs in a number of set expressions, e.g. *'ishshâ n^{e}bî'â*, a prophetess, and *'ishshâ zônâ*, a harlot.

Metaphorically, a noble woman represents wisdom, but a foolish woman (Prov 9:13) represents that which is opposed to wisdom.

The word is frequently used in the sense of "wife." The good wife is highly honored in the OT. He who finds one finds a source of blessing (Prov 18:22) and honor (Prov 12:4). A fruitful wife is a sign of blessing (Ps 128:3). Her honored position is evident in the fact that she is "from the Lord" (Prov 19:14). The classic picture of the ideal wife is set forth in Prov 31:10–31. A quarrelsome wife, however, may be a source of contention (Prov 19:13; 21:9, 19; 25:24; 27:15).

The legal role of the wife is clearly defined in the OT. Adultery is punishable by death for both parties (Deut 22:22). A woman suspected of adultery could be made to take an oath of innocence and subjected to a kind of lie detector test by her husband in the sacred precincts to determine her guilt or innocence (Num 5:11–31). Hebrew servants could have wives (Ex 21:3). If a servant's master gave him a wife, the servant stood in danger of being separated from his wife when his period of service ended (Ex 21:4–5). The newly married wife was not to be separated from her husband (Deut 24:5) and the widow was provided for in the Levirate system (Deut 25:5).

The role of the wife is used as a metaphor in a number of important passages. Adultery (Ezk 16:32) and divorce (Jer 3:1) figure strikingly in the prophetic message of denunciation. Israel was seen as the wife of the Lord, a figure expressive of the deepest love. Yet they spurned God, as a wayward wife spurns her husband. In Mal 2:14 the initiation of the marriage relationship between the Lord and his people is the Mosaic covenant.

Bibliography: Böhl, Franz M. Th., "The Position of Women in Ancient Babylonia and Israel," BS 77: 4–13, 186–97. Brooks, Beatrice Allard, "Some Observations Concerning Ancient Mesopotamian Women," AJSL 39: 187–94. Crook, Margaret B., "The Marriageable Maiden of Prov 31: 10–31," JNES 13: 137–40. Hoffner, H. A., "Symbols for Masculinity and Femininity," JBL 85: 326–35. Schofield, J. N., "Some Archaeological Sites and the Old Testament (Nuzu)," Exp T 66: 315–18. Yaron, Reuven, "Aramaic Marriage Contracts from Elephantine," JSS 3: 1–39. THAT, I, pp. 247–50.

T.E.M.

138 אסה (*'sh*) **Assumed root of the following.**
138a †אָסוֹן (*'āsôn*) ***mischief, evil, harm, hurt.*** (KJV translates "mischief"; ASV and RSV render similarly, "harm.")

The noun appears five times, always without the article. The passages in Genesis (42:4, 38; 44:29) relate to Jacob's concern for Benjamin's welfare. The references in Exodus (21:22–23) deal with injury to a pregnant woman.

C.L.F.

אָסוֹן (*'āsôn*). See no. 138a.
אֵסוֹר (*'ēsôr*). See no. 141a.
אָסִיף (*'āsîp*). See no. 140b.
אָסִיר (*'āsîr*), אַסִּיר (*'assîr*). See no. 141b,c.

139 אסם (*'sm*). **Assumed root of the following.**
139a אָסָם (*'āsām*) ***storehouse.*** Occurs only in Deut 28:8; Prov 3:10.

140 אָסַף (*'āsap*) ***gather, remove, gather in*** (harvest).

Derivatives

140a אֹסֶף (*'ōsēp*) ***gathering.***
140b †אָסִיף (*'āsîp*) ***ingathering, harvest.***
140c אָסֹף (*'āsōp*) ***what is gathered, store.***
140d †אֲסֵפָה (*'ăsēpâ*) ***a collecting, gathering.***
140e אֲסֻפָּה (*'ăsūppâ*) ***collection.***
140f †אֲסַפְסֻף (*'ăsapsūp*) ***collection, rabble.***

In the Niphal is translated "be gathered" (by death), "assemble," "be removed," "perish." The Pual is rendered "be gathered," whereas the Hithpael has the force of "gather themselves." (KJV, ASV, and RSV render similarly.) The verb has the same meaning in Ugaritic.

This verb occurs 199 times. Ugaritic attests a cognate root. The two principal words for "gather" are *'āsap* and *qābaṣ*. Transitively, the verb under consideration denotes "to bring together," "collect"; intransitively, "to come together," "assemble." The phrase "gathered to his fathers" is frequently used for "to die" or "death" (Gen 25:8, 17; 49:29, 33; Deut 32:50; II Kgs 22:20).

There are some scholars who suggest that this phrase intimates, albeit indistinctly and vaguely, an early belief in life after death with recognition of loved ones in the afterlife. It may, however, be a euphemism for death without clear theological import. The transitive force can denote the gathering of a host (Ps 27:10; cf. Isa 52:12).

An important use of the word is connected with the harvest for which the usual word is *qāṣîr*. Since Israel was an agricultural people, this harvest (*qāṣîr*) held for them great significance (Gen 8:22; 45:6). Events were counted from or related to harvests (Gen 30:14; Josh 3:15; Jud 15:1; Ruth 1:22; 2:23; I Sam 6:13; II Sam 21:9; 23:13). The three main feasts of the Jewish religious calendar answered to three harvest seasons (Ex 23:16; 34:21–22). The Feast of Passover was at the time of barley harvest, the feast of Pentecost was at the wheat harvest (Ex 34:22), and the Feast of Tabernacles at year's end came during fruit harvest. Between barley harvest and wheat harvest fall a few showers which increase the wheat yield (cf. Amos 4:7). From the time of wheat harvest until the fruit harvest there is no rain (II Sam 21:10; Jer 5:24). The Mosaic law surrounded the harvest with definite laws on gleaning (Lev 19:9), firstfruits (Lev 23:10), and the prohibition of harvesting a crop for which they had not labored (Lev 25:5).

The Gezer Calendar sets forth the harvest seasons in ancient Israel. Olives were harvested from the middle of September to the middle of November. Trees were beaten with long sticks (Deut 24:20; Isa 17.6). Flax was harvested in March–April by cutting it off at the ground, then allowing the stalks to soften (called retting) by dew or other moisture (Josh 2:6). In April or early May barley harvest took place with wheat harvest in May–June. The harvesting of figs, grapes, and pomegranates, summer fruits, was during August–September.

There are figurative usages also. Destruction of a harvest indicated God's punishment (Job 5:5; Isa 16:9; Jer 5:17). The "time of harvest" often denoted the period of destruction (Jer 51:33; Hos 6:11; Joel 3:13 [H 4:13]). The joy of harvest designated great rejoicing. The harvest of the Nile denoted an abundant ingathering (Isa 23:3). A harvest that was past indicated a lost and irretrievable opportunity (Jer 8:20).

A derived use of the verb occurs with the meaning of "withdraw" or "remove." When Saul heard the Philistine commotion in their camp (I Sam 14:19), he ordered the priest to withdraw his hand from the ark of God.

'āsîp. ***Ingathering, harvest*** (of grain and fruits). This noun appears twice, in Ex 23:16 and 34:22. The first passage deals with the three pilgrimage feasts in Israel's sacred calendar; the second treats the same feasts in summary fashion.

'ăsēpâ. ***Collecting, gathering,*** or ***collection.*** (KJV and ASV render "are gathered" [in the pit]; RSV translates "will be gathered together.")

This noun is a *hapax legomenon* (Isa 24:22), appearing in Isaiah's so-called apocalypse (chaps. 24–27) in connection with what some exegetes believe is an eschatological revelation. At least the resurrection is in view (Isa 25:8).

'ăsapsup. ***Rabble.*** (KJV, ASV similar with "mixed multitude"; RSV "rabble.") This masculine collective noun occurs once in Num 11:4 in reference to the motley collection of people who followed Israel from Egypt.

Bibliography: Albright, W. F., BASOR 92: 16ff.; Wright, G. E., *Biblical Archaeology,* Westminister, 1957, pp. 180ff.

C.L.F.

141 אָסַר (*'āsar*) ***tie, bind, harness, gird, imprison.*** (KJV, ASV, and RSV render similarly, tie, bind, imprison.)

Derivatives

141a אֵסוּר (*'ēsûr*) ***band, bond.***
141b †אָסִיר (*'āsîr*) ***bondman, prisoner.***
141c †אַסִּיר (*'assîr*) ***prisoners.***
141d אִסָּר (*'issār*) ***bond, binding obligation.***
141e †מָסֹרֶת (*māsōret*) ***bond.***
141f †מוֹסֵר (*môsēr*) ***band, bond.***

This term occurs thirty-four times in the OT. The root is attested in Ugaritic with the force of "to bind." With *milḥāmâ* the meaning is "to begin the battle," "make the attack." In the Niphal the rendering is "to be bound," "imprisoned"; in the Pual stem the translation is "to be taken prisoner." Another usage refers to binding oneself with an oath or obligation.

A number of Hebrew words indicate the concept of binding, such as *rākas* "to fasten" (Ex 28:28) and *ṣûr* "tie up" (Deut 14:25). It is employed in the sense of making one a prisoner (Jud 15:10; Ps 149:8 [H 9]). Imprisonment is often mentioned in the OT, showing that this was a common form of punishment among the Israelites and foreign nations (Gen 40:3; 42:19; Num 15:34; I Kgs 22:27; Jer 37:15, 21). Among the Hebrews there were no special prison buildings until probably the postexilic era. In Assyria and Egypt such buildings existed. In Israel rooms or pits connected with the royal palace or the homes of court officials served in this capacity.

There are several cases in which the liberty of individuals was restricted: Joseph's brethren were kept for three days (Gen 42:19); Shimei was restricted to the city of Jerusalem (I Kgs 2:36); the man who gathered sticks on the Sabbath was confined (Num 15:34); Micaiah was imprisoned by Ahab (I Kgs 22:27); Hanani by Asa (II Chr 16:10; Hoshea, after his fruitless attempt to form an alliance with Egypt, by Shalmaneser (II Kgs 17:4); Jehoiachin and Zedekiah in Babylon by Nebuchadnezzar (II Kgs 25:27; Jer 52:11).

The book of Jeremiah has much to say about imprisonment in Israel during the later years of the Davidic dynasty. The prophet was put in fetters, at the upper gate of Benjamin (Jer 20:2), because he had forewarned the people of Judah's fall. During the siege of the capital, Jeremiah was imprisoned in the court of the guard in the king's residence (32:2), apparently in the quarters of the sentry who guarded the palace. Finally, the prophet was accused of treason and confined in the house of Jonathan the scribe. It is thought that the place was not a private residence, but rather a building of that name which had been taken over to serve as a prison. This has greater cogency when one reads that the house had a dungeon and cells.

For a short time he was in the dungeon or pit (*bôr*) of Malchijah (Jer 38:6).

Prisoners were treated in conformity with the gravity of their offence. Samson was placed under hard labor (Jud 16:21) and physically mutilated by blinding. Adonibezek was incapacitated, his thumbs and large toes cut off (Jud 1:6). Special diet and garb were assigned prisoners (I Kgs 22:27; II Kgs 25:29). Punitive imprisonment was apparently unknown in the ancient near east, Greece, and Rome. In the Code of Justinian the custodial aspect of imprisonment was instituted with the position that "a prison is for confinement, not for punishment."

'āsîr. ***Prisoner, captive.*** (KJV, ASV, and RSV translate similarly.) Parallels are attested in Ugaritic, Arabic, and Aramaic. Fourteen references appear in the OT, of which two are marginal readings (Gen 39:20, 22). Contrary to Western concepts of imprisonment, ancient law did not mete out incarceration as a punishment. Prisons served as a temporary confinement until further review and deliberation of a case. Places of confinement differed; some were private houses (Jer 37:15), underground dungeons (Jer 37:16), the court of the guard (Jer 32:2), or perhaps even a cistern (Jer 38:6). In Gen 39:20, 22 Joseph, wrongly accused, is imprisoned with two of Pharaoh's chief officers. Out of this situation by the overruling of God, Joseph is elevated to a position second to Pharaoh. Samson the judge was imprisoned by his enemies, the Philistines, in order to wreak vengeance on him for his successful campaigns against them (Jud 16:21, 25). Isaiah employs the concept figuratively as he describes the activity of the King of Babylon in his imprisoning multitudes of the earth (Isa 14:17). The postexilic prophecy of Zechariah likens the exiles to liberated prisoners of hope (Zech 9:11). Interesting are the parallels of the word: solitary (Ps 68:6 [H 7]); poor or needy (Ps 69:33 [H 34]); those appointed to death (Ps 102:20 [H 21]); inhabitants of darkness and deep gloom (Ps 107:10).

'assîr. ***Prisoners*** (usually collective). KJV, ASV, and RSV render alike, "prisoners", except in Ex 6:24 where the translation is uniformly "Assir."

The root concept is found in Ugaritic. There are three references in the OT, all in the prophecy of Isaiah (10:4; 24:22; 42:7). Exodus 6:24, I Chr 6:22 [H 7] and 6:37 [H 22] have the proper noun, "Assir." In I Chr 3:17 the word *'assîr* is taken by some as the first son of Jeconiah. Others translate it "Jeconiah (the captive)" which seems to fit the context better. The OT mentions Egyptian, Assyrian, Judean, Babylonian, and Philistine prisoners. Solomon imprisoned Shimei ben Gera in the city of Jerusalem (I Kgs 2:36–37). The cities of refuge were provided for manslayers who were innocent of murder (Num 35). When Isaiah presented the bill of particulars of Israel's sins, he predicted that Assyria would be God's agent of wrath on Israel. Imprisonment and death would be the consequences (Isa 10:4). Isaiah in his well-known apocalyptic section (chaps. 24–27) foresaw the cataclysmic visitation of God upon the kings and leaders of the earth. They will be gathered as prisoners into the pit, confined there, and later punished with ultimate wrath (Isa 24:22). In the first of the Servant Songs, Isaiah predicts that Messiah will liberate Satan's prisoners, a figurative statement of Messiah's redeeming grace (Isa 42:7). Assir (Ex 6:24; I Chr 6:22 [H 7] 37 [H 22]), was a son of Korah, called son of Ebiasaph; he was named after his great-grandfather.

māsōret. ***Bond*** (construct). KJV and ASV are similar, with RSV giving rendering in footnote. The word appears only in Ezk 20:37 of Israel's judgment by God.

môsēr. ***Band, bond.*** (KJV renders "bands" where ASV and RSV translate "bonds.") The Ugaritic offers a parallel to this term. Eleven usages of this word are found in the OT. The English translation "band" (or "bond") is a rendering of more than one Hebrew word in the Scriptures. In its literal sense a band is anything that connects, encloses, confines, or strengthens. Figurative usage denotes that which chastens or restrains. Jeremiah (5:5) sets forth Israel's wickedness in which the rulers of the nation have overstepped the restraints of God. Jeremiah uses literal bonds to convey God's warning to Israel that they, as well as surrounding nations, will be brought under the domination of Nebuchadnezzar (27:2).

Spiritual liberation from sin is in view in the case of Ps 116:16. In Isa 52:2 the bonds mentioned are those of Zion's captivity. In a strikingly clear eschatological reference in Ps 2:3 the allied nations of earth are pictured as definitely opposed to the restraint and sovereign rule of God. A singularly beautiful protrayal of redeeming lovingkindness is found in Ps 107:14, where the literal and spiritual emphases of bonds interchange.

Bibliography: Elon, M., "Imprisonment," in *Encyclopedia Judaica,* VIII, 1972, pp. 1299–1303. Gordon, C. H., UT 19: no. 284. Sheehy, D. F., "Prisons," in *New Catholic Encyclopedia,* XI, 1967, pp. 791–793.

C.L.F.

אַף (*'ap*) I. See no. 133a.

142 אַף (*'ap*) ***II, also yea.*** (KJV, ASV, and RSV render similarly.)

The conjunction occurs over 120 times. It may denote that which is added to a preceding statement with the force of "also," "yea." A pointed example is found in the rebellious answer given to Moses in Num 16:14, "Also (moreover) you have not brought us into a land flowing with milk and honey." The conjunction is rare in prose; more often it is found in poetry as setting forth a new thought (I Sam 2:7). In elevated prose it appears in Lev 26:16 and following verses. With great intensity of feeling Isaiah builds up to a crescendo in Isa 48:12–13, 15 and elsewhere in chapters 40–48. What is often in view is something unexpected, "even," "indeed" (Job 14:3; 15:4). In both poetry and prose a previous statement is built into an a fortiori argument, "how much more" (after a positive sentence), or "how much less" (after a negative one). The usages may be summarized as additional use, "also"; emphatic, "I for my part"; antithetic, "but"; compounds, "yea, truly"; conditional, "when" *kî* follows the conjunction as in Prov 11:31, or interrogative as in Gen 3:1, "Is it indeed that God has said?"

C.L.F.

142.1 אֵפוֹד (*'ēpôd*), אֵפֹד (*'ēpōd*) ***ephod.*** (KJV, ASV, and RSV translate similarly.)

This word is found forty-eight times in the OT. Parallels are found in Assyrian and Ugaritic. In the Cappadocian texts *epadum* seems to mean a plaid robe. At Ras Shamra there was found a Ugaritic hymn (c. 1400 B.C.), which referred to an ephod, probably a garment of the goddess Anath. It is not certain that there is a correspondence to the Hebrew priestly garment. There is even some question as to the correctness of the translation of the passage. One scholarly view is that the OT ephod with the sacred ark was a kind of miniature temple. The ephod has even been compared to the tent-like shrine carried into battle by certain Arabian tribes. The prevailing view is still that the ephod was a garment for the high priest in Israel.

It was a sacred garment originally made for the high priest (Ex 28:4ff.; 39:2ff.). It was made of gold, blue, purple, scarlet and fine twined linen, fastened by two shoulder pieces and woven band for a girdle for the ephod. Two onyx stones, on which were engraved the names of the tribes of Israel, were placed on the shoulder pieces. The ephod may have extended below the hips or only to the waist. A breastplate with twelve precious stones in four rows was attached to the ephod with pure gold chains. Under the ephod was the blue robe of the ephod reaching to the feet of the priest.

Ephods were worn by others, also Samuel was girded with a linen ephod while ministering under Eli the priest (I Sam 2:18). The eighty-five priests at Nob were girded with linen ephods (I Sam 22:18). David was wearing a linen ephod when he accompanied the procession bringing the ark into Jerusalem (II Sam 6:14). Doubtless, the ephod of the high priest was more elaborate and ornamented than those worn by lay worshipers.

In time of crisis the will of the Lord was sought through the ephod (cf. David in I Sam 23:9; 30:7). In Israel both prophecy and the ephod were authorized means of ascertaining the will of God. The technical phrase for consulting the ephod with the Urim and Thummim is "to come before the Lord" (Ex 28:30; Jud 20:27; I Sam 14:18, 41).

When the Hebrews fell into idolatry, they used teraphim and graven images in conjunction with the ephod (Jud 17:5; 18:14, 15, 17, 20; Hos 3:4). It is safe to assume that in these instances the ephod was a priestly garment (cf. that made by Gideon, Jud 8:27), perhaps adorned with costly gems (as in the case of Micah, Jud 17:1–5).

After the captivity, the ephod did not serve the function described in the Pentateuchal legislation (Ezr 2:63; Neh 7:65). Some believe that the spiritual influence of the prophets served to overshadow this means of ascertaining the will of God.

Another form of the word is *'ăpūddâ,* found in Ex. 28:8; 39:5; Isa 30:22. It has been suggested that the robe with the golden bells may have been included in the word "ephod."

Bibliography: Albright, W. F., "Are the Ephod and the Teraphim Mentioned in Ugaritic Literature?" Basor 83:39ff. Albright, W. F., *Yahweh and the Gods of Canaan,* Doubleday, 1968, pp. 171, 174, 177, 179, 197, 200–205. Arnold, W. R., *Ephod and the Ark,* Harvard University, 1917. Foote, T. C., "The Ephod," JBL 21: 1–47. Grintz, Y. M., "Ephod," in *Encyclopedia Judaica,* 1972 vol. 6, pp. 804–806.

C.L.F.

142.2 אַפֶּדֶן (*'appedden*) ***palace.*** A Persian loan word.

143 אָפָה (*'āpâ*) ***bake.*** (KJV, ASV, RSV translate similarly.)

Derivative

143a מַאֲפֶה (*ma'ăpeh*) ***something baked*** (Lev 2:4).

In the Qal, *'āpâ* is translated as indicated; in the Niphal it is rendered "to be baked" (with leaven). There are twenty-five references in the OT. The verb is attested in Ugaritic. The participle of the Qal is used substantively and rendered throughout as "baker."

The term and its derivative refer specifically to the baking of bread and cakes made with flour and oil. Such baked food was a basic element in the daily diet of the Hebrews and their neighbors (Gen 19:3; I Kgs 17:12–13). Because bread was such an important commodity in the near east (cf. our "staff of life"), bakers were important officers, as in Egypt (Gen 40:1) and Assyria where the chief baker was singled out by an eponym. Baking was essential to the preparation of sacred meals (Gen 14:18) and certain bloodless offerings (Lev 21:6), especially in relation to the showbread of the sanctuary. The showbread and the baked offerings were an integral part of the worship of Israel (Lev 2:4ff.; 24:5). Bread was usually baked in an oven, a household duty of women. The Hebrew verb is often used synonymously with cooking in general (Ex 16:23).

C.L.F.

144 אֵפוֹ (*'ēpô*), אֵפוֹא (*'ēpô'*), אֵיפוֹא (*'êpô'*) ***then, so.***

It has been suggested that the word originally came from *pô* or *pōh,* a particle with a demonstrative force and a prosthetic aleph. The adverbial use of the particle is rendered "wholly," "so," "therefore." The word occurs fifteen times in the OT. When employed as an interrogative pronoun, it is translated "where." The particle is used in connection with interrogative pronouns and adverbs. In Gen 27:33 Isaac asks Esau, "Who then is he?" It is used with an interrogative adverb in Isa 19:12: "Where then are thy wise men?" Another use of the particle is in a command or wish, e.g. Job 19:23: "Would, then, that my words were written!" The term also appears after *'im.* Gen 43:11 reads, "If it be so, then, do this."

To summarize, the particle is found in sentences containing a question, command, or wish. It appears after interrogative particles; apart from the interrogative; before the interrogative; after an expression of a wish, *mî yitēn;* after the words *'im,* or *'im-lô'*, "if now"; following *'im* and apart from it; and in exhortations, meaning "then."

C.L.F.

אֲפוּנָה (*'apûnâ*). See no. 146c.
אָפִיל (*'āpîl*). See no. 145d.
אָפִיף (*'āpîp*). See no. 149a.

145 אפל (*'pl*). **Assumed root of the following.**
145a †אֹפֶל (*'ōpel*) ***darkness, gloom.***
145b אָפֵל (*'āpēl*) ***gloomy.***
145c †אֲפֵלָה (*'ăpēlâ*) ***darkness, gloominess.***
145d אָפִיל (*'āpîl*) ***late.***
145e מַאֲפֵל (*ma'ăpēl*) ***darkness.***
145f †מַאְפֵּלְיָה (*ma'pēlyâ*) ***deep darkness.***

'ōpel. ***Darkness, gloom*** (poet.), ***calamity,*** (fig.). ***spiritual darkness.*** (In Job 3:6 KJV renders "darkness," whereas ASV and RSV translate "thick darkness.") For the figurative usage the KJV translates, as do ASV and RSV, as in the case of the literal use.

There are nine instances of the occurrence of the word in the OT. Most appear in Job, two references in the Psalms, and one in Isa. This noun is used less frequently than *ḥōshek.*

Light and darkness are well-known opposites in Palestine. In that land the light does not fade gradually after twilight. Sunset is preceded by brightness, which is soon changed with the disappearance of the sun. Within an hour, sunset has given way to the darkness of night.

There are symbolic uses of darkness as there are of light. As light presages glory, blessing, purity, so darkness foreshadows disaster.

The light of God is required to reveal man's darkness and expel it (Job 34:21–22; Ps 139:11–12; Mic 7:8–9).

Job (3:6) bewails the day of his birth and the night in which he was conceived. For that night he wishes that only the deepest darkness might overtake it, so that it would not be reckoned among the months or years. He pleads for a little respite before he goes to the place where only darkness is the order of the realm (10:22). He wishes (23:17) that he could have been cut off before calamity overtook him, so that he might have been spared the agony. The prowess of man in his research into the secrets and phenomena of earth, characterized by darkness, is presented in Job 28:3, whereas in 30:26 Job laments that whenever he looked for a source of hope (light), it always turned into misfortune (darkness).

The Psalmist is grieved at the extreme enmity which the wicked harbor against the upright, because they use the cover of darkness to make their onslaughts (Ps 11:2). In a psalm that breathes the protection of God over his own, the Psalmist assures the trusting heart that no pestilence of the night will strike down the soul abiding in God (Ps 91:6).

Isaiah looks to a day of God's blessing on Israel when God himself will dispel their ignorance (29:18).

'ăpēlâ. ***Darkness, thick darkness, calamity, gloominess.*** KJV, ASV, and RSV are similar, "thick darkness" (with *ḥōshek*). The term is used literally, as when darkness fell upon the land of Egypt for three days during the time of the ten plagues (Ex 10:21–22). It is also used figuratively of calamity or distress. Darkness symbolizes moral failure and its punishment (Prov 4:9). Most of its ten usages occur in the prophetic books.

ma'pēlyâ. ***Deep darkness.*** (KJV renders "darkness"; ASV and RSV "thick darkness.") It occurs only in Jer 2:31 where Jeremiah remonstrates with Israel for their apostasy from God.

Bibliography: IDB, III, pp. 130–32. May, H. G., "The Creation of Light in Gen 1:3–5," JBL 58: 203–11.

C.L.F.

146 אפן (*'pn*). **Assumed root of the following.**
146a †אוֹפָן (*'ôpan*) אֹפָן (*'ōpān*) ***wheel.***
146b אֹפֶן (*'ōpen*) ***circumstance, condition*** (only in Prov 25:11).
146c אֲפוּנָה (*'apûnâ*) ***despair*** (meaning uncertain.) Occurs only in Ps 88:16.

'ôpan. ***Wheel.*** (KJV, ASV, and RSV render alike, "wheel.")

The noun for wheel, in the dual number, is attested in Ugaritic. Of the thirty-five references to wheel in the OT, twenty-five are found in the book of Ezekiel. The most frequent use of the term is in reference to the wheel of a chariot (Ex 14:25; Nah 3:2; Ezk 1:15ff.). The oldest wheels discovered are clay models of chariot wheels and parts of a potter's wheel (cf. Jer 18:3) from the fourth millennium B.C. Early wheels were made from wooden planks joined together by pegs. Lighter wheels came into use around 1500 B.C., along with horses. This gave the Egyptians a decided military advantage. The wheel was also used in connection with Solomon's temple. There the bronze stands had small chariot wheels with axles, hubs, rims, and spokes (I Kgs 7:33). These wheels formed the bases of the temple's lavers. Both Ezekiel (1, 10) and Daniel (7:9) had visions of God's throne set on a platform with wheels. The celebrated wheels within wheels of Ezk 1 had axles set at ninety degree angles somewhat like a gyroscope, so that the platform could go at once in any of the four directions, without a steering mechanism. The whole picture symbolized the omnipresence of the Lord, and the rapidity with which he executes judgment in his rule of the earth. Wheels were employed with machinery for drawing water (cf. Eccl 12:6, *galgal*). The rollers of a threshing wagon or cart are mentioned in Prov 20:26 and Is 28:27. Later Hebrew commonly uses *galgal* a synonym (q.v.) by metonymy for a wagon (Ezk 23:24).

C.L.F.

147 אָפֵס (*'āpēs*) ***fail, cease, come to an end.***

Derivatives

147a †אֶפֶס (*'epes*) ***ceasing.***
147b אֹפֶס (*'ōpes*), ***dual*** אָפְסַיִם (*'opsayim*) ***the extremities,*** i.e. the soles of the feet or the ankles (Ezk 47:3).

The KJV translates variously "faileth," "fail," "is at an end," "brought to nought"; ASV renders "faileth," "fail," and "brought to nought;" RSV prefers "is gone," "is no more," and "come to nought." The four OT references are Gen 47:15–16; Isa 16:4; 29:20. The root is common in the noun form "ends of the earth" or "extremities of the land."

'epes. ***Ceasing,*** then ***end, extremity, nonexistence, cessation of, nought.*** (KJV, ASV, and RSV render "ends of the earth"; when the word occurs as a particle the versions translate similarly.) The OT shows forty references to the term, including three more of the adverb *'apsî*, the final vowel being understood by some as the *yodh* paragogic. Ugaritic texts contain the word in connection with the end of a throne, that is, its top.

Isaiah's use of the word to express nonexistence is indeed vivid. When he describes the apocalyptic cataclysm of the last times which will overtake the enemies of the Lord, he declares that nobles and princes will not be there for the roll call (34:12). When extolling the transcendent greatness of the Lord of earth, the same prophet evaluates all the nations as nothing compared to Him (40:17). In the most scathing denunciations of idolatry on record, Isaiah castigates the idols of the pagan nations, especially of Babylon, as being nothing. Their work is nothing, and their images are nonentities (41:12, 24, 29). Reviewing national history, he relates that Egypt took advantage of Israel when they came to sojourn there. The Assyrians oppressed them for nothing, that is, without sufficient cause (52:4).

'epes occurs as a particle of negation mostly in poetry. It is then synonymous with the usual particle *'ên*. Such usage is found in Isaiah's pronouncement of woe on the nation's ungodly in his song to the vineyard. They launch an all-out drive for the acquisition of as much property as possible, so that there is no room left for others (5:8). Amos uses the word in a similar fashion in describing the decimation that will attend Israel's captivity (6:10).

Because Israel was despondent over their subjugation by the idolatrous Babylonians, and might have been led to think that the gods of the heathen were mightier than the God of Israel, Isaiah reminds them repeatedly there is no one in the supernatural or natural realm who is His equal (47:8, 10), a good rendering being, "I am, and there is no one else beside me." Hear the beautiful refrain in Isa 45:5, 6, 18, 21.

'epes is also used as an adverb of limitation. Israelites were permitted to receive interest from foreigners. Nevertheless, they were not to take it from their brothers in the land, lest some fall into poverty (Deut 15:4).

The plural denotes the extremities of the earth in relation to the power of God against his foes (Deut 33:17), or the worldwide extent of God's salvation (Isa 52:10), or the outreach of Messiah's kingdom (Zech 9:10). The ultimate bounds of the earth known to the ancient Hebrews were

India and Ethiopia (Est 1:1). There is no evidence that the Israelites, even when in apostasy, ever worshiped the earth, as did the people of Ugarit and Phoenicia. Earth was one of the brides of Baal and the source of the creation of heaven and earth.

Bibliography: BDB, *sub coce*. Gaster, T. H., "Earth," in *Encyclopedia Judaica,* 1972, pp. 338–40. *Myth, Legend and creation in the Old Testament,* Harper and Row, 1969, pp. 56, 98, 103, 144, 188, 294. Gordon, C. H., *Ugaritic Textbook,* 1965, no. 309 in Glossary. IDB, vol. II, pp. 2–3. KB, *sub voce.*

C.L.F.

אֶפַע (*'epa'*), אֶפְעֶה (*'ep'â*). See nos. 1791a,b.

148 אָפַף (*'āpap*) ***surround, encompass.***

149 *אָפַק (*'āpaq*) ***hold, be strong.***

Derivative

149a אָפִיק (*'āpîq*) ***channel*** (for water).

150 אפר (*'pr*) **I. Assumed root of the following.**

150a †אֵפֶר (*'ēper*) ***ashes.*** (KJV, ASV, and RSV render alike, "ashes.")

The word is found twenty-one times in the OT. It has a wide variety of uses. It is often employed parallel to the similar-sounding word *'āpār* (dust). It denotes that which is the result of burning. It is used figuratively for what is without value (Isa 44:20) or loathsome (Job 30:19). It signifies misery (Ps 102:9 [H 10]), shame (II Sam 13:19), humility before God (Gen 18:27; Job 42:6), and repentance and contrition (Dan 9:3; Mt 11:21). Ashes of a red heifer with so-called water of separation were used in the rite of purification (Num 19:9–10, 17). Ashes of sacrifices were mingled with running water to cleanse from pollution; they were also a sign of fasting (Isa 58:5; Jon 3:6). Sackcloth and ashes were the usual indications of repentance and humility, often coupled with fasting (Job 42:6; Est 4:1; I Macc 3:47). Ashes with dust were the customary signs of mourning (Isa 61:3). The mourner or penitent threw the ashes toward heaven, so that they fell back on himself, especially on his head, a custom attested among non-Hebrew also. In deep distress mourners sat on heaps of ashes (Job 2:8). Ashes on the head were also a token of humiliation and disgrace (II Sam 13:19). The king of Tyre (q.v.) mentioned in Ezk 28:18 was to be reduced to ashes by God's judgment.

Bibliography: De Ward, Eileen F., "Mourning Customs in 1, 2 Samuel," JJS 23:1–27,145–66. Richardson, TWB, p. 70.

C.L.F.

151 אפר (*'pr*) **II. Assumed root of the following.**

151a אֲפֵר (*'ăpēr*) ***covering, bandage.*** Occurs only in I Kgs 20:38.

151b אַפִּרְיוֹן (*'appiryôn*) ***sedan, litter, palanquin.*** Occurs only in Song 3:9.

151c †אֶפְרַיִם (*'eprayim*) ***Ephraim.***

'eprayim. *Ephraim.* (KJV, ASV, and RSV are similar, "Ephraim.") The name appears 139 times in the OT with various connotations, as will be shown below. The name is said to mean "double fruit," evidently from the presence of the dual ending. Ephraim was the younger of the two sons of Joseph and Asenath, who were born to them in Egypt. With his brother Manasseh he was adopted by Jacob, thus becoming the progenitor of an Israelite tribe. Jacob in blessing Ephraim above Manasseh (Gen 48) was predicting the coming prominence of the tribe that descended from him (Gen 41:50ff.; 48:20ff.). In Jacob's final blessing he included both grandchildren under the name of Joseph (40:22f.). At the Exodus the men of war from Ephraim totaled 40,500, but when they were mobilized a second time they were down to 32,500 (Num 1:33; 26:37). On the march in the wilderness, Manasseh and Benjamin joined Ephraim on the west of the tabernacle (2:18ff.). Hoshea the son of Nun was the Ephraimite among the spies sent into Canaan (13:8). When Moses blessed the tribes before his death, he pointed to the future ascendancy of this tribe (Deut 33:17).

Joshua, a member of this tribe, succeeded Moses as leader of the nation. Shechem and Shiloh, both in the territory allotted to the sons of Joseph, became the place of national assemblies and the focus of the people's worship. The leadership of Samuel the prophet further underscored the prominence of Ephraim. From the era of the conquest of Palestine the tribe was quite jealous of its prestige (Jud 7:24; 8:1; 12:1ff.). Their loyalty to and support of Saul as first king may be traced to the close ties between Joseph and Benjamin. However, they never appear to have been satisfied with the transfer of the royal prerogative to Judah in the rule of David (II Sam 2:8f.).

They saw in the revolt of Absalom an opportunity to weaken the influence of the tribe of Judah (II Sam 15:13). When Solomon's extravagance and the ineptness of Rehoboam brought about general disaffection with the Davidic dynasty, the Ephraimite Jeroboam took full advantage of the situation. From the disruption of the Solomonic kingdom to the captivity of Samaria (722/21 B.C.), Ephraim held such undisputed leadership that Ephraim and Israel were interchangeable as names of the northern kingdom.

The sons of Joseph had their allotment of territory in the central section of western Palestine, and it appears that the territory of Ephraim and Manasseh was held in common (Josh 16; 17:14). They did not expel the Canaanites from their cities, but subjugated them (Josh 16:10; 17:13). The area was quite productive, so the people enjoyed a prosperous life. Unfortunately, the measure of their material blessing was not paralleled by spiritual strength, but rather decline and moral decay (Isa 28:1, 4; Jer 31:18; Hos 9:13; 10:11).

As noted, the territory of Ephraim was the hill country of central Palestine. Around the central valley are ridges, valleys, and spurs. The area is one of the most fertile in all the land. Currently it is planted with olive, carob, and pomegranate trees, among others. Before the Conquest the region was wooded (Josh 17:18), and beasts of prey roamed there during the time of the monarchy (II Kgs 2:24).

The gate of Ephraim was a chief gate in the wall of Jerusalem (Neh 8:16; 12:39).

Bibliography: Aharoni, J., *The Land of the Bible,* Westminster, 1967, pp. 236–237. Ewing, W., "Ephraim," in ISBE, II, 1952, p. 963. Roth, Cecil, "Ephraim," in *Encyclopedia Judaica,* VI, pp. 806–9.

C.L.F.

152 אפת (*'pt*). **Assumed root of the following.**
152a †מוֹפֵת (*môpēt*) ***wonder, miracle, sign, portent.***

This masculine noun is of no certain etymology. No verb or other noun uses the same root letters. However, the meaning of *môpēt* is not questioned. Often it is parallel to *'ôt* (q.v.), which also means "sign," "symbol," "portent," "wonder," or "miracle" (Ex 7:3; Deut 4:34; 6:22; 7:19; 13:1ff.; 26:8; 28:46; 29:2; 34:11; Neh 9:10; Ps 135:9; Isa 8:18; 20:3; Jer 32:20, et al.). "Judgments" and "works" are parallel to *môpēt* in I Chr 16:12 and Ps 105:5. The LXX renders *môpēt* as *tērata* "prodigies," "marvels."

The first occurrences of môpēt in the OT are in Ex 4:21; 7:3,9; 11:9–10. In these verses it refers to Moses' rod changing into a snake (7:9), as well as to the ten major plagues on the Egyptians. Most of the usages in the Deuteronomy passages refer both to the miraculous punishments and the wonderful provisions God made for his people in the wilderness (e.g. water, manna, quails, and the pillar of fire). In this connection also note Neh 9:10; I Chr 16:12; Ps 78:43; 105:5, 27; 135:9; Jer 32:20.

Deuteronomy 13:1ff. and 28:46 are exceptions. In the former pericope *môpēt* refers to a "portent" or perhaps a prediction that a questionable prophet or dreamer gives. Depending on whether the *'ôt* (sign) or the *môpēt* (wonder) comes to pass, the would-be prophet is authenticated or condemned. The Deut 28:46 passage is in the curse section. Israel as a nation will become a "sign" or "wonder," i.e. a spectacle or demonstration of the rewards of disobedience. Psalm 71:7; Isa 8:18; 20:3; Ezk 12:6, 11; 24:24, 27; and Zech 3:8 use the word similarly. The psalmists or the prophets are themselves the object lesson.

Other miracles described by this word are the rending of the altar to authenticate the prediction about Josiah's advent (I Kgs 13:3, 5), the recovery of Hezekiah from mortal illness (II Chr 32:24, 31), and the restoration of Ezekiel's speech (Ezk 24:24, 27). Joel uses the word to describe celestial and terrestial manifestations of God's power in "the great and terrible day of the LORD" (2:30 [H 3:3–4]). Peter paraphrases this verse in Acts 2:19, using the Greek plural synonyms *terata* and *sēmeia.*

R.L.A.

אָצִיל (*'āṣîl*), אַצִּיל (*'aṣṣîl*). See no. 153b,c.

153 אָצַל (*'āṣal*) ***lay aside, reserve, withdraw, withhold.*** Denominative verb.

Parent Noun

153a †אֵצֶל (*'ēṣel*) ***beside, by, near.***

Derivatives

153b אָצִיל (*'āṣîl*) ***side, corner, chief.***
153c אַצִּיל (*'aṣṣîl*) ***joining, joint.***

'ēṣel. ***Beside, by, near.*** A preposition appearing fifty-nine times in the OT. There is no particularly outstanding or unique use of the word. It is used simply, as its meaning suggests, to indicate proximity: of place (by Gibeah, Jud 19:14; by En-rogel, I Kgs 1:9; beside the plains of Moreh, Deut 11:30; by Bethlehem, Jer 41:17); of position (beside the altar, Lev 1:16; the lion standing by the carcass, I Kgs 13:25; two lions standing beside the arms of the throne, I Kgs 10:19; beside his house, Neh 3:23); to some other person (lay my bones beside his bones, I Kgs 13:21; he came near where I stood, Dan 8:17; I remained there with the kings of Persia, Dan 10:13; brought them to their brothers, II Chr 28:15; the queen was sitting by him, Neh 2:6; beside Ezra, Neh 8:4).

Several times the preposition is used in a metaphorical context, at least three times in Prov. Proverbs 7:8 refers to the unsuspecting man who carelessly saunters through the street 'near' the corner where dame folly lives. As a matter of fact she lies in wait "at" every corner (7:12). Wisdom, on the contrary, has been "by" God's side from the beginning (8:30).

In the days of Samuel the Philistines captured the ark from the Israelites and attempted to place it in one of their temples "beside" Dagon (I Sam 5:2). The result was nothing short of disastrous.

And so it always has been. God challenges any false god I try to place beside him in my life.

V.P.H.

154 אָצַר (*'āṣar*) ***to store, lay up,*** used minimally in the OT, once in the Qal, Amos 3:10 (although KB³, p. 80 adds II Kgs 20:17/Isa 39:6); once in the Niphal (Isa 23:18); once in the Hiphil (Neh 13:13).

Derivative

154a †אוֹצָר (*'ôṣār*) ***treasure, treasury, storehouse.***

(Eighty times in the OT according to KB³ p. 23), most often in I Chr (thirteen times) and II Chr (eight times). It is unnecessary to accept the frequent emendation (as in RSV and JB) in Zech 11:13 of "cast it into the treasury (*'ôṣâr*)" for "cast it to the potter (*yôṣēr*)" in the celebrated passage about thirty pieces of silver (see Torrey in bibliography).

There are at least nine words in biblical Hebrew for "treasure" of which this is one. It is used in either a literal sense, referring to the treasure in the king's house or in the temple or one's individual acquisitions, and secondly in a cosmic sense, the source of God's possessions and blessing. Specifically there are ten references to "treasures/treasury of the king's house" (e.g. I Kgs 14:26) and nine references to "treasures/ treasury of the temple of the Lord" (e.g. I Kgs 7:51).

Many of these references are in a military context. A defeated nation was obliged to give up her treasures to the victor. Both Asa (I Kgs 15:18) and Joash (II Kgs 12:19) gave to the Arameans Benhadad and Hazael treasures from both the temple and the royal treasury. Nebuchadnezzar helped himself to both (II Kgs 24:13), as did the Egyptian Pharaoh, Shishak, much earlier (I Kgs 14:26).

At the individual level, treasure is to be happily accepted and used, not abused (Prov 8:21) but if it becomes an end in itself the consequences are dire (Prov 10:2; 15:16; 21:6, 20).

There are several references to divine storehouses, e.g. Ps 33:7; 135:7; Job 38:22. God's treasure house is in the heavens (Deut 28:12). In Jer 50:25 reference is made to God's "armory."

Bibliography: Torrey, C. C., "The Foundry at Jerusalem," JBL 55: 247–60. Wolf, C. U., "Treasure, Treasurer, Treasury," in IDB, IV, pp. 693–94.

V.P.H.

155 אַקּוֹ (*'aqqô*) ***wildgoat.*** Occurs only in Deut 14:5, in list of clean animals.

אֲרִאֵל (*'ărî'ēl*). See no. 159a.

156 אָרַב (*ārab*) ***to lie in wait, ambush.***

Derivatives

156a אֶרֶב (*'ereb*) ***a lying in wait.***
156b אֹרֶב (*'ōreb*) ***ambuscade.***
156c אָרְבָּה (*'orbâ*) ***artifice.***
156d †אֲרֻבָּה (*'ărūbâ*) ***window, sluice.***
156e מַאֲרָב (*ma'ărāb*) ***ambush.***

The verb is used forty times in the OT, most frequently in Jud (fourteen times) and Joshua (seven times). In the majority of these twenty-one instances, ambush as a method of warfare is described.

As Yadin has pointed out, there were five ways to conquer a fortified city: (1) penetration by force from above the fortifications; (2) penetration through the barriers; (3) penetration under the barriers (tunneling); (4) siege; (5) penetration by ruse.

There are at least two illustrations of this last method in the OT, both using the verb *'ārab*. One is the capture of Ai (Josh 8), the other is the holy war conducted against the Benjamites by their fellow Israelites for the shameful act of the former in condoning the actions of one of their own who had violated the Levite's daughter (Jud 20). In both instances the strategy is the same: (1) the positioning of an ambush behind the city; (2) the deceptive flight by the assault force to draw the defenders out of the city and after them in pursuit; (3) the storming of the city by the ambush party; (4) the "fleeing" assault force turns now to counterattack.

Frequently the enemies of the pious are described as those who "lurk," lie in wait for the unsuspecting: Ps 10:9; 59:3 [H 4]; Lam 4:19; Ezr 8:31. Even God is viewed as a "lurking" bear who has turned against his people (Lam 3:10). The verb may describe the actions of criminals before they strike: I Sam 22:8,13; Mic 7:2; Prov 1:11,18; 7:12; 12:6; 23:28. Against such there must be constant vigilance.

'ărūbâ. ***Window, chimney, floodgate.*** Twice the word is used to describe one of the two sources of the waters in the deluge (Gen 7:11; 8:2). In addition to rain from above there was also an auxiliary source, "the fountains of the great deeps," i.e. subterranean water. The phrase "windows of heaven," in the deluge context, is in some of the more recent Bible translations rendered "sluices," (NIV "floodgates"). There is no reason not to believe that the writer in Gen when using the phrase "window of heavens" was well aware of his own figurative language to describe the torrential downpour.

If God channels the waters of judgment and cleansing through these windows, he also sends his blessing through these same windows (Mal 3:10). Similarly compare II Kgs 7:2, 19 where

Elisha has made predictions of an incredible reduction in the price of food, much to the disbelief of the king's squire. Thus, such apertures are the means of God's cleansing or his blessing.

Two unique uses of *'ărūbâ* are (1) window, in the sense of a "chimney" through which smoke passes (Hos 3:13), and (2) the small opening in a pigeon loft (Isa 60:8).

The reference to "those who look out of windows are darkened" (Eccl 12:3) is probably not a poetical reference to the eyes which become dim with old age, but to some funereal practice (Dahood), or some disaster of unidentifiable nature (Sawyer).

Bibliography: Dahood, M., "Canaanite-Phoenician Influences on Qoheleth," Bib 33: 213–15. Gaster, T., "Cosmogony," in IDB, I, pp. 702–9. ______ "Old Testament Notes," VT 4: 79. Sawyer, J.F.A., "The Ruined House in Ecclesiastes 12: A Reconstruction of the Original Parable," JBL 94 519–31. Harris, R. L., "The Bible and Cosmology," JETS 5:15. Yadin, Y., *The Arts of Warfare in Biblical Lands,* McGraw-Hill, 1963, vol. I, pp. 16, 100, 110–11; vol. II, pp. 262–63.

V.P.H.

157 אָרַג (*'ārag*) ***weave.***

Derivatives

157a אֶרֶג (*'ereg*) ***loom.*** Only in Jud 16:14; Job 7:6.

157b †אַרְגָּמָן (*'argāmān*) ***purple.***

'argāmān. ***Purple,*** including most likely all shades of this color from deep red-black to violet. It is common in the English language to associate colors with moods or feelings. Thus traditionally purple is associated with anger, red with shame, yellow with cowardice, green with nausea, and so forth. The OT comes closest to this when it frequently expresses God's anger as "his nose turned red." Purple, however, is never used in this way.

As is well known, purple has been symbolically the dress of gods, royalty, and sometimes nobility. Classical sources certainly bear this out (Homer, *Iliad* 4, 141–145, and Suetonius, *Life of the Twelve Caesars* 6. 32 for the opinion of the infamous Nero on the subject). The same is said of the kings of Midian in the days of Gideon (Jud 8:26). Mordecai was similarly decorated by the Persian Ahasuerus (Est 8:15). Anyone who is capable of informing the distraught Belshazzar on the significance of the "writing fingers" is promised, among other things, that he will be dressed in purple (Dan 5:7, 16, 29). In the KJV the word is translated "scarlet." It is the Aramaic word *'arg^{e}wān,* some shade of red-purple. In the Apocryphal books it is recorded that purple clothing is worn by the high priest and prince (1 Macc 10:20, 62, 64; 11:58; 14:43; 2 Macc 4:38). The NT associates purple with imperial and pagan Rome, dressed as she was in this particular clothing (Rev 17:4; 18:16). In a fiendish attempt to make Jesus look as ludicrous as possible, his accusers dressed him in purple at his trial (Mk 15:17; Jn 19:2, 5). Jesus apparently dressed like everybody else and was indistinguishable at this point—so much so that his accusers had to hire Judas to point him out—no purple and no halo.

In the OT, it should be observed that purple is fairly well reserved for liturgical settings. The curtains in the temple were purple (Ex 26:1), as was the veil (Ex 26:31) and the ephod, a kind of a breastplate, of the high priest (Ex 28:6).

Such purple was obtained from mollusks along the eastern shores of the Mediterranean. The pigment was secreted by a gland in the lining of the stomach. The very name "Canaan" means "the land of purple" and the name "Phoenicia" is to be related to the Greek word *phoinos* "red-purple." It is in this kind of dye-work that Lydia, the first European convert to Christ, was employed, "a seller of purple" (Acts 16:14). Preparation of the royal purple of classical times is detailed in "The Magic Lure of Sea Shells," by P. A. Zahl and V. R. Boswell (*National Geographic,* 135: 401).

The root *argmn* appears in Ugaritic definitely with the meaning "gift to an exalted personage" but whether it may also mean "purple" is open to question (Rabin).

Bibliography: Jensen, L. B., "Royal Purple of Tyre," JNES 22: 104–118. Landsberger, B., "Ueber Farben Im Sumerisch-Akkadischen," JCS 21: 158–62. Rabin, Chaim, "Hittite Words in Hebrew," *Orientalia* 32: 116–18.

V.P.H.

158 אָרָה (*'ārâ*) ***I, pluck, gather.***

Derivatives

158a †אֲרִי (*ărî*), אַרְיֵה (*'aryēh*) ***lion.***

158b אֻרְיָה (*'ūryâ*) ***manger, crib.***

'ărî, 'aryēh. ***Lion.*** These are two of the seven words which are translated "lion" in the OT. There is no demonstrable difference between the two. Thus I Kgs 10:19 refers to the decorative lions (*'ărāyôt*) by the arms of Solomon's throne. For the twelve lions referred to in the following verse (10:20) *'aryēh* is used.

God is likened to a lion (Isa 38:13) who has broken the bones of Hezekiah, and similarly in the anonymous Lamentations (Lam 3:10). The "lion," however, can become the lion chaser against those who stalk Israel as a lion (Jer 49:19; 50:44). This is a natural figure of speech to designate Israel's enemies, a picture of pride, strength, and rapacity: Jer 4:7; 5:6 (Nebuchadnezzar?); Joel 1:6; Nah 2:11–13 [H 12–14]. But again, God can send lions against the lions: II Kgs 17:25–26. In the psalms of lament the writer's enemies are frequently described as lions: 7:2 [H 3]; 10:9; 17:12; 22:13, 21 [H 14, 22].

In the NT Satan is described as a "roaring lion" (I Pet 5:8), but even there he is outdone by the "lion out of the tribe of Judah" (Rev 5:5). The thrust here is not ferociousness, but regality.

Bibliography: TDOT, I, pp. 374–87. THAT, I, pp. 225–28. Glück, J. J., "*'ari* and *lavî* (*labî'*): an Etymological Study," ZAW 81:232–35. Porter, J. R., "Samson's Riddle: Judges XIV 14, 18," JTS 13: 106–109. Ullendorff, E., "Contribution of South Semitics to Hebrew," VT 6: 192–93.

V.P.H.

159 ארה (*'rh*) **II, Assumed root of the following.**
159a אֲרִיאֵל (*'ărî'el*) ***Ariel;*** אֲרִאֵיל (*'ări'el*) ***hearth.***

These two words can be considered together. The latter one is used in Ezk 43:15–16. It is a cultic object, an altar hearth that is superimposed on the base of the altar, having horns at its four corners. It may also be the top two sections of a three tiered altar. Comparison has been made with this word in Ezekiel and the expression in the Mesha Inscription, *'r'l dwdh,* which Mesha, the king of Moab, claimed to drag before his national god Chemosh. Was it an altar he dragged, or is *'r'l* a personal name, "my light is God," or what? It is difficult to be sure. Cf. II Sam 23:20 and I Chr 11:22.

In both of these verses in Ezekiel there is both a *Kethib* ("written") tradition and a *Qere* ("spoken") tradition. The *Kethib* is *'ărîēl* and the *Qere* is *'ărî'ēl.*

The word "Ariel" occurs in a prophetic oracle in Isa 29:1,2,7. It is a name given to Jerusalem. God will bring disaster upon Ariel (Jerusalem) and make her like an Ariel.

There are at least three possible etymologies for Ariel as used in Isa. One is to connect it with the Hebrew words *'ărî* and *'ēl,* "the-lion-of-God." The second is to connect it with a verb, not used in Hebrew, *'ārâ* "to burn" with a "l" afformative. The third is to relate it to the Akkadian word *arallû,* the name for both the netherworld and the world mountain. Although the etymology in Isaiah's oracle is unclear, the meaning is clear. Israel shall become, under the judgment of God, an Ariel, an altar hearth, that is, the scene of a holocaust. It will not be an animal that is burned, but Israel herself will be the victim. But, God's intervention will prevent total annihilation (29:7).

Bibliography: On the phrase *'r'l dwdh* in the Mesha Inscription: Andersen, F. I., "Moabite Syntax," Or 35: 90. Lipinski, E., "Etymological and Exegetical Notes on the Mešaᶜ," Or 40: 332–34.

On Ariel: Albright, W. F., "The Babylonian Temple Tower and the Altar of Burnt Offering," JBL 39: 137–42. May, H. G., "Ephod and Ariel," AJSL 56: 44–69. Feigin, S., "The Meaning of Ariel," JBL 39: 131–37. May, H. G., "Ephods" and "Ariel," AJSL 56: 44–69.

V.P.H.

אָרוּז (*'ārûz*). See no. 160e.
אֲרוֹן (*'ărôn*). See no. 166a.

160 ארז (*'rz*). **Assumed root of the following.**
160a †אֶרֶז (*'erez*) ***cedar.***
160b אַרְזָה (*'arzâ*) ***cedar panels*** (Zeph 2:14 only).
160c אָרוּז (*'ārûz*) ***firm, strong*** (Ezk 27:24 only).

'erez. *Cedar.* A tree of the pine family, one which grows best in a high and dry region. The Talmud (*Rosh Hashana* 23*a*), says that the inhabitants of Palestine called ten different trees cedar. It is, however, the *cedrus libani,* the cedar of Lebanon, that is most widely referred to when the word *'erez* is used in the Bible.

Not only the Israelites saw fit to make use of this timber. As far back as the reign of Ur-nammu—late 2000s B.C.—ancient kings from Mesopotamia came here to arrange for the export of the cedar of Lebanon to their home. Lebanon is called, in a text of Naram-sin, "the cedar mountain" (ANET, p. 268). In Egyptian literature, Wenamon, an official of the Temple at Amon at Karnak, is sent to Byblos to procure Lebanon's cedars for a ceremonial barge of the god Amon-Re. This takes place in the late Kingdom Period, at the close of the twentieth dynasty. In Canaanite poetry of the second millennium B.C. when a palace of Baal was to be built, workers went "to Lebanon and its timbers, to Shirion and its choicest cedars," (*llbnn wᶜṣh lšryn mḥmd arzh*) UT 16: Text 51:VI: 20–21.

The average height of such cedars is about eighty-five feet, though some have measured over one hundred feet. In trunk circumference the cedar may reach forty feet. Not infrequently the tree's horizontal spread of branches equals its height. It is also common for this tree to spread its roots among the rocks and thus secure a stronghold.

The Lebanon cedar in the Bible is used primarily in building. A particular oil in the cedar prevents destruction by dry-rot and insects. Such cedar was used on the inside of the temple (I Kgs 6:15, 18); the outside too (I Kgs 7:12); the altar of incense (I Kgs 6:20). Similar wood was used in the second temple (Ezr 3:7; Song 1:17(?)). In addition to buildings cedar was used in the making of ship masts (Ezk 27:5) and in religious rites (Lev: 14:4, 49, 51–52; Num 19:6).

It is only natural that this lofty, firmly-rooted tree should be used as a metaphor to describe a person's or nation's moral character. It can be used both positively and negatively. Balaam describes Israel as a "cedar beside the waters" (Num 24:6). She is both secure and prosperous. The opposite effect is achieved through the metaphor of Jer 22:23. Jehoiachin assumed his "nest among the cedars" made him inviolate and immune to judgment. Israel, by God's grace, has proliferated, as extensively as the branches of a cedar (Ps 80:10 [H 11]). Other strong "cedars," however, have flourished by violence, not by God's good grace (Isa 2:13; Ezk 31:3; Zech 11:1–2). Such cedars, strong as they may be, must be broken by God's power (Jer 22:7; Ps 29:5).

Bibliography: Haupt, Paul, "Heb. *'ärz,* Cedar, Ass. *irêšu,* Balsamic Juice," JAOS 45: 322–23. Shewell-Cooper, J. E., "Cedar," in ZPEB.

V.P.H.

161 אָרַח (*'āraḥ*) ***to wander, journey, keep company with.***

Derivatives

161a †אֹרַח (*'ōraḥ*) ***way, path.***
161b אֲרֻחָה (*'ărūḥâ*) ***meal, allowance*** (of food).
161c אֹרְחָה (*'ōrḥâ*) ***caravan.***

The verb is used five times in the OT. Job is accused of "keeping company" with the workers of iniquity (34:8). Normally it means "traveller," one who is on the move (Jud 19:17; II Sam 12:4; Jer 14:8, where it is applied to God; Jer 9:2 [H 1]).

'ōraḥ. ***Way, path.*** Although the word appears fifty-eight times in the OT, forty-five of them are limited to three books: Prov, nineteen times; Ps, fifteen times; Job, eleven times. Most often *'ōraḥ* is used in a figurative way, describing the way to life or to death. It often is parallel with the word *derek,* meaning "way, lifestyle." "Teach me your way (*derek*), O Lord, and lead me in a plain (?) path (*'ōraḥ*)," (Ps 27:11). "Do not enter the path (*'ōraḥ*) of the wicked, nor go in the way (*derek*) of evil men" (Prov 4:14; cf. Ps 139:3; Prov 2:8; 12:28; Job 6:18; Isa 30:11).

The contrast is between the way of sin/death and the way of obedience/life. These exhaust the options available to man. Man makes his own choice but he cannot choose his own consequences. The path of life (Ps 16:11; Prov 2:19; 5:6; 10:17; 15:24) corresponds with the path of integrity (Ps 27:11), the path of uprightness (Prov 2:13), the path of justice (Prov 2:8; 17:23; Isa 26:8; 40:14), the path of righteousness (Prov 8:20). Conversely, one is to spurn the path of evil (Ps 119:101) for it is a false path (Ps 119:104, 128).

To follow the path of truth and life is to follow God's own path (Ps 25:4, 10; 44:18 [H 19]; 119:115, where the word is a synonym for God's Torah; Isa 2:3).

The way which one chooses determines one's destiny. There is such a thing as the "road" of no return (Job 16:22). Bildad speaks of the "fate/path" of all that forget God (Job 8:13). Interestingly, the LXX translates *'ōraḥ* here as *ta eschata* "the end." Proverbs 1:19 indicates, "Such is the 'way/end' for those who are after dishonest gain," that consequences of evil behavior are intrinsic to that action and are not superimposed as a penalty. Thus the Bible can say that the way (*derek*) of the transgressor is hard.

When Jesus contrasts the two ways, the two doors and the two destinations in the Sermon on the Mount (Mt 7:13–14), he is basically repeating the concept of *'ōraḥ* and *derek,* as taught in Hebrew wisdom literature. Our Lord's reference to himself as "the way, the truth, the life" means that Jesus is the way to the truth about life. He is not the answer. That would be an oversimplification. He is the way that leads to the answer. Only after one steps out on the way does he discover that Jesus is the truth about life. Wisdom literature too challenges us to step out on the right way, the way of life, the way that leads to life.

V.P.H.

אֲרִי (*'ărî*), אַרְיֵה (*'aryēh*). See no. 158a,b.
אֲרִיאֵל (*'ărî'ēl*). See no. 159a.
אֻרְיָה (*'ūryâ*). See no. 158b.

162 אָרַךְ (*'ārak*) ***to be long.***

Derivatives

162a †אֹרֶךְ (*'ōrek*) ***length.***
162b †אָרֵךְ (*'ārēk*) ***long.***
162c †אָרֹךְ (*'ārōk*) ***long.***
162d אֲרוּכָה (*'ărûkâ*) ***healing.***

The verb is used only three times in the Qal stem: Gen 26:8; Ezk 12:22; 31:5. The remaining thirty-one occurrences are in the Hiphil stem, with the meaning "make long, prolong." As we will see, the verb is found most frequently in Deut, eleven times, mostly in the formula, "That (it may be well with you and that) you may 'prolong' your days in the land."

It cannot be denied that God intended for his creatures, among other blessings, the blessing of long life. Premature deaths in the Bible are the exception. *'ārak* is used first in this context of long life in the fifth commandment, "Honor your father and mother (caring for the elderly?) so that you may have a long life in the land the LORD your God has given you" (Ex 20:12).

It is in Deut that one finds the heaviest proliferation of the phrase, "That you may prolong your days/your days may be prolonged" (Deut 4:26, 40; 5:33 [H 30]; 6:2; 11:9; 17:20; 22:7; 25:15; 30:18; 32:47). In every instance the promise is prefixed by a moral contingency. It is only as Israel keeps God's laws and commandments (Deut 4:40) that she is guaranteed security in her land.

To be sure, longevity itself is not sacred. The antediluvians (Gen 5) were bad enough in the first century of their lives, worse in the second and third century of their lives, but by the eighth and ninth centuries they were so hopelessly incorrigible that God had to cleanse the earth. Long years did not produce repentance but hardness of heart.

The obituaries of the patriarchs reveal the same. At the end of Abraham's life (175 years) it is recorded that "he died at a ripe old age, an old man who had lived his full span of years" (Gen 25:7–8). Virtually the same is said of Isaac (180 years old, Gen 35:28–29). But, by contrast, Jacob says that his own life (130 years) consisted of only a few years and unhappy ones at that (Gen 47:8–9). This may be the Bible's way of saying that life's donation is more important than life's duration, not how long one lives, but how well one lives.

'ōrek. ***Length.*** Frequently as a measurement of some edifice such as the ark (Gen 6:15), the tabernacle or some part of the same, or a city. In the latter case one recalls Zechariah's vision of the man going forth to measure the "length" and breadth of Jerusalem about to be rebuilt (Zech 2:2 [H 6]). An angel calls the man back, for God is going to make Jerusalem larger than the human blueprint calls for. It will be a city without walls. The noun also is used often with the word "day(s)" to express a protracted period of time: Ps 21:4 [H 5]; 91:16; Prov 3:2, 16; Deut 30:20. "Length of days" might in some contexts signify the everlasting afterlife, according to Dahood (Ps 23:6; 91:16; Isa 53:10, *yā'ărîk*).

'ārēk. ***Long.*** Appears only in the construct form *'erek,* never in the absolute. It is used fifteen times. It is used ten times in connection with God, four times in connection with man (Prov 14:29; 15:18; 16:32; Eccl 7:8), once in connection with the wingspread of a bird (Ezk 17:3).

Applied to either God or man it is used most frequently in construct to the word *'appayîm,* and is translated "longsuffering, slow to anger/wrath." Literally, when the Bible says God is "longsuffering" (Ex 34:6; Num 14:18; Ps 86:15, etc.) it reads "God is long of nose." When he is angry, his nose becomes red and burns. It may be questioned whether in the living language the idioms had not already dropped their etymological associations and did not merely mean to be longsuffering and to be angry. When he is compassionate his nose becomes long, so long in fact that it would take forever to burn completely.

'ārōk. ***Long, protracted.*** Is used only three times. "There was a 'long' war between the house of Saul and of David" (II Sam 3:1; compare Jer 29:28; Job 11:9).

V.P.H.

163 אֲרָם (*ărām*) ***Aram, Syria.*** The latter translation is found in most English versions, the KJV for example.

The origins of the people called Arameans is clouded in mystery, but the prevailing view is that they were a group of western Semitic, Aramaic speaking tribes who infiltrated the Fertile Crescent as early as the third quarter of the second millennium B.C. Their original home was probably the Syro-Arabian desert.

It is not until much later, however, the last half of the tenth century B.C. to be specific, that the Arameans reached the climax of their political domination in Upper (northwest) Mesopotamia. The climax of Aramean power in Syria comes in the ninth century B.C., and parallels and interrelates with early developments in the divided monarchy.

Biblically and geographically, Aram is associated with Upper Mesopotamia in the Patriarchal period. Abraham is the brother of Nahor the grandfather of Aram (Gen 22:20–21). Both Isaac (Gen 25:20) and Jacob (Gen 28:5) marry Aramean wives. Jacob himself is described as a "wandering Aramean" (Deut 26:5). Finally we may note the extraordinary reference in Amos 9:7. Here it is related that God not only brought the Israelites from Egypt (south), but also the Philistines from Caphtor (the west) and the Arameans from Kir (northeast, Elam?). Once again one finds the scriptural affirmation that it is God who controls the movements and destinies of all nations.

After the three generations of these patriarchs no further references in the Bible are to be found until the time of Saul, a gap of five hundred years at the bare minimum. The Israelites first come into hostile contact with the Arameans towards the end of the eleventh century B.C. in the reign of Saul (I Sam 14:47, king(s) of Zobah), the action having shifted now to Syria (Damascus). This skirmish was to be an ominous harbinger of things to come between these two peoples. Although David was successful in subjugating the Arameans (II Sam 8:3; 10:6–19) they regained their autonomy a generation later under Rezon during Solomon's period of decline (I Kgs 11:23–25). Again, God had raised Rezon as a "satan" (adversary) against Solomon (I Kgs 11:23).

Asa, the third king of Judah, was the first to seek the support of these Arameans against Baasha king of Israel (I Kgs 15:16–22). Apparently the anomaly of the situation never dawned on Asa: squabbling believers appealing to unbelievers as a supportive force. Such policies of foreign alliance were to perturb the prophets to no small degree.

Perennial strife between the Arameans and the northern Israelites really begins during the reign of Ahab (874–853, I Kgs 20, 22). In the latter case Ahab is goaded into action by four hundred clergy of Baal. In opposition to these religious hirelings, a "four-hundred and first" prophet, Micaiah, urged non-involvement, but was ignored by Ahab. Such irruptions between these contiguous peoples, halted only by a common threat to both from the Assyrians, were to last for over a hundred years, down to the time of Jeroboam II (783–743 B.C., II Kgs 14:25, 28).

It is no coincidence that the literary prophets emerge precisely on the heels of this century-old war, a war that produced in Israel at least a society deeply divided between the impoverished masses and the wealthy few. It is to this cleavage, with all the accompanying social corruption, that the early prophets addressed themselves. The war and its aftermath had created more problems than it had solved.

Bibliography: DuPont-Sommer, A., "Sur les Debuts de l'Histoire Arameenne," Supp VT 1: 40–49. Gibson, J. C. L., "Light from Mari on the Patriarchs," JSS 7: 44–62. ———, "Observations on Some Important Ethnic Terms in the Pentateuch," JNES 20: 217–38. Kitchen, K. A., in NBD, pp. 55–59. Malamat, A., in *Peoples of Old Testament Times,* ed K. A. Kitchen Oxford, Clarendon, 1973, pp. 134–55. Mazar, Benjamin, "The Aramean Empire and its Relations with Israel," BA 25: 98–120. Tadmor, H., "The Southern Border of Aram," *Israel Exploration Journal* 12: 114–22. Unger, M. F., *Israel and the Arameans of Damascus,* James Clark, 1957.

V.P.H.

164 ארם (*'rm*). **Assumed root of the following.**
164a †אַרְמוֹן (*'armôn*) ***citadel, palace.***

This noun is always translated as "palace" in KJV except Prov 18:19 where the translation is "castle." It describes a fortified dwelling, usually a part of the royal complex. Speiser has connected Hebrew *'armôn* with the Assyrian root *ramû* which means principally "to found a dwelling, to dwell."

Of the thirty-two uses of *'armôn,* twenty-two of them are in the prophetic books, and eleven of these are found in Amos (1:4, 7, 10, 12, 14, etc.). In each the essence is that God will burn up "the palaces" of a certain individual or nation in divine judgment. It may be the Aramean Ben-Hadad (Amos 1:3); the Philistine city of Gaza (Amos 1:7); the Phoenician city of Tyre (1:10); of Edom (Amos 1:12); of Ammon (1:14). One cannot miss the holy war imagery in such passages. Because of its arrogance, the nation is deprived of one or some of its most imposing edifices.

This is not, however, something from which God guarantees immunity to his own. The citadels of Jerusalem too will be burned (Amos 2:5; cf. Hos 8:14). Israel's will suffer the same fate (Amos 3:11). God even hates her citadels (Amos 6:8) for they are filled with violence and extortion (Amos 3:10; cf. Lam 2:5, 7; Jer 17:27). Divine judgment does not spare the house of God; in fact, it begins there.

Bibliography: Speiser, E. A., "The Etymology of 'Armon'," JQR 14: 329.

V.P.H.

165 ארן (*'rn*) **I. Assumed root of the following.**
165a אֹרֶן (*'ōren*) ***fir or cedar.*** Occurs only in Isa 44:14.

166 ארן (*'rn*) **II. Assumed root of the following.**
166a †אֲרוֹן (*'ărôn*) ***ark, chest, coffin*** (ASV and RSV similar).

The LXX renders *kibōtos,* Vulgate *arca.* A masculine noun which occurs 193 times, it is assumed to derive from the root *'rn.*

The noun designates a box used for several purposes. The remains of Joseph were placed in a coffin in Egypt for eventual burial in Palestine (Gen 50:26). Sums of money for the repair of the temple were collected in a chest (II Kgs 12:10–11; II Chr 24:8, 10–11).

'ărôn is most frequently used for the ark of the covenant. Noah's boat, called an "ark" in the English Bible, is in Hebrew *ṭēbâ,* not *'ărôn.* As described in Ex, Bezaleel made the ark of acacia wood. There were gold rings on the corners through which staves were placed for carrying it (Ex 25:10–21; 37:1–9). In size the ark was 2½ by 1½ by 1½ cubits, and was overlaid inside and out with gold (Ex 25:11). It was surmounted by the mercy seat (*kappōret*) and cherubim with outstretched wings. The ark contained the tables of stone with the law (Deut 10:1–5; Ex 40:20), a pot of manna, and Aaron's rod which budded (Heb 9:4). The Damascus Document, fragments of which were found at Qumran, has the peculiar tradition that a copy of the Law was in the ark and it was sealed, which explains why David had not read it! (C.D.C. 5,3). The ark was set in the most holy place in the tabernacle.

In the wilderness the ark was carried by the Levites (Deut 10:8) before the line of march. A liturgical formula was recited when it was transported (Num 10:35–36). The ark was prominent at the crossing of the Jordan (Josh 3–4) and in the capture of Jericho (Josh 6–7). It was at Gilgal (Josh 7:6), Shechem (Josh 8:33), Bethel (Jud 20:27–28), and later Shiloh (I Sam 3:3). It was carried into battle against the Philistines at Aphek. They captured it (I Sam 4:3–11) but it caused plagues in the Philistine cities (I Sam 6:3–4). It was returned to Israel and for twenty years remained in the house of Abinadab at Kiriath-jearim. Finally David brought it up to Jerusalem (I Sam 7:1–2; II Sam 6:1ff.; Ps 132:1–8). Helping move the ark, Uzzah fell dead for touching it (II Sam 6:6–11). After that incident, it remained three months at the house of Obed edom. Later it was carried on a military expedition against the Ammonites (on one interpretation of II Sam 11:11), but it remained in Jerusalem at Absalom's revolt (II Sam 15:24f.). Solomon placed it in the holy of holies of the temple (I Kgs 8). The ultimate fate of the ark is a mystery. Jeremiah 3:16–17 may imply its existence as late as the time of Nebuchadnezzar. It was the subject of later Jewish legend (II Macc 2:4f.; *T. Sota* 13:1; *The Lives of the Prophets,* ed. Torrey, I, p. 36). There was no ark in either Zerubbabel's or Herod's temple (cf. Josephus, *Wars* 5.5.5).

Often designated "the ark" (*hā-'ārôn*), it is also "the ark of the Lord" (Josh 4:11, etc.) and "the ark of God" (I Sam 3:3, etc.). It is called "the ark of the God of Israel" by the Philistines (I Sam 5:2–11, etc.). The ark is most often "the ark of the covenant" (*'ărôn habbᵉrît,* Num 10:33, etc.; 184 times), "the ark of the testimony" (*'ărôn hā-'ēdût,* Ex 25:22, etc.; 13 times); "the ark of thy might" (Ps 132:8), and once "the holy ark" (*'ărōn haqqōdesh*; II Chr 35:3).

The Wellhausen school assigns the description of the ark to P and consequently considers it to be late. The effort to make the ark the empty throne of God is not based on concrete biblical evidence. First a container for the tables of stone, the ark was the visible sign of the presence of God at the sanctuary. But it was also an object carried into battle (Josh 6:11). As a powerful symbol of God's presence it had to be treated with proper respect. Calamity came to the Philistines, the men of Bethshemesh, and Uzzah for failure to show it proper reverence.

Bibliography: AI, pp. 297ff. Davies, G. Henton, "The Ark of the Covenant," in IDB, I, pp. 222–26. Gutmann, J., "The History of the Ark," ZAW 83: 22–30. Haran, M., "The Ark and the Cherubim: Their Significance in Biblical Ritual," *Israel Exploration Journal* 9: 30–38, 89–94. ———, "The Disappearance of the Ark," *Israel Exploration Journal* 13:46–58. Morgenstern, Julian, "The Ark, the Ephod, and the Tent," HUCA 17:153–265; 18:1–52. Richardson, TWB, p. 174. Tur-Sinai, N. H., "The Ark of God at Beth Shemesh (I Sam 6) and Peres Uzza (II Sam 6; I Chron 13)," VT 1: 275–86. Woudstra, Marten H., *The Ark of the Covenant from Conquest to Kingship,* Presbyterian and Reformed, 1965. TDOT, I, pp. 363–73.

J.P.L.

אַרְנֶבֶת (*'arnebet*). See no. 123a.

167 אֶרֶץ (*'ereṣ*) ***earth, land, city (-state), (under) world.***

According to KB³ (p. 87), this word appears approximately 2400 times in the OT. More specifically, THAT I, p. 229, remarks that *'ereṣ* is the fourth most frequently used noun in the OT, appearing 2504 times in the Hebrew sections and 22 times in the Aramaic sections.

The first two meanings listed above are far and away the most crucial. That is, *'ereṣ* designates either (a) "the earth" in a cosmological sense, or (b) "the land" in the sense of a specific territorial designation, primarily the land of Israel.

In the former meaning, we are informed first (Gen 1:9–13) that God created the earth on the third day. All is done here by the divine fiat. The earth is not the product of a primordial substance, as is the case in the Babylonian Enuma Elish where the earth is formed from part of the cadaver of the fallen and slain deity Tiamat. It is a sphere that is totally under the control of divine sovereignty. The earth is the Lord's (Ps 24:1). He is its King (Ps 47:2, [H 3]), and its Lord (Ps 97:5). As such the world is good, and is not to be written off as intrinsically evil, the work of a demiurge. Absolutely no tinge of an "escapist mentality" is to be found in the OT. The reader of Scripture cannot but notice how relatively silent the OT is about the next life or another world. By contrast this is a dominating motif in other ancient near eastern literature. Can this be one of the Bible's ways of accentuating the goodness of the earth, the here and now?

Because the earth is the Lord's, it is answerable to him. As sin escalated, God determined to destroy the earth (Gen 9:11). But ultimately our righteous God is not happy with mere judgment, for this simply destroys the wicked. It uncreates. The ultimate expression of righteousness is neither dis-creativity nor turning the clock back. It is redemptive righteousness that is ultimate righteousness. This is why we have the rainbow covenant. God's intention is to establish a new heaven and a new earth (Isa 65:17; 66:22; Rev 21:1).

The second major use of *'ereṣ* is to designate a particular territory. Here the references to Palestine are of special significance. The boundaries of this new land, promised to Abraham and his seed, are first spelled out in Gen 15:18. It is of interest that this promise has been fulfilled geographically only two times, briefly during the period of David, and again during the time of the Hasmoneans during the intertestamental period.

This land belongs to the Lord, as does the earth at large. It is his heritage (I Sam 26:19). The land is holy only because the God of holiness has given it to his people. There is nothing intrinsically sacrosanct about this land any more than there is about the city of Jerusalem or the temple. If God departs, the sanctity leaves too.

The world of the Bible is divided into two sections, Israel and the nations. One is holy, the other is impure. Although God governs everywhere, the area of his sanctity and self-revelation are limited to the boundaries of the land of Israel. In alien lands the people were not even capable of worshiping the Lord (Ps 137). This is illustrated in the book of Jonah. While it is said by the prophet himself that the Lord of heaven rules the sea and the dry land (1:9), yet he attempts to flee from the presence of God (1:3, 10). This can only mean that Jonah attempts to flee from the area of divine revelation. Here he hopes the land of God will not come upon him. No wonder then that the prophet's messages to the exiles ring with the call that God will bring his people back to this land. The meaning "underworld" (not given in BDB) is uncertain and appears to depend on the comparison of the usage of some verses of the Psalms with similar concepts in pagan literature.

Bibliography: *'ereṣ as underworld:* Cross, F., and Freedman, D., JNES 14: 247–48. Dahood, M., Bib 40: 164–66 and elsewhere. Holladay, W. L., VT 19: 123–24. *'ereṣ as city-state:* Dahood, M., Bib 44: 297–98. ______, Supp VT 16: 46–47. ______, Bib 50: 337. Watson, W. E. G., Bib 53: 92–93. *General:* Barr, JSS 20: 149–64. De Guglielmo, Antonine, "The Fertility of the Land in the Messianic Prophecies," CBQ 19:306–11. Delcor, M., "Les Attaches Litteraires, l'Origine et la Signification de l'Espression Biblique 'Prendre a Temoin le Ciel et la Terre'," VT 16: 8–25. Henrey, K. H., "Land Tenure in the Old Testament," PEQ 86: 5–15. Miller, Patrick, D., "The Gift of God," Interp 23: 451–65. Unger, Merrill F., "The Old Testament Revelation of the Creation of Angels and the Earth," BS 114: 206–12. Whitcomb, John C., "The Creation of the Heavens and the Earth," *Grace Journal* 8: 26–32. TDOT, I, pp. 388–404. THAT, I, pp. 228–35.

V.P.H.

168 אָרַר (*'ārar*) ***to curse.***

Derivative

168a מְאֵרָה (m^e*'ērâ*) ***curse.*** Used five times: Deut 28:20; Prov 3:33; 28:27; Mal 2:2; 3:9.

A striking fact is that there is such a proliferation of words in Hebrew which have been generally all translated "to curse." The list includes at least six: *'ārar, qālal, 'ālâ, qābab, nāqab, zā'am.* To group all of them together under the one general English equivalent, "to curse," is much too superficial. The distinctions between each have been thoroughly worked out in the monograph of Brichto (see bibliography).

The verb *'ārar* occurs sixty-three times in the OT, most of which are in the Qal (fifty-four). In this particular stem the most popular form by far is the passive participle (*'ārûr* and related forms). It is used forty times, Deut 27:15ff. and 28:16ff. accounting for eighteen of those. The verb is also used twelve times as an antonym of *bārak* "to bless" (Gen 9:25–26; 12:3; 27:29, etc.).

On the basis of Akkadian *arāru* "to snare, bind" and the noun *irritu* "noose, sling" Brichto, following Speiser, advances the interpretation that Hebrew *'ārar* means "to bind (with a spell), hem in with obstacles, render powerless to resist." Thus the original curse in Gen 3:14, 17, "cursed are you above all cattle" and "cursed is the ground for your sake" means "you are banned/anathematized from all the other animals" and "condemned be the soil (i.e., fertility to men is banned) on your account." Similarly, God's word to Cain, "you are cursed from the earth" means Cain is banned from the soil, or more specifically, he is banned from enjoying its productivity. Cf. also Josh 9:23; Jud 21:18; I Sam 26:19; II Kgs 9:34 (barred from proper burial); Mal 2:2. One recalls the passage where King Balak of Moab hires Balaam to "curse" the Israelites (Num 22:6ff.). The king wants the magician to say some word or recite some incantation that will "immobilize" the Israelites, giving the Moabite king the necessary opportunity to defeat his numerically superior foe. Of course such was not automatically effective. According to Kaufmann, "The Israelite idea stripped magical actions of their autonomous, metadivine potency and made them serve as vehicles for the manifestation of the will of God" (Y. Kaufmann, *Religion of Israel,* p. 84).

It will be observed that the majority of "curse" sayings with *'ārar* fall into one of three general categories: (1) the declaration of punishments (Gen 3:14, 17); (2) the utterance of threats (Jer 11:3; 17:5; Mal 1:14); (3) the proclamation of laws (Deut 27:15–26; 28:16–19. It is interesting that all these curse-sayings are a reflex of one violating his relationship to God. To illustrate from Deut 27:15–26, idolatry (v. 15), disrespect for parents (v. 16), deceiving one's neighbor (vv. 17, 24), manipulating the disadvantaged (vv. 18–19), sexual aberrations (vv. 20, 21, 22, 23), bribery (v. 5), and not observing God's law (v. 26) all bring the condemnation of the curse.

That curse formulae existed throughout the ancient world no one will deny. But the difference between them and those of the OT are adequately illustrated in this quote from Fensham: "The mechanical magical execution of the treaty-curse . . . stands in glaring contrast to the ego-theological approach of prophetic writings . . . the ego of the Lord is the focal point of the threat, the execution and punishment of a curse . . . Curses of the ancient Near East, those outside the Old Testament, are directed against a transgression on private property . . . but the moral and ethical obligation in connection with his duty to one God and love to his neighbour is not touched on" (pp. 173–74).

Bibliography: Blank, Sheldon H., "The Curse, Blasphemy, the Spell, and the Oath," HUCA 23:73–95. Brichto, H. C., *The Problem of "Curse" in the Hebrew Bible,* JBL Monograph Series, vol. XIII, 1963. Fensham, F. C., "Common Trends in Curses of the Near Eastern Treaties and Kudurru-Inscriptions Compared with the Maledictions of Amos and Isaiah," ZAW 75:155–75. Gerstenberger, Erhard, "The Woe-Oracles of the Prophets," JBL 81:249–63. Gevirtz, Stanley, "West-Semitic Curses and the Problem of the Origins of the Hebrew Law," VT 11:137–58. Lehman, Manfred R., "Biblical Oaths," ZAW 81:74–92. Richardson, TWB, p. 58. Scharbert, J., " 'Fluchen' und 'Segnen' im Alten Testament," Bib 39: 5–8. Speiser, E. A., "An Angelic 'Curse': Exodus 14:20," JAOS 80: 198–200. TDOT, I, pp. 405–18. THAT, I, pp. 236–40.

V.P.H.

169 אֲרָרַט (*'ărāraṭ*) ***Ararat,*** famous as the name of the mountain on which Noah's ark came to rest.

In the Scripture Ararat is both a land and a mountain. We are told in II Kgs 19:37 and Isa 37:38 that the sons of the Assyrian king Sennacherib fled to this land (in Akkadian, *Urarṭu*) after murdering their father. Urartu was an important nation around Lake Van in Armenia. It is now divided between Turkey, the Soviet Union, Iran, and Iraq. Its period of significance and power was from the ninth century B.C. until its destruction in the next century by the Assyrian Tiglath-Pileser III. In 612 B.C. it fell to the Medes. Cf. Jer 51:27.

A careful reading of Gen 8:4 shows that the Bible does not say that the ark landed on "Mount Ararat." What it does say is that the ark landed on "the mountains (*hārê*) of Ararat." Hence the NEB translates Gen 8:4 as "a mountain in Ararat." In this range what is now called Mount Ararat is easily the most imposing, rising to 16,900 feet above sea level. After surveying the historical and ancient textual evidence Cassuto concludes, "None of the identifications of the biblical Ararat with a specific mountain has any basis in the Scriptural text, for the expression *on the mountains of Ararat,* correctly interpreted, only connotes a mountain-unspecified-in the land of Ararat," (p. 105).

Debate still continues among "arkologists" whether or not there is an ark-or-anything-at the top of modern Mount Ararat. There are those who are both hopeful and optimistic (Montgomery, Morris) and those who are unconvinced and even cynical (Stiebing). The latter view says that the deluge story is an adaptation of its Babylonian counterpart, the Epic of Gilgamesh, in which it is said of Utnapishti's boat that "on Mt. Niṣir the ship landed/Mt. Niṣir held the ship fast, allowing no motion." Of course one need not be cynical, like Stiebing, to be reserved about what is being found on Mount Ararat. If the finds prove to be remains of the ark, this will be a wonderful confirmation; if they do not prove to be, the Gen story still stands.

Bibliography: Cassuto, U., *Commentary on Genesis,* II, Jerusalem: Central Press, 1964, pp. 103–105. Montgomery, J. W., *The Quest For Noah's Ark,* Minneapolis: Bethany, 1974. Morris, J. D., *Adventure on Ararat,* San Diego: Institute for Creation Research, 1973. Stiebing, W. H., "A Futile Quest: The Search for Noah's Ark," BAR 2: 1–2, 13–20. Westermann, C., *Genesis (Biblischer Kommentar Altes Testament*), 1973, pp. 594–96.

V.P.H.

170 אָרַשׂ (*'āraś*) ***betrothe.***

171 אָרַשׁ (*'ārash*). **Assumed root of the following.**

171a אֲרֶשֶׁת (*'ăreshet*) ***desire, request.*** This feminine noun occurs only in Ps 21:3.

172 אֵשׁ (*'ēsh*) ***fire.***

Derivative

172a †אִשֶּׁה (*'ishsheh*) ***fire offering.***

'esh appears over 375 times in the Bible. Preponderantly, these references are in the context of either God's revelation of himself to man (theophany) or man's approach to God (worship and sacrifice).

According to Gen 3:24, the climax of creation is a sword of fire (*lahaṭ haḥereb*) placed at the east of the garden of Eden. The only way man could get back in was to go through the fire. As a climax to God's covenant with Abraham, a flaming fire (*lappîd 'ēsh*) moves between the separated pieces of animals (Gen 15:17) as God's signature to the contract. The Lord appears to Moses in/as a flame of fire (Ex 3:2), a fire which purged the bush of every bug on it and a fire which protected the bush from any landing buzzard or browsing goat. Moses' response was one of fear and attraction. He was "lashed with terror, leashed with longing." The nocturnal pillar of fire preceding and following the people of God in the wilderness guarantees the faithful that they are led and followed by the divine presence. It is not hard to believe that the pulse rate and heartbeat of Moses considerably accelerated when he ascended Mount Sinai, engulfed in smoke (Ex 19:18). To take another portion of Scripture, look at the prophetic literature, the first chapter of Ezk for example. The prophet's life begins with a vision of God which is determinative for the rest of his life. It is a vision dominated by fire (Ezk 1:26–27). We can appreciate Ezekiel's problem. He is trying to explain something he has never seen before, i.e. God.

What does fire symbolize in the OT? For one thing it symbolizes judgment. It separates from the tree of life (Gen 3:24). Sodom and Gomorrah are consumed by fire (Gen 19:24). Nadab and Abihu, the sons of Aaron, are consumed by fire for offering "strange fire" (Lev 10:1ff.). Was it because they took the fire from a place outside the altar area, or were they under the influence of alcohol, or what? The strategic thing is that they were disobedient at the point of worship. A similar experience befell the sons of Korah (Num 16:1ff.). Ezekiel sees the angelic being scattering coals of fire over backslidden Jerusalem (Ezk 10:2).

On the other hand fire may symbolize cleansing. On the heels of the war with Midian (Num 31) the priest says that anything that passes through fire will be clean (Num 31:21–24). Isaiah saw the temple filled with smoke, saw God's glory and was purified (Isa 6). Cf. Mal 3:2 for the phrase "refiner's fire." This means then that to one fire means death and to another life. To one it means eternal judgment and to another eternal blessing. God's wrath is against all that is impure.

'ishsheh. ***Fire offering, offering made by fire.*** The etymology of this word (from *'ēsh* or something else) is debated (Driver). It can be applied to any offering which was wholly or partially consumed by fire. Thus it is applied to the burnt offering (Lev 1:9, 13); the cereal/grain offering (Lev 2:3); peace offering (Lev 3:3); the guilt offering (Lev 7:5); the consecration offering (Lev 8:28). It is used over sixty times in the OT.

Bibliography: Driver, G. R., "Ugaritic and Hebrew Words," in *Ugaritica VI,* Paris, 1969, pp. 181–84. Gradwohl, R., "Das 'Fremde Feuer' von Nadab und Abihu," ZAW 75: 288–96. Miller, Patrick D., "Fire in the Mythology of Canaan and Israel," CBQ 27: 256–61. Morgenstern, Julian, *The Fire upon the Altar,* Quadrangle, 1963. TDNT, VI, pp. 934–41. TDOT, I, pp. 418–28. THAT, I, pp. 242–46.

V.P.H.

173 אִשׁ (*'ish*) ***There is, there are.*** Softer form for the usual *yēsh.* Is used in II Sam 14:19 and Mic 6:10.

174 אשׁד (*'shd*). **Assumed root of the following.**
174a †אֶשֶׁד (*'eshed*) ***bottom, slope.***
174b אֲשֵׁדָה (*'ăshēdâ*) ***foundation.***

'eshed. ***Bottom, slope, lower part,*** which is the construct of *'āshēd* (itself not found in the OT), appears only in Num 21:15, "and the 'slope' of the valley/ravine."

This is in a quote from the otherwise unknown "Book of the Wars of the Lord," another witness to the fact that the OT did not exhaust the literary output of ancient Israel.

In the plural it is *'ăshēdôt*/*'ashdôt* "hillsides" (Josh 10:40; 12:8). One meets the transliteration "Ashdothpisgah" in the KJV in Josh 12:3; 13:20; Deut 3:17; 4:49. The reference is to the western slope of Mount Pisgah in Transjordan. From here Moses viewed the promised land before his death. [Probably also in Deut 33:2, cf. NIV. R.L.H.]

V.P.H.

175 אשׁה (*'shh*). **Assumed root of the following.**
175a אָשְׁיָה (*'oshyâ*) ***buttress.*** Occurs only in Jer 50:15.

אִשֶּׁה (*'ishsheh*). See no. 172a.
אִשָּׁה (*'ishshâ*). See no. 137a.

176 אַשּׁוּר (*ashshûr*) ***Asshur, Assyria,*** one of the sons of Shem, the eponymous ancestor of the Assyrians (Gen 10:22).

The land of Assyria took its name from the city of Assur, a city on the west bank of the Tigris in modern Iraq. The city in turn took its name from the deity Ashur who was primarily a warrior and a conqueror and whose symbol was an archer with a winged disk. The god is the symbol of the city and the state. Assur the god is Assur the state.

Assyria first emerges, albeit briefly, as an independent state on the heels of the Ur III dynasty, *c.* 2000 B.C. After this period of autonomy the Assyrian state fell under the control of foreign rulers for about five hundred years, first the Amorites, then the Hurrians.

The first person to claim the title "king of the land of Assyria" was Assuruballit (*c.* 1362–1327 B.C.). The empire reached its zenith in its earlier expansion under Tukultininurta I (*c.* 1244–1208 B.C.), the period of the conquest and the judges, but it had no apparent contact with Israel at this time. With the exception of the reign of Tiglath-pileser I (c. 1115–1077 B.C.) Assyria went once again into several centuries of weakness and eclipse. They were never a threat to Israel during the period of the United Monarchy.

It is, however, in the period of the divided monarchy, especially the ninth century B.C., that there takes place an Assyrian resurgence that is to present Israel with a threat she has never encountered before, something she never had to face from the earlier Philistines, Moabites, etc. That threat is the ominous appearance of a militant, hostile people with worldwide conquering ambitions. No longer is the concern simply border skirmishes. Now it is a fight for the right to existence. Surely it can be no accident or coincidence that shortly after this Assyrian resurgence there appears in Israel a new institution, the classical, literary prophets who will put these herculean nations into historical and theological perspective.

It is the Assyrian king Shalmaneser III (859–825 B.C.) who is the progenitor of this revitalization and the harbinger of still worse things to come for Israel. The initial sparks were lit at the battle of Qarqar (not mentioned in the Bible) on the Orontes River in Syria in 853 B.C. This was a confrontation between Shalmaneser and a coalition that included, among others, Syria and Israel (under Ahab). Any hopes Israel had for survival were virtually wiped out a century later by Tiglath-pileser III (745–727 B.C.). It is he who began the policy of incorporating the conquered territory into the empire as provinces. It was also he who used to a greater advantage than any before him the policy of transplanting conquered populations. Under Shalmaneser V Israel fell in 722 B.C., by now little more than a formality.

The literary prophets saw in these epochal events, culminating in 722 B.C., the first decisive fulfillment of their collective interpretation of history. Isaiah had viewed Assyria as the Lord's tool for chastening his people (5:26–29; 10:5–19). But interestingly, no specific Assyrian king is accorded a title as is the Babylonian Nebuchadnezzar ("my servant") or the Persian Cyrus ("my anointed one"). In the end Assyria destroyed God's people only after God's people had destroyed themselves.

V.P.H.

אָשׁוּר (*'ăshûr*). See no. 183c.
אֲשִׁישָׁה (*'ăshîshâ*). See no. 185d.
אָשְׁיָה (*'oshyâ*). See no. 175a.

177 אֶשֶׁךְ (*'eshek*) ***testicle.*** Occurs only in Lev 21:20, in phrase *m^e^rôaḥ 'āshek*.

178 אֶשְׁכּוֹל (*'eshkôl*) ***(grape) cluster.***

Three times the word is used in the Song of Solomon to describe the physical attraction between the lovers: she about him (Song 1:14); he about her (Song 7:7–8 [H 8–9]).

Such "clusters" of grapes were either delicious for eating (Mic 7:1; Deut 32:32) or for preparation in the making of wine (Isa 65:8). Such clusters were used in the beverage served to the Egyptian Pharaoh, as indicated by the dream of Joseph's cellmate, the chief butler (Gen 40:10).

Numbers 13:23–24 refers to the brook Eshcol, a body of water near Hebron (probably to the north), discovered by the Hebrew spies who had been despatched by Moses to reconnoiter the land of Canaan. The name was given to this brook because of the "clusters" of grapes that there were, clusters so large that they had to be carried on a pole between two men. A characteristic of the land of promise is its lushness and fertility, a land flowing with milk and honey. It will be the same in the eschatological day, a land in which there will be abundance of wine.

Herdner claims to have found the same root in a Ugaritic text, *'uṯkl,* but Gordon does not list such a word in his Ugaritic glossary.

Bibliography: Herdner, A., "Un nouvel exemplaire du rituel RS 1929 n^o^3," *Syria* 33: 104.

V.P.H.

179 אשׁל (*'shl*). **Assumed root of the following.**
179a אֵשֶׁל (*'ēshel*) ***tamarisk tree.***

180 אָשַׁם (*'āsham*) ***be desolate, be guilty, to offend, to acknowledge offense, to trespass.*** (ASV and RSV prefer the terms "guilt" and "guilty" more than "trespass," and NEB does not hesitate to use words like reparation, compensation, penalty and punishment.)

Derivatives

180a †אָשֵׁם (*'āshēm*) ***faulty.***
180b †אָשָׁם (*'āshām*) ***guiltiness.***
180c †אַשְׁמָה (*'ashmâ*) ***sin.***

The primary meaning of the word *'āsham* seems to center on guilt, but moves from the act which brings guilt to the condition of guilt to the act of punishment. In any particular passage it is often difficult to determine which thrust the word has. The word is used with its derivatives 103 times. Synonyms such as *'āwôn* and *rāsha'* often are translated with the word, "guilty," but normally their meanings are "iniquity" and "wicked," respectively. The word is used in Ugaritic in the cognate *'ṯm* (UT 19: no. 422; Ais WUS no. 474).

The verb *'āsham* occurs in the Pentateuch in Leviticus, chapters four, five and six, and in Numbers 5:6–7. The setting is cultic but also ethical. Any individual who had sinned was a guilty person. A procedure of obliterating guilt is outlined. Normally, restitution must be made according to cash values, plus a twenty percent cash penalty. An animal of specified value was brought to the priest, sin was confessed and the animal sacrificed in a specific manner. The goal was atonement and forgiveness.

In Jud 21:22 the verb seems to represent the consequences of breaking a vow. In II Chr 19:10, the first use of *'āsham* stresses guilt as a result of breaking the law of God; whereas, the second applies to the judges who must warn people that sin has consequences.

A contrast between punishment and redemption is apparent in Ps 34:21–22 [H 22–23]. In this instance, *'āsham* is the punishment itself. The sting of an inner guilt feeling is absent in Prov 30:10 also, for it points to the possible falseness of an accusation made against a slave.

An exhortation (Hos 4:15) not to offend (RSV "be guilty," NEB "guilt offering") is directed to Judah. Was Judah not to play the harlot like Israel, or not to incur guilt? Compare with 5:15 where Ephraim is depicted as being punished by God but they need to realize their offence (RSV "guilt"), that they were sinners. The next verse, 6:1, indicates possible salvation.

Hosea 10:2 says Israel is found faulty (RSV "bear their guilt," note NEB "they are mad"). Guilt is understood as the consequence of idol worship and of a divided heart (NEB "crazy"), but punishment was yet to come. In Hos 13:1, "offended" (RSV "guilty") points to acts of sin, but the next verse shows Israel still sinning and punishment is not mentioned until 13:3. Isaiah 24:6 and Joel 1:18 depict *'āsham* as the end result of sinning, even affecting animals.

Jeremiah (2:3) declared that those who devour Israel shall offend (RSV "became guilty," NEB "no one... went unpunished"). Is the meaning of *'āsham* the act of sin, the condition of guilt, or the end result of punishment? Since the last phrase in verse three speaks of a future evil, RSV would seem to be correct. The same is true of Jer 50:7.

In Ezk 6:6 guilt is the condition after punishment has happened. On the other hand, in 22:4, guilt is the consequence of idol worship but before punishment (cf. v. 15). So also 25:12, and Hab 1:11. In response to Zechariah's preaching, the rulers claimed they are not guilty (11:5), even while killing people. But lack of a guilt feeling will not forestall judgment.

Throughout these passages, *'āsham* varies in stress. It may denote acts of sin, responsibility for sin, punishment, and even the aftermath of punishment. Perhaps, one may hold that the *'āsham* connotes the totality of alienation from God, including its consequences.

'āshām. ***Guiltiness, offering for sin, sin, trespass, trespass offering.*** With a few exceptions this masculine noun denotes the trespass offering (RSV, NEB "guilt offering"). In Gen 26:10 Abimelek refers to a possible sin and its resulting guiltiness (RSV "brought guilt," NEB "make us liable to retribution"). The NEB probably has caught the basic meaning here. KJV has "trespass," in Lev 5:7,15 but more correctly ASV "trespass offering," RSV "guilt offering." All other twenty-two times in Lev the meaning is "trespass offering." The same is true of Numbers 5:7–8; 6:12; 18:9, of I Sam 6:3–4, 8, 17; of II Kgs 12:16, and of Ezk 40:39; 42:13; 44:29; 46:20 and of Isa 53:10. But in Ps 68:21 [H 22] *'āshām* is sin (RSV "wrongs," ASV "guiltiness"), and punishment is threatened. What of *'āshām* in Prov 14:9? KJV has "mocks at sin," RSV has "wicked," NEB has "too arrogant to make amends." None denote guilt, *per se*.

'ashmâ. ***Sin, cause of trespass, trespass offering.*** The KJV translates mostly "trespass" or "sin," i.e. the acts of sin, but marginal readings sometimes have "guiltiness" (ASV, RSV prefer "guilt" or "guilty") in Lev 4:3; 22:16. Joab argued that numbering of Israel was cause for trespass (ASV, "cause of guilt," RSV "bring guilt") in I Chr 21:3. In II Chr 24:18; 28:10,13; 33:23, KJV regards *'ashmâ* as "sin or trespass," but ASV and RSV sometimes prefer "guilt." Does the noun designate the acts of sin or liability to penalty before God? The same observation holds true of Ezr 9:6–7,13,15; 10:10,19, but all three versions agree that sins (RSV "wrongs") are intended in Ps 69:5 [H 6] and Amos 8:14, though RSV and NEB simply transliterate the Hebrew as though it were the name of a goddess.

'āshēm. ***Faulty, that which is faulty.*** The KJV translates this adjective in Gen 42:21 as "guilty" (ASV, RSV, same) and is the rare instance where a feeling of guilt is associated with the word. II Samuel 14:13 is more legalistic. David is faulty (ASV, "guilty," RSV "convicts himself"). And probably in Ezr 10:19 being "guilty" (KJV, ASV) is better than "guilt-offering" (RSV).

In summary, the root *'āsham* includes acts of sin, responsibility for them, punishment and its aftermath or, as an alternative, atonement. The word denotes any breach of God's covenant with Israel and any divine act of dealing with it, whether punishment or atonement.

Bibliography: Kellerman, Diether, "'Āšām in Ugarit?" ZAW 76: 319–22. Kidner, F. D., *Sacrifice in the Old Testament,* London: Tyndale, 1952. Morris, Leon, "'asham," EQ 30: 196–210. Richardson, TWB, pp. 207, 226–29. Ringgren, Helmer, *Sacrifice in the Bible,* Association Press, 1963. Snaith, N. H., "The Sin Offering and the Guilt Offering," VT 15: 73–80. TDOT, I, pp. 429–37. THAT, I, pp. 251–56.

G.H.L.

181 אַשָּׁף (*'ashshāp*) ***astrologer, enchanter, exorcist*** (JB), ***conjurer, necromancer*** (BDB).

The word *'ashshāp* describing some variety of occultist appears in both Hebrew and Aramaic. In the Aramaic form the middle letter is not doubled. All occurrences are in the book of Daniel (1:20 and 2:2 [Heb]; 2:10, 27; 4:4; 5:7, 11, 15 [Aramaic]). The Assyrian *âshipu* means the same.

The meaning of this word must be determined solely by context, since no etymology is apparent. Perhaps it is a loan word from Babylonia and related to the Assyrian *shiptu* ("conjuration"). Since the word is found only in Daniel, this is all the more likely. The Hebrew word *'ashpâ* is made from the same letters and means "quiver" (Job 39:23; Ps 127:5; Isa 22:6, 49:2; Jer 5:16; Lam 3:13), but any connection of meaning would be a guess although arrows were sometimes used in divination (Ezk 21:21 [H 27]).

In Dan 1:20 *'ashshāpîm* are parallel to *ḥarṭummîm* (magicians, q.v.), while in 2:2 they are also grouped with the *m^e kashsh^e pîm* (sorcerers) and *kaśdîm* (Chaldeans). The Aramaic word *gāz^e rîn* (soothsayers/astrologers) in the lists of Dan 4:7, 5:7, and 11 is the equivalent of the Heb *m^e kashsh^e pîm* used elsewhere.

Bibliography: Cornfeld, G., "Magic, Divination and Superstition," in *Pictorial Biblical Encyclopedia,* Macmillan, 1964.

R.L.A.

182 אשׁף (*'shp*). **Assumed root of the following.**

182a אַשְׁפָּה (*'ashpâ*) ***quiver for arrows.*** Derivation uncertain

182.1 אֶשְׁפָּר (*'āshpār*) ***date cake.*** Meaning uncertain.

183 אָשַׁר (*'āshar*) ***to go (straight), walk.***

Derivatives

183a †אֶשֶׁר (*'esher*), אָשָׁר (*'āshār*) ***happiness, blessedness.***

183b †אֹשֶׁר (*'ōsher*) ***happiness.***

183c †אַשּׁוּר (*'ăshûr*), אֲשֻׁר (*'ăshûr*) ***step, going.***

183d †אֲשֻׁר (*'ăshūr*) ***step, going.***

183e †אָשֵׁר (*'āshēr*) ***Asher.***

183f אֲשֻׁרִים (*'ăshūrîm*) ***boxwood.***

183g תְּאַשּׁוּר (*t^e 'ashshûr*) ***boxtree.***

183h אֲשֵׁרָה (*'ăshērâ*), אֲשֵׁרָה (*'ăshêrâ*) ***Ashera.***

The verb occurs in the Qal only in Prov 9:6, "go/walk in the way of understanding." In the Piel it is used eleven times with several nuances of which the most prominent is "to bless, called blessed": Gen 30:13; Mal 3:12, 15; Job 29:11; Ps 72:17; Prov 31:28; Song 6:9; similarly in two cases in the Pual, Ps 41:2 [H 3]; Prov 3:18. The relationship, if any, between Qal "to go" and Piel "to bless" is not apparent. Two derivatives each come from the meaning "bless," and "to walk."

There are two verbs in Hebrew meaning "to bless." One is *bārak* and the other *'āshar.* Can any differences between them be tabulated? For one thing *bārak* is used by God when he "blesses" somebody. But there is no instance where *'āshar* is ever on God's lips. When one "blesses" God the verb is *bārak,* never *'āshar.* One suggestion to explain this sharp distinction, i.e. that *'āshar* is reserved for man, is that *'āshar* is a word of envious desire, "to be envied with desire is the man who trusts in the Lord." God is not man and therefore there are no grounds for aspiring to his state even in a wishful way. Similarly God does not envy man, never desires something man is or has, which he does not have, but would like to have. Therefore God never pronounces man "blessed" (*'ashrê*) (Janzen). It should also be pointed out that when *bārak* is used the initiative comes from God. God can bestow his blessing even when man doesn't deserve it. On the other hand, to be blessed (*'ashrê*), man has to do something. Finally, *bārak* is a benediction, *'āshar* more of a congratulation. The former is rendered by *eulogētos* in the LXX and the latter by *makarios.*

To be "blessed" (*'ashrê*), man has to do something. Usually this is something positive. A "blessed" man, for example, is one who trusts in God without equivocation: Ps 2:12; 34:8 [H 9]; 40:4 [H 5]; 84:5 [H 6]; 84:12 [H 13]; 146:5; Prov 16:20. A "blessed" man is one who comes under the authority of God's revelation: his Torah, Ps 119:1; 1:2; Prov 29:18; his word, Prov 16:20; his commandment, Ps 112:1; his testimony, Ps 119:2; his way, Ps 128:1; Prov 8:32. The man who is beneficent to the poor is blessed (Ps 41:1 [H 2]); Prov 14:21). Note the negative approach of Ps 1, "blessed is the man who does not." He isolates himself and shuns the company of certain people, the ungodly. The psalm ends by noting that it is precisely these ungodly who will in the end be isolated. They will not stand in the judgment. They will be conspicuous by their absence for they will perish.

'esher. *Happiness, bliss.* Always occurs as *'ashrê,* usually defined as the masculine plural construct of the noun *'esher* (which form is nonexistent in the Hebrew Bible), "O the happiness(es) of." Perhaps "bliss" would be a better translation. It is used forty-four times in the OT, twenty-six of which are in the Psalter and eight in

Prov. It appears in the Pentateuch only in Deut 33:29, in the historical books only in I Kgs 10:8 (= II Chr 9:7), and in the prophets in Isa 30:18; 32:20; 56:2.

'ōsher. ***Happiness,*** a hapax legomenon, used in Gen 30:13, "What happiness is mine."

'ăshûr, 'ashshūr. ***Step, going, feet,*** the latter form occurring in Job 31:7 and Ps 17:11.

Both words are confined to Ps (six times), Job (two times), and Prov (once). Dahood (see bibliography) has argued for the existence of the word in Eccl 7:26, "The feet of her are dragnets" (*'ăsher* > *'ăshûrē*).

It should be observed that in the six Ps passages the noun is often used in parallel with a part of the body. In Ps 17:5 it is parallel with *pa'am* "foot"; in Ps 37:31 with *lēb* "heart"; in Ps 40:2 [H 3] with *regel* "foot" and again in 73:2; and finally in Job 31:7, here in conjunction with both *lēb* "heart" and *'ayin* "eye." All this lends credence to the possibility that *'ăshûr* also refers to some part of the body, feet, or legs.

In Scripture the word is used metaphorically, meaning something like "lifestyle." It may emphasize the believer's fidelity to God's way: Ps 17:5; 44:18 [H 19]; 73:2; Job 31:7; Prov 14:15. The word may also be used in a context affirming God's faithfulness in helping one to keep in his way: Ps 40:2 [H 3]; 37:31.

'āshēr. ***Asher,*** Jacob's second son by Zilpah, the handmaid of Leah. Chronologically he is Jacob's eighth-born son. The name is to be related to the verb *'āshar* in the Piel meaning of "to bless," the "happy, fortunate one," akin to the name Felix in the New Testament.

The specific etymology is found in Gen 30:13: "And Leah said, what fortune (*be'oshrî*, 'happy am I' in KJV) for the daughters will call me blessed (*'ishsherûnî*), and she called his name Asher (*'āshēr*)." Albright has discovered a related word, albeit feminine, analogous to Asher in a list of Egyptian slaves from the eighteenth century B.C. It appears there as *'sh-ra*. Further Pentateuchal references to Asher may be found in the blessing of Jacob (Gen 49:20) and in the blessing of Moses (Deut 33:24–26). The former passage underscores the fertility of the land as does the latter.

In the land partition section of Joshua the territory assigned to the tribe Asher comes third from the end (Josh 19:24–31) followed only by Naphtali and Dan. It was alloted territory in northwest Palestine, not far from the Phoenician cities of Tyre and Sidon. Biblical Israel does not appear to be homogeneous. Its systems of twelve tribes embraced populations with contrasting ways of life. Asher, along with Zebulon and Dan, were navigational. As such, they had more in common with the Phoenicians and the Philistines than they did with the inland Hebrews who were landlubbers. Their likenesses to each other would be akin to those of a man from Kansas and a man from Maine.

The Asher tribe never produced any religious or political leader throughout her history, not even during the days of the frequent appearances of the charismatic judges. Deborah even has to reprimand them for their unwillingness to participate in the fight against the Canaanites. They preferred to stay in more familiar surroundings, the seacoast, rather than to commit themselves to battling the enemy and making themselves vulnerable (and not only have the Asherites been guilty of this!).

'ăshērâ. ***Asherah.*** Both a Canaanite goddess and a wooden cult object in the OT. The word is translated "groves" in the KJV presumably on the basis of the LXX *alsos* and *nemus* in the Vulgate. Before examining the OT itself we turn to the famous Ugaritic texts from Ras Shamra. It is they which tell us who Asherah was. Her name is a feminine participle of the Ugaritic verb *'ṯr* (Heb *'āshar* "to go"). One of her titles is *rabbatu aṯiratu yammi,* "Lady Atirat of the Sea," or "the lady who treads on the sea." She is the consort or wife of the divine El, and as such enjoys the title *qaniyatu elima,* "progenitress/creatress of the gods." Her most famous son was Baal. A characteristic of all mythological literatures is "in the beginning there were two." In the Bible, however, we meet "in the beginning there was one." The issue is not simply arithmetic. The fact that one does not read about Mrs. God in Gen 1 and 2 may be one of the Bible's ways of stating that only God finds fulfillment in himself.

In one of the famous mythological texts from Ugarit, the Kret epic, it is predicted to Kret of his bride that "she will bear you seven sons/and an eighth (daughter) 'Octavia'/she will bear you the lad Yasib/who will suck the milk of Asherah." Hence, (divine) life is guaranteed and bequeathed.

To turn to the OT, there is no actual description of an Asherah there. Was it a tree, a pole, some kind of tree symbol, an image? It apparently was not a natural object but one that was constructed by man, an artifact. It was "made": I Kgs 16:33; II Kgs 17:16; 21:3; it was "set up": II Kgs 17:10; II Chr 33:19; Isa 27:9; it was "built": I Kgs 14:23. Only once is the verb "to plant" used, Deut 16:21, and here the meaning is "implant." The conclusion then is that in the OT Asherah stands for the Canaanite goddess represented by a carved wooden image implanted into the ground, usually adjacent to an altar dedicated to the god Baal and located on a hilltop under a leafy tree (Patai).

It is in the period of the divided monarchy that the Asherah cult flourished both in Israel and Judah, though its existence before is documented by the command in Ex 34:13, the prohibition of Deut 16:21, and the incident at the threshold of Gideon's life of service to God, Jud 6:25ff. Rehoboam's career marks the beginning of this in Judah (I Kgs 14:23). In the north the cult received its greatest momentum from the incentive of Jezebel who was responsible for the presence of "four hundred prophets of Asherah" (I Kgs 18:19). Even a reform-minded king such as Asa (I Kgs 15:13) or later Hezekiah (II Kgs 18:4) was unable to liquidate the movement. It was knocked down, but not knocked out. There was an almost inevitable resurrection even in the wake of reform. Compare son Manasseh's policy (II Kgs 21:7, even to the point of placing the image in the temple) on the heels of father Hezekiah's reform (II Kgs 18:4). Apostasy and idolatry just behind revival! What one generation attempts to get rid of a subsequent generation may trot back in, however reprehensible it may be. All too frequently this has been the pattern in the human race.

Bibliography: *'āshar, 'ashrê:* TDOT I, pp. 445–48. THAT I, pp. 257–60. Dahood, M., "Hebrew-Ugaritic Lexicography I," Bib 44: 298. Hillers, D. R., "Delocutive Verbs in Hebrew," JBL 86: 321–22. Kaser, W., "Beobachtungen zum altestamentlichen Makarismus," ZAW 82: 225–250. Lipínski, E., "Macarismes et psaumes de congratulation," RB 75: 321–67.

'āshēr: Albright, W. F., "Northwest-Semitic Names in Light of Egyptian Slaves from the Eighteenth Century B.C.," JAOS 74: 229. Witfall, W., "Asshur and Eber, or Asher and Heber?" ZAW 82: 110–13.

'ăshērâ: TDOT I, pp. 438–44. Albright, W. F., *Yahweh And The Gods of Canaan,* Doubleday, 1968, pp. 121–24. Barr, J., "Seeing the Wood For the Trees? An Enigmatic Ancient Translation," JSS 13: 11–20. Patai, R., "The Goddess Asherah," JNES 24: 37–52. Reed, W. L., *The Asherah In The Old Testament,* Texas Christian University, 1949.

V.P.H.

184 אֲשֶׁר (*'ăsher*) ***who, which,*** the relative particle used very frequently in the Hebrew Bible (Mandelkern's concordance uses almost twenty pages, small print, four columns to each page, to list all of the occurrences).

By contrast, the relative particle *she-* is used only sporadically in several books of the Bible, Jud, Ps, Song of Solomon for example. In Eccl the relative *she-,* however, is used almost as much as the relative *'ăsher* (eighty-nine times for the latter, sixty-eight times for the former according to BDB, p. 979*b,* but Dahood in Bib 33: 45 lists the ratio as 89/67).

Taking into consideration the prolific use of *'ăsher* in biblical Hebrew, it is of interest to observe that the equivalent has turned up only once in the Ugaritic texts: UT 16: Text 2060:34–35, *'aṯr iṯ bqṯ w stn ly* "find out what is available and write to me."

To be sure, the preponderant use of *'ăsher* is as a normal relative, usually with an expressed antecedent. But there are other nuances. Williams (see bibliography) lists seven syntactical uses of the particle and surely more could be added by other Hebrew grammarians. For example, one use of *'ăsher* is to express result: "'So that' if man could number the dust of the earth" (Gen 13:16). Another is to express purpose: "Keep his statutes . . . 'that' it may go well with you" (or is this result? Deut 4:40); "I am going out to the field to glean among the sheaves 'in order to' find favor in his eyes" (Ruth 2:2, a translation missed by both KJV and RSV; Sasson, *Interpretation* 30: 418). A third is to introduce a causal statement: "They plundered the city 'in reprisal for/because of' their sister" (Gen 34:27). A category not noticed by Williams is that in Ps 71:20, "'Although' you made me see troubles . . . you will restore me to life," a concessive use of *'ăsher* (note how the KJV inserts a word in italics to make sense once it has settled on the translation of *'ăsher* as "which").

On a number of occasions *'ăsher* is affixed to prepositions, for example *ba'ăsher* (nineteen times), but much more often with k^e*-ka'ăsher* (see the adequate outline of meanings in BDB, p. 455).

Bibliography: BDB, pp. 81–84. Archer, G., *A Survey of Old Testament Introduction,* Moody, 1964, pp. 465–66. Gaenssle, C., "The Hebrew Particle *'shr,*" AJSL 31: 3–66, 93–159. Gevirtz, S., "On The Etymology of the Phoenician Particle *'sh,*" JNES 16: 124–27. Gordon, C., *Ugaritic Textbook,* p. 369. Williams, R. J., *Hebrew Syntax: An Outline,* University of Toronto, 1967, pp. 77–78.

V.P.H.

185 אשש (*'shsh*). **Assumed root of the following.**

185a אֲשִׁישָׁה (*'ăshîshâ*) ***raisin-cake,*** which is consistently translated in the KJV as "flagons (of wine)."

The word occurs in Ugaritic as *'aṯiṯ,* but the precise etymology is obscure. Driver connects it with an Arabic root meaning "inflorescence of the grapevine" and together with the translation in Aquila (*oinanthē*) suggests that *'ăshîshâ* means: (1) the inflorescence of the palm studded with numerous flowers and a grape vine covered with berries, and (2) a raisin-cake resembling such a clump of berries pressed into a solid mass.

The word is used only five times in the OT. In II Sam 6:19 (= I Chr 16:3) we are told that David, in the process of bringing the ark to Jerusalem, gave out a bread roll, some dates (?), and a raisin-cake to his people. That such a food item was delectable is substantiated by the third use of *'ăshîshâ*, Song 2:5, "Feed me with raisin-cakes... with apples." See also Isa 16:7 (NIV).

The last reference is Hos 3:1, "As Yahweh loves the children of Israel although they turn to other gods and love raisin-cakes." The last part of this verse may also be translated, "To other gods who love raisin cakes." The meaning is not clear. Most likely the reference here is to similar "sacrificial cakes" (*kawwānîm*) that the people made for or offered to the "queen of heaven," i.e. Ishtar, the Assyrian goddess of fertility (Jer 7:18; 44:17–19). The point would be then that God's love for his own is a longsuffering love. Even participation in obnoxious pagan rites by the covenant peoples does not move God to abrogate his love for them.

Bibliography: Driver, G. R., "Hebrew Notes on 'Song of Songs' and 'Lamentations'" in *Festschrift Alfred Bertholet,* Tübingen: J.C.B. Mohr, 1950, p. 144.

V.P.H.

186 אֵת (*'ēt*) **I. Untranslated particle.**

An untranslated particle in Hebrew often described in grammars (somewhat superficially) as the sign of the direct object after a transitive verb. Its origin is unknown. The prevailing view is that *'ēt* was originally a noun meaning "essence, substance, self," a significance which it subsequently lost in the historical development of the language.

When *'ēt* is used to signify an accusative (*nota accusativi*) it is generally, though not always, in prose and when the object of the verb is determined by the definite article. More important than indicating an accusative, the function of *'ēt* is to emphasize the word to which it is attached.

For this reason one observes that *'ēt* is used not only with the accusative but with the subject (*nota nominativi*) of both intransitive and passive verbs. Copious illustrations could be offered but two will suffice. With *'ēt* as subject of an intransitive verb compare II Kgs 6:5: "The axe-head fell into the water" (*w^e'et-habbarzel nāpal 'el-hammāyîm*). With *'ēt* as subject of a passive verb compare Gen 17:5: "And your name (*'et-shimkâ*) shall no more be called Abram."

To summarize, *'ēt* was originally a substantive, and was used to emphasize the noun to which it was prefixed. In the course of time the emphatic meaning was lost and *'ēt* became a particle with no special meaning.

Bibliography: On a similar particle in other Semitic languages and texts: Andersen, F. I., "Moabite Syntax," *Orientalia* 35: 117–18. Leahy, T., "Studies in the Syntax of IQS," Bib 41: 152–54.

On Biblical Hebrew *'ēt:* Hoftijzer, J., "Remarks Concerning the Use of the Particle *'t* in Classical Hebrew," *Oudtestamentische Studiën* 14: 1–99. MacDonald, J., "The Particle *'t* in Classical Hebrew," VT 14: 263–75. Saydon, P. P., "Meanings and Uses of the Particle *'t,*" VT 14: 192–210. Walker, N., "Concerning the Function of *'eth,*" VT 5: 314–15.

V.P.H.

187 אֵת (*'ēt*) ***II, with, together with.***

On occasions there is a different nuance. To illustrate, "I have gotten a man 'from' (*'et-*) the Lord" (Gen 4:1). "The Lord... will fight for you (*lākem*), according to all he did 'for' you (*'it-t^ekem*) in Egypt" (Deut 1:30). "I have not sinned against you (*lak*) but you are doing evil 'against' me (*'ittî*) to fight against me (*bî*)" (Jud 11:27).

To return to the basic meaning "with," this preposition is used frequently in a particular theological context. This is (a) in the promises of God to man: "I am/will be with you"; (b) affirmations from man that God is indeed with them; (c) prayers of petition that God may be with them. The scripture then is replete with the idea that God calls his people to fellowship with himself, be it in the garden of Eden, in the odyssey of an Abraham, in a covenant situation at Sinai, in the tabernacle, in a wilderness, crossing a Jordan, entering a Canaan, and so forth. At this point we should observe that the NT is no different. It is Mark (3:13–15) who tells us that Jesus' primary reason for calling the twelve was "that they might be with him." The call to fellowship always precedes the call to service.

A glance, however, at biblical and post-biblical history shows that nothing is more difficult than walking with God. And we are not the problem—God is! Certainly Adam and Eve couldn't succeed at it long. By Gen 3, they are longing for a past that is gone forever. Look at the Israelites. By 586 B.C. the song of God had gone and Ezekiel saw God's presence leaving first the temple, then the city.

The reason lies in the nature of God, his holy and jealous love, and in the fact that everywhere God meets man, he places a moral demand on him. It is obedience and sensitivity to the Holy One that makes God and myself compatible.

Bibliography: Meek, Theophile J., "Translating the Hebrew Bible," JBL 79: 328–35. TDOT, I, pp. 449–63.

V.P.H.

אֵת (*'ēt*) III. See no. 192a.
אַתְּ (*'at*). See no. 189a.

188 אָתָה (*'ātâ*) ***to come.***

Derivative

188a אִיתוֹן (*'îtôn*) ***entrance.*** This masculine noun occurs only in Ezk 40:15.

The normal word for "come" is *bô'* which is used over twenty-five hundred times in the OT. By contrast *'ātâ* is used only twenty times, twenty-one times if one accepts the emendation proposed by Dahood for Ps 74:9, "Our signs we do not see, there is no longer a prophet, and no one has 'come' (*'ittānû* > *'ātānû*) who knows how long." Eighteen of the twenty are in the Qal and two in the Hiphil (Isa 21:14; Jer 12:9) with the meaning "to bring." In the Aramaic sections of the OT, *'ātâ* occurs exclusively for "to come" and there sixteen times. Observe also that all of the Hebrew occurrences are in poetic passages, never prose.

Nine times the root appears in Isaiah, mostly in the latter half except for 21:12, 14. No particular continuity marks the seven remaining passages: the coming of the future (41:23; 44:7; 45:11); the coming of Cyrus (41:25); those who come to debauch themselves (56:12); the coming of wild beasts to devour God's people (56:9; cf. Jer 12:9) humanity in general (41:5).

The verb is used to describe the "coming" of God only in Deut 33:2. It is used for "coming" to God in Jer 3:22. The root appears four times in Job: 3:25; 16:22; 30:14; 37:22.

Bibliography: Dahood, M., "Hebrew-Ugaritic Lexicography I," Bib 44: 299. Gordon, *Ugaritic Glossary,* no. 407. TDNT, V, pp. 861–65. THAT, I, p. 267.

V.P.H.

189 אַתָּה (*'attâ*) ***thou.*** (KJV, ASV, and RSV are similar, "thou.")

Ugaritic and other Semitic parallels are common. This second person singular pronoun occurs a few hundred times in the OT. It is appended to verbs for emphasis. Its use in oblique cases (genitive and accusative) is to afford stress to a preceding suffix.

Derivatives

189a אַתְּ (*'at*) ***thou*** (feminine).
189b אַתֶּם (*'attem*) ***you*** (masculine).
189c אַתֶּן (*'atten*) ***you*** (feminine).

C.L.F.

אָתוֹן (*'ātôn*). See no. 190a.
אָתוֹק (*'ātôq*). See no. 191a.
אַתִּיק (*attîq*). See no. 191b.

190 אתן (*'tn*) **Assumed root of the following.**
190a †אָתוֹן (*ātôn*) ***she-ass, she-donkey.***

The she-ass is prized as a valuable possession: Gen 12:16; 32:16; Job 1:3; 42:12. Pope observes that she-asses (*'ātôn*) are listed among Job's possessions but not male asses (*ḥămōr*). He observes, "Female asses are mentioned because they exceeded the male asses in number and in value, because of their milk and their breeding. They are also better for riding than male asses" (AB, *Job,* p. 7).

No wonder then that Kish dispatched his son Saul to find the she-asses that had wandered off (I Sam 9:3, 5, 20; 10:2, 14, 16). Saul, however, did not find what he was looking for (as Columbus). He did not find the she-donkeys but he did find a crown for his head. Similarly it is on the back of a donkey (*ḥămōr*), a colt, and the foal of a donkey (*ben-'ătōnôt*) that the Messiah will ride into Jerusalem (Zech 9:9). Speiser (AB, *Genesis,* p. 362) connects this verse with the phrase in Gen 49:11, *bᵉnî 'ătōnô,* "the young/foal of his she-ass" which he translates "purebred." He relates it to the phrase in the Mari texts *mar atānim* "choice, purebred ass."

Finally it is on an *'ātôn* that the diviner Balaam rides (Num 22ff.). The donkey even spoke to Balaam (Num 22:28; cf. talking snake in Gen 3:1ff.). It is unprofitable to pursue whether the ass gave forth an audible sound, or was merely an experience in the mind of Balaam, or both. What is important is that the story demonstrates that God's control over nature is so exhaustive and complete, and his word so powerful that he could use a dumb animal as the bearer of his word.

V.P.H.

אֶתְנָה (*'etnâ*) אֶתְנַן (*'etnan*). See nos. 2524a, 2529a.

191 אתק (*'tq*). **Assumed root of the following.**
191a אָתוֹק (*'ātôq*) ***gallery, porch.*** Occurs only in Ezk 41:15.
191b אַתִּיק (*'attîq*) ***gallery.*** Occurs only in Ezk 41:15–16; 42:3, 5.

192 אתת (*'tt*). **Assumed root of the following.**
192a אֵת (*'ēt*) ***III, plowshare.***

ב

ב

193 בְּ (b^e).

A very common preposition with a wide range of meanings. BDB list mainly: in, at or by, with (of accompaniment or of instrument), a verbal complement of specialized meaning, and, used with the infinitive construct, to introduce a temporal clause. Currently the Hebrew prepositions are recognized as having an even wider range of meaning. Ugaritic evidence indicates that b^e also often means "from," as does the preposition l^e (Gordon, UT 19: no. 435; Ais WUS 486).

R.L.H.

בִּאָה (*bi'â*). See no. 212a.

194 *בָּאַר (*bā'ar*) ***declare, make plain.***

Derivatives

194a †בְּאֵר (*b^e'ēr*) ***well, pit.***
194b †בְּאֵר לַחַי רֹאִי (*b^e'ēr laḥay rō'î*) ***well of the living one who sees me.***
194c †בְּאֵר שֶׁבַע (*b^e'ēr sheba'*) ***Beersheba.***
194d †בֹּאר (*bō'r*) ***cistern, pit, well.***
194e †בּוֹר (*bôr*) ***pit, cistern, well.***

This verb occurs only in the Piel stem. It describes writing on tablets of stone made clear and distinct (Deut 27:8) or some writing upon tablets which is legible at a hurried glance (Hab 2:2). In figurative use the verb means to make clear by explaining (Deut 1:5).

b^e'ēr. ***Well, pit.*** A feminine noun possibly from *bā'ar* "to make plain," but connection uncertain.

Wells for water were dug in the earth (Gen 21:30; 26:18, 21–22, 25) and the discovery of water was an occasion for rejoicing, celebrated in song (Gen 26:32; Num 21:17–18). Ordinarily water had to be drawn (Gen 24:11, 20), and so a flowing well ("living water") was a particularly good fortune (Gen 26:19). In a land where water was scarce, wells were a source of contention (Gen 26:19–21). Israel promised that they would drink no water from the wells of Edom and Ammon if they were allowed to pass through their territory (Num 20:17). When not in use, the well could be protected with a stone covering (Gen 29:2ff.). So covered, the well served as a hiding place for David's informers (II Sam 17:18–21). Water was drawn by women, and so the well served as a meeting place for the servant of Abraham and Rebekah (Gen 24:11ff.), Jacob and Rachel (Gen 29:2ff.), and Moses and Zipporah (Ex 2:15ff.).

b^e'ēr also designates slime or bitumen pit (Gen 14:10) and the pit as a place of destruction (Ps 55:23 [H 24]; 69:15 [H 16]).

b^e'ēr is also used figuratively. The strange woman is like a pit (Prov 23:27), but one's beloved is a well of living water (Song 4:15). A man's wife is his own well (Prov 5:15).

The noun is also used in place names such as Beersheba, Beer (Num 21:16), and Beerelim (Isa 15:8).

b^e'ēr laḥay rō'î. ***Well of the living one who sees me.*** This is the name of a particular site between Kadesh and Bered, as yet unidentified. It was the dwelling place of Isaac (Gen 24:62; 25:11) and the site of Hagar's deliverance from thirst (Gen 16:14). The name is connected with the phrase "thou art a God who sees" (Gen 16:13), but is the subject of much conjecture.

b^e'ēr sheba'. ***Beersheba.*** "*Well of Seven*" or "*Well of the Oath,*" it marked the southern extremity of Palestine, "From Dan to Beersheba," and its converse (Jud 20:1; etc.; I Chr 21:2, etc.). It was a sanctuary (Gen 21:33; 46:1–5; Amos 8:14; 5:5). Two explanations for the name are given in Genesis. One derives it from the oath (*shebu'â*) between Abraham and Abimelech attested by seven (*sheba'*) lambs (Gen 21:30–31). The second connects it with an oath (*shebû'â*) sworn by Isaac (Gen 26:31). [This is probably an example of a name explanation which was not intended to be etymological but a word play for interest and easier memory of the incidents. The place may have been called Beersheba before the incidents were described. Another clear example of such a non-etymological word play is Babel in Gen 11:9. Babel in Akkadian means "gate of God." But it sounds somewhat like the verb *bālal* "to confound." R.L.H.]

bō'r. ***Cistern.*** This is a masculine noun from the root *bōr* (Jer 2:13 and *Kethib* of II Sam 23:15–16, 20; see *bôr*). A cistern dug in rock which stored water in the rainy season. In time the water stagnated, and earthquakes cracked the rock and plaster. Jeremiah contrasts Jehovah, an artesian well, with idolatry, a stagnant, leaky cistern.

bôr. ***Cistern, dungeon, fountain, pit, well.*** (ASV and RSV similar.) *bôr,* related to *bō'r* (cistern, Jer 2:13), as well as to *b^e'ēr* (well) to which it is parallel (Prov 5:15), is a masculine noun perhaps from the root *b'r* which means "to write plainly." It occurs sixty-five times.

bôr may refer to a large pit in the earth. One of

David's mighty men slew a lion in a pit (II Sam 23:20; I Chr 11:22). In the dry climate of Palestine (already in pre-Israelite times, Deut 6:11; Neh 9:25), cisterns were hewn from rock and then plastered. They stored water collected during the rainy season for use in the dry season. The time when plastering began is uncertain. Frequent allusion is made to digging cisterns or wells (II Chr 26:10) and drawing water from them (II Sam 23:16). Drinking water from one's own cistern is Rabshakeh's promise of life as it ought to be (II Kgs 18:31; Isa 36:16). *bōr* is to be distinguished from "spring" (*ma'yān*; Lev 11:36). Israel's laws recognized the danger of animals falling into an open pit, and made the owner of the pit liable for damages in such cases (Ex 21:33–34). Such danger is also recognized in Qumran (CDC 11, 13) where it is specified that an animal was not to be lifted out on a Sabbath.

Pits or cisterns with their steep smooth sides made excellent prisons (cf. Isa 24:22). Hence Joseph's brothers held him prisoner in a pit until they sold him to the Midianites (Gen 37:20–29). In Egypt he was kept in a dungeon (Gen 40:15; 41:14). The last plague on Egypt affected even such prisoners (Ex 12:29). Jeremiah's opponents threw him into a pit, but Ebedmelech rescued him (Jer 38:6–13). *bêt habbôr* (house of the pit) may also be a general word for dungeon (Ex 12:29; Jer 37:16). Cisterns served as convenient dumping areas for corpses (Jer 41:7, 9), and they served as hiding places in times of danger (I Sam 13:6).

Well-known cisterns serve as geographical locations, e.g. the well of Bethlehem (II Sam 23:15–16), the well of Sirah (II Sam 3:26), the pit of Beth-eked (II Kgs 10:14), and the well at the threshing floor of Secu (I Sam 19:22).

In figurative usage, the wicked who lays a snare is like a man who digs a pit and falls into it (Ps 7:15 [H 16]). One's wife is his own cistern and he should find satisfaction with her (Prov 5:15). Death is the breaking of the wheel at the cistern (Eccl 12:6). Sarah is the pit (quarry) from which Israel was hewn (Isa 51:1–2). Experiencing great danger may be compared to being cast alive into a pit from which one may cry to the Lord (Lam 3:53, 55) and be delivered (Ps 40:2 [H 3]). Deliverance from captivity is being set free from the waterless pit (Zech 9:11).

The state of death is a going down to the pit (Ps 28:1). Hence the dead are those who go down to the pit (Ps 88:4 [H 5], 6 [H 7]; 143:7). The pit is in some sense a synonym of Sheol (q.v.; cf. Prov 1:12; Isa 14:15, 19; 38:18). Ezekiel, however, distinguishes between them (32:18–32). The Psalmist in distress pleads for deliverance from the pit (Ps 30:3 [H 4]) and likens his recovery to being drawn up from the horrible pit (Ps 40:2 [H 3]). Peoples like Tyre (Ezk 26:20), Egypt (Ezk 31:14, 16; 32:18), Assyria (Ezk 32:23), Elam (Ezk 32:24), Edom (Ezk 32:29), and Sidon (Ezk 32:30) are threatened with being brought down to the pit.

Bibliography: Heidel, A., "Death and the Afterlife," in *The Gilgamesh Epic and O. T. Parallels,* 2d ed., University of Chicago, 1949, pp. 137–223. Sutcliffe, Edmund F., *The Old Testament and the Future Life,* 2d ed., Newman Bookshop, 1947. Trump, Nicholas, J., *Primitive Conceptions of Death and the Nether World in the Old Testament,* Pontifical Biblical Institute, 1969. TDOT, II, pp. 463–65.

J.P.L.

195 בָּאַשׁ (*bā'ash*) ***stink, abhor.*** (ASV, RSV similar.)

Derivatives

195a בְּאֹשׁ (*be'ōsh*) ***stench.***
195b בָּאְשָׁה (*bo'shâ*) (stinking things) stinking or noxious weeds.
195c בְּאֻשִׁים (*be'ūshîm*) ***stinking or worthless things, wild grapes.***

When Moses struck the water of the Nile, the fish died and the river became foul (Ex 7:18, 21). After the plague of the frogs, the land was foul (stank). When some tried to save their allotted share of manna, it bred worms and emitted a stink (Ex 16:20). But the double portion gathered on the sixth day did not become foul (Ex 16:24). This term, stink, is also used by the Hebrew foremen of the Israelite slave force who complained to Moses and Aaron that they had made Israel's savour odious in Pharoah's presence (Ex 5:21).

Other usages for stink or foul: David cried out because his wounds were foul and festering on account of his folly (Ps 38:5 [H 6]). Jacob exclaimed to Levi and Simeon that their actions caused him to be odious to the people of Canaan with drastic consequences (Gen 34:30). Qohelet says that dead flies ferment and make perfumed oil stink (Eccl 10:1).

The idea of abhorrence is seen in David's decision to fight for the Philistines. They thought that David had made himself odious to the Israelites (I Sam 27:12). The affair of Absalom and his father's concubines was calculated to make Absalom abhorrent to David and to bring about misunderstanding between father and son (II Sam 16:21). Other shades of meaning are seen in the actions of wicked men who are loathsome (or act disgustingly, Prov 13:5).

Thus this word either describes objects that have a foul odor, bad relationships between people creating abhorrence, and the general principle that evil deeds are so rotten that they have a bad smell in God's nostrils.

L.G.

196 בָּבָה (*bābâ*) ***apple of the eye*** (i.e. pupil). Derivation uncertain.

197 בָּבֶל (*bābel*) ***Babel, Babylon.***

Babylon is the Greek spelling of the name which in Hebrew is uniformly "Babel." The words occurs some 290 times and refers to an ancient city on the eastern bank of the Euphrates about twenty miles south of Bagdad, near the modern village of Hilla in Iraq. Akkadian seems to derive the name from *babili(m)* or from another earlier Sumerian source. But in both cases it means "Gate of God." Genesis 11:9 gives the name as Babel (perhaps from *bālal* "to confuse") but probably intended as a parody, a word play referring to what happened when the languages were confused.

The first definite occurrence of bab-ili(m) is in the texts of the Third Dynasty of Ur (2300–2200 B.C., approximately Abraham's day), although the Scriptures state that Babylon along with Erech and Akkad was one of the earliest cities in the South (Gen 10:10).

The city figured prominently under Hammurabi placed by some at 1792–1749, by others at 1728–1686 B.C. and noted for his legal code. The might of Assyria prevented Babylon from being prominent (from the 1100s), although Tiglath-pileser III (745–727 B.C.) gave the city luster, ruling in it as Pulu, a name that occurs in the Bible as "Pul" (II Kgs 15:19). Merodach Baladan at about 700 B.C. represented a figure of resistance to Assyria and no doubt was looking for allies (Isa 39:1). The city was destroyed by Sennacherib in 689 B.C. because of rebellions, but the city was rebuilt by the succeeding Assyrian king, Esarhaddon (680–669 B.C.).

The Chaldeans moved into Babylonia (the area) under Nabopolassar in 626 B.C. and with his great successor Nebuchadnezzar II, proceeded to build the Neo-Babylonian empire. In 612, Assur, capital of Assyria, fell. Nebuchadnezzar conquered Judah in 606–605 (Dan 1) and annexed it in 587–586 (II Kgs 25). The empire extended its rule to the borders of Egypt and under Nebuchadnezzar, Babylon was a magnificent city. Less able rulers followed, and in 539 the Persians conquered Babylonia (Dan 5). The Persian empire fell two hundred years later. Babylon retained some importance under the Seleucids and succeeding Parthians, but it eventually fell into ruins.

Its first occurrence in the Bible pertains to the Tower of Babel episode in which man in a titanic social revolt attempted to throw off the rule of God and achieve unity and peace without God. The symbol of their unity was the tower, and the strength of their unity was their common language. As a result, God judged them by confusing their speech. According to the Sumerian Enmerkar Epic (141–46), at one time men praised Enlil "with tongue," possibly a reflection in secular history of this event.

Babylon's greatness and reputation is reflected in biblical sources (Isa 13; Mic 4:10), including Jeremiah's reference to Babylon's walls (51:12, 58), and of its religious system which venerated Marduk and/or Bel as gods of the city. Both names are known in the Bible (Isa 39:1?; Jer 50:2). Enuma Elish, the early Babylonian Genesis, mentions a pantheon of gods and goddesses. Even as late as the first century A.D., John referred to the religious system, Babylon, as the "Mother of harlots and of the abominations of the earth" (Rev 17:5). It is no wonder that God took Judah to Babylon so as to preserve a remnant of Judah by allowing them to experience first-hand the horrible folly of idolatry (for this reason more than half of all the biblical references are in Jer).

Whereas Nebuchadnezzar envisioned the proud city that usurped Jerusalem's headship as a head of gold (Dan 2), Daniel saw its true bestial character as a lion (Dan 7). Daniel based his prayer for Israel's release on Jeremiah's prediction that the captivity would last seventy years (Jer 25:11–12; 29:10; Dan 9:2ff.). But whereas Jeremiah predicted the length of the captivity, Isaiah foresaw the shape of Israel's exodus from Babylon through the conquest of Cyrus (Isa 41; 43:14; 45:1ff., etc.).

Bibliography: "Babylon," in *Encyclopedia Judaica,* IV, pp. 30–34. Jacobsen, T., "Babel," and "Babylon," in IDB, I, pp. 334–38. Wiseman, D. J., Babylon, O.T., ZPEB I, pp. 439–48. Kraeling, E. G. H., "The Towers of Babel," JAOS 40: 276–81. Parrot, A., *Babylon and the Old Testament,* Philosophical Library, 1958. Saggs, H. W. F., *The Greatness That Was Babylon,* Glasgow: McClelland, 1962. Siff, Myra, Harold Ginsberg, Israel Ta Shma, "Babel, Tower of," in *Encyclopedia Judaica,* IV. TDOT, I, pp. 466–69.

L.G.

בַּג (*bag*). Qere is *baz,* no. 225a.

198 בָּגַד (*bāgad*) ***deal (act) treacherously, deal deceitfully, (deal) unfaithfully, offend.*** (ASV and RSV similar except most of ASV and RSV use "treacherous[ly]" in place of "transgress[or].")

Derivatives

198a †בֶּגֶד (*beged*) ***I, treachery.***
198b †בֹּגְדוֹת (*bōgᵉdôt*) ***treacherous.***
198c †בָּגוֹד (*bāgôd*) ***treacherous.***
198d †בֶּגֶד (*beged*) ***II, garment.***

The various verb forms appear forty-seven times, twenty-one times using the participle as verbal noun to describe the one who deals treacherously. He is one who does not honor an agreement. The root in South Arabic means "to deceive."

The verb is used to denote unfaithfulness in several different relationships. It is used in connection with unfaithfulness in marriage. The object of the faithlessness may be the wife (Ex 21:8, a slave wife; Mal 2:14, wife of one's youth), or the husband (Jer 3:20). The latter passage also illustrates that the word is used to describe Israel's unfaithfulness to the Lord (Jer 9:2 [H 1]). In addition to the metaphor of unfaithfulness in marriage to describe Israel's revolt against the Lord, the Lord or his covenant is sometimes the explicit object of the verb (I Sam 14:33; Ps 78:57; 119:158). Even to question his justice is an act of treachery (Ps 73:15). Involved in unfaithfulness to the Lord's covenant may be unfaithfulness to one's brother (Mal 2:10ff). Thus the word is also used of breaching man-made treaties and the social responsibilities expected in normal human relationships. The men of Shechem dealt treacherously against Abimelech whom they had made their king (Jud 9). Job felt betrayed by his friends (Job 6:15), and in Jeremiah's time property rights were violated by treacherous men (Jer 12:6).

Wine (according to MT), or riches (according to 1Q Hab 8:3) may cause men to behave this way (Hab 2:5).

The treacherous are sometimes rewarded in kind (Jud 9; Isa 33:1). In any case the Lord will judge such false folk (Ps 25:3; Prov 2:22; 11:6; 21:18).

beged. ***Treachery.*** Appears twice, in Isa 24:16, as part of a play on words and in Jer 12:1 referring to treacherous dealers in treachery.

bōg^{e}dôt. ***Treacherous.*** (Zeph 3:4, RSV uses "faithless men"). It would seem that the idea of treacherous is more apropos since a strong rendering is needed to underscore false prophets as men of treachery who mislead an entire nation.

bāgôd. ***Treacherous*** (twice, Jer 3:7, 10).

beged ***II. Garment.*** The relation of this word to the above root is not clear. KB cite a corresponding semantic development in Arabic from the noun "dress" to a verb "disguise." But the details are not known.

beged is a general word and may be used in reference to any kind of garment, from the robes of the rich and mighty to the rags of the poor and the leper. It is used for the holy robes of the high priest and also for cloth used to cover the tabernacle furniture (Num 4:6–13) or a bed (I Sam 9:13).

Bibliography: TDOT, I, pp. 470–72. THAT, I, pp. 261–63.

L.G.

199 בַּד (*bad*) ***I, white linen.***

There is uncertainty as to the derivation of this noun. KB derive it from *bad* II (201a), a piece. It is used of the boy Samuel in his linen ephod (I Sam 2:18). The priests of Nob wore the linen ephod (I Sam 22:18). David danced before the Lord wearing a linen ephod (II Sam 6:14). The priests wore linen vestments, linen breeches, turbans, caps, tunics (Ex 28:42; 39:28; Lev 16:4). Angels appear clad in linen garments (Ezk 9:2–3; 10:2, 6).

L.G.

בַּד (*bad*) II. See no. 201a.
בַּד (*bad*) III. See no. 202a.

200 בָּדָא (*bādā'*) ***devise, invent (bad sense).***

201 בָּדַד (*bādad*) ***alone*** (three times only). (ASV and RSV same except in one instance, "no straggler," Isa 14:31.)

Derivatives

201a †בַּד (*bad*) ***II, alone, by itself, a part, besides.***
201b †בָּדָד (*bādād*) ***alone.***

The core concept is "to be separate and isolated." It can also connote the idea of dividing into parts. This verb underscores the idea of isolation, e.g. the lonely bird on the housetop (Ps 102:8), the donkey (simile of Ephraim) wilfully going alone to Assyria (Hos 8:9), and the lone army straggler.

bad ***II. Alone.*** This derivative is used over one hundred times, usually in the compound *l^{e}bad*. It may have a positive, a negative, or a neutral connotation. Positively, the word is used of the Lord's incomparability and uniqueness in his exclusive claim to deity as seen in his extraordinary works (Deut 4:35; 32:12; Job 9:8; Isa 44:24; Neh 9:6), or in his splendid exaltation (Ps 72:18; 148:13; Isa 2:11, 17). Also, positively, Balaam celebrated Israel's dwelling alone (Num 23:9), which seems to refer to his sole possession of the land of Canaan and to his security in it (cf. Jer 49:31).

But negatively, Israel's deplorable isolation is the result of the Lord's judgment on her (Isa 27:10; Mic 7:14; Lam 1:1). Commenting on the last passage Rudolph noted: "This is not the 'splendid isolation' of Num 23:9 and Deut 33:28, but the loneliness of a mother deprived of her children" (cited in TNDT, I, p. 476).

The word also has a negative connotation when a man is abandoned by his community or by God. Thus the unclean leper must suffer alone apart from human fellowship (Lev 13:46) and Jeremiah complained that because of his unique call he cannot sit at the company of merrymakers (Jer 15:17). The psalmists under the chastening hand of God felt alone—separated from men and abandoned by God (Ps 102:1–7 [H 2–8]).

This contrast between loneliness caused by abandonment and uniqueness in exaltation help one to better appreciate the Lord Jesus Christ who by enduring the loneliness of the cross secured a throne at God's right hand (Phil 2:6–11).

Then too it is not good for a man to live alone without a wife (Gen 2:18) and a man alone may be exposed to personal danger (II Sam 17:2). One feels the cold solitude of Jacob as he waits alone at night before his encounter with Esau, and finds himself reassured only after he secures the angelic benediction (Gen 32:24 [H 25]).

The word is used more neutrally in these famous passages: "Man does not live by bread alone" (Deut 8:3) and "against thee, thee only, have I sinned" (Ps 51:4 [H 6]).

As an adverb of limitation there is "through thee alone do we confess thy name" (Isa 26:13) while *l^e bad* followed by *min* becomes the preposition "apart from," "besides": the children of Israel . . . besides children (Ex 12:37), fortified cities . . . besides unwalled villages (Deut 3:5). There are cases where the *min* is prefixed, e.g. *mill^e bad* which might be an inverted *l^e bad min:* there is no other besides him (*mill^e badô,* Deut 4:35).

Still another rendering is that of a definite part, e.g. of each there shall be an equal part (*bad b^ebad* Ex 30:34), as well as the plural (*baddîm*) denoting: extended from something, e.g. strength (KJV; ASV "members," RSV "limbs," as from a man, Job 18:13); rods or branches of a vine (Ezk 17:6; 19:14); staves (RSV "poles") used in carrying the ark of the covenant (Ex 25:13), table of shewbread (Ex 25:27), or altar of burnt offering (Ex 27:6–7), altar of incense (Ex 30:4–5). It is also used of the bars of a fortress (Hos 11:6).

bādād. ***Alone*** (seven times), ***solitary*** (twice), ***desolate*** (Isa 27:10), ***solitarily*** (Mic 7:14), ***only*** (Ps 4:8).

The basic concept is solitariness: the leper is to live alone, in isolation (Lev 13:46), Israel dwells in safety alone (free from attack) (Deut 33:28), the Lord alone guided Israel (Deut 32:12).

L.G.

202 **בדד** (*bdd*) **II. Assumed root of the following.**

202a †בַּד (*bad*) ***III,*** ***liar*** (twice), ***lie*** (three times). Possibly from a root *bd'*.

The etymology of this word is uncertain. Its basic meaning is empty, idle talk. Moab's idle boasts were false (Isa 16:6). The term "empty talkers" described false prophets, e.g., oracle priests (diviners; Jer 50:36). The boaster's omens were idle talk (Isa 44:15).

L.G.

203 *בָּדַל (*bādal*) ***separate selves to, to be separated*** (Niphal), ***make a difference, divide, separate, sever*** (Hiphil; RSV translates "went over" in I Chr 12:8, "banned" in Ezr 10:8, and "designated" in Ezr 10:16).

Derivatives

203a בָּדָל (*bādāl*) ***piece, severed piece.***
203b מִבְדָּלָה (*mibdālâ*) ***separate place.***
203c †בְּדִיל (*b^edîl*) ***alloy, tin, dross.***
203d †בְּדֹלַח (*b^edōlaḥ*) ***bdellium.***

This verb, used only in the Niphal and Hiphil, has the basic connotation "to be separated" or "to separate," "to divide." This connotation occurs in such passages as Gen 1:6 where the firmament separated the waters; Gen 1:14, 18 where the celestial luminaries are seen as creating the distinction between night and day; and Ex 26:33 where the veil is pictured as separating the two areas of the temple.

The word occurs several times in contexts in which Israel's separation from foreigners is set forth (Ezr 6:21; Neh 9:2; 10:28 [H 29]). This was an ideal of the postexilic community reflecting their desire to preserve the ethnic integrity of the nation. In Lev 20:24 the word is used similarly except that it was God who separated Israel from the nations to a place of privilege. As a result Israel is to make a distinction (*bādal*) between clean and unclean animals (v. 25).

The word was also used in a somewhat technical sense as well. It could mean to discharge an army (II Chr 25:10) or to designate cities for special purpose (Deut 4:41; 19:2, 7) or individuals for service (I Chr 25:1; Ezk 39:14). In Ezr 10:8 it is used in the sense of "ban" with reference to unfaithful members of the postexilic community.

The concept of separation inherent in *bādal* was used to describe God's special activity in setting apart Aaron to the consecration of the holy things (I Chr 23:13) and the setting apart of the Levites (Num 16:9; Deut 10:8). Israel was set apart to be God's heritage (I Kgs 8:53).

The word also describes the separation from God that is the result of sin (Isa 59:2).

b^edîl. ***Plummet, tin*** (ASV similar, RSV "alloy.")

This word (to separate) denotes that which is separated from precious metal or metal ore and thus in Isa 1:25 refers to metal which in combination with precious metal reduces the precious metal to dross. It is used in that sense figuratively of Israel (Ezk 22:18). The word also means "tin" in a number of contexts. Tin with copper give the alloy bronze. Tin was therefore important in antiquity. Tarshish in Spain was apparently its main source. The expression "stone of tin" refers to a plummet in Zech 4:10 (but is not the word used in Amos 7:7–8).

b^{e}dōlaḥ. ***Bdellium.*** Possibly a stone (pearl?) or maybe a resin (so KB), *b^{e}dōlaḥ* was a product from the land of Havilah (Gen 2:12). The color of manna was compared to bdellium (Num 11:7). The derivation is uncertain.

T.E.M.

בְּדִיל (*b^{e}dîl*). See no. 203c.
בְּדֹלַח (*b^{e}dōlaḥ*). See no. 203d.

204 בָּדַק (*bādaq*) ***mend, repair.*** Perhaps a denominative from the following noun.
204a בֶּדֶק (*bedeq*) ***fissure, rent, breach.***

205 בהה (*bhh*). **Assumed root of the following.**
205a †בֹּהוּ (*bōhû*) ***void, waste, emptiness.***

Always occurring with *tōhû* "waste" (q.v.), *bōhû* describes the primordial condition of the earth, "void" at the beginning of creation (Gen 1:2), or "made empty" by God's judgment (Isa 34:11; Jer 4:23). It is probable that the descriptions in Isaiah of the desolations of Edom and those in Jeremiah of Israel borrow this phrase from the Genesis picture of a primordial chaos.

Bibliography: Young, Edward J., "The Interpretation of Genesis 1:2," WTJ 23: 151–78.

E.A.M.

בָּהִיר (*bāhîr*). See no. 211b.

206 בַּהַט (*bahaṭ*) ***a costly stone, perhaps porphyry.***

207 בָּהַל (*bāhal*) ***be disturbed, disturb, alarm, terrify; to hurry.*** (ASV renders "be troubled," "dismayed" but RSV frequently uses the more intensive "terrify," "panic," "alarm.")

Derivative

207a †בֶּהָלָה (*behālâ*) ***sudden terror, alarm.***

The verb *bāhal* occurs fifty times, eleven of which are in the Aramaic section of Daniel with similar meaning. Synonyms are *ḥārad* "tremble, be afraid," *pāḥad* "be afraid," and *yāgōr* a general word meaning "to fear." *yārē'* refers to a reverential fear. *bāhal* usually expresses an emotion of one who is confronted with something unexpected, threatening or disastrous (e.g. Israel at the news of Abner's death, II Sam 4:1; or the Benjamites when ambushed, Jud 20:41).

God disturbs nations, sometimes to the point of panic. Thus Edom was alarmed when she heard how God intervened in Israel's behalf at the Sea of Reeds (Ex 15:15). The Psalmist anticipates the panic which will descend on his enemies as God moves against them (Ps 6:10 [H 11]; 83:17 [H 18]). The day of the Lord especially will be marked by nations such as Babylon being alarmed (Isa 13:8). With the appearing of the chosen king, God will address the conspiring nations and "terrify (*bāhal*) them in his fury" (Ps 2:5). Thus, the preliminary psychological defeat of the enemy is part of God's acts in that war.

But individuals also know disturbance emotionally at the hand of God (cf. Job 23:15). *bāhal* is frequent in Daniel in connection with dreams and visions, both of the prophet (4:5) and of the king (5:6).

This connotation of fear from confrontation with the supernatural is seen in Saul's terror at the appearance of Samuel (I Sam 28:21) and Israel's fear in the presence of sudden death (Lev 26:16; Ps 78:33).

An additional meaning of *bāhal* "hurry," "be hasty," is found in narrative literature (e.g. II Chr 35:21; Est 2:9; Dan 2:25) and wisdom material, where it is associated with rash acts or haste in securing wealth (e.g. Eccl 5:2 [H 1]; 7:9; Prov 20:21 28:22).

behālâ. ***Sudden terror.*** In the four passages where *behālâ* is employed, God is always the agent bringing terror on Israel. God threatens terror (Lev 26:16), or is said to have brought *behālâ* on them (Jer 15:8; Ps 78:33) because of their disregard of him. It seems that both meanings of *bāhal* "alarm" and "haste" are brought together in the noun, *behālâ* "sudden terror."

E.A.M.

208 בהם (*bhm*). **Assumed root of the following.**
208a †בְּהֵמָה (*b^{e}hēmâ*) ***beast, animal, cattle.***
208b †בְּהֵמוֹת (*b^{e}hēmôt*) ***hippopotamus.***

b^{e}hēmâ. ***Beast, animal, cattle.*** (ASV and RSV similar.) Used 137 times, *b^{e}hēmâ* denotes four-footed animals and is distinguished from birds (Gen 6:7), fishes, and reptiles (I Kgs 4:33 [H 5:13]).

b^{e}hēmâ is in contrast to man (*'ādām*) (e.g. Ex 9:9–10) and though both are subsumed under living things (*ḥayyâ*), there is nowhere a classification of man as animal. *b^{e}hēmâ* can refer to both wild beast, though exclusive use as wild beast is less frequent (cf. Jer 7:33) and domestic animal. When referring to domestic animals, *b^{e}hēmâ* usually includes both large cattle (*bāqār*, q.v.) and sheep (*ṣō'n*), but not the "creeping things" (*remeś*) that creep along the ground. These are perhaps the smaller animals, lizards, rodents, etc.

b^{e}hēmâ, often collective, are God's creation (Gen 1:26) and are preserved by him through his provision (Ps 36:6 [H 7]; cf. 104:14).

Man's rule over the animal world is not to be interpreted as exploitation. Ruthless treatment of natural resources, including animals, brings judgment (Hab 2:17). Indeed, so intertwined is man's moral life with the world of nature that sins bring havoc also in the world of nature (Hos 4:1–4). Jeremiah states that human moral evil will bring about an absence of animals (Jer 9:10 [H 9]; cf. 9:4ff.). Righteous men have regard for beasts (Prov 12:10).

Several prohibitions relate to man with respect to beasts. He is not to make an image of God in their likeness (Deut 4:17). Human beings are not to have sexual intercourse with beasts on the penalty of death (Ex 22:10, 19 [H 9, 18]; cf. Lev 18:23). Certain animals, primarily but not only those that do not chew cud or have cloven hoofs, were unfit for food (Deut 14:4–8), likely for hygienic reasons (cf. Lev 11:46; 20:25, see R. L. Harris, *Man–God's Eternal Creation,* Moody, 1971, pp. 139–44).

In apocalyptic material, beasts become a symbol for bad nations, though another term is used there (e.g. Dan 7:7).

b^e^hēmôt. ***Hippopotamus*** (ASV "hippopotamus"; RSV "behemoth").

Though used only once (Job 40:15), *b^e hēmôt* has evoked considerable discussion. As an extension of the plural of *b^e hēmâ* (q.v.) akin to the superlative in the English, *b^e hēmôt* refers to a large beast, the brute beast *par excellence*. Judging from the description in Job 40:15, *b^e hēmôt* is a land animal in distinction to leviathan (*liwyātān,* q.v.), likely a sea monster, though some have regarded *b^e hēmôt* as a water creature.

The debate centers on whether *b^e hēmôt* is to be regarded as a natural animal, the hippopotamus, or whether there is a reference to an animal monster which in myths of the ancient middle east, so it is maintained, functioned as the adversary of the hero whom the hero, divine-like, overpowered. *b^e hēmôt* is best thought of as a large land animal whose habits are known and described but which, as is the custom in poetry, may symbolize another meaning here as the strange beast of mythology. It is possible therefore that an allusion to a mythological beast exists in the Job passage, but such allusion is not to be interpreted as legitimating these myths as true. (See the discussion of such mythological allusions under *ṭûaḥ*.) The pagan concept, if it is at all in view, is modified by the addition of "which I have made" (Job 40:15). The statement that *b^e hēmôt* is "first of the works of God" (Job 40:19) is a reference, not to chronology, but to the largeness of *b^e hēmôt* ("he ranks first among the works of God," NIV). [If *b^e hēmôt* is a real creature the description of a "tail like a cedar" is strange. Could it be that the word *zānāb* "tail" also can be used for other appendages—as the trunk of an elephant? In this case the elephant would be an even more likely candidate. R.L.H.]

The mention of *b^e hēmôt* heightens the impact of the passage which is that even the strongest creature is God's creation. The Greeks, it has been remarked, were arrested with the beautiful as expressive of deity; the Hebrews were impressed with the huge, even the ugly, as representing the power of deity.

E.A.M.

בְּהֵמוֹת (*b^e hēmôt*). See no. 208b.

209 בהן (*bhn*). **Assumed root of the following.**
209a †בֹּהֶן (*bōhen*) ***thumb, big toe*** (always used of both together).

Blood was applied to the thumb of the right hand and the big toe of the right foot at the consecration of the high priest (Ex 29:20) and his sons (Lev 8:23–24), and also to the right ear. The ritual would at least suggest that the priests were to hear, work, and walk for the Lord. Oil, in addition to blood, was similarly applied at the cleansing of lepers (Lev 14:14). In the conquest of Canaan. Adonibezek, the Canaanite king, was humiliated at his capture by the amputation of thumbs and big toes and thus rendered unfit to reign (Jud 1:6–7).

E.A.M.

210 בהק (*bhq*). **Assumed root of the following.**
210a בֹּהַק (*bōhaq*) ***harmless eruption of the skin*** (Lev 13:39).

211 בהר (*bhr*). **Assumed root of the following.**
211a †בַּהֶרֶת (*baheret*) ***white patch of skin*** (ASV "bright spot"; RSV "spot").

Found in Lev 13 and 14 only, *baheret* is a possible sign of a skin disease (*ṣāra'at,* q.v.). The checking of the symptom by the priest underscores the concern in the Bible for bodily hygiene.

E.A.M.

211b בָּהִיר (*bāhîr*) ***bright, brilliant, of light.***

212 בּוֹא (*bô'*) ***go in, enter.*** In the Hiphil, "bring." (ASV and RSV generally similar.)

Derivatives

212a †בִּאָה (*bî'â*) ***entrance.***
212b †מָבוֹא (*mābô'*) ***entrance.***
212c †תְּבוּאָה (*t^e bû'â*) ***produce.***

bô', the fourth most frequently occurring verb in the OT, is used 2570 times, for the most part with everyday meanings of "go, arrive, enter a house," or, more idiomatically, "to die" (go to the fathers) or for sexual relations (come in to her). A synonym is *hālak* "go"; an antonym is *yāṣā'* "go out."

Theologically the verb *bô'* appears in varied but significant contexts. Four aspects can be identified.

First, *bô'* is found with reference to YHWH as one who comes to his people. At the founding of Israel as a nation he came in thick clouds to Mount Sinai (Ex 19:9; 20:20). From Sinai he came with his ten thousands to fight for his people (Deut 33:2–5; Hab 3:3). In accordance with his promise that he would come to every place he chose to cause his name to be remembered (Ex 20:24), he came to Mount Zion with his ten thousands of holy ones (Ps 68:17 [H 18]). Thus he comes to fight for Israel throughout her history (Isa 30:27), which is an earnest that in the future he will give Israel an ultimate and universal victory over evil (Ps 96:13; 98:9). As in the past he fulfilled his promise to judge the nations (cf. Isa 19:1; Jer 25:31), so he will come in the future to judge the evildoers (Isa 66:15). He will come as a mighty warrior bringing back his people from the ends of the earth (Isa 40:9–11), and he will dwell in Jerusalem (Zech 2:10 [H 14]). The notion that the LORD is a God who comes with salvation is succinctly captured by Hosea: "Let us press on to know YHWH; his going forth is sure as the dawn; he will come to us as the showers, as the spring rains that water the earth" (6:3). This anticipation which characterizes the OT finds its fulfillment in part in Jesus Christ of whom it can be enthusiastically heralded, "Blessed be he who enters (*bô'* "cometh," ASV) in the name of the LORD" (Ps 118:26). God's coming to save is essentially an intervention and almost always regarded as imminent.

But he also comes to judge sinful Israel (Ps 50:3). In fact, one of the last prophecies of the OT is that YHWH will suddenly come to his temple as a refining fire (Mal 3:1).

But in addition to these statements regarding his personal coming, other texts reveal various ways in which he comes: in a dream to Abimelech (Gen 20:3); through messengers closely identified with him and yet distinct from him (Jud 6:11; 13:6–10); in connection with the ark (I Sam 4:6–7); and in the word of a prophet (Num 22:38; I Sam 2:27).

Secondly, "coming" (*bô'*) is associated with the promise-fulfillment motif. The verdict concerning the words (i.e. promises) of God by Joshua is that "all have come (*bô'*) to pass" (Josh 23:14). John Bright observes that as best he can tell, on every occasion when *bô'* is used of God's word or purpose, it has the force of "come to pass," "come true" (John Durkam & J. R. Porter, eds., *Proclamation and Presence,* John Knox, 1970, p. 206). The test of a true prophet is that his words must come to pass (Deut 18:22). Of course, the words of a false prophet may also come true, and thus one must examine the theological content of the word as well (Deut 13:3).

By bringing to pass either his threats or his promises YHWH demonstrates his dominion over history (Josh 23:15; II Kgs 19:25: Isa 31:2). Frequently the predictions use the causative Hiphil stem with *bô'* showing clearly that it is YHWH who is sovereignly guiding history (Ex 11:1; I Kgs 21:29; *passim*). In a passage that extols YHWH above graven images one reads, "Behold the former things have come to pass" (Isa 42:9). Gods are challenged to declare "things to come" (*bô'*) (Isa 41:22). The promise of land and progeny to the patriarchs is only one of many promise-predictions that have come to fulfillment and which argue for the superiority of YHWH.

A characteristic expression referring to the future, but not necessarily to the final days of the world history, is "days are coming" (participle of *bô'*). Although employed by Amos (8:11; 9:13) and Isaiah (27:6; 39:6), it is Jeremiah who most frequently uses it as an introductory phrase, sometimes to announce judgment (e.g. Jer 9:26 [H 24]; 19:6; 48:12; 49:2) but also to announce salvation (Jer 16:14), including the eatablishment of the new covenant (Jer 31:31) and the appearance of a kingly messiah (Jer 23:5).

In a word *bô'* is used in the announcements of threat and promise. Thus even as *bô'* is used in the announcement of judgment against Eli (I Sam 2:31) and against Hezekiah (II Kgs 20:17), the pre-exilic prophets use it in the form of a prophetic perfect with reference to the judgment coming upon Israel (Amos 8:2; Hos 9:7; Mic 1:9; 7:12). For Zephaniah it is the coming day of the Lord's fierce anger (2:2); for Jeremiah it is a day of calamity also for Egypt (46:22) and Babylon (50:27); for Ezekiel it is the day of distress (Ezk 7:7,10); and for Joel a day of destruction from Shaddai (Joel 1:15). This judgment will come because the people refused to repent (Isa 5:19; Jer 25:8–11; Zeph 2:3).

Our verb is also used in the proclamations of salvation that Israel will come back to the land (Mic 4:8; Isa 35:10; 51:11; Zeph 3:20; Ezk 11:16; 34:13). Ezekiel, moreover, saw the glory of the LORD coming into the new temple (43:4) and Haggai forsaw the wealth of all the nations coming to the temple (2:7). Ezra was among those of the Diaspora who came back to the house of God (3:8).

Thirdly, the word is used in connection with the coming "Messiah" who will bring salvation. Although Gen 49:10 is fraught with text-critical matters, it is at least certain that Jacob speaks of a ruler that will come from the tribe of Judah. Ezekiel and Zechariah further this hope for the "coming" one (Ezk 21:27 [H 32]; Zech 9:9f.). According to Zechariah this triumphant king is poor, and comes riding on a donkey, a symbol of his lowliness.

Finally, *bô'* is used with reference to the man who comes to the sanctuary in company with his community in order to pray and bring sacrifices (Deut 12:5; 31:11; II Sam 7:18; Isa 30:29; Jer 7:2, 10; Ps 5:7 [H 8]; 42:2 [H 3]). Whereas priests had to satisfy specific regulations in order to enter this sacred sphere (Ex 28:29f.; 29:30; etc.), all who enter must exhibit righteous behavior (Ps 15; 24). Foreigners also could come to pray (I Kgs 8:41), but eunuchs were excluded from the cultic community (Deut 23:1 [H 2]). When the people came to the sanctuary they also went to the priests (Deut 17:9). They also went to the prophet to inquire of the LORD (e.g. I Kgs 14:3, 5; II Kgs 4:42; Ezk 14:4, 7).

bi'â. ***Entrance.*** Used once, *bi'â* refers to an entryway within the temple area in which the offensive image of jealousy was erected (Ezk 8:5).

mābô'. ***Entrance, entry, setting*** (of sun). While *mābô'* refers concretely to the entrance of a city (Jud 1:24) or temple (II Chr 23:13) etc., it is used in an abstract sense in the phrase "going out and coming in" (II Sam 3:25) which in Hebrew idiom means "the whole range of a man's life" (cf. contexts: blessing Deut 28:6, surveillance I Sam 29:6, petition I Kgs 3:7, promise Ps 121:8, and judgment Isa 37:28).

t^e^bû'â. ***Produce, yield.*** (ASV often "increase"; RSV uses "increase" only once and prefers "produce," "harvest," "yield" or "gain." Both occasionally use "fruit.")

Used forty-two times with highest frequency in Lev, Deut and Prov, *t^e bû'â* refers to the yield of the ground, crops both in the form of grain and fruit. Poetic and prophetic literature extends this meaning to refer to "result." The yield (*t^e bû'â*) of wisdom is better than choice silver (Prov 8:19). The gain (*t^e bû'â*) of the wicked is sin and trouble (Prov 10:16; 15:6). Jeremiah identifies Israel as the firstfruit of YHWH's harvest (*t^e bû'â* Jer 2:3).

Three affirmations can be made concerning the produce of the ground. First, it is God who makes yield (*t^e bû'â*) possible. Israel was assured that even in the sabbatical and jubilee year the yield would be sufficient to meet the need (Lev 25:3ff., 12, 19ff.). God is praised for bringing about a fruitful yield (Ps 107:37; cf. Deut 33:14). He promises blessing in the form of productivity (Deut 16:15; cf. Isa 30:23).

Secondly, the ingathering of produce (*t^e bû'â*) was an occasion of celebration. There were two festivals of harvest in addition to the Festival of Unleavened bread. The feast of weeks (firstfruits of grain) was observed in May–June (Deut 16:9ff.). The end-of-the-year harvest in October, chiefly a fruit harvest, concluded with the observance of the festival of booths (Lev 23:39; cf. Deut 16:13ff.).

Thirdly, both in legal and wisdom literature the firstfruits of the produce (*t^e bû'â*) are designated for YHWH (cf. Prov 3:9; Deut 14:22). Israel was to tithe (*'āśar*) all the produce of the field annually. Every three years the agricultural tithe was designated particularly to the Levite, the sojourner, the fatherless, and the widow (Deut 26:12; cf. 14:28).

Bibliography: Blank, Sheldon H., "Some Observations Concerning Biblical Prayer," HUCA 32: 75–90. Driver, G. R., "Hebrew Notes," VT 1: 241–50. Speiser, E. A., " 'Coming' and 'Going' at the City Gate," BASOR 144: 20–23. TDNT, V, 861–65. TDOT, II, pp. 20–49. THAT, I, pp. 264–68.

E.A.M.

213 בּוּז (*bûz*) ***despise, hold as insignificant.*** (ASV and RSV usually similar, though RSV renders "scorn" in Song 8:7, Prov 30:17, and "belittle" in Prov 11:12.)

Derivatives

213a †בּוּז (*bûz*) ***contempt.***
213b †בּוּזָה (*bûzâ*) ***contempt.***

With derivatives, *bûz* appears twenty-four times, almost entirely in wisdom and poetic material. Synonyms are *bāzâ* "despise" and *nā'aṣ* "despise to the point of rejection." An antonym is *yārē'* "reverence," "regard," *bûz* is probably a by-form of *bāzâ* (q.v.).

One may despise (*bûz*) either people or their sayings, or, to include a closely related synonym, one may despise (*bāzâ*) also oaths (Ezk 17:16), birthrights (Gen 25:34), or even God (Mal 1:6). But to do so incurs God's wrath. To despise (*bûz*) wisdom is characteristic of fools (Prov 1:7; 23:9). Destruction is the end result for those who disregard, i.e. despise (*bûz*) the law (Prov 13:13).

Youth is counseled, "Do not despise your mother" (Prov 23:22). The seriousness of belittling a neighbor is evident from another proverb which depicts such action as betraying lack of sense (Prov 11:12) or as sinful (Prov 14:21). Scripture emphasizes the dignity of man (Ps 8:5; [H 6]) and whoever undercuts that dignity, whether for reasons of racial difference, economic standing, or even age is guilty of sin. For this reason there is punishment, e.g. for one who scorns parents (Prov 30:17). To despise one's neighbor is failure to love the neighbor as one loves himself. Jesus' reason for persons to refrain from despising children (*kataphroneō,* Mt 18:10) is that in heaven their angels behold the face of the Father, i.e. God has regard for them. It is sinful to despise the innocent.

bûz. *Contempt, put to shame.* (ASV and RSV similar, though RSV once "be laughed at" (Gen 38:23). The opposite of *bûz* is *hillēl* "praise" (Prov 12:8).

Contempt is characteristic of the wicked (Prov 18:3) and is often directed at the righteous (Ps 31:18 [H 19]), who then cry for God's mercy and intervention (Ps 123:3–4; cf. Ps 119:22). To be regarded by others as unimportant or insignificant is the luxury of those who are secure (Job 12:5) but it is irritable, if not hurtful, to those who are the objects of *bûz* and who understandably avoid it (Gen 38:23). Job was terrified by the "contempt of families" (clansmen?) so he sought God who would deal righteously with him (Job 31:34–35).

On the other hand, justice and the vindication of righteousness demands that the wicked be treated with contempt. Twice God is said to pour contempt (*bûz*) on princes. In the context of a description of God's greatness, Job uses the expression to indicate that God is not intimidated by princes (Job 12:21). The Psalmist calls on people to praise God for his deeds, among which is God's contempt on princes (Ps 107:40). Isaiah by faith warned the arrogant invading Assyrians that Jerusalem looked on their proud horde with contempt and scorn (II Kgs 19:21; Isa 37:22). This stance is consistent with the proverb "men with warped minds are despised" (Prov 12:8, NIV).

bûzâ. *Contempt.* Used in Nehemiah's prayer (Neh 4:4 [H 3:36]), *bûzâ* as illustrated by Tobiah's joking remark, is sufficient reason for a cry to God for intervention.

One may hold someone in such high regard in love that by contrast one despises (*bûz*) a house of wealth (Song 8:7). But apart from such usage of the verb, *bûz* is regarded as inappropriate, even sinful.

E.A.M.

214 *בּוּךְ (*bûk*) ***perplex, confuse.*** Occurs only in the Niphal.

Derivative

214a מְבוּכָה (*m^e bûkâ*) ***confusion, confounding*** (Mic 7:4).

215 בּוּל (*bûl*) ***Bul, the eighth month.*** Derivation uncertain. For other month names see no. 613b.

בּוּל (*bûl*). See no. 835d.

216 בּוּס (*bûs*) ***trample down*** (RSV and ASV similar).

Derivatives

216a †יְבוּסִי (*y^e bûsî*) ***Jebusite.***
216b מְבוּסָה (*m^e bûsâ*) ***downtreading, subjugation.***
216c תְּבוּסָה (*t^e bûsâ*) ***downtreading=ruin, downfall.***

This verb occurs twelve times. Often joined with "enemies," *bûs* is primarily destructive action (e.g. Zech 10:5), and differs from its synonyms *dārak* "march," "tread (winepress)," and *rāmas* "trample," "tread (clay)," which may, but need not, denote destruction.

God is often the subject who is either asked to trample down (*bûs*) the enemy (e.g. Ps 44:5 [H 6]) or who himself promises to trample down (*bûs*) peoples (Isa 63:6) such as the Assyrians (Isa 14:25). *bûs* is used anthropomorphically, but one should not miss the accompanying emotion of anger (cf. Isa 63:6).

Metaphorically, *bûs* is used of "desecration" (e.g. sanctuary, Isa 63:18).

y^ebûsî. *Jebusite(s).* Descendants of Canaan (q.v.; Gen 10:16), these peoples lived in the hill country of southern Palestine (Num 13:29), and occupied the area which during the time of King David was captured and became known as Jerusalem (II Sam 5:6; cf. Josh 18:28). As inhabitants of the hill country, they are associated with the Amorites (cf. Josh 15:63; 10:5).

The Jebusites are listed nine times as members of a six-nation group (Ex 3:8, 17; 23:23; 33:2; Deut 20:17; Josh 9:1; 11:3; 12:8; Jud 3:5), whose good land God was giving to Israel (Ex 13:5). God promised to drive out the Jebusites before Israel (Ex 23:23). They were to be destroyed so that Israel would not learn their abominable practices (Ex 34:11). But instead Israel, particularly the tribe of Benjamin, failed to expel them (Jud 1:21). Consequently the Jebusites eventually intermarried with the Israelites and became the occasion in part for Israel's idolatry and apostasy (Jud 3:5ff.).

That the stronghold of the Jebusites under David became the place for the temple as well as the capital illustrates not only the fulfillment of God's promise but also the decisive overturn of a pagan enclave to bring about God's glory.

In Josh 15:63 it says also that Judah failed to drive out the Jebusites who lived in Jerusalem. Jerusalem was on the border of Judah and Benjamin. Both failed. It is not to the contrary that Judah had once taken Jerusalem and fired the city (Jud 1:8). There was a spot which changed hands so often in the Korean war that it was called "heartbreak ridge"! These are the fortunes of war. The Jebusites were not dislodged until David's campaign (II Sam 5:6–9).

Although presented negatively as a group and

described as *nokrî* (foreigners, Jud 19:11), an individual Jebusite, such as Araunah (or Ornan, who offered his threshing floor to King David), is seen to be a man of generosity and grace (II Sam 24:18ff.; cf. I Chr 21:18ff.). Araunah is probably a Hurrian name meaning "lord," "nobleman" (see W. C. Kaiser, "Araunah," in ZPEB, I, pp. 257–58), which fits well with the presence of Hurrians (Horites) among the non-Israelite population of Jebus. Condemnation of a group does not preclude the uprightness of individuals within it. The view of some that the priest Zadok, inducted by David, was earlier a priest at a Jebusite sanctuary has insufficient evidence and is contrary to the biblical description (II Sam 8:17).

E.A.M.

217 בּוע (*bw'*). **Assumed root of the following.**
217a אֲבַעְבֻּעֹת (*'ăba'bū'ōt*) ***blisters, boils*** (Ex 9:9).

218 בּוץ (*bwṣ*). **Assumed root of the following.**
218a בֵּיצָה (*bêṣâ*) ***egg.***

219 בּוּץ (*bûṣ*) ***Byssus, a fine, costly white fabric.***

A synonym is *shēsh,* an Egyptian loan word which occurs from earlier literature as late as Ezk. *bûṣ* is found in late biblical writings only, including Chr. There are cognates in Akkadian and Phoenician. The word was borrowed into Greek as *byssus.*

bûṣ, a costly cloth, was a luxury import (Ezk 27:16), and therefore fit for the royal court (I Chr 15:27; cf. Est 1:6, Mordecai went to the Persian king draped with a mantle of this cloth, 8:15). The veil in Solomon's temple was made of *bûṣ* (II Chr 3:14) as were the garments of the priests (II Chr 5:12). Scripture does not exclude appreciation of finery.

Bibliography: Lambdin, Thomas O., "Egyptian Loan Words in the Old Testament," JAOS 73: 145–55.

E.A.M.

220 בּוק (*bwq*). **Assumed root of the following** (a by-form of בקק).
220a בּוּקָה (*bûqâ*) ***emptiness*** (Nah 2:11).
220b מְבוּקָה (*m^{e}bûqâ*) ***emptiness*** (Nah 2:11).

בּוֹקֵר (*bôqēr*). See no. 274b.

221 בּוּר (*bûr*) ***declare*** (?) ***explain, prove.***

Possibly a by-form of *bā'ar*. In Eccl 9:1, the Qal infinitive construct of *bûr* is used as a finite verb (see Bauer-Leander, p. 435; GKC sec. 113, no. 4a). In the Mishnah, "to make clear," "to prove" (Jastrow 197b). The root, form, and meaning are debatable. The LXX reads "my heart saw," KJV "to declare." The ASV and RSV, following the Vulgate, emend to *tûr* "to explore," "to examine."

J.P.L.

בּוֹר (*bôr*). See no. 194e.

222 בּוֹשׁ (*bôsh*) ***be ashamed, put to shame, disconcerted, disappointed.*** (ASV and RSV normally translate with the above, or in a few instances with "confound." Idiomatic usages such as "delay" and "cease" are discussed below.)

Derivatives

222a בּוּשָׁה (*bûshâ*) ***shame.***
222b בָּשְׁנָה (*boshnâ*) ***shame.***
222c בֹּשֶׁת (*bōshet*) ***shame.***
222d מָבוֹשׁ (*mābôsh*) ***private parts*** (ASV "secrets"). Occurs only in Deut 25:11 as masculine plural *m^{e}bûshîm.*

The primary meaning of this root is "to fall into disgrace, normally through failure, either of self or of an object of trust." Along with its derivatives, it occurs 155 times, all but 25 times in the prophets or the Psalms. No less than 38 occurrences are found in Jeremiah and 20 in Isaiah. The word is often paralleled with *kālam* "to be humiliated," and less frequently with *ḥātat* "to be shattered, dismayed." As these parallels suggest, the force of *bôsh* is somewhat in contrast to the primary meaning of the English "to be ashamed," in that the English stresses the inner attitude, the state of mind, while the Hebrew means "to come to shame" and stresses the sense of public disgrace, a physical state. Likewise, in Akkadian the G-stem of this root means "to come to shame" and the D-stem "to put to shame."

bôsh and its derivatives are used in five somewhat distinct ways. First, it is used idiomatically to express long delay or cessation. In Jud 3:25; II Kgs 2:17; 8:11 it is used to express the sense of confusion which either the waiter or the waited upon feel when a delay becomes excessively long. The two occurrences of the Polel form are also used to express this idiom, e.g. Ex 32:11 where the people of Israel say that Moses was "ashamed" (ASV and RSV "delayed") to come down from the mountain.

While the idiomatic use of *bôsh* to express cessation may be related to the above, it is more likely that it represents an interchange in meaning with *yābēsh* "to dry up." Four of the five occurrences of this usage are in Joel 1:10–17 where Hiphil forms indistinguishable from those of *yābēsh* are used. (Cf. Gesenius-Kautzsch-Cowley, 2d ed., p. 220.)

The second usage of *bôsh* expresses that sense of confusion, embarrassment, and dismay when matters turn out contrary to one's expectations. Thus, Job speaks of the shame of the caravaneers when they do not find water in the expected place (6:20). So also, Israel will be shamed when God cuts off the rain (Jer 14:3). In a more profound sense, Israel and the nations will be shamed by their idols when they fail them (Isa 42:17; Jer 22:22; Hos 10:6).

The third usage and the one that is most common carries the above thought further expressing the disgrace which is the result of defeat at the hands of an enemy, either in battle or in some other manner. In particular, the awful shame of being paraded as captives is thought of (Mic 1:11; cf. also Jer 2:26). Involved here are all the nuances of confusion, disillusionment, humiliation, and brokenness which the word connotes. The prophets normally use the word with this sense, promising Israel that unless she repents and turns from her idolatrous ways, she will certainly experience the shame of defeat and exile. (Cf. Isa 1:29; 30:5; Jer 2:36; 9:19 [H 18]; Ezr 9:6; Dan 9:7, etc.)

Intimately associated with this third use of the word is the question of trust. If Israel seeks to insure her own glory by refusing to trust in God but rather trusts in idols (Isa 1:29) or in foreign nations (Isa 20:5; 30:3,5), she will not get glory, but shame and disgrace. On the other hand, if one will humbly submit to God, he will find his true glory, for God will not let that person come to shame (Isa 29:22; Joel 2:26, 27; Zeph 3:19). It is this promise of which the Psalmist continually reminds God (Ps 25:3; 31:17 [H 18]; 37:19; 119:46).

Similarly, although Israel's enemies may triumph over her for a period, they must inevitably, because of their idolatry and their lack of trust in God, be brought to abject shame (Isa 41:11; Jer 46:24; 51:47.) Again, it is the Psalmist's fervent expectation that because he trusts in God, those who are attempting to destroy him must themselves be brought low in disgrace (Ps 6:10 [H 11]; 22:6; 40:14 [H 15]; 109:28).

Fourthly, shame results from imprudent or immoral action. This use is found in I Sam 20:30. From Saul's perspective Jonathan made a fool of himself not only by committing a grave injustice against the reigning king, but also by jeapordizing his mother's position who would become part of David's harem. Likewise Joab accused David of not thinking things through and thus acting foolishly (II Sam 19:5 [H 6]). But this usage is largely restricted to Proverbs. All the occurrences are Hiphil participles in references which describe explicitly or implicitly the actions of those who bring disgrace upon their parents or spouses (Prov 10:5; 12:4; 14:35, etc.).

The final use of *bôsh* is the one which coincides most closely with the common English connotation: a feeling of guilt from having done what is wrong. Jeremiah (6:15) is horrified that the people are not ashamed having committed abomination (idolatry). Similarly, Ezekiel (16:63) indicates that God's grace, manifested in the restoration, will not allay, but increase Judah's sense of shame. Not until then will she see what a terrible thing it was to trust idols instead of the living God. Ezra, discovering the situation in Jerusalem, cries out that he is ashamed because "our iniquities are higher than our heads."

Evidently this sense of horror over idolatry accounts for the transmutation of the names of Saul's sons Ishbaal (man of Baal) and Mephibaal (utterance of Baal) into Ish-*bosheth* (man of shame) and Mephi*bosheth* (utterance of shame, II Sam 2:8; 9:6, etc.). This substituion of "shame" for "baal" has a further development in the substitution of the vowels of boshet in other words. Thus, it is probable that molech is the word for "king" *melek* (i.e. the divine king) with the substitution of other vowels. Indeed, it may have been pronounced boshet. In the same vein, sikkut and kiyun may be vocalized from *shiqqûṣ* "abomination" (Amos 5:26).

In the few occurrences of the cognate in Ugaritic, it seems to be used in the final sense. E.g., Asherah rebukes Baal for killing Yam, saying, "Shame, shame." It is then said that Baal is ashamed and goes out (68:28–31).

Bibliography: TDOT, II, pp. 50–59. THAT, I, pp. 269–71.

J.N.O.

בַּז (*baz*). See no. 225a.

223 בָּזָא (*bāzā'*) ***divide, cut through*** (occurs only in Isa 18:2, 7).

224 בָּזָה (*bāzâ*) ***to despise, disdain, hold in contempt.*** (ASV and RSV similar.)

Derivative

224a בִּזָּיוֹן (*bizzāyôn*) ***contempt.***

bāzâ appears with its derivatives forty-three times in the OT. The basic meaning of the root is "to accord little worth to something." While this action may or may not include overt feelings of contempt or scorn, the biblical usage indicates that the very act of undervaluing something or someone implies contempt.

The use of *bāzâ* shows that disobedience to the Lord is based on "contempt, despising" of him. Thus David's adultery with Bathsheba is equated with contempt for the Lord (II Sam 12:10) and his word (v. 19). Likewise to "despise an oath" is equated with breaking the Lord's covenant (Ezk 16:59; 17:16, 18). A person who despises the Lord is devious in his ways (Prov 14:2). The opposite of *bāzâ* is *kābēd* "to honor" (I Sam 2:30), *yārē'* "to fear" (Prov 14:2), and *shāmar* "to keep" commandments (Prov 19:16).

The person who acts contrary to the community founded on the "fear of the Lord" must be cut off from it (Num 15:31); those who treat the Lord with contempt will themselves be held contemptible by him (Mal 1:6–7, 12; 2:9) and will die (Prov 19:16). Those who treated his messengers with disrespect experienced his wrath (II Chr 36:16).

The Lord also condemns to insignificance those who despise what he chose: Esau for despising the birthright (Gen 25:34), worthless fellows for despising Saul's election (I Sam 10:27), Goliath for despising David's youth (I Sam 17:42), and Michal for despising David's religious enthusiasm (II Sam 6:16).

Bibliography: TDOT, II, pp. 60–65.

B.K.W.

בִּזָּה (*bizzâ*). See no. 225b.

225 בָּזַז (*bāzaz*) ***to spoil, prey upon, seize, plunder.*** (ASV and RSV similar.)

Derivatives

225a †בַּז (*baz*) ***spoil.***
225b בִּזָּה (*bizzâ*) ***spoil, plunder, prey.***

The word and its derivatives occur seventy-seven times in the Hebrew Bible, of which occurrences seventeen are in Ezk, twelve in Isa, and twelve in the other prophetic books. It is always associated with warfare and violence, indicating the taking of goods or persons by force, usually as a concomitant of military victory.

This root is used in two ways. The first group of occurrences is found largely in the narrative literature. These usages simply report an event of plundering without indicating a necessary theological relationship. Such a usage appears in Gen 34:27, 29 where Jacob's sons are reported to have plundered Shechem. (Cf. also Est 3:13; I Sam 14:36, etc.)

The second group of usages is much larger than the first. In these occurrences plundering or being plundered is very closely connected to obedience to God. If Israel were obedient to God she would triumph over her enemies and would despoil them. This had been her experience during the latter part of the wilderness period and during the conquest of Canaan (Num 31:9, 32, 53; Josh 8:2, 27; etc.). God was pleased to give the spoil to them, only reserving to himself that which was designated *ḥerem,* devoted to God. By the same token, it is promised that in the latter days she will once again despoil her enemies (Isa 11:14; Zeph 2:9; etc.). God will act so mightily on Israel's behalf that even the lame will take spoil (Isa 33:23). However, this will not happen simply because Israel is Israel, but because she will then be obedient and because the fruit of her enemies' arrogance will have come to its full term (Ezk 26:5; 36:4; Jer 30:16).

In the meantime, however, a disobedient Israel and Judah were doomed to be spoiled not only by external enemies, but by one another (II Chr 28:8 [cf. v. 5]; Jer 20:5; Ezk 23:46; Amos 3:11). But at the end of time Israel will despoil those who spoiled them (Isa 42:22, 24; Jer 30:16; Ezk 39:10). To refuse to trust God was to be left helpless before ravening wolves (Ezk 34:8).

In the truest sense, it was through his final and utter obedience that Christ was able to spoil the principalities and powers and lead them on a triumphal march through heaven's gates (Col 2:15).

baz. ***Spoil, plunder, prey.*** This noun is used as an object (cognate accusative) of *bāzaz* six times (lit. "to spoil the spoil," cf. Ezk 29:19). It also appears in the name of Isaiah's son *Maher-shalal-hash-baz,* "The spoil speeds, the prey hastes," two times (Isa 8:1, 3). In general its range of usages duplicates the verb.

Bibliography: TDOT, II, pp. 66–68.

J.N.O.

בִּזָּיוֹן (*bizzāyôn*) See no. 224a.

226 בזק (*bzq*) **Assumed root of the following.**
226a בָּזָק (*bāzāq*) ***lightning flash*** (Ezk 1:14). Meaning uncertain.

227 בָּזַר (*bāzar*) ***scatter.***

בַּחוּן (*baḥûn*). See no 230c.
בָּחוֹן (*bāḥôn*). See no. 230d.
בָּחוּר (*bāḥûr*). See no. 231a.
בְּחוּרִים (*bᵉḥûrîm*). See no. 231b.
בָּחִיר (*bāḥîr*). See no. 231c.

228 בָּחַל (*bāḥēl*) ***I, to feel loathing.*** (RSV "detest.")

This word occurs once, in Zech 11:8. There it expresses the reaction of the flock, Israel, to the Good Shepherd. The use of the cognate in Syriac, "to be nauseated by," suggests the real force of the usage. Israel's abhorrence of her Covenant-Lord is expressed elsewhere in the OT through the use of such words as *gā'al* and *bāzâ* (q.v.).

J.N.O.

229 *בָּחַל (bāḥēl) *II.* Occurs only in the Pual, in Prov. 20:21, *naḥălâ m^eboḥelet* an "inheritance gotten by greed."

230 בָּחַן (bāḥan) ***to examine, try, prove.*** (ASV similar. RSV often translates "test.")

Derivatives

230a †בֹּחַן (bōḥan) ***testing.***
230b בַּחַן (baḥan) ***watchtower.***
230c בַּחוּן (baḥûn) occurs only with suffix, *baḥûnâyw,* their siege towers.
230d בָּחוֹן (bāḥôn) ***assayer.***

This root and its derivatives occur thirty-two times in the OT, chiefly in Job, Ps, and Jer. It often appears in parallel with *nāsâ* (נָסָה) and *ṣārap* (צָרַף), its meaning falling about midway between the two. *nāsâ* means "to put to the test, tempt" (in the archaic sense), while *ṣārap* means "to smelt, refine." *bāḥan* partakes of both of these in that it denotes examining to determine essential qualities, especially integrity. [Whereas *bāḥan* usually has God as its subject, *nāsâ* occurs almost equally with man as its subject. *ṣārap* when used in the religious sense has only God as subject and man as object. But *bāḥan* in contrast to the other two, is used almost exclusively in the spiritual or religious realm. Furthermore, whereas *ṣārap* and *nāsâ* denote attaining knowledge through testing, *bāḥan* seems to denote attaining knowledge intellectually or intuitively. Thus it seems to have the most spiritual connotations of these three synonyms. B.K.W.]

In only five of the occurrences is *bāḥan* used without explicit theological reference. These are found in Gen 42:15–16; Ezk 21:13 [H 18]; Job 12:11; 34:3.

All of the remaining occurrences (twenty-two times), except three, refer to God's examination of his people. In the exceptions, it is God who is tested. It is evident that this is abnormal procedure. In Ps 95:9 the people are reminded of the folly of testing God at Meribah. In Malachi, it is only because of the people's apathy that God calls them to test him (3:10, 15).

As is indicated in Hebrews (12:5–8), part of the privilege of being God's people is that of being tested (Jer 20:12; Ps 11:5; 139:23). Unlike the Egyptian doctrine where the heart is weighed after death, Yahweh continually assays the hearts of his people that in the end they may come forth as gold (Zech 13:9; Job 23:10).

bōḥan. ***Testing.*** Appears only in Isa 28:16 where it is used adjectivally with *'eben* "stone." In the NT (I Pet 2:4–6; Rom 9:33) this stone is interpreted as being Christ, the foundation stone of God's kingdom. Some writers believe that the word has nothing to do with "testing" being derived from a homonymous root meaning "fortress, tower," etc. Thus, this word would mean "strong, secure," etc.

Bibliography: TDOT, II, pp. 69–72. THAT, I, pp. 269–71.

J.N.O.

231 בָּחַר (bāḥar) ***to choose, elect, decide for.*** (ASV and RSV similar.)

Derivatives

231a †בָּחוּר (bāḥûr) ***young man.***
231b †בְּחוּרִים (b^eḥûrîm) ***youth.***
231c †בָּחִיר (bāḥîr) ***chosen.***
231d †מִבְחָר (mibḥār) ***choicest, best.***
231e †מִבְחוֹר (mibḥôr) ***choice.***

The root and its derivations occur 198 times with this meaning. The root idea is evidently "to take a keen look at" (KB), thus accounting for the connotation of "testing or examining" found in Isa 48:10 and in the usage of the Niphal stem in Proverbs (e.g. 10:20 "choice silver"). It has also been suggested that the root is related to the Arabic *bahara* "to cleave, till the ground, (in science) to penetrate," thus yielding some such meaning as "to distinguish." But the Akkadian *bêrum* "to choose" and much rarer "to test" is the most important Semitic parallel.

bāḥar is used only in a few instances without specific theological overtones. A typical example would be Gen 13:11, "Lot chose the plain." (Cf. also Ex 18:25; Deut 23:16 [H 17]; etc.). It is important to note, however, that it always involves a careful, well thought-out choice (cf. I Sam 17:40; I Kgs 18:25; Isa 1:29; 40:20).

Apart from these exceptions, the word is used to express that choosing which has ultimate and eternal significance. On the one hand God chooses a people (Ps 135:4), certain tribes (Ps 78:68), specific individuals (I Kgs 8:16; I Chr 28:5; I Sam 10:24; II Sam 6:21), and a place for his name (Deut 12:5; etc.). In all of these cases serviceability rather than simple arbitrariness is at the heart of the choosing. Thus Yahweh chose Israel to be holy and thereby to serve as his witness among the nations (Deut 14:6). But her election is not based on her own greatness but on the greatness of the Lord's love (Deut 7:7f.). The choice of Israel is confirmed by the exile and restoration, for in a new way Israel now bears witness of the Lord to the nations (Isa 41:8f.; 43:10; 48:10). The scriptural doctrine of divine capacity for choice demonstrates that purpose and personality, not blind mechanism, are at the heart of the universe. Since God carefully chooses certain ones for a specific task, he can also reject them if they deviate from that purpose (I Sam 2:27ff.).

bāḥûr ***I. Young man.*** (ASV and RSV similar.) *bāḥûr* and its derivative *b^eḥurîm* may both be understood to be derivatives of *bāḥar* "to choose," in that the picked or chosen men in a military context are usually the young men. But while *bāḥûr* "young man," may sometimes be confused with *bāḥûr* "chosen one" (cf. Ps 78:31 marg.), its meaning is generally quite distinct, especially when it is used antonymically with *zāqēn* "old man," or paralleled with *bᵉtûlâ* "virgin." As a result, most lexicographers see two different root meanings.

In the majority of its occurrences, this word is used in the context of God's judgment upon Israel. The point is made that even the young man, symbol of vigor, strength, and indeed, the continued existence of the nation, will be destroyed.

bāḥûr ***II. Elected, chosen.*** A Qal passive participle used almost entirely in military parlance, e.g. Jud 20:15–16, "Seven hundred thousand *chosen* men." It is used fifteen times thus, all but two in conjunction with enumeration.

bᵉḥûrîm. ***Youth*** (period of). An abstract plural noun (cf. Ges § 124d), appearing once in the masculine (Num 11:28, KJV and ASV "young men," ASV marg. and RSV "youth") and twice in the feminine, *bᵉḥûrôt* (Eccl 11:9; 12:1, all versions "youth").

bāḥîr. ***Chosen, elect.*** This derivative is used exclusively to indicate the relationship of the subject to God. It commonly occurs in a direct quotation of God, having the first singular possessive pronoun suffixed to it. Thus, God himself attests that this person or nation is his own personal choice. (Cf. Isa 42:1; Ps 89:3 [H 4]; etc.)

mibḥār. ***Chosen, choice.*** This word usually appears in construct with a following noun. As such it is often translated as a superlative (GKC § 133g). Cf. Gen 23:6, "In the choicest of our sepulchres." The idea seems to be that which has been examined and found to be best or most serviceable.

mibḥôr. ***Chosen, choice.*** Occurs twice. Its usage is similar to *mibḥār*.

Bibliography: Altmann, Peter, *Erwählungstheologie und Universalismus im AT,* Berlin: Topelmann, 1964. Berkouwer, G. C., *Divine Election,* Eerdmans, 1960. Clements, R. E., "Deuteronomy and the Jerusalem Cult Tradition," VT 15: 300–312. Palache, J. L., *Semantic Notes on the Hebrew Lexicon,* Brill, 1959. Richardson, TWB, p. 43. Rowley, H. H., *The Biblical Doctrine of Election,* London: Lutterworth, 1950. Wright, G. E., *The Old Testament Against Its Environment,* SCM, 1950, pp. 46–54. TDNT, IV, pp. 145–72. TDOT, II, pp. 73–87. THAT, I, pp. 275–99.

J.N.O.

232 בָּטָה (*bāṭâ*), בָּטָא (*bāṭā'*) ***speak rashly, thoughtlessly.***

Derivative

232a מִבְטָא (*mibṭā'*) ***rash utterance.*** Occurs only in Num 30:7, 9.

233 בָּטַח (*bāṭaḥ*) ***I, trust in, feel safe, be confident, careless.*** (ASV similar. RSV usually similar but occasionally "rely on.")

Derivatives

233a †בֶּטַח (*beṭaḥ*) ***safety.***
233b †בִּטְחָה (*biṭᵉḥâ*) ***trust.***
233c †בִּטָּחוֹן (*biṭṭāḥôn*) ***confidence.***
233d †בַּטֻּחוֹת (*baṭṭūḥôt*) ***security.***
233e †מִבְטָח (*mibṭaḥ*) ***trust.***

This is one of two words used in the OT to express trust or reliance upon, the other being *ḥāsâ* (q.v.). There is no clear cognate in the other Semitic languages although KB sees a connection with Arabic *baṭaḥa* "to be stretched out, taut" (cf. especially the VII stem). The basic idea would then have to do with firmness or solidity. Be that as it may, in Hebrew, *bāṭaḥ* expresses that sense of well-being and security which results from having something or someone in whom to place confidence. It is significant that the LXX never translates this word with πιστευω "believe in" but with ελπιζω "to hope," in the positive sense "to rely on God" or πειφομαι "to be persuaded," for the negative notion for relying on what turns out to be deceptive. This would seem to indicate that *bāṭaḥ* does not connote that full-orbed intellectual and volitional response to revelation which is involved in "faith," rather stressing the feeling of being safe or secure. Likewise, all the derivatives have the same meaning "to feel secure," "be unconcerned."

[The word *bāṭaḥ* has an ambivalent connotation when used of human relationships. The folk "living at ease" with their neighbors suffered for their credulity and gullibility, while those taking advantage of their careless posture are censured: cf. the false security of the Shechemites *vs.* the cruelty of Levi and Simeon (Gen 34:25), of Israel *vs.* Gog (Ezk 38:10–11). Proverbs 3:29 explicitly warns against taking advantage of a trusting neighbor. B.K.W.]

In general, the OT contrasts the validity of that sense of confidence which comes from reliance upon God with the folly of any other kind of security. It is made plain that all such trust will end in disgrace and shame (Ps 31:14 [H 15], see *bôsh*), whereas those whose hope is in God alone will be delivered from their enemies (Ps 22:4 [H 5]); their prayers will be answered (I Chr 5:20); they will walk in straight paths (Prov 3:5); will be given joy and gladness (Ps 16:9; 33:21); will know inner peace and absence of fear (Ps 4:8 [H 9]; Isa 26:3); etc. Hence, the repeated admonition to trust in the Lord (Prov 16:20; Isa 30:15; Jer 17:7).

The Psalms, which show the largest number of occurrences (50 out of a total of 181), are most consistently expressive of the values of trust in God. They also make the point that the cause for hope is not in one's merit with God or in some sort of "tit-for-tat" arrangement, but only because of God's *ḥesed* (q.v.), his unswerving loyalty, his gracious kindness. Ezekiel 33:13 makes it plain that no one dare hope for life on the basis of his own righteousness and Jer 7:4, 8, 14 show the folly of trusting in sacred formulas and structures. In this sense the OT foreshadows the NT in its proclamation that there is hope for those who accept God's gift of eternal life through Jesus Christ.

This hope in God is not a sort of querulous wishing, but a confident expectation. Unlike the pagan religions where unremitted anxiety was the rule, the Hebrew religion knew a God whose chief characteristic was faithfulness and trustworthiness (Deut 33:28; I Sam 12:11; Ps 27:3). This contrast between anxiety and confidence becomes all the more striking when one recalls that the pagan was never left without mechanisms whereby he felt he had some control over his destiny, while the devout Hebrew knew himself to be utterly without personal resources. But better to be utterly dependent on a gracious and dependable God, than left to one's own devices in a sea of fickle gods, vengeful demons, and inscrutable magical forces. In view of these facts God's sovereign control of man's destiny and God's total dependability, putting one's confidence in anything but God is seen to be utterly groundless. However, trust in God is not an automatic guarantee of protection from any and all harm. Nor is refusal to trust God necessarily the road to poverty and deprivation. In the face of his comforters' bland assurances, Job points out these apparent contradictions in some biting sarcasms (12:6; 24:23). Yet, even Job in his anguish must admit that any other source of security is ultimately valueless (31:24; cf. 39:11; cf. also Isa 50:10).

The OT considers these sources of false security in some detail in order to show by contrast the excellence of hope in God. The list includes man (Ps 118:8; 146:3; Prov 25:19; Jer 17:5); wickedness (Isa 47:10); violence and oppression (Ps 55:23 [H 24]; 62:10 [H 11]; Isa 30:12); riches (Ps 49:6 [H 7]; 52:7 [H 9]; Prov 11:28); idols (Ps 31:6 [H 7]; 115:8; Isa 42:17; Hab 2:18); military power (Deut 28:52; Ps 44:6 [H 7]; Isa 31:1; Jer 5:17; Hos 10:13); religion (Jer 7:4, 8, 14); one's own righteousness (Ezk 33:13; Hos 10:13); foreign alliances (Isa 36:4ff; Ezk 29:16). In particular the Bible heaps scorn upon those who live in complacency, never having evaluated the flimsy basis for such complacency (Isa 32:9–11; Ezk 30:9; Amos 6:1).

Perhaps the place where the central issues revolving around *bāṭaḥ* are seen most clearly in a brief compass is II Kgs 18 and 19 where the Assyrian Rabshakeh challenges the worth of Hezekiah's trust in God and where that trust is fully vindicated. The word occurs 20 times here and in the parallel passages (Isa 36–37; II Chr 32). In human relations, only one area of trust is commended: a husband in a wife of noble character (Prov 31:11, NIV).

beṭaḥ. ***Safety, security, carelessness.*** Used almost exclusively in adverbial constructions. Used frequently with *yāshab* "to dwell," e.g. Jer 23:6, where it is promised that God will deliver Israel in the future and make her dwell securely. In general, the word is used in two ways: the promise that those who are rightly related to God will dwell securely (Lev 25:18; Ps 16:9); and indication of the transitory nature of any security other than God's (Jud 18:7; Isa 47:8; Ezk 30:9).

biṭḥâ. ***Trust.*** Appears only in Isa 30:15, where it is used in a context which expresses resignation and cessation of one's own efforts.

baṭṭūhot. ***Security.*** Job 12:6 where Job in sarcasm says that those who provoke God are secure.

mibṭāḥ. ***Trust, confidence.*** Used in the same two ways as the previous. Appears only in poetic passages.

Bibliography: Eichrodt, W., Theology of the Old Testament, II, pp. 268–90. Kohler, L., "Hebräische Vokabeln," VT 55: 172–73. Rabin, Chaim, "Three Hebrew Terms from the Realm of Social Psychology," Supp VT 16: 219–30. TDNT, II, pp. 521–29; VI, pp. 191–92, 194–202. TDOT, II, pp. 88–93. THAT, I, pp. 300–304.

J.N.O.

234 בטח (*bṭḥ*) **II. Assumed root of the following.**
234a אֲבַטִּחִים (*'ăbaṭṭiḥîm*) ***watermelons*** (only in Num 11:5).

בִּטָּחוֹן (*biṭṭāḥôn*). See no. 233c.

235 בָּטַל (*bāṭal*) ***cease.*** Occurs only in Eccl 12:3.

236 בטן (*bṭn*) **I. Assumed root of the following.**
236a †בֶּטֶן (*beṭen*) ***womb, belly, body.*** (ASV and RSV similar, but both tend to translate "body" or utilize some periphrastic construction where KJV translates "belly.")

The basic meaning of this word according to the Semitic cognates is "interior"; in Hebrew it denotes the "lower abdomen" and has the same meaning in the Amarna tablets. As such it can refer to a woman's womb, or to the stomach, or be used in a figurative sense to express man's physical nature. It has a considerably broader range of meaning than *reḥem* "womb," with which it occasionally occurs in parallel. The reference to Ehud's plunging the sword into the *beṭen* of Eglon, king of Moab, suggests a touch of poetic justice, because this well-sated ruler, this "very fat man" lived off the spoils of his victims.

The prostration of one's *beṭen* on the ground expressed humiliation (cf. Ps 44:25 [H 26], Egyptian reliefs and the Amarna tablets).

The phrases "from the womb" and "fruit of the *beṭen*" are idiomatic, expressing "from birth" on the one hand and "issue from the body" or "children" on the other.

beṭen is used several times in the wisdom literature to express the deepest recesses of the person, and/or the seat of the desires (cf. Job 15:35; 20:20; Prov 18:8; 18:20; etc.). It is also used in parallel with *nepesh* "soul" to express the totality of the human person. "Body" is a rather colorless translation for the visceral quality of *beṭen* in these references (Ps 31:9 [H 10]; 44:25 [H 26]; Mic 6:7).

The references to God in connection with *beṭen* indicate that he is the one who shapes and forms the fetus (Job 3:3–11; 31:18; Ps 139:13; Jer 1:5; cf. Ps 51:15 [H 7]), who brings the child forth from the womb (Ps 22:9 [H 10]; Isa 46:3) and superintends its life from the earliest moments (Ps 71:6; Isa 49:1). The fruit of the womb is his reward (Ps 127:3; cf. Deut 7:13; 28: 4, 11; 30:9). The wicked, however, go astray "from the womb *mērāḥem* and speak lies" from birth *mibbeṭen* (Ps 58: 3 [H 4]). And God curses the womb of the adulteress (Num 5:21).

Probably as a polemic against the Babylonian notion that their gods called their kings from the womb, Isaiah proclaims that it was the Lord who formed the Servant and called him from the womb (Isa 44:2, 24; 49:5).

Bibliography: Dahood, M., "Hebrew-Ugaritic Lexicography," Bib 44: 301. Pederson, J., *Israel, Its Life and Culture,* London: Oxford, 1946, pp. 170–73. TDOT, II, pp. 94–98.

J.N.O.

237 בטן (*bṭn*) **II. Assumed root of the following.**
237a בָּטְנִים (*boṭnîm*) ***pistachio*** (Gen 43:11).

238 בָּיַי (*bāyay*), בַּי (*bay*) ***entreat.***
238a בִּי (*bî*) ***excuse me, please.*** Particle of entreaty.

239 בִּין (*bîn*) ***understand, consider, perceive, prudent, regard.***

There are seventeen other renderings in addition. (ASV almost the same; RSV varies the readings for the two most numerous, "understand" and "consider" by interchanging "perceive," "observe," "discern," et al.).

Derivatives

239a †בֵּין (*bên*) ***between.***
239b †בִּינָה (*bînâ*) ***understanding.***
239c †תְּבוּנָה (t^e*bûnâ*) ***understanding.***

The verb and its derivatives are used 247 times. Its main English usage is "understanding" or "insight." The background idea of the verb is to "discern," and this lies behind the derivative nouns and the close relation derived from the substantive *bayin* (see below) from which comes the preposition *bên* "between." The combination of these words, "discern between" is used in I Kgs 3:9, "That I may discern between good and evil." *bîn* includes the concept of distinguishment that leads to understanding.

The verb refers to knowledge which is superior to the mere gathering of data. It is necessary to know how to use knowledge one possesses (*Pirke Abot* 3:12). The verb *yāda'* (q.v.) can also mean "understanding" in the sense of ability (e.g. Esau as a skilful hunter). It can also mean "to be perceptive," (Ps 73:22). However, *yāda'* generally describes the process whereby one gains knowledge through experience with objects and circumstances. *bîn* is a power of judgment and perceptive insight and is demonstrated in the use of knowledge.

A person can perceive pertinent data with his senses: with his eyes he can discern (Prov 7:73, with his ears he can understand words (Prov 29:19). Understanding can also be said to feel (Ps 58:10) and discernment can even be sensed through taste (Job 6:30).

It is possible to hear without perceiving. Daniel did not understand what he had heard (Dan 12:8). It is said in a derogatory sense that the wicked cannot understand the knowledge he knows (Prov 29:7). Other instances emphasize an attentive observation or consideration: Moses accusingly asked the people to consider diligently the years of experience of all generations (Deut 32:7), and David perceived the destination of the wicked (Ps 73:17).

The Hiphil stem especially emphasizes ability to understand. Ezra read the word of God in the presence of men, women, and those able to understand, i.e. old enough (Neh 8:3). God can make a person understand his ways (Ps 119:34, 73). His angel came to give understanding to Daniel (Dan 10:14). The participial form refers to a teacher, i.e. one who gives discernment to his students (Ezra 8:16).

From a number of instances, insight or moral

understanding is a gift from God (Dan 2:21) and is not the fruit of empiricism. It is ethical discernment. A person prays for it (Ps 119:34) and since this insight is uniquely God's, he can reveal or conceal it (Isa 29:14). The seat of insight is the heart and it is the heart which discerns (or fails to discern) the works of the Lord (Ps 28:5), the fear of the Lord (Prov 2:5), righteousness and justice (Prov 2:9), and his will as his word is obeyed (Ps 111:10).

While understanding is a gift of God, it does not come automatically. The possession of it requires a persistent diligence. It is more than IQ; it connotes character. One is at fault if he doesn't have it and in fact, not to pursue it will incur God's punishment (Prov 2:1f; Ruth 1:21f.). When one acts on the objective presentations of God's revelation, he will attain the ideal of the significance of understanding.

bên. ***Between, among,*** et al. From *bayin,* a substantive that expresses the notion "interval," "space between." It appears many times (BDB selects only twenty-four entries), and in a number of situations of doubling where the second usage of *bîn* in separating a pair is not translated into English.

It is used as a preposition, "in the interval," "between," e.g. between the pieces (Gen 15:7), between your eyes (Ex 13:9), between the two walls (Isa 22:11), et al. In one unusual instance it is used with a singular between the Ulai, i.e. on its banks (Dan 8:16). To indicate the space separating two objects, *bên* is repeated: in the interval of Bethel and in the interval of Ai (Gen 13:3). Sometimes this result is accomplished by using *bên* followed by the preposition *l* indicating an interval with respect to the object, e.g. between you and between your God (Isa 59:2).

bên is also used of a temporal notion, during the interval of ten days (Neh 5:18), as well as with a number of other prepositions, in between, in among (Ezk 31:10), amongst (Isa 44:4), with preposition *min* (Gen 49:10, et al). There is also the plural *bênôt* between the wheels (Ezk 10:2) and the dual *bēnayim*, the man from the intervening space between two armies, Goliath, i.e. a champion (I Sam 17:4).

bên is also used with verbs of judging, knowing, teaching, etc., involving the notion of distinguishing, e.g. discerning between good and evil (I Kgs 3:9), judging between the nations (Isa 2:4).

bînâ. ***Understanding.*** This noun is used in a variety of ways. It refers to understanding, as in the prediction that Israel will never again be exposed to a foreign language difficult to understand (Isa 33:19), or in the statement that Daniel had understanding of every subject which Nebuchadnezzar asked (Dan 1:20). *bînâ* also refers to the very faculty of understanding. One is not to lean on his own understanding (Prov 3:5). A person should desist from his own understanding, thus trying to attain great wealth (Prov 23:4). People who have been involved in sin and iniquity are those of no understanding (Isa 27:11). People are encouraged diligently to seek this faculty of understanding (Prov 4:5, 7).

bînâ is also used as theobject of knowledge. Job inquired concerning the place of understanding (Job 28:12, 20) and then partially answered the question that to depart from evil is understanding (Job 28:28 where wisdom *ḥokmâ* [q.v.] and *bînâ* are close synonyms). Wisdom advises that a person should go in the way of understanding (Prov 9:6) and that the knowledge of the Holy One is understanding (Prov 9:10).

Understanding and wisdom (*ḥokmâ*) are personified (Prov 2:3; 7:4 but primarily in Prov 8:14f. where there are important implications). This personification also appears in Ecclesiasticus 24:9, 23, where the function of God's spirit mediated between God as wholly other, and the world (it would appear). The question has been asked as to whether wisdom is some aspect of a hypostasis with God, or if it is an abstract principle which has been made personal in the use of poetry. There is a mysterious objectifying of God's word-concept in wisdom by which the world exists as well as by whom we receive wisdom and power.

t^ebûnâ. ***Understanding.*** (ASV is similar but RSV uses "intelligence" in a few instances for "understanding.")

Synonymous with *bînâ,* it is used in the same variety of ways, although in different passages. By the act of understanding God shattered Rahab (Job 26:12). The faculty is such that a man of understanding walks in a path of uprightness (Prov 15:21). Then again, understanding can refer to the object of knowledge as when one gains understanding (Prov 3:13). *t^ebûnâ* is also personified as a woman lifting up her voice (Prov 8:1). Here understanding is parallel with wisdom and thus is seen as the teacher. In only one passage do *bînâ* and *t^ebûnâ* appear in synonymous parallelism: as one cries for discernment one must lift up his voice for understanding (Prov 2:3); the nouns refer to the object of knowledge.

Bibliography: Girdlestone, R., *Synonyms of the Old Testament,* Eerdmans, 1897, p. 74. Kidner, Derek, *Proverbs,* Inter-Varsity, 1964. Harris, R. L., "Proverbs," WBC, pp. 553–54. Orlinsky, Harry M., "The Biblical Prepositions Táḥaṭ, Bēn, Ba'ad, and Pronouns 'Anû (or 'Anū), Zo'ṭāh," HUCA 17: 267–92. TDOT, II, pp. 99–106. THAT, I, pp. 305–307.

L.G.

בֵּיצָה (*bêṣâ*). See no. 218a.

240 בִּירָה (*bîrâ*) ***palace.***

BDB suggests that it is a loan word from Akkadian. The cognate appears in Biblical Aramaic (Ezr 6:2). It is used of the temple in Jerusalem (I Chr 29:1, 19). In Neh 2:8, "palace" (KJV) is rendered "castle" (ASV) and "fortress" (RSV), while at Neh 7:2 the ASV and RSV use "castle." In Neh 1:1 and Est 1:2, 5; 2:3, 5, 8, et al., in Shushan the "palace," the ASV renders "palace" while the RSV uses "capital." The wording of the latter, *b^e shûshān habbîrâ*, suggests "in a fortress in the city" (BDB). The form *bîrānît* is identified as a plural form in GB.

L.G.

241 בַּיִת (*bayît*) ***house, household, home, place, temple, inward, family,*** et al. (ASV and RSV similar generally, except that RSV renders house (hold) instead of family.)

Derivatives

241a †בֵּית אֵל (*bêt'ēl*) ***Bethel.***
241b †בֵּית לֶחֶם (*bêt leḥem*) ***Bethlehem.***
241c בִּיתָן (*bîtān*) ***house, palace.***

The word is common to Aramaic, Arabic, Akkadian, and Ugaritic. By contrast *'ohel* is "tent," *me'ārâ* "cave," *bîrâ* "palace, castle," *hēkāl* "palace, temple," *ḥāsēr* "settlement," *môshāb* "dwelling," *mā'ôn* "refuge," *miqdāsh* "sanctuary," and *mishkān* "tabernacle."

It is used as a dwelling or habitation. Archeologists have uncovered some impressive houses with thick walls dating from the early Bronze Age (3000–2100 B.C.). At Debir were discovered thick walls of a house believed to be of the Middle Bronze period (2100–1500 B.C.). Lot's house at Sodom, also of the Middle Bronze Age, had well constructed walls which stopped the mob's assault. Other houses, not so well constructed, would not have lasted. For earlier house construction cf. Kenyon, K. M., *Archaeology in the Holy Land,* Praeger, 1961, pl. 5B and Mellaart, J., *The Neolithic of the Near East,* Scribners, 1975, esp. pp. 35–49.

The word is used of ordinary houses (Ex 12:7, et al.), dwelling houses (Lev 25:29), houses of solid materials with doorposts (Deut 11:20), walls (Lev 14:37) of stones, wood, and mortar (Lev 14:45). Possibly the walls were rectangular with a courtyard in front. For the door there was probably a wood beam as the lintel and two upright doorposts as jambs. There was also a room for domestic animals and a sleeping room. Cooking was usually done outside. Windows were probably open with a latticework covering while ceilings might have consisted of beams plastered with clay. Steps led to the roof. Larger houses or official buildings were supported by pillars (Jud 16:26f.). Albright shows a patrician house of the time of the monarchy with the first story enclosed on three sides and the second story supported on the fourth side by four pillars (*Archaeology of Palestine,* Penguin, 1960, p. 141). A house with seven pillars would be rich indeed (Prov 9:1; cf. NIV). Some of the better houses were built on the walls of a city (Josh 2:15) and also had roofs where people could relax (II Sam 11:12). The word "house" is also used to designate the temple and king's house in Jerusalem (I Kgs 5:3; 7:51) as well as Ezekiel's temple (Ezk 40f.).

bayit can be used in the construct to denote distinct buildings or parts of a large building. Thus it can be used of the king's house (I Kgs 10:12), a prison (Jer 37:15), a treasury (Isa 39:2), but most significantly of a temple: the house of a deity.

Many Canaanite place names stem from the temple of the deity located in it; e.g. Beth-Shemesh = Temple of the Sun-god, Shemesh, Beth-horon, Beth-shan. Israel by contrast named sites after persons: Hinnom, etc.

The most important house in Israel, of course, was the Lord's house, first mentioned in extra-biblical literature in the Arad ostraca. (See Y. Aharoni, BA, 31: 16f.) Because the Lord was uniquely present here, the Psalmist celebrated Zion and longed to appear before him in worship (Ps 26:8; 122:1). But when Israel made it a den of robbers, God threatened to destroy it, even as he had destroyed his residence at Shiloh (Jer 7).

Rooms of a large house can be called a *bayit*. Thus the word is used in construct to designate the drinking hall of Ahasuerus (Est 7:8), his harem (Est 2:3), and the winter house, a particular quarter of the palace in Jerusalem (Jer 36:22).

House is applied to places, e.g. place of my father's tombs (Neh 2:3), or Bethel as the king's house (Amos 7:13). *bayît* is used peculiarly as "place" (KJV), holders or receptacles, holders for the staves (rings, Ex 25:27), perfume boxes (Isa 3:20).

Importantly, house is applied to a household or family: Jacob's household (Gen 35:2), family of descendants as a corporate group, also Abraham's house (Gen 18:19) and David's house (II Sam 7:11), the Hebrew people as house of Jacob (Gen 46:27) and house of Israel (Ex 16:31), the father's house in sense of a clan or family (Num 1:2). In the OT there is a solidarity between a man and his house (Josh 2:12; 6:22; 7:1–5; I Kgs 7:15). So Joshua informs the Israelites that he and his house will serve the Lord (Josh 24:15).

By metonymy the word can denote what is in the house. This is the force of the tenth commandment prohibiting the coveting of a neighbor's house (Ex 20:17; cf. Gen 30:30; Num 22:18; 24:13, etc.).

Bibliography: Ahlstrom, G. E., "Der Prophet Nathan und der Tempelbau," VT 11: 113–27.

Dickie, A. C., "House," in ISBE, III, pp. 1434–38. Hyatt, J. Philip, "The Deity Bethel and the Old Testament," JAOS 59: 81–98. Landsberger, Franz, "The House of the People," HUCA 22: 149–55. Pope, Marvin H., "El in the Ugaritic Texts," Supp VT 2: 1–116, esp. p. 59f. Rainey, Anson F., "Family Relationship in Ugarit," Or 34: 10–22. Sellers, O., "House," in IDB, p. 657. Stigers, Harold G., "House," in ZPBD, pp. 217–21. Ward, William A., "Egyptian Titles in Genesis 39–50," BS 114: 40–59. TDOT, II, pp. 107–15. THAT, I, pp. 308–12.

bêt 'ēl. ***House of God.*** Indicates the city and sanctuary whose name is read in English as one word, "Bethel." It is mentioned sixty-five times, more than any other city except Jerusalem.

Bethel was a Canaanite and Israelite town, located ten to eleven miles north of Jerusalem, at the intersection of the north-south road along the crest of the hill line and the east-west road to the plains of Jericho and the coastal plain. It was on the north boundary of Benjamin (southern boundary of Ephraim).

The settlement at Bethel appears to have been established at the turn of the third millennium B.C. In the early patriarchal period the town was called Luz (Gen 28:19). When Jacob stopped there, he was at "the place" (Gen 28:11), possibly where Abraham had sacrificed (Gen 18:8) and where he had viewed the Jordan valley (Gen 13:9f.), east of the town. Four nearby springs made settlement inevitable. When Jacob awoke from his sleep, he set up a pillar of stones on which he had slept, poured oil on them, and called the place *bêt-'ēl,* emphasizing God's revelation of himself there. Jacob revisited the area when he was returning from Paddan-Aram to meet with God (I Sam 35:2–3, 7). It was there that Rebekah's nurse, Deborah, died and was buried under "the oak" nearby (Gen 35:8).

There is a lot of history associated with Bethel. It was a Canaanite royal city (Josh 12:16), was captured by Joshua (8:7), and allotted to Benjamin (18:22). Bethel was probably recaptured by the Canaanites early in the period of the Judges, but taken again by the house of Joseph (Jud 1:22f.) to remain Ephraimite territory (I Chr 7:28).

Later the ark was located in Bethel (Jud 20:18) and it became an important center of worship (I Sam 10:3). It was on Samuel's circuit when he judged Israel (I Sam 7:16). While remaining prosperous, it temporarily lost prominence when Saul's Gibeah and David's and Solomon's Jerusalem were in the fore. When the kingdom divided, Jeroboam I designated Bethel as the northern kingdom's main sanctuary, challenging the temple in Jerusalem and weaning the people away (I Kgs 12:26–33). The golden calf ritual and sanctuary at Bethel remained central as late as the time of Amos (3:14; 4:4; Hos 4:15). The northern revolt was thorough in every way, politically, etc., and especially in the synthesis of Yahweh worship and other cultic practices from Egypt, Canaan, and other middle eastern countries. God condemned the action, first in a warning by a man of God who pronounced doom upon Jeroboam (I Kgs 13) and by Amos and Hosea later who mocked Bethel as *bêt 'awen* (house of iniquity).

Apparently Bethel was spared when Samaria fell to Assyria (no archeological evidence suggests Assyrian destruction). It seems that priests still taught there after Samaria was destroyed (II Kgs 17:28). Josiah captured it, demolished the altar, and defiled the site (II Kgs 23:15), while the Babylonians destroyed the city in their second invasion (587–576 B.C.).

In the Persian period Bethel was included in the territory of Judah (Ezr 2:28; Neh 7:32). During the period of Hasmonean guerilla warfare, it was fortified by the Seleucids (I Macc 9:50; Josephus, *Antiquities,* 13.1.3). Vespasian captured it as he approached Jerusalem (Josephus, *Wars of the Jews,* 4.9.9).

Bethel is also associated with both sanctuary and deity. For the Canaanites *bêt-'ēl* was a city sanctuary dedicated to the deity *'ēl* (q.v.). *'ēl* was a general name for God in the ancient near east, but the Israelites identified *'ēl* with Jacob's experiences (Gen 28:10–22; 35). Babylonian documents by Nebuchadnezzar use the word in personal names, while some Jewish people at Elephantine (Elephantine Papyri) had names in combination with *bêt-'ēl,* indicating various attributes of God.

There is also a place by the same name not far from Beersheba (I Sam 30:27) in the territory of Simeon (which was an enclave in Judah), although there is probably a textual error since this appears as *b^{e}tûl* (Josh 19:4) and *b^{e}tû'ēl* (I Chr 4:30). The site of the city is still unknown.

Bibliography: Albright, W. F., *Archeology and the Religion of Israel,* Johns Hopkins, 1942, pp. 168–74. Albright, W. F. and J. L. Kelso, "The Excavation of Bethel," AASOR, 39: Fauer, Jose, "Idolatry," and Gershon Bacon, "The View of Kaufmann," in *Encyclopedia Judaica,* pp. 1227–33. Kelso, "The Second Campaign at Bethel," and "The Third Campaign at Bethel," BASOR, 137, 151. Rowley, H. H., *From Joseph to Joshua,* Oxford, 1950, pp. 19, 111, 138. Avi-Yonah, Michael, "Bethel," in *Encyclopedia Judaica,* IV, pp. 728–30.

bêt-leḥem. ***House of bread.*** In English it is read as one word, "Bethlehem," designating the city. It appears forty-three times; four times, as *bêt-hallaḥmî* "Bethlehemite," designating one belonging to Bethlehem. This name can refer to the place (house) of fighting (since the root *lḥm* refers also to fighting or to the place (house) of the god *laḥamu* (probably from the Amarna letters, where a complaint is registered that *bit laḥamu* was in the hands of the invaders), but all this etymology is uncertain.

The area is first mentioned in Scripture when Rachel was buried by Jacob on the way to Ephrath, specifically at Bethlehem (Gen 35:19). It is located about five miles south of Jerusalem in Judean territory.

The city with the surrounding area was the center of the tribe of Judah. A well-known family, descendants of Perez, settled there and in the Judges period some of the family included Boaz the ancestor of, and Jesse the father of David. This area produced the godly family of Ruth and Boaz.

Bethlehem unfortunately was the abode of the Levite who became the priest of Micah in Ephraim and later of the Danites (Jud 17; 18). Jewish people to this day despise this one for while he was a grandson of Moses, he became a shame. Therefore, in order to conceal his genealogy, the biblical text reads Manasseh (with an *n* above the line) instead of Moses (Jud 18:30). The Levite of Ephraim had a concubine from Bethlehem, and it was her death at the hand of the Levite that caused the civil war between Israel and Benjamin (Jud 19).

Bethlehem's prominence in the OT was in its association with David. It was his home (I Sam 17:12; 20:6) and there Samuel anointed him king (I Sam 16:1, 13). Possibly Bethlehem was one of the worship centers on Samuel's circuit. Some of David's kinsmen who were his personal warriors, sons of Zeruiah, were born there also. Near the end of Saul's reign the Philistines were quartered there (II Sam 23:14–16). It was the burial place of Asahel, brother of Joab (II Sam 2:32).

The succeeding history can be brief. Rehoboam fortified it (II Chr 11:16). Some of Gedaliah's murderers stopped at Bethlehem on their way to Egypt (Jer 41:16–17). Ezra 2:21 and Neh 7:26 record more than one hundred Bethlehemite emigrants, some of the leading citizens. Jews continued to live in Bethlehem in NT and post NT times and *Lam Rabbah* 1:15 records that a Roman garrison was quartered there to destroy any remnant of Bar Kokhba's army. Today no Jews live in Bethlehem.

Because of the messianic passage (Mic 5:2 [H 1]), early Jewish believers who recognized Jesus as Messiah, emphasized Bethlehem as his birthplace (Mt 2:1, 5: Lk 2:4, 15; Jn 7:42). Justin Martyr mentioned that the birthplace of Jesus was in a cave.

Thus the Son of God humbled himself to be born in a cave housing animals in a town so small and insignificant that when the land was distributed it was not even mentioned among the forty-six cities of Judah (Josh 15:20–63; Mic 5:2). In 325 Helena, mother of Constantine, had a church erected over the cave. It was destroyed in 529 A.D. in the Samaritan uprising against the Byzantines. Justinian (527–65) rebuilt it, and the Church of the Nativity today reflects the Justinian pattern. At the beginning of the 400s A.D., Jerome settled in Bethlehem and lived in a cave near the nativity cave. While in Bethlehem, Jewish scholars taught Hebrew to Jerome. His work in that cave, of translating the OT from Hebrew to Latin, became the basis of the Vulgate, in addition to his work of NT translation.

Bethlehem of Judah is not to be confused with a city of the same name in Zebulun (Josh 19:15). This is located about seven miles northwest of Nazareth.

Bibliography: Crowfoot, J. W., Early Churches in Palestine, Oxford, 1941, pp. 22–40. Masterman, E. W., "Bethlehem," in ISBE, I, pp. 449–50. Orni, Ephraim, "Bethlehem," in *Encyclopedia Judaica,* IV, pp. 739–45. Van Beek, G., "Bethlehem," in IDB, I, pp. 394–95.

L.G.

242 בָּכָא (*bākā'*) ***balsam tree*** (II Sam 5:23–24 = I Chr 14:14–15; Ps 84:7).

243 בָּכָה (*bākâ*) ***to weep, cry, shed tears.*** (ASV and RSV similar.)

Derivatives

243a †בֶּכֶה (*bekeh*) ***a weeping.***
243b †בְּכִי (*bᵉkî*) ***weeping.***
243c †בָּכוּת (*bākût*) ***weeping.***
243d בְּכִית (*bᵉkît*) ***weeping.***

This root occurs in all the major languages, including Arabic, Akkadian, and Ugaritic. It is used with approximately the same range of meaning. In Hebrew it means "to weep by reason of joy or sorrow, the latter including lament, complaint, remorse or repentance." The root is commonly paralleled with *dāmaᶜ* "to shed tears" and with *sāpad* "to mourn." But, whereas tears are associated with the eyes, weeping is associated with the voice; Semites do not weep quietly, but aloud. These parallelisms occur frequently in Ugaritic (Fisher). However, in Ugaritic, as in Akkadian and Arabic, the stress upon repentance which is seen in the conjunction of *bākâ* with *ṣûm* "to fast" is absent. Another synonym is *'ābal* which emphasizes the formal mourning for the dead.

Throughout the OT weeping is the natural and spontaneous expression of strong emotion. *bākâ* is especially prominent in the narrative literature although it also occurs frequently in the poetic and prophetic books. The total number of occurrences is 141.

The root is used in five different ways. Although weeping is usually associated with distress or sorrow, it is also a sign of joy. Interestingly enough, all occurrences of this usage appear in the Jacob narrative. Jacob wept for joy when he met Rachel after his journey from Canaan (Gen 29:11). So did Jacob and Esau when they met again after the long separation (Gen 33:4). Joseph and Jacob wept with each other when they met in Egypt (Gen 46:29), etc.

A much more frequent usage is crying in distress. Thus the baby Moses began to cry in the Pharaoh's daughter's presence (Ex 2:6). Similarly Esau wept in bitterness and frustration at the discovery of Jacob's fraud (Gen 27:38). Job says that he deserves punishment if he has committed any of a number of sins, among which is causing the "furrows of the land" to weep through abuse (Job 31:38). Israel wept because of the threat of the enemy (I Sam 11:4; 30:4; etc.); they wept in the exile (Ps 137:1; cf. Jer 31:15); and the Psalmist wept for those who despised God's law (Ps 119:136). The distress need not be one's own, for weeping may be a sympathetic reaction at the distress of another (cf. Job 2:12; 30:25; Isa 16:9; Jer 48:5; Ezk 27:31).

A specific form of distress is that which is on account of death. The form of the lament is seen clearly in I Sam 1 where David weeps for the slain Saul and Jonathon. The magnanimity of David which is shown in his weeping for Saul is seen again when he weeps for Abner, the enemy general (I Sam 3:32). It is evident at several points that the time of lament was carefully prescribed (Gen 50:4; Deut 34:8; etc.). Professional mourners were called to weep at times of death (II Sam 1:24; Jer 49:3; Ps 78:64; Job 27:15). This served the twofold purpose of insuring that the dead person was mourned properly and also that the mourning did not continue interminably.

This lamentation for the dead formed a specific part of the fertility cult, wherein the dead vegetation god was mourned in the fall of the year. Numerous references to this rite are found in the Ugaritic literature (e.g. texts 62; 67:VI, and cf. I Kgs 18:26–29 where a similar ritual was evidently performed). Ezekiel was horrified when he discovered that such practices were being carried on within the temple itself (8:14).

Another type of weeping would be that which is associated with pleading or complaint. Hannah wept with bitter tears as she pleaded with God for a son (I Sam 1:7–10). So also, Esther wept before the Persian emperor begging for her people's life (Est 8:3). Cf. also Hezekiah (II Kgs 20:3). This type of weeping can quickly become whining, as witness Samson's wife importuning him for the answer to his riddle (Jud 14:16) and the crying of the Israelites for meat (Num 11:4–20).

The final usage of "weeping" is unique to the OT. It is the weeping of repentance. In other cultures of the ancient near east weeping out of remorse or sorrow for punishment is known, but never sheer sorrow over having offended the deity. Both of these occur in the OT. An example of the former would be found in Jud 21:2 where the Israelites weep because of their folly in decimating Benjamin. On the other hand is the weeping of Josiah at the reading of the Law (II Kgs 22:19), or the weeping of Israel when she returns to her God (Jer 31:9; 50:4). When the Law was read to the returned exiles and they saw how far short they had fallen, they had to be reminded that a holy day was not for mourning (Neh 8:9; cf. also Ezr 10:1; Hos 12:4 [H 5]). Such weeping was that of Peter when he realized how he had denied his Lord (Mt 26:75). It may be said that there is no genuine repentance apart from a bitter sense of sorrow over one's sins, a sorrow so deep that it may quite properly issue in weeping. In the eschaton God will make an end to all weeping (Isa 65:19; cf. 25:8).

bekeh. ***Weeping.*** At Ezr 10:1 where the people wept greatly (lit. "multiplied weeping").

b^e^kî. ***Weeping.*** Occurs thirty times, five of which are cognate accusatives (cf. Jud 21:2).

bākût. ***Weeping.*** Name of the oak where Rebekah's nurse was buried (Gen 35:8).

Bibliography: Collins, T., "The Physiology of Tears in the OT," CBQ 33: 18–38, 185–97. DeWard, Eileen F., "Mourning Customs in 1, 2 Samuel," JJS 23: 1–27, 145–66. Fisher, L. R., *Ras Shamra Parallels,* vol. 1, Pontifical Biblical Institute, 1972, pp. 142–44. Hvidberg, F. F., *Weeping and Laughter in the Old Testament,* Brill, 1962. Westermann, C., "Struktur und Geschichte der Klage im AT," ZAW 25: 44–80. TDOT, II, pp. 116–20. THAT, I, pp. 313–15.

J.N.O.

בְּכוֹר (*b^e^kôr*). See no. 244a.
בִּכּוּרִים (*bikkūrîm*). See no. 244e.
בָּכוּת (*bākût*). See no. 243c.
בְּכִי (*b^e^kî*). See no. 243b.
בְּכִירָה (*b^e^kîrâ*). See no. 244d.
בְּכִית (*b^e^kît*). See no. 243d.

244 *בָּכַר (*bākar*) ***to be born first.*** (ASV and RSV similar.)

Derivatives

244a †בְּכוֹר (*b^e^kôr*) ***firstborn.***
244b בִּכְרָה (*bikrâ*) ***young camel.***
244c †בְּכֹרָה (*b^e^kōrâ*) ***birthright.***

244d †בְּכִירָה (b^e*kîrâ*) ***firstborn (of women).***
244e †בִּכּוּרִים (*bikkûrîm*) ***firstfruits.***
244f בִּכּוּרָה (*bikkûrâ*) ***firstfruits.***

Of the 158 occurrences of this root and its derivatives, only four are in verbal form and these are all in derived stems. This suggests that the basic idea in Hebrew is the nominal "the firstborn" and that the verb forms are derivative. In the Arabic, the root *bakara* means "to arise, to be first, to come early" and this is probably the root idea from which the Hebrew connotation has sprung.

b^ekôr. ***Firstborn, firstling, eldest (son).*** Arabic, Ethiopia, Aramaic, and probably Akkadian possess a nominal equivalent to Hebrew b^e*kôr* for "firstborn" indicating that this is the original meaning of the noun. This noun form accounts for 118 of the total occurrences of the root. In the singular and the plural constructions, masculine forms are used. However, in the four places where an absolute plural form is used it is always in the feminine בכ רוֹת: Deut 12:6; 14:23; Neh 10:37 [twice].

bikkûrîm. ***Firstfruits, firstripe.*** Only appears in masculine plural and refers especially to the first products of grain and fruit, (bread, Ex 23:16; grapes, Num 13:20; figs, Nah 3:12), a portion of which were to be given to the Lord as a thank offering and for the support of the priesthood (cf. Lev 2:14; Num 18:12–13).

b^ekōrâ. ***Birthright, primogenture.*** Appears only in feminine singular and always with this special meaning. Involves especially the legal claims of the firstborn to a double portion of the inheritance and to such other rights as might be his by virtue of his position as first born.

b^ekîrâ. ***Firstborn daughter.*** The feminine counterpart of b^e*kôr*. Appears only six times, five of which are in Gen. Of these, four are found in Gen 19 (vv. 31, 33, 34, 37) where Lot's firstborn daughter provokes her sister to join her in sexual relations with their father.

In Israel, as in much of the rest of the ancient near east, the firstborn son, Reuben, enjoyed a position of honor and favor. He is called "the first of the (procreative) strength" of the father (Gen 49:3). So noteworthy were departures from this rule, that they became, in C. H. Gordon's words, "worthy of saga." As such these departures constitute a literary theme in the Bible (Gen 25:23; etc.) and elsewhere (cf. Ug. Text 128: III:16). The Lord's choice of Abel over Cain, of Jacob over Esau, of Joseph and Judah over Reuben, of Ephraim over Manasseh, of Moses over Aaron, of David over his brothers, of Solomon over Adonijah, show that he is the Lord of sacred history and that he transcends cultural norms.

Many of the occurrences of b^e*kôr* simply delineate a particular son as the firstborn, indicating the importance attached to this position (esp. in I Chr, but frequently elsewhere). Among other rights, the firstborn was entitled to a double portion of the inheritance (Deut 21:17), to the father's blessing (Gen 27; cf. also 48:17–19), and to preferential treatment (Gen 43:33). If there were two sons, the firstborn would receive two-thirds of the inheritance, if three, two-fourths, etc. The firstborn could sell this inheritance (as in Nuzi law—cf. Gen 25:31–34). This concept is transferred to the prophetic gift in the case of Elisha to show his superiority over the other prophets (II Kgs 2.3ff.). Israel is called the Lord's firstborn (Ex 4:22; cf. Jer 31:9) to show that though it was the youngest of the nations, it occupied the position of leadership and privilege over them.

At the same time, however, the Israelites seem to have held the belief, in common with the rest of the ancient near east, that the deity, as lord of the manor, was entitled not only to the best but to the first share of all produce. This meant that the firstfruits of plant, animal and man were his. Commonly this meant that these could only be used in the practices of and support of the deity's temple. At any rate, they were forfeited to the deity. This is the basic meaning of the Lord's smiting the firstborn of Egypt. It is not Pharaoh, or the Egyptian gods who have the right to Egypt's firstborn. It is the Lord. He is the true owner of Egypt. This Egyptian experience became fundamental for the Hebrew concept of the firstborn (cf. Ex 11:5; Num 8:17; etc.).

It is with regard to the firstborn, however, that Hebrew practice differs sharply from the pagan. Both treat the first plants and animals as *tabu* and thus only available for sacrifice. The pagans carried this logic further, commonly sacrificing the eldest son as well. Although the Hebrews fell back into this custom during the divided monarchy (e.g. II Kgs 16:3) and perhaps may have even so interpreted the Lord's commandment to dedicate the firstborn (Ex 11:5; Ezk 20:26), the Old Testament exhibits a special loathing for child sacrifice (see the discussion under *tōpet*). Wherever it is reported, it is with horror (cf. Josh 6:26; II Kgs 3:27; Jer 32:35; Mic 6:7). Rather, the paradigm for treatment of the firstborn is found in the account of Abraham's near sacrifice of Isaac. It is redemption by means of substitution. As such, it foreshadows the substitutionary atonement of Christ. By rights, this child's life is forfeited to God. But God does not want to take the child's life, so he makes a way of escape. The chief means of substitution after Sinai was via the Levites. The Levitical family was consecrated to God in place of the firstborn (Num 3:1–45). The extra firstborn sons beyond the number of the Levites were redeemed at five shekels a head (Num 3:46–51). Apparently Num 18:15–16 refers to this transaction. Thereafter only the firstborn of animals was demanded (Deut 15:19).

Bibliography: AI, pp. 441–46; pp. 490–93. Gaster, T. H., "Sacrifices," in IDB, IV, p. 148. Kooy, V. H., "Firstborn," in IDB, II, pp. 270–72. Mendlesohn, I., "On the Preferential Status of the Eldest Son," BASOR 156: 38–40. Michaelis, W., "πρωτότοκος, πρωτοτοκεῖα," in TDNT, VI, pp. 872–76. Pedersen, J., *Israel, Its Life and Culture* III–IV, London: Oxford, 1940, pp. 300–22. Richardson, TWB, p. 83. TDOT, II, pp. 121–27.

J.N.O.

בַּל (*bal*). See no. 246d.
בֵּל (*bēl*). See no. 262c.

245 בָּלַג (*bālag*) ***gleam, smile.***

Derivative

245a מַבְלִיגִית (*mablîgît*) ***smiling, cheerfulness*** (Jer 8:18).

246 בָּלָה (*bālâ*) ***become old, worn out.***

Derivatives

246a †בָּלֶה (*bāleh*) ***worn out.***
246b בְּלוֹא (*bᵉlô'*) ***worn out things, rags.***
246c †תַּבְלִית (*tablît*) ***destruction.***
246d †בַּל (*bal*) ***not.***
246e †בְּלִי (*bᵉlî*) ***wearing out.***
246f †בְּלִימָה (*bᵉlîmâ*) ***nothingness.***
246g †בְּלִיַּעַל (*bᵉlîya'al*) ***worthlessness.***
246h בִּלְעֲדֵי (*bil'adê*) ***apart from, except, without.***
246i †בֵּלֶת (*bēlet*) ***not, except.***

bālâ appears sixteen times and is attested in the Ugaritic text by *bly* (Ut 19: no. 474, *blym alpm*, "The oxen are worn out," i.e. unfit for plowing).

Its basic meaning is used of the Israelites' garments which did not wear out (Deut 8:4; 29:4; Neh 9:21) in the wilderness. The Gibeonites claimed the reverse concerning their garments in Josh 9:13.

The same idea is used in a figurative expression relating to the heavens and the earth (Isa 50:9; 51:6; Ps 102:27). While other Scriptures teach the perpetuity of the heavens and earth, this one refers to their worn-out condition. The new heavens and new earth will consist of the old ones renewed; similarly, our resurrected bodies will have many features of continuity with our present bodies.

Men and women are said to waste away through age, cares, or sickness (Gen 18:12; Job 13:28; Ps 32:3; Lam 3:4). In the grave, the bodily form wastes away (Ps 49:15). Wicked men or an attacking enemy can wear out or exhaust the righteous (I Chr 17:9; cf. II Sam 7:10; Dan 7:25, Aramaic).

Finally, *bālâ* can mean "to wear out by use" or "to use to the full," as in Isa 65:22 or Job 21:13.

bāleh. ***Worn out.*** This adjective is used only twice, in Josh 9:4–5 and Ezk 23:43. The context in Joshua is the ruse employed by the Gibeonites. They showed Joshua their worn out sacks and wineskins (v. 4), and sandals and garments (v. 5). In Ezk 23:43, *baleh* is used figuratively. The adulteress (Judah) is worn out by her adulteries. The RSV finds the Hebrew obscure here and Eichrodt calls it untranslatable, but it is possible to translate it as "old in adulteries."

tablît. ***Destruction.*** A noun found only once, in Isa 10:25. Six MSS read *taklîtām* "consumption," but are probably confusing it with a more familiar term. Shortly the indignation of the Lord would end against Israel and be turned toward (*ᶜal*) the destruction of the invading Assyrians. The axe had forgotten that the Lord was swinging it (Isa 10:15).

bal. ***Not.*** An adverb appearing sixty-nine times. Both Phoenician and Ugaritic attest this negative. It is used mainly in poetry instead of *lo'*, which normally appears in prose.

In Isa 40:24, *bal* may gather the meaning "scarcely" or "hardly." Some argue, however for a "neither, nor" construction (Hahn, Koenig) or the negative may simply be used in a hyperbolic structure.

Some have argued that *bal* has a positive meaning as in Ugaritic (UT 19: no. 466, "I shall surely put," or II Aqht 1:21, "He surely has no son"). Also cf. Dahood AB on Ps 10:15: perhaps 15*b* could be rendered: "Search out his wickedness—surely you will find it."

bᵉlî. ***Wearing out.*** There are fifty-seven examples of this form. The only example of a substantive is found in Isa 38:17, "The pit of destruction," which refers to Sheol.

Usually it functions as an adverb of negation with adjectives or participles (II Sam 1:21; Ps 19:4; Hos 7:8). It is frequently joined to a substantive in the sense of "without" (Job 8:11; 24:10; 31:19, et al.). Rarely is it found with a finite verb (Gen 31:20; Isa 14:6).

When used with the preposition *min* it expresses the idea of causation and is rendered "from want of," "from lack of," or "because not." This combination occurs twenty times (e.g. Deut 9:28; Ex 14:11).

With the preposition *bᵉ* it means "without"

(Deut 4:42; 19:4). The preposition *l*[e] makes it "in a state of" or "without, regardless," (Isa 5:14; Job 41:25). Finally, with [c]*ad* it means "until" or "in that not" (Ps 72:7; Gen 31:20; Mal 3:10). These prepositional phrases account for over half of the uses and every context has its own nuance of meaning.

b[e]**lîmâ.** ***Nothingness.*** From *b*[e]*lîi* and *mâ:* "not-aught." Found only in Job 26:7. The Lord "hangs the earth upon nothing" (RSV), a remarkable vision of the earth being supported in space by the power of God.

b[e]**lîya'al.** ***Worthlessness.*** Belial from *b*[e]*lî* and *ya'al:* "not, without" and "to be of use, worth, or profit." Cf. Ugaritic *bl-mt,* "not-death" = "immortality" or *bl-mlk* "not-king" = "commoner." Others derive the name from *bl',* "to swallow," hence the "swallower." (Cf. F. Cross, D. N. Freedman, JBL 22 (1953) and D. Winton Thomas in *Biblical and Patristic Studies,* eds. J. N. Birdsall and R. W. Thomson, Freiburg, 1963, pp. 11–19). See however the discussion below on Ps 18:5.

The term appears twenty-seven times. The KJV and Vulgate treated it as a proper name in sixteen and eight instances respectively. The LXX renders it according to the context by the terms *paranomos, anomia,* and *aphrōn,* i.e. "lawless, lawlessness, witless."

Usually it occurs in such expressions as "son(s) of Belial" (Deut 13:14; Jud 19:22; I Sam 2:12; II Chr 13:7), a "daughter of Belial" (I Sam 1:16), "man or men of" (I Sam 25:25; II Sam 16:7; I Kgs 21:13; Prov 16:27), or a "worthless witness" (Prov 19:28). It appears alone in II Sam 23:6 and Job 34:18.

In Prov 6:12, the "worthless man" is equated with the "wicked man," *'îsh 'āwen.* He is a plotter of evil (Prov 16:27) as well as a "counsellor of villainy" (Nah 1:11) and a mocker of justice (Prov 19:28). In Psalms, *b*[e]*lîya'al* is used for torrents of perdition or destruction which overwhelmed the Psalmist (Ps 18:5; cf. II Sam 22:5), for the "deadly" thing (Ps 41:9), or for anything base (101:3). Many connect David's reference in Ps 18:5 to the mythological motif of the Canaanite god of death, *Mot* with his open mouth, the "swallower" in the netherworld. If this is a proper connection it is only the verbiage which is borrowed in the context and not the ideology. The LXX more realistically understands the metaphor of "streams" or "waves" in Ps 18:5 to be another of the frequent scriptural references to enemies rushing in like torrents.

This concept of Belial became a proper name for the prince of evil, Satan, in the pseudepigraphal literature, the Zadokite Document, and the War Scroll of the Dead Sea Scrolls. See also II Cor 6:15 and II Thess 2:3.

bēlet. ***Not, except.*** It is used as an adverb, conjunction, and with prepositions to express purpose 110 times. In the meaning "failure," it does not appear in the OT.

It appears as the adverb "not" with an adjective in I Sam 20:26, with a substantive in Isa 14:6, and with a finite verb in Ezk 13:3.

When it follows a negative, it takes on the meaning of "except" (Gen 21:26; Ex 22:19; Josh 11:19; Hos 13:4).

The form *biltî* likewise follows an expressed or an implied negative. In Num 11:6, Isa 10:4, and Dan 11:18 it is used in the sense of "except to," i.e. "there is nothing but to," hence nothing left. Note also Amos 3:3–4 "unless."

The form also appears following infinitives with three different prepositions: negation of *l*[e] "so as not, in order not" (Gen 4:15); negation of *min* "on account of not, because not," (Num 14:16; Ezk 16:28); and [c]*ad* "until not" (Josh 8:22).

Bibliography: Cooper, Jacob, "The End of the Material Universe," *Reformed Church Review* 7: 536–67. Dahood, M., *Proverbs and Northwest Semitic Philology,* Rome, 1963, p. 31. Goetze, A., "Ugaritic Negations," in *Studia Orientalia Ioanni Pedersen,* 1953, p. 123, n. 26. Hogg, J. E., "Belial in the OT," AJSL, 44: 56–58. Labuschagne, C. J., "Ugaritic BLT and BILTI in Isa X.4," VT 14: 97–99. O'Callaghan, Roger T., "Echoes of Canaanite Literature in the Psalms," VT 4: 164–76. Smith, Wilbur, "New Heavens and New Earth," in *Biblical Doctrine of Heaven,* Moody, 1968, pp. 223–36.

W.C.K.

247 *בָּלָה (*bālah*) ***trouble.*** Occurs only in the Piel (Ez 4:4).

Derivative

247a בַּלָּהָה (*ballāhâ*) ***terror, destruction.***

בְּלוֹא (*b*[e]*lô'*). See no. 246b.
בְּלִי (*b*[e]*lî*). See no. 246e.
בְּלִיל (*b*[e]*lîl*). See no. 248a.
בְּלִימָה (*b*[e]*lîmâ*). See no. 246f.
בְּלִיַּעַל (*b*[e]*lîya'al*). See no. 246g.

248 בָּלַל (*bālal*) ***mix, mingle, confuse, confound.***

Derivatives

248a בְּלִיל (*b*[e]*lîl*) ***fodder.***
248b בָּלַל (*bālal*) ***give provender. Denominative verb from*** *b*[e]*lîl.*
248c שַׁבְּלוּל (*shabb*[e]*lûl*) ***snail.***
248d †תֶּבֶל (*tebel*) ***confusion.***
248e †תְּבַלֻּל (*t*[e]*ballūl*) ***obscurity.***

A ritualistic term used of mixing oil into the flour or meal of the cereal offering until every particle of flour was mingled or anointed with oil (*bālûl bashshemen;* Ex 29:2, 40; Lev 2:4–5; and chap 7; and often in Num chaps 7, 15, 28, and 29).

An unusual form, expressing an extension of this idea, is found in Ps 92:11. The Psalmist exclaims, "I am anointed with fresh oil." While the verb is different, this idea is similar to the one in Ps 23:6.

A Hithpael form is found in Hos 7:8. There Ephraim "mixes himself among the peoples."

The only witness for the meaning of confounding is in the Tower of Babel narrative where the Lord said, "Let us go down and there confuse their language" (Gen 11:7). This incident provides the basis for a wordplay involving assonance (Gen 11:9). The place is named Babel because the Lord confused (*bālal*) the language of all the earth there. Babel itself does not mean "confuse"; it sounds enough like *bālal* for the paranomasia.

Probably the single example of the Hiphil in Isa 64:5 should be derived from the root *nābal* "fade away" rather than *bālal.*

The form in Judg 19:21 is a denominative of *b^e lîl* "fodder"; hence "to give provender."

tebel. ***Confusion.*** This word is only used twice in the OT. Both instances apply to a reversal of the divinely intended order of things in the sexual realm. Leviticus 18:23 calls bestiality a perversion (RSV) and Lev 20:12 uses this same term to apply to any sex relations with one's daughter-in-law, i.e. incest (RSV).

t^e ballūl. ***Obscurity.*** Only found in Lev 21:20. The NAB renders it "wall-eyed" while the NASB says "one who has a defect" (margin "slit") in his eye. The precise meaning remains unknown.

W.C.K.

249 בָּלַם (*bālam*) ***curb, hold in*** (Ps 32:9, only).

250 בָּלַס (*bālas*) ***gather figs, tend sycamore trees*** (Amos 7:14, only).

251 בָּלַע (*bāla'*) ***I, swallow down, swallow up.***

Derivatives

251a †בֶּלַע (*bela'*) ***swallowing.***
251b בִּלְעָם (*bil'ām*) ***Balaam.***
251c †בָּלַע (*bāla'*) ***II, confuse, confound.***

Used of men (Isa 28:4), fish (Jon 2:1), serpents (Ex 7:12), and animals (Gen 41:7, 24).

On two different occasions, the Lord caused the earth to open and swallow alive groups of men as a judgment: at the Red Sea (Ex 15:12) and at the Korah, Dathan, and Abiram rebellion (Num 16:30, 32, 34; 26:10; Deut 11:6; and Ps 106:17).

Frequently the word is used as a symbol of destruction and ruin: Lam 2:2, 5, 8; Isa 3:12; 49:19, etc.

bela'. ***Swallowing, devouring.*** This noun occurs only twice in the OT. In Ps 52:6, David uses it to refer with disgust to Doeg's "words that devour" (RSV Lit. "words of devouring"). In Jer 51:44, the Lord says that he will take from the mouth of the idol Bel "what he has swallowed" (RSV).

bil'am. ***Balaam.*** Mentioned fifty-one times in Num 22–24; also in Num 31:8, 16; Deut 23:5,6; Josh 13:22; 24:9–10; Mic 6:5; Neh 13:2; II Pet 2:15; Jude 11: Rev 2:14.

The older Gesenius lexicon analyzes the name as *bal* and *'am* "not-people" meaning "foreigner," i.e. (he who belongs) "not (to the) people." But this is impossible. To be preferred is the view of Simonis and Hengstenberg: *bela'* and *'ām* "destruction of people" which accords with his reputation as a charmer and conjurer. (Some have suggested that *Nikolaos* "conqueror of the people" in Rev 2:6,15 is a translation of this name.) However, Albright sees the name as Amorite *Yabil'ammu,* "the (divine) uncle brings" (AJSL 44:31ff.; JBL 63: 232, n.142).

While Balaam was the source of authentic revelation of God (Num 22–24), he was not thereby approved in all he did or said, as is shown by the devious advice which he gave to the king of Moab and Midian (Num 31:16; cf. Num 25: 1–3; Ps 106:28–29). Balaam was a heathen diviner. Balaak, according to ancient custom and belief, would not fight Israel without a propitious omen. Such omens were often cast again and again to get the right time to attack. By overpowering Balaam the Lord prevented Balak's attack.

bāla', *II. Confound, confuse.* The Psalmist prays in Ps 55:10, "Confuse, O Lord, divide their speech," all of which is reminiscent of *bālal* (Gen 11:7, 9) at the tower of Babel. Also cf. Ps 107:27; Isa 9:15; 19:3; and 28:7.

Bibliography: Albright, W. F., "The Oracles of Balaam," JBL 63: 207–33. Hengstenberg, E. W., "The History of Balaam and His Prophecies," in *Dissertations of the Genuineness of Daniel and the Integrity of Daniel,* Edinburgh: Clark, 1847, pp. 337–56. TDOT, II, pp. 136–38.

W.C.K.

בִּלְעֲדֵי (*bil'adê*). See no. 246h.
בִּלְעָם (*bil'ām*). See no. 251b.

252 *בָּלַק (*bālaq*) ***waste, lay waste.*** Does not occur in the Qal.

בֵּלֶת (*bēlet*). See no. 246i.

253 בָּמָה (*bāmâ*) ***ridge or height, high place, bamah*** (technical name for cultic platform).

A cognate is found in Akkadian and Ugaritic. *bāmâ,* which in eighty of the one hundred times refers to a worship area (or perhaps structure), has a basic meaning of "back," "ridge," or "height." So KB. In Ugaritic it means "back" of a person or animal (UT 19: no. 480). Where *bāmâ* refers to a worship area, ASV and RSV use "high place." The idiom of "treading on the heights" conveys the notion of possessing key terrain and thus signifies "being in firm control." To tread *bāmâ* is a promise given to Israel (Deut 33:29; cf. Isa 58:14); it is descriptive also of God (Mic 1:3).

A recent study relying heavily on Ugaritic and archeology, quite convincingly argues that the basic meaning is not "height" but "rib cage," "flank" with derived meanings of "hillsides," "cultic platform" (built of field stones), and by extension "altar" and even "sanctuary" (Vaughn). [Schrunk proposes as its primary meaning "cultic high place" or "cultic place" (see TDOT in bibliography).

The pagan cultic places were usually located on natural heights (I Sam 9:13ff.; 10:5; I Kgs 11:7; II Kgs 17:9, 29; 23:5, 8). They were supplied with idols (II Chr 33:19), an *'ăshērâ,* a wooden pole symbolizing the goddess of fertility and a *maṣṣēbâ,* one or more stone pillars symbolizing the male deity (II Kgs 3:2). The altar (II Kgs 21:3; II Chr 14:3 [H 2]) built of stones, was either separate from the *bāmâ* or part of it. The *bāmâ* contained a tent or room where the cultic vessels were stored and where the sacrificial meals were eaten (I Kgs 12:31; 13:32; II Kgs 17:29; 23:19). B.K.W.] All told, six activities may be traced: the burning of incense, sacrificing, the eating of sacrificial meals, praying, prostitution, and child sacrifice (cf. *bāmâ* in the valley, Jer 7:31).

Aside from the usage for a "height" or "lofty spot" *bāmâ* is essentially a place of worship. But what kind of worship? Critical thought in the past has argued that Israel normally worshipped in these local shrines until Josiah's reform centralized the worship in Jerusalem. All high places were legitimate and normal. The pejorative references to them are said to be due to post Josianic super-orthodox editors.

Prior to the monarchy during the time when the tabernacle of Shiloh was in ruins and prior to worship at the Jerusalem temple, worship was practiced at the *bāmâ,* chief of which was Gibeon, where God communicated with Solomon through a dream (I Kgs 3:2ff). Before him, Samuel frequented high places, officiating there (I Sam 9:12ff.).

After the building of Solomon's temple, references to *bāmâ* are pejorative, for building *bāmâ* represents Israel's sinful involvement in pagan worship. There is only one exception, during the upset days of Manasseh (II Chr 33:17). God's basic stance, already indicated in Lev 26:30, is one of "being against" *bāmâ.* "I will destroy your *bāmâ*" (Ezk 6:3; cf. I Kgs 13:2). Prior to their entry into the land, Israel was commanded to destroy pagan high places (Num 33:52; cf. II Kgs 17:11). The reason for God's judgment is that a *bāmâ* represents competing allegiances. In instances Israel substituted pagan deities for the worship of YHWH, but at other times, as in Samaria following the northern captivity, an attempt was made to worship both YHWH and other gods simultaneously (II Kgs 17:29). God's action against *bāmâ,* first threatened and then executed, stands as prime witness to the significance of the first command, "You shall have no other gods before me" (Ex 20:3).

God's displeasure with the *bāmâ* is cited at the first mention of the construction of a *bāmâ* in the nation of Israel. Solomon built high places for the gods Chemosh of Moab and Molech of the Ammonites in order to please his wives (I Kgs 11:7). Only in Josiah's time, three hundred years later, were these destroyed (II Kgs 23, a key chapter for information about *bāmâ*). The unnamed man of God protested Jeroboam's institution of *bāmâ* (I Kgs 13:2). The lengthy explanation in II Kgs 17 for the northern tribes' exile notes that the people built for themselves *bāmâ* "at all their towns" (II Kgs 17:9). Though the prophet Isaiah is silent about cultic *bāmâ,* likely because under Hezekiah they had been removed (II Kgs 18:4), Jeremiah in two prophetic judgment speeches announces that the *bāmâ,* which in his day was the place for human sacrifice, constituted part of the reason for the coming catastrophe (Jer 19:5; 32:35).

In fact worship at the high places seems to be a decisive or climaxing action of evil. At the time of Rehoboam, Judah initiated high places, thereby committing more sin than their fathers (I Kgs 14:22–23). Jeroboam's large enthusiasm for high places and his practice of placing priests there, "became a sin to the house of Jeroboam, so as to cut it off" (I Kgs 13:34).

Bibliography: Albright, W. F., "The High Place in Ancient Palestine," Supp VT 4: 242–58. Iwry, Samuel, "Massebah and Bamah in 1Q Isaiah A6[13]," JBL 76: 225–32. McCown, C. C., "Hebrew High Places and Cult Remains," JBL 69: 205–19. TDOT, II, pp. 139–44.

E.A.M.

בְּמוֹ (*b^e^mô*). See no. 153.

254 בֵּן (*bēn*) ***son, grandson, member of a group.***

Derivatives

254a †בִּנְיָמִין (*binyāmîn*) ***Benjamin.***
254b †בַּת (*bat*) ***daughter.***

Occurring almost five thousand times, *bēn* is basically but not exclusively a reference to the male offspring of human parents. It is also used idiomatically for children generally, for descendants, i.e. grandsons, for male offspring of beasts, for age designation (e.g. "son of eight days," Gen 17:12) and for people or items belonging in a category or group (e.g. "sons of prophets"). A synonym is *yeled* "child."

Along with other literature from the ancient near east, such as the Ugaritic epic of Keret, the OT places great value upon having a son. The original life from God and the image of God is passed on in the son (Gen 5:3; 9:6). A man achieves social continuance through his son (Deut 25:6; II Sam 18:8). It is against this value that the pain of the loss of an only son must be understood (Gen 22:2; Zech 12:10). The woman finds a great measure of fulfillment in childbearing (Gen 30:1; I Sam 1; Ps 113:9). A recurring motif from Genesis into the NT is the promise to childless parents, of a son (*bēn*). Features of such narratives include the appearance of a messenger, usually an angel, the promise, including either a description of the son's activities or his name, a response of surprise or even disbelief, and a report of the conception and birth (e.g. Gen 12:2; 17:6; Jud 13:7; II Kgs 4:16; Lk 1:13). Most striking is the promise to Isaiah: "Behold a young woman shall conceive and bear a son (*bēn*)" (7:14), see *'almâ* which some hold had immediate fulfillment, but which was unquestionably fulfilled eventually in the coming of Jesus Christ (Mt 1:23; cf. Isa 9:6 [H 5]).

Godly parents are fully rewarded in a wise son (Gen 27:46: Prov 10:1). Great emphasis is placed on the parents' responsibility to instruct the son in the Law (Ex 13:14; 20:10; Deut 11:19; Josh 4:6). On their part, sons are to honor their parents. In this connection it is important to note that the verb "honor" elsewhere in the OT takes as its object a person or that which has a sacral character.

Another motif involving *bēn* is the adoption procedure (cf. Gen 15:2ff.), which was especially common in Nuzi law. Moses was taken into Pharoah's daughter's house and "he became her son" (Ex 2:10). Certain statements which God directed both to people and to individuals are best appreciated in a figurative context associated with adoption or legitimation based on covenant promises, e.g. "Israel is my firstborn son" (Ex 4:22). Of David's descendant God declares, "He shall be my son" (II Sam 7:14) and of Israel it is to be said "sons of the living God" (Hos 1:10 [H 2:1]). Similarly of a king to be coronated, though with ultimate reference to Christ, "You are my son, today I have begotten you" (Ps 2:7; see *māshâḥ*). Clearly in these contexts *bēn* specifies an intimate relationship (cf. Ps 103:13). This functions to show the distance between Yahweh and his "son," the subordinate position of the "son," and his right to share God's authority.

A further motif is that of blessing/curse upon the son. The patriarchs such as Isaac and Jacob speak blessings upon their sons (Gen 27:28–29; 48:14ff.), but so does Moses bless Israel prior to his death (Deut 33:1). Punishment, on the other hand, is destined for sons of the third and fourth generation of parents who do evil (Ex 20:5; 34:7; cf. Jer 6:21).

An important motif is that of setting apart the firstborn male child (cf. *b^ekôr*) for the Lord. Of course children were not to be sacrificed as were the firstborn of animals, but children were to be redeemed (*pādâ,* q.v.) for a redemption price of five shekels (Ex 13:13; 34:20; Num 18:16). Furthermore, the naming of children by the prophets to convey a message should be noted (e.g. "Not-My-People" Hos 1:9; cf. Hos 1:3; Isa 7:3; 8:3).

One characteristic formula with the term *bēn* is "sons of Israel," a phrase that occurs 630 times and is rendered as "children of Israel" by ASV and as "people of Israel" or "Israelites" by RSV and NIV. It is comparable in idiom to "sons of Ammon," i.e. Ammonites. Another important formularic combination is "son of man" which is equivalent to "man" as the poetic parallelism makes clear (Num 23:19; Ps 8:4 [H 5]; Job 25:6; 35:8). *ben-ādām* ("son of man") occurs as a title for the prophet in Ezk (93 times), where the phrase designates simply "man" or "individual," but emphasizes the finiteness of the prophet *vis-a-vis* God's transcendence. Christ's appropriation of the title "Son of man" reaches back to its Aramaic usage in Dan 7:13 in which case (though interpretations vary) it underscores his identification with mankind and combines features of both suffering and glory. The "sons of God" ('ĕlōhîm) mentioned in Gen 6 are either angelic beings, or rulers, i.e. kings (cf. Ps 82:6), or more likely the godly line of Seth. In contrast to other religions, "sons of God" occurs seldom in the OT—this identical phrase only three other times—and generally signifies heavenly creatures (Ps 29:1 *'ēlîm* [with a parallel in 96:7]; Job 1:6 *'ĕlōhîm*; 38:7 *'ĕlōhîm*) or Israel (e.g. Deut 14:1; 32:19; also 32:8; cf. DSS).

binyāmîn. ***Benjamin.*** literally, "son of the right hand," or "son of the south."

Benjamin, the youngest son of Jacob and Rachel, is important in the story of his elder brother Joseph (Gen 42–45). The Benjamin tribe settled in central Palestine (Josh 18:21–28) between Ephraim and Judah, but did not totally drive out the Canaanites (e.g. Jerusalem, Jud 1:21).

The story of the brutal and shameful treatment given by the Benjamite city of Gibeah to the travelling Levite and his concubine, while illustrative of social conditions, reflects negatively on the Benjamites (Jud 19–21). Confronted with their evil, the Benjamites threw their support behind Gibeah. When clan or family loyalty blinds men from moral indignation the situation becomes vicious and the resulting civil war almost annihilated Benjamin.

The size of Benjamin receives occasional mention in Scripture. Though renowned for its valiant soldiers (Jud 20:15; cf. I Chr 8:40; Gen 49:27), its population was never large nor was its territory impressive in size (cf. Ps 68:27, NIV). Israel's first king protests his appointment noting that he is from the least of the tribes of Israel (I Sam 9:21; cf. Ps 68:27 [H 28]). Yet God's choice of Saul illustrates the principle that he not infrequently bypasses those of high station and reaches for those esteemed as insignificant (cf. Deut 33:12).

It should not go unnoticed that Samuel's ministry was mostly in the Benjamite region and that to the Benjamites belong not only Saul, but also Jeremiah (Jer 1:1), Esther (Est 2:5), and the apostle Paul (Rom 11:1).

The name Benjamin occurs in the Mari letters of the eighteenth century designating a particular tribe which appears to be somewhat nomadic. There it doubtless means "sons of the south." Jacob chose the name for his son because of the other meaning.

bat. *Daughter.* As in most Semitic languages, the primary meaning in the 587 occurrences of *bat* is that of female child in the household. Hebrew may use the compound *bānîm ûbānōt* "sons and daughters" to express "children" (approximately 110 times). As with son (*bēn*), *bat* in the plural may refer to membership in a group, as in "daughters of the Philistines," i.e. Philistine women. In expressions such as "Heshbon and her daughters," the reference is to satellite towns and villages (Num 21:25). Personified, *bat* specifies land or city as in, "O virgin daughter of Babylon" (Isa 47:1).

Although less emphasis is placed on daughters then sons (c. 585 references to 4850 respectively), they were greatly valued. The continuation of life depended on daughters—Eve is the "mother of all the living," and a daughter was valuable for her labor (Gen 24:15; 29:9; Ex 20:10). At marriage a bride price was paid to the daughter's father, but he normally restored it to her as a dowry (Gen 31:15). The dowry may even have been higher than the price (cf. W. Plautz, "Die Form der Eheschliessung im AT," ZAW 76: 298–18). The love of a father for an only daughter is illustrated by Jephthah's sorrow at the loss of his daughter (Jud 11:34–40; cf. II Sam 12:3). If there were no sons, a man's daughters inherited his property, provided they married within the same tribe (Num 27:1–11; 36:1–12).

The birth of a daughter brought about a mother's uncleanness twice the duration of uncleanness in the birth of a son. The daughters of the Canaanite culture brought about Israel's ruin (Num 25:1ff.; Deut 7:3; Jud 3:6; I Kgs 11:1, etc.), but the Aramean daughters of Abraham's family embraced the faith of their husbands (Gen 21:6; 24:58; 27:46; 29:32), though in the case of Jacob's wives it was less than perfect (Gen 31:1ff.; 35:2). Lot's daughters fled from Sodom with him leaving their husbands behind (Gen 19:14–16), though later they had incestuous relations with him (19:30ff.). Daughters accompanied their parents at religious festivities, and in the promised age they will share equally with sons in the Spirit's gifts (Joel 2:28 [H 3:1]). The prophets through personification make three theological affirmations. The first relates to the expression "daughter (of) Zion," understood not as a daughter belonging to Zion but as the daughter who is Zion, or as the aggregate of the city's inhabitants. While the expression appears in historical material (II Kgs 19:21) and hymnic poetry (Ps 9:14 [H 15]), among the prophets it is Isaiah who uses it most frequently in connection with what is known as Zion theology. Zion, a portion of Jerusalem, is a poetic way of referring to Jerusalem as a whole, and in some passages is a symbol for the whole land of Israel. Zion was God's choice. His presence, blessing, and protection is upon Zion, and, while thought therefore by the people to be inviolable, the prophets pronounced judgment on Zion. Yet they also declare that her "salvation comes" (Isa 62:11). E. J. Young holds that the expression "daughter of Zion" is also intended to be one of tenderness. (*Isaiah,* vol. I, p. 55)

Jeremiah speaks of the "daughter of my people," an expression found in his book and in Lam thirteen times but seldom elsewhere, and mostly in the context of approaching or realized calamity. Jeremiah notes the wound which his people sustained (Jer 8:19, 21), and describes his sorrow at the destruction of "the daughter of my people" (Jer 14:17; cf. Lam 2:11; 3:48). John Bright renders "My Daughter-My People" explaining that the nouns are in apposition and comments, "The term is a poetic, and endearing, personification of the people, and is a favorite with Jeremiah" (*Jeremiah,* 1965, p. 32). R. K. Harrison says, "This unusual term expresses Jeremiah's sense of God's kinship with Israel" (*Jeremiah,* p. 71).

Ezekiel develops an elaborate analogy on the

daughter motif by referring to Jerusalem as daughter of a Hittite (Ezk 16:45). This figure of speech enables the prophet to discourse on the upbringing of the daughter, to capitalize on the proverb, "Like mother, like daughter" (Ezk 16:44), to stress the increasing degradation of playing the harlot and finally to compare the sisters, Samaria and Sodom, who when compared to Jerusalem seem righteous.

Bibliography: Andersen, H. G., "Benjamin," in ZPEB I, 521–2. Berney, Leroy, "An Exegetical Study of Gen 6:1–4," JETS 13: 43–52. Bess, S. Herbert, "The Term 'Son of God' in the Light of Old Testament Idiom," *Grace Journal* 6: 16–23. Bright, J., *History of Israel,* Westminster, 1949, p. 70. Colerom, J. E., "The Sons of God in Genesis 6, 2," TS 2: 488–509. Cooke, Gerald, "The Israelite King as Son of God," ZAW 73: 202–25. ———, "The Sons of (the) Goddess," ZAW 76: 22–47. Delekat, C., "Zum Hebraischen Wörterbuch," VT 14: 7–66. DeBoer, P. A. H., "The Son of God in the Old Testament," OTS 18: 188–207. Emerton, J. A., "The Origin of the Son of Man Imagery," JTS 9: 225–42. Fensham, F. Charles, "The Son of a Handmaid in Northwest Semitic," VT 19: 312–22. Kline, Meredith G., "Divine Kingship and Genesis 6:1–4," WTJ 24: 187–204. Longenecker, Richard N., "Son of Man Imagery: Some Implications for Theology and Discipleship," JETS 13: 43–52. McKenzie, John L., "Divine Sonship and Individual Religion," CBQ 7: 32–47. ———, "The Divine Sonship of Man in the Old Testament," CBQ 7: 326–39. ———, "The Divine Sonship of Israel and the Covenant," CBQ 8: 320–31. ———, "The Divine Sonship of the Angels," CBQ 5: 293–300. Mendelsohn, I., "A Ugaritic Parallel to the Adoption of Ephraim and Manasseh," *Israel Exploration Journal* 9: 180–83. ———, "The Family in the Ancient Near East," BA 11: 24–40. Muilenberg, James, "The Son of Man in Daniel and the Ethiopic Apocalypse of Enoch," JBL 79: 197–209. Rainey, Anson F., "Family Relationships in Ugarit," Or 34: 10–22. Richardson, TWB, p. 230. Williams, James G., "The Prophetic 'Father'," JBL 85: 344–48. Winter, P., "Der Begriff 'Sohne Gottes' im Moselied Dt 32, 1–43," ZAW 67: 40–48. TDOT, II, pp. 148–58. THAT, I, pp. 316–24.

E.A.M.

255 בָּנָה (*bānâ*) ***build, rebuild.*** (ASV and RSV usually identical, but "rebuild" in the RSV is sometimes used where ASV uses "build," e.g. Ezk 36:36).

Derivatives

255a בִּנְיָה (*binyâ*) ***structure, building.***
255b בִּנְיָן (*binyān*) ***structure.***
255c מִבְנֶה (*mibneh*) ***structure.***
255d †תַּבְנִית (*tabnît*) ***pattern, plan.***

bānâ as construction refers to houses, cities, towers, altars, etc. and idiomatically to bring about increase in offspring (Gen 16:2). *bānâ* occurs 376 times in Qal and Niphal stems.

Synonyms are *kûn* "establish" (II Sam 7:13; Ps 89:4 [H 5]) and *'āśâ* "make." An antonym is *hāraṣ* "break down" (Jer 1:10; Ps 28:5).

The theological significance of the verb *bānâ* can be exposed by considering the use of the verb first with God and then with man as its subject.

1. God as Builder. YHWH is presented in Scripture as the master builder of both the created and historical order. The word is used metaphorically of his final creative act for man's good when he "built" the rib which he had taken from Adam into a woman (Gen 2:22). Elsewhere the biblical poets describe the ordered universe as a building which YHWH designed and built (Amos 9:6; cf. Ps 104:2–3).

YHWH, the wise, powerful and good architect of the created order is also the sovereign and moral master builder of temporal history. His sovereignty over history is seen in Joshua's prediction that it would cost a man his first born son to rebuild Jericho (Josh 7:26); Hiel the Bethelite fulfilled this grim prediction eight hundred years later (I Kgs 16:34). As the designer of history he tears down the edifices of the wicked while he builds his own kingdom. Concerning his sovereignty in tearing down the works of the ungodly, Job proclaimed: "With him are wisdom and might; to him belong counsel and understanding. Behold, he tears down, and it cannot be rebuilt" (Job 12:13–14a). Because of his righteous perfection the Psalmist foresaw: "Because they [the wicked] do not regard the works of the Lord nor the deeds of his hands, he will tear them down and not build them up" (Ps 28:5). At the time of his judgment he will destroy the cities of the godless so that they will never be rebuilt. This was the fate of the Canaanites (Deut 13:16 [H 17]), and of Tyre (Ezk 26:14). In a doxology Isaiah exclaimed: "O LORD, you are my God; I will exalt you, I will give thanks to your name . . .; a palace of strangers is a city no more; it will never be rebuilt" (Isa 25:1–2). In a word, that which is built through unrighteousness is unstable and will fall. Even Jerusalem will become a ruin because her leaders built Zion with bloodshed and Jerusalem with violence and injustice (Mic 3:10), and Jehoiakim will be buried like a stubborn donkey because he built himself a spacious house through unrighteousness and injustice (Jer 22:13–19; cf. Hab 2:12). YHWH subjected his chosen city to the same fate he inflicted on the Canaanites by giving its new houses to the enemy before Israel had ever used them (Deut 28:30;

Zeph 1:13). Though nations, such as Edom, may resolve to build in opposition to him his decrees, they will not succeed (Mal 1:4).

Other texts, however, affirm his sovereignty according to his righteous purposes in building up his kingdom through his elect. He also promised to build Jeroboam I an enduring house if he kept YHWH's statutes (I Kgs 11:38). Unlike David, however, Jeroboam I failed to behave as a true servant of YHWH.

In addition to building the houses of his faithful priests and kings, he is also the master builder of Zion and the temple. Even as in the days of Moses he gave instructions as to how his altars should be built (Ex 20:25; Deut 27:5). In the golden age of Israel's united kingdom, he chose the time, the place and the person to build his house (I Kgs 8:16–20). David promised Solomon that through YHWH's blessing, he would secure the necessary materials and craftsmen for its construction (I Chr 22:11; II Chr 2:7ff [H 6]). Thus he fulfilled his promise at the time he founded the nation to choose a place to put his name (Deut 12:5). A striking amount of detailed instruction is given about the building of these structures in which YHWH delights (cf. I Kgs 6; Ezk 40; Neh 3).

Moreover, though he chastens the house of David and Zion by tearing them down for a time, yet his purpose to bring salvation cannot be thwarted forever.

Jeremiah's use of the combination "build and plant," since it follows God's destructive act of judgment, illustrates that God in grace "builds again" (Jer 1:10; 18:7–10; 42:10). Impressive is YHWH's promise to the people destined for exile, "Again I will build you and you shall be built, O virgin Israel" (Jer 31:4; cf. 24:6; 33:7). In the metaphorical usages of this word pair it is always YHWH who is subject; and in Jeremiah, the object, when it is given, is always a group of people, primarily Israel. The word pair is linked with salvation history and emphasizes YHWH's initiative as well as his solicitude. Thus, he sent Cyrus to rebuild the temple (II Chr 36:23; Ezr 1:2–4) and promised to rebuild the house of David (Amos 9:11). (Perhaps as an indication of his intention to use Israel to bring universal salvation, he used the Phoenicians in building the first temple, and the uncircumcised Cyrus in building the second temple.)

Because God is sovereign over all, it is folly to build without his blessing. "Unless the LORD builds the house, they labor in vain who build it" (Ps 127:1). All houses and cities are at his disposal as he displayed when he promised to give to his elect cities and houses they did not build (Deut 6:10f; Josh 24:13) and threatened to destroy the cities of apostates (Deut 13:16 [H 17]). Siege equipment and fortifications are without profit apart from him (Ezk 17:17; cf. 21:22 [H 27]). David appropriately depended on God to build the walls of Jerusalem (Ps 51:18 [H 20]).

2. Man as Builder. Structures built by man are judged by God as either good or bad according as they conform to his character and purpose. Thus he accepted the altars built by Noah (Gen 8:20); the Patriarchs (12:7–8; 13:8; 18; 22:9; 26:25; 35:7); Moses (Ex 17:15; 24:4); Joshua (Josh 8:30). In contrast, he rejected the high places and altars to foreign gods built by Aaron (Ex 32:5); Solomon (I Kgs 11:7); Rehoboam (I Kgs 14:23); etc.

Cities, the most frequent object of *bānâ*, must also be evaluated by the same criteria. Thus he delights in the songs about Zion (Ps 122:3), but he found no delight in the city built by Cain (Gen 4:17) or in Assur's Nineveh (Gen 10:11). Though Tyre was famous for its beauty brought about by its expert craftsmen (Ezk 27:3ff), it was destroyed because of its sin (27:26ff). The same fate befell Samaria though it contained houses of dressed stone (Amos 5:1; cf. Isa 9:10 [H 9]) and decorated with ivory (I Kgs 22:39; Amos 3:15).

Building activity is frequently associated with God's saving activity. Under God's blessing, Solomon not only built up Zion but also built store cities and fortified others (II Chr 8:5). Ezekiel anticipates the day when Israel will again build houses (Ezk 28:26; 36:10, 33, 36), and the Psalmist calls upon heaven and earth to praise God because his servants will once again build the cities of Judah (Ps 69:35 [H 36]). The reader rejoices with the singers of Nehemiah's time who built for themselves villages around Jerusalem (Neh 12:29).

Houses became important in Israel's history when they became sedentary. The first notice that Jacob built a house and booths for his cattle occurs after he returned from Padan Aram and separated himself from Esau (Gen 37:18). Anticipating their settlement in the land, Moses instructed the people to make a parapet for their flat roofs lest someone might fall off (Deut 22:8); he excused a man from military service (20:5) who had not dedicated his new house.

The word is also used for women who build a family by bearing children. Rachel and Leah are mentioned in marriage blessing as having built the house of Israel (Ruth 4:11). Levirate marriage was instituted so a "house" or family would be built (Deut 25:9).

tabnît. ***Pattern, plan, form, image, likeness.*** (ASV and RSV often vary: e.g. ASV "pattern," RSV "plan," I Chr 28:11, 12, 18, 19; ASV "likeness" RSV "image" Ps 106:20). *tabnît* occurs twenty times.

Synonyms for *tabnît* are not easily differentiated from each other. *t^emûnâ* from the root *mîn* "kind" suggests "resemblance," "representation" (Num 12:8). *dᵉmût*, from the root *dāmâ* "like," is used in the sense of "copy," "likeness," or "image." *tō'ar* refers to "attractive form" (Gen 29:17; Jer 11:16). Wherever *tabnît* refers to structures it is best understood as "plan," e.g. David supplied Solomon with *tabnît* ("specifications," "blueprints") for temple items (I Chr 28:11, 19). In other contexts *tabnît* is better rendered "likeness" and is not essentially different from *tᵉmûnâ* (Deut 4:16–18; cf. Ex 20:4).

The tabernacle and its furnishings were to be made according to the *tabnît* (plan) God had shown Moses in the Mount (Ex 25:9, 40). Specifications for the tabernacle, the ark of the covenant, the table for the bread of the presence, etc. included dimensions, material, design, and even color (Ex 26:1) though not always were measurements indicated (cf. lampstand, Ex 25:31).

Bibliography: TDOT, II, pp. 166–80. THAT, I, pp. 325–26.

B.K.W.

256 בנט (*bnṭ*). **Assumed root of the following.**
256a †אַבְנֵט (*'abnēṭ*) ***girdle.*** (KJV, ASV, RSV render alike, "girdle(s).")

The word denotes the girdle of the high priest, the ordinary priests, and high officials. There are nine occurrences of this term in the OT; all but one (Isa 22:21) are found in Exodus and Leviticus. The *'abneṭ* was a ceremonial sash worn by the high priest and his assistants. It was made of embroidered linen in colors of blue, purple, and scarlet (Ex 28:4, 39–40). It was worn by high officials as well (Isa 22:21). *'abneṭ* is one of five OT words translated "girdle." Only one other refers to priestly apparel. Josephus affords some details of the girdle as used in his day. It was wrapped around the chest and after a number of twinings it was tied, hanging freely to the ankles. Such was the girdle which the high priest wore while performing no service. While he was offering sacrifices, in order to allow greater freedom of movement, he threw the sash to the left and wore it over his shoulder (Josephus, *Ant* 3.7.2). Some OT scholars think of the girdle as a loosely woven scarf. Although Deut 22:11 expressly forbids mixing wool and linen in a garment, it was permitted in this case, at least in the embroidery wool, although Ex 39:2*a* calls it a girdle of linen. The girdle was a usual part of the garments of the priests. The "girdle of the ephod" (*ḥēsheb hā'ēpōd*) was specially embroidered and worn by the high priest.

Bibliography: Levin, Moshe, *Melekhet Hammiskkan* (in Hebrew), Tel Aviv, 1968. Wright, G. E., "Israelite Daily Life," BA 18: 50–79.

C.L.F.

בִּנְיָה (*binyâ*). See no. 255a.
בִּנְיָמִין (*binyāmîn*). See no. 254a.
בִּנְיָן (*binyân*). See no. 255b.

257 בסר (*bsr*). **Assumed root of the following.**
257a בֹּסֶר (*bōser*) ***unripe or sour grapes.***

258 בעד (*b'd*). **Assumed root of the following.**
258a †בַּעַד (*ba'ad*) ***behind, through, round about, in behalf of.***

Used primarily as a preposition, *ba'ad* is significant theologically. First *ba'ad* occurs in conjunction with petition "in behalf of" (*ba'ad*) someone. Persons request a spiritual leader to pray (usually Hithpael of *pālal*) in their behalf, e.g. Pharaoh to Moses (Ex 8:28 [H 24]); people to Samuel (I Sam 12:19); Hezekiah to Isaiah (II Kgs 19:4); representatives to Jeremiah (Jer 21:2; 42:2). Or, assertions are made of spiritual leaders that they have or will intercede, e.g. Abraham (Gen 29:7) and Moses (Num 21:7; Deut 9:20). Jeremiah is commanded not to pray for (*ba'ad*) the people (Jer 7:16; 11:14). The preposition throughout underscores the mediating function of leaders, including prophets, in intercession.

Instructions given to priests include the expression "make atonement for (*ba'ad*)." Aaron is instructed to make atonement (*kāpar*, q.v.) for himself and his house (Lev 9:7). In the temple which Ezekiel describes, sin offerings are to be observed "to make atonement for" (*ba'ad*) the people (Ezk 45:17, 22). Descriptions of the ritual for the Day of Atonement repeated the same expression (Lev 16:6, 11, 17, 24). It is perhaps presumptuous to argue merely from *ba'ad* that sacrifice is to be understood as substitutionary. The whole ritual must be considered. Prayer is also spoken of as "making atonement for" (Ex 32:30). Yet there can be no doubt that sacrifice, supremely Christ's sacrifice, is "for the benefit of" and "in behalf of" others.

Non-theological usages include: away from, behind, out from or out through in various appropriate situations.

E.A.M.

בִּעוּתִים (*bi'ûtîm*). See no. 265b.

259 בָּעָה (*bā'â*) ***seek out, swell.***

bā'â suggests a search for what is covered or sealed (Isa 21:12; Ob 6). And it may suggest a swelling up as of boiling water (Isa 64:2) or the bulging of a wall (Isa 30:13). It has the same two meanings in Arabic.

E.A.M.

260 בעז (*b'z*). **Assumed root of the following.**
260a †בֹּעַז (*bō'az*) ***I, Boaz.***

A wealthy landowner from Bethlehem who figures prominently in the book of Ruth (Ruth 2:1–3). Through his considerate action for the widowed Ruth, Boaz exemplifies justice of which the Bible so often speaks (e.g. Deut 27:19). Since Boaz functions as a kinsman redeemer (*gōʼēl*, q.v.) his action has been regarded as pointing to Christ, the redeemer of mankind. As the great-grandfather of David, Boaz receives mention in geneaologies (I Chr 2:12) including those of Christ (Mt 1:5; Lk 3:32).

Boaz was also the name of one of the two large pillars flanking the entrance to Solomon's temple. Boaz stood to the north; the other pillar (*yākîn*) stood to the south (I Kgs 7:15–21). The majority of scholars believe that they had a purely decorative and symbolic function. But W. F. Albright suggested they were giant incense stands (*Archaeology and the Religion of Israel*, 1949, pp. 138–48). Others hold that they symbolized God's presence or that the pillars, together with the laver, symbolized Yahweh's lordship over the natural elements (land and water). R.B.Y. Scott appropriately notes that since the king "stood by the pillar" at important occasions (II Kgs 11:14; 23:3) the inscriptions may have dynastic significance. Boaz may recall: "In the strength (b^e*ʻōz*) of Yahweh shall the king rejoice" (Ps 21:1 [H 2]; JBL 58: 143ff.). Jean Ouellette, however, has recently argued that they were not freestanding but had a functional value ("The Basic Structure of Solomon's Temple and Archaeological Research," in *The Temple of Solomon*, ed. by Joseph Gutmann, Scholars Press, 1976). See also D. Ussishkin, "King Solomon's Palaces," BA 36: 84–88. See Busink, T. A., *Der Tempel von Jerusalem* (Leiden, 1970), pp. 312ff. for a convenient survey of the extensive scholarly literature on the subject.

E.A.M.

261 בָּעַט (*bāʻaṭ*) ***kick.***

בְּעִיר (b^e*ʻîr*). See no. 264a.

262 בָּעַל (*bāʻal*) ***possess, own, rule over, marry.*** (ASV and RSV usually similar, though RSV prefers "rule" to ASV "have dominion" [e.g. Isa 26:13]).

Derivatives

262a †בַּעַל (*baʻal*) ***owner, husband, Baal.***
262b †בַּעֲלָה (*baʻălâ*) ***female owner.***
262c †בֵּל (*bēl*) ***Bel.***

The verb with its derivatives, not counting its usage in compounds or as proper names, occurs more than one hundred times. One may own (*bāʻal*) a house (Ex 22:7), or rule over (*bāʻal*) territory (cf. I Chr 4:22). A man may take (*lāqaḥ*) a wife and marry (*bāʻal*) her (Deut 24:1).

A focus on the verb *bāʻal* from the theological standpoint leads to a consideration of marriage terminology employed by God in defining his relationship to his people. "For your Maker is your husband (*baʻal*), the Lord of hosts is his name" (Isa 54:5ff.). In Jer the existing marriage relationship becomes a motivation for repentance: "For I am a husband unto you" (Jer 3:14, ASV; RSV renders "I am your master"). In the justly famous new covenant passage the former covenant is described as a broken covenant, a situation which is the more sobering and shocking because "I was a husband (*baʻal*) to them, says Jehovah" (Jer 31:32, ASV; RSV similar; cf. Mal 2:11).

The future delights which God will have with his redeemed people are stressed in Isa where the land is said to be married (*bāʻal*, Niphal), apparently to YHWH. The name of the land, Beulah (passive participle of *bāʻal*), signifies both the intimacy and the joy of YHWH in conjunction with the land (*ʼereṣ*, q.v.; Isa 62:4). The background which such language gives to the NT concept of Christ as the bridegroom or husband of his people, the church, should be obvious (cf. Eph 5:21ff.). In any case one must not miss the close covenantal tie which this metaphor suggests, not only of love but of loyalty between God and his people.

baʻal. ***Owner, possessor, husband, Baal.*** Ugaritic also has the double use of master and the name of a deity. The root in most semitic languages means either "lord" or, when followed by a genitive, "owner."

In addition to *baʻal* as owner of things, the noun in the plural is used for citizens (*baʻalîm*) of a city (Josh 24:11). In Jud 9 where the noun occurs sixteen times, ASV consistently translates "men," but RSV in addition to "men" employs "citizens" (Jud 9:2) and "people" (Jud 9:46). *baʻal* can refer to partner or ally (Gen 14:13). Idiomatically *baʻal* as master of something characterizes the person (e.g. *baʻal* of wrath, Prov 22:24; of appetite, Prov 23:2; of dreams, Gen 37:19) or identifies occupation (e.g. officer, *baʻal* of the guard, Jer 37:13).

In addition to its appearance in compound names of people and places (e.g. Jerubbaal, Jud 9:16; Baalzephon, Ex 14:2), *baʻal* is the name of a great active god in the Canaanite pantheon and has other religious connotations.

The god Baal met in the OT is the West Semitic storm god, *bʻl* (sing.) and *bʻlm* (pl.), encountered in Egyptian texts (from fourteenth century B.C. on), Tell Amarna Letters (fourteenth century B.C.), Alalakh Tablets (fifteenth century B.C.), Ugaritic texts (fourteenth century B.C.), Amorite proper names from Mari, Tell al-Rimah, and

Chagar Bazar, and later in Phoenician and Punic texts. Both within the Bible and outside it the name appears either absolutely or in construct with place names; e.g. Baal-peor (Num 25:3, 5), Baal-berith (Jud 9:40), Baal-zebub (II Kgs 1:2). (Baal-zebub, "lord of flies," is a parody on his name found elsewhere, *b'l zbl,* "Prince Baal.") These names do not denote various gods with the epithet "lord," but local venerations of the same West Semitic storm and fertility deity called simply Baal, "Lord."

Scholars used to think that the plural form with the article, "the Baalim" denoted different local numina, but the plural form of the name occurs outside the Bible and the mention of "lovers" and "strangers" (Jer 2:25) suggest another use of the plural than that of a numerical plural. The article occurs frequently in Hebrew with proper names whose meaning is transparent.

Since the biblical writers did not intend to teach the Canaanite religion, we know more about Baal's roles, consorts, and cult from the extra-biblical literature than from the OT; but the picture of Baal presented in the OT comports well with the extra-biblical sources.

He was also called Haddu (=Hadad). He is above all the storm god who gives the sweet rain that revives vegetation. Dry years were attributed to his temporary captivity or even death. But at his revivification fields, flocks, and families became productive. In addition, he is a war god and fertility deity who consorts with Anat (is later equated with Astarte). Both by reciting the myth of his role in reviving life at the autumn new year festival and by magical ritual of sacred marriage represented in the cult by the king, the queen and a priestess, the West Semites hoped to ensure the earth's fertility. [This ritual is witnessed to in Babylon but not clearly in Canaan (cf. H. Frankfort *Kingship and the Gods*, also Kitchen, K. A., *Ancient Orient and the O.T.*, Inter-Varsity, 1966, p. 104). It should be noted that the identification of Baal as an annually dying and rising god with the Babylonian Tammuz has lately suffered. New Sumerian tablets published by S. Kramer show that Tammuz died once for all and C. H. Gordon has argued that Baal too had no annual death and resurrection. See the whole discussion with refs. in E. M. Yamauchi, "Tammuz and the Bible" JBL 84: 283–90. R.L.H.] Archaeological cultic objects with exaggerated sexual features, as well as the myths themselves, support the OT notices about the degraded moral features associated with the cult.

Throughout the period of the judges, Israel succumbed to this infectious cult (Jud 2:11ff.; 6:25) and had to be rescued from its tragic consequences by Yahweh's judges. During the period of the Omrides, Baal worship became the official state religion of the northern kingdom (I Kgs 16:31). Leah Bronner has presented convincing argument that Israel's miracles by Elijah and Elisha served as a polemic for God against the very powers attributed to this pagan nature deity, namely, fire (I Kgs 18:17ff.; II Kgs 1:9–16), rain (I Kgs 17:1; 18:41–46), food (I Kgs 17:1–6, 8–16; II Kgs 4:1ff.); children (II Kgs 4:14–17); revivification (I Kgs 17:17–23; II Kgs 4:18–37; 13:20–22, *The Stories of Elijah and Elisha as Polemics Against Baal Worship,* Leiden, 1968.) But their miracles did not rid the land of this degraded cult and it brought about the captivity of the northern kingdom (Hosea).

It also infiltrated the southern kingdom (II Kgs 11:18; 21:2ff.), and in spite of Josiah's reform (II Kgs 23:4ff.), brought the nation into exile (Ezk 16; 23, etc.).

The Hosea discourse describes how Israel, who received gifts of grain and oil from YHWH, used these for the worship of Baal (Hos 2:8 [H 10]). The chapter fairly turns on the term *ba'al,* not only in the mention of the Canaanite god(s) (e.g. Hos 2:8 [H 10]; 2:13 [H 15]; and 2:17 [H 19]), but in the imagery throughout of God as Israel's husband. Israel will call the Lord her husband (*'îsh,* Hos 2:16 [H 18]; cf. 2:2 [H 4]; 2:7 [H 9]) and no longer call him, apparently along with the list of other gods, my Baal (*ba'al*).

God's supremacy over Baal is constantly affirmed. However man's preoccupation from then and until this day is rather with sex and technology, than with devotion to the almighty God of history, who is also the covenant God.

B.K.W.

ba'ălâ. ***Female owner.*** Used infrequently, *ba'ălâ* signifies owner of something (e.g. a house, I Kgs 17:17). Or like *ba'al,* it is used to characterize a person (e.g. enchantress, lit. "possessor of charms," Nah 3:4; cf. I Sam 28:7). In contrast to *ba'al, ba'ălâ* is not used in the OT of a goddess except as the feminine form appears in names of localities (e.g. Josh 15:9).

bēl. ***Bel.*** The name of an earlier Babylonian god of heaven, parallel perhaps to the Sumerian Enlil, who at a later date was merged with Marduk. Bel ("lord," cf. Hebrew *ba'al*) was then added as title to Marduk. Bel, Babylon's patron deity, is incorporated in names like Belshazzar (Dan 5:1). The Babylonian form of the name is due to the loss of laryngeals in the Akkadian language.

Bel, the Babylonian form, is mentioned only three times in two prophets. Despite repeated statements that no gods beside YHWH exist, the OT mentions pagan deities in order to contrast certain aspects of Yahweh (cf 1 Cor 8:5–6).

Isaiah, strongly polemical concerning pagan gods and idols generally (cf. Isa 40:18f.; 41:20ff.;

45:20), names Bel and Nebo, both Babylonian deities, and describes them as unable to save their own statues in the hour of disaster.

In a passage that distinguishes most clearly between a god and the representation of him by an image, the writer contrasts the gods whose statues must *be carried,* with God who *carries* his people (Isa 46:1ff). Discussion of pagan deities emphasizes the contrast with YHWH. The statement about the defeat of Bel opens Jeremiah's oracle (Jer 50:2; cf. 51:44) and underscores another theme concerning pagan deities. Here and elsewhere the OT insists that no pagan deities are a match for YHWH; that YHWH is supreme and fully God.

Bibliography: Albright, W. F., "The North-Canaanite Poems of Al 'eyan Ba'al and the 'Gracious Gods'," JPOS 14: 101–40. ———, *Yahweh and the Gods of Canaan,* Doubleday, 1968. Ap-Thomas, D. R., "Elijah on Mount Carmel," PEQ 92: 146–55. Bronner, Leah, *The Stories of Elijah and Elisha as Polemics Against Baal Worship,* Leiden, 1968. Cassuto, U., "Ba'al and Mot in the Texts of Ugarit," BJPES 9: 45–51. ———, "Baal and Mot in the Ugaritic Texts," *Israel Exploration Journal* 12: 77–86. ———, "The Death of Ba'al: Table I *AB from Ras-Shamra," *Tarbiz* 12: 169–80. Dussand, R., "Le vrai nom de Ba'al," Rev Hist Rel 113: 5–20. Eissfeldt, O., "Ba'alshamen u. Jahwe," ZAW 16: 1–31. Mendelsohn, I., "The Family in the Ancient Near East," BA 11: 24–40. Morgenstern, Julian, "The Book of the Covenant, II," HUCA 7: 19–258. ———, "Beena Marriage (Matriarchate) in Ancient Israel and its Historical Implications," ZAW 47: 91–110. Oldenburg, Ulf, *The Conflict Between El and Baal in Canaanite Religion,* Brill, 1969. Pfeiffer, C. F., *Ras Shamra and the Bible,* Baker, 1962. Rainey, Anson F., "Family Relationships in Ugarit," Or 34: 10–22. Richardson, TWB, pp. 138–40. Worden, T., "The Literary Influence of the Ugaritic Fertility Myth on the Old Testament," VT 3: 273–97. Yamauchi, E. M., "Tammuz and the Bible" JBL 84: 283–90. Yaron, Reuven, "Aramaic Marriage Contracts from Elephantine," JSS 3: 1–39. TDOT, II, pp. 181–200. THAT, I, pp. 325–27.

E.A.M.

263 בָּעַר (*bā'ar*) ***I, to burn, consume, be kindled.*** (ASV and RSV similar.)

Derivative

263a †בְּעֵרָה (*bᵉ'ērâ*) ***fire.***

Of the several Hebrew words which are translated "to burn" two are most often used figuratively. These are *bā'ar* and *ḥārâ*. The others, such as *śārap, yāqad,* and *yāṣat* all have to do primarily with literal burning, whereas these two are commonly used to describe anger, passion, intrigue, etc. *ḥārâ* is confined almost totally to usage with anger, while *bā'ar* stresses the consuming and contagious qualities of fire especially in the religious context.

In the derived stems (Piel, Pual, and Hiphil) the root is normally used literally. As might be expected from the nature of the stems, the emphasis is upon "causing to burn," or setting afire (e.g. Ex 22:6 [H 5]). Almost all of these, however, are special cases and have to do with ceremonial burning. So the priests are commanded to burn wood on the altar continually (Lev 6:12 [H 5]; Neh 10:35); the lamps in the sanctuary are to be burning at all times (II Chr 4:20; 13:11). The prototypes of these are the theophanies in which the Lord's appearances are associated with the continuously burning bush (Ex 3:2–3) and the burning on Mt. Sinai (Deut 4:11; 5:23; 9:15), both of which seem to represent the very character of the righteous and purifying God (II Sam 22:9; Isa 10:17; Ezk 1:13; cf. also Isa 33:14; Heb 12:29). Thus *bā'ar* is used with "fire" when it is God's instrument to consume the wicked (Num 11:1; Isa 1:31; 9:18 [H 17]). To be of an alien nature to God is to be as dry tinder before a flame (Isa 10:17). This, the prophets promised, was to be rebellious Israel's experience before a Holy God (Isa 30:27; Jer 7: 20; Ps 83:14 [H 15]; etc.).

The word is also used to describe intense emotions (Ps 39:3 [H 4] Jer 20:9).

bᵉ'ērâ. ***Fire.*** Appears once in Ex 22:6 [H 5] where it is used as a cognate accusative with *bā'ar,* "the one who kindled the fire."

264 בָּעַר (*bā'ar*) ***II, be brutish.*** Denominative verb.

Parent Noun

264a †בְּעִיר (*bᵉ'îr*) ***beasts, cattle.***
264b †בַּעַר (*ba'ar*) ***brutish person.***

The verbal forms of this root may well be denominative from the noun form "beast." In turn, it is tempting to see a connection between that word and the Piel form of *bā'ar* "to graze." However, such a connection must remain highly tenuous. The root seems to contrast man's ability to reason and understand with the beast's inability to do so (Prov 30:2).

bᵉ'îr. ***Beasts, cattle.*** Does not seem to stress the brutish aspect of beasts, but is simply a synonym for *bᵉhēmâ* or *miqneh.*

ba'ar. ***A brutish person.*** Occurs five times in Psalms and Proverbs. Such a person is one who stubbornly refuses to accept God's grace (Ps 73:22). The use of the figure in Prov 30:2 shows Agur's humility.

Bibliography: TDOT, II, pp. 201–204.

J.N.O.

264.1 *בָּעַר (*bāʿar*) ***III, to put away, take away, feed on, waste.*** (ASV similar. RSV translates "purge" in Deut, elsewhere with a variety of words including "consume, destroy, exterminate, devour.")

This root occurs twenty-seven times, twice in the Hiphil and the rest in the Piel stem. Other lexicographers (cf. KB, GB, BDB) assumed that it was a derivative idea from the root meaning "to burn." Such a derivation would be easily understood, especially since *bāʿar* "to burn" seems to stress the consuming aspect of fire. However, most recent studies assume a separate root, especially since *bāʿar* "to burn" has a Piel form meaning "to kindle, set afire."

The most common usage of the word has to do with removing evil or evil influence from the land (20 times, 10 of which are in Deut). If a person has committed some flagrant sin (idolatry, murder, fornication, prostitution, adultery, intranational slavery) not only must he himself be removed, but through his execution the evil which he has set in train must be removed (Deut 13:1–5 [H 2–6]; II Sam 4:11; I Kgs 14:10 etc.). The necessity for this latter is seen in the provision made for purging the evil when a body is found and the murderer is not known (Deut 21:1–9). Evil cannot be explained away nor wished away. It must be dealt with and that in terms of life and death.

J.N.O.

265 *בָּעַת (*bāʿat*) ***to be overtaken by sudden terror, to terrify.*** (Niphal and Piel only.)

Derivatives

265a בְּעָתָה (*be*ʿ*ātâ*) ***terror, dismay.***
265b בִּעוּתִים (*biʿûtîm*) ***terrors, alarms occasioned by God.***

Half of the occurrences (of fifteen) are in poetry. Two synonyms are *pāḥad* "to tremble," and *ḥātat* "to be filled with terror." *bāʿat* is closest to *ḥātat,* though RSV more consistently and appropriately renders *bāʿat* with the stronger term "terrify." ASV occasionally uses "make afraid" (cf. Est 7:6; Job 13:11; 15:24).

Though men may be the occasion of terror (e.g. Est 7:6; cf. Job 13:11), it is primarily Yahweh that strikes terror. David is terrified (*bāʿat*) when confronted with the sword-carrying angel (I Chr 21:30). Saul was terrorized (*bāʿat*) by an evil spirit from Yahweh (I Sam 16:14). Visions, regarded as from God, bring terror, as shown in the account of Eliphaz (Job 4:14ff.) and Job's comment (Job 7:14).

The coming of God, even via the angel Gabriel, strikes terror into the heart of Daniel and this devout servant falls to his face (Dan 8:17). This experience is helpful in understanding the background against which Job makes his request, viz., that God not intimidate (*bāʿat*) him with his power and dread (Job 9:34; 13:21). The wicked have every reason to be terrified because they stretch forth their hand against God (Job 15:24f.).

bāʿat is the reaction of both saint and sinner who experience Yahweh. *bāʿat* underlines the greatness and overpowering aspect of God. Before such a God reverence and awe at the least are demanded.

E.A.M.

בֹּץ (*bōṣ*). See no. 268a.
בִּצָּה (*biṣṣâ*). See no. 268b.
בָּצִיר (*bāṣîr*). See no. 270f.

266 בצל (*bṣl*). **Assumed root of the following.**
266a †בָּצָל (*bāṣāl*) ***onion*** (Num 11:5).

267 בָּצַע (*bāṣaʿ*) ***to cut off, get, gain, be covetous, greedy, finish*** (Piel).

Derivative

267a †בֶּצַע (*beṣaʿ*) ***profit.***

bāṣaʿ and its derivative occur thirty-nine times in the OT. Dalman has argued that it is a technical term used by weavers to designate the action of cutting a piece of cloth free from the loom after it has been woven (cf. also KB). Isaiah 38:12 bears this out when it has Hezekiah contemplating the end of his life in such terms. Job (6:9) also asks that God would cut off his life. This explains the Piel meaning "to complete, finish." However, the more common connotation of the root is based on a slightly different aspect of "cut off." That is to cut off what is not one's own, or in the slang of our day, to take a "rip-off," thus to be greedy, covetous.

The derived uses in the cognate Semitic languages suggest that "to cut," "cut off," was the original meaning.

beṣaʿ. ***Profit, unjust gain, covetousness.*** Personal advantage derived from some activity. Used largely in the negative sense, as in the case of the racketeer who takes his "cut" from the profits of an otherwise legitimate business. In seven occurrences (out of a total of 23) the negative connotation is less apparent. E.g., Reuben queries his brothers as to the "profit" in killing Joseph (Gen 37:26) and Job's comforters argue that it is no *gain* to God even if Job were blameless (Job 22:3), etc. But the predominance of the negative usages indicates that it is very easy for the acquisition of personal gain to become the ruling motive of one's life, obscuring duty, honesty and the rights of others.

The contexts in which *bāṣaʿ* and *beṣaʿ* occur emphasize two points concerning the lust for personal gain. First, it is a special temptation to leaders, and those showing any predilection in that direction should be disqualified (Ex 18:21). The leader who succumbs to this temptation to use his position for his own ends will certainly play his people false (Ezk 22:27). Again and again in the OT, it was the desire of the leaders for personal gain which led Israel into disaster (cf. I Sam 8:3; Isa 56:11; Jer 8:10; 22:17, etc.).

Secondly, lust for personal gain is in direct opposition to unselfish devotion to God (Ps 10:3; 119:36; Isa 33:15) and must inevitably destroy the person who succumbs to it (Prov 1:19; 15:27; Hab 2:9). Perhaps its most disastrous result is its tendency to dull the hearing of God's word (Ezk 33:31).

Bibliography: Dalman, G. H., *Arbeit und Sitte im Palästina,* V, p. 123f. Delling, G., "πλεονέκτης," in TDNT, VI, p. 269f. TDOT, II, pp. 205–208.

J.N.O.

268 בצץ (*bṣṣ*). **Assumed root of the following.**
268a בֹּץ (*bōṣ*) ***mire*** (Jer 38:22).
268b בִּצָּה (*biṣṣâ*) ***swamp*** (Job 8:11; Ezk 47:11).

269 בָּצַק (*bāṣaq*) ***to swell*** (of feet) (ASV, RSV translate similarly.)

Derivative

269a בָּצֵק (*bāṣēq*) ***dough.***

bāṣaq occurs twice (Deut 8:4; Neh 9:21) in parallel passages where God's care of the Israelites during the wilderness period is recounted. Despite all their walking, wandering from place to place, their feet did not even swell nor did their clothes or sandals wear out (Deut 29:5 [H 4]).

J.N.O.

270 בָּצַר (*bāṣar*) ***to gather, restrain, cut off, fence, fortify.*** (ASV similar. RSV translates "fortified" where ASV and KJV read "fenced, walled," etc.)

Derivatives

270a בֶּצֶר (*beṣer*) ***precious ore.***
270b בָּצְרָה (*boṣrâ*) ***enclosure.***
270c בִּצָּרוֹן (*biṣṣārôn*) ***stronghold.***
270d בַּצֹּרֶת (*baṣṣōret*) ***dearth.***
270e בַּצָּרָה (*baṣṣārâ*) ***dearth, destitution.***
270f בָּצִיר (*bāṣîr*) ***vintage.***
270g מִבְצָר (*mibṣār*) ***fortification.***

KB holds that at least three separate but homophonous roots are involved here, one meaning "to gather," another meaning "to reduce" or "humble" (only Ps 76:12 [H 13]; KJV "to cut off"), and yet another having only Niphal and Piel forms, meaning "inaccessible," "impossible." There may be yet a fourth root, meaning "test, assay," as per Ugaritic 2067:3 (UT 19: no. 500; cf. Jer 6:27).

Of the seventy-three occurrences of *bāṣar* and its derivatives, all but eight have to do with fortification (or inaccessibility). Of these eight, seven have to do with the grape harvest. In Jer 6:9; 49:9 and Ob 5 it is indicated that when God in judgment gathers the harvest from Israel his vineyard, there will not even be gleanings left (contra Deut 24:21).

For the most part, the term "fortified (or fenced) city" is utilized as a term of designation, indicating the largest and most important habitation sites (ct. II Kgs 17:9). Such cities were very important strategically since they were almost impregnable until the perfection of siege techniques by the Assyrians (Jer 5:17). This fact was of special significance to the Israelite conquest (cf. Josh 10:20, etc.).

Since fortified cities were so strong, it was a great temptation for the Israelites to put their trust in them instead of in their God. Thus the prophets are at pains to show the folly of such trust (Isa 17:3; Lam 2:5; Hos 10:13–14, etc.). God alone is mankind's stronghold (cf. Ps 27:1, *mā'ôz*).

Bibliography: Dahood, M., *Ugaritic-Hebrew Philology, Biblia et Orientalia,* XVII, Pontifical Biblical Institute, 1965, p. 53.

J.N.O.

בִּצָּרוֹן (*biṣṣārôn*). See no. 270c.
בַּקְבֻּק (*baqbūq*). See no. 273a.
בְּקִיעַ (*b^e qîa'*). See no. 271c.

271 בָּקַע (*bāqa'*) ***to cleave, divide, break through, break up, rip up, tear.*** (ASV and RSV similar.)

Derivatives

271a †בֶּקַע (*beqa'*) ***half shekel.***
271b בִּקְעָה (*biq'â*) ***valley, plain.***
271c בְּקִיעַ (*b^eqîa'*), בָּקִיעַ (*bākîa'*) ***fissure, breach.***

This root with its derivatives appears seventy-three times in the OT. Cognates are found in Ugaritic (*bq'*), Arabic (*faqa'a*) and Ethiopic. The basic idea seems to be "a strenuous cleaving of recalcitrant materials" (Greenfeld, HUCA). As a result of the cleaving, the contents may "burst forth" (cf. Isa 58:8, etc.), but it is clear that this meaning is secondary and not primary as with such roots as פָּצַח (*pāṣaḥ*), or פָּרַץ (*pāraṣ*).

bāqa' is used in five situations, all of which express the forcefulness of the splitting action. Of these, only the first sees the splitting action as coming from within, as in the hatching of eggs (Isa 34:15; 59:5), the splitting of wineskins (Josh 9:4, 13), the dawn rending the heavens (Isa 58:8; cf. Mesha Insc. 1.15), etc.

The second usage expresses the splitting actions encountered in daily life as the splitting of wood (Gen 22:3; I Sam 6:14) or of stones (Ps 141:7).

Thirdly, the word is used with reference to the splitting of the earth. In all cases but I Kgs 1:40, where the splitting is attributed to the noise of jubilation over Solomon's coronation, this is the work of the Lord (Num 16:31, etc.). Two references here are of special importance, for they indicate that the earth will be split upon the return of the Lord (Micah 1:4; Zech 14:4). The creation will not be able to stand when the Creator returns in his glory.

Fourth, *bāqa'* is associated with warfare and violence. It is used several times to express the action of troops in breaking into a city, camp or territory (II Kgs 25:4; II Chr 21: 17; Ezk 30:16). The results of such a conquest were often horrifying. Captives and young children were frequently thrown from high places so that they were "split open" (KJV "dashed to pieces") on the rocks below (II Kgs 8:12; II Chr 25:12). Pregnant women were all too commonly "ripped up" (II Kgs 15:16; Amos 1:13, etc.).

The final usage is associated with water production and behind that lies creation. These creative activities were directly paralleled by God's redemptive actions on behalf of Israel. The One who first cleaved open brooks and springs (Ps 74:15) was able to do it again in the wilderness of Sinai (Ps 78:13; Isa 48:21). The One by whose knowledge the great deeps were first split up (Prov 3:20) (and again in Noah's day [Gen 7:11]) could once again exercise his mastery over the waters by dividing the waters of the Red Sea for his people (Ex 14:16; Isa 63: 12, etc.). In the Akkadian creation epic, Marduk is said to have split the body of Tiamat, the Great Deep, as the basis for creation. Whether some relation exists between the biblical and Akkadian material is difficult to ascertain (cf. Ps 74:12–17; Isa 51:9–11). In any case God's creation was pictured as *ex nihilo* and not as the result of some warfare of the gods. However, the burden of these passages is not simply that God is possessed of such terrible power as to split rocks and waters, etc., but that the possessor of such power is able to redeem a lost creation. Of this the Akkadian knows nothing. See the discussion under *tᵉhôm*, no. 2495a.

beqa'. ***Half-shekel.*** A "cloven" shekel. Appears only in Gen 24:22 and Ex 38:26. It is also to be understood in the weight of Solomon's gold shields (II Chr 9:16) which according to II Kgs 10:17 weighed three minas each (150 shekels, 300 beqas.

biq'â. ***Valley, plain.*** Originally a cleft in the mountains. Thus the plain of Megiddo (Zech 12:11) is that valley which lies between the Carmel range on the south and the highlands of Galilee on the north near the pass of Megiddo through the Carmel range. As such the word is to be distinguished from *'ēmeq* which means simply "low place." Of the twenty occurrences, eleven are used to designate places (as above). The remainder are often paralleled with "mountains," by which contrast, the entirety of the land is indicated (cf. Isa 40:4).

J.N.O.

272 בָּקַק (*bāqaq*) ***I, be luxuriant*** (Hos 10:1).

273 בָּקַק (*bāqaq*) ***II, empty.***

Derivative

273a בַּקְבֻּק (*baqbūq*) ***flask.***

274 *בָּקַר (*bāqar*) ***Seek, inquire*** (only in the Piel stem). (ASV and RSV generally similar except Prov 20:25 where RSV renders "reflect.")

Derivatives

274a †בָּקָר (*bāqār*) ***cattle, herd, ox.***
274b בּוֹקֵר (*bôqēr*) ***herdsman.***
274c †בֹּקֶר (*bōqer*) ***morning.***
274d †בַּקָּרָה (*baqqārâ*) ***a care, concern.***
274e †בִּקֹּרֶת (*biqqōret*) ***compensation.***

bāqar is found seven times. Much more frequent are synonyms *bāqash* "seek," "secure," and *dārash* "seek," "study," "seek (i.e. pray to) a deity."

bāqar, it is suggested, from the Arabic cognate, originally meant "split," "divide" and hence "discern." Its biblical use is largely in worship contexts, e.g. "checking" for ritual purity (Lev 13:36; cf. Lev 27:33) or "inquiry," in the sense of meditation, possibly self-searching (Ps 27:4; cf. II Kgs 16:15). Only in Ezk does *bāqar* refer to search of animals (Ezk 34:11–12).

In the Aramaic, *bᵉqar,* found only in Ezr, refers to "investigation," chiefly of records.

bāqār. ***Cattle, herd, ox.*** (ASV and RSV similar.) *bāqār* (180 times), often used collectively, is doubtfully to be linked with *bāqar* (see above) "to split," more particularly "to plow." It is used in the Mari letters, in Phoenician, Aramaic, and Arabic. Though *bāqār* refers to draught animals such as oxen, the term is used for domestic cattle, including bulls, cows, heifers, and calves. *bāqār* is distinguished from "flock" (*ṣō'n*) which denotes small cattle such as sheep and goats. *ṣō'n* and *bāqār* often denote all domesticated animals. *bᵉhēmâ* also refers to livestock generally including sheep and goats.

For the peoples of the ancient near middle east, including the Hebrews, cattle were a form of wealth. Indeed for the semi-nomadic patriarchs, wealth was measured in cattle. Hamor and Shechem of the hill country had cattle (Gen 34:28) and so did the patriarchs such as Abraham who were rich in cattle (Gen 13:2–7). Isaac was envied by the Philistines for his cattle (Gen 26:12–14). Nathan's parable described the rich man as one who owned *bāqār* (II Sam 12:2; cf. Eccl 2:7). Herds of cattle were a prize in war (Num 31:33; I Sam 27:9). In patriarchal times at least, cattle were given at the time of covenant making (Gen 21:27–31). *bāqār* are to be restored fivefold when stolen (Ex 22:1). Fertility among cattle was obviously important and the Canaanite gods, worshiped as fertility bringers, held an appeal to the Hebrews for that reason. But the Scriptures insist that increase of cattle is due to the Lord's blessing (Gen 24:35; Job 42:12).

As wealth, *bāqār* could be given as gifts (Gen 21:27). As a gesture of generosity Abraham prepared a calf for the angelic messenger (Gen 18:7). Joseph exchanged bread for cattle (Gen 47:17). David had royal herds (I Chr 27:29). *bāqār* were important in stewardship. A tithe of the herd (*bāqār*) was holy to the Lord (Lev 27:32). Of interest are the tallies recorded in Num 7:12ff. For Israel the tithe could hardly be an exclusively private affair about which the community was uninformed. The revival in Hezekiah's time brought a sense of stewardship and the voluntary gifts of *bāqār* (II Chr 31:6).

The existence of a family usually depended on its sheep and cattle. Thus Pharaoh felt secure in letting Israel go if they left their livestock behind (Ex 10:24). As part of the household, they participated in Nineveh's repentance (Jon 3:7) and the servants who tended them are mentioned after the animals (Gen 12:16; 26:14).

bāqār were given in sacrifice by the non-Israelite, Balak (Num 22:40). *bāqār* are designated by God as appropriate for sacrifice primarily no doubt because of the principle that the life of the flesh is in the blood (Lev 17:11), but perhaps also because *bāqār* represent a man's choice possession. Generally offerings were to be from the herd (*bāqār*), or flock (Lev 1:2; cf. Num 15), and for the most part, the animals were to be male, though not always (I Sam 16:2). Sometimes, as at the dedications, both a young bull from the herd (*bāqār*) and a ram from the flock were required (Ex 29:1; Lev 16:3). Burnt offerings for vows and free will offerings (Lev 22:17–19) but also sin offerings (Lev 4:3), required a male animal. The abundance of Solomon's sacrifice of *bāqār* at the temple dedication is a tribute both to his wealth and his piety (I Kgs 8:5, 63). The larger share of such offerings were eaten by the worshipers. The great numbers of sacrifices were commensurate with the crowds of people.

The *bāqār* were used as work animals for the settled farmer (I Sam 11:5; I Kgs 19:19; Job 1:14) and as a source of meat and sour milk (Deut 32:14; Isa 22:13) in all economies in Palestine as early as the late Stone Age (F. S. Bodenheimer, *Animal and Man in Bible Lands*, 1960, p. 36f.). As clean animals (Deut 14:4), they were used for food on special occasions (Gen 18:7; I Kgs 1:9) at the royal court (I Kgs 4:23 [H 5:3]) and in general as a vital food supply (Joel 1:18). It is of some interest that the larger cattle were evidently more used in ancient Palestine than now. Cattle require more pasture and feed than do sheep.

Note should be taken, in keeping with the theology of ecology, of God's concern for animals. The book of Jonah cites God's pity not only for human beings but also for livestock (Jon 4:11). *bāqār* and flocks at Nineveh were involved in the fast proclaimed by the king (Jon 3:7). The coming age of bliss is depicted as one in which there will be a change also in the habits of the animals, for "the lion will eat straw like an ox" (*bāqār*, Isa 11:7; cf. 65:25).

bōqer. ***Morning, dawn.*** (ASV and RSV similar.) Linked with the root *bāqar*, *bōqer* (c. 200 times) denotes the breaking through of the daylight and thus dawn or more usually morning. This noun is peculiar to Hebrew though the assumed root is not.

Frequent in narrative portions of the OT, *bōqer* denotes a time marker as in the expression, "Joshua rose early in the morning" (Josh 3:1). *bōqer*, when combined with evening (*'ereb*) may refer either to a full day (Gen 1:5), or in phrases "from evening to morning" designate night time (Lev 24:3), or "from morning to evening" (daytime; Ex 18:13). Occasionally *bōqer* refers to "the morrow."

In poetry, *bōqer* is more often mentioned than evening (*'ereb*). The voice of the worshiper will be heard in the morning, in praise (Ps 59:16 [H 17]) or in petition (Ps 88:13 [H 14]). The righteous are attentive to God in the morning through prayer and offerings (Ps 5:3 [H 4]); by contrast the wicked are also active but with evil schemes (Mic 2:1; cf. Isa 5:11).

bōqer may denote "early" or "promptly" as in "God will help her right early" (lit. "at the turning of morning," Ps 46:5 [H 6]; cf. Ps 90:14; 101:8), etc. but the case can not be proved. On the other hand in some of these passages *bōqer* may have a latent meaning, "the suitable time of salvation."

baqqārâ. ***Care, concern.*** A verbal form employed to compare God's care in his search for his flock with that of a shepherd (Ezk 34:12).

biqqōret. ***Compensation, scourging(?)*** (ASV "punishment"; RSV "inquiry.") If one may judge from an Akkadian root *baqāru* instead of *bāqar*, compensation is to be paid in a case involving a man and a betrothed, though unmarried, slave girl (Lev 19:20; the only occurrence of the term—see M. Noth, *Leviticus*).

Bibliography: Delekat, L., "Zum Hebräischen Wörterbuch," VT 14: 7–66. TDOT, II, pp. 209–28.

E.A.M.

276 *בָּקַשׁ (*bāqash*) ***to seek, require, desire*** (Piel and Pual only.)

ASV and RSV the same, except at I Sam 20:16 (RSV inferior); Est 2:21 (RSV superior); Dan 1:8 (no preference). Both are inadequate at Zeph 1:6 ("have not sought Jehovah, indeed have not sought him"; cf. Deut 4:29).

Derivative

276a †בַּקָּשָׁה (*baqqāshâ*) ***petition.***

Our root basically connotes a person's earnest seeking of something or someone which exists or is thought to exist. Its intention is that its object be found (*māṣā'*) or acquired (Ex 4:19). The object of this pursuit can be either specified or understood, either concrete or abstract. The specific meaning of *bāqash* is determined by its object in a given context. Unlike *dārash* (q.v.) its nearest synonym the activity of *bāqash* is seldom cognitive (but see Jud 6:29). Other words that are parallel (and hence, synonymous) are *rādap* "to pursue," *shā'al* "to ask," *pāqad* "to visit," *bāḥar* "to choose," etc. Cf. Ugaritic *bqt, UT* 19: no. 505. Phoenician *bqsh,* KAI, p. 5.

The first significant theological theme of *bāqash* is rooted in the concept expressed in Deut 4:29 (cf. Deut 6:6; Mt 22:37; *dārash*) whereby God binds his people to love and serve him as the first principle of their living. Pharoah was unable (or unwilling) to see the relationship between Moses' (Aaron's) request and the fact that its conditions were divinely stipulated (Ex 10:11). Hence, he was willing to let the men go "worship" their God, but considered the rest of their request to be an unwarranted ploy to escape slavery. God's covenants, however, require his people to seek him where and how he stipulates (Ex 33:7; cf. Isa 1:12). This "seeking" ultimately finds its object in the Lord (Ps 24:6; Zeph 1:6) and immediately in his covenantal provisions (Amos 8:12; Ps 34:14 [H 15]), promises (Ezk 7:26) and requirements (Zeph 2:3; Mic 6:8). Since false prophets direct "seekers" away from God (Lev 19:31) depriving them of true life, they are marked for capital punishment (Deut 13:10 [H 11]; cf. Gen 9:5). Israel eventually gave themselves to such false leaders but were repeatedly challenged to seek God wholeheartedly (Jer 29:13; 50:4; Deut 30:1–10). Their feigned pursuit of God (Ezk 7:25; Hos 5:6), his counsel (Ezk 7:26), and his word (Amos 8:12), was in vain since they did not seek him with pure hand (Ps 77:2 [H 3], *ngr*) and a clean heart (Ps 24:6). According to his grace God sought his people in their exile (judgment) reminding them of the ancient promise (Isa 45:19) and awakening them to repentance and restitution (Isa 51:1; 65:1). The NT attests the fullest sense of the preceeding (Rom 9:30; 10:20) when he not only appeared unexpectedly/suddenly in his temple (Mal 3:1; Jn 2:13ff.; Heb 12:22–24; 9:1–28), but resurrected the Gentiles to true life (Zech 8:21–22; Jer 31:31ff.). [Some will also hold that these spiritual fulfilments of the OT promises will be matched by literal fulfilments to Israel as well (Rom 11:26). R.L.H.]

It is noteworthy that Moses, who fled Egypt to escape those who were "justly" seeking to kill him (Ex 3:15; 4:19), had a confrontation with God whereby he sought his life (Ex 4:24). So, covenantal disobedience (Moses had not circumcised his son) deserved the death penalty, and the teaching also is (probably) that to exclude one's children from the covenant is tantamount to murder (cf. Gen 9:5). The idea of God "seeking" (requiring) one's life because of covenantal violation applies both to covenants God makes with man (e.g. creational covenant of life, Gen 9:5; the Mosaic covenant, Ezk 3:18, 20), and covenants sanctioned by God (I Sam 20:16; II Sam 4:11).

baqqāshâ. ***Petition, request.*** (ASV, RSV similar.) Our noun, modelled on a Pael infinitive (Aramaic), is a technical term (frequently synonymously parallel to *sh^e'ēlâ*) denoting a petition or request by a subject to a king that he grant a specific desire. It occurs seven times.

Bibliography: Sellers, O. R., "Seeking Good in the Old Testament," JBR 21: 234–37. TDOT, II, pp. 229–41. THAT, I, pp. 333–35.

L.J.C.

277 בַּר (*bar*) ***I, son.*** (ASV and RSV similar.)

The common Aramaic noun meaning "son" (Ezr 5:1; Dan 3:25; etc.). Occurs only three times without question in the Hebrew OT, the more common word being *bēn* (q.v.). Three of the occurrences are in one verse, Prov 31:2, which forms the introduction to the instruction of Lemuel. Typical of such literature, the instruction is addressed from a father to a son (cf. Prov 1:8; 2:1, etc.).

The final occurrence is much more problematic. It is found in Ps 2:12, "kiss the son lest he be angry." This has been taken to be a reference to Christ since earliest Christian times. However, with the exception of Syriac, none of the ancient versions contain the reading (e.g. LXX "accept correction"). Yet there is little agreement among the versions on the basis of which to reconstruct a Hebrew text, nor have any variants come to light at Qumran.

Secondly, it has been argued that since *bēn* appears in verse 7, *bar* in verse 12 must be a corruption. This assumes however that *bēn* and *bar* were never contemporary, one always having been used to the exclusion of the other. This assumes too much, given numerous uncertainties in our knowledge of the spread and usage of Aramaic.

The reading remains problematic, but until solid textual evidence comes to light, emendation is an unwarranted expedient. If the reading is accepted, the action involved probably is kissing the feet of the son, an act of homage well-attested in Babylonian and Egyptian sources.

Bibliography: Barnes, W. E., "The Psalms," I, in *Westminster Commentaries,* ed. W. Lock and D. C. Simpson, London: Methuen, 1931, p. 11f. Bertholet, A., "Eine Crux Interpretum," ZAW 28: 58–59 (cf. also p. 193). Briggs, C. A., "Psalms," I, in ICC, p. 23f. Dahood, M., "Psalms, 1–50," in AB, p. 13f. TDNT, VIII, pp. 340–62. TDOT, II, pp. 308–12.

J.N.O.

בַּר (*bar*) II, III. See nos. 288a,b.
בֹּר (*bōr*) I, II. See no. 288c,d.
בָּר (*bār*). See no. 288f.

278 בָּרָא (*bārā'*) ***I, create, make, Creator*** (Qal); ***choose, cut down, dispatch,*** (Piel); ***be created, be done*** (Niphal; RSV "yet unborn" in Ps 102:18 [H 19]; "clear ground" in Josh 17:15, 18; RSV and ASV "mark" in Ezk 21:19 [H 24]).

Derivative

278a †בְּרִיאָה (*b^erî'â*) ***new thing.***

The root *bārā'* has the basic meaning "to create." It differs from *yāṣar* "to fashion" in that the latter primarily emphasizes the shaping of an object while *bārā'* emphasizes the initiation of the object.

The question of the meaning of the root *bārā'* is complicated by its connotation in the Piel of "cut down" (Josh 17:15, 18; Ezk 23:47). This meaning may also obtain in the use of the word in Ezk 21:19 [H 24] where it need not connote carving a signpost, but simply the act of cutting down a branch or sapling as a marker). If this meaning attests to the concrete form of the Qal, the word may have meant "to form," "to fashion" in the sense of carving or cutting out. But it is possible that the Piel form may represent an entirely different root. KB (2d ed.) posits a second root used in the Piel meaning "to cut down." THOT (in loc.) follows KB (3d ed.) that there is one root with the basic meaning "separate," "divide." This would explain the usages of the Piel, but, as is often the case, is not decisive for the nuance of the meaning "create" in the Qal. And, since the word is used in such a distinctive sense in the Qal it is best to consider the meaning of the root solely on the basis of usage.

The word is used in the Qal only of God's activity and is thus a purely theological term. This distinctive use of the word is especially appropriate to the concept of creation by divine fiat.

The root *bārā'* denotes the concept of "initiating something new" in a number of passages. In Isa 41:20 it is used of the changes that will take place in the Restoration when God effects that which is new and different. It is used of the creation of new things (*ḥădāshôt*) in Isa 48:6–7 and the creation of the new heavens and the new earth (Isa 65:17). Marvels never seen before are described by this word (Ex 34:10), and Jeremiah uses the term of a fundamental change that will take place in the natural order (Jer 31:22). The Psalmist prayed that God would create in him a clean heart (Psa 51:10 [H 12]) and coupled this with the petition that God would put a new spirit within him (See also Num 16:30; Isa 4:5; 65:18).

The word also possesses the meaning of "bringing into existence" in several passages (Isa 43:1; Ezk 21: 30 [H 35]; 28:13, 15).

It is not surprising that this word with its distinctive emphases is used most frequently to describe the creation of the universe and the natural phenomena (Gen 1:1, 21, 27; 2:3, etc.). The usages of the term in this sense present a clearly defined theology. The magnitude of God's power is exemplified in creation. This has implications for the weak (Isa 40:26; cf. vv. 27–31) and for the unfolding of God's purposes in history (Isa 42:5; 45:12). Creation displays the majesty (Amos 4:13), orderliness (Isa 45:18), and sovereignty (Ps 89:12 [H 13]) of God. Anthropologically, the common creation of man forms a plea for unity in Mal 2:10. And man is seen as created for vanity in Ps 89:47 [H 48].

THOT argues that this word is used only in the P document and other late literature. Of course this view can only be sustained by dividing and post-dating the documents.

The limitation of this word to divine activity indicates that the area of meaning delineated by the root falls outside the sphere of human ability. Since the word never occurs with the object of the material, and since the primary emphasis of the word is on the newness of the created object, the word lends itself well to the concept of creation *ex nihilo,* although that concept is not necessarily inherent within the meaning of the word.

b^erî'â. ***New thing*** (RSV "something new"). The word connotes something new or extraordinary

(Num 16:30). It thus reflects a basic connotation of the root *bārā’* (Ex 34:10; Isa 48:6; Jer 31:22).

Bibliography: Anderson, Bernhard W., "The Earth is the Lord's," Interp 9: 3–20. Arbez, Edward P. and Weisengoff, John P., "Exegetical Notes on Genesis 1:1–2," CBQ 10: 140–50. Hanson, Howard E., "Num. XVI 30 and the Meaning of Bara'," VT 22: 353– 9. Knight, Harold, "The Old Testament Conception of Miracle," SJT 5: 355–61. Lane, William R., "The Initiation of Creation," VT 13: 63–73. Stuhmueller, Carroll, "The Theology of Creation in Second Isaias," CBQ 21: 429–67. Unger, Merrill F., "The Old Testament Revelation of the Creation of Angels and the Earth," BS 114: 206–12. TDNT, III, pp. 1005–28. TDOT, II, pp. 242–48. THAT, I, pp. 336–38.

T.E.M.

279 בָּרָא (*bārā’*) ***II, be fat.***

Derivative

279a †בָּרִיא (*bārî’*) ***fat, fatter, fed, firm, plenteous, rank.***

This word occurs with its basic connotation "fat" in Jud 3:17. While always retaining this original connotation it occurs with various nuances. It is used to describe healthy human beings (Dan 1:15), animals (Gen 41:2), and vegetation (Gen 41:5). It is used of the best portion of edible meats (Ezk 34:3) and also bears the secondary connotation of prosperity (Ps 73:4; Hab 1:16).

T.E.M.

בַּרְבֻּרִים (*barbūrîm*). See no. 288g.

280 בָּרַד (*bārad*) ***to hail.*** Probably a denominative verb.

Parent Noun

280a †בָּרָד (*bārād*) ***hail.***

Derivative

280b בָּרֹד (*bārōd*) ***spotted, marked.***

bārad is used as a verb in the Qal once (Isa 32:19).

bārād. ***Hail.*** Occurs twenty-nine times, of which twenty-two are in connection with the sixth plague in Egypt (Ex 9:18–33; Ps 18:13–14, etc.). Elsewhere, it is used either figuratively to describe destructive force, especially that coming upon disobedient Israel (Isa 28:2), or literally as a manifestation of God's power and glory (Ps 148:8).

J.N.O.

281 בָּרָה (*bārâ*) ***I, to eat.***

Derivatives

281a בִּרְיָה (*biryâ*) ***food*** (II Sam 13:5, 7, 10; Ezk 34:20).

281b בָּרוּת (*bārût*) ***food*** (Ps 69:22).

282 ברה (*brh*) **II. Assumed root of the following.**

282a †בְּרִית (*b^e^rit*) ***covenant*** (ASV and RSV); between nations: a treaty, alliance of friendship; between individuals: a pledge or agreement; with obligation between a monarch and subjects: a constitution; between God and man: a covenant accompanied by signs, sacrifices, and a solemn oath that sealed the relationship with promises of blessing for keeping the covenant and curses for breaking it.

The etymology of the word is uncertain. It may be related to the Akkadian word *burru* which means "to establish a legal situation by testimony with an oath" (CAD *baru,* p. 125); but some (O. Loretz, VT 16: 239–41) tie it to the Akkadian word *birtu* "a fetter" which is a derivative of the word meaning "between." L. Köhler claims the word was related to the root *brh* which has to do with the food and eating involved in the covenant meal (JSS 1: 4–7). The root is nowhere used as a verb in the OT nor is any other derivative of this root used, but the action involving covenant making employs the idiom "to cut a covenant" (Gen 15:18, etc.), that is making a bloody sacrifice as part of the covenant ritual. Köhler then would have the animal eaten in the covenant meal.

The covenant as a treaty or agreement between nations or individuals should be understood on the basis of whether the parties are equal or one is superior to the other. In Gen 14:13 Abraham and the Amorites were equal parties to a treaty but this is not true of Israel (under Joshua) and the Gibeonites (Josh 9). Here the oath aspect of the covenant is shown to be most important. Even though the Gibeonite vassals were subject to a curse for having lied (9:22–23), Joshua and Israel were still obligated to provide protection for them. Much later when Saul failed in this sworn covenant obligation, his family suffered punishment (II Sam 21).

It was common practice to set up a stela (stone) as a sign that a treaty had been established between two households or nations (cf. Jacob and Laban, Gen 31:44–47). On both sides appeal is made to the deity as a witness showing that the covenant is unalterable. Moreover, as in the case at Sinai, Jacob and Laban offered a sacrifice in the mountain and shared a common meal (Gen 31:54–55). Other signs which sealed such a treaty were used, such as a marriage between two royal houses (I Kgs 9:16). But the greatest tool for covenant making came to be the written document on which the words of the covenant, its terms in the form of promises and stipulations, were spelled out, witnes ed to, signed and sealed. Such covenant documents abound (cf. D. R. Hillers, *Covenant: The History of a Biblical Idea,* Baltimore, 1969). Behm concludes: "There is no firmer guarantee of legal security peace or personal loyalty than the covenant" (TDNT, II, p. 115; cf. Amos 1:9).

Apart from blood ties the covenant was the way people of the ancient world formed wider relationships with each other (*Treaty and Covenant,* D. J. McCarthy, Rome, 1963, p. 175). The accounts of the relationship between David and Jonathan are the only unequivocal mention of a compact between two individuals in the OT (I Sam 18:3; 20:8; 23:18). It is spoken of as "a covenant of the Lord" because the Lord witnessed the transaction and protected the legal order.

In Israel's monarchy the covenant relationship between the people and the king provided a kind of limited constitutional monarchy which was unique in the world in that early age (II Sam 3:21; 5:3; I Chr 11:3).

All of this covenant procedure provides the cultural setting in which God's relationship with his people is formulated. Modern studies on the meaning and the form of "covenant" in biblical theology have been vigorous since the appearance of George Mendenhall's *Law and Covenant in Israel and the Ancient Near East* (Pittsburgh, 1955; see also BA 17: 27–46, 49–76 and *Old Testament Covenant: A Survey of Current Opinions,* D. J. McCarthy, Richmond, 1972). McCarthy includes an excellent bibliography of covenant studies, pp. 90–108. For an evangelical theological treatment of this subject based on the source materials see the volumes entitled *Treaty of the Great King* (Grand Rapids, 1963) and *By Oath Consigned* (Grand Rapids, 1967) by M. G. Kline. Here Kline shows the suzerainty treaty found in the ancient near east is the key to understanding the form of God's covenant with ancient Israel. He maintains the Ten Commandments and the entire book of Deuteronomy and such sections as Joshua 24 are all based on a covenant pattern which has: 1. A preamble in which the suzerain is identified, 2. An historical prologue describing previous relations between the parties, 3. Stipulations and demands of the suzerain, 4. Swearing of allegiance with curses and blessings, that is Covenant Ratification, 5. Witnesses and directions for carrying out the treaty (*see Treaty of the Great King,* pp. 14, 28). In addition to the stipulations there may be a clause providing for the preservation and regular re-reading of the covenant.

The notion that a covenant between God and man did not exist in the formative stages of Israelite history as presented in Genesis and Exodus cannot be taken seriously any longer. Yahweh as a tribal deity in early Israel bound to his people by natural but not ethical ties, as a covenant relationship implies, is also a fading viewpoint.

D. J. McCarthy warns that the covenant concept in the OT presents a very rich and complex tradition and that the covenant is not primarily legalistic or moralistic but cultic, that is, tied to religious practice. He sees other analogies besides the treaty form as important, especially the family analogy—the father and son relationship in the Davidic Covenant (II Sam 7) and the husband and wife relationship as in Hosea. Covenant theology which puts all biblical revelation in the covenant framework now has the support of OT specialists like W. Eichrodt who make the covenant concept the central and unifying theme of the OT (*Theology of the Old Testament,* London, 1967, cf. also J. Barton Payne, *The Theology of the Older Testament*). Eichrodt finds that the covenant concept proves Israel's religion was historical, that is, not the imagination of later generations. It also gave Israel great assurance of a beneficent God at a time when the deities were considered arbitrary originators of evil. Some scholars hold that the *bᵉrît* was sometimes monergistic, that is a one-sided unconditional promise. This view is opposed by Eichrodt and Kline, although espoused by J. Begrich, ZAW 60: 1–11 and Murray, *The Covenant of Grace,* London, 1954. Kline maintains that all divine-human covenants in the OT involve sanction-sealed commitment to obey. The law and promise aspects of God's covenant relationship with his people do not violate each other. Deuteronomy 29:13–14 shows the Sinaitic Covenant was an extension of the Abrahamic Covenant, both of which are called here "a sworn covenant." The Sinai renewal merely stressed man's responsibility where the Abrahamic Covenant emphasized God's promise. Many agree with Hillers (*Covenant,* pp. 129–31) that the covenant (treaty) tradition is carried into the writings of the prophets in the so-called lawsuit (*rîb*) pattern. The prophets indict the people as covenant breakers, sometimes relating this to the covenant pattern by calling heaven and earth to witness (cf. Isa 1:2–3, 10–20; Jer 2:4–12; Mic 6:1–8; Ps 50).

The Priestly Covenant of Num 25:12–13, the Davidic Covenant of II Sam 7 and the New Covenant of Jer 31:31 are all administrative aspects of the same covenant, God's Covenant of Grace. This covenant reaches its climax at the Incarnation where Christ representing his people fulfilled all the stipulations of the covenant and bore the curse they deserved for breaking it (cf. F. C. Fensham, "Covenant, Promise and Expectation in the Bible," *Theologische Zeitschrift* 23:305–22).

Bibliography: Albright, W. F., "The Hebrew Expression for 'Making a Covenant' in Pre-Israelite Documents," BASOR 121:21–22. Begrich, J., "Berith. Ein Beitrag zur Erfassung einer alt. Denkform," ZAW 60: 1–11. Braulik, Georg, "Die Ausdrücke für 'Gesetz' im Buch Deuteronomium," Bib 51: 39–66. Brown, P. E., "The Basis of Hope," Interp 9: 35–40. Buis, Pierre, "Les Formulaires D'Alliance," VT 16: 396–411. Campbell, K. M. "Rahab's Covenant," VT 22: 243–44. Delcor, M., "Les Attaches Litteraires, l'Origine et la Signification de l'Expression Biblique 'Prendre a Temoin le Ciel et la Terre'," VT 16: 8–25. Coppens, J., "La Nouvelle Alliance en Jer 31, 31–34," CBQ 25: 12–21. Eichrodt, Walther, "Covenant and Law," Interp 20: 302–21. Fensham, F. Charles, "Clauses of Protection in Hittite Vassal-Treaties and the Old Testament," VT 13: 133–43. ______, "The Covenant as Giving Expression to the Relationship Between Old and New Testament," *Tyndale Bulletin* 22: 82–94. ______, "Did a Treaty Between the Israelites and the Kenites Exist?" BASOR 175: 51–54. ______, "The Treaty Between Israel and the Gibeonites," BA 27: 96–100. ______, "The Treaty Between the Israelites and the Tyrians," Supp VT 17: 70–87. Freedman, David Noel, "Divine Commitment and Human Obligation," Interp 18: 419–31. Frankana, R., "The Vassal-Treaties of Esarhaddon and the Dating of Deuteronomy," OTS 14: 122–54. Gerstenberger, Erhard, "Covenant and Commandment," JBL 84: 38–51. Hillers, Delbert R., "A Note on Some Treaty Teminology in the Old Testament," BASOR 176: 46–47. Kevan, E. F., "The Covenants and the Interpretation of the Old Testament," EQ 26: 19–28. Kitchen, K. A. *The Bible in its World,* Patermoster, 1977, esp. "The Covenant at Sinai and in Moab," pp. 79–85. Kline, Meredith G., "Dynastic Covenant," WJT 23: 1–15. Kutsch, Ernest, "Gesetz und Gnade," ZAW 79: 18–35. L'Hour, Jean, "L'Alliance de Sichem," RB 69: 5–36, 161–84, 350–68. Lang, G. H., "God's Covenants are Conditional," EQ 30: 86–97. Lincoln, C. F., "The Development of the Covenant Theory," BS 100: 134–63. ______, "The Biblical Covenants," BS 100: 309–23, 442–49, 565–73. McCarthy, Dennis J., "Berit and Covenant in the Deuteronomistic History," Supp VT 23: 65–85. ______, "Covenant in the Old Testament: The Present State of Inquiry," CBQ 27: 217–40. ______, "Hosea XII 2: Covenant by Oil," VT 14: 214–21. ______, "Three Covenants in Genesis," CBQ 26: 179–89. Mendenhall, G. E., "Covenant Forms in Israelite Tradition," BA 17: 50–76. Mitchell, John J., "Abram's Understanding of the Lord's Covenant," WTJ 32: 24–48. Muilenburg, James, "The Form and Structure of the Covenantal Formulations," VT 9: 374–67. Rand, James Freeman, "Old Testament Fellowship with God," BS 108: 227–36, 323–33; 109: 47–54, 151–63, 226–38. Robinson, T. H., "'Covenant' in the O.T.," Exp T 53: 298–99. Rogers, Cleon L. Jr., "The Covenant with Abraham and its Historical Setting," BS 127: 241–56. Rowley, H. H., "Moses and the Decalogue," BJRL 34: 81–118. Silving, Helen, "The State Contract in the Old Testament," JR 24: 17–32. Theil, Wilfried, "Sefer Berit," VT 20: 214–29. Thompson, J. A., The Significance of the Ancient Near Eastern Treaty Pattern," *Tyndale House Bulletin* 13: 1–6. Tsevat, M., "The Neo-Assyrian and Neo-Babylonian Vassal Oaths and the Prophet Ezekiel," JBL 78: 199–204. Tucker, Gene M., "Covenant Forms and Contract Forms," VT 15: 487–503. Van der Ploeg, J., "Studies in Hebrew Law," CBQ 12: 248–59. Weinfeld, M., "Covenant Terminology in the Ancient Near East and its Influence on the West, JAOS 93: 190–99. ______, "The Covenant of Grant in the Old Testament and in the Ancient Near East," JAOS 90: 184–203. ______, "Traces of Assyrian Treaty Formulae in Deuteronomy," Bib 56: 417–27. Whiteley, C. F., "Covenant and Commandment in Israel," JNES 22: 37–48. Widengren, George, "King and Covenant," JSS 2: 1–32. TDNT, II, 106–24, 126–29. TDOT II, pp. 253–78. THAT, I, pp. 339–52.

E.B.S.

בְּרוֹשׁ (*b^{e}rôsh*). See no. 289a.
בָּרוּת (*bārût*). See no. 281b.

283 ברז (*brz*). **Assumed root of the following.**
283a †בַּרְזֶל (*barzel*) ***iron.***

A loan word from Sumerian *BAR.ZIL via* Akkadian *parzillum* or possibly from Hittite. The use of terrestrial iron (as opposed to meteorite iron which has a different nickel content) has now been attested in the third and fifth millennia B.C. Thus it appears legitimately in Gen 4:22. The wide use of iron, the Early Iron Age, in Palestine evidently coincided with the coming of the Philistines about 1200 B.C. Their military successes were doubtless due in part to "the Philistine iron monopoly" (Albright, W. F., *Archaeology of Palestine,* Penguin, 1960, p. 110). This apparently was due to their use of iron tempering which they kept as a military secret from the Hebrews (I Sam 13:19). In twenty of the seventy-five occurrences of iron it is used in a figurative sense, usually in construct with other nouns to denote affliction (Deut 4:20; I Kgs 8:51; Jer 11:4), slavery (Deut 28:48; Jer 28:14), barrenness (Deut 28:23), and obstinacy (Isa 48:4).

Bibliography: Mellaart, J., *Anatolian Studies* 14: 111, 114. Kaiser, W. C., "The Literary Form of Genesis I–XI," in *New Perspectives on the OT,* ed. J. Barton Payne, Word, 1970, p. 55, nn. 30–33. Wright, G. E., "Iron in Israel," BA 1:5–8.

W.C.K.

284 בָּרַח (*bāraḥ*) ***flee, run away, chase, drive away, put to flight, reach, shoot (extend), hurry away.***

Derivatives

284a †בָּרִיחַ (*bārîaḥ*) ***fleeing.***
284b †בְּרִיחַ (*b^e rîaḥ*) ***bar.***
284c מִבְרָח (*mibraḥ*) ***fugitive.***

Basically *bāraḥ* means to go or pass through, and to flee or hurry. It occurs mostly in narratives, referring to flight from an enemy.

[In Phoenician-Punic, Donner and Röllig interpret a root *brḥ* to mean "to flee" or "to lose," while Cyrus Gordon proposes "to control, rule over." For Ugaritic and Hebrew, Gordon UT 19: nos. 514–516 proposes three homophonous roots: *brḥ* I, "to flee," *brḥ* II "evil" (= *bārîaḥ* in Isa 27:1; cf. Arabic *barḥ* "evil"), and *brḥ* III "shaft, bar" (= *bārîaḥ* in Jon 2:7). Although Gordon's analysis is contested, as seen below, it is obvious that more than one Semitic root may be behind the verbal, adjectival and nominal forms discussed in this entry. B.K.W.]

Almost all sixty-six uses of the verb refer to fleeing from an enemy, enemies, or a place. The first exodus is described as a "flight" from Egypt (Ex 24:5). Perhaps Isaiah's command to the exiles "to flee" Babylon (48:20) was a rhetorical device to arouse the exiles to the new miraculous opportunity to go home and rebuild Jerusalem. In some instances the flight is to a person or place (e.g. I Sam 22:20).

The verb has its basic meaning of "going through" in Ex 26:28; 36:33 where the middle bar holding together the boards of the walls of the tabernacle extend through the boards the length of the wall.

The causative form of the verb describes driving the residents of Gath out of their city (I Chr 8:13), the people of southern Palestine out of their valleys (I Chr 12:16), Nehemiah's driving away a son-in-law of Sanballat (Neh 13:28), leviathan who cannot be driven away by arrows, and a shameful son driving away his mother (Prov 19:26).

bāraḥ is used synonymously with *hālak* "go" (Ps 139:7), *mālaṭ* "escape" (I Sam 19:12, 18) and *nûs* "flee" (Jud 9:21).

bārîaḥ. Possibly an adjective meaning "fleeing," "crooked" or "piercing." In Isa 43:14 as a substantive it has been variously translated: nobles, KJV; the bars, RSV, NAB; prison bars, JB; and as they flee, NEB. It is used to describe a serpent in Job 26:13 as "crooked" KJV; "fleeing" RSV, JB; "fugitive" NAB; and "twisting" NEB. But in Isa 27, KJV translates *bārîaḥ* "piercing" and *ʿăqallātôn* as "crooked," while others translate *bārîaḥ* here as "fleeing" or "twisting."

[The passage in Isa 27:1 has a close parallel in Ugaritic (67 I:1–2) where it is applied to a "fleeing: serpent *ltn* (see discussion under *liw^e yatan*). Gordon (UT 19: no. 595) holds that there is a *baraḥ* II meaning "be evil," because of an Arabic root, but others question this, pointing out that the context of the Ugaritic reference is also unclear (L. Fisher, *Ras Shamra Parallels,* I, p. 36). The biblical authors use the name Rahab as a symbol for Egypt (Job 26:12 RSV; Ps 87:4; Isa 30:7, NIV), Leviathan may sometimes be so used. It seems to be the same as *ltn* with different vowels. It was some kind of serpent and obviously evil. Either adjective "fleeing" or "evil" would be applicable, but the meaning "fleeing" in Job 26:13 and Isa 27:1 seems satisfactory.

In Job 26:13 Gameroni (TDOT, II, p. 252) thinks it means a constellation presumably because of the parallel and a root *brḫ* in Akkadian meaning "to shine, to be radiant" and sometimes used with the determinative for star (CAD, II. 101). His suggestion, however is difficult to fit into the immediate clause. B.K.W.]

b^e rîaḥ. ***Bar, something thrust through.*** Refers to the bars which hold together the upright boards forming the walls of the tabernacle (Ex 26:26,27,28,29; 35:11; 36:31,32,33,34; 39:33; 40:18; Num 3:36; 4:31), and the bars to strengthen and lock city gates. The bars for the boards of the tabernacle were five on each side, set in gold rings and overlaid with gold.

The bars for the city gates were doubtless mostly timbers, though some are mentioned as bronze and others as iron. They invariably refer to cities as strongly defended or enclosed or lacking such defense if they are absent. When Jerusalem is destroyed her bars are broken (Lam 2:9) and when restored her gates are rebuilt with bars (Ps 147:13; Neh 3:3, 6, 13, 14, 15).

The bars of city gates are used figuratively for the stability of the earth (Job 38:10; Jon 2:7) or stubbornness (Prov 18:19). In Isa 15:5 some grammarians and commentators translate *b^e rîaḥ* either as fugitives or in Isa 15:5; Amos 1:5 NEB as nobles or great men.

mibraḥ. A masculine noun meaning "flight" or "fugitive" (Ezk 17:21) and so in KJV, but from contextual notions, NAB has "crack."

Bibliography: Rabin, C., "Bari^a h," JTS 47: 38–41. TDOT, II, pp. 249–52.

E.S.K.

בָּרִיא (*bārîʾ*). See no. 279a.
בְּרִיאָה (*b^e rîʾâ*). See no. 278a.
בִּרְיָה (*biryâ*). See no. 281a.

בָּרִיחַ (*bārîaḥ*). See no. 284a.
בְּרִיחַ (*berîaḥ*). See nos. 294a,b.
בְּרִית (*berît*). See no. 282a.
בֹּרִית (*bōrît*). See no. 288d.

285 בָּרַךְ (*bārak*) ***to kneel, bless, praise, salute, curse*** (used euphemistically). (ASV and RSV similar.)

Derivatives

285a †בֶּרֶךְ (*berek*) ***knee.***
285b †בְּרָכָה (*berākâ*) ***blessing.***
285c בְּרֵכָה (*berēkâ*) ***pool, pond.***

This root and its derivatives occur 415 times. The majority are in the Piel stem (214) which is translated "to bless." The Qal passive participle "blessed" occurs sixty-one times. The meaning "to kneel" appears only three times, twice in the Qal (II Chr 6:13; Ps 95:6) and once in Hiphil (Gen 24:11). On this basis some argue that *bārak* "to kneel" is a denominative verb from *berek* "knee" and is unrelated to *bārak* "to bless." However, there may have been a felt association between kneeling and the receiving of a blessing (cf. II Chr 6:13, also Arabic *baraka,* which shows the same range of meaning). To bless in the OT means "to endue with power for success, prosperity, fecundity, longevity, etc." It is frequently contrasted with *qālal* "to esteem lightly, curse" (cf. Deut 30: 1, 19).

berek. ***Knee.*** Used in relation to submission and obedience (Isa 45:23), fear and weakness (Nah 2:10 [H 11]), prayer (I Kgs 8:54), motherly care (the lap) (II Kgs 4:20), etc.

The great formula of blessing, the Aaronic benediction still used on some occasions in churches today, was primarily a prayer for the Lord's presence, grace, and keeping power. It was summed up in the expression "they shall put my name upon the children of Israel," i.e. God himself would be their God (Num 6:23–27).

In general, the blessing is transmitted from the greater to the lesser. This might involve father to son (Gen 49), brothers to sister (Gen 24:60), king to subjects (I Kgs 8:14). The blessing might be conveyed at departures on special occasions (II Chr 6:3) or upon introduction (Gen 47:7, 10). Its major function seems to have been to confer abundant and effective life upon something (Gen 2:3; I Sam 9:13; Isa 66:3) or someone (Gen 27:27f.; Gen 49). (In this respect, notice that Michal, despising her husband's blessing, was afflicted with barrenness, II Sam 6:20–23). It could, however, become merely a form. This was especially true of the greeting (I Sam 13:10; 25:14; Ps 118:26).

The verbal blessing, as just discussed, was normally futuristic. However, it could be descriptive, an acknowledgement that the person addressed was evidently possessed of this power for abundant and effective living (Gen 14:19; I Sam 26:25, etc.). This address becomes a formalized means of expressing thanks and praise to this person because he has given out of the abundance of his life. Very commonly, the Lord is addressed in this way. It is significant that *ḥesed* "kindness" and *'ĕmet* "faithfulness" are very frequently those attributes for which God is praised (e.g. Ps 31:21 [H 22]; 106:48). It is clear that for the OT the abundant life rests directly upon the loving and faithful nature of God.

Whatever may have been the ancient near eastern conception of the source of blessing, the OT sees God as the only source. As such he controls blessing and cursing (Num 22f.). His presence confers blessing (II Sam 6:11–20), and it is only in his name that others can confer blessing (Deut 10:8, etc.). Indeed, God's name, the manifestation of his personal, redemptive, covenant-keeping nature, is at the heart of all blessing.

As a result, those who are wrongly related to God can neither bless (Mal 2:2) nor be blessed (Deut 28) and no efficacious word can alter this. Those who are blessed manifest God's *ḥesed* and *'ĕmet* (Deut 15:14; I Sam 23:21; I Kgs 10:9; etc.). To rely upon the existence of the covenant between oneself and God without manifesting his nature is to bless oneself and to court disaster (Deut 29:18f.).

The transposition of blessing and cursing with life and death in Deut 30:19 and elsewhere reaches the heart of the OT concept of blessing. From Adam mankind has been under the curse of death, in all his works, in all his relationships. The power to beget life was understood by even the pagan to be a supernatural blessing (cf. Ug. 128:III:17; II Aq I:35; etc.). God demonstrates from Gen 12 onward that he alone has power to bestow this blessing. In the patriarchal narratives, blessing is linked very specifically to reproductive powers. The lesson is clear. God gives life. Neither god, nor man, nor rite can do so. Nor does God have to be cajoled to give his blessing. He wishes to give it to all who will trust him (Gen 12:3). From this base the understanding of God as the lifegiver is expanded to its ultimate expression in Jn 3:16f.; 10:10; etc.

berākâ. ***Blessing.*** Either the verbal enduement with good things or a collective expression for the good things themselves (Ezk 34:26; Mal 3:10, etc.). Sixty-seven occurrences.

Bibliography: Eichrodt, W., *Theology of the Old Testament,* II, tr. J. A. Baker, Westminster, 1967, pp. 349–51, etc. Guillet, J., "Le language spontané de la bénédiction dans l'Ancien Testament," *Recherches de science religieuse* 57: 163–204. Hempel, J., "Die israelitische

Anschauungen von Segen und Fluch im Lichte altorientalischer Parallelen," *Zeitschrift der Deutschen Morgenländischen Gesellschaft,* 79: 20–110. Mowinckel, S., *Psalmenstudien,* V, Amsterdam: Schippers, 1961. ———, *The Psalms in Israel's Worship,* II, tr. D. R. Ap-Thomas, Oxford: Blackwell, 1962, pp. 44–51. Murtonen, A., "The Use and Meaning of the Words lebārek and berākāh in the Old Testament," VT 9: 158–77. Pedersen, J., *Israel, its Life and Culture,* I–II, London: Oxford, 1926. Richardson, TWB, p. 33. Scharbert, J., "'Fluchen' und 'Segnen' im Alten Testament," Biblica 39: 1–26. "Die Geschichte der bāruk Formel," *Biblisches Zeitschrift* 17: 1–28. Towner, W. S., "'Blessed be Yahweh' and 'Blessed Art Thou, Yahweh'-The Modulation of a Biblical Formula," CBQ 30: 386–99. Westermann, C., *Der Segnen in der Bibel und im Handeln der Kirche,* Münich: Kaiser, 1968. TDNT, II, pp. 755–61. TDOT, II, pp. 279–307. THAT, I, pp. 353–75.

J.N.O.

286 ברם (*brm*). **Assumed root of the following.**
286a בְּרֹמִים (*b^{e}rōmîm*) ***variegated cloth*** (Ezk 27:24).

287 בָּרַק (*bāraq*) ***cast forth*** (lightning).

Derivatives

287a †בָּרָק (*bārāq*) ***I, lightning.***
287b †בָּרָק (*bārāq*) ***II, Barak.***
287c †בָּרֶקֶת (*bareqet*) ***a gem.***
287d †בָּרְקַת (*bār^{e}qat*) ***a gem.***
287e בַּרְקָנִים (*barqānîm*) ***briers.***

In MT *bāraq* occurs only once (Ps 144:6), but BDB and others suggest that the Hebrew text followed by LXX had *bāraq* also in II Sam 22:15 and Ps 18:14 [H 15] (KB also in Ezk 21:33). KJV seems to follow LXX in Ps 18:14 by translating "he shot out lightnings." RSV translates by "flash forth."

The verbal form of the root *brq* in Akkadian, Arabic and Ethiopic means "it lightens"; the Egyptian cognate denotes "glitter (of water)." Its Ugaritic and Hebrew nominal forms mean "lightning." Indeed, the Arabic verb *baraqa* may mean "to emit bolts of lightning (from a cloud)."

bārāq. ***Lightning, glittering, bright.*** The noun form is used much more widely than the verb. In the KJV it is fourteen times as "lightning," and, in a figure of speech, as "glittering" or "glitter" six times, and once as "bright."

Regarding the noun *bārāq,* BDB rightly distinguish its literal use to denote "lightning" from its metaphorical use to denote the "glitter" of a weapon: of a sword (Ezk 21:10, 15, 28 [H 15, 20, 33]), of a spear (Nah 3:3), of the metal tip of an arrow (Job 20:25) and of a chariot (Nah 2:4 [H 5]).

Its fourteen occurrences to denote "lightning" are theologically significant because in all of these instances lightning is associated with the LORD. This awe-inspiring phenomenon in the heavens reveals God's greatness and separation from mortal man and accompanies him in his theophanies.

To humble the intrepid fault-finder, Job, the LORD challenged him with the question: "Can you send forth lightnings?" (Job 38:35). Daniel was left without strength when the LORD appeared to him in a vision as a man whose face had the appearance of lightning (Dan 10:6ff.).

Lightning accompanied the LORD when he gave his righteous law to his people at Sinai (Ex 19:16). Elsewhere it is associated with his coming in judgment against his wicked enemies. In Ezekiel's famous vision, the lightning flashing forth from among the living creatures spoke of the LORD's righteous judgment on the earth (Ezk 1:13). Likewise Israel's poets describe the LORD of Hosts' epiphanies when he judges his enemies as being accompanied by lightning. Probably with reference to the LORD's numerous victories over his enemies by which he displayed his universal reign, the Psalmist celebrates the lightning that accompanied these victories (Ps 97:4; cf. Ps 135:7). More specifically his victory over Egypt at the Exodus (Ps 77:18 [H 19]), through David over his foes (II Sam 22:15 = Ps 18:14 [H 15]), and of Israel over Greece (Zech 9:14) are all heightened by being described as having occurred with lightning.

The association of lightning with the LORD also serves as a polemic against Baal, the principal Canaanite nature deity. The Ugaritic texts and artifacts portray Baal as the god of lightning, fire and rain. Thus one text reads: "Baal flashed his thunderbolts" (*'nt,* IV, 70), and another says: "He flashed lightning to the earth" (*Text 51,* V, 71). In a stele he is pictured as brandishing a club in one hand, and holding a stylized thunderbolt ending in a spearhead in the other (C. F. A. Schaeffer, *The Cuneiform Texts of Ras Shamra-Ugarit* (1936), plate XXXII, fig. 2). The stele indicates that Baal had power over the fire and lightning. It is against this background that one must read Jeremiah's warning: "Do not learn the ways of the nations, and do not be dismayed at the signs in the heavens. . . . But the LORD is the true God; he is the living God, an everlasting King; at his wrath the earth trembles. . . . The gods that have not made the heavens and the earth, these shall perish from the earth, and from under the heavens. . . . When the LORD utters his voice there is a tumult of waters in the heavens . . . ; he makes lightnings for the rain, and bringeth forth the wind out of his treasuries" (Jer 10:2–13; cf.

51:16). Indeed Baal has perished from the earth, but the LORD, the Creator-Redeemer continues to be worshiped as King.

bārāq. ***Barak.*** The name of the son of Abinoam, a military commander from Kedesh in Naphtali who was summoned by the prophetess Deborah to form an army of northern Israelites to wage war against the Canaanites.

The man Barak mentioned ten times in Jud 4 and three times in chapter 5 called out ten thousand men from the northern tribes of Zebulun and Naphtali and with this army routed and destroyed the Canaanite armies of Jabin under the command of Sisera. Though Barak has suffered in comparison with Deborah and Jael, two notable women of that time, his prowess and victory is extolled in the Song of Deborah and Barak, and in the New Testament book of Hebrews where he is listed in the roster of men of faith, doubtless as one who "conquered kingdoms" (Heb 11:32).

bāreqet. ***A gem, carbuncle?*** This noun occurs twice (Ex 28:17; 39:10) to designate the third gem in the first row of precious stones in the breastplate of the high priest.

bār^{e}qat. ***A gem, carbuncle.*** Doubtless the same noun as the one above with alternate vocalization. It is a gem in the covering of the prince of Tyre (Ezk 28:13). KJV translates these words as carbuncle but most moderns consider them to be emerald.

B.K.W.

בַּרְקָנִים (*barqānîm*). See no. 287e.

288 בָּרַר (*bārar*) ***purge, purify, choose, cleanse or make bright, test or prove.***

Derivatives

288a †בַּר (*bar*) ***II, pure, clean.***
288b †בַּר (*bar*) ***III, grain.***
288c בֹּר (*bōr*) ***I, lye, potash, alkali used in refining metals.***
288d †בֹּר (*bōr*) ***II, cleanness, pureness.***
288e בֹּרִית (*bōrît*) ***lye, alkali, potash, soap, used in washing.***
288f בָּר (*bār*) ***field.***
288g בַּרְבֻּרִים (*barbūrîm*) ***birds fattened for table of Solomon.***

Whereas BDB relate our verb to the Arabic *barra* "to be reverent, dutiful, devoted; to be kind, charitable, benevolent, virtuous, good," GB think that this Arabic word in turn goes back to the Arabic *barira,* "to be free, clear (with 'from' esp. of guilt or blame)." The Akkadian verb *barāru* means "to glitter" and its adjective *barru* means "pure" (of metal). The Ugaritic cognate means "to be pure, clean" and is related by Gordon to two other roots, *brr* I and *brr* II, meaning "metal" and "be free" respectively but he suggests that all the meanings may be derived from the one root (UT 19: no. 526). In Old South Arabic *brr* (causative) means "to purify." The Medieval Hebrew and Aramaic cognates meaning "to separate, select" are probably a secondary development, a meaning attested both in the OT and at Qumran. There is another Arabic root *bwr* "be uncultivated," possibly the root of the noun *bār* "field." Although the situation is obscure, we may present the derivatives under one root as does BDB.

"Purge" or "purify" is found in Ezk 20:38 where the Lord God says he will purge the rebellious transgressors out of scattered Israel. In Dan 11:35; 12:10 it is said that many people in the future will purify themselves. Zephaniah speaks of a pure language (3:9). But in Job 33:3, while KJV translates Elihu as saying that his lips know that they speak clearly, RSV and later translators render *bārar* as "sincerely." In David's Song of Deliverance *bārar* occurs twice, with a fine word play juxtaposing the Niphal and Hithpael "with the pure thou wilt show thyself pure" (*'im nābār titbārār*) (II Sam 22:27; Ps 18:26 [H 27]), and in his statement that the Lord had rewarded him according to the cleanness of his hands and recompensed him according to his cleanness in God's eyes (II Sam 22:21, 25; Ps 18:20 [H 21], 24 [H 25]).

The chronicler and Nehemiah use participial forms to indicate "choice" or "chosen" men or sheep (I Chr 7:40; 9:22; 16:41).

Isaiah uses *bārar* to depict the servant as the "polished" shaft of an arrow (49:2), a figure that Jeremiah also uses in 51:11. Here GB and Holladay CHL cite these passages under *brr* II "to sharpen" possibly related to the Arabic *bary* sharpen (a pen, etc.). The ministry of the servant would then be likened to a sharp arrow-equally fitting. Isaiah 52:11 declares that those who bear the vessels of the Lord should be "clean." An enigmatic command not to cleanse is found in Jer 4:11.

While KJV translates *bārar* as "manifest" in Eccl 3:18, ASV and modern versions speak of God proving or testing men so that they can see that they are like beasts.

bar. (Noun or adjective) ***kernel, grain of wheat;*** or ***clean, pure.*** The noun *bar* is fourteen times in various places a "kernel" or a "grain of wheat." In Ps 65:13 [H 14]; 72:16 it refers to grain standing in the field.

The psalmists use the adjective to describe those with a single mind toward God as "the *pure* in heart" (Ps 24:4; 73:1), and to praise the LORD's commands as *pure* (Ps 19:8). Zophar reproves Job for his claim that his ethical behavior is *pure* (free from moral fault) (Job 11:4—here it is parallel to *zkk* "to be bright, pure, clean"). Whereas in all these three passages the adjective denotes a quality of moral purity, the disputed *bar* in Prov 14:4 is translated by the NIV as "*empty*" with reference to a manger.

Bibliography: TDOT, II, pp. 308–12.

E.S.K.

289 ברשׁ (*brsh*). **Assumed root of the following.**
289a †בְּרוֹשׁ (*b^e^rôsh*) ***fir, cypress, juniper, pine.*** *b^e^rôt* is an Aramaic form of the same.

An evergreen anciently common in Palestine and Lebanon. KJV consistently translated "fir." Modern translators give fir, juniper, cypress and pine, but are not consistent. The word is attested also in Akkadian. The Aleppo Pine because of usefulness and size best fits the biblical data, though KB prefers Phoenician Juniper.

Hiram the Tyrian king sent *b^e^rôsh* and cedar to Solomon for temple construction. It was used for flooring the temple (I Kgs 6:15) and for the double doors of the entrance (6:34). The main temple was ceiled with *b^e^rôsh* overlaid with gold (II Chr 3:5).

The pines of Hermon were used for ships at Tyre (Ezk 27:5) and for making musical instruments (II Sam 6:5).

These trees are mentioned as the house of the stork in Ps 104:17. Isaiah says that Sennacherib destroyed the choice pine trees of Lebanon (II Kgs 19:23; Isa 37:24), that the pine trees will rejoice over Babylon's fall, and in a time of restitution the pine trees, among others, will be set in the desert (41:19) and will come up instead of the thorn (55:13).

When Israel returns to the LORD, Ephraim will say, "I am like a luxuriant pine tree" (Hos 14:8), but in Zechariah there is howling because "the pine is fallen" (11:2).

In Nah 2:4 *b^e^rôsh* evidently refers to a spear shaft, though recent translators, following LXX, read *pārāshîm* "horsemen."

E.S.K.

290 בשׂם (*bśm*). **Assumed root of the following.**
290a †בֹּשֶׂם (*bōśem*), בֶּשֶׂם (*beśem*), בָּשָׂם (*bāśām*) ***spice, sweet, sweet smell, sweet odor.*** Its cognates in Aramaic and Akkadian mean "be sweet," "be pleasant" respectively. KB derive Greek *balsamon* from the Arabic root *bshm*.

bōśem usually means "spice" but when used with a particular spice is "sweet" (KJV). In Ex 30:23,25 where the ingredients of the holy anointing oil are given, KJV has sweet cinnamon, and sweet calamus (RSV "sweet-smelling" cinnamon and "aromatic" cane; NEB "fragrant" cinnamon and "scented" cane). GB identifies the *qinn^e^mon beśem* and the *q^e^ nēh beśem* as fragrant pure cinnamon and *calamus odoratus* of the Greeks and Romans respectively.

Isaiah prophesies (3:24, KJV) that Zion will have instead of a "sweet smell," a stink (RSV, NEB, NAB "perfume"). Where KJV says that the girls of King Ahasuerus are purified six months with sweet odors (Est 2:12), NAB, NEB have "perfumes"; RSV, JB "spices."

Moses' request for materials for the tabernacle, its furnishings and its service included spices (especially for the anointing oil, Ex 25:6).

Spices were a significant part of the luxury and riches of the time. The Queen of Sheba gave Solomon an abundance of spices as a royal gift (I Kgs 10:2,10; II Chr 9:1,9,24), and Solomon received spices annually as tribute (I Kgs 10:25). Hezekiah showed his riches including spices to the envoys from Babylon as a token of his wealth (II Kgs 20:13), and spices are part of the merchandise coming to Tyre (Ezk 27:22). Levites returning from Babylon are made overseers of stores of spices.

Asa was laid in death on a bed of spices (II Chr 16:14).

Spices are often mentioned as alluring in the Song of Solomon (Song 4:10–16; 5:13; 6:2; 8:14). BDB, G-B, KB and Holladay HCHL all identify *bāśām* in Song 5:1 with the balsam shrub *Balsamodendrium Opolbasamun*. Some of these lexicons also think balsam is in view in 5:13; 6:2; and 8:14 (cf. Immanuel Löw, *Die Flora der Juden*, I,p. 299ff.).

E.S.K.

291 בָּשַׂר (*bāśar*) ***publish, bear*** (good) ***tidings, preach, show forth.*** (ASV and RSV similar.)

Derivatives

291a †בָּשָׂר (*bāśār*) ***flesh.***
291b בְּשֹׂרָה (*b^e^śōrâ*) ***tidings.***

This root and its derivative occur thirty times in the OT. Sixteen of these are in Samuel-Kings and seven are in Isaiah. The root is a common one in Semitic, being found in Akkadian, Arabic, Ugaritic, Ethiopic, etc. The root meaning is "to bring news, especially pertaining to military encounters." Normally this is good news, but (contra Friedrich, TDNT, II, p. 707) it need not necessarily be so (I Sam 4:17; II Sam 18:20 where *tōb* is specifically appended). The Akkadian bears this out, for the word is largely neutral there.

In the historical literature, the occurrences of *bāśar* cluster around two events: the death of Saul (I Sam 31:9; II Sam 1:20; 4:10), and the defeat and death of Absalom (II Sam 18:19f.) Although David received them differently, both were felt by the messenger to be good news.

This concept of the messenger fresh from the field of battle is at the heart of the more theologically pregnant usages in Isaiah and the Psalms. Here it is the Lord who is victorious over his enemies. By virtue of this success, he now comes to deliver the captives (Ps 68:11 [H 12]; Isa 61:1). The watchman waits eagerly for the messenger (Isa 52:7; cf. II Sam 18:25f.) who will bring this good news. At first, only Zion knows the truth (Isa 40:9; 41:27), but eventually all nations will tell the story (Isa 60:6). The reality of this concept is only finally met in Christ (Lk 4:16–21; I Cor 15:54–56; Col 1:5, 6; 2:13–15).

bāśār. ***Flesh*** (rarely ***skin, kin, body***). (ASV and RSV similar.) This word occurs 273 times in the OT. One hundred fifty-three of these are found in the Pentateuch. It seems to be a West Semitic root, no clear cognate existing in Akkadian (contra BDB and TDNT, cf. Chicago Assyrian Dictionary B 270a). In Arabic *bašara* means "skin" and there is a corresponding verb meaning "to peel off," etc. The Ugaritic cognate (*bšr*) occurs only four times, but it shows a range of meaning quite similar to that of the Hebrew. In Hebrew the word refers basically to animal musculature, but by extension it can mean the human body, blood relations, mankind, living things, life itself and created life as opposed to divine life.

bāśār occurs with its basic meaning very frequently, especially in the Pentateuch, in literature concerning sacrificial practices (e.g. Lev 7:17), but also in the prescriptions for dealing with skin diseases (Lev 13, etc.) The common paralleling with *'eṣem* "bone" to convey the idea of "body" denotes the central meaning of the word clearly (cf. Job 2:5, etc.).

But *bāśār* can be extended to mean "body" even without any reference to bones (Num 8:7; II Kgs 4:34; Eccl 2:3, etc.). As such it refers simply to the external form of a person. This is seen as one of the components of the human being, the others being especially *lēb* "heart" and *nepesh* "soul" (Ps 16:9; etc.). However, it would be inappropriate to think that the Hebrews conceived of a living soul inhabiting an otherwise dead body. Rather they saw the human reality as permeating all the components with the totality being the person.

Thus "soul" and "body" are directly paralleled in several places, notably in the Psalms (cf. 84:2 [H 3], "My soul longs, yea faints for the courts of the Lord, my heart and my flesh cry out for the living God"). In this way, to refer to someone as being of one's own "flesh and bone" (Gen 2:23) was to say more than that they shared the same bodily heritage. Again, to say that a man and woman become one flesh in the sexual embrace (Gen 2:24) is to say more than that they are united bodily.

If "body" can refer to man, it can also refer to mankind (Isa 66:16, 24, etc.) and even further to all living things (Gen 6:19, etc.). It is in this sense that "flesh" is seen in contrast to the spirit (*ruaḥ*) of God (Gen 6:3; Ps 56:4 [H 5]; Isa 31:3; 40:6; Jer 17:5). Flesh is transitory, weak, mortal. How then shall those who are fleshly exalt themselves against God? This does not mean that the OT uses "flesh" as the symbol of man's rebellion, however. The problem is not with man's flesh, it is with his "heart" (Ezk 11:19; 44:7), a will to rebel which forgets that it is only flesh (Eccl 5:5). To be sure, the basis for Paul's NT usage of "flesh" is present in the OT in the sense that the spiritual God is contrasted with fleshly man. However, the idea that the principle of sin is somehow resident in the flesh is an intertestamental idea.

Bibliography: Brueggemann, Walter, "Of the Same Flesh and Bone (Gen 2, 23a)," CBQ 32: 532–42. Burton, E. G., *Spirit, Soul and Flesh,* University of Chicago, 1918. Johnson, A., *The Vitality of the Individual in the Thought of Ancient Israel,* Cardiff: University of Wales, 1949, pp. 39–41. Lys, D., *La Chair dans l'Ancien Testament,* Paris: Editions Universitaires, 1967. Murphy, R. E., "Bsr in Qumran Literature and Sarks in the Epistle to the Romans," *Sacra Pagina* 2: 60–67. North, Robert, "Flesh, Covering and Response, Ex xxi 10," VT 5: 204–206. Pedersen, J., *Israel: Its Life and Culture,* I–II, London, Oxford, 1926, pp. 170–81. Richardson, TWB, p. 83. Sander, O., "Lieb-Seele-Dualismus im AT?" ZAW 77: 29–32. Scharbert, J., *Fleisch, Geist und Seele im Pentateuch,* Stuttgart Biblical Series: 19, Stuttgart: Katholisches Bibelwerk, 1967. TDOT, II, pp. 313–31. THAT, I, pp. 376–78.

J.N.O.

292 בָּשַׁל (*bāshal*) ***seethe, bake, boil, roast,*** and ***grow ripe.*** KJV translates *bāshal,* when it means boil, as seethe, sod, sodden or boil. A cognate verb in Akkadian, Ethiopic and Arabic (IV stem) means "cooked" and in Syriac and Akkadian means "ripe."

Derivatives

292a †בָּשֵׁל (*bāshēl*) ***cooked, boiled.***
292b מְבַשְּׁלוֹת (*meᵉbashshᵉlôt*) ***cooking places.***

In the more than a dozen places where *bāshal* is used to describe the preparation of cakes or animals in the sacrificial system, it can describe any kind of cooking procedure: "baking" (Num 11:8), "roasting" (Deut 16:7; II Chr 35:13) or "boiling" (Lev 8:31; Ezk 46:20, 24). This does not mean that the word is used indiscriminately. The passover must be roasted (*bāshal*) with fire (II Chr 35:13), but the holy offerings should be boiled (*bāshal*) in pots. Even clearer distinction is made in Ex 12:9 where boiling in water (*bāshal*) is contrasted with roasting with fire (*ṣālâ*), which is required for the passover.

The sons of Eli broke the law by demanding raw flesh as their part of certain sacrifices rather than accepting the boiled meat (I Sam 2:13, 15). Some women arranged to boil and eat their children during the Syrian siege of Samaria (II Kgs 6:29) and in the final siege of Jerusalem the same kind of gruesome event took place (Lam 4:10).

Where *bāshal* relates to a ripe stage (Gen 40:10; Joel 3:13 [H 4:13]), the reference seems to be to the harvest or grapes being ready for use, just as cooking makes the meat ready to be eaten.

bāshēl. ***Boiled.*** This adjectival form, occurs only twice in the sense of boiled (Ex 12:9; Num 6:19).

E.S.K.

293 בשן (*bshn*) **Assumed root of the following.**
293a †בָּשָׁן (*bāshān*) ***smooth, fertile, Bashan.*** Sixty occurrences.

The fertile country bounded by the Jabbok River on the south, the Sea of Galilee on the west, a line from Mount Hermon eastward on the north and the Hauran range on the east. This was the country of Og before capture by Israel under Moses. It became the territory for the half-tribe of Manasseh or Machir (Josh 13:30; 21:6). Golan was a city of refuge for that area (Josh 20:8). Levitical cities were also there (Josh 21:6). Though controlled by David and Solomon, it later was subject to changing rulership under the northern kingdom and Syria. Jeremiah prophesies that Israel will feed again in Carmel and Bashan (Jer 50:19).

Range animals and oak trees are subjects of figurative expressions. In the Song of Moses (Deut 32:14) reference is made to "rams of the breed of Bashan" and in Ps 22:12 "the strong bulls of Bashan," are a figure of the vicious enemies of the Messiah. Ezekiel prophesies that in the overthrow of Gog and Magog the flesh and blood of people and animals "as the fatlings of Bashan" shall be devoured by birds and beasts (Ezk 39:18).

Tyre made oars from "the oaks of Bashan" (Ezk 27:6). Isaiah 2:13 says the proud like the oaks of Bashan will be "brought low" in the day of the Lord.

E.S.K.

בֹּשְׁנָה (*bōshnâ*). See no. 222b.

294 בָּשַׁס (*bashas*). Occurs only in Amos 5:11, *bôshasᵉkem* "your trampling."

בֹּשֶׁת (*bōshet*). See no. 222c.
בַּת (*bat*) I, II. See nos. 254b, 298a.
בַּתָּה (*battâ*), בָּתָה (*bātâ*). See nos. 298 b, c.
בְּתוּלָה (*bᵉtûlâ*). See no. 295a.
בְּתוּלִים (*bᵉtûlîm*). See no. 295b.

295 בתל (*btl*). **Assumed root of the following.**
295a †בְּתוּלָה (*bᵉtûlâ*) ***virgin.***
295b †בְּתוּלִים (*bᵉtûlîm*) ***virginity.***

bᵉtûlâ. ***Virgin, maid, maiden;*** probably from an unused verb *bātal* "to separate." Although Hebrew lexicons and modern translations generally translate *bᵉtûlâ* as "virgin," G. J. Wenham ("Bᵉtûlāh 'A Girl of Marriageable Age,' VT 22: 326–48) and Tsevat (TDOT II, p. 338–43) contest this as the general meaning but prefer "a young (marriageable) maiden." But whereas Wenham does not concede the meaning "virgin" in any text, Tsevat allows this meaning in three out of its fifty-one occurrences (Lev 21:13f; Deut 22:19; Ezk 44:22). In any case, a strong case can be presented that *bᵉtûlâ* is not a technical term for *virgo intacta* in the OT, a conclusion that has important bearing on the meaning of *'almâ* in Isa 7:14.

The Cognate Languages. A study of the word in the cognate language sustains C. H. Gordon's contention that *bᵉtûlâ* in the near eastern languages by itself does not mean *virgo intacta* (JBR 21: 240–41).

The Egyptian word especially parallel to our Hebrew word is *ḥwn.t.* While the word may denote "girl," "virgin," it can also denote a young marriageable woman, or a young woman who has had sexual relations. Thus the word is used in the Pyramid Texts of the king's protectress who is explicitly called his mother, and of Isis, of whom it is said in a sarcophagus oracle that she is mysteriously pregnant. Tsevat concluded: "It can be stated that *ḥwn.t* is not used to denote biological virginity, but rather youthful vigor and potential motherhood" (P. 339).

The Akkadian cognate, *batultu,* denotes "primarily an age group: only in specific contexts . . . does it assume the connotation 'virgin' " (CAD II: 174). J. J. Finkelstein ("Sex Offences in Sumerian Laws," JAOS 86: 355:72) and B. Landsberger "Jungfräulichkeit: Ein Beitrag zum Thema 'Beilager und Eheschliessung' " in *Symbolae juridicae . . . M. David . . . edid.* J. A. Ankum . . ., II (Leiden, 1968, pp. 41–105) have underscored in independent studies that the word is normally best understood as "young (unmarried) girl." In fact, there is no one word for "virgin" in

Sumerian or Akkadian; that concept is expressed negatively by "who is not deflowered."

In Ugaritic *btlt* is a frequent epithet for Anat, Baal's wife, who repeatedly has sexual intercourse (cf. A. van Selms, *Marriage and Family Life in Ugaritic Literature,* London, 1954, pp. 69, 109).

In a Shiite tradition, Fatima, though the mother of Hasan and Hussein along with other children, bears the title *batūl* (C. Virolleaud, *Le Théâtre Persan,* Paris, 1950, p. 37). And in an Aramaic text from Nippur, Montgomery interprets the phrase, *btwlt* "travailing and not bearing," to denote a hapless wife suffering from miscarriages and other female complaints (*Aramaic Incantation Texts from Nippur,* Philadelphia, 1913, p. 131).

Tsevat concluded that the word "does not mean 'virgin' in any language exclusively (Aram.), mainly (Heb.), or generally (Akk. [and Ugar.?])" (p. 340).

OT usage. Whether *b^e^tûlâ* is used in a general sense, "young woman" or a more particular sense "virgin" cannot be decided for Ex 22:16f. [H 15f.]; Deut 22:28–29; Lev 21:2–3; etc. But in Lev 21:13–14 and Ezk 44:22 where *b^e^tûlâ* is contrasted with various classes of women who have had sexual experience, it seems probable that the concept of "virgin" is in view.

Wenham's argument that qualifying clauses of *b^e^tûlâ,* such as "that has had no husband" (Lev 21:2–3) or "whom no man had known" (Gen 24:16; Jud 21:12), are pointless if the word means "virgin" is less than convincing, for it cannot be decided whether these are non-restrictive or restrictive clauses, cf. II Sam 14:5 for a somewhat similar repetition.

But Wenham does call into question the conclusion that our word must mean "virgin" in Deut 22:13–21 because he offers a plausible interpretation assuming the general meaning of "nubile adolescence." In the first place, *b^e^tûlîm* "tokens of virginity" (vv. 14, 15, 17, 18) is morphologically the regular form for abstract nouns in biblical Hebrew designating age groups (cf. *n^e^'ûrîm* "youth" *z^e^qûnîm* "old age"). Moreover, according to him, the "tokens of virginity" called for by the elders are not the sheets of the wedding night but garments stained by blood during her last period, and by producing these the girl's parents could refute the jealous husband's complaint that his wife was with child by another man while she was still in her father's house. Finally, he argued that this interpretation admirably suits the sentence that if such tokens could not be produced she should be stoned to death "because she wrought folly in Israel by playing the harlot *in her father's house*" (Deut 22:21). Thus the "tokens" served as a test, proving that she was not pregnant when she was married. If she was not pregnant, she was presumed to be a virgin. If this interpretation of *b^e^tûlîm* is correct then this would further sustain the thesis that *b^e^tûlâ* is a "girl of marriageable age," since the onset of menstruation would be the clearest sign that she had attained that age.

Since Wenham has presented a strong case that the interpretation test is not one of virginity but chastity, one must concede that *b^e^tûlîm* or *b^e^tûlâ* does not clearly speak of virginity in this disputed text.

In eight places our word *b^e^tûlâ* is contrasted to or combined with the Hebrew word for young man (Deut 32:25; II Chr 36:17; Ps 148:12; Isa 62:5; Jer 51:22; Lam 1:18; 2:21; Zech 9:17). In these places the phrases signify no more than young men and women. In Ezk 9:6 it (in plural) refers to girls together with little children and women who will be killed because of Israel's wickedness.

But in Joel 1:8, where the *b^e^tûlâ* is called upon to lament the death of her *ba'al* "husband," it probably does not mean "virgin" for elsewhere *ba'al* is the regular word for "husband" and its usual translation by "bridegroom" in the versions is otherwise unattested. Likewise in Est 2:17 the *b^e^tûlōt* who spent a night with King Ahasuerus are not virgins, unless it is a "shorthand" for "those who had been virgins." In a parable Ezekiel speaks of Oholah and Oholibah playing the harlot and their *b^e^tûlîm* breasts being handled (23:3). Here too the notion of virginity would be inaccurate. Finally in Job 31:1 even the NEB translated our word by "girl" because it would not be sinful for Job to look on a virgin. Unless it is an epithet for a Canaanite goddess it probably designates a young married woman (cf. vv. 8ff).

Like Greek *parthenos,* Latin *virgo* and German *Jungfrau, b^e^tûlâ* originally meant "young marriageable woman" but since she was normally a virgin it was not difficult for this meaning to become attached to the word. This more technical meaning is a later development in Hebrew and Aramaic and is clearly its meaning by the Christian era. When the change took place is not clear.

What is clear is that one cannot argue that if Isaiah (7:14) in his famous oracle to Ahaz had intended a virgin he could have used *b^e^tûlâ* as a more precise term than *'almâ.*

b^e^tûlâ is used in a number of figurative expressions referring to cities or countries as young women: Zion (Isa 37:22); Babylon (Isa 47:1); Israel (Jer 18:13) etc. Cf. the frequent expression "the daughter of Zion."

Bibliography: Beegle, Dewey, M., "Virgin or Young Woman?" *Asbury Seminarian* 8: 20–34. Gordon, C. H. " 'Almah in Isaiah 7:14," JBR 21: 106. Knight, G. A. F., "The Virgin and the Old

Testament,'' RTR 12: 1–13. Young, Edwin J., ''The Immanuel Prophecy,'' WTJ 15: 97–124; 16: 23–50. TDNT, V, pp. 831–34. TDOT, II, pp. 338–43.

B.K.W.

296 *בָּתַק (*bātaq*) ***cut, cut off, cut down.*** Occurs only in the Piel, in Ezk 16:40.

297 בָּתַר (*bātar*) ***cut in two*** (Gen 15:10).

Derivative

297a בֶּתֶר (*beter*) ***part, piece.***

298 בתת (*btt*) **Assumed root of the following.**

298a בַּת (*bat*) ***a liquid measure, about twenty-two liters.*** See ZPEB, V, p. 916.

298b בַּתָּה (*battâ*) ***precipice, steep*** (Isa 7:19).

298c בָּתָה (*bātâ*) ***end, destruction*** (Isa 5:6).

ג

ג

גֵּא (*gē'*). See no. 299a.

299 גָּאָה (*gā'â*) ***rise up, grow up, be exalted in triumph.*** (RSV and ASV are similar.)

Derivatives

299a †גֵּא (*gē'*) ***proud.***
299b †גֵּאֶה (*ge'eh*) ***proud.***
299c †גֵּאָה (*gē'â*) ***pride.***
299d †גַּאֲוָה (*ga'ăwâ*) ***majesty, pride.***
299e †גָּאוֹן (*gā'ôn*) ***exaltation.***
299f †גֵּאוּת (*gē'ût*) ***majesty.***
299g †גַּאֲיוֹן (*ga'ăyôn*) ***proud.***
299h גֵּוָה (*gēwâ*) ***pride.***

The primary meaning of this root is "to rise." It occurs seven times in the OT. In two of these passages (Ezk 47:5; Job 8:11) the traditional rendition is preserved. The root also appears four times in the "Song at the Sea," i.e. Ex 15:1; 15:21. In this case we encounter a familiar phenomenon of the Hebrew language in which for emphasis the finite form of the verb is preceded by the infinitive absolute. Thus most of our versions translate the two verbal forms together as "triumphed gloriously." The sense is that God has "risen up (like a wave)" over his enemies. The seventh usage of this root is Job 10:16. The exact translation is problematical. Literally the passage reads, "If he lifts himself up, you (God) hunt me as a lion."

The basic idea of rising or growing is reflected in the following passages: (1) Isa 9:17 refers to an ascending "column" (*gē'ût*) of smoke, a metaphor of the effects caused by sin on anything it touches; (2) Ps 46:3 [H 4] refers to the "raging" or "tumult" (*ga'ăwâ*) of mountains in a scene of cataclysmic disturbance; (3) Ps 89:9 [H 10] talks of the "raging" (*gē'ût*) of the sea, a territory ruled by the Lord. Job 38:11, part of God's speech to Job, refers to "proud" (*gā'ôn*) waves. In connection with these references to frothing waters, one may also compare the phrase the "swelling jungle (*gā'ôn*) of the Jordan," in Jer 12:5; 49:19; 50:44; and Zech 11:3. The latter is a description of the area of rich and thick vegetation on both sides of the southern sections of the Jordan valley. (Cf. N. Glueck, *The River Jordan*, p. 63.) The jungle may be so called because of high growth or high water in flood. The Arabic name is the *Zor*.

The word "pride" (or its synonyms) can be used either positively or negatively in the Old Testament. In the positive category one can discern two applications of this. First would be those verses that speak of the land of Israel in terms of excellency, Ps 47:4 [H 5]; Ezk 24:21; Deut 33:29; Nah 2:3; Isa 4:2. In each of these cases the land's significance becomes such only because of her relationship to Yahweh. This is not an indigenous characteristic.

In the second place we could list those verses that speak of God's "pride/majesty/excellency": Ex 15:7; Isa 2:10, 19, 21; 24:14; Mic 5:3; Job 37:4; 40:10 (*gā'ôn*); Deut 33:26; Ps 68:35 (*ga'ăwâ*); Ps 93:1; Isa 12:5; 26:10 (*gē'ût*). In most of these passages the particular Hebrew word is translated in the LXX by *doxa* or an equivalent and not by *hubris*. Finally we may note the name of the spy sent out by Moses from the tribe of Gad, Geuel (Num 13:15), "El is majestic."

Preponderantly, however, it is in the negative sense that the OT uses this concept. The sections of the Bible that employ the term most frequently in a condemnatory context are (1) the prophets, Isa, Jer, and Ezk, and (2) Ps, Prov, and Job. There are fifty-three examples of this in these six books. The charge is laid often against noncovenant peoples such as: Moab (Isa 16:6); Egypt (Ezk 30:6); the Philistines (Zech. 9:6); Assyria (Zech 10:11) and so forth.

It is Israel, however, that comes under heaviest judgment. The attitude is as old as Sodom (Ezk 16:49 and cf. Ps 10:2). The precise charge is arrogance, cynical insensitivity to the needs of others, and presumption. It is both a disposition and a type of conduct (both of which are inextricably connected). Pride inevitably leads to destruction (Prov 15:25; 16:18; Jer 13:9; Isa 13:11, et al).

Thus we can observe that pride is not intrinsically wrong. It describes a part of God's character. It is to become a part of the life style of the believer (Job 40:10; Deut 33:29). Sin enters the picture when there is a shift of ultimate confidence from God as object and source to oneself as object and source.

gē'â. ***Pride.*** This word is found only in Prov 8:13.

gē'eh. ***Proud.*** The adjective is descriptive of the presumptuous man.

gē'. ***Proud.*** This word is found only in Isa 16:6 and is obviously to be related to *gē'eh* as the exact parallel in Jer 48:29 will indicate.

ga'ăyôn. ***Proud.*** Only in Ps 123:4.

Bibliography: Driver, G. R., "'Another Little Drink' in Isaiah 28:1–22," in *Words and Mean-*

ings, eds. P. Ackroyd and B. Lindars, Cambridge: The University Press, 1968, pp. 48–50. On the use of the root *g'h* in Ugaritic, 2 Aqht VI, 42–45, cf. S. Loffreda, "Raffronto fra un testo ugaritico (2 Aqht VI, 42–45) e Giobbe 40, 9–12," *Bibliotheca Orientalis* 8: 103–16. TDNT, VIII, pp. 299–305. TDOT, II, pp. 344–49. THAT, I, pp. 379–82. TWNT, VIII, pp. 299–302. M. Har-El, "The Pride of the Jordan," BA 41:68–69.

V.P.H.

גַּאֲוָה (*ga'ăwâ*). See no. 299d.
גְּאוּלַי (*g^e'ûlay*). See no. 300a.
גָּאוֹן (*gā'ôn*). See no. 299e.
גֵּאוּת (*gē'ût*). See no. 299f.
גַּאֲיוֹן (*ga'ăyôn*). See no. 299g.

300 גָּאַל (*gā'al*) ***I, redeem, avenge, revenge, ransom, do the part of a kinsman.*** (ASV and RSV similar, except that they translate "avenger of blood" instead of "revenger of blood.")

Derivatives

300a גְּאוּלַי (*g^e'ûlay*) ***redemption*** (Isa 63:4 only).
300b גְּאֻלָּה (*g^e'ūllâ*) ***redemption, right of redemption, price of redemption, kindred.***
300c גֹּאֵל (*gō'ēl*) ***I, redeemer.***

The participial form of the Qal stem of the verb has practically become a noun in its own right though it may properly be considered as merely a form of the verb.

The primary meaning of this root is to do the part of a kinsman and thus to redeem his kin from difficulty or danger. It is used with its derivatives 118 times. One difference between this root and the very similar root *pādâ* "redeem," is that there is usually an emphasis in *gā'al* on the redemption being the privilege or duty of a near relative. The participial form of the Qal stem has indeed been translated by some as "kinsman-redeemer" or as in KJV merely "kinsman." The root is to be distinguished from *gā'al* II, "defile" (which see).

The root is used in four basic situations covering the things a good and true man would do for his kinsman. First, it is used in the Pentateuchal legislation to refer to the repurchase of a field which was sold in time of need (Lev 25:25 ff.), or the freeing of an Israelite slave who sold himself in time of poverty (Lev 25:48ff.). Such purchase and restitution was the duty of the next of kin. Secondly, but associated with this usage was the "redemption" of property or non-sacrificial animals dedicated to the Lord, or the redemption of the firstborn of unclean animals (Lev 27:11ff.). The idea was that a man could give an equivalent to the Lord in exchange, but the redemption price was to be a bit extra to avoid dishonest exchanges. In these cases, the redeemer was not a relative, but the owner of the property. Thirdly, the root is used to refer to the next of kin who is the "avenger of blood" (RSV "revenger") for a murdered man. The full phrase "avenger of blood" is almost always used (cf. Num. 35: 12ff.). Apparently the idea is that the next of kin must effect the payment of life for life. As a house is repurchased or a slave redeemed by payment, so the lost life of the relative must be paid for by the equivalent life of the murderer. The kinsman is the avenger *of blood*. This system of execution must be distinguished from blood feuds for the *gō'ēl* was a guiltless executioner and not to be murdered in turn.

Finally, there is the very common usage prominent in the Psalms and prophets that God is Israel's Redeemer who will stand up for his people and vindicate them. There may be a hint of the Father's near kinship or ownership in the use of this word. A redemption price is not usually cited, though the idea of judgment on Israel's oppressors as a ransom is included in Isa 43:1–3. God, as it were, redeems his sons from a bondage worse than slavery.

Perhaps the best known instance of redemption of the poor is in the book of Ruth which is the most extensive OT witness for the law of levirate marriage. According to Deut 25:5–10, a widow without issue should be taken by her husband's brother to perpetuate seed and thus insure the succession of the land which was bound to the male descendants. The near relative here is called a *yābām*. The root *gā'al* is not used. In the situation in Ruth two things are mentioned, the field and the levirate marriage. The near kin was willing to buy the field, but not to marry Ruth.

The point is that when Naomi in her poverty had to sell the field the next of kin was obligated to buy it back for her. This he was willing to do for his brother's widow without issue. The land would presumably revert to him anyway at last. When he learned that he must marry Ruth and raise children who would maintain their inheritance, he refused and Boaz stepped in. But the two things, kinsman redemption and levirate marriage, are to be distinguished. The word *gō'ēl* "redeemer," does not refer to the latter institution.

In the famous verse Job 19:25 the word *gō'ēl* is translated "redeemer" in the AV and some have taken it to refer to the coming of Christ in his work of atonement. This would be expressed more characteristically by the Hebrew word *pādâ* (which see). This word in Job 19:25 is now more accurately referred to the work of God who as friend and kinsman through faith will ultimately redeem Job from the dust of death. The enigmatic "after my skin" of v. 26 could well be read with different vowels "after I awake" (see NIV footnote and Job 14:12–14 where Job's question about resurrection is climaxed by his hope that God will have regard for him at last and that Job like a tree will have a second growth—*ḥălîpâ,* v. 14, which answers to the *ḥālap* of v. 7). In any case Job expects with his own eyes to see God his *go'ēl* at last.

Bibliography: A. R. Johnson, "The Primary Meaning of the Root *g'l,*" Supp VT 1: 67–77. AI, 11–12, 21–23. Leggett, Donald A., *The Levirate Goel Institutions in the OT,* Presbyterian & Reformed Press. TDOT, II, pp. 350–55.

R.L.H.

301 גָּאַל (*gā'al*) ***II, defile, pollute.*** (ASV, RSV similar.)

Derivative

301a גֹּאֶל (*gō'ēl*) ***defiling,*** used only in Neh 13:29, the "defiling of the priesthood" by the faithless priests.

This root doubtless is to be distinguished from *gā'al* I, "to redeem." It appears that this root is a secondary formation from the similar root *gā'al* found also in Aramaic, meaning "abhor," "loathe." It is used twelve times.

The pollution specified by the verb is due to the blood of murder (Isa 59:3; Lam 4:14), the blood of vengeance (Isa 63:3), or by sin in general (Zeph 3:1; Neh 13:29). The word is used of the ceremonial pollution of imperfect sacrifices (Mal 1:7, 12), of the pagan king's diet (Dan 1:8), and of the uncertain lineage of the priests after the exile (Ezr 2:62; Neh 7:64). Thus the pollution specified is from any breach of moral or ceremonial law. The classification of Job 3:5 is uncertain. AV translates it "stain," taking it as *gā'al* II. ASV and RSV translate it "claim," taking it as *gā'al* I. The context perhaps favors the latter translation. The dark day of his birth is, according to Job's curse, to be "purchased" by darkness and dwelt in by the shadow of death.

R.L.H.

גַּב (*gab*). See no. 303a.
גֵּב (*gēb*) I. See no. 304a.
גֵּב (*gēb*) II, III. See nos. 323a,b.

302 גבא (*gb'*). **Assumed root of the following.**
302a גֶּבֶא (*gebe'*) ***cistern, pool*** (Isa 30:14; Ezk 47:11).

303 גבב (*gbb*). **Assumed root of the following.**
303a †גַּב (*gab*) ***back.***

The substantive is used thirteen times in the OT. Seven of these are in Ezk (1:18; 10:12; 16:24, 31, 39; 43:13). The word may be either masculine or feminine in gender. Thus, Ezk 1:18 reads: "As for their rings/rims (*gabbêhem*)... and their rings/rims (*gabbōtām*) were...." In the singular it is always masculine. In the plural it is masculine six times but feminine twice (Ezk 1:18 and Lev 14:9).

Although the meaning given above for *gab* was "back" this translation appears only in Ps 129:3. The poet, speaking for Israel, complains of the roughshod treatment to which she has been subjected by her enemies: "They have plowed upon my 'back'." Similar sentiment and phraseology are used in Isa 51:23 but there the word for "back/body" is *gaw,* a synonym for *gab.*

The basic meaning seems to be something like "curved" or "rounded." Job 15:26 mentions God's thicked-bossed shield (*gabbē māginnāw*) and the futility of Job's attempt to run headlong into it. In the visions of Ezekiel this word describes the rims (KJV-"rings") on the wheels of the chariot drawn by the four living creatures: Ezk 1:18; 10:12; and cf. I Kgs 7:33.

Three times in Ezk (16:24,31,39), Judah is condemned for building for herself, in the fashion of a harlot, a "vaulted chamber" (KJV "eminent place") and a lofty place (*rāmâ*). This may be a reference to an artificially constructed hill on which illegal cultic acts were performed (perhaps a word play between *rāmâ* and *bāmâ*). Thus the LXX translates *gab* here as *oikēma pornikon* "brothels."

gab appears in Job 13:12, "Your 'defenses' (KJV "strongholds") are 'defenses' of clay." In the context Job is refuting the idea that there is any substantiality to his critics' diagnoses and solutions.

Bibliography: Cohen, A., "Studies in Hebrew Lexicography," *AJSL* 40: 153–85, esp. 165–66, connects *gab* in Job 13:12 with the rabbinic root *gbb,* "to rake leaves," and translates Job 13:12*b* as "like useless bits of clay is your array of arguments." Guillaume, A., "The Arabic Background of the Book of Job," in *Promise and Fulfillment,* Edinburgh: Clark, 1963, pp. 106–27, esp. p. 112, translates Job 13:12*b* as "your replies are dusty answers."

V.P.H.

304 גבה (*gbh*). **Assumed root of the following.**
304a גֵּב (*gēb*) ***I, locust*** (Isa 33:4 only).
304b גּוֹב (*gôb*) ***locusts*** (Nah 3:17, only).
304c גֹּבַי (*gōbay*), גּוֹבָי (*gôbāy*) ***locusts*** (Amos 7:1; Nah 3:17).

305 גָּבַהּ (*gābah*) ***be high, exalted.***

Derivatives

305a גָּבֹהַּ (*gābōah*) ***high, exalted.***
305b גֹּבַהּ (*gōbah*) ***height, exaltation.***
305c גַּבְהוּת (*gabhût*) ***haughtiness*** (Isa 2:11, 17, only).

The root *gābah* and its derivatives are used ninety-four times in the OT. The verb appears in the Qal twenty-four times, meaning basically "to be high or lofty" and in the Hiphil ten times, meaning "to make high, to exalt." *gābōah* appears forty-one times, the noun *gōbah* seventeen times, and the noun *gabhût* twice. The root is used only three times in the Pentateuch (Gen 7:19; Deut 3:5; 28:52), but by contrast in the prophets cf. Isa, fourteen times; Jer, seven times; Ezk, twenty-two times.

As the root is used in its basic sense it describes the height of persons, objects, places, and natural phenomena. Thus, the verb *gābah* signifies the growing of a tree (Ezk 17:24; 31:5, 10, 14); the stem of a vine (Ezk 19:11); the heavens in respect to the earth (Ps 103:11; Job 35:5). Saul is described as being "taller" than any of his people (I Sam 10:23). It describes the high wall Manasseh built around Jerusalem (II Chr 33:14). It may mean "to fly high" as an eagle (Jer 49:16; Ob 4).

Similarly the adjective *gābōah* describes a high mountain(s) (Gen 7:19; Isa 30:25; 40:9; 57:7; Jer 3:6; Ezk 17:22; 40:2; Ps 104:18); high hills (I Kgs 14:23; II Kgs 17:10; Jer 2:20; 17:2); the high gates of Babylon (Jer 51:58); high battlements (Zeph 1:16); high towers (Isa 2:15); the high gallows intended for Mordecai (Est 5:14; 7:9); the horns in Daniel's vision (Dan 8:3). Similar documentation could be made for the use of the noun *gōbah*.

In several places the word is used in a very positive sense both with respect to man as a quality of life worthy of possession and as descriptive of God himself. In the former category compare God's word to Job, "Deck yourself with majesty (*gā'ôn*) and dignity (*gōbah*) (40:10; cf. 36:7) and II Chr 17:6, "Jehoshaphat's heart was lifted up ("encouraged") in the ways of the Lord." Secondly, God's position is said to be "on high" (Ps 113:5; Job 22:12) and his ways are "higher" than those of mankind (Isa 55:9).

The usual nuance behind the words under discussion is pride or haughtiness. Of interest is the negative usage of this word in connection with some part of the human body. For example, pride is linked with the heart in: Ezk 28:2, 5, 17; Ps 131:1; Prov 18:12; II Chr 26:16; 32:25 (all with the verb); Prov 16:5; II Chr 32:26 (with adjective and noun). Isaiah 2:11; 5:15 and Ps 101:5 connect pride with the eyes. Proverbs 16:18 and Eccl 7:8 tie pride with man's spirit, and Ps 10:4 with man's "nose"/countenance. On a few occasions individuals are said to be guilty specifically of this sin of pride: Uzziah (II Chr 26:16); Hezekiah (II Chr 32: 25–26); the prince of Tyre (Ezk 28:2, 17). Conversely, Isaiah speaks of the suffering servant who will be exalted (*rûm*), lifted up (*nāśa'*) and be very high (*gābah*) (52:13).

In the LXX the word is translated as *hupsos* or *hupsēlos*, but never as *hubris*.

Bibliography: TDOT, II, pp. 356–60. THAT, I, pp. 394–97.

V.P.H.

306 גבח (*gbḥ*). **Assumed root of the following.**
306a גִּבֵּחַ (*gibēaḥ*) ***having a bald forehead*** (Lev 13:41, only).
306b גַּבַּחַת (*gabbaḥat*) ***bald forehead*** (Lev 13, only).

גַּבְהוּת (*gabhût*). See no. 305c.
גְּבוּל (*gᵉbûl*), גְּבוּלָה (*gᵉbûlâ*). See nos. 307a,b.
גִּבּוֹר (*gibbôr*). See no. 310b.
גְּבוּרָה (*gᵉbûrâ*). See no. 310c.
גֹּבַי (*gōbay*). See no. 304c.
גְּבִינָה (*gᵉbînâ*). See no. 308b.
גְּבִיעַ (*gᵉbîa'*). See no. 309b.
גְּבִירָה (*gᵉbîrâ*). See no. 310d.
גָּבִישׁ (*gābîsh*). See no. 311a.

307 גָּבַל (*gābal*) ***to border.*** Denominative verb.

Parent Noun

307a †גְּבוּל (*gᵉbûl*) ***border.***
307b †גְּבוּלָה (*gᵉbûlâ*) ***border.***
307c גַּבְלֻת (*gablūt*) ***twisting.***
307d מִגְבָּלֹת (*migbālōt*) ***the twisted, i.e. cords.***

The verb appears only five times: Deut 19:14; Josh 18:20; Zech 9:2, Qal; Ex 19:12,23, Hiphil "to set bounds."

The root *gbl* is found in the place name Gebal or Byblos, the Phoenician maritime city on the coast of the Mediterranen, probably in the sense of Arabic Jebel "mountain"—mountains making a natural boundary.

gᵉbûl. ***Border, boundary, territory.*** Very frequently used in the books of the Old Testament in which a significant amount of attention and detail is devoted to geographical divisions such as the last half of Joshua.

This substantive appears 216 times in the OT. It is found most frequently in Josh (66 times); Ezk (39 times, and preponderantly in 40–48); and Num (25 times). The noun is used to designate either a geographical boundary or the territory as a whole. On a few occasions it is used in a figurative sense.

There are three major usages of *gᵉbûl*.

1. *gᵉbûl* indicates a boundary at one of the four major points on the compass: "south" Num 34:3; Josh 15:2,4; "north" Num 34:7; Josh 15:5;

"east" Num 34:10; Ezk 45:7; "west" Num 34:6; Josh 15:4,12.

2. A boundary formed by a body of water: Num 22:36, the Arnon; Josh 15:5, the sea.

3. A boundary of a land belonging to a nation or to a subdivision within that nation. Here it may take on the meaning of "border" as in the case of Egypt (I Kgs 4:21 [H 5:1]); Edom (Josh 15:1); Moab (Num 21:13); Ammon (Num 21:24).

The noun may also be translated by "territory" as in Gen 47:21 (Egypt); Jud 11:18 (Moab); Jud 1:36 (Amorite). We may also note the references to the expression "in (all) the *g^e bûl* of Israel: (Jud 19:29; I Sam 11:3,7; 27:1 *inter alia*) which are always to be translated "in (all) the territory of Israel," except for II Kgs 14:25. Hence the phrase is synonymous with the expression "the land (*'ereṣ*) of Israel."

4. The word can designate the boundary or farthest extension of possessions of individuals or groups of individuals: "area of your land" (Deut 19:3); "the boundary of their inheritance" (Josh 16:5), "the territory of their lot" (Josh 18:11), "the bounds of his city of refuge" (Num 35:26).

5. Whenever *g^e bûl* is used with a city name it is to be translated as "territory": Ashdod: I Sam 5:6; Tiphsah: II Kgs 15:16; Gaza: II Kgs 18:8; *inter alia*.

6. Figuratively the word is used to describe "the territory of darkness" (Job 38:20); "the territory of wickedness," (Mal 1:4); "the territory of God's holiness" (Ps 78:54).

In the ancient near east there was, at least on paper, a great respect for another's boundaries whether these were national boundaries or individual and private boundaries. To violate them is to violate something God has ordained. He has established the boundaries of all peoples (Deut 32:8). He has arranged the borders of the whole earth (Ps 74:17; 104:9). He has placed the sands as a boundary to the sea (Jer 5:22).

It is little wonder then that the Bible prohibits the moving of a neighbor's ancient landmark (*g^e bûl*) (Deut 19:14). Whoever does this is to be "cursed" (Deut 27:17). The offense, of course, was not violation of tradition, but stealing of real estate—and unalienable real estate at that. Nothing less than a biblical imprecation leveled against the violator is strong enough. Cf. also Hos 5:10; Job 24:2–4; Prov 22:28; 23:10. In such crimes the perpetrators are the strong and the wealthy and the victims the weak, the orphans and the widow. From the various scrolls found at the Dead Sea we have learned that those who defected from the Qumran sect were known as "removers of the landmark."

In light of the Ugaritic root *gbl* and the Arabic cognate several instances of Hebrew *g^e bûl* may be more accurately translated as "mountain": I Sam 13:18, "The mountain which looks over Zeboim," and Ps 75:54, "So he brought them to His holy mount, the mountain which his right hand had created."

g^ebûlâ. ***Border, boundary, landmark.*** With the exception of Isa 28:25 all usages of this word are in the plural.

Bibliography: Dahood, M., "Hebrew-Ugaritic Lexicography II," Bib 45: 383–412, esp. p. 396. Elon, M., "hassagat gevul," in *Encyclopedia Judaica,* VII, pp. 1460–66. Rabin, C., *The Zadokite Documents,* Oxford, Clarendon, 1954, pp. 4, 20, 42. Ross, J. F., "Landmark," in IDB, III, pp. 66–67. TDOT, II, pp. 361–66.

V.P.H.

308 גבן (*gbn*). **Assumed root of the following.**
308a גִּבֵּן (*gibēn*) ***humpbacked*** (Lev 21:20, only).
308b גְּבִינָה (*g^e bînâ*) ***curd*** (cheese, Job 10:10, only).
308c גַּבְנֹן (*gabnōn*) ***peak, rounded summit*** (Ps 68:16, only).

גַּבְנֹן (*gabnōn*). See no. 308c.

309 גבע (*gb'*). **Assumed root of the following.**
309a †גִּבְעָה (*gib'â*) ***hill.***
309b גָּבִיעַ (*gābîa'*) ***cup, bowl.***
309c †מִגְבָּעוֹת (*migbā'ōt*) ***turban.***
309d גִּבְעֹל (*gib'ōl*) ***bud.***

gib'â. ***Hill.*** The noun, used sixty times in the OT, may refer to a natural eminence smaller than a mountain but most often, as we shall see, it becomes a place of illicit worship. The same spelling is also used for the place name Gibeah, the Benjamite city and birthplace of Saul.

Of the sixty uses of *gib'â* in biblical Hebrew the heaviest clusters are to be found in the prophets (Isa thirteen times, Jer nine times; Ezk eight times). Particularly interesting here is the use of the phrase "on every high hill (*gib'â*) and under every green tree," or its variants, as a reference to the location of fertility cult practices in Israel and Judah.

This phrase occurs sixteen times in the OT. Some of these passages are: Deut 12:2; I Kgs 14:23; II Kgs 16:4; 17:10; Jer 2:20; 17:2; Ezk 6:13; Hos 4:13; II Chr 28:4. Each of these verses condemns a pagan Canaanite practice which has been adopted by the Hebrews.

If this unorthodox practice is to be equated with similar practices in which the Israelites engaged in connection with the "high place(s)" (*bāmâ*), then the reason for the prophetic denunciation becomes clear. There is nothing inherently wrong with worshiping God on "hills." The people's experience in the wilderness would substantiate that! But in this case it appears that the

Israelites adopted immoral cultic rites, popular among agricultural groups who pinned their faith to the Baal(s), the god of fertility and the giver of rain and crops, and to Asherah, the goddess of fertility. Why such indulgences were viewed by the prophets with abomination and horror is not difficult to surmise.

migbā'ôt. ***Turban, head gear,*** is used only four times: Ex 28:40; 29:9; 39:28; Lev 8:13, convex in shape perhaps, translated by the RSV as "cap." It is worn by the ordinary priests and is to be differentiated from the turban worn by the high priest (*miṣnepet*).

Bibliography: Albright, W. F., "The High Place in Ancient Palestine," Supp VT 4: 242–58. Hamlin, E. John, "The Meaning of 'Mountains and Hills' in Isa. 41:14–16," JNES 13: 185–90. Holladay, W. L., "On Every High Hill and Under Every Green Tree," VT 11: 170–76. McCown, C. C., "Hebrew High Places and Cult Remains," JBL 69: 205–19.

V.P.H.

גִּבְעֹל (*gib'ōl*). See no. 309d.

310 גָּבַר (*gābar*) ***prevail, be mighty, have strength, be great.*** (ASV and RSV similar.)

Derivatives

310a †גֶּבֶר (*geber*) ***man.***
310b †גִּבּוֹר (*gibbôr*) ***mighty man.***
310c †גְּבוּרָה (g^e*bûrâ*) ***might.***
310d גְּבִירָה (g^e*bîrâ*) ***lady, queen*** (masc. lord, Gen 27:29,37).
310e גְּבֶרֶת (g^e*beret*) ***lady, queen.***

This root and its derivatives occur 328 times in the OT, of which the verb accounts for but 26. The cognate is well attested in the semitic languages, appearing in Akkadian, Arabic, Aramaic, Phoenician, and Moabite. At present it is only known in a proper noun in Ugaritic. In general the same meaning is shared throughout. In Arabic the basic meaning of the root is "to rise, raise, restore," with the idea of being strong, or prevailing over coming only in the derived stems. That the Hebrew may share a similar range of meaning is seen in the Hithpael where the idea is not so much to make oneself prevail over God, as it is to raise oneself up in arrogance and stand in his face (Job 15:25; 36:9; Isa 42:13). The Hebrew root is commonly associated with warfare and has to do with the strength and vitality of the successful warrior.

In the first analysis, might and mighty men were causes for celebration in the OT. During much of the biblical period Israel was in a heroic age. Thus the feats and exploits of her champions were causes for delight and storytelling. Such an exploit was that of David's three mighty men as they broke through the Philistine lines to bring him water from Bethlehem (I Chr 11:15–19). I Samuel 1 is a lament for the fallen heroes, Saul and Jonathan, extolling their valiant deeds. Similarly II Sam 23 records the glories of various mighty men. I and II Chronicles contain many references to the mighty men of Israel, commonly employing the phrase *gibbôr ḥayil* "mighty man of valor" to describe them. Although Chr generally uses the term to express "warrior" or "soldier," there are indications that originally this was a technical term for men of a certain social class, "nobles" who had the privilege of bearing arms for their king (cf. Ruth 2:1; I Sam 9:1; II Kgs 15:20, etc. where "warrior" is too narrow a translation).

It is not surprising that in such a society God was often depicted as a warrior. God is the true prototype of the mighty man, and if an earthly warrior's deeds are recounted, how much more should God's be. Thus the psalmists recount God's mighty acts (106:8; 145:4,11,12; etc.) and in various places those attributes which a warrior-king might be expected to possess—wisdom, might, counsel and understanding—are attributed *par excellence* to God (Job 12:13; Prov 8:14). Isaiah (9:6; cf. 10:21) indicates that these will be the attributes of the Coming King, whose name is the Mighty God as well as the Prince of Peace, but he also makes it plain that justice and righteousness will accompany his might (cf. Ps 89: 13–14 [H 14–15]).

God's might draws the limits to man's might, for man's prowess is to be gloried in just so long as it does not overstep itself. When man sees his might as all he needs for successful living, he is deluded (Ps 33:16; 90:10; Eccl 9:11). When he, in the arrogance of his strength, pits himself against the Warrior-God, he will be destroyed (Ps 52; Jer 9:22; 46:5; etc.). Rather might must be tempered with wisdom (I Sam 2:9; Prov 16:32; 21:22) and the greatest wisdom of all is to trust God. Thus it is said that he is a *geber* (a male at the height of his powers) who trusts God (Ps 40:4 [H 5]). The man possessed of might who yet distrusts his own powers and instead trusts those of God is most truly entitled to the appellation "man" (Job 38:3; Jer 17:7; Mic 3:8). This is the "new man" of Paul, for he will have discovered that although transgressions have prevailed over him (Ps 65:3 [H 4]), the Lord's mercy will prevail over them (Ps 103:11) and that the Lord is indeed "mighty to save" (Ps 80:3).

geber. ***Man.*** As distinct from such more general words for man as *'ādām, 'ish, 'enôsh,* etc., this word specifically relates to a male at the height of his powers. As such it depicts humanity at its most competent and capable level. Sixty-six occurrences.

gibbôr. ***Mighty, strong, valiant, mighty man.*** (RSV often translates "warrior.") The heroes or champions among the armed forces. Occurs 156 times.

g^{e}bûrâ. ***Might.*** Refers especially to royal power. As such it is commonly ascribed to God. Sixty-three occurrences.

Bibliography: Fredriksson, H., *Jahwe als Krieger,* Lund: Gleerup, 1945. Kosmala, Hans, *Hebraer-Essener-Christen,* Brill, 1959, pp. 208–39. ______, "The Term *geber* in the Old Testament and in the Scrolls," Supp VT 17: 159–69. Kraeling, E. G., "The Significance and Origin of Gen 6; 1–4," JNES 6: 193–208. Miller, Patrick D., "The Divine Council and the Prophetic Call to War," VT 18: 100–107. ______, "God the Warrior," Interp 19: 39–46. Palache, J., *Semantic Notes on the Hebrew Lexicon,* Leiden: Brill, 1959, p. 18. Van der Ploeg, J., "Le sens de gibbor hail," RB 50: 120–25. Wright, G., *The Old Testament and Theology,* Harper, 1969, pp. 121–50. TDOT, II, pp. 367–81. THAT, I, pp. 398–401.

J.N.O.

311 גבשׁ (*gbsh*). **Assumed root of the following.**

311a גָּבִישׁ (*gābîsh*) ***crystal*** (Job 28:18, only).

312 גָּג (*gāg*) ***roof, housetop.***

This word appears thirty times in the OT and it usually signifies the highest point of an edifice, except for Ezk 30:3; 37:26 (the 'top' of the altar of incense) and Ezk 40:13 (the measuring of the outer court's east gate from the 'back' of one side to the 'back' of the other).

The roof that is referred to is flat, not peaked. This is obvious from several passages. The returned exiles erected booths and observed the feast of tabernacles o the roofs of their houses (Neh 8:16). Saul slept on the roof when, as a young lad, he visited Samuel (I Sam 9:25–26). It was from this vantage point that David spied Bathsheba bathing, and lust was spawned in his imagination (II Sam 11:2). Uriah's house was built most likely around a central courtyard which was left open to the sky. David's palace, the highest building of the complex, would command a view of the houses below. In the case of Samson (Jud 16:27) the roof was large enough to support 3,000 people. Rahab hid the spies among the stalks of flax on her roof (Josh 2:6,8). Probably she had laid out the flax to be retted by the dew.

Perhaps the Hebrew word means more than the roof itself. Proverbs 21:9 and 25:24 suggest (or affirm!) that it is better to accept solitariness and discomfort (in Hebrew, *pinnat gāg* "a corner of the housetop") than to put up with a nagging (NIV: quarrelsome) wife. This might well mean it is better, in such a situation, to be perched precariously on the corner of a roof (cf. the LXX *hupaithrou* "in the open air"). Or it may be a reference to a cramped attic such as a guest might use in an emergency (cf. I Kgs 17:19; II Kgs 4:10 though the root *gāg* is not used here).

The roof is a place where idolatry is invoked: Isa 15:3; 22:1; Jer 19:13; 32:29; 48:38. Three times (Ps 129:6; II Kgs 19:26; Isa 37:27) in the form of a curse, appears the formula "let them be like the grass on the 'housetops'." The analogy is to grass which springs up quickly on the flat roof of homes which are covered with packed earth. Having no depth of soil to take strong root in, the grass withers and dies (cf. Jesus' parable of the sower in Mt 13:3f.).

Bibliography: On the use of the root *gg* in Ugaritic, see Gordon, UT, 19: no. 556. Koehler, L., "Hebräischen Etymologien," JBL 59: 35–40, esp. pp. 37–38 derives both Hebrew and Ugaritic *gg* from Egyptian D*3*D*3* "head, roof."

V.P.H.

גַּד (*gad*) I, II. See nos. 313c,d.
גָּד (*gād*). See no. 313e.

313 גָּדַד (*gādad*) ***cut, invade.***

Derivatives

313a †גְּדוּד (*g^{e}dûd*) ***I, marauding band.***
313b †גְּדוּד (*g^{e}dûd*) ***II,*** גְּדוּדָה (*g^{e}dûdâ*) ***furrow, cutting.***
313c גַּד (*gad*) ***I, coriander.***
313d †גַּד (*gad*) ***II, fortune.***
313e †גָּד (*gād*) ***Gad.***

This verb is used eleven times in the OT. Seven of these are in the Hithpoel stem, and with two exceptions, they all refer to an act of self-laceration in an act of worship or to a custom of mourning. The most familiar passage will be the dramatic episode on Mount Carmel between Elijah and the prophets of Baal. In an attempt to invoke the power of Baal the prophets cried aloud and "cut themselves" after their custom with swords and lances (I Kgs 18:28). What exactly was the praxis behind these self-inflicted wounds is not sure. Everything has been suggested from the idea that this act was a substitute for human sacrifice to the idea that the effusion of blood established a covenant bond between the deity and the worshiper. More likely, since blood was so vital, the self-laceration was an act of imitative magic, and as the worshipers have relinquished a part of their essential self, so the deity will be prompted to unleash his power in whatever fashion it is called for at the moment (in this case, fire).

Since the Bible rejects the pagan idea that God can be coerced, it will also forbid such practices as are described in I Kgs 18:28. Thus, cf. Deut 14:1, "You shall not cut yourself." Three times there is a reference to this behavior in Jeremiah: 16:6; 41:5; 47:5, in the latter case with reference to the Philistines.

Two times in the Hithpoel stem the verb has nothing to do with the idea of cutting oneself. These are: (1) Jer 5:7, "And they 'trooped' to the houses of harlots," and (2) Mic 5:1 [H 4:14], "Now gather yourself in troops, O daughter of troops (*g^e dûd*)." (For the NIV footnote here, "Strengthen your walls, O walled city," cf. the Aram. *gûddā'* "wall"—Heb root *gādâ?*)

This reference from Micah is the usual nuance of *gādad* when it is used in the Qal: cf. Mic 6, Ps 94:21. Both times it is the invaded who speaks of the invader in a situation of uncertainty. Finally, we may note the use of the verb *gādad* in Gen 49:19 in connection with the "blessing of Jacob" upon Gad. The text reads: "As for Gad (*gād*), a troop (*g^e dûd*), shall raid him (*ye gûdennû*), but he shall raid (*yāgūd*) at the rear (*'āqēb*)." Obviously, this verse is full of puns as is illustrated by the deliberate alliteration.

g^edûd. ***A marauding band, troop.*** This noun appears thirty-two times in the OT excluding Ps 65:10 [H 11] where *g^edûd* is to be translated as "ridge," and is parallel to *t^elāmeyhā*, "its furrows," and Jer 48:37, *g^e dūdōt* "cuttings."

The word usually refers to those who take part in a military raid, but occasionally it may refer to the raid itself: II Sam 3:22. More often than not, the noun refers not to Israel's own troops but to those of her enemies: I Sam 30:8,15,23; I Kgs 11:24; II Kgs 5:2; 6:23; 24:2. In certain situations God may allow these unbelievers to inflict damage on his own people for chastisement (Jer 18:22).

A *g^edûd* could operate officially under royal sponsorship: II Sam 3:22 (David); II Sam 4:2 (Ishbosheth); II Chr 22:1 (Ahaziah); II Chr 25:9–10 (Amaziah); II Chr 26:11 (Uzziah). The function of such troops, perhaps mercenaries, was not to acquire land, but rather to put pressure for conformity on peoples already reduced to vassalage. In some cases these bands became primarily looters. This is the case of the "band" of the Amalekites mentioned in I Sam 30:8,15,23. There are a few references in the Bible to *g^e dûd* who operate independently; thus, "troop of robbers" in Hos 6:9; 7:1.

Two times the book of Job refers to God's *g^e dûd*: 19:12; 25:3, analogous to *Yahweh ṣ^e bā'ôt*, "Lord of hosts/armies." Job says that he himself was once like a king among his "troops" (Job 29:25).

gad ***II. Fortune.*** This word appears only twice in the OT. In Gen 30:11 it is a word play on the name of Gad. And Leah said, "Good fortune!", or as the KJV has it, "a troop comes" dividing the MT *bāgād* into something like *bā'/gad*. Speiser's translation in the Anchor Bible is "how propitious!" It seems preferable to translate it as an appellative and to connect it with such proper names as Gaddiel (Num 13:10), "El is my fortune"; Gaddi (Num 13:11), "my fortune"; Gadi (II Kgs 15:14–17); and the prophet Gad (I Sam 22:5).

The only other place where this word is used is Isa 65:11, "You who forsake the Lord... who set up a table for Gad (RSV "Fortune"), and fill cups of mixed wine for Meni (RSV, "Destiny")." Gad here seems to be a reference to a deity of fortune equivalent in meaning to the Greek Tyche. The rite described here is lectisterium, i.e. one in which food was spread before an image of the deity.

gād. ***Gad.*** The name of the first child born to Jacob by Zilpah, the maidservant of Leah and subsequently, one of the tribes to settle in the Transjordan area. His name is to be connected with *gādad/g^e dûd*. We have already discussed Gen 49:19 which points to Gad's capabilities in the area of military exploits. Deuteronomy 33:20 compares Gad to a crouching lion, ready to tear his victim to pieces. According to I Chr 5:18, Gad is "expert in war." Gad's leonine appearance is also stressed in I Chr 12:8. They were also as beautiful and swift as a gazelle.

V.P.H.

314 גדה (*gdh*). **Assumed root of the following.**
314a גָּדָה (*gādâ*) ***bank of river.***
314b †גְּדִי (*g^e dî*) ***kid.***
314c גְּדִיָּה (*g^edîyâ*) ***kids,*** only plural.

g^edî. ***Kid, a young goat.*** The etymology of the word is uncertain. In the husbandry of Israel a young male kid was the most expendable of the animals, less valuable than, say, a young lamb. The young males were used for meat; the females kept for breeding. Thus, a kid served admirably as a meat dish: Gen 27:9,16; Jud 6:19; 13:15; 15:1; I Sam 10:3; 16:20 (and cf. Lk 15:29, although as far as delicacy goes, not in the same class as a "fatted calf"). The kid could also serve as a present as in the case of what Judah gave to his daughter-in-law Tamar (Gen 38:17,20,23). When Isaiah gives us a glimpse of the eschatological age he says that "the wolf will lie down with the lamb (*kebeś*) and the leopard shall lie down with the kid (*g^e dî*, Isa 11:6).

Of special interest is the thrice repeated injunction against boiling "a kid in its mother's milk" (Ex 23:19; 34:26; Deut 14:21). Until recently the reason for this prohibition was enigmatic. This law is the basis for the Jewish Kashrut prohibition against preparing or consuming any food in which meat or milk or certain derivatives of the two are mixed.

Kids could be used for sacrifice as Num 15:11ff. indicates. But they could not be boiled in milk. The answer comes from the Canaanite Ugaritic texts, especially the story now popularly known as "The Birth of the Gods" or "The Story of Shahar ('dawn') and Shalim ('dusk')," in Gordon *UT*, 19: no 52. Lines 15, 16 of this story are:

15: *'l · 'iŝt · ŝb'd · ǵzrm · ṭb(ḫ* · g)d · *bḥlb · 'nnḫ · bḫm't*

15: Over the fire seven times the sacrificers cook a kid in milk, a lamb/mint (?) in butter.

The context indicates that a kid is cooked in milk at certain pagan sacrifices, possibly of first fruits, as part of a sacrificial meal to ensure good crops for the ensuing years. The Bible will repudiate this orientation to fertility cult practices. The blessing of fertile soil is from God, not magic.

Bibliography: Daube, D., "A Note on a Jewish Dietary Law," JTS 37: 289–91. Radin, M., "The Kid and Its Mother's Milk," AJSL 40: 209–18. TDOT, II, pp. 382–89. TWBAT, I, pp. 922–26.

V.P.H.

גְּדוּד (*g^{e}dûd*). I,II. See nos. 313a,b.
גָּדוֹל (*gādôl*). See no. 315d.
גְּדוּלָה (*g^{e}dûlâ*). See no. 315e.
גְּדוּפָה (*g^{e}dûpâ*). See no. 317a.
גְּדוּפִים (*g^{e}dûpîm*). See no. 317b.
גְּדִי (*g^{e}dî*). See no. 314b.
גְּדִיָּה (*g^{e}dîyâ*). See no. 314c.
גָּדִישׁ (*gādîsh*). See nos. 319a, 320a.

315 גָּדַל (*gādal*) ***grow up, become great or important, promote, make powerful, praise, (magnify), do great things.*** (ASV and RSV similar.)

Derivatives

315a †גָּדֵל (*gādēl*) ***becoming great, growing up.***
315b †גֹּדֶל (*gōdel*) ***greatness.***
315c גְּדִלִים (*g^{e}dilîm*) ***twisted threads.***
315d †גָּדוֹל (*gādôl*) ***great.***
315e †גְּדוּלָּה (*g^{e}dûllâ*) ***greatness.***
315f †מִגְדָּל (*migdāl*) ***tower.***
315g מִגְדּוֹל (*migdôl*) ***tower.***

The root is used for physical growth of people and other living things as well as for the increase of things tangible and intangible whether objects, sounds, feelings or authority. It overlaps in meaning with *rābab* and *rābâ* but unlike these roots it never refers to being numerous, only to being great in size, importance etc. It is combined with the divine name to form personal names, the most frequent form being Gedaliah meaning "the LORD is great" (II Kgs 25:22–25). In I Sam 26:24 the word means to set a high value on one's life. In Job 2:13 it is used for expressing intense grief while in I Kgs 10:23 it refers to the importance (greatness) of a king. It often speaks of God's greatness (II Sam 7:22) and Messiah is described as one who "will be great unto the ends of the earth" (Mic 5:4 [H 3]).

The meaning "cause to grow" or "rear" children, plants etc. is limited to the Piel stem. In both Piel and Hiphil stems, however, it bears the meaning "to magnify" or "consider great." This is how the psalmists frequently use the word, calling on the worshiper to ascribe greatness to the Lord and to his name (Ps 35:27; 40:16 [H 17]; 70:4 [H 5]).

In Ezk 38:23 the verb is used reflexively to show how God magnifies himself by means of his acts in nature and in history, to show the nations that he is the Lord. But in Isa 10:15 the same form is employed to show how evil man attempts to magnify himself against the Lord and in Dan 11:36–37 this is precisely the word used to describe what the Antichrist will do at the end of the age as he seeks to show himself omnipotent.

gādēl. ***Becoming great, rich*** (Gen 26:13), growing up (I Sam 2:26).

gōdel. ***Greatness*** of a king or a tree (Ezk 31:2,-7,18), the arm of God (Ps 79:11), the mercy of God (Num 14:19), and of God himself (Deut 3:24; 5:21 [H 24]; 9:26; 11:2; 32:3; Ps 150:2). Isaiah uses the word for the pride (insolence) of the human heart (Isa 9:8; 10:12).

gādôl. ***Great,*** an adjective with somewhat the same range of meanings as the verb (above) meaning "many" in number and other intensified concepts like "loudness," in sound, being old in years, great in importance.

g^{e}dûllâ. ***Greatness,*** especially as an attribute of God.

migdāl. ***Tower,*** probably deriving from early times when the tower was the largest (greatest) structure in a town.

Bibliography: TDOT, II, pp. 390–415. THAT, I, pp. 402–408.

E.B.S.

316 גָּדַע (*gāda'*) ***hew down, cut off, cut in two, shave off.***

Derivative

316a †גִּדְעוֹן (*gid'ôn*) ***Gideon.***

The verb *gāda'* frequently refers to the hewing down of idols (Ezk 6:6; Deut 7:5; 12:3; II Chr 14:2; 31:1; 34:4, 7). In Deut 7:5 and II Chr 14:2; 31:1 the objects that are to be hewn down are the Asherah poles, cult objects in honor of this Canaanite fertility goddess. Isaiah uses the verb to describe the cutting down of the king of Babylon who makes himself a god (Isa 14:12). The wicked treasurer Shebna is likened by Isaiah to a securely fastened peg that will be hewn down. On the other hand Isaiah predicts that the iron bars of cities will be cut in two so Cyrus can conquer them (Isa 45:2). In other places the verb simply means to cut down trees (Isa 9:9; 10:33). Isaiah also uses it to mean shave off the beard as a sign of mourning (Isa 15:2).

gid'ôn. ***Gideon,*** the judge (Jud 6–8). Several other proper names are derived from this root: Gideoni from the tribe of Benjamin (Num 1:11; 2:22; 7:60, 65) and Gidom, a place in the territory of Benjamin (Jud 20:45).

We may safely assume that Gideon's name came from the fact that he was a *gibbôr ḥayil* which is rendered "a mighty man of valor" in KJV. This term could also be rendered "a hero of the army." His name, Gideon, is connected with this occupation, that is, he was a "hacker" or "one who hewed down" the enemy. He was certainly not living up to his name at first when the angel of the LORD appeared to him in Jud 6:11, 12. But Gideon's breaking down the altar of Baal was much in keeping with his name. But then as a taunt to the followers of Baal his name was changed to Jerubbaal ("let Baal plead"). He became one of the major judges or rulers of Israel after his long-remembered victory over Midian (Isa 10:26; Ps 83:11).

E.B.S.

גִּדְעוֹן (*gid'ôn*) See no. 316a.

317 גָּדַף (*gādap*) ***revile men, blaspheme God.***

Derivatives

317a †גְּדוּפָה (*g^e dûpâ*) ***taunt.***
317b †גִּדּוּפִים (*giddûpîm*) ***reviling words.***

The verb appears to derive from a root which means to cut or to wound.

Psalm 44 tells us what the believer's attitude should be when God allows him to become an object of "scoffing and derision" (v. 13 [H 14]) from "the voice of him who reproaches and reviles" (v. 16 [H 17]). "While all this happened to us," the Psalmist says to the Lord, "We did not forget you, nor were we untrue to your covenant. Our hearts did not turn aside, nor did our steps leave your way ... No, for your sake we are killed all day long and considered as sheep to be slaughtered" (vv. 17 [H 18], 18 [H 19], 22 [H 23]). This latter verse contains the very words Paul quoted in Rom 8:36 when he presents the ultimate spirit of Christian triumph over the world, the flesh and the devil, saying, "Nay in all these things we are more than conquerors through him that loved us" (v. 37).

The root *gādap* also means "to blaspheme," that is revile God. The classic illustration of this is in the parallel passages in II Kgs 19:22 and Isa 37:23. There the servants of the king of Assyria stood outside the walls of Jerusalem and preached a whole sermon of blasphemy in the Hebrew language against the God of Israel. The LORD's oral response came through his prophet in Isa 37:22–36 (II Kgs 19:21–34). His historical response came through his angel that destroyed the army of Sennacherib.

g^edûpâ. ***Taunt.*** Compare Ezk 5:15 where of Jerusalem the prophet says, "She shall be a reproach and a taunt ... to the nations round about...."

giddûpîm. ***Reviling words.*** God warns through the prophet Isaiah that he will allow Israel to be abused with reviling words (Isa 43:28). But God also comforts the nation when it becomes the object of such abuse (Isa 51:7). He even promises to punish those nations that do it. Through Zephaniah he says, "I have heard ... the revilings of Ammon ... they shall become as Gomorrah" (Zeph 2:8).

Bibliography: TDOT, II, pp. 416–18.

E.B.S.

318 גָּדַר (*gādar*) ***wall up or off.***

Derivatives

318a גָּדֵר (*gādēr*) ***wall.***
318b גְּדֵרָה (*g^e dērâ*), גֶּדֶרֶת (*g^e deret*) ***wall.***

319 גדשׁ (*gdsh*) **I. Assumed root of the following.**

319a גָּדִישׁ (*gādîsh*) ***heap, stack*** (Ex 22:5; Jud 15:5; Job 5:26).

320 גדשׁ (*gdsh*) **II. Assumed root of the following.**

320a גָּדִישׁ (*gādîsh*) ***tomb*** (Job 21:32, only).

321 גָּהָה (*gāhâ*) ***be cured, healed.*** Based on Aramaic usage the root means "to be set free from guilt, pain or disease" (cf. Hos 5:13).

Derivative

321a גֵּהָה (*gēhâ*) ***a cure, healing.*** This noun is used in Prov 17:22. "The happy heart brings about a good cure," or "A happy mind is good medicine" (Beck).

322 גָּהַר (*gāhar*) ***bend, crouch*** (I Kgs 18:42; II Kgs 4:34–35).

323 גּוּב (*gûb*) ***dig*** (II Kgs 25:12).

Derivatives

323a גֵּב (*gēb*) ***II, pit, ditch, trench*** (e.g. Jer 14:3; II Kgs 3:16).

323b גֵּב (*gēb*) ***III, beam, rafter*** (I Kgs 6:9, only). Meaning uncertain.

גּוֹב (*gôb*). See no. 304b.

324 גּוֹג (*gôg*) ***Gog*** is the ruler of the land of Magog and prince of Rosh, Meshech and Tubal (Ezk 38 and 39). Gog is also the name of a Reubenite in I Chr 5:4.

324a †מָגוֹג (*māgôg*) ***Magog,*** the name of the land ruled by Gog (q.v.).

Ezekiel envisions this prince as the leader of a vast horde of armed troops that includes people from Persia, Cush, Put, Gomer, and Beth-togarmah. They will march against Israel at a time when the people of God have returned to their land and live in peace completely undefended. But this will all be allowed by the Lord that he might display his holiness among them. The people of God will not have to fight, for God himself will destroy the armies of Gog (Ezk 38:19–23). Revelation 20:7–9 places this event after "the thousand years are over," when "Satan will be released . . . and deceive all the nations . . . Gog and Magog, and mobilize them for war."

All attempts to trace the origin of the name Gog must be held to be tentative. Some see the name in Gyges of Lydia who drove away the Cimmerians (Gomer). Others see it in a name mentioned in Assyrian records, Gâgu, the chief of a mountain tribe north of Assyria (cf. BDB). It is not important theologically that we be able to trace the name linguistically or identify it historically. Most Christians intrepret these passages eschatologically. Precise interpretations differ. Some see the passage as highly symbolic of the final struggle between the Church and the forces of evil. Others taking it quite literally say the nation Israel will be attacked after the millenium when Satan is released only to be finally destroyed by being cast into the lake of fire. Others consider the references in Rev 20:7–9 to be allusions, not decisive as to the time of fulfilment and they identify the time of fulfilment as the battle of Armageddon before the millennium.

Magog. ***Magog.*** It is used in Ezk 32:2; 39:6 and Rev 20:8 in this eschatological sense. However, in the table of nations in Gen 10 (paralleled by I Chr 1:5) Magog is the name of a nation that descended from Japheth (v. 2). Here Magog has some connection with others related to Japheth, such as Gomer (Cimmerians?), Madai (Medes?), Javan (Ionians), Tubal, Meshech, and Tiras, some of whom are also mentioned in Ezk 38 and 39. They are all people who lived north of Israel, more or less, and who are of non-semitic origin.

Bibliography: TDOT, II, pp. 419–25.

E.B.S.

325 גּוּד (*gûd*) ***invade, attack*** (e.g. Gen 49:19; Hab 3:16).

גַּו (*gaw*). See no. 326a.
גֵּו (*gēw*). See no. 326b.

326 גוה (*gwh*). **Assumed root of the following.**

326a גַּו (*gaw*) ***back.***
326b גֵּו (*gēw*) ***back, midst.***
326c גֵּוָה (*gēwâ*) ***back.***
326d †גְּוִיָּה (g^e*wîyâ*) ***body, corpse.***
326e †גּוֹי (*gôy*) ***nation, people.***

g^ewîyâ. ***Body, carcass, corpse, dead body.*** The term refers to a body as an object, whether dead (as in the case of the lion's body, Jud 14:8–9, and Saul's corpse, I Sam 31:10,12), or else as alive (Egyptians so speak of themselves in Gen 47:18). Living bodies of creatures (Ezk 1:11, 23) and the angelic "man" (Dan 10:6) appear in visions; thus the objectivity of a vision is supported.

gôy. ***Gentile, heathen, nation, people.*** ASV and RSV differ and agree in various instances, e.g. Gen 10:5; *goy* appears twice. Both translate "nations" in one instance, but RSV has "peoples" in the other. It is difficult to ascertain the exact definition of the term. However, if one takes the various usages into consideration, as well as some seemingly related terms, *gaw, gēw, gēwâ,* the back part of the body; *gew,* Aramaic for midst; and g^e*wîyâ*, living body or corpse (see below), one must conclude that the basic idea is that of a defined body or group of people, or some specific large segment of a given body. The context will generally indicate the specific quality or characteristic which is to be understood.

[The synonym *ʿam* is used largely for a group of people or for people in general. However sometimes, especially in poetic parallel with *gôyim,* it may refer to a nation, whether a foreign nation or Israel. *gôyim* on the other hand more usually refers to nations, especially the surrounding pagan nations. l^e*ʾōm* is mainly used as a poetic synonym of either of the above words in either of their usages. R.L.H.]

The term *gôy* is used especially to refer to specifically defined political, ethnic or territorial groups of people without intending to ascribe a specific religious or moral connotation. Thus, in Gen 10:5 the writer speaks of defined groups of people according to their territories. When God speaks to Abraham about Egypt as a strong nation the term *gôy* is used. Elisha prayed that invading Syria, this *gôy,* might be blinded (II Kgs 6:18). In this general ethnic sense the term may even be used of Abraham's seed. Thus God said to Abraham, "I will make of you a great nation," i.e. a political, territorial, identified people (Gen 12:2; 17:20; 21:18). In Ex 33:13 Moses, referring to Israel, a distinct body of people, says, "This *gôy* (i.e., nation) is thy people (*'am*)." In Deut 4:6–7, Moses speaks of the Israelite nation as a political, ethnic body (*gôy*) which is a wise and understanding people (*'am*), existing as, and recognized by other nations as, a specific national identity (Ps 83:4 [H 5]). It is necessary to stress that the Scriptures speak of Israel's existing as a distinct nation in Moses' time because of the widespread misapprehension that Israel became a nation only after entering Canaan. Israel was a nation in Moses' time, just as it was in Joshua's time (Josh 3:17; 4:1; 5:6). So also in Jeremiah's time and thereafter, in spite of the exile (Jer 31:36).

The term (*gôyim*) is used in a number of specific ways. When a number of specific nations are referred to, it is this plural form that is used and the translators have rendered it as "nations" (Gen 10:31; Jud 2:23; Isa 61:11) or as "people" (Zech 12:3, KJV). The plural form is employed also to refer to the people dwelling in and around Canaan; these were definite ethnic, political, territorial groups, whom Israel as a nation was to dispossess (Deut 4:38; Josh 23:13) or among whom, for testing and judgment, Israel was to live (Jud 2:21, 23). But the plural form is also used occasionally to refer to the various national entities that were to proceed from Abraham (Gen 17:4–6). Sarah also was to be a mother of nations (Gen 17:16).

Once the descendants of Abraham had become a distinct, recognized, political, and ethnic group of people who were in a specific covenant relationship with Yahweh, the term *goy* and *gôyim* increasingly takes the meaning of "gentiles" or "heathen," in reference to the non-covenant, non-believing peoples considered as national groups. However, Israel is still repeatedly spoken of as *goy* also, e.g. when Israel is spoken of as taking possession of territory (Josh 3:17) or when foreigners speak of her (Deut 4:6). Israel is spoken of as an holy nation (gôy,) because of her covenant status, her redemption and circumcision (Josh 5:8). However, the rule is that the uncircumcised are the *goyim* (Jer 9:25).

The surrounding nations exhibit their heathen character by their wickedness (Deut 9:4–5), their abominations (Deut 18:9; II Chr 33:2), and the making of their own gods (II Kgs 17:29). These nations are said to rise up against God and oppress his covenant people, yet the Lord holds them in derision (Ps 59:8 [H 9]) and causes them to perish (Ps 10:16). Moses, and the prophets particularly, warned Israel that if they lived and worshiped as the *gôyim,* they would share in the judgment due the heathen (Deut 32:28; Isa 1:4; Mal 3:9).

It must not be concluded from the fact that the surrounding nations, the *gôyim,* although referred to as gentiles and heathen, are to be considered *per se* as helplessly lost, without God and hope. Rather, they are eventually to participate in all the blessings God promises to give to Abraham and his progeny upon condition of faith. The covenant people of Israel are God's people, but through them the *gôyim* are destined to be blessed of God in future days (Gen 12:1–3). In the meantime God will use the nations to punish his unfaithful covenant people (Jer 4:7; Hab 1:5ff.); on the other hand they will some day contribute to the glory of Israel (Isa 60:10ff.; Hag 2:6ff.). They too are invited to seek the Messiah that he may be a light to them (Isa 11:10; 42:6). Indeed, the *gôyim* are to join in the great procession to Mount Zion (Isa 2:2ff.) and of their children it is said that this one and that one were born in her (Ps 87:4 [H 5]). Thus there will be basically just one people of God, made up of believers from every tribe, tongue, people and nation; however, in OT times, it was through the covenant people, the *'am,* that the blessings of God were revealed to and bestowed upon the *gôyim.*

Bibliography: Cody, Aelred, "When Is the Chosen People Called a Goy?" VT 16: 1–6. Girdlestone, R. B., *Synonyms of the Old Testament,* Eerdmans, 1951. Moran, William L., "'A Kingdom of Priests'," in *The Bible in Catholic Thought,* Herder and Herder, 1962, pp. 7–20. Rost, L., "Die Bezeichnungen fur Land und Volk im Alten Testamentum," in *Festschrift Otto Procksch,* Leipzig, 1934. Speiser, E. A., "'People' and 'Nation' of Israel," JBL 79: 157–63. Watts, John D., "The People of God," Exp T 67: 232–37. TDNT, II, pp. 364–69. TDOT, II, pp. 426–37.

G.V.G.

גֵּוָה (*gēwâ*). See nos. 299h, 326c.

327 גוז (*gûz*) ***bring, cut off.*** (ASV and RSV similar.)

gûz conveys the idea (in various Semitic languages, such as Arabic *ǧâza*) "to pass." The life of aged people passes away (Ps 90:10). A wind made the quail pass over (Num 11:31). In the OT this verb refers to an acting source other than man.

G.V.G.

גּוֹזָל (*gôzāl*). See no. 337c.
גּוּחַ (*gûaḥ*). See no. 345.
גְּוִיָּה (*g^e wîyâ*). See no. 326d.
גּוֹי (*gôy*). See no. 326e.
גּוֹלָה (*gôlâ*). See no. 350a.

328 גָּוַע (*gāwa'*) ***be dead, die, give up the ghost, perish, yield up the ghost, ready to die.***

It is often used in connection with *mût* (Gen 25:8,17; 35:29; cf. 49:33; Num 20:29; Job 3:11, 14:10; Lam 1:19). In Num 17:12f. [H 17:27f.] it is parallel to *'ābad*.

Abraham was "well on in years," i.e. facing death, when he sent Eliezer to Padan-Aram to find a wife for Isaac (Gen 24:1; 25:8). Isaac "knew not the day of his death" when he attempted to bless Esau (Gen 27:2). Speiser suggests that Isaac did not necessarily consider that his end was near, but was in effect making a will using legal terminology paralleled in Nuzi. However, he had death in prospect. Jacob expired after setting out certain prospects for his sons (Gen 49:1,33).

Job was prepared to die if anyone could bring charges against him (Job 13:19) and promised his false friends that he was ready to maintain his integrity until he died (Job 27:5). God's afflictions, when resisted, end in death, a fate Israel at first feared after the Lord had vindicated Moses and Aaron against their complaint (Num 17:12–13 [H 27:27–28]), but a fate they later longed for when the water failed at Zin (Num 20:3). Achan died because of his iniquity (Josh 22:20), and all life is dependent upon God (Ps 104:29).

Bibliography: TDOT, II, p. 438. Speiser, E. A., "I Know Not the Day of My Death," *Oriental and Biblical Studies*, Univ. of Penn., 1967, pp. 89–96.

H.G.S.

329 *גּוּף (*gûp*) ***shut, close.*** This verb occurs only once, in the Hiphil (Neb 7:3).

Derivative

329a גּוּפָה (*gûpâ*) ***body, corpse.***

330 גּוּר (*gûr*) ***I, abide, be gathered, be a stranger, dwell (in/with), gather together, remain, sojourn, inhabit, surely, continuing.***

Derivatives

330a †גֵּר (*gēr*) ***sojourner.***
330b גֵּרוּת (*gērût*) ***lodging (place).***
330c †מָגוֹר (*māgôr*) ***I, sojourning place.***
330d מְגוּרָה (*m^e gûrâ*) ***storehouse, granary.***
330e מַמְּגֻרוֹת (*mamm^e gūrôt*) ***storehouse, granary.***

The root means to live among people who are not blood relatives; thus, rather than enjoying native civil rights, the *gēr* was dependent on the hospitality that played an important role in the ancient near east. When the people of Israel lived with their neighbors they were usually treated as protected citizens; foreigners in Israel were largely regarded as proselytes.

Often because of famine the people of Israel lived as protected citizens outside the promised land: Abraham in Egypt (Gen 12:10); Israel in Egypt (47:4); Isaac with Abimelech of Gerar (26:3). In the case of the Patriarchs, however, they became "protected" citizens in the promised land through the call of God (Gen 17:8; 20:1; 23:4). Hebrews 11:9,13 describes them as pilgrims and strangers, evidence that they did not regard themselves as members of the sinful world. Many passages illustrate this meaning. Abraham, Isaac, and Jacob only sojourned in Canaan (Ex 6:4), although Isaac and Jacob were born there. The land had not been given to them because the iniquity of the Amorites was not yet full (Gen 15:16). The Israelites are called sojourners (*gērîm*) in Egypt (Deut 10:17–19; Ex 22:20); being outsiders at the beginning and virtual slaves at the end of their stay.

Jacob describes his stay with Laban as a sojourn, for he expected to return to Canaan. Lot dwelled in Sodom, but when he quarrelled with the men of Sodom he was scornfully called a sojourner, i.e. a foreigner, one without voice in community affairs (Gen 19:9).

Israel in exile in Mesopotamia was said to sojourn there (Ezr 1:4) because exiled from their covenant home. wthe Canaanites became *gērîm* after the conquest (Ex 20:10; 22:20; 23:9), because their sin had voided any privileges conferred upon them under the common grace of God. Even Israel is termed a sojourner in the sense that their tenure in the land was effective only as long as they honored the Covenant.

In the age to come the wolf will be the protected citizen of the lamb (Isa 11:6). Evil never enjoys that status with God (Ps 5:4 [H 5]); but the Psalmist regards himself as such before the Lord (Ps 39:1–13; I Chr 29:15). Indeed, even after the Conquest Israel is still a sojourner in the land, for the land belongs to the Lord (Lev 25:23).

gēr. ***Alien, sojourner, stranger,*** referring to someone who did not enjoy the rights usually possessed by the resident. The clearest sense of the noun *gēr* is seen when used of Israel in their sojourn in Egypt (Ex 23:9; Gen 15:13). Moses named his son Gershom in memory of his stay in

Midian (Ex 18:3), for he had been exiled from both Egypt and Canaan. Abraham, Isaac and Jacob lived as strangers in Canaan (Ex 6:4) meaning that they had no property rights there.

The *gēr* in Israel was largely regarded as a proselyte. He was to be present for the solemn reading of the Law (Deut 31:12) showing that he was exposed to its demands. The law concerning "unleavened bread" applied to him as well as the native (Ex 12:19), and a circumcised *gēr* could keep Passover (Ex 12:48f.; Num 9:14). He was also included in the festival of the Great Day of Atonement (Lev 16:29) and was expected to celebrate the Feast of Booths (Deut 16:14). With the native he was threatened with the death penalty if he offered a sacrifice to a foreign god (Lev 17:8f.) and was forbidden to eat blood (17:10,12,13). Though in contrast to the native he was allowed to eat what had died or was torn (Deut 14:21), like the native Israelite he underwent special cleansing (Lev 17:15f.). He was also included in the rites of cleansing with the ashes of the red heifer (Num 19:10). The laws of sexual chastity applied to him as well as the native (Lev 18:26) along with the Sabbath laws (Ex 20:10; 23:12). In a word he was to show the same fidelity to the Lord (Lev 20:2).

He also enjoyed many of the same rights as the native and was not to be oppressed (Ex 22:21 [H 20]; Lev 19:3; Jer 7:6; 22:3). He is mentioned in connection with the poor (Lev 19:10; cf. 23:22) and with orphans and widows (Deut 14:29; 16:11, 14; 24:17; 26:13; 27:19). With them he shared the sheaf left in the field (24:19) and the gleanings in the olive trees and in the vineyards (24:20–21) along with the tithe every three years (14:27; 26:12). He was to be treated righteously in judgment (1:16; 24:17; 27:19) and the six asylum cities were also cities of refuge for him (Num 35:15). In a word the Lord loves the *gēr* (Deut 10:18). Israel should not oppress him because they themselves were oppressed and know his soul (Ex 22:21; [H 20]; Deut 10:19). They were to love him as themselves (Lev 19:34).

David employed them as stonecutters (I Chr 22:2) and they served in the army (II Sam 1:13). Solomon made them stonecutters and burdenbearers (II Chr 2:17f. [H 16f.]). In the curse formulae of Deut 27 it is predicted that the social order would be reversed and the *gēr* become the head, the Israel the tail.

māgôr. ***Dwelling, pilgrimage, where they sojourn, wherein one is a stranger.*** It occurs only in the plural, *m^e gûrîm*. This is used of the places where Abraham, Isaac, and Jacob dwelled in their pilgrimage (Gen 36:7). Job's figure of an empty house as a judgment (Job 18:19) indicates it has become a place of pilgrimage, a temporary abode. Psalm 119:54 shows a similar usage. The point seems to be that wherever man lives, his existence is essentially transient, and dependent on the grace of God. But when he lives in obedience to the divine will, his life is full of expectancy and assurance of that eternal life to come (cf. Heb 11:9–10,13–14,16).

Bibliography: TDNT, V, pp. 8–28, 842–51; VI, pp. 728–42. TDOT, II, pp. 439–49. THAT, I, pp. 409–12. Levison, Nahum, "The Proselyte in Biblical and Early Post-Biblical Times," SJT 10: 45–56. Marmorstein, Emile, "The Origins of Agricultural Feudalism in the Holy Land," PEQ 85: 118–23. Neufeld, Edward, "The Prohibitions against Loans at Interest in Ancient Hebrew Laws," HUCA 26: 355–412. North, Robert, "Biblical Jubilee and Social Reform," *Scripture* 4: 323–35.

H.G.S.

331 גּוּר (*gûr*) ***II.*** (The RSV variously translates seven occurrences of this root as band selves together, gather together, gash, stir up wars, stir up strife.)

Derivatives

331a גּוֹר (*gôr*) ***whelp.***
331b גּוּר (*gûr*) ***whelp, young.***

In Arabic this root means "to act wrongfully against." It is probably a subordinate form of *gārâ* "to attack."

The root means to stir up trouble or difficulties for someone or among people.

In Isa 54:15 the infinitive absolute with the imperfect occurs, but is indistinguishable in form from *gûr* I (q.v.), so that it could be translated either "gather together" or "stir up strife." The "crowd together" of KD favors the former. But cf. NIV "attack."

The RSV translation of "band together" in Ps 56:6 [H 7]; 59:3 [H 4] would be more expressively translated as "stir up strife," along with "they have waited for my life." Cf. the Arabic expression *ğâr 'al* "to act wrongfully against" with Ps 59:3 *gûr*.

In Ps 140:2 [H 3] the RSV "stir up strife" agrees well with the other half of the parallelism, "plan evil things in their heart."

In Hos 7:14, the RSV translates *yitgôrārû* as "gash" as though from *gādâ*, which is based on reading daleth for resh.

H.G.S.

332 גּוּר (*gûr*) ***III, be afraid, fear, stand in awe.*** It is probably a by-form of *ygr* "to be afraid." The RSV translates in addition "be in great dread, tremble."

Derivatives

332a †מָגוֹר (*māgôr*) ***II, fear, terror.***
332b †מְגוֹרָה (*m^e gôrâ*) ***fear, terror.***

This root means to be intimidated before a stronger or superior being or thing. It is used of fear toward men, animals and God. The Moabites feared the Israelites when the Moabites appeared on the horizon, because of their great numbers (Num 22:3).

Judges are instructed not to fear "the face of men," i.e. not to let the social position of any adversary in litigation intimidate them nor sway them in judgment (Deut 1:17).

The threats of a false prophet were not to turn the people from God (Deut 18:22).

Although David was only a stripling, the gifts bestowed on him impressed and then frightened Saul (I Sam 18:15).

Job rejects the implied charge of secret sin, avowing his innocency and claiming that he would see God in the flesh; therefore his slanderers should fear judgment (Job 19:29).

Leviathan strikes fear in even the mighty men of the earth (Job 41:25 [H 17]).

The Lord is pictured as fearing the boasters of the heathen if they chasten Israel (Deut 32:27). But Samaria is to fear the consequences of the idols in Bethel (Hos 10:5).

māgôr, m^e^gôrâ. ***Fear, terror.*** This noun, "horror," in KB, occurs less frequently than *yārē'* or *pāḥad*. *māgôr* has the more extreme sense of terror, in contrast to *yārē'* which is more restrained (Ps 31:13, [H 14]; cf. Ps 111:10 and 19:9 [H 10]; Jer 20:4; cf. Prov 14:26. Deliverance from the terror of human caprice rests in God (Ps 34:4 [H 5]; cf. v. 1 [H]; cf. also the familiar phrase in Jeremiah, *māgôr missābîb,* terror on every side, 6:25, etc.).

H.G.S.

גּוֹרָל (*gôrāl*). See no. 381a.
גּוּמָּץ (*gûmaṣ*). See no. 362a.

333 גושׁ (*gwsh*). **Assumed root of the following.**
333a גּוּשׁ (*gûsh*) ***clod, lump*** (Job 7:5, only).

גֵּז (*gēz*). See no. 336a.

334 גִּזְבָּר (*gizbār*) ***treasurer*** (Ezr 1:8, only).

335 גָּזָה (*gāzâ*) ***cut, cut off, sever.***

Derivative

335a †גָּזִית (*gāzît*) ***a cutting, hewing***

The word is used especially of hewn stones. This kind of stone was forbidden on the original altar prescribed in Ex 20:25. Lifting up a tool to shape the stones of the altar was polluting it. The reason was not that iron was a tabu metal as some have suggested on the basis of Deut 27:5 (note that Ex does not mention iron), but simply that a graven and ornamental altar might become the object of worship instead of the Lord of the altar. A similar idea is present in I Kgs 6:7 where the shaping of the stones of the temple was to be done before they were brought to the site. "So that there was neither hammer nor axe nor any tool of iron heard in the house, while it was being built." Such stones were used in Solomon's palace (I Kgs 7:9, 11) as in all large buildings of OT times (Amos 5:11; Isa 9:10). The only reference to hewn stone in Ezekiel's visionary temple is in 40:42 where four tables of hewn stone were prescribed for preparing the burnt offering.

E.B.S.

גִּזָּה (*gizzâ*). See no. 336b.

336 גָּזַז (*gāzaz*) ***shear*** (a sheep), ***mow*** (grass), ***cut off*** (hair or a nation).

Derivatives

336a †גֵּז (*gēz*) ***shearing.***
336b †גִּזָּה (*gizzâ*) ***fleece.***

gēz. ***shearing*** or ***mowing.*** Amos 7:1 may refer to either but Ps 72:6 clearly refers to mowing.

gizzâ. ***fleece.*** Used only of Gideon's fleece in Jud 6:37–40.

Job tore his garments and cut off his hair as a symbol of mourning when he received word of the violent death of his children. Likewise Micah (1:16) calls on the nation, and Jeremiah (7:29) calls on Jerusalem to cut off the hair and be bald in mourning over pending destruction. Nahum uses the verb *gāzaz* to describe the cutting off (destruction) of Assyria. Isaiah uses the term to illustrate the meekness with which the Suffering Servant receives punishment in behalf of those who have gone astray into sin. "Like a ewe that is dumb before those who shear her so he does not open his mouth" (Isa 53:7).

E.B.S.

גָּזִית (*gāzît*). See no. 335a.

337 גָּזַל (*gāzal*) ***seize, tear off, pull off, take away by force, rob.***

Derivatives

337a גָּזֵל (*gāzēl*) ***robbery*** (Lev 5:21; Ps 62:11; Isa 61:8), ***something plundered*** (Ezk 22:29).
337b גְּזֵלָה (*g^e^zēlâ*) ***robbery*** (Ezk 18:7), stolen goods (Ezk 33:15; Isa 3:14; Lev 5:23).
337c גּוֹזָל (*gôzāl*) ***young*** (of birds). Derivation uncertain.

In Jud 9:25 the picture is one of people who lie in wait and rob those who come along the road.

This root has in its meaning the violence that goes beyond mere stealing or taking another's belongings but includes robbing by force, tearing off. One of the most violent horrors of the ancient world was the practice of flaying people, that is, literally skinning them alive. It was one of the atrocities committed by the armies of Assyria. Although using the verb somewhat figuratively the prophet Micah has such flaying in mind when he uses this verb in Mic 3:2, "You who hate good and love evil, who tear the skin from off them . . . and who flay their skin."

In other contexts the verb refers to deeds of similar horror. For example, tearing a fatherless child from the breast (Job 24:9), seizing by violence wells of water (Gen 21:25), houses (Job 20:19), and fields (Mic 2:2). As noted above, Eccl uses the root to speak of political violence, the tearing away of justice and righteousness in a country (5:8). Proverbs 4:16 describes the truly wicked people as "those who are robbed of their sleep unless they do evil and cause someone to fall."

Bibliography: TDOT, II, pp. 456–60.

E.B.S.

338 גזם (*gzm*). **Assumed root of the following.**
338a †גָּזָם (*gāzām*) ***locust.***

A name derived from the verb *gāzam* "to cut off." It occurs in but three passages: Joel 1:4; 2:25; Amos 4:9. The KJV translates it as the "palmerworm," i.e. a processional caterpillar like a "palmer" or a pilgrim with a palm branch. The LXX translates the term as *kampē* "caterpillar."

The *gāzām* may be an immature locust in a certain stage of development. Ordinarily locusts do not attack olive leaves until everything else has been consumed. Thus Amos 4:9 describes a situation of complete devastation.

E.M.Y.

339 גזע (*gz'*). **Assumed root of the following.**
339a גֶּזַע (*geza'*) ***stock, stem*** (Isa 11:1; 40:24; Job 14:8).

340 גָּזַר (*gāzar*) ***cut down, cut off, cut in two, divide, snatch, decree.*** (ASV and RSV similar.)

Derivatives

340a †גֶּזֶר (*gezer*) ***part.***
340b †גְּזֵרָה (*g^e zērâ*) ***separation.***
340c גִּזְרָה (*gizrâ*) ***cutting, separation.***
340d מַגְזֵרָה (*magzērâ*) ***cutting instrument, ax.***

The root with its derivatives occurs forty-one times, sixteen of which are represented by the proper noun Gezer, a Levitical city on the border of Ephraim. Like its synonym *kārat,* this root has the basic meaning "to sever."

The verb describes the division of an object into parts (I Kgs 3:25; II Kgs 6:4) and even the chewing of food (Isa 9:19). When followed by the preposition *min* (from) it connotes a violent severance from a former way of life. The cutting off might be from the fold (Hab 3:17), worship (II Chr 26:21), the protective care of God (Ps 88:5 [H 6]), or life itself (Isa 53:8). The Niphal without the preposition refers more generally to death or destruction (Ezk 37:11; Lam 3:54). In Est 2:1 and Job 22:28 the verb has the connotation common in Aramaic, of making a pronouncement; cf. our English word "decide" from the Latin, "to cut off from."

gezer. ***Part, piece, in sunder.*** Used only in the plural of the halves of animals (Gen 15:17) and the divided portions of the Red Sea (Ps 136:13).

g^ezērâ. ***Separation, not inhabited.*** Used in Lev 16:22 of the "land of separation" (ASV and RSV "solitary land") into which a live goat was taken and abandoned on the day of atonement.

It was so called because the area was cut off from water (KB) or from habitation. Later Jewish teachers interpreted *g^e zērâ* to mean a precipice from which the goat was to be hurled down.

J.E.S.

גָּחוֹן (*gāḥôn*). See no. 342a.

341 גחל (*gḥl*). **Assumed root of the following.**
341a †גַּחֶלֶת (*gaḥelet*) ***coal, burning coal, coals of fire, hot coals.*** (ASV and RSV similar except once "hot embers" and once "glowing coals.")

Wood coals (as opposed to *peḥem,* black coals, charcoal) were used for cooking (Isa 44:19), heating (Isa 47:14), and burning incense (Lev 16:12). Burning coals are figurative of lightning (Ps 18:9), a single heir of a dying house (II Sam 14:7), strife (Prov 26:21), shame (Prov 25:22), and divine judgment (Ps 120:4; 140:10 [H 11]).

Bibliography: TDOT, II, pp. 461–65.

J.E.S.

342 גחן (*gḥn*). **Assumed root of the following.**
342a גָּחוֹן (*gāḥôn*) ***belly, of reptiles*** (Gen 3:14; Lev 11:42).

343 גַּיְא (*gay'*) ***valley.***

Several Hebrew words are used to designate the various kinds of valleys which are part of the topography of Canaan. The larger plains are called *biq'â* and *'ēmeq. naḥal* suggests a valley which has a gully. *gay'* seems to be restricted to elongated and flat-bottom depressions.

Perhaps the most famous valley in the OT is the

Valley of Hinnom just south of Jerusalem. Here Moloch was worshiped with immolations of children (II Chr 28:3; 33:6). After Josiah abolished this practice and desecrated the valley (II Kgs 23:10), it came to be associated with the judgment of sinners (Jer 7:32; 19:6). Later the place was made a garbage dump. The NT writers transliterated *gay' hinnōm* (via Aramaic) into Greek and applied the term *géenna* to the place of eternal punishment.

gay' is used figuratively of an obstacle which must be overcome (Isa 40:4) and of a grave danger which one might experience (Ps 23:4). In OT eschatology the "valley of passengers" (RSV "travelers") east of the Dead Sea is designated as the burial site for the hostile armies of Gog (Ezk 39:11, 15). A valley-like escape route is provided for the people of God at the Second Coming of Christ (Zech 14:4–5).

J.E.S.

344 גיד (*gyd*). **Assumed root of the following.**

344a גִּיד (*gîd*) ***sinew*** (e.g. Gen 32:33; Isa 48:8).

345 גִּיחַ (*gîaḥ*), גּוּחַ (*gûaḥ*) ***burst forth.***

Derivative

345a †גִּיחוֹן (*gîḥôn*) ***Gihon.*** A proper noun derived from a root signifying "to burst forth or draw forth" (BDB), and hence has the meaning "the Gusher" or "the Bubbler."

Gihon is used once of a river and five times of a spring of water. The second-named of the four tributaries which joined to form the river of Eden is called Gihon (Gen 2:13). It is said in the KJV to compass the whole land of Ethiopia (ASV and RSV Cush). While *kûsh* in the OT usually refers to Ethiopia, the reference here is to the land of the Kassites located east of the Tigris. The verb *sābab* rendered "compass" (KJV, ASV) or "flow around" (RSV) is better rendered "to wind through or meander." The primeval Gihon river must have been one of the several rivers which descend from the eastern mountains to join the Tigris river in the Mesopotamian plain. Most likely the Gihon is to be identified with either the Diyala or the Kerkha river.

By the spring Gihon, on the eastern side of Jerusalem, Solomon was proclaimed king (I Kgs 1:33ff.). From earliest times this spring was a prominent part of the waterworks of Jerusalem. Hezekiah constructed a rock hewn tunnel which carried the water of Gihon into the fortifications of the city (II Chr 32:30). Gihon is usually identified with the Spring of Steps which gushes intermittently throughout the day.

Bibliography: Harris, R. L., "The Mist, the Canopy and the Rivers of Eden," JETS 4: 177–79. Simon, J., *Jerusalem in the Old Testament*, Brill, 1952. Speiser, E. A., "The Rivers of Paradise," in *Oriental and Biblical Studies*, University of Pennsylvania, 1967, pp. 23–34. TDOT, II, pp. 466–68.

J.E.S.

גִּיחוֹן (*gîḥôn*). See no. 345a.

346 גִּיל (*gîl*) ***rejoice, be glad.***

Derivatives

346a †גִּיל (*gîl*) ***I, rejoicing.***
346b גִּיל (*gîl*) ***II, circle, age.***
346c †גִּילָה (*gîlâ*) ***rejoicing.***

Root meaning is "to circle around" from which such ideas as "to circle in joy" are readily derived. The root meaning is more applicable to vigorous, enthusiastic expressions of joy; but, in the OT, it and its derivatives serve as poetic and prophetic terms for various kinds of joy.

gîl most often refers to rejoicing at God's works or attributes. Typical examples are rejoicing at God's work in general (Ps 118:24), his restoration of his people (Isa 49:13), his delivering from enemies (Ps 9:14 [H 15]) and protection from enemies (Ps 31:7–8), God's glory and judgment (Ps 97:8), and God's rule (I Chr 16:31). Other occasions for such rejoicing are a wise son (Prov 23:25), a beautiful bride (Song 1:4), dividing the spoils (Isa 9:3 [H 2]), and the enemy's misfortune (Ps 13:4 [H 5]). The wicked rejoice in evil (Prov 2:14).

"Rejoice with trembling" (Ps 2:11, ASV) may allude to the physical movement associated with the term's root meaning.

gîl. ***Joy, rejoicing, gladness*** (in the prepositional phrase, "for joy," it may be translated "greatly" or "exceedingly," Prov 23:24). This term expresses a wide range of joys ranging from the exuberant joy of an oriental wedding procession (Ps 45:15 [H 16]) to the quieter joy of the discouraged whose woes are ended by death (Job 3:22). Other joys expressed by this term are those of the satisfied father (Prov 23:24), the worshiper of God (Ps 43:4), and God-given prosperity (Ps 65:12 [H 13]). It also expresses the joy removed by judgment (Isa 16:10; Joel 1:16).

gîl. ***Age*** (from "to circle"; KJV "sort"). Refers to Daniel's circle of contemporaries (Dan 1:10).

gîlâ. ***Joy, rejoicing.*** Feminine of *gîl* above. Twice refers to the joys to come when God restores his people (Isa 35:2; 65:18).

J.P.L.

347 גיר (*gyr*). **Assumed root of the following.**

347a גִּר (*gir*) ***chalk, lime*** (Isa 27:9, only).

גַּל (*gal*). See no. 353a.
גֵּל (*gēl*). See no. 353b.

348 גלב (*glb*). **Assumed root of the following.**
348a גַּלָּב (*gallāb*) ***barber*** (Ezk 5:1).

גַּלְגַּל (*galgal*). See no. 353i.
גִּלְגָּל (*gilgāl*). See nos. 353j,k.
גֻּלְגֹּלֶת (*gūlgōlet*). See no. 353l.

349 גלד (*gld*). **Assumed root of the following.**
349a גֶּלֶד (*geled*) ***skin*** (of man, Job 16:15).

350 גָּלָה (*gālâ*) ***uncover, remove.***

Derivatives

350a †גּוֹלָה (*gôlâ*) ***captivity.***
350b †גָּלוּת (*gālût*) ***captivity.***
350c גִּלָּיוֹן (*gillāyôn*) ***table, tablet.***

Hebrew *gālâ* in its transitive meaning "to uncover" has its closest connections with Northwest Semitic (cf. Phoenician in the Ahiram Inscription, "... and *uncovered* this sarcophagus," and Imperial Aramaic in the Word of Ahiqar, "Do not *reveal* your secrets to your friends") and with Arabic *ǧalā* "to make/become clear."

In its intransitive meaning "to remove, go into exile" it is remotely related to the Ugaritic verb of motion *gly* "to leave" (Gordon) or "to arrive at" (Aistleitner), as well as to the Arabic *ǧalā* "to emigrate." It occurs as a loan word with this meaning in late Aramaic and Akkadian.

The meaning "to uncover" occurs in the Qal, Niphal, Piel, Pual and Hithpael stems, and the meaning "to depart, to go into exile" occurs in the Qal, Hiphil and Hophal stems.

In the light of this evidence it must remain at this point an open question whether we are dealing with one or two roots. In any case, we will discuss the verb under these two main meanings: "to uncover," and "to depart, to go into exile."

"*To uncover.*" In the Qal the verb is used frequently with the organs of sense as the object: the ear (I Sam 9:15, *passim*) and the eye (Num 24:4).

The idiom "to uncover the ear" means simply "to show, to reveal" and occurs with either man or God as its subject. With man as its subject it occurs in connection with Saul to Jonathan (I Sam 20:2), of Jonathan to David (I Sam 20:12–13), of aides to Saul (I Sam 22:8), of priests to Saul (I Sam 22:17); of Boaz to the nearer kinsman (Ruth 4:4). With God as its subject: to Samuel (I Sam 9:15); to David (II Sam 7:27 = I Chr 17:25) to ordinary humans (in the Elihu speech—Job 33:16; 36:10). Since it is used of men as well as of God, it must not be thought of as a technical term for God's revelation. To Samuel he reveals himself directly (cf. Isa 22:14) and to David he sometimes mediated his revelation through the prophet Nathan. To ordinary folk he reveals himself in dreams or visions (Job 33:16) and in trying experiences (Job 36:10).

Amos used *gālâ* with *sōd* "secret" as its object in this classic statement about God's revelation to his prophets: "Surely the LORD God will do nothing but he *revealeth* his secret unto his servants the prophets" (Amos 3:7). (The verb also has *sōd* as its object in Prov 20:19.)

When God revealed himself to Balaam it is said that Balaam's eyes were "uncovered," "opened" (Num 24:4,6). It appears that in this manner Balaam saw something which he otherwise could not see.

In addition to these private disclosures, the Qal of *gālâ* is used for widespread communication. During the intrigue and contest between Haman and Mordecai the letters of the king were published to all the people of the provinces proclaiming what both Haman (Est 3:14) and Mordecai (8:13) had written. The Qal passive participle is used in Jer 32:11, 14, to denote an "open" document in contrast to a sealed one.

In the Niphal the action happens to the subject itself in either a passive or reflexive way. Thus in a passive sense it means "to be uncovered": of nakedness (Ex 20:26; Isa 47:3), of skirts (Jer 13:22), and of foundations (II Sam 22:16 = Ps 18:16) where it is parallel to the Niphal of *rā'â* "to be visible." Thus it also means "to be known" (Isa 23:1) and "to be revealed"—of a word from God to Daniel (Dan 10:1).

In the reflexive sense it means "to expose oneself" (three times of David in II Sam 6:20) or "to show/reveal oneself," of Jonathan to the Philistines (I Sam 14:8), of the gates to death to Job (Job 38:17) and of God. With God it is used to designate his theophany to Jacob (Gen 35:7; cf. Gen 28). The word is also used of God's revelation three times in the stories of Samuel's childhood: of his revelation to Eli's fathers (I Sam 2:27), to Samuel (I Sam 3:21; cf. I Sam 3:7). Here, as in the idiom "to uncover the ear" and in Amos' classic statement it denotes the revelation of God to a prophet.

The Niphal participle with a passive notion is used in Deut 29:28 to denote God's open threats and promises revealed to Israel in that book. According to Isa 40:5 the glory of the LORD—his triumphant victory on earth through his rule in Israel—will be revealed to all flesh. It has the same meaning in Isa 56:1. It is used in Isa 53:1 for the revelation to mankind of God's work through the Suffering Servant.

Thus, though not a technical term for divine revelation, the verb *gālâ* frequently conveys this meaning.

Likewise in the Piel it always denotes "to uncover" something which otherwise is normally concealed. Thus it means "to open" the eyes—to see an angel (Num 22:31) or wonderful things in the law (Ps 119:18); "to make known, revealed, manifest": of Jeremiah in his complaint to the Lord (Jer 11:20; 20:12), of the LORD in his revelation of peace and truth to Israel (Jer 33:6) and his righteousness to them (Ps 98:2); "to betray": of fugitives (Isa 16:3), of secrets (Prov 11:13; 25:9); "to uncover, expose": of Esau's hiding place (Jer 49:10), the mysteries of darkness (Job 12:22), foundations (Mic 1:6), sin (Job 20:27; Lam 2:14; 4:22), and feet (Ruth 3:4,7).

But it is used most frequently in this stem for designating proscribed sexual activity. It occurs twenty-four times in Lev 18 and 20 in the expression "to uncover the shame" which denotes sexual intercourse in proscribed situations, usually incest, also Deut 22:30 [H 23:1]; 27:20. It is also used of uncovering or removing that which covers: the woman's skirt (Isa 47:3; Nah 3:5), of Judah's protective covering (Isa 22:8), and Leviathan's outer armor (Job 41:13 [H 5]). In many passages, then, it has the connotation "to shame."

Alongside of Lev 18 and 20 it occurs in the prophetic complaint that Israel has "uncovered her nakedness," a metaphor denoting that she threw off her loyalty to the Lord. Against this, the Lord or her former lovers will "expose the nakedness" = "to shame" of the faithless nation (Hos 2:12; Ezk 16:36); cf. the threat against Nineveh (Nah 3:5) and against Babylon (Isa 47:3).

"*To remove, go into exile.*" The basic meaning of the intransitive *gālâ* appears in Ezk 12:3 where the prophet receives the commandment "go forth" and in the lament of Phineas's travailing wife: "The glory of Israel is departed." A similar meaning is found in Isaiah's lament: "The mirth of the land is gone" (Isa 24:11) and in this description by Zophar of the fate of the wicked: "The increase of his house shall depart" (Job 20:28). It also has this simple meaning "to depart" in Prov 27:25 and Hos 10:5.

In the remaining twenty passages in the Qal it has the more precise meaning "to be led into captivity." In addition it occurs thirty nine times in the Hiphil with the meaning "to carry away into exile" and seven times in the passive Hophal with a similar meaning as in Qal. The verb figures prominently in the announcement of judgment by Amos (1:5; 5:5,27; 6:7; 7:11,17) and Jeremiah (13:19; 20:4; 22:12; 27:20; cf. Lam 1:3; see also Isa 5:13).

In several passages the Lord is designated as the subject who leads Israel into captivity (Jer 29:4,7,14; Ezk 39:28; Amos 5:27; Lam 4:22; I Chr 5:41—the only place where the human agent [Nebuchadnezzar] is explicitly mentioned; cf. of other people in II Kgs 17:11). Usually, however, Israel (Judah) or its glory is the subject of the verb.

The Lord's judgment of leading Israel out of the land into captivity functions as an appropriate contrast to his carrying out his promise to give them the land as a gift at the beginning of their history. Likewise, his repeated promises to the fathers to give them the land stand out sharply against his repeated warnings through the prophets to lead them out of the land. In II Kgs 17:11 Israel's expulsion from the land is explicitly paralleled with the fate of the Canaanites whom he expelled in favor of Israel when they entered the land.

It is instructive to note that the verb never occurs in Deuteronomy. In this book the threat of eviction from the land is expressed by other expressions such as "to perish quickly (*'bd*) from upon the land" (Deut 4:26; 11:17), and *pûṣ* (Hiphil) "to scatter." If the putative Mosaic addresses contained in Deuteronomy are in fact of late origin, as is commonly alleged, it seems strange that *gālâ*, the common term for eviction from the land in the ninth to seventh century prophets, does not occur.

gôlâ. ***Captivity, captive, those carried away,*** or ***removing.*** This feminine noun referring to anyone carried away captive or to captivity itself occurs forty-one times scattered throughout the prophets and Kgs, Chr, Ezr, Neh, and Est. The reference for the most part is to the Babylonian captivity of the kingdom of Judah, which was the result of their sinful disobedience to God.

gālût. ***Captivity, captive,*** or ***carried away captive.*** In the fifteen occurrences of the feminine noun *gālût,* reference is made to a group of captives (Isa 20:4; 45:13; Jer 24:5; 28:4; 29:22; 40:1; Amos 1:6,9; Ob 20) or a period of captivity variously specified as the captivity of Jehoiachin (II Kgs 25:27; Jer 51:31; Ezk 1:2) or our captivity (Ezk 33:21; 40:1), almost all of which refer to the captivity of Judah in Babylon.

Bibliography: TDOT, II, pp. 476–88. THAT, I, pp. 415–17.

B.K.W.

גֻּלָּה (*gūllâ*). See no. 353c.
גִּלּוּל (*gillûl*). See no. 353h.
גְּלוֹם (*gᵉlôm*). See no. 354c.
גָּלוּת (*gālût*). See no. 350b.

351 גָּלַח (*gālaḥ*) ***poll, shave, shave off.***

(ASV and RSV similar, except "cut" replaces "poll.") The root seems to mean "to be bare, smooth, naked." It is broader in meaning than *qāraḥ* which refers to baldness of the head. The verb occurs twenty-two times in the intensive stems.

Among Semites shaving off hair or the beard was a sign of lamentation and distress (Jer 41:5; cf. Amos 8:10). Israelite priests, however, were forbidden to follow these mourning customs (Lev 21:5; Ezk 44:20). Sometimes shaving symbolized purification, as in the case of a person cured of a skin ailment (Lev 13:33; 14:8) or a captive woman who was about to marry an Israelite (Deut 21:12). At the time of his consecration, a Levite was to "cause a razor (*he'ĕbîr ta'ar*) to pass over his whole body" (Num 8:7). Opinions differ as to whether he was to merely trim his hair or shave it off completely. When a Nazirite terminated his vow, the hair of his head was shaved off and burned in the fire of the altar (Num 6:18–19).

Under other circumstances, shaving of the beard was considered a great indignity (II Sam 10:4). A different custom, however, prevailed in Egypt (Gen 41:14). It is not altogether clear why Absalom shaved his head periodically (II Sam 14:26).

Used figuratively, shaving referred to the complete stripping of a land by the enemy (Isa 7:20).

Bibliography: Fensham, F. Charles, "The Shaving of Samson: A Note on Judges 16:19," EQ: 97–98.

J.E.S.

גִּלָּיוֹן (*gillāyôn*). See no. 350c.
גָּלִיל (*gālîl*) I, II. See nos. 353e,f.
גְּלִילָה (*g^e lîlâ*). See no. 353g.

352 גלל (*gll*) **I. Assumed root of the following.**
352a גָּלָל (*gālāl*) ***account.*** Occurs only in the construct state with the preposition *b^e*, *biglal* "on account of," "for the sake of."

353 גָּלַל (*gālal*) ***II, commit, remove, trust, run down, seek occasion, wallow, roll,*** and ***roll down, away*** or ***together.***

Derivatives

353a †גַּל (*gal*) ***heap, wave.***
353b גֵּל (*gēl*) ***dung.***
353c †גֻּלָּה (*gūllâ*) ***basin, bowl.***
353d גָּלָל (*gālāl*) ***dung.***
353e †גָּלִיל (*gālîl*) ***I, turning, folding.***
353f גָּלִיל (*gālîl*) ***II, cylinder, rod, circuit.***
353g גְּלִילָה (*g^e lîlâ*) ***circuit, boundary, territory.***
353h †גִּלּוּל (*gillûl*) ***idols.***
353i †גַּלְגַּל (*galgāl*) ***wheel, whirl, whirlwind.***
353j גִּלְגָּל (*gilgāl*) ***I, wheel.***
353k †גִּלְגָּל (*gilgāl*) ***II, Gilgal.***
3531 †גֻּלְגֹּלֶת (*gūlgōlet*) ***skull, head.***
353m †מְגִלָּה (*m^e gillâ*) ***roll.***

gālal means to roll some object on, upon, away, in, against, from, together, unto, or down. This figure is used for rolling oneself on the Lord and so to trust the Lord (Ps 22:8 [H 9]) or to commit one's behavior or life to the Lord (Ps 37:5; Prov 16:3) or remove such non-material things as reproach and contempt (Ps 119:22).

The physical act of the rolling of something or someone (*gālal*) appears in only four episodes and possibly two or three observations. The first is in the story of Jacob meeting Rachel at the well in Paran, mentioning the necessity of rolling the stone from the well and of Jacob doing this (Gen 29:3,8,10).

When Joshua caught the five Amorite kings in a cave during the Gibeonite battle, he ordered his men to roll great stones on the mouth of the cave to incarcerate them until the battle's end (Josh 10:18).

Saul, knowing his hungry people were eating meat with blood still in it, directed his men to roll a great stone to him upon which the animals could be slaughtered (I Sam 14:33).

After Joab had thrust his sword treacherously through Amasa, Amasa wallowed in his blood in the road (II Sam 20:12).

Jeremiah in a figure likens Babylon to a mountain when he says of her, "I will roll thee down from the rocks" (30:14). Surely the wise man writes metaphorically, "He that rolleth a stone, it will return upon him" (Prov 26:27). When Isaiah employs the verb in two effective figures: the heavens shall be "rolled together like a scroll" (34:4) and "garments rolled in blood" (9:5), depicting warfare in contrast to the reign of the prince of peace.

Joshua used *gālal* symbolically when he said, after the circumcision of the Israelites, "This day have I rolled away the reproach of Egypt" (Josh 5:19) and the place was named Gilgal—a word play on *gālal*.

Close to the meaning of rolling an object is Amos's metaphor, "But let judgment run down as waters and righteousness as a mighty stream" (Amos 5:24).

Other uses of *gālal* are more remote from rolling an object. Among the indignities that Job suffers is the action of young men who rolled themselves upon him—probably as an army breaking through defenses (Job 30:14). Joseph's brothers fear that Joseph is seeking occasion (*gālal*) against them to enslave them (Gen 43:8).

gālal becomes trust, commit or remove in four places. The thought is to "roll one's trouble" upon someone or away from oneself (cf. KB). Those who stigmatize the victim of Ps 22 says, "He trusted on the Lord that he would deliver him, let him deliver him" (v. 8 [H 9]) while in Ps 37:5 and Prov 16:3 we are urged to commit our works and way unto the Lord. In Ps 119:22 the Psalmist requests, "Remove from me reproach and contempt: for I have kept thy testimonies."

gal. ***Heap, wave, billow*** and ***spring.*** A masculine noun apparently coming from the idea of rolling, piling or heaping one thing upon another. It is used of a heap of stones as the wreckage of a city (II Kgs 19:25) or as a memorial (Gen 31:46–52). In the same fashion water pushed up into waves or billows (Ps 42:7 [H 8]; Isa 48:18; Jer 5:22; Jon 2:3) and the bubbling up of a spring can be indicated by *gal* (Song 4:12).

The parting place of Laban and Jacob was a heap of stones which Jacob's men piled up as a witness to the covenant between Laban and himself. Jacob called the place Galeed "the heap of witness" (Gen 31:46–52). Laban's name for it means the same thing in Aramaic. A great heap of stones was placed over the remains of Achan and his family (Josh 7:26). The king of Ai received the same treatment after his capture (Josh 8:29) and so did Absalom after he was killed (II Sam 18:17).

The Lord sent a message through Isaiah and Hezekiah to Sennacherib telling him that the Lord used him to make "fenced cities into ruinous heaps" (II Kgs 19:25; Isa 37:26).

Isaiah praises the Lord because it was he who "made of a city an heap" (25:2), and Jeremiah says both Jerusalem and Babylon will become heaps (51:37) while Hosea declares that Gilgal's "altars are as heaps in the furrows of the field" (12:11).

gūllâ. ***Springs, bowls*** or ***pommels.*** Rolling water in Josh 15:19; Jud 1:15 describes springs or pools (or possibly so called from being round pools).

At the top of the pillars in front of the temple bowl-like capitals or mouldings were placed (bowls I Kgs 7:41, but pommels II Chr 4:12,13); cf. bowl on Menorah (Zech 4:2,3). In Eccl 12:6 "the golden bowl be broken" describes death in old age.

gālîl. ***Folding*** or ***rings.*** An adjective describing the leaves of the doors of the temple in Jerusalem (KJV "folding," but variously translated in modern versions) (I Kgs 6:34).

A masculine noun translated "rings," to which decorative hangings were fastened (Est 1:6). In Song 5:14 the bridegroom's hands are gold "rings" (KJV; KB, BDB cylinder or rod).

gillûl. ***Idols, images.*** One of about ten basic words for idol in the OT. The word means logs, blocks, shapeless things (BDB). Thus it is used as a polemic against pagan religion. This masculine plural form occurs sparingly (nine times) outside of Ezk (thirty-eight times).

In Lev 26 KJV Moses at Sinai warns the Israelites about turning from the Lord and worshiping idols, saying if this happens, the Lord will throw their carcasses on the carcasses of their idols (26:30). The NEB freely translates, "I will pile your rotting carcasses on the rotting logs that were your idols." In Deut Moses speaks in this vein when he renews the covenant and refers to the idols (*gillûlîm*) of Egypt, and those of wood, stone, silver and gold which they saw on their journey (29:17).

Asa, a grandson of David, removed out of the land all the idols that his father Abijam had made (I Kgs 15:12). To the contrary Ahab did very abominable things at the instigation of Jezebel in following idols as the Amorites did (I Kgs 21:26).

The northern kingdom is indicted for serving idols, specifically disobeying the Lord's command not to do so (II Kgs 17:12). Later, Manasseh was more wicked than the Amorites in making Judah sin with his idols, and Amon his son did the same (II Kgs 21:11, 21). Josiah, however, in obedience to the Lord put away these idols after he had read the book which Hilkiah found in the temple (II Kgs 23:24).

Jeremiah says that Babylon's images (*gillûlîm*) would be destroyed. Here *gillûlîm* translated images (only place in KJV) is parallel with *ʿăṣabbîm* translated idols or images and cognate with a verb meaning to grieve or cause sorrow.

Ezekiel who has thirty-eight of the forty-seven occurrences of *gillûlîm* denounces idolatry as infidelity and prostitution (16:36; 37:23). Good Israelites have not "lifted up their eyes to idols," while the wicked have done so (18:6,12,15). Ezekiel reminds the people that God told them not to defile themselves "with the idols of Egypt." Nevertheless "their heart went after" them (20:7,8,16,18,24). They were not to "pollute themselves" with idols (20:31). In dramatic irony the prophet says: "Go ye, serve ye everyone his idols" (20:39). Again he declares that Israel works against herself by idolatry and defiles herself (22:3,4; 23:7). They are polluted with idols of Babylonia and Assyria (23:30) and have followed heathen idolatry to the extent of killing their children in sacrifice to idols and so they will "bear the sins of their idols" (23:39, 49), but the Lord will destroy the idols of Egypt (30:13).

When Ezekiel hears that Jerusalem is destroyed, he says that the people do not possess the land because of their idolatry (33:25; 36:18, 25). Only twice more does Ezekiel refer to idols and in quite a different vein. He predicts that Judah and Israel will be united in their land and will not defile themselves any more with idols (37:23). In the restoration the priests and Levites who went astray will be punished by a lowering of rank and given a less important activity in the new sanctuary. Only the Zadokite priests who remained true to the Lord will serve in the high office of priest (44:10,12). [There is not any one word for "idol" in the OT. The idols are named variously by the prophets depending on the characteristization they felt would be most effective at the time. Five words are mainly used: 1) *gillûl* "logs, blocks" (though KB suggests that it is a pejorative word calling the idols dung pellets); it is used the most often, but mainly in Ezk. 2) *pesel,* "carved image." 3) *massēkâ* "cast image." 4) *maṣṣēbâ* "standing stone image." 5) *ʿāṣāb* "thing of grief." It is of interest that the first four are characterizations arising from the physical nature of the image, especially referring to how it was made. The prophets scorned the idols as things made by the hand of men. Indeed, that phrase is sometimes used as a substitute for the word idol (e.g. Isa 2:8). They did not admit that the idol was a mere representation of the god. They declared that the material object itself was the pagan's god—and with the prevailing animism, they were doubtless correct. In this vein, Isaiah pours scorn on the idolater who uses half a log for firewood and the other half to make a god (Isa 44:9–20).

Other words for idols are: *ṣelem* "image," which emphasizes its representational character (used seven times); *sēmel* of uncertain etymology (used five times); *tᵉrāpîm,* apparently meaning a "thing of shame" used for Laban's household gods stolen by Rachel; *mippᵉleṣet* "thing of horror"; *'ĕlîl* "empty or meaningless thing"; and *'āwen* "sinful thing" BDB (KB suggests, a "thing of mystery" from a possible etymology, but BDB is better on the basis of the usage of *'āwen*). Also to be mentioned are the *'ăshērâ,* which are indeed cult objects, perhaps sacred poles, but are more symbols of the goddess *'ăshērâ* rather than idols in the normal sense. R.L.H.]

galgal. ***Wheel.*** Nine times in KJV, but Isa 17:13 is "a rolling thing" and Ps 77:18 [H 19] in the heavens. Modern translations in Ps 77:18 [H 19] generally, use whirlwind (NEB has "thistle down" in Ps 83:13 [14]); NIV has tumbleweed).

Various wheels are: those for war chariots (Isa 5:28; Jer 47:3; Ezk 23:24; 26:10), for drawing water (Eccl 12:6) and wheels of Ezekiel's vision of departure of God's glory (Ezk 10:2,6,13) though more often Ezekiel uses another word for these wheels of his vision (see *'ôpān*).

gilgāl ***II. Gilgal*** (a circle of stones?). There seem to be five places called Gilgal. Deuteronomy 11:30 locates Ebal and Gerizim "over against Gilgal" which appears to be near Shechem.

The Gilgal of Elijah and Elisha is near Bethel (II Kgs 2:1; 4:38). Here Elisha purifies the "death in the pot" food for the sons of the prophets.

The king of the nations of Gilgal is thought to have lived on the border of the plain of Sharon.

A border city of Judah mentioned in Josh 15:17 is on the road from Jericho to Jerusalem (Josh 18:17).

The Gilgal most often referred to was the first camping place after the Israelites crossed the Jordan. It was east of Jericho (Josh 4:19), but its exact location is still uncertain. Muilenburg proposed Khirbet el-Mefjir on the basis of the OT, the onomastica in Josephus and Eusebius and the archaeological remains (BASOR 140: 11–27). Here a pile of twelve stones from the Jordan memorialized their crossing. Here also that generation was circumcised and "rolled away the reproach of Egypt," the first Passover in the new land was celebrated and the manna ceased (5:9–12). The Gibeonites came to Joshua's headquarters here and later Joshua divided part of the country by lot in Gilgal (Josh 9:6; 10:6,7,9,15,43; 14:6).

In Jud 2:1 the angel of the Lord goes up from Gilgal to Bochim to prophesy against the Israelites. Gilgal is on Samuel's circuit (I Sam 7:16; 10:8) and remains an important center during the time of Saul (I Sam 11:14,15; 13:4,7,8,12,15; 15:12,21,33) and David (II Sam 19:15,40).

Hosea and Amos refer disparagingly to the sinful and wicked worship at Gilgal in their day (Hos 4:15; 9:15; 12:12; Amos 4:4; 5:5).

[In harmonizing the accounts of the conquest found in Joshua with the ensuing settlement of the land presented in Judges, Y. Kaufmann makes the salient point that Joshua's wars aim to destroy and exterminate the enemy and not to occupy the land. He wrote: "Joshua separates the *wars* entirely from the *occupation of the territory.* He keeps the people *in camp* [for some time at Gilgal] for the whole duration of the war. No matter where the army fights, it always returns to the camp. . . . He is compelled to prevent the people from occupying its portions until the end of the war, because he cannot be sure that he will be able to muster them for the general war if they are engaged in claiming land" (*The Biblical Account of the Conquest of Palestine,* 1953, p. 92). B.K.W.]

gūlgōlet. ***Skull, head*** or ***person.*** The Akkadian cognate, i.e. *gulgullu* and *gulgullâti.* In KJV every man, poll, skull, or head. Usually used for counting people (Ex 16:16; 38:26; Num 1:2, 18; 3:47; I Chr 23:3, 24). But it also refers to the breaking of Abimelech's skull (Jud 9:53), Jezebel's skull (II Kgs 9:35), and Saul's head when it was fastened to the wall of the temple of Dagon (I Chr 10:10). Cf. the Aramaic Golgotha in the Gospels (Mt 27:33; Mk 15:22; Jn 19:17).

mᵉgillâ. ***Volume, roll*** (KJV), ***scroll.*** *mᵉgillâ* occurs with *sēper* "book," the scroll of the book (Jer 36:2,4: Ezk 2:9, Ps 40:7 [H 8]).

Jehoiakim cut and burned Jeremiah's scroll (Jer 36). Ezekiel sees a scroll at his call (2:9; 3:1–3) and Zechariah a flying scroll containing God's curse against wickedness (5:1,2). Ezra mentions the scroll recording Cyrus's decree to rebuild the temple (6:2).

Egyptian scrolls and probably many of those used in Palestine were made of papyrus (note how easily Jeremiah's scroll burned). The Dead Sea Scrolls were made of skins stitched together. The book (codex) came into use in the first and second centuries after Christ. The Scroll was written "within" (recto) and, when necessary, "without" (verso) (cf. Ezk 2:10).

E.S.K.

354 גָּלַם (*gālam*) ***to wrap up, fold, fold together*** (II Kgs 2:8; only).

Derivatives

354a גְּלוֹם (*g^elôm*) ***wrapping, garment*** (Ezk 27:24, only).

354b גֹּלֶם (*gōlem*) ***embryo*** (Ps 139:16, only).

354c גַּלְמוּד (*galmûd*) ***hard, barren*** (i.e. Isa 49:21; Job 15:34).

גַּלְמוּד (*galmûd*). See no. 354c.

355 *גָּלַע (*gāla'*) ***to expose, lay bare.*** Occurs only in the Hithpael (e.g. Prov 17:14; 18:1).

356 גִּלְעָד (*gil'ād*) ***Gilead.***

Derivative

356a †גִּלְעָדִי (*gil'ādî*) ***Gileadite.***

Gilead sometimes refers to the area in Transjordan between the Arnon and Jabbok rivers, sometimes to that between the Jabbok and the Yarmuk and sometimes to the whole area.

Laban overtook Jacob as Jacob returned to Canaan at Mount Gilead (Gen 31:21, 23, 25), and Ishmaelites from Gilead bought Joseph and took him to Egypt (Gen 37:25).

Because Gilead was good pasture land, Gad and Reuben got the southern part (Num 32:1, 26, 29). Moses gave northern Gilead to Machir, son of Manasseh (Num 32:39,40). This allocation is corroborated in Deut 3:13,15,16; 4:43.

Sihon, King of the Amorites, ruled over half Gilead (Josh 12:2) and Og, King of Bashan, over the other half (12:5). Joshua 13:25 says that Moses gave Gilead to Gad, but verse 31 says half was given to Machir.

The song of Deborah and Barak makes a disparaging reference to the men of Gilead for their failure to join in the battle against Jabin King of Hazor (Jud 5:17).

Jair, a Gileadite, judged Israel for twenty-two years (Jud 10:4).

The men of Gilead, seeking a man to lead them against the Ammonites, appealed to Jephthah whose father was Gilead and whose half-brother had thrust him out of the country years before (Jud 11:1,2; 10:8–18, 11:5–29). Jephthah, successful in defeating the Ammonites, incurred the opposition of the Ephraimites in the process, so the Ephraimites fought him. During this fray the Gileadites identified the Ephraimites by their inability to pronounce shibboleth properly (Jud 12:4,5,7 see E. A. Speiser, "The Shibboleth Incident," *Oriental and Biblical Studies,* Univ. of Penna., 1967, pp. 143–50).

The men of Gilead served in the war against Benjamin (Jud 20:1). However, because no men from Jabesh-gilead fought in those battles, the Israelites killed all its citizens except four hundred young unmarried women, to provide wives for some Benjamites who survived the war (Jud 21.8–14).

Gilead was ruled by Ishbosheth during David's reign in Hebron (II Sam 2:9), but David took refuge there during Absalom's rebellion and the battles leading to Absalom's death were fought in Gilead (II Sam 17:26). Gilead was among the places in which David's sinful census was taken.

Jabesh-gilead had cause to favor Saul because he broke an Ammonite siege and saved the men and the city from debasing humiliation and agony (I Sam 11:1,9). The men of Jabesh-gilead, in turn, rescued the bodies of Saul and his sons from the wall of Beth-shan (I Sam 31:11; II Sam 2:4, 5; I Chr 10:11). Later David brought the bones of Saul and Jonathan up from Jabesh-gilead and buried them in the sepulchre of Saul's father.

Ramoth-gilead was prominent in the wars with the Syrians and Ahab was killed near there (I Kgs 4:13; 22:3–29; II Chr 18:2–28). Ahab's son Joram was wounded at Ramoth-gilead (II Kgs 8:28; II Chr 22:5). A young prophet is sent by Elisha to Ramoth-gilead to anoint Jehu king (II Kgs 9:1, 4, 14; I Chr 6:80). Later Jehu loses Gilead to Hazael (II Kgs 10:33) and still later Tiglath-pileser captures Gilead from Pekah (II Kgs 15:29).

Jeremiah cries out, "Is there no balm in Gilead?" to emphasize the availability of the Lord's healing (8:22). Gilead's balm itself, however, will not heal the people (46:11). In any case its balsam was proverbial. Rich woodlands covered its hills and served as a symbol of luxury along with Lebanon and Carmel (Jer 22:6; 50:19; Zech 10:10). Its goats also were famous (Song 4:1; 5:5).

Amos curses the Ammonites for ripping up the pregnant women of Gilead (1:13), and the people of Damascus because they threshed Gilead with iron threshing instruments. Hosea says that Gilead is a wicked city (6:8).

When Israel returns from captivity Gilead will be possessed again (Ob 19; Zech 10:10) and they will feed in Gilead (Mic 7:14) and be satisfied there (Jer 50:19). In Ezekiel's vision of reconstruction, Gilead is on the eastern border.

Mention is made of Gilead the Gadite (I Chr

5:14) and Gilead son of Machir son of Manasseh (Num 26:29,30; 27:1; 36:1; Josh 17:1,3).

gil'ādî. ***Gileadite.*** The patronymic occurs eleven times (Num 26:29; Jud 10:3; 11:1,40; 2:7; II Sam 17:27; 19:31; I Kgs 2:7; II Kgs 15:25; Ezr 2:61; Neh 7:63).

Bibliography: Kraus, Hans-Joachim, "Gilgal," VT 1:181–99. Mauchline, John, "Gilead and Gilgal: Some Reflections on the Israelite Occupation of Palestine," VT 6:19–33. Muilenburg, J., "The Site of Ancient Gilgal," BASOR 140: 11–27. Baly, Denis, *The Geography of Palestine* Harper, 1957, pp. 225–31.

E.S.K.

357 גָּלַשׁ (*gālash*) ***to sit, sit up, possibly to recline.*** Occurs only in Song 4:1; 6:5.

גַּם (*gam*). See no. 361a.

358 *גָּמָא (*gāmā'*) ***swallow (liquids).*** Occurs in the Piel (Job 39:24) and Hiphil (Gen 24:17).

Derivative

358a גֹּמֶא (*gōme'*) ***rush, reed, papyrus*** (e.g. Isa 18:2; Job 8:11).

359 גמד (*gmd*). **Assumed root of the following.**

359a גֹּמֶד (*gōmed*) ***cubit*** (Jud 3:16, only).

359b גַּמָּדִים (*gammādîm*) ***valorous men*** (Ezk 27:11).

גְּמוּל (*g^e^mûl*). See no. 360a.

360 גָּמַל (*gāmal*) ***to deal, to recompense, to ripen*** (ASV: do, deal, requite, reward; RSV: deal, requite, deal bountifully.)

Derivatives

360a †גְּמוּל (*g^e^mûl*) ***recompense.***
360b †גְּמוּלָה (*g^e^mûlâ*) ***recompense.***
360c †תַּגְמוּל (*tagmûl*) ***benefit.***
360d †גָּמָל (*gāmāl*) ***camel.***

This verb occurs in the Qal and Niphal stems. In the Qal it signifies to render either good or evil to someone. In some passages the two are contrasted (Prov 31:12; I Sam 24:17 [H 18]); in others evil is done (Gen 50:15,17; Prov 3:30); in still others good is done (Isa 63:7). At times the idea is to deal bountifully with (Ps 13:6; 116:7, etc.), or to deal out reward (II Sam 19:36 [H 37]). At times there is a recompense or a requital in a bad sense (Ps 7:4 [H 5]); Deut 32:6; Ps 137:8).

The Qal form may mean to wean a child (I Sam 1:23–24; I Kgs 11:20; Hos 1:8) so that one reads of the weaned child (*gāmûl*; Ps 131:2) or the child weaned from milk (*g^e^mûlê mēḥālāb*).

gāmal in the Qal may also mean to bear ripe almonds (Num 17:8 [H 23]) or to ripen, of grapes (Isa 18:5).

gāmal occurs in the Niphal three times, twice of the weaning of Isaac (Gen 21:8) and once of Samuel (I Sam 1:22).

g^e^mûl. ***Recompense, reward, benefit, dealing.*** This noun occurs eighteen times. It is the recompense given by God (Isa 3:11; 35:4; 59:18; 66:6; Jer 51:6; Lam 3:64; Ob 15; Joel 3:7 [H 4:7]) and by man (Joel 3:4 [H 4:4]; Ps 137:8); the benefits God has given (Ps 103:2; II Chr 32:25), and the deeds one does (Jud 9:16; Prov 12:14; Isa 3:11). The Psalmist invokes God, the God of recompense (Jer 51:56; cf. Deut 28), to give the wicked his due (Ps 28:4; 94:2).

g^e^mûlâ. ***Dealing, recompense.*** This feminine noun is used of the reward which David offered to Barzillai in return for a favor which he showed to David when he was fleeing from Absalom (II Sam 19:37). A plural form in the prophets describes God's retribution to his adversaries (Isa 59:18), in particular to Babylon, for the Lord is a God of recompense (Jer 51:56).

tagmûl. ***Benefit.*** This is an abstract masculine noun (GKC 85*r*) from the root *gāmal.* It occurs in the plural with an Aramaic suffix, *tagmûlôhî* (GKC 91*l*; Ps 116:12). The ASV renders "benefits," and the RSV, "bounty." Having recovered from an illness, overwhelmed with God's goodness toward him, the Psalmist asks what he should return for such benefits. He answered with self-dedication, sacrifice, and payment of vows.

gāmāl. ***Camel.*** LXX, *kamēlos.* A beast of burden mentioned throughout the OT, from the patriarchal accounts to the postexilic age. Used primarily for riding (Gen 24:61,63; 31:17; I Sam 30:17; Isa 21:7) and carrying loads, camels were also milked (Gen 32:15–16). Camel flesh is considered edible by Arabs. But Israel's dietary laws prohibited it, since the camel chews the cud, but has no parted hoof (Lev 11:4; Deut 14:7).

The camel's ability to go long periods without water suited him for the spice trade (II Chr 9:1), carrying food some distances, transporting products of Gilead to Egypt (Gen 37:25), transporting tribute (II Kgs 8:9f.; I Chr 12:41, and transporting gifts to the Lord (Isa 60:6). Caravans were of various sizes (Gen 24:10). Making the camels kneel (Gen 24:11), unloading them, and providing food for them (Gen 24:32) was a regular part of the trip. Drawing water for camels at a well at a stopping place was a big task; Rachel's willingness to do it showed her character and answered Eliezer's prayer (Gen 24:10, 19, 20, 44, 46).

Raiders rode camels (Jud 6:5; 7:12; 8:21,26) and often seized the camels of their enemies (Job

1:17; Jer 49:29, 32; I Sam 15:3; 27:9; II C r 14:15 [H 14]); Isa 30:6). One episode lists a booty of fifty thousand camels (I Chr 5:21). Sennacherib lists camels among the booty he took from Judah. Camels were a means of rapid escape (I Sam 30:17). Rabbah of Ammon is threatened with becoming a pasture of camels (Ezk 25:5).

The wealth of men like Abraham (Gen 12:16; 24:35), Jacob (Gen 30:43), and Job was counted (along with other livestock) in the number of their camels. Job had three thousand before his affliction, but six thousand afterward (Job 1:3; 42:12). David had a special overseer of camels (I Chr 27:30). Like other livestock, camels were victims of the plague in Egypt (Ex 9:3; cf. Zech 14:15). Those who returned from exile are said to have had 435 camels (Ezr 2:67; cf. Neh 7:68).

Albright has argued that the camel was not extensively domesticated until the Iron Age (about 1200). He holds that the patriarchal references are somewhat anachronistic and that the common nomad of that day depended on the ass (SAC, p. 164–65). He does, however, allow that "partial and sporadic domestication may go back several centuries earlier." J. P. Free gathered evidence of earlier use of domesticated camels, though his proof need not be pressed to say that ass nomadism was not the more common (J. P. Free, JNES 3: 187–93.) K. Kitchen since then has brought out additional evidence to demonstrate that the camel was domesticated already in the Early Bronze Age (see Andre Parrot, *Syria* 32: 323).

Bibliography: Free, Joseph P., "Abraham's Camels," JNES 3: 187–93. Isserlin, B. S., "On Some Possible Occurrences of the Camel in Palestine," PEQ :50–53. Lambert, W. G., "The Domesticated Camel in the Second Millennium: Evidence from Alalakh and Ugarit," BASOR 160: 42–43. THAT, I, pp. 426–28.

J.P.L.

361 גמם (*gmm*). **Assumed root of the following.**
361a †גַּם (*gam*) ***again, alike.***
361b מְגַמָּה (*m^e gammâ*). ***Meaning uncertain, perhaps "hordes"*** (Hab 1:9).

gam. ***Again, alike, as, but, even, likewise, in like manner, so much as, then, though, with, yea.*** A particle occurring over 750 times, *gam* denotes addition. It is often repeated in a sentence, in which case the most frequent translations are both... and; either... or; nay... neither; so... and. Sometimes in English translations *gam* is completely ignored.

gam has at least ten distinctive usages in the OT. (1) Sometimes *gam* simply serves as a particle of addition or accumulation (Gen 7:3). (2) When two or more persons or objects are viewed as functioning together, *gam* may serve as a comprehensive particle (Jud 9:49; Prov 17:15). (3) Like the connective particle waw, *gam* may function conjunctively to join two nouns (Joel 1:12) or two verbs (Ps 137:1) or two clauses (Jud 5:4). (4) Like *'ap*, *gam* may serve as an intensive particle at the beginning of an emphatic statement (Prov 17:26; Joel 2:29 [H 3:2]). (5) As an emphatic particle *gam* is used to stress a particular word within the sentence, especially pronouns and nouns with pronominal suffixes (Gen 4:26; 10:21; 27:34).

(6) In addition *gam* has a correlative use which indicates correspondence between two actions (Gen 20:6). (7) Sometimes *gam* has a consequential force and is used to introduce an action which is a logical consequence of some antecedent action. *gam* is frequently used to introduce the just and appropriate response of God to transgression (Jud 2:21; Jer 4:12) or repentance (II Sam 12:13). In the same sense *gam* is used to indicate man's reasonable response to God's grace (Josh 24:18; I Sam 1:28). (8) *gam* also has an adversative use in which it introduces contrariety or antithesis (Ezk 16:28; Ps 129:2). (9) In its confirmatory use *gam* serves to underscore or confirm a direct statement or an impression which has just been made (Gen 29:30; Hos 9:12). (10) *gam* is also used to indicate a climax (Gen 27:33; Deut 23:3–4). [An interesting use of *gam* apparently for emphasis is in the series of uses of *gam hû'* in I Sam 19:19–24. Saul had sent messengers to Ramah three times to arrest David. Each time the messengers saw Samuel and the others prophesying they also prophesied, or, better, even they prophesied. Finally, Saul "also he" went and "also he" prophesied and "also he" lay down naked all night. But the use of *gam hû'* does not necessarily mean that the others also stripped themselves when they prophesied, nor that such behavior is inherent in prophesying. The phrase may be used here for emphasis and mean that even Saul prophesied and even Saul stripped himself. Probably KJV is too extreme in saying that he lay down naked. He had thrown off his royal robes and especially his sword and armor thus allowing David to get away with a twelve hour start! Saul's action was a special case for a special purpose and the *gam* merely emphasizes this fact. R.L.H.]

J.E.S.

362 גמץ (*gmṣ*). **Assumed root of the following.**
362a גּוּמָץ (*gûmāṣ*) ***pit*** (Eccl 10:8; Prov 26:27).

363 גָּמַר (*gāmar*) ***cease, come to an end, fail, perfect, perform.*** (ASV similar; RSV renders "fulfill" instead of "perfect" or "perform.")

Derivative

363a גֹּמֶר (*gōmer*) ***Gomer, a proper name.***

gāmar occurs only five times (all in the book of Psalms), and has the basic meaning "to complete or finish." It is similar in meaning to *'āpēs, pāsas* II, and *shābat*. Negatively, the verb refers to the abrupt and seemingly permanent termination of that which previously existed.

The Psalmist is concerned that godly men have ceased to be in the land (Ps 12:1 [H 2]). He prays that God will terminate wickedness (Ps 7:9 [H 10]) and wonders if the promise made to Abraham has been permanently canceled. Positively, *gāmar* refers to how the Lord finishes or accomplishes in the life of his saints all that he undertakes (Ps 57:2 [H 3]; 138:8).

Gomer was the name of Hosea's unfaithful wife (Hos 1:3). His relationship to her was symbolic of God's relationship to wayward Israel. Japheth's eldest son also bore the name Gomer doubtless from a non-semitic original (Gen 10:2–3). His descendants are usually identified as the Cimmerians who moved onto the stage of history from the area north of the Black Sea in the eighth century B.C. Gomer is named as one of the confederates of Gog in the eschatological battle against the people of God (Ezk 38:6).

Bibliography: Dahood, Mitchell, "The Root GMR in the Psalms," TS 14: 595–97.

J.E.S.

גַּן (*gan*). See no. 367a.

364 גָּנַב (*gānab*) ***carry away, steal, steal away.*** (ASV and RSV similar except the latter renders once "outwit" and twice "cheat.")

Derivatives

364a גְּנֵבָה (*gᵉnēbâ*) ***theft, thing stolen.***
364b גַּנָּב (*gannāb*) ***thief.***

Basically the verb means "to take that which belongs to another without his consent or knowledge." It is restricted to acts of theft done secretly. The related verbs *gāzal* and *'āshaq* emphasize the violent aspect of seizing the property of another. *gānab* and its derivatives occur some sixty times.

The eighth commandment condemns stealing (Ex 20:15; Deut 5:17) including burglary (Ex 22:2) and kidnapping (Ex 21:16). Thievery was regarded with the utmost disdain in Israel (Lev 19:11; Jer 2:26; cf. Prov 6:30). In one case alone is *gānab* commended (II Kgs 11:2).

Punishment for theft in Israel was not as severe as that of some neighboring nations, where the death penalty was inflicted. The Law required the thief to return to his victim twice the amount he had stolen (Ex 22:7). Thus the thief lost the exact amount he had hoped to gain. The penalties were doubled and more if the thief slaughtered or sold a stolen animal. Only in the case of kidnapping (Ex 21:16) or theft of "devoted things" (Josh 7:11, 25) was a thief executed.

gānab is used figuratively to describe wind sweeping something away unexpectedly (Job 21:18; 27:20). In the Hithpael the word is used to depict the thief-like movements of military deserters (II Sam 19:4). "To steal the heart" is an idiom which means "to deceive." It is correctly rendered by the RSV in Gen 31:20 ("outwit") but missed by both RSV and ASV in Gen 31:26–27 and II Sam 15:6.

J.E.S.

גַּנָּה (*gannâ*). See no. 367b.

365 גנז (*gnz*). **Assumed root of the following.**
365a גְּנָזִים (*gᵉnāzîm*) ***chests*** (meaning uncertain, Ezk 27:24); ***treasury*** (Est 3:9; 4:7).

366 גַּנְזַךְ (*ganzak*) ***treasury*** (I Chr 28:11). Persian loan word.

367 גָּנַן (*gānan*) ***defend.*** (ASV and RSV also render "put a shield about," and "protect.")

Derivatives

367a †גַּן (*gan*) ***enclosure, garden.***
367b גַּנָּה (*gannâ*) ***garden.***
367c †מָגֵן (*māgēn*) ***shield.***
367d †מְגִנָּה (*mᵉginnâ*) ***covering.***
367e *†מָגַן (*māgan*) ***deliver up.*** Denominative from *māgēn*. Occurs only in the Piel.

The verb and its derivatives occur about 130 times. The basic idea of the verb is to cover over and thus shield from danger.

gānan is used only in reference to the protective guardianship of God. Of its eight occurrences, six have to do with the Assyrian crisis in the days of Hezekiah. Isaiah assured the king that God would care for Jerusalem like a mother bird hovering with wings spread over her young in the nest (Isa 31:5). God would protect Jerusalem in this crisis for his own sake and for the sake of David (Isa 37:35). The deliverance of Jerusalem would demonstrate to the world that God was faithful to his promises and mighty to deliver his people from their oppressors. Zechariah twice uses the same verb to describe the divine protection of God's people in their wars against the sons of Greece (9:15) and of Jerusalem in the last days (12:8).

gan, gannâ. ***Garden.*** A garden (*gan, gannâ*) is a plot of ground protected by a wall or a hedge.

These areas were often irrigated (Isa 58:11) and were used to cultivate flowers, fruits, and vegetables (Song 5:1; 6:2). During the hot summer months such gardens provided a refuge from the stifling heat (Song 5:2; 8:13). The king's residence probably included an elaborate garden or private park (II Kgs 25:4). Frequently gardens were used as burial places (II Kgs 21:18, 26). Isaiah condemned the people of his day for turning their gardens into centers for pagan worship (Isa 1:29; 65:3; 66:17). An enclosed and fruitful garden became the figure of a chaste woman (Song 4:12) and of national prosperity (Num 24:6; Jer 29:5; Amos 9:14). The destruction of such gardens typified desolation (Amos 4:9).

The primeval garden of Gen 2–3 is perhaps the most famous garden in the OT. This garden was located in an area called Eden (q.v.; Gen 2:8, 10) and consequently came to be known as the garden of Eden (Gen 2:15; 3:23–24). A careful study of the geographical details of Gen 2 suggests that the garden was located near the mouth of the Persian Gulf. It is not unlikely that the original site lies under the waters of the gulf. In later times this garden, known also as the "garden of the LORD," came to be used as a symbol of land that was covered with lush vegetation (Gen 13:10; Isa 51:3; Ezk 36:35; Joel 2:3). In one passage the "garden of God" represents the created world and the trees of the garden, the kings of the earth (Ezk 31:8–18). A primeval garden appears in Ezk 28:12–19. This passage is notoriously difficult. It is probably best regarded as a mocking allusion to a corrupt Canaanite version of the Eden story.

māgēn. ***Shield, buckler, defense, ruler, armed, scales,*** now also ***suzerain*** is suggested. The noun *māgēn* refers to an object which provides covering and protection to the body during warfare. Of the six Hebrew words rendered in KJV as "shield" or "buckler" only *māgēn, ṣinnâ,* and possibly *sheleṭ* refer to what may properly be called shields. It is obvious that *māgēn* and *ṣinnâ* refer to different types of shields, but English versions have not consistently maintained the distinction, rendering both words indiscriminately as "shield" or "buckler." *māgēn* refers to the smaller and more common type of round shield carried by light infantry and officers. *ṣinnâ* is the rectangular shield which covered the whole front of the body.

In view of the fact that God is always the one who protects (*gānan*) his people, it is no surprise that he is so often called the shield (*māgēn*) of Israel. He is the shield about his servants (Gen 15:1), the house of Aaron (Ps 115:10), the nation of Israel (Deut 33:29) and all those who walk uprightly and put their trust in him (Prov 2:7; 30:5). The word *māgēn* is also used figuratively of princes as protectors of the realm (Ps 89:18 [H 19]; 47:9 [H 10]; Hos 4:18).

Though not specifically listed in the vocabulary of Gordon (UT 19) or Aistleitner (AisWUS), *māgēn* may also mean "suzerain." Dahood has argued the case convincingly in AB, Ps I (p. 17 and elsewhere, see indices). He argues from the meaning of *māgan* "bestow a gift" amply witnessed in Punic and Ugaritic (UT and AisWUS in loc.), that the noun refers to the giver of gifts, the suzerain, the benefactor (from the suzerain's viewpoint!). He remarks that the Carthaginian generals were called *māgōn,* translated into Latin by *imperator.* There are indeed places especially in the Pss, where the translation "suzerain" fits very well, though it is difficult to be sure, for a suzerain claims to be both a benefactor and a protector. So a passage like Ps 89:18 could be "shield" used figuratively of a prince, or could be translated directly as "suzerain."

m^eginnâ. ***Sorrow.*** Occurs only once in the expression "sorrow of heart," a figure for obstinacy or blindness of heart (Lam 3:65). The ASV translates it "hardness of heart" and the RSV "dullness of heart."

māgan. ***Deliver, deliver up.*** (RSV "bestow," "hand over"; ASV "cast off"). A denominative from *māgēn* used only three times, all in the Piel, or, according to Dahood, a separate verb. The idea is that a person is so hemmed in that there is no way of escape from the particular danger envisioned. This verb is synonymous with the Piel of *sāgar.*

J.E.S.

368 גָּעָה (*gā'â*) ***low*** (of cattle, Job 6:5; I Sam 6:12).

369 גָּעַל (*gā'al*) ***abhor, loathe, be vilely cast away, fall.***

Derivative

369a גֹּעַל (*gō'al*) ***loathing.***

This root indicates an intense aversion which is expressed often in punitive or adverse action.

If Israel kept the Lord's law, the Lord would not abhor them but continue to dwell among them (Lev 26:11), but if they abhorred the divine statutes, then God would bring judgments on the people (26:15). The attitude which the Lord would hold toward those on whom he would visit judgment is expressed by this root (26:30), indicating a rejection of those persons. The divine abhorrence is paralleled on the part of the people by their abhorrence and their contempt for the Lord's statutes and ordinances (26:43). But the Lord's abhorrence of them would not extend to their destruction in the land of their exile or to forgetting them (26:44). The judgment predicted in Lev 26 finds its fulfillment in the time of Jeremiah who used this word to describe the Lord's attitude toward Israel when he afflicted them in accordance with the cursing formulae of the covenant. The abhorrence of the sanctity of marriage obligations is the root from which arises progressively deeper transgressions illustrated by the worsening spiritual state of the "daughters" Sodom and Jerusalem in comparison with their "father," the Hittite and their "mother," the Amorite (Ezk 16:45). David implies that the vile death of Saul and Jonathan is inconsistent with their status (II Sam 1:21), except that rejection of God may result in that kind of death.

B.K.W.

370 גָּעַר (*gā'ar*) ***corrupt, rebuke, reprove.***

Derivatives

370a †גְּעָרָה (*ge'ārâ*) ***rebuke.***
370b †מִגְעֶרֶת (*mig'eret*) ***rebuke.***

This root indicates a check applied to a person or peoples through strong admonitions or actions.

Jacob rebukes Joseph when he relates the dream of sun, moon, and eleven stars bowing to him (Gen 37:10). Aggressive nations flee before God when he checks their deed against his people (Isa 17:13). God rebukes Satan's attempt to hinder worship in Jerusalem (Zech 3:2).

Ruth is not prevented from gleaning in Boaz's fields even though she is from Moab (Ruth 2:16). God prevents the normal action of water and wave when he rolls back the Red Sea (Ps 106:9).

geʿārâ. ***Rebuke, rebuking.*** The seas cannot prevent the revelation of secrets buried in their depths, for God's rebuke can roll them back to expose all that is there (II Sam 22:16). *ge'ārâ* describes the rejection of wise counsel by the scoffer (Prov 13:1). It likewise describes the power in the command of God to dry up the sea (Isa 50:2), to make the heavens tremble (Job 26:11), to overthrow the warrior (Ps 76:6 [H 7]), and to destroy morale which results in flight before the enemy (Isa 30:17). Wise rebuke is effective in the hearts of those who accept it (Prov 17:10; Eccl 7:5), but the scoffer rejects wise counsel. In contrast to the rich man who may have to ransom his life, the poor man does not even hear a threat (Prov 13:8).

mig'eret. ***Rebuke*** (RSV frustration). This noun is used once in parallelism with the words cursing and vexation (*hamm'ērâ* and *hamm*e*hûmâ*, Deut 28:20), indicating the fruitless conclusion of the activities of a people which turns away from God.

Bibliography: Macintosh, A. A., "A Consideration of Hebrew גער," VT 19: 471–79. THAT, I, pp. 429–30.

H.G.S.

371 גָּעַשׁ (*gā'ash*) ***shake, quake*** (e.g. Ps 18:8; II Sam 22:8).

גַּף (*gap*). See no. 373c.

372 גפן (*gpn*). **Assumed root of the following.**
372a גֶּפֶן (*gepen*) ***vine, vine tree.***

It has the same meaning in Ugaritic. In Akkadian it denotes a "shrub, plant with tendrils." This root designates the grape vine of whatever species (cf. Job 15:33; Jer 8:13).

Noah was the first after the flood to grow grapes, though this word is not used in that connection. The vine was cultivated in predynastic Egypt, and pictures of grape vines were shown laden with grapes.

The planting and care of a vineyard (*kerem* q.v.) is described in Isa 5:1–6, which indicates the grapes could be good (sweet) or wild (sour). Ground was prepared by gathering out the stones, the larger ones used to make up the encircling walls. Sometimes the vineyard was the only source of income, which would explain Naboth's refusal to sell to Ahab (I Kgs 21:1–4).

The Lord's favor is expressed in the gift of vines and vineyards (Hos 2:15 [H 14, 17]). The vine figures in visions (Gen 40:9–10) and parables (Jud 9:12), indicating its prominence; it is figurative for a fruitful wife (Ps 128:3). Vineyards could be rented. (These are not *gepen*). The grapes were preserved as raisins as well as being made into wine.

Behm notes that the metaphor of the vine is common in Israelite and Judaic literature. "It is used," he writes, "for the people of Israel in Hos 10:1; Jer 2:21, Ez 15:1ff.; 19:10ff; Ps 80:9ff. . . .; for the messiah which is like a vine"; for wisdom in Sir. 24:17; for the wife in Ps. 128:3' " (TDNT, I, p. 342). It is against the failure of Israel to produce the fruit that the Lord was looking for, namely, justice and righteousness (Isa 5:1–6), that Jesus' proclamation that he is the true vine must be interpreted (John 15:1ff.).

Bibliography: Brown, J. P., "The Mediterranean Vocabulary of the Vine," VT 19: 146–70. Forbes, R. J., *Studies in Ancient Technology* 3: 70–78.

H.G.S.

373 גפף (*gpp*). **Assumed root of the following.**
373a גַּף (*gap*) ***body, self*** (Ex 21:3–4); ***height, elevation*** (Prov 9:3).

374 גֹּפֶר (*gōper*) with עֵץ (*'ēṣ*) ***gopher wood.*** Meaning unknown.

The only use of this word in the OT occurs in Gen 6:14. Because it is similar to *kāpar* "to cover over," some have believed that the *g* is miswritten for *k*, and that therefore *gōper* should be translated resinous wood, like fir or pine (cf. BDB; A. Heidel, *Gilgamesh Epic and O.T. Parallels*, Univ of Chicago Press, p. 233). If the word were derived from Akkadian *gipāru*, it might be a Sumerian loan word (Heidel, ibid.), but the equivalent in Hebrew would be *gipâr*. Hebrew *gōper* presumes an Akkadian form *gūpru* (analogues: *kūpru: kôper*, Gen 6:14). *gūpru* has been found in two or three passages (Heidel, p. 234) but with the meaning "tables"; and once in the Old Babylonian version of the Gilgamesh Epic, Tab II, col 2, line 33 (ibid, p. 28; *Orientalische Literaturzeitung* 24: col 269). The use of the wood in Noah's ark (q.v.) may be explained as follows: the word "nests" (KJV "rooms") should perhaps be translated "reeds" since other uses of the root for this word are in the singular, and since construction in general is under consideration. If "reeds" were accepted, it would follow that gopher wood was the framework with reed interlacing. Actually the brief biblical account can hardly be used to give the details of construction. (cf. Ullendorf, E. "The Construction of Noah's Ark," VT 4: 95–96).

H.G.S.

375 גָּפְרִית (*goprît*) **brimstone** (e.g. Gen 19:24; Ps 11:6; NIV, sulfur).

גִּר (*gir*). See no. 347a.

376 גרב (*grb*). **Assumed root of the following.**
376a גָּרָב (*gārāb*) ***itch, scab*** (Lev 21:20; 22:22; Deut 28:27).

גַּרְגַּר (*gargar*). See no. 386c.
גַּרְגְּרוֹת (*garg^erôt*). See no. 386d.

377 *גָּרַד (*gārad*) ***scrape, scratch.*** Occurs only once, in the Hithpael (Job 2:8).

378 גָּרָה (*gārâ*) ***stir up, be stirred up, contend, meddle, strive.***

Derivatives

378a גָּרוֹן (*gārôn*) ***neck, throat.***
378b תִּגְרָה (*tigrâ*) ***contention, strife.***

The root is often used in connection with warfare. Thus Israel was commanded to involve himself in battle with Sihon, the Amorite, so that the Amorites should be dispossessed and his land taken by the Israelites (Deut 2:24). Warfare is also explicitly in view in Israel's relation with Moab at the time of the Conquest (Deut 2:9), and implied in its relation with Edom and Ammon (Deut 2:5,19). However, Israel was prohibited from involving himself in battle with Edom, Moab and Ammon because they were blood relatives. Involvement in war is also the purpose of Amaziah of Judah in his challenge to Jehoash of Israel, that Amaziah (per Johoash) might increase his territory (II Kgs 14:9–10). Likewise the uses in Dan 11 clearly point to warfare: in this case between Egypt and Syria (vv. 10, 25).

The word is used apart from war to denote the opposition of God's people to those who forsake God's law (Prov 28:4). A characteristic of the proud (Prov 28:25) or angry (15:18) is to stir up strife. Blinded by her strife against God, Babylon is caught unawares in a snare (Jer 50:24).

Psalm 39:10 [H 11] has the only use of *tigrâ*, descriptive of the blow of God's hand levelled against David.

B.K.W.

גֵּרָה (*gērâ*) I, II. See nos. 386a,b.
גָּרוֹן (*gārôn*). See no. 378a.
גְּרוּשָׁה (*g^erûshâ*). See no. 388b.

379 *גָּרַז (*gāraz*) ***cut, cut off.*** Occurs only once, in the Niphal (Ps 31:23).

Derivative

379a גַּרְזֶן (*garzen*) ***axe*** (e.g. Deut 19:5; I Kgs 6:7).

380 גרטל (*grṭl*). **Assumed root of the following.**
380a אֲגַרְטָל (*'ăgarṭāl*) ***basin, basket*** (Ezr 1:9; II Kgs 10:7).

381 גרל (*grl*). **Assumed root of the following.**
381a †גּוֹרָל (*gôrāl*) ***lot, portion.***

Occurs seventy-seven times (without Prov 19:19 Kethiv; Qere *gdl*) and is always translated "lot" or "lots" (KJV). Probably the noun is related to Arabic *ǧarwal* "pebble" (KB) and by metonomy came to be used for "lot" because little stones were used in lasting lots. BDB call attention here to Greek *psēphos* = "pebble," "vote," and *kuamos* = "bean," "lot." It refers then to some article like a stone which was thrown or allowed to fall in a way to determine a choice. In some cases not only the lot itself but what was chosen is called lot (Jud 1:3), and one's circumstances or even life as a whole is one's lot (Ps 16:5). Recompense or reward may be one's lot (Isa 17:14; Dan 12:13).

While the Hebrew OT uses six verbs meaning throw, give or fall describing the method of determining choice by lot, KJV translates each of them as casting lots (Lev 16:8; Josh 18:6, 8; Prov 16:33; Isa 34:17; Joel 4:3). The lot is said to come up, out, upon, or for a person or thing.

Nowhere does the OT explain either what a lot

is or how casting lots was accomplished. Prov 16:33 mentions that "the lot is cast into the lap" and Micah speaks of casting "a cord by lot" (2:5); but these observations provide no real clues to the nature of the lot nor to the method of casting lots. Quite possibly we ought to assume differing techniques for various places, times and occasions. Its exact connection with Urim and Thummir is not known.

The use of the lot to determine the mind and the will of God continues throughout the OT and is explicitly declared to be in his control in Prov 16:33: "The lot is cast into the lap; but the whole disposing thereof is of the LORD."

One of the most important uses of the lot occurred in the division of the land of Palestine among the Israelites after the conquests of Moses and Joshua. Under Moses direction, Reuben, Gad, and a half-tribe of Manasseh received land east of the Jordan. Under Joshua the land west of the Dead Sea, the Jordan and the Sea of Galilee was distributed by lot to the remaining tribes. This casting of lots was done partly at Gilgal (Josh 14–17) and partly at Shiloh (Josh 18, 19). The Levites were granted cities for themselves in various tribal areas. These cities also were apportioned by lot (Josh 21).

The retention of family patrimonies is illustrated in the case of Zelophehad's daughters who were not to marry outside their tribe so that their inheritance would not be taken from the lot of their father's tribe (Num 36:1–2). By metonymy the word is used for the portion of land assigned to a tribe or family and therefore becomes an equivalent for *naḥălâ* "inheritance," *ḥeleq* "portion," *yᵉrūshshâ* "possession," *'ăḥūzzâ* "possession," etc. From this the noun comes to denote in general "portion, fate, destiny" (cf. Isa 17:14; 34:17; 57:6; Jer 13:25; Ps 16:5). At the end of the days the resurrected man will stand in his lot (Dan 12:3).

On the day of atonement the destiny of two goats was determined by lot (Lev 16:8–10)—one lot for the LORD and the other lot for the scapegoat. The goat on which the LORD's lot fell was offered on the altar, while the sins of the Israelites were confessed over the other goat and the goat was sent away into the wilderness. This act indicated that the sins were taken away—removed from the Israelites. After this fashion atonement and removal of their sins was effected.

Victors cast lots in dividing the spoils of the booty in general, of Jerusalem (Ob 11), of the honorable men taken in Thebes (Nah 3:10), of the ravaged people of Israel (Joel 3:3 [H 4:3]) and of the Messiah's clothing (Ps 22:18 [H 19]; cf. Jn 19:24). Lots were also cast for assignment to service: of the men to fight against Gibeah (Jud 20:9), of the priests to serve in the temple (I Chron 24:5), of the people to dwell in Jerusalem (Neh 11:1) and of those to supply wood for the altar fire (Neh 10:34 [H 35]). In addition, it was used to discover God's will for the detection of a guilty person: of Achan (Jos 7:14) (?) and of Jonah (Jon 1:7). Rooted in the awareness that God controlled Israel's history and the individual's portion, the lot served to settle disputes (Prov 18:18).

The casting of the lot to decide governmental or judicial matters was practiced by other ancient peoples, as by Haman in the time of Esther. It was by a decision called casting Pur (lot, *gôrāl*) that Haman, the enemy of the Jews, determined a proper time for their massacre, whereupon he sent word throughout the provinces ruled by Ahasuerus that the Jews should be destroyed (Est 3:7; 9:24). But because Mordecai with the help of Esther was able to frustrate this attempt of Haman, the day of Purim became a time of rejoicing rather than one of sadness. Throughout the book the providential timing of events decisively favors the Jews against Haman.

Bibliography: J. Lindlom, "Lot-casting in the OT." VT: 12: 164–66.

E.S.K.

382 גָּרַם (*gāram*) ***lay aside, leave, save.*** Occurs only in Zeph 3:3.

Derivatives

382a גֶּרֶם (*gerem*) ***bone*** (Prov 17:22), ***strength,*** (Gen 49:14), ***self*** (II Kgs 9:13).

382b *גָּרַם (*gāram*) ***break bones.*** This denominative verb occurs only in the Piel (Num 24:8; Ezk 23:34).

383 גרן (*grn*). **Assumed root of the following.**

383a גֹּרֶן (*gōren*) ***barn, barnfloor, corn, floor, threshingfloor, threshing place, void place.*** This word signifies the place where grain was threshed from the stalk and chaff.

The threshing floor when full was at once the symbol of plenty and wealth and the target of raiders (I Sam 23:1). It was vulnerable to attack, because it had to be open to breezes which facilitated winnowing the grain. The threshing place of Arauna, which David bought and where Solomon later built the temple, was such a place. If near the town, the *gōren* was a communal thing and therefore near the gate (I Kgs 22:10, a "void place"). Ruth finds Boaz on the threshing floor, presumably guarding the newly harvested sheaves or threshed grain.

The blessing of God is symbolized by the full threshing floor (Joel 2:24). From it was taken the heave offering to the Lord (Num 15:20) and the tithe of the increase (over what was planted 18:30).

The sheaves were spread out on the hard surface and either trampled by animals or by a sledge or roller machine to separate the kernels from the stalks, the whole being turned over a sufficient number of times to effect the separation.

Bibliography: Ahlstrom, G. W., "Der Prophet Nathan und der Tempelbau," VT 11: 113–27. Gray, John, "Tell El Fara by Nablus: A 'Mother' in Ancient Israel," PEQ 84: 110–13. ______, "The Goren at the City Gate: Justice and the Royal Office in the Ugaritic Text 'AQHT," PEQ 85: 118–23. Lambert, W. G., "Two Akkadian Cognates," JJS 5: 40–41. Marget, Arthur W., "גרן נכון in II Sam 6,6," JBL 39: 70–76. Smith, Sidney, "The Threshing Floor at the City Gate," PEQ 78: 5–14. Wright, G. E., *Biblical Archaeology,* 1957, p. 182.

H.G.S.

גָּרַס (*gāras*). See no. 387.

384 גָּרַע (*gāra'*) ***clip, diminish, restrain, take from, withdraw, abate, do away, keep back.***

Derivative

384a מִגְרָעָה (*migrā'â*) ***recess.***

This root signifies a reduction of quantity of things or of social or religious activities.

The Israelites, during their bondage in Egypt, were not permitted to lower their production of bricks, even when they were forced to gather their own straw (Ex 5:7–8). The inevitable reduced count was attributed to idleness on their part (5:17).

Women were not allowed to marry outside their tribes if they were heirs to property, in order to avoid diminishing the tribe's economic standing (Num 36:1–7). A person who had become unclean from contact with a corpse was not prohibited from eating the Passover, but was to do so a month later (Num 9:7). The ordinances of God must not be diminished or added to in their smallest parts that Israel might have the larger blessing (Deut 4:2; cf. Rev 22:18–19). The many progeny promised to the faithful would be cut down if they turned away from God (Ezk 5:11).

Whereas Eliphaz accuses Job of repressing meditation before God and limiting wisdom to himself, Job learns that God does not forsake (withdraw from) the righteous, which widens his perspective. (Job 36:7).

In the marriage relationship the rights of a secondary wife to food, clothing or conjugal relations may not be diminished (Ex 21:10).

H.G.S.

385 גָּרַף (*gārap*) ***sweep*** (Jud 5:21, only).

Derivatives

385a אֶגְרֹף (*'egrōp*) ***fist*** (Ex 21:18; Isa 58:4).

385b מֶגְרָפָה (*megrāpâ*) ***shovel*** (Joel 1:17, only).

386 גָּרַר (*gārar*) ***drag, drag away*** (e.g. Hab 1:15; Prov 21:7).

Derivatives

386a גֵּרָה (*gērâ*) ***I, cud*** (e.g. Lev 11; Deut 14).

386b גֵּרָה (*gērâ*) ***II, gerah, a weight, a twentieth part of a shekel*** (e.g. Ex 39:13; Lev 27:25).

386c גַּרְגַּר (*gargar*) ***berry*** (Isa 17:6, only).

386d גַּרְגְּרוֹת (*garg^erôt*) ***neck*** (e.g. Prov 1:9; 3:22).

386e מְגֵרָה (*m^egērâ*) ***saw*** (I Kgs 7:9; II Sam 12:31).

387 גָּרַשׂ (*gāraś*) ***be crushed*** (Ps 119:20; Lam 3:16 there spelled with samekh).

Derivative

387a גֶּרֶשׂ (*gereś*) ***a crushing*** (Lev 2:14, 16).

388 גָּרַשׁ (*gārash*) ***cast up, drive out/away, divorce, expel, put away, thrust out, trouble.***

Derivatives

388a †גֶּרֶשׁ (*geresh*) ***thing put forth.***
388b †גְּרוּשָׁה (*g^erûshâ*) ***act of expulsion.***
388c †מִגְרָשׁ (*migrāsh*) ***suburb.***

The root denotes an effective separation between persons or groups, expulsion. Ugaritic attests the meaning "to drive out."

Adam and Eve were driven from the garden of Eden and prevented from returning by the angel with the flaming sword (Gen 3:24). Cain was expelled from God's presence and forced to become a defenseless wanderer among men (Gen 4:14), the penalty of his fratricide. Israel was to dispossess the Canaanites from the promised land and eject them (Ex 23:31). Balak hoped to expel the Israelites (Num 22:11) by force. David used the word to describe his flight from Saul (I Sam 26:19) because it was affected by violent means (hence the word *gārash,* forcible or violent expulsion). The men who petitioned Pharoah to release the Israelites were driven from his presence (Ex 10:11), probably whipped away by the royal bodyguard and his officers. It would appear that although the context must supply the method, the word does include some idea of the use of physical means. An illustration of the means used is seen in Josh 24:12, where the hornet is the means (figuratively) of spurring on the exodus of the Canaanites from before Israel. Of course the word of authority of king or judge was sufficient to effect expulsion from office. I Kings 2:27 states Solomon expelled Abiathar from the priesthood because of machinations against David. Deuteronomy 24:1–4 deals with the bill of divorcement which separated husband and wife.

gārash expresses the execution of divine wrath in respect to the Canaanites' expulsion from the land (Ex 23:31) and later on, Israel's (Hos 9:15). Envy is the cause of the expulsion of Jephthah by his brothers (Jud 11:7). Fear and consternation led Pharoah at last to expel the Israelites (Ex 11:1; 12:31).

gārash is applied figuratively to the wicked in Isa 57:20. They will not always be hidden, but as the sea casts up flotsam and jetsam on the beach, so will the wicked be exposed. Paul (Gal 4:29–30) refers to the expulsion of Hagar (Gen 21:10) allegorically, describing the basic difference between those who work for salvation and those who believe God's promises, inferring that in the same way the former will be ejected from the kingdom of God.

geresh. ***Thing put forth, produced.*** A poetic term, used of produce arriving in its season, as if produced by the sun or moon (Deut 33:14).

g^erûshâ. ***Act of expulsion, a violence.*** Used of oppressive actions against peoples (Ezk 45:9).

migrāsh. ***Suburb, cast out.*** Descriptive of a principle city or town and used of the subordinate villages as separate entities around a principle city. Perhaps derived from *gārash* "drive," then the pasture land to which the flocks were driven. The relation to the root is unclear.

H.G.S.

389 *גָּשַׁם (*gāsham*). This denominative verb occurs in the Pual "be rained upon" (Ezk 22:24), and in the Hiphil "cause or send rain" (Jer 14:22).

Parent Noun

389a גֶּשֶׁם (*geshem*) ***rain, shower*** (e.g. Gen 7:12; Amos 4:7).

390 גֹּשֶׁן (*gōshen*) ***Goshen.*** A district in Egypt.

It is synonymous with the "land of Ramesses" (Gen 47:6,11). The location of the district depends on the location of the city of Avaris (also called Tanis), capital of the Hyksos dynasty. Later known as Pi-Ramesses, Avaris was the seat of the pharoahs during the time of Joseph. Therefore, the district of Goshen must have been near Pi-Ramesses, which some have located in the ruins of Khata'naQantir on the Bubastite Nile. The city Tanis on Lake Menzaleh is not a likely candidate since it was not founded until the Twenty-first Dynasty (1065 B.C. and later). The direct land connection to Asiatic areas of the capital city implied in the Joseph narrative would not be true of the latter Tanis.

It has been shown that the name "Goshen" is found in the name Phacusa (modern Faqus). This name, read by some from the Egyptian as *šśmt,* is actually to be read *gšmt,* Hebrew *goshem,* Greek *gesem.* According to the narrative of Abbess Astheria, Gaqus is only four miles from Pi-Ramesses (thus locating it), which places Goshen close to the Egyptian seat of government.

Bibliography: Uphill, E. P., "Pithom and Raamsees: Their Location and Significance," JNES 27: 291–316; 28: 15–39. Stigers, H. G., *Genesis,* Moody, 1975. Van Seters, John, *The Hyksos: A New Investigation,* Yale, 1966. Kitchen, K. A., "Raamses," in ZPEB, V, p. 14. ———, *The Bible in its World,* Paternoster, 1977, pp. 76–78.

H.G.S.

391 *גָּשַׁשׁ (*gāshash*) ***feel with the hand, stroke.*** This verb occurs only once, in the Piel (Isa 59:10).

גַּת (*gat*). See no. 841a.
גִּתִּית (*gittît*). See no. 841b.

ק

ד

392 דָּאֵב (*dā'ēb*) ***become faint, languish*** (Jer 31:13, 25; Ps 88:10).

392a דְּאָבָה (*d^e'ābâ*) ***faintness, dismay*** (Job 41:14).

392b דְּאָבוֹן (*d^e'ābôn*) ***faintness, languishing*** (Deut 28:65).

דְּאָבוֹן (*d^e'ābôn*). See no. 392b.

393 דָּאַג (*dā'ag*) ***be afraid, careful.***

Derivative

393a †דְּאָגָה (*d^e'āgâ*) ***care, anxiety.***

The root *dā'ag* signifies anxiety, with a shading toward the meaning of fear in some cases.

Saul left off searching for his father's asses because he feared that his father would feel anxiety, arising out of the time spent in the search (I Sam 9:5; 10:2). Jeremiah portrays the attitude of a man who trusts in God in the midst of invasion as untroubled (non-anxious) by such events (17:8, paraphrasing Ps 1), for he draws nourishment and strength from divine resources.

Zedekiah refuses to surrender to the Babylonians (Jer 38:19) because he is concerned about the Jews who have gone over to the Babylonians, fearing that they will harm him.

Isaiah asks the harlot, Israel, who it was that brought such fear and worry on her that she turned to idolatry without thinking of the Lord (Isa 57:11).

d^e'āgâ. ***Care, carefulness, fear, sorrow, heaviness.*** The tribes which settled east of the Jordan expressed a proper anxiety that their children would forget God. Therefore they set up an altar, not for sacrifice, but rather to remind future generations of their duty to serve the Lord together with the tribes living west of the Jordan.

H.G.S.

394 דָּאָה (*dā'â*) ***fly swiftly, dart through the air*** (e.g. Deut 28:49; Ps 18:11).

Derivatives

394a דָּאָה (*dā'â*) ***bird of prey*** (Lev 11:14; Deut 14:13).

394b דַּיָּה (*dayyâ*) ***bird of prey*** (Isa 34:15).

דֹּב (*dōb*). See no. 396b.

395 דבא (*db'*). **Assumed root of the following.**

395a דֹּבֶא (*dōbe'*) ***rest*** (Deut 33:25). Meaning uncertain.

396 דָּבַב (*dābab*) ***move gently, glide, glide over.***

Derivatives

396a †דֹּב (*dōb*) ***bear.***

396b †דִּבָּה (*dibbâ*) ***defaming, evil report.***

dōb. ***Bear, Ursinus Syriacus (the Syrian bear).*** When deprived of its cubs this animal is a dangerous creature (II Sam 17:8; cf. Prov 17:12); at times it roars out in frustration (Isa 59:11). On occasion they attacked people (cf. Amos 5:19); once they attacked in fulfillment of Elijah's curse on people who were insolent toward God (II Kgs 2:24).

The bear is used as a metaphor for the activity of both the wicked and of God. In the former use it denotes the wicked as essentially bestial—cruel, insensitive, self-seeking, and without a spiritual consciousness (Prov 28:15; cf. other passages where the wicked are described as bestial: Ps 22:12ff.; Dan 7:1–8). In the latter usage it denotes the ferocity of God's wrath unleashed against sinful Israel (Lam 3:10; Hos 13:8).

dibbâ. ***Defaming, evil report, infamy, slander.*** This word refers to defamation, perhaps whispered slander, if the connection is with the root *dābab* "to move gently." It is used for a report of evil character (Gen 37:2). The fainthearted spies give a bad report on Canaan (Num 13:32). The utterance of *dibbâ* marks the fool (Prov 10:18). Israel is a *dibbâ*, a public scandal, and will be judged by God (Ezk 36:3).

The root in Akkadian means "to speak, charge, plot"; in an Aramaic compound "to slander"; in Egyptian "lawsuit."

H.G.S.

דִּבָּה (*dibbâ*). See no. 396b.
דְּבוֹרָה (*d^ebôrâ*). See no. 399f.
דְּבִיר (*d^ebîr*). See no. 399g.

397 דבל (*dbl*). **Assumed root of the following.**

397a דְּבֵלָה (*d^ebēlâ*) ***lump of pressed figs*** (e.g. I Sam 39:12; I Chr 12:40).

398 דָּבַק (*dābaq*) ***cleave, cling, stick to, stick with, follow closely, catch, keep close to, join to, overtake.***

Derivative

398a †דֶּבֶק (*debeq*) ***joints, soldering.***

dābaq is used quite often in the OT of physical things sticking to each other, especially parts of the body. Job says that his bone cleaves to his skin (19:20) and that formerly the tongue of leading men cleaved to the roof of their mouths when he was present (29:10). This figure of the tongue cleaving to the roof of the mouth in silence occurs also in Ps 137:6 and Ezk 3:26. In another place Job asserts his innocence by saying that nothing cleaved to his hands Job 31:7—a figure well-known in the modern world.

In God's description of leviathan, he mentions that "the flakes of his flesh are joined together" (Job 41:23 [H 9]), referring to the plates of a crocodile's skin or the scales of a snake(?).

Elsewhere it is said of an unfortunate situation: "My bones cleave to my skin" (Ps 102:5 [H 6]) and "The tongue of the sucking child cleaveth to the roof of his mouth for thirst" (Lam 4:4), a figure also employed in Ps 22:15 for the suffering Messiah in his thirst (cf. Lk 23:36).

Parts of the body are said to stick to various objects. Psalm 44:25 says "our belly cleaveth unto the earth" and Ps 119:25, "My soul cleaveth unto the dust." Of one of David's mighty men it is said that he slew Philistines until "'his hand clave unto the sword" (II Sam 23:10).

dābaq also carries the sense of clinging to someone in affection and loyalty. Man is to cleave to his wife (Gen 2:24). Ruth clave to Naomi (Ruth 1:14). The men of Judah clave to David their king during Sheba's rebellion (II Sam 20:2). Shechem loved Dinah and clave to her (Gen 34:3) and Solomon clave in love to his wives (I Kgs 11:2).

Most importantly, the Israelites are to cleave to the Lord in affection and loyalty (Deut 10:20; 11:22; 13:4 [H 5]; 30:20; Josh 22:5; 23:8) if his blessing is to be theirs. In Jer 13:11 it is said that the Lord caused the Israelites to cleave to him, and Hezekiah is approved because he clave to the Lord. In these verses parallel words and phrases that describe this proper attitude to the Lord are: fear, serve, love, obey, swear by his name, walk in his ways, and keep his commandments.

dābaq also means to keep close to someone, and doubtless this sense is included in references admonishing God's people to cleave to him. But God is never the subject of the verb.

Boaz counsels Ruth to keep "fast by my maidens" (2:8, 21) and so she did (v. 23). In the causative form, *dābaq* means to pursue or even overtake someone, usually in a hostile sense. Laban overtakes Jacob in Gilead (Gen 31:23), and Micah overtakes the children of Dan (Jud 18:22), but the Israelites "pursued hard" after a group of the Benjamites (Jud 20:45) and later, after the Philistines (I Sam 14:22). Also, the Philistines "followed hard" upon Saul (I Sam 31:2; I Chr 10:2).

Sickness or pestilence or evil, too, is said to overtake or adhere to people (Gen 19:19; Deut 28:21, 60; II Kgs 5:27). But the iron and the clay of the toes of the image in Dan 2 will not stick to (KJV "cleave") each other (v. 43).

debeq. ***Joints, soldering.*** Occurs only three times; twice as the joints of the protective armor worn by Ahab when attempting to thwart God's prophecy of his death (I Kgs 22:34; II Chr 18:33) which BDB translates attachment of appendage between armor plates, and as soldering in Isa 41:7 describing the construction of idols. Reference is obviously to one thing attached to another.

Bibliography: THAT, I, pp. 421–32.

E.S.K

399 דָּבַר (*dābar*) ***to speak, declare, converse, command, promise, warn, threaten, sing, etc.***

Derivatives

399a †דָּבָר (*dābār*) ***word, speaking, speech, thing, etc.***
399b †דֶּבֶר (*deber*) ***pestilence.***
399c דֹּבֶר (*dōber*) ***pasture.***
399d דֹּבְרוֹת (*dōbrôt*) ***floats, rafts.***
399e †דִּבְרָה (*dibrâ*) ***cause, reason, manner.***
399f דְּבוֹרָה (*d^e bôrâ*) ***bee.***
399g דְּבִיר (*d^e bîr*) ***I, oracle.***
399h †דְּבִיר (*d^e bîr*) ***II, Debir, a city in Judah.***
399i †דִּבֵּר (*dibbēr*) ***speaker, word.***
399j †דַּבֶּרֶת (*dabberet*) ***words.***
399k מִדְבָּר (*midbār*) ***I, mouth.***
399l †מִדְבָּר (*midbār*) ***II, wilderness.***

Some lexicographers distinguish two roots for the Hebrew *dbr:* I. "to be behind, to turn back" related to Arabic *dub*[*u*]*r* with the same meaning and Akkadian *dabāru* "to push back." Derivatives of this root include *d^e bîr* "back chamber," *dōber* "(remote place) pasture," *dōberôt* "raft [dragged behind the ship]," and *midbār* "steppe." II. "word," mostly found in the noun *dābār* "word, thing" and the verb in Piel "to speak, address." Etymologically related to *dbr* II are *dibrâ* "thing," and *dibbēr* a rare nominal form of the verb, and *midbār* "mouth" with instrumental *mem.* Although Seeligman (VT, 14: 80) derives *dabberet* "word" from root I, it appears more plausible to see it as a derivative of root II. While BDB and GB do not differentiate *dbr* as occurring as a verb in two different roots, KB assigns *dbr* to root I in the Piel for Job 19:18; II Chr 22:10 and in Hiphil for Ps 18:47 [H 48] and 47:3 [4]. We will limit our discussion of the verb to the putative root II.

No convincing etymology for *dbr* has been offered to this time. Akkadian possesses the vocable *dabābu*—noun and verb—with meanings strikingly similar to those of Hebrew. As a substantive it means "speech," or "legal matter" and as a verb "to speak" (CAD. D.2–14). But Hebrew also has a root *dbb* attested in the noun *dibbâ* "whispering, slander." It is questionable whether the similarity between Akkadian *dbb* and Hebrew *dbr* is due to chance or to a true etymological connection.

The root occurs in the Lachish ostraca and in the Siloam Tunnel Inscription. Outside of Hebrew it occurs in Phoenician-Punic with the same meaning as Hebrew and in Biblical Aramaic in a nominal *dibrâ* "matter."

dābar is probably a denominate verb from *dābār,* as it is used almost exclusively in the Piel, Pual, Hithpael, and Qal participle. Ugaritic evidence shows no use of *dābar* "to speak" (nor of *'āmar* "to say"), but does have instance of the use of *midbar* II, wilderness.

In any language the words which represent the basic verb for speaking and the noun for "word" cannot but be of supreme importance. The verb *dābar* and the noun *dābār* have these important spots in the Hebrew Bible. Procksch in TWNT states that the noun is the basic form and the verb stems from it.

These two words occur more than 2500 times in the OT, the noun more than 1400 times and the verb more than 1100. The source of the words is unclear though they are common in Semitic languages.

Some words cover much territory, spreading into many areas of thought and in the process compounding problems for communicators—especially for those who try to translate ideas into other languages. In the KJV *dābar* is translated by about thirty different words and *dābār* by more than eighty. Some of these are synonyms but many are not. All, however, have some sense of thought processes, of communication, or of subjects or means of communication. The noun *dābār* stretches all the way from anything that can be covered by the word thing or matter to the most sublime and dynamic notion of the word of God.

Many synonyms are found in Ps 119 where the message from God is eulogized. Doubtless the most important synonyms are *'āmar* "to say" and the masculine and feminine *'ēmer* and *'imrâ* which are almost always translated "word." In his discussion on synonyms for the word of God, Girdlestone mentions *'āmar* "to say," *millâ* "word," *nā'am* "utter," *peh* "mouth," tôrâ "law," *dāt* "edict," *ḥōq* "statute," *ṣāwâ* "command," *piqqûdîm* "charge," *'ōraḥ* "way," *derek* "path," *mishpaṭ* "judgment," and *'ôd* "testimony."

In this list of synonyms, the first four refer to the ordinary use of the root *dābār*. The word *'āmar* "to say" is very like *dābar* but is usually followed by the thing said. *millâ* "word" was long called a late Aramaizing synonym, but now is recognized as simply a poetic and less common expression for WORD. *nā'am* is mostly restricted to the nominal form *n^e'ūm* meaning a prophetic oracle. The word *peh* "mouth" is a mere figurative use of the organ of speech for the speech. The rest of the words in Girdlestone's list, edict, statute, command, etc. are variant expressions for the authoritative word indicated by *dābār* (or *'ōmer* or *'imrâ*) in some contexts.

[Although *'mr* "to say" is the closest synonym to *dbr,* its basic meaning stands out clearly against *dbr* (Piel). In the case of *'mr* the focus is on the content of what is spoken, but in the case of *dbr* primary attention is given to the activity of speaking, the producing of words and clauses. While *'mr* cannot be used absolutely (without giving the content of what is said), *dibber* can be so used (cf. Gen 24:14; Job 1:16; 16:4, 6). Moreover, while *'mr* can have a diversity of subjects by personification (land, animals, trees, night, fire, works, etc.), *dbr* almost always has personal subjects or designations of their organs of speech (mouth, lips, tongue, etc.). They are also distinguished with respect to the one addressed. While in the case of *'mr* it is sufficient to use the weaker preposition *l^e*, *dbr* normally demands the stronger preposition *'el* (about ten times more frequently than *l^e*). These differences, however, do not detract from the importance of what is said as the object of *dbr* which includes most matters pertaining to moral and ideal values. As in some other verbs used mainly in the Piel, the Qal occurrences are almost exclusively in the active participle and designate mostly one who speaks something as a commandment or on account of an inner compulsion. Thus it is used with: truth (Ps 15:2), lies/falsehood (Jer 40:16; Ps 5:6 [H 7]; 58:3 [H 4]; 63:11 [H 12]; 101:7), right (Isa 33:15; 45:19; Prov 16:13), well-being (Est 10:3), folly (Isa 9:17 [H 16]), insolence (Ps 31:18 [H 19]). It is also used of angels who bear God's message (Gen 16:13; Zech 1:9,13,19 [H 2:2, etc.) and of speech of abiding relevance (Num 27:7; 36:5). B.K.W.]

In the KJV some of the less common translations of the *dābar* include: "answered" (II Chr 10:14) as parallel to *'ānâ* "answer" in v. 13 (where Rehoboam answers his critics); "uses entreaties" (Prov 18:23); "give sentence" or "give judgment" in Jer 4:12 and 39:5 (with *mishpāṭîm*); "publish" (Est 1:22) and "be spoken for" (Song 8:8). The KJV has "subdues" in Ps 18:47 where some such notion is necessary to parallel "avenge" in the first part of the sentence. This psalm occurs also in II Sam 22 and there (v. 48) the Hebrew word for "bring down" is used in the place of *dābar*. This corroborates the rare meaning of "subdue" for *dābar* in Ps 18:47 and Ps 47:3. Modern translations also give this meaning in these passages.

A most important declaration, which is reiterated over and over again (about 400 times), in the OT use of *dābar,* is that God "spoke." The Pentateuch is loaded with such statements as "The LORD said," "The LORD promised" and "The LORD commanded," all translations of *dābar*.

God's spokesmen are often challenged as Moses was challenged by Miriam and Aaron saying, "Hath the LORD indeed spoken only by Moses?" (Num 12:2). But the LORD always supports his word and his spokesman.

dābār. ***Word, speaking, speech, thing, anything, everything*** (with *kōl*), ***nothing*** (with negatives), ***commandment, matter, act, event, history, account, business, cause, reason,*** and in construction with prepositions: ***on account of, because that.*** This noun is translated in eighty-five different ways in the KJV! This is due to the necessity of rendering such a fertile word by the sense it has in varying contexts. As "word" *dābār* basically means what God said or says.

The decalogue, "the ten words" (Ex 34:28; Deut 4:13; 10:4), are ten declarations or statements, as in Deut 10:4, the ten words (*d^e^bārîm*) which the Lord spoke (*dibbēr*). The ten words are commandments because of the syntactical form of their utterance. The ten words are what God said; they are ten commandments because of how God said them.

The *dābār* is sometimes what is done and sometimes a report of what is done. So, often in Chr, one reads of the acts (*dibrê*) of a king which are written in a certain book (*dibrê*). "Now the acts of David the king... are written in the book of Samuel the seer, and in the book of Nathan the prophet, and, in the book of Gad the seer." In the KJV of II Chr 33:18 acts, words, spake and book are all some form of *dābar*/*dābār*. And in the next verse, sayings is added to this list! The Hebrew name for Chronicles is "the book of the words (acts) of the times" (*sēper dibrê hayyāmîm*). Here "words (acts) of the times" is equal to "history"—"annals."

The revelatory work of God is often expressed by "the word of the Lord came" to or upon a person (I Chr 17:3 and often in the prophets). Jehoshaphat says of Elisha that "the word of the Lord is with him" (II Kgs 3:12). When prophecy was stilled as in Samuel's childhood, "The Word of the LORD was precious" (KJV; RSV "rare"). But Moses says that Israel has the word very near, because he refers to the book of the law which had recently been given to them, as the immediately preceding context shows. In II Sam 16:23 the counsel of Ahithophel is said to be like the counsel of an oracle (KJV, RSV). Here *dābār* is "oracle," though *massā'*, KJV "burden," is often used for oracle in modern translations.

[Gerleman notes that the singular construct chain *d^e^bar YHWH* "the word of the LORD" occurs 242 times and almost always (225 times) the expression appears as a technical form for the prophetic revelation (THAT, I, p.439). He also notes that the plural construct chain *dibrê YHWH* "the words of the LORD" occurs seventeen times and much more frequently than the singular construction after verbs of speaking *ngd* [Hiphil] (Ex 4:28); *spr* [Piel] "to recount" (Ex 24:3); *dbr* [Piel] "to tell" (Num 11:24; Jer 43:1; Ezk 11:25); *'mr* "to say" (I Sam 8:10), *qr'* "to cry out" (Jer 36:6, 8; THAT, I:439). In seven passages the *d^e^bar YHWH* has a juristic character (Num 15:31; Deut 5:5; II Sam 12:9; I Chr 15:15; II Chr 30:12; 34:21; 35:6). B.K.W.]

Certain characteristics of the word of the Lord are enunciated in Ps. Among them are: "The word of the Lord is right" (33:4), "settled in heaven" (119:89), "a lamp unto my feet and a light unto my path" (119:105) and "true" (119:160).

The efficaciousness of the word of the Lord is often cited by certain phrases like "according to the word of the Lord" (I Kgs 13:26), or "I will perform my word" (I Kgs 6:12).

The chronicler says that the Lord stirred up Cyrus "that the word of the LORD spoken by the mouth of Jeremiah might be accomplished" (36:22). Through Isaiah the LORD says that his word will be like the rain and the snow making the land productive. "It shall not return unto me void, but it shall accomplish that which I please, and it shall prosper in the thing whereto I sent it" (Isa 55:11). Jeremiah also promises that the Lord's Spirit and word shall never depart from his people and is "like a fire" and "a hammer that breaketh the rock in pieces" (Jer 23:29).

[In addition, the word of the Lord is personified in such passages as: "The LORD sends his message against Jacob, and it falls on Israel" (Isa 9:8 [H 7]); "He sent his word and healed them" (Ps 107:20); "He sends his command to the earth" (Ps 147:15). Admittedly, because of the figure it appears as if the word of God had a divine existence apart from God, but Gerleman rightly calls into question the almost universal interpretation that sees the word in these passages as a Hypostasis, a kind of mythologizing. Gerleman suggests that this usage is nothing more than the normal tendency to enliven and personify abstractions. Thus human emotions and attributes are also treated as having an independent existence: wickedness, perversity, anxiety, hope, anger, goodness and truth (Ps 85:11f.; 107:42; Job 5:16; 11:14; 19:10) (THAT, I, p. 442). B.K.W.]

deber. ***Pestilence, murrain,*** and ***plague.*** This masculine noun is commonly mentioned together with such words as famine, evil, blood, judgment, sword, and noisome beast (KJV; RSV "evil beast"). Jeremiah in his predictions of dire events quite often combines sword, famine, and pestilence (14:12;21:7,9; 24:10; 27:8,13; 29:17–18; 32:24,36; 34:17; 38:2; 42:17,22; 44:13).

Any kind of pestilence which results in death is meant. Aside from about five instances, all uses of *deber* relate to pestilence as sent by God as punishment. Solomon in his prayer at the temple dedication speaks of the possibility of pestilence as a basis for prayer (I Kgs 8:37; II Chr 6:28). However, God in his response says, "If I send pestilence" (I Chr 7:13). Jehoshaphat speaks like Solomon but he puts the statement on the possibility of pestilence as a basis for prayer towards the temple in the mouth of the people (II Chr 20:9). Psalm 91:3, 6 refers to God saving from evil pestilence. All other references are statements of historical occurrences, or threats or prophecies of punishment from the Lord.

dibrâ. ***Cause, sake, intent, order, estate, end, regard.*** *dibrâ* occurs seven times (Job 5:8; Ps 110:4; Eccl 3:18; 7:14; 8:2; Dan 2:30; 4:17). In Ps 110:4 *dibrâ* is usually translated "order of Melchisedek" but in NEB "succession."

For the compound *'al dibrat* see M. Dahood Bib 33: 47f.

dibbēr. ***Speaking or one who speaks*** (?). A form in Jer 5:13 which is uniformly translated as *dābār* "The word is not in them."

dabberet. ***Words.*** A feminine singular noun; cognate of *dābār* found only in Deut 33:3. Probably a poetic collective for all Moses said.

d^ebîr. ***Oracle, sanctuary, Debir.*** As a proper noun Debir is: (1) the name of a king of Eglon who joined the southern coalition against the Gibeonites and the Israelites under Joshua, (2) the name of a prominent Canaanite city, formerly called Kirjath-sepher (Josh 15:15, 49; Jud 1:11), (3) a city of the Gadites east of Jordan (Josh 13:26) and (4) another city on the northern border of Judah (Josh 15:7).

d^ebîr also refers to the holy of holies and is translated sixteen times in KJV and ASV as "oracle," but RSV and modern versions translate as sanctuary, inner sanctuary, inner temple, inner room and other such terms. It is not used of the holy of holies of the wildnerness tabernacle.

Debir (Kirjath-sepher) was a prominent city in the Judean hills near Hebron. Joshua totally destroyed Debir in the southern campaign (Josh 10:38–39; 11:21; 12:13) but either the city was rebuilt and retaken by Othniel or else the destruction by Joshua is a general statement and Othniel actually took the town. Judges 1:11 says that Caleb gave Achsah his daughter to Othniel as wife because he conquered Debir in battle. Debir was later given to the sons of Aaron (Josh 21:15).

midbār. ***Wilderness or desert.*** *midbār* is used to describe three types of country in general: pastureland (Josh 2:22; Ps 65:12 [H 13]; Jer 23:10), uninhabited land (Deut 32:10; Job 38:26; Prov 21:19; Jer 9:1), and large areas of land in which oases or cities and towns exist here and there. The wilderness of Judah has at least a half-dozen cities in it. The wilderness of Jordan (the alluvial plain) contains cities, and the wilderness of Sinai has within it a number of oases. *midbār* is also used figuratively (Hos 2:5; Jer 2:31).

The largest tracts called *midbār* are Sinai, the Negeb, the Jordan Valley, and the Arabian desert.

Specific wilderness areas are: Beer-sheba (Gen 21:14), Paran (Gen 21:21; Num 10:12; 12:16; 13:3, 26; I Sam 25:1), Sin (Ex 16:1; 17:1; Num 33:11–12), Sinai (Num 1:19, etc; Ex 19:1–2; Lev 7:38); Zin (Num 13:21 etc.; Deut 32:51; Josh 15:1), Beth-aven (Josh 18:12), Judah (Jud 1:16; Ps 63 title), Ziph (I Sam 23: 14, 14; 26:2), Maon (I Sam 23:24–25), Gibeon (II Sam 2:24), Damascus (I Kgs 19:15), Edom (II Kgs 3:8), Jeruel (II Chr 20:16) Shur (Ex 15:22; 16:1; Num 1:19 etc.), Etham (Num 33:8), Kedemoth (Deut 2:26), Tekoa (II Chr 20:20), Kadesh (Ps 29:8; Ps 63 title), and Egypt (Ezk 20:35).

The wilderness is often described negatively as without grapes, fountains, pools of water, rivers, pleasant places—or as in a notable statement: "Can God furnish a table in the wilderness?" (Ps 78:19).

Bibliography: Braulik, Georg, "Die Ausdrücke für 'Gesetz' im Buch Deuteronomium," Bib 51: 39–66. McKenzie, John L., "The Word of God in the Old Testament," TS 21: 183–206. Milik, J. T., "Deux Documents Inédits du Désest de Juda," Bib 38: 245–68. Mowinckel, S., "The 'Spirit' and the 'Word' in the Pre-exilic Reforming Prophets," JBL 53: 199–227. ______, "The Decalogue of the Holiness Code," HUCA 26: 1–27. ______, "A Postscript to the Paper 'The Spirit and the Word in the Pre-exilic Reform Prophets'," JBL 56: 261–65. O'Connell, Matthew J., "The Concept of Commandment in the Old Testament," TS 21: 351–403. Ouelette, Jean, "The Solomonic D^ebîr according to the Hebrew Text of I Kings 6," JBL 89: 338–43. Plossman, Thomas, "Notes on the Stem d-b-r," CBQ 4: 119–32. Richardson, TWB, pp. 232, 283–85. THAT, I, pp. 433–42.

E.S.K.

400 דבשׁ (*dbsh*). **Assumed root of the following.**
400a †דְּבַשׁ (*d^ebash*) ***honey.***
400b דַּבֶּשֶׁת (*dabbeshet*) ***hump*** (of camel).

d^ebash. ***Honey.*** Of the fifty-three occurrences of *d^ebash,* seventeen are in "the land flowing wih milk and honey" and are anticipatory of the land God was to give to Israel, or reminiscent of that anticipation.

Si-nuhe, an Egyptian official of the Middle Kingdom who went into voluntary exile in Syria-Palestine, gives this description of the land in the

Patriarchal period: "It was a good land, named Yad. Figs were in it and grapes. It had more wine than water. Plentiful was its honey, abundant its olives. Barley was there, and emmer. There was no limit to any (kind of) cattle" (ANET, p. 19).

Honey was among the products Jacob sent to Egypt for grain (Gen 43:11). It was even more prized then than today because, since they had no sugar, it was their chief sweetener.

Manna tasted "like wafers made with honey" (Ex 16:31).

No honey was to accompany meat offerings; it was not to be burned on the altar (Lev 2:11), but it was included in the tithes and firstfruits (II Chr 31:5).

Moses' song says that God made Israel to "suck honey out of the rock" (Deut 32:13; cf. Ps 81:16 [H 17]). Honey was part of Samson's riddle which his wife enticed him to tell her and reported to her people (Jud 14:8–9, 18).

Jonathan's taste of honey brought Saul face to face with defiance from his army and consequent frustration of his vow (I Sam 14:25–29, 43).

The wicked shall not see "brooks of honey and butter," says Zophar. Pleasant words and love are as honey and the honeycomb (Prov 16:24; 24:13; 25:16, 27; Song 4:11; 5:1). In Ps 19:10 [H 11] and 119:103 God's words are sweeter than honey and the honeycomb, and Ezekiel found that the scroll God gave him was in his mouth "as honey for sweetness" (Ezk 3:3).

The child Immanuel will have butter and honey to eat (Isa 7:15) and in a happier day to come everyone left in the land will have the same (7:22).

E.S.K.

דָּג (*dāg*). See no. 401a.

401 דָּגָה (*dāgâ*) ***multiply, increase.***
401a †דָּג (*dāg*) ***fish.***
401b †דָּגָה (*dāgâ*) ***fish.***
401c דִּיג (*dîg*) ***fish for, catch.*** Denominative verb.
401d דַּוָּג (*dawwāg*), דַּיָּג (*dayyāg*) ***fisherman.***
401e דּוּגָה (*dûgâ*) ***fishing, fishery.***

dāg, dāgâ. ***Fish.*** The masculine *dāg* and the feminine *dāgâ* appear in the OT with no apparent difference in meaning. Fish are referred to as creatures low in intelligence or in control of their destiny (Gen 9:2; I Kgs 4:33; Job 12:8; Eccl 9:12; Hab 1:14; Gen 1:26, 28; Ex 7:18, 21), or as food (Num 11:5, 22; Neh 13:16). The word was used for a gate in Jerusalem, the fish gate (II Chr 33:14; Neh 3:3; 12:39; Zeph 1:10). In biblical times they were caught by spears (Job 41:7), hooks (cf. Job 41:1, 2; Isa 9:8) and nets (Hab 1:15; Eccl 9:12). See pictures in ANEP, p. 34.

Fish without fins and scales were unclean for Israel. Albright has suggested that this law protected Israel from the parasites and diseases carried by mudburrowing fish, clams, snails, etc. (Albright, YGC, p. 178; Harris, R. L., *Man-God's Eternal Creation,* Moody, p. 140).

A graven image in the likeness of any fish is prohibited (Deut 4:18). God's wrath will extend to fish (Ezk 38:20; Hos 4:3; Zeph 1:3), but in the new age waters from the temple will heal the Dead Sea so it will have many fish of many kinds (Ezk 47:9, 10).

The Lord prepared a great fish to teach Jonah the impossibility of fleeing from him (Jon 1:17; 2:1, 11). The identity or biological classification of this great water monster is unknown, as Jonah does not give us details about the miracle. See ZPEB, V, p. 925.

E.S.K.

דָּגוֹן (*dāgôn*). See no. 403b.

402 דָּגַל (*dāgal*) ***look, behold*** (Song 5:10, only).

Derivatives

402a דֶּגֶל (*degel*) ***standard, banner*** (e.g. Num 1:52; 2:3, etc.).
402b דָּגַל (*dāgal*) ***carry, set up a standard*** (Ps 20:6; Song 6:4, 10).

403 דגן (*dgn*). **Assumed root of the following.**
403a †דָּגָן (*dāgān*) ***grain.***
403b †דָּגוֹן (*dāgôn*) ***Dagon.***

dāgān. ***Grain,*** translated "corn" in the KJV in all forty occurrences except Num 18:12 and Jer 31:12 where it is translated "wheat." "Corn" is old English for cereal grain.

dāgān does not specify what grain is meant, but it was a desirable and valuable crop. In descriptions of the productivity of the land, grain (KJV "corn"), wine (*tîrôsh,* q.v.), oil and livestock are usually mentioned, but "grain, new wine and oil (NIV)," or just corn and wine occur as the fresh products of the field. Grain as well as other products was to be tithed and the tithes given to the priests and Levites (Num 18:12; Deut 18:4) who were to make a heave offering of the tithes (Num 18:27). Tithes of grain were not to be eaten in their homes but only "before the LORD" (Deut 12:17; 14:23).

The increase of grain, wine, oil and livestock came as blessing from God consequent upon the people's obedience (Deut 7:13; 11:14). A decrease or cessation of such productivity was punishment for disobedience (Deut 28:51; Lam 2:12; Hos 2:11; Joel 1:10, 17; Hag 1:11).

After his reform Hezekiah built storehouses to hold the abundance of grain, wine, and oil (II Chr

31:5; 32:28). The prophets predict that grain, wine, oil and livestock will be abundant in the age of blessing (Jer 31:12; Ezk 36:29; Joel 2:19; Zech 9:17).

E.S.K.

dāgôn. **Dagon.** The name of the god of the Philistines referred to only twice aside from the eleven occurrences in I Sam 5 where the story of the capture of the ark of the covenant is told.

Scholars debate whether Dagon is etymologically related to Heb. *dag* "fish" and was thus a fish-god, or to Heb. *dāgān* "grain" and thus a vegetation deity, or to Arabic *dagga, dágā, dagana*, "to be cloudy" "rainy" and thus a storm-god. No modern scholar since the turn of the century follows Jerome and Kimchi who suggested on the basis of popular etymologizing that he was a fish-god. Many moderns follow Philo Byblios and W. F. Albright who view him as a grain-god, but Albright thinks that the Heb. word for grain was derived from the name of the god and not vice-versa (*Archaeology and the Religion of Israel*, 1953, pp. 77, 22).

F. J. Montalbano, however, though recognizing the weakness of the Arabic evidence, brings together strong evidence, at least for Mesopotamia, that Dagon was a storm-god. "Canaanite Dagon: Origin, Nature," *CBQ* 13: 381–97). His evidence includes: 1.) An Akkadian text from the time of Hammurabi says: "Dagan is Enlil" (the Sumerian storm-god). 2.) At Larsa he is mentioned alongside of Enlil and called one of the great gods, a title not given to fertility deities in Mesopotamia 3.) On a seal from the Neo-Sumerian period (2070–1960) his name appears before that of his wife *Sha-la-ash* possibly the same as *Sha-la*, wife of Adad, the weather-god. 4.) Gelb had earlier concluded that Dagan of the Hurrians is none other than the Hurrian weather-god Teshup. But Montalbano thinks that the West Semites assumed him into their pantheon as a god of grain, even though at Ugarit he was identified as the father of Hadad, the celebrated storm-god in the Levant. The evidence for this thesis is the fact that in one of the Ugaritic texts, the name of the god is synonymous with the word for grain. The association of a weather-god with grain is obvious.

We first encounter Dagon in our literary sources from Mesopotamia in an important historical inscription of Sargon in which he tells us that he stopped at Tutuli (on the Upper Euphrates) to worship Dagan. Naram-Sin, grandson of Sargon, attributes his conquest from the Euphrates to the coast of Syria to Dagan. From this point on throughout the history of Mesopotamia we find proper names compounded with the element Dagan. Hammurabi (1728–1530) calls himself: "The warrior of Dagan, his creator . . . ," and at Mari, Zimri-Lim offers him rich gifts in response to a revelation from Dagan enabling him to defeat the Benjaminites. Shamsi Adad I (1748–1716), king of Assyria, built a temple to Dagan at the site sixty km north of Mari. Moreover, his name is frequently invoked by the Assyrian kings in the later Assyro-Babylonian inscriptions (900–640).

In the West, Dagan is mentioned among the gods at Ebla (2400–2250 B.C.). We may mention here "Dagan of Tuttul," "Dagan of Sivad," "Dagan of Canaan" exactly like "Dagan of the Philistines." Note also the mention of Canaan at this early period (Giovanni Pettinato, "The Royal Archives of Tell Mardikh-Ebla," BA 39: 48). Paolo Matthiae lists Dagan as one of the great gods at Ebla ("Ebla in the Late Early Syrian Period," BA 39: 110). At Ugarit on the north Syrian coast archaeologists have uncovered two commemorative stelae bearing his name, and in their texts Baal is called "Dagan's son" twelve times; four times his name appears alone.

In Palestine he was the principal deity of the Philistines during the biblical period. He was worshipped by them at Gaza (Jud 16:21–23), Ashdod (I Sam 5:2–3; I Macc 10:83–85) and at Beth-shan (I Sam 31:10; I Chr 10:10). According to Sanchuniathon he played a prominent place in the Phoenician pantheon. Other shrines belonging to him are indicated by their place names. There was a Beth-Dagan in Judah (Josh 10:41), another in Asher (Josh 19:27). The name appears in the list of towns conquered by Rameses III (1197–1167), although this may be copied from an earlier one of Rameses II (1301–1234). This *Byt-dgn* is probably the same as the one spoken of by Sennacherib (704–681) as *bit-daganna* located in the plain of Sharon. Mazar unearthed a Philistine temple at Tel Qasile whose artifactual remains, including two pillars separated by a space the length of a very large man's arm span and in front of the altar, comports most favorably with the literary description of Dagan's temple at Gaza (Jud 16:23–31) (IEJ 24: 77–88).

Thus Dagan's cult was prominent in Assyria, Babylonia, Syria and Palestine from at least 2400 B.C. on through the pre-exilic period. Against this history the LORD's victories over Dagan through Joshua (Josh 19:27), Samson (Jud 16) and above all through his ark containing his moral law (II Sam 5) becomes the more glorious and significant in his history of establishing his rule on the earth through Israel.

Bibliography: Delcor, M., "Jahweh et Dagon," VT 14: 136–54. Montalbano, F. J., "Canaanite Dagon: Origin, Nature [with complete Bibliography]," CBQ 13:381–97.

B.K.W.

404 דָּגַר (*dāgar*) ***gather together as a brood*** (Jer 17:11; Isa 34:15).

405 דַּד (*dad*) ***breast, teat, nipple*** (e.g. Prov 5:19; Ezk 23:3, 21).

406 *דָּדָה (*dādâ*) ***move slowly.*** Occurs in the Piel (Ps 42:5) and Hithpael (Isa 38:15; Ps 42:5).

דֹּדָה (*dōdâ*). See no. 410b.

407 *דָּהַם (*dāham*) ***astonish, astound.*** Occurs only once, in the Niphal (Jer 14:9).

408 דָּהַר (*dāhar*) ***rush, dash*** (Nah 3:2, only).

Derivatives

408a דַּהֲרָה (*dahărâ*) ***rushing, dashing*** (Jud 5:22, only).
408b תִּדְהָר (*tidhār*) ***elm*** (Isa 41:19).

409 דּוּב (*dûb*) ***pass away*** (Lev 26:16; I Sam 2:33).

דַּוָּג (*dawwāg*). See no. 401d.
דּוּגָה (*dûgâ*). See no. 401e.

410 דוד (*dwd*). **Assumed root of the following.**
410a †דּוֹד (*dôd*) ***beloved, uncle.***
410b דֹּדָה (*dōdâ*) ***aunt.***
410c †דָּוִד (*dāwid*), דָּוִיד (*dāwîd*) ***David.***
410d דּוּדַי (*dûday*) ***mandrake.***
410e דּוּד (*dûd*) ***pot, jar.***

dôd. ***Beloved, love, uncle.*** Of fifty-eight occurrences in KJV thirty-eight are "beloved" (all in Song except Isa 5:1), eight are "love" and seventeen "uncle." *dôd* is used by the Shulamite for her lover, or by those who speak of him. He calls her *ra'yâ* "companion" or "love" (lover).

Isaiah refers to the Lord as "beloved" in his Song of the Vineyard (5:1).

dôd as "love" itself is extolled or described by "thy love is better than wine" (Song 1:2), "We will remember thy love more than wine" (1:4), "How fair is thy love" and "How much better is thy love than wine" (4:10) and "There will I give thee my love" (7:12).

Ezekiel speaks of the Lord's kindness toward Israel when "thy time was the time of love" (16:8). But the Babylonians "came to her into the bed of love," and defiled her (23:17).

In Prov 7:18 the harlot says to the foolish young man, "Come, let us take our fill of love until the morning."

dôd is "uncle" in Lev 20:20 where lying with one's aunt is prohibited (see *gālâ*). This uncovers his "uncle's nakedness." Among those who should redeem a man sold to another because of poverty are "his uncle or his uncle's sons" (Lev 25:49). Other references to "uncle" are simple identifications.

dāwîd. ***David, dawid*** David son of Jesse, king of Israel. The name is conjectured to come from *dôd* "beloved" but the etymology is uncertain. It has been compared with the Mari term *dawidum* "leader," but this too is unsure JNES 17: 130.

Most of the more than a thousand occurrences of the name appear in the historical books which tell of his life and reign: Sam, Chr, and Kgs. Because of his prominence, the ideal nature of his person and reign, and the messianic covenant made with him, references to him occur also in Ps, Prov, Eccl, Song, Isa, Jer, Ezk, Hos, Amos, and Zech.

His name is mentioned in the superscriptions of seventy-five psalms and also thirteen times in the body of individual psalms. References in the superscriptions indicate Davidic authorship or to the inclusion of certain psalms in an earlier Davidic collection.

The name of David first occurs in I Sam 16:13 in the narrative of Samuel's semi-private anointing of him to be king. His life can be divided into the early years which include his anointing by Samuel, his service to Saul (soothing Saul's spirit by his music), and his defeat of Goliath; the years of his exile while being pursued by Saul, during which he gathers a private army to himself and solidifies his control over a large part of Judah; the seven years of his rule over Judah as king with Hebron as his capital, and of growing influence over the north; and then the thirty-three years of his rule over all Israel, with its successful wars, extension of Israel's boundaries, religious and administrative centralization in Jerusalem, and growing influence and affluence in the world of that day.

The theological impact of David's life is of utmost importance. Though he is obviously a man of his time in the brutality of warfare and the arrogance of authority, he is, nevertheless, the epitome of devotion to his Lord and to the ideals of the revealed word of God. This is shown not only in the Psalms but also in the narratives of the historical books. It is David who brings the ark into Jerusalem and makes every attempt to establish the religious life revealed through Moses. It is David who leads the people devotionally by his Psalms constantly directed to faith and obedience to the Lord. It is David who makes preparation for the construction and service of the temple, even though the actual construction is denied him.

However, the greatest theological significance of David rests in his recognition of the relationship of the anointed king to the Lord. Out of this understanding comes the doctrine of the messiah (from *māshaḥ* "to anoint"). David was a perfect recipient of the covenant which promised not only an eternal dynasty, but a son who would also be "son of God" ruling forever over the kingdom of God (II Sam 7:11–16; I Chr 17:10–14). Specific references to David as prefiguring the Messiah are: Ezk 34:23–24; 37:24–25; Hos 3:5; Jer 30:9. There are in addition figurative expressions for great David's greater Son, the "stem" or "branch" or "root of Jesse" (Isa 11:1, 10). The "righteous Branch" of David (Jer 23:5; 33:15), the tabernacle (*sukkâ*) of David (Amos 9:11) and the tabernacle (*'ōhel*) of David (Isa 16:5).

The name of David is used in these descriptive phrases: city of David (II Sam 5:7, 9), house of David (II Sam 3:1, 6), throne of David (II Sam 3:10; I Kgs 1:37), sepulchre of David (Neh 3:16; II Chr 32:33), tower of David (Song 4:4), musical instruments of David (Neh 12:36), God of David (II Kgs 20:5), and mercies of David (II Chr 6:42; Isa 55:3).

Bibliography: Ap-Thomas, D. R., "Saul's 'Uncle'," VT 11: 240–45. Stamm, J. J., "Der Name des königs David," Supp VT 7: 165–83.

E.S.K.

דּוּדַי (*dûday*). See no. 410d.

411 דָּוָה (*dāwâ*) ***infirmity.***

Derivatives

411a †דְּוַי (*dᵉway*) ***languishing.***
411b דָּוֶה (*dāweh*) ***faint.***
411c †מַדְוֶה (*madweh*) ***disease.***
411d †דַּוָּי (*dawway*) ***faint.***
411e דְּיוֹ (*dᵉyô*) ***ink.***

Ugaritic *dw* and Arabic *dawiya* mean "to be sick."

In Lev 12:2 the discharge after the birth of a baby is said to render a woman unclean. Contact with a corpse also rendered unclean. The latter required purification through sprinkling with water mixed with the ashes of a red heifer (Num 19:14–19). The avoidance of contamination by menstrual discharge was part of the general avoidance of discharges from the body, many of which are dangerous as the results of infection. This general avoidance of contamination contributed to the public health of Israel. At the same time, it received religious sanction being administered by the priests. All uncleanness became a type of sin which had to be cleansed by redemption. Watchfulness against contamination is inculcated by the law concerning menstruation (Lev 15). As the context shows, the danger envisioned in the law is the unnatural discharge due to sickness. Those who demanded sexual intercourse at that time were liable to punishment (Lev 20:18). But the details of the law are not clear—whether it refers to relations within marriage (it does not say "his wife") or to a particular case of rape or adultery.

dawway. ***Faint,*** indicating a temporary weakness of body or soul. The meaning of faint for *dawway* (Isa 1:5) is appropriate, since Israel has poured out her strength in idolatry. The doom facing Israel makes Jeremiah faint (Jer 8:18) because he can see no relief for his people.

dᵉway. ***Languishing, sorrowful.*** Job, who is counselled to accept his afflictions as proper retribution for secret sin, rejects the counsel as loathsome (*dᵉway*, 6:7), seeing no reason for these afflictions.

madweh. ***Disease.*** Ugaritic *mdw* "illness." In Deut 7:15 and 28:60 *madweh* accents the loathsome character of the diseases of Egypt: elephantiasis, dysentery, and opthalmia (Kline, *Treaty of the Great King,* p. 69).

H.G.S.

412 דּוּחַ (*dûaḥ*) ***cast out, purge, wash.***

The root signifies cleansing through washing.

The sacrificial ritual in Solomon's temple, unlike that of the tabernacle, provided separate facilities for cleansing offerings. There were five lavers on the north and five on the south in which the burnt offerings (*'olâ*) were washed before being placed on the altar (II Chr 4:6). The legs and internal organs of the burnt offering were washed in order to remove contamination from contact with the feces in slaughter and dismemberment.

Isaiah (4:4) picks up this image in describing the future cleansing of Israel. God will wash away their sins, transgression and idolatry when through affliction and judgment they repent and turn to him.

Nebuchadrezzar's destruction of Judah and Jerusalem is called a purging in Jer 51:34.

The picture of washing is repeated in the NT, becoming the central thought in the phrase "washing of regeneration" (Tit 3:5) through which the old man of sin is cleansed away.

H.G.S.

דְּוַי (*dᵉway*). See no. 41*a*.
דַּוָּי (*dawway*). See no. 411d.
דָּוִיד (*dāwîd*). See no. 410c.

413 דּוּךְ (*dûk*) ***pound, beat*** (in mortar, Num 11:8).

Derivative

413a מְדֹכָה (*mᵉdōkâ*) ***mortar.***

414 דּוּכִיפַת (*dûkîpat*) ***unclean bird, perhaps hoopoe*** (Lev 11:19; Deut 14:18).

415 דום (*dwm*). **Assumed root of the following.**
415a †דּוּמָה (*dûmâ*) ***silence.***

415b †דּוּמִיָּה (*dûmîyâ*), דֻּמִיָּה (*dūmîyâ*) ***silence, repose.***
415c †דּוּמָם (*dûmām*) ***silent.***

dûmâ. ***Silence.*** In Ugaritic it means "to keep silence"; in Arabic "to last," "to be motionless" (of water); and in Ethiopic "to be stupified."

The word connotes the "silence of death." The Psalmist praises the Lord for his narrow escape from the land of silence (Ps 94:17) and notes that the Lord's glory is not enhanced by those whose praise is silenced in death (115:17).

dûmîyâ. ***Silence, repose.*** Sometimes it is good to keep silence, but at other times it is bad. The Messiah laments that since God apparently fails to answer his prayer, he finds no rest or relief from his situation (Ps 22:12). David found that when he kept silent out of fear of his enemies, his distress grew worse (Ps 39:2). It would be wrong to keep silence when praise is due, so praise awaits God in Zion (Ps 65:1). On the other hand, it is good to wait on God in silence (Ps 62:1). However, the form here may be taken from *dāmâ* "to be like" (so KJV). Perhaps, "Praise awaits you O God in Zion" (NIV, footnote "befits").

dûmām. ***Dumb, silent.*** Used to describe dumb idols (Hab 2:19). Sometimes silence is brought about by judgment, but at other times it is the fruit of faith. Thus Babylon must henceforth be silent because God has ended her glory (Isa 47:5). But an attitude of non-complaint should characterize those who trust in God (Lam 3:26).

דּוּמִיָּה (*dûmîyâ*). See no. 415b.
דּוּמָם (*dûmām*). See no. 415e.
דּוֹנַג (*dônag*). See no. 444a.

416 דּוּץ (*dûṣ*) ***spring, leap, dance*** (Job 41:14, only).

417 דוק (*dwq*). **Assumed root of the following.**
417a דָּיֵק (*dāyēq*) ***bulwark, sidewall*** (e.g. II Kgs 25:1; Ezk 4:2).

418 דּוּר (*dûr*) ***heap up, pile, dwell.***

Derivatives

418a דּוּר (*dûr*) ***circle, ball.***
418b †דּוֹר (*dôr*), דֹּר (*dōr*) ***generation.***
418c מְדוּרָה (*m*ᵉ*dûrâ*) ***pile*** (of wood, etc.).

Occasionally there is a Hebrew word wherein etymology, as a route to discovery of ancient thought patterns, is all-important in discovering the true life-situation in which the word must be understood. Such is the case here. Authorities all agree that *dôr,* the noun, is derived from *dûr,* the verb. The simple primitive sense, not expressly found in any biblical text, is to move in a circle, surround. Since ashes, grain, meal, etc., when heaped up form a circle on the floor, ancient Semites used this word for "to heap up" or "to pile something"—thinking graphically of the shape of the heap at its base, rather than as we, of the height or outline of the elevation created. Also, since houses were usually a group of rooms surrounding a central court, and perhaps since some very early houses were circular, the word was employed with the meaning, to dwell. This analysis is provided strong support by the fact that *dûr,* a noun appearing only twice, and likewise from *dûr* (verb) must be translated a ball (Isa 22:18), round about (Isa 29:3) and pile (Ezk 24:5). In this manner an original meaning of "go in a circle" (as attested by its appearance in cognate Arabic and Assyrian, and inferred by *a posteriori* reasoning for a common link between the ideas of pile and dwell), though apparently out of use in OT times, provide the basis for a word of important theological meaning.

dôr, dōr. ***Generation.*** By a thoroughly understandable figure, a man's lifetime beginning with the womb of earth and returning thereto (Gen 3:19) is a *dôr;* likewise from the conception and birth of a man to the conception and birth of his offspring is a *dôr.* A period of extended time and several other related meanings would be inevitable in a language prone to metaphors.

Thus the following analysis of the actual use of *dôr* in the OT unfolds quite naturally.

1. The circle of a man's lifetime, from birth to death. This is the apparent meaning at Gen 15:16, where four generations cover an epoch of 400 years (cf. Gen 15:13). This conforms to the long length of life among the Hebrew patriarchs (Keil, *Commentary* p. 216). "In the times of the patriarchs it was reckoned at a hundred years.... So among the Romans the word *seculum* originally signified an age or generation of men and was later transferred to denote a century" (Gesenius *Lexicon,* trans. Edw Robinson, 26th ed., 1891). This idea is present in the passages which speak of a generation as passing away, rather than as being succeeded by another (Deut 1:35; 2:14).

2. More frequently, of the circle of a man's life from his conception and birth until the conception and birth of his offspring. Familiar examples are in the recurring phrase, "Even to the tenth generation" (Deut 23:2 [H 3]; 3 [H 4]) and "the children of the third generation" (Deut 23:8 [H 9]). Extended uses listed below rest on this.

3. A period or age of time. *dôr* is used in various combinations to express this: *dôrôt sh*ᵉ*lāmîm* (Is 51:9); *dôr wādôr* (Deut 32:7); *l*ᵉ*dōr dōr* (Ex 3:15), *b*ᵉ*kol dōr wādōr* (Ps 45:18); *'ad dōr wādōr* (Psa 100:5); *b*ᵉ*dōr dōrîm* (Ps 102:25).

There are others. In some *dôr* indicates an age or period of past time (Isa 51:9), future time (Ex 3:15), past and future (Ps 102:24). Many occurrences are employed to indicate endless time, i.e. eternity, often paralled with other concrete terms as *'ôlām* "forever" (Ps 89:1 [H 2]) or *'im shemesh* and *w^e lipnê yārēaḥ*, literally, "with the sun and before the moon."

4. One group—as opposed to a single person—as related to another by natural descent (Jud 2:10). This is a group of posterity, as in the case of "four generations" of Job's offspring (Job 42:16) and in references such as "throughout their generations" (Gen 17:7, 9) and "throughout your generations" (Gen 17:12; see also Ex 12:14, 17, 42 et al.).

5. A special use of the fourth sense above is to mean simply "contemporaries," viz. "and of his generation, who considered"? (Isa 53:8); cf. Gen 6:9 *dōrōtāyw* "in his own generation and those immediately contiguous" (BDB).

6. By a natural transition this word is used widely with a metaphorical sense to indicate a class of men distinguished by a certain moral or spiritual character. Thus God is "in the generation of the righteous" (Ps 14:5) and those whose "hands" and "heart" are clean are "the generation of them" that seek God's face (Ps 24:6). The wicked "fathers" of Israel were "a stubborn and rebellious generation; a generation that set not their heart aright" (Ps 79:13). This usage is frequently employed (see Prov 30:11, 12, 13, 14; Jer 2:31; 7:29).

This usage via LXX becomes, in the word *genea*, a Hebraism of frequent striking occurrence in the mouth of Jesus in the Greek NT (e.g. Mt 11:16; 12:29,45; 16:4; 17:17, etc.). John the Baptist and Jesus employed *gennēma, genēma* similarly (Mt 3:7; 12:34; 23:33; Lk 3:7).

In the LXX dôr is most frequently rendered *genea*, rarely *genēsis;* never *gennēma genēma* (Hatch and Redpath, *Concordance to the LXX*).

In the OT, the chronological use is predominant, (number three above) though the metaphorical (number five) is the most significant theologically.

It ought to be noted that this word in the chronological sense is only one of the many biblical terms for time demonstrating that revelation presents time as a durative, measurable phenomenon. Duration may not be excluded from the biblical idea of time.

Bibliography: Ackroyd, P. R., "The Meaning of Hebrew דור Considered," JSS 13: 3–10. Neuberg, Frank J., "An Unrecognized Meaning of Hebrew DÔR," JNES 9: 215–17. THAT, I, pp. 443–44.

R.D.C.

419 דּוּשׁ (*dûsh*), דִּישׁ (*dîsh*) ***tread, thresh.***

Derivatives

419a דַּיִשׁ (*dayish*) ***threshing.***
419b מְדֻשָׁה (*m^e dūshâ*) ***that which is threshed.***
419c דִּישֹׁן (*dîshōn*) ***a clean animal.***

Aramaic is the same, and in Akkadian it is "to tread on" (of threshing oxen). This root basically means "to thresh." Only two references to actual threshing occur (I Chr 21:20; Isa 28:27–28). Hosea (10:11) uses *dûsh* to indicate an attitude.

Isaiah 28:27 mentions that different methods were used for different size grains, threshing for larger sizes, and the rod for tapping out the cummin.

The instruments of threshing are seldom mentioned, although Isaiah speaks of the cart wheel (28:28) and the threshing sledge with teeth (41:15). Grain was separated from chaff by winnowing, when the wind was favorable. The fan (30:24) or the whisk broom was used to sweep away the dust as it settled out or blew away. Finally the grain was passed through a sieve to separate the dirt (cf. Amos 9:9; Isa 30:28; Lk 22:31).

dûsh is also used figuratively. The breaking action of threshing speaks of the defeat of the adversaries of Hazael of Damascus (II Kgs 13:7). *dûsh* is used in Gideon's threat against the elders of Succoth (Jud 8:7), and of the subjugation of Gilead by Syria (Amos 1:3). It is also used of Israel's victory over her enemies (Mic 4:13; Isa 41:15). On the latter verse, see E. J. Hamlin, JNES 13: 185–90. Hamlin argues that in Isa 41:15ff. the mountains and hills are mentioned because they were the sites of pagan worship.

H.G.S.

420 דָּחָה (*dāḥâ*) ***chase, overflow, thrust, totter, sore, drive away/out, be outcast, cast down.***

Derivatives

420a דְּחִי (*d^e ḥî*) ***falling.***
420b מִדְחֶה (*midḥeh*) ***ruin.***

This root connotes "to pursue and cast down" with the intent to harm. Twice it occurs as an intensive infinitive absolute. In Arabic it means "to drive."

The Psalmist pictures Israel as one who was being pushed hard by his foes in order to bring about his downfall (Ps 118:13). On one occasion David likens himself to a tottering wall as he is being assaulted by the wicked (Ps 62:3 [H 4]). On another occasion he complains that the wicked are attempting to trip his feet, i.e. to bring about his downfall (Ps 140:4 [H 5]). But elsewhere he praises God for keeping his feet from falling (Ps 56:13 [H 14]; cf. 116:8). Jeremiah predicts that the pursuit of wickedness by the wicked prophets and priests will lead finally to slippery paths in darkness where they will be driven and fall (Jer 23:12), and the sage avers that whereas the righteous find a refuge at the time of death, the wicked are brought down to final ruin at the time of their calamity (Prov 14:32). He also concludes that a flattering tongue works havoc (Prov 26:28). David prays that the angel of God will pursue the wicked and bring them to destruction (Ps 35:5). Isaiah envisions the day when the outcasts of Israel will be gathered together from the Diaspora (Isa 11:12; 56:8).

H.G.S.

421 *דָּחַח (*dāḥaḥ*) ***to be thrust down.*** Occurs only once, in the Niphal (Jer 23:12).

דְּחִי(*dᵉḥî*). See no. 420a.

422 דחן (*dḥn*). **Assumed root of the following.**

422a דֹּחַן (*dōḥan*) ***millet*** (Ezr 4:9, only).

423 דָּחַף (*dāḥap*) ***drive, hasten*** (e.g. Est 3:15; 6:12).

Derivative

423a מַדְחֵפָה (*madḥēpâ*) ***thrust*** (Ps 140:12, only).

424 דָּחַק (*dāḥaq*) ***thrust, crowd, oppress*** (Joel 2:8; Jud 2:18).

425 דַּי (*day*) ***sufficiency, enough,*** combined with prepositions: בְּדַי, מִדַּי, etc.

דִּיג (*dîg*). See no. 401c.
דַּיָּג (*dayyāg*). See no. 401d.
דַּיָּה (*dayyâ*). See no. 394b.
דְּיוֹ (*dᵉyô*). See no. 411e.

426 דִּין (*dîn*) ***judge, contend, plead.***

Derivatives

426a דִּין (*dîn*) ***judgment.***
426b דַּיָּן (*dayyān*) ***judge.***
426c מָדוֹן (*mādôn*) ***strife, contention.***
426d מְדִינָה (*mᵉdînâ*) ***province.***

This word, with its derived noun *dîn* is nearly identical in meaning with *shāpaṭ* (q.v.) and its derived noun *mishpāṭ* (q.v.). It appears only twenty-three times, a fraction of the times *shāphaṭ* and *mishpāṭ* appear. Of the twenty-three appearances, five are in parallel with *shāpaṭ* (Jer 5:28; 22:16; Prov 31:8; Ps 7:8 [H 9]; 9:8 [H 9]) and twice more it is associated in the text with *mishpāṭ* (Ps 72:2; Jer 21:12). Thus nearly a third of its occurrences show how closely the idea of *dîn* was identified or associated with the root *shāpaṭ*. The verb also occurs in Ugaritic and in parallel with *ṯpṭ* (the cognate of *shāpaṭ*) (Fisher, RSP, vol. 1, p. 166). Likewise a similar—nearly identical as far as it goes—list of terms is associated with *dîn*, demonstrating the near identity of meaning: with *mêshārîm* "uprightness," "equity" (Ps 96:10; cf. Ps 75:2); and with *gāsha'* (Ps 54:1 [H 3]; cf. Ps 72:4). As with *shāpaṭ* it represents God's government as both among his *people* [Israel] and among all peoples (Ps 135:14 "people"; Ps 7:8 [H 9] "peoples" cf Ps 72:2; Ps 9:8 [H 9]). As far as the small number of occurrences allows a test, the range of meanings is exactly the same: to govern, in the whole range of activities of government: legislative, executive, judicial or otherwise. See the discussion of *shāpaṭ* and *mishpāṭ*. The difference between the terms is simply that *dîn* is poetic, probably also an archaic and more elegant term. Of the twenty-three occurrences, only one is outside the Protestant grouping of poetical and poetical-prophetic literature. The exception is the single passive form—a Niphal participle (II Sam 19:9 [H 10]).

The chief theological significance of this word is that apparently like *shāpaṭ* it embodies the idea of government, in whatever realm, in all its aspects.

Bibliography: Speiser, E. A., "YDWN, Gen 6_3," JBL 75: 126–29. THAT, I, pp. 448–50.

R.D.C.

דָּיֵק (*dāyēq*). See no. 417a.
דִּישׁ (*dîsh*). See no. 419.
דַּיִשׁ (*dayish*). See no. 419a.
דִּישׁוֹן (*dîshôn*). See no. 419c.
דַּךְ (*dak*). See no. 429a.

427 *דָּכָא (*dākā'*) ***be crushed, contrite, broken.***

Derivatives

427a †דַּכָּא (*dakkā'*) ***I, contrite, crushed.***
427b דַּכָּא (*dakkā'*) ***II, dust (that which is crushed).*** According to Ps 90:3, God turns man back into dust.

dākā' is used in the Piel and Pual, and twice in the Hithpael (Job 5:4; 34:25). This verb is used only in poetry. (Cf. *dākak, dākâ,* and Akkadian *dakāku.*)

dākā' and its derivatives are applied only to people except for Ps 89:10 [H 11], which mentions the crushing of Rahab, probably a reference to God's victory over Egypt. God is frequently the subject of the verb. He is the one who crushes the oppressor (Ps 72:4) and the wicked (Job 34:25), but he does not crush the prisoner underfoot (Lam 3:34). Job requests God to crush him and put an end to his misery (6:9). According to

Isa 53:10, God did crush his servant. Verse 5 indicates that he "was crushed for our iniquities." This emphasizes the emotional and spiritual suffering of the Savior as he became sin for us (cf. Ps 51:8 [H 10]).

Several times it is the wicked or the enemies who are crushing the righteous (Ps 94:5; 143:3). Even the leaders of Israel were guilty of crushing their people (Isa 3:15). The poor and needy were sometimes crushed in court (Prov 22:22; cf. Job 5:4).

Man's frailty is seen in the brevity of life, as he returns to the dust (Ps 90:3). Job 4:19 contrasts man with the angels and notes that he is crushed more easily than a moth.

dakkā' I. ***Contrite, crushed.*** "Crushed" can also have the positive nuances of "humble, contrite." God is close to those who are brokenhearted and contrite (Isa 57:15; Ps 34:18 [H 19]). He condemns Israel for her failure to humble herself even after Jerusalem's collapse (Jer 44:10).

H.W.

428 דָּכָה (*dākâ*) ***be crushed, broken, contrite.***

Derivative

428a דֳּכִי (*dŏkî*) ***crushing, dashing*** (Ps 93:3, only).

This verb is a by-form of the verb *dk'*, which also means "to crush," and of *dûk* "to pound, beat." It is used only in Ps, twice in the Niphal (38:8 [H 9]; 51:17 [H 19]) and twice in the Piel (44:19 [H 20]; 51:8 [H 10]). The form in Ps 10:10 is disputed, though it is possibly a use of the Qal. Most versions render it "he crouches" (KJV, ASV), although "he is crushed" is also plausible.

The verb appears only in laments and is consistently used of one who is physically and emotionally crushed because of sin or the onslaught of an enemy. In Ps 51:8 [H 10] and probably 38:8 [H 9], the psalmist speaks of his bones being broken because of involvement in sin. Psalm 51 refers to David's adultery with Bathsheba and the subsequent conviction of sin that he experienced. In verse 17 [H 19] he notes with some consolation that God does not despise a broken and contrite ("crushed") heart. The same parallel (using *dk'*) occurs in Ps 34:18 [H 19]. In Ps 74:21 "oppressed" is parallel to "the afflicted" and "needy."

In Ps 44:19 [H 20] the situation seems to refer to a military defeat in which the nation has been "crushed." No sin is mentioned in the entire psalm, and yet the land has been humiliated, and overrun with jackals (cf. Jer 9:11). Proverbs 26:28 notes that a liar hates the people he crushes.

H.W.

429 דכך (*dkk*). **Assumed root of the following.**

429a דַּךְ (*dak*) ***crushed, oppressed*** (e.g. Ps 74:21; Prov 26:28).

429b דַּכָּה (*dakkâ*) ***crushing*** (Deut 23:2, only).

דָּל (*dāl*), דַּל (*dal*). See nos. 431a, 433a.

430 דָּלַג (*dālag*) ***leap*** (e.g. Zeph 1:9; I Sam 5:5).

431 דָּלָה (*dālâ*) ***draw*** (water).

431a דָּל (*dāl*) ***door.***

431b דָּלָה (*dālâ*) ***door.***

431c דְּלִי (*d^e lî*) ***bucket.***

431d דָּלִיּוֹת (*dālîyôt*) ***branch, bough.***

431e †דֶּלֶת (*delet*) ***door.***

delet. ***Door, gate, leaf*** (of a door). This noun is used eighty-six times in the OT and in all but one passage it refers to the door on a house, a room of the house, a temple, or the gates of a city. Sometimes it is used metaphorically (Song 8:9; Job 3:10; 38:8; 41:14 [H 6]; Ps 78:23). In one passage, Jer 36:23, it seems to describe some kind of tablet on which Baruch took dictation from Jeremiah. This latter meaning of *delet* is now confirmed by evidence from Ugaritic and Phoenician in which *dlt* may mean both "door" and "tablet." Also in the Lachish letters (in Hebrew, sixth century B.C.), letter no. 4, line 3, is the phrase *ktbty 'l hdlt* "I have written upon the tablet." One can also compare the Greek word *deltos* "writing tablet."

Doors in biblical times were made of strips or planks of wood bounded by metal strips, usually bronze or iron. Actually the door was an assemblage including beside the door itself the following: two doorposts (*m^e zûzâ*) which are the door's vertical sides; a lintel (*mashqôp*), the door's upper horizontal side; and a sill or a threshold (*sap*), the door's lower horizontal side. Wider doorways such as those used in city gates or large buildings had a third vertical column on which two doorleaves, one attached to each of the doorposts, converged when shut. This is implied by the number of times *delet* is used in the dual in the Bible. The door, which usually opened inward, did not have hinges like ours. The butt edge of the door consisted of an upright post which swung in sockets. The lower socket was usually a hollowed stone. The upper socket consisted of a metal frame or a hollow made in the lintel.

delet is to be differentiated from other words of approximately the same meaning. In relation to *sha'ar* "gate," *delet* represents only the swinging door, while *sha'ar* denotes the entire structure of the gate (Neh 3:1,6,13–15). In relation to *petaḥ* "door, entrance," *petaḥ* is the entrance to the house. *delet* is a device for closing and opening the entrance. Also, *delet* is used only in connection with a built house. Thus compare God's word to Cain, "Sin is crouching at the door (*petaḥ*," Gen 4:7). "And the Lord appeared to Abraham... as he sat by the door (*petaḥ*) of his tent" (Gen 18:1).

One will recall that God told his people, just before the exodus from Egypt, to smear the doorposts (*mᵉzûzâ*) and the lintel (*mashqôp*), but not the door itself, with blood (Ex 12:7). The death angel would pass over those houses in which such steps had been taken.

In Deut 6:4ff. and 11:20 there is a reference to the ancient and still prevailing custom of hanging the *mᵉzûzâ* to the doorpost. In contemporary Judaism the *mᵉzûzâ* refers not to the doorpost itself but to the parchment scroll which is affixed to the doorpost. On one side of the scroll is the appropriate words from Deut. On the back of the parchment is the Hebrew word *shadday*, which is not only a name for God, "Almighty," but is also an acronym for *shômēr daltôt yiśrā'ēl* "Guardian of the doors of Israel." How appropriate it is then in the NT for Jesus to say, "I am the door of the sheep" (Jn 10:7).

V.P.H.

דַּלָּה (*dallâ*). See nos. 433b,c.

432 דָּלַח (*dālaḥ*) ***make turbid*** (Ezk 32:2).

דְּלִי (*dᵉlî*). See no. 431c.
דָּלִיּוֹת (*dālîyôt*). See no. 431d.

433 דָּלַל (*dālal*) ***to be low, hang down.*** The RSV and ASV translate the same except when rendering the verbal form.

Derivatives

433a †דַּל (*dal*) ***one who is low.***
433b דַּלָּה (*dallâ*) ***I, thrum.***
433c דַּלָּה (*dallâ*) ***II, poorest, lowest.***

This root connotes lowness as a state or a goal. It occurs sixty-two times. Used metaphorically, the verb describes a state of deprivation which in its extremity issues in a cry to God. It sometimes refers to physical distress (Jud 6:6). The noun *dallâ* I describes hair (Song 7:5 [H 6]) and thread hanging from a loom (Isa 38:12). *dālal* is apparently applied to miners suspended by ropes (Job 28:4) and the legs of the lame (Prov 26:7) which "hang down (and nothing more)." It also describes dried up streams (Isa 19:6).

dal. ***One who is low.*** This root occurs most frequently in the adjectival form. Unlike *'ānî, dal* does not emphasize pain or oppression; unlike *'ebyôn,* it does not primarily emphasize need, and unlike *rāsh,* it represents those who lack rather than the destitute. We might consider *dāl* as referring to one of the lower classes in Israel (cf. II Kgs 24:14; 25:12). In *dāl* the idea of physical (material) deprivation predominates. Compare, also, *dallâ* denoting the opposite of fatness (Gen 41:19), and the poorest and lowest of Israel whom the Babylonians left behind (II Kgs 24:14). Gideon cites the weakness (*dal*) of his clan when he questioned God's call to him to deliver Israel (Jud 6:15, cf. II Sam 3:1). *dal* describes the appearance of Amnon as he pined for Tamar (II Sam 13:4).

dal denotes the lack of material wealth (Prov 10:15) and social strength (Amos 2:7). Such people are contrasted with the rich (Ex 30:15; Ruth 3:10) and the great (Lev 19:5). God enjoins their protection (Ex 23:3; Lev 14:21; Isa 10:2), and promises to them justice (Isa 11:4). Only infrequently is *dal* used of spiritual poverty (cf. Jer 5:4), and in most cases such usages parallel *'ebyôn,* needy (Isa 14:30).

L.J.C.

434 דָּלַף (*dālap*) ***drop, drip*** (Job 16:20; Ps 119:28; Eccl 10:18).

Derivative

434a דֶּלֶף (*delep*) ***a dropping*** (Prov 19:13; 27:15).

435 דָּלַק (*dālaq*) ***hotly pursue*** (e.g. Gen 31:36; Ob 18).

Derivative

435a דַּלֶּקֶת (*dalleqet*) ***inflammation*** (Deut 28:22).

דֶּלֶת (*delet*). See no. 431e.

436 דָּם (*dām*) ***blood.***

This important word appears 360 times in the OT, most often in Lev (88 times) and Ezk (55 times), followed by Ex (29 times), Deut (23 times), and Ps (21 times). These occurrences can be divided roughly in a two-to-one ratio, into two general categories: (1) the shedding of blood through violence and havoc resulting usually in death, as in war or murder; (2) the shedding of blood, always resulting in death, in a sacrifice to God.

The theological debate today centers around the significance of what is symbolized by the biblical word, "blood" in a context of sacrifice. Briefly, two suggestions have been made. One is that blood symbolizes life. The blood of the victim is the life that has passed through death. Thus, to say that one is saved by "the blood of Christ" means that we are saved by Christ's life, by participating in his life. Much emphasis is placed here on several OT verses which all say substantially the same thing: "The life of the flesh is in the blood" (Gen 9:4; Lev 17:11,14; Deut 12:23).

The second interpretation and the one adhered to in this article, emphasizes that blood in the OT denotes not life, but death, or more accurately, life that is offered up in death. Having said this, it should be pointed out that there is absolutely nothing in the OT akin to the morbid preoccupation with the sinister deities of the netherworld such as one finds in the blood rituals of Israel's neighbors where the emphasis is also on "blood-death."

The three passages quoted above should present no problem. Rather than saying that blood is life they simply say that blood is the source of life, the means by which life is perpetuated. To remove the blood is to terminate life. Hence, in the OT a threefold prohibition emerges from this: (1) the sanctity of life; a man may not shed the blood of another man. In such cases of homicide it is the responsibility of one of the kinsmen to act as a "blood redeemer" (*gô'ēl hā-'ādām*) for the deceased by killing the slayer (Num 35:19; Deut 19:12). In such cases where God is the avenger of blood the verb used is never *gā'al* but *nāqam*—take vengeance (Deut 32:43); or *dārash*—seek, require (Gen 9:5). Related to this are those instances where an individual has committed an infraction of the moral law that necessitates the death penalty. The expression used in the Bible to describe such a person is, "His blood is upon him" (Lev 20:9,11–13,16,27) or "his blood shall be upon his head" (Josh 2:19; I Kgs 2:37).

(2) The second principle that emerges from the relationship between blood and life is that before a sacrifice of an animal could be offered to God, all of its blood must be drained and disposed of either on the altar, the ground, or elsewhere (Lev 1:5; 4:6; Deut 12:24; Ex 12:7). (3) Eating blood is prohibited (Lev 3:17; 17:10–13; I Sam 14:31–35; Ezk 33:25). The reason is simple enough. Atonement for sins was made by the sacrifice of the life of animals as a substitution for one's own life; and the shedding of blood was the most important element in the expiation of sin. Hence, the prohibition on human imbibing. It was too sacred for ordinary man to handle.

There can be no doubt that theologically the primary teaching of the OT about the blood is its role in the forgiveness of sins. God promises atonement for sin and cleansing by the blood of a guiltless substitute. How logical it will be then for the NT to take this concept to its fullest fulfillment and extension. We are reconciled to God by the death of his Son, and we shall be saved by his life (Rom 5:10).

Bibliography: Dewar, L., "The Biblical Use of the Term 'Blood'," JTS 4: 204–208. Koch, M., "Der Spruch 'Sein Blut bleibe auf seinem Haupt' und die israelitischen Aüffassung vom vergossenen Blut," VT 12: 396–416. McCarthy, D., "The Symbolism of Blood and Sacrifice," JBL 88: 166–76. ———, "Further Notes on the Symbolism of Blood and Sacrifice," JBL 92: 205–10. Morris, L., "The Biblical Use of the Term 'Blood'," JTS 3: 216–27. ———, JTS 6: 77–82. Reventlow, H., "Sein Blut Komme über sein Haupt," VT 10: 311–27. Richardson, TWB, p. 33. Steinmuller, J., "Sacrificial Blood in the Bible," Bib 40: 556–67. Stibbs, A., *The Meaning of the Word 'Blood' in Scripture,* 3d ed., London: Tyndale, 1962. Wood, Bryant, G., "'In the Blood is Life'—A Common Belief in Ancient Times," *Bible and Spade* 2: 105–14. TDNT, I, pp. 172–77. THAT, I, pp. 448–50.

V.P.H.

437 דָּמָה (*dāmâ*) ***I, be like, resemble.***

Derivatives

437a †דְּמוּת (*d^e mût*) ***likeness.***
437b דִּמְיוֹן (*dimyōn*) ***likeness.***

This verb appears thirty times in Biblical Hebrew and twice in Biblical Aramaic (Dan 3:25; 7:5). In the Qal stem the verb is used mostly in reference to man and by man, either in the form of a direct statement (Ps 144:4; 102:6 [H 7]; Isa 1:9) or in the form of a rhetorical question (Ezk 31:2,18; cf. v. 8, in connection with the Egyptian Pharaoh). A similarly structured question is found in Isa 46:5 with God expressing his own incomparability. The verb is also an ideal one for the author of the Song of Solomon where the respective lovers search for appropriate figures of speech to convey their depth of love for each other: 2:9, 17; 7:8; 8:14; 1:9 (Piel).

In the Piel stem the verb assumes the meaning "to compare, imagine, think, intend." Of special interest here are those references in the latter chapters of Isaiah where the Lord says of himself that there is nothing or nobody to whom he can be compared (Isa 40:18,25; 46:5; cf. Ps 50:21 where God chides the people for attempting to make him in man's image). The corollary of this theme in Isaiah would be something like, "I am the Lord, and besides me there is no savior" (Isa 43:11). The point of these verses in Isaiah is not that God says no one is comparable to him in appearance or being, but that no one is comparable to him in ministry and function.

d^emût. ***Likeness.*** Although this substantive is used only twenty-six times in the OT, it is a very important word. It appears in the theophanic section of Ezekiel (1:5,10,13,16,22,26,28; 10:1,10,21,22), and quite often in juxtaposition with *k^e marê* "like the appearance of." Ezekiel is very careful never to say that he saw God, *'ĕlōhîm* (as did Isaiah in his prophecy, Isa 6:1, the object or content of Isaiah's vision is *'ădōnāy*), but only that he saw the likeness of God or the likeness of the entourage that surrounds God. In such practice he is comparable to Daniel (Dan 10:16) and

John in the Apocalypse (Rev 1:13), and perhaps Heb 7:3 (the introduction of Melchizedek). All of the above references in Ezekiel refer to visual similarities, but Isa 13:4 shows that *dᵉmût* can be used also for audible similarities, and structural similarities in the sense of being a pattern or model (II Kgs 16:10, parallel with *tabnît*).

Finally we note two important passages in which man is said to be created in "(the image and) likeness of God" (Gen 1:26; 5:1), and one passage where Adam fathered a son, Seth, "in his likeness" (Gen 5:3).

Our purpose here is not to examine per se the doctrine of *imago Dei*. The studies on this have been legion. Specifically, we shall attempt to ascertain the relationship between *ṣelem* ("image," q.v.) and *dᵉmût* ("likeness") in Gen. Nowhere else in the OT do these two nouns appear in parallelism or in connection with each other. The following suggestions have been made. (1) Roman Catholic theology has maintained that "image" refers to man's structural likeness to God, a natural image, which survived the Fall and "likeness" refers to man's moral image with which he is supernaturally endowed; and it is this likeness that was destroyed in the Fall. (2) The more important word of the two is "image" but to avoid the implication that man is a precise copy of God, albeit in miniature, the less specific and more abstract *dᵉmût* was added. *dᵉmût* then defines and limits the meaning of *ṣelem* (Humbert, Barr). (3) No distinction is to be sought between these two words. They are totally interchangeable. In Gen 1:26, which is God's resolution to create, both words are used. But in v. 27, the actual act of creation, only *ṣelem* is used, not *dᵉmût*. The two words are so intertwined that nothing is lost in the meaning by the omission of *dᵉmût*. Also, the LXX translates *dᵉmût* in Gen 5:1 not by the usual *homoiosis* but by *eikon*, the Greek counterpart for Hebrew *ṣelem* (Schmidt). (4) It is not *ṣelem* which is defined and limited by *dᵉmût* but the other way around. Two things are important here: (a) the similarity between *dᵉm*ut and the Hebrew word for "blood" *dām;* (b) in Mesopotamian tradition the gods in fact created man from divine blood. Genesis then represents a conscious rejection of and polemic against pagan teaching by asserting that *ṣelem* specifies the divine similarity to which *dᵉmût* refers, viz., man's corporeal appearance and has nothing to do with the blood that flows in his veins (Miller). (5) The word "likeness" rather than diminishing the word "image" actually amplifies it and specifies its meaning. Man is not just an image but a likeness-image. He is not simply representative but representational. Man is the visible, corporeal representative of the invisible, bodiless God. *dᵉmût* guarantees that man is an adequate and faithful representative of God on earth (Clines).

Bibliography: Ausselin, David Tobin, "The Notion of Dominion in Genesis 1–3," CBQ 16: 277–94. Barr, J., "The Image of God in the Book of Genesis—A Study of Terminology," BJRL 51: 11–126. Clines, D.J.A., "The Image of God in Man," *Tyndale Bulletin* 19: 53–103. Humbert, P., *Études sur le récit du paradis et de la chute dans la Genèse,* Neuchâtel: Sécretariate de l'Université, 1940. Jenni, E., in THAT, pp. 451–56. Labuschagne, C. J., *The Incomparability of Yahweh in the O.T.,* Leiden: Brill, 1966. Miller, J. M., "In the 'Image' and 'Likeness' of God," JBL 91: 289–304. Piper, J., "The Image of God: An Approach from Biblical and Systematic Theology," *Studia Biblica et Theologica* 1: 15–32 (arguing for the ontological, substantialistic interpretation of the "image of God" doctrine). Schmidt, W. H., *Die Schöpfungsgeschichte der Priesterschrift,* Neukirchen-Vluyn: Neukirchener Verlag, 1964. Wynkoop, M. B., *A Theology of Love,* Beacon Hill Press, 1972, esp. chaps. 6–7 (arguing against the ontological interpretation of the "image of God" doctrine). Buswell, J. O., *A Systematic Theology,* vol. I, pp. 232–42. Richardson, TWB, p. 226.

V.P.H.

438 דָּמָה (*dāmâ*) ***II, cease, cut off, destroy, perish.***

Derivative

438a †דֳּמִי (*dŏmî*) ***rest, silence.***

The root under consideration is used almost exclusively in prophetical books or context. Thus, the verb is found outside this genre only in II Sam 21:5 and Ps 49:12,20 [H 13, 21]. The verb means to come to an end, but it is always a violent end that is indicated: Isa 15:1; Jer 47:5; Hos 4:5–6; 10:15.

In a different context, however, this verb is used by Jeremiah in his aspiration that his tears shed for his people not "cease" (Jer 14:17; cf. Lam 3:49). Isaiah also uses the verb (in the Niphal perfect) in his familiar, "Woe is me for I am 'undone'" (6:5).

dāmâ is used seventeen times in the OT and twelve of these are in the Niphal stem.

dŏmî. ***Rest, silence,*** occurs four times: Isa 62:6–7; Ps 83:1 [H 2]; Isa 38:10. The latter reference presents some problem in translation as evidenced by the KJV "cutting off" and the RSV "noontide" plus the lack of unity among the ancient versions. It may be that the origin of *dŏmî* here is not *dāmâ* II, but rather *dāmam* II, "to mourn, wail"; so, "I said in my sorrow I have."

Bibliography: On the use of *dŏmî* in Isa 38:10 cf. Dahood, M., "Textual Problems in Isaiah," CBQ 22: 400–409, esp. p. 401. On the relation of the roots *dûm/dāmâ/dāmam,* all meaning basically "cease, be silent," cf. G. R. Driver, "A

Confused Hebrew Root (דמם,דמה,דום) in *Sepher N.H. Tur-Sinai*, Publicationes Societatis Invest. Script, VIII, 1960.

V.P.H.

דֻּמָּה (*dûmmâ*). See no. 439b.
דְּמוּת (*d^e^mût*). See no. 437a.
דֳּמִי (*dŏmî*). See no. 438a.
דִּמְיוֹן (*dimyōn*). See no. 437b.

439 דָּמַם (*dāmam*) ***I, be silent, still; wait.***

Derivatives

439a דְּמָמָה (*d^e^māmâ*) ***whisper,*** (I Kgs 19:12; Job 4:16; Ps 107:29).
439b דֻּמָּה (*dûmmâ*) ***one silenced, destroyed*** (Ezk 27:32, only).

dāmam is cognate to the Ugaritic *dmm* "be silent." It occurs twenty-nine times in the Qal, and five times in the Niphal. It is found primarily in poetry.

dāmam is often found in a context of catastrophe and mourning. Aaron and Ezekiel had to keep quiet in spite of the death of loved ones (Lev 10:3; Ezk 24:17). The elders of Judah sit silently with dust on their heads (Lam 2:10). Sometimes the notion of stress is absent, however, as in Job 29:21.

Judgment upon nations brings the meaning close to "destroy." The cities of Moab (Jer 48:2) and the island fortress of Tyre (Ezk 27:32) are silenced, and men of war are brought to the silence of death. Jeremiah applies this to the troops of Damascus (49:26) and Babylon (50:30; cf. Isa 23:2). The only Hiphil use of the verb refers to the Lord dooming Israel (Jer 8:14). The wicked (I Sam 2:9; Ps 31:17 [H 18]) and the Egyptians at the Red Sea (Ex 15:16) are also silenced in death.

In I Sam 14:9 the concept of "waiting" or "standing still" appears. This seems to be the meaning when Joshua asks the Lord to make the sun "stand still" and the moon "stop" so he could pursue the Amorites (Josh 10:12–13). Those interpreters who explain this miracle in terms of the silencing of the sun's heat have a more difficult time, especially in view of the parallelism with the moon.

Several times in the Psalms this verb is used of being still before the Lord in quiet meditation (4:4 [H 5]; 131:2). We are to rest in the Lord and wait patiently for him (Psa 37:7). Yet God's rescue from trouble did lead the Psalmist to end his silence and sing praises to the Lord (Ps 30:12). [H 13]).

440 דָּמַם (*dāmam*) ***II, wail*** (Isa 23:2).

441 דמן (*dmn*). **Assumed root of the following.**
441a דֹּמֶן (*dōmen*) ***dung*** (e.g. Jer 8:2; Ps 83:11).
441b מַדְמֵנָה (*madmēnâ*) ***dung pit*** (Isa 25:10, only).

442 דָּמַע (*dāma'*) ***weep*** (Jer 13:17, only).

Derivatives

442a דֶּמַע (*dema'*) ***juice*** (Ex 22:28, only).
442b †דִּמְעָה (*dim'â*) ***tears*** (e.g. Ps 80:6; Eccl 4:1).

dim'â. ***Tears.*** Occurs twenty-three times, mostly in poetry in Jeremiah and Psalms. Cognate to Ugaritic *dm't* and Akkadian *dimtu*. It is a collective noun, but the plural *d^e^mā'ôt* is found in Ps 80:5 [H 6] and Lam 2:11.

"Tears" usually occurs in a context of mourning and lamenting. Jeremiah wept profusely because of the crushing of Judah (Jer 14:17) and the ensuing captivity (13:17). His eyes became a "fountain of tears" (Jer 9:1 [H 8:23]) and a "river" (Lam 2:18) as he wept over his slain countrymen. Isaiah drenched the land of Moab with tears as he mourned their judgment (16:9), but Ezekiel was not allowed to weep even when his wife died (24:16). The Psalmist wept because of his enemies (6:6 [H 7]; 56:8 [H 9]) but rejoiced when God rescued him from death (116:8).

Several times tears are associated with prayer (Ps 39:12 [H 13]; Lam 2:18). God answered Hezekiah's tearful prayer and healed him of a fatal illness (II Kgs 20:5 = Isa 38:5). In Jer 31:16 the promise of Israel's return from captivity brings an end to their tears (cf. Ps 126:5), and Isaiah looks forward to that blessed day when God will "wipe away tears from all faces" (25:8).

Twice, tears are regarded as food and drink (Ps 42:3 [H 4]; 80:5 [H 6]), and the concept of measuring the amount of tears (80:5) is found also in Ugaritic: "His tears drop like shekels to the ground" (Keret 1:28).

H.W.

443 דַּמֶּשֶׂק (*dammeśeq*) ***Damascus.***

In Amos 3:12 the Hebrew text reads *d^e^mesheq*, which the ancient versions translated as "Damascus" but modern commentators generally translate by piece, part, corner, etc. In Chronicles and in Aramaic, Damascus is spelled *darmeseq*. The name in Egyptian is *tymshqw* and in Akkadian *dimashqi*.

Damascus, a very ancient city, is recognized in the Bible from the time of Abraham who pursued a Mesopotamian raiding party to Hobah near Damascus where he rescued Lot (Gen 14:15). Abraham's steward was Eliezer of Damascus (Gen 15:2).

The city was situated in an oasis on the plain east of Mount Hermon and watered by the Abana and Pharpar rivers.

Damascus is not mentioned again in the OT until David extends his kingdom northward and conquers Syria and the Syrians of Damascus (II Sam 8:5,6: I Chr 18:5,6). From David's time until Damascus is overcome by Assyria, tension between Syria (often referred to by its capital city, Damascus) and Israel results in sporadic warfare with victory sometimes on one side and sometimes on the other.

Rezon, a leader among the Syrians of Zobah, fled with his followers to Damascus, became king there and was a problem to Solomon during Solomon's reign (I Kgs 11:24). However, Ahab later dominates that area sufficiently to effect a treaty which gave him control of certain areas of Damascus (I Kgs 20:34). About this time Naaman, captain of the Syrian army is healed by Elisha (II Kgs 5:12ff.).

Elisha goes to Damascus, as the Lord instructed him (I Kgs 19:15), and informs Hazael that Ben-hadad the king would die and that Hazael would become king in his place and ravage Israel (II Kgs 8:7ff.).

Later Jeroboam II regains control of Damascus (II Kgs 14:28).

When Ahaz is king of Judah, Syria and Israel unite in warfare against Judah. This occasions Isaiah's famous prophecy of a virgin conceiving a son whose name would be Immanuel which was a sign that the Lord would be with Judah and the coalition of Israel and Syria would be destroyed by Assyria. Ahaz, however, does not accept the sign and sends the silver and gold in the temple at Jerusalem and the treasures of his palace (cf. II Chr 16:2; 24:23) to Tiglath-pileser of Assyria who then conquered Damascus and took its people captive to Kir (II Kgs 16:8, 9). Ahaz on a visit to Tiglath-pileser in Damascus became attracted to an altar and set up one like it in the temple at Jerusalem and sacrificed to the gods of Damascus (II Chr 28:23).

Isaiah prophesied that Jerusalem would be destroyed like Damascus (7:8; 8:4; 10:9; 17:1–3).

Amos too prophesies against Damascus (1:3, 5), and declared that Israel would go into captivity beyond Damascus (5:27).

In the closing years of the kingdom of Judah, Jeremiah prophesies that judgment would fall on Damascus (49:23, 24, 27).

In the last OT references, Ezekiel and Zechariah mention Damascus in describing the borders of the land after the return from captivity (Ezk 47:16,17,18; 48:1; Zech 9:1). Ezekiel also mentions Damascus as a merchant in his description of the glory of Tyre (27:18) and in the description of the bride in the Song of Songs it is said, "Thy nose is as the tower of Lebanon which looketh toward Damascus" (7:4).

Bibliography: Reider, J., "דמשק in Amos 3, 12," JBL 67: 245–48. Unger, Merrill F., "Some Comments on the Text of Genesis 15:2, 3," JBL 72:49–50.

E.S.K.

444 דנג (*dng*). **Assumed root of the following.**
444a דּוֹנַג (*dônag*) ***wax*** (e.g. Mic 1:4; Ps 22:15).

דֵּעַ (*dēa'*). See no. 848a.
דֵּעָה (*de'â*). See no. 848b.

445 דָּעַךְ (*dā'ak*) ***go out, be extinguished*** (e.g. Isa 43:17; Prov 20:20).

דַּעַת (*da'at*). See no. 848c.

446 דפה (*dph*). **Assumed root of the following.**
446a דֳּפִי (*dŏpî*) ***blemish, fault*** (Ps 50:20, only).

447 דָּפַק (*dāpaq*) ***beat, knock*** (Gen 33:13; Song 5:2; Jud 19:22).

448 דָּקַק (*dāqaq*) ***crush, grind, break in pieces.***

Derivatives

448a †דַּק (*daq*) ***thin, fine, gaunt.***
448b דֹּק (*dōq*) ***veil, curtain.*** Occurs only in Isa 40:22, where the heavens are likened to a thin veil.

dāqaq occurs mostly in the Qal and Hiphil. It is used both literally and figuratively (contrast *dk', dkh*). Three times it is used alongside the word "threshing" (Isa 28:28; 41:15; Mic 4:13).

The verb and the adjective *daq* refer one time each to food. In Isa 28:28 there is a description of grinding grain to make bread. In Ex 16:14 manna is called "thin" or "fine flakes" that looked like frost. Two passages refer to the fragrant incense used by the priests. A special blend of spices and frankincense was ground into powder and placed in front of the "testimony" (Ex 30:36). On the Day of Atonement, Aaron was to take burning coals and two handfuls of finely ground incense into the holy of holies (Lev 16:12).

The adjective occurs six times in Gen 41, which relates the dream of Pharaoh interpreted by Joseph. Pharaoh was perplexed by the seven ugly and "gaunt" ("leanfleshed," KJV) cows (vv. 3, 4) and by the seven "thin" heads of grain scorched by the east wind (vv. 6, 7, 23, 24). Physical appearance is also the point of Lev 21:20, where dwarfs are disqualified from the priesthood (cf. Lev 13:30).

A number of passages refer to grinding to powder idols and images. The most famous is the incident of the golden calf, in which an angry Moses put the powder into water and made the people drink it (Ex 32:20; Deut 9:21). This became the pattern for King Asa of Judah, who cut up an Asherah pole, crushed it and had it burned in the Kidron Valley (II Chr 15:16). Josiah followed suit, grinding up Asherah poles in Jerusalem (II Kgs 23:6) and Bethel (II Kgs 23:15). He did the same with the pagan altars and images throughout the country, scattering the powder on the graves of their devotees (II Chr 34:4, 7).

Metaphorically, the Scriptures speak of trampling the enemy, grinding them as fine as dust. With the Lord's help, Israel will be able to crush many nations in battle (Isa 29:5; 40:15; Mic 4:13), just as David was able to pound his enemies into submission (II Sam 22:43). Isaiah underscores the insignificance of the nations compared with an almighty God by calling them mere "dust on the scales" (40:15, NASB).

daq. ***Thin, fine, gaunt.*** Occurs mostly in the Pentateuch (eleven out of fourteen uses) and, like the verb, often has a negative sense. Can be applied to people, animals, and things.

In I Kgs 19:12 *daq* refers to the "gentle whisper" through which God spoke to Elijah after the prophet had fled to Mount Sinai.

H.W.

449 דָּקַר (*dāqar*) ***pierce, pierce through, thrust through.***

Derivative

449a מַדְקָרָה (*madqārâ*) ***piercing, stab*** (Prov 12:18, only).

dāqar is used six times in the Qal, once in the Niphal, and three times in the Pual—all three participial forms in the writings of Jeremiah (37:10; 51:4; Lam 4:9). Normally the piercing results in death. But in Jer 37:10 the term refers to men who are seriously wounded. The weapon associated with *dāqar* is usually the sword, though a spear is the instrument in Num 25:8.

Several times *dāqar* refers to a disgraceful death. In its only occurrence in the Pentateuch the term is used of the blow, inflicted by the priest Phinehas, that killed an Israelite man and a Midianite woman (Num 25:8). It was this drastic action that stopped the plague against the Israelites resulting from idolatry and immorality connected with the worship of the Baal of Peor. In two instances Israelite rulers asked their servants to pierce them through to avoid dying in disgrace. Abimelech wanted to avoid the charge that a woman killed him (Jud 9:54), and Saul feared abuse at the hands of the Philistines (I Sam 31:4 = I Chr 10:4). The alleged contradiction as to the death of Saul in II Sam 1:9 is probably due to the Amalekite's stretching the truth so as to get credit for Saul's death and to obtain a reward. He got more than he asked for!

The term appears twice in Zechariah, again with the connotation of disgrace. In 12:10 it refers to the nation of Israel finally turning to Christ, "the one they have pierced," at the second coming. The next chapter predicts that in that day no false prophet will be allowed to live, for his own parents will pierce him through (13:3).

Four times *dāqar* is used in connection with the armies of Babylon. The Chaldean forces will be successful against Judah (Jer 37:10; Lam 4:9), but they too will fall before the invading armies of the Medes and Persians (Isa 13:15; Jer 51:4).

H.W.

דּוֹר (*dōr*), דַּר (*dar*). See nos. 418b, 454a.

450 דרא (*dr'*). **Assumed root of the following.**

450a דֵּרָאוֹן (*dērā'ôn*) ***aversion, abhorrence*** (Isa 66:24; Dan 12:2).

דֵּרָאוֹן (*dērā'ôn*). See no. 450a.

451 דרב (*drb*). **Assumed root of the following.**

451a דָּרְבָן (*dorbān*) ***goad*** (I Sam 13:21, only).

451b דָּרְבֹנָה (*dorbōnâ*) ***goad*** (Eccl 12:11, only).

דָּרְבָן (*dorbān*). See no. 451a.

452 דרג (*drg*). **Assumed root of the following.**

452a מַדְרֵגָה (*madrēgâ*) ***steep place, steep*** (Song 2:14; Ezk 38:20).

דַּרְדַּר (*dardar*). See no. 454e.
דָּרוֹם (*dārôm*). See no. 454d.
דְּרוֹר (*d^e^rôr*) I, II. See nos. 454b,c.

452.1 דָּרְיָוֶשׁ (*daryāwesh*) ***Darius.***

Darius was the name of three kings of Persia mentioned in the OT and of Darius the Mede mentioned in Dan 5:30; chap. 6; and 11:1, whose identity is in dispute.

Darius I, the Great, son of Hystaspes, was king from 521 to 486 B.C. During his time the second temple was finished (516 B.C.). The work on the temple began under Cyrus the Great (559–530) in about 539 B.C. The work was halted by the opposition and stopped also during the reign of Cambyses (530–532). But Darius was a new ruler, not Cambyses's son and the work was begun again under the urging of Haggai and Zechariah and the leadership of Zerubbabel the governor and Joshua the high priest. It was finished in 516 under the patronage of Darius who ruled in 521–486. This is the one mentioned in Ezr 4:5, 24 and in Haggai and Zechariah. After the reigns of Xerxes (Ahasuerus of Esther, 486–465) and Artaxerxes I (464–424) of the times of Ezra and Nehemiah came Darius II (Ochus, 424–404). This was the Darius of Neh 12:22. In Neh 12 a line of Levites is given from the returnee Jeshua as: Joiakim, Eliashib, Joiada, Jonathan, Jaddua. These span the period 539–404 B.C., a not unlikely situation. There is no need to call this Darius of Neh 12 the king Darius III, Codomannus (335–331 B.C.). Josephus indeed says that Jaddua was high priest in the days of Darius III. But there could have been two Jadduas, as we know there were two Sanballats (Wonder, A.W., "Sanballat" in WBE, II, p. 1517). Or Josephus, who was a much later author, might have confused the two kings Darius II and III.

Darius the Mede of Dan 5:30, chap. 6; 11:1 remains a problem of identification. Daniel says he took the kingdom of Babylon after Belshazzar's fall, but history says Cyrus the Great conquered Babylon. Many find here in Dan a mistake confusing Cyrus the Great and Darius the Great. It would be an odd mistake for a book so accurate in other ways. There are two suggested solutions. J. C. Whitcomb in his book *Darius the Mede* (Eerdmans, 1963), argues in considerable detail that the description of this Darius fits Gubaru a sub-king of Babylon under Cyrus. D. J. Wiseman suggests on the basis of a tablet of that period referring to Cyrus (evidently) as king of the Medes, that Darius the Mede was just a second name that Cyrus used for his Median subjects. There is nothing improbable in this, but more evidence is needed to render a decision. See Wiseman, D. J., *et al., Notes on Some Problems in the Book of Daniel,* 1965, pp. 9–16.

R.L.H.

453 דָּרַךְ (*dārak*) ***tread, bend; lead*** (Hiphil).

Derivatives

453a †דֶּרֶךְ (*derek*) ***way, road.***
453b מִדְרָךְ (*midrāk*) ***treading or stepping place*** (Deut 2:5).
453c †דַּרְכְּמוֹן (*darkᵉmôn*) ***unit of measure, perhaps drachma.***

Primarily used in the Qal stem, though several examples of the Hiphil also occur. Normally appears in poetic materials, often in the prophetic books and in Psalms. God is frequently the subject of this verb, especially when used in a metaphorical sense.

The basic concept behind *dārak* has to do with setting foot on territory or objects, sometimes with the sense of trampling them. In Deuteronomy and Joshua the verb is used of taking possession of the promised land. Israel will receive as an inheritance all the land that the sole of her foot will tread (Deut 1:36; 11:24; Josh 1:3; 14:9). Once, it is the Assyrian army that invades Israel and tramples its citadels (Mic 5:5 [H 4]). This concept of "marching" is likely seen in Jud 5:21 also. Psalm 91:13 refers to treading or trampling the lion and the cobra.

A frequent idiom is "treading upon the high places of the earth," indicating control of the enemy (Deut 33:29; cf. Hab 3:15) or, when used of God, his sovereignty as Creator of heaven and earth (Amos 4:13; cf. Job 9:8). In Mic 1:3 God comes down from heaven to judge his sinful people. Some interpreters feel that in these passages the "high places" refer to the mountaintops, as the Lord sweeps across the face of the earth.

Another standard idiom is to "tread" or "bend" the bow (*dārak qeshet*); that is, one steps on the bow in order to bend it and string it. An army that is equipped and ready for action has drawn swords, sharp arrows, and bent bows (Isa 5:28; 21:15). Babylon is the target of archers because of her sinfulness (Jer 50:14), and in Zech 9:13 the Lord bends Judah as his bow in order to attack Greece. Because of Israel's sin, however, the Lord bent his bow against His people (Lam 2:4), and even Jeremiah felt as if he were God's target (Lam 3:12).

The righteous and the afflicted often find that the wicked bend their bows and aim at them (Ps 11:2; 37:14). Sometimes the bow of the wicked is compared to their tongue (Jer 9:3 [H 2]), which lets fly "bitter speech" as their arrows against the godly (Ps 64:3 [H 4]; cf. Ps 58:7 [H 8]).

Eight times in the prophetic books reference is made to "treading grapes" or "treading the winepresses," for the normal method of gaining juice from the grapes was to trample them with one's bare feet. Treading grapes is sometimes associated with joy and gladness, anticipating the drinking of the fruit of the vine (Amos 9:13, Jud 9:27). Joyful shouting accompanied the treading of grapes (Isa 16:10; Jer 48:33). Apparently olives were crushed in similar fashion on occasion (Mic 6:15; Job 24:11). The prophets more often connect the crushing of the grapes with judgment, and in this imagery, the grape-juice symbolizes the blood of those who are being trampled (Isa 63:2–3; Lam 1:15). The shouting of those who tread the grapes becomes a war cry against the enemy (Jer 25:30).

When the verb occurs in the Hiphil stem, it consistently refers to God as he leads the righteous in straight paths. This can mean the road from the wilderness or from Babylon (Ps 107:7; Isa 42:16; cf. Isa 11:15) or, more commonly, the metaphorical path of uprightness or truth (Prov 4:11, Ps 25:5, 9). The best path is to follow God's commandments (Ps 119:35).

derek. ***Way, road, journey, manner, work.*** Related to the verb *dārak* "to tread, trample"; hence, it refers first to a path worn by constant walking. Genesis 3:24 mentions the "way to the tree of life," blocked after the fall of man. Hagar was on the road to Shur when an angel met her (Gen 16:7). This could also be translated "on the way" to Shur (cf. Gen 38:21; Ex 4:24). Sometimes *derek* can refer to a major highway, such as the king's highway (*derek hammelek*) running north and south in Transjordan (Num 20:17; 21:22). The "way of the sea" (Isa 9:1 [He 8:23]), known later as the Via Maris, extended from Gaza to Damascus. Exodus 13:17 mentions the road along the coast from Egypt through Philistine country.

derek can also mean "journey," usually one of several days' duration. Joseph prepared supplies for his father's journey to Egypt (Gen 45:23), and the Gibeonites tricked Joshua by claiming to have completed "a very long journey" (Josh 9:13). Elijah mocked the prophets of Baal as he suggested their god might be "on a journey" (I Kgs 18:27). In Gen 24:21 Abraham's servant thanks God for making his journey (or "mission") to Mesopotamia successful.

More numerous are the metaphorical uses of *derek*. It often refers to the actions and behavior of men, who either follow the way of the righteous or the way of the wicked (Ps 1:6). The way of the righteous is closely linked with "the way of the Lord." Parents are to command their children "to keep the way of the Lord" (Gen 18:19; cf. Prov 22:6), which is found in the statutes and commands of God's law (I Kgs 2:3). God's ways are much higher than man's ways, and the wicked is urged to forsake his sinful way (Isa 55:7–9).

God sent the flood because men "had corrupted their ways" (Gen 6:12) and even after the giving of the law, Israel quickly deviated from the way of the Lord (Deut 9:16) though they were assured that their ways would not be successful (Deut 28:29). During the divided kingdom, the rulers of Israel consistently walked in the way of Jeroboam and ignored God (I Kgs 16:26). They took a path that seemed right, but in the end it led to death (Prov 14:12).

In Prov 30:19 the behavior of a man courting a maiden is compared with the uncanny movement of an eagle in the sky, a snake on a rock, and a ship in the sea.

Occasionally *derek* means "manner" or "custom." Lot's daughters committed incest with their father because they thought that, after the destruction of Sodom, the normal "custom" of marriage was impossible (Gen 19:31). Later in Genesis, Rachel excused herself from rising in her father's presence because "the manner of women (her menstrual period) is upon me" (31:35).

Twice in Job and once in Proverbs *derek* refers to God's work in a creation context. In Job 40:19 the mighty Behemoth is called "the first of the works of God." The identical idiom (*rē'shît-derek*) in Prov 8:22 may refer to personified wisdom as the first of God's works also. In Job 26:14 the evidence of God's power in creation and in history is called "the fringes of His ways" (NASB) or "the outer fringe of his works" (NIV).

"Ways" has the unusual sense of "sexual favors" in Jer 3:13 and Prov 31:3.

The cognate noun in Ug, *drkt*, is clearly used to mean "dominion, thrones of dominion" (Ais WUS no. 792; UT 19: no. 702 "rule, dominion"). The relation between the meaning "road" and "dominion" is not clear, but it may be seen in the meaning cited by Gordon (UT id.) "to march." The idea of "tread" could extend to tread down in authority or to tread upon a road or way. In any case there are OT passages which seem to be elucidated by the translation "dominion, power, force, authority." Pope finds two in Job: 17:9 and 26:14 ("Job" AB, in loc.); Dahood argues for such a meaning in a number of places in the Psalms and elsewhere (Bib 38: 306–20). The places he suggests in his "Psalms" AB include: Ps 1:1, 6; 67:2 [H 3]; 77:13 [H 14]; 90:16; 101:2; 102:23 [H 24]; 119:37; 138:5 and 146:9. Some of these are convincing; some are not. The meaning is allowed in HCHL and should doubtless be adopted in a few OT contexts.

dark[e]**môn.** ***Drachma, dram*** (KJV), daric (RSV). This word is used only in Ezr 2:69 and Neh 7:69–71 with reference to gold contributed either to rebuilding the temple (Ezr 2:69) or Jerusalem. The heads of families gave sixty-one thousand of these coins to Zerubbabel, while the governor, heads of families, and the rest of the people contributed a total of forty-one thousand to the work under Nehemiah.

If "drachma" is the correct translation, one can compare the Greek genitive plural *drachmōn*. Greek drachmas dating from the Persian period have been uncovered at Beth-zur (cf. J. P. Free, *Archaeology and Bible History*, p. 253). There is no doubt that the Greeks were involved in trading in the fifth century (Albright, W. F., *Archaeology of Palestine;* p. 143). The drachma was a silver coin, however, whereas the term in question refers only to gold. This factor has led some to identify *dark*[e]*mōnîm* with *'ădarkōnîm,* the Persian "daric" mentioned in I Chr 29:7 and Ezr 8:27. The daric was a gold coin named for King Darius. Whatever the correct etymology may be, the coin probably weighed about eight and one-half grams. See no. 28.1.

Bibliography: Archer, G. L., "Coins," in ZPEB, I, p. 903.

H.W.

454 דרר (*drr*). **Assumed root of the following.**

454a דַּר (*dar*) ***pearl or mother of pearl*** (Est 1:6). Meaning uncertain.

454b †דְּרוֹר (*d^e rôr*) ***I, release, freedom.***
454c דְּרוֹר (*d^e rôr*) ***II, swallow*** (Ps 84:4; Prov 26:2).
454d †דָּרוֹם (*dārôm*) ***south.***
454e דַּרְדַּר (*dardar*) ***thistles*** (Hos 8:10, only).

d^e rôr. ***Release, freedom.*** Cognate to Akkadian *andurāru* "freedom, liberty." A technical expression referring to the release of Hebrew slaves and of property every 50 years in the year of Jubilee (Lev 25:10—the verse inscribed on the Liberty Bell). Slaves were allowed to return to their families, and land that had been leased due to poverty was restored to its original owners. The only reference to this release in Israelite history occurred during the reign of Zedekiah when Jerusalem was under Babylonian siege (about 587 B.C.). Zedekiah made a covenant with the people and "proclaimed freedom" to the slaves (Jer 34:8). When the siege was temporarily lifted, however, the people changed their minds and took back their slaves (34:11). Because of their hypocrisy, the prophet Jeremiah announced that the people would be "set free"—to the sword, pestilence, and famine (vv. 15–17).

Isaiah uses the term once (61:1) in announcing good news to the afflicted, including a proclamation of liberty to captives. This text, portraying the reversal of Jerusalem's material and spiritual fortunes, was quoted by Christ in the synagogue in Nazareth with reference to his own ministry. But the townspeople refused to believe his claim.

The last occurrence of *d^e rôr* is in Ezk 46:7, where the future prince is allowed to give a gift of property to his servants until the year of release.

dārôm. ***South.*** Used sparingly and mostly in poetry, except for a cluster of references in Ezk 40–42, which describe the future temple in detail. A number of gates, rooms, or doorways faced south or were on the south side (40:24, 27, 44; 41:11; 42:12–13). In Ezk 20:46 [H 21:2] *dārôm* appears along with two other synonyms for "south," *têmān* and *negeb,* as the Lord commands the prophet to preach against this section of the land of Israel.

The word occurs only once in the Pentateuch, in the blessing of Moses in Deut 33:23. There, the inheritance of the tribe of Naphtali is described as "the sea and the south" (NASB) or "southward to the lake" (NIV). In Eccl 1:16 and Job 37:17 *dārôm* refers to the wind, which blows in turn to the south and north. Job notes that the south wind can bring uncomfortably hot conditions. Ecclesiastes 11:3 also deals with rain and winds that may fell a tree either to the south or the north.

H.W.

455 דָּרַשׁ (*dārash*) ***to seek with care, inquire, require.*** ASV and RSV usually the same with the RSV superior at several places, e.g. Isa 8:19; 19:3; Ps 9:12 [H 13]; Ezr 7:10, etc., and inferior at Deut 17:9; Ps 10:4; II Chr 25:15. Both are inadequate at Zeph 1:6.

Derivative

455a †מִדְרָשׁ (*midrāsh*) ***record.***

Our word is distinguished from its frequent parallel and equivalent *bāqash* (q.v.) (*dārash-bāqash*, Ps 38:12 [H 13]; Ezk 34:6; *bāqash-dārash,* Jud 6:29; Deut 4:29) inasmuch as it 1. means "to seek with care" (I Sam 28:7), 2. is often cognitive (its end is "to know"), and 3. seldom governs an infinitive. For other synonyms see *bāqash*. Cf. Ugaritic *drsh* (UT 19: no. 709). Our verb occurs 164 times.

The meaning "to seek with care" (cognitive) occurs in Lev 10:6, where Moses seeks to find out in detail what happened to the sin-offering, and in II Sam 11:3 where David seeks to find out who Bathsheba was (cf. Deut 23:6 [H 7]; Jer 29:7). Israel is told to seek carefully the place God would choose (Deut 12:5) and justice (Isa 1:17; cf. 16:5!). In the eschaton Jerusalem, the place no one seeks (Jer 30:17), will be the place "sought out" (Isa 62:12; or "cared for," Deut 11:12). Furthermore, it is the Gentiles who would seek out the messianic king (Isa 11:10). His place of rest (Num 10:33; Deut 12:9) is glorious.

Closely related to the above is the meaning "to care for." The Psalmist retorts "no man cares for my soul" (Ps 142:4 [H 5]). Israel is told to seek the welfare of the city of their exile (Jer 29:7). Perhaps I Chr 15:13; II Chr 1:5 refer to "care" for the ark and the brazen altar.

Another theological theme develops from Deut 4:29 (cf. *bāqash*) where Israel is warned of future defection and admonished to wholehearted worship (Deut 6:6; Mt 22:37). The Chronicler evaluates the history of Israel in terms of their "seeking" God (I Chr 22:19; 28:9; II Chr 31:21, etc.) or idols (II Chr 25:15). Isaiah reports Israel's refusal to seek God in spite of divine chastening (Isa 9:13 [H 12]; cf. Jer 10:21). God reminds them of the ancient promise (Isa 55:6; Jer 29:13, Hos 10:12). He reproves them for "seeking" him while continuing in their transgressions (Isa 58:2) but promises blessings in the eschaton for those who seek him in truth (Isa 65:10). Interestingly, even those who do not seek shall find God (Isa 65:1; Isa 11:10; Rom 10:20).

To seek God also connotes an inquiry after knowledge, advice, insight, into a particular problem (Gen 25:22). Such inquiry could be made through a prophet, i.e. a divine spokesman (Ex 7:1; Ex 18:15ff.; I Sam 9:9; Jer 21:2, etc.), or through a priest using "lots" (*shā'al;* Deut 17:9). Seeking the word of a false deity often involved complex rituals (Deut 12:30; II Chr 25:15 (?); II

Sam 11:3; Ezk 21:21 [H 26]). Closely related to this is the "legal" use of our verb, viz., to seek divine judication (Ex 18:15; Deut 17:4, 9; cf. Mt 18:5–20; I Cor 6; I Tim 3) by consulting divinely authorized "judges."

Finally, our root is used of divine vengeance on those who take a life. God will diligently seek restitution of a life for a life (Gen 9:5; cf. *bāqash*). In at least one instance this stipulation is evoked and divinely executed (II Chr 24:22, 24; Ps 9:12 [H 13]; 10:4). To fail in declaring God's work puts a "shepherd" (a minister) under this divine sentence (Ezk 33:6). All pronouncements from divine messengers (prophets) require human acceptance and obedience whether miraculously attested or not (Deut 13:1ff.) if they are consistent with previous revelation even if they add thereto (Deut 18:22; Jn 7:40; Acts 3:22f.). Ultimately, God requires justice, lovingkindness, and a humble walk (Mic 6:8; cf. Ezk 20:40).

midrāsh. ***Record.*** ASV and RSV only differ at II Chr 13:22. Our word represents a written historical record (a place to "search out something"). It is used in later Jewish study to refer to fanciful or recondite exegesis. It occurs twice.

Bibliography: Lust, J., "On Wizards and Prophets," Supp VT 22: 133–42. Sellers, O. R., "Seeking God in the Old Testament," JBR 21: 234–37. THAT, I, pp. 460–66.

L.J.C.

456 דָּשָׁא (*dāshā'*) ***sprout, shoot, grow green*** (Joel 2:22; Gen 1:11; Jer 50:11).

Derivative

456a †דֶּשֶׁא (*deshe'*) ***young, new grass, green herb, vegetation.*** Cognate to Akkadian *dīshu* "spring grass, new pasture" (CAD, p. 163).

Used as a cognate accusative in Gen 1:11, where the earth sprouts "vegetation" or "grass" on the third day of creation. God makes the grass grow as food for animals (Jer 14:5; Job 6:5; 38:27), and this tender, green grass grows characteristically after the rains have come (Deut 32:2; II Sam 23:4). In time of drought the grass dies out (Isa 15:6).

Metaphorically, the growth of this tender grass is compared with the rule of a just king in II Sam 23:4. The bones of a happy man are said to "flourish like the new grass" (Isa 66:14). In Ps 23:2 the Lord has his sheep lie down in green pastures and enjoy an ideal resting place. Perhaps the rest follows a time of feeding on the tender grass.

When it is linked with *yereq* "green plants," *deshe'* refers to grass that easily withers and is gone. The enemies of Assyria are short of strength, like the green herb (II Kgs 19:26 = Isa 37:27). In Ps 37:2 the godly are told not to envy wicked men, because they fade quickly like the grass (cf. Isa 15:6).

H.W.

457 דָּשֵׁן (*dāshēn*) ***be(come) fat, prosperous; to anoint.***

Derivatives

457a דֶּשֶׁן (*deshen*) ***fatness, fat ashes*** (e.g. Lev 1:16; Ps 63:6).

457b דָּשֵׁן (*dāshēn*) ***fat*** (Isa 30:23; Ps 92:15; 22:30).

The verb *dāshēn* is used only in poetry except for the Pentateuch, once in the Qal stem (Deut 31:20), usually in the Piel or Pual. Refers to the "fatty ashes" left after the burning of sacrificial animals (Ex 27:3; Num 4:13). God's judgment on Edom is compared to a great sacrifice as both God's sword and the ground are covered with "fat" (Isa 34:6–7).

Since fat animals were considered the healthiest and the fat was regarded as the best part of sacrificial animals (cf. Ps 20:3 [H 4]), the metaphorical usage of "prosperous" or "rich" is easily understood. The righteous man is described as a fruitful tree, "full of sap" in his old age (Ps 92:14 [H 15]). In Proverbs, the generous man, the diligent man, and the one who trusts in the Lord are all called "fat" or "prosperous" (11:25; 13:4; 28:25). Good news "gives health to the bones" (Prov 15:30). Psalm 23:5 refers to the head "anointed (made fat) with oil" as a description of the blessing of God.

In Deut 31:20 comes the warning that when God's people are "satisfied and prosperous (fat)" they will forsake him and worship other gods.

H.W.

458 דָּת (*dāt*) ***decree, law, edict, regulation.***

This loanword from the Persian *dāta* is found twenty times in Est, once in Ezr (8:36), and several times in the Aramaic sections of Ezr and Dan. It is spelled the same in Hebrew and Aramaic. Since all three books deal with kings of Persia, the use of this foreign term is readily explained. It overlaps the use of *tôrâ, mishpāṭ,* and *ḥōq* in Hebrew. The relationship between "decree" and "law" was very close, and "the laws of the Medes and Persians" could not be changed (Est 8:8; cf. Dan 6:12 [H 13]).

Essentially, the law was what the king wanted. His wishes quickly became law, as illustrated by the fact that the "word of the king" is connected with the law four times in Est (2:8; 4:3; 8:17; 9:1). This is illustrated in the episode involving Queen Vashti, who refused to display her beauty to the king's guests. An edict was issued ending Vashti's reign as queen, and this immediately became part of the "laws of the Medes and Persians" (1:19). Such edicts were written down and sent throughout the kingdom for all to know (1:20; 3:14).

A second and more important edict was prepared by Haman to the effect that all Jews could be killed on the thirteenth day of Adar (3:14). This dire threat moved Mordecai and Esther to plead for the lives of their people. Haman's murderous intentions were nullified by a counter decree authored by Mordecai that gave the Jews the right to defend themselves (8:13–14). At Esther's request, this edict was extended an extra day to give the Jews more time to destroy their enemies.

Esther's courage in approaching King Ahasuerus without invitation illustrated the severity of Persian law. She knew that, according to the law, if the king did not extend the scepter to her, she would die (4:11, 16). Vashti's experience was just the opposite. By refusing to come when summoned, she left herself open to the condemnation of the law (1:13, 15, 19).

Actually, Haman charged the Jews with practicing different laws—laws allegedly incompatible with those of the Persians (3:8). "Laws" in this sense comes close to the meaning of "customs" and "religious practices." Daniel's enemies attempted to bring about his downfall by driving a similar wedge between "the law of his God" and the law of King Darius (Dan 6:5, 8 [H 6, 9]).

Another less technical use of "law" occurs in Est 2:12, where a twelve-month period of purification was prescribed before a woman was taken to the king. Like all other "laws," these regulations were strictly followed.

The meaning of "law" in 1:8 is more difficult, since the point seems to be that each person could drink as much as he wished. Apparently "law" could be understood as the king's order giving this individual freedom to his banquet guests.

In the only occurrence of *dāt* in Hebrew outside the book of Esther, it refers to the decrees given by Artaxerxes supporting Ezra's efforts to strengthen the returned exiles in Jerusalem (Ezr 8:36; cf. 7:12–24).

H.W.

ה

ה

459 הַ (*ha*) ***the.***

All West Semitic languages since the first millenium B.C. (Hebrew/Aramaic/Phoenician) plus Arabic have in their language a morpheme that functions as a definite article. In none of these languages is the definite article a separate word, as in English, but rather it is prefixed to the word it determines, except in Aramaic where it is affixed (i.e. postpositive). The definite article is not differentiated according to gender (like the French *le/la* or the Greek *ho/hē/to*) nor according to number (*le/les*). The one form, *ha,* covers masculine and feminine, singular and plural. Nor is there in Biblical Hebrew any word for the indefinite article "a/an." Occasionally the latter may be expressed by the numeral "one" *'eḥād:* I Sam 6:7, "a new cart."

Most likely the definite article was originally a demonstrative pronoun, with an early form of something like *hal-* or *han-* although the article itself cannot be traced back morphologically to such an earlier form. In Biblical Hebrew, then, the "l" or "n" of *hal/han* assimilates to the first consonant producing doubling (gemination) of that consonant, so, *hal/n-shemesh* "the sun," becomes *hashshemesh.* When a guttural is the first consonant of the determined word the vowel of the article will change, involving either compensatory lengthening or dissimilation.

The article is added not only to substantives but also to adjectives if the latter are used attributively and not predicatively, for example: the couplet *hā'îsh haṭ-ṭôb* equals "the good man," but the couplet *hā'îsh ṭôb* equals "the man (is) good." The article may also be added to, strange as it seems, verbs. In such instances it appears to assume the force of a relative. Cf. I Chr 26:28, "All that Samuel had dedicated (*hahiqdish*)"; Josh 10:24, "The chiefs of the men of war who went with him (*hehāl*^{e}*kû'*)." The article may also be appended to a preposition as in "the thigh and that which was upon it (*w*^{e}*he'ālehâ*, I Sam 9:24).

There are several instances where the Hebrew avoids the definite article but smooth English translation demands its inclusion. To express a genitival relationship the Hebrew, where nouns (or adjectives) are involved, places the first word (the *nomen regens*) in the construct case in relation to the second word, the absolute one (the *nomen rectum*). The grammatical rule is that the word in the construct case never has the definite article except for a few anomalous occurrences. The absolute noun, if it is definite, has the article according to normal usage. The construct is definite or indefinite according to the definiteness of indefiniteness of the absolute. Thus, the phrase "(the) horse of the king" would be written *sûs ham-melek,* never *has-sûs ham-melek.*

Conversely, there are a number of places where the Hebrew adds the article but smooth English translation demands its exclusion. An illustration of this would be the OT references to Satan. Preponderantly when the OT is referring to Satan as a superhuman adversary of both God and man he is referred to as "the satan." This is true of the fourteen times he is mentioned in Job 1 and 2, and also in Zech 3:1–2 (twice). Thus, Job 1:7 reads literally, "The Lord said to the satan." The thrust of the article in these passages is to show that "sātān" is not a name, but only a title. The only passage that refers to "Satan," a name, is I Chr 21:1 (i.e. without the appended article), and one must compare this verse in Chr with its parallel in II Sam 24:1 (cf. GKC 126,e). On the other side of the coin scholars have used this rule of proper names being definite *sui generis* to argue that the Hebrew word *t*^{e}*hôm* "deep" in Gen 1:2 is really a veiled reference to the Babylonian Tiamat or is at least the philological equivalent. She is the female dragonesque personification of the primordial saltwater ocean in Babylonian traditions about creation of the world. *t*^{e}*hôm* (q.v.) is, indeed, never used in the Bible with the definite article, something characteristic of proper names in the Bible. Yet, at all points, this hardly seems adequate proof to make an equation. Dahood comes to the conclusion that "Biblical *t*^{e}*hôm* equals Ug *thm,* and does not derive directly from Babylonian sources, as urged by earlier generations of scholars" (AB, *Psalms* III, p. 36).

It may be added that the article is rare in biblical poetry—a usage akin to Ugaritic which has no clear article at all.

Bibliography: Most of the standard Hebrew grammars supply information on the morphology and syntax of the definite article, but cf. especially Gesenius' *Hebrew Grammar,* Oxford: Clarendon Press, par. 126. Honeyman, A. M., "Ugaritic and Semitic Usage," JAOS 75: 121–22, who contends that Ugaritic *hn* is the ancestor of the Canaanite definite article. Lambdin, T., "The Junctural Origin of the West Semitic Definite Article," in *Near Eastern Studies in Honor of William Foxwell Albright,* ed. H. Goedicke, Baltimore: Johns Hopkins, 1971, pp. 315–33.

V.P.H.

460 הֲ (*hă*). Interrogative particle.

hă is prefixed to the first word of a sentence or a clause, mostly involving direct questions. Depending on the first consonant, and the vowel of the word to which this particle is appended, the interrogative *hă* may become *ha*/*he*/*ha* with a following *dagesh forte*.

As a rule the simple question in Hebrew is introduced by the interrogative *hă*. Sometimes, however, this particle is not present and yet the interrogative sentence is quite obvious. For example, "Shall Saul reign over us?" (I Sam 11:12) lacks any interrogative indicator.

When *hă* appears in a question that question is not asking primarily for information but rather is a rhetorical question to which usually a negative answer is expected ("Am I my brother's keeper?" Gen 4:9) and occasionally a positive answer.

This becomes most clear in prophetic literature, and we shall use as an example Jeremiah. In many instances the particle is used parallel with *'im*. Jeremiah 18:14 reads, "Does the snow of Lebanon leave (*hă*)? Do the mountain waters run dry (*'im*)?" These two questions obviously require negative answers. Yet the prophet continues in v. 15 to say that God's people have forgotten him. Thus, two rhetorical questions are used to intensify the severity of God's wrath on this unnatural cleavage between himself and his people. Jeremiah may use the double rhetorical question (*hă . . . 'im*) to rephrase a generally accepted presupposition and then challenge it (2:14,31; 3:5; 8:4), or to express traditional religious dogma (8:19,22; 14:19,22).

Of special interest is Jeremiah's use of the formula *hă—'im—maddû'*. Cf. 2:14, "Is Israel a slave (*hă*)? Is he a homeborn servant (*'im*)? Why (*maddû'*) has he become a prey?" And for the same formula in Jeremiah cf. 2:31; 8:4–5; 8:19; 8:22; 22:28; 49:1. In each case the first two questions establish the presuppositions of his sermon and an agreement with his audience but the third question draws the implications of the agreement just established. Like Job, Jeremiah is a man of dispute.

Bibliography: GKC, par. 100 k-n (for morphology); par. 150 a-i (for syntax). On the use of questions in Jeremiah, Brueggemann, W. M., "Jeremiah's Use of Rhetorical Questions," JBL 92: 358–74. Holladay, W. L., "The So-Called 'Deuteronomic Gloss' in Jer. VIII: 19b," VT 12: 494–98.

V.P.H.

461 הֵא (*hē'*) ***lo! behold!*** (Gen 47:23; Ezk 16:43).

462 הֶאָח (*he'āḥ*) ***aha!*** (e.g. Ps 35:21, 25; Ezk 25:3).

הַבְהַב (*habhab*). See no. 849b.

463 הָבַל (*hābal*) ***act emptily, become vain.*** Denominative verb.

Parent Noun

463a †הֶבֶל (*hebel*) ***vapor, breath.***

The denominative verb appears five times in the OT, four times in the Qal and once in the Hiphil (Jer 23:16). Of particular interest here are the parallel verses Jer 2:5 and II Kgs 17:15: They went after vanities and "became vain." (NIV: "They followed worthless idols and became worthless themselves.") Two inexorable principles are illustrated here: (1) every man takes on to some degree the character and nature of the God he worships; (2) the characteristic of all false gods is that they destroy their worshippers.

hebel. ***Vapor, breath, vanity.*** This substantive is translated almost exclusively by the KJV as "vanity." Except for the passages in Eccl, where the RSV concurs with the KJV, the RSV generally leans to the translation "breath" or "worthless." The noun appears seventy-one times in the OT. Thirty-six times it is used in Eccl, where it occurs at least once in each of the twelve chapters except chapter ten.

The proper name, Abel, the second son of Adam, is also written *hebel*. Whether or not there is a connection between this and the substantive under discussion is another matter. Most of the Hebrew lexions have connected "Abel" with the cognate Akkadian word *ablu*/*aplu* "son." One will note that Abel is named in Gen 4 without any explanation, a fact that can hardly be without significance since almost all the proper names in Genesis are explained by assonances.

The basic meaning of *hebel* is "wind" or "breath." This is illustrated best in Isa 57:13, "The wind (*rûaḥ*) will carry them off, a breath (*hebel*) will take them away," and Prov 21:6, "The getting of treasures by a lying tongue is a fleeting vapor (*hebel niddāp*)." The verb *nādap*, meaning "to drive," is most often used in connection with the wind as the driving force (e.g. Ps 1:4; 68:2 [H 3]).

There are three basic categories or contexts in which *hebel* is used. First, it is used as a designation for false gods worshiped by the people of God and hence is usually translated in this context by the RSV as "idols": Deut 32:21; I Kgs 16:13, 26; II Kgs 17:15; Jer 2:5; 8:19 (parallel to *pesel*); 10:8, 15; 51:18; Jon 2:9; Ps 31:6 [H 7].

Secondly, the term represents the individual and sometimes exasperating sentiments of individuals: Isa 49:4 where the servant Israel says, "I have labored in vain (*rîq*), I have spent my strength for nothing (*tōhû*) and vanity (*hebel*)."

Job complains about the brevity and uncertainty of his life (7:16). Cf. the similar idea in the Psalter: Ps 39:5,6, 11 [H 6,7, 12]; 62:9 [H 10]; 78:33 (in which *hebel* is parallel to *behālâ,* from the root *bāhal* "to hasten"): 94:11; 144:4 (*hebel* parallel to *ṣēl*). Hence, *hebel* seems to mean here "short-lived."

Third is the cluster of references found in Eccl (thirty-six). These may be grouped into several subdivisions. First are those passages in which the author states his inability to find fulfillment in work, both in his failure to be creative and in his lack of control over the privilege of free disposition of his possessions; this is "vanity": 2:11, 19, 21, 23; 4:4, 8; 6:2. Second are those verses in which the author struggles with the idea that the connection between sin and judgment, righteousness and final deliverance is not always direct or obvious. This is an anomaly about life and it is "vanity": 2:15, 6:7–9; 8:10–14. The meaning of *hebel* here would be "senseless." Thirdly are those verses in which the author laments the shortness of life; this is "vanity": 3:19; 6:12; 11:8, 10. Life, in its quality, is "empty" or "vacuous" (and thus unsubstantial), and in its quantity is "transitory."

Rather than the above observations being final conclusions about life by the author of Eccl, perhaps they reveal something of his method and his concealed premise. He may be attempting to demonstrate man's inability to find meaning to life unaided by divine revelation and interruption. This solo quest will always end in futility.

Bibliography: Gordis, R., *Koheleth: The Man and His World,* 3d ed., Schocken, 1968. Guillaume, A., "Paranomasia in the Old Testament," JSS 9: 282–90, esp. pp. 282–83 for a proposed Arabic etymology for the proper name Abel. Kinlaw, D. F., "Ecclesiastes" in *The Wesleyan Bible Commentary,* II, Eerdmans, 1968. Meek, T. J., "Translating the Hebrew Bible," JBL 79: 328–35, esp. pp. 330–31. Staples, W. E., "The 'Vanity' of Ecclesiastes," JNES 2:95–104. THAT, I, pp. 467–69.

V.P.H.

464 הָבְנִי (*hobnî*) ***ebony*** (Ezk 27:15, only).

465 הָבַר (*hābar*) ***divide*** (Isa 47:13, only).

466 הגג (*hgg*). **Assumed root of the following.**

466a הָגִיג (*hāgîg*) ***murmuring, whisper, musing*** (Ps 5:2; Ps 39:4). From the hypothetical root *hgg,* but closely related to *hāgâ.*

467 הָגָה (*hāgâ*) ***I, utter, mutter, moan (mourn,*** KJV***), meditate, devise, plot.***

Derivatives

467a הֶגֶה (*hegeh*) ***a rumbling, growling, moaning*** (Job 37:2; Ezk 2:10; Ps 90:9).

467b הָגוּת (*hāgût*) ***meditation, utterance*** (Ps 49:3 [H 4], only).

467c †הִגָּיוֹן (*higgāyôn*) ***meditation.***

hāgâ occurs primarily in poetry, especially in Ps and Isa. It is used in the Qal, except for Isa 8:18 (Hiphil).

The basic meaning of *hāgâ* and its cognates is a low sound, characteristic of the moaning of a dove (Isa 38:14; 59:11) or the growling of a lion over its prey (Isa 31:4). It is sometimes used in mourning contexts, such as the moaning over the judgment upon Moab (Isa 16:7; Jer 48:31) or the whispering of the enemy after the collapse of Jerusalem (Lam 3:62). Wizards are known to whisper and mutter in their occult practices (Isa 8:19). In distress the psalmist sighs and cries out to God for help (5:1 [H 2]).

Often the term refers to the plots originating in the heart of wicked men or nations which then are given expression in lying and deceitful words (Ps 2:1; Prov 24:2). The wicked words uttered are described as coming both from the heart (Isa 59:13) and from the tongue (Isa 59:3). The righteous can also "devise" or "ponder" a proper answer (Prov 15:28) and then talk about wisdom (Ps 37:30) or God's righteousness (Ps 35:28; 71:24). In Ps 19:14 [H 15] "the meditation of my heart" is parallel to "the words of my mouth," as the psalmist compares his own speech with what God communicates in nature and in Scripture.

Another positive use relates to meditating upon the Word of God, which, like the plots of the wicked (Ps 38:12 [H 13]), goes on day and night (Josh 1:8; Ps 1:2). Perhaps the Scripture was read half out loud in the process of meditation. The psalmist also speaks about meditating upon God (63:6 [H 7]) and his works (77:12 [H 13]; 143:5).

higgāyôn. ***Meditation, whispering, melody.*** The noun *higgāyôn* refers to the music of a harp in Ps 92:3 [H 4]. Possibly a musical notation is meant by the "Higgaion" in Ps 9:16 [H 17], but "meditation" is an alternate interpretation. For other such terms see *selâ.*

H.W.

468 הָגָה (*hāgâ*) ***II, remove, drive out.***

This verb occurs only three or four times, depending on one's handling of II Sam 20:13. Proverbs 25:4–5 uses the infinitive absolute *hāgô* to begin successive verses. A comparison is made between the beneficial effects of removing dross from silver and removing the wicked from the king's presence. The results will be a purer vessel and a more righteous government. Isaiah also uses the Qal stem to describe the way God "drove" Judah out of her land (27:8). The "fierce blast" is compared with the hot east wind that blows in from the desert. In all three of these examples the removal is difficult to effect but nonetheless necessary to produce purity.

The form *hōgâ* in II Sam 20:13 is treated as a Hiphil of *yāgâ* by BDB, but KB feels that the root is properly *hāgâ*. It refers to the removal of the dead body of Amasa from the road after Joab had treacherously murdered the man David had appointed to replace him.

H.W.

הָגוּת (*hāgût*). See no. 467b.
הָגִיג (*hāgîg*). See no. 466a.
הִגָּיוֹן (*higgāyôn*). See no. 467c.
הָגִין (*hāgîn*). See no. 469a.

469 הגן (*hgn*). **Assumed root of the following.**
469a הָגִין (*hāgîn*) ***appropriate, suitable*** (Ezk 42:12). Meaning uncertain.

470 הגר (*hgr*). **Assumed root of the following.** This root, meaning "flee" is found in the Arabic name for Mohammed's famous flight, the Hegira.
470a †הָגָר (*hāgār*) ***Hagar.*** (ASV and RSV the same.)

Hagar is the name of Sarah's Egyptian maid, the mother of Ishmael by Abraham. The name is Semitic, not Egyptian.

The information about Hagar is recorded in Gen 16 and 21. Sarah, childless at age 75, offered Hagar to Abraham to bear a child for her. This was customary as we learn from tablets from ancient Nuzi (cf. "New Kirkuk Documents Relating to Family Laws," *The Annual of the American Schools of Oriental Research,* X, 1930, p. 32). Rachel and Leah also gave their maids to Jacob to bear children for them (Gen 30:1–13).

After Hagar conceived, she felt superior to Sarah, who then mistreated her, causing her to flee. During her flight an angel promised her posterity, and told her to return to the household.

Ishmael was fourteen when Sarah bore Isaac. Soon afterwards Hagar and Ishmael were sent away for good. When Hagar feared that they would die of thirst, God promised her that he would make of Ishmael a great nation, and then showed her a well of water. They lived in Paran, and Hagar obtained a wife for Ishmael from Egypt.

[It may be noted that the dangerous condition in which Hagar found herself in the desert near Beersheba (Gen 21:14–21) was quite possibly due to accident. Abraham sent her away and she went south, presumably on the way to Shur (the road to Egypt) which she had traveled before (Gen 16:7). It will be remembered that she was an Egyptian. According to the Hebrew of Gen 21:14, she apparently lost her way (*tā'â* "err," cf. Ps 119:176 "like a lost sheep" and Isa 53:6). The penalty for getting lost in the desert is severe. Her deliverance came supernaturally. Abraham's action in sending Hagar away seems harsh, but was actually in accord with common Mesopotamian law (particularly the Code of Hammurabi). Hagar's child was legally Sarah's. Nuzi law specifies that in such a situation the natural son of the legal wife would be given the right of the firstborn. But it seems that Hagar was not satisfied with all this. So vicious animosity arose. In this case Abraham's reliance on common law instead of God's promise bore bitter fruit. R.L.H.]

Paul (Gal 4) used the relationship of Sarah and Hagar in an allegory, Hagar representing the bondage of children born after the flesh and self-effort, and Sarah, the free wife of Abraham, representing the believers of the new covenant of promise and grace.

Bibliography: TDNT, I, pp. 55–56.

C.P.W.

471 הדד (*hdd*). **Assumed root of the following.**
471a הֵידָד (*hêdād*) ***shout, shouting, cheer.***
471b הֵד (*hēd*) ***shout.*** Occurs only in phrase *hēd hārîm* "shout on mountains" (Ezk 7:7).
471c †הֲדָד (*hădād*) ***Hadad.*** (ASV, RSV the same.)

hădād. ***Hadad.*** The name of several royal Edomites, including two kings who are listed among the kings of Edom: A son of Bedad who defeated Midian (Gen 36:35–36; I Chr 1:46–47), and a later king (I Chr 1:50–51; and the variant spelling, *hădar,* Gen 36:39).

Hadad was the name of an adversary of Solomon, possibly the same as the second king mentioned above (I Kgs 11:14–21, 25; with variant spelling *'ădad,* 11:17). When Joab, David's general, slaughtered the Edomites, Hadad, a young Edomite of royal stock, was taken by his father's servants to Egypt. Here he married the sister of Pharoah's wife. He remained in Egypt, nurtured by Pharoah, until David and Joab died. He then returned to Edom to stir up trouble for Solomon.

The name Hadad is the name of an ancient Semitic storm god. The Edomite name "Hadad" mentioned above may be an abbreviation of names compounded with Hadad. It is used as one component of several compound names: Ben-hadad, king of Syria (I Kgs 15:18), Hadedezer, king of Zobah (II Sam 8:3) and Hadadrimmon, a compound divine name, but perhaps a place in Megiddo (Zech 12:11). Hadad may be the same as the Ugaritic *hd,* an alternate name for Baal (see

UT 19: no. 749), and the Babylonian Adad, Addu.

Bibliography: On Ben-hadad King of Syria, see A. Malamat, "The Arameans," in *Peoples of OT Times*, ed. Wiseman, D. J., Oxford, 1973, p. 152, note 24.

C.P.W.

472 הָדָה (*hādâ*) ***stretch out (hand).***

473 הָדַךְ (*hādak*) ***tread down.***

474 הדם (*hdm*). **Assumed root of the following.**

474a הֲדֹם (*hădōm*) ***stool, footstool.*** Always refers to the footstool of the Lord (Ps 110:1; Isa 66:1, etc.).

475 הֲדַס (*hădas*) ***myrtle*** (tree), e.g. Isa 41:19; Neh 8:15, Zech 1:8).

476 הָדַף (*hādap*) ***cast away (out), drive, expel, thrust (away).*** (ASV similar, RSV also stab, thwart.)

The basic meaning is to "push," "push away." It is used eleven times in the OT, always negatively. The object is usually a person or persons, often an enemy.

The enemy may be a national power, as Israel's enemies which the Lord would drive from the land (Deut 6:19; 9:4; Josh 23:5), and Egypt which the Lord would drive before her enemies (Jer 46:15). Whether the Egyptian army, its leadership, or the bull god Apis (RSV following the LXX) is the object here, a military defeat of Egypt is to be understood.

The object may also be an individual, as God promises to thrust the steward, Shebna, out of office (Isa 22:19), or as Gehazi attempts to push a woman away from Elisha (II Kgs 4:27). Bildad pictures the wicked man as being thrust from light into darkness (Job 18:18). The word aiplies to the action of a manslayer (hence RSV"stab," Num 35:20,22).

The word, used figuratively of people, refers to fat sheep pushing the weak ones (Ezk 34:21). According to Prov 10:3 the Lord pushes aside (RSV "thwarts") the desire (KJV "substance") of the wicked.

C.P.W.

477 הָדַר (*hādar*) ***honor, adorn, glorify.***

Derivatives

477a הֶדֶר (*heder*) ***splendor, glory*** (occurs only in Dan 11:20).

477b †הָדָר (*hādār*) ***ornament.***

477c הֲדָרָה (*hădārâ*) ***adornment, glory.***

The verb occurs seven times in Biblical Hebrew (with one dubious reading in Isa 45:2 where for MT *hădûrîm* IQIsa[a] has *hărārîm*) and three times in Biblical Aramaic.

The verb is used mostly in describing man's relationship to man. The youthful are to honor the elderly (stated positively in Lev 19:32 and negatively in Lam 5:12). Hence, behind the word lies the idea "to show respect." Other ideas involved include showing "partiality" (to the poor, who is caught up in a legal crisis, simply because of his poverty, not because of his innocence: Ex 23:3). On the other hand there are prohibitions regarding fawning over the wealthy, courting their attention, or excusing their actions whenever they are reprehensible; Lev 19:15; Prov 25:6. In just one passage (Isa 63.1) the verb is used (in its passive participial form) in connection with a description of God's appearance which is "glorious."

In the Aramaic passages the verb always means "to honor/glorify (God)." In Dan 4:34 [H 31], it is parallel with the verbs *b[e]rak, sh[e]baḥ;* in Dan 4:37 [H 34] with *rûm, sh[e]baḥ;* in Dan 5:23 with *sh[e]baḥ*.

hādār. ***Ornament, splendor, honor.*** This substantive appears twenty-nine times in the OT of which sixteen are in the Psalms.

The noun *hādār* is associated with: (1) the glory of nature as it reflects the goodness of God (Lev 23:40; Ps 111:3, Isa 35:2); (2) man (Isa 53:2, the suffering servant, "comeliness"); man as he is created by God (Ps 8:6); the elderly man's gray hair (Prov 20:29); the ideal wife (Prov 31:25). (3) It is applied to cities: Jerusalem (Isa 5:14); Zion (Lam 1:6); and the areas of Persia, Lud, and Put (Ezk 27:10); (4) to the Joseph tribes (Deut 33:17) and perhaps to all of Palestine (Dan 11:20, *heder*). Several of these passages deal with the departure of this glory from God's people. The children of God have no indigenous glory of their own. If God departs the glory departs. Hence, this is a gift from God but it is still revocable.

Most frequently the substantive is applied to either (a) the king and his royal majesty or (b) God himself. In the former category we may note the following passages: Ps 21:5 [H 6]; 45:3–4 [H 4–5]); Prov 14:28 (*hădārâ*). It is not only an endowment for royalty, but it is also an activity worthy of royalty, as illustrated by Nebuchadnezzar (Dan 4:34 [Aram 31] and 4:37 [Aram 34]) and Belshazzar (Dan 5:23).

In the following passages the term is descriptive of God: Ps 29:4; 90:16; 96:6 (= I Chr 16:27); 104:1; 111:3; 145:5, 12. Of special interest here is the parallel connection between the phrases "the glory of his (God's) majesty," *hădar g[e]'ōnô*, and "the fear/terror (*paḥad*) of the Lord" (Isa 2:10, 19, 21). The prophet warns the Judeans to "hide" from both. This entreaty follows on the heels of a devastating list of sins which must be judged. Obviously Isaiah does not counsel the people to hide in hopes that they might escape the searchlight of God. What he does say is that the people are so reprobate and backslidden that they cannot possibly fellowship with a God of pure light and majesty. Thus, this is not advice; it is an imprecation.

The phrase *hădrat qōdesh* merits special comment. It appears four times in the OT: Ps 29:2; 96:9; I Chr 16:29; II Chr 20:21, plus the related phrase in Ps 110:3, *hadrê qōdesh*. Each time the RSV translates this couplet "holy array" with the exception of Ps 110:3 where it opts for the translation "holy mountains" (reading a different text). So, "worship the Lord in holy array," (e.g. Ps 9:2). A parallel to "holy array" would be *bigdê qōdesh*, "holy garments," in Lev 16:4. Also in several instances the verb *hādar* (Isa 63:1) and the substantive *hādār* (Ps 104:1, Job 40:10; Prov 31:35) are connected with the verb *lābash* ("to clothe"), and Ezk 16:14 with the verb *śûm/śîm*, perhaps a reference to some kind of an investiture ceremony.

On the other hand, the KJV consistently translates the couplet, "the beauty of holiness." Now, in the light of Ugaritic evidence, a third option presents itself. In the Kret epic A: lines 154, 155 we read:

Krt · yh̲ṯ · wḥlm
'bd · il · whdrt
Krt looked and it was a dream
the servant of El and it was a
(divine) appearance

In our biblical passages then, the major emphasis is on the Lord and his appearance, not on the worshipper except as the realization of God's actual presence evokes awe. A third translation could be: "prostrate yourselves before the Lord when he appears in holiness."

Bibliography: On the phrase *hădrat qōdesh*, cf. Ackroyd, P. R., "Some Notes on the Psalms," JTS 17: 392–99, esp. pp. 393–96. Cross, F. M., "Notes on a Canaanite Psalm in the Old Testament," BASOR 117: 19–21, esp. p. 21. Caquot, A., "In splendoribus sanctorum," *Syria* 33: 36–41. Dahood, M., *Psalms*, AB, vol. 3: 116. Donner, H., "Ugaritismen in der Psalmenforschung," ZAW 79: 322–50, esp. pp. 331–33. Gordon, UT: no. 752. Vogt, E., "Der Aufbau von PS 29," Bib 41: 17–24, esp. p. 24. THAT, I, pp. 469–72.

V.P.H.

478 הָהּ (*hāh*) ***alas!*** (Ezk 30:2).

479 הוֹ (*hô*) ***ah!*** (Amos 5:16).

480 הוּא (*hû'*), הִיא (*hî'*) ***he, she, it, himself, herself, the same, which (is), that (is), who, et al.*** (ASV and RSV similar.)

This is the third person singular, independent nominative pronoun, "he," "she," "it."

For the most part Hebrew does not (as does English) require the use of an independent pronoun to precede a finite verb when the noun-subject is omitted. When it does appear it is usually for emphasis or in another type of construction.

One such construction is a nominal sentence or clause, that is a sentence which has no finite verb, but a noun or an adjective (including the participle as a verbal adjective) acts as the predicate. (The English must include a form of the verb "to be." In this construction the pronoun is necessary if the noun subject is omitted: with a noun predicate, "it (is) my master" (Gen 24:65), with an adjective predicate, "he was faint" (Gen 25:29), with a participial predicate, "he (was) sitting at the door of the tent" (Gen 18:1).

When such a nominal sentence or phrase is connected with preceding material it may be translated as if the pronoun were a relative: "Bela, which is Zoar," (Gen 14:2), "Esau, who is Edom" (Gen 36:1). Occasionally the pronoun follows the predicate: thus, "unclean it," to be translated "it is unclean" (Num 19:15), "twenty gerahs it," "it is twenty gerahs" (Num 18:16). This is especially true in dependent clauses such as those introduced by *kî*, meaning "that," "for," "because": "for unclean he," that is "he is unclean" (Lev 13:11), "because many they (were)" (Num 22:3). This is also common with *'ăsher*, meaning "which," "that": "from the beast which not clean it (is)" (Gen 7:2), "which not from your seed he (is)" (Gen 17:12), often called the resumptive pronoun.

Sometimes in a nominal sentence the pronoun stands between the subject and the nominal predicate where the English would have a form of the verb "to be": "And Joseph, he (was) the ruler" (Gen 42:6), "you (are) he, God" (II Sam 7:28). The pronoun, which is redundant in English, is not in this case, a substitute for the verb "to be" but is used to indicate emphasis, *'attâ hû'*: It is you that. Also after an interrogative the pronoun may be added for emphasis, "who (is he that) will condemn me?" (Isa 50:9).

The pronoun may be used before a finite verb when a phrase separates the subject from the verb: "The woman whom thou gavest to be with me, she gave me" (Gen 3:12), and "one that shall come . . . he shall inherit (from) you" (Gen 15:4). Unless there is reason for emphasis this use is redundant in English and not generally translated.

The pronoun is also used to tie in an additional subject added after the predicate, "And Joseph returned to Egypt, he, and his brethren, and all" (Gen 50:14).

With the article, the pronoun may function as the demonstrative adjective, "that" (corresponding to *zeh* "this"), "that place" (Gen 21:31), "in that day" meaning "the same day" (Gen 15:18).

hû' may be used simply for emphasis: "I know that *he* can speak" (Ex 4:14), or "the Lord, *he* (is) God" (Ps 100:3). The emphasis may be expressed in English by "himself," "the Lord himself will require it" (Josh 22:23). When it is used to reinforce a preceding suffix pronoun, it is difficult to translate in writing, because the English equivalent is to put stress on that pronoun, "what *he* saith," that is, what Hushai says in contrast to what Ahithophel has said (literally, "what is in *his* mouth," II Sam 17:5).

The *w* and *y* are not merely vowel letters as shown by the Ugaritic pronouns *huwa* "he" and *hiya* "she" (*hw* and *hy*).

Unexplained is the usage in the Pentateuch and a few other places where *hw'* means either "he" (vocalized *hû'*) or "she" (vocalized with a perpetual qere *hî'*). In the past this has led some to feel that the original pronoun for both genders was *hw'* but Ugaritic denies this conclusion. Apparently the situation is due to some dialect or vagary of a scribal school.

Bibliography: Montgomery, J. A., "The Hebrew Divine Name and the Personal Pronoun *hū'*," JBL 63: 161–63.

C.P.W.

481 הָוָא (*hāwā'*) ***fall*** (Job 37:6, only).

482 הוד (*hwd*). **Assumed root of the following.**
482a †הוֹד (*hôd*) ***splendor, majesty, vigor, glory, honor.***

The noun is used twenty-four times in the OT, appearing most frequently in the Psalter (eight times). Quite often it is found in juxtaposition with the related word, *hādār*, also meaning "majesty" or "honor," always in the order *hôd wᵉhādār:* Ps 21:6; 45:3 [H 4] 96:6 (= I Chr 16:26); 104:1; 111:3; Job 40:10 (seven times). The LXX translates *hôd* by *doxa* (nine times), by *exomologēsis* (four times), plus sundry other words. So far no related root in other Semitic languages has been found for *hôd*. It is uniquely a Hebrew word.

This substantive is used as a characteristic or attribute of: (a) man: Num 27:20, Moses and Joshua; Prov 5:9, the wise son; Dan 10:8, Daniel (translated by the KJV as "comeliness" and by the RSV as "radiant appearance"); Hos 14:7, the northern Israelites after their repentance and restoration to divine blessing; Jehoiakim (Jer 22:18); (b) animals, specifically the horse: Job 39:20; Zech 10:3; (c) plants, the olive: Hos 14:7.

Preponderantly the substantive is connected with God. His majesty can be seen in the creation: Ps 8:2, "God's glory is chanted above the heavens," or "by" the heavens if we are dealing here with the music of the spheres; Ps 148:13, God's glory is above the earth and heaven; Hab 3:3, "God's glory covers the heaven." When the biblical writers look at the work of God's hand in the universe they can do nothing but speak of God's glory: Ps 145:4. This glory is part of God's wardrobe (Ps 104:1). It can be heard (Isa 30:30; Ps 8:2). God bequeaths this to the man who lives in fellowship with him: Ps 21:6; I Chr 29:25 (Solomon). This attribute is applied finally to the Messiah who shall build the temple and bear royal honor (Zech 6:13).

In addition to the parallel with *hādār* noted above we may note the following: in I Chr 29:11 *hôd* is grouped with the following Hebrew words, all descriptive of God's nature: *gᵉdullâ* (greatness); *gᵉbûrâ* (power); *tip'eret* (glory); *nēṣaḥ* (victory). In Job 40:10 besides *hādār*, *hôd* is used in conjunction with the words *gā'ôn wāgōbah* (majesty and excellency). In Hab 3:3–4 *hôd* is used along with *tᵉhillâ* (praise); *nōgah* (brightness) and *'ōz* (power).

Finally we may note the use of the *hôd* in such proper names as Hodiah (Neh 8:7), "Yahweh is my splendor"; Hodevah (Neh 7:43), "Yahweh is majesty"; Abihud (I Chr 8:3), "my father is majesty": Ammihud (I Chr 9:4), "my kinsman is majesty," and perhaps the Benjamite judge Ehud.

Bibliography: Although the root *hôd* has not appeared in any Semitic languages other than Hebrew there are, nevertheless, words in these languages that mean "awe-inspiring splendor." Compare, for example, in Babylonian, Oppenheim, A. L., "Akkadian pul(u)ḫ(t)u and melammu," JAOS 63: 31–34. Cassin, E., *La splendeur divine*. Introduction à l'étude de la mentalité mésopotamienne, Paris: La Haye, Mouton & Co, 1968. Mendenhall, G. E., *The Tenth Generation*, Baltimore: John Hopkins, 1973, Chapter 2, "The Mask of Yahweh." THAT, I, pp. 472–74.

V.P.H.

483 הָוָה (*hāwâ*) ***I, fall.*** (ASV, RSV. So KJV, by confusion with *hāwâ* II see below, renders the verb as "be.")

Derivatives

483a †הַוָּה (*hawwâ*) ***calamity.***
483b †הַיָּה (*hayyâ*) ***calamity.***
483c †הֹוָה (*hōwâ*) ***disaster.***

The single OT occurrence of *hāwâ* I (Job 37:6) is an imperative, describing physical falling. Its form, *hĕwē'*, has been called "an Arabizing usage" (BDB, p. 217); but more likely the aleph is to differentiate it from *hāwâ* II (KB, p. 227).

The verb *hāwâ* I depicts the literal fall of rain and snow (Job 37:6). But its derived nouns speak metaphorically of a fall in fortune. So *hayyâ* identifies the calamities that descend on Job (Job 6:2; 30:13); and *hōwâ,* those to fall suddenly upon Babylon (Isa 47:11) or upon Judah, "disaster upon disaster" (Ezk 7:26). The commonest noun, *hawwâ,* advances from an identifying of the fact of troubles (Ps 57:1), such as those brought upon parents by an unwise son (Prov 19:13), to the cause for troubles, i.e. moral failure. Psalm 5:9 [H 10] may therefore be rendered either, "Their heart is destruction" (RSV) or "wickedness" (KJV, ASV). Other psalms describe a throne of "iniquity" (Ps 94:20) and "wickedness" which rulers devise (Ps 52:2 [H 4] evidently Saul himself was the "mighty man" of v. 1 [H 2], not the underling Doeg, cf. J. A. Alexander, *The Psalms,* II, p. 13). But a good man can perceive these "perverse things" (Job 6:30). In Scripture all such lapses are subject to God's sovereign control and can be overcome by sincere faith (Ps 38:12–13; 94:19–20).

hawwâ. ***Calamity, wickedness, evil desire,*** ASV, RSV, also craving, lust; KJV "mischievous desire, naughtiness," Prov 10:3; 11:6; Mic 7:3. Derives from *'āwâ* "to desire" (q.v.). KB, p. 228.

hayyâ. ***Calamity.*** A Kethib variant on *hawwâ* in Job.

hōwâ. ***Disaster.*** KJV, ASV, "mischief," in its archaic sense of calamity.

J.B.P.

484 הָוָה (*hāwâ*) ***II,*** the older form and rare synonym of *hāyâ* (q.v.), ***be, become.*** (ASV and RSV similar, but RSV, lie, Eccl 11:3.)

Derivatives

484a †יהוה (*yhwh*) ***Yahweh.***
484b †יָהּ (*yāh*) ***Yahweh.***

The root signifies either existence, e.g. of a tree trunk, being at rest where it falls (Eccl 11:3), or development, e.g. of Nehemiah's alleged scheme to become king of Judah (Neh 6:6). Only three other instances of *hāwâ* II are preserved in the Hebrew OT (Gen 27:29; Eccl 2:22; Isa 16:4), though *hāwā'* remains as the standard form of the verb "to be" in biblical Aramaic.

Yahweh. The Tetragrammaton YHWH, the LORD, or Yahweh, the personal name of God and his most frequent designation in Scripture, occurring 5321 times (TDNT, III, p. 1067) in the OT (KJV and ASV, the LORD, or, in those contexts where the actual title "Lord" also occurs, GOD, except KJV, Jehovah, in seven passages where the name is particularly stressed (Ex 6:3; Ps 83:18 [H 19]; Isa 12:2; 26:4] or combined with other elements, such as Jehovah Jireh [Gen 22:14; cf. Ex 17:15; Jud 6:24; ASV, consistently Jehovah]).

yāh. A contracted form of Yahweh. Occurs fifty times (rendered in English as above, except KJV, Jah, in Ps 68:4 [H 5], where the name is particularly stressed).

Also numerous proper nouns compounded with shortened forms of the divine name "Yahweh," e.g.: *yᵉhônātān,* Jehonathan, "Yahweh has given"; abbreviated *yônātān* "Jonathan," a substitute name for the same person (compare I Sam 13:2–3 with 14:6, 8; II Sam 17:17, 20 with I Kgs 1:42–43); and *yᵉhôshāpāṭ,* Jehoshaphat, "Yahweh has judged"; alternatively *yôshāpāṭ,* "Joshaphat," applied only to two subordinates of David (I Chr 11:43; 15:24).

The theological importance of *hāwâ* II stems from its derived nouns, which identify the personal name of deity, Yahweh, or its contractions.

The tetragrammaton YHWH is not ordinarily written with its appropriate Hebrew vowels. But that the original pronunciation was YaHWeH seems probable, both from the corresponding verbal form, the imperfect of *hāwâ,* anciently *yahweh,* and from later representation of YHWH in Greek *iaoue* or *iabe.* An apocopated form of *hāwâ* in the imperfect, that occurs in Eccl 11:3, is *yᵉhû'* (otiose aleph, GKC, p. 211). This in turn may account for the shorter name *YHW* in the fifth century B.C. Elephantine papyri and the initial elements *yᵉhô-, yô-,* and *yē-* (KB, p. 369) in such names as Jehozadak, "Yahweh (is) righteous," or Joel, "Yahweh (is) God."

[An alternative possibility for the original pronunciation of the Tetragrammaton should be mentioned. Actually, there is a problem with the pronunciation "Yahweh." It is a strange combination of old and late elements. The first extra-Biblical occurrence of the name is in the Moabite Stone of about 850 B.C. At that time vowel letters were just beginning to be used in Hebrew. If YHWH represents a spelling earlier than 900 B.C. (as would seem likely), the final "*h*" should have been pronounced. The pronunciation Yahweh assumes the ending of a lamed-he verb, but these verbs in Moses' day ended in a "*y*" (cf. for *bānâ* the Ug. impf. *ybny*). So the ending "*eh*" is a late form. But in Hebrew in late times a "*w*" that began a word or syllable changed to "*y*" (as in the pe-waw verbs and the verb *hāyâ* itself). So the "*w*" of Yahweh represents a pre-mosaic pronunciation but the final "*eh*" represents probably a post-davidic form.

In view of these problems it may be best simply to say that YHWH does not come from the verb *hāwâ* (presumably *hawaya* in its early form) at all. There are many places in the OT where it is now recognized that the parallel of a name and its meaning is not necessarily etymological. For instance, I Sam 1:20 probably does not mean that the name Samuel is derived from the verb *shāma‘* "to hear." Genesis 11:9 does not mean that Babel comes from the verb *bālal* "confusion" but only that the two words sound somewhat alike. Likewise Jacob is said to mean both "heel" (Gen 25:26) and "supplanter" (Gen 27:36). There are many other examples of this device which is to be taken as a paranomasia, a play on words, rather than as an etymology. Therefore we may well hold that YHWH does not come from the verb *hāwâ* which is cited in the first person *'ehyeh* "I will be," but is an old word of unknown origin which sounded something like what the verb *hāwâ* sounded in Moses' day. In this case we do not know what the pronunciation was; we can only speculate. However, if the word were spelled with four letters in Moses' day, we would expect it to have had more than two syllables, for at that period there were no vowel letters. All the letters were sounded.

At the end of the OT period the Elephantine papyri write the word YHW to be read either *yāhû* (as in names like Shemayahu) or *yāhô* (as in names like Jehozadek). The pronunciation *yāhô* would be favored by the later Greek form *iaō* found in Qumran Greek fragments (2d or 1st centuries B.C.) and in Gnostic materials of the first Christian centuries. Theodoret in the fourth century A.D. states that the Samaritans pronounced it *iabe.* Clement of Alexandria (early 3d century A.D.) vocalized it as *iaoue.* These are quite late witnesses and seem to contradict the much earlier Jewish witness of Elephantine and the name elements, none of which end in "*eh.*"

As to the meaning of the name, we are safer if we find the character of God from his works and from the descriptions of him in the Scripture rather than to depend on a questionable etymology of his name. See further the writer's remarks in "The Pronunciation of the Tetragram" in *The Law and the Prophets,* J. H. Skilton, ed., Presbyterian & Reformed, 1974, pp. 215–24. R.L.H.]

Among the commonest names with this element are *y^e^hônātān* "Jonathan," the name of seventeen different OT characters (ISBE, III, pp. 1580, 1730). These include Moses' treacherous (great)grandson Jonathan (Jud 18:30, ASV), David's faithful friend Jonathan, the son of Saul (I Sam 18:1), and David's young courier Jonathan the son of Abiathar (II Sam 15:27; I Kgs 1:42). *y^e^hôshāpāt* "Jehoshaphat," identifies six individuals (ISBE, III, pp. 1581–1582, 1743), including Israel's recorder under David and Solomon (II Sam 8:16; I Kgs 4:3) and Judah's fourth king after the division, 872–848 B.C. The name reappears in Joel's prediction of the Valley of Jehoshaphat (Joel 3:2, 12 [H 4:2, 12]), where God will overcome the nations gathered to oppose his advent in glory. But rather than designating the site of King Jehoshaphat's ancient victory (Beracah between Hebron and Bethlehem, II Chr 20:26), this title seems to identify a spot beside Jerusalem (Joel 3:17 [H 4:17]), traditionally the Kidron, below Olivet (Zech 14:4). It may be less a place name than prophecy's description of the event of *y^e^hôshāpāṭ* "Yahweh has judged."

y^e^hôshûă‘-yēshûă‘ designates ten Hebrew leaders (ISBE, III, pp. 1622, 1743) from Moses' successor Joshua (KJV, Jehoshua in Num 13:16; I Chr 7:27) to the post-exilic high priest Jeshua (Ezra 3:2; Neh 12:10). The former's name was changed from the Hiphil infinitive, Hoshea, "salvation," to Joshua, with its deeper spiritual connotation of "Yahweh (is) salvation" (Num 13:8, 16). Both men are called "Jesus" in Greek (Acts 7:45; I Esd 5:48), i.e., *yeshûa‘* is our Lord's Hebrew name, "for he will save his people from their sins" (Mt 1:21). This may be a shortened form with the divine element omitted, meaning "he will save."

The shortened independent form of the divine name, Yah, occurs primarily in poetry and in the exclamation, Hallelu-*yah,* praise Yahweh. It serves also as a terminal element in proper nouns like Elijah: *'ēlîyâ* (or *'ēlîyāhû*), "God (is) Yahweh."

In the post-biblical period, reverence for the ineffable name "Yahweh" caused it to be supplanted in synagogue reading (but not in writing) with the noun *'ădōnāy,* "my master," or Lord. Next, when medieval Jewish scholars began to insert vowels to accompany the consonantal OT text, they added to YHWH the Masoretic vowel points for *'ădōnāy;* and the actual writing became an impossible *YăHōWāH,* the ASV "Jehovah."

God's name identifies his nature, so that a request for his "name" is equivalent to asking about his character (Ex 3:13; Hos 12:5 [H 6]). Critical speculation about the origin and meaning of "Yahweh" seems endless (cf. L. Köhler, *OT Theology,* pp. 42–46; IDB, II, pp. 409–11); but the Bible's own explanation in Ex 3:14 is that it represents the simple (Qal) imperfect of *hāwâ* "to be," I am [is] what I am. The precise name Yahweh results when others speak of him in the third person, *yahweh* "He is." Albright, it is true, has championed a causative rendering, "I cause to be, I create" (*From the Stone Age to Christianity,* 2d ed., 1946, p. 198; D. N. Freedman, JBL, 79: 151–56); but this is rightly criticized as "conjuring up a nonexistent Hiphil form" (N. Walker, JBL, 79: 277).

Some have gone on to suggest that the Qal meaning of Yahweh must be God's unchangeableness toward his people (Ex 3:15; G. Vos, *Biblical Theology,* p. 134). But, as Moses himself indicated (Ex 3:13), the fact that he was the ancient God of the fathers was insufficient to answer Israel's need at that time; and, in any event, the OT has little to say concerning abstractions such as "the changelessness of deity" (though in the NT Jesus did use Ex 3:14 to introduce the thought of his eternal divine existence, Jn 8:58). God's immediately preceding promise to Moses had been, "Certainly I will be with you" (Ex 3:12). So his assertion in verse 14 would seem to be saying, "I am present is what I am." Indeed, the fundamental promise of his testament is, "I will be their God, and they will be my people" (Ex 6:7, etc.; contrast Hos 1:9); thus "Yahweh," "faithful presence," is God's testamentary nature, or name (Ex 6:2,4; Deut 7:9; Isa 26:4).

The use of Yahweh as a divine name goes back to earliest times (Gen 4:1,26; 9:26), although the documentation for its employment among other early cultures appears questionable (IDB, II, p. 409). In Ex 6:3 the Lord explains to Moses that by his name Yahweh he had not been "known" to the patriarchs, meaning "know" (see *yāda'*) in its fullest sense: the name was in use (Gen 12:8; 15:2, 7, 8) but was not appreciated in the redemptive significance that it acquired under Moses (J. A. Motyer, *The Revelation of the Divine Name*). For even the so-called P document, which critics have hypothesized as contradicting the Bible's claims to the earlier use of Yahweh (ibid., pp. 3–6), utilizes it in premosaic proper nouns (Jochebed, Ex 6:20; Num 26:59).

Commencing with the later judges (I Sam 1:3), the name Yahweh is often combined with *ṣᵉbā'ôt,* "hosts" (armies, q.v.). The Tetragrammaton occurs in every OT book except Eccl and Est. It appears in the ninth century Moabite inscription of Mesha (line 18). From the eighth century onward the element "Yau-" is employed in Aramaic names and in Mesopotamian references to Hebrew rulers. Only in pre-NT times was God's personal name replaced with the less intimate title *'ădōnāy* (Gr., *kurios)* "Lord."

Scripture speaks of the Tetragrammaton as "this glorious and fearful name" (Deut 28:58) or simply "*the* name" (Lev 24:11). But it connotes God's nearness, his concern for man, and the revelation of his redemptive covenant. In Genesis 1—2:3, the general term *'ĕlōhîm* (q.v.) "deity," is appropriate for God transcendent in creation; but in 2:4–25 it is Yahweh, the God who is immanent in Eden's revelations. In 9:26–27, Elohim enlarges Japheth, but Yahweh is the God of Shem; the latter is especially used in references to the God of Israel. In Ps 19 the heavens declare the glory of El (vv. 1–6); but the law of Yahweh is perfect, and Yahweh is "my strength and my redeemer" (vv. 7–14 [H 8–15]; cf. G. T. Manley, *The Book of the Law,* p. 41). Yet the distinction is not pervasive: Psalms 14 and 53 are practically identical except for the divine names employed; book I of the Psalter (Ps 1–41) simply prefers Yahweh, and book II (42–72), Elohim. Ultimately the connotations of the name Yahweh are fulfilled in the "covenant of peace," when the God who has been present from the first will be fully present at the last (Isa 41:4); cf. Ezekiel's stress upon God's "sanctuary in the midst of them forevermore" (Ezk 37:26) and his eschatological city's being named *YHWH shāmmâ* "Yahweh is there."

Bibliography: Abba, R., "The Divine Name Yahweh," JBL 80:320–28. Albright, W. F., *Yahweh and the Gods of Canaan,* pp. 168–72. Freedman, D. N., "The Name of the God of Moses," JBL 79: 151–56. Harris, R. L., "The Pronunciation of the Tetragram," in *The Law and the Prophets,* ed. J. H. Skilton, Presbyterian and Reformed, 1974, pp. 215–24. Jacob, E., *Theology of the OT,* Harper, 1958, pp. 48–54. Motyer, A. J., *The Revelation of the Divine Name,* London: Tyndale, 1959. Payne, J. B., *Theology of the Older Testament,* Zondervan, 1962, pp. 147–54. TDNT, III, pp. 1058–81.

J.B.P.

485 הוֹי (*hôy*) ***ah! alas! ho! O! woe!*** (ASV and RSV similar.)

An interjection, usually of lamentation. It occurs fifty times in the prophets and once elsewhere. Six usages refer to mourning for the dead (as I Kgs 13:30), and forty involve negative warnings or threats of God's physical chastisement. But in Isa 55:1 it introduces a positive invitation to come and buy good things without money or price (cf. Zech 2:6–7).

Bibliography: Clifford, R. J., "The Use of *hôy* in the Prophets," CBQ 28: 458–64. Gerstenberger, Erhard, "The Woe-Oracles of the Prophets," JBL 81: 249–63. Wanke, Gunther, "*'ôy* and *hôy,*" ZAW 78: 215–18. THAT, I, pp. 474–76.

C.P.W.

הוֹלֵלָה (*hôlēlâ*). See no. 501a.
הוֹלֵלוּת (*hôlēlût*). See no. 501b.

486 הוּם (*hûm*) ***be moved, ring again, make a (great) noise.*** (Instead of destroy, ASV discomfit, RSV throw into confusion; for make a noise, RSV be distraught; for ring again, RSV be in an uproar. Otherwise ASV and RSV similar.)

Derivative

486a מְהוּמָה (*mᵉhûmâ*) ***destruction, discomfiture, trouble, tumult, vexed, vexation.*** (The ASV and RSV are similar but do not use destruction or vexed. The RSV also uses panic, confusion, disturbance.) The meaning of this noun is "confusion," "disturbance," "turmoil."

The basic meaning of this root seems to be a severe disturbance, i.e. "to disturb greatly," "stir," "discomfit."

The verb is used six times, once in the Qal (Deut 7:23). Here, used with the cognate accusative, it refers to God as greatly disturbing (afflicting) the enemies until they are destroyed. In the Niphal the verb refers to the excitement of a city that is "stirred up" (Ruth 1:19; I Kgs 1:45), or of a camp (I Sam 4:5). The subject is the earth (or land) which "is shaken" or "resounds" from the shouting of excited people. The Hiphil may be translated "stir," "make a disturbance" (Ps 55:2 [H 3]; Mic 2:12), but opinion on how to translate these passages, is divided.

In ten of twelve of its occurrences the noun depicts the action of the Lord against Israel's enemies (Deut 7:23), or against Israel herself (Deut 28:20).

The root *hûm* is doubtless a by-form of *hāmam* and possibly of *hāmâ* (q.v.).

C.P.W.

487 *הוּן (*hûn*) ***be ready.*** (ASV be forward, RSV think it easy.)

Derivative

487a †הוֹן (*hôn*) ***enough, riches, substance, wealth.*** (ASV and RSV similar.)

The verb is used only once (in the Hiphil, Deut 1:41). Here it means to "consider it easy," "think lightly of," possibly to "dare." It is used to characterize the Israelites' attempt to conquer Canaan after God had told them that they must wait. P. C. Craigie comments here: "There was a fine balance in the nature of the covenant that they constantly failed to grasp. First, they could not really trust in the Lord, who would fight for them and protect them. Then, when they rose to shallow confidence in the Lord, they forgot the seriousness of their task" (*The Book of Deuteronomy,* Eerdmans, 1976, p. 106).

hôn. ***Enough, riches, substance, wealth.*** The noun means "wealth," but its use is poetic. It is used twenty-six times, in Prov (nineteen times) and in Ezk, Ps, and Song.

The basic meaning of the noun is "goods" or "substance" in sufficient quantity to be considered "riches" or "wealth" (Prov 3:9, etc.). If, as is assumed, this noun is actually derived from the verb above, the meaning of "goods" or "wealth" may have developed from the idea of that which is usually considered necessary to make life "easy." The word is used opposed to *dal* "poor," "weak," "helpless" (Prov 19:4; 28:8). *Hôn* is used in conjunction with *ʿōsher,* the common word for "riches" (Ps 112:3; Prov 8:18). The usual word for "property" or "goods," *rᵉkûsh,* is mostly limited to prose passages.

In Ps 44:12 [H 13] the translation "for naught" or "for a trifle" (RSV) is from *bᵉlōʾ hôn* "without riches." God has sold his people without even asking a price for them. The translation "enough" in Prov 30:15–16 is necessary from the context. The idea may be that of "sufficiency" but in this case not of wealth.

The attitude of the OT toward *hôn* is ambiguous. There is a good and a bad kind of wealth. The robber looks for wealth (Prov 1:13), but the good man honors the Lord with his wealth (Prov 3:9). Riches do not deliver in the day of wrath (Prov 11:4) but knowledge brings precious and pleasant riches (Prov 24:4). The riches of Tyre are condemned (Ezk 27:12) but in Ps 112:3 riches are the reward of the godly man (see *ʿāshar*).

C.P.W.

488 *הוּת (*hût*) ***shout at.*** Occurs only once, in the Poel (Ps 62:4).

489 הָזָה (*hāzâ*) ***sleep.*** (ASV and RSV, dream.)

This word is used only in Isa 56:10. It is used of sleeping dogs which represent the false leaders of Israel. The most probable meaning is "dream." Some assume the form to be a scribal error for *ḥōzeh* "seer" and some MSS so read, but the LXX supports the MT.

C.P.W.

490 הִי (*hî*) ***lamentation, wailing*** (Ezk 2:10, only).

הִיא (*hîʾ*). See no. 480.
הֵידָד (*hêdād*). See no. 471.
הֻיְּדוֹת (*hūyᵉdôt*). See no. 847a.

491 הָיָה (*hāyâ*) ***to be, become, exist, happen.***

This verb appears 3,540 times in Biblical Hebrew, and all of these are in the Qal stem except for twenty-one uses of the Niphal. The verb is related to another Hebrew word meaning "to become," *hāwâ* (only five times: Gen 27:29; Isa 16:4; Eccl 2:22; 11:3; Neh 6:6), and the same verb in Biblical Aramaic, *hăwâ* (71 times). In Akkadian its phonetic equivalent, *ewû,* means "to turn oneself into, to become like." To express being or existence Akkadian uses not *ewû* but *bashû* (much like Ugaritic and Phoenician *kûn*).

Very seldom in the OT is *hāyâ* used to denote either simple existence or the identification of a thing or person. This can be illustrated by a quick glance at almost any page of the KJV on which one will find numerous examples of words such as "is, are, was, were," in italics, indicating that these are additions by the translators for the sake of smoothness, but not in the Hebrew itself. In such cases the Hebrew employs what is known grammatically as a nominal sentence, which we may define most simply as a sentence lacking a verb or a copula, for example: I (am) the Lord your God; the Lord (is) a sun and shield; the land (is) good; and in the NT, blessed (are) the poor. This almost total lack of *hāyâ* as a copula or existential particle has led some to use this phenomenon as confirming evidence that "static" thought was alien to the Hebrews, the latter thinking only in "dynamic" categories (see Boman in the bibliography below).

An alternative way in Hebrew to express existence besides the nominal sentence is by the particles *yēsh* (positive) and *'ayin* (negative), really another type of nominal sentence "perhaps 'there are' fifty righteous in the city"; " 'there is' no God." Both of these words are more substantival in nature than they are verbal, and in function they resemble the French *il y a* and the German *es gibt*.

There are instances, however, where *hāyâ* is used with a predicate adjective: (a) in the description of a past situation which no longer exists, "The earth was (*hay^{e}tâ*) formless and void" (Gen 1:2); (b) in historical narration, "The serpent was (*hāyâ*) more subtil than any beast of the field" (Gen 3:1); (c) in the expression of a gnomic truth, "It is not good that man should be (*hĕyôt*) alone" (Gen 2:18). Notice the juxtaposition of the verbal sentence, with *hāyâ* and a nominal sentence without it: "You shall be (*tihyû*) holy for I (am) holy (*qādôsh 'ănî*, Lev 19:2). Boman would account for the absence of a copula in the latter part of this phrase by stating that the predicate (holy) is inherent in the subject (God) and hence the copula is unnecessary. He would also add that the first "be" really means "become." To jump from this observation, however, to the conclusion that the basic meaning of "to be" in the Bible is "to become" seems to be unwarranted.

Of special import is the use of the verb *hāyâ* in covenant formulae: I will be your God and you will be my people (Jer 7:23; 11:4; 24:7; 31:33, etc.), and in the context of God's promises of blessings and judgements: and I will make of you a great nation . . . and you shall be a blessing (Gen 12:2). A frequent, although perhaps misleading, translation of *hāyâ* is, as we have noted above, "to come." This can be seen in connection with God's spirit "coming" upon an individual (Jud 11:29; I Sam 19:20), and in those places where God's word "came" to someone (Gen 15:1; I Sam 15:10; II Sam 7:4; Jer 36:1).

A final and brief word may be said about the meaning and interpretation of Jehovah/Yahweh. It seems beyond doubt that the name contains the verb *hāyâ* "to be" (but also see article YHWH). The question is whether or not it is the verb "to be" in the Qal, "He is," or the Hiphil, "He causes to be," a view championed by W. F. Albright. The strongest objection to this latter interpretation is that it necessitates a correction in the reading of the key text in Ex 3:14: "I am that I am." Most likely the name should be translated something like "I am he who is," or "I am he who exists" as reflected by the LXX's *ego eimi ho ōv*. The echo of this is found surely in the NT, Rev 1:8. More than anything perhaps, the "is-ness" of God is expressive both of his presence and his existence. Neither concept can be said to be more important than the other.

Bibliography: Barr, James, *The Semantics of Biblical Language*, Oxford University Press, 1961, esp. pp. 58–72, in opposition to Boman's emphasis on the "dynamic" versus "existential" character of *hāyâ*. Boman, T., *Hebrew Thought Compared With Greek*, trans. J. L. Moreau, London: SCM, 1960, esp. pp. 38–49. DeVaux R., "The Revelation of the Divine Name YHWH," in *Proclamation and Presence*, eds. J. I. Durham and J. R. Porter, London: SCM, 1970, pp. 48–75, with citation of the appropriate bibliography of studies on the meaning of the Tetragrammaton. Preuss, H. D., "Ich will mit dir sein," ZAW 80: 139–73. Schild, E., "On Exodus iii 14: 'I am that I am'," VT 4: 296–302. THAT, I, pp. 477–85.

V.P.H.

הַיָּה (*hayyâ*). See no. 483b.

492 הֵיךְ (*hêk*) ***how.*** (ASV and RSV the same.)

This secondary spelling of *'ek* also introduces a question showing indignation or astonishment (GKC 148). The former is evidenced in I Chr 13:12 in David's self indignation, and the latter in Dan 10:17. The Ugaritic cognate is *'k* (UT 19: no. 147). Our word occurs twice.

L.J.C.

493 הֵיכָל (*hêkāl*) ***palace, temple, nave, sanctuary.***

ASV and RSV similar with improvements by the latter in I Kgs 6:3; II Chr 36:7, but inconsistencies in II Kgs 23:4, etc. As in extra-biblical literature this loanword from Sumerian/Akkadian (*É.GAL/ekallu;* Ugaritic *hkl*, UT 19: no. 763) essentially represents a king's dwelling quarters, i.e. a palace. In the Bible it is not necessarily of stone (Ps 18:6 [H 7]), nor of gigantic proportions (I Kgs 6:3). Our word has a rich variety of synonyms: *'armôn* (*harmôn*, Amos 4:3; *'almôn*, Isa 13:22), a large luxurious dwelling place, which, however, are not used of the house of God; *bîrâ*, perhaps a Persian loanword for "palace, citadel"; *m^{e}ṣād*, stronghold, fort, etc. Other words for God's dwelling place are: *bêt* (Gen 33:17 where a booth *sukkôt* is called a *bêt*), also called an *'ōhel* (I Sam 2:22), *miqdāsh* (any place sanctified by God from the land of Palestine, Ex 15:17, to the sanctuary itself, Lev 16: 33; see *qōdesh*); *bāmôt*, hilltops or mountain tops (II

Sam 1:19; Deut 32:13) which often served as the locations for worship, whether legitimate (I Sam 9:12; I Kgs 3:4) or illegitimate (Lev 26:30). Especially note the mythological use (e.g. Amos 4:13); finally see *mishkān* (dwelling place in general) and *māqôm* (God's chosen place; see *qûm*). Our word occurs eighty times.

Extra-Palestinian applications of *hêkāl* refer solely to the domicile of a king (II Kgs 20:18, hence, RSV in Amos 8:3; Hos 8:14; II Chr 36:7). Within Israel it refers to the dwelling place of the great king, God (Ezr 3:6). Akkadian (CAD,E,I, p. 52) *ekallu* represents the royal palace, royal property, or the main room (reception hall?) of a private house. Interestingly, the OT exhibits similar connotations. Let us especially note that our word does not occur in the OT until I Sam, the document appearing after the kingship was established in Israel. This meaning (God's palace) occurs in the psalmists' prayers when they describe the life of blessedness (Ps 65:4 [H 5]). Figuratively, David prays that he, too, may dwell in God's house/temple (Ps 27:4). He surely does not ask for a change in God's law whereby he, a non-priest, could enter (indeed, dwell in) the temple. So it is a state of blessedness for which he prays, that he might always be in God's favor. No doubt, it is God's earthly palace/temple toward which David directs his prayer, although it is God himself whom he addresses (Ps 5:7 [H 8]; 138:2). God is not limited spatially to the temple (I Kgs 8:27). However, God's chosen place is his temple and it is to be respected in proportion to the respect due to the Creator (Jer 7:4). Disparaging it will bring divine judgment (Jer 50:285. God himself will raise up a servant to restore his temple (Cyrus, Isa 44:28), foreshadowing the founding of God's perfect temple by a man named "branch" (Zech 6:12; cf. Isa 11:1; Jer 23:5; 33:15; for the church as this temple, compare Mal 3:1/Mt 3:10–12; I Cor 3:3–15, II Cor 6:16). Paul uses the word *naos,* which can refer to the entire building (Arndt, p. 535).

It is to be noted that the term *hēkal* is applied to God's house while it was still a tent (I Sam 1:9; 3:3). In Ps 27, the temporary structure where David placed the ark is called a house (*bēt*), a temple (*hēkāl*), a booth (*sukkâ*), and a tent (*'ōhel*).

Our word is also applied to the entire property of God. Hence, David states that everything in God's temple says, "glory" (Ps 29:9).

hêkāl also refers to the main room of the temple as such. First, God's divine reception hall (I Kgs 6:3; 7:50; II Chr 4:7) was where Samuel slept as a lad (I Sam 3:3). Since only priests were to enter this area, perhaps the lad was not as young as commonly thought (Num 4:3). Godless kings placed idols therein (II Chr 29:16). It was this holy place that Uzziah profaned (II Chr 26:16). Later, the enemies of Nehemiah sought to trick him into entering. Had he done so, they would have been able to discredit him (Neh 6:10ff).

Finally, God's true temple and throne are in heaven (Ps 11:4; Mic 1:2; Hab 2:20; Jon 2:4 [H 5], 7 [H 8]). In Isaiah's vision (Isa 6:1ff.), the heavenly sanctuary had no separation between the throne of God (ark, i.e. holiest place) and the altar upon which coals burned (the holy place). Truly this bespeaks the perfect state wherein there is no mediator except God.

For a different view, see K. D. Schunck, "Zentralheiligtum, Grenzheiligtum, und Höhenheiligtum in Israel," *Numen* 18: 132–40.

Bibliography: Kapelrud, Arvid S., "Temple Building, a Task for Gods and Kings," Or 32: 56–62. Richardson, TWB, pp. 173, 209. Ussishkim, D., "King Solomon's Palaces," BA 36: 78–106. Wright, G. R., "Shechem and the League Shrines," VT 21: 572–603. Wright, G. E., "Solomon's Temple Resurrected," BA 4: 17–30. ______, "The Significance of the Temple in the Ancient Near East," BA 7: 41–88. Zeitlin, Solomon, "The Temple and Worship," JQR 51: 209–41.

L.J.C.

הֵילֵל (*hêlēl*). See no. 499a.

494 הִין (*hîn*) **hin.** (ASV and RSV the same.)

Perhaps borrowed from Egyptian *h( )n(w)* or *hn(n)w,* a liquid measure of approximately one pint, which is however one-eighth of a hin. A "hin" is a unit of liquid measure. Post-biblical sources make it one-sixth of a bath or twelve logs. The bath is a liquid measure equal to the ephah (q.v.) which is used for dry measure. The bath probably was about twenty-two liters, twenty-three and one-fourth liquid quarts, about six gallons.

The word is used twenty-two times in the OT. It is used twenty times to measure the oil and wine (once "strong drink") used for sacrifices (Num 15, 28, et al.). Fractional parts, one-half, one-third, and one-fourth, as well as a full hin are used, but never more than one. As an object lesson, Ezekiel was allowed to drink only one-sixth of a hin (about two-thirds of a quart) of water each day to represent conditions in Jerusalem under a long siege (Ezk 4:11). The Mosaic law called for the use of a "just hin" (Lev 19:36), as it demanded just measures and weights of every kind.

Bibliography: AI, pp. 195–209. Huey, F. B., "Weights and Measures," in ZPEB.

C.P.W.

495 הָכַר (*hākar*) Occurs only in Job 19:3, in phrase *lō'-tēbōshû tahk^{e}rû-lî.* Meaning

dubious, perhaps "shamelessly you attack me" (NIV).

הַכָּרָה (*hakkārâ*). See no. 1368e.

496 *הָלָא (*hālā'*) ***removed far off.*** This denominative verb occurs only once, in the Niphal (Mic 4:7).

Parent Noun

496a הָלְאָה (*hāl'â*) ***out there, onwards, further*** (e.g. Gen 19:9; Jer 22:19).

הִלּוּל (*hillûl*). See no. 500a.

497 הַלָּז (*hallāz*) הַלָּזֶה (*hallāzeh*) הַלֵּזוּ (*hallēzû*) ***this (one) there, yonder.***

This secondary rare demonstrative pronoun intensifies the designation. The shortened form can be either masculine (Jud 6:20) or feminine (II Kgs 4:25), while the form *hallēzû* is feminine (GKC 34f). These forms might have been developed from the regular *zeh* plus the definite article plus the emphatic lamed (Nötscher, VT 3: 372–80).

L.J.C.

הָלִיךְ (*hālîk*). See no. 498b.

498 הָלַךְ (*hālak*) ***go, walk.*** ASV and RSV similar with the latter sometimes improving on the former.

Derivatives

498a הֵלֶךְ (*hēlek*) ***traveler.***
498b הָלִיךְ (*hālîk*) ***step.***
498c †הֲלִיכָה (*hălîkâ*) ***going, way, traveling company.***
498d מַהֲלָךְ (*mahălak*) ***walk, journey.***
498e †תַּהֲלוּכָה (*tahălûkâ*) ***procession.***

Our word denotes movement in general, although usually of people. Hence, it can be applied with various connotations (including Josh 17:7), and in various contexts. Especially, we ought to notice the imperative ejaculatory use (Gen 37:13, 20; Gen 19:32; 31:44), the use of the infinitive to extend the action of another verb (Gen 8:3, 5; see GKC,113u), and the use of the finite to concretize the action of another verb (Gen 27:14; 50:18; II Kgs 3:7; Isa 2:3). Synonyms are: *rûṣ* "run," *bô* "come, enter," *yāṣā'* "go out," *'ālâ* "ascend," and *shûb* "return." Its antonyms are: *yāshab* "sit," and *'āmad* "stand." Our root occurs 1562 times. It is a common Semitic root (Akkadian *alāku,* CAD. A.I, pp. 300–28; Ugaritic *hlk,* UT 19: no. 766).

The specific application of this verb to various kinds of going may be translated variously: e.g., the "creeping" of a snake (Gen 3:14), the "prowling" of foxes (Lam 5:18), the "sailing" of ships (Gen 7:18), the "flowing" of water (Gen 2:14), the "llaying" of trumpets (Ex 19:19), the "walking" of men (Ex 14:29), etc. In another special use this verb signifies the end of, e.g. rain (Song 2:11), dew (Hos 6:4), wind (Ps 78:39), grief (Job 16:6), human life (Gen 15:2; Josh 23:14), etc.

This verb can be applied both tosupposed gods (Ps 115:7) and to the Lord God. Although other verbs are generally used in theophanic accounts (Frank Schnutenhaus, "Das Kommen und Erscheinen im Alten Testament," ZAW 76: 1–22) there is at least one clear use of *hālak* in such a context (Gen 18:33). Perhaps Gen 3:8 is also a theophanic context, although the participle may go with *qôl* rather than with "Lord God," in which case the translation would be "the voice of the Lord God which was going through the garden on the wind of the day." Conceived anthropomorphically, God walks on the clouds (Ps 104:3) or in the heavens (Job 22:14). More frequently, and more importantly *hālak* is applied to Yahweh's coming to his people in judgment or blessing (II Sam 7:23; Ps 80:2 [H 3]), especially during the wilderness wanderings (e.g. Ex 33:14; 13:21). In this latter context, note the new Exodus (Isa 45:2). As the people followed the ark of God through the desert so they followed it in ritual (infrequently expressed by *hālak;* cf. Josh 3:6; Num 10:32–36).

Apostasy is described as their "going after" other/false gods (Ex 32:1; Jer 5:23), pursuing one's own evil counsel (Jer 7:24; Ps 1:1), or heart (Jer 11:8), or walking in darkness (Isa 9:2 [H 1]), and meets with God's judgment (Lev 26:24). The truly pious follow God's leading in all that they do (i.e., they keep his commandments, I Kgs 3:14; Ps 119:1ff.). This idea can be expressed by *hālak* alone (without *'aḥărê* plus words such as *ṣᵉdāqôt* (Isa 33:15), etc. The Hithpael is used in this connection to emphasize the continuity of the action. Striking examples of men who so lived before God are Enoch, Noah, Abraham, etc. (Gen 5:22; 6:9; 17:1).

hălîkâ. ***Goings, doings, procession, travelers.*** ASV and RSV translate variously with the latter giving superior renderings. This noun (GKC84ᵃ1) concretizes various connotations of the verb whether conceived as the process of going (Ps 68:24 [H 25]; Nah 2:5 [H 6]; Hab 3:6; Ugaritic *hlk. kbkbm*; Albright, BASOR 82: 49), or the process of life (Prov 31:27), or the thing that goes (Job 6:19). For cognates see Akkadian *alaktu* (CAD A.I., pp. 297–300). Our word occurs six times.

tahălûkâ. ***Procession.*** ASV and RSV the same. This *hapax legomenon* (GKC 85r) concretizes the formal ritualistic "going."

Bibliography: Blank, Sheldon H., "Some Considerations Concerning Biblical Prayer," HUCA 32: 75–90. Speiser, E. A., "The Durative

Hithpa'el: A Tan-Form," JAOS 75: 118–21. THAT, I, pp. 486–92.

L.J.C.

499 הָלַל (*hālal*) ***I, shine.*** (ASV and RSV similar.)

Derivative

499a †הֵילֵל (*hêlēl*) ***Helel.***

Our root represents the giving off of light by celestial bodies. Perhaps the Ugaritic phrase *bnt. hll* (daughter of Helel?) as a name for *kṯrt* (UT 19: no. 769) exhibits a similar meaning. The root occurs five (maybe six, KD Job 25:5) times.

The verb is used by Job in highly poetic passages to describe the shining of the sun (29:3; 31:26). In both instances the parallels make the meaning clear. Also, Isa 13:10 contrasts this aspect of heavenly bodies and the darkening of the sun and moon. These heavenly bodies are symbolically/figuratively darkened as a sign of blessing (Isa 60:19; Joel 2:31 [H 3:4]) and/or judgment whether historical (Isa 13:13; Ezk 32:7) or eschatalogical (Joel 2:10). All the uses of our verb appear in contexts with mythological connections. This is not to say that biblical writers assumed the validity of pagan myth. Indeed, as Job (41:18 [H 10]) seeks to make clear, God alone exists as deity. The pagan gods are creations of their own minds (Isa 2:8). Leviathan is a toy in God's hands, i.e., he mocks the pagan religions. Interestingly, in Job 41:18 [H 10] the line parallel to that in which our verb appears alludes to *shaḥar* (q.v.; cf. J. W. McKay, "Helel and the Dawn-Goddess," VT 20: 456ff.) which is probably to be understood as the name of a goddess. McKay (op. cit.) contends that in the allusion in Isa 14:12–15 there is a Canaanite version of the Greek Phaethon myth as mediated and influenced by Phoenician culture during the "heroic age." The development of the Canaanite version is complex and has affinities with the Ugaritic myth involving Athar, son of Athirat, who was unable to occupy the throne of Baal. It was Phaethon who attempted to scale the heights of heaven and as the dawn star was ever condemned to be cast down into Hades (*sh*^{e}*'ôl,* q.v.). Even if one does not accept McKay's argument, it is important to note the following philological oddities: (1) *har mô'ēd* (Isa 14:13) and Ugaritic *ģr.ll* ("The Mount of Lala") where there assembled the *pḫr. m'd,* ("The Assembled Body" ANET, p. 130—UT 16: Text 137:20) and (2) the name *ṣāpôn* (Isa 14:13) which is well known in Ugaritic as the mountain of the gods. The God of Israel is not enthroned on Saphon; he reigns from heaven itself (cf. *hêkāl*). Any interpretation of Isa 14 which does not take into account the mythological allusion does i justice to what is said there. [It may be helpful to add that this much-discussed passage with possible parallels to pagan mythology is actually in form a quotation from a heathen king. It is natural for a heathen king to boast that he would exalt his throne above the gods or above the mountain where he believed the gods assembled. R.L.H.]

hêlēl. ***Helel.*** This proper name is a *hapax legomenon* describing the King of Babylon (Isa 14:12).

L.J.C.

500 *הָלַל (*hālal*) ***II, praise, boast*** (only in Piel, Pual and Hithpael). (ASV and RSV usually the same.)

Derivatives

500a †הִלּוּל (*hillûl*) ***rejoicing, praise.***
500b †מַהֲלָל (*mahălāl*) ***praise.***
500c †תְּהִלָּה (*t*^{e}*hillâ*) ***praise.***

This root connotes being sincerely and deeply thankful for and/or satisfied in lauding a superior quality(ies) or great, great act(s) of the object. Synonyms are: *yādâ* (Hiphil) "to praise," "give thanks"; *rānan* "to sing or shout joyfully"; *shîr* "to sing (praises)"; *bārak* (Piel) "to praise," "bless"; *gādal* (Piel), "to magnify"; *rûm* (Polel), "to exalt"; *zāmar* (Piel), "to sing, play, praise"—all of which see. For cognates see Akkadian *alālu.* 1. *atlalu* "to shout, brag, boast; 2. *šululu* "to hail, acclaim, utter a cry, to generally express joy" (*CAD* A.I., pp. 331ff.); and Ugaritic *hll* (UT 19: no. 769). Our root occurs 206 times.

This root can be used of exalting human beauty (Gen 12:15; II Sam 14:25) or human understanding (Prov 12:8). The noun *t*^{e}*hillâ* is used of the renown of cities (Jer 48:2). Also *hālal* can bespeak the praise given to a good homemaker (Prov 31:28, 31), a wise diplomat (I Kgs 20:11), which comes from a king (Ps 63:11 [H 12]), etc. However, our root usually refers to praising deity, even false deities (Jud 16:24).

The most frequent use of our root relates to praising the God of Israel. Nearly a third of such passages occur in the Psalms. The largest number of these are imperative summons to praise. The frequency and mood emphasizes the vital necessity of this action. The centrality of the cultus to Israel's national *élan* further confirms that necessity, as does the fact that psalmody in Israel's religion was so strongly linked to David the idyllic king. The themes surrounding and included in the verbal expressions of praise (the psalms) show that it is imperative that God in his deity (Ps 102:21 [H 22]) be recognized and that the fullness thereof be affirmed and stated. This is to be offered in an attitude of delight and rejoicing. Belief and joy are inextricably intertwined. Secondly, it is significant that most of these occurrences are plural (except Ps 146:1; Ps 147:12, collective). This shows us, as does the use of the psalms in the worship that praise of Jehovah was especially, though by no means uniquely (Ps 146:1), congregational. This praise could involve choirs and musical instruments, too. It could be expressed in speaking (Jer 31:7), singing (Ps 69:30 [H 31]), and with dancing (Ps 149:3). Such praise was an essential element of formal public worship. It is important to note the strong relationship between praise and intellectual content. The entire creation both terrestrial (Ps 148:1ff.) and heavenly (Ps 148:2) are summoned to praise God. This does not, however, imply that such activity was anything other than intelligent. Such personifications (Rom 8:20ff.) emphasize the responsibility of all creation to joyfully render to God his due (Ps 150:6). Praise and cultus are constants in man's obligation and privilege before the Creator and Savior (Ps 106:1). Interestingly, during the Exile, public worship was sustained, but apart from the temple. In order to emphasize their diminished "joy" in worship the pious hung up their harps (Ps 137:2), and resumed playing in worship upon their restoration (Ps 147:7). Furthermore, the messianic age is to attest the singing of a new song (Isa 42:10; cf. Rev 5:9). The NT worshiping community came into the self-awareness that they were the temple of God (I Cor 3:16; see *hêkāl*). Temple worship is most joyful and expressed both in old and new songs.

Our verb is also used in the voluntive sense whereby the pious declares his intention to praise God. These declarations are either at the beginning (Ps 145:2) or end (Ps 22:22 [H 23]) of a psalm, although usually *yādâ* (Hiphil) is used in such psalms. Even the individual praise is in a cultic context (Ps 22:22 [H 23]; 35:18). t^e*hillâ* can also be used in such psalms (145:1; 9:14 [H 15]; 109:1). This individual affirmation exhibits acceptance of the imperative mood voiced in *hālal*. Here, too, the importance of that activity for life is emphasized by its sustained verbal expression (Ps 63:5 [H 6]; 34:2 [H 3]). To so publicly exalt God's person (Deut 10:21; Jer 17:14) and work (Ps 106:2) is tantamount to an affirmation of life itself. The historical books (i.e. Chronicles) assume such a resolution and especially note the arrangement and establishment of the cultic order and ascribe the establishment of the musical worship to David.

Another use of our root reflects on the nature and content of praising God. He is the unique and sole object and the content of true praise (Ps 65:1 [H 2]; 147:1; cf. Jer 17:14). God is further and inseparably joined to praise (Ps 109:1; Deut 10:21; Ps 22:3 [H 4]). Moreover, human existence and praising the true God are closely related (Ps 119:175). Upon death this cultic public praise, of course, ceases (Ps 115:17; cf. sh^e*'ôl,* and L. Coppes "Sheol, What is It?" *Covenanter Witness* 92: 14–17). The fullest richness of human life produces continual praise (Ps 84:4 [H 5]).

The profane connotation (in the sense of a laudable quality) is sometimes applied to God. This is especially expressed in the Hithpael and the noun t^e*hillâ*. One's only and continual boast (glorying) is to be in God (Ps 105:3). Indeed, if one is pious he will so glory in God (Ps 64:10 [H 11]; note its parallel *śāmaḥ*). God's praise (paralleled by *hôd*) fills the earth (Hab 3:3). t^e*hillâ* is also parallel to *kābôd* (Isa 42:8) and God declares that he will not allow another to receive his due. Yet, God's praise is proclaimed (Isa 42:10), recounted (Ps 78:4), and ever increasing (Ps 71:14). His praise considered in this objective sense is closely tied to his historical acts of deliverance in behalf of his elect (Ex 15:11; Ps 78:4; 106:47) showing God's covenantal interest in and work in history. He is not simply abstract being-in-itself, nor transcendent (Job 38–41).

The prophets declare Israel to be the "glory" (t^e*hillâ*) of God when she is in a divinely exalted and blessed state (Isa 62:7; Jer 13:11). The prophets also summon the elect, indeed the whole world (Isa 61:11) to praise and rejoice over the promised salvation (Isa 43:21). The foreseen fulfillment (Isa 62:7) extends to the messianic state (Joel 2:26).

hillûl. ***Festal jubilation.*** ASV and RSV the same in Jud 9:27, but RSV is better in Lev 19:24. These joyous festivals of praise among Jews and Canaanites apparently took place upon the fourth year's harvest. This firstfruits' rite sanctified the vineyard or field with a sacrificial meal (KD, *Joshua, Judges, Ruth,* p. 366f.).

mahălāl. ***Praise.*** ASV and RSV the same. This noun represents the degree of praise or lack thereof rendered to one by others (Prov 27:21, KD). It is that by which a man is tried and is likened to the crucible in which silver or gold is tried.

t^ehillâ. ***Praise, praiseworthy deeds.*** ASV and RSV similar. This noun represents the results of *hālal* as well as divine acts which merit that activity. This latter use occurs both in the singular (Ps 196:47) and plural (Ex 15:11; Ps 78:4). Parallel words are *kābôd* "honor" (Isa 41:8), and *shēm* "name" (Ps 48:10 [H 11]; Isa 48:9). Our word occurs fifty-seven times.

Bibliography: TDNT, VIII, 493–98. THAT, I, pp. 493–501.

L.J.C.

501 הָלַל (*hālal*) ***III, to be insane.*** ASV and RSV similar with the latter sometimes striking closer to the root meaning.

Derivatives

501a הוֹלֵלָה (*hôlēlâ*) ***madness.***
501b †הוֹלֵלוּת (*hôlēlût*) ***madness.***

This root stresses the irrational aspect of insanity whereas *shāga'* (q.v.) emphasizes the behavioral aspect. Consequently, our root is parallel to *siqlût/śiqlût* "foolishness, folly," *keśel* "folly," and is an antonym of *ḥokmâ* "wisdom." Our root occurs sixteen times.

The basic meaning of the root emerges most clearly in Eccl 2:12. Significant connotations are revealed in I Sam 21:13 [H 14] and Jer 25:16 (cf. 51:7) where an insane man and a drunkard respectively are described. Furthermore, most instances exhibit an application to irrational thought processes (e.g., Eccl 1:17). Our root, interestingly, is applied to the wicked (*rāsha'*) in the Psalms (5:5 [H 6]; 73:3; 75:4 [H 5]; cf. Eccl 7:25) describing the loud boisterous nonsensical behavior and mindset (KD on Ps 5:5 [H 6]). Sin (especially idolatry, Jer 50:38), therefore, is irrational in view of the nature of God, the creation, and mankind (Eccl 10:13), and yet it fills the heart of man (Eccl 9:3). The sovereign Jehovah dispenses the wine of wrath causing men to act even more insanely (Jer 51:7; 25:16) than normally, as do drunkards. He controls and frustrates false prophets (Isa 44:25) and leaders (Job 12:17).

hôlēlôt, hôlēlût. ***Madness.*** This noun, constructed on the Qal participle form, signifies the state of being *hālal*. It occurs five times and only in Eccl.

L.J.C.

הַלְמוּת (*halmût*). See no. 502a.

502 הָלַם (*hālam*) ***hammer, strike down*** (e.g. Jud 5:22; Isa 16:8).

Derivatives

502a הַלְמוּת (*halmût*) ***hammer, mallet*** (Jud 5:26).
502b יַהֲלֹם (*yahălōm*) ***precious stone,*** perhaps jasper (Ex 28:18; 39:11; Ezk 28:13).
502c מַהֲלֻמוֹת (*mahălūmôt*) ***strokes, blows*** (Prov 18:6; 19:29).

503 הֲלֹם (*hălōm*) ***hither*** (e.g. Ex 3:5; Jud 18:3).

504 הֵמָּה (*hēmmâ*), הֵם (*hēm*), הֵנָּה (*hēnna*) ***they, these, the same, who,*** et al. (ASV, RSV similar.)

This is the third person plural independent nominative pronoun, "they." It is the plural form of *hû'* (*hî'*) which should be consulted for a more detailed treatment, as the usage is similar.

Though not required preceding a finite verb, it is used in nominal sentences or clauses, "they (are) crying out" (Ex 5:8), or with the pronoun following the predicate, "entangled, they, in the land", i.e. "they are entangled in the land" (Ex 14:3), and with *kî,* meaning "that," "for," "for few they (are)" (Josh 7:3).

The pronoun may be used before a finite verb when a phrase separates the subject from the verb, "the priests . . . that kept the charge of my sanctuary when . . . , they shall come near" (Ezk 44:15).

The pronoun is used when adding an additional subject after the predicate, "the handmaids came near, they and their children" (Gen 33:6), and as a resumptive pronoun in a relative clause.

hēm (seldom *hēmmâ*) is used with the article (*bayyāmîm hahēm*) as a demonstrative adjective, "in those days" (Deut 17:9). Unlike the singular, the third person plural forms occasionally combine with prepositions, "by them" (Hab 1:16, etc.). *hēnna* is the feminine form.

As in the singular, the plural is used for emphasis and sometimes is translated "themselves," "but every small matter they would do the judging themselves" (Ex 18:26).

C.P.W.

505 הָמָה (*hāmâ*) ***cry aloud, mourn, rage, roar, sound; make noise, tumult; be clamorous, disquieted, loud, moved, troubled, in an uproar.*** (RSV also growl, howl, be in turmoil, moan, thrill, yearn, beat wildly, thunder, et al.; ASV similar.)

Derivatives

505a †הָמוֹן (*hāmôn*) ***abundance, tumult.***
505b הֶמְיָה (*hemyâ*) ***sound, music.***

This root, used thirty-four times, means "cry out," "make a loud noise," or "be turbulent." It is a strong word, emphasizing unrest, commotion, strong feeling, or noise.

This verb is difficult to translate uniformly and the translation will vary from passage to passage and translator to translator. Thus in Isa 17:12 the KJV has "make a noise," ASV "roar," RSV "thunder." Subjects include people (Ps 77:3 [H 4]), waves (Jer 5:22), cities (I Kgs 1:41), the heart (Jer 4:19), and the bowels (Song 5:4, RSV "heart was thrilled"; Jer 31:20, RSV "heart yearns"). The translation "concourse" (Prov 1:21) is inferred from the commotion.

hāmôn. ***Abundance, company, many, multitude, noise, riches, rumbling, sounding, store, tumult.*** (ASV similar, RSV also troops, rushing, wealth, music, populous.) This noun, although variously translated means "multitude" or "host," with emphasis on unrest, turbulence, or noise.

In sixty-four of eighty-four occurrences the "multitude" is people, often troops. Sometimes the emphasis is on the sound of a multitude, hence "noise" (Isa 31:4), "tumult" (II Sam 18:29), or "rumbling" (Jer 47:3). The KJV "sounding of thy bowels" (Isa 63:15) is better translated "yearning of thy heart" (ASV, RSV). The RSV "orgies" (Jer 3:23) assumes the purpose of multitudes on the mountains (KJV "multitude of mountains"). The Valley of Hamon-gog (Ezk 39:11, 15) means the Valley of the multitude of Gog where the slain of God will be buried after their attack on Israel from the north.

The root *hāmâ* may be related to *hāmam* or *hûm* whose meanings are similar.

C.P.W.

הָמוֹן (*hāmôn*). See no. 505a.
הֶמְיָה (*hemyâ*). See no. 505b.

506 הָמַל (*hāmal*). **Assumed root of the following.**
506a הֲמֻלָּה (*hămūllâ*), הֲמוּלָּה (*hamûllâ*) ***rainstorm, roaring or rushing sound*** (Jer 11:16; Ezk 1:24).

507 הָמַם (*hāmam*) ***break, consume, crush, destroy, discomfit, trouble, vex.*** (ASV similar except scatter for break, RSV does not use break, consume or vex, but adds throw into confusion or panic, rout.)

The basic meaning of this word seems to be "to give attention to" in the negative sense, that is, "harass," "trouble," often with the purpose of creating panic.

This verb is used thirteen times. Ten times God is the subject. Of these, five times the object is Israel's enemy whom God strikes with panic for their sake. (See I Sam 7:10; Ex 14:24; Ex 23:27; Josh 10:10; Jud 4:15; and also II Chr 15:6 with a more general subject.) Thus it denotes an important aspect of holy war.

The verb is used parallel to "scatter" in II Sam 22:15, Ps 18:14 [H 15], and Ps 144:6 (parallel passages). God uses arrows and lightnings to trouble his enemies. (Some would translate *hāmam* as "set in motion" referring to the arrows and lightning.) The word is also used to indicate the effect of a cart wheel on grain (Isa 28:28). But some make wheel the object and translate "set in motion."

The word describes God's treatment of the Israelites over forty until they died in the wilderness. He made sure of their death (Deut 2:15). Other subjects of this verb are: Nebuchadnezzar, against Jerusalem (Jer 51:34), and Haman against the Jews (Est 9:24).

The root *hāmam* is related to the verb *hûm* of similar meaning.

Bibliography: THAT, I, pp. 502–503.

C.P.W.

508 המס (*hms*). **Assumed root of the following.**
508a הֶמֶס (*hemes*) ***brushwood*** (Isa 64:1).

509 המר (*hmr*). **Assumed root of the following.**
509a מַהֲמֹרָה (*mahămōrâ*) ***flood*** (Ps 140:11, only).

510 הֵן (*hēn*) ***behold, if, lo, though.*** (ASV and RSV similar.)

An interjection demanding attention, "look!" "see!" and sometimes in context, "if." It is used one hundred times. It is, at least in some uses, a short form of *hinnēh* (q.v.). It or *hinnēh* or both are in Ugaritic reflected in the *hn* of similar meaning.

hēn is mainly used to emphasize the information which follows it, "behold, I have bought you" (Gen 47:23), although sometimes the emphasis is on a person, "behold my servant" (Isa 42:1). The information may be only an assumption, "Behold, they will not believe me" (Ex 4:1). When the assumption is a condition it is translated "if," e.g. "if I shut up heaven . . . , or if I command the locusts" (II Chr 7:13). In this passage *hēn* is parallel to *'im,* meaning "*if* I send pestilence." The KJV uses "though" to introduce a condition in Job 13:15, "though he slay me" (but ASV and RSV, "behold, he will slay me"). "If" is also used in the sense of "whether," "and see if there be such a thing" (Jer 2:10). This usage for "if" may be not the equivalent of "behold" but derived from the Aramaic *hēn* which means "if" exclusively. The Ugaritic *hn* apparently is not used for "if."

Over half of the instances of this word are in Isa and Job, with the others mainly confined to the Pentateuch. This is in contrast to the use of *hinnēh* which is evenly distributed throughout the OT.

510a †הִנֵּה (*hinnēh*) ***behold, lo, see.*** (ASV and RSV "if.") An interjection demanding attention, "look!" "see!" It occurs over a thousand times. See also the shorter form, *hēn.*

510b הֵנָּה (*hinnēh*) ***hither.*** When used in pairs, "here and there." Derivation uncertain.

hinneh is sometimes used as a predicator of existence according to T. O. Lambdin: "It differs from *yesh* in that it emphasizes the immediacy, the here-and-now-ness, of the situation (*Introduction to Biblical Hebrew,* Scribner's Sons, 1971, p. 168).

hinnēh may be used to point out things (pillar and heap, Gen 31:51; covenant, Gen 17:4), but more often it is used to point out people, "behold my maid" (Gen 30:3). Often pronouns are attached as suffixes, especially the first person singular: "See me standing" (i.e. "behold I stood," Gen 41:17), or for emphasis the pronoun is repeated, "And I, behold I am bringing" (Gen 6:17), and often the idiom, "Behold me!" (i.e., "here I am," I Sam 3:4f.).

Then too, according to Lambdin, "Most hinneh clauses occur in direct speech . . . and serve to introduce a fact upon which a following statement or command is based" (ibid., p. 169). Thus, "Behold your handmaid is in your charge; do to her" is equivalent to "since your handmaid is" (Gen 16:6). With the first person suffix followed by a particle it is used often in the prophets as a statement of what God will do, "Behold, I am going to proclaim liberty . . . to the sword" (Jer 34:17). Especially with the participle it may point out what is just on the verge of happening (Ex 4:23, 7:17 etc.).

In a few instances *hinnēh* is used to emphasize one specific possibility and may be translated "if," "and if . . . the disease is checked" (Lev 13:5, RSV).

An important fact or action may follow introductory words: "As for Ishmael . . ., behold I have blessed him" (Gen 17:20), "In my dream and behold I stood" (Gen 41:17). The pronoun may be omitted if understood, "Behold, between Kadesh and Bered," i.e. "it," referring to a well, was thus located (Gen 16:14).

Bibliography: Labuschagne, C. J., "The Particles *hēn* and *hinnēh*," OTS 8: 1–14. Ward, William A., "Comparative Studies in Egyptian and Ugaritic," JNES 20: 31–40.

C.P.W.

הֵנָּה (*hēnnâ*). See no. 504.
הִנֵּה (*hinnēh*). See nos. 510a,b.

511 הַס (*has*) ***be silent, hold peace, tongue, (keep) silence, still.*** (ASV and RSV similar.)

An interjection with imperative force meaning "be silent," "hush." It is used seven times: to command people to refrain from speaking (Amos 6:10) or weeping (Neh 8:11); to demand awesome or respectful silence before the Lord (Hab 2:20); in grief for the dead (Amos 8:3).

C.P.W.

512 הָפַךְ (*hāpak*) ***turn, overturn.***

Derivatives

512a †הֶפֶךְ (*hepek*) ***contrary.***
512b †הֲפֵכָה (*hăpēkâ*) ***overthrow.***
512c †הֲפַכְפַּךְ (*hăpakpak*) ***crooked.***
512d †מַהְפֵּכָה (*mahpēkâ*) ***overthrow.***
512e †מַהְפֶּכֶת (*mahpeket*) ***stocks.***
512f †תַּהְפֻּכָה (*tahpūkâ*) ***perversity.***

This root together with its derivatives appears 118 times in the OT. The verb accounts for the majority of these, being used ninety-four times (Qal, fifty-five times; Niphal thirty-four times; Hophal, once; Hithpael, four times).

The root *hāpak* figures prominently in connection with three themes of Scripture. First, it is found in association with the expression of God's anger and wrath upon unrepentant Sodom and Gomorrah: Gen 19:21, 25, 29; Deut 29:23 [H 22]; Isa 13:19; Jer 20:16; 49:18; 50:40; Amos 4:11; Lam 4:6. Perhaps the use of this verb will shed light on the exact nature of the catastrophe. That it was a volcanic eruption seems unlikely. On the other hand, to translate *hāpak* in these instances as "annihilate" would suggest the disastrous effects of an earthquake, accompanied by lightning which ignited the natural gases of the Jordan Valley area, producing the terrible inferno (and cf. Job 28:5).

By extension, God promises the same treatment to Jerusalem (II Kgs 21:13); Nineveh (Jonah 3:4); the unbelieving nations (Hag 2:22, parallel with *shāmad*) and generally "the wicked" (Prov 12:7). Man is also capable of "overthrowing" (i.e. reducing to vassalage) another city (I Chr 19:3; II Sam 10:3) or even mountains (Job 28:9, something God does too, Job 9:5).

The second theme of Scripture in the development of which *hāpak* appears frequently is the miracles surrounding Israel's exodus from Egypt and her pilgrimage in the wilderness. Most often the verb describes God's actions in turning the Nile into blood (Ex 7:17, 20; Ps 78:44; 105:29, and cf. the reference to the streams of Edom becoming pitch in Isa 34:9). The mind of Pharaoh and his servants was "changed" upon hearing of the escape of the Israelites (Ex 14:5); God even "turned" the hearts of the Egyptians to hate his people (Ps 105:25). To make Israel's escape good God "turned" the sea into dry land (Ps 66:6). The Lord "turned" a strong west wind which drove the locusts into the Red Sea (Ex 10:19). God had "turned" the rod into a serpent (Ex 7:15). He "turned" the rock unto a pool of water (Ps 114:8). While passing through the territory of Moab Israel was the intended recipient of a curse from the hired professional seer Balaam, but God "turned" Balaam's curse into a blessing (Deut 23:5 [H 6]; Neh 13:2).

The third theme is the biblical description of the symptoms of leprosy as described in Lev 13. In this one chapter the root *hāpak* appears nine times (vv. 3, 4, 10, 13, 16, 17, 20, 25, 55), mostly in connection with the hair turning white as a sign of leprosy.

Elsewhere it is of interest to note that *hāpak* in the translation "to turn" is neutral in meaning, as is one of its synonyms *shûb*. That is, it may mean to turn (from) good to bad with either God or man as the subject. "I will turn your feasts into mourning" (Amos 8:10). "Against me he turns his hand" (in judgment as opposed to blessing, Lam 3:3). With man as the subject cf. "you have turned into a degenerate vine (Jer 2:21); "those whom I love have turned against me (Job 19:19); "you have turned justice into poison" (Amos 6:12). It may indicate a change in attitude from joy to chagrin (with man, Lam 1:20; with God, Hos 11:8).

On the other hand, *hāpak* may be used positively in the sense of turning the doleful into the joyful, the bad into the good. Cf. "I will turn their mourning into joy" (Jer 31:13 and also Ps 30:11 [H 12]). "He turned the curse of Balaam into a blessing" (Deut 23:5 [H 6] and Neh 13:2). "He (i.e. Saul) shall be changed into another man" (I Sam 10:6). This root is used to describe the aboutface in the fortunes of the diasporic Jews living in Babylon in the days of Persian hegemony: Est 9:1, 22.

hepek. ***Contrary, contrariness, perversity,*** a substantive that occurs three times in the OT: Ezk 16:34 (twice) in a graphic description of Judah's life of harlotry; and in Isa 29:16 "o your distortions" (of Israel).

hăpēkâ. ***Overthrow,*** a noun only in Gen 19:29 in connection with Sodom and Gomorrah.

mahpēkâ. ***Overthrow.*** Five of its six uses refer to God's action on Sodom and Gomorrah, the exception being Isa 1:7.

mahpeket. ***Stocks,*** Jer 20:2–3; 29:26; II Chr 16:10. It may not be clear what shape these ancient stocks took. Probably they were quite different from those of colonial days, but the details are not certain.

tahpūkâ. ***Perversity.*** Of its nine uses eight are in Proverbs (and cf. Deut 32:20). This substantive is always translated by the KJV as "froward" or "frowardness" except Prov 23:33 and in the RSV by "perverse, perverted, perverseness." It is a sin connected mostly with the mouth (Prov 2:12; 10:31–32; 16:30) and also with the heart (Prov 6:14); the eyes (Prov 16:30); and the mind (Prov 23:33).

Bibliography: On *hāpak* and the direct object *yd* "hand" in Lam 3:3; I Kgs 22:34; II Kgs 9, 23; II Chr 18:33, see Fitzgerald, A., "Hebrew *yd* = 'Love' and 'Beloved'," CBQ 29: 368–74. On the expression *nhpk b* in Job 19:19, see Penar, T., "Job 19:19 in the Light of Ben Sira 6, 11," Bib 48: 293–95. On *hāpak* in connection with the Sodom and Gomorrah incident, see Sarna, N., *Understanding Genesis,* McGraw-Hill, 1967, esp. pp. 137–42.

V.P.H.

513 הֹצֶן (*hōṣen*) ***weapon*** (Ezk 23:24). Meaning and derivation uncertain.

הַר (*har*). See no. 517a.
הַרְאֵל (*har'ēl*). A form of no. 159a (q.v.).

514 הָרַג (*hārag*) ***destroy, kill, murder, slay, murderer, slayer, out of hand*** (Num 11:15). Used a total of 172 times, it is usually translated "slay."

Derivatives

514a הֶרֶג (*hereg*) ***slaughter.***
514b הֲרֵגָה (*hărēgâ*) ***slaughter.***

The root includes the ideas of murder and judicial execution, as well as the killing of animals.

The first use of the word (Gen 4:8) reports Cain's crime, shedding Abel's blood which "cried to God," i.e. for vengeance. David ordered the execution of the murderers of Ishbosheth (II Sam 4:11–12). The same word is used for both murder and judicial execution in agreement with the command of Gen 9:6. The murderer is to be executed on the grounds that failure to do so signifies consent to the crime and breaks the covenant with God. Furthermore it denies God's image in man.

If a householder killed a robber who broke into his home during the night, he would not incur blood guilt, since the nocturnal housebreaker would not stop at murder to accomplish his purpose.

Parallels to biblical laws on murder are few in the literature of Mesopotamia. There loss of life could be compensated for through payment of a fine. Only in aggravated cases was the death penalty imposed.

There is much overlapping in the use of the various words for "kill." This word is seldom used of killing animals. Usually it is used of killing men and numerous times of violent killing in war or intrigue. It is never used for the killing of sacrificial animals and very seldom for the killing of animals for food. The word is common in the histories of the judges and the monarchy as the thing represented was itself all too common. Numbers of these instances refer to murder (for which *rāsaḥ* is more characteristic, cf. Ex 20:13), but many refer to such items as Jezebel's killing the prophets of the Lord (I Kgs 18:13), Levi and Simeon's slaughter of the Shechemites (Gen 34:26), and Joab's killing of Abner (II Sam 3:30). The word is used sometimes of God's judicial judgments, e.g. the slaying of Egypt's firstborn (Ex 13:15), but such uses are rare. In the angel's slaughter of Sennacherib's army, the word *nākâ* is used. Usually *hārag* is used of violent killing of men by other men—sometimes with justification, often, alas not!

Bibliography: Amran, D., "Retaliation and Compensation," JQR 2: 191–211. Daube, D., "Error and Accident in the Bible," *Revue Internationale des Droits de l'Antiquite* 2: 393–416. Pritchard, J. B., ed., ANET, pp. 161–97, for a comparison of biblical and ancient near eastern laws. Saalschutz, *Das Mosaische Recht mit Beruchsichtigung des späteren Judischen,* II, 1848, pp. 437–592.

H.G.S.

515 הָרָה (*hārâ*) ***bear, be with child, conceive, progenitor, be conceived, conceive.***

Derivatives

515a הָרָה (*hārâ*) ***pregnant.***
515b הָרִיָּה (*hārîyâ*) ***pregnant.***
515c הֵרָיוֹן (*hērāyôn*) ***conception, pregnancy.***

Three words are used in relation to the birth process: *hārâ* "conceive," *yālad* "bear, give birth" and *ḥûl* "to labor in giving birth." Another word for conceive is *yāḥam,* used more, however, of animals in heat (but cf. Ps 51:7). The first describes the inception and the latter two the termination of the process.

Generally *hārâ* is used to state the results of sexual intercourse. In this respect there is often a connection with some phase of the redemptive program of God. That is, the conceptions of which the OT speaks concern children who were to play an important part in redemptive history. Although a secondary issue in the structure of Genesis, the record of the conception of Ishmael (Gen 16:4–5) may be considered a memorial to the folly of using men's ways to achieve the purposes of God: "the promised seed is not of nature but of grace" (Dodds, *The Book of Genesis,* London: 1896, p. 148). Sarah's faith could not stand the strain of delay.

The successive births of Cain, Abel, and Seth, set out for us the hope of personal redemption. All did not go in the way of Cain, and the message of grace was preserved until and through Noah. The selective, monergistic power of God is demonstrated in the conception of Isaac (Gen 21:2), demonstrating that the power of God alone is able to bring about his redemptive purposes, for both Abraham and Sarah were too old to have children. Men must trust solely in God's power, not in their own desperate attempts.

Rebekah was barren, and Isaac prayed for her to conceive (25:21). Isaac presumably expected children early in his marriage, almost as a matter of course, for he lived under God's promise that Abraham would become the father of many nations (Gen 17:4). But only when he resorted to God in prayer was Rebekah granted conception, emphasizing again that the creation of the holy line is in God's hands.

In the case of Jacob, it became a matter of almost too many children. The story of the births of his eleven sons in Padan-Aram is only sketched (Gen 29:32ff.). But the same principles hold. First, there is no doubt about the identity of the inheritors of the land of promise. Second, the people who carry the oracles of God are clearly defined. Third, it is clear that through the faith delivered to Abraham the true people of God are to be known in all time.

The creative power of God is finally manifested in the birth of the Messiah, for he was to be begotten of God the Spirit in the womb of the virgin (Isa 7:14), thus completing God's long work of redemption. The birth of the virgin's son, in light of the context, stands as a rebuke to the ideas of Ahaz to secure safety for Israel, and the divine character of the son proclaims that peace and safety will come only as God himself rules the earth.

[It is now alleged that the phraseology of Isa 7:14 is found in Ugaritic (UT 16: nos. 77, 11.5, 7), and that it is only a formula announcing the arrival of a royal heir to be born naturally. This is not quite the case. In the Ugaritic passage the verb *hry* "be pregnant" is not used at all. The text does speak of a virgin (*btlt*) who will later bear a child naturally. Interestingly, the Ugaritic line in poetic parallelism uses the word for "virgin" cognate to the Hebrew *'almâ* (q.v.) of Isa 7:14. The case is different in Isa 7:14. There the prophet speaks of a pregnant virgin, using the participle (or adj.) of *hārâ*. The announcement is similar to Gen 16:11 addressed to Hagar who had conceived and was pregnant. As far as the grammar goes, this could refer to a pregnant virgin either contemporary or in the future, but the reference to virginity shows that the pregnancy is miraculous. R.L.H.]

The birth of Samuel (I Sam 1:20) also demonstrates the redemptive power of God. Hannah's desire for children is used by God to provide a spiritual leader for his people in a time when a dedicated priest and teacher of the law was needed. In a like manner, even in the face of Pharoah's edict, the birth of Moses, and his survival in the royal household, appears to be the almost ironic frustration of the royal will by the God of heaven, to further his redemptive program.

A figurative use of the root is indicated in that the origin of lies is in the heart, the soul of men, the first step in overt sin. The birth pangs of a pregnant woman are used as a simile to describe the terroristic seizure of man's soul as the judgment of God is poured out (Isa 26:17).

H.G.S.

הֵרוֹן (*hērôn*). See no. 515c.
הָרִיָּה (*hārîyâ*). See no. 515b.

הֵרָיוֹן (*hērāyôn*). See no. 515c.
הֲרִיסָה (*hărîsâ*). See no. 516b.
הֲרִיסוּת (*hărîsut*). See no. 516c.

516 הָרַס (*hāras*) ***beat down, break, break down, break through, destroy, overthrow, pluck down, pull down, throw down, ruined, destroyer, utterly.***

Derivatives

516a †הֶרֶס (*heres*) ***overthrow, destruction.***
516b †הֲרִיסָה (*hărîsâ*) ***ruin.***
516c †הֲרִיסוּת (*hărîsût*) ***overthrow, destruction.***

This root means to destroy by tearing down, e.g. city walls, houses, and fortresses.

Its first usage occurs in Ex 15:7, referring to the destruction of the Egyptian armies in the Red Sea. At Sinai Moses was instructed to erect barriers around the mountain to prevent the people from breaking through and approaching too closely (Ex 19:21, 24). A breakthrough would be a destructive action against God's sanctity.

Gideon begins his work of deliverance by destroying his father's altar to Baal (Jud 6:25) when his father called the people's attention to the impotence of such idols (vv. 28–35). In Elijah's day it was the people who tore down the altars of the Lord (I Kgs 19:10, 14) but in the following revival the Baal worship was destroyed in Israel at least for a time.

As to the Canaanites, Israel was to destroy them (Ex 23:24) and break up their idols, thus striking at their morale and defeating them.

Objects of destruction included walls (Ezk 13:14), foundations (Ezk 30:4), barns (Joel 1:17), cities (II Kgs 3:25; I Chr 20:1), either by God (Lam 2:2; Ex 15:7), or men (I Chr 20:1). The foolish woman pulled down her house by her sins (Prov 14:1) and the king who took a gift (which influenced his judgment) and destroyed the kingdom he was born to uphold. It was a policy of warfare to destroy cities which did not surrender when their walls had been breached (I Chr 20:1; cf. Deut 20:10–14). The wicked ideas sinners advance in the cities bring about their destruction (Prov 11:11) by sapping morality and the will to resist the intruder. The slothful's neglect can bring about the deterioration of the garden walls which mark off property (Prov 24:31).

Part of Jeremiah's work was to pull down so that the true work of God could be built in its place (Jer 1:10).

heres. ***Overthrow, destruction,*** the result of destructive activities (only in Isa 19:18) applied in a word play to the Egyptian city On (Heliopolis city of the Sun-*ḥeres*), differing only in the shift from *h* to *ḥ*.

hărîsâ, hărîsût. ***Overthrow, destruction.*** The latter word is the abstract form, "ruined."

H.G.S.

517 הרר (*hrr*). **Assumed root of the following.**

517a †הַר (*har*) ***hill*** (sixty-one times) ***hill country*** (once) ***mount, mountain*** (486 times). RSV uses mount where it is appropriate.

The antiquity, majesty, power and height of mountains reaching up to the heavens above the clouds naturally led people to associate mountains with gods. The peoples of ancient Mesopotamia thought that on Kammer Duku, the bright mountain in the east, the gods fixed destiny on New Year's Day, and that on Mashu in the West, heaven and the underworld met, thus providing entrance to the realm of the dead. In Syria-Palestine the mountains were worshipped and were the sites for pagan worship. According to the Ras Shamra texts, Zaphon, modern Mons Cassius north of Ras Shamra, was worshipped and regarded as the abode of Baal.

The OT uses mountains with theological intention in at least four ways. First, the Lord is greater than the mountains: he establishes them (Ps 65:6 [H 7]; 90:2), weighs them (Isa 40:12), breaks them in pieces (I Kgs 19:11; Hab 3:6), grinds and threshes them in pieces (Isa 41:15), sets them on fire (Deut 32:22; Ps 83:14 [H 15]; 104:32), melts them (Mic 1:4; Isa 63:19), and removes them (Job 9:5). Isaiah portrays the coming of the Lord and the return of the exiles by the levelling of hills (Isa 40:4; 45:2; 49:11).

Second, the mountains are a symbol of power: Babylon is called a destroying mountain (Jer 51:25); the opposition to Zerubbabel is likened to a mountain that will become a plain (Zech 4:7), and the kingdom that will endure for all eternity is symbolically portrayed as a mountain that fills the earth (Dan 2:44).

Third, the Lord gives his people a sense of his nearness by choosing mountains for his worship and revelation. Moses and Elijah pray on a mountain (Ex 17:9; I Kgs 18:42); blessings and curses are invoked from Mount Ebal and Gerizim (Deut 11:29; 27:12f.; Josh 8:33), worship is offered on various mountains (cf. Gen 22:2; Josh 5:3; I Sam 9:12ff; I Kgs 3:4) and the ark is set on a hill (I Sam 7:1; II Sam 6:3).

But above all the Lord chose Sinai and Zion as the places where he reveals himself. On Mount Sinai the Law was given and the national worship established. It was to Horeb that Elijah fled for new supplies of strength and grace. On Zion he put his name and this became the final and central place of worship (Ex 15:17; Deut 12:1). Here the tribes assembled in worship (Ps 122; 133).

There is in the OT more than a hint that the

earthly Zion is but a symbol of what in the NT becomes explicitly the heavenly Jerusalem. The Mountain of God in Ps 68 [H 16] is taken by both BDB and Dahood (Psalms II, in AB) as general, "a great mountain," but still the picture is of God's ascent on high and so the great heavenly mountain (cf. Eph 4:8–10). In the last days Zion will be the exalted source of God's law and center of his rule, the heavenly Jerusalem on earth (Isa 2:2–3; Mic 4:1–2).

Fourth, employing the imagery of its neighbors, the OT denotes the divine abode by reference to the mountain in the extreme north (Ps 48:2). In Isa 14:12ff. and Ezk 28:11–19 the pagan kings of Babylon and Tyre respectively are described as seeking to become gods by ascending the mythological divine mountain. But as Foerster rightly notes: "But the decisive pt. is that here the pagan myth is used ironically in songs mocking the downfall of pagan rulers." Elsewhere pagan mythology is deliberately pushed into the background (TDNT, V, p. 483). Some understand these kings to be allusions to Satan and see the mountain in the north as a symbol of Heaven.

Bibliography: Hamlin, E. John, "The Meaning of 'Mountains and Hills' in Isa 41:14–16," JNES 13: 185–90. TDNT, V, pp. 479–83.

B.K.W.

518 *הָתַל (*hātal*) ***deceive, mock.*** This verb occurs only once, in the Piel (I Kgs 18:27).

518a הֲתֻלִים (*hătūlîm*) ***mockery*** (Job 17:2, only).

הָתַת (*hātat*). See no. 488.

ז

ו

519 וָ (*wā*) וְ (w^e), וּ (*û*) ***and, so, then, when, now, or, but, that,*** and many others. (ASV and RSV similar.) The vocalization varies.

This is an inseparable prefix which is used as a conjunction or introductory particle which can usually be translated "and."

The fundamental use of the prefix is that of a simple conjunction "and," connecting words ("days and years," Gen 1:14), phrases ("and to divide" Gen 1:18), and complete sentences (connecting Gen 2:11 with verse 12). However it is used more often and for a greater variety of constructions than is the English connector "and."

It is often used at the beginning of sentences, for which reason the KJV begins many sentences with an unexplained "and." This use may be explained as a mild introductory particle and is often translated "now" as in Ex 1:1 where it begins the book (KJV, ASV; the RSV ignores it completely; cf. Gen 3:1, 4:1).

The item following the prefix is not always an additional item, different from that which preceded: "Judah and Jerusalem" (Isa 1:1), pointing out Jerusalem especially as an important and representative part of Judah; "in Ramah, and in his own city" (I Sam 28:3), the two being the same place, hence the translation "even" as explanatory. When the second word specifies the first the construction is called a "hendiadys," i.e., two words with one meaning. For example, "a tent and a dwelling" in II Sam 7:6 means "a dwelling tent."

The prefix may mean "or" or the negative "nor" (Ex 20:10), or, if it connects opposing ideas, it may mean "but" (Gen 3:3; 4:2). It may add an additional subject in a way not acceptable in English, "I will fast, and my maidens" (Est 4:16). The noun can also denote purpose as in English, e.g. "Divide and conquer." Used twice, the meaning may be "both... and" (Num 9:14). For "a weight and a weight" (Deut 25:13) is meant "different weights." It is used to connect two ideas in a proverb, "Cold waters to a thirsty soul, and good news from a far country" (Prov 25:25), that is, they are alike. These usages are not really different meanings of the conjunction. They derive from the fact that Hebrew is more paratactic than English. We subordinate some clauses and specify relationships. Hebrew often puts clauses and phrases side by side leaving the sense and juxtaposition to specify the precise relationship.

The prefix is often used to introduce a circumstantial clause and is better translated "when," "since," "with," etc., "Why is thy countenance sad, and (i. e. "seeing," "since") thou art not sick?" (Neh 2:2). The prefix is often to be translated "then" as a consequent introducing the second part of a conditional sentence, "Buf if he wash not..., then he shall bear his iniquity" (Lev 17:16)—the so-called *waw* of the apodosis.

A common use of this prefix is with a short form of the prefixed conjugation of the verb in a special construction with the letter following the prefix (usually) doubled. This form, generally called the "waw consecutive," usually denotes sequence in past narrative. But sometimes the action is not successive in a strict sense. It may denote logical sequence (cf. Gen 2:1; 23:20; Deut 3:8) or action that is actually prior to the preceding verb, i.e. it functions as a pluperfect (cf. Gen 19:27; Num 1:48; II Sam 12:27; I Kgs 12:13; *passim*). W. Martin refers to this last usage as "dischronologized narrative ("Dischronologized Narrative in the Old Testament," Vetus Testamentum, Congress Volume, Rome, 1968: 179–86). This use explains the apparent contradiction between Gen 1:24–26 and Gen 2:19. The latter passage means "and the Lord had formed."

[The origin and even meaning of this waw consecutive has been much discussed. The treatment in GKC is in accord with that in S. R. Driver, *Use of the Tenses in Hebrew*. In brief, it says that this form is found only in sequences and it takes its meaning from the lead verb. A lead verb in the perfect will be followed by this form which represents a continuation of that past action viewed as incomplete from the standpoint of the past horizon. Similarly for the sequence of an imperfect verb continued by a waw consecutive with a perfect.

An alternative view was presented by Zellig S. Harris, *The Development of the Canaanite Dialects* (New Haven: American Oriental Society, 1939), pp. 47–49. He argued that this waw preserved an old Ugaritic past tense which by accident is similar to the newly-developed imperfect.

G. H. Gordon shows rather convincingly that the alleged old past tense in Ugaritic was identical with a form like the Hebrew imperfect. But it is admitted by all, that this preformative tense in Ugaritic had both a narrative past and an imperfect usage. R. Laird Harris (*Introductory Hebrew Grammar,* Eerdmans, 1950, pp. 33–34) would modify Zellig S. Harris's view to hold that the waw consecutive is a preservation of the old

Ugaritic narrative meaning of the imperfect tense which was used in a past sense with or without the waw. In poetic Hebrew also the imperfect shows this narrative past sense with or without the waw. Cf. the sequence of tenses in Ps 18:4–12.

G. Douglas Young has argued that this waw is a reflection of Egyptian usage ("The Origin of the Waw Consecutive," JNES 12: 248–52).

A waw with the usual pointing (simple shewa) is used with the imperfect and called the waw conjunctive. The meaning of this form also is debatable. It does not seem usually to refer simply to the future—that would call for a waw consecutive with the perfect. Rather it normally throws the verb into the subjunctive and expresses result, purpose, volition, etc. It often has a cohortative "a" attached.

The same conjunction is used commonly in Ugaritic but apparently as a separate word, as it is often separated from the following word by a word divider. M. Dahood alleges also an emphatic, an explicative and a vocative waw (*Psalms* III, in AB, pp. 400–402). R.L.H.]

Bibliography: Blake, Frank R., "The Hebrew Waw Conversive," JBL 63: 271–95. Meek, Theophile J., "Translating the Hebrew Bible," JBL 79: 328–35. Pope, Marvin, "'Pleonastic' Wāw before Nouns in Ugaritic and Hebrew," JAOS 73: 95–98. Young, G. D., "The Origin of the *wāw* Conversive," JNES 12: 248–52. Wernberg Møller P., "'Pleonastic' Waw in Classical Hebrew," JSS 3: 321–26.

C.P.W.

520 וָו (*wāw*) ***hook.*** (ASV and RSV the same.)

The basic meaning of the word is hook, peg. It is used thirteen times in the OT, but only in the plural and only in Ex 26, 27, 36 and 38. It is used for the silver and gold hooks to which the curtains in the tabernacle were fastened. Although not used in the OT as such, the word also refers to waw, the sixth letter in the Hebrew alphabet, probably because of its shape.

C.P.W.

521 וזר (*wzr*). **Assumed root of the following.**

521a †וָזָר (*wāzār*) ***strange*** (ASV "laden with guilt," RSV "guilty").

The KJV translators read *wā* "and" with *zar* (participle of *zûr*) "strange," but BDB, KB and others translate "guilty" (Prov 21:8 only). It may be related to an Arabic cognate meaning "to bear a burden" or to another meaning "to be guilty."

C.P.W.

וָלָד (*wālād*). See no. 867a.

ז

ז

522 זאב (*z'b*). **Assumed root of the following.**
522a זְאֵב (*z^e'ēb*) ***wolf*** (e.g. Gen 49:27; Jer 5:6).

זֹאת (*zō't*). See no. 528.

523 זבב (*zbb*). **Assumed root of the following.**
523a †זְבוּב (*z^{e}bûb*) ***flies.***

Found only six times in the OT, including four occurrences as part of the compound name "Baal-zebub." Eccl 10:1 uses the word as part of a proverb: "Dead flies make a perfumer's oil stink." In Isa 7:18 the fly (or "flies") is symbolic of the troops of Egypt, which will descend upon the land of Israel at the Lord's invitation and devastate the land. One of the plagues of Egypt will now strike the Hebrews.

In II Kgs 1, Ahaziah king of Israel sent messengers to inquire of the Philistine deity Baal-zebub, the god of Ekron. Ahaziah had been injured in a fall and wanted to know if he would recover (1:2). At God's command, Elijah confronted the messengers, rebuked them for consulting a foreign god and predicted the death of Ahaziah (1:3, 6). Later Elijah personally told the king that his lack of faith in the God of Israel sealed his doom (1:16).

Since Baal-zebub means "lord of flies," interpreters believe that "flies" may involve a mocking alteration of z^{e}bûl, "prince," "high place," or "dais." In Ugaritic literature, Baal is referred to as a prince. The change from "prince" to "flies" would parallel the use of "bosheth," "shame," in place of "Baal" in such names as Ish-bosheth and Mephibosheth. In the NT "Beelzebub" is called "the prince of the devils." Most Greek manuscripts have "Beelzeboul," though the Syriac and similar manuscripts use "Beelzeboub."

H.W.

524 זָבַד (*zābad*) ***bestow upon, endow with*** (Gen 30:20).

Derivative

524a זֶבֶד (*zebed*) ***endowment, gift*** (Gen 30:20).

זְבוּב (*z^{e}bûb*). See no. 523a.
זְבוּלוּן (*z^{e}bûlûn*). See no. 526b.

525 זָבַח (*zābaḥ*) ***sacrifice, slaughter.***

Derivatives

525a †זֶבַח (*zebaḥ*) ***sacrifice.***
525b †מִזְבֵּחַ (*mizbēaḥ*) ***altar.***

The verb *zābaḥ* is mainly used of killing animals for sacrifices. Most often in Qal, though the Piel occurs nineteen times in connection with idolatrous sacrifices on the high places (Hos 11:2; II Kgs 12:3). Three times the Piel refers to the prolific and legitimate sacrifices of Solomon (I Kgs 8:5; II Chr 5:6) or Hezekiah (II Chr 30:22).

zebaḥ. ***Sacrifice.*** Generic noun often linked with offerings (Ps 40:6 [H 7]) or burnt offerings (I Sam 6:5; Ex 10:25). It is frequently used in connection with peace offerings (*sh^{e}lāmîm*, cf. Lev 3:1; 17:5), but on occasion it is distinguished from peace offerings (Num 15:8; Josh 22:27). Often *zebaḥ* is a cognate accusative to *zābaḥ*, but sacrifices can also be "made" (Num 6:17; I Kgs 12:27), "brought" (Amos 4:4; Deut 12:6) or "brought near" (Lev 7:11).

mizbēaḥ. ***Altar.*** A place of sacrifice. Used 401 times, mainly in the Pentateuch and historical books. Altars of stone (Josh 8:31), of earth (Ex 20:24), of wood and bronze (Ex 38:1), and of wood and gold (Ex 30:1–6) are found. Sometimes altars are given names, such as Jacob's altar at Shechem ("El the God of Israel," Gen 33:20), Moses' at Rephidim ("The Lord is my banner," Ex 17:15), or Gideon's in Ophrah ("The Lord is peace," Jud 6:24). There are many references to illegitimate altars, often in connection with sacred pillars (Ex 34:13) and high places (II Kgs 23:15).

The importance of sacrifices is seen early in Genesis. After the flood, Noah built an altar and sacrificed "clean" animals and birds to the Lord. Abram worshiped the Lord who had appeared to him by building an altar at Shechem when he arrived in the promised land (Gen 12:7–8). Other altars were built by the patriarchs Isaac and Jacob at Beersheba and Bethel to commemorate God's blessing (Gen 26:25; 35:7). Isaac was laid on an altar at Mount Moriah by his father Abraham, but his place was taken by a ram in what proved to be the clearest OT example of the meaning of substitutionary sacrifice. The sacrifice of the Passover lamb and resultant sparing of all the firstborn sons conveyed the same meaning (Ex 12:27).

Genesis also records the sacrifice offered by Jacob when he concluded a covenant with Laban (31:54). The meal symbolized the friendship between the parties and their intention to keep their promises. When Israel entered a covenant with the Lord, Moses built an altar at the foot of Mount Sinai and offered burnt offerings and peace offerings (Ex 24:4–5). Psalm 50:5 refers to "those who made a covenant with me by sacrifice."

At Mount Sinai Moses received instructions about the altars and sacrifices connected with the Tabernacle. The altar designed for the animal sacrifices was the bronze altar, or "altar of burnt offering." It was about seven and one-half feet square and four and one-half feet high, with horns on each corner, made "of one piece" with the altar. It was made of acacia wood and overlaid with bronze (Ex 38:1–2). A bronze grating, poles and utensils were accessories of the altar (Ex 30:28; 35:16). The sacrifices were burned on the altar, and the priests put some of the blood on the horns, then poured out the rest at the base of the altar (Lev 4:7, 25). This great altar was set in the courtyard, in front of the doorway of the tabernacle (Ex 40:7).

The other altar was called the "altar of incense" or the "gold altar" (Ex 39:38; 40:5). It was about eighteen inches square and a yard high, with four horns and a gold molding. It too was made of acacia wood, but overlaid with gold (Ex 30:1–6). The blood of the guilt offering was placed on the horns of this altar (Lev 4:7). Because of its fragrant incense, this altar was placed in the holy place, in front of the sacred curtain.

The purification of the altar of burnt offering is sometimes linked with the consecration of the entire tent of meeting (Ex 29:44). Blood was sprinkled on the altar to make atonement for it as well as for the most holy place on the Day of Atonement (Lev 16:20, 33; cf. 8:15). There are also several references to the dedication of the altar. Special offerings were presented (Num 7:10, 11, 84) and the altar was anointed with oil (Ex 40:10). When Aaron and his sons were consecrated, the anointing oil was sprinkled on the altar seven times (Lev 8:11).

King Solomon built an altar of burnt offering thirty feet square and fifteen feet high (II Chr 4:1). Even this was not large enough for the offerings at the dedication of the temple (I Kgs 8:54), the "house of sacrifice" (II Chr 7:12).

Solomon's successors sometimes neglected the altar, but good kings like Asa (II Chr 15:8) and Hezekiah cleansed it (II Chr 29:18). Ahaz replaced the altar with a model patterned after one he had seen in Damascus (II Kgs 16:14–15). Uzziah also sinned by usurping the place of a priest and burning incense on the altar of incense (II Chr 26:16).

Several other significant altars are mentioned in Scripture. Joshua built one of uncut stones on Mount Ebal as Israel renewed her covenant with God (Josh 8:31). The two and a half tribes who lived in Transjordan made a special "memorial" altar near the Jordan River, one "not for burnt offering or for sacrifice" (Josh 22:11, 26). David set up an altar on Mount Moriah, the site of the temple, when an angel appeared to him there (II Sam 24:25). And Elijah took twelve stones—one for each tribe—and repaired the altar of the Lord on Mount Carmel (I Kgs 18:30–32).

The horns of the altar were considered a place of refuge, even for a murderer (Ex 21:14). Adonijah took hold of the horns of the altar and Solomon spared his life (I Kgs 1:50–51). But when Joab did the same thing, Solomon ordered his death (I Kgs 2:28).

The centrality of sacrifices in the worship of Israel led to a perfunctory parade of animals to the altar, and God had to warn his people that the burning of fat and the outpouring of blood did not automatically win his favor. "To obey is better than to sacrifice" (I Sam 15:22) and God delights "in loyalty rather than sacrifice" (Hos 6:6). Isaiah charges that God is "fed up" with all their hypocritical offerings (1:11). Righteousness and justice are more important than sacrifice (Prov 21:3). Only when hearts are right with God are sacrifices acceptable and the means of bringing great joy (Neh 12:43). In the Psalms, thanksgiving and a broken spirit are regarded as sacrifices that honor God (Ps 50:14, 23; 51:17 [H 19]).

Unfortunately, Israel was constantly tempted to get involved in pagan sacrifices. God warned them to tear down Canaanite altars and smash their sacred pillars (Ex 34:13; Deut 7:5), but instead the Israelites tore down God's altars and killed his prophets (I Kgs 19:10). On the verge of entering the promised land, Israel was invited to sacrifice to the gods of Moab, and the resulting idolatry and immorality was one of the worst chapters in their history (Num 25:2ff.). In Palestine the Israelites quickly fell prey to Baal worship, building altars and even temples to this Canaanite deity (Jud 6:30; Hos 11:2; I Kgs 16:32). Jehu led a massive attack on Baalism after the disastrous reign of Ahab (II Kgs 10:19), and Josiah tore down the altars (including incense altars) of Baal in his great reform (II Chr 34:4, 7). Jeroboam I is renowned for the altar he built at Bethel and the sacrifices to the golden calves (I Kgs 12:32). Not until the days of Josiah (c. 621 B.C.) was this shrine dismantled (II Kgs 23:15). Among other perversions, Ahaz sacrificed to the gods of Damascus (II Chr 28:23) and Amon offered sacrifices to the carved images of Manasseh (II Chr 33:22).

Frequently, the biblical writers condemn the high places, where the people (I Kgs 22:43 [H 44]) and sometimes the kings (II Kgs 16:4) sacrificed and burned incense. Though these "hill shrines" could claim some legitimacy prior to the construction of the temple (cf. II Chr 1:3), the strong tendency was to worship Baal or the golden calves.

Pagan worship sometimes involved sacrifice to demons (Lev 17:7; Deut 32:17), including the offering of their children to the idols of Canaan (Ps 106:37–38). Such horrible rituals are cited by Ezekiel as one of the major reasons for God's judgment on the nation (16:20–21).

While the primary use of *zābaḥ* and *zebaḥ* concerns the killing of animals for sacrifice, occasionally the idea of "slaughter" occurs without any sacrificial context. The Israelites were permitted to slaughter animals and eat meat in their home towns (Deut 12:5, 21). Ahab slaughtered a large number of sheep and oxen to provide a sumptuous meal for Jehoshaphat and the people with him (II Chr 18:2). When Elisha gave up farming to become Elijah's associate, he killed a pair of oxen and shared the food with the people (I Kgs 19:21).

The ideas of "slaughter" and "sacrifice" are powerfully combined in passages portraying divine judgment. Josiah "slaughtered/sacrificed" priests of the high places on the very altars they served (II Kgs 23:20; cf. I Kgs 13:2). The day of the Lord is described as a "sacrifice" as princes and armies are destroyed. A time of slaugher was in store for Israel (Zeph 1:7, 8), Egypt (Jer 46:10) and Edom (Isa 34:6, see *dāshēn*). The flesh of the armies of Gog and Magog will be sacrificed on the mountains of Israel to provide a great feast for the birds and animals (Ezk 39:17–19).

Other futuristic passages present the nations in a more favorable light. Isaiah 19:21 declares that one day the Egyptians will know the Lord and will bring sacrifices and offerings to him (cf. II Kgs 5:17). In Israel the priests are promised a perpetual role in presenting sacrifices on behalf of the people (Jer 33:18; Ezk 44:11).

Bibliography: Kidner, F. Derek, *Sacrifice in the OT*, London: Tyndale, 1951. AI, pp. 415–510.

H.W.

526 זָבַל (*zābal*) ***exalt, honor.*** Used only in Gen 30:20 in a word play on the name Zebulun.

Derivatives

526a †זְבֻל (*z^e^bul*) ***habitation, height.***
526b †זְבוּלוּן (*z^e^bûlûn*) ***Zebulun.***

z^e^būl. ***Habitation, height, exalted abode.*** This noun is found only five times. The vowel is invariably defective. Probably cognate to Ugaratic *zbl* "prince (ship)" (cf. UT 19: no. 815).

The term *z^e^būl* first occurs in I Kgs 8:13 (= II Chr 6:2) when, at the dedication of the temple, Solomon addressed the Lord and said, "I have built thee an exalted house" (RSV). The expression *bêt z^e^būl* is rendered "an house to dwell in" (KJV) and "a magnificent temple" (NIV)

In two passages *z^e^būl* is associated with heaven. Isaiah 63:15 pleads with God to look down from his holy and glorious "habitation" ("lofty throne," NIV) and intervene on behalf of his exiled people. In Hab 3:11 there is a reference to Joshua's long day when the sun and moon stood still "in the heavens" ("in their habitation" KJV; cf. Josh 10:12–13).

The last occurrence is found in Ps 49:14 [H 15], a passage that bemoans the fate of fools. Even the wealthy ones are destined for the grave "far from their princely mansions" (NIV) or "so that they have no habitation" (NASB).

Each of these references has some link with "splendor" or "majesty" ane the basic meaning of the word may be "eminence" (cf. Speiser, *Genesis* in AB, p. 231). One of the titles for Baal in the Ugaritic corpus is *zbl b'l arṣ* "Prince Lord of Earth." The god of Ekron mentioned in II Kgs 1:2–6, Baal-zebub, "Lord of flies," may be an intentional perversion of "Baal-zebul" (cf. *z^e^bûb*).

z^e^bûlûn. ***Zebulun.*** The name of the sixth son of Leah and the tenth son of Jacob. "Zebulun" may mean "honor" (cf. Gen 30:19, 20) and has been related to Akkadian *zubullû*, "bridegroom's gift" by Speiser (*Genesis*, in AB, p. 231; also cf. *z^e^būl*).

The tribe of Zebulun was the fourth largest both at the start and the conclusion of the wilderness wanderings (Num 1:31; 26:26). In lists of the twelve tribes, Zebulun normally followed Issachar (Num 1:9; 2:7), but in the blessing of Moses, Zebulun is named first (Deut 33:18). Zebulun joined the disgraced Reuben in pronouncing the curses from Mount Ebal (Deut 27:13).

Zebulun's tribal allotment is given in Josh 19:10–16. Her territory lay on the northern edge of the Jezreel Valley, north of Manasseh and Issachar and south of Asher and Naphtali. Both Gen 49:13 and Deut 33:19 link Zebulun with the seashore. Perhaps this refers primarily to the trade between the Mediterranean and the Sea of Galilee which enriched Zebulun.

Zebulun was one of the tribes which failed to drive out the Canaanites (Jud 1:30) but her warriors were highly praised for their courageous role in the victories over Sisera and the Canaanites (Jud 4:6, 10; 5:14, 18) and later the Midianites (Jud 6:35; cf. Ps 68:27 [H 28]). When David became king over all Israel, Zebulun sent him a large contingent of 50,000 troops and abundant supplies (I Chr 12:33 [H 34], 40 [H 4]). During Hezekiah's reign, some from Zebulun accepted his invitation to celebrate the Passover in Jerusalem (II Chr 30:10–19). The tribe is also named with Naphtali as recipients of the honor to come upon Galilee at the advent of Christ (Isa 9:1 [H 8:23]).

H.W.

זָג (zāg). See no. 527a.
זֵד (zēd). See no. 547a.
זָדוֹן (zādôn). See no. 547b.

527 זוג (zwg), זיג (zyg). **Assumed root of the following.**
527a זָג (zāg). ***Name of some insignificant product of the vine, forbidden to Nazirites*** (Num 6:4).

528 זֶה (zeh), זֹאת (zō't) ***this, such.***

The regular demonstrative pronoun, sometimes used as a collective (Lev 11:4; Jud 20:16). The singular form can be used with numerals, as in "these ten times" (Num 14:22; cf. "these many years" in Zech 7:3). When it modifies a noun in the *nomen rectum* it normally follows the other adjectives. If it precedes an adjective, as in Hag 2:9, *habbayit hazzeh ha'aḥărôn,* the final adjective, "the latter," most likely modifies the *nomen regens.* Hence, the verse should probably be translated "the latter glory of this house" rather than "the glory of this latter house." Rarely *zeh* is used with proper nouns, especially in the phrase "this Jordan" (Gen 32:10 [H 11]; Deut 3:27; Josh 1:2, 11). "This Lebanon" also occurs (Josh 1:4).

zeh is frequently used independently to mean "this one" or "this man" in a way that directs pointed attention to the individual. In Gen 5:29 Noah is singled out as "this one" who "shall give us rest," and in Isa 66:2 the Lord says, "To this one I will look, to him who is humble and contrite of spirit." Micah 5:5 [H 4] emphatically declares, "And this One [God] will be our peace."

Several times the individual in question is referred to in a sarcastic or contemptuous manner. When Saul was anointed king, the skeptics said, "How shall this man save us?" (I Sam 10:27). The Philistine Achish complained to his men that he already had enough madmen, when "this one" (David) pretended to be insane to escape from the Philistines (I Sam 21:15 [H 16]). David himself referred to stingy Nabal as "this fellow" whose property David had apparently guarded in vain (I Sam 25:21).

In Jud 5:5 and Ps 68:8 [H 9] God is spoken of as "*zeh Sînāy*" "the One of Sinai," a usage similar to Arabic *ḏû* "the owner of" or "the one belonging to." God had revealed himself to Israel in mighty power at Mount Sinai, so when he took action again on behalf of his people, they thought of him in terms of his revelation par excellence at Sinai (cf. the rare Hebrew demonstrative and relative *zû*).

The derogatory use of *zeh* is also seen in verses where it may be translated "such." When Bildad describes the calamities that strike the ungodly, he says, "Surely such are the dwellings of the wicked" (Job 18:21). Job himself laments the frailty of man and asks God, "Do you fix your eye on such a one?" (Job 14:3).

zeh is also attached enclitically to a variety of interrogative pronouns in order to strengthen them. The Lord emphatically asks, "Where (*'ê zeh*) is the house you will build for me? (Isa 66:1). An all-powerful God can hardly be contained in a temple made by man. Often, this type of question involves strong emotions. Compare Moses' cry to God, "Why didst thou ever (*lāmmâ zeh*) send me? (Ex 5:22), or the complaint of the Israelites to Moses, "Why did we ever leave Egypt? (Num 11:20). In these examples, "ever" is an attempt to translate *zeh.*

zeh (or its feminine *zō't*) is also used in combination with prepositions. For example, *bāzō't* can mean "in spite of this" (Lev 26:27; Ps 27:3). The form *bāzeh* means "here" in Gen 38:21–22 and Num 23:1, probably elliptical for "in this place."

H.W.

529 זהב (zhb). **Assumed root of the following.**
529a †זָהָב (zāhāb) ***gold.***

This is the most basic of several Hebrew words for gold, though it is modified by a number of adjectives that refer to different kinds of gold. Most references to gold relate to the tabernacle or to Solomon's temple and palace.

"Good" gold is mentioned in connection with the garden of Eden in Gen 2:12. Pure gold (*ṭāhôr*) appears several times in Exodus. The ark of the covenant was overlaid with pure gold, and a gold molding was around it (Ex 25:11). The lampstand was hammered (*miqshâ*) out of pure gold with its base, shaft and branches (37:17, 22). The cherubim were also hammered out of gold (25:18). Gold thread was used for the high priest's ephod (Ex 28:6).

In the Solomonic era pure gold is called *sāgûr,* perhaps cognate to Akkadian *sakru.* It may have been gold hammered into thin foil for gilding. The holy of holies was overlaid with this pure gold (I Kgs 6:20) and the lampstands were made out of the same gold (I Kgs 7:49). The vessels Solomon used in the house of Lebanon were of pure gold also (I Kgs 10:21 = II Chr 9:20). Solomon made shields out of beaten gold (*shaḥûṭ*), alloyed with another metal to make them harder (I Kgs 10:16). His throne of ivory was overlaid with "refined gold" (*mûpāz,* I Kgs 10:18). Much gold was brought from the region of Ophir during Solomon's fabulous reign (I Kgs 9:28; cf. Ps 45:9 [H 10]).

The Israelites were warned not to make idols of silver or gold, but the worship of the golden calf was a constant problem (Ex 32:3–4; I Kgs 12:28). When God plagued the Philistines for their possession of the ark of the covenant, they made 5 golden hemorrhoids or ulcer models (cf. 'ōpel) and 5 golden mice as a guilt offering to the Lord (I Sam 6:4).

In the Psalms the word of God is regarded as more desirable than gold (Ps 19:10 [H 11]), and his law is better than thousands of pieces of gold and silver (119:72, 127). God himself is described as coming "in golden splendor" in Job 37:22.

H.W.

530 *זָהַם (*zāham*) ***be foul, loathsome.*** Occurs only in the Piel (Job 33:20).

531 *זָהַר (*zāhar*) ***I, shine, send out light.*** (ASV and RSV similar.)

Derivative

531a זֹהַר (*zōhar*) ***shining, brightness.***

Close parallels occur in Aramaic and Arabic. It is used only once in the OT (Hiphil stem) and is employed to say that wise people, who turn many to righteousness, "shall shine" like the brightness of heaven (Dan 12:3).

L.J.W.

532 *זָהַר (*zāhar*) ***II, teach, warn, admonish.*** (ASV and RSV similar.)

Both BDB and KB hold this to be a second root, while older editions of Gesenius take the meaning here represented as a secondary meaning of the same root, and related to the first meaning. The root is used twenty-one times, all in the Hiphil and Niphal stems, the latter being the passive of the former.

The meaning "teach" is probably basic to the root, but is not used frequently. A clear example occurs when Jethro, Moses' father-in-law, advises Moses to limit himself to such a duty as to "teach" the people the laws (Ex 18:20). The most frequent meaning is "warn," which is used fourteen times in two chapters alone, Ezk 3 and 33, the classic portions dealing with the responsibility of watchmen to warn people under their care (cf 3:17–21; 33:3–9). The meaning "admonish" is illustrated in the proverbial statement that it is better to be a poor, wise child than an old, foolish king, who will no longer "be admonished" (Eccl 4:13).

The Zohar is the name of the influential mystical commentary on the Pentateuch written by Moses Leon in the 13th Century A.D.

L.J.W.

533 זִו (*ziw*) ***name of the second month, apparently in the Canaanite system.*** For other names of months, see no. 613b.

זוּ (*zû*), זֹו (*zô*). See no. 528.

534 זוּב (*zûb*) ***flow, gush, issue, discharge.*** (ASV and RSV similar, except that RSV uses "discharge" in place of "issue.")

Derivative

534a זוֹב (*zôb*) ***issue, discharge.***

The basic idea is a movement of liquid, flowing from one location to another. The root is used only in the Qal stem. It occurs fifty-four times, including both the verb and noun.

The word usually occurs in one of three contexts. 1. The movement of water in a stream. Water is said to have "gushed" forth from the rock struck by Moses in the wilderness (Ps 70:20; cf. Ps 105:41; Isa 48:21).

2. A characteristic description of Palestine: it is said to be "flowing" with milk and honey. This phrase occurs many times in the OT (e.g. Ex 3:8, 17; 13:5; 33:3; Deut 6:3; 11:9, etc.).

3. A discharge, pathological or normal, from the genito-urinary tract. With three exceptions, Lev 22:4; Num 5:2; II Sam 3:29, all usages appear in Lev 15. It is used in verses 2–15, 32–33 (verb eleven times, noun seven) to refer to a diseased "discharge" from a man (possibly including diarrhea); in verses 19–24 (verb once, noun once) to the discharge of a woman's menstrual period; and in verses 25–30 (verb once, noun five times) to an unnatural discharge of blood from a woman.

L.J.W.

זוּד (*zûd*). See no. 547.

534 זוה (*zwh*). **Assumed root of the following.**

534a זָוִית (*zāwît*) ***corner*** (Ps 144:12; Zech 9:15; Lev 1:5).

534b מָזוּ (*māzû*) ***garner*** (Ps 144:13).

535 זוז (*zwz*) **I. Assumed root of the following.**

535a †זִיז (*zîz*) ***moving things.***

535b †מְזוּזָה (*m^e^zûzâ*) ***doorpost, gatepost.***

zîz. ***Moving things, wild beasts.*** This noun is used three times, twice to mean "moving things" (AV, ASV "wild beasts"; RSV "all that moves") of the field (Ps 50:11; 80:13 [H 14]), and derivation from the above root is probable. The third occurrence, in Isa 66:11, means "abundance" (so KJV, ASV, and RSV), and likely comes from another unused root (so BDB; although KB favors a different unused root, yielding the translation, "breast").

m^e^zûzâ. ***Doorpost, gatepost.*** A noun used eighteen times. Its relation to the above root is uncertain. The word is used once for the gateposts of Gaza, which Samson carried away together with the gate (Jud 16:3). It is used once for the gateposts of the tabernacle court, beside which apparently was a customary seat for the aged Eli (I Sam 1:9). It is also used for the gateposts of the Temple, both those built by Solomon (I Kgs 6:31, 33) and those described by Ezekiel (41:21).

The Israelites applied blood to the two *m^ezûzîm* of their homes at the time of their deliverance from Egypt (Ex 12:7, 22–23). Thus they saved their firstborn from death (Ex 12:29).

Bibliography: Thornes, D. W., "The meaning of zîz in Ps 80:13," Exp T 76: 385.

L.J.W.

536 זוז (*zwz*) **II. Assumed root of the following.**

536a זִיז (*zîz*) ***abundance, fulness*** (Isa 66:11, only).

זָוִית (*zāwît*). See no. 534a.

537 זול (*zwl*) **I. Assumed root of the following.**

537a †זוּלָה (*zûlâ*) a noun, probably from the unused root, *zûl* ***"remove,"*** used as a preposition and conjunction, meaning "***except, only, save that,***" stemming from the basic idea of "removal."

It occurs sixteen times, once as a conjunction (Josh 11:13) and often as a preposition (Deut 1:36; Ps 18:31 [H 32]; Isa 45:21, etc.).

L.J.W.

538 זול (*zûl*) ***II, lavish*** (Isa 46:6, only).

539 *זון (*zûn*) ***feed.*** This verb occurs only once, in the Hophal (Jer 5:8).

Derivative

539a מָזוֹן (*māzôn*) ***food, sustenance*** (Gen 45:23; II Chr 11:23).

540 זוע (*zûa'*) ***tremble, quiver, be in terror.*** (KJV "vex").

Derivatives

540a †זְוָעָה (*z^ewā'â*), זַעֲוָה (*za'ăwâ*) ***horror.***

Contextual evidence does not permit the assigning of a dogmatic or precise meaning to this term and its derivatives; but ideas such as "trembling" and "fear" are possible in all cases. It apparently describes the tremors of the jaw in old age (Eccl 12:3). It refers to Mordecai's failure to "tremble" before Haman (Est 5:9) though some less specific, courteous movements characteristic of near eastern manners may there be denoted. A causative form (Pilpel) is translated as "making to tremble" (Hab 2:7).

z^ewā'â, za'ăwâ. ***Horror*** (KJV "vexation, removing"). A term used to describe God's people as a result of God's judgment. The severity and extent of God's judgment is such that they become a "horror" to the observing nations (Deut 28:25; Jer 15:4; 34:17). In other contexts the extent of judgment and horror are amplified by derision (II Chr 29:8) and being an object of plunder (Ezk 23:46).

A.B.

541 זור (*zûr*) ***I, be a stranger.*** (ASV and RSV similar.)

KB gives the basic meaning as "turn aside." BDB cites the similar but apparently not related root *sur* that has this meaning.

Apart from its participial use, the word appears only four times in Qal, twice in Niphal, and once in Hophal. Typical is Job 19:13, where Job states that his former friends have become "estranged" from him. The Niphals and Hophals are passive.

zûr is principally used in the participial form, *zār,* appearing sixty-nine times. It carries the force of a noun, and is so listed by KB. It is used for some action strange to the law (Lev 10:1), and for one who is a stranger to another household (Deut 25:5), to another person (Prov 14:10), and to another land (Hos 7:9). The basic thought is of non-acquaintance or non-relatedness. The feminine form, "The Strange Woman," often in Prov is the adulteress.

Bibliography: Sniders, L. A., "The Meaning of *zr* in the Old Testament," OTS 10: 1–154.

L.J.W.

542 זור (*zûr*) ***II, be loathsome.***

Derivative

542a זָרָא (*zārā'*) ***loathesome thing.***

This verb is used only once (Job 19:17), but is taken by BDB, KB and some modern versions to come from a root different from *zûr* I "be a stranger" because the Arabic cognate is spelled with *d* instead of *z* as is the case with the Arabic cognate of *zûr* I.

543 זור (*zûr*) ***III, press down and out.*** (ASV, RSV similar.)

Derivatives

543a †זֵר (*zēr*) ***circlet, border.***
543b זַרְזִיר (*zarzîr*) ***girded, alert.***
543c מָזוֹר (*māzôr*) ***wound.***

The root appears only four times, all in Qal. Gideon "thrust together" (pressed) the test fleece, to see if it contained water (Jud 6:38).

zēr. ***Circlet, molding, crown.*** The basic idea seems to be of something around the edge of a central body, as though pressed out from it. The word is used ten times in the OT, each in reference to the "crown" (AV, ASV) or "molding" (RSV) around the Ark (Ex 25:11), the table of showbread (Ex 25:24–25), and the altar of incense (Ex 30:3–4). It is not used for a king's crown.

L.J.W.

544 *זָחַח (*zāḥaḥ*) ***remove, displace.*** Occurs only in the Niphal (Ex 28:28; 39:21).

545 זָחַל (*zāḥal*) ***I, shrink back, crawl away*** (Deut 32:24; Mic 7:17).

546 זָחַל (*zāḥal*) ***II, fear, be afraid*** (Job 32:6, only).

547 זִיד (*zîd*) זוּד (*zûd*) ***boil, act proudly, presumptously, rebelliously.*** (ASV and RSV similar.)

Derivatives

547a †זֵד (*zēd*) ***proud, arrogant.***
547b †זָדוֹן (*zādôn*) ***pride, insolence.***
547c †זֵידוֹן (*zêdôn*) ***proud, raging.***
547d †נָזִיד (*nāzîd*) ***boiled food, pottage.***

Because the root form does not appear in the OT, its spelling, whether with middle yod or waw, is not certain. The verb appears only in the Qal and Hiphil stems, with no clear distinction in meaning between them. In the sphere of the physical, it means "to boil"; in the sphere of personality, "to act in a proud manner." With its derivatives, the word appears a total of forty times in the OT.

The verb is used only once in reference to boiling (Gen 25:27–34). The text states that Jacob "boiled" (KJV "sod") pottage (v. 29).

The verb form is used eight times in reference to the personality, and three of the derivatives are used only in that connection. The basic idea is pride, a sense of self-importance, which often is exaggerated to include defiance and even rebelliousness. For instance, in Prov 11:2, the "proud" person is set over against the humble (cf. Prov 13:10). A similar use is found in Jer 49:16; 50:31–32; Ezk 7:10, with the added implication that God is strongly opposed to such pride.

zîd is frequently used to refer to three specific aspects of pride. One is presumption. Because a person is proud he presumes too much in his favor, especially in the sense of authority. For instance, the false prophet was one who presumed to speak in the name of God, assuming authority to do so, without having been called (Deut 18:20; cf. v. 22 for use of the noun derivative). False gods, too, are spoken of as presuming authority for themselves (Ex 18:11); and Babylon is said to have claimed too much for herself as against the Holy One of Israel (Jer 50:29). Egyptians assumed the same in subjecting the Israelites to bondage (Neh 9:10).

The second aspect is rebellion or disobedience. Because the person is proud he asserts his oan will to the point of rebelling against one in authority over him. The Israelites so asserted themselves against God when they chose to fight the Canaanites, even though God told them not to do so (Deut 1:43). The same thought is contained in Neh 9:16, 29. Eliab, David's older brother, accused him of having pride in coming to the Philistine battle scene (I Sam 17:28, where *zādôn* is used with the sense of *hybris*).

The third, closely related to the second, carries the additional element of willful decision. If a person so asserted himself and killed his neighbor, his own life was required as punishment. If the slaying was unintentional, however, a place of refuge was available for him (Ex 21:14). Indeed, if a person willfully disobeyed the priest, whether murder was involved or not, he had to die (Deut 17:12–13, where both *zîd* and *zādôn* appear). This seems to explain David's distinction between "hidden" (KJV "secret") and "presumptuous" sins (Ps 19:12–13 [H 13–14]). He prays that he may be cleansed from the "hidden," thus admitting his guilt in that respect; but asks that he may be kept from the "presumptuous."

zēd. ***Proud, arrogant, presumptous.*** An adjective, which refers twelve times to people and once to sins.

zādôn. ***Pride, insolence.*** A noun used eleven times. The adjective and noun forms of *zîd* are used in contexts having pride in view as opposed to God, which is a major sin. Persons so characterized are parallelled with those who "work wickedness" and "tempt God" (Mal 3:15 [H 13]), and with "all who do wickedly." As a result, they will be burned like stubble in the day of God's impending punishment (Mal 4:1 [H 3:19]). Frequently, such people are depicted as opposing those who try to do the will of God (Ps 19:14; Ps 119:51, 69, 78, 122; Jer 43:2).

zêdôn. ***Proud, raging.*** The one instance of this adjectival form refers figuratively to "proud" (RSV "raging") water, which represents overwhelming trouble (Ps 124:5). The thought seems to be of power asserted against a person which brings him to the point of death.

nāzîd. ***Boiled food, pottage.*** A noun, used six times. All six usages refer to "pottage" or boiled food (Gen 25:29, 34). Three are used of boiled food which, having become poisoned by poisonous ingredients mistakenly added, had to be made edible by Elisha's miracle (II Kgs 4:38–41). The sixth employment is by Haggai (2:12), who uses it to designate a kind of food, along with bread, wine, oil, and meat.

L.J.W.

זֵידוֹן (*zêdôn*). See no. 547c.
זִיז (*zîz*). See no. 535a, 536a.
זִיקָה (*zîqâ*). See no. 573.
זֵירוֹן (*zêrôn*). See no. 582d.

548 זַיִת (*zayit*) ***olive tree, olive*** (derivation uncertain)

The olive was and is a common and valuable tree in the Near East, famous for its fruit, oil and wood. The oil especially was a staple, being used in diet as shortening (Lev 2:4–6), in lamps for light (Ex 27:20) and in ritual for anointing (Ex 29:7). Kings and priests were anointed with olive oil. Elijah anointed Elisha to succeed him as a prophet. Oil was used also medicinally and as a perfume (Ps 104:15; Ezk 16:9). The practice of anointing kings is rarely attested outside of Israel, but deVaux cites it for Hittite kings (AI p. 104). Anointing of kings is rather clearly a symbol of endowment with the Spirit of God (I Sam 10:1, 10; 16:13). Such a symbol would also fit well the anointing of priests (which deVaux puts quite late because of his views on the P document, "Everyone admits that all these texts were edited after the Exile" [id. p. 105]!). The seven-branched lampstand with its oil-fed lamps is also interpreted as symbolizing the Spirit of God (Zech 4:2–6). It is possible that the symbolism of oil for spirit was not difficult for the ancient Hebrew because daily he observed the oil of his lamps disappearing into the air of his room. And the Hebrew word for "wind" and "spirit" is the same. It is obvious that the NT word Messiah—Christ derives from the OT word for the anointed king, also messiah. But it should be noted that the OT uses the word "messiah" for the expected Figure quite sparingly. Instead, it speaks of him usually as the Shoot of David, the Son of David, the Tabernacle of David, the Branch of David, the Branch, or just David (Ezk 34:23; 37:24). This usage is reflected also in the DSS in The Messianic King and the Florilegium (Gaster, T. H. *The Dead Sea Scriptures*, rev. ed. Doubleday, 1964, pp. 334, 338). But in Ps 2:2 and Dan 9:25, 26 and possibly in a few other Pss the royal title becomes a title of great David's greater Son which the NT and some other pre-Christian literature pick up and use extensively. See further *mashîaḥ*.

Bibliography: Harris, R. L., "Messianic Promises in the OT," in Buswell, J. O., *A Systematic Theology of the Christian Religion*, II, Zondervan, 1963, pp. 543–51. AI, pp. 102–106.

R.L.H.

זַךְ (*zak*). See no. 550a.
זְכוֹכִית (*zᵉkôkît*). See no. 550b.
זָכוּר (*zākûr*). See no. 551f.

549 זָכָה (*zākâ*) ***be clear, clean, pure.***

Cognate of *zākak* and Akkadian *zakû*. Used only in poetry and always in a moral sense. The Piel means "to make or keep clean, pure," the Hithpael, "to make oneself clean" (only in Isa 1:16).

The term appears twice in Job (15:14; 25:4), and both times Job's comforters are asking how a man can be pure in the sight of God. In each verse *zākâ* is parallel to *ṣādaq* "be righteous." A similar question appears in Prov 20:9 where the admission is made that no one has kept his heart pure and sinless. Those who walk in accord with God's word can live pure lives, however (Ps 119:9). The psalmist also notes that at times the wicked appear to be happier and more prosperous than the one who keeps his heart pure (73:13), but in the end the wicked are ruined. In Isa 1:16 God warns the people of Judah that they must wash and make themselves clean or face severe judgment.

Twice the verb is used of God. In Ps 51:4 [H 6] David admits that God was "justified" when he judged David for his sin with Bathsheba. The interpretation of Mic 6:11 is difficult. Is God asking if he should "justify wicked scales" (NASB) or "acquit a man" (RSV, NIV) who uses dishonest scales? The thought seems to be that God will not "declare pure" such a sinner.

H.W.

550 זָכַךְ (*zākak*) ***be bright clean, pure.***

Derivatives

550a זַךְ (*zak*) ***pure, clean.*** Used of olive oil and incense in Ex and Lev, while in Job and Prov it is used metaphorically, only.

550b זְכוֹכִית (*zᵉkôkît*) ***glass*** (Job 28:17).

zākak is probably a by-form of *zākâ*, which sometimes occurs in close proximity to *zākak* (Job 15:14–15; 25:4–5). Both verbs are also used parallel with *rāḥaṣ* "to wash" (cf. Job 9:30, Isa 1:16).

The references in the Pentateuch deal with the tabernacle. The olive oil for the lamps in the holy place had to be pure, and these lamps were kept burning continually, i.e. every night (Ex 27:20; 30:7–8, NIV, Lev 24:2). Exodus 30:34 mentions that pure frankincense was combined with fragrant spices to make a special blend of incense. The same quality of frankincense was placed with each row of loaves on the table of showbread in the holy place (Lev 24:7).

Job's miserable comforters deny that he is pure and upright (Job 8:6), though Elihu reminds Job that he seems to feel that he is "pure and without sin" (33:9). Twice, man's status is compared with nature. According to Job 15:15 and 25:5 not even the heavens or the stars are pure in God's eyes, so how can man claim to be flawless? Yet, Lam 4:7 states that prior to the siege of Jerusalem her princes were "purer" (KJV, RSV, NASB) or "brighter" (NIV) than snow and "whiter than milk." The description of their diseased and shriveled bodies in v. 8 may indicate that the "whiteness" and "purity" related to strong and healthy bodies rather than to their moral and spiritual condition.

Several passages in Prov relate purity to conduct. A man may think that his ways are "innocent" (NIV) or "pure" (RSV), but the Lord examines the motives (16:2). In contrast to the deceit of the wicked, the behavior of the "pure" (RSV) or "innocent" (NIV) is right (21:8). Even a child can demonstrate a godly character by conduct that is pure and right (20:11).

In Job 11:4 Zophar questions Job's claim that his "beliefs" or "teachings" are pure or flawless, making him pure in God's sight. Job protests his own innocence in in 16:17, for he has not engaged in violence and his prayer was pure.

H.W.

551 זָכַר (*zākar*) ***think (about), meditate (upon), pay attention (to); remember, recollect; mention, declare, recite, proclaim, invoke, commemorate, accuse, confess.***

Derivatives

551a †זֵכֶר (*zēker*) ***remembrance.***
551b †זִכָּרוֹן (*zikkārôn*) ***memorial.***
551c †זְכַרְיָהוּ (*zᵉkaryāhû*) זְכַרְיָה (*zᵉkaryâ*) ***Zechariah.***
551d †אַזְכָּרָה (*'azkārâ*) ***memorial portion.***
551e †זָכָר (*zākār*) ***male.***
551f †זָכוּר (*zākûr*) ***male.***

There are three groups of meanings: 1) for completely inward mental acts such as "remembering" or "paying attention to," 2) for such inward mental acts accompanied by appropriate external acts, and 3) for forms of audible speaking with such meanings as "recite" or "invoke." Cognate evidence indicates that the third group of meanings is closest to the verb's root meaning. This range of meanings shows the same blending or overlapping between mental states and external acts seen also in other Hebrew terms (e.g. Hebrew *shāma'* "to hear").

Most examples of the Qal of *zākar* refer to inner mental acts, either with or without reference to concomitant external acts. Examples of internal mental acts are the Jews' recollection of Jerusalem (Ps 137:1) and their remembrance that they had been slaves (Deut 5:15). "Remembering" is contrasted with "forgetting" (Ps 74:22–23). "Meditating" or "thinking about" is likely the issue when Job "meditates" upon the well-being of the wicked (Job 21:6–7) and when the Psalmist "meditates" upon God (Ps 63:6 [H 7]). When God is challenged to "remember" the meaning is better taken as "pay attention to" since nothing ever escapes God's omniscience (Ps 89:47 [H 48]). It is frequently difficult to decide which of the above meanings best fits a particular passage.

Numerous passages add to the above meanings the additional implication of taking appropriate action. God's remembrance of his covenant results in delivering his people (Ex 2:24) or in preserving them (Lev 26:44–45). Conversely, remembering sin may be tantamount to withholding favor (Hos 7:1–2). Remembering Hezekiah's past faithfulness resulted in healing (II Kgs 20:3), and remembering Noah was to make the waters to subside (Gen 8:1). For God not to remember iniquity was to forgive and to withhold further judgment (Ps 79:8–9).

For men also "remembering" results in action. "Remembering" may imply repentance (Ezk 6:9) or observing the commandments (Num 15:40) especially that of the Sabbath (Ex 20:8). For the ends of the earth, remembrance is repentance (Ps 22:27 [H 28]). In political relations, not remembering a treaty is to break it (Amos 1:9). (See BDB for a nearly exhaustive list of such usages.) Some such cases are clear examples of distinct causes and effects; but in some other cases the relation between the remembering and the concomitant action is so close that they are virtually identified in the mind of the writer. (Cf. the close relation between "to hear" and "to obey" in biblical Hebrew.)

There are relatively few cases in which Qal forms clearly refer to audible speaking. Audible speech is referred to in Nah 2:6 (RSV "summoned," KJV "recount"). A recitation of mighty men comparable to the recitations of heroes found in Homer is likely. The widow asked for an audible invocation or oath from David for the protection of her remaining son (II Sam 14:11). Jonah's "remembering" in the sea creature's belly could well be taken as an audible "invoking" in prayer (Jon 2:8). If the possibility of meanings such as "recite" or "invoke" is accepted, the "remembering" of God's wonderful works could be a public recitation of those deeds (I Chr 16:12; cf. v. 8: "make known his deeds"; see also Ps 105:5; RSV "remember") and perhaps should be translated as "recite the wonderful works. . . ."

The category of psalms which recall God's great deeds may provide examples of such recitations (Ps 104, 105, 106).

The Hiphil of *zākar* is generally translated in two ways: 1) to "mention," "invoke," or "declare" and 2) "to cause to remember," i.e. the causative of "to remember." For the first group of meanings, the Hiphil designates audible invoking of God's name (Ex 23:13; note "out of your mouth"). It refers to the ritual invoking of the names of false deities (Josh 23:7; note other ritual elements in the context: "swear," "serve," and " bow down"). It expresses Joseph's desire that the chief butler mention him to Pharaoh (Gen 40:14). In Isa 49:1, the contextual parallel, "called," indicates that audible mentioning is related to "named my name." Audible mention of the ark led to Eli's death (I Sam 4:18). Official proclaiming may be thus designated; the RSV correctly translates this term as "proclaim" in Isa 12:4. Psalm 20:7 [H 8] (RSV "boast") refers to a public outcry, though its exact meaning is not clear. The Hiphil participle designates the office of the "Recorder" (II Chr 34:8); this could signify the man who "proclaims" or "makes known" by written records rather than by audible statements.

However, for the second group of meanings, "to cause to remember," there are no indisputable examples. The passages thus translated can be translated as examples of the group of meanings discussed above. The act of remembering desired by Absalom (II Sam 18:18) could easily have been an audible ceremony of filial respect. The small group of passages involving bringing sins to remembrance probably refers to public, legal accusation (I Kgs 17:18; possibly Num 5:15). God, elsewhere, challenges his people to accuse him (Isa 43:26; RSV "put me in remembrance") so that the case may be publicly argued. For the chief butler, this term describes public confession of personal fault (Gen 41:9). "Proclaiming" God's name fits the context of Ps 45:17 (RSV "cause to be celebrated"). Likewise, some public statement (RSV "extol") is proper for Song 1:4. (The exact meaning of the Hiphils in psalm headings—38, 70—remains unclear, though they are usually taken as meaning "to invoke"; cf. I Chr 16:4 where, if the meaning is invoke, it probably refers to the liturgical practice of using such psalms as 38 and 70.) On the basis of the above examples, the present writer concludes that the meaning "to cause to remember" for the Hiphil is dubious.

The Niphal provides the passive for both the Qal and the Hiphil. It expresses "being remembered" (Job 24:20). "Being remembered" may be followed by the appropriate act of "being delivered" (Num 10:9). It is possible that the harlot sang in order "to be noticed" or "to have attention paid to her" (Isa 23:16) as much as "to be remembered." The passive idea "to be invoked" occurs (Hos 2:17 [H 19] RSV, "They shall be mentioned by name no more"; Zech 13:2, RSV "be remembered").

zēker. ***Remembrance, commemoration, invocation, invocation, name*** (RSV "memorial name"). The range of meanings of this noun indicates that it is a general verbal noun for the whole range of meanings of the verb *zākar.* It refers to the mental act of memory; the loss even of the memory of a group expresses the total destruction of the group involved such as the Amalekites (Ex 17:14), the wicked (Job 18:17), or men in general (Eccl 9:5). It may designate the observing of a commemorative feast (Est 9:28). "Noticing" or "paying attention to" fits well the permanent "remembrance" of the righteous (Ps 112:6; "He is not moved, the just is for [God's] attention eternally"—literal translation)

Other contexts deal with various forms of audible or public expression. It refers to God's "invocation" by which God is to be invoked (Ex 3:15; NASB "memorial name"). God's "invocation" serves as a euphemism for the term "God" (Ps 30:4 [H 5]; 97:12; and perhaps Ps 102:12 [H 13]; RSV "name" in all such cases). If the translation "name" is insisted on, it should be understood as "invocation name" rather than "memorial name." Two passages use this term to refer to the "recitation" of God's great deeds, "They shall bubble forth the recitation of your abundant goodness" (Ps 145:7; writer's translation; RSV "pour forth the fame") and "he has made the recitation of his wonderful works" (Ps 111:4; writer's translation; RSV "caused his wonderful works to be remembered").

zikkārôn. ***Memorial, reminder, token, record.*** The *zikkārôn* is an object or act which brings something else to mind or which represents something else. As such it may be a "memorial," a "reminder," a historical "record," or a physical "token" which calls to mind a deity. The Passover feast was a memorial (Ex 12:14) of a great historical event. The Feast of Unleavened Bread was like a reminder between the eyes (Ex 13:9). Korah's censers were a reminder of an important truth (Num 17:5). The "book of records" (Est 6:1; KJV) was a written reminder of Mordecai's deeds, and the maxims (Job 13:12, RSV) of Job's friends, like all proverbs, were reminders of the abstract truths which they expressed. In Isa 57:8, the "token" (RSV "symbol"), which reminded the worshiper of his god, was probably an idol image but the term emphasizes its character as a reminder over its character as a representation. In Eccl 1:11; 2:16 the point is that there are no records or objects to serve as reminders (cf. RSV "remembrance") of the wise man, the fool, things to come, or things past; the reference is not to the mental act of remembering.

z^ekaryâ, z^ekaryāhû. ***Ya or Yahu (i.e. Yahweh) remembered. Zechariah.*** Over twenty people are so named in the OT (see BDB for a complete listing) of whom three will be discussed here.

1) Zechariah, the son of Jehoiada, he priest, who rebuked the religious apostasy of Joash and was consequently martyred in the court of the temple (II Chr 24:20; *c.* 800 B.C.).

2) The teacher who exerted a favorable influence on king Uzziah (II Chr 26:5; *c.* 750 B.C.).

3) Zechariah, the son of Berechiah, the son of Iddo (Zech 1:1, 7) whose ministry of arousing the people to rebuild the temple (*c.* 520 B.C.) and of commenting on the world scene of his day is recorded in the book carrying his name. It is likely that the phrase "son of Iddo" is a clan designation rather than a designation of relatively near paternity. The clan of Iddo is clearly singled out in the restored community (Neh 12:12, 16; note "father's house" = "clan"). It has been conjectured that he was too young for the prophetic office prior to 520 B.C. (NBD) and that he was high priest at that time (JewEnc); but neither conjecture has firm support.

By NT times, a man named Zechariah had become a well-known martyr Mt 23:35; Lk 11:51). The designation "son of Berechiah" indicates that Zechariah, the prophet, is referred to. However, doubts as to the originality of this designation, and the place and manner of Zechariah's death indicate that the prominent martyr could be the son of Jehoiada. Or, the NT martyr may be a man otherwise unknown.

'azkārâ. ***Memorial portion*** (KJV "memorial"). Technical term for that portion of the cereal offering (*minḥâ*, q.v.) which was burned as God's share (Lev 2:2, 9, 16). Its derivation indicates a meaning such as "memorial" or "remembrance." It also refers to the "memorial" which was burned from the shewbread (Lev 24:7). This particular "memorial" refers to the frankincense alone since the bread itself was eaten by the priests rather than being burned (v. 9; see KB for other views).

A.B.

zākār. ***Male, man, man child, mankind*** (ASV similar; RSV translates "man child" by "son" in Isa 66:7, Jer 20:15 and "mankind" by "male" in Lev 18:22; 20:13). The word *zākār* denotes the male of humans or animals. It is used in Gen 1:27 in its basic sense where it occurs with "female" (n^e *qēbâ*) describing the creation of mankind. The word occurs frequently with *n^e qēbâ* denoting the sexes of humans (Gen 5:2; Lev 12:7, etc.) as well as of animals (Gen 7:3, 9, 16, etc.). In short it is used for the male sex when sexual distinctions are in view.

The word is used of males who are participants in the rite of circumcision (Gen 17:10; 34:15; Ex 12:48 etc.) and frequently connotes male persons of the Israelite society who were counted in censuses (Num 1:2; 3:15; Ezra 8:3, etc.).

The word *zākār* occurs in passages prohibiting sexual congress between males (Lev 18:22; 20:13) and is used of the male partner in sexual intercourse (Num 31:18, 35; Jud 21:12). Ezekiel uses the term of male images with which the disobedient Israelites committed idolatrous fornication (16:17). The word is also used of the male sex as incapable of childbearing (Jer 30:6).

Males were the object of slaughter (Gen 34:25; Num 31:7) and the objects of vows to the Lord (Lev 27:3, 7). The word is used of male descendants (Josh 17:2) as well as male infants (Lev 12:2; Jer 20:15).

It also is used for male animals that were used in the rite of sacrifice (Ex 12:5; Lev 1:3, 10; Deut 15:19 etc.).

zākûr. ***Male, men children.*** This word which occurs with suffixes in Hebrew, always refers to males as such. In three occurrences (Ex 23:17-34:23; Deut 16:16) it refers to the participation of male Israelites in the religious feasts and in one occurrence (Deut 20:13) it is used of the male population of any city conquered by the Israelites.

T.E.M.

Bibliography: Blau, J., "Reste des I-Imperfekts von ZKR, Qal," VT 11: 81–86. Childe, Brevard, *Memory and Tradition in Israel*, SCM, 1962. Richardson, TWB, pp. 142–43. THAT, I, pp. 507–17.

זִכָּרוֹן (*zikkārôn*). See no. 551b.
זְכַרְיָהוּ (*z^e karyāhû*). See no. 551c.

552 זלג (*zlg*). **Assumed root of the following.**
552a מַזְלֵג (*mazlēg*) ***the pronged fork, a sacrificial instrument*** (I Sam 2:13).
552b מִזְלָגָה (*mizlāgâ*) ***sacrificial implement belonging to altar in tabernacle*** (Ex 27:3) ***and temple*** (I Chr 28:17).

זַלְזַל (*zalzal*). See no. 553a.

553 זָלַל (*zālal*) ***I, shake, quake.*** (ASV and RSV use "quake," whereas KJV uses "flow down," taking the word as coming from another root, *nāzal* ("to flow down") in the three places where it appears.

Derivative

553a זַלְזַל (*zalzal*) ***(quivering) tendrils.***

The three uses of the word refer to the quaking of a mountain (Jud 5:5; Isa 64:1 [H 63:19; 64:2]).

BDB and KB agree that *zālal* is the root of the word. KB classify the two roots *zālal* as one.

L.J.W.

554 זָלַל (*zālal*) ***II, be light, worthless, make light of, squander, be a glutton, be vile.*** (ASV and RSV translate similarly, except that "be a glutton" is used more consistently.)

Derivative

554a †זֻלּוּת (*zûllût*) ***worthlessness.***

The word is used twice intransitively, meaning "worthless, insignificant." As such it is contrasted with *yāqār* "precious," in Jer 15:19. It is used with a transitive meaning four times, to mean "make light of" something, so that the object comes to be squandered. These times are thought to refer to a gluttonous person (Deut 21:20; Prov 23:20–21; 28:7). Only in the second passage is food mentioned. It is possible that the reference is not to the amount of food eaten (i.e. gluttony) but to the manner of banqueting (KJV "riotous eaters of flesh"). The general condemnation of gluttony as a sin rests largely upon the interpretation of this word in these few places. It is probable that in Deut 21:20 the capital crime referred to is a vileness beyond gluttony. If this is the root rather than *zûl* employed in Lam 1:8 (so BDB), then it is used once in the Hiphil, meaning "make light of" in the sense of "despise."

zûllût. ***Worthlessness, vileness.*** This noun is used once and means "vileness," that which is exalted among men when the wicked prowl about (Ps 12:8 [H 9]).

L.J.W.

555 זלעף (*zl'p*). **Assumed root of the following.**

555a זַלְעָפָה (*zal'āpâ*) ***raging heat*** (e.g. Ps 119:53; Lam 5:10).

זֻלּוּת (*zûllût*). See no. 554a.
זִמָּה (*zimmâ*). See no. 556b.
זְמוֹרָה (*z^e môrâ*). See no. 559b.
זָמִיר (*zāmîr*). See nos. 558b, 559a.

556 זָמַם (*zāmam*) ***purpose, devise, consider.***

Derivatives

556a זָמָם (*zāmām*) ***plan, device (bad sense,*** Ps 140:9).
556b זִמָּה (*zimmâ*) ***plan, device, wickedness.*** Used in a negative sense everywhere except Job 17:11.
556c †מְזִמָּה (*m^e zimmâ*) ***purpose, plot.***

zāmam is found only in the Qal stem. It is used mainly of the Lord carrying out his purposes in judgment against wicked nations or of wicked men who devise schemes against God and the righteous.

Outside of Zech 1:6 and 8:14 and Job 42:2 the references to both the verb and noun where God is the subject occur in the writings of Jeremiah. The passages are divided between God's purpose in punishing Israel (Jer 4:28; 23:20; 30:24; Lam 2:17; Zech 1:6) and in judging Babylon (Jer 51:11–12), the instrument, ironically, he used to punish Israel! For both nations, God's purpose involved severe destruction. Zechariah 8:14–15 contrasts God's purpose to do harm with His new purpose to do good to Jerusalem. According to Job 42:2, no purpose of God can be thwarted.

When referring to men, both the verb and noun usually speak of evil plans and schemes. In Gen 11:6 the extent of human scheming is seen in the plan to build the tower of Babel. The only other occurrence in the Pentateuch is in Deut 19:19, where a false witness earns the punishment he had intended another to receive. In Psalms and Proverbs the wicked plot against the righteous man, gnashing at him with their teeth (Ps 37:12) or scheming to kill him (Ps 31:13 [H 14]; cf. Prov 30:32). Pride drives an evil man to persecute the godly partly because in his thinking (*m^e zimmôt*) there is no God (Ps 10:4). Job complains about the thoughts of the comforters who are ruining his reputation (Job 21:27).

Twice, the noun is linked with the verb "to do" (Ps 37:7; Jer 11:15) implying that an "evil deed" may be the meaning intended. Yet the idea may be that the wicked are "carrying out" evil schemes, thus preserving the basic mental frame of reference behind *zāmam*.

In Ps 17:3 occurs the one positive use of the term. There the psalmist purposes that his mouth will not involve him in sin.

The book of Proverbs contains the broadest range of meaning relative to this term. There is a sharp division between the negative concept of "men who devise evil" and the positive notion of "discretion." The former occurs only in conjunction with the nouns "man" (*'îsh*, Prov 12:2; 14:17) and "possessor" (*ba'al*, Prov 24:8), and in each case the plural *m^e zimmôt* is used. A "man of schemes" or "who devises evil" is readily condemned and hated (Prov 12:2; 14:17).

The singular form *m^e zimmâ*, however, receives the consistently positive meaning of "discretion" the five times it appears. This use occurs in Prov 1:4; 5:2; 8:12, where it is linked with "knowledge" and "prudence." In Prov 2:11; 3:21 "discretion," like her sisters, "understanding" and "sound wisdom," guards one's life from harm. Hence, within Proverbs 1–8 "discretion" ranks as one of the key terms for wisdom employed by the author.

The verb occurs only twice, in Prov, once with the normal meaning of "plot" (Prov 30:32), and once in the sense of "consider" (31:16). This latter meaning is found in the epilogue of the book, a poem honoring the woman who exemplifies wisdom at its best. This excellent wife "considers a field and buys it." Instead of spending her time dreaming up wicked schemes, she makes plans that will bring great benefit to her family.

H.W.

557 זָמַן (*zāman*) ***be fixed, appointed*** (of time, Ezra 10:14; Neh 10:35; 13:31).

Derivative

557a זְמָן (*z^{e}mān*) ***appointed time, time.*** (Neh 2:6; Eccl 3:1; Est 9:27).

558 *זָמַר (*zamar*) ***I, sing, sing praise, make music.***

Derivatives

558a †זִמְרָה (*zimrâ*) ***song, music.***
558b †זָמִיר (*zāmîr*) ***song.***
558c †מִזְמוֹר (*mizmôr*) ***psalm.***

zāmar occurs only in the Piel. It is cognate to Akkadian *zamāru* "to sing, play an instrument." It is used only in poetry, almost exclusively in Ps.

The vast majority of occurrences of the verb and its derivatives focus upon praising the Lord. The people of Israel lift their voices and their instruments to praise their God as long as they live (Ps 104:33; 146:2). Several times this praise is directed toward the "name" of the Lord, for the "name" stands for God himself (Ps 66:4; 18:49 [H 50]; 135:3).

The song of praise first occurs in Ex 15:2, where Moses celebrates the victory over the Egyptians at the Red Sea. The verb is used in Jud 5:3, the song of triumph written by Deborah to commemorate the crushing defeat of Sisera and his mighty chariots (cf. Ps 68:4 [H 5]; 32 [H 33]). Music rises from the faithful to praise God for "what he has done" (Ps 9:11 [H 12]), for the "glorious things" or "wonderful acts" he has accomplished (Isa 12:5; Ps 105:2). The Lord's "love and justice" evokes praise in Ps 101:1, and according to Ps 119:54 God's "decrees are the theme of my song" (NIV).

In Isa 24:16 the words of a song are "Glory to the Righteous One." Psalm 47:7 [H 8] notes that since God is the King of all the earth, men are to sing to him a "maskil," a term of uncertain meaning also found in the heading to Ps 45.

A number of terms are found parallel to *zmr*, including *shîr* "to sing" (Jud 5:3; Ps 27:6; 101:1; 104L33) *rānan*, "to shout for joy" (Ps 71:23; 98:4), *yādâ*, "to praise" (Ps 57:9 [H 10]; 33:2), and *hālal*, "to praise" (Ps 149:3). The close relationship between *zmr* and "praise" is reflected in the fact that the Hebrew name for the book of Psalms (which translates the Hebrew *mizmôr*) is "Praises" (*t^{e}hillîm*). When it is parallel to another verb, *zāmar* almost always comes last. In Ps 98:5 the imperative *zamm^{e}rû* and the cognate *zimrâ* begin and end the verse to form a kind of "inclusio."

Sometimes *zāmar* is directly linked with a musical instrument, as is *zimrâ* (see above). The lyre (Ps 71:22), the ten-stringed lyre (Ps 33:2; 144:9), the harp (Ps 98:5) and the tambourine (Ps 149:3) are all used to "make music" in praising the Lord. The parallel line in Ps 149:3 speaks about praising the Lord with dancing. In light of these references, singing may not always be implied when *zāmar* or its cognates occurs.

Two passages refer to songs in a negative sense. In Isa 25:5 the Lord shows his faithfulness to the poor and needy by silencing "the song of the ruthless." In Amos 5:23 the Lord refuses to listen to the songs and music of Israel's festivals, for the nation has abandoned justice and righteousness.

zimrâ. ***Song, music.*** Three times out of seven it is used in connection with either the harp or tambourine (Ps 81:2 [H 3]; 98:5, Amos 5:23). In the song of Moses occurs the well-known line, "The Lord is my strength and song" (Ex 15:2). The whole verse is repeated in Isa 12:2 and Ps 118:14.

zāmîr. ***Song.*** Used in the plural except for Isa 25:5. In II Sam 23:1 David is called "the sweet psalmist of Israel" (KJV, RSV) or "Israel's singer of songs" (NIV).

mizmôr. ***Psalm.*** Appears in fifty-seven psalm headings, usually in conjunction with a name or a title. In thirty-four psalms it follows *lam^{e}naṣṣēaḥ*, "for the director of music," and twenty-three of the same headings also have *l^{e}dāwid*, "of David." Five times it is preceded by *shîr*, "a song," and eight times *shîr* follows (cf. Ps 65 and 66). In Psalm 98:1 *mizmôr* stands alone in the title. For other such musical terms see *selâ*.

H.W.

559 זָמַר (*zāmar*) ***II, trim, prune*** (Lev 25:3–4, Qal; Isa 5:6, Niphal).

Derivatives

559a זָמִיר (*zāmîr*) ***trimming, pruning.*** (Song 2:12, only.)
559b זְמוֹרָה (*z^{e}môrâ*) ***branch, twig, shoot*** (e.g. Num 13:23; Ezk 8:17).
559c מַזְמֵרָה (*mazmērâ*) ***pruning knife.*** (Isa 2:4; 18:5; Mic 4:3).
559d מְזַמֶּרֶת (*m^{e}zammeret*) ***snuffers*** (e.g. II Kgs 25:14; Jer 52:18).

560 זמר (*zmr*) **III. Assumed root of the following.**
560a זִמְרָה (*zimrâ*) ***choice products.*** (Gen 43:11, only). Meaning dubious.

560b זֶמֶר (*zemer*) ***mountain sheep*** (Deut 14:5, only). Meaning dubious.

561 זַן (*zan*) ***kind, sort*** (Ps 144:13; II Chr 16:14). Derivation uncertain.

562 זָנַב (*zānab*) ***cut off.*** Denominative verb.

Parent noun

562a †זָנָב (*zānāb*) ***tail.***

A noun, probably from the unused root, *zānab* (meaning unknown), signifying "tail." It is employed ten times and in some well-known contexts. For instance, Moses was told to take the serpent by the "tail" (Ex 4:4). Samson tied the three hundred foxes in pairs by their "tails" (Jud 15:4). It is used figuratively for the idea "lowest in rank." God warned Israel that, if they did not remain faithful to him the stranger would be the head and Israel only the "tail" (Deut 28:44). It is also used figuratively to mean "end, stump." The two enemy kings besieging Jerusalem were likened to the "tails" (ends, stumps) of firebrands (Isa 7:4). [The usage in Job 40:17 presents a problem if behemoth is a hippopotamus as is often supposed. Is it possible that here the word means appendage in general and may refer to the trunk of an elephant which more appropriately may be likened to a cedar? R.L.H.]

L.J.W.

563 זָנָה (*zānâ*) ***commit fornication, be a harlot, play the harlot.*** (ASV and RSV similar.)

Derivatives

563a †זְנוּנִים (*zᵉnûnîm*) ***fornication.***
563b †זְנוּת (*zᵉnût*) ***fornication.***
563c †תַּזְנוּת (*taznût*) ***fornication.***

KB identify a second root using these consonants, meaning "be angry" (Jud 19:2). Evidence for understanding this one usage to mean "be angry," when "play the harlot" is quite possible, is lacking. Most authorities (BDB included) hold to one root only. The verb appears eighty-nine times in the Qal stem, once in the Pual, and nine times in the Hiphil. Five of the Hiphil instances call for the causative meaning. The basic idea of the word is "to commit illicit intercourse" (especially of women).

This verb is used in both literal and figurative senses. Figuratively, the thought may concern forbidden international intercourse, of one nation (especially Israel) having dealings with other nations. It may also refer to religious intercourse, of Israel worshiping false gods.

The literal meaning is illicit heterosexual intercourse. The word regularly refers to women; it refers only twice to men (Ex 34:16; Num 25:1). The participial form is regularly used to designate the harlot (Gen 34:31). Such persons received hire (Deut 23:19), had identifying marks (Gen 38:15; Prov 7:10; Jer 3:3), had their own houses (Jer 5:7), and were to be shunned (Prov 23:27). Rahab, who hid the spies sent by Joshua, is called by this term. The contention that she was merely an innkeeper is based on finding the root of this participal in *zûn* "to feed," rather than *zānâ;* but for this little evidence exists.

Certain distinctions exist between *zānâ* and the parallel root *nā'ap* "to commit adultery." *nā'ap* commonly refers to men rather than women. *nā'ap* connotes sexual intercourse between a married person and someone other than his/her spouse (Lev 20:10). The two words are set in significant contrast in Hos 4:13–14, where "daughters" are said to "commit whoredom" (ASV and RSV "play the harlot," *zānâ*) and "spouses" to "commit adultery" (*nā'ap*). A few times the woman, with whom the act is done, is definitely identified as married (Lev 20:10; Jer 29:23). Never is the person said to be unmarried. The words are sufficiently parallel, however, that they can be used for the same person (Hos 3:1, 3, concerning Gomer; Ezk 16:32–36, concerning Israel as an unfaithful nation). A third distinction is that *nā'ap* is not used to designate the professional prostitute. A similarity between the two roots is found in the fact that both are used in a figurative as well as a literal sense; and also that, in the figurative, they are employed for the same basic concepts.

zānâ also refers figuratively to Israel as committing national harlotry (Ezk 16:26–28). Tyre (Isa 23:17) and Nineveh (Nah 3:4) are also mentioned in this way. The thought seems to be of having relations with these nations for the sake of political and monetary benefit, although in the case of Nineveh the added element of alluring, deceitful tactics leading on to oppressive dominance is implied.

Still a third figurative meaning is found in Isa 121, where the Israelites' departure from God's approved moral standards is called harlotry.

The three derivatives are used as almost exact synonyms, each being employed both literally and figuratively. The third (*taznût*) is unusual in that it is employed only by Ezekiel, and that in only two chapters: 16 (nine times) and 23 (eleven times). Although Ezekiel uses also the other two derivatives (total of five times), his preference for *taznût* is clear.

Bibliography: Brooks, Beatrice A., "Fertility Cult Functionaries in the Old Testament," JBL 60: 227–53. Gordis, Robert, "Hosea's Marriage and Message: A New Approach," HUCA 25: 9–35. Rabinowitz, Jacob J., "The 'Great Sin' in Ancient Egyptian Marriage Contracts," JNES 18:73. Richardson, TWB, p. 16. Rowley, H. H., "The Marriage of Hosea," BJRL 39: 200–33.

Tushingham, Douglas A., "A Reconsideration of Hosea, Chapters 1–3," JNES 12: 150–59. Wiseman, D. J., "Rahab of Jericho," Tyndale House Bulletin 14: 8–11. TDNT, VI, pp. 584–90.

L.J.W.

זְנוּנִים (*z^e nûnîm*). See no. 563a.
זְנוּת (*z^e nût*). See no. 563b.

564 זָנַח (*zānaḥ*) ***I, reject, spurn, cast off.*** (ASV and RSV similar, except that RSV prefers at times "spurn" or "reject.")

Related to an Arabic root meaning "be remote, repelled," *zanaḥ* carries the basic meaning of strong dislike or disapproval. The word is used sixteen times in the Qal and three in the Hiphil, with no clear distinction in meaning. The Qal is used in Ps 43:2, as the Psalmist cries out to God, "Why dost thou cast me off?" The RSV uses "rejected" in Ps 60:1 [H 3], as David states, "O God, thou hast rejected (KJV "cast off") us." The Hiphil use is employed by David, as he instructs Solomon that, if Solomon should forsake God, then God would "cast (him) off forever" (I Chr 28:9).

L.J.W.

565 זָנַח (*zānaḥ*) ***II, stink, emit stench.*** (ASV and RSV have "become foul"; whereas KJV uses "turn far away," after root I.)

Both BDB and KB understand this as a second root. It is used only once, in the Hiphil, describing the Nile River as made to "stink" in a future day of judgment at the hand of God (Isa 19:6).

Bibliography: Yaron, Reuven, "The Meaning of ZANAḤ," VT 13: 237–39.

L.J.W.

566 *זָנַק (*zānaq*) ***leap.*** This verb occurs only once, in the Piel (Deut 33:22).

זֵעָה (*zē'â*). See no. 857b.
זַעֲוָה (*za'ăwâ*). See no. 540a.
זְעֵיר (*z^e'êr*). See no. 571a.

567 *זָעַךְ (*zā'ak*) ***extinguish.*** Occurs only in Job 17:1 (Niphal).

568 זָעַם (*zā'am*) ***be indignant, express indignation, denounce.*** (ASV and RSV similar.)

Derivative

568a †זַעַם (*za'am*) ***anger, indignation.***

The basic idea is experiencing or expressing intense anger. The word is parallel to *qāṣap,* except that its expression takes a more specific form, especially of denunciation. The word appears eleven times in the Qal stem and once in the Niphal.

The verb is used to indicate both the state of being indignant and the activity giving expression to that state. It is used in reference to man, but more often to God. Isaiah foretells a day when God's "indignation" will be experienced by Israel's enemies (Isa 66:14). In Num 23:7–8, *zā'am* is used in parallel with the verbs *'ārar, nāqab,* and *qābab,* each meaning "to curse," as first Balak, king of Moab, bids Balaam, "Come, curse (*'ārar*) me Jacob, and come, defy (*zā'am*) Israel." Then Balaam replies, "How shall I curse (*nāqab*) whom God hath not cursed (*qābab*)? Or how shall I defy (*zā'am*) whom the Lord hath not defied (*zā'am*)?"

za'am. ***Anger, indignation.*** This noun is used twenty-two times. It is regularly translated "indignation," referring more often to God than to man. *za'am* is used in parallel with *qāṣap,* as Jeremiah states that the earth shall tremble at God's wrath (*qeṣep*), and the nations shall not be able to bear his "indignation" (*zā'am*) (Jer 10:10; cf Ps 102:11).

Bibliography: Brichto, Herbert C., *The Problem of "Curse" in the Hebrew Bible,* in *Journal of Biblical Literature* Monograph Series, Vol. 13, Society of Biblical Literature and Exegesis, 1963, pp. x, 232. Scharbert, Josef, "Fluchen und Segnen im Alten Testament," Bib 39: 1–26.

L.J.W.

569 זָעַף (*zā'ap*) ***fret, be sad, be wroth.***

Derivative

569a †זַעַף (*za'ap*) ***storming, indignation.***
569b זָעֵף (*zā'ēp*) ***out of humor, vexed.***

The root of this verb, according to the Aramaic cognate *z^e'ap* "to storm, rage against," means to storm, blow, or breathe hard. It is so used in Jon 1:15 of the raging sea. KB suggests "be embittered against," "be dejected," BDB adds "be enraged."

A person who storms within himself is enraged. One with an inner storm can be sad, troubled in appearance (Dan 1:10).

The baker and butler had reason to be troubled in heart; their dreams were real but uninterpreted. Uncertainty caused unrest; they fretted and were crestfallen (Gen 40:6). The wise man of Prov, however, points to a far more tragic storm in a man's heart: it is of the fool whose folly brings him into well-deserved ruin resulting in an unreasonable rage in his heart against God (Prov 19:3). The Chronicler (II Chr 26:19) tells of King Uzziah's strength and pride which led him to desecrate the temple and the altar of incense. When rebuked, Uzziah *was wroth* and when he expressed this rage of his heart in the temple sanctuary he was immediately stricken with leprosy (II Chr 26:19).

The biblical testimony is that there is no peace, health, or happiness for the man with a storm in his heart.

zaʿap. The noun is used to describe the state king Asa was in when he was rebuked by the prophet Hanani (II Chr 16:10). Because Asa had relied upon neighboring kings and not upon the Lord, the prophet, sent of the Lord, told him he had done foolishly. To have folly pointed out was to cause a storm in the king's heart. This inner rage led Asa to commit atrocities. He remained hardened, so much so that four years later, when he was diseased, he refused to seek the Lord. This rage of a man's heart is as the roaring of a lion, it is fierce and awesome (Prov 19:12). It is comparable to a sea in a raging storm (Jon 1:15).

The term is used twice of the Lord's attitude. The Assyrians who rejoiced as they ravished Israel, are to see the raging, storming character of God's anger against them (Isa 30:30). Micah says he will endure the Lord's rage brought on by enemies but he is also assured the Lord will bring forth light and deliverance when the storm of his rage is spent.

G.V.G.

570 זָעַק (*zāʿaq*) ***cry, cry out, call.*** (ASV and RSV similar.)

Derivative

570a †זְעָקָה (*zeʿāqâ*) ***cry, outcry.***

The basic meaning of this root is "to cry for help in time of distress." It is used mainly in the Qal, but occurs a few times in the Niphal and Hiphil, where it carries distinctive meanings. It is parallel in meaning to *ṣāʿaq*. The two roots are doubtless mere variants, as is not unusual with such similar sibilants.

In the Qal stem, the word is used almost exclusively in reference to a cry from a disturbed heart, in need of some kind of help. The cry is not in summons of another, but an expression of the need felt. Most frequently, the cry is directed to God. When the Israelites were being invaded annually by the Midianites, they expressed this cry (Jud 6:6–7). Occasionally it is directed to a false deity (Jer 11:12), and once to a king (II Sam 19:29). A few times the word is used for a cry not directed to anyone, but simply as a note of alarm. All the city of Shiloh so cried out when told that the Ark had been captured by the Philistines (I Sam 4:13). The cry may be sounded in behalf of another person (Isa 15:5). It may be in lament at bad news (Jer 47:2); or it may be a cry of protest (Job 31:38). In only one instance is the idea of summons involved, and that is when Jephthah called for Ephraimites to assist him against the Ammonites (Jud 12:2). This is still a cry for help.

The Niphal stem is used six times and always of assembling people together. They are thus considered to be "called ones" (Josh 8:16).

The Hiphil stem occurs seven times, but only once with the causative meaning (Jon 3:7). Four times it carries the idea of assembly, thus corresponding to the Niphal meaning, but in the active mood (II Sam 20:4–5). Once it is used to express an outcry of alarm, much like one of the uses of the Qal, and once simply to get another's attention in order to convey a message (Zech 6:8).

The distinction between *zāʿaq* and *ṣāʿaq* seems to be that *ṣāʿaq* was used earlier. This is only a relative distinction, however, because *zāʿaq* is also found in the Pentateuch, and *ṣāʿaq* also appears in postexilic writings. But a tally of the number of times each occurs, during the early and later periods, supports the general distinction. In writings, which likely were penned no later than the time of the united monarchy, *ṣāʿaq,* in both its verb and noun forms, is found some forty-four times (out of a total seventy-six), while *zāʿaq* appears only thirty-six (out of a total eighty-nine). In postexilic writings, *ṣāʿaq* occurs only twice, while *zāʿaq* appears eight times. In Jeremiah, Ezekiel, and Zechariah, the score is twenty-one to seven in favor of *zāʿaq*.

In meaning, the two roots are very close. Both signify the same basic sense of a cry for help out of a situation of distress. Both show such a cry being voiced to God, to false deities, and to people, although *ṣāʿaq* is used several times for the last, while *zāʿaq* is only once. The Niphal uses of the two are parallel in meaning. Some difference occurs in the Hiphil, in that *ṣāʿaq* appears only once, in one of the meanings of *zāʿaq,* namely of calling together an assembly.

zeʿāqâ. ***Cry, outcry.*** The noun derivative is used eighteen times, and sixteen of them correspond closely to the idea of the Qal stem, i.e. they designate a cry for help in the face of to the idea of the Qal stem, i.e. they designate a cry for help in the face of distress. For instance, the word is used for the cry directed to Nehemiah by Jews who were being oppressed by their wealthy neighbors (Neh 5:6). Mordecai gave this cry when he heard of Haman's plot against the Jews (Est 4:1). *zaʿaq* is also used in an abstract reference to the foolish clamor of a poor ruler (Eccl 9:17), and to the outcry against Sodom that had come to God's notice (Gen 18:20).

L.J.W.

571 זער (*zʿr*). **Assumed root of the following.**
571a זְעֵיר (*zeʿêr*) ***a little.***
571b †מִזְעָר (*mizʿār*) ***a little, a trifle, a few.***

mizʿār. ***Smallness, a little, a few.*** This word occurs only four times, in Isaiah. Three usages are in conjunction with *meʿaṭ* (of the same meaning). Used together, in two instances, they give literally, "a trifle, a little" time, calling for the stressed translation, "a very little while" (Isa 10:25; 29:4). The two other usages concern numbers. In Isa 16:14, for example, where it is employed again with m^{e}*'aṭ*, a literal rendition gives, "a little, small" remnant. Cf. the root *ṣā'ar* of similar meaning. This word may be merely a phonetic variation.

L.J.W.

572 זֶפֶת (*zepet*) **pitch** (Ex 2:3; Isa 34:9).

573 זֵק (*zēq*) ***missile, spark*** (Prov 26:18; Isa 50:11).

זֵק (*zēq*). See no. 577a.
זְקוּנִים (z^e*qûnîm*). See no. 574e.

574 זָקֵן (*zāqēn*) ***be, become old.***

Related Terms

574a †זָקָן (*zāqān*) ***beard, chin.***
574b †זָקֵן (*zāqēn*) ***old.***
574c †זֹקֶן (*zōqen*) ***old age.***
574d †זִקְנָה (*ziqnâ*) ***old age.***
574e †זְקוּנִים (z^e *qûnîm*) ***old age.***

zāqēn is probably a derivative of *zāqān* (beard). It is a stative verb which in the Qal denotes the state of being which follows being young (Ps 37:25). We meet the phrase "old and advanced in years" (Gen 24:1; Josh 13:1; cf. I Sam 17:12) or "old and full of days" (I Chr 23:1). It refers to both men and women. During this period of life prospects of marriage (Ruth 1:12) and childbearing cease (Gen 18:12–13; II Kgs 4:14). Grey hair appears (I Sam 12:2). There is a failing of sight (Gen 27:1; cf. I Sam 3:2; 4:15), metabolism and mobility (I Kgs 1:1, 15), and there is danger of falling (I Sam 4:18). A description of the onset of age in poetic symbols is found in Eccl 12:1–5. Death is an imminent prospect (Gen 19:31; 24:1; 27:1–2; Josh 23:1–2). Leadership must be relinquished (Josh 13:1; I Sam 8:1, 5; I Chr 23:1). Yet one in this state is to be respected (Lev 19:32) and not despised (Prov 23:22).

The Hiphil of the verb denotes the aging of persons (Prov 22:6) and of a tree root (Job 14:8).

Age sixty seems to separate the mature from the aged (Lev 27:1–8), although evidently the Levites retired at fifty (Num 4:3, 23, 30). The Psalmist suggests seventy years as a normal life span and eighty as unusual (Ps 90:10). In the period of the Kings a man of eighty is accounted a man of very great age (II Sam 19:32 [H 33]).

zāqān. ***Beard.*** A masculine noun from the root *zākēn*. Ugaritic *dqn*, Ais WUS No. 782. The chin whiskers of a man (II Sam 20:9) and of a lion (I Sam 17:35) could be seized. To be cleansed, the leper had to shave his beard (Lev 14:9). Israelites and priests (Lev 19:27; 21:5) were forbidden to cut the corners of the beard. In times of distress the beard was plucked (Ezr 9:3) or shaved (Isa 15:2; Jer 41:5; 48:37). Ezekiel was commanded to shave as a symbol of coming destruction of Jerusalem (Ezk 5:1). The odd expression in Ps 133:2 (KJV) does not mean that Aaron's beard went down to the skirts of his garments, but that the anointing oil did.

zāqēn. ***Aged, ancient, ancient man, elder, senator, eldest, old, old man, old woman.*** The LXX renders *presbuteros*. *zāqēn* is an adjective derived from *zāqēn* "to be old," which is a denominative verb from *zāqān* "beard."

zāqēn, used either as an attributive adjective or as a substantive, describes the person (male or female) who, contrasting with the youth (*na'ar;* Gen 19:4; cf. Ps 37:25) has reached the stage in life called old age. The semitism "old and full of years (days)" is sometimes met (Gen 25:8; 35:29; Job 42:17). The normal Hebrew society not only had boys and girls playing in the streets but there were also old men and women leaning on their staffs (Zech 8:4). "Young" and "old" make up the total of society (Ex 10:9; Josh 6:21; II Chr 36:17; Est 3:13).

The old man is to be honored (Lev 19:32; cf. Lam 5: 12). The young wait to speak until the old have spoken (Job 32:4). Their value as advisors (cf. Ezk 7:26) is recognized in the account of Rehoboam's rejecting their counsel in favor of that of the young men (I Kgs 12:6ff.). On the other hand, the advice of the elders saved Jeremiah's life (Jer 26:17). The old man is adorned by his grey hair (Prov 20:29) and his children are his crown (Prov 17:6).

zāqēn as a substantive, usually plural, is a technical term occurring about one hundred times. Only the context can determine whether old men or the ruling body is intended in any particular case. The OT is not clear concerning the age required to qualify one to be a *zāqēn* or details of appointment to this group.

There are elders within a house, e.g. Pharaoh's (Gen 50:7; Ps 105:22) or David's (II Sam 12:17). The ruling body of the Hebrew city as well as of a people like the Moabites and Midianites (Num 22:4, 7) and the Gibeonites (Josh 9:11) were the elders. The institution was known to the Hittites, to Mari, and to the Babylonians from the Hammurabi period onward. Elders and commanders (*śarim*) frequently are combined to make up a governing body. Elders sitting at the gate of the city (Deut 21:19; 22:15; Prov 31:23; Lam 5:14) settled many questions such as disputed virginity (Deut 22:15); ratification of property settlements (Ruth 4:9, 11); and trying of murder cases (Deut 19:12; 21:1ff.; Josh 20:4).

Already in the Pentateuch we encounter the

"elders of Israel" (Ex 3:16; 18:12). They witnessed the striking of the rock (Ex 17:5–6). In the wilderness a group of seventy witnessed the covenant ceremony (Ex 24:1, 9). They adjudicated cases while Moses was on the mountain (Ex 24:14). Elders laid their hands on the head of the sin offering when the whole congregation had sinned (Lev 4:15). They received the spirit at the tent of meeting (Num 11:16, 24–25). Twenty-five elders witnessed the fate of Datham and Abiram (Num 16:25). Ten men made up a deciding body (Ruth 4:2). Elders stood with the judges before the ark at the reading of the law (Josh 8:33; cf. 23:2; 24:1).

The elders of Israel requested a king from Samuel (I Sam 8:4). Even after the establishment of the monarchy, the choice of a king rested with the elders of Israel so that David made a covenant with them before they anointed him at Hebron (II Sam 5:3). Absalom obtained their favor (II Sam 17:4, 15) and David returned to rule after the revolt only with the permission of the "elders of Judah" (II Sam 19:11 [H 12]). They continued as an advisory body to the king in later history (I Kgs 20:7) and retained independent authority (I Kgs 21:8). Josiah summoned them for the reading of the newly discovered law (II Kgs 23:1).

The elders continued to be influential even during the Exile (Jer 29:1; Ezk 8:1; 14:1; 20:1) and in the postexilic community (Ezra 10:8, 14). The role continued in modified forms in the synagogue and in the church. But those who ruled in the community of Qumran were not the "elders."

zōqen. ***Old age.*** A masculine noun derived from the root *zāqan,* (Gen 48:10), it refers to age as a quality. Unlike Moses' (Deut 34:7), Jacob's senility brought failing eyesight.

ziqnâ. ***Old, old age.*** This feminine noun, derived from the root *zākan,* occurs in the absolute and construct states. It is used for the advanced age of Sarah, Solomon, and Asa (Gen 24:36; I Kgs 11:4; 15:23). It represents a time of increasing infirmity to which God's care extends (Ps 71:9, 18; Isa 46:4).

z^e^qûnîm. ***Old age.*** This masculine noun refers to a state of being (Gen 21:2, 7; 37:3; 44:20). In the case of Abraham, it points to the unusualness of Isaac's birth. It explains Jacob's favoritism toward Joseph and Benjamin.

Bibliography: Bornkamm, G., "Presbuteros," in TWNT, VI, pp. 651–83. Evans, Geoffrey, "Ancient Mesopotamian Assemblies," JAOS 78: 1–11. Jacobson, Thorkild, "Primitive Democracy in Ancient Mesopotamia," JNES 2: 159–72. McKenzie, Donald A., "Judicial Procedure at the Town Gate," VT 14: 100–104. McKenzie, John L., "The Elders in the Old Testament," Bib 40: 522–40. Malamat, Abraham, "Kingship and Council in Israel and Sumer," JNES 22: 247–53. Noth, Martin, *The History of Israel,* London: Black, 1958, pp. 107–108. Pedersen, Johannes, *Israel,* vols. I-II, London: Oxford, 1940, pp. 36ff. TDNT, VI, pp. 655–61.

J.P.L.

575 זָקַף (*zāqap*) ***raise up*** (Ps 145:14; 146:8).

576 זָקַק (*zāqaq*) ***I, refine, purify.*** (ASV and RSV similar.)

The basic idea is of making something pure (cf. *ṣārap,* which connotes testing something to determine its degree of purity). The root is used twice in Qal, once in Piel, and four times in Pual. The Qal appears in Job 28:1, which speaks of a place for gold where they "fine" (RSV "refine") it. The Piel occurs in Mal 3:3, which says that God will "purge" (RSV "refine") Levites like gold and silver. The Pual of *zāqaq* always occurs as a participle. For instance, a part of that which David collected for building the temple is described as "refined" gold (I Chr 28:18). Every instance but two refers to the refining of metals, which, of course was done by fire. win Isa 25:6 the refining of wine is referred to which probably was done by decanting, not filtering (as KB suggest), cf. Jer 48:11. The reference in Job 36:27 is difficult. Pope ("Job" in AB) translates "that distill rain from the flood." Could the process of evaporation here be referred to metaphorically as a refining?

L.J.W.

577 זקק (*zqq*). **Assumed root of the following.**

577a זִק (*zēq*) ***fetter*** (e.g. Nah 3:10; Isa 45:14). Derivation uncertain. GB, unlike BDB, derive from *znq* because of Arabic and Syriac cognates.

577b אָזִק (*'ăzēq*) ***manacle*** (Jer 40:1, only).

זֵר (*zēr*). See no. 543a.

זָרָא (*zārā'*). See no. 542d.

578 *זָרַב (*zārab*) ***be burned, scorched.*** Occurs only in the Pual.

Derivative

578a †זְרֻבָּבֶל (*z^e^rūbābel*) ***Zerubbabel, a name.***

Zerubbabel was a grandson of King Jehoiachin (I Chr 3:16–19), taken captive by Nebuchadnezzar in 597 B.C. (II Kgs 24:11–16); hence an heir to the throne of Judah. He is frequently called a "son of Shealtiel" (Salathiel, Ezr 3:2, 8; Neh 12:1; Mt 1:12, etc.), but a son of Pedaiah, brother of Shealtiel, in I Chr 3:17. Shealtiel likely died childless.

Either his nephew, Zerubbabel, was considered his legal heir, and hence called his son (Ex 2:10), or else Pedaiah fulfilled his levirate duty in marrying the widow of Shealtiel, in which instance the first child would be considered son of the deceased (Deut 25:5–10).

Zerubbabel was the civil leader (called *paḥat* "governor," Hag 1:14; 2:2, 21) of the Jews who returned from the Babylonian exile, under Cyrus' permission, *c.* 537 B.C. leading the first returning band of exiles. Rebuilding of the Temple was begun *c.* 536 B.C. (Ezr 3:8–13), but it ceased (Ezr 4:24) shortly after the foundation was completed. Sixteen years later (520 B.C., Darius's second year, Hag 1:1; Zech 1:1), the two prophets Haggai and Zechariah, began to preach and urge resumption of the building. Zerubbabel, along with Joshua, the high priest, responded (Ezr 5:1–2; Hag 1:12). The work was completed in the spring of 515 B.C. Besides leading the rebuilding, Zerubbabel restored both the courses of the priests and Levites (Ezr 6:18) and the provision for their maintenance (Neh 12:47). Nothing is known of the man after the completion of the Temple; nor is there any record of his death.

[It is commonly supposed today that Zerubbabel who was of the seed royal had kingly pretensions. He is supposed to have led an independence movement which was quickly put down by the Persians and Zerubbabel met an untimely death. There is no direct evidence for this theory. It assumes that Zech 6:11 does not present Joshua the high priest as typical of the Messiah, but that the original reading was "Zerubbabel" who was the object of the prophecy. The view does not envision Zerubbabel as both king and priest. It favors the translation "There will be a priest by his throne" (RSV). Cf. the NEB footnote to v. 11 "possibly an error for Zerubbabel." The view is advanced in Kraeling, E. *Commentary on the Prophets, II, Daniel to Malachi,* Nelson, 1966, pp. 299–300. R.L.H.]

L.J.W.

זְרֻבָּבֶל (*zᵉrūbbābel*). See no. 878a.

579 זָרָה (*zārâ*) ***fan, scatter, cast away, winnow; disperse, compass, spread, be scattered, dispersed.***

Derivative

579a מִזְרֶה (*mizreh*) ***pitchfork.***

The basic thought of the verb is to stir up the air to produce a scattering and spreading effect. However, the simple act of scattering or spreading is also suggested, e.g. Moses scattered gold dust on water (Ex 32:20). Unfaithful priests have dung spread upon their faces (Mal 2:3).

The term *zārâ* is used in various verbal forms to indicate a scattering or dispersing for reasons of purification or chastisement. Grain is cleansed of chaff by using a fan to blow it away. God's covenant people require a purifying also, but it will be a chastening experience; hence the Lord is said, metaphorically, "to fan" his people (Jer 15:7), with the result that they will be scattered as chaff to various distant places. Moses warned this would happen if Israel forsook the covenant (Lev 26:33). Jeremiah (49:32) and Zechariah (1:19; 2:2) both referred to how Israel was dispersed by the Gentile invaders among foreign nations. It was also foretold that those nations used to chastise Israel, would some day themselves be fanned and completely scattered for all time to come (Isa 41:16).

The dispersion of Israel is referred to by various synonyms which express other aspects or nuances of God's chastening process; cf. *nāpaṣ* "dash, scatter"; *pûṣ* "dash, scatter"; *pāraṣ* "break out, disperse"; *pārad* "spread"; and *pāzar* "scatter."

[The difficult usage in Ps 139:3 may be a semantic extension of this root in the sense of "examine" or, as BDB suggest and KB and Dahood (in AB, *Psalms III*) affirm, may be a denominative verb *zārâ* "to measure" from the noun *zeret* "span." R.L.H.]

G.V.G.

זֵרוּעַ (*zērûaʻ*). See no. 582b.
זְרוֹעַ (*zᵉrôaʻ*). See no. 583a.
זַרְזִיף (*zarzîp*). See no. 584a.
זַרְזִיר (*zarzîr*). See no. 543b.

580 זָרַח (*zāraḥ*) ***arise, rise, rise up, shine.*** (ASV and RSV similar.)

Derivatives

580a זֶרַח (*zeraḥ*) ***dawning, shining.***
580b †אֶזְרָח (*'ezrāḥ*) ***native.***
580c †מִזְרָח (*mizrāḥ*) ***place of sunrise, east.***

BDB does not list "to shine" as one of the meanings, but KB gives "shine forth," "flash forth."

zāraḥ means "to rise, come up," and is used in three ways. 1) It refers to the breaking forth of the symptoms of leprosy (*ṣaraʻat* q.v.; II Chr 26:19). 2) It is used of the sun as appearing, without specific reference to the diffusion of its light (Eccl 1:5; Jn 4:5), (and thus it is a reference to the time of day), or else as [radiating] its light in the morning (II Sam 23:4). 3) It is also used in a figurative sense to speak of salvation, light, glory resulting from God's coming into a man's life (Ps 112:4; Isa 58:10; 60:1). The thought is that as the sun appears in the morning without man's effort, but nevertheless floods his surroundings with light and dispels the darkness, so the Lord is sovereign in the bestowal of his salvation, which brings light and glory. The term is used twice of God himself appearing to bring salvation (Isa 60:2) and righteousness to his people (Mal 4:2 [H 3:20]). In both cases there is a prophecy concerning the coming of Jesus Christ as Saviour and Lord.

'ezrāḥ. ***A native, one rising from his own soil.*** This noun refers to one arising from his native soil. In the Mosaic legislation the term is used frequently to indicate the specific native origin (Num 15:29, like a tree, Ps 37:35) of the descendants of the Patriarchs who belong to the promised land (Ex 18:19).

mizrāḥ. ***East, the sun rising.*** This noun is closely related to *zāraḥ*. Used in relation to the sun rising, it refers specifically to the place or area of sunrise. It is often translated "east." It is used in a strictly locative sense (Isa 41:2; Josh 11:8) but also figuratively in prophecies of woe (Amos 8:12) and of blessedness (Zech 14:4).

G.V.G.

581 זָרַם (*zāram*) ***pour forth in floods, flood away*** (Ps 90:5, Qal; Ps 77:18, Poel).

Derivatives

581a זֶרֶם (*zerem*) ***flood of rain, downpour*** (e.g. Isa 4:6; Hab 3:10).
581b זִרְמָה (*zirmâ*) ***issue*** (i.e. semen, Ezk 23:20).

582 זָרַע (*zāra'*) ***I, scatter seed, sow.***

Derivatives

582a †זֶרַע (*zera'*) ***sowing, seed, offspring.***
582b זֵרוּעַ (*zērûa'*) ***sowing, thing sown.***
582c זֵרֹעַ (*zērōa'*) ***vegetable.***
582d זֵרְעֹן (*zēr'ōn*) ***vegetable.***
582e †יִזְרְעֶאל (*yizr^e'e'l*) ***Jezreel.***
582f מִזְרָע (*mizrā'*) ***place of sowing.***

This verb appears fifty-six times: forty-six times in the Qal, once in the Pual, six times in the Niphal, and three times in the Hiphil. The etymology of *zr'* is most puzzling, for while it appears in Arabic, Syriac, and Ugaritic, pointing to a Protosemitic *zr'* and seems to be a conflation of the two roots of *zr'* "to sow" and *ḏrw* "to scatter," this does not agree with the fact that the *ḏ* of *ḏr'* does not remain in Ugaritic, but appears as *dry*. (Cf. UT, 5: nos 3–4; 19: nos. 702, 705; but notice 19:733 *ḏr'* "arm.")

Literally, *zāra'* refers to the action of sowing seed in the fields (Gen 26:12; Isa 37:30). It is used with the accusative of the type of seed sown, e.g. sowing wheat (Jer 12:13), or with the accusative of the field sown (Ex 23:10; Lev 25:3). Occasionally, it is also followed by the double accusative of both seed and field (e.g. Lev 19:19; Deut 22:9, "You shall not sow your field with two kinds of seed"). In this prohibition, a reference is made, no doubt, to the Canaanite ritual inducing fertility. Finally, this verb is also used of sowing salt in a captured city (Jud 9:45).

Metaphorically, the action denotes the Lord's sowing (planting or establishing) Israel in the land of Palestine in a future day (Hos 2:25) or of his confession that though he has scattered (i.e. sown) Israel among the countries of the earth, he will also gather them one day in the future (Zech 10:9). *zāra'* is also used figuratively in connection with moral actions: to sow justice (Prov 11:18), righteousness (Hos 10:12), light, i.e. happiness (Ps 97:11), wickedness (Prov 22:8), trouble (Job 4:8), and wind (Hos 8:7). In Isa 17:10 the verb depicts Israel as practicing idolatry by sowing plants or slips to an alien god, while in Ps 126:5 it is a figure of the grief of hard work followed by joyous results. It can also refer to reigns of kings and princes under the figure of trees (Isa 40:24). Finally, in the Niphal it refers to a woman being made pregnant (Num 5:28) or bearing a child (Hiphil Lev 12:2).

zera'. ***Sowing, seed, offspring.*** This noun is used 224 times. Its usages fall into four basic semantic categories: 1. The time of sowing, seedtime; 2. the seed as that which is scattered or as the product of what is sown; 3. the seed as semen and 4. the Seed as the offspring in the promised line of Abraham, Isaac, and Jacob or in other groups separate from this people of promise.

The primary meaning comes from the realm of agriculture. Seedtime or sowing, as over against the time of harvest, will recur according to a promised pattern which God guaranteed to Noah after the flood (Gen 8:22; cf. Lev 26:5). This sowing or planting takes place in the fields (Ezk 17:5) and thereby accords well with the Akkadian *zēru* "cultivated land." The seed itself which is planted in these fields has the same name (Gen 47:19, 23; Lev 11:37–38; Num 24:7; Deut 28:38; Isa 55:10; Amos 9:13). The product produced has the same designation (e.g. the seed of the herbs and trees in Gen 1:11–12, 29 or the seed that is gathered into the barn in Job 39:12; cf. Deut 14:22; Isa 23:3). Thus, the whole agricultural cycle is practically summed up in the word *zera'*; from the act of sowing to the seed planted, to the harvest taken. *zera'* is used figuratively in referring to Judah's idolatry (Isa 17:11). They are planting "pleasant plants" along with "strange slips." This refers either to the Ugaritic *n'mn* of the Tammuz-Adonis cult or to the folly of planting thorns and thistles and expecting a crop of flowers or vegetables.

zera' refers to semen in Num 5:28, "she shall

be made pregnant with seed." Frequently it occurs in the expression "flow of semen" (Lev 15:16, 32; 22:4). It is also used as the accusative of mode and translated euphemistically as "lying carnally with a woman" (Lev 15:18; 18:20; Num 5:13). Note the same use in the promise of Jer 31:27. The Lord will sow the houses of Israel and Judah with the seed of man and the seed of beast in the latter days.

The most important theological usage is found in the fourth category. Commencing with Gen 3:15, the word "seed" is regularly used as a collective noun in the singular (never plural). This technical term is an important aspect of the promise doctrine, for Hebrew never uses the plural of this root to refer to "posterity" or "offspring." The Aramaic targums pluralize the term occasionally, e.g. the Targum of Gen 4:10, but the Aramaic also limits itself to the singular in the passages dealing with the promised line. Thus the word designates the whole line of descendants as a unit, yet it is deliberately flexible enough to denote either one person who epitomizes the whole group (i.e. the man of promise and ultimately Christ), or the many persons in that whole line of natural and/or spiritual descendants.

Precisely so in Gen 3:15. One such seed is the line of the woman as contrasted with the opposing seed which is the line of Satan's followers. And then surprisingly the text announces a male descendant who will ultimately win a crushing victory over Satan himself.

This promise to Eve was enlarged and made more specific in the Abrahamic Covenant. God would grant a land and a numerous offspring through Abraham's son Isaac and his offspring: Gen 12:7; 13:15–16; 15:13,18; 16:10; 17:7–10,12,19; 22:17–18; 24:7; 26:3–4,24; 28:4,13–14; 32:13; 35:12; 48:4. This whole line builds and the promise continues in Ex 32:13; 33:1; Deut 1:8; 11:9; 34:4; Josh 24:3.

The same can be said for David and his offspring. The promise is continued in II Sam 7:12; made parallel to the term "Messiah" in Ps 18:50 [H 5] (see II Sam 22:51); and repeated in Ethan's commentary on the Davidic covenant of II Sam 7 in Ps 89:4,29,36 [H 5,30,37].

This corporate solidarity found in the seed of Eve, Abraham, and David receives theological comment in Isa 41:8; 43:5; 44:3; 45:19,25; 48:19; 53:10; 54:3; 59:21; 61:9; 65:9; 66:22; Jer 31:36–37; 33:26; II Chr 20:7.

yizr^{e}‘e'l. ***Proper name meaning God sows or God will sow; Jezreel.*** There are five different usages of this name. Three are geographical locations: 1. a town in Issachar at the foot of Mount Gilboa (Josh 19:18; I Kgs 21:1ff.); 2. a town in Judah from which one of David's wives came (I Sam 25:43); and 3. the valley of Jezreel which connected the Esdraelon valley on its west side and the Jordan River valley on its east side.

Jezreel is also the name of one of Judah's descendants (I Chr 4:3).

The most important theological usage is the name given to the first child born to the prophet Hosea and Gomer (Hos 1:4–5). The prophet names his son "Jezreel," which in Hos 2:23 [H 25] involves a play on the meaning of the verb *zāra‘* "to sow" and "to scatter." However, in 1:4 the reference is to the historical incident of Jehu's bloody path to the throne (II Kgs 9:30–10:11). According to Hos 1:3, Gomer bore this son to Hosea; therefore he was not conceived in harlotry. We must reject the view that God told the prophet to take a woman who was a harlot with children already born out of wedlock. Rather, the command in Hos 1:2 involves the figure of speech known as zeugma, in which the main verb(s) ("go, marry") control two objects grammatically, but only one logically. The expression is elliptical, for one must supply the verb "and beget children." The stigma of the mother's later action is passed on to the children so that they too are called the children of harlotry, but they are not such literally. Finally, what may be considered a statement of purpose, Hos 1:2, is more probably a construction signifying result and therefore is in this regard like Isa 6:9–12.

In spite of Israel's apostasy and spiritual harlotry, matched by the later physical harlotry of Gomer, God will sow Israel again one day in her land in the latter days (Hos 1:11 [H 2:2]).

Bibliography: TDNT, VII, pp. 538–44.

W.C.K.

583 זרע (zr‘) **II. Assumed root of the following.**

583a †זְרוֹעַ (z^{e}rôa), זְרֹעַ (z^{e}rōa‘) ***arm, shoulder, strength.***

583b אֶזְרוֹעַ (’ezrôa‘) ***arm.***

The etymology of this root is not entirely clear, but it appears in Akkadian, Ugaritic, Arabic, Aramaic, and Ethiopic.

The literal meaning of "arm" is the rare usage for this word, occurring in just over a dozen of some ninety references, e.g. Jud 15:14; 16:12; II Sam 1:10. Twice it refers to the shoulder of a sacrificed animal (Num 6:19; Deut 18:3).

Most frequently, *z^{e}rôa‘* is used metaphorically. The "arm of flesh," symbolizing man's strength, is impotent compared to God's power (II Chr 32:8). In the plural, "arms" is equivalent to military or political forces or armies (Dan 11:15, 22, 31). Thus to "break the arms" of an enemy is a figurative expression (I Sam 2:31; Job 22:9; 38:15; Ps 10:15; 37:17; Jer 48:25; Ezk 30:21–22, 24–25) for destroying the enemies' strength, power, or violence, and therefore their capacity to make war.

More frequently still the arm is used as an anthropomorphic figure of God's power. The most vivid of these instances occurs in Isa 30:30 in which the lightning stroke is pictured as the "descending blow of his arm." God reveals the power of his "outstretched arm" in creation (Jer 32:17) and in his deliverance of Israel from Egypt (Ex 6:6; 15:16; Deut 4:34; Ps 77:15 [H 16]; Isa 63:12). In a similar way, that arm or power of the Lord will bring another deliverance in the last day (Ps 98:1; Isa 40:10; 51:9ff.; 52:10; 63:5; Ezk 20:33f.). In the meantime, underneath Israel are the Lord's everlasting arms for the protection and preservation of his people (Deut 33:27; Ps 89:13 [H 14]; Isa 33:2). These same arms were used on behalf of individuals on two occasions (II Chr 6:32; Isa 40:11). In Isa 53:1 the "arm of the Lord" is used as a metonymy for the redemptive word which the Lord achieved through his servant.

Bibliography: Ginsberg, H. L., "The Arm of YHWH in Isaiah 51–63 and the text of Isa 53: 10–11," JBL 77: 152–56. THAT, I, pp. 522–23.

W.C.K.

584 *זָרַף (*zārap*) ***drip.*** This verb occurs only once, in the Hiphil (Ps 72:6).

Derivative

584a זַרְזִיף (*zarzîp*) ***drop, dripping*** (Ps 72:6, only).

585 זָרַק (*zāraq*) ***scatter, sprinkle, strew.*** (ASV similar, RSV "throw upon.")

Derivative

585a †מִזְרָק (*mizrāq*) ***bowl, basin.***

The verb *zāraq,* meaning "to toss, throw, scatter in abundance" (cf. BDB) appears thirty-five times; its synonym *nāzâ* appears twenty-four times. Both are translated "sprinkle" with but few exceptions; e.g. "scatter" seed (Isa 28:25); "strew" idol-dust on graves (II Chr 34:4); streaks of gray in a man's hair (Hos 7:9). The LXX translates *zāraq* as "pour," when it refers to the blood of the sacrifices upon the altar.

zāraq is used in religious ceremonies for two specific purposes. 1) By sprinkling blood at the solemnizing of an inviolable bond between God and man (T. Lewis, in ISBE, 2487). The sprinkling of the blood on the people and the altar (Ex 24:6–8) confirmed the altar as the open way for the sprinkled, i.e. confirmed covenant people, to a holy, righteous yet loving God (cf. also II Kgs 16:15). 2) Sprinkling was an integral aspect of the purification rite. Blood was sprinkled to indicate or confirm sanctification (Ex 29:20; Lev 1:5), as well as for hygienic purposes which had a definite religious meaning (Lev 17:6).

Finally, *zāraq* is used in other deeply religious ways. It speaks of judgment: Moses *threw* dust in the air to bring the plague of boils upon Egypt (Ex 9:8). Ezekiel uses *zāraq*, of sprinkling clean water (36:25) in connection with the Lord's regenerating work in the hearts of his exiled covenant people.

mizrāq. ***Basin, bowl.*** Twice this noun is used to refer to drinking-bowls (Amos 6:6; Zech 9:15) and thirty times to basins used in various religious settings and ceremonial rituals. They were considered of great significance because sacrificial blood was sprinkled, spattered, or splashed from them.

G.V.G.

586 *זָרַר (*zārar*) ***sneeze.*** This verb occurs only in the Poel (Job 41:10; II Kgs 4:35).

587 זֶרֶת (*zeret*) ***span*** (e.g. Isa 40:2; Ex 25:10).

ח

ח

חֹב (*ḥōb*). See no. 589a.

588 חָבָא (*ḥābāʾ*) ***hide.*** (ASV and RSV similar.)

Derivatives

588a מַחֲבֵא (*maḥăbēʾ*) ***hiding place,*** only in Isa 32:2, *maḥăbēʾ rûaḥ* (construct state).

588b מַחֲבֹא (*maḥăbōʾ*) ***hiding place,*** only in I Sam 23:23.

ḥābāʾ, in twenty-five of its thirty occurrences, refers to people hiding in fear of death. Thus the five kings of the southern confederacy hid themselves in a cave out of fear of Joshua (Josh 19:27), and Adam and Eve hid themselves out of consciousness of their alienation from the Lord God (Gen 3:8). Other occasions include Saul hiding from the public (in modesty?) when he was made king (I Sam 10:22). Young men "hid themselves" in respect or awe from Job (Job 29:8, RSV "withdrew"). Jacob fled "secretly" from Laban ("hid himself to flee," Gen 31:27). The most notable use is in Gen 3:8,10 where Adam and Eve hid themselves from the Lord after their sin. The context says that they hid in fear, possibly remembering the threat of certain death for their transgression and sensing their guilt in the presence of the righteous God.

Twice the thing hid is not a person. In Job 29:10 the nobles "hid" their voices (ASV, RSV "voice . . . was hushed," KJV "held their peace"). In Job 38:30 the waters "hide themselves" as a stone, that is, water as such disappears as it becomes ice (RSV "become hard").

In the Hiphil the use of this verb is transitive as Rahab "hid" the spies (Josh 6:17, 25, et al.). The single occurrence of the Hophal is passive of this use, as people are hidden in prisons (Isa 42:22). The use in the Niphal, the Hithpael, and the single occurrence of the Pual (Job 24:4) is generally intransitive with a few instances of passive use such as Joash "hidden" from Athaliah (II Kgs 11:3 and II Chr 22:12).

ḥābâ (q.v.) is probably a variant spelling of *ḥābāʾ* and the two should be considered together.

C.P.W.

589 חָבַב (*ḥābab*) ***love*** (Deut 33:3).

Derivative

589a חֹב (*ḥōb*) ***bosom*** (Job 31:33).

590 חָבָה (*ḥābâ*) ***hide.*** (ASV the same, RSV also "conceal.")

Derivative

590a חֶבְיוֹן (*ḥebyôn*) ***hiding, hiding place,*** only in Hab 3:4.

This word means "hide," used intransitively for people hiding, usually in fear for their lives. The exception is II Kgs 7:12 where an army is presumed to be hiding in ambush. The use is Niphal except in Isa 26:20, which uses the Qal. It is probably a variant spelling of *ḥābāʾ* and should be considered with it.

C.P.W.

חַבּוּרָה (*ḥabbûrâ*). See no. 598g.

591 חָבַט (*ḥābaṭ*) ***beat (off, out), thresh.*** (ASV, RSV similar.)

The word is used regarding the harvesting or preparation of certain crops: olive trees beaten (Deut 24:20), wheat threshed (Jud 6:11), barley (Ruth 2:17). Certain spices are "beaten out" with a stick (Isa 28:27). The only other usage is figurative, referring to God's action in regathering Israel to her homeland (Isa 27:12).

C.P.W.

חֶבְיוֹן (*ḥebyôn*). See no. 590d.

592 חָבַל (*ḥābal*). ***The words "bind," "pledge," and "travail" are united in BDB under one root.***

It appears that there are several words, one originally beginning with *ḥ* meaning "bind" (root I in KB) which has an Arabic and Ugaritic cognate; a second beginning originally with *ḥ* meaning "pledge" (root II in KB) which has a cognate in Arabic in the Ishtafel stem; a third beginning originally with *ḥ* meaning "destroy" (root III in KB) which has a cognate in Arabic; and a fourth beginning originally with *ḥ* meaning "travail" (root IV in KB). The fifth, "advise," has no Arabic equivalent. The analysis of KB, similar to GB, will be followed.

592a †חָבַל (*ḥābal*) ***I, bind*** (verbal form not used in the OT).

Derivatives

592b †חֶבֶל (*ḥebel*) ***I, cord, rope, band, company*** (ASV and RSV similar).

592c חֹבֵל (*ḥōbēl*) ***sailor,*** used of the Tyrian masters of the sea in Ezk 27:8, 27–29 and of Jonah's shipmaster (Jon 1:6).

592d חִבֵּל (*ḥibbēl*) ***mast,*** used only in Prov 23:35. Exact meaning uncertain.

ḥebel I. ***Cord, rope, snare, tackling, line, lot, portion, region, country, coast, band, company.***

The basic use of the noun *ḥebel* is as "cord" or "rope." It may be a strong, utilitarian kind of rope for letting spies out of a window (Josh 2:15), for letting Jeremiah in and out of the cistern (Jer 38:6), for laying waste a city (II Sam 17:13), or for bracing a ship's mast and securing the sail (hence "tackling" Isa 33:23). It may be decorative, of fine linen (Est 1:6), or used on the head for mourning (I Kgs 20:31). It may be used as a snare or trap (Job 18:10). The figurative use in connection with death (Ps 116:3) or Sheol (II Sam 22:6) may represent death as a snare, or binding. Alternatively these forms may be considered to be from *ḥēbel,* "pain" (as of childbirth see below). In most occurrences these two nouns are indistinguishable by form. The KJV translates these and other passages "sorrows." Other figurative uses include: the "silver cord," speaking of life (Eccl 12:6), "with cords of a man," that is, "compassionately" (Hos 11:4), the "cords" or "snares" of sin (Prov 5:22, RSV "toils"), et al.

The cord may be used to measure, as David measured two lines of Moabites for death and one to be spared (II Sam 8:2). Specifically, a measuring line is *ḥebel middâ* (Zech 2:1). Land is measured, or divided by line (Amos 7:17; Ps 78:55). From this, *ḥebel* comes to mean the area measured, a portion or lot (lot meaning "obtained by chance"), especially the inheritance of a tribe (Josh 17:5f), or of an individual (Ps 105:11). It also denotes a "country" or "region" (Deut 3:4f.). If the region is near the sea it is translated "coast" (Zeph 2:5, 6,7). The KJV translates *ḥebel* as coast also in Josh 19:29, but the ASV margin and the RSV take the word in this context to be a proper name.

ḥebel is to be translated "band" or "company" in I Sam 10:5, 10. Possibly this is true of Ps 119:61, "bands of wicked men," but "snares" also fits the context. The use of *ḥebel* meaning "band" or "company" is attested in Ugaritic where it is used for a flock of birds as well as a company of people. Its use as "rope" is also attested. (See Cyrus H. Gordon, UT, 19: no. 832.)

ḥebel is a symbol of captivity or subjection (I Kgs 20:31f.) and is used figuratively of the snares for the wicked (Job 18:10; Prov 5:22, the enslavement of sin) or set by the wicked (Ps 140:5 [H 6]; 119:61). The Psalmist describes his situation before the Lord's deliverance as one in which he was bound by the cords of death (Ps 18:5 [H 6]; 116:3).

C.P.W.

593 חָבַל (*ḥābal*) ***II, lay to pledge, take a pledge of, withhold.*** (ASV and RSV similar but do not use "withhold"). The verb, as used in the OT, means "to hold as pledge or security." It is used only in the Qal (eight times) and possibly in the Niphal (Prov 13:13).

Derivative

593a †חֲבֹל (*ḥăbōl*) ***pledge.***

Used three times in Ezk, it refers to a pledge taken (or registered) to guarantee a loan. Another word used for pledge is *'ērābôn* (q.v.) which has come over into Greek and appears in the Gr. NT as *arrabōn* "earnest" (Eph 1:14).

The details of taking a pledge are not entirely clear. E. A. Speiser in a very helpful article draws a close parallel between the law in Lev 25:35–54 ("Leviticus and the Critics," in *Oriental and Biblical Studies,* University of Pennsylvania, 1967, pp. 123–42). He remarks that "in Mesopotamia, interest was normally discounted in advance. The technical term for such advance deduction was *ḥūbullû* (not loan without interest as the term is sometimes erronneously rendered, but loan with interest already deducted)." Speiser holds that the Lev passage (which calls the loan *neshek,* q.v.) shows that the Israelites gave discounted loans, then, if the creditor could not pay, he was seized to work off the loan. However, at this point no more interest would be charged—that second interest would be *neshek* "usury." Speiser, following Koschaker, also suggests that the cloak taken in pledge (Ex 22:26 [H 25])—or the shoes that confirm a contract (Ruth 4:7; Amos 2:6)—is not a security for a loan, but a token exchange validating the transaction. Apparently it was taken in evidence and then was to be returned promptly ("Of Shoes and Shekels," *idem,* pp. 154–55).

C.P.W.

594 חָבַל (*ḥābal*) ***III, destroy, spoil; deal corruptly, be corrupt, offend.*** (ASV also be consumed; RSV also be broken ruined.)

Derivative

594a †חֶבֶל (*ḥebel*) ***destruction.***

The main use of this verb is in the Piel, meaning to "ruin," "destroy." In the Qal the meaning is "act corruptly."

The use of this verb in the Qal, "be very bad," is limited to Job 34:31, "offend," and Neh 1:7, "act corruptly," against God in both instances. *ḥābal* may occur in the Niphal stem in Prov 13:13, "be destroyed" or "bring destruction on oneself." Some, however, take this form to be from *ḥābal* I, "to take a pledge."

The Piel use, "destroy" or "ruin," may be intensive of the Qal, "act corruptly." The destruction may be carried out by God (Eccl 5:5), a nation (Isa 13:5), a knave or villain (Isa 32:7), or "the little foxes that spoil the vines" (Song 2:15). The verb is used with the cognate *ḥebel,* destruction, in Mic 2:10.

The Pual, "be destroyed," is used just twice: in reference to the oppressive yoke of the Assyrians (Isa 10:27), and in Job's complaint that his spirit "is broken" (RSV; ASV "consumed"; KJV, "breath is corrupt").

ḥebel II "destruction" (Mic 2:10 and possibly Job 21:17), is related to *ḥābal* III.

In most forms *ḥēbel* (see below) is not distinguishable from *ḥebel* except by context. For this reason there is some disagreement as to which word is involved in many of the contexts, and some of the analysis is arbitrary. It seems best to classify under *ḥēbel* only those contexts which refer to the pains of childbirth, whether literal (Isa 26:17) or figurative (Jer 13:21). Other uses (including Job 21:17 "snares") should be considered as from *ḥebel* I or II. The singular of this word is used only in Isa 66:7. The KJV translates *ḥēbel* most often as "sorrows" and includes a number of instances which may be just as easily classified with *ḥebel* (Ps 18:4–5 et al [H 5–6]).

C.P.W.

595 *חָבַל (*ḥābal*) ***IV, bring forth, travail.*** Used only in the Piel. The initial consonant, as shown by the Arabic cognate, was originally *ḥ*. It is used only in Ps 7:15 and Song 8:5.

Derivative

595a †חֵבֶל (*ḥēbel*) ***pain, pang, sorrow.*** (ASV and RSV similar.) This noun means "pain," specifically that of childbirth. In most forms *ḥēbel* is indistinguishable from *ḥebel* (above). The word occurs with this definition only eight times.

596 חָבַל (*ḥābal*) ***V.*** This verb is represented in the OT only in its derivative.

Derivative

596a †תַּחְבֻּלָה (*taḥbūlâ*) ***good advice, (wise) counsel.*** (RSV (wise) guidance, skill, counsel; ASV similar.)

The noun is used six times, always in the plural. BDB and many commentators, however, relate this word to *ḥbl* I as a nautical term, rope-pulling and hence steering (a ship), used figuratively of wise counsel (Prov 1:5, 11:14; 20:18; 24:6).

taḥbūlâ is "direction" or "guidance" (perhaps from the pulling of a rope to guide or direct). It is used for God's giving "direction" to the clouds (Job 37:12), or the "guidance" or "counsel" of the wicked (Prov 12:5). In general the word means "wise guidance" or "good counsel" (although the RSV translates "skill" in Prov 1:5). It is used only in Prov except for the reference in Job (above).

596.1 חֲבַצֶּלֶת (*ḥăbaṣṣelet*) ***meadow saffron or crocus*** (Song 2:1; Isa 35:1).

597 חָבַק (*ḥabaq*) ***embrace, fold*** (ASV, RSV similar).

Derivative

597a חִבֻּק (*ḥibbūq*) ***fold*** (hands).

ḥābaq basically designates an expression of love by the position or action of one's hands or arms. Three specific aspects of love are referred to.

The first use of the term expresses the idea of embracing someone else to show fondness or affection. Thus, Laban embraced his nephew Jacob (Gen 29:13) and Joseph his brothers in Egypt after revealing his identity (Gen 48:10). The "great woman" (or prophetess) of Shunem was promised a newborn son whom she could lovingly hold in her arms (II Kgs 4:16). Job uses the term of one who seeks a rock of safety to find comfort and security (24:8).

The second use of *ḥābaq* describes the embrace of lovers. This embrace can designate virtuous love (Song 2:6) or the adulterous embracing of a stranger's bosom.

Finally, the idea of folding of hands is an implicit designation of self-love. This folding of the hands (the noun *ḥibbūq* is used twice, Prov 6:10; 24:33) is an evidence of sloth and lack of concern. However, the Preacher says the fool folds his hands and eats meat, while the worrying, striving man sees only wind (Eccl 4:5). The point is that neither the sloth nor striving of the self-loving one are conducive to a lasting peace.

G.V.G.

598 חָבַר (*ḥābar*) ***be joined, coupled, league, heap up, have fellowship with, be compact; be a charmer.*** BDB adds "to unite, tie a magic knot," (RSV has "joined forces," ASV "joined together" and other such variations).

Derivatives

598a †חֶבֶר (*ḥeber*) ***company, association, spell.***

598b חֶבְרָה (*ḥebrâ*) ***association, company.***

598c †חָבֵר (*ḥābēr*) ***united, associate, companion.***

598d †חֲבֶרֶת (*ḥăberet*) ***consort, i.e. wife,*** only in Mal 2:14.

598e †חֹבֶרֶת (*ḥōberet*) ***a thing that joins or is joined, only of the curtain pieces of the tabernacle, as joined together*** (Ex 26:10; 36:17).
598f חַבָּר (*ḥabbār*) ***associate, partner in a trade or calling,*** only in Job 40:30.
598g חַבּוּרָה (*ḥabbûrâ*), חַבֻּרָה (*ḥabbūrâ*), חַבְרָה (*ḥabrâ*) ***stripe, blow.***
598h חֲבַרְבֻּרָה (*ḥăbarbūrâ*) ***stripe, mark,*** only in Jer 13:23.
598i †חֶבְרוֹן (*ḥebrôn*) ***Hebron.***
598j †מַחְבֶּרֶת (*maḥberet*) ***thing joined, place of joining.***
598k מְחַבְּרָה (*m^e ḥabb^e râ*) ***binder, clamp, joint.***

In Ugaritic the term appears as a name for a town, meaning "community," and it is thought to be related to the common Semitic root meaning "to be joined" (UT 19: no. 924) and translated as "bind" in Assyrian.

The main idea of *ḥābar* in the OT is "to join or unite" two or more things. However, the root idea of the term "to bind" also appears, especially in the concept "charm." Only in Deut 18:11 does this term appear in a verbal form to express the idea of charming, i.e. casting a spell or tying up a person by magic. The act of charming is set forth as an idolatrous act and diametrically opposed to receiving revelation from God through his appointed prophets (Deut 18:15).

The verb *ḥābar* in the sense of "join" is used with four specific references. 1) Objects were joined together, e.g. curtains in tabernacle construction to make one complete side (Ex 26:3), shoulder pieces in coupling together the parts of the priests' holy garments (Ex 28:7), wings of the living creatures touching one another (Ezk 1:9). 2) Men were joined together in political and military activities. Five nations of the Sodom-Gomorrah confederacy united for military purposes against invaders from the east (Gen 14:3) but their union led to a common defeat. Jehoshaphat made a political union with wicked Ahaziah of Israel for commercial purposes but it was denounced by God's prophet (II Chr 20:35–37). Daniel saw kings joining themselves together in a league (Hithpael) (RSV "make alliance") which was doomed to failure (Dan 11:6, 28). 3) Men are joined in a general manner as belonging to the race of the living (Eccl 9:4) and in a specific way as a group of people who are formed into a strong unified city (Ps 122:3). 4) Men of Judah wrongly joining with faithless Israel in military and political ventures (II Chr 20:35) displeased God; men joining themselves to idols and idol worshipers did so much more (Ps 94:20). God's heartrending complaint against Ephraim is that he is joined to idols (Hos 4:17). To be joined to idols means to have forsaken God.

ḥeber. *Company, association, spell, enchantment, companion; grandson.* a variant of *ḥābēr*, *ḥeber* reflects the sense of "bind, cast a spell," except in a few places (Prov 21:9). The usual translation is "enchantments" referring to the means the charmers employed to influence people or the result of their charming efforts (Deut 18:11). All aspects were divinely forbidden to covenant people.

The meaning "companion" is found three times in Jud 4. The meaning "grandson" (perhaps from the close connection between son and grandson genetically) occurs in Gen 46:17; Num 26:4; I Chr 4:18; 7:31; 8:17.

ḥāber. *Companion, associate, knit together* (RSV "associated with" him; ASV "companion" for fellows).

This word is used as an adjective and noun to refer to the very close bond that can exist between persons (cf. UT 19: no. 834). In Aramaic the term indicates the close relationship between Daniel and his three friends because of their common faith and loyalty to God (Dan 2:13–18). The Psalmist expressly states that the fear of God is the common bond between "companions" (Ps 119:63).

The term *ḥābēr* is also used to express the very close relationship that exists between people in various walks of life. Israelites were "united as one man" (RSV) in their war against the Benjamites because of their outrageous crime (Jud 20:11). Men can be very closely joined together as thieves (Isa 1:23), as destroyers (Prov 28:24), and as corrupt priests likened to ambushing robbers (Hos 6:9).

ḥăberet. *Consort, wife, companion.* This feminine noun, synonym of wife (Mal 2:14), indicates the type of a close relationship which the root *ḥābar* expresses.

ḥōberet. *Coupling.* A feminine noun, it refers to the actual joint of, or joining piece between, two parts of the tabernacle (Ex 26:10) and temple (II Chr 34:11).

ḥebrôn. *Hebron.* This proper name is said to be related to the verb *ḥābar* and thus its meaning could be considered as "confederacy, association, league" or possibly as "charmer" or "enchanting." Certain scholars have endeavored to link the name Hebron to certain organized or united military activities. But even though it is true that Abraham, the father of the Israelites, lived in its area (Gen 23), and that David lived there, united the people of Israel, and reigned there for seven and a half years (II Sam 5), and also that Absalom tried to unite the people in a revolt there against David, these episodes do not indicate necessarily that the place was named Hebron because of these various activities.

Hebron was perhaps the highest town in Palestine (elevation 3,040 feet). Abraham built his third altar in its vicinity (Gen 13:18), lived and buried his dear one there (Gen 23). It was given to Caleb as part of his inheritance (Josh 14:13–14). It continued to have religious significance in Israel because it became a city of refuge (Josh 1:13), and it was the scene of the establishment of the Davidic theocratic monarchy (II Sam 2:4; 5:3). It remained a worship center (II Sam 15:7, 8) even after David transferred his capital to Jerusalem. It may be noted that in those years the tabernacle at Shiloh was destroyed and the temple of Solomon not yet built. There were then different acknowledged places of God-honoring worship of which Hebron was one, Gibeon another and there were others.

maḥberet. This feminine noun is not translated by one specific word. It refers to the things joined, e.g. curtain pieces of the tabernacle (Ex 26:4–5) or the shoulder pieces of the priestly garment (Ex 39:20). It also refers to the actual place where the joining of two or more pieces took place.

G.V.G.

חֲבַרְבֻּרָה (*ḥăbarbūrâ*). See no. 598h.
חֶבְרוֹן (*ḥebrôn*). See no. 598i.
חֲבֶרֶת (*ḥăberet*). See no. 598d.
חֹבֶרֶת (*ḥōberet*). See no. 598e.

599 חָבַשׁ (*ḥābash*) ***bind, saddle, bandage, govern.***

Used in the Qal, Piel, and Pual stems. Cognate with Ugaritic *ḥbsh* (UT 19: no. 835); Akkadian *abāshu;* Arabic *ḥabasa* "to confine, to restrict." It occurs thirty-three times.

ḥābash means "to bind on" one's headgear in Ex 29:9; Lev 8:13; Ezk 24:17. Jonah speaks of the seaweeds which were "bound" around his head (Jon 2:5 [H 6]).

It is used frequently of "saddling" an ass: Gen 22:3; Num 22:21; II Sam 17:23; I Kgs 13:13, etc.

In Ezk 27:24 a passive participle is used for a decoration of "twisted" cordwork.

ḥābash is often used of "binding" on a bandage, and thus of medicating and healing the wounded.

In Job 34:17 *ḥābash* has the sense of "rule" or "govern."

In Job 40:13 *ḥābash* is taken in the sense of the Arabic *ḥabasa* "to imprison" by the NAB. The NEB aptly translates "shroud them in an unknown grave."

Many scholars (Dhorme, Dahood, Pope, Rowley) and some translations (JB, NAB, NIV) interpret *ḥibbēsh* in Job 28:11 as representing *ḥippēś* "searches," instead of KJV "bindeth" or NEB "dams up," on the basis of the Vulgate, Aquila, and Ugaritic evidence. Instead of damming the floods, the miner would be represented as searching out the sources of the rivers.

E.Y.

600 חבת (*ḥbt*). **Assumed root of the following.**
600a חֲבִתִּים (*ḥăbittîm*) ***flat cakes or bread wafers*** (I Chr 9:31, only).
600b מַחֲבַת (*maḥăbat*) ***flat plate, pan, or griddle*** (e.g. Lev 2:5; 6:14; Ezk 4:3).

חֲבִתִּים (*ḥăbittîm*). See no. 600a.
חַג (*ḥag*). See no. 602a.
חָגָא (*ḥāgā'*). See no. 602b.

601 חגב (*ḥgb*). **Assumed root of the following.**
601a †חָגָב (*ḥāgāb*) ***grasshopper or locust.***

The word may be derived from a root which in Arabic means "to cover" or "to conceal," alluding to the covering of the ground or the concealing of the sun by locust swarms. The term *ḥgb* appears in Ugaritic (UT 19: no. 836). In the Talmud the word becomes the general term for locust.

The word appears five times. The KJV translates it four times as "grasshopper" and once as "locust" in II Chr 7:13.

ḥāgāb occurs at Eccl 12:5 in a difficult passage which describes the progressive senility of a man. The NEB has "the locust's paunch is swollen," and the NAB "the locust grows sluggish," which portrays the stiffness of the aged. On the basis of Arabic cognates, some hold that the word here is a term for the hip.

See also *'arbeh.*

E.Y.

602 חָגַג (*ḥāgag*) ***celebrate, keep (hold) a (solemn) feast (holy day).*** (ASV and RSV similar.)

Derivatives

602a †חַג (*ḥag*) ***feast.***
602b חָגָא (*ḥāgā'*) ***reeling*** used only in Isa 19:17. (Derivative from *ḥāgag* unsure.)

The basic idea of this root is "keep a feast" or "celebrate a holiday" but the word usually refers to the three main pilgrimage-feasts of Israel. The verb is used sixteen times while the derivative *ḥag* (below) is used sixty-one times.

Most often the verb (sometimes with its cognate accusative) is used specifically for the celebration of one of the three main pilgrim-feasts (Ex 23:14), the Passover together with the Feast of Unleavened Bread, the Feast of Weeks or Harvest of Firstfruits, and the Feast of Booths (Tabernacles) or Feast of Ingathering.

The Passover, instituted at the Exodus (Ex 12),

commemorated God's sparing the Israelites when the first-born of Egypt died. It was the fourteenth day of the first month (Abib or Nisan, about April). It was followed on the fifteenth day by the Feast of Unleavened Bread which was held for a week with a special feast on the final day (Ex 13:3–10; Lev 23:4–8; Deut 16:1–8). The two are usually considered as one feast. By this feast Israel not only expressed heartfelt joy for the Lord's deliverance, but was reminded of its devotion to the Law (Ex 13:9).

The Feast of Weeks or Harvest of Firstfruits later known as Pentecost because it was held fifty days after the first day of Unleavened Bread (fifteenth day of Nisan), although properly fifty days after the waving of the sheaf of the firstfruits (which was done on a Sabbath, therefore Pentecost fell on Sunday) (Lev 23:9–21), done at the beginning of the harvest (Deut 16:9–11). The feast, then, commemorated the first fifty days of harvest.

The Feast of Ingathering was held for a week starting the fifteenth day of the seventh month (Ethanim or Tishri, about October) to celebrate the end of the harvest period (Ex 23:16). This was in conjunction with the Feast of Booths (Tabernacles) or Succoth which commemorated the time when the children of Israel lived in tents. For a week all native Israelites were to live in booths to remind them of a different era (Lev 23:33–43; Deut 16:13). The two feasts were considered one, and with the Day of Atonement and New Year's the seventh month was especially feastive. Today it is called the time of the high holy days.

The verb is used more generally in Ps 42:4 [H 5] and Nah 2:1, but the reference is probably to one or all of the above feasts. It is also used by Moses in his request to Pharoah that the children of Israel might leave to hold a feast.

David found his enemies, the Amalekites, "spread abroad . . . eating and drinking and feasting" (I Sam 30:16), that is, they were acting as if they were holding a feast. The ASV and RSV translate "dancing." More difficult to translate is Ps 107:27. The context pictures sailors on a storm-tossed ship, staggering like drunken men. A parallel to staggering in this context would hardly be feasting, but the actions of one feasting or dancing at a feast might be descriptive of the sailors, hence the translation "reel (to and fro)."

ḥag. ***(Solemn) feast, feast day.*** The noun means "pilgrim feast" or simply "holiday," i.e. a day or season of religious joy. The Arabic cognate, *haǧǧun,* is used to refer to a pilgrimage to Mecca.

The use of this noun is limited mainly to the three pilgrim-feasts mentioned above. Four times it is used for each of tte three in a single context (Ex 23:15–16; 34:18–22; Deut 16:16; II Chr 8:13). Otherwise the noun applies most often (twenty times) to the Feast of Booths (Ingathering), secondly (eleven times) to the Feast of Unleavened Bread (or Passover) and once to the Feast of Weeks (Deut 16:10).

ḥag is used for the feast instituted by Jeroboam I to take the place of the Feast of Booths (I Kgs 12:32–33). The term is used on two occasions for specific feasts which are left unnamed (Jud 21:19; Ps 81:3 [H 4]). There are nine references to feasts in general.

In Ex 23:18 the phrase "fat of my feast" is parallel to "blood of my sacrifice." The term feast is used of the sacrifice connected with the feast, hence the KJV translation here is "sacrifice." The KJV and ASV translate *ḥag* as "sacrifice" also in Ps 118:27 on the basis that since it is bound and the altar is mentioned, it must be an animal. The RSV "festal procession" assumes the binding to be decorative and figurative. The term is used by Moses to refer to the feast he requested from Pharoah to be allowed to hold (Ex 10:9). It is also used for the feast held in honor of Aaron's calf (Ex 32:5).

The term *mô'ēd* "appointed time," is also used for "feast," but is a broader term including sabbaths, new moons, etc.

[Critical scholars debate the development of these feasts. Eissfeldt puts it, "Thus, for example, in J and in E (Ex. 34:18a, 22; 23:15a,a,16) the connections of the three agricultural festivals with nature is quite clear. These connections remain recognisable in D too (Deut. 16:3a, 9–11, 13–15), no matter whether the statements made here are original or not and also in H (Lev. 23:9–12, 15–21, 39–43)" (*Old Testament Introduction,* trans. P. R. Ackroyd, Harper, 1965, p. 207). The matter is treated extensively from a similar viewpoint by DeVaux (AI, pp. 484–501).

It is indeed true that these feasts have an agricultural aspect. This is emphasized, as Eissfeldt says, in Ex, Lev, and Deut. DeVaux argues that a feast like Passover was not agricultural, but became attached to the agricultural feast of unleavened bread at a late date. All this is supposition. It is rather natural that the institution of the Passover in Ex 12 does not emphasize the agricultural. The further provisions given in view of entering the land do.

Apparently the Passover season with the sheaf of firstfruits (Lev 23:10) signalized the beginning of barley harvest. The feast of weeks in June would be at the end of the wheat harvest. The feast of booths or ingathering would celebrate the grape harvest as well as olive, dates, and other fruit. These feasts were pilgrimage festivals, i.e. all males had to come to the sanctuary and bring their contribution which were given in kind (Ex 23:15). R.L.H.]

Bibliography: Haran, Menahem, "zebah hayyamim," VT 19: 11–22. Lewy, Hildegard and Julius, "The Origin of the Week and the Oldest West Asiatic Calendar," HUCA 17: 1–152. Morgenstern, Julian, "Supplementary Studies in the Calendars of Ancient Israel," HUCA 10: 1–148. Richardson, TWB, pp. 211–13. Segal, J. B., "The Hebrew Festivals and the Calendar," JSS 6: 74–94. Snaith, Norman H., "Time in the Old Testament," in *Promise and Fulfillment,* ed. F. F. Bruce, Edinburgh: T. & T. Clark, 1963, pp. 175–86. Stewart, Roy A., "The Jewish Festivals," EQ 43: 149–61.

C.P.W.

603 חגה (*ḥgh*). **Assumed root of the following.**
603a חֲגָוִים (*ḥăgāwîm*) ***places of concealment, retreats*** (Song 2:14; Jer 49:16; Ob 3).

חֲגוֹר (*ḥăgôr*). See no. 604a.
חָגוֹר (*ḥāgôr*). See no. 604b.

604 חָגַר (*ḥāgar*) ***gird.***

Derivatives

604a †חֲגוֹר (*ḥăgôr*) ***girdle, belt.***
604b חָגוֹר (*ḥāgôr*) ***girded*** (Ezk 23:15, only).
604c †חֲגוֹרָה (*ḥăgôrâ*) ***girdle, belt.***
604d מַחֲגֹרֶת (*maḥăgōret*) ***girding, sash***

ḥāgar is cognate with Akkadian *agāru* "to surround," Ugaritic *ḥgr* "to gird" (UT 19, no. 837), and Arabic *ḥağara* "to restrain." It appears in the Bible forty-four times.

The verb is used of girding the girdle and other garments in Ex 29:9, Lev 8:7, 13, etc. It is used of girding about the loins the sackcloth, the garment of coarse goats' hair used in mourning or in penitence: II Sam 3:31; I Kgs 20:32; Isa 22:12, 32:11; Lam 2:10.

ḥāgar is often used of the girding on of a sword as in I Sam 17:39; Ps 45:3 [H 4]. In I Sam 25:13 NEB and JB translate "buckle on" the sword. In Jud 18:11 the armed men are literally "girded" with weapons.

The proverbial statement in I Kgs 20:11, literally "let not him who is girding boast as he who is ungirding," means, as the Targum indicates, "Let not him who is girding himself and going down into the battle boast himself as the man who has conquered and is coming up from it." The NEB substitution, "The lame must not think himself a match for the nimble," is hardly appropriate.

The custom of tucking up one's long flowing robes into the girdle before strenuous activity or walking quickly has given us the expression "to gird up one's loins"."

An important use of the term appears in Ps 76:10 [H 11], where the KJV reads: "Surely the wrath of man shall praise thee: the remainder of wrath shalt thou *restrain* (lit, gird)." This means that God girds on himself as a garment the last futile efforts of man's wrath. This is the general sense of the RV, RSV, NASB, and JB.

On the other hand, the NEB and the NAB repoint *'ādām* "man" as *'ĕdôm* "Edom" and *ḥēmōt* "wrath(s)" as *ḥămāt* "Hamath," a city in Syria, and follow the LXX's *heortasei,* which presupposes the verb *ḥāgag* "make festival" instead of *ḥāgar.* The NAB reads: "For the wrathful Edom shall glorify you and the survivors of Hamath shall keep your festivals." The NIV is: "Your wrath against men brings you praise, and the survivors of your wrath are restrained."

The appearance of the verb *yaḥgᵉrû* in II Sam 22:46 seems to be a textual error for *yaḥrᵉgû* "they came out."

ḥăgôrâ, ḥăgôr. ***Girdle, belt.*** The feminine form *ḥăgôrâ* is used five times and the masculine form *ḥăgôr* is used three times.

The *ḥăgôrâ* was mankind's first garment, loincloths (KJV, RSV "aprons") hastily improvised from fig leaves by Adam and Eve (Gen 3:7).

The *ḥăgôrâ* as worn by women was not an undergarment, as the word "girdle" connotes in modern usage, but a valuable ornamented belt or sash like the Japanese *obi* (Isa 3:24; Prov 31:24).

With men the *ḥăgôrâ* (*ḥăgôr*) was the accoutrement on which the sword was hung (I Sam 18:4). The phrase designating young men fit for military service is "all who were able to put on the *ḥăgôrâ*" (II Kgs 3:21; KJV "armour," NEB "arms"). This military belt was highly prized as a trophy of war (II Sam 18:11); Cyrus Gordon believes that this verse reflects a tradition of belt wrestling.

For an illustration of belt wrestling see ANEP, fig. 219. For synonyms see *'abnēṭ, 'ēzôr, ḥēsheb, mēzaḥ.*

Bibliography: Gordon, Cyrus H., "Belt-Wrestling in the Bible World," *The Hebrew Union College Annual,* 1950–51, pp. 131–36; plates I-V. Hönig, H. W., *Die Bekleidung des Hebräers,* Zürich: Brunner, Bodmer, 1957, pp. 26–27, 76–77.

E.Y.

חַד (*ḥad*). See no. 605a.

605 חָדַד (*ḥādad*) ***be sharp, keen*** (e.g. Hab 1:8; Isa 44:12).

Derivatives

605a חַד (*ḥad*) ***sharp*** (e.g. Ezk 5:1; Isa 49:2).
605b חִדּוּד (*ḥaddûd*) ***sharpened, pointed*** (Job 41:22).

606 חָדָה (*ḥādâ*) ***I, be (come) sharp*** (Prov 27:17).

607 חָדָה (*ḥādâ*) ***II, rejoice*** in the Qal stem, and make glad or gladden in the Piel stem.

Derivative

607a חֶדְוָה (*ḥedwâ*) ***gladness, joy.***

The verb is used but once in the Piel in Ps 21:7, "Thou hast made him exceeding glad with thy countenance" (KJV).

It is used in the Qal in Ex 18:9 to describe Jethro's rejoicing when he heard the report of Moses. Another occurrence has been suggested at Jer 31:13 by reading the MT *yaḥdāw* "together" as *yaḥdū* "shall be merry," a reading supported by the LXX and adopted by the RSV, the JB ("will be happy"), and the NEB ("shall rejoice"). The MT reading is upheld by the NAB ("as well") and by J. Bright.

Bibliography: Bright, John, *Jeremiah,* Doubleday, 1965, p. 274. Dahood, M., "Ugaritic and the Old Testament," *Ephemerides Theologicae Lovanienses* 44:51.

E.Y.

608 חָדָה (*ḥādâ*) ***III, see, gaze;*** Niphal ***appear.***

In addition to the common Hebrew *ḥāzâ*, reflecting Ugaritic *ḥdy*, M. Dahood in numerous articles and books has proposed that we should also recognize many instances in which the Hebrew text has preserved the variant *ḥādâ* "to see."

These suggestions have not been incorporated in any recent translations but some of his more plausible proposals have been listed in Koehler-Baumgartner's lexicon (cf. HCHL).

In Ps 33:15 where the KJV has, "He fashioneth their hearts "alike" *yaḥad,* Dahood would suggest, "The creator "inspects," *yaḥd(eh),* their intention." In Ps 49:10 [H 11] instead of the KJV, "*Likewise* the fool and the brutish person perish," Dahood renders, "If he 'gazes' upon fools." Instead of the RSV translation of Job 34:29, " 'whether' it be a nation or a man," he would propose, "Upon nations and men he 'gazes.' "

In Gen 49:6 and Job 3:6 instead of reading the verbs as forms of *yāḥad* "to be united or joined," Dahood would see them as Niphals of *ḥādâ* and render them "appear."

Bibliography: Dahood, M., "Some Ambiguous Texts in Isaias," CBQ 20: 46–48. ——, "Hebrew-Ugaritic Lexicography," *Bib* 45: 407–8. ——, "Ugaritic Lexicography," in *Mélanges Eugène Tisserant,* I, Vatican: Biblioteca Apostolica Vaticana, 1964, p. 88. ——, *Psalms I,* in AB, Doubleday, 1966. Ginsberg, H., "Lexicographical Notes," in *Hebräische Wortforschung,* Leiden: Brill, 1967, pp. 71–72. Smick, E., "Suggested New Translations of Old Testament Poetry," BETS 11: 90–91.

E.Y.

חַדּוּד (*ḥaddûd*). See no. 605b.
חֶדְוָה (*ḥedwâ*). See no. 607a.

609 חָדַל (*ḥādal*) ***I, cease, stop, forbear, desist, forego.***

Derivatives

609a †חֶדֶל (*ḥedel*) ***cessation.***
609b †חָדֵל (*ḥādēl*) ***fleeting, rejected.***

The word is cognate with the Arabic *ḫadala* "to leave, forsake"; the root is unknown in Ugaritic. The verb occurs fifty-five times.

ḥādal most often means to cease doing something, as in Gen 11:8; Jud 15:7; Job 3:17; I Sam 12:23; Jer 44:18; 51:30.

It can mean to "forbear" or "refrain" from doing something, as in Job 16:6. The question put to the oracle in I Kgs 22:6 was, "Shall I go . . . to battle or shall I forbear?" In II Chr 25:16 the imperative means "stop" (RSV), "be quiet" (JB).

In the parable of the trees in Jud 9:9, 11, 13 *ḥādal* means "shall I give up."

In Num 9:13 the word means "neglect" or "fail."

In Job 19:14 the verb can have either a transitive sense: Job's relatives have failed or deserted him (RSV, NAB), or an intransitive sense: they have fallen away (NEB).

In Ex 24:12 *ḥādal* means "to leave alone." Job twice asks that God leave him alone (Job 7:16; 10:20). The prophet in Isa 2:22 advises his hearers, "cease ye from man" (KJV), i.e. "have no more to do with man" (NEB).

ḥādal is used eight times in the absolute sense of "cease" or "come to an end."

ḥedel. ***Cessation.*** In Isa 38:11, the sole occurrence, the word *ḥedel* is usually emended to read *ḥeled* "world." Inasmuch as 1QIs[a] has the same form as the MT, Dahood suggests that *ḥedel* is correct and means "cessation."

ḥādēl. ***Fleeting, rejected.*** Appears three times in three different senses. In Ezk 3:27 it means "one who forbears," or refuses to heed the prophet. In Ps 39:4 [H 5] translated "frail" (KJV), the word means "fleeting" or "short lived."

In Isa 53:3 the Messiah is described as "rejected of men" (KJV, RSV, JB, NIV), "avoided by men" (NAB). The alternative suggestion of Thomas, "forsaking men," is followed by the NEB, "he shrank from the sight of men." Calderone suggests "senseless," from a root *ḥādal* II "to be fat" (q.v.). Neither is a preferable alternative.

Bibliography: Dahood, Mitchell, "*ḥedel* 'Cessation' in Isaiah 38, 11," Bib 52: 215–16. Gordis, Robert, "Studies in Hebrew Roots of Contrasted Meanings," JQR 27: 33–58. Thomas, D. Winton, "Some Observations on the Hebrew Root *ḥdl*," Supp VT 4: 8–16.

E.Y.

610 חָדַל (*ḥādal*) ***II?, to be fat, to be prosperous.***

Citing the Arabic *hadula* "to become fat, plump." Thomas and Calderone have suggested that in some passages *ḥādal* may reflect an altogether different root. This may be plausible for I Sam 2:5 which would read, "The hungry grew fat." Job 14:6 would then read "that he may be filled with food" instead of "that he may rest."

In Prov 19:27 Calderone would read "grow prosperous . . . by hearing instruction"; in Prov 23:4 "by your wisdom grow prosperous."

Bibliography: Calderone, Philip J., "*ḤDL*-II in Poetic Texts," CBQ 23: 451–60. ———, "Supplementary Note on *ḤDL*-II," CBQ 24: 412–19.

E.Y.

611 חדק (*ḥdq*). **Assumed root of the following.**

611a חֵדֶק (*ḥēdeq*) ***brier*** (Mic 7:4; Prov 15:19).

612 חָדַר (*ḥādar*) ***surround, enclose.*** Occurs only in Ezk 21:19, as a Qal feminine singular participle, *haḥōderet lāhem* "that which surrounds them."

Derivative

612a †חֶדֶר (*ḥeder*) ***chamber, innermost or inward part, parlor, within.*** (ASV and RSV similar except that they do not use the last three words.)

The word means a "compartment" or "room" (within a building) which affords privacy. The KJV usually translates this word as "chamber," using "room" in the sense of "space." A general word for "chamber" is *lishkâ*. Another term, *'ălīyyâ*, refers to a cool "roof-chamber." *ḥeder* is used thirty-nine times, including seven figurative usages.

ḥeder mainly designates a room where people, even rulers, can find privacy (Gen 43:30, Joseph: I Kgs 1:15, David; Jud 3:24, Eglon). It may be that the *ḥeder* to which Eglon went was a room within the roof chamber (*'ăliyyâ*), not the roof chamber itself. Specifically *ḥeder* is used in reference to the ruler's bedroom (*ḥădar mishkāb*), where frogs were to enter (Ex 8:3 [H 7:28]). Ishbosheth (II Sam 4:7), and the King of Syria (II Kgs 6:12) were murdered there. *ḥeder* is the room of the bridegroom (Joel 2:16), the birthplace of a bride and the place to which she brings the bridegroom (Song 3:4), and the room in which Samson planned to meet with his wife (Jud 15:1).

It is a place to hide: for people in general (Isa 26:20), men lying in wait for Samson (Jud 16:9, 12), Joash hidden from Athaliah (KJV "in the bedchamber," *ḥădar hammiṭṭôt* II Kgs 11:2 same as II Chr 22:11), Benhadad hiding from Ahab (I Kgs 20:30). The last passage actually reads "a room in a room" and is translated "inner chamber." The same phrase is used by Micaiah when telling the false prophet Zedekiah where he would hide (I Kgs 22:25, same as II Chr 18:24) and by Elisha when telling the prophet where to take Jehu to anoint him (II Kgs 9:2). The *ḥeder* is a place where one can do evil in secret: Amnon (II Sam 13:10f.), the elders of Israel (Ezk 8:12).

More generally the word is used for inner rooms of the temple complex (KJV parlours, I Chr 28:11) and for storerooms (Prov 24:4). In Deut 32:25 it is used in contrast with "outside," hence KJV "within." (Terrors and destruction are to come in both places.) It is not used for the holy of holies of the tabernacle or temple.

The word is used four times figuratively, referring to chambers within the belly. "The words of a whisperer go down to the 'innermost parts of' the belly" (Prov 18:8; 26:22). The same area is searched (Prov 20:27), and made clean by stripes (Prov 20:30). The phrase, "chambers of death" (Prov 7:27), may possibly refer to an afterlife but more likely refers to tombs or the graveyard. It is parallel to "Sheol" (cf. "The Meaning of the Word Sheol," JETS 4: 129–35.

The word is also used figuratively of the chamber from which a stormwind (*sûpâ*, q.v.) comes (Job 37:9). The KJV translates *ḥeder* as "south" for the assumed source of the stormwind, but RSV is probably more accurate in rendering: "From its chamber comes the whirlwind." "Chamber of the south" (Job 9:9) may name a constellation or be the confines of one.

C.P.W.

613 חָדַשׁ (*ḥādash*) ***renew, repair.*** (ASV and RSV also restore.)

Derivatives

613a †חָדָשׁ (*ḥādāsh*) ***new, new thing, fresh.***

613b †חֹדֶשׁ (*ḥōdesh*) ***month, monthly, new moon.***

ḥādash is used in the sense of "repair" or "rebuild" referring to cities (Isa 61:4), the temple (II Chr 24:4, 12), and the altar (II Chr 15:8). It is also used figuratively. Under Samuel the kingdom was renewed at Gilgal (I Sam 11:14). David wanted a right spirit, equivalent to a clean heart, renewed within him (Ps 51:10 [H 12]). The prophet asked for renewal as of old (Lam 5:21). God renews the face of the ground, that is, gives it new life (Ps 104:30), and he renews one's youth (Ps 103:5). Job complained that God was bringing new witnesses against him (Job 10:17).

The use of the verb as well as its derivatives is attested in Ugaritic (see UT 19: no. 843.)

ḥādāsh. ***New, new thing, fresh.*** This adjective, usually attributive, describes, as in English, a variety of physical objects (e.g., house, wife, cords, sword, garment, cruse, meal offering, king, gate, etc.). It is also used for non-material things as name (Isa 62:2), song (Ps 149:1), covenant (Jer 31:31), God's mercies (Lam 3:23), heart, and spirit (Ezk 36:26). While suffering, Job longed for the time when his glory was "fresh" in him (Job 29:20).

ḥōdesh. ***Month, monthly, new moon.*** Although this word properly means "new moon," it is commonly used as an equivalent to our word "month" because the month began when the thin crescent of the new moon was first visible at sunset. It was used along with the more rare *yeraḥ,* from *yārēaḥ* meaning "moon." (Note especially I Kgs 6:1, 37, 38; 8:2 where the terms are used interchangeably. Although *yeraḥ* is never used as a numbered month, its use as a named month is attested in Ugaritic as well as the OT. See UT 19: no. 1151.) The Hebrew calendar used a lunar month fitted into a solar year. This was done by adding an extra month approximately once every three years because it was about eleven days less than the solar year. In early Israel the first of each month, or new moon, was determined by observation and proclaimed officially by the blowing of trumpets. The month was considered to be thirty days (note Gen 7:11; cf. 8:3–4), unless the new moon was observed earlier.

Only four of the names of the months used in Israel's earlier history are recorded in the Old Testament: Abib, the first month (Ex 13:4), Ziv (Zif), the second month (I Kgs 6:1), Ethanim, the seventh month (I Kgs 8:2), and Bul, the eighth month (I Kgs 6:38). Most often the months were designated by number. (Note especially I Chr 27:1–15 where all twelve are listed by number.) Later the Babylonian names were incorporated into Hebrew. Of these, seven are used in the Old Testament: Nisan, the first month (Neh 2:1), Sivan, the third (Est 8:9), Elul, the sixth (Neh 6:15), Kislev, the ninth (Zech 7:1), Tebeth, the tenth (Est 2:16), Shebat (Sebat), the eleventh (Zech1:7), and Adar, the twelfth (Est 3:7).

The first month, Abib/Nisan, began in the spring with the vernal equinox. This was commanded in Ex 12:2, 18. But according to Ex 23:16 and 34:22 the Feast of Ingathering (held in the seventh month, Lev 23:39) was held at the end of the year (perhaps the agricultural year). The Feast of Trumpets (Lev 23:23–25; Num 29:1–6) was held on the first day of the seventh month and is now celebrated as the Jewish New Year (Rosh Hashanah). Thus there is evidence of an older alternate calendar year starting in the fall. The use of *ḥōdesh* "to devour those who sinned" (Hos 5:7) may be that they will be swallowed up in another month. But possibly the vain offering of the unrepentant is his own downfall (cf. KD), or perhaps the participation in a pagan new moon celebration is his downfall (cf. IB).

When *ḥōdesh* refers only to the beginning of the month, it is naturally translated "new moon," which was a feast day. It is one of the "appointed feasts" and is listed with the Sabbath and the pilgrim feasts as involving burnt offerings (II Chr 8:13 et al.), and is also characterized by the blowing of trumpets (Ps 81:3 [H 4]; Num 10:10). Since it was a feast, David's absence from Saul's table at the new moon was especially noticeable (I Sam 20:5f.).

Bibliography: Morgenstern, Julian, "The Three Calendars of Ancient Israel," HUCA 1: 13–78. ———, "Supplementary Studies in the Calendars of Ancient Israel," HUCA 10: 1–148. Wright, G. Ernest, "Israelite Daily Life," BA 18: 50–79. THAT, I, pp. 524–29.

C.P.W.

614 *חוּב (*ḥûb*) ***make guilty.*** Used but once in the Piel stem. In Dan 1:10 with the word *rō'sh* it means to endanger one's head (KJV, ASV, RSV). The NEB paraphrases the clause, "It will cost me my head."

Derivative

614a חוֹב (*ḥôb*) ***debt.*** Occurs only in Ezk 18:7.

E.Y.

615 חוּג (*ḥûg*) ***describe a circle, compass.*** Used only once, having the object *ḥōq* expressed (Job 26:10).

Derivatives

615a חוּג (*ḥûg*) ***circuit, circle, compass.***

615b †מְחוּגָה (*m*^e^*ḥûgâ*) ***compass.*** Occurs only in Isa 44:13.

In Job 26:10 the Creator has "compassed the waters with bounds" (KJV), or according to the more literal rendering of the RSV, "He has described a circle upon the face of the waters." This may mean the establishment of a boundary in the distance as the NEB, "He has fixed the horizon," or at the shore (cf. Job 38:8, 11). This is also the thought found in the use of the noun in Prov 8:27, "He set a compass upon the face of the depth" (KJV), which the NEB renders, "He girdled the ocean with the horizon."

Job 22:14 (KJV) declares that God "walketh in

the circuit of heaven" (*ḥûg shāmayîm*); the "vault" of heaven is the expression used by the RSV, NAB, and NEB. The JB translates, "He prowls on the rim of the heavens."

Isaiah 40:22 (KJV) asserts that the Creator sits upon the "circle of the earth" (*ḥûg hā'āreṣ*), a rendering retained by the ASV, RSV, and JB. The NAB has, "He sits enthroned above the vault of the earth," which the NEB amplifies as the "vaulted roof of the earth." NIV: "He sits enthroned above the circle of the earth." The poets of the OT describe their universe phenomenologically, i.e. as it appears to them standing on the earth and looking above and about. This perspective differs from that of modern scientific thought, which assumes a perspective beyond the earth. Both are accurate and useful according to their own perspectives.

Some have held that Isa 40:22 implies the sphericity of the earth. It may, but it may refer only to the Lord enthroned above the earth with its obviously circular horizon. Note the remarkable concept given in Job 26:7.

m^eḥûgâ. ***Compass.*** Occurs only in Isa 44:13 where it describes an instrument used by a carpenter as he fashions an idol. The LXX renders this as *metron* "measure" or "rule." Most versions (AV, ASV, RSV, NAB) translate the word as "compass," NIV "compasses," but the JB uses "dividers" and the NEB "calipers."

E.Y.

616 חוּד (*ḥûd*) ***propound a riddle.*** Denominative verb.

Parent Noun

616a †חִידָה (*ḥîdâ*) ***riddle, difficult question, parable.***

A derivation has been suggested from Aramaic *'ăḥad* "hold fast, cover," for the Aramaic *'aḥîdâ* "riddle" (cf. Dan 5:12). The *ḥîdâ* is an enigmatic saying, question, or story whose meaning must be determined by the audience.

It is used seventeen times. The KJV translates it nine times as "riddle," five times as "dark" sentences, speeches, or sayings, twice as "hard questions," and once as "proverb."

It is used eight times in Jud 14 of "riddles" propounded by Samson to the Philistine guests at his wedding. These were conundrums involving a contest of wits, a source of entertainment popular among Arabs today. Cf. the contest of the guardsmen in I Esd 3: 4–24.

At a higher social level the *ḥîdôt* in I Kgs 10:1 (II Chr 9:1) were "difficult questions" posed by the Queen of Sheba to test Solomon's reputation for wisdom. Josephus (*Antiquities* 8.5.3 [143]) describes Hiram of Tyre sending Solomon "tricky problems and enigmatic sayings."

The Psalmist in Ps 49:4 [H 5] speaks of the "riddle" of life, death, and redemption.

In Num 12:8 the "dark speeches" denote the indirect revelations ordinarily given by the Lord, in contrast to the face-to-face mode of communication granted to Moses.

See also *māshāl,* which occurs together with *ḥîdâ* in Ps 49:4 [H 5]; Ps 78:2; Prov 1:6; Ezk 17:2; and Hab 2:6.

Bibliography: Rinaldi, G., "Alcuni termini ebraici relativi alla letteratura," *Bib* 49:274–76.

E.Y.

617 חוה (*ḥwh*) **I. Assumed root of the following.**

617a חַוָּה (*ḥawwâ*) ***tent village*** (e.g. Deut 3:14; Josh 13:30).

618 חָוָה (*ḥāwâ*) ***II, show, tell, make known.***

Derivative

618a אַחְוָה (*'aḥwâ*) ***declaration,*** only in Job 13:17.

ḥāwâ is used in the Piel stem five times in Job and once in Psalms.

In Job it is used of the condescending efforts of Eliphaz and Elihu to instruct Job: 15:17; 32:6, 10, 17; 36:2. Cf. Sir 16:25.

In Ps 19:2 [H 3] night after night "imparts" (NAB) or "reveals" (NASB) knowledge.

The corresponding verb in Aramaic is used in the Pael and (H)aphel stems fourteen times in Daniel.

Scholars have cited the use of the verb in Job as an Aramaism.

The verb appears often in the Elephantine Aramaic papyri, and in the Genesis Apocryphon (2:5, 6, 21; 5:9; 22:3).

Bibliography: Vogt, Ernestus, *Lexicon Linguae Aramaicae Veteris Testamenti,* Pontifical Biblical Institute, 1971, pp. 60–61. Wagner, Max, *Die Lexikalischen und Grammatikalischen Aramaismen in alttestamentlichen Hebräisch,* Berlin: Töpelmann, 1966, p. 53.

E.Y.

619 חָוָה (*ḥāwâ*) ***III, exclusively in the Eshtaphal stem,*** *hishtaḥăwâ* ***"to prostrate oneself"; "to worship."***

Formerly this was analyzed as a Hithpael of *shāḥâ* (q.v.). Cognate with the Ugaritic *ḥwy* "to bow down" (UT 19: no. 847), used in parallel with *kbd* "to honor," the verb occurs 170 times, in the majority of cases of the worship of God, gods, or idols.

The verb in its original sense meant to prostrate oneself on the ground as in Neh 8:6 "worshipped" (KJV, RSV) but more correctly "prostrated themselves" (NEB, JB, NAB) as the phrase *'ārṣâ* "to the ground" requires.

Prostration was quite common as an act of submission before a superior. Vassals in the Amarna letters write, "At the feet of the king . . . seven times, seven times I fall, forwards and backwards." (Cf. ANEP, fig. 5.) Jehu or his servant bows down on his knees with his forehead touching the ground before Shalmaneser III on the Black Obelisk (cf. ANEP, fig. 351).

Muslims perform their *salaḥ* or prayer by an elaborately prescribed *suğûd* (cf. Heb *sāgad* "to bow down") in which the forehead must touch the ground.

The Greek word *proskuneō,* which is used to translate *hishtaḥăwâ* 148 times in the LXX, had a semantic development similar to the Hebrew word. Like it *proskuneō* can mean either "prostration" or "worship." Whether the *proskunēsis* which Alexander the Great received implied "worship" or simply "obeisance" was uncertain to his contemporaries, as it has been to scholars.

Prostration was a common act of self-abasement performed before relatives, strangers, superiors, and especially before royalty. Abraham bowed himself before the Hittites of Hebron (Gen 23:7, 12). He also bowed before the three strangers who visited him at Mamre (Gen 18:2), as did Lot before the two angelic visitors who came to him at Sodom (Gen 19:1). Neither realized at the time that they were before superhuman beings. Balaam, however, perceived that it was an angel who blocked his way, and he "fell prostrate" (JB, Num 22:31).

Following Egyptian protocol, Joseph's brothers made obeisance before him (Gen 42:6; 43:26, 28), thus fulfilling his dream (Gen 37:7, 9, 10).

Because of the infidelity of Eli's sons his posterity will be reduced by God's judgment (I Sam 2:36) "to crouch" (KJV); "to grovel" (NAB); "to beg him on their knees" (JB), i.e. to a state of beggary. At En-dor Saul recognized the revivified Samuel and "did obeisance" (I Sam 28:14, RSV).

It was in open defiance of Persian court etiquette that Mordecai refused to bow or to prostrate himself before Haman (Est 3:2, 5; cf. Herodotus 1.134; 3.86; 8.118). The Targum and Midrash explain Mordecai's refusal on the basis of an alleged idol on Haman's robe. Mordecai may have bridled at the thought of bowing before an Amalekite or Agagite (Est 3:1; cf. I Sam 15:32–33).

The verb is used in I Chr 29:20 with two phrases, literally as the KJV: "worshipped the Lord and the king." The NEB renders: "prostrating themselves before the Lord and the king" (cf. NAB); the JB has "went on their knees to do homage to Yahweh and to the king." The RSV supplies a second verb, "worshiped the Lord, and did obeisance to the king." Thus the Egyptians will bow themselves before Moses, petitioning him to leave, and kings and princesses will bow down before redeemed Zion (Ex 11:8; Isa 45:14; 49:23).

The verb is used less frequently of an individual's worship of the Lord. Abraham on his way to sacrifice Isaac says that he is going to worship (Gen 22:5). The distraught Saul asks for forgiveness that he might worship (I Sam 15:25, 30–31). It is used most often of particular acts of worship, e.g. of Abraham's servant who "bowed his head and worshipped" (Gen 24:26, 48), and of Gideon (Jud 7:15) upon experiencing God's grace. Such acts often involved actual prostration "to the earth" as in the case of Abraham's servant (Gen 24:52), Moses (Ex 34:8), Joshua (Josh 5:14), and Job (Job 1:20).

In Exodus there are three cases of spontaneous communal worship: when the people heard that the Lord had spoken to Moses (Ex 4:31), when they received instructions for the Passover (Ex 12:27), and when they saw the pillar of cloud (Ex 33:10). In II Chr 20:18 Jehoshaphat and the people "fell down before the Lord, worshiping the Lord" (RSV), when they heard his promise of victory.

Commands or invitations to worship are given to Moses, Aaron, and the elders in Ex 24:1, "Come up to the Lord . . . and worship afar off" (RSV), and on the occasion of the firstfruits, "you shall set it down before the Lord your God, and worship before the Lord your God" (Deut 26:10; unless indicated otherwise, subsequent citations will be from the RSV). The Psalmist exhorts, "O come, let us worship and bow down, let us kneel before the Lord, our Maker" (Ps 95:6).

After the death of Bathsheba's child David went into his chapel to worship (II Sam 12:20). His son, Solomon, completed the temple (II Chr 7:3), which became the focus of organized worship. Though there were rival sanctuaries, as archaeology has confirmed, Hezekiah insisted that worship should be conducted "before this altar in Jerusalem" (II Kgs 18:22; Isa 36:7; II Chr 32:12; cf. 29:29–30). The Psalmist declares, "I will worship toward thy holy temple" (Ps 5:7 [H 8]; cf. 138:2). Jeremiah spoke to those who worshipped in the temple of their need to repent (Jer 7:2; 26:2). As they did not repent, Nebuchadnezzar destroyed the temple, but Ezekiel beheld in a vision a new temple in which the prince and his people would worship (Ezk 46:2, 3, 9).

The Psalms and the prophets foresee the day when the gentiles will also worship. Those who will worship the Lord include: "all the earth" (Ps 66:4); "all flesh" (Isa 66:23); all the nations (Ps 22:27 [H 28]; 72:11; Zeph 2:11; Zech 14:16–17); kings and princes (Isa 49:7; cf. Ps 72:11); "all the fat ones" (RV; Ps 22:29 [H 30]), which the RSV interprets as "all the proud" and the JB as "all the prosperous" of the earth.

Before the Lord, not only men worship but also the *b^e nê 'ēlîm* (Ps 29:1–2) "sons of the mighty" (RV), literally "sons of God," probably angels (cf. Ps 89:6 [H 7] but also Ps 96:7). Nehemiah 9:6 declares that the host of heaven worship the Lord who created the heavens, the earth, and the seas. According to Ps 97:7 even "all gods bow down before him."

The second commandment forbids the worship of any graven images or other gods (Ex 20:5; 34:14; Deut 5:9). The Israelites were warned not to worship the gods of the Amorites, Hittites, etc. (Ex 23:24; Ps 81:9 [H 10]).

Nevertheless Israel repeatedly worshiped other gods (Deut 29:26 [H 25]; Jud 2:12, 17; Jer 13:10; 16:11; 22:9). These gods included those of the Moabites (Num 25:2), those of the Edomites (II Chr 25:14), Ashtoreth of the Sidonians, Chemosh of Moab, Milcom of the Ammonites (I Kgs 11:33), and Baal of Sidon (I Kgs 16:31; 22:53 [H 54]).

In an interesting passage the verb is used both of "worship" and of "bowing" without an attitude of worship. After Naaman's healing and his conversion to the monotheistic worship of the Lord (II Kgs 5:17), the Syrian officer asked Elisha, "In this matter may the Lord pardon your servant: when my master (i.e. the king) goes into the house of Rimmon *to worship* there, leaning on my arm, and *I bow myself* in the house of Rimmon, when *I bow myself* in the house of Rimmon, the Lord pardon your servant in this matter" (II Kgs 5:18, RSV). Elisha did not object and said, "Go in peace."

A problem passage is Gen 47:31 where Jacob before dying "bowed himself upon the head of the bed (*miṭṭâ*)." The LXX, however, reads, "And Israel worshiped, leaning on the top of his staff," rendering the consonants as *maṭṭeh* "staff." The Syriac and Itala agree; Heb 11:21 cites the LXX. In this context Speiser suggests, "The term 'to bow low' need not signify here anything more than a gesture of mute appreciation. . . ." Cf. also I Kgs 1:47 where the dying David bows down in bed.

See also *kākap, kāra', qādad, sāgad, 'ābad.*

Bibliography: Ap-Thomas, D. R., "Notes on Some Terms Relating to Prayer," VT 6: 229–30. Cranfield, C. E. B., "Divine and Human Action," Interp 12: 387–98. Davies, G. Henton, "Worship in the OT," in IDB, IV, pp. 879–83. Driver, G. R., "Studies in the Vocabulary of the Old Testament," JTS 31: 279–80. Rowley, H. H., Worship in Ancient Israel, London: S. P. C. K., 1967. Watts, John D. W., "Elements of Old Testament Worship," JBR 26: 217–21. TDNT, VI, pp. 758–63. THAT, I, pp. 530–32.

E.Y.

620 חוח (*ḥwḥ*). **Assumed root of the following.**
620a חוֹחַ (*ḥôaḥ*) ***brier, bramble.***
620b †חָח (*ḥāḥ*) ***hook, ring, brooch.***

ḥāḥ occurs seven times. It means "brooches" (KJV "bracelets") in the list of personal ornaments dedicated to the Lord's service (Ex 35:22).

In all the other passages it refers to hooks or rings used to capture and control men, employing the methods normally used to handle animals. The warning against Sennacherib (II Kgs 19:28; Isa 37:29) may possibly be drawn from actual practice, as we have an Assyrian relief of captives with a ring through the lips (ANEP, fig. 447; cf. fig. 524).

E.Y.

621 חוט (*ḥwṭ*). **Assumed root of the following.**
621a †חוּט (*ḥûṭ*) ***thread, string, cord.*** It appears seven times.

Abraham refused to accept from the king of Sodom so much as a "thread to a sandal strap" (Gen 14:23; cf. Genesis Apocryphon 22:21). This synecdoche, substitution of a part for the whole, in this case using small insignificant objects for totality, is found in a slightly different form in the Aramaic papyri (Cowley 15:25) *mn ḥm 'd ḥwṭ* "from straw to string."

Rahab's sign to the Israelites (Josh 2:18) was a cord made of scarlet thread. Samson was able to snap off the Philistine ropes like a "thread" (Jud 16:12).

See also *pātîl, ḥebel, 'ăbōt.*

Bibliography: Speiser, E. A., "A Figurative Equivalent for Totality in Akkadian and West Semitic," JAOS 54: 200–203.

E.Y.

622 חֲוִילָה (*ḥăwîlâ*) ***Havilah,*** the name of a number of tribes and places. It may be derived from *ḥôl,* and may mean "a sandy area."

The Pishon, the first-mentioned of the four rivers that went forth from the Garden of Eden, flowed through the "Havilah," a land of gold (Gen 2:11). It is not possible to establish where this was. Suggestions have ranged from India, Colchis, and Arabia, to northern Ethiopia and eastern Sudan. (See the discussion under *'ēd.*)

In the table of nations Havilah is listed with the sons of Cush (Gen 10:7; I Chr 1:9). Another Havilah is listed with the sons of Joktan (Gen 10:29; I Chr 1:23). The former tribe, "African" Havilah, may have been located on the coast of Eritrea and Somaliland in northeast Africa, corresponding to the classical *Abalitai/Aualitai* located south of the straits of Bab el-Mandeb. The latter tribe, "Arabian" Havilah, may have been located in the area of Yemen in Southwest Arabia where a Sabaean inscription locates *Haulān.*

A fourth Havilah is the area which makes up the eastern terminus of a route whose western terminus is Shur in northwest Sinai. The Ishmaelites settled in the territory between these termini (Gen 25:18). Saul pursued the Amalekites from Havilah toward Shur (I Sam 15:7). Eratosthenes cited by Strabo (16.4.2) lists the *Chaulotaioi* next to the Nabataeans in describing the route from Petra to Babylon; Pliny (6.32.157) also lists the *Avalitae* as neighbors of the Nabataeans. This Havilah may therefore be the area in northwest Arabia, east of the Sinai and Petra and northwest of Teima and the great Nafud Desert.

Bibliography: Simons, J., *The Geographical and Topographical Texts of the Old Testament,* Brill, 1959, pp. 40–41. Wissman, I. and Höfner, M., *Beiträge zur historischen Geographie des vorislamischen Südarabien,* Wiesbaden: Steiner, 1953, pp. 239–41. Yahauda, A. S., *The Language of the Pentateuch,* London: Oxford University, 1933, pp. 190–91.

E.Y.

חַח (*ḥāḥ*). See no. 620b.

623 חוּל (*ḥûl*) ***I, travail, be in anguish, be pained, dance, whirl, writhe, fear, tremble.*** (RSV "rage"; otherwise, RSV and ASV adopt same range of meanings, though individual verses may be interpreted differently).

Derivatives.

623a †חֹל (*ḥōl*) ***sand.***
623b †חִיל (*ḥîl*) ***pain, agony, sorrow.***
623c †חִילָה (*ḥîlâ*) ***pain (?).***
623d חֵל (*ḥēl*), חֵיל (*ḥêl*) ***rampart, fortress.***
623e חֵילָה (*ḥêlâ*) ***rampart, fortress.*** Occurs only in Ps 48:14.
623f †חַלְחָלָה (*ḥalḥālâ*) ***writhing.***
623g †מָחוֹל (*māḥôl*) ***dance, dancing.***
623h †מְחוֹלָה (*mᵉḥôlâ*) ***dance.***

The verb contains two basic ideas: 1) whirling around in circular movements (reflected in the derivatives *māḥôl* and *mᵉḥolâ*) and 2) writhing in labor pains (reflected in *ḥîl* and *ḥîlâ*). These may be taken as two distinct roots of similar form (KB) or as two emphases of the same root (BDB). This article adopts the latter point of view. Like several other verbs of movement (*e.g. ḥārad* and *pāḥad*) its meaning may also include those emotions and attitudes associated with the movements. (Note: *Englishman's Hebrew and Chaldee Concordance* erroneously lists forms from *ḥûl* II and *yāḥal* under this word.)

Physical movements of various sorts are in mind in referring to dancing (Jud 21:21), quaking movements of mountains (Hab 3:10), and, perhaps, the whirling (?) movements of a sword (Hos 11:6; RSV "rage" reflects this interpretation). Twice abstract quantities are figuratively viewed as physical entities which move or whirl about until they land on their targets: the curse on Joab is thus viewed (II Sam 3:29; "May it whirl around," writer's translation) as in God's anger, Jer 23:19; "swirl" (NASB). Another example of such figurative representation of an abstract quantity as a real, concrete, entity is the "sin" which crouched at the door for Cain (Gen 4:7).

This verb expresses the writhing movements of labor contractions (Isa 45:10) though it may recall the joys of bearing denied to the barren (Isa 54:1) as well as pain. Several times it describes those who are in anguish in witness of God's judgment (Isa 23:5; Ezk 30:16; Joel 2:6; Mic 4:10). In such cases the idea of inner mental anguish may displace the idea of writhing in pain as when Egypt is in anguish at the news of Tyre's fall (Isa 23:5). Jeremiah's complaint that those who have been judged have not felt anguish (Jer 5:3) refers to mental anguish or remorse. It also describes the anguish of the good man oppressed by the wicked (Ps 55:4 [H 5]).

Contextual parallels show that it can refer to writhing or trembling in terror (Ps 77:16 [H 17]; Jer 5:22). The same idiom underlies poetic similes in which the earth writhes or trembles (Ps 97:4; 114:7).

Several difficult passages must be noted. The interpretation that Saul was "wounded" by the Philistine archers (I Sam 31:3; RSV, KJV) has no support from other usages of "*ḥûl*"; its best support is the possibility of repointing the text so as to read the Hebrew word *ḥālal* "to pierce" (*wayyāḥōl*). As the text is pointed, "be terrified" or "harassed" (i.e. "put into anguish") is preferable. Two passages command the earth to "tremble" (RSV, ASV) or "fear" (KJV) before God (I Chr 16:30; Ps 96:9). However, unlike the two contexts in which the earth trembled above, these contexts are completely filled with positive acts of worship (I Chr 16:28, 29, 31; Ps 96: 7, 8, 10). For this reason, it is better in these contexts to interpret *ḥûl* with a term of positive worship, either as "dance" (i.e. the *mᵉḥôlâ* as a religious dance) or a joyful "trembling" in worship. The usage of this term in Lam 4:6 (RSV "laid") remains unclear.

The Hiphil is causative, "to make to writhe" or "to cause to be in anguish" (BDB; Ps 29:8, note: other possible Hiphils are better derived from *yaḥel:* Gen 8:10; Jud 3:25; Lam 3:26). The Hophal is passive, "to be born" (Isa 66:8, ASV, RSV).

Most Polels are best taken as intensive in meaning rather than causative. Giving birth (Job

39:1), the writhing of "shades" (RSV) or of the "deceased" (KJV; Job 26:5), and dancing (Jud 21:23) are all thus expressed in an intensive form. In the intensive form, "giving birth" is broadened into "forming" or "creating" (Ps 90:2; cf. also Prov 26:10 as translated in the KJV). In a similar idiom, the north wind "brings forth" rain (Prov 25:23). A single Polel seems to be causative; Ps 29:9 in which the text as pointed is translated, "maketh the hinds to calve" (ASV) although the RSV translation ("makes the oaks to whirl," NIV "twists the oaks") demands only a minor change in pointing and gives a better poetic parallel.

The Pulal is the passive of the Polel, "to be born" (Job 15:7; Ps 51:5 [H 7]). This idiom may be used to refer to creation or origins on a cosmic scale (Prov 8:24–25).

The Hithpolel occurs twice describing the whirling tempest (Jer 23:19) and the writhing of a man in pain (Job 25:20). These are more easily taken as intensive, though they could be construed as reflexive with some ingenuity. Similarly the Hithpalpel is intensive when it describes the great agitation or writhing of Esther upon learning of the decree against her people (Est 4:4).

ḥōl. ***Sand.*** Generally used as a simile for a great number or for vastness in some other respect. The number of grains of sand often is the measure for the number of God's people. Abraham was promised that they would be like the sand in number (Gen 22:17) as was Jacob (Gen 32:13). It describes their number under Solomon (I Kgs 4:20) and Israel's number in other times of special blessing (Isa 48:19, Hos 1:10 [H 2:1]). Israel's number as the sand of the sea is contrasted with the small number which will survive judgment (Isa 10:22).

Sand also illustrates the quantity of grain (Gen 41:49), armies (Jud 7:12), and quail sent to feed the Hebrews (Ps 78:27). Extent of judgment is shown by the number of widows being as the sand (Jer 15:8). Twice sand illustrates weight rather than discrete number (Job 6:3; Prov 27:3). It reminds of God's sovereignty in marking the bounds of the seas (Jer 5:22). It is not clear whether the phrase "captives like sand" (Hab 1:9) refers to the number of captives or to their being as unimportant or valueless as sand. Limitless quantity may be the significance of sand in the "hidden treasures of sands" (Deut 33:19).

ḥîl. ***Pain, agony, sorrow.*** Used four times before impending disaster to describe pain or agony such as that experienced by a woman in labor (Jer 6:24, 22:23, 50:43; Mic 4:9). In two passages, contextual parallels indicate a meaning of writhing in terror (Ex 15:14; Ps 48:6 [H 7]). In both cases, the physical writhing expresses the inner terror aroused by knowledge of God's great deeds.

ḥîlâ. ***Pain(?), agony(?)*** (KJV "sorrow"). Apparently a feminine form of the preceding word and thus similar in meaning. Used in an unclear context from which no distinct meaning can be derived (Job 6:10).

ḥalḥālâ. ***Writhing, agony, terror.*** Writhing either in anguish (Isa 21:3) or in terror (Ezk 30:9).

māḥôl. ***Dance, dancing.*** The dance may symbolize joy; joy as contrasted with mourning (Ps 30:11 [H 12]; Lam 5:15) and the joys which will come with God's future blessings (Jer 31:4, 13). The dance, also, is an acceptable means of praise (Ps 149:3; 150:4).

m^eḥôlâ. ***Dance, dancing.*** No clear distinction in meaning from māḥôl. It expresses joy and celebration of military victories (Ex 15:20; Jud 11:34; I Sam 18:6). Or a purely religious dance may be referred to (Ex 32:19; Jud 21:21). Evidence does not permit a clear interpretation of the "dance of the two camps" (Song 6:13 [H 7:1]).

A.B.

624 חוּל (*ḥûl*) ***II, be firm, endure.*** (So ASV; RSV "prosper" for "be firm"; KJV see *ḥûl* I.)

Derivative

624a †חַיִל (*ḥayil*) ***might.***

The basic meaning of this verb is "be firm," "strong." It is used just twice: God's "ways are firm" (Ps 10:5), and the "prosperity (of the wicked) will not endure" (Job 20:21). Other similar forms are considered to be *ḥûl* I.

ḥayil. ***Might, strength, power; able, valiant, virtuous, valor; army, host, forces; riches, substance, wealth; et al.*** (ASV and RSV similar with some variation.) The basic meaning of the noun is "strength," from which follow "army" and "wealth." It is used 244 times.

In the sense of "strength," "power," or "might" in general, *ḥayil* is used about twenty times: of God (Ps 59:11 [H 12]), from God (Ps 18:32 [H 33]), physical strength of a man (Eccl 10:10), or even of plant life (Joel 2:22).

As wealth is often related to power, *ḥayil* is thus used to mean "wealth" about thirty times, being translated "wealth," "riches," "substance," or "goods." It may be the wealth of a nation (Tyre, Ezk 28:4–5), an individual (e.g. Job, Job 31:25), the wiiked (Job 15:29), or from God (Deut 8:18, etc.).

Approximately eighty-five times *ḥayil* is used as an attribute of people. It follows *'îsh* "man" ("valiant man," I Kgs 1:42), sometimes *bēn*, "son" ("valiant man," II Sam 17:10), and most often follows *gibbôr* "mighty (man)" ("mighty man of valor"). The individual designated seems to be the elite warrior similar to the hero of the Homeric epic, and it may be that the *gibbôr ḥayil* was a member of a social class. Although in most contexts his military prowess was involved, he was wealthy enough to bear special taxes (II Kgs 15:20, translated because of context, "mighty men of wealth"). The use in I Kgs 1:52 indicates that the *ben ḥayil* (translated "worthy man") was also to be honorable or reputable. Adonijah's life was in danger because of his treachery, not because of lack of strength or wealth. *ḥayil* also designates men of ability: to care for Joseph's sheep (Gen 47:6, translated "men of activity"), or to judge the people (Ex 18:21, 25, translated "able men"). When the term is used of a woman (Ruth 3:11; Prov 12:4; and 31:10) it is translated "virtuous" (ASV, RSV "worthy" or "good"), but it may well be that a woman of this caliber had all the attributes of her male counterpart.

The use of *ḥayil* to designate a class of people is seldom found outside the historical books from Josh to II Chr. Moreover the translation sometimes obscures its occurrence, such as: "men of activity," "able men," "worthy man," "men of wealth," "man of power" (I Sam 9:1), "man of might" (II Kgs 24:16), "strong men" (I Chr 26:7, 9), and even "meet for the war" (KJV, Deut 3:18).

ḥayil follows *'āśâ* "do" or "make" in an idiom translated "do worthily" (Ruth 4:11), "virtuously" (Prov 31:29) for women, and "do valiantly" (Ps 60:12 [H 14], et al.) for men.

Resulting from the meaning "strength," *ḥayil* is used over one hundred times (about half of which are in Jer and Ezk) in the sense of "army," "host," or "forces." In this connection it is also translated "band of men" (I Sam 10:26), "band of soldiers" (Ezra 8:22), and for some reason "war" meaning "army" in the phrase "captains of war" (KJV, II Chr 33:14).

In a related sense *ḥayil* is used for the entourage which accompanied the queen of Sheba when she visited Solomon (I Kgs 10:2; II Chr 9:1; variously translated "company," "train," "retinue").

C.P.W.

625 חום (*ḥwm*). **Assumed root of the following.**

625a חוּם (*ḥûm*) ***darkened, dark brown or black*** (Gen 30:32, 33, 35, 40).

חוֹמָה (*ḥômâ*). See no. 674c.

626 חוּס (*ḥûs*) ***pity, spare.*** The ASV and RSV translate about the same.

The basic meaning of *ḥûs* is "to look with pity" often with the added nuance "spare." It refers to the feeling which goes out toward one who is in trouble (cf. KB, p. 282). It should be distinguished from *ḥāmal* "to spare," and *rāḥam* "to love, have mercy upon," although the distinctions sometimes fade. The word occurs twenty-four times.

This word is used primarily in Deut and the prophets, especially Ezk. The people are told not to feel sorry for murderers (Deut 19:13), those who bear false witness (Deut 19:21), or a woman who seizes the genitals of a man who is engaged in a fight (cf. Deut 25:12). These all deserve their punishment so must not be spared out of pity. In Deut 13:8 it is used in a negative sense with *ḥāmal*. Thus God describes how he wants his people to react toward the idolator: let not your eye pity and do not spare; they have earned their reward! So, they were not to feel sorry for the Canaanites (Deut 7:16); they were not to be spared. In Ezk the people are reminded that they received favorable treatment at their birth (as a nation) from God alone who pitied them (*ḥûs*) and spared them (*ḥāmal*) from certain destruction (16:5). They are reminded of their subsequent lack of obedient and loving response when they continually engaged in idolatry. Therefore, God intones the judgment of Deut 13:8 [H 9] (Ezk 5:11; 7:9, et al.), viz. death. The translations both render *ḥûs*, as "spare," and *ḥāmal* "pity." But there appears to be no apparent reason for this switch in meaning, especially since Ezekiel's usages clearly recall Deut 13:8 [H 9] (where both ASV and RSV render *ḥûs* "pity," and *ḥāmal* "spare"). Jeremiah uses *ḥûs* twice with both *ḥāmal* and *rāḥam;* cf. *rāḥam.*

The basic meaning of *ḥûs* surfaces in Ezk 24:14 where it appears after "go back" and before "repent" apparently being parallel with both. All three are spoken by God who refuses to cancel the coming judgment. So, our word denotes God's refusal to spare the people out of pity from the anticipated judgment. Similarly in Jon 4:10 God reminds the prophet that he felt sorry for the gourd even as God felt sorry for and spared the creatures (babes and cattle, KD, in. loc.) of Nineveh. Pharaoh tells Joseph's family to abandon most of their material possessions and not to attach themselves to them emotionally, i.e. have no regard (*ḥûs*) for them (Gen 45:20).

Sometimes *ḥûs* is hard to distinguish from *ḥāmal* "to spare," as in Ezk 20:17 where it is parallel to "I destroyed them not" (cf. Ps 72:13 where it is parallel to "save"). Elsewhere it appears to approach *rāḥam,* the inner feeling of compassion arising out of a natural bond (or, with God, due to adoption). Cf. Neh 13:22 where God is asked to remember on the basis of *ḥûs* and lovingkindness.

L.J.C.

חוֹף (*ḥôp*). See no. 710a.

627 חוץ (*ḥwṣ*). **I. Assumed root of the following.**
627a †חוּץ (*ḥûṣ*) ***outside, outward, street.***
627b †חִיצוֹן (*ḥîṣôn*) ***outer.***

ḥûṣ. ***Abroad, field, forth, highway, out, outside, outward, street, without.*** (ASV and RSV similar.)

This noun, which occurs 164 times, basically means "outside." This may be the outer surface of the structure or object involved or it may be the area away from it. The word is often combined with various affixes and is translated adverbially, "(to the) outside." It often refers specifically to the area which is "outside," especially the "streets."

ḥûṣ is used approximately fifty-four times in reference to a community, either a city, or the earlier Israelite camp. In the Pentateuch it is often used with respect to the camp. Lepers must remain outside the camp (Num 5:3; 12:14); a part of the sin offering was burned outside the camp (Lev 4:12). Similarly *ḥûṣ* may refer to the "outside" of a city, specifically, outside the walls. Lot and his family were placed outside Sodom (Gen 19:16); merchants lodged outside Jerusalem over the Sabbath (Neh 13:20). As a specific area outside the city it is translated "field(s)": as a place where sheep are born (Ps 144:13, KJV "streets"), as a synonym for *śādeh* "field" (Prov 24:27).

The word also is used about thirty-five times in conjunction with a structure, such as a tent (Lev 14:8), a house (Ex 12:46; Josh 2:19), a temple (Ezk 41:25), or just outside any structure in the rain (Ezr 10:13). The "outside" within a city would be a street and *ḥûṣ* is thus translated about fifty times, especially in the plural (Jer 5:1; 11:13, et al.). The reference to streets in I Kgs 20:34 probably involves trading, hence the RSV translation "bazaar." It is used parallel to *r^e ḥôb* "plaza." It may be identified as a specific street, as that of the bakers (Jer 37:21).

"Outside" may be within a building but outside a particular room or enclosure (Ex 26:35). It may be the outer surface of an object such as the ark of the covenant (Ex 25:11), or Noah's ark (Gen 6:14), in which case it is used in opposition to *mibbayit,* "on the inside" (from *bayit* "house"). The word may mean "outside" an immediate family or clan (Deut 25:5; Jud 12:9).

The use in Eccl 2:25, KJV "more" (than I), is difficult. If this is the meaning, *ḥûṣ* must mean outside in the sense of "beyond." The RSV (and ASV marg.) "apart" (from him) translates *ḥûṣ* and fits the context but must substitute "him" (God) for the pronoun, following the LXX.

The word is part of the placename, Kirjath-huzoth (Num 22:39), "city of streets," an unidentified town in Moab.

ḥîṣôn. ***Outer, outward, utter, without.*** (ASV similar, but does not use "utter"; RSV, "outer," "outside.") An adjectival form of *ḥûṣ,* its basic meaning is "outer," "outside."

It is used twenty-five times, seventeen times in Ezk 40–46, where it usually refers to the outer court. Most of the other usages refer to the location of structures. Twice (I Chr 26:29; Neh 11:16) the word is applied to the business duties of officials. This use may be figurative, designating the secular nature of the work. The KJV "utter" meaning "outer," now obsolete, has been replaced in newer versions.

C.P.W.

628 חוץ (*ḥwṣ*) **II. Assumed root of the following.**
628a חַיִץ (*ḥayiṣ*) ***party-wall, i.e. a thin wall*** (Ezk 13:10).

629 חוק (*ḥwq*), חיק (*ḥyq*). **Assumed root of the following.**
629a †חֵיק (*ḥêq*) ***hollow, bosom, bottom, midst*** (RSV "embrace," once "lap").

Basic idea is that of a hollow or cavity from which the ideas of a hollow formed by a fold of a garment at the breast (BDB) and the hollow of the lap are derived.

Literal hollows are best exemplified by the hollow bottom of Ahab's chariot in which the blood gathered (I Kgs 22:35). However, the significance of the literal "bosoms" of Ezk 43:13, 14, 17 is difficult to discern. Suggestions are "blood-channel" (KB), "moulding" (KB), hollow bottom of altar" (BDB), "bottom" (ASV), and "base" (RSV). Giving into the bosom is a euphemism for sexual relations (Gen 16:5; RSV "embrace").

A variety of abstract, figurative ideas are expressed by this term. Family intimacy may be emphasized (Deut 28:54; Mic 7:5). Tender care or concern may be expressed as in the poor man's care for his only sheep (II Sam 12:3), the widow's care for her sick son (I Kgs 17:19), and God's carrying his people in his arms in his bosom (Isa 40:11). Giving the old king's wives into the new king's bosom showed the new king's authority (II Sam 12:8; cf. also II Sam 16:20–23). Naomi formally laid Ruth's child "in her bosom" as a symbol that this child was her (and her husband's) legitimate heir (Ruth 4:16).

The "bosom," like other physical terms (e.g. "bones," "kidneys," and "heart") may serve as an emphatic, intimate term for the person himself. Judgment "into the bosom" marks the object of judgment with special intimacy (Isa 65:6; cf. Jer 32:18, NASB) Anger lodging in the bosom of fools (Eccl 7:9), fire in the "bosom" (Prov 6:27), and prayer returning to the bosom of the one who prays (Ps 35:13; KJV, ASV) are other typical examples of this motif (cf. also Ps 89:50 [H 51]; Job 19:27, lit. "my kidneys in my bosom are finished").

A.B.

630 חָוַר (*ḥāwar*) ***be, grow white, pale*** (Isa 29:22, only).

Derivatives

630a חוּר (*ḥûr*) ***white stuff*** (Est 8:15; 1:6).
630b חוּרָי (*ḥûrāy*) ***white stuff*** (Isa 19:9).
630c חֹרִי (*ḥōrî*) ***white bread or cake*** (Gen 40:16).

חוּרָי (*ḥûrāy*). See no. 630b.

631 חוּשׁ (*ḥûsh*) ***I, hurry, make haste, hasten.***

Derivative

631a חִישׁ (*ḥîsh*) ***quickly.*** Used only in Ps 90:10, of the passing away of human life.

ḥûsh is cognate with Akkadian *hāshu* "to move quickly" and Ugaritic *ḥsh* "hurry" (UT 19: no. 849). The verb occurs twenty times in the Qal and Hiphil stems.

Isaiah 5:19 denounces those who say insincerely, "Let him make haste, led him speed his work that we may see it." Although God sometimes tarries, he declares, "I am the Lord; in its time I will hasten it" (Isa 60:22).

It is for this reason that the psalms so often plead urgently, "Hasten to help me" or "Hasten to me" (Ps 22:19 [H 20]; 38:22 [H 23]; 40:13 [H 14]; 70:1, 5 [H 2, 6]; 71:12; 141:1).

Isaiah (8:1, 3) was instructed to give his son the name *Mahēr-shālāl-ḥāsh-baz,* "Speed-spoil-hasten-plunder," signifying the imminent fall of Damascus and Samaria before the Assyrians. An Egyptian name of the Eighteenth Dynasty, *is ḥ'ḳ,* similarly means "Hasten, Seize Booty."

Bibliography: Humbert, Paul, "Mahēr Šalāl Ḥāš Baz," ZAW 50: 92–92.

E.Y.

632 חוּשׁ (*ḥûsh*) ***II, be agitated, worry about, enjoy (?).***

Cognate with Akkadian *ḫāshu* "to worry"; Aramaic *ḥăshash* "to suffer, to worry"; Syriac *ḥash* "to feel"; and Arabic *ḥassa* "to feel." It appears in two passages, and possibly a third. Zophar in Job 20:2 does not speak of the "haste" within him (KJV, RSV), but of his "agitation."

Ecclesiastes 2:25 is taken "enjoy" by many commentators so that it inquires, "Apart from God who can eat or have enjoyment?" on the basis of Eccl 2:24 and the Akkadian *ḫashāshu* "to be happy." Ellermeier, however, holds that the verb means "to worry," in the sense that God is responsible not only for situations which we enjoy but also those which cause us to worry.

In Isa 28:16 instead of "he who believes will not be in haste," Driver suggests "will not be agitated." Or the letters *ḥsh* may be in error for *bsh* "be ashamed" (cf. LXX and Rom 9:33; I Pet 2:6).

Bibliography: Driver, G. R., "Studies in the Vocabulary of the Old Testament II," JTS 32: 253–54. Ellermeier, Friedrich, "Das Verbum ḥûsh in Koh 2:25," ZAW 75: 197–217.

E.Y.

633 חָזָה (*ḥāzâ*) ***I, look, see, behold, prophesy, provide.***

Derivatives

633a †חָזוֹן (*ḥāzôn*) ***vision.***
633b †חֹזֶה (*ḥōzeh*) ***seer.***
633c חָזוֹת (*ḥāzôt*) ***visions.*** Occurs only in II Chr 9:29).
633d †חָזוּת (*ḥāzût*) ***vision.***
633e חִזָּיוֹן (*ḥizzāyôn*) ***vision.***
633f מַחֲזֶה (*maḥăzeh*) ***vision.***
633g מֶחֱזָה (*meḥĕzâ*) ***light, place of seeing, window.*** Occurs only in I Kgs 7:4–5.

Like the word "behold" in English, this word is employed almost exclusively in poetry or exalted prose. It is used exclusively in Qal, but appears in all parts of that stem: This word, appearing about fifty times, is apparently an exalted term in rather frequent use.

ḥăzâ, ḥăzā' in the Aramaic portions of Dan and Ezr (about thirty times) are entirely parallel to the Hebrew.

The word *rā'â,* used approximately fourteen hundred times in the OT, presents a similar range of literal, metaphorical, and extended usages as is true also of the English words "look," "see" and "behold."

Any word meaning to see with the eyes, the most vivid form of sensation, seems bound to be employed for almost any sensation (by eyes, ears, nose, tongue, skin) as well as any mental or spiritual perception. Notice how at least two different senses are attributed to eyes in the prize mixed metaphor of all literature: The children of Israel complain to Moses and Aaron, "You have made our savor to stink in the eyes of Pharaoh" (Ex 5:21). In the case of *ḥāzâ* the bare literal sense is rare. Metaphorical and special senses are more common, as follows:

1. The literal sense, perception with physical organs of sight (Job 27:12; Prov 22:29; 29:30).

2. The special way in which a lover gazes at his (her?) beloved (Song 6:13 [H 7:1]).

3. To "see to" something, i.e. provide (from

Lat *pro-video* "see to"). The idea is to secure needful things against a foreseen need or occasion (Ex 18:21; ASV margin of Isa 57:8 refers to Israel's providing objects for idolatrous worship).

4. This word is carried to the realm of pure spiritual understanding in two outstanding passages (Job 36:25 and Ps 63:2 [H 3]).

5. Metaphorically of God's awareness of either evil or good actions among men (Ps 11:4; 17:2).

6. Immediate vision of God by select persons specially chosen (Ex 24:9–11).

7. The revelatory vision granted by God to chosen messengers, i.e. prophets. Such apparently was the experience of Balaam the son of Beor (Num 24:4, 16). This vision of the prophets took place sometimes in the waking state, but also in "the spirit" (see Num 24:2). Sometimes the experience of "seeing" a revelatory dream is designated by *ḥāzâ* and *ḥăzā'* (Aram). See Dan 2:26, 4:5, 9 [H 2, 6] etc.

8. The vision of God which every saint shall have after death, without reference to any bodily organ of sight is designated by *ḥāzâ* in two very important passages (Ps 17:15; Job 19:26–27, possibly also Ps 11:7; Isa 33:17).

9. Because of the importance of the revelatory vision as means of the prophets' special knowledge of divine things, the word sometimes means to speak as a prophet (Isa 30:10, "*Prophesy* not unto us right things"). It might be that this active sense (prophesying, to speak as a prophet), rather than the passive one of receiving prophetic revelation, may be the sense of Isa 1:1 ("which he saw," etc.) and other similar passages (Isa 2:1; 13:1; Lam 2:14; Ezk 13:8; Amos 1:1, etc.). To speak even as a false prophet may be designated by *ḥāzâ* (Zech 10:2). The active sense is close to certain in this last case. The close association of *ḥāzâ* and derived forms *ḥōzeh, ḥāzôn* etc. with prophecy is shown by the way the "seer" is on occasion defined by the technical term *nābî'* (II Sam 24:11). See especially Ezk 12:27.

ḥāzôn. ***Vision.*** This word has a range of usage similar to that of *ḥizzayôn, maḥăzeh,* and other derivatives of *ḥāzâ*. Like *ḥāzôt,* it is used in the titles of certain prophetic books (Nah and Isa).

ḥōzeh. ***Seer,*** derived from *ḥāzâ*. Of the twenty-two occurrences eleven are connected with the name of a particular person, indicating his office as prophet (Gad, II Sam 24:11; I Chr 21:9; I Chr 29:29; II Chr 29:25; Heman, I Chr 25:5; Iddo, II Chr 9:29, 12:15; Hanai, II Chr 19:2; Asaph, II Chr 29:25; Jeduthun, II Chr 35:15; Amos is addressed as a *ḥōzeh*). The identity of office between *nābî'* (several MSS) and *ḥôzeh* (in apposition) is shown by II Kgs 17:13. This is enforced by Amos 7:12 where Amos is addressed as an *ḥōzeh* who prophesies, *viz. ḥōzeh... tinnābē'*. Isaiah 29:10 further unites *ḥōzeh* with *nābî'*. It seems therefore that *ḥozeh* is simply a more elegant word than *rō'eh,* of near identical meaning (cf. I Sam 9:9). Three words then can designate an OT "prophet," *viz.* "Now the acts of David the king... are written in the history of Samuel the seer [*rō'eh*], and in the history of Nathan the prophet [*nābî'*], and in the history of Gad the seer [*ḥōzeh*]" (I Chr 29:29).

Whatever the derivation of these three words, Scripture specifies that *nābî'* means spokesman for God (Ex 7:1–2; cf. Ex 4:16; Jer 23:16; Isa 1:20; Zech 7:12; Amos 3:8; 7:16). *rō'eh* and *ḥōzeh* preserve awarefess that God sometimes made revelation to the prophets by visions, i.e. "seeing."

See excellent discussion in H. E. Freeman, *An Introduction to the OT Prophets,* Moody, 1968, pp. 37–41.

ḥāzût. ***Vision, conspicuousness.*** (Five times in OT). In three of the occurrences it is scarcely distinguishable in meaning from the second meaning of *ḥizzāyôn* (q.v.)—a prophetic deliverance, message, oracle. Twice, in Daniel, it has the adjectival sense of conspicuousness (Dan 8:5, 8).

ḥizzāyôn. ***Vision.*** This is one of several nouns derived from *ḥāzâ*. It is very close to *maḥăzeh* (which appears only three times, Gen 15:1; Num 24:4, 16; Ezk 13:7, always of true or alleged revelatory visions). Of the nine times *ḥizzayôn* is used in the OT, five refer to the prophetic function. As with *ḥāzâ* (to see, have vision) it may designate the oracle-message from God, e.g. Nathan's prophetic "words" to David (II Sam 7:17) are called an *ḥizzāyôn* (specifically *hadd^{e}bārîm hā'ēlleh* is equated with *hāḥizzāyôn hazzeh*). The speakers in the discourses of Job four times use the word, apparently in the same sense (Job 4:13; 7:14; 20:8; 33:15).

Bibliography: Pfeiffer, R. H., "Wisdom and Vision in the O. T.," ZAW 11: 93–101. Richardson, TWB, p. 277. Rowley, H. H., "Ritual and the Hebrew Prophets," JSS 1: 338–60. Scott, R. B. Y., "Oracles of God," Interp 2: 131–42. THAT, I, pp. 533–37.

R.D.C.

634 חזה (*ḥzh*) **II. Assumed root of the following.**

634a †חָזֶה (*ḥāzeh*) ***breast of an animal sacrifice.*** The word appears thirteen times in Ex, Num, and especially Lev.

The breast portions of the "ram of Aaron's ordination" (Ex 29:26, 27; cf. Lev 8:29), of the "peace offerings" (Lev 7:30–31, 34; 9:20, 21) and of the Nazirite offering (Num 6:20) were "waved" (Num 6:20; Lev 7:34; 10:14–15; etc.), that is, in a horizontal movement symbolizing their presentation to God. They then became the portions of the priests.

Although the Hebrew word is used only of animals, the Aramaic cognate *ḥădēh* appears once in its plural form as the breasts of the image seen by Daniel (Dan 2:32). In the Genesis Apocryphon 20:4 the dual *ḥdyh* is used in the description of Sarah, "How lovely are her breasts."

E.Y.

חָזוֹן (*ḥāzôn*). See no. 633a.
חָזוֹת (*ḥāzôt*). See no. 633c.
חָזוּת (*ḥāzût*). See no. 633d.

635 חזז (*ḥzz*). **Assumed root of the following.**
635a חֲזִיז (*ḥăzîz*) ***thunderbolt, lightning flash*** (Job 28:26; Zech 10:1).

חִזָּיוֹן (*ḥizzāyôn*). See no. 633e.
חֲזִיז (*ḥăzîz*). See no. 635a.
חֲזִיר (*ḥăzîr*). See no. 637a.

636 חָזַק (*ḥāzaq*) ***be(come) strong, strengthen, prevail, harden, be courageous, be sore*** (meaning be severe). (ASV and RSV similar.)

Derivatives

636a †חָזָק (*ḥazaq*) ***strong.***
636b †חֶזְקָה (*ḥezqâ*) ***strength*** (once in the masc. form *ḥēzeq*).
636c †חֹזֶק (*ḥōzeq*) ***strength.***
636d †חָזְקָה (*ḥōzqâ*) ***force.***

The basic meaning of this word in the Qal stem is "be(come) strong." In general, the Piel is causative of the Qal, "make strong," "strengthen." The Hiphil is "take hold of," "seize," while the Hithpael stem is "strengthen oneself," hence, "take courage." The use of *ḥāzaq* is similar to *'āmēṣ* and *'āzaz* except for the Hiphil which is more like the Qal of *'āḥaz*. This verb is used 291 times.

The Qal form, used eighty-two times, means to "be strong" or "become strong." In most cases it can be so translated, but often the variety of contexts encourages or necessitates a variety of renditions. Most often the word is used for strength in battle (I Kgs 20:23). The admonition to be strong in combat may simply be an exhortation to be of good courage (and is so translated in II Sam 10:12).

In Gen 41:56 "strong" is used in the sense of "severe" (RSV; KJV and ASV "sore") in reference to a famine. Similarly a battle may be "severe" (II Kgs 3:26). "To be stronger than" in context comes to mean "prevail," as the word of David "prevailed" against Joab (II Sam 24:4), David against the Philistine (I Sam 17:50), and Jotham over the Ammonites (II Chr 27:5). When used of Pharoah's heart the meaning is "harden" (Ex 7:13f.).

[The hardening of Pharoah's heart is an old problem, one that is more theological than linguistic. The verb *ḥāzaq* is used twelve times in the narrative (Ex 4–14), mostly with the Lord as the agent, but four times in the passive or stative sense ("Pharaoh's heart was hardened"). Also, the verb *kābēd* is used five times, both with the Lord as the agent, with Pharaoh as the agent, and in the passive sense. The verb *qāshâ* is used once with the Lord as the agent. There is no discernible difference here in the usage of these words. It is clear that Pharaoh was an unrepentant sinner at the start (chapter 5). It is perhaps enough to point this out and remark that all of God's hardening of an obstinate sinner was judicial and done that God's deliverance should be the more memorable. And this, too, was in God's plan (Ex 9:16), though it is also inexplicably true that Pharaoh sinned freely and was therefore terribly guilty (cf. Acts 4:25–28). R.L.H.]

Other resultant meanings include "be sure" (Deut 12:23), "be steadfast" (Josh 23:6, RSV), "catch hold" (II Sam 18:9, Absalom's head in the oak; the causative of this is common usage in the Hiphil), "recover" (Isa 39:1, Hezekiah from sickness), "stout," (of peoples' words against God, Mal 3:13).

The Qal form of the verb is used twice (II Chr 28:20; Isa 28:22) in the Piel sense of "strengthen."

The basic meaning of the Piel stem (used sixty-four times) is causative of the Qal, to "make strong," "strengthen." As with the Qal it is used often in the context of battle or combat. Often the object of the verb is the hands or the arms of an individual. "To strengthen the hands" may mean "to aid" (Ezra 1:6), or, more often, "to encourage" (I Sam 23:16). The person encouraged may be the object of the verb (II Sam 11:25; Isa 41:7). Strengthen may be translated simply "help" (II Chr 29:34).

The Piel is used sixteen times in the sense of "repair" (II Kgs 12:5f.). As in the Qal, when the object of the verb is the heart (ten times), the verb is translated "harden" (Ex 4:21f.). It is used twice in the sense of "fasten" (or "support") as with nails (Isa 41:7; Jer 10:4).

The Hiphil frequently (sixty-three times) means "take hold," i.e. "grasp," "seize." It is used thirty-four times in Neh in the sense of "repair," referring to the rebuilding the wall of Jerusalem. Other uses are varied: "prevail" (Dan 11:7), "support" (Lev 25:35), "receive" (II Chr 4:5), "retain" (Jud 7:8), "constrain" or "urge" (II Kgs 4:8), "confirm" (Dan 11:1), "strengthen" (II Sam 11:25), "aid", i.e. "strengthen the hand" (Ezk 16:49), "join" (Neh 10:29), "hold" (Neh 5:16).

The Hithpael (used twenty-seven times) is translated in a variety of ways but is usually reflexive of some use of the Qal stem, i.e. "strengthen oneself," "encourage oneself."

ḥāzāq. ***Strong, mighty, hard.*** This adjective means "strong" in the sense of "powerful" (including the power to resist). Of its fifty-seven occurrences, twenty-three refer to a "strong hand," most often to God's power, as in the Exodus. The word refers also to the strength of a man (Caleb, Josh 14:11), the wind (Ex 10:19; I Kgs 19:11), and a sword (figurative, Isa 27:1). Although the word often refers to God's powerful hand it does not seem to be used as a substitute for deity (as *'elyôn* is).

It is translated variously because it occurs in many different contexts. Applied to the blast of a trumpet the word is translated "loud" (Ex 19:16). When applied to sickness (I Kgs 17:17) or famine (I Kgs 18:2), it is appropriately translated "severe" (RSV; the ASV reads "sore"). The KJV also refers to "sore war" (I Sam 14:52), but translates a similar phrase "hottest battle" (II Sam 11:15). The RSV uses "hard(est) fighting" in both references.

When referring the face, forehead, or heart *ḥāzāq* implies an unyielding stubbornness or strong resistance (Ezk 2:4; 3:7–8, variously translated: "stiffhearted," "stubborn," "impudent," etc.). It is also used as a substantive, "mighty one," "strong one" (Ezk 34:16; Job 5:15).

ḥezqâ. ***Strength, strengthen self, strong, was strong.*** (ASV and RSV similar.) A noun, used four times meaning "strength," but translated as a verb in some contexts.

ḥōzeq. ***Strength.*** (ASV and RSV the same.) The noun, used five times, means "strength," always in the sense of "military prowess."

ḥōzqâ. ***Force, mightily, repair, sharply.*** (ASV similar, but RSV "violently.")

C.P.W.

637 חזר (*ḥzr*). **Assumed root of the following.**
637a חֲזִיר (*ḥăzîr*) ***swine, boar*** (e.g. Lev 11:7; Deut 14:8).

638 חָטָא (*ḥāṭā'*) ***miss, miss the way, sin, incur guilt, forfeit, purify from uncleanness.***

Derivatives

638a †חֵטְא (*ḥēṭ'*) ***sin.***
638b †חַטָּא (*ḥaṭṭā'*) ***sinners.***
638c †חַטָּאָה (*ḥaṭṭā'â*) ***sin, sinful thing.***
638d †חֲטָאָה (*ḥăṭā'â*) ***sin, sin offering.***
638e †חַטָּאת (*ḥaṭṭā't*) ***sin, sin offering.***

The root occurs about 580 times in the Old Testament and is thus its principle word for sin. The basic meaning of the root is to miss a mark or a way. It is used two or three times in Ugaritic to mean "sin" (UT 19: no. 952, Ais WUS 1019).

The verbal forms occur in enough secular contexts to provide a basic picture of the word's meaning. In Jud 20:16 the left-handed slingers of Benjamin are said to have the skill to throw stones at targets and "not miss." In a different context, Prov 19:2 speaks of a man in a hurry who "misses his way" (RSV, NEB, KJV has "sinneth"). A similar idea of not finding a goal appears in Prov 8:36; the concept of failure is implied.

The verb has the connotation of breach of civil law, i.e. failure to live up its expectations, in Gen 40:1. Compare the international overtones of II Kgs 18:14, and the accusatory thrust of the word, fault, in Ex 5:7. The Egyptians had failed to supply straw for brick-making. Serious breakdown in personal relationship is highlighted by the verb, negatively in I Sam 19:4, and 24:12 but by confession of Saul in 26:21. Compare Jud 11:27.

The KJV does not catch the nuance of the verb in Job 5:24, but RSV does with "miss nothing" and NEB does with "nothing amiss," NIV "nothing missing." The verb, *ḥāṭā'*, here means anything less that the total. A corollary in personal relationships is found in Gen 43:9; 44:32. Judah proposes that he "bear the blame" (KJV, REV) or be "guilty" (NEB) if he fails to fulfill his promise. Extended to religious obligations, the form, *ḥāṭā' min,* in Lev 4:2 designates a failure to observe God's laws and in Lev 5:16 denotes action which gives less than is due, a failure of full duty.

When *ḥāṭā'* is followed by *lĕ,* a failure to respect the full rights and interests of another person is involved, e.g. Gen 20:9; Jud 11:27; II Chr 6:22, or of God as well, e.g. Ex 10:16; I Sam 2:25. Often God is the object.

But *ḥāṭā'* followed by *bĕ* denotes strong opposition. See Gen 42:22; I Sam 19:4f.; Job 2:10; Neh 9:29. In summary, one may say that *ḥāṭā'* plus *lĕ* is quite personal, whereas *ḥāṭā'* plus *bĕ* is more physical.

In the many instances in which the verb occurs in the Qal stem the object is either God or his laws, or else the verb is intransive. In so acting, man is missing the goal or standard God has for him, is failing to observe the requirements of holy living, or falls short of spiritual wholeness. The participle seems to designate the sinner in Prov 13:22; Isa 65:20 and all instances in Eccl. But in Isa 1:4 it designates the quality of being less than acceptable to God.

Thus like other words related to the notion of "sin" it assumes an absolute standard or law. But, whereas *pesha'* signifies a "revolt against the standard," and *'āwâ* means either "to deviate from the standard" or "to twist the standard," *ḥāṭā'* means "to miss, to fall short of the standard. The Greek word *anomia* "sin," consists of the privative prefix with the word for "law," thus "without law." Therefore judgment is implied, for the law in fact is binding even if the sinner thinks himself to be "without law."

In the Piel stem, the verb has a privative connotation, as in Gen 31:39 where Jacob had to "bear the loss" for any animal which could not be accounted for. In a religious sense, the majority of the Piel forms denote a cleansing or purifying ceremony during which sin is done away with, e.g. Ex 29:36; Lev 14:29, 52; Num 19:19; Ps 51:7 [H 9] and all instances in Ezekiel. See also the same meaning in the Hithpael stem (Num 8:21; 19:12–13, 20; 31:19–20, 23; Job 41:25 [H 17]). In Lev 9:15 and II Chr 29:24 this verb form means "to make a sin offering."

In the Hiphil stem, the verb means "to lead someone else into sin." Exodus 23:33 warns the Israelites against allowing the Canaanites to lead them into sin. The sin of Jeroboam was a standard by which the evil kings of northern Israel were judged (I Kgs 14:16; 15:30, etc.); cf. Neh 13:26. The verb seems to have the sense of guilt in Deut 24:4. Idolatry is the sin against which the warnings are primarily directed.

ḥēṭ'. ***Sin, punishment.*** This masculine noun is an act of *ḥāṭā'* which means that it is the failure to hit the mark, a turning away from obedience, a lack of wholeness or of acceptance before God. The noun appears thirty five times in the Old Testament.

On a secular level the noun refers to a breach of civil law or the regulations of a monarch, as in Gen 41:9 and Eccl 10:4.

In a number of instances (Num 27:3; all occurrences in Deut; II Kgs 10:29; Ps 103:10; Isa 38:17; Lam 1:8; Dan 9:16) the noun either designates or implies an act of disobedience to God. Deut 21:22 and 22:26, refer to a sin of death, i.e. a sin that must be punished by death.

Since Hebrew does not have a distinctive word for guilt, some of the words for sin carry this concept. This noun is one which sometimes functions in this manner. The KJV often indicates the thought by the phrase, "bear sin." Examples may be found in Lev 20:20; Num 9:13; Isa 53:12 and Ezk 23:49. RSV would add Lev 19:17 to this list, and would translate the noun as "guilt" in Hos 12:8.

The noun includes the concept of punishment in Lam 3:39.

ḥāṭṭā'. ***Sinners, sinful.*** Another masculine noun, *ḥaṭṭā'* appears eighteen times in the Old Testament. It designates a habitual sinner who is subject to punishment because of his or her practices. In one instance, I Kgs 1:21 the word is secular in orientation and refers to a probable penalty. A quality of sinfullness is found in Num 32:14.

ḥaṭṭā'â. ***Sin, sinful thing.*** This feminine noun is used only three times. In Ex 34:7 it is linked with *'āwôn* and *pesha'* as forgiveable, and also has an abstract meaning in Isa 5:18. An Aramaic form is in Ezr 6:17 with the meaning of sin-offering.

ḥăṭā'â. ***Sin, sin offering.*** Another feminine noun is *ḥăṭā'â* appearing eight times and normally carrying an abstract connotation. In all occurrences except in Ps 32:6 (where it means "sin offering") the word means "sin." In Gen 20:9; Ex 32:21; 30, 31; and II Kgs 17:21 it is modified by the adjective *gādôl* and usually refers to idolatry. In Ps 32:1 and 109:7 the noun designates sin as such.

ḥaṭṭā't. ***Sin, sin offering.*** The most extensively used noun form is the feminine *ḥaṭṭā't* which occurs almost two hundred and ninety times. In Gen 18:20 the noun refers to the condition of sin. In Gen 31:36; 50:17 it is paired with *pesha'* another common term for sin. In Lev and in Num the noun appears many times alternating in meaning between sin, the reality of disobedience to God, and sin-offering, the means of removing the guilt and penalty of sin before the Lord through the sacrificial system. In this context, the noun is closely associated with *'āshām,* which is often translated as "guilt-offering."

Both the noun and the verb are for emphasis in Deut 9:18. The noun is used for Israel's particular sin, the golden calf (9:21) and is paired with *pesha'* in v. 27. In Deut 19:15 with *'āwôn* which is often translated as iniquity. This pairing of *ḥaṭṭā't* with other words for sin is fairly frequent in wisdom and prophetical writings. The meaning sin offering appears quite often in II Chr, Ezra, Neh and Ezk. The term has the sense of guilt in II Chr 28:13; Ps 32:5; of punishment in Lam 4:6 and Zech 14:19; of purification in Num 8:7; 19:9, 17.

In the majority of cases *ḥaṭṭā't* denotes sin/s against man, e.g. I Sam 20:1; Ps 59:3, or against God, mainly in the historical and prophetical literature.

Man can only deal with sin through the sacrificial offerings coupled with confession and turning from sin to God. God may deal with sin by punishing those who continue in their sin (Josh 24:19; I Kgs 14:16; Neh 9:37; etc.); by forgiving sins as indicated in I Kgs 8:36; II Chr 6:25, 27; Ps 32:5; Jer 36:3; and by purging sin as in Ps 51:2; Isa 6:7; Zech 13:1.

Since sin was understood in the ancient near eastern religions as a violation of the status quo in cultic, political, and social life, each country with peculiar emphases, the pagan people could only strive to conteract its consequences by magical practices. In Israel, the people learned by revelation that sin was disobedience of God's will and exploitation or disregard of the rights of other people. Sin was declared to be an extremely serious matter and could only be taken care of by a creative and gracious act of merciful forgiveness by God. And the cure was effective, bringing about a new life of joy and fruitfulness.

For the people of Israel there was hope for a change of life, both as individuals and as a nation, because God was willing to turn away from his wrath toward sin (primarily idolatry but also social sins) and do wonderful things for those who would contritely turn from sin, confess, make restitution and surrender to God and his way of salvation. Many a song in the Psalms declares the reality of release from the burden of sin's guilt and penalty.

Bibliography: Coggan, F. D., "The Meaning of *ḥṭ'* in Job 5, 24," *Journal Manchester Egyptian Oriental Society* 17: 53–56. Gelin, Albert, *Sin in the Bible,* Desclee, 1964. Hartman, Louis F., "Sin in Paradise," CBQ 20: 26–40. Kidner, F. D., *Sacrifice in the Old Testament,* London: Tyndale, 1952. Milgrom, J., "The Function of the *ḥaṭṭa't* Sacrifice," *Tarbiz* 40: 1–8. ______, "Sin-offering or Purification-offering" VT 21: 237–39. Porubcan, Stefan, *Sin in the Old Testament,* Herder, 1963. Quell, G., *Sin,* London: Adam and Charles Black, 1951. Rabinowitz, Jacob J., "The 'Great Sin' in Ancient Egyptian Marriage Contracts," JNES 18: 73. Richardson, TWB, p. 207. Ringgren, H., *Sacrifice in the Bible,* Association, 1963. Smith, C. R., The *Bible Doctrine of Sin,* London: Epworth, 1953. Snaith, Norman H., "Sacrifices in the Old Testament," VT 7: 308–17. ______, "The Sin-offering and the Guilt-offering," VT 15: 73–80. Staples, W. E., "Some Aspects of Sin in the Old Testament," JNES 6: 65–79. Unger, Merrill F., "The Old Testament Revelation of the Beginning of Sin," BS 114: 326–33. Zink, J. K., "Uncleanness and Sin," VT 17: 354–61. TDNT, I, pp. 268–293. THAT, I, pp. 541–48.

G.H.L.

חַטָּאת (*ḥaṭṭā't*). See no. 638e.

639 חָטַב (*ḥāṭab*) ***I, cut or gather wood, usually firewood*** (e.g. Ezk 39:10; Deut 19:5).

640 חטב (*ḥṭb*) **II. Assumed root of the following.**

640a חֲטֻבוֹת (*ḥăṭūbôt*) ***dark-hued stuffs*** (Prov 7:16).

חֲטֻבוֹת (*ḥăṭūbôt*). See no. 640a.
חִטָּה (*ḥiṭṭâ*). See no. 691b.

641 חָטַם (*ḥāṭam*) ***hold in, restrain*** (Isa 48:9).

642 חָטַף (*ḥāṭap*) ***catch, seize*** (Jud 21:21; Ps 10:9).

643 חטר (*ḥṭr*). **Assumed root of the following.**

643a חֹטֶר (*ḥōṭĕr*) ***branch or twig*** (Isa 11:1), rod (Prov 14:3).

חִידָה (*ḥîdâ*). See no. 616a.
חַי (*ḥay*). See nos. 644a,b.

644 חָיָה (*ḥāyâ*) ***live, have life, remain alive, sustain life, live prosperously, live forever.*** Also ***be quickened, revive from sickness, discouragement, or even death.***

Derivatives

644a †חַי (*ḥay*) ***I, living.***
644b חַי (*ḥay*) ***II, kinsfolk.***
644c †חַיָּה (*ḥayyâ*) ***I, living thing.***
644d חַיָּה (*ḥayyâ*) ***II, community.***
644e חָיֶה (*ḥayeh*) ***having the vigor of life, lively.***
644f †חַיִּים (*ḥayyîm*) ***life.***
644g חַיּוּת (*ḥayyût*). ***Occurs in the phrase*** **'almānôt ḥayyût** "widowhood of livingness," i.e. grass widow, one who was separated from her husband.
644h †מִחְיָה (*miḥyâ*) ***preservation of life.***

As a verb this root appears in three stems in Hebrew. The Qal conveys the basic meaning "to live or have life" whereas the two derived stems overlap in their meaning of "giving or restoring life."

Throughout the OT the possession of life is an intrinsic good, "All that a man has will he give for his life" (Job 2:4), and "a living dog is better than a dead lion" (Eccl 9:4). "Long life is in Wisdom's right hand" (Prov 3:16). Against this estimation of life one can appreciate the depths of Job's despair when he desired to surrender his life (Job 3:17ff.).

Physical life originally came from God (Gen 2:7). After the Fall, death entered man's experience. The fruit of the tree of life would have endowed man with immortality (Gen 3:22). God continues to be the source of life (Ps 36:9; 139:13ff.) and the Lord of life and death (Num 27:16; Deut 32:39; Job 12:10).

The OT speaks of life as the experience of life rather than as an abstract principle of vitality which may be distinguished from the body. This is because the OT view of the nature of man is holistic, that is, his function as body, mind, spirit is a unified whole spoken of in very concrete terms. Life is the ability to exercise all one's vital power to the fullest; death is the opposite. The verb *ḥāyâ* "to live" involves the ability to have life somewhere on the scale between the fullest enjoyment of all the powers of one's being, with health and prosperity on the one hand and descent into trouble, sickness, and death on the other. Sometimes the Psalmist calls on the Lord to be saved alive from the very brink of the pit (Ps 30:3 [H 4]). He asks to be "preserved alive" and "revived" so that he can enjoy "the land of the living." Some have been extreme in maintaining that this "land of the living" is heaven, while others have gone too far in maintaining that the Israelites did not understand man as having a spirit but simply as being an animated body. Some have quoted verses like Isa 26:14, "The dead do not live," to prove that Israel's view was that death is total. There are indeed some verses that say the living, not the dead, praise the Lord, but these verses are expressions of simple physical observation. The fact is that in contrast to Mesopotamian ideas of creation where man was made to be mortal, in the OT man was created to immortal life, not as a spirit but as a whole man, body and soul ("Life," ZPEB, III, p. 927). The entrance of death was viewed as unnatural.

The OT word *ḥāyâ* has a range of meaning which includes "to prosper, to sustain life," or "to nourish" (Gen 27:40; Gen 45:7; II Kgs 18:32; I Sam 10:24; II Sam 12:3) or "to restore to health, to heal, recover" (Josh 5:8; II Kgs 1:2; 8:10).

In contrast to the ancient near east, where men sought to link themselves with forces of life thought of in terms of nature deities, by magical recitations of myth accompanied by appropriate magical ritual, in the OT life is decided by a right relationship to the righteous standards of the Word of God. Moses places the people in a state of having to decide between life and death by laying the word of God before them (Deut 30:15–20). Israel is called upon to choose life, "for this word is not a vain thing for you; because it is your life" (Deut 32:47). Bultmann notes that Ezekiel "frees life from all false supports and obligations and relates it wholly and utterly to the Word of God (Ezk 3:18ff.; 14:13ff.; 18:1ff.; 20:1ff.; 33:1ff.)" (TDNT, II, p. 845). In Prov, man is again called upon to make a decision for life, by embracing Wisdom (Prov 2:19; 5:6; 6:23; 10:17; 15:24). By cleaving to God, the righteous have life (Hab 2:4; cf. Amos 5:4, 14; Jer 38:20).

But there is also the somewhat less concrete meaning where one "lives" by the words of God, "not by bread alone" (Deut 8:3; Ps 119:50, 93). Some would insist that this refers to prosperity as the gift of obedience rather than to the spiritual quality of life, as Jesus seems to have interpreted Deut 8:3. But considering again the biblical unity of man's nature, it obviously refers to both.

While it may be difficult to show any developed concept of incorporeal immortality in the OT, there are a number of passages where the verb *ḥāyâ* means "to restore to life," which would imply the overcoming of death. Since OT terminology uses death and life in a wide spectrum of nuances, in some passages it is difficult to tell whether extreme trouble or illness or what we would call death is meant. (The reader should keep in mind that modern medicine, despite its technological sophistication, has trouble defining actual death.) Two such passages are II Kgs 13:20–21, where a man's body "revives" or is "restored to life" upon touching the bones of Elisha. The other is I Kgs 17:17–24 where Elijah "restores to life" the body of the widow's son. Both of these passages appear to be dealing with resurrection from death, but one would have some difficulty from the terminology alone proving whether they were resurrected or merely revived. But the people involved in II Kgs 13:20–21 are treating the man as dead that is, burying him and the boy "had no breath left in him." So in each case the person was received back to life from what the Hebrews called "death."

Psalm 49, while using the word *ḥāyâ* only twice (vv. 9, 18 [H 10, 19]) is very instructive in what it says about the Psalmist's attitude toward living and dying. He teaches that evil men perish. There is no way for them to be redeemed so that they can go on living forever and never see death (vv. 7–8 [H 8–9]). But the Psalmist is not totally negative about death. He expresses his faith in God's promise to redeem his life from the power of the grave (Sheol) for he says, "God will receive (take, snatch, as Enoch and Elijah, see *lāqaḥ*) me" (v. 15 [H 16]). This passage should be linked with Ps 17:15, "I will be satisfied when I wake in your likeness" and also to Ps 16:11 where "the path of life" and overcoming of death is predictive of the resurrection of Jesus Christ (Acts 2:24–29). Bultmann adds, "There is a remarkably plain expression that the relationship of grace will persist, that fellowship initiated by God cannot be destroyed in Ps 73:23ff. One may say that here the OT belief in the hereafter finds its purest formulation. This expectation is neither magical nor mythical not speculative nor mystical. It is a certainty which is produced in the righteous by the concept of grace alone" (TDNT, II, p. 848).

One of the meanings of the word *ḥayyîm*, "endless life," has been generally recognized in the past only as a very late usage of the word. (See BDB on Dan 12:2, p. 313). M. Dahood (*Psalms* I, II, III, in AB, 16, 17, 17a) has brought the Ugaritic literature to bear on the early meaning of this word.

Though Dan 12:2 is often cited in the lexicons as the usage of *ḥayyîm* to mean eternal life, Dahood sees it so used in the Psalms. He refers to the Ugaritic antecedent in 2 Aqht VI. 27–29 (AB pp. 91, 170)

"Ask for eternal life (*ḥym*)
And I will give it to you,
Immortality (*bl·mt*)
And I will bestow it on you.
I will make you number years with Baal,
With gods you will number months."

Proverbs 12:28 uses *'al-māwet* (no death) as the parallel of *ḥayyîm* (life). The Ugaritic *bl·mt* translated "immortality" above is an equivalent expression. The RSV says that the Hebrew is uncertain and proceeds to give a translation based on an emended text. However, Ewald, Bertheau, Franz Delitzsch, and Saadia, the Judeo-Arabist of the Middle Ages, said *'al-māwet* means "immortality." The KJV wisely translated it "no death," NIV, "immortality." They have all been proved correct by the Ugaritic *bl·mt* as used in the above citation. Dahood translates the verse:

"In the path of virtue is eternal life (*ḥayyîm*),
And the treading of her way is immortality (*'al-māwet*)."

M. Pope (JBL 85: 455–66) objects to this translation on the basis that the synonymous parallelism goes against the larger context which consists of a series of couplets in antithetical parallelism and "therefore death not immortality is the proper antithesis." But is there here a larger context? Are not these proverbs a list of independent thoughts? Indeed it is not unusual of the proverbs to shift from one form of parallelism to another (cf. 17:21–22; 19:4–5, etc.). Pope states that *ḥayyîm* as eternal life is not justified by the parallelism of *ḥym* and *bl·mt* in Ugaritic because, the hero's, Aqhat's, reply shows he did not believe immortality could be had by a mortal and he therefore accuses the goddess Anat of lying to him. The implication is that since the Ugaritic hero didn't believe humans could have immortality, the writers of the Old Testament must share the same skepticism. The point is not what the Ugaritians believed but that they used the word *ḥym* for eternal life, whereas the Hebrew lexicons generally list only Dan 12:2 as using *ḥayyîm* distinctively to denote eternal life because of its alleged Maccabean origin.

Another similar use of *ḥayyîm* is in Prov 15:24 where it is put in antithesis with Sheol:

"The path of life above belongs to the wise,
because he turns away from Sheol below."

Whether this passage has relevance on this subject depends on how one interprets Sheol (q.v.) here and in other places in the OT. Sheol often means only "the grave" in OT usage. If that is the meaning here, then *ḥayyîm* as its antithesis need mean only "this earthly life." But if Sheol can mean "netherworld," then *ḥayyîm* here may mean "life after death." The writer holds that Proverbs entertains the concept that "death" (*māwet*) and Sheol involves more than the grave. Prov 2:18–19 parallels death with the place where "the shades" (*r^e pā'îm*) are. And Prov 9:18 parallels Sheol in the same way. This at least opens the possibility that in Prov 15:24 "the path of life above" can mean eternal life in heaven in contrast with Sheol below where the shades dwell.

Some OT scholars would reject this notion, even though they might admit *ḥayyîm* could mean "endless life" on earth. But we are reminded of the repeated OT idea that God dwells in heaven (Deut 4:36, 39: I Kgs 8:27; Job 22:12; Ps 20:6 [H 7], 80:14 [H 15], etc.) where his throne is (Ps 11:4) and that the Psalmist longs to see his face (Ps 17:15). Amos (9:2), a prophet the critics accept at face value from the eighth century, considers both heaven and Sheol as places where people might conceivably go. Although Dahood may be extreme in his application of this meaning for *ḥayyîm*, his critics may be equally extreme in rejecting the notion entirely. For example, in what sense does the king receive eternal life in God's presence (Ps 21:4–6 [H 5–7])? And in what sense does Mount Zion abide forever (Ps 125:1)? The answer is similar in either case. The earthly Mount Zion has a counterpart in heaven (cf. Ps 123:1) and the king's prosperity on earth is only the beginning of all God's eternal goodness to him (Ps 16:11). It is very interesting (Ps 30:5) to see the temporal contrast between the Lord's anger and his favor. His anger is for a moment but his favor is for "life-eternal" not just a "lifetime" as in the RV.

ḥay. ***Living, alive.*** This adjective is often used as an epithet of God (Josh 3:10; Hos 2:1; Ps 42:3, etc.) but also of man, animals, and vegetation in contrast to what is dead or dried up. The plural form describes flowing or fresh water (Gen 26:19; Lev 14:5–6; Num 19:17, etc.). Jesus used a word play on this meaning (Jn 4:10).

ḥayyâ. ***Living thing, animal.*** The term is used mostly of wild animals in contrast to domestic animals. Psalm 104:25 uses it of creatures that live in water. Ezekiel in chapter 1 employs the term to describe the "living creatures" of his vision, which were composite in nature, having features of both man and animals. More rarely it means anything that lives (Ezk 7:13).

ḥayyîm. ***Life,*** as an abstract idea, meaning the state of being alive as opposite to being dead. Life at its best, health, endless life.

miḥyâ. ***Preservation of life*** (Gen 45:5), the appearance of new flesh (Lev 13:10), food, subsistence (Jud 6:4, 17:10).

Bibliography: Greenberg, Moshe, "The Hebrew Oath Particle *hay/he*," JBL 76: 34–39. Gruenthaner, Michael J., "The Old Testament and Retribution in this Life," CBQ 4: 101–110. Lehman, Manfred R., "Biblical Oaths," ZAW 81: 74–92. O'Connell, Matthew J., "The Concept of Commandment in the Old Testament," TS 21: 351–403. Richardson, TWB, pp. 127–28. Rust, Eric C., "The Destiny of the Individual in the Thought of the Old Testament," *Review and Expositor* 58: 296–311. Sawyer, John F. A., "Hebrew Words for the Resurrection of the Dead," VT 23: 218–34. TDNT, II, pp. 843–61. THAT, I, pp. 549–56.

E.B.S.

חַיּוּת (*ḥayyût*). See no. 644g.
חַיִּים (*ḥayyîm*). See no. 644f.
חִיל (*ḥîl*). See no. 623b.
חַיִל (*ḥayil*). See no. 624a.
חֵיל (*ḥêl*). See no. 623d.
חִילָה (*ḥêlâ*). See no. 623e.
חִין (*ḥîn*). See no. 694c.
חַיִץ (*ḥayiṣ*). See no. 628a.
חִיצוֹן (*ḥîṣôn*). See no. 627b.
חֵיק (*ḥêq*). See no. 629a.
חִישׁ (*ḥîsh*). See no. 631a.
חֵךְ (*ḥēk*). See no. 692a.

645 חָכָה (*ḥākâ*) ***to wait; to wait for.***

Cognate with Akkadian *ḫakūm* "to wait for" which occurs in a Mari text (*Archives Royale de Mari* 4. 22.9). It occurs thirteen times in the Piel stem and once as a Qal participle (Isa 30:18). The KJV translates the word as "wait," except in II Kgs 7:9, 9:3 as "tarry" and in Job 3:21 as "long for."

Bandits are said to wait in ambush (Hos 6:9). Job speaks in despair of those who wait for or yearn for death (Job 3:21).

The book of Daniel closes with a blessing for those who would wait for the fulfillment of the prophecies (Dan 12:12). Habakkuk 2:3 urges believers to wait for the vision though it tarries. The Lord declares, "Wait for me" (Zeph 3:8). The expressions "to wait for the Lord" in Isa 8:17 and "to wait for him" in Isa 64:4 [H 3], connote an attitude of earnest expectation and confident hope.

See also *qāwâ*.

Bibliography: Thomson, J.G.S.S., "Wait on the Lord," Exp T 65: 196–98. Wagner, M., "Beiträge zur Aramaismenfrage im alttestamentlichen Hebräisch," Supp VT 16: 361–62. TDNT, IV, pp. 583–85; VI, pp. 193–202.

E.Y.

646 חכל (*ḥkl*). **Assumed root of the following.**
646a חַכְלִילִי (*ḥaklîlî*) ***dull*** (from wine, Gen 49:12).
646b חַכְלִילוּת (*ḥaklîlût*) ***dullness*** (of eyes in drunkenness (Prov 23:29).

חַכְלִילִי (*ḥaklîlî*). See no. 646a.
חַכְלִילוּת (*ḥaklîlût*). See no. 646b.

647 חָכַם (*ḥākam*) ***be wise, act wise(ly).*** (ASV and RSV similar except in one instance RSV uses "shrewdly.")

Derivatives

647a †חָכְמָה (*ḥokmâ*) ***wisdom.***
647b †חָכָם (*ḥākām*) ***wise(man).***

The verb is used twenty-six times and most of the passages appear in the Qal stem meaning "be wise," etc. In the Piel stem the meaning is "making wise" or "teaching." Of all the words denoting intelligence, the most frequently used are this verb and its derivatives, which occur some 312 times in the Hebrew OT. About three-fifths of the usages are found in Job, Prov, and Eccl.

[The main synonyms are *bîn, bînâ,* and *tᵉbûnâ*. The verb *bîn* is used more widely to mean "consider," "discern" "perceive," but the nouns are close synonyms to *ḥokmâ* and are used especially in Prov and Job. In the well-known verse Prov 4:7, "understanding" is not a higher stage than "wisdom," but a poetic synonym used for emphasis. The root *śākal* is also widely used for ordinary intelligence and skill. It is often used for that wisdom which brings success—even prosperity. This wisdom was possessed by David (I Sam 18:14) and will characterize the Messiah (Jer 23:5; Isa 52:13). But the Hiphil participle is used particularly in Prov as another synonym of *ḥokmâ*. This word, *maśkîl,* is also used extensively to designate a type of psalm. *tûshîyâ,* like *śākal,* has the double meaning of wisdom and the success which is the effect of wisdom. R.L.H.]

The essential idea of *ḥākam* represents a manner of thinking and attitude concerning life's experiences; including matters of general interest and basic morality. These concerns relate to prudence in secular affairs, skills in the arts, moral sensitivity, and experience in the ways of the Lord.

The subject wisdom was discussed throughout the ancient near east. Mesopotamian wisdom, which originated with the Sumerian, emphasized human experiences, character, and counsel regarding practical advice. The problems of death and suffering were discussed. Egyptian wisdom included the concept of *ma'at* ("truth," "intelligence," "justice"), according to which one order existed in the whole universe. J. A. Wilson characterizes it as a created and inherited rightness, which tradition built up into an orderly stability (*The Culture of Ancient Egypt,* University of Chicago, 1951, p. 48). Gods and men were subject to this order of conduct, which was taught by the priests. Some have felt that much of the OT royal wisdom, which great leaders imparted to their students, was borrowed from Egyptian wisdom (e.g. Prov 23:13f. borrowed from the teachings of Amenemope, although it is more likely that an original source reflects a revelation of wisdom.) Ugaritic literature also has a form of maxims concerning the father-son relationship possibly reflecting Canaanite wisdom. A later Arabic derivative of the verb denotes "to restrain from acting in an evil manner."

The wisdom of the OT however, is quite distinct from other ancient world views although the format of wisdom literature is similar to that of other cultures. Reflected in OT wisdom is the teaching of a personal God who is holy and just and who expects those who know him to exhibit his character in the many practical affairs of life. This perfect blend of the revealed will of a holy God with the practical human experiences of life is also distinct from the speculative wisdom of the Greeks. The ethical dynamic of Greek philosophy lay in the intellect; if a person had perfect knowledge he could live the good life (Plato). Knowledge was virtue. The emphasis of OT wisdom was that the human will, in the realm of practical matters, was to be subject to divine causes. Therefore, Hebrew wisdom was not theoretical and speculative. It was practical, based on revealed principles of right and wrong, to be lived out in daily life.

In the historical and prophetical books, the word *ḥokmâ* is sometimes used just to refer to ordinary intelligence and skill (Ex 35:35; Dan 1:4), but even there sometimes the divine and moral wisdom is in view.

The wisdom literature, while sometimes using wisdom as prudence and cleverness, majors on ethical and spiritual conduct. Because God revealed himself to Israel, their sacred literature has the effect of a divine imperative; *ḥākam* refers to godly cleverness and skill, which results in practical action. The one who hears (Prov 8:33; 23:19; 27:11), will be industrious, will know how to talk, and his will, will be in captivity to God's. He will have life. This wins divine approbation.

ḥokmâ. ***Wisdom.*** The usages of *ḥokmâ* cover the whole gamut of human experience. Wisdom is seen in the skill of technical work in making garments for the high priest (Ex 28:3), craftsmanship in metal work (Ex 31:3, 6), as well as the execution of battle tactics (Isa 10:13). Wisdom is required from government leaders and heads of state for administration (Deut 34:9; II Sam 14:20), including pagan leaders as well as Israelites (Ezk 28:4–5). The Messiah demonstrates wisdom and discernment in his function as leader of his people (Isa 11:2).

Wisdom is expressed in shrewdness. The woman of Tekoa averted a town's bloodshed in her clever plea for its safety (II Sam 20:22). But a shrewd person is not to boast of his gift (Jer 9:22). The ostrich displays traits lacking shrewdness when she acts in her silly selfish manner (Job 39:17). The gift of shrewdness can be used in an ungodly way to deny the omniscience of God (Isa 47:10).

Prudence, an aspect of wisdom, is expressed by those who speak with wisdom (Ps 37:30; Prov 10:31), and who use time carefully (Ps 90:12). This kind of wisdom in the practical affairs of life is derived from the revelation of God (Isa 33:6).

The source of all wisdom is a personal God who is holy, righteous, and just. His wisdom is expressed against the background of his omnipotence and omniscience. By his wisdom God numbered the clouds (Job 38:37), founded the earth (Prov 3:19), and made the world (Jer 10:12). Wisdom, being found in God, is regarded as a divine attribute (Job 12:13). He alone knows wisdom in its truest sense (Job 28:20, 23). The wisdom of God is not found in man's speculation. He alone must provide this wisdom for man's guidance so that man can live the best possible moral and ethical life (Prov 2:6; Job 11:6).

In proverbial fashion, the Bible personifies divine wisdom so that it seems to be a hypostasis of God, but stops just short of giving it separate existence. This wisdom was brought forth before all things (Prov 8: 22–31). She has built a house and prepared a banquet for those who will listen to her (Prov 9:1f.). She even teaches in public places (Prov 1:20; 8:1, 6, 11–12). By her instruction her students receive a divine spirit (Prov 1:2), the naive become wise, politicians become wise, and those who receive from her wealth are crowned with honor and riches (Prov 8:1–21).

This personification of wisdom is unique. While there were gods and goddesses in the ancient near east who were thought to possess the gifts of wisdom it is unlikely that any existed by the name of wisdom. The figure of wisdom in the OT never came to be regarded as a deity independent of the Lord although some such expressions occur in Prov 8. These have often been taken as an adumbration of Christ. Wisdom did attain a degree of personification, with features which were by no means abstract. Wisdom should not be regarded as God but it does belong to God; it is one of his attributes. Wisdom has a personal existence in the living word of the NT, but wisdom is not the Logos herself (Delitzsch, *Proverbs*, p. 183). That Wisdom is personified as a woman in Prov 1–9 is partly explained by the fact that the noun is feminine. There the Lady Wisdom is contrasted with the woman Folly who is personified sin. Note the studied contrast of Prov 9:4–6 and 9:16–18. This personification of wisdom is not found outside these chapters.

Wisdom for man is not only to make one humanly wise, but also to lead him to fear the Lord, for this is the beginning of all wisdom (Job 28:28). True wisdom for man involves knowing the Holy One. So, men are to listen to the wisdom of God with attentive ears (Prov 2:2). In fact, inner happiness only comes when man attains this wisdom (Prov 3:13) through a strenous search (Prov 2:4), which is actually a search for God himself (Prov 2:5). Skeptics will never find this wisdom and will never know the full meaning of life (Prov 14:6f.). In the great poem of Job 28 wisdom in this special biblical sense is practically defined as trust in God and the avoidance of sin. (Cf. the emphasis on *ḥokmâ* as referring to moral wisdom in contrast to sinful folly in R. L. Harris, "Proverbs," in WBC, pp. 553–54.)

ḥākām. ***Wise(men); cunning (man).*** Reflects the usages of *ḥokmâ* in describing the wise man. He is skilful in various kinds of technical work, e.g. as artisans (of tabernacle and temple furniture, Ex 35:10), and goldsmiths (Jer 10:9). The wise man knows how to administer the affairs of state (I Kgs 5:21) and is also shrewd, e.g. the wise woman of Tekoa handling a delicate matter before Solomon (II Sam 14:2). The plural also indicates the learned and shrewd men, astrologers, magicians of many nations: Egypt (Gen 41:8), Babylon (Isa 44:28), Persia (Est 6:13). Prudence also describes the wise person's attitude to kings (Prov 16:14), his prudence in conforming to the word of God (Deut 4:6), or a lack of it in ignoring God's will (Hos 13:13).

The wise man constituted a third office, using wisdom in harmony with the function of the other two offices (Jer 18:18). Thus the wise man gave practical advice based on divine revelation as well as his own experience and observation.

Bibliography: Albright, W. F., "Some Canaanite-Phoenician sources of Hebrew Wisdom," in *Wisdom in Israel and in the Ancient Near East,* ed. M. Noth and D. Winton Thomas, Brill, 1960. Blank, S. H., "Wisdom," in IDB, pp. 852–61. Crenshaw, J. L., "Method in Determining Wisdom Influence upon 'Historical' Literature," JBL 88: 129–42. Gordis, Robert, "The Social Background of Wisdom Literature," HUCA 18: 77–118. Harris, R. L., "Proverbs," in WBE. Hubbard, D. A., "The Wisdom Movement and Israel's Covenant Faith," *Tyndale Bulletin* 17: 3–33. Irwin, William, "Where Shall Wisdom Be Found?" JBL 80: 133–42. Knox, Wilfred, "The Divine Wisdom," JTS 38: 230–37. Kramer, Samuel Noah, "Sumerian Wisdom Literature: A Preliminary Survey," BASOR 122: 28–31. Malfroy, Jean, "Sagesse et Loi dans le Deuteronome Études," VT 15: 49–65. Marcus, R., "The Biblical Hypostases of Wisdom," HUCA 23: 157–71. Montgomery, J. W., "Wisdom as Gift," Interp 16: 43–57. Murphy, Roland E., "Assumptions and Problems in Old Testament Wisdom Research," CBQ 29: 407–12. Pfeiffer, R. H., "Wisdom and Vision in the O.T.," ZAW 11: 93–101. Priest, John F., "Where is Wisdom to be Placed," *Journal of Bible and Religion* 31: 276–82. Reines, C. W., "Koheleth on Wisdom and Wealth," JSS 5: 80–84. Richardson, TWB, p. 282. Scott, R. B. Y., *The Way of Wisdom,* Macmillan, 1971. Talmon, S., "'Wisdom' in the Book of Esther," VT 13: 419–55. Van Imschoot, P., "Sagesse et Esprit dans l'A. T.," RB 47: 23–49. Whybray, R. N., *Wisdom in Proverbs,* London: SCM, 1965. TDNT, VII, pp. 476–514. THAT, I, pp. 557–66.

L.G.

חֹל (*ḥōl*). See nos. 623a; 661a.
חֵל (*ḥēl*). See no. 623d.

648 חָלָא (*ḥālā'*) ***I, be diseased, suffer.***

Derivative

648a תַּחֲלֻאִים (*taḥălū'îm*) ***diseases.*** The word occurs five times, always in the plural.

Derived from *ḥālâ, ḥālā'* is cognate with the Akkadian *halu* "sickness, grief." It occurs once in the Qal stem (II Chr 16:12) and once in the Hiphil stem (Isa 53:10).

In II Chr 16:12 we are told that Asa developed a serious foot disease, perhaps gout or gangrene (NEB). Although medical treatment and physicians are not condemned as such (cf. Isa 38:21; Jer 8:22), Asa was at fault because he consulted the physicians rather than the Lord. Furthermore, we do not know what forbidden rites these "physicians" (*rōpa'îm*) may have practiced.

In Isa 53:10 the Lord is pleased to "put him to grief" (RSV; cf. also KJV , NASB), literally "make him sick." That is, it pleased the Lord that his Servant should suffer. The NAB renders, "But the Lord was pleased to crush him in infirmity" (cf. JB "with suffering"). The NEB renders a reconstructed text.

taḥălū'îm. ***Diseases.*** Jehoram died of "sore diseases," which may have been a kind of dysentery resulting in a prolapse of the rectum. According to II Chr 21:19, Jehoram died "in great agony" (RSV; JB and NAB, "in great pain"). The NEB reads, "Painful ulceration brought on his death."

Jeremiah 14:18 speaks of the "diseases of famine" (RSV), which KJV paraphrases "them that are sick with famine." Severe malnutrition causes numerous diseases.

The Psalmist praises the Lord who forgives all his iniquities and heals all his diseases (Ps 103:3). Here, as in Isa 53, sin and sickness are closely related. Sin and sickness are related to guilt and punishment. Moreover, both are hopeless states which only God can relieve. In Isa 53 they find solution in the vicarious death of the Servant of the Lord.

Bibliography: Harrison, R. K., "Disease," in IDB, I, 847–51.

E.Y.

649 חלא (*ḥl'*) **II. Assumed root of the following.**
649a חֶלְאָה (*ḥel'â*) ***rust*** (Ezk 24:6, 12).

650 חלב (*ḥlb*) **I. Assumed root of the following.**
650a חָלָב (*ḥālāb*) ***milk, sour milk, cheese.***

Cognate with Akkadian *hilpu,* Ugaritic *ḥlb* (UT 19: no. 862), and Arabic *ḥalab*. The word occurs forty-four times in the Masoretic text.

Human milk is mentioned in Isa 28:9; the weaned child would have been about three years old (cf. II Macc 7:27).

The *ṭᵉlēh ḥālāb* which was offered by Samuel (I Sam 7:9) was a "sucking lamb," i.e. an "unweaned lamb" (NAB).

The Israelites utilized the milk of cows, goats, and sheep (Deut 32:14; Prov 27:27). Because of the warm climate, people of the Near East generally utilized the milk not as milk or butter, but as sour milk or curds (yogurt).

When Sisera came to Jael's tent she opened a skin bottle of milk. Fresh milk shaken in such a skin would be curdled by the bacteria left on the inner surface, and would then be served as sour milk (Jud 4:19; 5:25) or *ḥem'â,* which is not "butter." Called *leben* in Arabic, it is still served to guests by bedouins. Cf. Gen 18:8.

When the sour milk was twisted tightly in a cloth (Prov 30:33), curds were produced. Cf. Isa 7:22. David brought food for his brothers, and ten cheeses, literally "cuts of milk," for their commander (I Sam 17:18).

The Israelites were commanded not to "seethe," i.e. boil a kid in its mother's milk (Ex 23:19; 34:26; Deut 14:21). Since a Ugaritic text (UT 16: Text no. 52:14) specifies, "They cook a kid in milk," the biblical injunction may have been directed against a Canaanite fertility rite. Later Jewish interpretation held that this involved the prohibition of eating meat and dairy dishes together.

Milk is used in a number of symbolic or metaphoric expressions. The Lord promised to bring the children of Israel into a land flowing with milk and honey (Ex 3:8, 17, etc.). The image is of a fertile land with pastures and flowers which would present a sharp contrast to the desolate Sinai wilderness. Some protested that Moses had not brought them to such a land but had instead taken them out of such a land, namely Egypt (Num 16:13).

Milk is used in other expressions which speak of prosperity and fertility (Deut 32:14; Joel 3:18 [H 4:18]).

The process of embryonic development is compared in Job 10:10 to the coagulation of milk. Cf. Ps 139:13–16; Eccl 11:5; Wisd 7:1–2; II Macc 7:22–23.

Zion in its future glory will suck the "milk of nations" and "the breast of kings" (Isa 60:16, RSV).

For Job's description of the prosperous man (Job 21:24), most authorities prefer to follow the versions in reading *ḥēleb* "fat" for *ḥālāb* "milk" (MT, KJV). The difficult word is *'ăṭîn* (KJV "breasts") which occurs only here. The LXX translates it *egkata* "entrails" and the Vulgate *viscera*. It has been conjectured that the word represents Aramaic *'ăṭam* "flank," hence "thighs" or "haunches." The RSV translates "his body full of fat"; the JB "his thighs all heavy with fat"; and the NAB "his figure is full," NIV "his body well nourished."

See also *ḥem'â, ḥēmâ, maḥămā'ōt, ḥēleb.*

Bibliography: Fisher, Loren R., ed., *Ras Shamra Parallels I,* Pontifical Biblical Institute, 1972, pp. 29–32, 182. Gaster, Theodor H., *Customs and Folkways of Jewish Life,* Sloane, 1955, pp. 211–14. Kosmala, H., "The So-Called Ritual Decalogue," *Annual of the Swedish Theological Institute* 1: 50–57, 60–61.

For figures of milk and milking, see ANEP, figures 76, 97, 99, 100, 600.

E.Y.

651 חלב (*ḥlb*) **II. Assumed root of the following.**
651a †חֵלֶב (*ḥēleb*) ***fat.***

Cognate with Punic *ḥlb,* Syriac *ḥelba,* Ugaritic *ḥlb,* Arabic *ḥilbun* "midriff fat." It occurs ninety times, usually referring to the fat of animal sacrifices, especially in Lev where it appears forty-five times. It is to be distinguished from *ḥālāb* "milk" which has a Ugaritic cognate *ḥlb* and Arabic *ḥalab*.

The KJV translates *ḥēleb* as "fat" or "fatness," except for "marrow" in Ps 63:5 [H 6], "grease" in Ps 119:70, metaphorically, "the best" in Num 18:12, 29–30, 32, and "the finest" in Ps 81:16 [H 17]; 147:14.

The fat of sacrificial animals, specifically the fat surrounding the kidneys and intestines, was burned by the priests (Lev 3:3–4, 10, 14–16). In some cases the fat tail of the broadtail sheep, which can weigh up to ten pounds, was offered (Lev 3:9; Ex 29:22).

The fat was burned in the following offerings: 1. the "burnt offering" (KJV) or holocaust (Lev 1:8, 12 where *peder* "suet" is used); 2. the "peace offering" (KJV) or "communion sacrifice" (JB, Lev 3:9ff.; 7:15ff.); 3. the "sin offering'' (Lev 4:8–10); and 4. the ''trespass offering'' (KJV, Lev 7:3–4).

Like the blood, the fat was not to be eaten (Lev 3:17; 7:23, 25). Whether this prohibition applied to all animal fat or just the portions specified is a matter of dispute; cf. NAB footnote on Lev 7:23. The fat of an animal that had died of natural causes or had been torn by other animals could be used for grease (Lev 7:24).

Various theories have been offered to explain why the fat was sacrificed with the blood. There is, of course, the functional reason that fat burns well with little odor and would thus be a good practical representative portion of the peace offerings which were offered in large numbers at festival gatherings and which were eaten by priests and people. Some see in fat the seat of life, the symbol of strength, or the food of gods (cf. Ezk 44:7). In contrast to the pagan gods, who were dependent upon sacrifices for their sustenance (cf. *The Gilgamesh Epic* 11. 159–61), Jehovah declares, ''Will I eat the flesh of bulls or drink the blood of goats?'' (Ps 50:13).

Abel's sacrifice of the firstlings of the flock and of their fat (Gen 4:4) indicated his desire to offer the best to God. The offering of the fat, which was the tastiest part, symbolized the worshiper's desire to offer the best to God.

Such offerings were therefore welcomed by God (Isa 43:24). But the mechanical offering even of fat was no substitute for obedience (I Sam 15:22).

A number of passages describe the selfish, rebellious man who reveals his gluttony in his obese features. In Job 15:27 the godless man has hidden his face in fat. (In Ps 17:10 the wicked have shut up their *ḥēleb*, perhaps not to be read as ''fat'' here but as ''midriff,'' as in the cognate Arabic word, as this was considered the seat of the emotions.) The eyes of the wicked ''swell out with fatness'' (RSV) or ''gleam through folds of fat'' (NEB) (Ps 73:7). The heart of the godless is ''gross like fat'' (Ps 119:70, RSV). When Jeshurun, i.e. Israel, waxed fat and sleek he forsook God (Deut 32:15; cf. Jer 5:28). (For Job 21:24 see *ḥālāb*.)

ḥēleb is used idiomatically for the best of the land (Gen 45:18), as is the English expression ''the cream of the crop.''

In Ezk 34:3 the NEB, JB, and NAB follow the LXX and the Vulg. in reading *ḥālāb* ''milk'' instead of *ḥēleb*.

Bibliography: Heller, J., ''Die Symbolik des Fettes im AT,'' VT 20: 106–8.

See also *bārā', bārî', dāshēn, mishman, mashmanîm, peder, shāman, shāmēn.*

E.Y.

652 חֶלְבְּנָה (*ḥelbᵉnâ*) ***a kind of gum*** (Ex 30:34).

653 חלד (*ḥld*). **Assumed root of the following.**
653a †חֶלֶד (*ḥeled*) ***duration of life, the world.***

Zophar admonishes Job that if he (Job) will do right and put away evil his ''life will be brighter than the noonday'' (Job 11:17). The Psalmist laments over how fleeting his life is. ''You made my day like a few handbreadths; my life is as nothing in your presence'' (Ps 39:5 [H 6]). Psalm 89:47 [H 48] strikes a similar note, ''Remember, how short (of what duration) my life is.''

The other meaning of *ḥeled* is related to the former. The world is used not meaning just the earth, but rather the total scene of life and action on the earth. Psalm 49:1 uses the word clearly with this meaning ''Hear this all you people; listen, all who live in the world.'' The translation of Ps 17:14 is more difficult but most agree *ḥeled* also means ''world'' in this verse. The meaning is either ''by your hand, O Lord, destroy them from the world'' or ''save me (v. 13) by your hand, O Lord, from men of the world.''

E.B.S.

654 חלד (*ḥld*). **Assumed root of the following.**
654a חֹלֶד (*ḥōled*) ***weasel*** (Lev 11:29).

655 חָלָה (*ḥālâ*) ***I, be or become sick, weak, diseased, grieved, sorry, et al.*** (ASV and RSV similar.)

Derivatives

655a †חֳלִי (*ḥŏlî*) ***sickness.***
655b †מַחֲלֶה (*maḥăleh*) ***disease.***
655c מַחֲלָה (*maḥălâ*) ***sickness.***
655d †מַחֲלוּי (*maḥălûy*) ***sickness.***

The basic meaning of this root is ''to be(come) sick'' or ''faint.'' The verb is used fifty-nine times. Due to the nature of the verb there is seldom any difference in translating with the auxiliary ''be'' or ''become.''

In many contexts (e.g. Gen 48:1; Ezk 34:16) no distinction need be made between ''sick'' or ''weak,'' the latter resulting from the former. But in Jud 16:7, 17 sickness cannot be involved because ''to be weak'' (in opposition to *kōaḥ*, strength) here is explicitly stated to be ''as another man'' or ''like any man.'' The other uses of this verb could be construed always to imply a sickness of some sort but this is often not necessary. Thus in Isa 57:10 the word is applied to what is probably the natural result of a long journey (ASV and RSV, ''be faint''; KJV, ''grieved'').

To be ''sick'' includes the condition brought about by physical injury or wounding: by beating (Prov 23:35 KJV: ASV and RSV ''hurt''), from battle wounds (II Kgs 8:29), from a fall (II Kgs 1:2). It is used in a general sense (like the English) for illness, regardless of cause, sometimes leading to death: Jacob (Gen 48:1), Hezekiah (II Kgs 20:1). It is used more specifically of disease: as with Asa's feet (I Kgs 15:23). It is used of animals such as those which are unsuitable for sacrifice (Mal 1:8, 13).

The verb is also used in the sense of "sick of heart" or "mind," as a girl sick with love (Song 2:5; 5:8). Saul complained that nobody was "sick," i.e. "felt sorry" for him (I Sam 22:8).

The non-physical form of sickness is more evident in the Niphal. Amos speaks of those who are "at ease in Zion" but "are not grieved (i.e. "made sick") for the afflication of Joseph" (Amos 6:6) and Isaiah speaks of a "day of being sick" (translated "day of grief," Isa 17:11). But the Niphal is also used for the "diseased" (Ezk 34:4) and "faint" (Jer 12:13). In the latter reference Jeremiah uses the word for the effort to sow wheat (which results in reaping thorns). The KJV and ASV translate "put themselves to pain," but the RSV, "tire themselves out." The Niphal participle is also used in the sense of "severe" when referring to wounds or blows (Jer 10:19).

The Hiphil "make sick" is used four times in various contexts. Micah 6:13 should probably be understood "I have made thy smiting sick" in the sense of "sore" or "severe." (The RSV rejects the Hebrew text here.) The Hiphil is used in reference to feelings ("hope deferred makes the heart sick," Prov 13:12), and to sickness that comes from wine (Hos 7:5).

Isaiah 53:10 (KJV) reads, "Yet it pleased the Lord to bruise him; he has put *him* to grief," i.e. "he has made him sick" in the sense of mental anguish. But it could be in a physical sense, i.e. "he has wounded him." This would parallel the corresponding passive (Hophal) which is used three times, always in the sense of "I am wounded (made sick)" from battle injuries (I Kgs 22:34; II Chr 18:33, Ahab; II Chr 35:23, Josiah).

The Hithpael is used just three times—all concerning Amnon, in the sense of "make oneself sick." He made himself sick with inordinate desire (II Sam 13:2), and then made himself appear sick (vv. 5–6).

The Piel is causative in Deut 29:22 (but the KJV translates "hath laid" to avoid a cognate to the noun "sickness"). The only other Piel is an infinitive translated "infirmity" (Ps 77:10 [H 11], KJV, ASV) or "grief" (RSV, ASV marg.). For other Piel forms see *ḥālâ*, II. The Pual is used once: "become (or) be made weak" (Isa 14:10).

ḥŏlî. ***Sickness, disease, illness.*** This noun follows the verb in meaning "sickness" whether from physical causes (the fall of Ahaziah, II Kgs 1:2), or from disease (in Asa's feet, II Chr 16:12; in the bowels of Jehoram, II Chr 21:15). It may be applied figuratively to a nation (Hos 5:13). It is used to describe a given situation as a calamity (Eccl 6:2, RSV, "affliction").

The word is translated "grief" in Isa 53:3–4, although it may be better translated "sickness" (margin of ASV and RSV), whether physical or spiritual. The parallel is *mak'ôb,* meaning "pain," but translated "sorrow." Jeremiah (chaps 6–7) uses the term to describe the spiritual depravity of Jerusalem (KJV, "grief"). The KJV also translates "grief" in Jer 10:19 (RSV, affliction), but the use in context is similar to Eccl 6:2 (above), perhaps to be translated "calamity."

maḥăleh. ***Disease, infirmity.*** Used twice (II Chr 21:15; Prov 18:14).

maḥălûy. ***Sickness or wound.*** Used only in II Chr 24:25 of the condition of Joash as a result of conflict with Syrians.

C.P.W.

656 *חָלָה (*ḥālâ*) ***II, beseech, entreat, pray, make prayer, suit, application.*** (ASV and RSV similar.)

Derivative

656a †מַחֲלַת (*maḥălat*) **Mahalath.**

This word is used sixteen times, always in the Piel stem, and always with p^e*nê* "the face of." With p^e*nê* the meaning is "entreat," "seek the favor of." The use of *ḥlh* in this construction is similar to that of the Hithpael of *ḥānan,* "entreat favor."

Thirteen of the sixteen usages refer to the favor being sought of the Lord. Usually this involves a prayer for mercy or help in the threat of danger. The danger may be the hand of God (Ex 32:11, as a result of the golden calf), or of enemies (II Kgs 13:4, the Syrians against Jehoahaz).

As applied to others, Zophar tells Job that if he would "be good" people would entreat his favor (Job 11:19, KJV "make suit unto you"). In Prov 19:6 we are told that "many will entreat the favor of the liberal man (KJV prince)." According to Ps 45:12 [H 13], the rich shall entreat the bride of the King, who is identified in Heb 1:8–9 as the Son of God.

Some would call attention to the invariable use with p^e*nê* and urge that the idiom means to stroke the face of someone and thus mollify him, but this seems to be extreme etymologizing. The origin of the idiom may not be clear. The meaning, however, as determined by usage is plain. Other words for "to pray" are *ḥānan* and *pālal* (q.v.).

C.P.W.

māḥălat. ***Mahalath.*** This technical musical term of uncertain meaning is found in the headings of Ps 53 and 88 [H 53:1 and 88:1]. Most versions simply transliterate the term. The NASB suggests a connection with *ḥālâ* "to be weak, sick," hence a sad tune. Others relate it to *meḥōlâ,* a round dance. In Ps 88, where it is joined with "Leannoth," the NIV says it may possibly be a tune, "The Suffering of Affliction." For other such terms see *selâ.*

H.W.

657 חלה (*ḥlh*) **III. Assumed root of the following.**

657a חֲלִי (*ḥălî*) ***ornament*** (Prov 25:12; Song 7:2).

657b חֶלְיָה (*ḥelyâ*) ***jewelry*** (Hos 2:15).

חַלָּה (*ḥallâ*). See no. 660b.
חַלּוֹן (*ḥallôn*). See no. 660c.
חֲלוֹם (*ḥălôm*). See no. 663a.
חֲלוֹף (*ḥălôp*). See no. 666b.
חֲלוּשָׁה (*ḥălûshâ*). See no. 671b.
חַלְחָלָה (*ḥalḥālâ*). See no. 623f.

658 חָלַט (*ḥālaṭ*) ***catch, pick up (a word).*** Used only in I Kgs 20:33.

חֳלִי (*ḥŏlî*). See no. 655a.
חֲלִי (*ḥălî*). See no. 657a.
חֶלְיָה (*ḥelyâ*). See no. 657b.
חָלִיל (*ḥālîl*). See no. 660d.
חָלִילָה (*ḥălîlâ*). See no. 661c.
חֲלִיפָה (*ḥălîpâ*). See no. 666c.
חֲלִיצָה (*ḥălîṣâ*). See nos. 667a, 668a.

659 חלך (*ḥlk*). **Assumed root of the following.**

659a †חֶלְכָה (*ḥēlkâ*) ***hapless, unfortunate person, poor*** (KJV).

The word is used only as a noun and only in one context, Ps 10:8–14. The psalm is about the treachery of the wicked who lie in wait to destroy their unfortunate victims. The wicked man thinks God will overlook this but he does not (vv. 11–14). The hapless are exhorted to commit themselves to the Lord who is the helper of the fatherless. The root appears to be used three times, although some suggest the usage in v. 10 has another meaning (scoundrel, cf. Holladay, *A Concise Hebrew and Aramaic Lexicon,* p. 105). It is true that the spelling in v. 10 is slightly different but the root is no doubt the same. It is possible that the word in v. 10 is the so-called "abstract plural." The verse may be rendered, "He (the wicked) crushes (him); he sinks low and falls into helplessness because of his strength."

E.B.S.

660 חָלַל (*ḥālal*) ***I, wound (fatally), bore through, pierce.*** Survives in Arabic *ḥalla* "pierce through." Occurs ninety-six times, including derivatives.

Derivatives

660a †חָלָל (*ḥālāl*) ***slain, fatally wounded.***
660b †חַלָּה (*ḥallâ*) ***cake (if pierced).***
660c †חַלּוֹן (*ḥallôn*) ***window*** (if taken as a piercing or hollow in the wall).
660d חָלִיל (*ḥālîl*) ***flute, pipe.***
660e חָלַל (*ḥālal*) ***play the pipe.*** Denominative verb.
660f †מְחִלָּה (*meḥillâ*) ***hole.*** Occurs only in Isa 2:19 (parallel to cave in rocks).

The verb itself is used only eight times and mainly in poetry. It usually means a fatal wounding of persons, as does the adjective *ḥālāl.* Twice it refers to the fleeing serpent, parallel to the Lord's action in smiting Rahab to death (Isa 51:9; Job 26:13; though in the latter passage KJV assumes *ḥālal* "create").

In the messianic passage Isa 53:5, "wounded" (KJV marg. "tormented"; JB "pierced through") follows the divine smiting (v. 4). The Poel form used (*meḥôlāl*) is similar to that in Isa 51:9; cf. "pierced by the sword" (Pual, Ezk 32:26). The quotation in Jn 19:12 ("they shall look on him whom they have pierced") is from Zech 12:10 but this v. uses another verb (*dāqar*) "pierced through fatally" (usually in retribution). In Jer 51:4 and Lam 4:9 *dāqar* is used as a synonym of ḥālal.

There is no need to read Ps 77:11 as "my sickness" (*ḥălōtî*) instead of "my wounding" (*ḥalōtî*), an idea already expressed in Ps 109:22 (RSV here "stricken," but the context is of death). Proverbs 26:10 is to be read with RSV "an archer who wounds everyone" rather than the hypothetical KJV "the great (God) who formed (created) all things."

ḥālāl. ***Slain, fatally wounded.*** The rendering "pierced" rests on its probable derivation from *ḥālal* I. This adjective is used eighty-seven times, one-fourth of which are qualified with "by the sword." That the action was fatal is confirmed by the context and circumstantial evidence in most instances. It included the act of wounding and the resultant groans. The wounds were inflicted usually in war, but also in persecution (Ps 69:26 [H 27]) or hunger (Lam 4:9), and ended in death. For this reason KJV sometimes equivocates (marg.) between "wounded" and "slain" (e.g. I Chr 10:1). (In Lev 21:7, 14 the fem. *ḥălālâ* refers to a woman who had been violated.)

ḥallâ. ***Cake.*** This feminine noun occurs fourteen times and is a technical term for a special type of baked cake made of fine flour (Lev 2:4) and oil (Lev 7:12; Num 6:15). It has been considered as having some characteristic perforations (*Ringbrot*) on the basis of a supposed etymology from *ḥālal* I. This cake was part of the firstfruits offering (Num 15:20) and was placed on the altar

(Lev 8:26) as part of the burnt offering (Ex 29:23). It was, however, eaten by participants as part of the communion (peace) offering (II Sam 6:19; Ex 29:2; Num 6:19).

ḥallôn. ***Window.*** This noun (masculine and feminine) occurs thirty-four times and its meaning in the OT is not in doubt. It is usually taken as an opening "pierced" in the wall (from *ḥālal* I). It was an opening in a building which provided light and air, usually high up in the wall and below the eaves for security purposes. The etymology is uncertain and cannot be connected with the Syrian portico architectural feature (*bīt ḫilāni;* cf. Akk *ḫitlanni,* Hittite *hilammar*).

Windows are found in many types of building in both inner and outer walls. They were not glazed and seldom shuttered. They served as air vents as in the ark (Gen 8:6). They could be set in square frames (I Kgs 6:4) and were large enough for a person to be lowered through them (Josh 2:15; I Sam 19:12; II Cor 11:33). Exceptionally a person, as a thief, might enter through them (Joel 2:9) although they were protected by bars or latticework (Jud 5:28; Prov 7:6; cf. II Kgs 1:2). Through these a person could be seen from street level and look out (II Kgs 9:30–32), although to identify this "woman at the window" with cult practices and representations in art is hazardous.

The phrase "windows of heaven" (KJV, RSV) translates another term (*'ărubbâ,* q.v.) which should be translated "sluices, floodgates" (as JB and NIV). Like the eyes (Eccl 12:3), the furnace (Hos 13:3), or the dovecot (Isa 60:8) these could be opened (Gen 7:11) or shut (Gen 8:2). So figuratively God controls the irrigation to let fall a destructive flood (Gen 8:2; cf. Isa 24:18) or the shower of plenty (II Kgs 7:2) a symbol of blessing (Mal 3:10).

m^eḥillâ. ***Hole.*** This feminine noun occurs only once, in Isa 2:19, where it is parallel to cave in rocks.

D.J.W.

661 חָלַל (*ḥālal*) ***II, profane, defile, pollute, desecrate; begin*** (Hiphil only).

Derivatives

661a †חֹל (*ḥōl*) ***profaneness, commonness.***
661b †חָלָל (*ḥālāl*) ***II, profaned, dishonoured, unhallowed.***
661c †חָלִילָה (*ḥālîlâ*) ***far be it (from me etc.), God forbid that*** emphatic substantive used as negative particle or interjection.
661d †תְּחִלָּה (*t^eḥillâ*) ***beginning, first.***

The etymology and basic meaning of this root are not known. Comparison with Arabic *ḥll* "to free from lawful obligations" and with the use in Ugaritic (only once, *Ugaritica* V, 3. 11.6, "profanation of hands" UT Supplement p. 552) may indicate its semantic range.

It and its derivatives are used eighty-three times. *ḥālal* is associated with uncleanness (*ṭum'â*) and similar terms with which the physical, ritual, and ethical issues overlap.

The root *ḥll* is used to mark the act of doing violence to the established law of God (Zeph 3:4), breaking the covenant (Ps 55:21), or the divine statutes (Ps 89:31 [H 32]). Thus to profane is to misuse the name of God (Lev 18:21), the Sabbath (Ex 31:14) or the holy place, and so desecrate it.

The Levitical laws had as one aim to safeguard the priests against defilement in character, body, or ritual. They could be made personally unholy by contact with the dead (Lev 21:4). In regard to sexual relationships, the rules were quite strict. The priest might only marry a virgin of his own people (Lev 21:7–15). In ritual the priest must not make holy things unholy by partaking of sacrifices outside the prescribed period (when food would have become polluted naturally, Lev 19:8). The holy place itself was to be protected by prohibiting entry to "aliens uncircumcised in heart and flesh" (Ezk 44:7).

The original use of the word may have been in reference to sexual relations, since it is used of Reuben's defilement of his father's line (Gen 49:4) or of intercourse within the near kin relations forbidden by law. Such actions were considered fornication and prostitution. The word may therefore be used of any action which controverts God's planned order.

God himself was said to "profane" his own inheritance by giving it over to Babylon when his people broke the law and were exiled (Isa 47:6), and likewise his priests when they were sent off to Chaldea (Isa 43:28). In this he was acting to prevent his Name from being profaned, i.e. considered unholy, by heathen nations, even though it meant that the sanctuary, crown, and kingdom of Judah were "profaned."

The Hiphil theme of the verb is only used twice; of the Name ("I will not let my holy Name be profaned any more," Ezk 39:7) and of the need of man not to "break" his word (KJV "violate") when it was a vow or pledge involving the Lord's name (Num 30:3). For this reason the frequent use of the Hiphil (106 times) as "to begin" is probably not to be derived from the same root (see *t^eḥillâ* below) unless possibly it developed from the concept of freeing oneself of the obligation to act in a certain way by setting about the business of getting free.

ḥōl. ***Profaneness, commonness, common.*** This masculine noun is used seven times. First, to describe a non-sacred place (Ezk 42:20; 48:15) or anything non-holy, i.e. in distinguishing between the holy and the common, even between the clean and the unclean (Lev 10:10; Ezk 22:26; 44:23). Second, in I Sam 21:5–6 it describes "common" bread as opposed to the bread of the presence (KJV "in a manner common"; RSV "even when it is a common journey"). Here again it is used to describe the opposite of "holy."

ḥālāl. ***Unhallowed, profaned, dishonoured.*** This adjective (see *ḥālal* II) occurs four times. In each case the emphasis is on real or symbolic breaking of the sexual laws. In Lev (21:7, 14) it is used of women associated with (perhaps synonymous with) women who are harlots. In the list of persons a Levite may not marry it follows a widow or divorcee (here also possibly synonyms). It similarly describes Israel as the "unhallowed, wicked one" (RSV; cf. KJV "profoundly dishonoured one"; RV "deadly wounded" taking it from *ḥālal* I).

ḥālîlâ. ***Far be it (from me, etc); God forbid (that I, etc.).*** This expression, occurring nineteen times introduces a strong negation or deprecation of an act. It is spoken by a king or person of high official standing or by persons collectively in a solemn legal situation. Its use is attested only until the monarchy. Job 27:5; 34:10 reiterates a context similar to that in which Abraham uses it to God, Gen 44:7. It is used by God himself (I Sam 2:30), to him (Gen 18:25), and about him (Job 34:10). The full, and possibly stronger expression, with the force of an oath includes the name of God (as the Lord lives, may it not be, etc.—I Sam 14:25; 24:7; II Sam 20:20).

Since it is usually associated with *ḥālal* II it may mean *ad profanum*. But this is by no means certain. It may be a reduplicative form (cf. Akk *ḫâlu* "drip blood," and so the life ebbs away) calling down a curse on the person who would commit a prohibited action; but this is unlikely in the light of its use by God himself.

t^e^ḥillâ. ***Beginning, first*** (in a series). This feminine noun, derived from the Hiphil of *ḥālal* discussed above, is used twenty-two times in three categories. First, it marks the first of a series of occurrences, the outset, as of a journey (Gen 13:3; 41:21) or the first in order of attack (Jud 1:1). Secondly, and most commonly, it refers to the "beginning" of a specified time, e.g. the barley harvest (Ruth 1:22), the growth of vegetation (Amos 7:1), or the occupation of Samaria by Babylonian deportees (II Kgs 17:25). It is used of the first words of a prayer (Dan 9:23) or of the first words of a godless man's speech (Eccl 10:13). Thirdly, in an abstract sense, it denotes the "first principle" of wisdom, which is the fear of the Lord (Prov 9:10).

Bibliography: Blank, Sheldon H., "Isaiah 52,5 and the Profanation of the Name," HUCA 25: 1–8. Richardson, TWB, p. 272. THAT, I, pp. 570–75.

D.J.W.

662 חָלַם (*ḥālam*) ***I, be healthy, strong*** (Job 39:4, Qal; Isa 38:16, Hiphil).

663 חָלַם (*ḥālam*) ***II, dream.***

Derivative

663a חֲלוֹם (*ḥălôm*) ***dream.***

Apparently derived from the verb *ḥālam* "to dream" and certainly equivalent in every way to *ḥēlem* "dream," in the Aramaic portion of Dan. This article will treat the Hebrew and Aramaic *ḥēlem* as precisely equivalent. Whether the verb *ḥālam* "to be strong," is a homonym or if there is a more primitive meaning for *ḥālam* "be strong" is moot, but it is interesting that if "be strong" is the primitive source, it came to mean "to dream" by virtue of the fact that erotic dreams of males at puberty, accompanied by seminal emissions connect the idea of "be strong" with "to dream." Evidence is the cognate Arabic. KB unites the two roots under one entry. There is no other Hebrew word for a dream in the OT.

Use of the word easily falls under two categories: (1) Ordinary dreams, such as all people have periodically during sleep. They can be frightening (Job 7:14); are transitory (Job 20:8; Isa 29:7–8); and have natural causes (Eccl 5:2). This is significant theologically as establishing the point that authors of scripture endorse no general theory of psychic or religious significance of dreams.

There are, however, a number of cases which show that it may have been a general belief among Israelites and their neighbors that dreams sometimes do have religious significance. Pharaoh's imprisoned butler and baker thought so (Gen 40) as also some Hebrew warriors of Gideon's time (Jud 7:13–15). (2) Revelatory dreams, in which God conveys information to mankind. These in the case of "lying prophets," are bogus to start with, i.e. invented by their human originators (see Jer 23:14–40). "They speak a vision of their own heart, and not out of the mouth of the Lord" (v. 16). "I have not sent these prophets, yet they ran: I have not spoken to them, yet they prophesied" (v. 21). Of genuine revelations by dreams there are several grades. In some God appears (under what figure or form we do not know) and in a straightforward way informs the sleeping recipient. Of this sort is the dream of Abimelek, king of Gerar (Gen 20:3–7) and of Jacob at Bethel (Gen 28:10–19). Of another sort are dreams wherein the divine disclosure is through symbolic things, persons, and actions. The dreamer is puzzled and requires the aid of a human interpreter. The interpreter (prophet) is the primary agent of revelation, the dream being only the occasion (Gen 40, 41; Dan 2:4). In some, as above the dream is inexplicable without help from God, but the agent of explanation is a divine messenger (angel) who appears within the dream (or vision) state of the subject. An example is in Dan 7 (see v. 16). Sometimes the prophet-dreamer awakens and, remembering his dream, is puzzled by it, and the divine messenger (angel) comes to him in his ordinary wakeful state to explain the meaning of the dream (Dan 8, see vv. 15–27).

Both dreams and visions (see *ḥōzeh* and *ḥāzôn*) were frequent modes of divine communic tion to the prophets of Israel. Numbers 12:6–8 is specific to this point. It is by no means clear that such were the exclusive modes of divine communication, even though dreams and visions were characteristic. (See Isa 1:1 and contrast Jer 1:1–2—"vision" *versus* "word" and "words.") Hebrews 1:1 suggests many modes of communication.

"Dream" seems to designate the sleeping state of prophetic receptivity and "vision" the individual segment within the dream. Dan 7, for example speaks of "a dream" in which there were several "visions of his head upon his bed" (v. 1; see vv. 2, 7, 13).

Visions and dreams did not as such render the one who claimed to have them an authentic bearer of divine truth unless the person (prophet) presented his credentials. The dream definitely was *not* his credential. (See Deut 18, 13.) Discerning saints mourned the absence of these prophets, their dreams and visions, and their "signs" (I Sam 3:1; cf. v. 20; Ps 74:9).

Bibliography: "Dream," in *Dictionary of New Testament Theology,* ed. Colin Brown, vol. I. Oppenheim, L., *The Interpretation of Dreams in the Ancient Near East,* 1956. Ruble, Richard, L., "The Doctrine of Dreams," BS 125: 360–64.

R.D.C.

664 חַלָּמוּת (*ḥallāmût*) ***a tasteless plant, purslane (?).*** Derivation and meaning uncertain.

665 חַלָּמִישׁ (*ḥallāmîsh*) ***flint.***

The word is used only five times in the OT. It is a quadraliteral root which probably comes from an unknown non-semitic source. In the Num 20 account of Moses' bringing water from the rock another root (*sela'*) is used. But in Deut 8:15 where this event is referred to again the words *ṣûr ḥallāmîsh* "the rock of 'flint' " are used. The poetry of Ps 114:8 divides the terminology of Deut 8:15 putting one of the words on each side of the parallelism: "who turned the rock (*ṣûr*) into standing water//the 'flint' into a fountain of water."

Job uses the word in his wisdom poem (chapter 28) to speak of the technological ability of men who can "put their hands on the flint and overturn mountains by the roots" (v. 9) but still cannot find wisdom. Deuteronomy 32:13 uses the word metaphorically to tell how God materially blessed his people. The Lord made his people "such honey out of the rock and oil out of the 'flinty' rock." Isaiah uses the word in a forceful simile of firm determination based on faith in the Lord God. "For the Lord God will help me . . . therefore have I set my face like a flint and I know that I will not be ashamed" (50:7).

Bibliography: Landsberger, B., "Akkadisch-Hebräische Wortgleichungen," Supp VT 16: 176–204.

E.B.S.

666 חָלַף (*ḥālap*) ***pass on, or away, pass through, change;*** Piel and Hiphil usually "change" garments, wages, etc.

Derivatives

666a חֵלֶף (*ḥēlep*) ***in exchange for.***
666b חֲלוֹף (*ḥălôp*) ***passing away, vanishing, appointed to destruction.***
666c חֲלִיפָה (*ḥălîpâ*) ***change (of garments), replacement.***
666d מַחֲלָף (*maḥălāp*) ***knife (which cuts through?).***
666e מַחְלָפָה (*maḥălāpâ*) ***braids, locks (of hair).***

The Ugaritic has a cognate to the last derivative *mḥlpt* "lock of hair" (Aistleitner WUS no. 1035). The Arabic *ḫalafa* is used for "replace," "succeed." From this usage comes the title of the Turkish ruler, the Caliph.

In the Qal the usage of the verb is illustrated by Jud 5:26. Jael pierced through Sisera's temples (cf. Job 20:24). Whirlwinds, conquerors, ghosts pass through or by (Isa 21:1; 8:8; Job 4:15). The verb is also used for the growth of grass (Ps 90:5–6) and for the second growth of a tree (Job 14:7).

This last usage is of special interest for it bears on Job's concept of a future life. In despair, Job had longed for death (3:11–15). Then he pleads for relief from God who seemed about to destroy him (10:8–9). Then in a difficult verse he affirms his hope (13:15) and his assurance of vindication (13:18). In chap. 14 he gives explicit consideration to life after death. First, he cites the case of a tree which when cut down will put forth a second growth (v. 7, Hiphil of *ḥālap*). Not so with man. Of more value than a tree, he dies and does not rise. Job finds this unthinkable and raises the poignant question, "If a man dies, will he live again?" He answers his own cry with a declaration of faith drawn from his tree illustration. Job will wait for his "second growth" (v. 14, *ḥălîpâ*) to come. He is sure that God will have respect for, will long for Job the creation of his own hands. Interpreted by consideration of the key word *ḥālap* the passage prepares for the more famous passage on the subject, Job 19:23–27.

Bibliography: Harris, R. L., "The Book of Job and Its Doctrine of God," *Grace Journal* 13: 28–29.

R.L.H.

667 חָלַץ (*ḥālaṣ*) ***I, draw off, take off, withdraw*** (Qal); ***rescue, be rescued,*** (Piel, Niphal).

Derivatives

667a חֲלִיצָה (*ḥălîṣâ*) ***what is stripped off a person, as plunder, in war.*** Occurs only in II Sam 2:21 and Jud 14:19.

667b מַחֲלָצָה (*maḥălāṣâ*) ***robe of state.***

This verb is used with the meaning given above in the Qal stem only four times in the Bible (Deut 25:9; Isa 20:2; Lam 4:3; Hos 5:6). In Lev the word has this meaning twice in the Piel (Lev 14:40, 43). The other meaning, to rescue, is found only in poetic material in Job, Ps, and Prov. In these books the verb is found sixteen times meaning "rescue," mostly in the Psalms. This OT poetic usage is reflected in Phoenician theophoric names such as *ḥālaṣba'al* (Baal has rescued). The two meanings are within the same semantic range. The Psalmist is in trouble and calls on the Lord to "rescue" him, "deliver" him, "pull him out" of his distress. In Ps 7:4 [H 5] the Psalmist himself is the agent rather than the object of rescue. Here he touches on the lofty theme of doing good to one's enemies, asserting, "Yes, I have 'rescued' him that without cause is my enemy." The words of Jesus on loving one's enemies (Mt 5:43, 44) is not wholly a NT theme.

Bibliography: Thomas, D. W., "A Note on Jud. 14, 18," JTS 34: 165.

E.B.S.

668 חָלַץ (*ḥālaṣ*) ***II, equip for war, put on a warrior's belt, gird or arm oneself, make ready for battle, invigorate, make strong.***

Derivatives

668a †חֲלִיצָה (*ḥălîṣâ*) ***belt.***

668b †חֲלָצַיִם (*ḥălāṣayim*) ***loins.***

With these meanings the root is used mostly in the Qal, occasionally in the Niphal and only once in the Hiphil.

The widest usage of this root is the meaning "to arm" or "equip for war." In Num 32:21 etc. and in Josh 4:13; 6:7, 9, 13, where the Israelites are preparing themselves to invade the promised land as armed soldiers, the passive participle of this verb is employed. The participle describes the soldiers of David (I Chr 12:23–24), of Jehoshaphat (II Chr 17:18; 20:21), of Pekah (II Chr 28:14) and of the king of Moab (Isa 15:4).

ḥălîṣâ. ***Belt.*** A soldier's (hero's) belt with which he girded himself. Cf. Akkadian *ḫaliṣu* belt, leatherstrap (CAD, vol. 6, p. 43). Although other Hebrew words also apply (*ḥăgôr, 'ēzôr*) this one fits well with the figure in Eph 6:14, "Stand firm then, with the belt of truth buckled around your waist" (NIV). Since this was the symbol of the soldier's prowess in battle, its removal was proof that he was defeated. The belt wrestling which was practiced in the OT world (cf. ANEP 218, 219) is reflected in the two passages where this noun is used. In II Sam 2:21 where probably a belt wrestling joust is in progress Abner tries in vain to get Asahel to take on a young man and "take his belt." In Jud 14:19 Samson takes on thirty Philistines and strips them of their belts.

ḥălāṣayim. ***Loins,*** as the seat of vigor and place from which one's seed comes (Gen 35:11; I Kgs 8:19). Several usages stress the girding of the loins (Job 38:3; 40:7; Isa 5:27; 11:5; 32:11).

E.B.S.

669 חָלַק (*ḥālaq*) ***I, share, divide, allot, apportion, assign.*** RSV and KJV also "assign."

Derivatives

669a †חֵלֶק (*ḥēleq*) ***share, part, territory.***

669b †חֶלְקָה (*ḥelqâ*) ***share, piece, portion, plot*** (KJV parcel) of land, field.

669c חֲלֻקָּה (*ḥălūqqâ*) ***part, portion,*** only in II Chr 35:5.

669d †מַחֲלֹקֶת (*maḥălōqet*) ***share, division, allotment.***

The word has legal connotations similar to *naḥălâ*, "give as a possession" but with the more specific implication of what is granted. It differs radically from the many Hebrew roots for "divide" used in the sense of "to break into parts." The verb, used only in Qal and Piel (sixty-two times) is used including its derivatives some 194 times.

The verb is commonly used of parcelling out shares (RSV "allotments") of land (Num 26:53), whether by lot (Num 26:53), inheritance (Prov 17:2), or other forms of division (Prov 29:24). It can be used of any division, whether of food at a feast (II Sam 6:18), clothing (Ps 22:19), or the spoils of war (Prov 16:19). Thus people may be divided into unspecified groups (Gen 14:15; though this might be derived from an equivalent to Arabic *ḥlq* "encircle"), two factions (I Kgs 16:21), or specific divisions as in the case of the priests and Levites for temple service (see *maḥălōqet*).

God makes the division. The question is asked if it is he who "distributes" pains in his wrath (Job 21:17) which "divides" (KJV; "scatters" RSV) the wicked. The "divided" heart of Hos 10:2 is perhaps to be translated "false" or "flattering" heart; (see *ḥālaq* II). It is God who gives a share of (RSV "allots") sun, moon, and stars as guides (not deities for worship) to all peoples (Deut 4:19). Since some Jewish commentators consider this to condone idolatry among the gentiles, they and the Vulgate translate *ḥlq* here as an equivalent of the Arabic *ḫalaqa* "create." God is the source of light which is "distributed" (RSV Job 38:24). Although the verb is not directly used of the Lord's allocation of land to his people, the use of the noun (see *ḥēleq*) shows that it was ultimately his.

ḥēleq. ***Share, part, territory.*** KJV, RSV also "portion, tract." This word occurs sixty-two times. It is used as a synonym of "lot" (*gôrāl*) when it is a share of booty divided among the victors (Gen 14:24) or of offerings among the priests (Lev 6:10). More commonly it refers to a share in an inheritance. Early in the OT the word is used with a technical nuance of share of land given to all the tribes when they entered the land. In this use the term is parallel with "inheritance" (*naḥălâ*). On the principle that "the land is the Lord's inheritance," the land share came to be regarded as synonymous with "share of land" (*ḥebel*) given out by lot to the tribes. Some think that those living outside the designated "land of God," i.e. east of Jordan (Josh 22; cf. Ezk 48) were thought to have been denied their "share in the Lord" (Josh 22:25–27; Zech 2:16). Thus the land, as part of the covenant promise of God, was given to his people as their possession (Mic 2:4) and share in God's righteousness (Neh 2:20).

But Aaron and the Levites, dedicated to God's service, had no such share of land. For them "the Lord is your share and your inheritance" (Deut 10:9; Num 18:20). Cf. the statement in the messianic Psalm 16:5, "The Lord is the portion of my inheritance, you maintain my lot (*gôrāl*). This special relationship resulted in arrangements for the maintenance of the temple personnel from the offerings and not from any land which they worked themselves.

This relationship with God and people was defined in a spiritual concept "the Lord is my share" (Ps 73:26), "the Lord is the portion of his people" (Deut 7:9), just as he is their refuge (Ps 142:5 [H 6]) and so their sufficiency. The Levites and, by extension, the God-fearer, find here "a full and complete expression of all that his relationship with God guarantees him" (G. von Rad, *The Problem of the Hexateuch*, 1966, p. 263).

In view of the spiritual implications of the word it is small wonder that it formed a popular element in Israelite personal names, e.g. Hilkiah.

ḥelqâ. ***Share, share (of territory), piece, portion or plot*** (of land; KJV "parcel"), field. Cf. Aramaic *ḥălāq;* Akkadian *eqlu* "field."

The major share or tenure of land in the OT derived from tribal allotments (see *ḥēleq*), so that this feminine noun *ḥelqâ* most commonly denotes the "share" or division of land made to the various tribes of Israel after the Conquest. Thus God was seen to have granted the best share as the commander's choice (Deut 33:21). The multiple ownership of land is already attested in Jacob's need to buy land ("a share of a field") from several sons of the Shechem family (Gen 33:19; Josh 24:32). Later on, Boaz appears to have farmed only part of Elimelech's land (Ruth 2:3; 4:3). By the time of the monarchy the term had become the general one for "field" (II Kgs 3:19), but often with the implication of inheritance (II Kgs 9:21). Jeremiah sees the land of Israel as God's field (12:10; cf. I Cor 3:9). The "portion" of Job 24:18 may well mean "field" because of the parallelism with "vineyard," in which case every use of this noun can be translated "field" in the ancient sense. The noun *ḥăluqqâ* is used for "share" in II Chr 35:5 only and the Aramaic *ḥălāq* in Ezr 4:16; Dan 4:12, 20.

It was not an uncommon practice in the ancient near east to name fields by some incident as an alternative to the owner's name. Helkath-hazzurim (II Sam 2:16) near Gibeon where Ishbosheth's men were killed by David's forces under Joab was the "field of sword-edges" or possibly, reading *haṣṣorîm*, the "field of plotters."

maḥălōqet. ***(Tribal) allotment (of land), division, course.*** This feminine noun from *ḥālaq* I is used thirty-two times. The KJV also translates "portions" and JB "borders." It is used in Joshua (11:23; 12:7; 18:10) of the distinctive shares of land given by Joshua to Israel, an idea reiterated in Ezk 48:29. In exilic and postexilic times the term is used frequently (twenty-six times in Chr) of the technical groupings or subdivisions of the priests and Levites for the work in the Jerusalem temple and, more rarely, of the military divisions arranged by David (I Chr 23:6, etc.) both of which originated in the Mosaic legislation (Ezr 6:18).

Bibliography: Kamhi, D. J., "The Root HLQ in the Bible," VT 23: 236–39. THAT, I, pp. 576–78.

D.J.W.

670 חָלַק (*ḥālaq*) ***II, be smooth, slippery thus figuratively, flatter.*** Cf. Ugaritic *ḥlq*,

Arabic *ḥalaqa* "be smooth." Including derivatives, it occurs twenty-eight times.

Derivatives

670a חֵלֶק (*ḥēleq*) ***smoothness, flattery, seductiveness (of speech).***
670b †חָלָק (*ḥālāq*) ***smooth.***
670c †חֶלְקָה (*ḥelqâ*) ***smoothness, flattery.***
670d חַלֻּק (*ḥallūq*) ***smooth.*** Occurs only once, in the plural construct (I Sam 17:40).
670e חֲלַקָּה (*ḥălaqqâ*) ***smoothness, fine promises.*** Occurs only as plural abstract (Dan 11:32).
670f †חֲלַקְלַקּוֹת (*ḥălaqlaqqôt*) ***smoothness, slipperiness, flattery, fine promises.***
670g †מַחְלְקוֹת (*maḥlᵉqôt*) ***smoothness.***

The verb refers once to the literal process of smoothing metal to make an idol by hitting it on an anvil with a forge hammer (Isa 41:7). Its principal use (Qal and Hiphil) is of smooth speech or flattery, i.e. words which were smoother than butter and like oil (Ps 55:21 [H 22]). This use of the tongue is always condemned (Ps 5:9 [H 10]) and ends in the speaker being himself entrapped (Prov 29:5). It is characteristic of the seductive woman who is to be avoided (Prov 2:16; 7:5). The enigmatic man who "flatters himself in his own eyes" (Ps 36:2 [H 3]) may possibly be better translated, "His God will destroy him with a glance when he uncovers his impious slander" (cf. Dahood, M. "Psalms" I, AB, p. 271), taking this from *ḥālaq* III "perish." Ugaritic *ḫlq* "perish" is parallel to *mt* "die" (UT 19: no. 969) and Akkadian *ḫalâqu* "disappear." "Their heart is divided" (Hos 10:2 KJV) is better taken as "is false" (RSV) that is, figurative of the fickle heart.

ḥālāq. ***Smooth.*** This adjective is used to describe the smooth skin of Jacob as opposed to hairy Esau (Gen 27:11), and smooth stones in a wadi (Isa 57:6), some of which ("smooth ones of stones," i.e. possibly "the smoothest") David used to kill Goliath (I Sam 17:40, *ḥalluq*). A distinctive feature of the bald cliffs by the Dead Sea was called the "bare (smooth) mountain" (Josh 11:17; 12:7 KJV: RSV translates as a name, Mt. Halak). Some commentators associate this with Arabic *ḫlq* "high." Figuratively the adjective describes the mouth of the flatterer (in parallel with the "lying tongue" Prov 5:3; cf. 26:28). One day divination which flatters would, like the false vision, be done away from Israel (Ezk 12:24).

ḥelqâ. ***Smooth part, smoothness, flattery.*** This noun is used five times and denotes something smooth (Isa 30:10), like the neck (Gen 27:16) or slippery places where one is likely to fall (Ps 73:18).

ḥălaqlaqqôt. Similar in meaning to *ḥelqâ*. It is used as an abstract to describe the way of the evil person, which will be dark and slippery (Ps 35:6). Since the parallel is darkness, some see this as a rare use of *ḫlq* (cf. Arabic *'aḫlawlq* "darkness" or *ḥālaq* "destruction." See also *ḥālaq* II). As smooth speech this noun is clearly used of seductive words or flattery (Prov 6:24) by which some attempted to win kingdoms, a concept emphasized in Dan (11:21, 34).

maḥlᵉqôt. ***Smoothness.*** This feminine plural noun occurs only in I Sam 23:28 in the place name Sela-hammahlekoth (so KJV). If from *ḥālaq* II, it could be the "rock of smoothness," i.e. slippery rock (so BDB), but this may not be a proper name. [Though there is a town in Pennsylvania called "Slippery Rock"!—EDITOR] If taken from *ḥālaq* I it is assumed that it was "rock of divisions" as the place where Saul and David parted. However the word is used elsewhere in this sense only of the division of priests (see *maḥălōqet*). The "rock of escapes" (so RSV) can be supported from Akkadian *ḫalāqu* "escape."

Bibliography: Kamhi, D. J., "The root *ḥlq* in the Bible," VT 23: 235–39.

D.J.W.

חֲלַקְלַקּוֹת (*ḥălaqlaqqôt*). See no. 670f.

671 חָלַשׁ (*ḥālash*) ***be weak, prostrate*** (e.g. Ex 17:13).

Derivatives

671a חַלָּשׁ (*ḥallāsh*) ***weak*** (Joel 4:10).
671b חֲלוּשָׁה (*ḥălûshâ*) ***weakness, prostration*** (Ex 32:18).

חָם (*ḥām*). See no. 674a.
חַם (*ḥam*). See no. 677b.
חֹם (*ḥōm*). See no. 677a.

672 חמא (*ḥm'*). **Assumed root of the following.**
672a חֶמְאָה (*ḥem'â*) ***curd*** (modern *leben*).

673 חָמַד (*ḥāmad*) ***desire, delight in.*** Cf. Ugaritic *ḥmd* "be pleasant," but also covet, lust after (ASV and RSV similar but in the positive contexts [eleven of twenty-one] prefer the less ambiguous delight in"). The Arabic *ḥamida* means praise and the name Mohammed comes from the root.

Derivatives

673a †חֶמֶד (*ḥemed*) ***desirable, pleasant*** (marg., things of desire).
673b †חֶמְדָּה (*ḥemdâ*) ***desire,*** also an adjective, ***pleasant, precious.***

673c †חֲמוּדוֹת (*ḥămûdôt*) **desirableness, preciousness.**
673d †מַחְמָד (*maḥmad*) **pleasant thing.**
673e †מַחְמֹד (*maḥmōd*) **pleasant thing.**

From its initial occurrences, the verb *ḥāmad* describes on the one hand God's "pleasant" trees in Eden (Gen 2:9); but on the other, the tree forbidden to Adam, which became sinful when "desired" (the same Niphal participle) to make one wise (3:6). Similarly, the noun *ḥemed* identifies both "pleasant" fields (Isa 32:12; marg., fields of "desire") and "desirable" young Assyrians, pagans (Ezk 23:6, 12, 23), who proved to be Israel's downfall.

Positively, Ps 39:11 [H 12] speaks of man's "beauty," KJV (part. pass.; ASV marg., collective, "delights"; RSV, "what is dear to him"); cf. the noun *ḥămuddîm* "pleasant things," or luxuries (Lam 1:11; cf. Prov 21:20). When Haggai therefore predicts that "the desire of all nations shall come" (2:7), he probably is not referring to the Messiah (as in v. 9*b*) but rather to the contributions of precious things (ASV; *ḥemdâ*) for refurbishing Zerubbabel's temple (the same noun, II Chr 36:10). The Shulammite sits by her beloved "with great delight," *ḥāmad*, Piel (Song 2:3; literally, "May I delight and sit"); she says that he is altogether "lovely," *maḥmad*, a "desire" (5:16). God himself "desired" Jerusalem for his abode (Ps 68:16 [H 17]; cf. 106:24; Jer 3:19; 12:10), and the Lord's ordinances are more to be "desired," *neḥmādîm*, than gold (Ps 19:10 [H 11]; see Ezr 8:27, copper items called *ḥămûdôt* "preciousness," like gold).

Even when scoffers "delight" in their mockery (Prov 1:22*b*), the act as such, of delighting, appears to them good, paralleling "love" (1:22*a;* cf. 12:12; Job 20:20). To Judah, correspondingly, images became "delectable" things (Isa 44:9; ASV, "delighted in"; see 2:16), "desired" (1:29); but this reaction "is primarily psychological and only secondarily ethical" (RTWB, p. 64).

Negatively, however, the Tenth Commandment prescribes, "Thou shalt not *ḥāmad,* covet" (Ex 20:17), which refers to an "inordinate, ungoverned, selfish desire" (BDB, p. 326). Israel was not to "desire" (Deut 7:25; ASV, RSV, "covet") the gold adorning idols, to lust after prostitutes (Prov 6:25), or to covet fields (Mic 2:2; cf. Ex 34:24). Achan's sin at Jericho was that he desired the spoil (*ḥāmad* Josh 7:21). When Aramean officers described what ever was *maḥmad* "pleasant," in their eyes (I Kgs 20:6) they sought the most desirable treasures of Samaria as plunder.

In religion, "the desire (*ḥemdâ*) of women" (Dan 11:37) would probably refer to the deity Tammuz-Adonis (KB, p. 308; Ezk 8:14; ICC, Dan, in loc.). Though God's anointed king appears as the desire of Israel (I Sam 9:20; contrast II Chr 21:20), Isaiah must predict for the messianic servant an absence of beauty, that we should desire (*ḥāmad*), "be drawn to" him (53:2).

ḥemed, ḥemdâ. ***Desirable, pleasant*** (marg., things of desire). More frequently feminine *ḥemdâ* (seventeen as opposed to five occurrences of *ḥemed*) "desire"; also adjective, "pleasant," "precious."

ḥămûdôt. The quality of desirableness, preciousness, rendered "a man greatly beloved" (Dan 9:23; 10:11, 19), "pleasant (KB, p. 309, delicate) bread" (10:3), "goodly raiment" (Gen 27:15), or "precious jewels" (II Chr 20:25), but also true plurals, pleasant or precious things (Dan 11:38, 43). Occurs nine times.

maḥmad. Concretely, a pleasant thing (four out of thirteen times) or person, e.g. either Ezekiel's wife, "the 'desire' of his eyes," or his contemporaneous temple (Ezk 24:16, 21, 25); also adjectival renderings: beloved, lovely, pleasant.

maḥmōd. Only plural, *maḥămuddîm,* pleasant things; (Lam 1:7, 11).

Bibliography: Büchsel, F., in TDNT, III, pp. 169–70. Coates, J. R., "Thou Shalt not Covet [Ex 20:17]," ZAW 11: 238. Gamberoni, J., "Desire," in *Sacramentum Verbi,* vol. I, Herder & Herder, 1970, pp. 206–209. THAT, I, pp. 579–80.

J.B.P.

674 חמה (*ḥmh*). **Assumed root of the following.**
674a †חָם (*ḥām*) ***father-in-law.***
674b †חָמוֹת (*ḥāmôt*) ***mother-in-law.***
674c חוֹמָה (*ḥômâ*) ***wall.***

ḥām. ***Father-in-law.*** ASV and RSV the same. This noun denotes the father of one's husband. Its Akkadian cognate is *emu* (CAD E. p. 154ff.) which usually represents a male relative: father-in-law, son-in-law, or wife's/sister's son. Our word occurs four times.

ḥāmôt. ***Mother-in-law.*** The feminine of the above noun. Its Akkadian cognate is *emētu* (CAD E, p. 149). Our word occurs eleven times.

That our word signifies the father-in-law (mother-in-law) is clear not simply on the basis of the Akkadian cognates, but from the Bible itself. In Gen 38:13, 25, it is evident that Judah, who was beguiled by Tamar to fulfill his levirate duty, was the father of her two deceased husbands. Equally clear is the use in I Sam 4:19, 21, where the wife of Phinehas, Eli's son dies grieving over her family and giving birth to a son, Ichabod. The feminine noun stands opposite *kallāt* in Ruth 2:23, and clearly signifies mother-in-law. Interestingly, Micah (7:6) decries the deep moral corruption evidenced in the breakdown of societal bonds, especially the bond between mother-in-law and daughter-in-law.

L.J.C.

חֵמָה (*ḥēmâ*). See no. 860a.
חַמָּה (*ḥammâ*). See no. 677c.
חֲמוּדוֹת (*ḥămûdôt*). See no. 673c.
חָמוֹץ (*ḥāmôṣ*). See no. 681a.
חַמּוּק (*ḥammûq*). See no. 682a.
חֲמוֹר (*ḥămôr*). See no. 685a.
חָמוֹת (*ḥāmôt*). See no. 674b.

675 חמט (*ḥmṭ*). **Assumed root of the following.**
675a חֹמֶט (*ḥōmeṭ*) ***a kind of lizard*** (Lev 11:30).

חָמִיץ (*ḥāmîṣ*). See no. 679c.
חֲמִישִׁי (*ḥămîshî*). See no. 686d.

676 חָמַל (*ḥāmal*) ***spare, have compassion on.***

Derivatives

676a †חֶמְלָה (*ḥemlâ*) ***mercy.***
676b †מַחְמָל (*maḥmal*) ***object of deep love.***

The ASV and RSV translations reflect the breadth of this root and the subsequent difficulty in rendering it. Basically, this root connotes that emotional response which results (or may result) in action to remove its object (and/or its subject) from impending difficulty. It should be distinguished from *ḥûs* and *rāḥam*. It occurs forty-five times.

The idea of "sparing" is clearly seen in Jer 50:14 where God instructs Cyrus's armies to "spare no arrows." Obviously, there is no inward emotional element of compassion upon the arrows involved in this sparing. Job confesses that his pain spares not (Job 6:10). On the other hand, the jealous man when taking revenge spares not (Prov 6:34), i.e. holds nothing back, is merciless. The wicked takes delight in his evil and holds it in his mouth (Job 20:13). He spares it and will not let it go (ASV).

In Deut 13:8 [H 9] this word is used negatively with *ḥûs* to describe how God wants his people to react to idolators. Samuel evokes this judgment: spare not the Amalakites (the idolators) who refused passage to Israel (I Sam 15:3, 9, 15). Destroy them completely! But Saul disobeyed. Cyrus is directed not to spare Babylon (Jer 51:3; cf. Hab 1:17). In these cases there is to be no emotion which would hinder thorough-going destruction. Things will be so bad in the captivity that even natural affection would be absent and brother would not spare brother (Isa 9:19 [H 18]; the people would turn to cannibalism! What a contrast to the restitution when God will spare his people (Mal 3:17 in which *ḥāmal* is difficult to distinguish from *rāḥam,* q.v.).

This root can also apply to the emotion leading (or tending to lead) to the action of sparing. In Ex 2:6, Pharoah's daughter sees baby Moses, and she has compassion on him (ASV), i.e. her heart is moved with love. Israel rebuffed God's persistent admonitions, bringing his wrath on themselves. God had been patient because he had compassion (loving concern) upon them (II Chr 36:15f.). Ezekiel (16:5) reminds Jerusalem that only God pitied (see *ḥûs*) and had compassion (*ḥāmal*) on her as on a baby, saving her from certain destruction (cf. Moses and Pharoah's daughter).

This root can also express the emotion of pity (cf. *ḥûs*). Nathan tells the parable of (II Sam 12:4) the rich man who spares taking his own sheep (RSV "was unwilling"), having no pity on the poor man (v. 6). This change in meaning is clear from the context. He lacked that feeling of concern which would lead him to spare the poor man the grief of losing his only and beloved lamb. God says Israel's teachers fatten their "lambs" for slaughter and have no twinge of feeling (pity) when their "lambs" are slaughtered (Zech 11:5). Just so, God during the Exile appeared to have no feeling toward his people (Lam 2:2, 3:43), but they brought this on by their own idolatry (cf. Deut 13:8 [H 9]). This shows us how terrible was the sin which resulted in the Exile; how deeply God hates idolatry. Contrast with this just how wonderful is the age of restitution (Mal 3:17; Joel 2:18).

Finally, this root is used of God's reaction when his name was profaned by those who scoffed Israel in captivity. He states that he has concern (RSV) or regard (ASV) for his name; i.e. he cannot allow his name (and, therefore, his person) to appear powerless to deliver his people. Therefore, he says that he will bring his people back (Ezk 36:21).

ḥemlâ. ***Mercy.*** This Qal infinitive absolute is used twice to describe God's mercy in delivering and/or protecting from danger. God was merciful to Lot's family in leading them by the hand from Sodom (Gen 19:16). In Isa 63:9 *ḥemlâ* is parallel to *'āhab,* love, as God's feeling sorry for Israel issuing from his love.

maḥmal. ***Object of deep love.*** In Ezk 24:21 the sanctuary is described as the object of Israel's pride, and pleasure, and deep longing (*ḥāmal*). Hence, the sanctuary is what they love and want to preserve from destruction or defilement.

L.J.C.

677 חָמַם (*ḥāmam*) ***be hot, warm.*** ASV and RSV similar; however, cf. Isa 57:5.)

Derivatives

677a †חֹם (*ḥōm*) ***heat, hot.***
677b †חַם (*ḥam*), חַמִּים (*ḥammîm*) ***warm.***
677c †חַמָּה (*ḥammâ*) ***sun, heat.***
677d †חַמָּן (*ḥammān*), חַמָּנִים (*ḥammānîm*) ***incense altars.***

This root refers to physical heat, i.e. warmth produced, by the sun, the human body, clothing, and an oven. It appears in most Semitic languages (Akkadian *emmu,* CAD E, p. 150f.; Ugaritic *ḥm,* UT 19: no. 870). Some uses of *ḥōreb* and *shārab* parallel the meaning "heat produced by the sun," or "skin." Heat in an emotional sense is usually represented by *ḥēmâ* and its derivatives (cf. Isa 57:5; Jer 51:39; Ps 39:3 [H 4]). Our root occurs thirty-five times.

ḥōm. ***Heat, hot.*** This noun represents a thing typified by heat: viz. a season (Gen 8:22; Job 24:19; Jer 17:8; KB), and bread (I Sam 21:6 [H 7] used adjectivally). The infinitive of *ḥāmam* appears with the same form as this noun. The noun occurs four times.

ḥam, ḥammîm. ***Warm.*** This adjective modifies its subject applying to it the quality resulting from *ḥāmam.* It occurs twice.

ḥammâ. ***Sun, heat produced by the sun.*** This noun usually (except Ps 19:6 [H 7]) is a poetic alternative for *shemesh* (sun). It can make one black (i.e. tanned), as can mourning (Job 30:28). In the time of judgment it is darkened (Isa 24:23), and it is made more luminous in the time of redemption (Isa 30:26), even though a single historical occasion might produce both results. Significantly our word is paralleled to *shaḥar* (q.v.; also see *hālal* and *l*ᵉ*banâ* (q.v.), and may be an infrequently recognized Canaanite name of the sun god (Song 6:10). Our word occurs six times.

ḥammānîm. ***Incense altars.*** This noun represents small (II Chr 34:4) cultic objects used in pagan worship and is paralleled to *'ashērîm* (Isa 17:8). Nabatean and Palmyra inscriptions substantiate the proffered identification. Perhaps the small stone cup-shaped objects discovered through Palestinian excavations are *ḥammānîm* (AI I, p. 286). The word occurs eight times.

Bibliography: Lewy, Julius, "The Old West Semitic Sun-God Hammu," HUCA 18: 429–81. Wright, G. E., "'Sun-Image' or "Altar of Incense'?" BA 1: 9–10.

L.J.C.

חַמָּן (*ḥammān*). See no. 677d.

678 חָמַס (*ḥāmas*) ***wrong, do violence to, treat violently.*** Used seven times in the Qal, once in the Niphal. The Arabic cognate means to be hard, strict, severe.

Derivatives

678a †חָמָס (*ḥāmās*) ***violence, wrong.***
678b תַּחְמָס (*taḥmās*) ***a name of the male ostrich.***

This noun and verb are together used sixty-seven times and mostly translators seem satisfied with the word "violence" in some form (KJV, RSV, NIV). It may be noted, however, that the word *ḥāmās* in the OT is used almost always in connection with sinful violence. It does not refer to the violence of natural catastrophes or to violence as pictured in a police chase on modern television. It is often a name for extreme wickedness. It was a cause of the flood (Gen 6:11, 13, parallel to "corrupt"). Other usages are: a "malicious" witness (Ex 23:1; Deut 19:16 NIV); "cruel" hatred (Ps 25:19); oppression and violence (Ps 72:14 NIV); violence is risen up into a rod of wickedness (Ezk 7:11, a rod to punish wickedness, NIV). The aspect of sinfulness is illustrated also by the verb which twice refers to "transgression" of God's law (Ezk 22:26; Zeph 3:4).

Of special interest is the enigmatic reaction of Sarah to her handmaid's mocking. She says to Abraham, "My wrong be upon thee" (Gen 16:5). Speiser (*Genesis,* AB, pp. 116–8) takes it as an objective construction "the injustice done to me,... *ḥāmās* 'lawlessness, injustice'... is a strictly legal term which traditional 'violence' fails to show adequately." It could be that Sarah is declaring Abraham responsible or it could even suggest that she is saying that it is up to him to correct that injustice.

R.L.H.

679 חָמֵץ (*ḥāmēṣ*) ***I, be sour, leavened.***

Derivatives

679a †חָמֵץ (*ḥāmēṣ*) ***that which is leavened.***
679b חֹמֶץ (*ḥōmeṣ*) ***vinegar.***
679c חָמִיץ (*ḥāmîṣ*) ***seasoned.*** Occurs only in Job 30:24.
679d מַחְמֶצֶת (*maḥmeṣet*) ***anything leavened.*** Occurs only in Ex 12:19–20.

The verb occurs five times in the Qal stem, two times in the Hiphil, and once in the Hithpael stem.

This root designates the action and result of yeast, *ś*ᵉ*'ôr,* bread dough which is *leḥem ḥāmēṣ.* The basic meaning is to become fermented or sour. Hosea 7:4 has a brief description of a baker working on leavened dough until it was ready for the oven. This idea of becoming sour is extended to a person's negative attitudes in Ps 73:21 and probably in Ps 71:4 where it is translated "cruel."

The main religious significance of the word is tied to its exclusion from certain cultic practices of the Hebrews. The Hiphil participle of the verb is used in a strong command that anyone who eats leavened bread during the Passover feast is to be cut off from Israel (Ex 12:19–20). Ex 12:39 notes that Passover bread was not leavened because the Hebrews went out quickly from Egypt thus having no time to raise the dough. Thus it had the symbolic value of teaching Israel that having been redeemed from Egypt they should leave their old life quickly and set out toward the promised land by faith.

ḥāmēṣ. ***Leaven, leavened bread.*** This is the primary word for food which is in process of fermenting or has fermented. Normally, it is limited to the grain foods: wheat, barley, and spelt. In the Old Testament these grains are theologically significant because when ground and mixed with yeast, their use is prohibited in certain religious activities. In the discussion of the verb form, it was noted that anyone who ate leavened bread during the passover could be excommunicated. The noun is used in this context (Ex 12:15) and reference is made in Ex 13:3, 7 that no leavened bread is permitted in house or on table during the Passover because of the Exodus event and God's act of bringing the Hebrews out of Egypt quickly (see also Deut 16:3).

Leavened bread was also prohibited in connection with the offering of sacrifices involving blood (Ex 23:18; 34:25). Neither it nor honey could be burned with a meal offering (Lev 2:11) and it cannot be baked with the fire offering (Lev 6:15). But leavened bread could be eaten with the thank-offering (Lev 7:13; Amos 4:5) and with the firstfruit offerings (Lev 23:17).

In later Jewish thought leavened bread became a symbol of corruption and impurity, as also in Jesus' teachings (Mt 16:2; Mk 8:15) and in one remark by Paul in I Cor 5:8.

Bibliography: Beak, H. F., "Leaven," in IDB, III, pp. 104–5. Lewis, J. P. "Leaven," ZPEB, III, pp. 901–903. White, H. A., "Leaven," in *A Dictionary of the Bible,* III, Charles Scribner's Sons, 1903, p. 90. "Ḥamez," in *Encyclopaedia Judaica,* VII, pp. 1235–36.

G.H.L.

680 חָמַץ (*ḥāmaṣ*) ***II, be red*** (Isa 63:1; Ps 68:24).

681 חָמַץ (*ḥāmaṣ*) ***III, be ruthless*** (Ps 71:4).

Derivative

681a חָמוֹץ (*ḥāmôṣ*) ***the ruthless*** (Isa 1:17).

682 חָמַק (*ḥāmaq*) ***turn away*** (Song 5:6, Qal; Jer 31:22, Hithpael).

Derivative

682a חַמּוּק (*ḥammûq*) ***curving, curve*** (Song 7:2).

683 חָמַר (*ḥāmar*) ***I, ferment, boil, foam.***

Derivatives

683a †חֶמֶר (*ḥemer*) ***wine.***
683b †חֵמָר (*ḥēmār*) ***bitumen.***
683c †חֹמֶר (*ḥōmer*) ***cement.***
683d חָמַר (*ḥāmar*) ***smear with asphalt*** (Ex 2:3, only).

This root is sometimes confused with another one with identical consonants which means reddish (root III).

The verbal form of this root is illustrated in Ps 46:4 in which "waters . . . be troubled" (KJV, or "foamed," RSV). An extension to human emotions is found in Lam 1:20; 2:11, and to "wine . . . red" (KJV; "foaming," RSV). The verb probably means red (RSV; "foul," KJV) in Job 16:16.

ḥemer. ***Wine.*** A masculine noun, which occurs only in Deut 32:14 and Isa 27:2.

ḥēmār. ***Bitumen, asphalt.*** This masculine noun may have arisen from the trait of asphalt seething, or swelling up from the ground or coming to the top of the Dead Sea and/or its reddish-brown color. This material was used in Babylon as mortar (Gen 11:3), was abundant in the Dead Sea area (Gen 14:10) and was imported to Egypt (Ex 2:3) for mortar and a sealant.

ḥōmer. ***Cement, mortar, clay.*** This noun was also a term for the reddish clay of that area, particularly Palestine. See Isa 29:16; 45:9 (personified); Jer 18:4; and cf. Job 30:19; Isa 10:6. In one instance clothing is likened to clay (Job 27:16).

Job extended this term to designate human bodies in 4:19; 10:9; 13:12 and then to liken, metaphorically, men in their creaturely relationship to their Maker to the potter-clay relation. Along this same line, Isa 45:9 personifies clay which rebels against the potter, to make the point that idolatry is unnatural and illogical.

[Or this passage may mean that mere man, the clay, must not question the ways of the Sovereign of history, the Potter. The specific challenge in view here may be one's questioning the Lord's use of the uncircumcised Persian king, Cyrus, to serve both as his shepherd to restore Israel and as his anointed one to shatter gentile opposition to his people (Isa 44: 28—45:1), and thereby bring forth God's righteousness (Isa 45:8). B.K.W.]

This motif appears also in Isa 64:7 as a humble affirmation of man's creature relationship to God. Jeremiah was told by God to go to the potter's shop to watch him form clay into vessels (Jer 18:1–4), then God likened Israel and nations to clay in the hands of a potter. The crucial difference lies in man's ability to say "yes" or "no" and God's right to respond with grace or judgment. Paul brought into his arguments the same metaphor to demonstrate God's sovereignty over man (Rom 9:20–23).

G.V.G.

684 חָמַר (*ḥāmar*) ***II, heap up.*** This root is confused with the first root by some translators in Hab 3:15, e.g. "heap," KJV; "surging," RSV.

Derivatives

684a חֹמֶר (*ḥōmer*) ***I, heap.***
684b †חֹמֶר (*ḥōmer*) ***II, homer.***
684c †חֲמֹר (*ḥămōr*) ***heap.***

The verbal form is present in OT if the form in Hab 3:15 is a participle. The nominal form is duplicated in the plural for emphasis in Ex 8:10, coming from the masculine noun, *ḥōmer.* The Hebrew measure of capacity, the *ḥōmer,* possibly comes from the act of heaping grain in a container or pouring liquid into a jar. As a dry measure, the homer held 10 ephahs equal to 6¼ bushels figuring the ephah at 22 liters. As a liquid measure, the homer held ten baths (22 liters) equal to 58 gallons (see the discussion of measures under "ephah"). These measures are mentioned in several religious contexts (Lev 27:16; Num 11:32; Ezk 45:11, 13–14).

The masculine noun, *ḥămôr,* appears in Jud 15:16 in a redundant manner to emphasize the magnitude of Samson's victory over the Phistines.

685 חָמַר (*ḥāmar*) ***III, be red.*** The verbal form possibly is found in Job 16:16.

Derivative

685a חֲמוֹר (*ḥămôr*) ***(he)-ass.***
685b יַחְמוּר (*yaḥmûr*) ***roebuck.***

It is uncertain whether this masculine noun comes from the root meaning red since few donkeys in the Middle East are reddish in color. From earliest history this animal has served man as beast of burden, as transportation, and as field animal. They are among those creatures listed as unclean for food (Lev 11:1–8; Deut 14:3–8) but II Kgs 6:25 says its flesh was eaten in time of desperate famine. The strength of the beast is metaphorically applied to Issachar (Gen 49:14) and its burial to the ignominious death of King Jehoiakim (Jer 22:19).

In contrast to the mule and horse which were associated with war, the donkey was associated with peace and humility (II Sam 19:27) and thus related to the Messiah in Zech 9:9; Mt 21:5, 7. There is a tinge of contempt in Ezk 23:20, which refers to the genital organ of an ass.

The donkey and ox could not plow together (Deut 22:10) but they both benefitted in the Sabbath rest (Deut 5:14). The offspring was subject to the law of firstlings (Ex 13:13) but among the Hebrews the donkey could not be a sacrifice in the cultic rites although an ass was killed at Mari in covenant-making ceremonies (McCarthy, D. J., *Treaty and Covenant,* Pontif. Biblical Inst., 1963, p. 53). In an interesting way the Lord used a donkey to frustrate Balaam in some of his schemes (Num 22–24).

Bibliography: Cohon, Samuel, "Ass," in ISBE, I, pp. 287–88. McCullough, W. S., "Ass," in IDB, II, pp. 260–61. McKenzie, J. L., "Ass" in *Dictionary of the Bible,* I, Bruce, 1965, pp. 62–63.

G.H.L.

686 *חָמַשׁ (*ḥāmash*) ***I, take one fifth.*** This denominative verb occurs only in the Piel (Gen 41:34).

Parent Noun

686a חָמֵשׁ (*ḥāmesh*), חֲמִשָּׁה (*ḥamishshâ*) ***five.***
686b חֹמֶשׁ (*ḥōmesh*) ***fifth part*** (Gen 47:26 only).
686c חֲמִשִּׁים (*ḥămishshîm*) ***fifty.***
686d חֲמִישִׁי (*ḥămîshî*), חֲמִישִׁית (*ḥămîshît*) ***fifth*** (ordinal number).

687 חמשׁ (*ḥmsh*) **II. Assumed root of the following.**
687a חֹמֶשׁ (*ḥōmesh*) ***belly*** (e.g. II Sam 2:23; 3:27).

688 חמשׁ (*ḥmsh*) **III. Assumed root of the following.**
688a חֲמֻשִׁים (*ḥămūshîm*) ***in battle array*** (e.g. Ex 13:18; Josh 1:14).

689 חמת (*ḥmt*). **Assumed root of the following.**
689a חֵמֶת (*ḥēmet*), חֶמֶת (*ḥemet*) ***waterskin*** (Gen 21:14–15, 19).

חֵן (*ḥēn*). See no. 694a.

690 חָנָה (*ḥānâ*) ***decline, bend down, encamp, lay siege against.***

Derivatives

690a חָנוּת (*ḥānût*) ***cell*** (as having curved roof). (Only in Jer 37:16.)
690b †חֲנִית (*ḥănît*) ***spear.***
690c †מַחֲנֶה (*maḥăneh*) ***camp.***

690d תַּחֲנָה (*taḥănâ*) ***encamping or encampment.*** Occurs only in II Kgs 6:8.

The verb is used 143 times in the OT, 74 times in Num alone. The latter statistic is what one would expect in a biblical book dealing to a large degree with the travels of God's people from place to place, or from one camp to another.

maḥăneh. ***Camp.*** In the OT a "camp" is a temporary (never permanent) protective enclosure for a tribe or army. It is derived from the verb *ḥānâ* "to bend, curve," and hence it may be that the Hebrew camp (or the ancient semitic camp, since the word was not limited to the Hebrews) was originally circular in layout. Possibly such a circular camp, i.e., tents erected in a protective circle around the cattle, may derive from early semi-nomadic days. Or the word may derive from the circular lines of a besieging force.

A glance, however, at the camp described in the early chapters of Num (1:47—2:34; 3:14–16; 10:11–28) reveals that the Israelite camp is set up in a square around the tent of meeting tabernacle. In a schematic arrangement three tribes, each with their own insignia, were stationed on the four sides of the tabernacle, with special positioning for the Levites.

To choose a camp site when one is or expects to be continually hounded by antagonistic forces is not easy. The Bible indicates that at least two factors were in mind when a camp site was chosen: (1) the availability of water (Josh 11:5; Jud 7:1, and hence the advantage to camping at an oasis rather than at a site dependent on the flow of a river); and (2) lines of natural defense which formed a barricade (I Sam 17:3; 26:3).

Most important, the camp, as described in the Pentateuch, assumes its significance simply because it is adjacent to the tabernacle, the dwelling place of God's presence. As a result certain conditions must be observed and maintained. For one thing, cleanliness in the camp is imperative (Num 5:1–4; Deut 23:10–14). The dead were buried outside the camp (Lev 10:4–5). The lepers were banished from the camp (Lev 13:46). For coming in contact with anything dead the penalty was exclusion from the camp for seven days (Num 31:19). Criminals were executed outside the camp (Lev 24:23, and cf. Heb 13:12, "Jesus also suffered outside the gate"). The camp is too close to God's presence to allow sin or impurity to intrude. The idea of "God's camp" is also applied to the permanent temple as seen in II Chr 31:2.

The LXX translation for *maḥăneh, parembolē*, is also applied in the NT to the church (Rev 20:9), "the camp of the saints."

ḥănît. ***Spear.*** A lethal weapon, the spear was short and capable of being thrown (I Sam 18:11; 20:33, translated here by the KJV as "javelin," but it is the word *ḥănît*). Even its butt could be used as a weapon (II Sam 2:23). Most frequently, this weapon is mentioned as being Saul's personal weapon: I Sam 18:10; 19:9, 10; 22:6; 23:21; 26:7, 16, 22; II Sam 1:6; I Chr 11:23. Possibly this signifies authority. Thus, in Ugaritic text 125:47 the son of King Krt on an important mission carries his spear, presumably as a mark of royal status.

Goliath also had a spear (I Sam 17:7; 21:9; I Chr 20:5). In his duel, or battle of champions, with David, David is prompted to say: "the Lord saves not with a sword and with a spear" (I Sam 17:47). These are not the kinds of weapons with which God stocks his arsenal (cf. II Cor 10:4). Surely this idea is uppermost in the eyes of the prophets as they anticipate the coming age of peace when men shall "beat their swords into ploughshares and their spears into pruning hooks" (Isa 2:4; Mic 4:3).

Bibliography: AI, I, pp. 241–46. Yadin, Y., The Art of Warfare in Biblical Lands, I-II, 1963. Unger, M. F., *Unger's Bible Dictionary*, Moody, 1957, pp. 169–70.

V.P.H.

חַנּוּן (*ḥannûn*). See no. 694d.
חָנוּת (*ḥānût*). See no. 690a.

691 חָנַט (*ḥānaṭ*) ***spice, make spicy, embalm.***

Derivatives

691a חֲנֻטִים (*ḥanūṭîm*) ***embalming,*** only in Gen 50:3.

691b †חִטָּה (*ḥiṭṭâ*) ***wheat.***

The substantive comes from the root *ḥānaṭ*, meaning perhaps "to project" or "to mature" because the grains project from the place of the ear of the wheat when it ripens. In the Bible it is referred to thirty times, and all but seven of these are in the plural. The singular is feminine in form and the plural is masculine in form.

It is planted in Palestine after the autumn rains have softened the ground sufficiently for plowing, thus in November–December, and is harvested in the spring, April–June. The "wheat-harvest" (*q^{e}ṣîr ḥiṭṭîm*) is mentioned in Gen 30:14; Ex 34:22; Jud 15:1; Ruth 2:23; I Sam 6:13; 12:17. Of the species of cereals referred to in the Bible wheat (*ḥiṭṭâ*) is usually considered the most valuable. Note that of the seven species with which Israel is blessed as she enters her new land, wheat is placed first (Deut 8:8). There is even a tradition in the Talmud that the tree of knowledge of which Adam and Eve partook was a *ḥiṭṭâ* (Sanhedrin 70b).

This wheat was "harvested" (Ruth 2:23; I Sam 6:13). It was "threshed" (Jud 6:11; I Chr 20:21); "cleaned" (II Sam 4:6). It also figures prominently as a part of Solomon's obligation regarding the alliance he made with Hiram the king of Phoenician Tyre. In addition to olive oil Solomon was to give wheat (I Kgs 5:11 [H 25]; II Chr 2:10, 15 [H 9,14]) to Hiram.

The Psalmist twice uses the word symbolically of God's care and provision: Ps 81:16 [H 17]; 147:14. God promises the "finest of wheat" (*ḥēleb ḥiṭṭâ*), literally "the kidney fat of wheat" (cf. Deut 32:14). Thorns are the opposite of wheat (Job 31:40; Jer 12:13).

Jesus, of course, resorted to the analogy of the "grain of wheat" in John 12:24 to press home the necessity for his own death. Paul in I Cor 15:36f. employs the same analogy to say that the body cannot be transformed into the new life of the resurrection unless it dies.

Bibliography: Feliks, J., "Wheat," in *Encyclopaedia Judaica,* vol. XVI, 480–481. Kislev, M. E., "Ḥiṭṭa and Kussemet: Notes on their Interpretations," *Lěšonénu* 37: 83–95 (in Hebrew). Trever, J. C., "Wheat," in IDB IV, pp. 839–40.

V.P.H.

חַנֻטִים (*ḥanūṭîm*). See no. 691a.
חָנִיךְ (*ḥānîk*). See no. 693a.
חֲנִינָה (*ḥănînâ*). See no. 694e.
חֲנִית (*ḥănît*). See no. 690b.

692 חנך (*ḥnk*) **I. Assumed root of the following.**

692a †חֵךְ (*ḥēk*) ***palate, mouth.*** ASV and RSV similar, although RSV twice renders "speech" for ASV "mouth" (Prov 5:3; Song 5:16).

Half of the occurrences of *ḥēk* are in Job where, rendered often as "mouth," it is set in context of taste or speech.

Theologically, the term is significant in two connections. As an organ vital for speech *ḥēk,* like mouth (*peh,* q.v.) is linked with true and false statements. Wisdom, personified, commends herself to mankind by saying, "All the words of my mouth (*ḥēk*) are righteous" (Prov 8:7). Job claims innocence because under provocation he has not permitted his mouth (*ḥēk*) to sin.

The expression, "tongue cleaving to mouth," apart from denoting thirst, is an idiom in the Hebrew for being speechless. Ezekiel's dumbness may indicate the gravity of the impending destruction of Jerusalem or perhaps the importance of waiting to speak Yahweh's word only. The idiom was used in imprecations and oaths (cf. Ps 137:6).

E.A.M.

693 חָנַךְ (*ḥānak*) ***II, dedicate, inaugurate.*** ASV and RSV similar.)

Derivatives

693a †חָנִיךְ (*ḥānîk*) ***trained servant.***
693b †חֲנֻכָּה (*ḥănūkkâ*) ***dedication.***
693c חַכָּה (*hakkâ*) ***hook fastened in jaw, fish hook.***

The verb occurs infrequently (five times) with the object "house," either private (Deut 20:5) or religious (e.g. I Kgs 8:63). Although usually rendered "dedicate" a more accurate translation is "begin" or "initiate." See Prov 22:6 for *ḥānak* translated as "train" (a child). Synonyms are *qādēsh* "to set apart," a notion not inherent in *ḥānak,* and the phrase *mālē' yad* "fill the hand," thought by some to mean "filling the hand (with an offering?) for Yahweh" (cf. Jud 17:5, 12; Ex 29:24f.), a phrase used with respect to "people."

ḥānak is best understood as "inaugurate." There is not in the term itself the notion that dedication is to someone or to something, though that concept is present in the synonyms. With one exception (Prov 22:6, where the meaning is "start"; cf. NEB), *ḥānak* and its derivates refer to an action in connection with structures such as a building (1 Kgs 8:63), wall (Neh 12:27), an altar (Num 7:10), or an image (Dan 3:2).

ḥānak is almost certainly a community action which in the case of cult structures involves offerings. The ceremony of dedication (*ḥănūkkâ*) for Solomon's altar extended over seven days (II Chr 7:9). Dedication of Solomon's temple as well as the temple at Ezra's time was marked by numerous sacrifices (I Kgs 8:63; Ezr 6:17).

Judging from Israelite practice, the initial use of a religious structure was given special significance. The completion of a project was observed with an inauguration of the structure, an event appropriately accompanied by sacrifice and joy. Rites of inauguration have their place. Elsewhere, with the use of other vocabulary, greater emphasis is given to the consecration of people to God.

ḥānîk. ***Trained servants, trained men*** (RSV). A hapax legomenon in Gen 14:14. Now translated as "armed retainer" used by Palestinian chieftains as mentioned in the Egyptian Execration Texts (nineteenth-eighteenth centuries B.C. and in a fifteenth century B.C. cuneiform inscription from Taanach, Israel. It is of textual significance that this hapax has good second millennium parallels. No point is to be made of the number of armed retainers born in Abraham's house (318). Nor is it accurately to be compared to the Scarab of Amenophis III which records that the princess Gilukhipla arrived from Naharaim (Haran) with 317 women of the harem (A. DeBuck, *Egyptian Reading Book I,* 1948, p. 67).

ḥănūkkâ. ***Dedication, inauguration.*** The term

occurs eight times in Hebrew and twice in each of the Aramaic portions of Ezra and Daniel.

The noun is most famous because of its intertestamental use for the reestablishment of worship in the temple after the excesses of Antiochus Epiphanes. This Hanukkah feast is mentioned in Jn 10:22. It falls in late December.

Bibliography: Albright, W. F., JBL 58:96. ______, BASOR 94:24. Lambdin, Thomas O., JAOS 73:150. Reif, S. C., "Dedicated to חנך," VT 22: 495–501.

V.P.H.

חִנָּם (*ḥinnām*). See no. 694b.

693.1 חֲנָמֵל (*ḥănāmēl*) ***sleet.***

694 חָנַן (*ḥānan*) ***I, be gracious; pity;*** in Hithpael stem ***to beseech, implore.***

Derivatives

694a †חֵן (*ḥēn*) ***favor, grace.***
694b †חִנָּם (*ḥinnām*) ***freely, for nothing.***
694c חִין (*ḥîn*) ***grace.*** Occurs only in Job 41:4.
694d †חַנּוּן (*ḥannûn*) ***gracious.***
694e †חֲנִינָה (*ḥănînâ*) ***favor.***
694f †תְּחִנָּה (*tᵉḥinnâ*) ***supplication.***
694g †תַּחֲנוּן (*taḥănûn*) ***supplication.***

Cognate with Akkadian *enēnu, ḫanānu* "to grant a favor," Ugaritic *ḥnn* "to be gracious, to favor" (UT, 19: no. 882), and Arabic *ḥanna* "to feel sympathy, compassion."

It is used in the Qal stem fifty-six times, in the Hithpael seventeen times, in the Hophal once, in the Piel once, in the Polel twice, and in the Niphal once.

The verb *ḥānan* depicts a heartfelt response by someone who has something to give to one who has a need. Ap-Thomas's suggestion that the verb comes from a biliteral root "to bend, to incline," i.e. to condescend, is not convincing. According to Flack the verb describes "an action from a superior to an inferior who has no real claim for gracious treatment."

In reaction to earlier studies, Neubauer in his recent monograph defines the verb as God's intervention to save and to help his faithful servant or nation with the emphasis on loyalty rather than on grace and love. He arrives at this conclusion by an extrapolation from social relations to theological relations. His attempt to read such a nuance into the various occurrences of *ḥānan* and its derivatives leads to forced interpretations.

The LXX translates the verb with *oikteireō* "to pity or have compassion," with *eleō* "to show mercy or sympathy," or in the Hithpael stem with *deisthaō* "to supplicate."

The verb is used in social or secular contexts as well as theological ones. It often has the sense of showing kindness to the poor and needy.

Job begs his friends, "Pity me, pity me" (Job 19:21).

The Hithpael stem means "to beseech," as in Gen 42:21 where the brothers recalled how Joseph had pleaded with them. The Syrian captain besought Elijah for his life and for the lives of his soldiers (II Kgs 1:13). Esther implored the king with tears (Est 8:3; cf. 4:8).

The apparent Niphal in Jer 22:23, *nēḥant,* is probably a textual error for a form derived from the verb *'ānaḥ* as shown by the LXX, Peshitta, and Targum. Modern translations follow the LXX *katastenaxeis* and render "you will groan."

The overwhelming number of uses in the Qal stem, some forty-one instances, have Yahweh as the subject. The plea *ḥonnēnî,* "be gracious to me," appears nineteen times in the Psalms. The Psalmist asks Yahweh to show him favor in view of his loneliness (Ps 25:16 [H 17]), his distress (Ps 31:9 [H 10]), his transgressions (Ps 51:1 [H 3]) where the favor he asks for is that God will erase the indictment against him, etc. Cf. Isa 33:2.

The Lord graciously gave Jacob his children (Gen 33:5) and prospered him (Gen 33:11). Joseph's benediction upon Benjamin (Gen 43:29), and Aaron's benediction (Num 6:25) ask for God's gracious dealing.

Amos (5:15) urges his hearers to establish justice that the Lord might be gracious to them. In the final analysis the Lord is sovereign in acting graciously to those whom he selects (Ex 33:19).

The Hithpael is used in supplications to God: by Moses who begs to see the Promised Land (Deut 3:23); by Solomon in dedicating the temple (I Kgs 8:33, 47, 59; 9:3; II Chr 6:24, 37); by the Psalmist (Ps 30:8 [H 9]; 142:1 [H 2]); and by Hosea (12:4 [H 5]) of Jacob's appeal to the angel who wrestled with him. Job, who is advised by Bildad to supplicate God (Job 8:5), concedes that though he were righteous this would be his only recourse (Job 9:15).

Instead of taking *ḥannôt* as an infinitive in Ps 77:9 [H 10], "Hath God forgotten to be gracious?" (AV), Dahood suggests taking it as a substantive, parallel to *raḥămāyw* "bowels." He translates, "Have *the inmost parts* of God dried up?"

The verb *ḥānan* and its derivatives are components of the names of fifty-one persons. These include: Baalhanan, Elhanan, Hananel, Hanani, Hananiah, Hannah, Hanun, Henadad, Jehohanan, Johanan, Tehinnah. Cf. the Punic names Hanno and Hannibal.

The woman's name Hannah has given us Anna, Ann, Nan, Nancy, Anita (Spanish) and Annette (French). Johanan has given us the name John: Jean (French), Giovanni (Italian), Juan

(Spanish), Johann, and Hans (German), Jan (Dutch), and Ivan (Russian).

For synonyms of *ḥānan,* etc. see especially *ḥesed* and *raḥûm.*

ḥēn. ***Favor, grace, charm,*** etc. This word occurs sixty-nine times, including forty-three times in the phrase "to find favor in the eyes of," seven times with the verb "to give," and three times with the verb "to obtain" (Est 2:15, 17; 5:2), which leaves fourteen independent uses of the word.

The word never appears with the article or in the plural; it has the personal suffix once in Gen 39:21.

The vast majority of occurrences are secular and not theological in significance. In contrast with the verb *ḥānan,* the focus of attention is not on the giver, but on the recipient, of what is given. In contrast with the frequent occurrences of the verb and other derivatives, in the Psalms *ḥēn* occurs but twice in Ps 84:11 [H 12] "the Lord will give favor" (RSV), and in Ps 45:2 [H 3] of the "grace" on the lips of the bridegroom.

ḥēn appears thirteen times in Proverbs, often with an aesthetic significance of charm or beauty.

As Neubauer has stressed, many of the passages in which this phrase is found concern the relations of a superior to an inferior, e.g. a king to his subject. But it is too much to hold that the phrase is a *terminus technicus* so that Jacob in Gen 32:5 [H 6]; 33:8, 10, 15, is actually acknowledging himself a vassal of Esau.

The phrase is found in the crucial passage on the justification of divorce in Deut 24:1 which was the basis for the debate between Hillel and Shammai. Rabbi Akiba held that a man might divorce his wife "even if he found another fairer than she, for it is written: 'if she find no favor in his eyes.' "

In theological usage Noah and Moses are said to have found grace in the sight of the Lord (Gen 6:8; Ex 33:12). It was the Lord who caused Joseph to find favor with the chief jailer (Gen 39:21), and the Israelites favor with the Egyptians (Ex 3:21; 11:3; 12:36). In Num 11:15 Moses is saying to the Lord no more than, "Do me a favor and please kill me."

In Zech 12:10 the house of David and the inhabitants of Jerusalem will have poured upon them "the spirit of *ḥēn* and *taḥănûnîm.*" The Targum reads "a spirit of mercy and compassion"; Unger takes this as the Holy Spirit.

The shouts of acclamation at the completion of Zerubbabel's temple in Zech 4:7, literally, "*ḥēn, ḥēn,*" are interpreted by Unger to mean, "What gracefulness (beauty) it has!" Sellin has suggested, "Bravo, bravo!"

In a number of passages *ḥēn* means "charm" or an attractive personality which creates a favorable impression. In the Aramaic Proverbs of Ahiqar we have the phrase *ḥn gbr hymnwth* "for a man's charm is his truthfulness" (ANET, no. 132, p. 429). It is the heeding of wisdom which produces this favor: Prov 3:4; 13:15; Eccl 9:11; 10:12. The woman with this grace or charm, not just physical beauty (Prov 11:16; cf. 11:22), is worthy of honor.

The woman who fears the Lord is praised, in contrast to one who posseses merely deceitful charm and vain beauty (Prov 31:30). Nahum 3:4 compares Nineveh to a prostitute who is *ṭôbat ḥēn,* which the LXX renders *kalē kai epicharis* and the Vulgate *speciosae et gratae,* i.e. "beautiful and pleasing." Cf. NAB "fair and charming"; NEB "fair-seeming."

ḥinnām. ***Freely, for nothing, unjustly, without cause, in vain.*** Cf. Latin *gratis,* English *gratuitously.* This adverb occurs thirty-two times. It has no inherent religious significance.

It can mean "for nothing" as in Gen 29:15. In Ex 21:2, 11 it is used of the Hebrew slave freed; in Num 11:5 of the food which was eaten for free in Egypt; in Isa 52:3 of the Jews who have sold themselves into slavery "for nothing."

In Prov 23:29 the alcoholic has wounds "without cause" (KJV) or rather "for nothing" (NAB). The NEB paraphrases, "Who gets the bruises without knowing why?"

The Psalmist complains that his enemies plan evil for him "without cause" (Ps 35:7; "unprovoked," NEB). Cf. Ps 109:3; 119:161.

The word *ḥinnām* is used in several senses in Job. Satan asks (Job 1:9) whether Job fears God "for nothing," that is, without an ulterior purpose. God responds (Job 2:3) by replying to Satan that he has incited him against Job "without cause" or "without justification." Job (Job 9:17) later complains that his wounds have been multiplied "for no reason" (JB). Eliphaz accuses Job of taking someone's pledge "unjustly" (Job 22:6).

The word can also mean "in vain," as in Prov 1:17 of the bird net set in vain. In Ezk 6:10 Yahweh warns that he has not spoken in vain.

Dahood has suggested that *ḥinnām,* e.g. in Ps 35:7, should be translated "secretly, stealthily" from the Ugaritic *ḥnn.* The traditional rendering, however, makes good sense.

The Aramaic verb which is cognate with Hebrew *ḥānan* is used in the Peal stem in Dan 4:27 [Aram 24] in Daniel's advice to Nebuchadnezzar "to show mercy" to the poor, and in the Hithpael stem in Dan 6:11 [Aram 12] of Daniel's supplication.

ḥannûn. ***Gracious.*** This word occurs thirteen times, eleven times in combination with *raḥûm* "merciful, compassionate." The LXX usually translates it *eleēmōn* "merciful." The adjective describes the gracious acts of Yahweh. His grace is revealed together with his righteousness, as most of the passages which speak of him as *ḥannûn* also speak of his judging evil, e.g. Joel 2:13.

All occurrences of *ḥannûn* refer to God (Ex 22:27 [H 26]; 34:6; II Chr 30:9; Neh 9:17, 31; Ps 86:15; 103:8; 111:4; 116:5; 145:8; Joel 2:13; Jon 4:2). In Ps 112:4, the RSV supplies "the Lord" as the one who is gracious, but the description is probably of the righteous man who shares the characteristics of his God.

Perhaps the most striking use of this word is the great proclamation of the name of God to Moses on Mount Sinai (Ex 34:6). The verse is alluded to repeatedly in later writings (Num 14:18, but does not use this phrase; Ps 86:15; 103:8, 145:8; Joel 2:13; Jon 4:2).

ḥănînâ. ***Favor, pity.*** It occurs but once in Jer 16:13. The LXX translates it *eleos* "pity, mercy." Because of Judah's apostasy the Lord says that he will no longer grant his pity.

tᵉḥinnâ. ***Supplication, mercy.*** The word occurs twenty-four times and means a prayer for grace on all but two occasions when it means "mercy." Half of all the occurrences appear in Solomon's prayer at the dedication of the temple (I Kgs 8–9; II Chr 6).

In Josh 11:20 *tᵉḥinnâ* designates the "mercy" of the victor for the vanquished, and in Ezr 9:8 Yahweh's "grace" (KJV) or "mercy" (NAB) for the remnant of his people. In both cases the LXX has *eleos* "mercy."

taḥănûn. Always used in the plural *taḥănûnîm*. ***Supplications.*** Similar in general to the preceding but representing less a formal entreaty (used only once in II Chr 6:21 in Solomon's prayer) than the outpourings of a troubled soul; used in parallel to "weepings" in Jer 3:21, 31:9. It is used seven times in the Psalms, all except once in the phrase *qôl taḥănûnay* "the voice of my supplications" (KJV), "my cry for mercy" (NEB).

Bibliography: Ap-Thomas, D. R., "Some Aspects of the Root ḤNN in the Old Testament," JSS 2: 128–48. Flack, E. E., "The Concept of Grace in Biblical Thought," *Biblical Studies in Memory of H. C. Allemen,* ed. J. M. Myers, Augustin, 1960, pp. 137–54. Lofthouse, W., "Ḥen and Ḥesed in the Old Testament," ZAW 51: 29–35. Reed, William L., "Some Implications of ḤĒN for Old Testament Religion," JBL 73: 36–41. Richardson, TWB, pp. 80, 100. Snaith, N. H., *The Distinctive Ideas of the Old Testament,* London: Epworth, 1944, pp. 127–31. Torrance, T. F., "The Doctrine of Grace in the Old Testament," SJT 1: 55–65. TDNT, IX, pp. 376–81. THAT, I, pp. 587–96.

E.Y.

695 חָנַן (*ḥānan*) ***II, be loathsome*** (Job 19:17, only).

696 חָנֵף (*ḥānēp*) ***be defiled, polluted, profaned, corrupt.*** (ASV similar; RSV in most cases uses "pollute" for the KJV renderings.)

Derivatives

696a †חֹנֶף (*ḥōnep*) ***hypocrite.***
696b †חָנֵף (*ḥānēp*) ***hypocrite.***
696c חֲנֻפָּה (*ḥănūppâ*) ***profaneness, pollution,*** only in Jer 23:15.

The core notion is of inclining away from right whereas in Arabic it may mean to incline to a right state. In Aramaic the root means "to act falsely toward," "act with hypocrisy"; in Akkadian (Amarna letters) "exercise ruthlessness toward" (BDB). The verb appears eleven times, seven of which are in the Qal stem.

The verb can refer to land being polluted for various reasons. In the Qal stem there is mentioned the transgression of laws, violation of statutes and the breaking of the covenant, all of which pollute the land (Isa 24:5). Breaking of marriage vows to marry another precludes a return to the first mate; in the same way a favored people who drifted back and forth between devotion to idols and the Lord, pollutes the land (Jer 3:1). The evidence of immorality and other gross wickedness of the Canaanite fertility cult was to be seen on every hilltop in the land, thus polluting it (Jer 3:2, 9). Because of many sins Zion was in danger of God's discipline by being polluted by pagan nations (Mic 4:11).

The Hiphil stem describes the pollution of land. The murderer who had shed innocent blood was regarded as polluting the land (Num 35:33).

Prophet and priest could be polluted. Their evil actions were to be found even in the house of the Lord and their pollution polluted the temple (Jer 23:11). Daniel's prediction regarding Antiochus Epiphanes indicated that he was to flatter (but actually pollute) those who had already broken the covenant. Some misguided rulers would actually serve their interests in the corruption of the sanctuary but the counterforce of those who knew God (the Maccabees) would take action against this evil (Dan 11:32).

The adjective denotes a godless man, a man who forgets God (Job 8:13) and lives in opposition to all that is right (Job 17:8; Isa 9:17; 10:6). Of the thirteen times it is used, it appears eight times in Job, emphasizing the action and tragedy of the godless. Any hope which the godless have will perish (Job 8:13). The godless can never come into the presence of God (Job 13:16). Association with the godless is a barren experience (Job 15:34). The godless have their pleasures but momentarily (never forever, Job 20:5). The godless should not hold governmental positions lest the people fall into a trap (Job 34:30). The man who forgets the fear of God is godless, a menace to society. He will be judged.

David demonstrates the upside-down character of the godless. Those who had turned against him were likened to the coarse jesting at godless banqueting tables (Ps 35:16). The character of the godless, being and actions, God will judge. Retribution will come so swiftly that even the godless will tremble and be terrified (Isa 33:14).

ḥōnep. ***Hypocrisy,*** Isa 32:6. The fool (worst word, *nābāl* q.v.) with whom no one can reason, is the one who practices ungodliness or profaneness.

ḥānēp. ***Hypocrite, hypocritical.*** (ASV, RSV, and NIV usually translate this word as "godless," possibly the better rendering from the core idea.)

L.G.

697 *חָנַק (*ḥānaq*) ***strangle.*** Occurs in the Niphal (II Sam 17:23) and the Piel (Nah 2:13).

Derivative

697a מַחֲנָק (*maḥănāq*) ***strangling.***

698 חסד (*ḥsd*) **I. Assumed root of the following.**

698a †חֶסֶד (*ḥesed*) kindness, lovingkindness, mercy and similar words (KJV). (RSV usually has steadfast love, occasionally loyalty, NASB lovingkindness, kindness, love, NIV unfailing love.)

698b †חָסִיד (*ḥāsîd*) ***holy one, godly, saint.*** RSV faithful, godly one, loyal. NIV, saint, godly.

698c חֲסִידָה (*ḥăsîdâ*) ***stork*** (perhaps because it was thought to be kind to its young).

For centuries the word *ḥesed* was translated with words like mercy, kindness, love. The LXX usually uses *eleos* "mercy," and the Latin *misericordia*. The Targum and Syriac use frequently a cognate of *ṭob*. The root is not found in Akkadian or Ugaritic. The lexicons up through BDB and GB (which said *Liebe, Gunst, Gnade,* love, goodness, grace) are similar. KB however is the "mutual liability of those . . . belonging together."

In 1927 Nelson Glueck, shortly preceded by I. Elbogen, published a doctoral dissertation in German translated into English by A. Gottschalk, *Hesed in the Bible* with an introduction by G. A. LaRue which is a watershed in the discussion. His views have been widely accepted. In brief, Glueck built on the growing idea that Israel was bound to its deity by covenants like the Hittite and other treaties. He held that God is pictured as dealing basically in this way with Israel. The Ten Commandments, etc. were stipulations of the covenant, Israel's victories were rewards of covenant keeping, her apostasy was covenant violation and God's *hesed* was not basically mercy, but loyalty to his covenant obligations, a loyalty which the Israelites should also show. He was followed substantially by W. F. Lofthouse (1933), N. H. Snaith (1944), H. W. Robinson (1946), Ugo Masing (1954), and many others.

There were others, however, who disagreed. F. Assension (1949) argued for mercy, basing his views on the OT versions. H. J. Stoebe (doctoral dissertation 1951, also articles in 1952 VT and in THAT) argued for good-heartedness, kindness. Sidney Hills and also Katherine D. Sakenfeld (*The Meaning of Ḥesed in the Hebrew Bible, a New Inquiry*), held in general that *ḥesed* denotes free acts of rescue or deliverance which in prophetic usage includes faithfulness. For this historical survey and references see Sakenfeld pp. 1–13 (hereafter called Sak.); also LaRue in the book by Glueck (here called G.)

The writer would stress that the theological difference is considerable whether the Ten Commandments are stipulations to a covenant restricted to Israel to which God remains true and to which he demands loyalty, or whether they are eternal principles stemming from God's nature and his creation to which all men are obligated and according to which God will judge in justice or beyond that will show love, mercy and kindness.

On the meaning of our word *ḥesed* it is convenient to start, as G. and Sak. have done, with the secular usage, i.e. between man and man. Glueck argues that *ḥesed* is practiced in an ethically binding relationship of relatives, hosts, allies, friends and rulers. It is fidelity to convenantal obligations real or implied. Sakenfeld goes over the same material and concludes that indeed a relationship is present (love almost necessitates a subject—object relation) but that the *ḥesed* is freely given. "Freedom of decision" is essential. The help is vital, someone is in a position to help, the helper does so in his own freedom and this "is the central feature in all the texts" (p. 45).

Glueck certainly seems to find obligation where there is none. Stoebe gives an extensive treatment of *ḥesed* in THAT (pp. 599–622) and remarks (p. 607) that I Kgs is an instance where *ḥesed* is unexpected. Benhaded was defeated. He could claim no obligation. He hoped for mercy, kindness. Stoebe cites the men of Jabesh also (II Sam 2:5). Saul had died in defeat. The care of Saul's body seems clearly to have been a free act of kindness.

Also Laban's willingness to send Rebekah to Isaac was not from any covenant obligation (though G. cites the appeal to providence in v. 50). It was a kindness to a long-lost relative. He could easily have said "no." The beautiful story of Ruth is tarnished by considering Ruth's action as motivated by contractual obligations. The Lord had no obligation to get the widows new husbands in Moab (1:8–9). Ruth went with Naomi from pure love. Boaz recognized her action as goodness in 2:11–12 and calls it *ḥesed* in 3:10. Even Glueck inclined toward kindness here. The action of Rahab was kindness (Josh 2:12). Her loyalty would naturally and legally be to her king and city. The angels in Gen 19:19 were hardly bound by covenant obligation—or any obligation—to Lot. Indeed the basis of their action is said in v. 16 to have been their compassion (cf. Isa 63:9). In Gen 21:23 Abimelech cites his previous *ḥesed* as grounds for making the covenant with Abraham which required further *ḥesed*. Glueck makes something of I Sam 20:8, 14, 15 where David and Jonathan swore friendship. This covenant, says G. was the basis of the *ḥesed*. Here, perhaps, is G's major mistake. He forgets that covenants arise on the basis of a relationship and that the obligations are often deeper than the covenant. Verse 17 shows that Jonathan's love moved him to make the covenant. When Jonathan died, David lamented for him out of love, not obligation (II Sam 1:26). David's *ḥesed* to Saul's house is said to be for the sake of Jonathan, not because of a legal obligation (II Sam 9:1, 3, 7). Glueck seems to miss the mark widely when he says it was neither grace nor mercy; it was brotherliness required by covenantal loyalty. Such a view has failed to see the depth of David's character. Stoebe calls it the spontaneous proof of a cordial friendly attitude (*herzlich freundlich Gesinnung*). Other examples must be omitted, but they are similar. All parties agree that in Est 2:9, 17 the word is used of favor, kindness, but some try to make this usage unusual being post-exilic.

When we come to the *ḥesed* of God, the problem is that of course God was in covenant relation with the patriarchs and with Israel. Therefore his *ḥesed* can be called covenant *ḥesed* without contradiction. But by the same token God's righteousness, judgment, fidelity, etc. could be called covenant judgment, etc. The question is, do the texts ascribe his *ḥesed* to his covenants or to his everlasting love? Is not *ḥesed* as Dom Sorg observed (see Bibliography) really the OT reflex of "God is love"?

A prominent early usage is in God's declaration of his own character: Ex 20:6 parallel to Deut 5:10 and also Ex 34:6–7. These passages are discussed by G., Sak. and Stoebe from the viewpoint of documentary division first. But aside from this Sak. emphasizes the freedom of God's *ḥesed*. in all these passages. She notes the proximity to words for mercy in Ex 34:6–7 and remarks that it is "this aspect of God's *ḥesed* (as his mercy) which takes on greater importance in exilic and postexilic writing"—of which she envisions a good bit—(p. 119). However, she considers Ex 20 and Deut 5 as in a "covenantal context" (p. 131) and holds that "those who are loyal (loving) will receive *ḥesed* while those who are disloyal (hating) will be punished" (p. 131). She is led into this covenantal emphasis by the prior idea that since secular treaties speak of love, brotherhood and friendship between suzerain and vassal, that therefore these are covenant words and show that a covenant was at least implied. This view forgets that love is a covenant word because kings borrowed it from general use to try to render covenants effective. They tried to make the vassal promise to act like a brother, friend and husband. It does not follow that God's love is merely a factor in a covenant; rather the covenant is the sign and expression of his love. McCarthy more acceptably says, "the form of the Sinai story in Ex 19–24 which is reflected in the text without later additions does not bear out the contention that the story reflects an organization according to covenant form." His view is that the power and glory of Yahweh and the ceremonies conducted effected the union "more than history, oath, threat and promise" (McCarthy, D. J., *Treaty and Covenant*, Pontif. Bib. Inst., ed. of 1963, p. 163).

The text itself of Ex 20 and Deut 5 simply says that God's love (*ḥesed*) to those who love him (*'āhab*) is the opposite of what he will show to those who hate him. The context of these commands is surely God's will for all mankind, although his special care, indeed his covenant, is with Israel. That *ḥesed* refers only to this covenant and not to the eternal divine kindness back of it, however, is a fallacious assumption.

The text of Ex 34:6–7 is fuller and more solemn, coming as it does after the great apostasy. It was a tender revelation of God's self to Moses. Sakenfeld is right here "that forgiveness must always have been latent [at least!] in the theological usage of *ḥesed*" even before the exile (p. 119). The association with divine mercy is surely patent in the words and in the context of the occasion of the apostasy. The word *raḥûm* with its overtones of mother love, and *ḥannûn* "grace" combined with the phrase "slow to anger" all emphasize the character of God who is love. He is great in *ḥesed* and *'emet* (of which more later). He keeps *ḥesed* for thousands which is immediately related to forgiveness of sin. That all this simply says that God keeps his oath seems trivial. The oath is kept because it is the loving God who speaks the oath.

Sakenfeld nicely brings together the several passages dependent on Ex 34:6–7. They are: Num 14:18–19; Neh 9:17; Ps 86:15; 103:8; 145:8 (cf. 9 and 10); Joel 2:13; and Jon 4:2. Of these passages, only Ps 86:15 includes the word *'emet* after *ḥesed*. They all speak of the love of the Lord and some mention his forgiveness. None specifically ground the *ḥesed* in covenant.

The phrase *ḥesed* and *'emet* "truth" mentioned above is thought by some to argue for the concept of loyalty or fidelity in *ḥesed*. It occurs some twenty-five times with about seven more in less close connection. Most agree it is a hendiadys and one noun serves to describe the other. Therefore the phrase means "faithful love" or "true kindness" or the like. Kindness and faithfulness is a fair equivalent hendiadys in English. The combination hardly seems to further the idea of fidelity to a covenant in the word *ḥesed*. If the term already meant that, why would the qualifier "faithful" be added? Usually, as in the usage of *ḥesed* alone, there is no covenant expressed to which fidelity is due. It is alleged in I Kgs 3:3, but although God's *ḥesed* to David in making his son king was indeed according to covenant; it was also according to his love which lay back of his covenant. The text does not ascribe it to covenant loyalty. Stoebe points out in Ps 89 that the covenant of v. 3 is based on the *ḥesed* of v. 2 [H 4 and 3] (THAT, p. 615).

Another pair of nouns is covenant, *b^erît*, and *ḥesed* used seven times with some other instances of use in near contexts. The main instance is Deut 7:9, 12 which has echoes in I Kgs 8:23; II Chr 6:14; Neh 1:5; 9:32; and Dan 9:4. It itself is called by Stoebe (THAT, p. 616) a paraphrase of Ex 34:6. He remarks that Deut 7:8 already bases all God's favor on his love. If this pair be translated "covenantal love" or "covenant and love," it should be remembered that the love is back of the covenant. This point is illustrated by Jer 2:2 where the *ḥesed* of Israel's youth is likened to the love of a bride. The love of a bride is the basis of the promise, not the result.

It should be mentioned that *ḥesed* is also paired about fifteen times with nouns of mercy like *raḥûm*, e.g. Ps 103:4; Zech 7:9 (and cf. Ex 34:6–7 above), *ḥēn*, e.g. Gen 19:19; Ps 109:12, *tanḥûm*, Ps 94:18–19, etc. These instances usually stand as paired nouns not really in an adjectival relation. The implication is that *ḥesed* is one of the words descriptive of the love of God.

So, it is obvious that God was in covenant relation with Israel, also that he expressed this relation in *ḥesed*, that God's *ḥesed* was eternal (Note the refrain of Ps 136)—though the *ḥesed* of Ephraim and others was not (Hos 6:4). However, it is by no means clear that *ḥesed* necessarily involves a covenant or means fidelity to a covenant. Stoebe argues that it refers to an attitude as well as to actions. This attitude is parallel to love, *raḥûm* goodness, *ṭôb*, etc. It is a kind of love, including mercy, *ḥannûn*, when the object is in a pitiful state. It often takes verbs of action, "do," "keep," and so refers to acts of love as well as to the attribute. The word "lovingkindness" of the KJV is archaic, but not far from the fulness of meaning of the word.

ḥāsîd. ***Holy one, saint.*** Whether God's people in the OT were called *ḥāsîd* because they were characterized by *ḥesed* (as seems likely) or were so called because they were objects of God's *ḥesed* may not be certain. The word is used thirty-two times, twenty-five of them in the Pss. It is used in sing. and pl. Once, Ps 16:16, it refers to the Holy One to come. The word became used for the orthodox party in the days of the Maccabeans.

Bibliography: Dentan, R. C., "The Literary Affinities of Exodus 34:6ff.," VT 13: 34–51. Freedman, D. N., "God Compassionate and Merciful," *Western Watch* 6: 6–24. Glueck, Nelson, *Hesed in the Bible,* trans. by A. Gottschalk, Hebrew Union College Press, 1967. Kuyper, Lester J., "Grace and Truth," *Reformed Review* 16: 1–16. Sakenfeld, Katherine D., *The Meaning of Hesed in the Hebrew Bible: A New Inquiry,* Scholars Press, 1978. Snaith, N.H., *The Distinctive Ideas of the Old Testament,* Schocken, 1964, pp. 94–130. Sorg, Dom Rembert, *Ḥasid in the Psalms,* Pro decimo Press, 1953. Stoebe, H. J., "Die Bedeutung des Wortes Ḥäsäd im Alten Testament," VT 2:244–54. Yarbrough, Glen, "The Significance of *ḥsd* in the Old Testament," Unpublished Ph.D. Dissertation, Southern Baptist Theological Seminary, 1959. TDNT, I, pp. 696–701. THAT, I, pp. 599–622.

R.L.H.

699 *חָסַד (*ḥāsad*) ***II, be reproached, ashamed.*** This verb occurs only once, in the Piel (Prov 25:10).

Derivative

699a חֶסֶד (*ḥesed*) ***shame, reproach*** (Lev 20:17; Prov 14:34).

700 חָסָה (*ḥāsâ*) ***seek refuge, flee for protection*** and thus figuratively ***put trust in*** (God), ***confide, hope in*** (God or person). ASV, RSV similar.

Derivatives

700a חָסוּת (*ḥāsût*) ***refuge, shelter,*** only in Isa 30:3.

700b מַחְסֶה (*maḥseh*) ***refuge, shelter.***

The root is probably to be distinguished from *bāṭaḥ* "rely on," "take refuge in" as denoting more precipitate action. The etymology is doubtful. With derivatives the root is used fifty-six times, predominantly in the Psalms and similar poetic and hymnic literature.

While it is used literally of taking shelter from a rainstorm (Isa 4:6; 25:4; Job 24:8) or from any danger in the high hills (Ps 104:18), it is more often used figuratively of seeking refuge and thus putting confident trust whether in any god (Deut

32:37) or in the "shadow" (protection) of any major power such as Egypt (Isa 30:2; cf. the plant in the parable of Jud 9:15).

This idea of taking refuge may well derive from the common experience of fugitives or of men at war, for whom the adjacent hills provided a ready "safe height" or "strong rock" to which the often helpless defender could hurry for protection. In this way the noun *maḥseh* "place of refuge" is used as a snyonym of *mā'ôz* "stronghold," *miśgāb* "secure height," or *mānôs* "place of escape."

As is the case with the parallel terms, the "rock" (*ṣûr*, Ps 62:7), "rock of my refuge" (*ṣûr maḥsî* Ps 94:22), "the shield, cover" (*māgēn*, Ps 144:2; Prov 30:5), or the "wings" denoting protection (Ruth 2:12; Ps 17:8; 36:7 [H 8]), the "Refuge" is used as an epithet for God. He above all is the Refuge (*maḥseh*, Ps 14:6; 46:1 [H 2]; 62:8; 91:9), the Shelter (Ps 61:3 [H 4], KJV), the "strong Refuge" (Ps 71:7), and Fortress (Ps 91:2). God is ever the sole refuge of his people. Trust in him (godliness) protects the individual by its solidarity (Prov 14:26; Jn 4:10). The Qal stem of *ḥāsâ* is primarily used of man putting trust in God as his Rock (II Sam 22:3), Strength (Ps 18:2 [H 3]), and Stronghold (NEB "sure refuge," Nah 1:7). It is always better to trust in God rather than to trust (*bāṭaḥ*) in princes (Ps 118:8–9). He acts as the shield or cover (*māgēn*) of all who take refuge in him (II Sam 22:31; Ps 18:30 [H 31]).

The analogy of taking refuge in God may occasionally refer to the temple of God in Jerusalem where the afflicted of his people could always find refuge (Isa 14:32 RSV: cf. Ps 61:4). This was a development of the ancient custom whereby the fleeing criminal could seize the horns of the altar and so find safety from revenge (I Kgs 1:50). The interpretation of Prov 14:32 ("the righteous hath hope in his death," KJV) is difficult but should probably be emended from *b^{e}môtô* ("in his death") to *b^{e}tummô* (interchanging the "m" and "t") to read "seeks refuge in his integrity" (so LXX), as opposed to the wicked who is driven away in his wickedness.

"To seek refuge" stresses the insecurity and self-helplessness of even the strongest of men. It emphasizes the defensive or external aspect of salvation in God, the unchanging one in whom we "find shelter" (F. D. Kidner, *The Psalms*, 1973, *ad loc* Ps 46:1). David could view the cave to which he had fled as a stronghold, whereas others would see it as a trap.

The result of taking refuge in God is to be "blessed" (Ps 2:12) and be "saved" (Ps 17:7). Such a person should rejoice (Ps 5:11 [H 12]), find goodness (Ps 31:19 [H 20]) and "possess the land" (Isa 57:13).

The root occurs in proper names. An ancestor of Baruch and Seraiah is called Mohseiah (*maḥ^{e}sēyâ*, "the Lord is a refuge," Jer 32:12; 51:59). Hosah, a Levite listed as the gatekeeper of the western and Shellecheth gate of the temple (I Chr 16:38) had sixteen sons and brothers in similar service (26:10–11, 16). Hosah was also the name of a place in Asher (Josh 19:29).

Bibliography: Delekat, L., "Zum Hebräischen Wörterbuch," VT 14: 7–66. Tsevat, M., "A Study of the Language of the Biblical Psalms," JBL Monograph 9: 4ff., 48ff.

D.J.W.

חָסוּת (*ḥāsût*). See no. 700a.
חָסִיד (*ḥāsîd*). See no. 698b.
חָסִיל (*ḥāsîl*). See no. 701a.
חָסִין (*ḥăsîn*). See no. 703c.

701 חָסַל (*ḥāsal*) ***finish off, consume.*** Used of the locusts destroying crops (Deut 28:38).

Derivative

701a †חָסִיל (*ḥāsîl*) ***locust.***

The word is derived from the verb *ḥāsal* "to consume" (Deut 28:38). It occurs six times. The LXX mistakently translates it four times as *erusibē* "smut," and twice as *brouchos* "unwinged locust." The KJV translates it as "caterpillar." KB's suggestion of "cockroach" is erroneous. The word appears in Ugaritic as *ḥsn* "grasshopper," parallel to *irby* "locust" (UT 19: no. 883).

In Joel 1:4 and 2:25, *ḥāsîl* is used as the "consuming" young locust.

See also *'arbeh*.

E.Y.

702 חָסַם (*ḥāsam*) ***stop up, muzzle*** (Deut 25:4; Ezk 39:11).

Derivative

702a מַחְסוֹם (*maḥsôm*) ***muzzle*** (Ps 39:2).

703 חסן (*ḥsn*). **Assumed root of the following.**

703a †חֹסֶן (*ḥōsen*) ***riches, treasure.***

703b חָסֹן (*ḥāsōn*) ***strong*** (Amos 2:9; Isa 1:31).

703c חָסִין (*ḥăsîn*) ***strong, mighty*** (Ps 89:9).

ḥōsen. ***Riches, treasure.*** (ASV and RSV similar, KJV also "strength.") The word is used five times. The meaning is "wealth," usually "physical prosperity." The exception is Isaiah's reference to the Lord as a "wealth of salvations, wisdom, and knowledge" (Isa 33:6). The KJV translates "strength" here and also (with the LXX) in Jer 20:5 (see *hûn*).

C.P.W.

704 חַסְפַּס (*ḥaspas*) ***scale-like*** (Ex 16:14, only). Derivation uncertain.

705 חָסֵר (*ḥāsēr*) ***lack, have a need, be lacking.***

Derivatives

705a חֶסֶר (*ḥeser*) ***poverty*** (occurs twice).
705b חֹסֶר (*ḥōser*) ***want, lack*** (occurs twice).
705c †חָסֵר (*ḥāsēr*) ***needy, lacking.***
705d חֶסְרוֹן (*ḥesrôn*) ***deficiency*** (occurs once).
705e מַחְסוֹר (*maḥsôr*) ***need, poverty.***

The earliest occurrence of this verb describes the decrease of the waters which prevailed over the earth at the flood (Gen 8:3, 5). The lack is seen in the decrease of the numbers of the righteous in Sodom, i.e. the lack of five from the fifty seen in the decrease of the numbers of the righteous in Sodom, i.e. the lack of five from the fifty Abraham first proposed (Gen 18:28).

ḥāsēr is most frequently used to express the sufficiency of God's grace to meet the needs of his people. They never lack. In the wilderness, when the people followed God's command they never lacked manna (depending on God's daily supply; Ex 16:18). Moses reminded them of this just before they entered Canaan (Deut 2:7) and this became their basis of hope in Canaan (Deut 8:9).

This proved to be so for those who trusted the Lord, e.g. the widow (I Kgs 17:14), the Psalmist David (Ps 23:1), all who seek the Lord (Ps 34:10 [H 11]), and those who worship the Lord (Isa 51:14). He who has a good, God-fearing wife will see his abundance from God through her (Prov 31:11).

Conversely, the lack of bread or other blessings points to God's disfavor because of lack of faith (Isa 32:6; Ezk 4:17).

Ultimately, because of the faithlessness of the people, not only would they sense the lack of blessings but would even credit it to their not serving the pagan gods of Canaan (Jer 44:18). We see how God gave them up to their reprobate minds.

The root occurs in other Semitic languages such as Aramaic, Arabic, and Ethiopic, not, however, so far, in Ugaritic.

ḥāsēr. ***Lacking, in need of.*** (The same generally in ASV and RSV.) This adjective is in form the same as the verb *ḥāsēr* (see above). It is used primarily, however, in reference to the lack of wisdom and understanding. Thus it occurs most frequently in the wisdom literature and primarily in Prov (thirteen times out of nineteen).

The adjective occurs a few times in the sense of the lack of things, as does the verb e.g., lack of madmen (I Sam 21:15 [H 16]); lack of bread (II Sam 3:29; Prov 12:9); lack of oil (I Kgs 17:16).

The primary use of this adjective is in expressing man's predicament spiritually of lacking wisdom or understanding which leads to God. Those who lack understanding commit sin (Prov 6:32); deserve the rod (Prov 10:13); belittle their neighbors (Prov 11:12); follow what is worthless (Prov 12:11); rejoice over folly (Prov 15:21); make foolish vows (Prov 17:18); and are sluggards with a field full of weeds (Prov 24:30). If a ruler, he becomes a cruel oppressor (Prov 28:16). Although he may lack nothing of material things, one without God has no power to enjoy it all (Eccl 6:2). In short, if anyone lacks wisdom he shows himself to be a fool everywhere, even in public (Eccl 10:3).

Yet, if one realizes this lack, he can gain wisdom by looking to the provider of wisdom, the Lord (Prov 9:4). One who lacks can be admonished by God's wisdom to seek wisdom (Prov 9:16).

J.B.S.

חֶסְרוֹן (*ḥesrôn*). See no. 705d.
חַף (*ḥap*). See no. 711a.

706 *חָפָא (*ḥāpā'*) ***do secretly.*** *ḥāpā'* occurs only once, in the Piel (II Kgs 17:9).

707 חָפָה (*ḥāpâ*) ***cover, overlay.*** (ASV has "overlay" in Chr passages where RSV uses "covered" or once "ceiled.")

The Qal is used to express the covering of the head or face in a time of shame such as the shame of Haman (Est 6:12; 7:8) or the shame of David and those with him in his flight from his son Absalom (II Sam 15:30; cf. also Jer 14:3–4).

The Piel is used to express the overlaying of one object with another as in the gold overlays in the construction of the Lord's house (II Chr 3:5, 7, 8–9).

In each case, the idea seems to be that of hiding the less attractive underneath the more attractive. This is borne out by the cognate languages, especially Arabic, which use the root chiefly to express the act of hiding. It does not occur in Ugaritic.

Bibliography: Gordis, Robert, "Studies in Hebrew Roots of Contrasted Meanings," JQR 27: 33–58.

J.B.S.

חֻפָּה (*ḥuppâ*). See no. 710b.

708 חָפַז (*ḥāpaz*) ***hasten, flee, fear, be terrified*** (RSV often prefers "be frightened" or "flee" for KJV "make haste."

Derivative

708a †חִפָּזוֹן (*ḥippāzôn*) ***haste (?).***

There is no clear distinction between Qal and Niphal forms in meaning. In two contexts it parallels terms meaning fear (Deut 20:3, "tremble"; Ps 48:5 [H 6], RSV "took to flight"; KJV "hasted away"). Some contexts give support, though less than decisive support, for a meaning of "hasten" (i.e. in terror). The hasty flight of Mephibosheth's nurse (II Sam 4:4) and the hasty retreat of the Aramaeans (II Kgs 7:15) are examples. Once, the term serves as a poetic parallel for "fled" (Ps 104:7). "Being in terror" suits well the context of Ps 116:11 (RSV "consternation"), Ps 31:22 [H 23] (RSV "alarm"), and I Sam 23:26 ("David was fearful so that he went away" writer's translation). The meaning of this term in Job 40:23 is unclear (KJV "hasteth"; RSV "frightened"). "Flee in terror" may summarize its meanings.

ḥippāzôn. ***Haste (?), fear (?), fleeing (?).*** A technical term of uncertain meaning which describes the manner in which the Hebrews were to eat the first Passover (Ex 12:11) and the manner in which they left Egypt (Deut 16:3). In these contexts either "in haste" or "in fear" is possible. The poetic parallel to "flight" (Isa 52:12 in RSV) suggests a meaning such as "hasty flight" or "fearful flight."

J.P.L.

חִפָּזוֹן (*ḥippāzôn*). See no. 708a.

709 חפן (*ḥpn*). **Assumed root of the following.**

709a חֹפֶן (*ḥōpen*) ***hollow of hand*** (e.g. Eccl 4:6; Ezk 10:7).

710 חָפַף (*ḥāpap*) ***I, cover, shelter, shield.***

Derivatives

710a חוֹף (*ḥôp*) ***shore, coast.***
710b †חֻפָּה (*ḥūppâ*) ***canopy.***

The verb *ḥāpap* occurs only in Moses' blessing (Deut 33:12), describing the security of Benjamin. He is loved by the Lord "who shields (KJV "covers") him all the day."

ḥūppâ. ***Canopy, chamber.*** (RSV same; ASV uses "covering" in Isa 4:5.) It is used three times in the OT. In Isa 4:5 the idea of protection seems paramount, and *ḥūppâ* is in close conjunction with *sūkkâ*, a word for "booth" or "shelter" (v. 6). This important passage describes the future glory of Zion in terms of the wilderness wandering. Just as the pillar of cloud and fire shielded Israel from the Egyptians, a protective canopy will provide shade and refuge from storms for Mount Zion.

Twice *ḥūppâ* is related to a wedding. In Joel 2:16 it is parallel to *ḥēder,* which means "bedroom, inner chamber." The bride is instructed to go from her bedroom, the groom from his canopy to plead that the Lord might spare his people from judgment. Normal joys are interrupted during this spiritual crisis.

There is some question as to whether the canopy was a special tent where the marriage was consummated, or whether it was a protective covering over the wedding ceremony itself. Psalm 19:5 [H 6] compares the sun rising in its strength to a bridegroom coming out of his canopy. This expresses the joy of youthful love as the groom anticipates a new life with his bride, perhaps specifically referring to the sun's course as a happy wedding procession (cf. MT 25: 6–10).

H.W.

711 חפף (*ḥpp*) **II. Assumed root of the following.**

711a חַף (*ḥap*) ***innocent, pure*** (RSV), occurs only at Job 33:9, where Elihu accuses Job of claiming to be "innocent," "pure," "blameless" (NEB). Derived from the verb *ḥāpap* "to rub, to cleanse," the word means "clean."

E.Y.

712 חָפֵץ (*ḥāpēṣ*) ***I, take delight in, be pleased with, desire.***

Derivatives

712a †חָפֵץ (*ḥāpēṣ*) ***delighting in.***
712b †חֵפֶץ (*ḥēpeṣ*) ***delight.***

The basic meaning is to feel great favor towards something. Its meaning differs from the parallel roots, *ḥāmad, ḥāshaq,* and *rāṣâ,* in that they connote less emotional involvement. *ḥāmad* and *ḥāshaq* are usually translated "desire," and *rāṣâ* "accept," favor being based on need, or judgment of approval. In the case of *ḥāpēṣ*, the object solicits favor by its own intrinsic qualities. The subject is easily attracted to it because it is desirable. A fourth root, *gîl,* somewhat parallel, connotes even greater emotional involvement. Here the subject gives expression to his delight in a joyful attitude and conduct. The root *ḥāpēṣ* is used more frequently than the other words, a total of 123 times, including the verb and its derivatives.

ḥāpēṣ occurs only in the Qal stem, and it means "to experience emotional delight." This delight may be felt by men or by God. Men are said to experience it in respect to women. Shechem, son of Hamor, had "delight" in Jacob's daughter Dinah (Gen 34:19). The contestants in King Ahasuerus's beauty contest did not return to him after the first viewing unless he had "delight" in them (Est 2:14). Men also experience it with other men. When King Saul wanted David to marry his daughter Michal, he instructed his servants to inform David that the king had "delight" in him (I Sam 18:22).

This delight may be experienced in respect to matters and things. Joab used the word when he asked David why he persisted in having a census taken, or the army mustered (see *pāqad*), i.e. why he had "delight" in it (II Sam 24:3). The word is also used in reference to people delighting in certain activities. King Ahasuerus asked Haman what should be done to the man whom the king "delighted" to honor (Est 6:6). Still another use of the word is in an absolute sense, as in a repeated expression of Song: "Nor awake (my) love, until he please" (2:7; 3:5; 8:4).

The word is used of God having delight in certain people. In David's song of deliverance, he says that God provided for him because he "delighted" in him (II Sam 22:20). The Queen of Sheba expressed a blessing to God because he "delighted" in Solomon (I Kgs 10:9). God is said to experience this delight toward good works of men. For instance, he "delights" in his sabbath being kept and his law observed (Isa 56:4), in "mercy" and "knowledge of God" (Hos 6:6), and in "truth" (Ps 51:8). In respect to himself, God engages in activities in which he takes "delight" (Ps 115:3; 135:6). Samson's father, Manoah, feared death for himself and wife because the Angel of the Lord had appeared to them, but his wife replied that had God "delighted" to do this, he would not have received their sacrifices.

ḥāpēṣ. ***Delighting in, having pleasure in.*** This adjective, used similarly to the verb, occurs in ten passages, nine of which depict man's activity. With men who "delight" in God's righteous cause, God is said to be pleased (Ps 35:27). Nehemiah prays that God would be attentive to the prayer of those who "delighted" to fear his name (Neh 1:11).

ḥēpeṣ. ***Delight, pleasure.*** The noun *ḥēpeṣ* is used more frequently, thirty-nine times, and in varying contexts. It is used in such expressions as "land of delight" (Mal 3:12) or "words of delight" (Eccl 12:10), where it speaks of the pleasure which the "land" or "words" give. Of the righteous man, Ps 1:2 says his "delight" is in the law of the Lord. Persons can be objects of this delight, when they please other persons (Ps 16:3). *ḥēpeṣ* may be used for that which a person wishes strongly to do or have. For instance, Solomon gave the Queen of Sheba all her "delight" (I Kgs 10:13). Job indicates that he had not withheld the poor from their "delight" (Job 31:16). The word is used further in reference to a person's great interest, his business. An interest of Israel was in fasting, and this is said to have been her "delight" (Isa 58:3). Isaiah writes that the "delight" of God will prosper in the hand of Christ (53:10).

The word is also used in reference to that in which God finds delight. The Persian king, Cyrus, would perform that in which God had "delight" (Isa 44:28).

Bibliography: Staples, W. E., "The Meaning of Ḥēpeṣ in Ecclesiastes," JNES 24: 110–12. THAT, I, pp. 621–22.

L.J.W.

713 חָפֵץ (*ḥāpēṣ*) ***II, bend down.***

This root must be distinguished from *ḥāpēṣ* I, "take delight in," because of its one use in Job 40:17: "He bends down his tail like a cedar." The root is found also in Arabic, where it means "lower, depress." This word has no Hebrew derivative and is uncertain in meaning. Pope *Job* in AB, posits "arches" as suitable for the tail. The problem is that many take this to refer to a hippopotamus which has a small tail. Could the word "tail" mean appendage? In that case the appendage could be the trunk stretched out (Lisowsky) like a cedar.

L.J.W.

714 חָפַר (*ḥāpar*) ***I, dig, search for.*** (ASV and RSV similar.)

Derivative

714a חֲפַרְפָּרָה (*ḥăparpārâ*) ***mole,*** only in Isa 2:20 (one word in the DSS and some Greek witness).

The basic idea is to dig in the ground for some reason; and, on this count, the word is quite parallel to *kārâ*. It can also mean to search for an object. It is used twenty-two times, in the Qal stem. The word is used often for digging a well. It is so employed in connection with Abraham (Gen 21:30), and Isaac (Gen 26:15, 18, 19, etc.). It is used for digging a pit as a trap (Ps 7:15 [16]); for digging in quest of a hidden object (Jer 13:7); and even for a horse's pawing as he grazes (Job 39:21). The idea of searching is employed less often, but is clearly meant. For instance, the word is used in connection with the work of Joshua's spies, sent to search out Jericho (Josh 2:2–3). It is used regarding the eagle as it "seeketh" (searches for) its prey (Job 39:29).

L.J.W.

715 חָפֵר (*ḥāpēr*) ***II, be ashamed, feel abashed, be confounded.*** (ASV and RSV similar.)

The basic idea concerns the loss of self-possession through humiliation, embarrassment, or confusion. It is close in meaning to the root *bôsh*. In fact, in fourteen of its seventeen usages, it is parallel with *bôsh*. *bôsh* is used more frequently, which suggests that *ḥāpēr* is mainly a word of amplification. A typical example of both appearing in the same context occurs as Micah predicts a day when "seers" will "be ashamed" (*bôsh*) and "diviners" will "be confounded" (*ḥāpēr*, Mic 3:7). No discernible difference in meaning exists between the two roots in such a context. Both words include the connotation of disappointment, as used in Job 6:20; Job there speaking of "companies of Sheba" coming and looking in vain for water and thus experiencing *bôsh* and *ḥāpēr*.

One Hiphil usage is clearly causative in nature; a son being said to "cause shame" (*bôsh*) and "bring reproach" (*ḥāpēr*) on his parents, when he does not respect them properly (Prov 19:26). Two Hiphils speak of manifesting shame; for instance, Israel being urged not to fear because she would not "be ashamed" (*bôsh* and would not "be put to shame" (*ḥāpēr*); the thought being that the land would not display a scene of hardship and destruction (Isa 54:4).

L.J.W.

חֲפַרְפָּרָה (*ḥăparpārâ*). See no. 714a.

716 חָפַשׂ (*ḥapaś*) ***search, search for, disguise oneself.***

Derivative

716a †חֵפֶשׂ (*ḥēpeś*) ***plot.***

ḥāpaś is used primarily in the Piel and Hithpael (eight times each), rarely in Qal, Niphal, and Pual (six times). "To disguise oneself," i.e. "to have oneself be searched for," is the regular Hithpael usage.

The few occurrences in the Qal stem use "search" in a metaphorical sense. One can search for wisdom (Prov 2:4), or probe one's behavior (Lam 3:40), doing some serious soul-searching (Prov 20:27).

The Piel is used for concrete situations, i.e. searching through a house for plunder (I Kgs 20:6) or for prophets of Baal (II Kgs 10:23). God will search out the wicked of Jerusalem (Zeph 1:12), even as Saul searches for the fugitive David (I Sam 23:23; Amos 9:3). A lost cup and lost idols are the objects of searches by Joseph (Gen 44:12) and Laban (Gen 31:35).

In the difficult Ps 64:6 [H 7], some mental searching is in progress. The wicked are devising "a well conceived plot," perhaps a "well researched" scheme to trap God's servant. Three times in the verse the root *ḥāpaś* appears.

The Hithpael "disguise oneself" usually refers to kings who effect the disguise by laying aside their royal garb. Saul fooled the witch of Endor (I Sam 28:8), but neither Ahab (I Kgs 22:30 = II Chr 18:29) nor Josiah (II Chr 35:22) survived the battles which they had entered in disguise. Once, a prophet pulled a headband over his eyes to keep Ahab from recognizing him (I Kgs 10:38).

ḥēpeś. ***Plot, shrewd device.*** This masculine noun occurs in Ps 64:6 [H 7] only, in conjunction with the Pual participle.

H.W.

717 *חָפַשׁ (*ḥāpash*) ***be free.***

Derivatives

717a חֹפֶשׁ (*ḥōpesh*) ***saddle cloths,*** only in Ezk 27:20. Meaning dubious.

717b †חֻפְשָׁה (*ḥūpshâ*) ***freedom,*** only in Lev 19:20.

717c †חָפְשִׁי (*ḥopshî*) ***free.***

717d חָפְשִׁית (*ḥopshît*) ***freedom, separateness,*** only in II Kgs 15:5=II Chr 26:21.

ḥāpash occurs only in the Pual stem in Lev 19:20, referring to a female slave who is pledged to a husband but commits fornication with another man. Both she and the man who violated her are to be punished. They are not put to death, since she is not free and presumably could not defend herself.

ḥūpshâ. ***Freedom.*** This feminine noun appears only in Lev 19:20, referring to a slave girl who had not been freed.

ḥopshî. ***Free.*** An adjective, probably related to Ugaritic *ḫbṯ* "soldier" or "free commoner" (UT 19: no. 930), and the *ḫubshu* of the Amarna letters. The majority of its sixteen occurrences refer to freedom from slavery. A male or female Hebrew slave was to be freed in the seventh year without payment (Ex 21:2, 5). In fact, the owner was to supply the released slave with provisions of grain and wine and animals from the flock (Deut 15:12–13, 18). Evidently owners were reluctant to follow this command. During the siege of Jerusalem in the reign of Zedekiah, Hebrew slaves were given their freedom, but when the Babylonians temporarily withdrew, the owners quickly reclaimed their slaves. Jeremiah blasted this hypocrisy (Jer 34:9–11, 14, 16).

If a man knocked out a slave's tooth or destroyed his eye, the slave was set free as compensation (Ex 21:26–27). Isaiah speaks of letting the oppressed go free during a genuine fast (58:6).

Sheol is a place where the slave is finally free from his master (Job 3:19), but the "freedom" of death is equated with being cut off from the Lord in the difficult Ps 88:5 [H 6].

David's father was released (*ya'ăśeh ḥopshî*) from taxes or other obligations as a reward for David's slaying Goliath (I Sam 17:25).

Bibliography: Albright, W. F., "Canaanite Ḥofši, 'free', in the Amarna Tablets," JPOS 4: 169. ______, "Canaanite Ḥapši and Hebrew Hofši Again," JPOS 6: 106. Gordis, Robert, "Studies in Hebrew Roots of Contrasted Meanings," JQR 27: 33–58. Henry, K. H., "Land Tenure in the Old Testament," PEQ 86: 5–15. Mendelsohn, I., "The Canaanite Terms for 'Free Proletarian'," BASOR 83: 36–39.

H.W.

חָפְשִׁי (*ḥopshî*). See no. 717c.
חָפְשִׁית (*ḥopshît*). See no. 717d.
חֵץ (*ḥēs*). See no. 721b.

718 חָצֵב (*ḥāṣēb*) ***dig, divide, hew, hewer, make, mason.*** (ASV and RSV similar except that RSV translates "set up" in Prov 9:1, "flashes forth" in Ps 29:7, and occasionally "stonecutters.")

Derivative

718a מַחְצֵב (*maḥṣēb*) ***hewing.*** Always occurs in the phrase *'abnê maḥṣēb* "hewn stones."

The basic meaning of the word is "to hew," "to cut or dig by blows with a tool or instrument." It is used in this basic sense in Isa 10:15 of cutting with an axe and in Job 19:24 of engraving with an instrument of iron. It is used most often in the sense of hewing out cisterns or digging wells (Deut 6:11; Isa 5:2; Jer 2:13; Neh 9:25; II Chr 26:10) and is used once with the connotation of hewing out a tomb (Isa 22:16).

The word also has the sense of "to mine" or "quarry," as in mining for copper (Deut 8:9) and quarrying for stone (II Chr 2:2, 18 [H 1, 17]). In the participial form the word connotes "stonecutters" or "masons" (e.g. I Chr 22:2).

It may be used in the sense of "to fashion," as with pillars (Prov 9:1), and "to hew a carcass" (Isa 51:9).

Metaphorically the verb connotes the devastating effect that the words of the prophets had on Israel (Hos 6:5). It is also used to describe the hewing of the nation of Israel as from a mass of rock (Isa 51:1). In Ps 29:7 it is used of the cleaving of fire, apparently a reference to forked lightning which was caused by the voice of the Lord.

T.E.M.

719 חָצָה (*ḥāṣâ*) ***divide, live half (of one's life).***

Derivatives

719a חֵצוֹת (*ḥēṣôt*) ***division, middle.***
719b †חֲצִי (*ḥăṣî*) ***half.***
719c חֵצִי (*ḥēṣî*) ***arrow,*** an alternative form of *ḥēṣ*.
719d מֶחֱצָה (*meḥĕṣâ*) ***half, of spoils,*** only in Num 31:36, 43.
719e †מַחֲצִית (*maḥăṣît*) ***half, middle.***

This verb occurs primarily in the Qal stem, eleven times, and also four times in the Niphal. It is used of dividing up quantities of all sorts, including groups of people.

The concept of "dividing" is applied to things, people, and time. Precise quantities are sometimes specified, such as "half a hin" of oil or wine which accompanied an offering (Num 15:9–10; 28:14). Every time a census was taken, exactly half a shekel (*maḥăṣît*) was paid per person (Ex 30:13). When Israel defeated the Midianites, they divided the plunder equally between the warriors and the rest of the congregation (Num 31:27, 29f., 42, 47). The width of each board of the tabernacle was one and one-half cubits (Ex 26:16).

Half of the blood of an offering was poured in basins, the other half sprinkled on the altar (Ex 24:6). To insult David, the Ammonites shaved off half the beards of his servants and cut off their clothes "in the middle," i.e. at the hip (II Sam 10:4). The Jordan River was divided by Elijah and then Elisha (II Kgs 2:8, 14), and the Mount of Olives will be split in half from east to west at the Lord's return (Zech 14:4).

Groups of persons are divided also. Jacob divided the children among his wives at Esau's approach (Gen 33:1), and Gideon split his three hundred into three companies (Jud 7:16; 9:43). "Half the people of Israel" joined Judah in reinstating David as king (II Sam 19:40 [H 41]), and during a civil war in Israel, half followed Tibni while half supported Omri (I Kgs 16:21). The empire of Alexander the Great was divided into four parts (Dan 11:4). Also in Gen 33:1 the division is into *four* groups, not the *two* which is the more common usage. Ezekiel envisions the day when Judah and Israel will no longer be two separate kingdoms (37:22).

The "half-tribe" of Manasseh" is a technical term referring to the part of the tribe that settled in Transjordan. Usually *ḥăṣî* is used, (Num 32:33; Josh 1:12) but sometimes *maḥăṣît* (Josh 21:25; I Chr 6:71 [H 55]).

References to time include the expression "in the middle of the night." While some translations render this "midnight," it was not necessarily midnight when the Angel of the Lord slew the firstborn in Egypt (Ex 12:29). Nor did Samson carry off the gate of Gaza at precisely twelve o'clock AM (Jud 16:3). The Psalmist prays that God will not remove him "in the midst of my days" (102:24 [H 25]). It is rather the wicked who "will not live out half their days" (Ps 55:23 [H 24]). Fortunes illegally obtained will disappear in the middle of one's life (Jer 17:11).

The important reference in Dan 9:27 to "the middle of the week" apparently signifies the midpoint of the seven-year period called "the Great Tribulation" (Dan 12:1, 7 [cf. v. 11]; Rev 11:3). The last half of this period appears to be detailed as 1290 days in Dan 12:11.

ḥăṣî. ***Half, middle.*** This masculine noun occurs 123 times and shows a broad range of usages.

maḥaṣît. ***Half, middle.*** *maḥăṣît,* a feminine noun, is used fourteen times. It is a close synonym of *ḥăṣî.*

H.W.

חֲצוֹת (*ḥēṣôt*). See no. 719a.
חֲצִי (*ḥăṣî*). See no. 719b.
חֵצִי (*ḥēṣî*). See no. 719c.
חָצִיר (*ḥāṣîr*). See nos. 723b, 724a, 725a.

720 חצן (*ḥṣn*). **Assumed root of the following.**
720a חֵצֶן (*ḥēṣen*) ***bosom of a garment*** (Ps 129:7).
720b חֹצֶן (*ḥōṣen*) ***bosom*** (Neh 5:13; Isa 49:22).

721 חָצַץ (*ḥāṣaṣ*) ***divide.***

Derivatives

721a חָצָץ (*ḥāṣāṣ*) ***gravel.***
721b †חֵץ (*ḥēṣ*) ***arrow.***
721c *חָצַץ (*ḥāṣaṣ*) ***shoot arrows*** (Piel only, Jud 5:11). Perhaps this verb is derived from *ḥeṣ.*

ḥēṣ. ***Arrow.*** Most of its fifty-six uses occur in poetry. Arrows are deadly weapons normally shot from a bow, but Uzziah built a catapult that could shoot arrows or stones (II Chr 26:15). Powerful armies were armed with sharp arrows (Isa 5:28), though God kept Assyria from shooting a single arrow at Hezekiah's Jerusalem (II Kgs 19:32 = Isa 37:33). Israel's army (Num 24:8) and kings (Ps 45:5 [H 6]) possessed sharp arrows also. The spelling *ḥēṣî* derived from *ḥāṣâ* is also used.

Arrows were consulted by the king of Babylon as a means of divination, along with idols and livers (Ezk 21:21 [H 26]). Elisha had King Joash shoot an arrow and strike the ground with his arrows (II Kgs 13:15, 17–18) to symbolize victory.

Wicked men shoot their arrows to fell the righteous (Ps 11:2). Often this refers metaphorically to the bitter, violent words hurled at the godly (Ps 57:4 [H 5]; 64:3 [H 4]; Jer 9:7). God is the one who nullifies these dangerous arrows (Ps 58:7 [H 8]; 91:5) and makes his arrows drunk with the blood of his enemies (Deut 32:42).

Yet God's arrows of judgment are aimed at Israel (Deut 32:23), and the Psalmist, Job, and Jeremiah all complain about God's arrows sunk deep into them (Ps 38:2 [H 3]; Job 6:4; Lam 3:12). In theophanies, flashes of lightning are often referred to as arrows (Ps 18:14 [H 15]; 144:6; Hab 3:11).

Psalm 127:4 compares children to the arrows in a soldier's hand, and in Isa 49:2 the Servant of the Lord is called a select (polished?) arrow.

Toward the end of the OT period, the Persian armies depended heavily on their archers. They carried large quivers on their backs and were trained to shoot with great rapidity.

H.W.

חֲצֹצְרָה (*ḥăṣōṣrâ*). See no. 726a.
חצצר (*ḥṣṣr*). See no. 726b.

722 חצר (*ḥṣr*) **I. Assumed root of the following.**
722a †חָצֵר (*ḥāṣēr*) ***court, enclosure.***

Cognate with Ugaritic *ḥẓr* and its dialectal variant *ḥṭr* (UT 19: nos. 855, 852*a*) "court"; cf. Aramaic *ḥuṭrā,* Phoenician *ḥṣr,* Arabic *ḥaẓīrat* "an enclosure for sheep." It occurs in the singular 120 times, in the feminine plural 20 times, and in the masculine plural 5 times. The LXX usually translates it *aulē,* and occasionally *epaulis* or *skēnē.*

Near Eastern houses were built around a court. Such a court might contain a well (II Sam 17:18). The plague of frogs died out from the houses, the courtyards (KJV "villages"), and the fields (Ex 8:13 [H 9]).

Most of the references to courts concern sacred or royal buildings. Ahasuerus's palace in Susa had an "outer" and an "inner" court. Haman waited in the "outer" court (Est 6:4), for no one was permitted to enter the "inner" court without the king's permission (Est 4:11).

The numerous references in Ex and Num are to the court of the tabernacle, a large rectangular space one hundred cubits by fifty cubits. They describe in particular the hangings and the pillars around its periphery. The court was functional, allowing space for the worshipers to gather, to slaughter animals, and to eat. It was symbolic of the worshiper approaching God and yet God being set apart in the temple itself.

Solomon's building complex at Jerusalem included: the "inner" court of the temple (I Kgs 6:36; 7:12); the court of the palace (I Kgs 7:8), perhaps the "middle" court of II Kgs 20:4 (following the Qere); and the "great" court covering the entire area of the complex (I Kgs 7:9, 12).

The temple that Ezekiel beheld in his visions had an outer and an inner court (Ezk 40:17–19). The people assembled in the outer court, which was surrounded by thirty rooms (Ezk 40:17). On the sabbath and the new moon the gate of the inner court was opened sothat the prince could worship at its threshold (Ezk 46:1–3).

Although many have asserted that Solomon's temple had only one court, Ezekiel's vision and other references (I Kgs 6:36; 7:12; II Kgs 21:5; 23:12; II Chr 4:9; 33.5) indicate that the first temple had an inner court of priests and an outer court. The second temple of the New Testament era had a court of the gentiles and an inner court which was subdivided into courts of the women, Israel and the priests.

Even in the OT era the Psalmist had invited the nations to come into the courts of the Lord (Ps 96:8). The Psalmist declares that he longs for the courts of the Lord (Ps 84:2 [H 3]), for even a day in his courts is better than a thousand elsewhere (Ps 84:10 [H 11]).

E.Y.

723 חצר (*ḥṣr*) **II. Assumed root of the following.**
723a †חָצֵר (*ḥāṣēr*) ***village.***
723b חָצִיר (*ḥāṣîr*) ***settled abode, haunt*** (Isa 34:13; 35:7).

ḥāṣēr. ***Village, settlement.*** Cognate with the Akkadian *haṣārum* found at Mari; cf. Arabic *ḥaḏara* "to dwell" and S Arabic *ḥḏr* "enclosed camp." It occurs forty-six times (thirty-two times in Joshua), always in the masculine plural. The LXX usually translates it *kōmē,* occasionally *epaulis.*

In some cases the *ḥāṣēr* may have been no more than a settlement of the tents of Bedouins (Gen 25:16; Isa 42:11). In contrast to cities, villages were unwalled (Lev 25:31). In the distribution of land in Joshua, 114 cities are allotted to Judah together with daughter or satellite villages (Josh 15:32, 36, 41, 44).

Bibliography: Orlinsky, H., "*Ḥāṣēr* in the Old Testament," JAOS 59: 22–37. Wolf, C. U., "Village," in IDB, IV, p. 784.

E.Y.

724 חצר (*ḥṣr*) **III. Assumed root of the following.**
724a †חָצִיר (*ḥāṣîr*) ***grass.***

Derived from a root "to be green"; cf. Arabic *ḥaḍira.* It appears as *ḥṣr* in the Old Aramaic Sefire I.A 28 text, and in the Akkadian treaty of Ashurnirari V (Rev 4.20) as *ṣēri* "green" in the sense of grass.

In Palestine grass grows rapidly after the winter and spring rains. It wilts just as rapidly before the heat of summer or the blistering *khamsin,* the dry desert wind.

Because of its ephemeral nature, grass is often used as a symbol of the transitoriness of man's existence: the wicked will soon wither like the grass (Ps 37:2); men are like the grass which flourishes in the morning but fades in the evening (Ps 90:5; cf. Ps 103:15). The fleeting nature of man, which is like that of the grass, is contrasted with the abiding character of God's Word (Isa 40:6–8; cf. Jas 1:10–11). Inasmuch as it is the Creator who comforts us we are not to be afraid of mortal man who is like the grass (Isa 51:12).

The flat roofs of the Palestinian houses would often sprout some grass which would wither even before it grew much because it had no depth of soil. So Israel's enemies would wither before the Lord (II Kgs 19:26; Isa 37:27; Ps 129:6).

725 חצר (*ḥṣr*) **IV. Assumed root of the following.**
725a †חָצִיר (*ḥāṣîr*) ***leek.***

From a root "to be narrow," as the leek looks like an elongated onion. It appears but once, in Num 11:5 in the list of Egyptian foods which the Israelites missed in Sinai. The *Allium porrum,* called *iaqet* by the Egyptians, is featured in such texts as the Medinet Habu calendar, the Ebers papyrus, the Tale of the Shipwrecked Sailor, etc. Pliny (*Natural History* 19.33) mentions that the most esteemed leeks come from Egypt, and says that Nero ate nothing but chives, i.e. chopped leeks, on certain days of the month.

See also *deshe', yereq, 'ēśeb.*

Bibliography: *Fauna and Flora of the Bible,* London: United Bible Societies, 1972. Shewell-Cooper, W. E., "Flora," in ZPEB, II, pp. 571,578.

E.Y.

726 חצר (*ḥṣr*) **V. Assumed root of the following.**
726a †חֲצֹצְרָה (*ḥăṣōṣrâ*) ***trumpet.***
726b *חצצר (*ḥṣṣr*) ***sound the trumpet*** This denominative verb occurs only in the Piel and the Hiphil. (*Qere* *חָצַר).

ḥăṣōṣrâ. ***Trumpet.*** Perhaps from a root "to be narrow," describing its shape, the word occurs twenty-nine times, always in the plural except Hos 5:8. Of these occurrences sixteen are in I and II Chr. It is translated by the LXX *salpigx* and by the Vulgate *tuba,* both "trumpet."

The trumpet was made of beaten silver (Num 10:2). According to Josephus in *Antiquities* 3.12.6 (291), "In length a little short of a cubit, it is a narrow tube, slightly thicker than a flute. . . ." The trumpets of Herod's temple are depicted on the Arch of Titus and on silver denarius coins of Bar Cochba. Early Egyptian examples were found in Tutankhamon's tomb. It should be distinguished from the *shôpār,* the curved ram's horn trumpet.

Moses was commanded to make a pair of trumpets (Num 10:2). The number of trumpets was increased to 7 (I Chr 15:24) and to 120 (II Chr 5:12).

With the possible exception of their use at the

coronation of Joash (II Kgs 11:14; II Chr 23:13), trumpets were used by the priests (Num 10:8; I Chr 15:24; 16:6; II Chr 23:13; cf. Sir 50:16).

Trumpets were used for a variety of purposes. They were used to summon the tribes, or their leaders, and to signal the breaking of camp (Num 10:2–4). Trumpets were blown while the burnt offering was being offered in Hezekiah's rite (II Chr 29:27–28; cf. Num 10:10).

Although the ram's horn (*shôpār*) was usually employed for military purposes, priests sometimes used the trumpets in times of war so that the Lord would respond (Num 10:9; 31:6; II Chr 13:12, 14).

In Hos 5:8 the prophet commands the blowing of the horn and the trumpet as a signal of the enemy's approach.

The trumpets must have emitted a high, shrill sound. The signals depended upon the number of trumpets used, the types of sounds, and their sequence. The *t*ᵉ*rû'â* (RSV "alarm") seems to have been a rapid succession of three notes (*Mishnah*, Rosh ha-Shanah 4.9). At the first "alarm" the camps on the east set out, etc. (Num 10:5). The ordinary way of blowing the trumpet (*tāqa'*) produced a sustained sound. Mazar's excavation discovered in 1968 a fragment from Herod's temple with the inscription "for the house of the blowing (of the trumpet)," designating where the priest stood on the parapet to blow the trumpet: *LBYT HTQY'H*.

See also *shôpār, qeren, yôbēl*.

Bibliography: Finesinger, Sol Baruch, "Musical Instruments in the OT," HUCA 3: 21–75, esp. pp. 61–63. Yadin, Yigael, *The Scroll of the War of the Sons of Light against the Sons of Darkness*, London: Oxford University, 1962, pp. 87–113. TDNT, VII, pp. 76–85.

E.Y.

חֹק (*ḥōq*). See no. 728a.
חֵק (*ḥēq*). See no. 629a.

727 חָקָה (*ḥāqâ*) ***carved, portrayed, set a print*** (ASV and RSV similar, also render "set a bound").

The root is parallel to *ḥāqaq* "engrave" and occurs four times in the OT: three times as Pual participle and once as a Hithpael form. The doors of the temple were adorned with carved work (*hammeḥuqqeh*, I Kgs 6:35). Ezekiel saw the idols of Israel portrayed by carving on the walls of the temple chamber (Ezk 8:10). Oholibah in her idolatry saw men portrayed on the wall (Ezk 23:14).

The Hithpael form (Job 13:27) is difficult to interpret. GKC 54*f* suggests the meaning, "to draw a line for oneself." The verb was rendered *aphikou* ("to reach unto") by the LXX and *considerasti* ("consider") by the Vulgate. Older interpreters paralleled the verse to Job 14:15, deriving the meaning that God had limited Job by drawing a line about his feet that he could not cross. That act may be compared to Solomon's limitation of Shimei (I Kgs 2:36–37). Hence the KJV: "Thou puttest a print for the souls of my feet," and ASV and RSV: "Thou markest a line about the soles of my feet." The NEB and M. Pope in *Job*, AB assume a custom of cutting a brand into the heels of a slave so that the heels make identifiable tracks in the earth. Similarly, it is impossible for Job to escape.

J.P.L.

728 חָקַק (*ḥāqaq*) ***engrave, portray, decree, inscribe, govern.*** (ASV and RSV similar, but ASV translates the participial form as "governor," and RSV uses "commander" when the context is military.)

Derivatives

728a †חֹק (*ḥōq*) ***statute.***
728b †חֻקָּה (*ḥūqqâ*) ***enactment.***

ḥāqaq occurs in the Qal, Polel, and Hophal stems a total of nineteen times, and has the primary meaning of cutting in or engraving in stone as hewing a tomb in the rock (Isa 22:16) and as drawing a picture on a brick (Ezk 4:1) or a wall (Ezk 23:14). It may also describe writing on the palm of one's hand (Isa 49:16) or in a book (Isa 30:8; Job 19:23). It is set alongside *kātab* ("write") in Isa 30:8. God has drawn a circle upon the face of the deep and has marked out the foundations of the earth (Prov 8:27, 29).

This root occurs in the Polel stem. *ḥāqaq* refers to enacting a decree (Isa 10:1; Prov 8:15; cf. Jer 31:35), hence the participial form (*m*ᵉ*ḥōqēq*) designates a ruler, lawgiver (Gen 49:10; Isa 33:22), or commander (Jud 5:9, 14). The root may also parallel *shēbeṭ* ("staff") designating the ruler's staff which is the symbol of ruling (Num 21:18; Ps 60:7 [H 9]; 108:8 [H 9]).

Genesis 49:10 is a significant messianic passage (see R. L. Harris, "Excursus" in J. O. Buswell, *Systematic Theology of the Christian Religion*, II, Zondervan, 1963, p. 544). Whether *m*ᵉ*ḥōqēq* is translated "lawgiver" (KJV) or "ruler's staff" (RSV), it is clearly a symbol of rule and therefore promises the kingship to Judah. Critical authors attempt to date this prediction after the event, but Gen 49 is widely admitted to be earlier than the monarchy. The LXX reading makes the verse even clearer by taking "between his feet" as a euphemism for "loins." The king would belong to Judah's descendants. Interestingly, a fragment from the Dead Sea Scrolls quotes this verse and applies it to "the coming of the legitimately anointed (king), the scion of David" for whom they hoped (T. H. Gaster, *The Dead Sea Scriptures*, rev. ed., Doubleday, 1964, p. 334).

The Pual participle describes that which is decreed.

ḥōq. ***Statute, custom, law, decree*** (ASV and RSV translate also ordinance, due and bound.) The masculine noun *ḥōq* is from the root *ḥāqaq* which means "to scratch" or "to engrave," hence "to write." It occurs 128 times, and its feminine counterpart *ḥūqqâ* occurs 102 times.

It was a common practice among the ancients to engrave laws upon slabs of stone or metal and to set them up in a public place (e.g. the code of Hammurabi, engraved on diorite stone). But this root is not limited to the writing of laws on stone. The LXX chiefly used three words to render *ḥōq: prostagma* "order" or "injunction," *dikaiōma* "regulation" or "requirement," and *nomimon* "commandment." The use of *ḥōq* in Qumran is similar to that in the OT.

ḥōq occurs in sequences with other words for law: *d*ᵉ*bārîm* (words), *tôrâ* (law), *mishpāṭ* (judgment), *'ēdût* (testimony), and *miṣwâ* (commandment). These words are used almost indiscriminately. In a few cases *ḥōq* and *mishpāṭ* are used as if intended to summarize two kinds of Israelite law (Ex 15:25; Josh 24:25; Ezr 7:10). But efforts to distinguish clearly between their connotations have not been entirely successful. Albrecht Alt has suggested such a distinction in his categories of casuistic and apodictic laws. But he admits that *ḥōq* is not limited to the apodictic form. More recent efforts to make *ḥōq* designate that to which men must respond in obedience is in general true, but fits only some of the cases.

As "rule" or "prescription" *ḥōq* may designate duties imposed by God (Ex 18:16) or man (Gen 47:26; II Chr 35:25; Jud 11:39). In the case of the latter, it conveys the import of "statute" or "custom," as in the phrase "statutes of your fathers" (Ezk 20:18; I Sam 30:25). The verb most frequently used with *ḥōq* is *shāmar* "to keep," which stresses the concept that *ḥuqqîm* (plural) are precepts and rules to be obeyed. When used in connection with *b*ᵉ*rît* (covenant) it denotes the demands which God made upon his covenant people. The decree of the Lord gives the king his rights and duties over the people of God (Ps 2:7).

ḥōq at times designates a legal right. Joseph gives Pharoah a fifth of the land's produce (Gen 47:26). Isaiah (10:1) alludes to iniquitous decrees by which the poor were legally fleeced. Even natural laws such as the "bound" of the sea (Prov 8:29) give the sea its right of sway. There are regulations for the heavenly bodies (Ps 148:6), the rain (Job 28:26), and the sea (Jer 5:22; Job 38:10).

ḥōq at times designates "privilege" or "due." The Egyptian priests had a right which exempted them from selling their land (Gen 47:22). The priest's share in the sacrifice was a perpetual right (Ex 29:28; cf. Lev 24:9), established by God's decree.

ḥōq as "custom" is demonstrated in the case of the memorial for Jephthah's daughter (Jud 11:39). It is also seen in the demand that Israel not walk in the customs (*ḥūqqâ*) of Canaan (Lev 18:3, 30; 20:23).

ḥūqqâ. ***Enactment, statute, ordinance manner.*** (ASV and RSV similar, but when dealing with pagan rites render the root "custom" (Lev 18:30; 20:23; II Kgs 17:8; Jer 10:3).

A feminine noun from the root *ḥāqaq* "enscribe" or "engrave." *ḥūqqâ* is used in the combination *ḥūqqôt 'ôlām* (perpetual statute) to designate an ordinance from God which is perpetually binding, e.g. the regulations of Passover (Ex 12:14), Unleavened Bread (Ex 12:17; cf. 13:10), Booths (Lev 23:41), Day of Atonement (Lev 16:29, 31, 34), the Aaronic priesthood (Ex 29:9), the perpetual light (Ex 27:31; Lev 24:3), the priest's linen clothing (Ex 28:43), blowing of trumpets (Num 10:8), laws for the sojourner (Num 15:15), and laws of uncleanness (Num 19:10, 21).

Certain prohibitions are also called perpetual statutes, e.g. against eating of fat and blood (Lev 3:17), against a priest drinking wine and strong drink when entering the tent of meeting (Lev 10:9), against sacrificing to devils (satyrs?) (Lev 17:7), against eating certain foods (Lev 23:14), against Levites inheriting land (Num 18:23).

There are also ordinances of Passover (Ex 12:43; Num 9:12, 14; cf. 9:3); the altar (Ezk 43:18); the house of the Lord (Ezk 44:5); the law (Num 31:21; 19:2); judgment (Num 27:11); life (i.e. leading to life, Ezk 33:15), and the statutes of Omri (i.e. the customs of Omri, Mic 6:16).

In certain passages *ḥūqqâ* parallels judgment (*mishpāṭ* II Sam 22:23; Ps 18:22 [H 23]) and commandment (*miṣwâ,* Deut 6:2; 28:15, 45; 30:10). It occurs in legal sequences "commandments, statutes, and ordinances" (Deut 8:11; 30:16); "commandments, statutes, and ordinances" (Deut 8:11; 30:16); "commandments, testimonies, and statutes" (Jer 44:23); and "charge, statutes, ordinances, and commandments" (Deut 11:1; cf. I Kgs 2:3).

Bibliography: Blank, Sheldon H., "The LXX Renderings of Old Testament Terms for Law," HUCA 7: 259–60. Braulik, Georg, "Die Ausdrücke für 'Gesetz' im Buch Deuteronomium," Bib 51: 39–66. Falk, Zeev W., "Hebrew Legal Terms," JSS 5: 350. Jones, G. H., "The Decree of Yahweh (Ps II.7)," VT 15: 336–44. Morgenstern, Julian, "The Book of the Covenant, II," HUCA 7: 19–258. ______, "The Decalogue of the Holiness Code," HUCA 26: 1–27.

Van der Ploeg, J., "Studies in Hebrew Law," CBQ 12: 248–59, 416–27; 13: 28–43, 164–71, 296–307. Victor, Peddi, "A Note on ḥōq in the Old Testament," VT 16: 358–61. THAT, I, pp. 626–32.

J.P.L.

729 חָקַר (ḥāqar) ***search, investigate, examine.***

Derivatives

729a †חֵקֶר (ḥēqer) ***searching, inquiry.***
729b מֶחְקָר (meḥqār) ***range*** (as place to be explored). Only in Ps 95:4 (cf. Job 38:16).

ḥāqar is used primarily in the Qal stem, but also four times in the Niphal, and once in the Piel (Eccl 12:9). It can refer to initial phases of a search or the end result, but always connotes a diligent, difficult probing.

A concept common to wisdom literature, which is concerned with investigating legal cases (Prov 18:17) and the plight of the needy (Job 29:16), searching out a particular subject (Job 5:27; 8:8; 28:27), or examining proverbs (Eccl 12:9). A search can have as its object information about a city (II Sam 10:3 = I Chr 19:3) or a country (Jud 18:2) or even mining prospects (Job 28:3). Sometimes the search is fruitless, e.g. the attempt to find out the weight of the bronze used for the temple (I Kgs 7:47) or to search out the foundations of the earth (Jer 31:37).

Often a person's character or feelings are being probed. Jonathan sought to "sound out" his father's attitude toward David (I Sam 20:12). The Lord is the one who searches and knows us (Ps 139:1; Job 13:9). He probes the heart and examines the mind (Jer 17:10), and if there is sin and unfaithfulness, he is not deceived (Ps 44:21 [H 22]).

ḥēqer. ***Searching, inquiry.*** This noun is used of the "heart-searching" of the tribe of Reuben, which failed to aid Deborah and Barak against the Canaanites (Jud 5:16).

Usually, the emphasis is on the impossible. The heart of kings is unsearchable (Prov 25:3). Six of its ten usages refer to the unsearchable nature of God, e.g. his greatness (Ps 145:3) and his understanding (Isa 40:28). His miraculous deeds are inscrutable (Job 5:9; 9:10), and the number of his years past finding out (Job 36:26).

H.W.

חֹר (ḥōr). See nos. 757a, 758a.
חֻר (ḥūr). See no. 758b.

730 חרא (ḥr') **Assumed root of the following.**
730a חֶרֶא (ḥere') ***dung*** (Isa 36:12; II Kgs 18:27), i.e. *ḥ^erê yônîm* "dove's dung."
730b מַחֲרָאָה (maḥărā'â) ***draught house*** (II Kgs 10:27).

731 חָרֵב (ḥārēb) ***I, dry up; be in ruins; lay waste; make desolate.***

Derivatives

731a †חָרֵב (ḥārēb) ***dry, desolate.***
731b †חֹרֶב (ḥōreb) ***I, dryness, desolation.***
731c †חֹרֵב (ḥōreb) ***II, Horeb.***
731d †חָרְבָּה (ḥorbâ) ***ruins.***
731e †חָרָבָה (ḥārābâ) ***dry land.***
731f †חֲרָבוֹן (ḥērābôn) ***drought.*** Used only in Ps 32:4, as a metaphor of fever heat.

ḥārab is used in the Qal, Niphal, Pual, Hiphil, and Hophal stems. Cognate with Akkadian *ḫarābu* "be desolate"; Ugaritic *ḫrb* "become dry" (UT 19: no. 1000); Arabic *ḫariba* "be void of water and vegetation." The verb occurs thirty-seven times, including twelve times in Isa. BDB divides into two roots: be dry and be in ruins. We follow KB which takes this word as one root with a semantic extension.

The verb *ḥārab* originally meant "to be dry." Secondarily it and its derivatives denoted, on the one hand, the heat which caused dryness, and on the other, the desolation of waste areas, the devastation caused by wars.

The verb is used in the Qal stem of the waters which dried up after the flood (Gen 8:13), and in the Pual stem of the bowstrings which had not been dried which were used to tie up Samson (Jud 16:7). Gideon sought to test the Lord with the fleece which was alternately wet then dry (*ḥōreb*, Jud 6:37, 39–40). In Isa 48:21 *ḥorbâ* means "deserts."

The verb in the Hiphil stem is used of Sennacherib's boast that his warriors were so numerous that they had dried up rivers with the soles of their feet (II Kgs 19:24; Isa 37:25). Job 14:11 compares the drying up of a river to death.

One of the characteristics of the might of Yahweh is his ability to dry up the seas and the rivers (Isa 44:27; 50:2; Nah 1:4). He dried up the Sea of Reeds (AV, "Red Sea") for the passage of the Israelites (Ps 106:9; Isa 51:10).

When Judah forsook the Lord's living waters, Jeremiah called upon the heavens to be appalled, literally "be exceedingly dried up," at such perfidy (Jer 2:12).

In some passages *ḥōreb* refers to "heat" rather than to "dryness." Jacob complained to Laban, that he had been consumed by the heat (KJV "drought") of the day and the cold of the night (Gen 31:40). Jehoiakim's corpse was to be exposed to the heat of the day and the cold of the night (Jer 36:30). Job complains, "My bones are burned with fever" (JB, Job 30:30).

In Isa 4:6; 25:4–5 the Lord's protection is likened to the refreshing shade from the heat, provided by the clouds.

Especially in the writings of Isa, Jer, and Ezk who both foresaw and witnessed the devastations of invading Assyrian and Babylonian armies, the word *ḥārab* and its derivatives denote desolation and ruin.

A rare use of the word in an earlier period is its occurrence as a Hiphil participle to describe Samson as the "ravager" (Jud 16:24, RSV) of the Philistine country.

In the postexilic period Nehemiah is saddened to learn that Jerusalem is still in ruins (Neh 2:3, 17), but Ezra thanks God for his grace in permitting the Jews to repair the temple's ruins (Ezra 9:9).

However, when the Jews' dedication to rebuilding the temple flagged, the prophet Haggai rebuked them with a paronomasia or play on words. He proclaimed that because the Lord's house had remained "in ruins" (*ḥārēb,* Hag 1:4, 9) the Lord would bring a "drought" (*ḥōreb,* Hag 1:11) upon the land.

Yahweh warned that he would bring desolation upon his own people if they turned to idols (Lev 26:31, 33). Such desolation was sent in turn against Israel (Amos 7:9), and Judah (Jer 7:34; 22:5; 25:9; Ezk 6:6) because of their disobedience and apostasy.

In Judah's case the desolation was to be limited in time (Jer 25:11), and remedial in purpose (Ezk 12:20; Zeph 3:6–7). Jer 33:10 promises that in the desolate place "without man or inhabitant or beast" voices of gladness would be heard once more. Ezk 36:38 prophesies that the waste cities will be filled with "flocks of men" and Ezk 36:35 that the desolate land will blossom like the "garden of Eden."

But it is above all the prophet Isaiah who voices the promise of a resurrection from the ruins of God's judgment. It is the Lord who will raise up the ruins of Jerusalem (44:26). Their desolate places will one day be too limited for the increased population (49:19). The Lord will comfort Zion's waste places and transform them into an Eden (51:3). Jerusalem's ruins will break forth into singing (52:9), as they will be rebuilt (58:12; 61:4).

In Zeph 2:14 the Hebrew reads, "Desolation (*ḥōreb*) is on the threshold." Following the Vulgate and the LXX, which reads *korakes* representing the Hebrew *'ōrēb,* the RSV, JB, and NAB translate "raven" and the NEB "bustard" as an indication that Nineveh will become the lodging place of wild birds and animals.

See also *dālal, yābēsh, shā'â, shāmam.*

ḥārēb. ***Dry, waste, desolate.*** The adjective occurs twice in the sense of "dry" (Lev 7:10; Prov 17:1) and eight times in the sense of "desolate."

ḥōreb. ***Dryness, drought, heat, desolation.*** This noun occurs sixteen times. Compare the proper noun Horeb.

ḥōreb. ***Horeb.*** An alternative name for Mount Sinai, derived from *ḥārab* and signifying a desolate region. It occurs seventeen times, including nine times in Deut. The documentary hypothesis suggests that this name for the mountain of God is characteristic of D and E (Ex 3:1; 17:6; 33:6), while Sinai is used in the J and P sections (see, however, Deut 33:2).

In some passages Horeb seems to designate an area larger than Mount Sinai (Deut 4:10; 9:8; 18:16). Moses struck the rock in the region of Horeb (Ex 17:6), but not on Mount Sinai which the Israelites did not reach until later (Ex 19:1).

Suggestions as to the location of Horeb/Sinai have included: 1. a volcanic mountain al-Hrob in Midian southeast of Aqaba; 2. Jebel el-Halal, thirty miles west of Kadesh-barnea; 3. Sinn Bishr (2000 feet), thirty miles southeast of Suez; and 4. one of three peaks in southern Sinai.

Deuteronomy 1:2 indicates that it was an eleven-day journey from Horeb to Kadesh-barnea. Elijah in his flight went forty days and forty nights to Horeb (I Kgs 19:8). Both references would fit a location in southern Sinai, as would the identification of Paran with the Wadi Feiran.

Peaks in southern Sinai identified with Horeb/Sinai include: 1. Jebel Serbal (6825 feet), identified as early as Eusebius; 2. Ras eṣ-Ṣafṣafeh (6739 feet) with a considerable plain below it; and 3. Jebel Musa (7363 feet), the favored site looming over St. Catherine's Monastery, established by Justinian in the sixth century.

The Psalmist recalls how the Israelites made a calf at Horeb (Ps 106:19). When Solomon installed the ark, it contained only the two tables of stone which Moses placed in it at Horeb (I Kgs 8:9; II Chr 5:10). One of the last exhortations of the OT is the injunction to remember the law of Moses which the Lord had commanded him at Horeb (Mal 4:4 [H 3:22]).

ḥorbâ. ***Waste or desolate places, ruins.*** The word occurs forty-two times, including twenty-six times in the plural, mostly in Isa, Jer, Ezk.

ḥārābâ. ***Dry land.*** The word occurs eight times. In all but two cases (Gen 7:22; Hag 2:6) the land has been made dry by God's miraculous intervention: at the Sea of Reeds (KJV "Red Sea," Ex 14:21); at the Jordan (Josh 3:17, 4:18; II Kgs 2:8); and at the Nile as a threat by Yahweh (Ezk 30:12).

ḥērābôn. ***Heat or drought.*** Occurs but once at Ps 32:4. The Psalmist declares that before he confessed his sin his strength had been dried up by the "heat" or the "drought" of summer.

Bibliography: Hyatt, J. P., *Exodus*, London: Oliphants, 1971, pp. 203–207. Phythian-Adams, W. J., "The Mount of God," *Quarterly of the Palestine Exploration Fund* 1930: 135–49, 193–209. Rothenberg, Beno, and Aharoni, Yohanan, *God's Wilderness*, Thomas Nelson, 1962.

E.Y.

732 חָרַב (*ḥārab*) ***II, slay, fight.***

Derivative

732a †חֶרֶב (*ḥereb*) ***sword.***

Cognate with Arab *ḥaraba* "to plunder" and *ḥarbu* "war, battle." It occurs only in the following passages: in the Qal at Jer 50:21,27 in the sense of "slay" (RSV); in the Niphal at II Kgs 3:23, "The Kings have surely fought together" (RSV; the KJV reads "the kings are surely slain").

ḥereb. ***Sword, dagger;*** rarely knife or a chisel. Cognate with Akkadian *ḫarbu;* Ugaritic *ḥrb* "sword," "knife" (UT 19: no. 893); Egyptian *ḥrp;* Arabic *ḥarbatu* "javelin"; Greek *harpē* "sickle"; Latin *harpe* "sickle."

ḥereb, which occurs 407 times, is the most frequently mentioned weapon in the OT. The LXX translates it 195 times as *rhomphaia* "sword"; 165 times as *machaira* "short sword," "dagger," "knife"; 8 times as *xiphos* "straight sword"; and 4 times as *egcheiridion* "dagger."

From archeological and iconographic evidence we know that the common swords of the third and early second millennia B.C. were rather short, straight swords made of bronze. In the second millennium a curved sickle-shaped sword, called by the Egyptians *khopesh* "foreleg," became popular. Yadin believes that the expression "to smite with the edge of the sword," e.g. in Joshua's campaigns, refers to this type of smiting sword. Examples have been recovered from Shechem and Gezer.

At the end of the second millennium, the Philistines and other Sea Peoples introduced the long, straight sword made of iron (cf. I Sam 13:19), which could be used to cut and to stab. Such iron swords have been found at Beit Dagon and Tell el-'Ajjul (see illustrations in Yadin cited in the bibliography).

Swords were worn in a "sheath" (*ta'ar,* I Sam 17:51), which was hung on a "girdle" (see *ḥāgar* and *ḥăgôrâ*). This was normally worn on the left side.

Apparently the tempering of iron to make steel usable for swords was a military secret kept from the Israelites by the Hebrews. This advantage was held by the Philistines until David's day. The I Sam 13:19–22 passage preserves a very accurate analysis of the days when the Philistines had the long iron swords and the Israelites had only the short bronze daggers.

Ehud, a left-handed man, was able to conceal his weapon in his girdle on the right side. He made for himself a two-edged short sword, about eighteen inches long, with a small hilt (Jud 3:15–16, 21–22).

In the days of the united monarchy the Israelites adopted the heavy swords of the Philistines, which could penetrate armor (I Sam 17:5, 38, 51; 21:9). As it was also pointed for stabbing, such a sword was used by Saul to commit suicide (I Sam 31:4).

Once in Ps 89:43 [H 44] the expression *ṣûr,* literally "rock, flint" of "his sword" denotes the edge of the sword, reflecting an archaic practice when blades were made of flint; cf. Akkadian *ṣurru, ṣurtu* "flint," "blade."

The usual Hebrew expression translated "edge of the sword" is *pî-ḥereb,* literally "mouth of the sword" (Ex 17:13; Num 21:24; Josh 6:21, etc.). The Hebrew phrase, literally "a sword of mouths" occurs in Ps 149:6 and Prov 5:4. This phrase is translated "two-edged" sword, following the LXX *distomos,* literally "double-mouthed," but meaning "two-edged." (Cf. Heb 4:12; Rev 1:16; 2:12.) The sword is said "to devour" its victims (Deut 32:42; II Sam 2:26; 11:25; etc.).

In Ezk 21 there is a vivid description of the "sword of Yahweh" at work as an instrument of his judgment. In vv. 1–7 [H 6–12] his sword is unsheathed for action. Then in the furious Song of the Sword (vv. 8–17 [H 13–22]) we see the sword polished, then brandished, and even addressed as a living object (v. 16 [H 21]). Though it is the king of Babylon who wields the sword against Judah (vv. 18–27 [H 23–32]) and against Ammon (vv. 28–32 [H 33–37]), it is actually Yahweh himself who exercises the divine judgment (v. 17 [H 22]).

In the following passages the word is used as a metonymy for "war": Lev 26:25; II Chr 29:9; Jer 14:15; 24:10; Ezk 7:15; 33:2ff. etc.). In Ps 22:20 [H 21] *ḥereb* is used as a metaphor for a violent end.

In a different simile harsh words and sharp tongues are likened to swords. Proverbs 12:18 describes rash words as being like "sword thrusts" (RSV). The Psalmist's enemies have tongues like "sharp swords" (Ps 57:4 [H 5]). The wicked "whet their tongues like swords" (Ps 64:3 [H 4]). Cf. Ps 55:21 [H 22] where malicious words are compared to "drawn swords" and Ps. 52:2 [H 4] a "sharp razor."

Succumbing to a temptress is as fatal as an encounter with a "two-edged sword" (Prov 5:4).

The "flaming sword" in the hands of the cherubim who guarded Eden has been explained by Cassuto and von Rad as the objectification of lightning (cf. Ps 104:3–4). It is rather the symbol of God's holiness and judgment.

In a few passages *ḥereb* may represent a tool or knife rather than a sword or dagger. In Jer 5:17 a foreign enemy will batter down the cities with the *ḥereb*, a phrase omitted by the NEB and JB as an incongruous addition. Inasmuch as we have Assyrian reliefs of sappers undermining the walls of a besieged town with their daggers, the phrase is not so incomprehensible. The same practice may be in mind in Ezk 26:9, where the KJV translates "with his axes"; cf. NAB "weapons."

Although Ezekiel (Ezk 5:1) may very well have used a sharp sword to shave himself, a smaller "blade" (JB) would have been handier.

The instruments used for circumcision were "flint knives" (Josh 5:2–3; cf. Ex 4:25). For an Egyptian depiction of the rite of circumcision using such a knife, see ANEP fig. 629. The early stone altars to Yahweh were not to be built or engraved with the use of a "tool" (Ex 20:25; Deut 27:5).

There are some passages in which the reading *ḥereb* in the text poses problems. In a list of natural calamities in Deut 28:22 the preferable vocalization (cf. LXX, Vulg.) is *ḥōreb* "drought" (RSV). In Lam 5:9 the *ḥereb* of the desert is read as *ḥōreb* "heat" by the NEB and NAB.

Job 5:15 says that God saves *mēḥereb mippîhem,* literally "from a sword, from their mouth." The NAB takes this as a form of the common expression "the edge of the sword," but the RSV, NEB, and JB omit *mēḥereb* from their translations.

In Isa 1:20 the NEB has chosen to revocalize *ḥereb* as *ḥārûb,* a word which does not appear in the OT, but is known from later Jewish texts, and translates: "Locust beans (i.e. carobs) shall be your only food."

Bibliography: Meek, Theophile J., "Archaeology and a Point in Hebrew Syntax, BASOR 122: 31–33. Wever, J. W., "Sword," in IDB, IV, pp. 469–70. Yadin, Yigael, *The Art of Warfare in Biblical Lands,* London: Weidenfeld and Nicolson, 1963, pp. 134–36, 140–45, 172–75, 194–95, 204–9, 222–23, 228, 232–37, 340–41, 344–45, 348–50, 358–59, 384–85, 420–25, 438. ——, "Warfare in the Second Millennium B.C.E.," in *The World History of the Jewish People: II, Patriarchs,* ed. Benjamin Mazar, Rutgers, 1970, pp. 129–33.

E.Y.

חֶרְבוֹן (*ḥērābôn*). See no. 731f.

733 חָרַג (*hārag*) ***quake*** (Deut 32:25; Ps 18:46).

734 חרגל (*ḥrgl*). **Assumed root of the following.**
734a †חַרְגֹּל (*ḥargōl*) ***a kind of locust.***

Its etymology is uncertain. The word occurs only in Lev 11:22 in the list of leaping insects considered edible. The LXX renders it *akris* "locust" (NEB "green locust"). Both KJV "beetle" and RSV "cricket" are hardly correct, since those insects are omnivorous and thus not suitable for food.

See *'arbeh.*

735 חָרַד (*ḥārad*) ***quake, move about, (be) startled, tremble, (be) afraid;*** causative stems to (cause to) move, terrify (RSV emphasizes terror and panic).

Derivatives

735a †חָרֵד (*ḥārēd*) ***afraid, trembling.***
735b †חֲרָדָה (*ḥărādâ*) ***quaking, trembling.***

The root meaning is "to shake," from which meanings such as "tremble" and "fear" are derived. Physical shaking describes the quaking of Mount Sinai (Ex 19:18). Geographic quaking serves as a poetic figure for human trembling (Isa 10:29, 41:5; Ezk 26:18). Physical movement may be the point of this verb and *ḥărādâ* as well in II Kgs 4:13 referring to the solicitous moving-around of typical Near Eastern hospitality (cf. however "be *anxiously* careful" and "*anxious* care" suggested by BDB). "Come trembling" (Hos 11:10–11) probably emphasizes the notion of bird-like (v. 11!) movements and may refer to movements of joy or terror.

Most occurrences refer to trembling from emotional agitation before an unusual circumstance. Isaac trembles upon perceiving Jacob's deception (Gen 27:33). Adonijah's guests react similarly when they learn that Solomon has been crowned (I Kgs 1:49). Boaz's startled awakening in the night is described by the same word (Ruth 3:8; RSV "startled"). It can describe a military force either as passively demoralized (I Sam 13:7) or as broken into outright panic (I Sam 14:15).

The Hiphil functions causatively meaning "to cause to move" or "to frighten." It describes throwing an army in terror (Jud 8:12; II Sam 17:2). Most Hiphil usages occur in two recurring idioms: the description of desolation as the absence of anyone to frighten away the wild animals (Deut 28:26; Isa 17:2; Jer 7:33) and the description of security as the absence of anyone to terrorize (Job 11:19; Jer 30:10; Ezk 34:28).

ḥārēd. ***Afraid, trembling.*** Root meaning may appear in describing the fearful of Gideon's army as "trembling" (Jud 7:3). Eli's anxiety concerning the ark is described as "his heart trembled" (I Sam 4:13). Four passages speak of trembling before God's word or commandment. In Isa 66:2, 5, these are the penitent and faithful; in Ezr (9:4, 10:3) it refers, perhaps as a technical term, to those leaders who perceive God's word of judgment and support Ezra's reforms. In all four passages a meaning of "awe" or "reverence" is indicated (cf. similar usages of *pāḥad* and *yārē'*).

ḥărādâ. ***Quaking, trembling, fear, care (?)*** (RSV "panic"). Primarily describes human trembling before some strange or fearsome event. Typical examples are the terror of Daniel's companions before a vision (Dan 10:7) and the trembling of the nations at Tyre's downfall (Ezk 26:16). The terror of a demoralized army is called the "panic of God" (I Sam 14:15; RSV "great panic"; note: while this expression may mean "great panic" it may also emphasize the miraculous, divine origin of the panic!). It is not clear whether the "cry of panic" (RSV Jer 30:5; KJV "voice of trembling") refers to the shout which causes panic or the terrified cry of those in panic. For "care" in II Kgs 4:13 see below.

A.B.

736 חָרָה (*ḥārâ*) ***burn, be kindled*** (of anger). (ASV and RSV similar, except that RSV avoids the translation "wroth," usually employing "angry.")

Derivatives

736a †חָרוֹן (*ḥārôn*) ***heat, burning*** (of anger).

736b †חֳרִי (*ḥŏrî*) ***heat, burning*** (of anger).

This word is related to a rare Aramaic root meaning "to cause fire to burn," and to an Arabic root meaning "burning sensation," in the throat, etc. The Hebrew verb is always used in reference to anger. The meaning of the root differs from such words for "anger" as *'ānap, zā'am,* and *qāṣap,* in that it emphasizes the "kindling" of anger, like the kindling of a fire, or the heat of the anger, once started. The verb and its derivatives are used a total of 139 times.

ḥārâ is used in reference to the anger of both man and God, and in parallel ways. In respect to man, the noun *'ap* "anger," frequently occurs as subject, "anger was kindled." For instance, the "anger" of Potiphar, Joseph's master in Egypt, "was kindled" toward him, over his wife's false accusation (Gen 39:19). An equally common usage is without a subject, thus giving a medio-passive meaning, "It was kindled." Of Jacob it is said that, "It was kindled to him," meaning that his anger was kindled when he learned that Laban had pursued him.

In respect to God, the noun *'ap* is employed as subject in Num 11:1. The "anger" of the Lord "was kindled" toward Israel because of further murmuring. An instance of the medio-passive voice is found in II Sam 22:8 (cf. Ps 18:7 [H 8]), according to which the "foundations of heaven moved and shook, because it was kindled to God." Only once is the subject of the verb "God" (man is never the subject), in Hab 3:8, "Was the Lord displeased against rivers?" (literally, "Was the Lord kindled against rivers?").

In the Niphal stem, the root appears three times, and each, in contrast to that just noticed for the Qal stem, either has or implies a personal subject, referred to in a passive sense. For instance, in Song 1:6 the Shulamite bride says that the sons of her mother "were angry" (literally, "were kindled") with her.

In the Hiphil stem, the root appears only twice and neither in a causative sense. In Job 19:11, it is used in the same way and meaning as in Qal, when the subject *'ap* is employed. In Neh 3:20, it carries the unusual sense of intensifying an idea; Baruch, a worker on the wall of Jerusalem, being said to have "earnestly" (literally, "in a burning manner") repaired his part of it.

The Hithpael stem occurs four times, always meaning, "Fret not yourself" (Ps 37:1, 7–8; Prov 24:19). The reflexive thought is: "Do not kindle yourself" in respect to the wicked, etc. Again, a personal subject is implied.

An unusual feature regarding the root is that two instances of the Tiphel (causative) stem occur (Jer 12:5; 22:15). Both imply the existence of a personal subject, the one speaking of a person "competing" (literally, "burning to outrace") with horses; and the other of "competing" (literally, "burning to outshine") with other people for status by living in cedar.

ḥārôn. ***Heat, burning*** (of anger). This noun derivative, which occurs forty-one times, is used only in reference to God. A frequent use finds it followed by *'ap,* giving the translation, "The fierceness (literally, "burning") of the anger of Yahweh" (Num 25:4). Many times it is followed simply by *'ap* with a suffix, giving "the fierceness ("burning") of his (your, my, etc.) anger" (Deut 13:18). A few times the word itself carries the suffix, without the use of *'ap,* but these are infrequent. It may be added in respect to Jer 25:38 that *ḥārôn,* as here shown in some texts, is better taken as a variant for *ḥereb* "sword."

ḥŏrî. ***Heat, burning*** (of anger). This noun bearing the same meaning as *ḥārôn,* is used twice of God and four times of man. It is always followed by *'ap.* For instance, Jonathan left the presence of his father, Saul, in "the fierceness (burning) of anger" because of Saul's attitude toward David (I Sam 20:34).

Bibliography: Blank, Sheldon H., "'Doest Thou Well to be Angry?'" HUCA 26: 29–41. THAT, I, pp. 633–34.

L.J.W.

חָרוּז (*ḥārûz*). See no. 737a.
חָרוֹן (*ḥārôn*). See no. 736a.

חָרוּל (ḥārûl). See no. 743a.
חָרוּץ (ḥārûṣ). See nos. 752a,b, 753a.

737 חרז (ḥrz). **Assumed root of the following.**
737a חָרוּז (ḥārûz) ***string of beads*** (Song 1:10).

חַרְחֻר (ḥarḥūr). See no. 756b.

738 חרט (ḥrṭ) **I. Assumed root of the following.**
738a †חֶרֶט (ḥereṭ) ***graving tool.***
738b †חַרְטֹם (ḥarṭōm) ***magician.***

ḥereṭ. ***Graving tool, pen.*** Aaron used a *ḥereṭ* to shape the golden calf (Ex 32:4). Some modern versions paraphrase the expression to give the idea of casting or molding (cf. JPS, JB, NEB).

The only other occurrence of the word is in Isa 8:1 where God commands the prophet to write the name of Maher-shalal-hash-baz on a tablet with "a man's *ḥereṭ*." The Berkeley translation has "common script." The Amplified has "a graving tool *and* in ordinary characters [which the humblest man can read.]" The Jerusalem Bible has "ordinary writing," NEB has "common writing," and NAB has "ordinary letters," the NIV "ordinary pen."

ḥarṭōm. ***Magician, diviner, scribe.*** This word, describing some variety of occultist, appears in both Hebrew (*ḥarṭummîm*) and Aramaic (*ḥarṭummîn*). It is the word for Egyptian "magicians" (Gen 41:8, 24; Ex 7:11, 22; 8:3, 14–15; 9:11) and for the Babylonian "magicians" (Dan 1:20; 2:2, 10, 27; 4:4, 6; 5:11). The last five references are in the Aramaic section of Daniel. Only 2:10 uses *ḥarṭōm* in the singular.

According to Gen 41:8, the pharaoh summoned all the *ḥarṭummîm* (magicians) and *ḥăkamîm* (wise men). The word is parallel to *mᵉkashshᵉpîm* (sorcerers), *'ashshāpîm* (enchanters, q.v.), and *kaśdîm* (Chaldeans) in Dan 2:2. In the Aramaic list of Dan 2:27 *gāzᵉrîn* (soothsayers) replaces *mᵉkashshᵉpîm,* while *ḥakkîmîn* (wise men) replaces *kaśdîm*.

Because it seems related to the word *ḥereṭ* (q.v.) meaning "stylus" or the like, some translations take *ḥarṭōm* to mean "scribe." (See *Young's Literal Translation,* the ASV marg., the 1913 *Improved Edition Bible,* and the Berkeley Version in the Gen and Ex passages.)

It may, however, be a loan word from Egyptian. It consists of four radicals, unlike most Semitic words, which have three. There is an Egyptian word *ḥrj-tp* which may mean "magicians" or "priests," although it usually means "governor," "chieftain," "adviser."

Bibliography: Cornfeld, G., "Magic, Divination and Superstition," in *Pictorial Biblical Encyclopedia,* Macmillan, 1964. Loewenstamm, Samuel E., "The Making and Destruction of the Golden Calf," Bib 48:481–90. Ward, William A., "Egyptian Titles in Genesis," BS 114: 40–59. Zuck, Roy B., "The Practice of Witchcraft in the Scriptures," BS 128: 352–60.

R.L.A.

739 חרט (ḥrṭ) **II. Assumed root of the following.**
739a חָרִיט (ḥārîṭ) ***bag, purse*** (II Kgs 5:23; Isa 3:22).

חַרְטֹם (ḥarṭōm). See no. 738b.
חֳרִי (ḥŏrî). See no. 736b.

740 †חֹרִי (ḥōrî), חוֹרִי (ḥôrî) ***Horite, Hori.*** (ASV and RSV translate the same.)

This noun appears to be a loan word. Formerly it was thought to be related to the root *ḥrr* III, having to do with a hole or cave, though usually *ḥrr* refers to a small hole. Now it is generally considered to be the Hebrew spelling for Akkadian *ḫurru* (Ug. *ḫry*). It is to be distinguished from *ḥōrî* "white bread or cake." It occurs ten times, twice as a personal name.

The extrabiblical sources clearly attest the presence of Hurrians in Palestine after 1550 B.C. (cf. the Ug. texts, the Amarna tablets, cuneiform tablets from Taanach and Shechem, and certain Egyptian writings; Noth, *The Old Testament World,* pp. 233, 240ff.). During the second half of the second millennium the Egyptians knew SW Asia as *Ḫr*. Hurrian names appear in Near Eastern inscriptions of this period (confirmed by Hurrian tablets from Boghazköy). Albright says that in the Old Testament the names of the Horites are Hurrian; therefore, "there can be no doubt that this (i.e., Hurrian) is the language spoken by the biblical Horites" (*From the Stone Age to Christianity,* 1947, p. 36).

Our problem is that the biblical Horites were residents of Edom, not Palestine. The Horites appear to be the Hurrian inhabitants of Edom (Gen 36:20), who were driven out of the region by Esau's descendants (Deut 2:12, 22). It has been suggested, therefore, that the Horites are the non-Palestinian Hurrians, and the Hivites are the Palestinian Hurrians (Thomas, *Archaeology and Old Testament Study,* p. 81). This would explain how Zibion could be a Hivite (Gen 36:2) and the son of Seir the Horite (Gen 36:20). If so, they occupied some places in central Palestine, including Shechem (Gen 34:2) and Gibeon (Josh 9:6–7). The LXX reading "Horite" strengthens this suggestion.

The Hurrians are to be distinguished from the Subarians, the Sumerians, the Semites, and the Indo-Europeans. They originated in the mountains E and NE of Mesopotamia which they gradually infiltrated. By the fifteenth century B.C. they boasted a kingdom, Mittani. During this era their nobles seem to have been Indo-European (as attested by their names).

Bibliography: Albright, W. F., *From the Stone Age to Christianity,* Doubleday, 1947. Gelb, I. J., *Hurrians and Subarians,* 1949. Noth, M., *The Old Testament World,* I, Edinburgh: Clark, 1964. Speiser, E. A., *Introduction to Hurrian,* ASOR Annual, 1941. Thomas, D. Winton, *Archaeology and Old Testament Study,* Oxford: Clarendon, 1967.

L.J.C.

חָרִיט (*ḥārîṭ*). See no. 739a.
חִרְיוֹנִים (*ḥiryônîm*), i.e. *h^e^rê yônîm*. See no. 730a.
חָרִיץ (*ḥārîṣ*). See no. 752c.
חָרִישׁ (*ḥārîsh*). See no. 760c.
חֲרִישִׁי (*ḥărîshî*). See no. 760e.

741 חָרַךְ (*ḥārak*) ***I, set in motion, start*** (Prov 12:27).

742 חרך (*ḥrk*) **II. Assumed root of the following.**
742a חֲרַכִּים (*ḥărakkîm*) ***lattice or other opening through which one may look*** (Song 2:9).

743 חרל (*ḥrl*). **Assumed root of the following.**
743a חָרוּל (*ḥārûl*) ***a kind of weed, perhaps chickpea*** (e.g. Prov 24:31; Zeph 2:9).

744 *חָרַם (*ḥāram*) ***I, ban, devote, destroy utterly.*** (ASV and RSV similar, except that both prefer "devoted" or "devoted thing" in passages not dealing with destruction.)

Derivatives

744a †חֵרֶם (*ḥērem*) ***devoted thing, ban.***
744b †חֶרְמוֹן (*ḥermôn*) ***Hermon.***

The root *ḥrm* is used only in the causative stems; forty-eight times in the iphil and three in the Hophal. The basic meaning is the exclusion of an object from the use or abuse of man and its irrevocable surrender to God. The word is related to an Arabic root meaning "to prohibit, especially to ordinary use." The word "harem," meaning the special quarters for Muslim wives, comes from it. It is related also to an Ethiopic root, meaning "to forbid, prohibit, lay under a curse." Surrendering something to God meant devoting it to the service of God or putting it under a ban for utter destruction.

The idea of devoting an object for service to God appears in Lev 27:28. Whatever is devoted to the Lord, whether man, animal, or property, is considered most holy by God and is therefore not to be sold or redeemed by substituting something else. According to Num 18:14 and Ezk 44:29, all such objects are to be given to the priests for the support of the religious ceremonies. The gold, silver, bronze, and iron from Jericho, for instance, were so designated (Josh 6:19, *qōdesh layhwh*).

Usually *ḥāram* means a ban for utter destruction, the compulsory dedication of something which impedes or resists God's work, which is considered to be accursed before God. The idea first appears in Num 21:2–3, where the Israelites vowed that, if God would enable them to defeat a southern Canaanite king, they would "utterly destroy" (i.e. consider as devoted and accordingly utterly destroy) his cities. This word is used regarding almost all the cities which Joshua's troops destroyed (e.g. Jericho, Josh 6:21; Ai, Josh 8:26; Makkedah, Josh 10:28; Hazor, Josh 11:11), thus indicating the rationale for their destruction. In Deut 7:2–6, the command for this manner of destruction is given, with the explanation following that, otherwise, these cities would lure the Israelites away from the Lord (cf. Deut 20:17–18). Any Israelite city that harbored idolators was to be "utterly destroyed" (Deut 13:12–15; cf. Ex 22:19).

A man who was the object devoted to God came under the same ban. Leviticus 27:28–29 states that he was to be put to death. He could hardly be assigned to ceremonial service, for this was the work of Levites. To make this regulation agree with the sixth commandment (Ex 20:13; cf. 21:20), however, the thought must be that the persons so devoted were captives in wars such as those of Jericho or others under the ban, e.g. the Amalekites (I Sam 15:3).

Because the root *qādash* "to be holy," also carries the thought of setting apart from ordinary use in surrender to God (especially in the Piel), we must distinguish objects set apart because "devoted," from those set apart because "holy." In a text discussed above, Lev 27:28–29, the two were brought together in that the devoted object was considered most holy by God. This suggests that the two were closely related, and this was true in respect to objects devoted for ceremonial service. But in respect to the objects to be destroyed, they were considered to be offensive to God and injurious to his work. Objects to be set apart because holy were pleasing to him and useful.

A few times the root is used in respect to foreign nations "utterly destroying" a city or country (cf. II Kgs 19:11; II Chr 20:23). Light on this may come from the Mesha inscription. On line 17 King Mesha (cf. II Kgs 3:4) uses the word as he explains that he slaughtered all the inhabitants of Nebo because he made the city a "devoted" city to his god Chemosh.

ḥērem. ***Devoted thing, devotion, ban.*** This noun derivative is used twenty-eight times in the OT to refer either to the object devoted or to the ban itself. The story of Jericho's fall to Israel provides clear examples of the first use. The whole city is called a "devoted thing" (Josh 6:17), and all Israelites are warned to keep themselves from the "devoted thing," which likely is a reference to items within the city all of which had to be burned if flammable and if not, given to God. When Achan disobeys and takes of these items, Israel's army is defeated by the people of Ai, and God says that Israel has now become a "devoted thing" itself until the "devoted thing" (Achan in his sin) is destroyed from its midst (Josh 7:12–13). So, then, Jericho the heathen city was "devoted" because it stood in the way of God's work through Israel in making conquest of Canaan. Israel became "devoted" because of sin which entered and made the nation unusable in God's work. Achan in his sin became "devoted" because he was the reason for Israel's hindrance as the people of God.

Also note passages using *ḥērem* to refer to the ban itself. According to I Kgs 20:42, Benhadad, the Syrian king, was a man under the "ban" of God. In Isa 34:5, Edom is said to have been a people under the "ban" of God. The kingdom of Judah was given to the "ban" in that Babylonia was permitted to bring the captivity on her (Isa 43:28).

ḥermôn. ***Hermon.*** The name of Mount Herman, meaning "sacred." Also called *śiryôn* and *śᵉnîr* (Deut 3:9) or *śî'ōn* (Deut 4:48).

Bibliography: Malamat, Abraham, "The Ban in Mari and in the Bible," in *Biblical Essays*, pp. 40–49. Richardson, TWB, p. 68. THAT, I, pp. 635–38.

L.J.W.

745 חָרַם (*ḥāram*) ***II, slit, mutilate.*** (ASV uses "flat"; RSV "mutilated.")

Derivative

745a †חֶרֶם (*ḥerem*) ***net.***

ḥāram is related to the Arabic root meaning "to slit" or "to perforate" the partition between the nostrils, for the insertion of a ring. It is used only once, in Lev 21:18. The form is a passive participle, and it describes a face (nose) as "mutilated," one of the deformities which would disqualify a priest from service.

ḥerem. ***Net.*** This noun is used nine times. Its meaning comes from the idea of something perforated. It is used twice in reference to the net of a hunter (Mic 7:2; Eccl 7:26); and seven times to the net of a fisherman (Ezk 26:5, 14; 32:3; 47:10; Hab 1:15–17).

L.J.W.

חֶרְמוֹן (*ḥermôn*). See no. 744b.

746 חֶרְמֵשׁ (*ḥermēsh*) ***sickle*** (Deut 16:9; 23:25 [H 26]). Derivation uncertain.

747 חָרָן (*ḥārān*) ***Haran.***

Haran was the city in which Abraham and his family settled after they left Ur (Gen 11:31–32). After the death of Terah, Abraham's father, Abraham and his family began their journey to Canaan (Gen 12:1). Haran is called the "city of Nahor" in Gen 24:10 because Nahor, Abraham's brother, settled there. Haran was the home of Laban, the brother of Rebekah. Rebekah encouraged Jacob to flee to Laban's home at Haran when Esau allegedly threatened his life (Gen 27:43). Jacob's fortunes improved greatly during his long stay with Laban. The account of Jacob's arrival at Haran is recorded in Gen 29:1–8.

Rabshekah, in his boastful challenge to Hezekiah, mentioned Haran among cities destroyed by the Assyrians (II Kgs 19:12; Isa 37:12). Ezekiel 27:23 cites it as a center of trade. The city was an Assyrian provincial capital for some time, as well as the capital of Ashur-urballit after the destruction of Nineveh.

T.E.M.

748 חרס (*ḥrs*). **Assumed root of the following.**

748a חֶרֶס (*ḥeres*) ***sun*** (Job 9:7; Jud 14:18).

חֶרֶס (*ḥeres*). See nos. 748a, 759b.

חַרְסוֹת (*ḥarsôt*). See no. 759c.

749 חָרַף (*ḥārap*) ***I, reproach, blaspheme, defy, jeopardize, rail, reproach, upbraid.***

Derivative

749a חֶרְפָּה (*ḥerpâ*) ***reproach.***

Basically, the word means "to reproach," with the specific connotation of casting blame or scorn on someone.

The connotation of casting blame is evident in Job 27:6 where Job protests that his heart does not reproach him for any of his days. In Prov 27:11 the wisdom teacher desires that his pupil may be wise so that the teacher may not incur blame from others. In Neh 6:13 the word seems to be used in the sense of "defame," i.e. impute blame or guilt to someone in order to harm his character.

In most instances the word is used in the sense of casting scorn. In Ps 74:10 the word occurs in parallelism with *nā'aṣ* (scorn, condemn) and in Prov 14:31 it is the antithesis of *kābēd* (honor) and may be understood as disgrace or dishonor. In Jud 5:18 the people of Zebulon are described as scorning their lives even to death.

In contexts where an adversary reproaches with scorn or insults, "taunt" is an acceptable translation (Jud 8:15; Ps 119:42). Where one is pictured as treating another with contempt or scorn the word may bear the nuance of "mocking" (II Kgs 19:22). The connotation "defy" is evident in contexts where one sets at naught the strength of an enemy (I Sam 17:10ff.).

T.E.M.

750 חָרַף (*ḥārap*) ***II, spend harvest time.*** This denominative verb occurs only in Isa 18:6.

Parent Noun

750a חֹ֫רֶף (*ḥōrep*) ***harvest time, autumn.***

751 *חָרַף (*ḥārap*) ***III, acquire.*** This verb occurs only once, in the Niphal (Lev 19:26).

752 חָרַץ (*ḥāraṣ*) ***I, bestir oneself, decide, decree, determine, maim, move.*** (RSV similar except that it translates "growl" and "mutilate" in Ex 11:7.)

Derivatives

752a †חָרוּץ (*ḥārûṣ*) ***I, sharp, diligent.***
752b חָרוּץ (*ḥārûṣ*) ***II, trench, moat,*** only in Dan 9:25.
752c חָרִיץ (*ḥārîṣ*) ***a cut, thing cut, sharp instrument.***
752d חַרְצַנִּים (*ḥarṣannîm*) ***an insignificant vine product, grape seeds(?).***

Basic to the meaning of *ḥāraṣ* are the concepts "to cut or sharpen" and "to decide." (The former meaning is represented in the noun *ḥārûṣ* and the Akkadian cognate *ḫarāṣu* which means "to cut," "cut off," "deduct" as well as "to determine" and "to clarify.")

The connotation "to cut" is most clearly seen in Lev 22:22 where the word occurs in a proscription against the use of maimed animals for sacrifice.

Other usages of the word with the connotation of "cut" occur in more metaphorical passages. In Josh 10:21 the word is used in an expression which means "to speak against." The translation "moved" (KJV; ASV; RSV) has little support either in the Hebrew or Akkadian usage. The expression literally means "to sharpen the tongue" and evidently connotes speaking against another with hostility. The same meaning seems to be inherent in the use of the word in Ex 11:7 where it is used of a dog and expresses the idea of angry growling. In II Sam 5:24 David was commanded to "be sharp" when he heard a sound in the trees, i.e. he was to act quickly. (The Chronicler renders the command as "go out to battle.")

The concept "decide, determine" is clearly evident in I Kgs 20:40 where one decided his own judgment. In all other instances the word connotes the concept of "determined" and refers to something which cannot be changed. Perhaps the basic idea of "cut" is evident here in that that which is incised cannot be altered.

ḥārûṣ. ***Decision, pointed things, sharp, threshing instrument, wall.*** The concept of sharpness inherent in the verb is evident in the noun *ḥārûṣ* when it is used of a threshing sledge (Isa 28:27; 41:15; Amos 1:3; Job 41:30 [H 22]). Metaphorically the word was used of "sharpness" as an attribute, i.e. diligence (Prov 10:4; 12:24, 27; 13:4; 21:5).

The concept of "cut" is evident in its reference to a moat (Dan 9:25). The word is used metaphorically of a strict decision in the sense that something which is cut or incised cannot be altered (Joel 3:14 [H 4:14]).

753 חרץ (*ḥrṣ*) **II. Assumed root of the following.**
753a חָרוּץ (*ḥārûṣ*) ***III, gold*** (e.g. Zech 9:3; Prov 3:14).

754 חרצב (*ḥrṣb*). **Assumed root of the following.**
754a חַרְצֻבָּה (*harṣūbbâ*) ***bond, fetter*** (Isa 58:6), ***pang*** (Ps 73:4).

חַרְצַנִּים (*ḥarṣannîm*). See no. 752d.

755 חָרַק (*ḥāraq*) ***gnash or grind the teeth*** (e.g. Job 16:9; Lam 2:16).

756 חָרַר (*ḥārar*) ***I, be burned, charred.*** The ASV translates "burned" except in Ps 69:3 [H 4]. The RSV concurs in all places except Isa 24:6 where it renders "scorched," and in Ps 69:3 [H 4] where it renders "parched."

Derivatives

756a חָרֵר (*ḥārēr*) ***parched place.*** Only in Jer 17:6, referring figuratively to the life of the godless.
756b חַרְחֻר (*ḥarḥūr*) ***violent heat, fever,*** only in Deut 28:22.

Basically this root connotes the product left from burning (cf. Ugaritic *ḥrr* "roast"). It is to be distinguished from *ḥrr* II, having to do with nobility or being freeborn, and *ḥrr* III, having to do with a hole. It is not to be confused with *ḥārâ* "to burn" (usually of anger). *ḥārar* "burned, charred" is mostly a poetic root. It is used twelve times.

This root describes the inhabitants of the earth who were objects of God's wrath (Isa 24:6), what is left after fire has worked on bone (Ezk 24:10–11), metal, or wood (Ezk 15:4; Ps 102:3 [H 4]). It can also be used of the inward effect of fever (Job 30:30), and of the parching of a throat due to excessive weeping (Ps 69:3 [H 4]). It occurs once in the Pilpel stem (indicating rapidly repeated action), setting forth the contentious man's continual agitation (kindling) in fostering and sustaining strife (Prov 26:21).

757 חרר (*ḥrr*) **II. Assumed root of the following.**
757a †ח׳ר (*ḥōr*) ***noble*** (usually occurs in the plural).

The ASV and RSV translate the same except in Eccl 10:17 where the RSV renders "free-man" (ASV "nobles"), and Isa 34:12. *ḥōr* is usually connected with the root *ḥrr* II, which (concluding on the basis of Semitic cognates) has to do with being or becoming free. There is a possible connection between *ḥōr* "noble" and the root *ḥwr* "be or grow pale, white" (the princes of Israel have fair complexions, Lam 4:7). Distinguish from *ḥōr,* "hole" and from *ḥōr* "white cloth." Our word occurs thirteen times.

The *ḥōrîm,* along with the elders, were leaders of cities (I Kgs 21:8) who had authority to bring a man to trial. They were of sufficient prominence to escape hand-to-hand warfare and were found in the inner palace during the Babylonian seige. They were slain before Zedekiah's eyes, along with the princes (Jer 39:6), according to prophecy (Isa 34:12). Later the *ḥōrîm* were listed beside the priests and rulers (*s*^{e}*gānîm*) as the leaders of Israel during the postexilic reconstruction (Neh 4:14 [H 8], 19 [H 13]). They appear to be the heads of the people, perhaps equivalent to the *śarîm* "princes" (cf. Ezr 9:2). Since the word occurs in contexts where Israel has close contact with Aramaic-speaking peoples, it might well be an Aramaic loanword.

The *ḥōrîm* supervised construction of the wall during the reconstruction (Neh 4:14 [H 8]). They had sufficient funds to loan to the common people (Neh 5:7). They controlled farming and merchandising (Neh 13:17). They had ready access to the ruling body (Jer 39:6; Neh 6:17) and were a body to be reckoned with.

ḥōrîm seems to be almost synonymous at times with *śarîm* (cf. Jer 27:20 and II Kgs 24:14). If it is synonymous, then monarchical usage denotes administrators and heads of influential families, i.e. men of position, while postexilic usages embrace "influential people." On the basis of an identification with *śarîm,* these *ḥōrîm* were not "nobles" in the sense of a landed aristocracy.

Bibliography: McKenzie, John L., "The Elders in the Old Testament," Bib 40: 522–40. Van der Ploeg, J., "Les Chefs du Peuple d'Israel et leurs Titres," RB 57: 57–58.

L.J.C.

758 חרר (*ḥrr*) **III. Assumed root of the following.**
758a חֹר (*ḥōr*), חוֹר (*ḥôr*) ***hole*** (e.g. II Kgs 12:9 [H 10]; Song 5:4).
758b חֻר (*ḥūr*), חוּר (*ḥûr*) ***hole*** (Isa 42:22; 11:8).

759 חרשׂ (*ḥrś*). **Assumed root of the following.**
759a †חֶרֶשׂ (*ḥereś*) ***earthenware.***
759b חֶרֶס (*ḥeres*) ***an eruptive disease*** (Deut 28:27).
759c חרסות (*ḥrswt,* Kethib), חַרְסִית (*ḥarsît,* Qere) ***potsherds*** (Jer 19:2).

This word, which occurs seventeen times, represents the potter's product (Isa 45:9) which is dried and fired (Ps 22:15 [H 16]), or even glazed (Prov 26:23). Bottles (*baqbūq*), bowls (*k*^{e}*lî*), and pots/pitchers (*nēbel*) are made of it. It is in vessels made of *ḥereś* that documents were stored (Jer 32:14). *ḥereś* can apply generally to a vessel (Prov 26:23), or it can mean pieces of potsherd at least large enough to use to carry a coal from a hearth or dip water for a drink (Isa 30:14). Hence, *ḥereś* is the baked clay so commonly unearthed by archaeologists.

Being porous, it absorbed the fat of holy things and the uncleanness of unclean things. Thus it was to be broken when contacted by either holiness or uncleanness (Lev 6:28 [H 21]; Num 15:12). A clay vessel was to be used in the trial of jealousy (Num 5:17) and in leprosy purification rites, symbolizing man's commonness before God. The Psalmist prophetically compares the Messiah's strength to a dried up and baked piece of clay (potsherd, Ps 22:15 [H 16]). During the exile the "most precious" royalty of Israel became as valueless and common as clay pots (Lam 4:2). God reminds the people of their relative worthlessness and vulnerability by comparing them to clay vessels (Isa 45:9). Jeremiah (19:1) bought (and subsequently broke) an earthenware pot to symbolize how Israel had so absorbed sin that they had to be destroyed according to God's law regarding polluted pottery (Lev 11:33).

L.J.C.

760 חָרַשׁ (*ḥārash*) ***I, engrave, plow, devise.***

Derivatives

760a †חָרָשׁ (*ḥārāsh*) ***engraver.***
760b חֲרֹשֶׁת (*ḥărōshet*) ***carving.***
760c חָרִישׁ (*ḥārîsh*) ***plowing, plowing time.***
760d מַחֲרֵשָׁה (*maḥărēshâ*), מַחֲרֶשֶׁת (*maḥăreshet*) ***ploughshare.***
760e חֲרִישִׁי (*ḥărîshî*) ***harsh.*** Used only in Jon 4:8. Meaning uncertain and uncertain to which root *ḥārash* it is related. KJV "vehement," NIV "scorching."

The basic idea is cutting into some material, e.g. engraving metal or plowing soil. The word is used twenty-six times, of which twenty-three are in the Qal stem, two in the Niphal, and one in the Hiphil. The Ugaritic noun *ḥrsh* means "craftsman." Another Ugaritic word *ḥrṯ* cognate to Hebrew *ḥārash* means "to plow." This would argue for two overlapping roots in Hebrew.

ḥārash is used a few times for engraving metal. For instance, one of the expert craftsmen from Tyre, whom King Solomon summoned to work on the temple, is described as a "worker" ("engraver," a participle) in brass (I Kgs 7:14). More often the word is used for plowing the ground. Elisha, when Elijah called him to service, is said to have been "plowing" with twelve yoke of oxen (I Kgs 19:19). One of the Mosaic laws was that a person should not "plow" with an ox and an ass together (Deut 22:10).

The idea of "plowing" is also used figuratively. It symbolizes wicked activity (Hos 10:13), Israel being charged with having "plowed" iniquity. It stands for oppression in Ps 129:3, as the Psalmist cries out, "The plowers plowed upon my back." A third usage is to mean "devise," usually in connection with evil. For instance, a proverb states, "Devise not evil" against your neighbor (Prov 3:29). *ḥārash* refers to both evil and good in Prov 14:22. Those who "devise evil" are said to err and those that "devise good" to receive mercy and truth. *ḥārash* occurs twice in the Niphal concerning Micah's prediction (Jer 26:18 quoting Mic 3:12) that Jerusalem would be "plowed" like a field. The one Hiphil usage shows no clear difference in meaning from Qal, as Saul is said to have "practised" ("devised") evil against David (I Sam 23:9).

ḥārāsh. ***Engraving, carpenter, smith, mason.*** Whereas the verb majors on plowing soil, its noun derivative, occurring thirty-five times, stresses engraving, usually metal, but also wood or stone. Gold brought from Uphaz is said in Jer 10:9 to be the work of the "workmen" ("engravers"). David states that in preparation for the building of the temple he had gathered gold and silver to be worked on by the hands of "artificers" ("engravers") of the day (I Chr 29:5). Frequently, however, the word refers to more than the work of engraving. For instance, the gold calf, erected in Israel by Jeroboam, is said to have been made by "workmen," the context implying all the activity involved with making it, such as casting the metal as well as engraving it (Hos 8:6). In Isa 40:19, *ḥārāsh* is used for the "workman" who melts a graven image. It is also properly translated "smith," in I Sam 13:19, which refers to people who could sharpen iron implements. This verse is now elucidated by reading *ḥārāsh* as ironsmith. Coppersmiths were long active in Israel, but the Philistines had brought in the iron age and kept the working and specifically the tempering of iron a military secret. The new long iron swords were denied to the Israelites. Only the Philistine smiths could sharpen the plow points which they did by heating, beating them out and tempering again (Finegan, LAP, p. 149). See *ḥereb.*

ḥārash is used a few times in reference to wood and stone. In the days of the good high priest Jehoiada, money is said to have been given to the "carpenters" ("workers of wood") and builders for repairing the temple (II Kgs 12:12). The skilled work necessary to cut the names of the twelve tribes on two onyx stones is said to have been that of an "engraver" in stone (Ex 28:11). *ḥārash* refers to both stone and wood in II Sam 5:11 (I Chr 14:1 same), as Hiram, king of Tyre, is said to have sent "carpenters" ("workers of wood") and "masons" ("workers of stone") to David for the construction of a palace in Jerusalem.

The word is used numerous times without indicating any type of material. For instance, Nebuchadnezzar is said to have taken captive to Babylon all the "craftsmen" and smiths of Judah. The word is used also to describe the work of Bezaleel and Aholiab, specially chosen to lead in the tabernacle construction, an endeavor which no doubt involved materials of various kinds (Ex 35:35; 38:23). In one instance, the word is used to refer to a person "skilled" in respect to bringing destruction (Ezk 21:36).

Bibliography: Mendelsohn, I., "Guilds in Ancient Palestine," BASOR 80: 17–21. ______, "Guilds in Babylonia and Assyria," JAOS 60: 68–72.

L.J.W.

761 חָרֵשׁ (*ḥārēsh*) ***II, be silent, speechless, deaf.*** (ASV and RSV similar.)

Derivatives

761a †חֵרֵשׁ (*ḥērēsh*) ***deaf.***
761b חֶרֶשׁ (*ḥeresh*) ***silently, secretly,*** only in Josh 2:1.

The basic idea is of non-communication, expressed by either not speaking or not hearing. That is, the word may refer to the subject being silent, or to the object being deaf. The root *dāmam* is parallel in meaning to *ḥārēsh* as "being silent."

The verb is used only seven times in the Qal, thirty-eight in the Hiphil, and once in the Hithpael. In the Qal, it usually concerns silence in speaking. It always refers to God. For instance, David calls upon God not to keep "silence" toward him in a time of need (Ps 35:22). The Psalmist prays similarly in Ps 83:1 [H 2], employing *ḥārēsh* and *dāmam* in parallel. Only o ce is the Qal stem used definitely to mean "be deaf,'' namely, in Mic 7:16, where the prophet speaks of nations being ''deaf'' in respect to Israel in a future day. Used in the Hiphil stem, it usually concerns silence in speaking, but, in contrast to the Qal, almost always refers to man. The meaning is quite the same, however. For instance, Abraham's servant is said to have ''held his peace'' (''remained silent'') as he observed Rebekah, wondering if she was God's choice as Isaac's wife. Only in Job 11:3 does the Hiphil carry a clear causative meaning. Once the Hiphil means ''be deaf''; namely, when the people urged Samuel to ''cease not'' (literally, ''do not be deaf'') to cry to God for them, as the Philistines were drawing near. The word appears once in the Hithpael, with the expected reflexive meaning (Jud 16:2).

ḥērēsh. ***Deaf.*** Though the verb is seldom used in reference to non-hearing, the derived adjective carries this sense in each of its nine usages, calling for the translation ''deaf'' (Ex 4:11; Lev 19:14; Ps 38:13 [H 14] etc.).

L.J.W.

762 חרשׁ (*ḥrsh*) **III. Assumed root of the following.**

762a חֹ֫רֶשׁ (*ḥōresh*) ***wood, wooded height*** (e.g. Isa 17:9; Ezk 31:3).

763 חרשׁ (*ḥrsh*) **IV. Assumed root of the following.**

763a †חֶ֫רֶשׁ (*ḥeresh*) ***magic art or possibly mechanical art.***

This noun is used only in Isa 3:3. BDB favors the meaning ''magic art,'' citing Aramaic and Ethiopic roots in support. KB and Gesenius agree. Accordingly, the phrases ''skillful magician'' and ''expert enchanter'' are parallel. KD and E. J. Young favor ''mechanical art,'' and interpret the two phrases as contrasts: ''skillful artificer'' and ''expert enchanter.'' Ugaritic uses the noun *ḥrsh* in the area of magic and sorcery (Aisleitner WUS no. 976).

L.J.W.

764 חָרַת (*ḥārat*) ***grave, engrave*** (Ex 32:16).

חָשִׂיף (*ḥāśip*). See no. 766a.

765 חָשַׂךְ (*ḥāśak*) ***withhold; keep in check; refrain.***

The ASV and RSV translate similarly, each attempting to render the same idea. The root refers to the free action of holding back something or someone (also used intransitively, Ezk 30:18; Job 16:5. See G. R. Driver, *JTS* 34: 380). The actor has the power over the object. This root is to be distinguished from *mānaʿ* ''to withhold, deny.'' Ug. *ḥśk* means ''take hold of.'' Our root occurs twenty-eight times.

Elisha spared Naaman, i.e. restrained, stopped him from paying for his cure (II Kgs 5:20). A somewhat different connotation occurs where Job remarks that comforting words can dull the edge of grief, keeping it under control and holding it back (Job 16:5–6). In Jer 14:10 the people are condemned because they did not control themselves but wholeheartedly gave in to evil. Interestingly, God tells Isaiah (Isa 58:1) to be equally unbridled in denouncing this sin. In the eschatological age God's unrestricted blessings stand in stark contrast to man's present sin. Those who are in the most helpless position (the barren, since God alone controls the womb, cf. *reḥem/raḥam*) are to construct dwellings without restraint in anticipation of that blessing (Isa 54:2).

God may restrain man's sinfulness. Thus he keeps Abimelech from taking Sarah (Gen 20:6), and David from killing Nabal (I Sam 25:39). So the Psalmist beseeches God to keep him from presumptuous sin (Ps 19:13 [H 14]).

L.J.C.

766 חָשַׂף (*ḥāśap*) ***strip, lay bare.***

Derivatives

766a חָשִׂיף (*ḥāśîp*) ***little flocks*** (I Kgs 20:27). Meaning uncertain.

766b מַחְשֹׂף (*maḥśōp*) ***a laying bare, a stripping*** (Gen 30:37).

The ASV and RSV generally agree in concept but vary a little as to wording. The basic meaning here is to strip off a covering so as to bare what is covered. *ḥāśap* occurs almost exclusively in poetical literature and is very similar to (if not equal to) the more common *gālâ*. This root occurs nine times (or ten times; see Ps 29:9).

This word is used to describe the armies who like locusts that strip trees of leaf and bark, will devastate Israel (Joel 1:7). So God in judgment will strip Edom (Jer 49:10). Judgment and disgrace result in having one's clothes stripped off below the waist (as with captive slaves, Isa 20:4, or harlots, Jer 13:26). God brings such extreme humility even upon his own people (Jer 13:26). It is also used of the action of the Lord as he *bares* his arm to effect salvation before the eyes of all the earth (Isa 52:10).

Ugaritic (*ḥśp*) suggests another radical meaning of *ḥāśap*, viz. to draw out a liquid from a large vessel ''to scoop'': cf. Isa 30:14; Hag 2:16.

L.J.C.

767 חָשַׁב (*ḥāshab*) ***think, plan, make a judgment, imagine, count.*** (ASV and RSV mainly

similar, though RSV avoids the translations "imagine" and "count.")

Derivatives

767a חֵשֶׁב (*ḥēsheb*) ***ingenious work.***
767b חֶשְׁבּוֹן (*ḥeshbôn*) ***reckoning, account.***
767c חִשָּׁבוֹן (*ḥishshābôn*) ***device, invention.***
767d †מַחֲשָׁבָה (*maḥăshābâ*) ***thought, device.***

The basic idea of the word is the employment of the mind in thinking activity. Reference is not so much to "understanding" (cf. *bîn*), but to the creating of new ideas. The root appears mainly in the Qal stem, but also in both Niphal and Piel, and once in Hithpael. The verb alone appears 121 times.

Six clear variations of the basic thought of this root can be distinguished in the OT. The most frequently used is that of "planning," "devising." This variation is employed in reference to both man and God, and it appears in both Qal and Piel. Israelites, for instance, are warned not to "devise" evil against a brother (Zech 7:10). In one verse, Gen 50:20, there is reference to both man and God, as Joseph uses the word twice; first in saying that his brothers "meant" (planned) evil in their earlier treatment of him, but that God "meant" (planned) it for good.

The next most frequent use is in the sense of "making a judgment." This too is employed in reference to both man and God, and it appears in Qal and Niphal. The well-known text, Isa 53:4, uses it: "We did esteem (judge) him stricken, smitten of God, and afflicted." God is the subject as Job exclaims, "He counts (judges) me for his enemy" (33:10). The uses in Niphal are simply the passive of Qal.

A third use, rather infrequent, is that of merely running thoughts through the mind, meditating (Qal and Piel). Malachi speaks commendably about those who feared the Lord and "thought" about his name (3:16). The Piel is employed (without any clear distinction in meaning) as David shows surprise, in respect to the identity of man, that God should take "account" (have thoughts) of him (Ps 144:3).

A fourth variation means "to impute," actually a specialized sense of "to make a judgment." This variation occurs three times in Qal and three in Niphal, the latter simply being the passive. It refers to both God and man. Shimei, after having blatantly cursed David, beseeches David not to "impute" sin unto him (II Sam 19:20). More significantly, God is spoken of as imputing. Abraham believed God and God "counted" (imputed) it to him for righteousness (Gen 15:6; Rom 4:3). David states that the man is blessed to whom the Lord "imputes" not iniquity (Ps 32:2; Rom 4:8).

A fifth variation means "to invent," a use found only in the Qal. It is employed of Bezaleel, chosen by God to be head builder of the tabernacle, describing a part of his work as "devising" (inventing) artistic productions, using gold, silver, and brass (Ex 31:4; 35:32, 35). Uzziah, king of Judah, placed in Jerusalem, war machines "invented" by clever men (II Chr 26:15).

The last variation means "accounting," "bookkeeping," used only in the Piel. In the time of the aged high priest, Jehoiada, when repairs were being made on the temple, the word is used to say that the priests "reckoned" (accounted) not with the workmen in connection with money for the project, because the workers were honest. In the Mosaic legislation, the word is used several times in respect to the "accounting" necessary for figuring the fluctuating value of properties and produce, in the light of an approaching year of Jubilee (Lev 25:27, 50, 52; 27:18, 23). The one use of the Hithpael is simply a reflexive of the second variation noted, "to make a judgment" (Num 23:9).

maḥăshābâ. ***Thought, device.*** This noun derivative appears in three basic meanings: "thought," "plan," and "invention," all three corresponding to basic variations noted for the verb. It is used to mean "thought" in Gen 6:5, "Every imagination of the 'thoughts' of his heart was "evil." The second, "plan," occurs when the Israelites are made to say, in contrast to God's will for them, that they would follow their own "devices (plans) and do as they wanted" (Jer 18:12). The third is used in reference to a skilled worker, whom Hiram of Tyre sent to Solomon to work on the temple. He was described as being able to work out any "invention" necessary for the task (II Chr 2:14).

L.J.W.

חֶשְׁבּוֹן (*ḥeshbôn*). See no. 767b.
חִשָּׁבוֹן (*ḥishshābôn*). See no. 767c.

768 חָשָׁה (*ḥāshâ*) ***silent, inactive, still.***

The ASV tends to translate "hold one's peace" where the RSV renders "keep quiet." The basic meaning of the root is "to keep quiet," i.e. to be inactive, especially with reference to speaking; it is used also of wares (Ps 107:29). This is a poetical root which strongly parallels *ḥārash* and *dāmam* (cf. Isa 42:14).

The Psalmist gives insight into the nature of sin by reporting that his silence in the face of aggravation left him with sin within (Ps 39:2 [H 3]; cf. v. 8 [H 9], also Mk 7:20).

Among the prophets, only Isaiah uses this word. God, comparing himself to a warrior, says that formerly he was silent, but now he will speak against the sin of his people (Isa 42:14). When he did not speak they ignored him (Isa 57:11; cf. Rom 2:4). Now he will speak in judgment (Isa 65:6). The judged, however, are to remonstrate against his silence as the cause of their affliction. In the eschaton the Servant of the Lord pledges himself to tireless activity until the righteous of Jerusalem shine forth as brightness (62:1). He will appoint watchmen upon her gates to call out continually to God on her behalf (64:6) until God responds. Restoration does not rest upon man either as to instigation (man needs a mediator) or accomplishment (justification is an act of God).

L.J.C.

חָשׁוּק (*ḥāshûq*). See no. 773b.
חִשּׁוּק (*ḥishshûq*). See no. 773d.
חִשּׁוּר (*ḥishshûr*). See no. 774b.

769 חָשַׁךְ (*ḥāshak*) ***be dark, darkened, black, dim, hidden.*** Denominative verb.

Parent Noun

769a †חֹשֶׁךְ (*ḥōshek*) ***darkness.***
769b חָשֹׁךְ (*ḥāshōk*) ***obscure, low,*** only in Prov 22:20.
769c †חֲשֵׁכָה (*ḥăshēkâ*) ***darkness.***
769d †מַחְשָׁךְ (*maḥshāk*) ***darkness.***

Little doubt surrounds the meaning of this denominative verb coming from the noun *ḥōshek* (darkness). It occurs eighteen times, seventeen times in poetical books. Exodus 10:15 is the only occurrence of *ḥāshak* in a prose passage. There it refers to the plague of darkness over Egypt. Elsewhere the word is used to indicate judgment or curse. (See Job 3:9; 18:6; Ps 105:28; Isa 5:30; 13:10; Jer 13:16; Ezk 30:18; Amos 5:8; 8:9; Mic 3:6.)

The author of Eccl used *ḥāshak* to describe the dim vision that comes with old age: "Those who look out the windows shall be darkened" (12:3*b*). Lamentations 5:17 uses the word similarly. The Psalmist may be praying down the curse of blindness on his enemy when in Ps 69:23 he asks that their eyes "be darkened."

In Lam 4:8 *ḥāshak* refers to the sun-blackened skin of the exiles.

A cognate accusative appears in Ps 139:12: "For you darkness itself is not dark" (NAB). Only Job 38:2 clearly conveys the idea of hiding in it. There God asked the patient hero the immortal question, "Who is this who darkens counsel without knowledge?"

ḥōshek. ***Dark, darkness, obscurity, night, dusk.*** The noun *ḥōshek* is the common word for "darkness," and in about half of its eighty occurrences it means literally the opposite of light.

Genesis 1:2 uses *ḥōshek* referring to the primeval "darkness" which covered the world. In verse 4 the celestial luminaries divided the "darkness" from the light (cf. v. 18). And in verse 5 the "darkness" was called "night." Elsewhere *ḥōshek* is equal or parallel to "night," as in Josh 2:5; Job 17:12; 24:16; and Ps 104:20.

This word is used for the plague of "darkness" on the Egyptians (Ex 10:21–22; Ps 105:28). It also accompanied God's appearance on Mt. Sinai (Ex 14:20; Deut 4:11; 5:23).

In several places it refers to the "darkness" of the grave (I Sam 2:9; Job 10:21; 18:18; 34:22; Ps 88:12 [H 13]; Eccl 6:4).

The word occurs far more frequently in Job, Psalms, and Isaiah than in all the other books together. Often it has a figurative meaning as noted in the paragraph above. Among those meanings are "ignorance" (Ps 18:28 [H 29]; 107:10; Isa 9:2 [H 1]); "evil" (Isa 5:20); "hiddenness" (Ps 18:11 [H 12]; 139:11–12); "blindness" (Job 12:25; 22:11; Isa 29:18); and "judgment" (Job 3:4; Ps 35:6; Isa 47:5; 59:9). The few times the other prophets use *ḥōshek* it is mostly in this last sense (cf. Ezk 32:8; Joel 2:2, 31 [H 3:4]; Amos 5:18, 20; Nah 1:8; Zeph 1:15).

ḥăshēkâ. ***Dark, darkness, dark places.*** Like the verb (*ḥāshak,* q.v.) and masculine nouns (*ḥōshek,* and *maḥshāk,* this feminine noun also means "darkness" in the few places where it occurs.

The first appearance of *ḥăshēkâ* "darkness" and the only one in a prose section is in Gen 15:12. There it is a supernatural "darkness" paralleled by the Hebrew word *tardēmâ* meaning "deep sleep" or "torpor."

Psalms 82:5 and 139:12 both use *ḥăshēkâ;* in fact, 139:12 also has *ḥōshek.* Both refer to a darkness that cannot hide or limit God.

The word appears twice in Isaiah. In 8:22 it is parallel to *ṣarâ* (distress), *mᵉʿûp ṣûqâ* (anguished gloom), and *ʾăpēlâ mᵉnuddāḥ* (thick blackness). In 50:10, as in Ps 82:5, it is figurative for "ignorance," "evil," or "unbelief."

This word may occur in Mic 3:6, but since grammarians cannot distinguish between this feminine noun and a feminine form of the verb in the third person singular of the verb *ḥāshak,* there is a difference of opinion. The sense of the verse is not altered, however, in either case.

maḥshāk. ***Dark, darkness, dark place, hiding place.*** The noun *maḥshāk* appears only in poetical passages. In Ps 88:6 [H 7] *maḥshāk* is parallel to "grave" (cf. Ps 143:3; Lam 3:6) and is used in connection with wickedness (Ps 74:20; Isa 29:15), terror (Ps 88:18 [H 19]), and blindness (Isa 42:16).

R.L.A.

770 *חָשַׁל (*ḥāshal*) ***shatter.*** Used only once, in the Niphal.

770.1 חַשְׁמַל (*ḥashmal*) ***a shining substance, amber or electrum.***

771 חַשְׁמַן (*ḥashman*) ***ambassadors.*** Occurs only in Ps 68:31 [H 32]. Meaning and derivation uncertain.

772 חשׁן (*ḥshn*). **Assumed root of the following.**
772a †חֹשֶׁן (*ḥōshen*) ***breastpiece.*** (KJV and ASV are similar, "breast-plate"; RSV renders it "breastpiece.")

It occurs twenty-three times in the OT. Arabic cognates indicate that the word means "beauty," pointing to its value and importance among the holy garments of the high priest. It was made of the same materials as the ephod (Ex 28:15). It was a square pouch a span (about three inches) on a side, with gold rings at the corners. On it were twelve gems on which were engraved the names of the tribes of Israel. Gold cords fastened the upper rings to the gems on the shoulders of the ephod. The breastplate symbolized the unity of the nation, the dependence of the people on the person and ministry of the high priest, their presence before God as a beloved people, and the channel of the revelation of God's will. With it were the Urim and Thummim whereby the will of God was conveyed to the people (Ex 28:15–30). The LXX designates it as the "oracle of judgment" for "breastplate of judgment" or "breastplate of the (oracular) decision," in Hebrew. It was considered the most important item among the distinctive garments of the high priest. Josephus's account of the breastplate is elaborate, but not entirely reliable (*Antiquities of the Jews* 3.7.5)

Bibliography: AI, p. 350f.

C.L.F.

773 חָשַׁק (*ḥāshaq*) ***be attached to, love.*** The ASV and RSV basically agree with the AV, improving Deut 10:15, Ps 91:14, Isa 38:17 (but RSV "desired to build" is hardly adequate in I Kgs 9:19 = II Chr 8:6).

Derivatives

773a †חֵשֶׁק (*ḥēsheq*) ***desire, thing desired.***
773b חָשׁוּק (*ḥāshûq*) ***fillet or ring clasping a pillar of the tabernacle.***
773c *חָשַׁק (*ḥshq*) ***to furnish with fillets or rings.*** Denominative verb used only in the Piel and Pual.
773d חִשּׁוּק (*ḥishshûq*) ***spoke of a wheel*** (I Kgs 7:33).

ḥāshaq emphasizes that which attaches to something or someone; in the case of emotions (to which the biblical usage is limited) it is that love which is already bound to its object. It should be distinguished from *'āhab* "love," *'āwâ* "desire, wish," *ḥāmad* "desire, take pleasure in." Also, contrast *ḥāshaq*, II "to join, furnish with fillets or rings." Our root occurs twelve times.

This root may denote the strong desire of a man toward a beautiful woman (Gen 34:8) who could, however, be put away if she did not live up to expectations (Deut 21:11–14).

A deep inward attachment (in a positive sense) is descriptive of God's love of Israel (Deut 10:15). He was bound to them of his own volition (love) and not because of anything good or desirable in them (Deut 7:7). It is to God's attachment (love) that Hezekiah attributes his deliverance (Isa 38:17). This is the love that will not let go. If a man has such an attachment toward God he will be delivered (Ps 91:14).

ḥēsheq. ***Desire, thing desired.*** In I Kgs 9:1, 19 (II Chr 8:6) the temple and palace, as well as other structures necessary for the functioning of the kingdom, are described as *ḥēsheq* to Solomon. These were not constructed merely for his own pleasure. But he was emotionally bound to them by his love of pleasing God (cf. I Kgs 9:1).

L.J.C.

774 חשׁר (*ḥshr*). **Assumed root of the following.**
774a חַשְׁרָה (*ḥashrâ*) ***collection, mass*** (II Sam 22:12).
774b חִשּׁוּר (*ḥishshûr*) ***hub of a wheel*** (I Kgs 7:33).

775 חשׁשׁ (*ḥshsh*). **Assumed root of the following.**
775a חֲשַׁשׁ (*ḥăshash*) ***chaff*** (Isa 5:24; 33:11).

776 חֵת (*ḥēt*) ***Heth.***

A son of Canaan and the eponymous ancestor of the *ḥittî* (Gen 10:15; I Chr 1:13). The name occurs fourteen times, twice in the phrase "daughters of Heth" (Gen 27:46), and ten times in the phrase "sons of Heth" (Gen 23:3, 5, 7, 10 [twice], 16, 18, 20; 25:10; 49:32). It is plain from the collocation of this phrase with *ḥittî* (cf. Gen 23:10; 25:9, 10; 49:30, 32) that they are equivalent.

776a †חִתִּי (*ḥittî*) ***Hittite.***

An ethnic term which is apparently but not certainly cognate with Hittite *ḪATTI*, Egyptian, *ḫt*, Akkadian *ḫattû*, Ugaritic *ḫt*, *ḫty* (UT 19: nos. 1021, 1024). The name is transliterated by the LXX as *khettaios*. The name occurs forty-eight times, including twenty times in lists of the inhabitants of Canaan along with such groups as the Amorites, Canaanites, Girgashites, Jebusites, and Perizzites.

Leaving out of account the geographical list-ings (Num 13:29; cf. Gen 10:15; I Chr 1:13) and the expanded list of Gen 15:19f., the Hittites occupy the first place five times (Deut 7:1; 20:17; Josh 9:1; 12:8; II Chr 8:7), and second place ten times (Ex 3:8, 17; 13:5; 23:23; Josh 3:10; Jud 3:5; I Kgs 9:20; Ezr 9:1; Neh 9:8). In prominence the Hittites are second only to the Canaanites.

In the patriarchal narratives of Gen the Hittites occupy the areas of Hebron and Beersheba. Numbers 13:29 reports that together with the Jebusites and the Amorites they held the hilly areas. Abraham bought the cave of Machpelah for the burial of Sarah from Ephron the Hittite (Gen 23:10).

Esau grieved his parents by marrying the daughters of Heth, apparently in the Beersheba region (Gen 26:34; 27:46). These women are also considered "daughters of the land" and "daughters of Canaan" (Gen 27:46; cf. 28:1; 36:2).

From the period of the Conquest and the Judges, apart from the lists there are but two independent occurrences of the word. In Josh 1:4 Joshua is promised "all the land of the Hittites to the Great Sea." As the reference to the Hittites is omitted by the LXX, it may possibly be a gloss. In Jud 1:26 a man of Luz (Bethel), who aided the Israelites against his own city, departed to the land of the Hittites. Hittites are also mentioned in connection with David and Solomon (I Sam 26:6; I Kings 11:1 etc.).

In a passage decrying the abominations of Jerusalem, Ezekiel (Ezk 16:3, 45) declares that the city's father was an Amorite and her mother a Hittite.

An analysis of the names of nine individuals who are called Hittite indicates that they all have Semitic names: Ephron (Gen 23:10); his father Zohar (Gen 23:8); Esau's wives, Judith, Basemath, Adah (Gen 26:34; 36:2); and Ahimelech (I Sam 26:6). Uriah (II Sam 11:3) may be a name derived from the Hebrew word *'ûr* "light, fire," or from the Hurrian word *iwri* "lord."

In nonbiblical references the name Hittite can have a number of meanings. In rare instances it can designate the aboriginal Hattian people of Anatolia. Usually, it designates the Indo-Europeans (Nesites and Luwians) who invaded Anatolia *c.* 2000 B.C. and established a mighty empire which flourished *c.* 1700–1200 B.C. The remnants of this empire in the form of the kingdoms of Carchemish, Hamath, etc. in northern Syria are called Neo-Hittite by scholars. The Assyrians and the Babylonians in the first millennium B.C. used the term *māt Ḫatti* "land of Hatti" to designate Syria and Palestine.

It is fairly clear that the references to the Hittites in the days of David, Solomon, and Elisha (1000–900 B.C.; cf. II Kgs 7:6) are probably to the Neo-Hittites of Syria. Some scholars such as Montgomery, Noth, Gurney, and Van Seters believe that even earlier references reflect anachronistic allusions to the Neo-Hittites.

On the other hand, in spite of the inconclusive nature of the external evidences, other scholars such as Bruce, Gordon, Kitchen, Simons, and North maintain that the patriarchal Hittites may very well have stemmed from the imperial Hittites of the second millennium B.C. The name of Tidal (Gen 14:1) has been compared with the royal Hittite name Tudhalia. M. Lehmann has suggested that Gen 23 reveals acquaintance with a Hittite legal background. A Hittite text of Murshili II mentions a migration of the people of Kurushtama from Anatolia into Egyptian territory *c.* 1350 B.C., which might conceivably be Palestine.

E. Speiser, followed by Gelb and Gray, believe that the designation *ḥittî* may be a textual error for *ḥōrî* (q.v.) or "Hurrians." As noted above, Uriah's name may be Hurrian. We know that there were many Hurrians in central Palestine in the second millennium B.C.; in the Amarna period (fourteenth century) the king of Jerusalem bore the name Abdi-Ḫepa (or Warad-Ḫepa if the first half of the name be read also as Hurrian), i.e. "Slave of the Hurrian goddess Ḫepa." The Masoretic text and the LXX confuse the names Hittites, Hurrians, and Hivites more than once.

H. Hoffner has argued that the simplest solution is to regard the Hittites of the patriarchal stories and of the lists as an indigenous Canaanite tribe, whose name is homonymous with the imperial Hittites, but who are quite independent of them.

Bibliography: Bruce, F. F., "Hittites," in NBD, pp. 528–29. Gelb, I. J., "Hittites," in IDB, II, pp. 612–15. Gurney, O. R., *The Hittites,* rev. ed., Penguin, 1966. Hoffner, H. A., "The Hittites and Hurrians," in *Peoples of Old Testament Times,* ed. D. J. Wiseman, Oxford: Clarendon, 1973, pp. 197–228. ______, "Some Contributions of Hittitology to Old Testament Study," *Tyndale Bulletin* 20: 27–55. Lehmann, Manfred R., "Abraham's Purchase of Machpelah and Hittite Law," BASOR 129: 15–18. North, Robert, "The Hivites," Bib 54: 43–62. Speiser, E. A., *Genesis,* in AB. Tucker, Gene M., "The Legal Background of Genesis 23," JBL 85: 77–84. Van Seters, John, "The Terms 'Amorites' and 'Hittites' in the Old Testament," VT 22: 64–81.

E.Y.

חַת (*ḥat*). See nos. 784a,b.

777 חָתָה (*ḥātâ*) ***snatch up, usually fire, coals.***

Derivative

777a †מַחְתָּה (*maḥtâ*) ***snuffdish, firepan, tray, censer.***

This feminine noun seems related to the root *ḥth* meaning "to take" or "to catch," referring to fire (cf. Ps 52:5 [H 7]; Prov 6:27; 25:22; Isa 30:14). (The noun *m^e ḥittâ* differs only in the vowels and dagesh and means "destruction" or "ruin.")

maḥtâ first occurs in connection with the description of the tabernacle and its tools for service. They were made of gold (Ex 25:38; 37:23; Num 4:9) and were parts of or used with the seven-branched lamp. Some, used with the altar, were bronze (Ex 27:3; 38:3; Num 4:14). Of course in a culture which had no matches, firepans or in common life potsherds would be used to carry the coals to light one fire from another.

According to I Kgs 7:50 and II Chr 4:22, Solomon made new firepans for the temple, which were later taken as booty by the conquering Babylonians (II Kgs 25:15; Jer 52:19). These are the bronze tools associated with the altar.

In Lev 10:1, 16:12, and Num 16, *maḥtâ* refers to something other than the utensils used with the lampstand or the altar. Most translate *maḥtâ* in these places as "censer." Numbers 16 describes the rebellion of Korah. The earth swallowed up the rebels but their "censers" were beaten out as a plating for the altar (16:39–40 [H 17:4–5]).

R.L.A.

חִתָּה (*ḥittâ*). See no. 784d.
חִתּוּל (*ḥittûl*). See no. 779b.
חַתְחַת (*ḥatḥat*). See no. 784e.
חִתִּי (*ḥittî*). See no. 776a.
חִתִּית (*ḥittît*). See no. 784f.

778 *חָתַךְ (*ḥātak*) ***are determined*** (KJV); decreed (ASV, RSV, Amplified, JB, NAB); settled (Berkeley Version); marked out (NEB).

This verb appears only in the passive stem (Niphal), and only in Dan 9:24, the famous "seventy weeks" passage. In rabbinic Hebrew the root *ḥtk* basically means "cut," hence the translation "decreed" in most versions. (See Marcus Jastrow, *Dictionary of the Targumin, the Talmud Babli and Yerushalmi, and the Midrashic Literature,* I, Pardes, 1950, p. 513.)

R.L.A.

779 *חָתַל (*ḥātal*) ***entwine, enwrap.*** Occurs only in the Pual and Hophal (Ezk 16:4).

Derivatives

779a חֲתֻלָּה (*ḥătūllâ*) ***swaddling band-*** (Job 38:9).
779b חִתּוּל (*ḥittûl*) ***bandage*** (Ezk 30:21).

780 חָתַם (*ḥātam*) ***affix a seal, seal up.*** This verb occurs in the Qal, Niphal, and Hiphil.

Derivatives

780a †חוֹתָם (*ḥōtām*) ***seal, signet*** (ASV, RSV the same except RSV has signet ring in Hag 2:23).
780b †חוֹתֶמֶת (*ḥōtemet*) ***a signet seal.***

The basic meaning of this root is "to seal." Various kinds of documents were authenticated by affixing seal impressions from stamp or cylinder seals. The one was stamped into clay or wax while the other was rolled across it, leaving an impression. Letters (I Kgs 21:8), decrees of kings (Est 3:12; 8:8, 10; Dan 6:17–18), covenants (Neh 10:1 [H 2]), land purchase deeds (Jer 32:10, 11, 44), and books (Dan 12:4) were sealed. Also an unintelligible prophecy is said in a simile to be sealed (Isa 29:11).

Hence sealing designates that which is securely enclosed (Dan 12:9) by lying under a seal (Dan 12:9), e.g. the stars (Job 9:7), a treasure (Deut 32:34), or one's transgression (Job 14:17). Isaiah was to seal up his teaching in his disciples, that is, to keep it securely (Isa 8:16). A sealed fountain is a metaphor for a chaste woman (Song 4:12).

The root also signifies to close up the hand of man so that he cannot work in winter (Job 37:7) and signifies that which is closed up (Job 24:16) as when a man's running sore or discharge of the urinary tract is stopped (Lev 15:3).

ḥōtām. ***Seal, signet.*** This masculine noun, from the root *ḥātam* "to seal," refers to a seal made of engraved stone impressed in clay or wax to authenticate a document. If it were a cylinder seal like those used in Mesopotamia it would be suspended around the neck on a string (Gen 38:18). A stamp seal such as was more common in Palestine would be carried, or worn on a finger (Jer 22:24). However *ṭabaʿat* is the ordinary word for signet ring. Jezebel used Ahab's seal to authenticate the order of Naboth's death (I Kgs 21:8; cf. sir 42:6). Numerous stamp seals and cylinder seals have been found in archeological excavations in Palestine.

The stones and gold plate on the priest's garment were engraved as a jeweler engraved signets (Ex 28:11, 21, 26; 39:6, 14, 30). As distinctive property of its owner, a seal could prove that Judah had been with Tamar (Gen 38:18; but v. 25 has *ḥōtemet*). "The signet on the right hand" is a figure for that which is particularly precious to one (Jer 22:24; Hag 2:23).

In figures of speech the beloved desires to be as the seal on the heart and upon the arm (Song 8:6). One speaks of morning changing the earth like clay under the seal (Job 38:14) the figure probably being derived from the rolling of a cylinder seal over clay; of Leviathan's back shut up closely as with a seal (Job 41:15 [H 7]); and of a king as the signet of perfection (Ezk 28:12).

ḥōtemet. *Signet.* Used for impressing documents, the cylinder seal was widely known in the ancient near east. As a mark for personal property, the seal, practically a signature, was undisputable evidence that Judah had been with Tamar (Gen 38:25; cf. v. 18).

Bibliography: Tufnell, O., "Seals and Scarabs," in IDB, pp. 254–59. Huey, F. B. "Seal," in ZPEB, V, pp. 319–24.

J.P.L.

781 חתן (*ḥtn*). **Assumed root of the following.**

781a חֹתֵן (*ḥōtēn*) ***wife's father, father-in-law.*** KB use the word *ḥōtēn* in the sense of son-in-law. The Ug is *ḫtn*. UT 19: no. 1025; vb. "to marry," noun: "son-in-law" (KJV, ASV, and RSV, "father-in-law.") The word appears twenty-two times, of which all but four citations refer to Jethro, priest of Midian, Moses' father-in-law. KB reverse the persons calling Moses the son-in-law.

781b *חָתַן (*ḥātan*) ***make oneself a daughter's husband.*** Denominative verb.

Parent Noun

781c †חָתָן (*ḥātān*) ***daughter's husband, bridegroom.***

781d חֲתֻנָּה (*ḥătūnnâ*) ***marriage, wedding,*** only in Song 3:11.

The denominative verb occurs only as a Hithpael "make oneself a daughter's husband," "become somebody's son-in-law." (KJV, ASV, and RSV render alike in Josh 23:12, "make marriages.")

Joshua, in his final address to Israel, explicitly warned them against contracting marriages with the native Canaanites lest the latter become a snare to the people of God (Josh 23:12–13). Once Solomon was established on the throne of Israel, he began the well-known practice of contracting marriages for political purposes (I Kgs 3:1). The nation had been admonished on this very score with regard to the nations already resident in the land of promise (Deut 7:3). The questionable value of contracted marriages to settle problems between peoples had already been witnessed in the case of the sons of Jacob and Shechem the Hivite, who had violated the sanctity of Jacob's household. Saul the king enticed David to become his son-in-law to satisfy his inordinate jealousy (I Sam 18:26–27). Examples of the relationship of sons-in-law to a father-in-law are seen in the history of Jacob (Gen 29–31) and Moses (Ex 2:20–22; 4:18).

ḥātān. ***Daughter's husband, bridegroom.*** The first designation shows the relationship to the bride's father; the second, to the bride. (KJV, ASV, and RSV translate alike.) Some twenty references to the noun are found in the OT. The root appears in Ugaritic as noun and verb.

Married life was the normal state among the Hebrews. The family was the basic social unit. Marriage had important family and tribal consequences. If a woman proved unsatisfactory to her husband, she would return to her father's house, with an aftermath of strained relations between the families (Jud 14:20; I Sam 18:19). The natural procedure, then, was for the families involved to contract the conditions for the union. This did not rule out automatically the consent of the couple (Gen 24:8), and love matches were possible also (Gen 29:20; 34:3; Jud 14:1; I Sam 18:20). The husband was his bride's master (Isa 62:4), but this was not an absolute norm (Gen 21:10ff.). When the husband was incorporated into the tribe of his wife, the children were considered as belonging to her tribe or family (cf. Jacob and Laban, Gen 31:31, 43; Moses and Jethro, Ex 2:21; 4:18).

Betrothal among the ancient Israelites was a binding agreement, considered a part of marriage (Gen 24:58, 60). Dowry was paid to the parents of the bride, and this was the central element in the betrothal. In Jacob's case it took the form of a stipulated number of years of service; for David it involved a specific task for Saul (I Sam 18:25). The betrothal consisted of a settlement of the terms of the marriage in the presence of witnesses. The union could take place some months or even years after the betrothal. Unfaithfulness of a betrothed couple was considered adultery (Deut 22:23; see also Mt 1:19).

At the time of the marriage the wedding procession was the first part of the ceremonies (Ps 45:15). The friends of the bridegroom (Jn 3:29) went, as a rule by night, to take the bride and her party to the groom's home (Mt 9:15), an event marked by much joy (Jer 7:34). The marriage supper took place in the home of the groom, a feast as elaborate as means permitted. No formal religious ceremony was part of the marriage ceremony, unlike our custom. The union was consummated in the bridal chamber or tent (Gen 24:67).

The biblical basis for marriage is in Gen 2:18, 24. It is to be monogamous (Gen 2:24). Polygamy was common (Jud 8:30; II Sam 5:13), but the assumption underlying references in Ps 128; Prov 12:4; 31:10–31 is monogamy. The prophets used marriage as a figure of God's love for Israel (Isa 61:10; 62:5; Hos 2:21–22; Song). Marriages which involved close relations (but not first cousins) were forbidden (Lev 18, 20). Children were a blessing and barrenness a misfortune (Psa 127:3–5). Little is known about the marriage ceremony. The act is referred to simply as "taking a wife" (Ex 2:1). Some type of feast as a celebration took place (Gen 29:22). Processions for the bride and groom were a chief part of the celebrations.

Bibliography: Burrows, M., *The Basis of Israelite Marriage,* American Oriental Society, 1938. Epstein, L. M., *Marriage Laws in the Bible and the Talmud,* Harvard University Press, 1942. Goodman, P. & H., *The Jewish Marriage Anthology,* Jewish Publishing Co., 1965. Kahana, K., *The Theory of Marriage in Jewish Law,* Brill, 1966. Neufeld, E., *Ancient Hebrew Marriage Laws,* Longmans, 1944.

C.L.F.

חֲתֻנָּה (*ḥătūnnâ*). See no. 781d.

782 חָתַף (*ḥātap*) ***seize, snatch away*** (Job 9:12).

Derivative

782a חֶתֶף (*ḥetep*) ***prey*** (Prov 23:28).

783 חָתַר (*ḥātar*) ***dig, row*** (e.g. Jon 1:13; Amos 9:2).

Derivative

783a מַחְתֶּרֶת (*maḥteret*) ***breaking in, burglary*** (Jer 2:34).

784 חָתַת (*ḥātat*) ***(be) broken, abolished, afraid, dismayed*** causative stems: to break, terrify, dismay, (RSV "be in panic," "to panic"; ASV "cracked").

Derivatives

784a †חַת (*ḥat*) ***I, terror, fear.***
784b חַת (*ḥat*) ***II, shattered, dismayed.***
784c †חֲתַת (*ḥătat*) ***terror,*** only in Job 6:21.
784d †חִתָּה (*ḥittâ*) ***terror,*** only in Gen 35:5.
784e †חַתְחַת (*ḥatḥat*) ***terror,*** only in Eccl 12:5.
784f †חִתִּית (*ḥittît*) ***terror.***
784g †מְחִתָּה (*mᵉḥittâ*) ***destruction, ruin, terror.***

The basic idea is "to be broken" from which other abstract and secondary ideas are derived such as "be abolished" or "be in panic." Four ranges of meanings are attested for this word and its derivatives: 1) literal breaking, 2) abstract destruction, 3) demoralization, and 4) terror.

Both Qal and Niphal forms of the verb are stative. Both may refer either to being broken or to derived ideas such as fearing or being demoralized. They can be slightly distinguished in that the secondary significance of the Qal form refers to the broader idea of demoralization or dismay in general while the Niphal form has clearly assumed the meaning of "to fear."

For the Qal form, literal breaking is indicated in describing the "cracked" condition of land under drought (ASV Jer 14:4; RSV "dismayed"). The "destruction" of Misgab (Jer 48:1; RSV "fortress" for "misgab") may preserve the root meaning.

However, most of its usages refer to secondary meanings. It describes the terror or panic of military leaders whose courage has been broken (Isa 31:9). With the broader meaning of "demoralized," usually translated "dismayed," it may describe defeated nations (Isa 20:5; Jer 48:20, 39), gods of defeated nations (Jer 50:2) or classes of people (Jer 8:9). In harmony with its meaning, the typical parallel for the Qal form of this verb is *bôsh* "to be ashamed" as in most examples cited above. Demoralization, stemming from frustration, may be expressed by this verb as applied to Job's three friends after they gave up arguing with Job (Job 32:15).

The Niphal signifies breaking or destruction in reference to people: Ephraim is shattered (Isa 7:8), and God's enemies will be broken to pieces (I Sam 2:10). However, God's righteousness shall never be broken (Isa 51:6).

The meaning "to fear" is several times attested in passages where the Niphal parallels other terms for "fearing." It describes the terror of the Hebrew army at Goliath's challenge (I Sam 17:11) and it appears in the negative command not to fear (Deut 1:21; Josh 8:1). Like other verbs of fearing (cf. *yārē'* and *pāḥad*) it can refer to awe or reverence as in revering God's name (Mal 2:5).

Other derived stems develop the meanings noted above. The Piel is causative, "You terrified me" (Job 7:14; note: most authorities regard the Piel of Jer 51:56 as a textual error and translate it passively or statively, "bones are broken"). The Hiphil is causative, meaning "to break" (Isa 9:4 [H 3]; "hast broken") and "to terrify" (Job 31; 34; note also the difficult passage, Hab 2:17).

ḥat. ***Dread, fear.*** Twice refers to the internal emotion of fear (Gen 9:2; Job 41:33 [H 25]). II, broken, demoralized. Once describes the broken bows of the mighty (I Sam 2:4) and once describes emotional demoralization (Jer 46:5; usually translated "dismayed").

ḥătat. ***Calamity*** (KJV "casting down"; ASV "terror"). Describes Job's state (Job 6:21). "Calamity" or "misfortune" drawn from the idea of "breaking" best fits the context.

ḥittâ. ***Terror, fear.*** Used once (Gen 35:5) for the supernatural terror cast upon the surrounding cities after the massacre of Shechem.

ḥatḥat. ***Fears, terrors.*** Occurs only in the plural, referring to the fears of old age (Eccl 12:5).

ḥittît. ***Terror.*** Used only in Ezk 32:24–32 to describe the terror cast upon the nations by Tyre and by the military power of the other nations listed there.

m^e^ḥittâ. ***Destruction, ruin, terror*** (KJV, ASV "dismaying"; RSV "horror"). Three meanings: 1) Literal physical ruins (Ps 89:40); 2) Destruction in an abstract sense may be described (e.g. Prov 10:14; 18:7); and 3) An external object of terror (Jer 17:17; 48:39). In several passages it is unclear whether abstract ruin or an external terror is described (e.g. Prov 10:15; 10:29). There are no clear examples in which this term refers to the internal emotion of terror.

A.B.

מ

ט

785 *טֵאטֵא (*ṭēʾṭēʾ*) ***sweep.*** Occurs only in the Pilpel, in Isa 14:23, *weṭēʾṭēʾtîhā bᵉmaṭʾăṭēʾ hashmēd* "and I will sweep it with the broom of destruction."

Derivative

785a מַטְאֲטֵא (*maṭʾăṭēʾ*) ***broom.*** Occurs only in Isa 14:23.

טְבוּל (*ṭᵉbûl*). See no. 788a.
טַבּוּר (*ṭabbûr*). See no. 790a.

786 טָבַח (*ṭābaḥ*) ***slaughter, butcher, slay, kill ruthlessly.*** (ASV and RSV similar.)

Derivatives

786a †טֶבַח (*ṭebaḥ*) ***slaughter, slaughtering, animal.***
786b †טִבְחָה (*ṭibḥâ*) ***slaughtered meat, flesh, slaughter, meat.***
786c †טַבָּח (*ṭabbaḥ*) ***cook, body guard, guardsman.***
786d †טַבָּחָה (*ṭabbāḥâ*) ***female cook.***
786e †מַטְבֵּחַ (*maṭbēaḥ*) ***slaughter.***

The primary literal meaning of this root is "to deliberately slaughter or butcher an animal for food," but this concept is most often employed metaphorically to depict the slaying of men. The synonym *zābaḥ,* though similar in its basic nuance, conveys the additional idea of "slaughter for sacrifice" from which the offerer often partakes. *hārag* (q.v.) and *shāḥaṭ* (q.v.) are found in parallelism with *ṭābaḥ; hārag* conveys the sense of killing with violence in war or conflict while *shāḥaṭ* emphasizes beating the subject in order to kill it or, since the Akk *shaḫāṭu* means "flay," "to kill for sacrifice" which often included skinning.

The central meaning of the root occurs only three times (Gen 43:16; Ex 22:1 [H 21:37]; I Sam 25:11). The root is predominantly used metaphorically, portraying the Lord's judgment upon Israel and upon Babylon as a slaughter. The emphasis is placed upon Israel's leaders, the "shepherds," who ironically are being slain. This carnage is executed by Nebuchadnezzar's invasion in 586 B.C. (Jer 25:34; Ezk 21:10 [H 15]) which leaves slaughtered corpses in Jerusalem's streets (Lam 2:21). Cursing upon Israel was promised in the Mosaic covenant (Lev 26; Deut 28), where God declares that he will ultimately curse Israel's rebellion by depriving her of her own herds which will be confiscated and slaughtered for food by foreigners (Deut 28:26, 31). Though Babylon is the "sword" used by God to "slaughter" Israel in judgment, Babylon too will perish as a lamb led to slaughter through the Lord's wrath (Jer 51:40). This comparison to a lamb brought to slaughter emptasizes two aspects of judgment depicted by this root. First, the slaughtered victim is unaware of the consequences of the course which he is following, as implied by Jeremiah's self-description as a lamb led by the men of Anathoth to slaughter, unconscious of their plans (Jer 11:19; cf. Jer 51:40). This is vividly portrayed by *ṭebaḥ* when it is employed to describe a young man who does not realize the consequences of being seduced by a prostitute (Prov 7:22). Second, the element of planning by the executioner is clearly present in contexts where this root is employed (cf. Jer 11:19; Prov 7:22). Psalm 37:14 portrays the wicked plotting to "slay" the upright.

A unique use of *ṭebaḥ* and *ṭābaḥ* is provided in Prov 9:2 when "wisdom" is personified as one preparing "wisdom" as her food (*ṭābḥâ ṭibḥāh*) for foolish mankind to eat.

ṭebaḥ. ***Slaughter, slaughtering, animal.*** **ṭibḥâ.** ***Slaughtered meat, flesh, slaughter, meat.*** **maṭbēaḥ.** ***Slaughter, place of slaughter.***

These three derivatives are employed to represent the slaughtered victim. The sense of an animal being slain is conveyed only by *ṭebaḥ* in Gen 43:16 and *ṭibḥâ* in I Sam 25:11 (as cognate accusatives). Otherwise, *ṭebaḥ* is employed primarily to represent people as the slaughter victim, especially by God's judgment (cf. two exceptions discussed above in Prov 7:22; 9:2). All nations will ultimately experience the Lord's vengeance demonstrated in their slaughter (Isa 34:2) through Babylon's campaigns (of 586 B.C. and following) and at the end time. Israel will be slain by the Lord's "sword," Babylon (Ezk 21:10, 15 [H 15, 20]—note the relation to *hārag,* "slay" *ḥălālîm* and *reṣaḥ* "slaughter" in Ezk 21:11, 14, 22 [H 16, 19, 27]); Edom, Moab, Ammon, and Babylon will be brought down to the slaughter by the Lord (Isa 34:6; Ezk 21:28 [H 33]; Jer 50:27; cf. *maṭbēaḥ* in Isa 14:21). *ṭebaḥ* emphasizes God's justice whereby he purposes to punish those who refuse to respond to his call (Isa 65:12)—those who have failed to understand that the ultimate consequences of failing to listen when God speaks, is physical destruction.

ṭebaḥ is employed to describe the Messiah's death for sin, emphasizing his silence by the comparison to a lamb when it is slaughtered (Isa 53:7). Although a lamb is silent because it is ignorant of its destiny, certainly the Messiah was fully cognizant of the Father's will in his death, the horribleness of which is conveyed by the figure of "slaughter."

The noun *ṭibḥâ* is used (in parallel to *hārag*)in Jer 12:3 for the judgment of the wicked and in Ps 44:22 [H 23] for Israel's affliction which the righteous endure because of their stand for the Lord. Apparently *'ebḥâ* (Ezk 20:15 [H 21]) is an error or an alternate for *ṭibḥâ*.

ṭabbaḥ. ***Cook, bodyguard, guardsman.*** **ṭabbābâ.** ***Female cook.*** These two derivatives convey the idea of a "cook" who slaughters and prepares meat: *ṭabbāḥ,* for a masculine "cook" (only in I Sam 9:23–24) and *ṭabbāḥâ,* used only once in I Sam 8:13 for a female "cook." The normal use of *ṭabbāḥ* (twenty-nine times) describes a "body guard" or "guardsman." Genesis employs the term with *śar* and *sārîs* to describe Potiphar and the prison warden, chief officials in Egypt. The basic nuance of "executioner" lies behind the development of the noun, though both in the Joseph account in Egypt (Gen 37–41) and in the function of Nebuzaradan, the "chief (*rab*) of the guard" of Nebuchadnezzar in II Kgs 25 and Jer 39–52, the sense of the term has become that of "chief official." This is supported by the parallel officials mentioned in Jer 39:13—"the chief of the soothsayers" and "the chief of the eunuchs"—and by the cognate Aramaic noun in Dan 2:14 which describes a high court official commissioned to execute the Babylonian wise men. This passage may argue that the function of "execution" is still the duty of officials receiving this title. Whether in Egypt or Babylon, the official with this title is the king's representative to execute discipline, judgment, and leadership.

Bibliography: TDNT, VII, pp. 929–33.

R.H.A.

787 טָבַל (*ṭābal*) ***I, dip, plunge.*** (ASV and RSV similar.)

The verb conveys the immersion of one item into another: bread in vinegar (Ruth 2:14), feet in water (Josh 3:15), a coat in blood (Gen 37:31). *baptō* is the common LXX rendering of this root.

"Dipping" is employed in Israel's religious ritual of cleansing. (See I Sam 14:7 for dipping in the literal sense). In the sin offering, whereby the sinner's (individual or national) iniquity is atoned, the priest dips his finger into the blood of the sacrificial animal and sprinkles it before the veil or places it upon he altar's horns (Lev 4:6, 17; 9:9). The sinner is identified with the animal's blood shed as a representation of the death paid for the sin. Hbrews 9:19–22 draws on this figure of cleansing by blood. Similarly, bllod was placed on the doorposts at Passover, representing the lamb's blood shed substitutionally for the first born (Ex 12:22). Identification is also conveyed in the cleansing ritual for lepers (Lev 14:6, 16, 51; II Kgss5:14) and the dead (Num 19:18). Hyssop, or the priest's finger, is dipped in water or oil, cleansing agents, and sprinkled upon the unclean object to identify it as cleansed.

Job 9:31 employs the root to represent Bildad "plunging" Job into the filthy pit of accusations. Blessing is depicted by "dipping" one's feet in oil (Deut 33:24; cf. Job 29:6).

Bibliography: TDNT, I, pp. 535–36.

R.H.A.

788 טבל (*ṭbl*) **II. Assumed root of the following.**

788a טְבוּל (*ṭᵉbûl*) ***turban.*** Occurs only in Ezk 23:15.

789 טָבַע (*ṭāba'*) ***sink, sink down, drown, settled or planted.*** (ASV and RSV translate "fastened" and "shaped" respectively for "settled" or "planted.")

Derivative

789a †טַבַּעַת (*ṭabba'at*) ***ring, signet-ring.***

The central meaning is "to sink into something." The literal meaning of the root is clearly pictured by the stone which sank in Goliath's skull (I Sam 17:49). However, the root is normally employed metaphorically. To be "sunk in the mire" (Jer 38:6) portrays the idea of one trapped in a given circumstance, whether in indecision and entanglement (Jer 38:22), in predicaments of sin (Ps 9:15 [H 16]), or in despair over affliction and distress (Ps 69:2, 14 [H 3, 15]). God's work of creation is described in terms of "sinking" a foundation (Job 38:6—parallel to "laying a cornerstone") and establishing the mountains (Prov 8:25). Destruction is conveyed by this root in the collapse of Jerusalem's gate ("sunk into tte ground," Lam 2:9) and the drowning of the Egyptian army in the Reed Sea (Ex 15:4).

ṭabba'at. ***Ring, signet ring.*** This term denotes an official seal-ring of the Pharaoh or king which makes decrees official by its imprint (Gen 41:42; Est 3:10, 12; 8:2, 8, 10). The synonym *ḥōtām* (q.v.) has this same nuance and implies that the Messiah, represented by Zerubabbel, will be God's official seal and certainty of all his decrees (Hag 2:23). This meaning, or that of an ordinary finger ring, is used in Ex 35:22, Num 31:50, and Isa 3:21. The noun is employed twenty-eight times in Ex to describe the rings used for poles (or bars) which hold the tabernacle together, which carry the furniture, or which enable the high priest's breastplate to be fastened to the ephod.

R.H.A.

790 טבר (*ṭbr*). **Assumed root of the following.**
790a טַבּוּר (*ṭabbûr*) ***highest part, center.*** Occurs in Jud 9:37; Ezk 38:12.

791 טֵבֵת (*ṭēbet*) ***tenth month (December–January).*** This noun, a loan from Akkadian, occurs in Est 2:16. (For other month names see no. 613b.)

טָהוֹר (*ṭāhôr*). See no. 792d.

792 טָהֵר (*ṭāhēr*) ***be pure, clean.***

Derivatives

792a †טֹהַר (*ṭōhar*) ***clearness.***
792b †טְהָר (*ṭᵉhār*) ***cleanness.***
792c †טָהֳרָה (*ṭŏhorâ*) ***purification.***
792d †טָהוֹר (*ṭāhôr*) ***clean, pure.***

The root *ṭhr* is cognate with Ugaritic *ṭhr* (variant *ẓhr*), used of gems of lapis lazuli (UT 19: no. 1032); cf. S. Arabic *ṭhr* "pure" and Arabic *ṭahara* "to be pure, clean." The verb occurs ninety-four times in the Qal, Piel, Pual, and Hithpael stems. It is used almost exclusively of ritual or moral purity. Once, however, in the Piel it refers to the cleansing of the skies by the winds in Job 37:21, "sweeps the clouds away" (NAB), and once as a Piel participle it refers to the purifying of silver (Mal 3:3).

All told *ṭāhēr* and its derivatives occur 204 times. In the great majority of cases they appear in the priestly literature: about forty-four percent in Lev and Num, about sixteen percent in Ex (especially of the pure gold for the cult), and about fourteen percent in Chr and Ezk.

The LXX generally translates *ṭāhēr* and its derivatives by *katharizō, katharos, katharismos,* etc. "to purify," "pure," "purity."

In a material sense the adjective *ṭāhôr* is used to describe the pure gold of the appurtenances of the tabernacle in numerous passages in Ex: of the ark (25:11), the mercy seat (25:17), the table (25:24), various vessels (25:29), the lampstand, AV "candlestick" (25:31); the plate (28:36), the incense altar (30:3), etc. Garments for Aaron were made with cords as of pure gold (Ex 39:15); cf. Ex 37 *passim.* The lampstand of gold is also described as a pure lampstand (Ex 31:8; 39:37).

Also made of pure gold were the appurtenances of the temple (I Chr 28:17), its inner decorations (II Chr 3:4), and Solomon's throne (II Chr 9:17). The "pure table" of the showbread (II Chr 13:11) is interpreted by the RSV to be a "table of pure gold."

The Lord commanded Moses to make perfumed incense which would be "pure and holy" (Ex 30:35).

The price of wisdom is above that of pearls, topaz, and pure gold (Job 28:18–19). The words of the Lord are pure words, (JB) "without alloy," as silver (Ps 12:6 [H 7]).

In Zechariah's vision (Zech 3:5) the high priest Joshua was to exchange his filthy garments for rich apparel, including "a clean turban" (AV, "fair mitre"). Its glistening purity would be emblematic of his newly sanctified state.

The word *ṭāhēr* is used of the purification of the booty taken in war either by fire or by "the water of impurity" (Num 31:23). The verb and its derivatives are most frequently used of the purification necessary to restore someone who has contracted impurity (see *ṭāmē'*) to a state of purity so that he could participate in the ritual activities (Lev 22:4–7).

After the birth of a child a mother had to wait a certain period and then bring certain offerings to be cleansed "from the flow of her blood" (Lev 12:7–8). A man who had a discharge waited seven days, then washed his clothes and bathed in order to be clean (Lev 25:13). The identification of the discharge (see *zûb*) is uncertain. Was it diarrhea? Or did it include any running sore?

A "leprous" man who had been healed had to go through an elaborate ceremony to be declared clean (Lev 14): Two live "clean" birds had to be provided. The priest killed one bird, dipped the living bird in its blood, sprinkled the man with the blood, declared him clean, and then released the bird (vv. 4–7). The man then had to wash his clothes, shave, and bathe (v. 8), and repeat all this a week later (v. 9). The priest then sacrificed the man's offerings of lambs, cereal and oil, and anointed parts of the man's body with blood and oil (vss. 11–20). Less expensive offerings were prescribed for the poor (vss. 21–32). The leprous man healed by Jesus was instructed to show himself to the priest and offer for his cleansing what Moses had commanded (Mk 1:44; Mt 8:4; Lk 5:14; cf. Lk 17:14). A house which was "leprous" was purified through a similar process (Lev 14:48–53). See *ṣāra'at* "leprosy, disease."

For the purification from the defilement of death either by contact with a corpse, a tomb, etc., special "waters of impurity" prepared with the ashes of a red heifer had to be sprinkled (Num 19): After the heifer had been burned, a clean person had to gather the ashes and place them outside the camp in a clean place (v. 9). The defiled man was to be sprinkled with this water on the third and the seventh day of his week of impurity (vss. 11, 12). He would then wash his clothes, bathe, and then be clean (ve. 19).

Soldiers who killed in warfare also required such purification (Num 31:19). In Ezekiel's vision of Gog, Israel would spend seven months burying the multitude of corpses to cleanse the land (Ezk 39:12, 14, 16).

Priests and Levites, in particular, had to be

cleansed to fulfil their ritual functions. Moses was commanded to sprinkle "the water of expiation" (RSV) upon the Levites to cleanse them (Num 8:5–22). Later the duty of the Levites included the cleansing of all that was holy in the temple (I Chr 23:28). During Hezekiah's reform they purified the temple (II Chr 29:15).

In the post-exilic period when the temple was rebuilt the priests and the Levites purified themselves so that the passover could be celebrated (Ezr 6:20). Likewise at the dedication of the wall of Jerusalem the priests and the Levites purified themselves, the people, the gates, and the wall (Neh 12:30, 45). When Nehemiah returned to Jerusalem a second time he cleansed the temple chambers which had been defiled by Tobiah (Neh 13:9), and ordered the purification of the Levites and the priests from everything foreign (Neh 13:22, 30). When the Lord returns he will purify the sons of Levi as a refiner (*mᵉṭahēr*) of silver (Mal 3:3).

Ritual purity was intended to teach God's holiness and moral purity. Lev 16:30 (RSV) declares, "For on this day shall atonement be made for you, to cleanse you; from all your sins you shall be clean before the Lord." Hauck says: "Because the religion of Israel emphasises so strongly the holiness of God, it develops the concept of purity with corresponding energy. The law works out a whole series of regulations. Some purifications are preparatory. They set man in a necessary state of holiness for encounter with God (Ex 19:10; Num 8:15). Some are expiatory. They restore forfeited purity by lustrations (Lev 16:1ff., 19:23ff.; Ezk 39:12; II Chr 29:15; 34:3, 8 (TDNT, III: 416).

It was not the ritual purification from the officiating priest which ultimately mattered, but the forgiveness from God which rendered men clean before him. Hezekiah prayed for those who sincerely sought the Lord though they may not have observed all the rules for ritual cleansing: "For a multitude of the people... had not cleansed themselves, yet they ate the passover otherwise than as prescribed. For Hezekiah had prayed for them, saying, 'The good Lord pardon every one who sets his heart to seek God... even though not according to the sanctuary's rules of cleansing'" (RSV, II Chr 30:18–19).

Ritual sanctification and purification could be practiced by idolaters in preparation for their cults (Isa 66:17). On the other hand, whereas faithless Israel brought forth unsatisfactory offerings to the Lord (Mal 1:7–10), the Gentiles would one day offer a pure offering (Mal 1:11).

Not external appearance but an inward attitude is what is required for true purity. "He who loves purity of heart... will have the king as his friend" (Prov 22:11). Following the LXX, the RSV of Prov 15:26 reads: "The thoughts of the wicked are an abomination to the Lord, the words of the pure are pleasing to him." The Heb. reads, "pleasant words are pure." [Citations are from the RSV below.]

True purity cannot be achieved by any man on his own. Rather, "There are those who are pure in their own eyes but are not cleansed of their filth" (Prov 30:12). Eliphaz asks, "Can a man be pure before his Maker?" (Job 4:17).

Only God can cleanse. There are those, to be sure, who will not be cleansed. The Lord asks Jerusalem, "How long will it be before you are made clean?" (Jer 13:27). But for others, the Lord promises: "I will cleanse them from all the guilt of their sin against me" (Jer 33:8).

The Lord promises cleansing in a number of key passages in Ezekiel: "I will sprinkle clean water upon you, and you shall be clean from all your uncleannesses, and from all your idols I will cleanse you" (36:25; cf. 36:33). "They shall not defile themselves any more with their idols....; but I will save them... and will cleanse them" (37:23).

That such cleansing was not just intended for the people of God in the future but for individuals is demonstrated by that most personal of Psalms (Ps 51), in which the writer, identified in the superscription with David after his sin with Bathsheba, cries out: "Wash me thoroughly from my iniquity" (vs. 2 [H 4]); "Purge me with hyssop, and I shall be clean" (vs. 7 [H 9]); "Create in me a clean heart, O God" (vs. 10 [H 12]).

See also: *bar, bōr, bārar, zāk, zākâ, zākak, kābas, nāqî, rāḥaṣ;* for impurity see *ṭāmē'*.

ṭōhar. ***Clearness; purification.*** This substantive is used but once in Ex 24:10 of the clearness of the sky, "clear blue" (NEB), and twice of ritual purification in Lev 12:4, 6.

ṭᵉhār. ***Cleanness, purity.*** This *hapax legomenon* occurs in Ps 89:44 [H 45] in a passage which speaks about the Lord's power to cast the king's throne to the ground. The AV renders it, "Thou has made his *glory* to cease." Some Hebrew MSS read **miṭhār,* perhaps "purity, splendor." The NAB reads "luster." Following the conjectural emendation *maṭṭeh* are the RSV "the scepter," JB "his glorious scepter"; cf. NEB "his glorious rule."

ṭŏhorâ. ***Purification, cleansing.*** This noun is used thirteen times, always of ritual purity.

ṭāhôr. ***Pure, clean.*** The adjective occurs ninety-four times and is used in a material sense as of "pure" gold, in a ritual sense, and in an ethical sense.

Bibliography: Girdlestone, R. B., *Synonyms of the Old Testament,* Eerdmans, reprint, 1953, pp. 142–46. Gispen, W. H., "The Distinction between Clean and Unclean," *Oudtestamentische Studiën* 5: 190–96. Rinaldi, Giovanni, "Note Ebraiche: Lev. c. 12 (טָהֵר; טָהֳרָה)." *Aegyptus* 34: 50–55. Huppenbauer, Hanswalter, "טהר und טהרה in der Sektenregel von Qumran," *Theologische Zeitschrift* 13: 350–51. Vaux, Roland de, *Ancient Israel,* 1961, pp. 460–64. Milgrom, Jacob, "The Biblical Diet Laws as an Ethical System," *Interpretation* 17: 288–301. Hauck, F. and Meyer, R., "καθαρός," in TDNT, III, pp. 413–23. Noth, Martin, *Leviticus,* SCM, 1965. Snaith, N., *Leviticus and Numbers,* Nelson, 1967. Paschen, Wilfried, *Rein und Unrein,* Kösel-Verlag, 1970. Neusner, Jacob, *The Idea of Purity in Ancient Judaism,* Brill, 1973, pp. 7–31. Levine, Baruch, *In the Presence of the Lord,* Brill, 1974, pp. 77–91. Harris, R.L., Man—God's Eternal Creation, Moody, 1971, pp. 139–44.

E.Y.

793 טוֹב (*ṭôb*) ***(be) good, beneficial, pleasant, favorable, happy, right.*** Hiphil "to do good," etc.

Derivatives

793a †טוֹב (*ṭôb*) ***good*** (adjective and noun).
793b †טוּב (*ṭûb*) ***good things, goodness.***
793c טוֹבָה (*ṭôbâ*) ***good, welfare.***

This root refers to "good" or "goodness" in its broadest senses. Five general areas of meaning can be noted: 1) practical, economic, or material good, 2) abstract goodness such as desirability, pleasantness, and beauty, 3) quality or expense, 4) moral goodness, and 5) technical philosophical good. This article is organized as follows: 1) the verb *ṭôb,* 2) the adjective *ṭôb* together with its substantival uses, 3) the noun *ṭûb.* It is frequently difficult to distinguish between verbal and adjectival derivatives from *ṭôb*. This difficulty is insignificant for present purposes since both usages deal with the same range of meanings.

The verb frequently occurs with an impersonal subject, "It is good . . ." This idiom may describe a state of happiness or well-being as in describing the illusory well-being of the Hebrews in Egypt (Num 11:18), the well-being of a slave with a good master (Deut 15:16), and Saul's restful contentment resulting from David's music (I Sam 16:16). To be good to someone or in their eyes indicates that person's desire or will. It was good in God's eyes (i.e. God's will) to bless Israel (Num 24:1). Job asks God if it was God's will to oppress (Job 10:3). Balaam saw the tents of Israel as good, meaning, beautiful or fair (Num 24:5). Pleasantness or desirability is meant when the woman's love is "better" than wine (Song 4:10). Wine being "good" indicates the joy produced by drinking (Est 1:10).

The Hiphil means to actively engage in good, in contrast to the stative meaning of the Qal. It can refer to doing practical good to someone else, as the Hebrews promised to Hobab (Num 10:29, 32) or it can refer to doing the right thing. Both Jehu (II Kgs 10:30) and David (I Kgs 8:18) are thus praised. (Some alleged Hiphils of this verb are better classified under *yāṭab* q.v.).

ṭôb. ***Good, pleasant, beautiful, delightful, glad, joyful, precious, correct, righteous.*** (The nouns *ṭôb* and *ṭôbâ* are treated as substantival usages of the adjective, since there is no distinction in meaning between them.) Hebrew idiom often uses *ṭôb* where English idiom would prefer a more specific term such as "beautiful" or "expensive."

"Good" is well attested referring to practical or economic benefit. Good fruit (Gen 2:9) and the grain of Pharaoh's dream (Gen 41:5, 36) were good for eating. The "good" of Joseph's enslavement (Gen 50:20) included such practical benefits as food and national survival. Practical administrative disadvantages were involved in Moses' judging which was "not good" (Ex 18:17). Other practical goods denoted by this term are: the promise of victory denied to Ahab (II Chr 18:7); hospitality and friendship (Gen 26:29); beneficial counsel (II Sam 17:7, 14); general economic prosperity (I Kgs 10:7); agricultural prosperity (Hos 10:1, ASV); and God's intentions (Amos 9:4). The violent life (Prov 16:29) and deeds which undermined the morale of the nation (Neh 5:9) are called "not good." The "good" of labor may refer to the practical gain from work (Eccl 3:13; but cf. RSV "pleasure").

"Good" is used in respect to a wide variety of abstract perspectives. A good name is better than descendants in respect to fame and reputation (Isa 56:5). David's loyalty to Achish, his feudal lord, is described as "good" (I Sam 29:9, RSV "blameless"). Elihu challenged his companions to determine what was good in respect to truth or validity (Job 34:4). For the wise men, slowness of anger was more desirable than the violent strength of the warrior ideal (Prov 16:32). Likewise, the poor wise child was "better" than the stubborn king (Eccl 4:13).

Esthetic or sensual goodness may be denoted. It describes the beauty, or desirability, of the "daughters of men" to the "sons of God" (Gen 6:2), Rebekah's beauty (Gen 24:16), and Bathsheba's beauty (II Sam 11:2). English idiom prefers "handsome" when this term describes men (I Sam 16:12). Sensory delight is at issue in describing the "sweetness" of cane (Jer 6:20), and in Namaan's judgment that the waters of Damascus were "better" than the muddy waters of the Jordan (II Kgs 5:12). Sensual desirability is included in describing one vintage as better than another (Jud 8:2).

"Good" frequently means "happy." It describes the happy occasion of a royal wedding (Ps 45:1 [H 2]). A happy feast can be described as a "good day" (Est 8:17; RSV "holiday"; cf. I Sam 25:8). The "good heart" describes happiness (II Chr 7:10; Prov 15:15). Happiness may be induced by alcohol (Eccl 9:7).

A related idiom is the usage of "good in [one's] eyes" to express preference or will. Examples are the escaped slave's preference for a domicile (Deut 23:16; RSV "where it pleases him") and Zelophehad's daughters' preferences for husbands (Num 36:6). God's will may be thus expressed (I Sam 3:18). It describes perverted, sinful desires (Gen 19:8; Jud 19:24). In such cases, the idiom is without moral significance.

ṭôb may include ideas of superior quality or relative worth. As such it describes the "pure" gold of Havilah (Gen 2:12) and high quality perfumed oils (Song 1:3; RSV "anointing oils"). Quality craftsmanship is thus designated (Isa 41:7), as is quality or nobility in human character, as when Moses is described as "goodly" (i.e. "noble"; Ex 2:2).

An important usage of this term refers to moral goodness. The command, "Depart from evil and do good" (Ps 34:14 [H 15]) clearly contrasts "good" with moral evil. The "good way" which God will teach his reluctant people refers to moral life (I Kgs 8:36). "Good" and "right" *yāshār,* often occur as parallel terms for moral goodness (II Chr 14:1; 31:20).

Finally, Eccl uses *ṭôb* in the sense of the philosophical *summum bonum.* Ecclesiastes 2 tells the reader that there is no higher good than the life of hedonistic pleasure (v. 24) and, in this context, raises the question of what is the "Good" which man should seek. Other references could be interpreted similarly (Eccl 3:22; 8:15).

Some usages blend two or more of the areas ofmeaning discussed above. The "good land" of the Old Covenant included practical, economic, and esthetic overtones (Deut 1:25; Josh 23:13). Likewise, the concept of God as "good" is rich with the overtones of all possible meanings of the term "good" (I Chr 16:34; Ps 145:9). In light of the above discussion, each individual usage must be clearly examined to see which of the above meanings are possible.

A number of literary expressions need special treatment. "Good and evil" serves as an idiom of universality (Num 24:13; II Sam 13:22). Some have suggested that the tree of knowledge of good and evil involves no more than this idiom of universality (Gen 2:9), but the total context of early Gen is based upon a moral significance for the phrase. To acknowledge the word of another as "good" was to indicate assent or acceptance; moral judgment is not the issue (II Kgs 20:19; cf. I Sam 20:7). The "good eye" indicates generosity (Prov 22:9; RSV "bountiful eye"). In Eccl, "to see Good" is translated as experiencing the good things or the joys of life (Eccl 5:17; RSV "find enjoyment"; Eccl 6:6; RSV "enjoy no good").

ṭûb. ***Goods, prosperity, goodness, fairness, graciousness.*** The same categories of meaning are found as for the adjective above except for the technical philosophical usage. It refers to material things in Joseph's dealings with his family (Gen 45:18, 20, 23) and in the goods taken in seeking a bride for Isaac (Gen 24:10), though the latter case involves quality as well as economic value. For abstract meanings, "goodness of heart" refers to joy (Deut 28:47; Isa 65:14). Esthetic beauty is involved in Hos 10:11 (lit. "fairness of neck"; possibly also Zech 9:17). The "goodness" of God which can be appealed to for forgiveness (Ps 25:7) is something akin to kindness or graciousness. "Goodness" of taste and knowledge may refer to correctness (Ps 119:66; lit. "correctness of taste and knowledge"). From context (vv. 17–20) God's moral goodness is the object of praise in Ps 145:7. These examples show that the meanings of this term are nearly as broad as those of the adjective; thus the full range of possible meanings for the adjective must be considered in exegeting this term.

Bibliography: TDNT, I, pp. 13–15. THAT, I, pp. 652–63.

A.B.

794 טָוָה (*ṭwh*) ***spin.*** This verb refers to the work of the women in spinning curtains for the tabernacle (Ex 35:25–26).

Derivative

794a מַטְוֶה (*maṭweh*) ***that which is spun,*** i.e. yarn (Ex 35:25).

795 טוּחַ (*ṭûaḥ*) ***coat, plaster, overlay, besmear.*** (ASV and RSV also render the term by "daub.")

Derivatives

795a טִיחַ (*ṭîaḥ*) ***a coating,*** only in Ezk 13:12.

795b †טֻחוֹת (*ṭūḥôt*) ***inward parts.***

The primary meaning of this root is to cover over one item with another. It is employed to describe the silverplating of temple stones (I Chr 29:4) and the process of cleansing a house infected with a plague ("leprosy?") (Lev 14:42–48). The priests remove the infected plaster and stones which harbored the disease and repair the house with new stones and plaster. False prophets use *ṭûaḥ* figuratively to "cover-up" God's truth (Ezk 13:10–15) or politicians' wickedness (Ezk 22:28).

ṭūḥôt. ***Inward parts.*** This noun (found twice in the OT) describes an object covered over, hidden, or concealed. Ps 51:6 [H 8] clearly communicates the sense of "inward being"—inner man covered by the body. *ṭūḥôt* is parallel to *sātum,* a "closed up place," and to the seat of the sin nature (v. 5), denoting the residence of truth or faithfulness, referred to elsewhere as "heart" (Ps 15:2; cf. I Sam 12:24). There is no agreement concerning the etymology of this term in Job 38:36, and the meaning of the word poetically parallel to it is debated. *ṭūḥôt* is understood as 1) man's inward being" (cf. Ps 51:6 [H 8]), 2) "clouds" (in the sense of that which is covered), or 3) "Thot," the Egyptian ibis bird (parallel to the sense of "cock" for *śekwî*). The context describes man's inability to direct storm and rain clouds. Verse 36 implies that God is the source of wisdom implanted either in the inner man (perhaps the best rendering), or in a cloud to make it give rain, or in the ibis. [For discussion of the third view, that *ṭūḥôt* is the Egyptian god of wisdom and *śekwî* either "cock" or the planet Mercury (coptic *souchi,* so Pope, "Job," in AB, p. 302); cf. Albright's remarks in YGC pp. 244–8. He argues from UG that *ṭuḥôt* does indeed refer to Thot, but that *śekwîy* means "mariner" (Ug *Thkt* "ship," UT 19: no. 2680). He says that *souchi,* Coptic for "Mercury," is a mistake of modern Coptic students. The possible reading then would be, "Who puts wisdom in Thot (or the ibis, symbol of Thot) or who gives understanding to the mariner?" On the whole, the first view as indicated above is probably preferable. R.L.H.]

R.H.A.

796 טוט (*ṭwṭ*), טיט (*ṭyṭ*). **Assumed root of the following.**

796a †טִיט (*ṭîṭ*) ***mire, mud, damp dirt, clay.*** (ASV is similar; RSV also employs "bog.")

The term represents wet dirt, sediment, or building clay. *yāwēn* has a similar meaning; *repesh* has the nuance of "sludge." *'āpār* is employed in antithetical parallelism to *ṭîṭ*—the dry dirt versus the wet. The meaning of the verbal root is unknown (BDB), although there is an Akkadian cognate *ṭîṭu.*

There are two basic literal meanings: "mud," or "mire," which settles in a cistern (cf. Jer 38:6) and clay employed for bricks (Nah 3:14). Twice the literal meaning is used in similes. Leviathan is represented as a crocodile whose scales leave marks in the "wet dirt" (Job 41:30 [H 22]), and the restlessness of the wicked is pictured as a turbulent sea stirring up the "mud" from the bottom (Isa 57:20).

Figuratively, this noun is employed to portray God's deliverance of believers from enemies (II Sam 22:43) or his judgment upon foes (Mic 7:10; Zech 10:5) by trampling them like "mud" or dust in the streets. The figure of one sinking into the "mire" at the bottom of a cistern is used to depict the instability, loneliness, and helplessness of one in distress (Ps 40:2 [H 3]; 69:2, 14 [H 3, 15]). The abundance of "mud" in the ancient streets is employed to describe Tyre's wealth in gold (Zech 9:3).

R.H.A.

טוֹטָפוֹת (*ṭôṭāpôt*). See no. 804a.

797 *טוּל (*ṭûl*) ***hurl, cast.*** Does not occur in the Qal.

Derivative

797a טַלְטֵלָה (*ṭalṭēlâ*) ***a hurling.*** Occurs only in Isa 22:17.

טוֹפַּח (*ṭôpaḥ*), also טֹפַח (*ṭōpaḥ*). See no. 818c.

798 טור (*ṭwr*). **Assumed root of the following.**

798a טוּר (*ṭûr*) ***row.***

798b טִירָה (*ṭîrâ*) ***encampment, battlement.***

799 טוּשׂ (*ṭûś*) ***rush, dart.*** Occurs only in Job 9:26, *k*ᵉ*nesher yāṭûś 'ălê 'ōkel* "like eagles swooping down upon their prey" (NIV).

800 *טָחָה (*ṭāḥâ*) ***hurl, shoot.*** Occurs only in Gen 21:16 (in the Pa'lel), *harḥēq kimṭaḥăwê qeshet,* literally "making distant like shooters of a bow" i.e. about a bowshot off.

טֻחָה (*ṭuḥâ*), טֻחוֹת (*ṭuḥôt*). See no. 795b.
טְחוֹן (*ṭ*ᵉ*ḥôn*). See no. 802a.
טְחוֹר (*ṭ*ᵉ*ḥôr*). See no. 803a.

801 טָחַח (*ṭāḥaḥ*) ***be besmeared.*** Occurs only in Isa 44:18.

802 טָחַן (*ṭāḥan*) ***grind, crush.*** (ASV and RSV similar.)

Derivatives

802a טְחוֹן (*ṭ*ᵉ*ḥôn*) ***grinding mill.*** Occurs only in Lam 5:13.

802b טַחֲנָה (*ṭaḥănâ*) ***mill.*** Occurs only in Eccl 12:4.

ṭāḥan means to reduce to powder by rubbing between two harder objects (cf. Ex 32:20; Num 11:8; Deut 9:21).

Figuratively *ṭāḥan* portrays extreme political oppression against the poor (parallel to *dākā'*, Isa 3:15), wifely submission through performance of normal domestic duties (Job 31:10), humility to perform menial tasks resulting from judgment (Isa 47:2), and teeth (Eccl 12:3).

R.H.A.

803 טחר (*ṭḥr*). **Assumed root of the following.**
803a †טְחוֹר (*ṭᵉḥôr*) ***hemorrhoid, tumor.*** (ASV similar; RSV employs "ulcer" in Deut 28:27 [26].

A swelling or tumor. UT, 19: no. 1034 (*ṭḥr*) gives no meaning. *ṭᵉḥôr* (always plural) is the Qere reading for *'ōpel* six times; *ṭᵉḥôr* is employed outright twice (I Sam 6:11, 17). The verbal root is not found in Hebrew, but it means "eject" in Arabic and "strain at stool" in Aramaic (BDB).

ṭᵉḥôr, as the Qere reading, was probably employed as a euphemism for *'ōpel* by the Masoretes. Deuteronomy 28:27 relates *'ōpel* to the general term *shᵉḥîn* "boils" or "eruptions," and to other skin diseases—scurvy and itch. These are physical disorders which Yahweh will bring upon Israel in judgment for disobedience to the Mosaic covenant. Many render the term "tumor" in I Sam 5–6 from its description as a "plague" (*maggēpâ*) and its association with "mice," known for carrying bubonic plague characterized by swellings in the lymph glands of the groin, armpits, etc. (I Sam 6:3–4). This malady was able to be visualized by images. The Philistines made golden images of the "tumors" and "mice" as trespass-offerings (*'āshām*) for the guilt incurred by their invasion of Yahweh's rights. These images of Yahweh's judgment upon the Philistines were given as restitution for their guilt (I Sam 6:3) to secure healing in perhaps a homeopathic way.

R.H.A.

804 טטף (*ṭṭp*). **Assumed root of the following.**
804a †טוֹטָפוֹת (*ṭôṭāpôt*) ***frontlets, bands, marks.*** (ASV and RSV employ only "frontlets.")

Always plural. Denotes a mark or sign placed on the forehead between the eyes as a memorial. It is debated whether the verbal root is *ṭṭp* (BDB), "encircle," or *ṭpp* "strike" or "tap."

The placing of "frontlets" upon the forehead is always associated with making "signs upon your hand." A common means of identifying slaves in the ancient near east was to mark their hands and/or their foreheads. Perhaps these "frontlets" were marking Israelites as the Lord's servants who were to be identified by allowing the Law to permeate their thoughts and actions. The literal "marking" (whatever the form) had its primary sense in the figurative equation with God's commandments as the "frontlets"—the statutes of the feast of unleavened bread (Ex 13:1–10), the regulations of the firstborn (Ex 13:11–16), and the overall stipulations of the Mosaic covenant (Deut 6:8; 11:18). These "frontlets" were to be "memorials" on the forehead (cf. the substitution of *zikkārôn* for *ṭôṭāpôt* in Ex 13:9), reminding the Israelite to think upon the commandments of the Lord and to keep them. Later Jewry took these "frontlets" in a literal ostentatious way and were rebuked by Jesus (Mt 23:5). They tied little boxes on their foreheads and wrists and placed scripture verses in them as a reminder. One of these phylacteries was found in the caves of Qumran.

טִיחַ (*ṭîaḥ*). See no. 795a.
טִיט (*ṭîṭ*). See no. 796a.
טִירָה (*ṭîrâ*). See no. 798b.
טַל (*ṭal*). See no. 807a.

805 טָלָא (*ṭālā'*) ***patch, spot.***

806 טלה (*ṭlh*). **Assumed root of the following.**
806a †טָלֶה (*ṭāleh*) ***lamb.*** (ASV and RSV similar.) A "young lamb" (cf. I Sam 7:9). The root *ṭlh* is unknown (BDB).

God's tenderness and gentleness is displayed by shepherding his kingdom subjects as new "lambs" (Isa 40:11). Millennial perfect environment—without fear or harm—is portrayed by a defenseless lamb feeding with its perennial destroyer.

R.H.A.

טַלְטֵלָה (*ṭalṭēlâ*). See no. 797a.

807 טלל (*ṭll*) **I. Assumed root of the following.**
807a †טַל (*ṭal*) ***dew.***

Ugaritic *ṭl* "dew" and verb *ṭll* "to fall" (of dew); UT 19: no. 1037. This masculine noun is from the assumed root *ṭālal*. The great difference between temperatures of night and day in Palestine causes heavy dews, which keep vegetation alive during the summer drought. The amount varies in different regions, but in Gaza there is dew 250 nights of the year. The Bible often notices this feature. One spending the night out of doors was "wet with dew" (Song 5:2). Considered a gift from the sky (Deut 33:28; Prov 3:20), dew was withheld by God for disobedience (Hag 1:10); was withheld along with rain by Elijah's prayer (I Kgs 17:1); but was given in times of God's favor (Zech 8:12). Hence dew was considered a blessing (Gen 27:28) and the lack of it was a privation (Gen 27:39) or a curse (II Sam 1:21). Job is unable to answer who has begotten it (Job 38:28).

Morning dew in the wilderness was accompanied by manna which remained when the dew had evaporated (Ex 16:13–14; Num 11:9). The sign to Gideon, dew being on the fleece but not on the surrounding ground, was then reversed, the ground being wet and the fleece dry (Jud 6:37–40), which would be just as unusual.

Figuratively, God's and the king's favor (Prov 19:12), man's speech (Deut 32:2), and the blessings of unity of brethren (Ps 133:3) are compared to the fall of dew. God's quiet watching is as a cloud of dew (Isa 18:4). Job's former prosperity is compared to dew on branches (Job 29:19). An unexpected attack (II Sam 17:12), Jacob's influence among the nations (Mic 5:7 [H 6]), and the vigor of youth (Ps 110:3) are all also compared to dew. Israel in their unfaithfulness were like the dew that goes away early (Hos 6:4; 13:3).

Bibliography: Baly, Denis, *The Geography of the Bible,* 1957, pp. 43–45.

J.P.L.

808 *טָלַל (*ṭālal*) ***II, cover over, roof.*** Occurs only in the Piel stem (Neh 3:15; Gen 19:8).

809 טָמֵא (*ṭāmēʾ*) ***become unclean.***

Derivatives

809a †טָמֵא (*ṭāmēʾ*) ***unclean.***
809b †טֻמְאָה (*ṭūmʾâ*) ***uncleanness.***
809c טָמְאָה (*ṭomʾâ*) ***uncleanness,*** only in Mic 2:10.

ṭāmēʾ is cognate with Jewish Aramaic *ṭᵉmāʾ*, Syriac *ṭamaʾ*; cf. Egyptian Arabic *ṭamy* "alluvial mud" from *ṭamā* "to flow over." The verb occurs 155 times in the Qal, Niphal, Piel, Pual, Hithpael, and Hothpaal stems. It occurs but once in the Pual stem in Ezk 4:14 and once in the Hothpaal in Deut 24:4.

All told, *ṭāmēʾ* and its derivatives occur 279 times, about 64 percent in Lev and Num, and 15 percent in Ezk. The LXX translates these words by *akathartos* 121 times, *akatharsia* 38 times, and *miainō* 94 times, respectively "unclean," "uncleanness," and "to defile."

Animals and foods were considered clean or unclean by their nature. Persons and objects could become ritually unclean. Personal uncleanness could be incurred through birth, menstruation, bodily emissions, "leprosy," sexual relations and misdeeds and contact with death. Priests and levites were especially concerned with the issues of cleanness and uncleanness.

The greatest uncleanness was idolatry which defiled the temple and the land. The prophets, in denouncing moral uncleanness, used ritual uncleanness as a metaphor for the wickedness which only God can cleanse.

Most of the ordinances dealing with ritual uncleanness appear in Lev 11–15: chapter 11 deals with clean and unclean animals, chapter 12 with birth, chapters 13–14 with "leprosy," and chapter 15 with emissions and menstruation.

Leviticus 7:19–21 stipulates that one who had come into contact with anything unclean was not to eat of the sacrifice. An unclean person who presumed to do so should be cut off. (An unclean person could eat unconsecrated meat [Deut 12:15, 22].) The unclean person had to be sent outside the camp, as the Lord dwelt in its midst (Num 5:1–4; cf. Lev 15:31).

Genesis 7:2 speaks of clean and unclean animals which Noah took into the ark, and Gen 8:20 of the clean animals which he sacrificed to the Lord. The unclean animals which are listed in Lev 11 included the camel, the hare, and swine (vv. 1–8); sea creatures without fins or scales, e.g. eels (vv. 9–12); birds such as the raven and the vulture which eat carrion (vv. 13–19); most insects except the locust (see *ʾarbeh*, vv. 20–23); crawling animals such as weasels, mice, and lizards (vv. 29–31). Cf. Deut 14:3–21.

Objects such as earthernware vessels, ovens, food and drink which had been contaminated, for example, by a mouse had to be broken or discarded (Lev 11:33–35).

It was in order not to defile themselves with non-kosher food that Daniel and his friends in Babylon determined to eat vegetables and water (Dan 1:8; cf. I Macc 1:62–63; II Macc 7).

After giving birth to a son, a woman was considered unclean for seven days until his circumcision and then for thirty-three more days in the "blood of purification" (Lev 12:2–4). For a daughter she was to be unclean for eighty days (Lev 12:5). Birth was not only a mysterious process but one which involved ritual uncleanness (cf. Gen 8:21; Job 14:1, 4; 15:14; 25:4).

Sexual relations per se resulted in ritual uncleanness until sunset. Both the man and the woman had to bathe in water to be cleansed (Lev 15:18). Intercourse was forbidden during a woman's menstrual uncleanness (Lev 15:24; 18:19).

A woman's normal menstruation rendered her unclean for seven days (Lev 15:19–24). When David noticed Bathsheba bathing on her roof, she was "purifying herself from her uncleanness" (II Sam 11:4).

A woman with a discharge of blood beyond her normal period was considered unclean until seven days after such a flow ceased (Lev 15:25–28). Thus the woman with the issue of blood who was healed by Christ, continually conveyed uncleanness to all about her. But instead of Jesus being defiled, the woman was cleansed (Mt 9:20ff.; Mk 5:25ff.; Lk 8:43ff.).

A man who had a discharge or emission from his "flesh" was rendered unclean for seven days

(Lev 15:2–13). Though the description of the emission is not explicit, it was probably an abnormal discharge from the penis, but may have included any abscess, diarrhea or running sore.

The disease represented by the Hebrew word *ṣāraʻat* in Lev 13–14 was apparently not true leprosy, *elephantiasis graecorum* or as it is called today, Hansen's Disease. The LXX and Vulgate, however, translated it *lepra;* cf. RSV "leprous disease," NEB "malignant skin disease." The "leprosy" (KJV) of Lev 13–14 seems to refer to epidermal maladies including boils, rashes, impetigo, and ringworm. They were ritually and medically contagious. Of more significance, perhaps, were the contagious and dangerous diseases with skin symptoms, such as scarlet fever and smallpox.

Upon the appearance of "leprosy" the patient was to be examined by the priest after a quarantine of a week or two (Lev 13:4–5). If declared unclean, he was to wear torn garments, leave his hair disheveled, cover his upper lip, and cry, "Unclean! Unclean!" until he recovered (Lev 13:45–46; cf. Lam 4:14–15). Once cured he was to present himself to the priest who would declare him cleansed (Lev 14:1–32; see *ṭāhēr*).

The word *ṣāraʻat* is also used of a mold, mildew, or fungus which spread in garments (Lev 13:47–59) and the walls of a building. Garments were burned if the "leprosy" persisted, and the building had to be broken up (Lev 14:45) if the "leprosy" rmained.

Death was especially defiling. A priest was not to defile himself with the dead, except his closest relatives (Lev 21:1–3; Ezk 44:25). The high priest was not to defile himself even for his father or mother (Lev 21:11).

Those who had become unclean through contact with the dead were to eat the Passover a month later (Num 9:6–11). Touching a grave conveyed impurity (Num 19:16). This led to the later custom of whitewashing sepulchres to warn passersby of their presence (cf. Mt 23:27; Acts 23:3).

To cleanse such defilement, the priest employed the water of the ashes of the red heifer (Num 19:1–22, see *ṭāhēr*).

One who had to be particularly wary of becoming unclean through contact with a corpse or even by entering a room where a dead man lay (Num 6:6) was the Nazirite. If someone suddenly fell dead beside him and contacted him, he became unclean and had to be cleansed and begin the days of his Nazirite vow over again (Num 6:9–12). The Nazirite Samson also had to beware of eating anything unclean (Jud 13:4, 7, 14).

Priests were to teach the distinction between what was clean and what was unclean (Lev 10:10; cf. Ezk 22:26; 44:23). Priests were not to approach the holy elements while they were unclean (Lev 22:1–9). Aaron was to make atonement for the uncleannesses of the people by killing the goat of the sin offering (Lev 16:15–16).

God's temple was to be guarded against defilement. Jehoiada stationed guards at the temple so that no one who was unclean could enter (II Chr 23:19). Alas, it was the priests under Zedekiah who made the temple unclean (II Chr 36:14). Because of Israel's apostasy the Lord permitted his temple to be defiled by the heathen (Ps 79:1), abominations (Jer 7:30; 32:34), slayings (Ezk 9:7), idolatry, adultery, and human sacrifice (Ezk 23:37–39).

The land was defiled if an executed criminal was left on the tree overnight (Deut 21:23; cf. Gal 3:13). The sacrifice of innocent children polluted the land with blood (Ps 106:38).

Idolatry defiled the land (Ezk 36:18; cf. Gen 35:2). The Lord asked Judah, "How can you say, 'I am not defiled, I have not gone after the Baals?' " (Jer 2:23). Israel had defiled herself by the idols which she had made (Ezk 22:4; cf. 14:11; 36:25; 37:23).

Inasmuch as the people had made themselves unclean through their idolatry (Ezk 20:7, 18, 30, 31), Yahweh would defile them through their gifts (Ezk 20:26), that is, by the horrible practice of child sacrifice. The Israelites would be exiled and forced "to eat" unclean food in Assyria (Hos 9:1–4). Amaziah, the priest who opposed Amos, was to die in an unclean land (Amos 7:17).

What was the basis for the various regulations concerning uncleanness? Baruch Levine has gone so far as to suggest that impurity was the "actualized form of demonic forces" which even threatened God himself. Impurity in this view has a quasi-independent power.

Certain elements of impurity were associated with contagious disease and death. The laws of uncleanness gave Israel a very effective quarantine for public health. Some matters of impurity were aesthetically repulsive. Other elements may originally have been associated with idolatry.

Whatever theories are adduced to explain the laws of uncleanness, the Scriptures themselves emphatically associate them with the holiness of God. The so-called Law of Purity (Lev 11–16) was placed side by side with the Law of Holiness (Lev 17–26). In the passages which list unclean foods, the holiness of Yahweh is emphasized as the reason for avoiding unclean foods.

The regulations regarding uncleanness set Israel apart from other nations. These were object lessons or adumbrations (Heb 8:5; 10:1) of God's holiness which could not co-exist with the uncleanness of sin.

Especially in the prophets, the ideas of ritual uncleanness were used as metaphors of moral uncleanness. Haggai used the contagion of the defilement of death to denounce the immoral behavior of Israel which contaminated even their offerings (Hag 2:13–14). The behavior of Judah is likened by Ezekiel to the impurity of a woman in her menses (Ezk 36:17).

Hosea (5:3; 6:10), Jeremiah (2:23; 13:27), and above all Ezekiel (23:7, 13, 17; 24:13; 43:7) denounced the infidelity of Israel as defiling adultery or harlotry. Cf. Ps 106:39.

Micah decried as impurity crimes of injustice (Mic 2:10; cf. 2:1–7). Isaiah realized that he was a man of "unclean lips" (Isa 6:5) and confessed, "We have all become like one who is unclean, and all our righteous deeds are like a polluted garment" (Isa 64:6 [H 5]).

Unfortunately the prophets' ethical perception of the precepts of uncleanness was replaced by an increasing preoccupation with ritual minutiae. The last division of the Mishnah, the *Tohoroth* and its twelve tractates, deals with the casuistry of uncleanness.

It was in protest against their exaggerated emphasis upon ritual cleanness that Jesus denounced the hypocrisy of the Pharisees (Mt 15:10–20; 23:25–28). By his fiat Jesus declared all foods clean (Mk 7:19, RSV; cf. I Tim 4:4–5). It was supremely ironic that the Jewish leaders who denounced Jesus were so scrupulous that they did not step into Pilate's judgment hall lest they be defiled and become unfit to eat the Passover (Jn 18:28).

See also *gā'al* II, *ḥālal, ḥānēp*. For purity and purification see *ṭāhēr*.

Bibliography: See under *ṭāhēr*.

E.Y.

810 *טָמָה (*ṭāmâ*) ***stopped up.*** Occurs only in the Niphal, in Job 18:3 or possibly by-form for *ṭāmē'* "be unclean."

811 טָמַן (*ṭāmēn*) ***hide, conceal, bury.*** (ASV and RSV sometimes translate "lay" or "lay up" when traps are hidden.)

Derivative

811a †מַטְמוֹן (*maṭmôn*) ***treasure.***

The primary meaning of this root is "to hide an object so that it cannot be found." The normal sense of the root has developed also a specific nuance of "hiding by burial," especially of important or precious items (Gen 35:4; Ex 2:12; Josh 7:21–22; II Kgs 7:8). The OT hymnic and wisdom literature normally employ the root to convey the concept of one being ensnared or trapped by the devices of the wicked or enemies, whether literally or figuratively. The emphasis is upon 1) the unknown secrecy of these snares of life that lie in wait and 2) the petitions and expectations of the righteous to be delivered from ensnarement by an omniscient God who knows their paths and sees the traps (cf. Ps 31:4 [H 5]; 142:3 [H 4]). Job invokes similar snares upon the wicked (Job 18:10; 20:26; 40:13). Job also employs the verb to portray the inner sin that lies hidden from man's sight (Job 31:33). Isaiah commands Israel to hide herself for safety and security in the time of Yahweh's judgment (Isa 2:10).

maṭmōn. ***Treasure; hidden treasure*** (ASV and RSV render it "stones" in Jer 41:8). This derivative, similar to the passive participle in Deut 33:19, conveys the idea of a treasure precious enough to be hidden (normally silver and riches, but even food stuffs). Figuratively the word portrays the preciousness of an item which is greatly desired: wisdom, discernment (Prov 2:4), and death (Job 3:21).

R.H.A.

812 טנא (*ṭn'*). **Assumed root of the following.**

812a טֶנֶא (*ṭene'*) ***basket.***

813 *טָנַף (*ṭānap*) ***soil, defile.*** Occurs only in the Piel stem, in Song 5:3.

814 טָעָה (*ṭā'â*) ***wander astray, stray, err.*** (ASV translates "seduce" and RSV renders "misled" due to the Hiphil form.)

The basic meaning is "to deviate from what is right." *ṭā'â* is employed once (Ezk 13:10) of false prophets who lead Israel into error by condoning evil practices (which the Mosaic covenant condemned) and declaring "peace" when judgment was imminent.

R.H.A.

815 טָעַם (*ṭā'am*) ***taste, eat; perceive.*** (ASV and RSV similar.)

Derivatives

815a †טַעַם (*ṭa'am*) ***taste.***

815b מַטְעָם (*maṭ'ām*) ***tasty food, dainties.***

The primary meaning of the root is "to try, or to evaluate, with the tongue, normally with a view to consumption if the flavor is suitable." Akkadian *ṭēmu* has a similar semantic range. A major difference between this verb and *bîn* is that *bîn* emphasizes understanding as well as decision making. *bîn* is also more comprehensive, including perception through all the senses. The synonym *nākar* stresses recognition and acknowledgment.

The root is employed in three basic situations. First, it is used for the act of eating food, an act which also incorporates the normal process of "tasting" the flavor (I Sam 14:24, 29, 43). Close to this first usage is the second—the concept of "tasting" to ascertain flavor (II Sam 19:35 [H 36]). This sense is employed in comparison with the function of the ear testing words (Job 12:11; 34:3), showing how the final meaning of this verb developed—the idea of evaluation and decision, i.e. perception. "Discernment" is made by the wife as she experiences the profits of her labor to be good (Prov 31:18) and by the Psalmist who discovers God's faithful protection to be good when he decides to take refuge in Yahweh (Ps 34:8 [H 9]).

ta'am. ***Taste, discretion, judgment, discernment, decree.*** (ASV and RSV translate "behavior" in I Sam 21:13 [H 14] and in Ps 34 superscription, the ASV translates "reason" in Prov 26:16 and "understanding" in Job 12:20.)

Though the derivative noun is employed to convey the more basic idea of "flavor" (Ex 16:31; Num 11:8), its predominant usage is to denote "discretion" and "discernment." Good "judgment" comes only from God's commandments (Ps 119:66) and is in the sovereign control of God (Job 12:20). A woman with discretion is praised (I Sam 25:33), while a woman without godly discernment is like a pig with a gold ring in its snout (Prov 11:22).

A variant meaning of this noun is discovered when David changes his "conduct" and acts like a madman before Achish (I Sam 21:13 [H 14]). David made a decision to act differently when he appraised the need of the situation. He changed his "discretion" or "behavior." Another variant meaning is "decree." This occurs when a judgment has been made and then formalized (Jon 3:7). The Aramaic influence of *ṭ*^{e}*ʻēm* may have affected this usage by the Assyrian king.

R.H.A.

816 טָעַן (*ṭāʻan*) ***I, load.*** Occurs only in Gen 45:17.

817 *טָעַן (*ṭāʻan*) ***II, pierce.*** Occurs only in the Pual, in Isa 14:10.

טַף (*ṭap*). See no. 821a.

818 טָפַח (*ṭāpaḥ*) ***extend, spread (out).***

Derivatives

818a טִפֻּחִים (*ṭippūḥîm*) ***dandling,*** only in Lam 2:20.
818b טֶפַח (*ṭepaḥ*) ***span, hand breadth.***
818c טֹפַח (*ṭōpaḥ*) ***span, hand breadth.***
818d מִטְפַּחַת (*miṭpaḥat*) ***cloak.***

The basic meaning is "to stretch, expand, or draw out a surface." *ṭāpaḥ* stresses "space," while *nāṭâ* emphasizes the stretching "action" and "direction," *pāraś* accentuates "unfolding" often, to cover something, *pāśâ* conveys "contagion," and *shāṭaḥ* highlights "dispersement."

The root describes the creation of heaven's expanse, demonstrating God's sovereign, omnipotent, and external attributes (Isa 48:13).

ṭōpaḥ. ***Span, hand-breadth.*** *ṭōpaḥ* is interchangeable with *ṭepaḥ* and identical in meaning. The root of the plural form is uncertain (perhaps from *ṭapḥâ*) (KB).

The derivatives are linear measurements equivalent to the hand's width at the base of the fingers. The *ṭōpaḥ* (about 3 inches) is apparently the difference between the common and the long cubit in Ezk 40:5. In contrast, *zeret* "span," (q.v.) equals the distance between the thumb and the little finger when extended. *ṭepaḥ* and *ṭōpaḥ* are primarily used to convey measurements of tabernacle and temple structures and furnishings. David compares life's brevity to a few handbreadths (Ps 39:5 [H 6]). The architectural sense in I Kgs 7:9 is uncertain; perhaps it is a "covering" or a "border" (cf. Ex 25:25).

R.H.A.

טֹפַח (*ṭōpaḥ*), also טוֹפַח (*ṭôpaḥ*). See no. 818c.

819 טָפַל (*ṭāpal*) ***smear or plaster over.***

820 טִפְסַר (*ṭipsar*) ***scribe, marshal.*** Probably a loan word from Sumerian through the Akkadian *dup sharru.*

821 טָפַף (*ṭāpap*) ***trip, take quick little steps,*** only in Isa 3:16.

Derivative

821a †טַף (*ṭap*) ***children, little children, little ones.*** (ASV and RSV translate "families" and "dependents" respectively in Gen 47:12.)

The primary meaning is "human beings from the ages of 0 to 20, with stress on the younger ages" (cf. Num 14:29–31). A similar root, *ʻôlēl,* stresses "infancy." Another synonym, *bēn,* portrays a much larger classification for "people" which may be limited to "sons." *ṭap* is always employed in the singular in the generic sense. The verbal root from which this noun derives is thought by some to be *ṭpp* (BDB), others *ṭnp* (KB) with the verb *ṭāpap* "trip along" being a denominative verb.

This noun is commonly employed to represent the remaining element of mankind apart from men and women (e.g. Josh 8:35), though sometimes it is limited to those *bānîm* of Israel who have not yet known good or evil (Deut 1:39; cf. II Chr 20:13; 31:18) or to females who have not had sexual relations (Num 31:17–18). The term is used frequently in military contexts where the "little children" are to be protected or taken as spoils of war—a specific stipulation of the Law

(Deut 20:14). "Little ones" are slaughtered when a nation is exterminated (Jud 21:10). When God's judgment comes upon Israel, all the wicked, including "little children," will experience the Lord's wrath (Ezk 9:6).

R.H.A.

822 טָפַשׁ (*ṭāpash*) ***be gross.***

823 טָרַד (*ṭārad*) ***pursue, chase, be continuous.***

824 טרה (*ṭrh*). **Assumed root of the following.**
824a טָרִי (*ṭārî*) ***fresh.***

טְרוֹם (*ṭ^erôm*). See no. 826.

825 *טָרַח (*ṭāraḥ*) ***toil, be burdened.*** Occurs only in the Hiphil, in Job 37:11, *'ap-b^erî yaṭrîaḥ 'āb* "he burdens with moisture the cloud(s)."

Derivative

825a טֹרַח (*ṭōraḥ*) ***burden.***

טְרִי (*ṭ^erî*). See no. 824a.

826 טֶרֶם (*ṭerem*) טְרוֹם (*ṭ^erôm*), ***not yet, before that.*** Adverb of time. Not found in cognate languages.

827 טָרַף (*ṭārap*) ***tear, rend.*** (ASV and RSV translate the Hiphil as "feed" in Prov 30:8.)

Derivatives

827a טָרָף (*ṭārāp*) ***fresh plucked,*** only in Gen 8:11.
827b טֶרֶף (*ṭerep*) ***prey, food, leaf.***
827c †טְרֵפָה (*ṭ^erēpâ*) ***animal torn (by beasts).***

The primary meaning of this root is "to seize a creature with predaciousness, tear the flesh, and consume it." A similar root, *gāzal,* q.v. emphasizes "tearing away and gaining possession;" *pāraq* stresses "partition," as in tearing apart;" *qāra'* is similar to *pāraq* and is used primarily for "tearing of garments."

While the root is employed to convey the primary meaning, the very is predominantly used to illustrate the predatory nature of people who continually conquer and destroy others. The tribes of Benjamin and Gad, respectively, are likened to a ravenous wolf (Gen 49:27) and a lioness (Deut 33:20); the kings of Israel and Judah are viewed as young lions destroying their people (Ezk 19:3, 6), while Assyria and Edom are pictured as ferocious lions in their conquests (Nah 2:12 [H 13]; Amos 1:11). Israel's false prophets are depicted as lions ravening the Israelites, taking their treasures as payment for prophecies which devoured their lives. Israel's princes were ravenous wolves which preyed upon the people, shedding blood for dishonest gain (Ezk 22:25, 27). God's judgment is likened to a beast tearing its prey (Ps 50:22), though God will ultimately heal his people's wounds of judgment (Hos 6:1). In Yahweh's kingdom, Israel will be an instrument of judgment like unto a predacious lion (Mic 5:8 [H 7]).

ṭ^erēpâ. ***An animal torn (by beasts), torn flesh.*** (ASV translates "prey" in Neh 2:12 [H 13].) *ṭ^erēpâ* is predominantly used in the Mosaic covenant stipulations: 1) When one kept his neighbor's domestic animal and that animal was slain by a wild beast, no restitution was to be made to the neighbor, for the animal's death was accidental (Ex 22:13 [H 12]). 2) The Law forbade the eating of flesh from an animal torn by beasts (Ex 22:31 [H 30]), especially by the priests when they ministered, for a priest would die if he profaned the holy things (Lev 22:8). Ezekiel practiced this principle (Ezk 4:14), and this law will also be valid for millennial priests (Ezk 44:31). 3) The consumption of fat from a torn animal was prohibited, though this fat may be used for other purposes (Lev 7:24). 4) If one ate torn flesh, provisions for cleansing were stipulated (Lev 17:15; cf. Lev 22:8). 5) Each prohibition concerning the consumption of a torn animal is found in a context forbidding the eating of blood because torn animals are not bled properly and would therefore fall under this ban as well.

R.H.A.

י

י

828 יָאַב (*yā'ab*) ***long for, desire.*** Occurs only in Ps 119:131.

829 יָאָה (*yā'â*) ***befit, befitting.*** Occurs only in Jer 10:7.

830 יָאַל (*yā'al*) ***I, be foolish, become fools, act foolishly, show wicked folly.*** (ASV and RSV similar, except that RSV translates "have no sense" in Jer 5:4.)

The primary meaning of this root is "to exhibit a moral behavior which demonstrates a lack of understanding of God's righteous ways." It is similar in meaning to *nābal.*

The term involves both an ignorance of God's ways and an active insensibility and opposition to the known righteous behavior which God desires of his people for their own good.

When the Lord is dealing with foreign nations, the emphasis of this root lies upon the lack of understanding of God's purposes and ways. The princes of Egypt have led their people astray because they did not understand the Lord's purposes for Egypt (Isa 19:13). Parallel terms in the context indicate that these leaders were "deceived" (*nishsh*^{e}*'û*) and "scoundrels" (*'ĕwilîm*) who were morally bad. Likewise, the Lord judged the Babylonian diviners because their words and boastings were empty of God's righteous ways (Jer 50:36).

The common usage of this root when it is used to describe Israelites concerns a failure to behave morally according to their understanding of God's righteous revelation. Miriam deliberately acted contrary to God's revealed truth when in jealousy she questioned Moses' humility and leadership (Num 12:11). Jeremiah claims that the people of Jerusalem, being weak (*dallîm*), behaved improperly when they did not seek to do God's truth or justice, but rather swore falsely, refused to repent, and obstinately rejected correction and instruction (Jer 5:4).

Foolishness, therefore, as conveyed by this term, does not stress the inability to act intelligently, but rather the moral failure to behave according to God's prescribed holy conduct.

R.H.A.

831 יָאַל (*yā'al*) ***II, shew willingness; be pleased; be determined; undertake to do; begin or make a beginning.*** (ASV and RSV similar, though both also translate "taken upon" and "be content"; ASV in addition renders "would" and RSV translates "persist.")

The primary meaning of this verb is "to make a volitional decision to commence a given activity." *Archomai* is normally employed in the LXX to translate this Hebrew term.

This volitional decision to begin an act clearly indicates the function of one's mind to initiate. This causative aspect of the verb is highlighted by the fact that it only occurs in the Hiphil form. The verb concentrates on the volitional element rather than upon emotional or motivational factors. It stresses the voluntary act of the individual's will to engage in a given enterprise, not what may have brought him to that decision.

This basic concept is expressed in three ways in the OT. First, the verb is employed in a context of politeness or modesty, as when Abraham declares that he "would like to speak" (Gen 18:27, 31). The individual has determined to act, but they state their decision politely. Men employ this verb in this manner to offer invitations (Jud 19:6) and to encourage (cf. II Kgs 5:23; 6:3; Job 6:28).

Second, the essential idea found in this root may take the form of "willingness." One is "willing to initiate an action" (cf. Ex 2:21; Josh 7:7; Jud 17:11). David, humbled by the import of the Davidic covenant, modestly petitions God to "be willing" to bless David's descendants (II Sam 7:29). Samuel is reminded that the Lord will not forsake Israel, for he "was willing" (or pleased) to make Israel his people (I Sam 12:22). In both incidents, the Lord took the initiative to choose Israel as his own People and the descendants of David as the Messianic line. God must, therefore, bless them both.

Finally, the central meaning of this verb takes the nuance of "determination" and "resolve." Both the Canaanites and the Amorites made the decision to begin to retain their residence in the land of Canaan with resolve (cf. Josh 17:12; Jud 1:27, 35). Likewise, Ephraim was determined to begin to walk in the ways of man which were in contrast to the stipulations of the Mosaic covenant (Hos 5:11). Because of this stubborn volition of Ephraim, the Lord judged her.

Theologically, this verb strongly supports the concept of man's freewill, for man can make decisions to initiate any given action (within human control), but God holds him responsible for that volitional decision.

R.H.A.

832 יְאֹר (*y*^{e}*'ōr*) ***Nile; Nile-canals; river; stream; canal.*** (Normally ASV translates "river" and RSV translates "Nile.")

The primary meaning is "a river or stream which forms a definite channel through the land, usually referring to the Nile and/or its canals." The term is probably an Egyptian loan-word from *'io'r, 'iotr*. Synonyms are: *nāhār*, a general term for a larger "river;" (often the Euphrates) *naḥal*, denoting a "dry wady;" *'āpîq*, describing a "stream-bed;" and *peleg* sometimes suggesting an "artificially-cut canal."

This noun is employed five basic ways. First, it refers to the river Nile. In judgment contexts, the drying up of the Nile portrays Egypt's life-source being severed (Isa 23:3); the Nile's dominance over the land of Egypt is compared to the comprehensiveness of Egypt's judgment (Isa 19:6–8; Ezk 29:3–10) and that of others (Isa 23:10); the fluctuation of the Nile is likened to the rise and fall of nations (Jer 46:7–8; Amos 8:8). Second, the Nile's canals are depicted by the plural of this term, often describing the vastness of Egypt (Isa 7:18). Third, this noun sometimes conveys the general idea of "river" (Isa 33:21). Fourth, Daniel employs the term in reference to the Tigris river (or Hiddekel, cf. Dan 10:4 and Dan 12:5–7). Fifth, Job uses this noun to describe man's ability to cut rock channels (Job 28:10; cf. *peleg*).

Bibliography: TDOT, VI, pp. 596–601.

R.H.A.

833 *יָאַשׁ (*yā'ash*) ***despair.*** Occurs only in the Niphal and Piel stems.

יאתון (*y'twn*) Kethib. See no. 188a.

834 *יָבַב (*yābab*) ***cry shrilly.*** Occurs only in the Piel stem, in Jud 5:28.

יְבוּל (*y^{e}bûl*). See no. 835c.
יְבוּסִי (*y^{e}bûsî*). See no. 216a.

835 יָבַל (*yābal*) ***bring, carry, lead, conduct.*** (ASV same; RSV translates "bear" in Ps 60:29 [H 30].)

Derivatives

835a יָבָל (*yābāl*) ***watercourse, stream, as irrigating.*** Occurs only in Isa 30:25 and 44:4, as the plural construct, *yiblê (-māyim)*.
835b יוּבַל (*yûbal*) ***stream,*** only in Jer 17:8.
835c †יְבוּל (*y^{e}bûl*) ***produce (of the soil).***
835d †בּוּל (*bûl*) ***produce, outgrowth,*** only in Job 40:20; Isa 44:19.
835e †יוֹבֵל (*yôbēl*), יֹבֵל (*yōbēl*) ***trumpet.***
835f יַבַּל (*yabbal*) ***runnings, suppurating,*** only as the feminine singular *yabbelet*, as a substantive in Lev 22:22.
835g אוּבַל (*'ûbal*) ***stream, river,*** only in Dan 8:2, 3, 6.
835h †תֵּבֵל (*tēbēl*) ***world.***

The primary meaning of this root is "to cause to transport an object from one place to another." The verb occurs only in the causative stems. Ugaritic is similar. The Akkadian *wabālu* "to bring" also has a by-form *tabālu* with the same meaning.

The root conveys two essential nuances. First, the basic sense of "bring" is used when the object of the verb is inanimate. The object is normally 1) a gift (*shay*) offered in homage to Yahweh in response to his presence (Ps 76:11 [H 12]), especially in time of judgment (Isa 18:7) and in his temple (Ps 68:29 [H 30]), or 2) a present given to others. Israel's deportation to Assyria is viewed as a present to Assyria (Hos 10:6), and Israel brought oil to Egypt as a bribe (Hos 12:1 [H 2]). Passively, this nuance is employed to depict the expansion of Tyre (Isa 23:7).

Second, when the object is people, the sense of this root is normally "lead." This verb conveys Yahweh's leading in three ways. First, he will lead Israel back to Canaan in Israel's future restoration. Then, in the millennial kingdom, Yahweh will lead Israel in paths where they will not stumble (Jer 31:9). Second, all who seek Yahweh will be led by him into the blessings of the Davidic covenant (Isa 55:12). Third, Yahweh will lead Israel into judgment (Ps 60:9 [H 11]; 108:10 [H 11], et al.). It is also significant that the Messiah, himself, is to be led as a lamb to slaughter on behalf of the sins of the people (Isa 53:7).

y^{e}bûl. ***Produce (of the soil), increase.*** (ASV and RSV also translate "fruit." RSV uses "possessions" in Job 20:28.) *y^{e}bûl* primarily refers to the produce which grows up directly from the ground. The synonym *p^{e}rî* indicates the "fruit" of trees as well as other plants (cf. Ezk 37:24). *t^{e}bû'â* emphasizes the "yield" or "income" of the product. *y^{e}bûl* is primarily associated with the blessings and cursings of Yahweh. In the Mosaic covenant, the land is blessed or cursed in response to Israel's obedience or disobedience to the covenant (Lev 26:4, 20; Deut 11:17; 32:22), though ultimately she will receive the blessings of the land in the millennium (Ezk 34:27; Zech 8:12). Judgment is often manifested through the destruction of a nation's produce by Yahweh or by another nation (Jud 6:4; Ps 78:46; Hag 1:10). Figuratively, even the production of one's house may depart during judgment (Job 20:28).

yôbēl. ***Trumpet, ram's horn, jubilee.*** This noun is most likely derived from the root *yābal* (BDB), though some think the root is more appropriately *ybl* "toss" or the Phoenician *ybl* "ram." From usage, it appears that two roots may be represented in the singular noun form. The horn employed to call assemblies and announce one's presence in Ex 19:13 and Josh 6 most likely derives from the Phoenician *ybl* "ram," since the horn is probably made from the ram's horn. This term is distinct from *shōpār* which is the general and most common word for any kind of trumpet or horn. Some think the *yôbēl* in Josh 6 refers to the same "horn" that is employed at the beginning of the year of jubilee. On the other hand, this noun in Lev and Num is never translated, but transliterated by the word "jubilee." The context of these passages is the "year of jubilee" when the land lies fallow, all possessions (especially the land, its produce, and slaves) revert to the original owners, and produce is provided for the people by Yahweh's blessing upon the land in the previous year, therefore it seems that the derivation of "jubilee" is probably from *yābal* "to bring (forth)." The produce is "brought forth" to provide for the fallow jubilee year, and property is "brought" or "returned" to the original owners. The "year of jubilee" begins with the blast of the *shōpār* on the Day of Atonement each fiftieth year. It is a year that is holy (separated) unto Yahweh (Lev 25:10–15).

bûl. ***Produce (of a tree), food.*** (ASV translates Isa 44:19 "stock" and RSV renders it "block.") *bûl* is only employed twice in the OT. In Isa 44:19 the reference is used to depict an idol constructed from wood (or product of a tree). This term in Job 40:20 refers to the edible product of trees.

tēbēl. ***World.*** This noun is used in three basic situations. First, the noun is employed to represent the global mass called earth, including the atmosphere or heavens (cf. Ps 89:12; II Sam 22:16; et al.). *tēbēl* is often in parallelism or apposition with *'ereṣ* (I Sam 2:8; Isa 26:9; 34:1; et al.) when *'ereṣ* is used in its broadest sense of "the world." The "world" was created by God, not false gods (Jer 10:12; Ps 93:1) and it belongs solely to him (Ps 24:1). God's eternality is illustrated by his existence before the creation of the "world" (Ps 90:2) and his wisdom (perhaps a personification of Christ) was present prior to the world's creation (Prov 8:26, 31). Creation itself gives a "worldwide" witness to God's glory (Ps 19:4 [H 5]) which should result in Yahweh's praise (Ps 98:2). Yahweh will judge this "world," making it empty (Isa 24:4), though in the millennium God will cause Israel to blossom and fill the whole world with her fruit (Isa 27:6).

Second, *tēbēl* is sometimes limited to "countries" or "the inhabitable world." This meaning is more closely related to the root meaning. It refers to the world where crops are raised. This is observed in the judgment message against the king of Babylon (not Satan) for violently shaking the "world" or "inhabitable world" (Isa 13:11; 14:17). Lightning is said to enlighten the "world"—undoubtedly referring to a limited land area (Ps 77:18 [H 19]; 97:4).

Third, *tēbēl* may also refer to the inhabitants living upon the whole earth. This is demonstrated by the parallelism of *tēbēl* with *lᵉ'ūmîm* (Ps 9:8 [H 9]) and *'ammîm* (Ps 96:13; 98:9). The context of these references is Yahweh's judgment upon the world's inhabitants—a judgment both executed in righteousness and instructive of Yahweh's righteousness (Isa 26:9; 34:1).

In several passages the sense of *tēbēl* as the global earth in combination with its inhabitants is clearly observed. Everything belongs to Yahweh as his creation (Ps 50:12). Yahweh alone controls this world (Job 34:13; Nah 1:5) and his power is over all the earth which always responds to his presence (Job 37:12; Ps 97:4).

Bibliography: TDNT, VII, pp. 75–85.

R.H.A.

836 יָבַם (*yābam*) ***perform the duty of a brother-in-law.***

Parent Noun

836a †יָבָם (*yābām*) ***husband's brother, brother-in-law***

836b †יְבֵמָה (*yᵉbēmâ*) ***brother's wife, sister-in-law.***

The primary meaning of this denominative verb is "to assume the responsibility to marry one's widowed sister-in-law in order to raise up a male heir to the deceased brother." The verbal root is probably a Piel denominative verb derived from the noun *yābām* ("brother-in-law") (BDB) but which developed its specific nuance from the brother-in-law's function in the law of levirate marriage. The Ugaritic root means to "beget, create" with the noun derivative, *ybmt,* meaning possibly "progenitress," used as an epithet of the goddess Anath (cf. Dahood, *Biblica* 46: 313; UT 19: no. 1065).

The verbal root is only employed in two contexts in the OT: Gen 38 and Deut 25. In Gen 38:8 the root is used by Judah to encourage his son, Onan, to marry Tamar, Onan's sister-in-law, and to go in to her and raise up "seed" to his brother, Er. The context clearly indicates that this meant that Onan was to have sexual relations with Tamar in order to beget a male descendant to carry on Er's name.

This principle, illustrated in Gen 38, is known as "the law of Levirate marriage." This law, delineated in Deut 25:5–10, was designed to provide a male heir to a man who died without a son so that that deceased man might have his "name" continued ("build up his . . . house") in Israel and have his property retained in his name. The law was only applicable when a man died without having a male heir. The first son born to the union of the widow and her brother-in-law carried on the name of the son's "legal" father (his mother's first husband), even though he was conceived by proxy. The importance of keeping the name in the family is stressed when the law forbids the widow to marry outside her husband's family. Of course, the custom kept the title to the property within the clan.

The act of assuming the responsibility to perform this duty for the deceased brother is the essence of the meaning of *yābam*. If the brother-in-law refused to perform this duty of raising up a male heir to his deceased brother, then before the elders the widowed sister-in-law would publicly disgrace her brother-in-law by taking his shoe off his foot and spitting in his face. From that moment on, he would be known throughout Israel as "the house of him who has his shoe loosed."

yābām. ***Husband's brother, brother-in-law.*** (ASœ v and RSV the same.) This masculine noun is employed only in the Deut 25 passage to refer to the "brother-in-law" who is to perform the duty for his deceased brother described above. One of the best known examples of the execution of the law of levirate marriage is in the book of Ruth where Boaz performs this duty for his deceased relative by marrying Ruth and raising up heirs for his kinsman who had died. However, another separate biblical principle is also integral to the argument of the book of Ruth—that of the kinsman redemption whereby Boaz redeemed the land that Naomi had to sell in her poverty. *yābām* refers to the performing of the duty described in the law of levirate marriage whereas *gō'ēl* is used to depict the function of the "redemption" of property.

In the book of Ruth the nearest kinsman was willing to purchase the property which Naomi had had to sell in her poverty, but when he discovered that he must also perform the duty of levirate marriage and marry Ruth, he refused to perform either responsibility. It was at this point that Boaz assumed these duties.

y^ebēmâ. ***Brother's wife, sister-in-law.*** (RSV and ASV the same.) UT 19: no. 1065 renders the term "widowed sister-in-law" and also proposes "progenitress (of heroes)." Variant vocalizations are *y^ebāmâ* and *y^ebāmeh*. *y^ebēmâ* is employed in the Deut 25 context to designate the widowed "sister-in-law." In the book of Ruth, the term is used outside the context of levirate marriage just to refer to Ruth's "sister-in-law," Orpah (Ruth 1:15).

E. A. Speiser "Of Shoes and Shekels" in *Oriental and Biblical Studies* Univ of Pennsylvania, 1967, pp. 151–56.

R.H.A.

837 יָבֵשׁ (*yābēsh*) ***be or become dry, be dried up, make dry, wither.*** (ASV, RSV same.)

Derivatives

837a †יָבֵשׁ (*yābēsh*) ***dried, dry.***
837b †יַבָּשָׁה (*yabbāshâ*) ***dry land.***
837c יַבֶּשֶׁת (*yabbeshet*) ***dry land,*** only in Ps 95:5; Ex 4:9.

The primary meaning of this root is "to be or become dry without moisture from necessary or normal fluids." The synonym *ḥārab* is almost equivalent to *yābēsh* though *ḥārab* is employed more frequently to indicate bodies of water becoming dry, whereas *yābēsh* is employed more often to portray dryness of vegetation.

Though the verbal root is employed to convey the concepts of plants withering for lack of internal moisture and land becoming parched for lack of rain, the root is used primarily in the OT to communicate four basic theological truths. First, this verb is employed to describe two important OT miracles: the dryness of the earth's surface which God caused after the Noahic flood (Gen 8:7, 14) and the dryness of the ground upon which the children of Israel walked as they crossed the Reed Sea in the exodus from Egypt and the Jordan river in the conquest of Canaan (Josh 2:10; Ps 74:15). The second theological verity is closely related to the first. This root is used to portray certain attributes of God. God's immutability is observed in his drying up the Jordan river just as he previously dried up the Reed Sea (Josh 4:23). The sovereignty of God is emphasized in his ability to cause plants and lands to dry up at his command (Isa 40:24; Ezk 17:24; et al.). God's omnipotence is clearly seen in the miracles mentioned above (cf. Job 12:15).

The third truth communicated by this verb is judgment. The literal judgment of Yahweh in which he makes a land barren by withholding rain and drying up all water and produce in that land is common throughout the OT. This type of judgment is poured out upon Moab (Isa 15:6); Egypt (Isa 19:5–7; Zech 10:11), Babylon (Jer 50:38; 51:36), and most of all Israel and Judah (Jer 12:4; Isa 42:15; Joel 1:20; et al.). Israel's scattering until the end times is symbolized by "dry bones" (Ezk 37:11). Individuals who oppose God are sometimes judged by the withering of a limb (I Kgs 13:4; Zech 11:17), and those who forget God will perish like a withered plant (Job 8:12; 15:30; 18:16).

Finally, the frailty of mankind and life is compared to grass that withers (Isa 40:7–8). The brevity of man's normal lifespan is likened to grass that grows up in the morning but withers and dies by the evening (Ps 90:6). This, in turn, is contrasted to the enduring quality of God's Word (Isa 40:7–8). The failure of man's vitality and strength is compared to the dryness of a potsherd in a Messianic psalm (Ps 22:15 [H 16]) while the distress of man (Ps 102:4, 11 [H 5, 12]) and his death (Job 14:11) are likened again to grass that withers. A broken spirit can even produce psychosomatic illnesses ("dries up the bones," Prov 17:22).

yābēsh. ***Dried, dry.*** Though identical in form with the verbal root, this word is probably a participial form frozen as an adjective—all three forms are alike in many of the stative verbs.

yābēsh is primarily employed figuratively. The Lord's judgments are likened to the burning of dry fuel (Ezk 20:47 [H 21:3]; Nah 1:10). Other concepts conveyed by the figure of "dryness" are harassment (Job 13:25), captive Israel (Ezk 37:2, 4), Yahweh's sovereignty (Ezk 17:24), desire for food (Num 11:6), and the sterility of an eunuch (Isa 56:3).

yabbāshâ. ***Dry land, dry ground.*** The synonym *ḥārābâ* is equivalent in meaning, whereas *ṣiyyâ* stresses "drought."

yabbāshâ emphasizes "dry land" in contrast to bodies of water (cf. Jon 2:11). Two basic theological events are partially described by this noun: the separation of the "dry land" from the waters in creation (Gen 1:9–10) and the crossing of the Reed Sea and the Jordan river in the exodus and conquest respectively (Ex 14:16–29; Neh 9:11).

R.H.A.

יַבֶּשֶׁת (*yabbeshet*). See no. 837c.

838 יָגַב (*yāgab*) ***till, be husbandman.***

Derivative

838a יָגֵב (*yāgēb*) ***field.***

839 יָגָה (*yāgâ*) ***I, suffer, grieve, afflict.*** (ASV, RSV similar.)

Derivatives

839a †יָגוֹן (*yāgôn*) ***grief, sorrow, anguish.***
839b †תּוּגָה (*tûgâ*) ***grief, sorrow, heaviness.***

The primary meaning is a mental troubling resulting from affliction. *yāgâ* stresses mental sorrow in affliction. *kā'ab* accentuates the pain. *ʻānâ* emphasizes humbling.

In Lam the root describes Jerusalem's grief resulting from God's judgment in 586 B.C. Jerusalem's great iniquities occasioned this judgment which God desired not to bring. Israel will also suffer in the end-time judgments (Zeph 3:18). Such "sorrow" will ultimately be removed and placed upon Israel's tormentors because of God's faithfulness and compassionate restoration of Israel (Lam 3:32–33; Isa 51:11, 23; cf. *yāgôn* in Isa 35:10).

yāgôn. ***Grief, sorrow, anguish.*** Is employed to portray both individual sorrow experienced in times of difficulty (*e.g.* David when pursued by enemies, Ps 31:10 [H 10]) and national grief (Ezk 23:33). Grievous judgment demonstrates God's power (Ps 107:39), though God is "grieved" over Israel's rebellion (Jer 8:18).

tûgâ. ***Grief, sorrow, heaviness.*** This noun stresses the emotional sadness of grief. Such grief comes to a foolish son's parents (Prov 10:1) and to the perverse man's heart (Prov 14:13). Only God's Word brings relief from this state of mind (Ps 119:28).

R.H.A.

840 *יָגָה (*yāgâ*) ***II, thrust away.*** Occurs only in the Hiphil, in II Sam 20:13.

יָגוֹן (*yāgôn*). See no. 839a.
יָגוֹר (*yāgôr*). See no. 843a.
יָגִיעַ (*yāgîaʻ*). See no. 842d.

841 יגן (*ygn*). **Assumed root of the following.**
841a †גַּת (*gat*) ***winepress, wine vat.***
841b גִּתִּית (*gittît*). Meaning unknown. Probably a musical instrument.

Probably derived from *ygn* (BDB). The primary meaning is "a vat for treading out juice from grapes" (synonymous with *pûrâ*). *yeqeb* describes the container that receives juice from the *gat*.

The Law prohibited the use of winepresses on the sabbath (cf. Neh 13:15). God's judgment is compared to the treading of grapes (cf. Lam 1:15; Isa 63:2).

The word is at least as old as the Amarna letters, where it appears in the form *Gi(n)t-* in place names.

R.H.A.

gittît. ***Gittith.*** This is a musical term of uncertain meaning, perhaps related to the Philistine city Gath and occurring in the heading of three Psalms (8, 81, 84). Each time it is connected with the preposition *ʻal* "upon," "according to," or even "in the fashion of." Since *gat* is also the word for "winepress," some feel it refers to the celebration of the grape harvest at the Feast of Tabernacles. All three psalms are joyful hymns of praise. Other interpreters think "Gittith" signifies either a tune or an instrument well-known at Gath. David spent several months as a vassal of the king of Gath and could have become familiar with it then. For other such terms see *selâ*.

H.W.

842 יָגֵעַ (*yāgēaʻ*) ***toil, labor, grow or be weary.*** (ASV, RSV similar.)

Derivatives

842a יָגָע (*yāgā'*) ***gain (product of labor),*** only in Job 20:18.
842b יָגֵעַ (*yāgēa'*) ***weary, wearisome.***
842c †יְגִעָה (*ye gi'â*) ***wearying.***
842d יָגִיעַ (*yāgîa'*) ***weary,*** only in Job 3:17, as a plural construct in the phrase *ye gî'ê kōaḥ* "weary of strength" i.e. toil-worn.
842e יְגִיעַ (*ye gîa'*) ***toil, product.***

The primary meaning is "to work until one is tired and exhausted." The two synonyms *yā'ēp* and *lā'â* (q.v.) tend to stress the nuance of "weariness." The adjective *yāgē(a)'* is identical in form and is translated "weary, wearisome, toilsome."

The root is used to convey two basic thrusts: 1) an emphasis on the toil of work, and 2) the weariness that results from labor. God meant that toil should result in the benefits of the end product. This is especially true in farming (Josh 24:13). However, whenever Israel "toiled" in idolatry and "grew weary" of God's ways (Isa 57:10; Mal 2:17), she reaped the product of her labor: God's judgment. This judgment often took the form of drought, famine, and devastation, so that Israel was unable to harvest the fruits of the land. This, in turn, caused Israel to complain that her "labor" in the land was only in vain (Isa 49:4). The Lord promises, however, that in the millennium Israel will no longer labor in vain, but she will reap the fruit of the land—the product of her labors (Isa 62:8; 65:23). A similar type of judgment is brought upon Babylon because of her "labor" in sorcery (Isa 47:12, 15). However, there is no deliverance for Babylon (Jer 51:58; Hab 2:13).

The Scriptures warn against toiling for wealth, for the labor of a fool only wearies him (Prov 23:4; Eccl 10:15).

Because Israel "grows weary" of the Lord's ways by practicing idolatry, they will also "become weary" of God's judgments (Lam 5:5). Men grow physically weary and emotionally weary, but the Lord never "grows weary" in His works and ways (Isa 40:28–31; Ps 6:8 [H 7]). The Lord is "wearied" only by the iniquities of man (cf. Isa 43:24).

y^egîa'. ***Toil, labor, product, gain.*** (ASV and RSV similar, though RSV translates "wealth" in Isa 45:14.)

This noun denotes the work of creatures that yields a product. It is primarily employed to describe the fruit of labor in agriculture and animal husbandry. It is the blessing of God for one to eat the produce of his own labor (Ps 128:2), but if Israel turned from God's ways and "worked" iniquity (Isa 55:2; Hos 12:8 [H 9]), God promised to judge her with famine (Deut 28:33; cf. Jer 3:24; Hag 1:11). In this sense the noun emphasizes the end product of "labor" being destroyed, while the verb stresses the action of "toil" that produced the final fruit. Egypt was judged in like manner (Ps 78:46) through the plagues. Nehemiah warns of similar discipline (Neh 5:13), while David's imprecations against his enemies consist of analagous judgments (Ps 109:11).

R.H.A.

843 יָגֹר (*yāgōr*) ***be afraid, fear, dread.***

Derivative

843a יָגוֹר (*yāgôr*) ***fearing,*** only in Jer 22:25; 39:17.

The basic meaning is "to fear something with great dread" (similar to *pāḥad* q.v.). *yārē'* (q.v.) has nuances of "reverence." Probably a byform of *gûr* "be afraid" (q.v.).

The root primarily describes "fear" of God's discipline when one has disobeyed, or thinks he has disobeyed, God's ways (Deut 28:60; Job 9:28; Ps 119:39). Moses "fears" when the golden calf is built (Deut 9:19).

R.H.A.

844 יָד (*yād*) ***hand, power, monument, axle, tenon, stay side, part, time.*** (ASV and RSV similar.)

The primary meaning of this noun is "the terminal part of the arm used to perform functions of man's will."

This term is employed literally of man's hand which does normal work functions (Gen 5:29), good or bad (Gen 4:11). The law of *lex talionis* ("hand for a hand") is a penalty involving destruction of bodily parts for bodily parts harmed by another (cf. Harris, R. L., *Man—God's Eternal Creation,* Moody, 1971, pp. 117–18).

Significant theologically is the manifold way in which the word "hand" is employed idiomatically. These idioms arise from the versatility of the hand. The phrase "into (or "under") someone's hand" conveys authority involving responsibility, care, and dominion over someone or something. One may be under the custody of this authority. In the Amarna letters, the Canaanite gloss *ba-di-ú* means "in his hand." Mankind is to have the rest of creation "under his dominion" (Gen 9:2). Sarah's authority over Hagar (Gen 16:6, 9), Joseph's over Potiphar's house (Gen 39:3–8), that of Moses and Aaron over Israel (Num 33:1), and David over Aram (I Chr 18:3) are all expressed by this phrase. Yahweh is to have authority over our lives. We place our hearts and spirits into his care, sovereignty, and judgment (Ps 31:5, 15; [H 6, 16]; II Sam 24:14). Moreover, this idiom portrays "victory over someone" when one is "delivered into one's hands." Deliverance, on the contrary, is described as being "delivered out of one's hands." Often Yahweh promised Israel that he would "deliver her enemies into her hands" (Gen 49:8; Josh 6:2) and that he would deliver Israel "out of her enemies' hands" (Ex 3:8). Refuge cities provided "deliverance" for the innocent slayer "from the hand" of the revenger of blood (Num 35:15).

The hand symbolized "power" or "strength" (Deut 8:17). Deuteronomy 32:36 described Israel's loss of power by saying "their hands were gone." Moses' hand was poignantly used to portray power in the plagues against Egypt (Ex 10:12–25). The most notable use of this metaphor is its conveyance of God's power. I Chronicles 29:12 declares that in Yahweh's hand is power and might (cf. Ps 89:13 [H 14]). His hand is not "short" (or "weak") (Isa 59:1), but mighty. A predominant demonstration of his power was his deliverance of Israel from Egypt (Ex 13:3–16; Num 33:3). All the world witnessed Yahweh's power through this event (Josh 4:24). His hand created the world (Ps 8:6; 95:5) and works truth and justice (Ps 111:7). He upholds and guides the righteous with his hand (Ps 37:24; 139:10). He continually lifts up his hand on our behalf (Ps 10:12). A corollary idea is that of "ability" to accomplish a task. The phrases "hand reaches" or "hand finds" denote the ability to do or obtain something (Lev 14:21–32).

"Possession" is a common function of the hand. Therefore, "in one's hands" often bears that connotation. The Ishmaelites had Joseph in their possession ("hands," Gen 39:1). Yahweh declared that he would take David's kingdom from his son (I Kgs 11:12, 31–35).

"Submission" is indicated by the phrase "to give one's hands under" someone else. Solomon's officials "submitted" to him (I Chr 29:24). Yahweh exhorted Israel to "submit" to him and not rebel.

"To stretch out the hand" conveys two ideas. It expresses the "attacking" of an object (Josh 8:19, 26); second, it describes the psalmist's yearning for the Lord (Ps 143:6).

"Putting one's hand to" something expresses "work" and the activity in which that person is involved (Deut 2:7; 30:9). "Strengthening the hands" is helping someone (cf. Jonathan helping David; I Sam 23:16).

Obstinate rebellion is described by the phrase "high hand" (Num 15:30). Contrarily, the same expression conveyed God's mighty deliverance of Israel from Egypt (Ex 14:8). "Shaking the hand" symbolized God's warning and destruction of judgment (Isa 10:32; 19:16). Contempt is likewise visualized by this symbol (Zeph 2:15).

"Laying hands on" has four basic connotations. First, this phrase was employed to depict killing (Gen 37:22, 27). Second, it was used in the ritual ceremony of blessing (cf. Gen 48:17). Third, commissioning for a specific office or task was normally accompanied by the laying on of hands (cf. Moses' inauguration of Joshua and Acts 13:1–3). Fourth, the important theological concept of substitution was continually portrayed through the laying of hands upon a sacrificial animal. On the Day of Atonement, the high priest transferred the nation's sins to the goat ("substitution"), by laying his hands upon the goat. Individuals depicted their sins as transferred to and borne by the sacrificial animal through this expression (Ex 29:10–19; Lev 1:4). Ultimately this figure was fulfilled in Christ's bearing of our sins upon the cross (Col 2:14).

The "uplifted hand" expressed several nuances. First, it symbolized prayer as one lifted up his hands toward the sanctuary (Ps 28:2). Second, the uplifted hand periodically accompanied a public blessing (Lev 9:22). Third, it was common for one to lift up his hand in an oath. When Abram vowed not to take spoils of war, he lifted up his hand to the king of Sodom. Another means of expressing a vow was to place the hand under the thigh of the other person as Abram's servant did when swearing that he would be faithful to Abram's charge (Gen 24:2, 9). The most significant vows of scripture are those anthropomorphically made by God. The oath most remembered in the scripture by this accompanying sign is God's unconditional and eternal covenant promise to make a nation from Abram and bless the world through that nation, Israel (Gen 12:1–3; cf. Ex 6:8; Num 14:30). God also swore to avenge the blood of his servants (Deut 32:40).

Consecration was depicted by the idiom "fill the hands." Some suggest that the sense of filling means the hands were full and had no time for other business, though others think that "filling" was with a sacrificial portion since this phrase was predominately used in the commissioning of priests (Ex 29:9–35; 16:32). Ritual cleansing was portrayed by "washing the hands" (Lev 5:11), making the person ritually righteous (II Sam 22:21). This symbolic action also denoted "absolution from guilt" (Deut 21:6–7; cf. Mt 27:24).

To give to one was to "open the hand" (Deut 15:8, 11), whereas to "shut the hand" was to withhold (Deut 15:7). God opens his hand to satisfy the desire of every living thing (Ps 145:16).

One who "slacks his hand" (or withdraws his hand) "gives up" (Josh 10:6); the slothful "buries his hand in a dish" (Prov 19:24). The silent places the "hand to the mouth" (Prov 30:32).

"Hand" is interestingly employed to mean an "ordinance" (Ezr 3:10) or a "monument" (cf. ritual stelae at Hazor) used perhaps to establish a covenant or as religious commemorations (I Sam

15:12; Isa 56:5). The Law was symbolically placed on the hand of the Israelite to remind him of its centrality in life (Deut 6:8). The instrumentality of giving ordinances and God's word was expressed with "by the hand of."

Perhaps the joining of hands led to the use of *yād* to denote "axles" which held the wheels of the molten sea together (I Kgs 7:32–33) and the "stays" (tenons) to fasten the boards of the tabernacle or temple (Ex 26:17–19; I Kgs 7:35–36). The hand hanging at the side most likely precipitated the use of *yād* for "side, coast, or border" (Ex 2:5; Num 2:17; 34:3). The spreading of the hands denoted "space" (Gen 34:21), while "hand" also meant "part" or "time" (Gen 43:34; 47:24). A different root, *ydd,* "to love," may be the basis for translating *yād* "penis" in the context of Isa 57:8, 10 (cf. UG 19: no. 1072).

Bibliography: TDOT, IX, pp. 426–29. THAT, I, pp. 667–73.

R.H.A.

845 יָדַד (*yādad*) ***I, cast a lot.***

846 ידד (*ydd*) **II. Assumed root of the following.**

846a †יָדִיד (*yādîd*) ***beloved, lovely.***
846b †יְדִידוֹת (*ye dîdôt*) ***love song.***
846c יְדִידוּת (*y^edîdût*) ***beloved one.***

yadîd. ***Beloved, lovely.*** The basic meaning of the noun is "one greatly loved" by God or by man. The noun is derived from the verb "love" (*ydd*) (BDB; KB).

This noun is primarily employed to describe the nation of Israel (or Judah) and individuals as those who are greatly loved by the Lord. Such love by God brings protection (cf. Benjamin; Deut 33:12) and prosperity (Ps 127:2) upon the beloved people. This love demonstrates the reason for God's continual faithfulness to his people Israel, even when they were disobedient and unfaithful (Jer 11:15). It is upon the basis of this love of God for Israel that she petitions for the Lord to hear and deliver her from judgment (Ps 60:5 [H 7]; 108:6 [H 7]). Isaiah describes the Lord, the vinedresser of unfaithful Israel, as his beloved (Isa 5:1), showing his great love for the Lord. The psalmist rejoices in the temple dwellings as "lovely" (or "beloved"), i.e. the place where he delights to worship the Lord.

y^edîdôt. ***Love (song); (song of) love.*** The primary meaning of this noun is "love" or "beloveds." The form is grammatically equivalent to the feminine plural of *yādîd,* being understood as that form by BDB, but listed separately by KB.

This noun is employed only once in the OT, being used to describe a song of love, or a song of beloveds, which they most likely sang for the groom or the couple as a wedding song at their wedding (Ps 45:1). The plural form probably indicates the broad use of this psalm as a wedding hymn.

R.H.A.

847 יָדָה (*yādâ*) ***confess, praise, give thanks, thank.*** (ASV, RSV similar, except that RSV also uses "acknowledge" and "extol.") In the Qal and Piel it means "throw, cast."

Derivatives

847a הֻיְּדוֹת (*hūyy^e dôt*) ***songs of praise,*** only in Neh 12:8.
847b †תּוֹדָה (*tôdâ*) ***confession, praise.***
847c †יְדוּתוּן (*ye dûtûn*), יְדֻתוּן (*ye dūtûn*) ***Jeduthun.***

The primary meaning of this root is "to acknowledge or confess sin, God's character and works, or man's character." The basic difference between this verb and its synonym, *hālal,* is that the latter term tends to stress "acclaim of," "boasting of," or "glorying in" an object, while *yādâ* emphasizes "recognition" and "declaration" of a fact, whether good or bad. The LXX normally renders *yādâ* with *exomologeō.*

The root verb is employed three basic ways. First, it was used to convey the acknowledgment or confession of sin, individually or nationally. The basic idea was clearly observed in David's personal confession described in Ps 32:5 in which the poetic parallelism demonstrates that confession was making known the sin to God and not hiding it. It is important to note that the confession of sin is to be made to God. The epitome of national confession is found in the Day of Atonement ceremony when the high priest laid his hands on the head of the goat, thereby symbolically transferring the nation's sins on to the goat, while the high priest confessed aloud all the sins of the nation of Israel (Lev 16:21). The Hithpael form is normally employed when this verb is used to convey the confession of national sins. This stem was also employed when the great confessions of Israel's sins were made by Daniel (Dan 9:4, 20), Ezra (Ezr 10:1), Nehemiah (Neh 1:6), and the people of Israel (Neh 9:2–3) during and after the Babylonian captivity. National confessions of sin were normally public. God greatly desires that we acknowledge our sins before him (cf. I Jn 1:9) in order to maintain a proper relationship with him.

Second, this verb was predominatly employed to express one's public proclamation or declaration (confession) of God's attributes and his works. This concept is at the heart of the meaning of praise. Praise is a confession or declaration of who God is and what he does. This term is most often translated "to thank" in English versions, but such is not really a proper rendering according to Westermann:

> In the Old Testament . . . there is as yet no verb that means only "to thank." *Hōdāh,* which is usually translated as "to thank," is not used in the Old Testament a single time for an expression of thanks between men. Thus it is clear from the start that this *hōdāh* cannot be equated with our "to thank," which can be directed equally to God and to man. In those places in the O.T. where our "thank" as something taking place between men is most clearly found, the verb used is *bērēk,* which does not have the primary meaning of "praise" but means "bless."
> In view of these facts, it is clear that the O.T. does not have our independent concept of thanks. The expression of thanks to God is included in praise, *it is a way of praising.* (Westermann, Claus. *The Praise of God in the Psalms.* Richmond: John Knox Press, 1965, pp. 26–27.)

The best rendering of the term is "confession," for the person confesses or declares God's attributes and works, as seen abundantly in the psalter (cf. Ps 89:5 [H 6]; Ps 105; Ps 106; Ps 145) and elsewhere (cf. I Chr 29:13). Therefore, *yādâ* is one of the key words for "praise." It is continually found in Hebrew poetry in parallelism with such praise terms as *hālal* "to praise," *zāmar* "to praise with musical instruments," *rûm* "to exalt," *zākar* "to remember," *kābad* "to glorify," and *nāgad* "to declare." Thanksgiving follows praise, for when one declares God's attributes and works, he cannot help but be thankful for these. Praise leads regularly to thanksgiving. [Westerman has drawn attention to an important point. However, it may be doubted if his formulation be necessary in all particulars. If, sometimes, thanks is included in praise, then those numerous instances where *yādâ* is used to praise God *for* some act or thing may well be equated to our concept giving thanks, especially if a basic meaning of the root is "to acknowledge" as BDB suggests. R.L.H.]

Praise normally has Yahweh, or his Name, as its object (Ps 97:12; 99:3; 136:1–3, 26). Only the living, not the dead, praised God (Isa 38:18–19; Ps 6:5 [H 6]; 30:9 [H 10]; 88:10 [H 11]). Initiators of praise included righteous individuals (Ps 140:13 [H 14]), the people of Israel (Ps 106:47), the nations (Ps 45:17 [H 18]), all the kings of the earth (Ps 138:4), the heavens (Ps 89:5 [H 6]), and the wrath of men (Ps 76:10 [H 11]). They all confessed God's great character and his wondrous works. Praise of Yahweh was public, found among the nations (II Sam 22:50) and in the great assembly of the people of Israel (Ps 35:18). When an individual, or a people, came to praise Yahweh, they gave praise orally by word or song (Ps 109:30; 28:7), often accompanied with musical instruments (II Chr 5:13; Ps 33:2; 43:4). Such praise was normally given in the tabernacle (or temple) (Ps 100:4; 122:4) under the direction of those Levites appointed by David strictly for the ministry of celebration through praise and confession of Yahweh's person (I Chr 16:4). This was a major aspect of worship which was to be carried on every morning and evening in the tabernacle (I Chr 23:30). This praise was to be given wholeheartedly (Ps 86:12; 111:1) with an upright heart (Ps 119:7) in accordance with Yahweh's righteous ways (Ps 7:17 [H 18]). Such praise was to be continual—forever (Ps 30:12 [H 13]).

Third, *yādâ* was also employed to convey man's praise of man, the confession of some truth about a man (Ps 49:18 [H 19]). The name "Judah," meaning "praise," comes from this root, for Judah's brothers would praise (or confess) him (Gen 29:35).

tôdâ. ***Confession, praise, sacrifice of praise, thanks, thanksgiving, thank-offering.*** This cognate noun, being derived from *yādâ,* basically means "confession," either of sin or of God's character and works. The term was employed uniquely in reference to the sacrificial system of Israel. One could bring a "thank-offering" (or "praise-offering") in which he would make declarations of praise to God and/or confession of sin to God as he offered his sacrifice. When the accompanying confession concerned sin, the offering was classified as a "peace-offering" and was so offered in order that the individual may be accepted before God (cf. Lev 7:12–15; 22:29). Such an offering and confession glorified God, showing his righteousness in contrast to the person's sin (Ps 50:23), and was a means by which one ordered his way aright.

When the sacrifice was accompanied with praise (confession) of God, it was especially a time of joy (Ps 95:2; Jer 17:26; 33:11). God was magnified by such praise (Ps 69:30 [H 31]). Psalm 100 is a typical psalm of praise for this type of occasion as indicated both in its superscription as well as in its content. Singing appears to have been a common means through which one confessed God's greatness (Ps 147:4). It also seems that in given situations many made vows that they would come to the tabernacle (or temple) and offer a sacrifice of praise and confession when God delivered them from their present circumstance (Ps 56:12 [H 13]; 116:17; cf. Jonah in Jon 2:10 and Manasseh in II Chr 33:16).

There are instances where confession is made without sacrifice. The returned exiles from Babylon gave praise; Israel praised God for the rebuilding of the walls of Jerusalem (Neh 12:31–40); Achan confessed his sins to Yahweh before Joshua (Josh 7:19–21).

y^e^dûtûn. ***Jeduthun.*** The name of one of the three leaders of the musical guilds in the tabernacle (and the temple) under king David (I Chr 9:16; 25:1–7; II Chr 5:12; 29:14; 35:15). These perpetual guilds were appointed to celebrate, confess, and praise Yahweh with song and musical instruments. The primary instrument of Jeduthun's guild was the harp, though the trumpet, lyre, and cymbals were perhaps used as well (I Chr 16:42; II Chr 5:12). In the superscriptions to Psalms 39, 62, and 77, the reference to "Jeduthun" is most likely a reference to him and his guild as the musical performers who were to render the psalm instrumentally and/or vocally. It is therefore interesting that the name "Jeduthun" is most likely derived from *yādâ,* one of the major terms for praise (cf. BDB, pp. 392–393).

R.H.A.

יְדוּתוּן (*y^e^dûtûn*). See no. 847c.

848 יָדַע (*yāda'*) ***know.*** (RSV, ASV similar.)

Derivatives

848a דֵּעַ (*dēa'*) ***knowledge, opinion.***
848b †דֵּעָה (*dē'â*) ***knowledge.***
848c †דַּעַת (*da'at*) ***knowledge.***
848d †יִדְּעֹנִי (*yidd^e^'ōnî*) ***familiar spirit.***
848e †מוֹדַע (*môda'*), מֹדַע (*mōda'*) ***relative.***
848f †מֹדַעַת (*mōda'at*) ***kindred, kinship,*** only in Ruth 3:2.
848g †מַדָּע (*maddā'*) ***knowledge.***
848h †מַדּוּעַ (*maddûa'*), מַדֻּעַ (*maddūa'*) ***why?***

This root, occurring a total of 944 times, is used in every stem and expresses a multitude of shades of knowledge gained by the senses. Its closest synonyms are *bîn* "to discern" and *nākar* "to recognize." The root is found in Akkadian, Ugaritic, and the Qumran materials. In addition to "know," the KJV uses the archaic forms "wot" and "wist."

yāda' is used of God's knowledge of man (Gen 18:19; Deut 34:10) and his ways (Isa 48:8; Ps 1:6; 37:18), which knowledge begins even before birth (Jer 1:5). God also knows the fowl (Ps 50:11).

yāda' is also used for man's knowledge and for that of animals (Isa 1:3).

The participle occurs in phrases describing skill in hunting (Gen 25:27), learning (Isa 29:11–13), lamentation (Amos 5:16), sailing the sea (II Chr 8:18), and playing an instrument (I Sam 16:16).

In certain contexts it means "to distinguish." "To know good and evil" (Gen 3:5, 22) is the result of disobeying God. To distinguish between these is necessary for the king (II Sam 19:36). A child cannot distinguish between the left and right hands (Jon 4:11) nor between good and evil (Deut 1:39; Isa 7:15). The context of the latter passage and the similar statement in Isa 8:4 may indicate that the reference is to a child's not being able to distinguish what is beneficial and harmful. While ordinarily gained by experience, knowledge is also the contemplative perception possessed by the wise man (Prov 1:4; 2:6; 5:2; Eccl 1:18).

yāda' is used to express acquaintance with a person in such statements as "do you know Laban?" (Gen 29:5; Ex 1:8; II Sam 3:25). The Pual participle designates kinfolk (II Kgs 10:11, etc.) and acquaintances (Job 19:14; Ruth 2:1, etc.). *yāda'* is also used for the most intimate acquaintance. God knows Moses by name and face to face (Ex 33:17; Deut 34:10). He knows the Psalmist's sitting and arising (Ps 139:2).

yāda' is also used for sexual intercourse on the part of both men and women in the well-known euphemism "Adam knew Eve his wife" and its parallels (Gen 4:1; 19:8; Num 31:17, 35; Jud 11:39; 21:11; I Kgs 1:4; I Sam 1:19). It is used to describe sexual perversions such as sodomy (Gen 19:5; Jud 19:22) and rape (Jud 19:25).

In addition to knowledge of secular matters *yāda'* is also used of one's relation to the divine, whether acquaintance with other gods (Deut 13:3, 7, 14) or with Jehovah (I Sam 2:12; 3:7). The heathen do not know God (Jer 10:25) and neither does Israel, according to the prophets (Jer 4:22). The plagues of Egypt were sent so that the Egyptians might know that Jehovah is God (Ex 10:2, etc.). He will destroy (Ezk 6:7) and restore Israel so that they may know that he is God (Isa 60:16). The prophet Ezekiel, in particular, uses the phrase "that you may know" in his threats (Ezk 6:7, 10, 13, 14; 7:4, 9, 27, etc.).

dē'â. ***Knowledge.*** This feminine noun is translated *gnōsis* in the LXX, and *scientia* in the Vulgate. The Lord is a God of all knowledge (Job 36:4; I Sam 2:3). The wicked question his knowledge (Ps 73:11). He is the object of man's knowledge, and Isaiah envisions an earth full of the knowledge of the Lord (Isa 11:9). The prophet preaches knowledge (Isa 28:9) and the ideal ruler rules by it (Jer 3:15). The noun may be only another form of *da'at* (see below). The masculine noun *dēa'* is quite similar.

da'at. ***Knowledge, cunning*** (ASV and RSV similar). This feminine noun is from the root *yāda'* "to know." The root expresses knowledge gained in various ways by the senses. The noun occurs ninety-three times in the Old Testament, most frequently in the wisdom literature, with forty-one instances in Prov, ten in Job, and nine in Eccl. It is used forty-two times in the Qumran materials and is also used in Ugaritic and Akkadian.

da'at is a general term for knowledge, particularly that which is of a personal, experimental nature (Prov 24:5). It is also used for technical knowledge or ability such as that needed for building the tabernacle and temple (Ex 31:3; 35:31; I Kgs 7:14). *da'at* is also used for discernment (Ps 119:66). Both deeds committed unintentionally (Deut 4:42; 19:4; Josh 20:3, 5; *b^e lî da'at*) and mistaken opinions are "without knowledge" (*lō' da'at*, Prov 19:2).

da'at is possessed by God (Job 10:7; Ps 139:6; Prov 3:20), from whom nothing can be hidden (Ps 139:1–18). He teaches it to man (Ps 94:10; 119:66; Prov 2:6). It appears parallel with wisdom (*ḥōkmâ*) and understanding (*t^{e}bûnâ*), instruction (*mûsār*), and law (*tôrâ*). Wisdom is used in series with "science" (*maddā'*, Dan 1:4) and is the opposite of "folly" (*'iwwelet*, Prov 12:23; 13:16; 14:18; 15:2). Hence *da'at* is the contemplative perception of the wise man (Prov 1:4; 2:6; 5:2; Eccl 1:18).

da'at is also used for moral cognition. Thus the tree in the Garden of Eden was a tree of the knowledge of good and evil (Gen 2:9, 17). By eating its fruit man came to know in a way comparable to the knowledge of God (see above). This important reference may also be taken as the figure of speech known as merism to indicate objective awareness of all things both good and bad. In this sense the sinful pain did become like God (Gen 3:22). Cassuto says, "Before they ate of the tree of knowledge, the man and his wife were like small children who know nought of what exists around them" (U. Cassuto, *Genesis*, vol. I, p. 112).

Particularly distinctive is the prophetic concept of "knowledge of God" (*da'at 'ĕlōhîm*) which is particularly prominent in Hosea (4:1, 6; 6:6; cf. Prov 2:5). Knowledge of God is derived from those outstanding historical events in which God has evidenced and has revealed himself to chosen individuals such as Abraham and Moses. These revelations are to be taught to others. "Knowledge of God" appears in parallel with "fear of the Lord" (*yir'at YHWH* Isa 11:2; cf. 58:2; Jer 22:16) as a description of true religion. The man who has a right relation with God confesses him and obeys him. To do justice and righteousness and to judge the cause of the poor and the needy is to know God (Jer 22:15–16). On the other hand where there is no knowledge of God there is swearing, lying, killing, stealing, committing adultery and breaking all bonds (Hos 4:1–2). Such will bring destruction upon a people (Hos 4:6; cf. Isa 5:13). Knowledge of God is more pleasing to him than sacrifice (Hos 6:6). The prophetic view of the messianic age is of a time in which the knowledge of God covers the earth as water covers the sea (Hab 2:14; cf. Isa 11:9).

yidd^e'ōnî. ***Wizard*** (KJV and some modern translations); fortune-teller (Berkeley Version, NAB); familiar spirit (JPS, NEB); spirit (NEB, NAB); magician (JB); and sorcerer (JB). Since the root of *yidd^e'ōnî* is the verb *yāda'* "to know," implied in the title, therefore, is esoteric knowledge not available to the ordinary person.

yidd^e'ōnî always occurs parallel to *'ôb* (witch, q.v.). It may be a description of an *'ôb* or it may be the masculine counterpart. (Similarly, "witch" and "wizard" are a feminine and masculine pair in English.) As the Hebrew word *yidd^e'ōnî* is related to knowledge, so the English word "wizard" is related to wisdom.

God forbad his people to consult the *yidd^e'ōnî* (Lev 19:31; 20:6, 27; Deut 18:11) as well as other diviners. Despite the fact that Saul outlawed them, he still consulted an *'ôb* "spirit" according to I Sam 28. How the Israelite kings dealt with these spiritists was a significant factor in characterizing the king as good or evil (II Kgs 21:6; 23:24; II Chr 33:6). Isaiah spoke of them with utter scorn (8:19; 19:3).

mōda'. ***Kinsman.*** The LXX follows the Kethib, rendering this feminine noun as *gnōrismos* "acquaintance," from a Piel participial form. The Vulgate and English versions follow the context where Boaz is a kinsman (Ruth 2:1; cf. 2:20; 3:2, 12; 4:3).

mōda' is used figuratively in Prov 7:4, paralleling sister, to describe wisdom.

mōda'at. ***Kindred, kinsman.*** The LXX renders this feminine noun as *gnorismos* "acquaintance," but the Vulgate translates *propinquus* "kindred." The English versions follow the Vulgate and context (Ruth 3:2; cf. 2:20; 4:3). For the Levirate marriage custom, see Gen 38; Deut 25:5; Mt 22:23, and cf. *yābam*.

madda'. ***Knowledge, science, thought.*** This masculine noun is used in contexts with wisdom (*ḥokmâ*). Solomon's request was for wisdom and knowledge (II Chr 1:10–12). The Hebrew children surpassed others in knowledge (Dan 1:4, 7; KJV and ASV, "science"; RSV, "learning"). It is paralleled with that done in secret, hence "thought" (Eccl 10:20). It also occurs in Sir 3:13; 13:8.

J.P.L.

maddûa'. ***Why? wherefore? on what account?*** (ASV and RSV are similar.) BDB and KB suggest that it is a contraction of *mâ yadûa'* "what being known," i.e. "from what motive." It is variously translated in the LXX by *tís, dia tí, hína tí, hína tí toûto, tí hotí, hôs tí*. Hence, this interrogative adverb is used to inquire about a motive (cf. Gen 26:27), as an indirect question (cf. Ex 3:3), or as a rhetorical device, as in Isa 5:4f., "When I looked for good grapes, why did it only yield bad?" (NIV).

Bibliography: Baumann, E., "*yada'* und seine Derivate," ZAW 28: 25–41, 110–41. Davies, T. W., *Magic, Divination* and *Demonology,* reprint, KTAV, 1969. Dentan, Robert C., *The Knowledge of God in Ancient Israel,* Seabury, 1968. McKenzie John L., "Knowledge of God in Hosea," JBL 74: 23ff. Piper, O. A., "Knowledge," in IDB, pp. 42–44. Richardson, TWB, pp. 121–22. Thomas, D.W., "Additional Notes on the Root *yd'* in Hebrew," JTS 15: 54–57. TDOT, I, pp. 696–703. THAT, I, pp. 682–700.

P.R.G.

יִדְּעֹנִי (*yidd^{e}'ōnî*). See no. 848d.
יָהּ (*yāh*). See no. 484b.

849 יָהַב (*yāhab*) ***give, ascribe, come!*** Aramaic *y^{e}hab* "give."

Derivatives

849a †יְהָב (*y^{e}hāb*) ***lot.***
849b †הַבְהָב (*habhab*) ***gift.***

yāhab is used some thirty-three times, only in the Qal imperative. The Aramaic is used twenty-eight times in different tenses. The more common synonym is *nātan* rendered by *didōmi* "give," in LXX. Yet *didōmi* is also used, almost exclusively, for the Aramaic *y^{e}hab*. Our word emphasizes the notion of presenting or setting an object or person somewhere. The LXX renders the noun *y^{e}hāb* with *merimna* (Ps 55:22 [H 23]) "what has been given you" (KJV "burden").

The verb is used only in the Qal imperative in the following ways: (1) as an interjection "Come! Come now!" (Gen 11:3, plus four times) translated in LXX by the adverb *deute,* mostly used as a hortatory particle (cf. Isa 1:18, LXX). (2) The basic idea is expressed by "give!" It is used with the object of what is to be given with indirect object expressed, in Gen 29:21 "give me my wife" the idea being of having her presented to Jacob, in Deut 1:13 of giving, i.e. presenting men for appointment. The notion of choosing or nominating would be involved here. A development of the above is "set!" "place!" as in II Sam 11:15, "Set/place Uriah on the front of the battle!"

(3) The most theologically important meaning is used in the command to "give" (KJV) or "ascribe" (ASV, RSV) glory to the name of the Lord (Deut 2:3; Ps 29:1–2; 96:7–8; I Chr 16:28–29). It is interesting to note that though these passages are practically the same, the LXX renders I Chr by *didōmi* "give" and the Ps passages with *pherō* which basically means "to bring, present, bear" whether a burden or a gift. "Ascribe" with the synonyms "attribute" or "credit" would suggest "inferring of cause, quality, authorship" (Webster). Hence the passages would demand everyone to acknowledge the Lord Yahweh as the great king and offer such ascription of glory and greatness as is commensurate with his majesty. Cf. Rev 21:24 which alludes to Isa 60:11 where the kings of the earth shall bring (*pherō*) their glory to the new Jerusalem.

In the Aramaic portions of Daniel and Ezra, the cognate has the more general meaning of Heb *nātan* "give." In Biblical Aramaic the verb *y^{e}hab* in the simple stem is not used in the imperfect and the verb *n^{e}tan* is used only in the imperfect. In many of these passages, the sovereignty of God is set forth as the giver of wisdom (Dan 2:21, 23), life (Dan 7:12), kingdoms, power, strength and grandeur (Dan 2:37–38; 5:18–19), deliverance from physical danger (Dan 3:28) and the one who is in control of the destinies of people and nations (Ezr 5:12, Dan 7:12, 25, 27).

y^{e}hab. ***Gift, lot (what is given).*** The two derived nouns (see also *habhab*) are considered corrupt or unexplained in KB. *y^{e}hāb* in Ps 55:22 [H 23]) is translated "burden" (KJV, ASV, RSV) with the additional marginal note "what he has given you" (RSV taking the word as a perfect of the verb). Instructive is the LXX *merimna* "care, anxiety, burden" in this passage, used four times for *d^{e}'āgâ* "anxious care." In Sir 34:1 and 42:9 it is linked with sleeplessness. The thought then would be God's providence, whether it forbodes evil or good, should not induce fear or brooding anxiety, but contrariwise should cause one to turn in quiet confidence to the Lord who gives a new perspective on life. God then does not guarantee our desire, but rather he is the one who knows our needs better than we ourselves.

habhab. ***Gift.*** Hosea 8:13, they sacrifice flesh for the sacrifices of "mine offerings" and eat it, KJV; "they love" sacrifice, they sacrifice flesh and eat it, RSV; as for the sacrifices of "mine offerings," ASV; they "bring" sacrifices, Modern Language Bible; as for "my sacrificial gifts," NASB, similarly NIV. KB considers this corrupt, and would emend both here and in 4:18 to a form of *'āhab* "love." The RSV considers both passages unclear, and then follows KB. But the form *habhab* is not an unusual reduplication.

P.R.G.

850 *יָהַד (*yāhad*) ***become a Jew.*** Denominative verb.

Parent Noun

850a †יְהוּדִי (*y^{e}hûdî*) ***Jew, Jewish.***
850b יְהוּדִית (*y^{e}hûdît*) ***Jewish.***
850c †יְהוּדָה (*y^{e}hûdâ*) ***Judah.***

yāhad occurs only once, in Est 8:17, "Many among the peoples of the land became Jews" where it is a Hithpael participle. We here note Sennacherib's use *Ya-ú-di* for the land of Judah and *Ḫa-za-qí-a-ú Ya-ú-da-ai* "Hezekiah the Jew."

y^e^hûdî. ***Jew, Jewish,*** an adjective used fourteen times. Its plural *y^e^hûdîm* "Jews, men of Judah" is used seventy-one times substantively.

y^e^hûdît. ***Jewish*** is the feminine adjective used six times in the expression "in the Jewish language" as in Isa 36:11, 13 and Neh 13:24.

y^e^hûdâ. ***Judah*** (ASV and RSV similar). This proper noun is used of persons and of a territory. It occurs over eight hundred times, not including derivatives. The original meaning of the root is lost, not being found either in Ugaritic or Assyrian. In Gen 29:35 and 49:8 an explanation is made by using *yādâ* in the Hiphil meaning "to give thanks, laud, praise." However, these names of Jacob's sons should often be considered a play on words rather than definition or derivation. In the one case Leah names her fourth son, saying, "This time I will give thanks to Yahweh." In the second, Jacob's blessing on him makes the pun "Judah, your brothers shall praise you" and then continues with the specific promises.

Judah was the name of the fourth son of the patriarch Jacob, born of Leah. It is the name of several individuals in the postexilic period (Ezr 3:9; 10:23; Neh 11:9; 12:8, 36). Judah takes a secondary position in the patriarchal account.

However, Gen concludes with a significant promise anticipating the prominence of Judah in later covenantal history. The episode of Judah and Tamar (Gen 38) contrasts with the ethical, indeed, the covenantal standard of behavior of Joseph (Gen 39:9) who recognized that adultery with Potiphar's wife was above all else sin against a holy God. However, God's sovereign grace was operating in Judah's life, both in his becoming a leader among his brothers (Gen 43:3; 44:14; 46:28) as well as being the foremost in repentance and confession for his sin against Joseph (Gen 43:8f.; 44:16–34). Jacob's blessing promised leadership, victory, and kingship (Gen 49:8–12) anticipating the royal line established by covenant with David and ultimately the Lord Jesus Christ who was to combine in his person the suzerain king and the anointed one (Messiah). See the discussion of v. 10 under *shēbeṭ*.

Throughout the Pentateuch, little prominence is given to Judah's descendants, other than leading the vanguard in the wilderness wanderings (Num 2:9). Clearly, Judah is now the name of a tribe which does not figure strongly until David ben Jesse was anointed king over Judah, then over all Israel (II Sam 2:4; 5:3). The significant religious contribution was the establishment of Jerusalem (in the territory of Judah) as "the place where Yahweh your God chooses to put his name" (Deut 12:5, 11, 14, 18, 21, 26, etc.; cf. II Sam 7:5–6, 13).

Following Solomon's apostasy (I Kgs 11:1–13) God divided Israel (ten tribes) from Judah which from the days of Joshua included the territory of Simeon (Josh 19:9). Although the prophets spoke of the people of Israel and the sons of Judah as people of God because of a covenantal relationship (cf. *'ammî* "my people") stemming from the times of Abraham, Isaac, Jacob and Moses (e.g. Amos 2:4, 6; 3:1f.; 9:14; Hos 1:11 [H 2:2]; 12:13); nevertheless the covenant relationship continued through Judah alone after the disastrous fall of Samaria and the northern kingdom. The name "Israel" is used more specifically of the covenanted people of God, denoting the totality of the elect who are united to Yahweh, but Micah and Isaiah and other writers after the fall of Samaria use the term "Israel" when speaking of Judah which essentially is a political name. Cf. Isa 5:7; 8:18; Mic 2:12; 3:1, 8–9; 4:14; 5:1. But Judah as a nation was to last a little over one hundred years more before her overthrow in 586 B.C. The prophets continually were calling the people of God to return to true covenant relationship (e.g. Jer 4:4). With the Babylonian exile, Judah continues its basic identification, though a people no longer in their own land. During this period the people of God are called *y^e^hûdî* notably in Zech 8:23 and Dan 3:8, 12. A small percentage returned to their homeland during the Persian period, yet both groups ultimately participated in God's providential workings. The remnant restored to the land became the channel through which the promised Messiah came, born in David's natal city Bethlehem. The people of the dispersion provided a bridge for the apostolic proclamation and the reception of the Gospel. In this connection special reference should be made to Est 8:17, "many among the peoples [in each and every province] became Jews," with the several NT references to proselytes, i.e. Acts 2:10; 10:1f., and synagogues, i.e. Acts 13:14ff; 13:43; 14:1.

Many believe that Judah and Israel will be restored to covenantal favor by the sovereign steadfast faithfulness of Yahweh. Explicit statements by Hosea (1:9, 10 [H 2:1]; 3:5; 14:4), Amos (9:8–12), Jeremiah (33:3–26), and Ezekiel (37:16–28) should be compared to Paul's teaching (Rom 9–11) and John's revelation (Rev 7:4–8).

Bibliography: TDOT, III, pp. 359–65.

P.R.G.

יְהוּדָה (*y^e^hûdâ*). See no. 850c.
יְהוּדִי (*y^e^hûdî*). See no. 850a.
יְהוּדִית (*y^e^hûdît*). See no. 850b.
יהוה (*yhwh*). See no. 484a.

851 יהר (*yhr*). **Assumed root of the following.**
851a יָהִיר (*yāhîr*) ***proud, haughty;*** (ASV; RSV adds "arrogant").

LXX translates with *alazōn*. Used only twice in the OT, Prov 21:24 and Hab 2:5. Both the Hebrew parallels and the Greek translation clarify the meaning. In Prov the parallel words are *zēd* "presumptuous, haughty" and *lēṣ* "scoffer" (q.v.) which are further described as "one who acts with insolent pride" (*zādôn*). In Hab "the haughty, arrogant man" is one who, betrayed by wine, is motivated by greed. In short, his confidence is not in the Lord who is in control of the destinies of all men.

In Wisdom 5:8 *alazoneia* ("what has our arrogance profited us?") is set in contrast to the ways of the Lord and thus separates from God.

The NT usage of *alazoneia* focuses more clearly the meanings involved. In Rom 1:30 and II Tim 3:2 the word appears in lists of characteristics which describe the unregenerate who deserve to die for these sinful practices. I John 2:16 declares that the "pride of life" does not originate from the Father. Rather, it comes from the sinful heart which arrogantly and defiantly replaces the sovereign God. Contrawise, he who truly loves the Father and exalts him as sovereign, exhibits his faith commitment by doing his will. James puts it clearly in perspective when he speaks of the arrogant man who makes his decisions as if he could dispose of the future without taking into account that God is sovereign in all the affairs of life in the final analysis. "Instead you ought to say, 'If the Lord will we shall live and we shall do this or that.' As it is, you boast in your arrogance. All such boasting is evil" (4:15–16). Ribbeck is quoted as defining the *alazōn* as one who "makes more of himself" than the reality justifies, "ascribing to himself either more and better things than he has, or even what he does not possess at all," and who "promises what he cannot perform" (in TDNT, I, p. 226).

In short, *yāhîr* reflects an egocentric, arrogant person.

P.R.G.

יָהִיר (*yāhîr*). See no. 851a.
יַהֲלֹם (*yahălōm*). See no. 502b.
יוּבַל (*yûbal*). See no. 835b.
יוֹבֵל (*yôbēl*). See no. 835e.

852 יוֹם (*yôm*) ***day, time, year.***

Derivative

852a †יוֹמָם (*yômām*) ***by day.***

The ASV and RSV translate *yom* similarly with the latter frequently representing the sense more accurately (exception: Gen 2:17; 3:5 attest the same Hebrew construction, yet the RSV confuses the reader by rendering them differently).

Our word is the "most important concept of time in the OT by which a point of time as well as a sphere of time can be expressed." The word is also common in Ugaritic. It can denote: 1. the period of light (as contrasted with the period of darkness), 2. the period of twenty-four hours, 3. a general vague "time," 4. a point of time, 5. a year (in the plural; I Sam 27:7; Ex 13:10, etc.). Especially note the following special meanings: *b^{e}yôm* (frequently "when"; *b^e* can be replaced by *min* or *'ad*), *hayyôm* (frequently "today," or some particular day), *bîmê* "in the time of," *y^{e}mê* "as long as" (Deut 11:21; Gen 8:22). Akkadian *ūmu* "day," is often combined with *ina* "in," in the form *inūma, enūma* to mean "when" (e.g. *enūma elish*), exactly as Hebrew *b^{e}yôm*. There is no real synonym to our word although compare *'ēt* ("time") and *'ôlām* ("eternity") in some contexts (Ezk 21:25 [H 30]; Num 13:20, etc.). Other Hebrew words sometimes translated "day" are: *'ôr* "light," *bōqer* (the usual Hebrew word for "morning" the period of light before noon; Jud 19:26), *shaḥar* (the Northwest Semitic word for "morning-goddess," see *shaḥar, hālal,* UT 19: no. 2399; Gen 32:25). Finally, *yôm* used adverbially (*kōl-hayyôm,* Job 1:5; Gen 6:5) parallels *tāmîd* ("continually") in meaning g)num 4:7). Antonyms of our word are: *lay^{e}lâ* (Gen 8:22), and *'ereb* (Gen 1:5; cf. Dan 8:14). Our word, a common Semitic root (UT 19: no. 1100), and the concept of time surrounding it do not present a unique Hebrew understanding of time (Jenni, THAT I, *yôm,* "tag"). The root occurs 2355 times.

It is important to note that the daytime was not divided into regular hourly divisions, but according to natural phenomena (Ex 18:13; Gen 43:16; 15:12; 18:1, etc.). The night, however, was divided into three watches (perhaps Lam 2:18; Jud 7:19; Ex 14:24). Furthermore, there is apparently a certain duality in the determination of the beginning and ending of the day with the former being sometimes evening (Est 4:16; Dan 8:14), and sometimes morning (Deut 28:66–67; AI, I, pp. 180ff.).

"Day" is surrounded by many theological themes related to God's sovereignty. God, being eternal, antedates (Isa 43:13; Dan 7: 9) and transcends time (Ps 90:4). Time ("days") was created by God (Gen 1) and is under his control (Ps 74:16). Especially, note Joshua's miraculous "day" (SOTI, p. 259 ff.). Man is called to recognize this sovereignty by conforming life to the time divisions established by God (Ex 20:11; 31:17, etc.). God assured the regularity of time (Gen 8:22), but this does not mean that regularity is a law to which God is subject. Indeed, it will someday be divinely suspended (Zech 14:7). Like cosmological and terrestrial time man's lifespan is ordered (Ps 90:10), determined (Ps 139:16), and controlled (Deut 30:20; Ps 55:23 [H 24]); 91:16; Isa 38:5) by God. The Bible gives repeated indications of God's interest in and concern for time and its events (Gen 26:33; 24:55). Moreover, a unique (to the ancient world) and ever-present philosophy of history is exhibited therein.

[The myth makers of the Ancient Near East did not conceive of time in terms of a horizontal, linear ordering of events reaching from a historical beginning to a final consummation of all things. Rather, they regarded time as cyclical, the annual reordering and revitalizing of the universe. Their creation myths were recited at annual New Year's festivals as magical words to accompany a magical ritual in order to reactualize the original cosmology, the passage from chaos to cosmos. In mythopoeic thought time has no significance and history no meaning.

But Genesis 1 betrays a totally different notion about time. Here time is conceived as linear and events occur successively within it. Moreover, from the biblical viewpoint man's behavior in the present determines his state in the future. Time is the defined arena in which it will be demonstrated that righteousness is rewarded with life and evil is punished with death. Such a viewpoint invests man's time with the greatest moral value and history serves as an instrument whereby God's character can be displayed B.K.W.]

Special notice should also be given to the theological significance of several constructions and phrases. *yôm 'ăsher* "the day when" is used preponderantly to introduce events with particular importance in the history of salvation (Deut 4:32; Num 15:23, etc.; see also the use with *shā*). The period "forty days and forty nights" frequently signifies a time of reformation (Gen 7:4; Ex 16:35; 24:18) and/or trial (Jon 3:4). The word *hayyôm* sometimes signifies a redemptive time (if not moment) when repentance is divinely summoned (Ps 95:7), salvation divinely bestowed (Ps 118:24), or adoption divinely effected (Ps 2:7). For the meaning of the phrase "days of old," see *qādam*. One of the most debated occurrences of *yôm* is its use in reference to creation. The difficulties in exegesis there are complicated by many factors (see E. J. Young, *Studies in Genesis One*, Presbyterian and Reformed, 1964, pp. 43ff.). Like Young, this writer believes the days of Gen 1 to be intentionally patterned, chronological, of indeterminable length, initiated with 1:1, intended to show step-by-step how God "changed the uninhabitable and unformed earth of verse two into the well-ordered world of verse thirty-two," and "straight-forward, trustworthy history" (ibid., p. 103ff.). Another much debated phrase is the "day of the Lord." It can be used eschatalogically or noneschatalogically. It is a day of judgment and/or blessing (Isa 2). Hence, the eschatalogical meaning embraced by this idea entails all of prophetic eschatology (George A. Gay, "Day", Baker Dictionary of Theology, p. 156; Jenni, op. cit., loc. cit.; K. D. Schunck, "Der Tag Jahwehs," VT 14: 319–30). Similar expressions are *bayyôm hahû'* "in that day" which can refer to ordinary expected events (Isa 21:6) or can be eschatological and *'aḥărît hayyāmîm* which can refer to events in the general future (Deut 31:29) or to the eschaton (Harris, R. L., "The Last Days in the Bible and Qumran," in *Jesus of Nazareth Savior and Lord*, C. F. H. Henry, ed., Eerdmans (1966)).

yômām. ***By day.*** This adverb modifies the verbal activity by specifying that it occurred while it was yet light. Its antonyms are *layᵉlâ* (Ex 13:21) and *bā'ereb* (Ezk 12:3–4). Our word occurs fifty-one times.

Bibliography: TDNT, II, pp. 943–48. THAT, I, pp. 707–26.

L.J.C.

יוֹמָם (*yômām*). See no. 852a.

853 יון (*ywn*) **I. Assumed root of the following.**
853a יָוֵן (*yāwēn*) ***mire*** (Ps 40:3; 69:3).

854 יון (*ywn*) **II. Assumed root of the following.**
854a †יוֹנָה (*yônâ*) ***dove, pigeon*** used thirty-two times, exclusive of the personal name or psalm title (56:1).

Translated in LXX by *peristera*, the field or rock dove which in Lev is translated "young pigeon." From ancient times this was domesticated for food and as a carrier pigeon. This should be distinguished from *tôr* "turtledove," LXX *trugōn*. The term *yônâ*, however, may be used generically for all the different species.

The *yônâ* is used in the Levitical code as a sacrifice by the poor instead of the more costly bull or sheep in the burnt offering (Lev 1:14) or in the case of the sin offering, "if he cannot afford a lamb, then he shall bring to the Lord his guilt offering for that which he has sinned, two turtledoves (*tôr*) or two young pigeons (*yônâ*), one for a sin offering and the other for a burnt offering" (Lev 5:7). Furthermore, in the rites of purification, a woman who had given birth was to bring a lamb and a young pigeon or a turtledove for the dual sacrifice, but "if she cannot afford the lamb, then she shall take two . . . young pigeons" (Lev 12:6, 8). Cf. Lk 2:24 where Mary fulfills her obligation after the manner of the poor. The doves still represented a valuable personal possession.

The dove was so familiar to an Israelite household that its habits were an excellent source of similies or metaphors. Its cooing was used in similies for mourning or lamenting, e.g. Hezekiah's "I moan like a dove" (Isa 38:14). Cf. Isa 59:11; Nah 2:7 [H 8]. In Ps 55:7 David wishes he had "wings like a dove," to fly away from the troubles prevailing upon him. Cf. Jer 48:28. The meaningless flights back and forth serve as simile for Ephraim's vacillation between Assyria and Egypt, i.e. "like a silly dove" (Hos 7:11). Hosea also uses the figure of the returning migration of doves as a figure depicting the return of exiles from Assyria.

P.R.G.

855 יָוָן (*yāwān*) ***Greece, Ionia, Ionians.*** Transliterated Javan. Appears eleven times in the OT, plus once in a disputed passage, Ezk 27:19. A loan word.

In the geneologies of Gen 10 and I Chr Javan is listed as one of the sons of Japheth along with Gomer, Magog, Tubal, Meshech, and others. Gomer's sons are listed, followed by the sons of Javan, including Tarshish and Kittim among others. The names mentioned above are recognized immediately as significant place names appearing elsewhere in Scripture. Furthermore Gen 10:5, 20, 30–31 explicitly mentions that these genealogies are by nations. Finally, the LXX by translating with *Iōuan* would clearly identify this name with Ionia, one of the republics of Greece.

When Isaiah speaks of "Javan" among a group of nations, he refers to them as distant coastlands that have not known of the Lord's glory (Isa 66:19). We note in passing that in the prophets, LXX translates with *Hellas* or *Hellēnes*. Ezekiel refers to Javan as one of the nations which traded with Tyre (27:13). Further, Daniel has several references to Greece. Although not specifically named in chapters 2 and 7, it seems to be included as one of the four empires. However, it is explicitly mentioned in 8:21, "the shaggy goat represents the kingdom (lit. king) of Greece, and the large horn that is between his eyes is the first king."

That here we have a reference to Alexander the Great is clear from the following verse which refers to the "four kingdoms which will arise from his nation."

In 10:20 Daniel refers to the guardian angel of Greece with whom the angelic being struggled as he came to assist Daniel. Daniel also refers to Greece in a tremendous battle confrontation with the army of the Persian empire (11:2). Henceforward, there follows a series of identifiable historical episodes down to the time of the Seleucid Antiochus Epiphanes who apparently stands as a type of the eschatological Antichrist.

Zechariah refers once to Greece in 9:13, "And I will stir up your sons, O Zion, against your sons, O Greece." It is not quite clear if this is a historical reference within the fifth century or to the Seleucid wars in the second century, or possibly to a future eschatological occasion.

P.R.G.

יוֹנָה (*yônâ*). See no. 854a.
יוֹנֵק (*yônēq*). See no. 874a.
יוֹנֶקֶת (*yôneqet*). See no. 874b.
יוֹסֵף (*yôsēp*). See no. 876a.
יוֹרֶה (*yôreh*). See no. 910a.
יוֹתֵר (*yôtēr*). See no. 936d.

856 *יָזַן (*yāzan*). Occurs only in the Pual, in Jer 5:8, possibly meaning "furnished with weights," i.e. testicles, as if from *'āzan* II, but dubious. GB derive from *zûn,* Syriac "feed," therefore "well-fed."

857 יזע (*yz'*). **Assumed root of the following.**
857a יֶזַע (*yeza'*) ***sweat.*** This masculine noun occurs only in Ezk 44:18, "they must not wear anything that makes them perspire" (NIV).
857b זֵעָה (*zē'â*) ***sweat.*** A feminine noun occurring only in Gen 3:19, "by the sweat of your brow, you will eat your food."

יִזְרְאֶל (*yizr^e'el*). See no. 582e.

858 יָחַד (*yāḥad*) ***be united, be joined.*** (ASV, RSV similar.) Occurs three times in the Qal, once in the Piel.

Derivatives

858a †יָחִיד (*yāḥîd*) ***only, only begotten son.***
858b †יַחַד (*yaḥad*) ***unitedness.***
858c יַחְדָו (*yaḥdāw*) ***together.***

yāḥîd. ***Only, only begotten son, beloved, solitary.*** Appears eleven times (KJV twice uses "darling," RSV renders "my life" following the poetic parallel with *napshî* or Ps 22:20, [H 21]; 35:17 (NIV "my precious life") and "desolate" in Ps 68:6 [H 7] (ASV follows KJV). LXX translates it seven times with *agapētos* "beloved" and four times with *monogenēs* "only begotten." The Ugaritic cognate is *yḥd.*

Theologically, *yāḥîd* is important as it impinges on NT Christology. The word basically refers to an only child (cf. Ug *yḥd* "either 'a person without kith or kin' or 'an only son' subject to military service only under extenuating circumstances," UT 19: no. 410). Jephthah's daughter is described accordingly, "now she was his one and only child, besides her he had neither son nor daughter" (Jud 11:34). Consider the pathos elicited in Amos 8:10 where the judgment of God is described as "a time of mourning for an only son'' (cf. Jer 6:26; Zech 12:10). However, in Gen 22 Abraham is told, ''take now your son, your only son (*yāḥîd*), whom you love (*'āhab*), Isaac, and go to the land of Moriah.'' Here the LXX uses *agapētos* ''beloved'' rather than *monogenēs* ''only begotten'' as in Jud 11:34. *monogenēs* may be more specific. If so, it could not apply to Isaac who had Ishmael as a half brother. It must be pointed out, however, that even *monogenēs* may ''be used more generally without reference to its etymological derivation in the sense of 'unique', 'unparalleled,' 'incomparable,' '' (TDNT, IV, p. 738; see especially nn. 5–6).

In what sense is Isaac a *yāḥîd = agapētos?* Obviously, an only child is especially dear to parents. It is tempting to see here the idea of ''incomparable'' and ''without parallel'' anticipating the Messiah in his ''unique'' relationship to the Father who claims him as *ho huios mou ho agapētos* ''my beloved Son'' (Mt 3:17; 17:5 and parallels). This expression finds its equivalence in John's *ho monogenēs huios* ''the only begotten son'' i.e. ''the unique son'' (Jn 1:14, 18; 3:16, 18; I Jn 4:9). The supreme act of God is evidence of his love for the world. This was prophetically typified by Abraham's willingness to sacrifice Isaac. In Ps 22:20 and 35:17 *yāḥîd = monogenēs* is variously translated ''my darling,'' ''my only life,'' referring to the uniqueness of the soul.

[There is thus warrant for the idea that the term *monogenēs* in John does not refer to derivation of the Son from the Father as in human families, but to the uniqueness and love of the Trinitarian relationship. The doctrine of eternal generation of the son never meant such derivation. Indeed it was adopted against the Arian theology that the son had a ''beginning'' and was ''made.'' R.L.H.]

Another use of *yāḥîd* is ''solitary,'' ''isolated,'' ''lonely.'' It is used of men, as when David cries out ''turn to me and be gracious to me, for I am lonely and afflicted'' (Ps 25:16). God expresses his concern for such in Ps 68:5–6 [H 6–7], ''A father of the fatherless and a judge for the widows . . . God makes a home for the lonely; he leads out the prisoners into prosperity.'' Dahood, by vocalizing MT *yaḥēd* as *yāḥîd* in Ps 86:11, translates, ''Yahweh, teach me your way, that I may walk faithfully to you alone; teach my heart to revere your name.'' (Cf. Ps 88:17 [H 18] ''they close in on me alone'' as in contrast to ''encompassed me altogether.'') He then comments, ''The king pledges fidelity to Yahweh alone since he alone is God, as affirmed in the preceeding verse'' (AB, *Psalms*, II, p. 295). Generally, *yaḥad* describes the community in action, doing things together. In Ps 34:3 [H 4]; Isa 52:9, the community extols the praise of God together. This unanimity especially for the people of God is beautifully underscored by the LXX's use of *homothumadon* (''with the same emotion,'' i.e. ''with the same mind'') ''unanimously.'' Demosthenes urges the people to set aside personal feelings replacing it by *homothumadon* to resist Philip. Hence, personal feelings are not to be considered in ''unity.'' The NT stresses the inner unanimity of the church, as in Rom 15:4–5, ''May God . . . grant you to be of the same mind with one another according to Christ Jesus, that *with one accord* you may with one voice glorify the God and Father of our Lord Jesus Christ.'' See also Acts 1:14; 2:1, 46; 4:24; 5:12, 15:25.

yaḥad. ***Unitedness,*** as adverb when accusative ***in union, together, altogether,*** also adverb **yaḥdāw** ***together, alike,*** both appearing altogether 134 times. LXX primarily translates with *homothumadon* ''with one mind, unanimously.''

P.R.G.

יַחְדָּו (*yaḥdāw*). See no. 858c.
יָחִיד (*yāḥîd*). See no. 858a.
יָחִיל (*yāḥîl*). See no. 859a.

859 יָחַל (*yāḥal*) ***wait, hope.***

Derivatives

859a יָחִיל (*yāḥîl*) ***waiting,*** used only in Lam 3:26.
859b †תּוֹחֶלֶת (*tôḥelet*) ***hope.***

yāḥal occurs eighteen times in the Piel, fifteen times in the Hiphil and three in the Niphal with the idea of ''tarrying'' and ''confident expectation, trust.'' The LXX translates it nineteen times with *elpizō* and *epelpizō* ''to hope.'' ASV and RSV translate similarly.

In the three instances where *yāḥal* is used in Niphal it has the simple concept of waiting for a short period of time, e.g. Noah ''waited yet another seven days'' before sending the dove (Gen 8:12). Cf. Ezk 19:5. This notion also is expressed in the Piel (Job 14:14) and the Hiphil (I Sam 13:8). However, *yāḥal* is used of ''expectation, hope'' which for the believer is closely linked with ''faith, trust'' and results in ''patient waiting.'' The sense of expectation may be positive, i.e. hoping for good in the future. Ezekiel 13:6 is a case in point, where people rely on the declarations of the false prophets ''yet they hope for the fulfillment of their word.'' Cf. Ps 71:14, ''But as for me, I will hope continually.'' Since *yāḥal* is primarily translated by *elpizō* in the LXX with the good in view, the opposite notion (Heb *zᵉwāʻâ* ''fear'' or ''dread'' in Isa 28:19) is translated *elpis ponēra*, lit. ''hope of evil.'' This *yāḥal* ''hope'' is not a pacifying wish of the imagination which drowns out troubles, nor is it uncertain (as in the Greek concept), but rather *yāḥal* ''hope'' is the solid ground of expectation for the righteous. As such it is directed towards God. The

Psalmist twice commands: "O Israel, hope in the Lord, for with the Lord there is lovingkindness (Heb *ḥesed*), and with him is abundant redemption" (Ps 130:7; cf. 131:3).

In times of despair, the Psalmist encourages himself by saying, "Hope in God, for I shall yet praise him, the help of his presence" (Ps 42:5 [H 6]; also 42:11 [H 12]; 43:5).

However, no greater testimony to such confident expectation is given than when Job cries out, "Though he slay me, I will hope in him. Nevertheless, I will argue my ways before him" (Job 13:15). However ASV and RSV render the verse, "Behold, he will slay me; I have no hope" following MT Kethib reading instead of the Qere which is supported by the LXX and other versions, in which case, Job's impatience demonstrates his refusal to "patiently wait" for the Lord (cf. Job 6:11). Nevertheless, *yāḥal*, "hope" is a close synonym to *bāṭaḥ* "trust" and *qāwâ* "wait for, hope for," as in Mic 7:7, "But as for me, I will wait for the God of my salvation. My God will hear me." The last phrase clearly demonstrates the confidence of the righteous in God's future action at a time when sin is being judged. But further, the verse reflects not only the ground of faith, the Lord himself, but the saving activity of his God. In short, that which is hoped for is not some desideratum arising from one's imagination, but in God himself and whatever he should propose to accomplish. One is reminded of the Christian's confidence as expressed in Rom 8:28–29. Hence the godly may confidently rest on God's word, e.g. "Those who fear thee shall see me rejoice, because I have hoped in thy word" (Ps 119:74, NASB weakens this "because I wait for thy word"). Cf. also 119:43, 81, 114, 147; 130:5. He may also be confident about God's faithful convenant love, e.g. "Behold, the eye of the Lord is on those who fear him, on those who hope for his loving kindness (*ḥesed*, Ps 33:18). Cf. also Lam 3:21, 24.

Not only does "hope" bring relief from present problems, but also in the eschatological sense "hope" in God's help and ultimate salvation will bring to an end all distress. One needs to look at Isa 51:5 where God promises his omnipotent help, "My righteousness is near, my salvation has gone forth, and my arms will judge the people; the coastland will wait for me, and for my arm they will wait expectantly." Cf. also Jer 29:11; 31:17; Mic 7:7.

tôḥelet. ***Hope.*** [This word may refer in two verses of Prov to a confidence in a future life. In Prov 10:28 the joyful *tôhelet* of the righteous is contrasted with the no hope (*tiqwâ*) of the wicked. The previous verse concerns long life and sudden death so the questions of eternity are in view. Proverbs 11:7 seems to support this idea; at death the hope of the wicked is gone. The words *'aḥărît* and *tiqwâ* (q.v.) are open to similar interpretations in Prov 23:18; 24:14, 20. There, the righteous man is said to have an *'aḥărît* (NIV "future hope") in contrast to the wicked who has none and whose lamp will be snuffed out. Solomon, like Job, found the resolution of the antimomies of this existence in the judgments of a future life. R.L.H.]

Bibliography: TDNT, IV, pp. 583–85; VI, pp. 193–202. THAT, I, pp. 727–29.

P.R.G.

860 *יָחַם (*yāḥam*) ***be hot;*** Piel, ***conceive.***

Derivative

860a †חֵמָה (*ḥēmâ*) ***heat, hot displeasure, indignation, anger, wrath, poison, bottles*** (ASV and RSV use various synonyms).

The noun *ḥēmâ,* according to BDB, is derived from the verb *yāḥam* "be hot," which is used only in Piel and means "to be in heat" or "to conceive." That the noun *ḥēmâ* is derived from the verb *ḥāmam* "be or become warm," "become hot," is also entirely possible, for its various derivatives (*ḥōm, ḥam, ḥammâ*) all mean heat as from the sun or a fire. Ugaritic uses the word *ḥm* "heat," but does not use either verb (UT 19: no. 870). Actually, the two verbs may be by-forms; their meanings are similar. However, since *ḥēmâ* is used in the OT of heat within a person, i.e. his heart, mind, etc., the word could well be related to the root *yāḥam* which refers primarily to conception.

The OT has a number of synonyms for *ḥēmâ* and each has its specific emphasis (see *qāṣap* for a discussion).

The term *ḥēmâ* is used a few times to indicate physical heat in the sense of a fever or of poison causing fever (Deut 32:24, 33). However, the term is used, as a rule, to convey the concept of an inner, emotional heat which rises and is fanned to varying degrees. The context usually gives a clue as to which translation should be preferred, whether anger, hot displeasure, indignation, wrath, rage or fury. Thus, in Ps 37:8, in a progressive parallelism, the Psalmist says, "Cease from anger (*'ap*), yes from intense, hot anger (*ḥēmâ*). (Cf. also Jer 20.)

The OT speaks of man's *ḥēmâ.* Esau's reaction to his brother's deception was one of intense heat (Gen 27:44), so also could a king's reaction be to the death of his warriors (II Sam 11:20). Naaman went away in a rage (II Kgs 5:12). Ahasuerus was furious with Haman (Est 7:7, 10). A man's jealousy is the source of his "rage" (Prov 6:34). The prophets spoke of the fury of the oppressors (Isa 51:13) and Ezekiel of his own hot anger or fury (Ezk 3:14). These examples indicate a variety of reasons for this "heat in men," and show that rage and fury could be considered the legitimate translation in many instances.

In various places where *ḥēmâ* appears it refers to God's reaction to his unfaithful covenant people (Deut 9:19; Jer 42:18). God is aroused to great heat because he, as a jealous God, sees the people he loves disobey him and appeal to, or consort with, sinners or "no gods." He then expresses his rage or pours out his fury (Ezk 36:6). Other nations who violate his intentions and Word, also experience God's displeasure by the pouring out of God's fury (Jer 10:25; Nah 1:2, 6). God's indignations and fury are abated and appeased when he has poured them out in judgment (Jer 42:18). Remorse and repentance would not avert it (II Kgs 22:13–17). However, Phinehas, jealous with God's jealousy, having killed the lawbreaker, did turn God's heat away from Israel (Num 25:11). The point seems clear, once God is provoked to *ḥēmâ,* satisfaction of some kind must be made by the execution of judgment upon the cause of it.

G.V.G.

יַחְמוּר (*yaḥmûr*). See no. 685b.

861 יחף (*yḥp*). **Assumed root of the following.**
861a יָחֵף (*yāḥēp*) ***barefoot.***

862 *יָחַשׂ (*yāḥaś*) ***enroll or be enrolled.*** Denominative verb used in the Hithpael.

Parent Noun

862a יַחַשׂ (*yaḥaś*) ***genealogy.***

863 יָטַב (*yāṭab*) ***be good, be well, be glad, be pleasing.***

Derivative

863a מֵיטָב (*mêṭāb*) ***the best.***

yāṭab is used forty-two times in the Qal imperfect and sixty-three times in the Hiphil. The Hiphil infinitive is used adverbially, "diligently, thoroughly." For Qal perfect the OT uses *ṭôb* (q.v.).

When David prays in Ps 51:18 [H 20], "Do good in thy good pleasure unto Zion," he acknowledges that the covenant Lord is the source of all that is good and pleasing to mankind. This "doing good" is not capricious, but based on the covenant relationship revealed to the patriarchs (which was in turn based on God's free mercy and choice), e.g. when Jacob prepares to face Esau, he prays, "O God of my father Abraham... O Lord, who said to me, 'Return to your country and to your relatives, and I will prosper you' (lit. will do good with you). I am unworthy of all the lovingkindness (*ḥesed* "covenant love"; q.v.) and of all the faithfulness which thou hast shown to thy servant" (Gen 32:9 [H 10]). The prosperity in view (see also v. 12 [H 13]) is in the context of covenantal relation as evidenced by the name Lord (*yhwh*), lovingkindness (*ḥesed*), faithfulness (*'emet* "truth") and servant (*'ebed*). This helps to understand God's dealing well with the midwives (Ex 1:20), and Solomon (I Kgs 1:47). God's "doing good" to his people pervades the book of Deut in the frequently repeated formula "that it may go well with you" (4:40; 5:16, 29 [H 26]; 6:3, 18; 12:25, 28; 22:7) and often in Jer (7:23; 38:20; 40:9; 42:6).

Conversely, the covenanted servant's response is ever to be well pleasing to his Lord. Hence, Solomon's prayer is commended as "pleasing in the sight of the Lord" (lit. "be good in the eyes of"). Cf. Ps 69:31 [H 32]. Jeremiah laments over the decadent Jews in 4:22, "They are stupid children,... they are shrewd to do evil, but to do good they do not know," and Isaiah (1:17) calls them to a radical decision of repentance, "Learn to do good, seek justice, reprove the ruthless, defend the orphan," etc. Cf. Gen 4:7, Jer 13:23 and the various calls of the prophets to "amend your ways and your doings" (e.g. Jer 7:3; 26:13).

This vertical relationship is the theological basis for the horizontal relationship between men, as in Gen 34:18, "their words pleased Hamor." See Neh 2:5–6. This pleasing interpersonal relationship makes a joyful or glad heart. Cf. Eccl 7:3; Prov 15:13; 17:22.

All of these notions converge on the Lord Jesus Christ who as the God-Man epitomizes them, for "he went about doing good" (i.e. healing, etc.) ever pleasing the Father who had sent him.

[Aside from the usages in which *yāṭab* refers to God's beneficent attitude and dealings with his people, the verb seems to refer to beneficence in general whether or not it is associated with fidelity and righteousness of character. E.g. it is used in connection with the trickery of Jacob's sons at Shechem [Gen 34:18], of Pharaoh's pleasure at Jacob's coming to Egypt (Gen 45:16), of the idolatrous priest's pleasure, at joining the Danites (Jud 18:20), of David's agreement with Joab to stay away from the battle (II Sam 18:4 [H 5]). The word is also used in the sense of doing something well or diligently. It is even used of going to excess in sin (Mic 7:3)! R.L.H.]

P.R.G.

864 יַיִן (*yayin*) ***wine.***

Probably a loan word. It has cognates in Indo-European: Greek *oinos,* Latin *vinum,* German *Wein.* It also appears in the Semitic languages, Akkadian *īnu,* Arabic *wayn* (meaning "black grapes"), and Ugaritic *yn* (UT 19: no. 1093). The word is used 140 times, 12 of these in combination with *shēkār* (KJV "wine and strong drink"; NIV sometimes "wine and beer"). Its intoxicating properties are mentioned at least twenty times. It is mentioned as a common drink, an element in banquets and as the material used in libation offerings. These are called "drink offerings" in KJV, RSV, NIV, etc., but they were not drunk. The related Hebrew verb (*nāsak*) means "to pour out." These offerings were poured out on the sacrifices on the brazen altar (Ex 29:40 and 30:9), but in sarcasm the heathen gods are spoken of as eating the food and drinking the drink offerings given them (Deut 32:38).

Wine was forbidden to priests while ministering (Lev 10:9—there is a hint that Nadab and Abihu in Lev 10:1–7 desecrated the sanctuary in drunkenness). Nazirites also and Samson's mother-to-be were to drink no wine or *shēkār* (NIV "fermented drink"; Jud 13:4; Num 6:3). The Israelites "ate no bread and drank no wine" during the forty years in the wilderness, (Deut 29:6). Kings were to avoid it so as to govern with a clear head (Prov 31:4–5). Solomon warns against the use of wine because of its final tragic consequences (Prov 23:30–31).

Abundance of wine, however, is taken as a symbol of affluence (Gen 49:11–12; I Chr 12:40; Ezk 27:18). There are places that speak of the lift to the feelings that wine brings (Zech 10:7; II Sam 13:28; Est 1:10; Ps 104:15; Eccl 9:7–10; 10:19; Isa 55:1). It may be questioned whether in these verses wine is commended because of this lift or if the verses use the freedom from inhibition of incipient drunkenness as a symbol of plenty and blessing—cf. Nathan's reference to David's polygamy as a symbol of God's giving him great riches (II Sam 12:8).

Wine is also used in symbolic ways of the drink that wisdom mingles (Prov 9:2), of the Lord's wrath (Jer 25:15, etc.) of disaster (Ps 60:3 [H 5]) of Babylon's judgment (Jer 51:7) of violence (Prov 4:17) and of desire (Song 1:2; 4:10).

Wine was the most intoxicating drink known in ancient times. All the wine was light wine, i.e. not fortified with extra alcohol. Concentrated alcohol was only known in the Middle Ages when the Arabs invented distillation ("alcohol" is an Arabic word) so what is now called liquor or strong drink (i.e. whiskey, gin, etc.) and the twenty per cent fortified wines were unknown in Bible times. Beer was brewed by various methods, but its alcoholic content was light. The strength of natural wines is limited by two factors. The percentage of alcohol will be half of the percentage of the sugar in the juice. And if the alcoholic content is much above 10 or 11 percent, the yeast cells are killed and fermentation ceases. Probably ancient wines were 7–10 per cent. Drunkenness therefore was of course an ancient curse, but alcoholism was not as common or as severe as it is today. And in an agricultural age, its effects were less deadly than now. Still, even then it had its dangers and Prov 20:1 and 23:29–35 are emphatic in their warnings. To avoid the sin of drunkenness, mingling of wine with water was practiced. This dilution was specified by the Rabbis in NT times for the wine then customary at Passover. The original Passover did not include wine (Deut 20:6).

Related words are *shēkār,* probably beer, *'āsîs* perhaps wine from other fruit juices (Song 8:2), *tîrôsh* (q.v.) apparently the fresh juice from the vineyard, never by itself associated with intoxication.

R.L.H.

865 *יָכַח (*yākaḥ*) ***decide, judge, prove, rebuke, reprove, correct.*** (ASV, RSV similar.)

Derivatives

865a †תּוֹכֵחָה (*tôkēḥâ*) ***reproof, rebuke.***
865b †תּוֹכַחַת (*tôkaḥat*) ***argument, reproof.***

yākaḥ does not occur in the Qal. It is used fifty-four times in the Hiphil, and three times in the Niphal.

The juridical notion of *yākaḥ* is clearly established by one of its early uses: Laban, having caught up with Jacob and having searched in vain through all Jacob's belongings for his valuable amulets, is scolded by Jacob, "What is my sin, that you have set in hot pursuit after me? Though you have felt through all my goods, what have you found? Set it here before my relatives and yours, that they may decide (i.e. judge) between us two" (Gen 31:36f.). Then referring to Laban's dream the night before, he claims, "God has seen my affliction... and rebuked you last night." NASB translates, "So He rendered judgment last night"; NIV "rebuked" (v. 42). See also I Chr 12:18; Job 9:33 where "daysman" is used, but ASV and RSV "umpire." Yet other usages are also witnessed, e.g. Gen 24:14, 44, "appointed."

The forensic use is clearest in the covenant lawsuit context. See Huffmon, JBL 78: 286–95. Psalm 50:8, 21, Hos 4:4, and Mic 6:2 are considered cases where Yahweh in his covenant relation with a people who have repeatedly broken the covenant, now brings a lawsuit against them after the pattern of Deut 32. Dahood translates Ps 50:21*c,* "I will accuse you and draw up a case before your eyes" (AB, 16, p. 304, but ASV "reprove," NIV, "I will rebuke you and accuse you to your face"). He refers to Job 40:2 where the nuance of the participle *môkîaḥ* "he who accuses" God (RSV "he who argues") is clearly present as understood by the ancient versions.

However, the most familiar passage where *yākaḥ* occurs is in Isa 1:18 which is within a covenant lawsuit. Following a record of rebellion where Yahweh, the plaintiff, condemns Judah for their self-designed religious festivals (1:10–15), Isaiah issues a call to repentance (1:16–20). Within this context then we should understand the expression "let us reason together" (KJV, NIV as meaning "let us debate our case in court." Micah 6:2 supports this notion, speaking of "the indictment of Yahweh," then of Yahweh's case against his people" (*rîb* "lawsuit, case") in parallel with the phrase "with Israel he will dispute" (RSV and ASV "will contend," NIV "is lodging a charge," BDB "will argue"). This judicial element, which is the primary meaning of *yākaḥ,* has a clear theological basis as seen in Isa 11:3, where the activities of "the Stem of Jesse, the Branch" is spoken of as one who "will not judge (*shāphaṭ*) by what his eyes see, nor make a decision by what his ears hear." The parallelism underscores our thesis. In addition, v. 4 uses the same two words, "But with righteousness he will judge the poor, and decide with fairness for the afflicted of the earth" in connection with the ever loving concern for the innocent party, the poor, the widow, the orphan, who are oppressed by the greedy and ruthless (cf. Isa 1:17, 23; Mic 6:8). But it is precisely because of the covenant that Yahweh acts in such a manner, that he requires his people to exhibit in their lives this element of the *imago dei.*

It is not without significance that Lev 19:17 enjoins the people of God to confront their neighbors when they sin, "thou shalt surely rebuke your neighbor" (ASV), "you may surely reprove" (NASB). RSV weakens it considerably with "you shall reason with." This in view of the command "you shall be holy, for I the Lord your God am holy" (v. 2). But this confrontation has two reasons attached: to avoid developing a hatred for the neighbor, and to avoid complicity in his sin. Verse 18 further amplifies the action with the second great commandment, "You shall love your neighbor as yourself." Confrontation, rebuke, correction is to be considered, therefore, as an integral part of brotherly love.

To rebuke, to correct, to convince or convict would not only imply exposure of one's sin but also to call a person to repentance. It has a theofugal motion which points away from sin and to repentance toward God. Hence the tremendous implication for discipline in the church—not only to purify the Body of Christ, but also to restore the wayward to holy living and covenantal service (cf. Mt 18:15; Eph 5:11; I Tim 5:20; II Tim 4:2, etc.).

Furthermore, when one examines the many passages that speak of God's loving correction (e.g. Prov 3:12, "For whom Yahweh loves he reproves"; Job 5:17), one finds the parallel term *yāsar* "to instruct, discipline" or *mûsār* "discipline, instruction" (Ps 6:1 [H 2]; Job 5:17; Prov 3:11 [H 12]; 10:17; 12:1; 13:18; 15:5, etc.). It is evident that there is a pedagogic force to *yākaḥ* and *yāsar*. But whereas *yāsar* has the notion of paternal chastisement (as evidenced by the LXX's translating *paideuō*), *yākaḥ* denotes education and discipline as a result of God's judicial actions. "This embraces all aspects of education from the conviction of the sinner to chastisement and punishment, from the instruction of the righteous by severe tests to his direction by teaching and admonition" (Buchsel, in TDNT, II, p. 473). [For a somewhat varying view of the covenant lawsuit motif, see the articles on *mishpāṭ* and *rîb*. R.L.H.]

tôkēḥâ. ***Reproof, rebuke, correction*** (only four occurrences). Translated in LXX as *elegchos* "refutation, correction" (ASV and RSV "rebuke, punishment").

tôkaḥat. ***Argument, reproof, correction.*** Often used in parallel with *mûsār* (q.v.) "discipline, instruction, discipline."

Bibliography: THAT, I, pp. 730–31.

P.R.G.

866 יָכֹל (*yākōl*) ***be able, prevail, overcome*** (ASV and RSV similar.)

yākōl is translated in the LXX mostly by *dunamai* "I can, am able" which is used in a rather weak sense as in contrast to *ischuō* "be strong, powerful." *yākōl* is used of ability or capacity in a physical, ethical, or religious sense. The negative particle is used in about 85 percent of the 199 times it occurs in the OT. Whereas the Hebrew word expresses only a weak ability, the Aramaic *ye kīl* seems to express greater power.

The basic meaning "to be able" is used primarily of man. It refers (with the negative) to lack of self control, as Joseph not being able to restrain himself (Gen 45:1; cf. v. 3); or to inability to control circumstances as Moses' mother no longer being able to hide him (Ex 2:3; see also Gen 13:6; Ex 7:21). It is also used of capacity in virtue of ability, again, negatively of the magicians not having the ability to replicate the miracles of Moses (Ex 9:11) and of the tribes of Israel "not being able to drive out" the enemy out of their newly inherited territory (e.g. Josh 15:63; 17:12; Jud 2:14; cf. also Deut 31:2; Isa 36:14; Lam 1:14).

In the moral or religious sense, there is the limitation of prohibition, often translated "you may not" such as in Deut 17:15, "You may not put a foreigner [as king] over yourselves" (cf. also Deut 7:22; 12:17; 16:5; 21:16, etc., all in Qal imperfect). Perhaps the most impressive example of God's command as delimiting the power of man is Balaam's statement, "Though Balak were to give me his house full of silver and gold, I could not do anything... contrary to the command of Yahweh" (Num 22:18; cf. 24:13, ASV "I cannot go beyond the word of Jehovah my God").

However, *yākōl* is correctly translated "prevail, overcome" when used of men in wrestling or battling. A prominent example would be Jacob's wrestling with the Angel of Yahweh (Gen 32:25ff.). The Angel does not overcome Jacob, and then Jacob's name is changed to "Israel, for you have striven with God and with me and have prevailed." In I Sam 17:9, Goliath puts alternatives before Saul's army. "If he is able to fight with me and kill me, then we will become your servants, but if I prevail against him and kill him, then you shall become our servants and serve us."

yākōl is also used of the gods. In II Chr 32:13–15, Sennacherib sardonically gloats over the inability of the various gods of the nations to protect them from his mighty army. But his equating the God of Israel with the national deities proves to be his downfall (cf. v. 19), for Yahweh of hosts, the sovereign God of the universe, is indeed able to deliver his covenant people from Sennacherib. He is the God of history, creating and sustaining the world, and his power and will affect the destinies of nations and of individual lives. This power of God is assumed by Moses when he intercedes for the Israelites who deserve to be destroyed. But what would the heathen nations say, that "Yahweh could not bring this people into the land he promised by oath, therefore he slaughtered them in the wilderness" (Num 14:16; Deut 9:28). But it is precisely "by thy great power (*bᵉkōḥăkâ haggādōl*) and thine outstretched arm" (Deut 9:29) that Yahweh exhibits his mighty power to deliver and to redeem his people.

God's sovereign power is in clear focus in Daniel's Aramaic cognate *yᵉkīl*. In Dan 3:17f. the three friends of Daniel make an eloquent confession of faith, "Our God, whom we serve is able to deliver us from the furnace of blazing fire" (cf. 3:29, Nebuchadnezzar's statement contrasting God's power against that of heathen gods). Nebuchadnezzar, from his personal experience, affirms God's sovereign power to control the destinies of proud and powerful individuals (4:37, [Aram 34]; cf. Dan 6:20 [Aram 6:21]).

With reference to the concept of power, strength, and omnipotence of God, several synonymous nouns or adjectives should be noted: *ḥayil* "ability, power, competence, strength" as in Ps 84:7 [H 8], "They go from strength to strength." A stronger synonym is *kōaḥ* "strength, power" which is used of God's power in creation (Jer 10:12; 51:15; Ps 65:7) and governance of the universe (Ps 29:4). As noted above, in Deut 9:26–29, the Israelites were redeemed by the great *kōaḥ* of Yahweh, a much stronger term than the root *yākōl* would imply, for here it expresses the great deployment of God's power. Finally when referring to a person "who can do something" (seeking to express power, might, or dominion) such as a ruler, the Hebrew uses *gibbôr* "strong, mighty, valiant man" (Jud 6:12); *ḥāzāq* "strong, stout, mighty (one)" (Isa 28:2; Amos 2:14); *śar* "chief, ruler, captain, prince" (Dan 11:5).

Bibliography: Grundmann, in TDNT, II, pp. 284ff.

P.R.G.

867 יָלַד (*yālad*) ***bear, beget, bring forth, gender, travail.*** The Ugaritic *yld* is similar.

Derivatives

867a וָלָד (*wālād*) ***child*** (Gen 11:30).

867b †יֶלֶד (*yeled*), יַלְדָּה (*yaldâ*) ***child, son, youth.***

867c יַלְדוּת (*yaldût*) ***youth, childhood.*** This noun, which occurs only three times, may indicate the time when one is young, or the quality of being young.

867d †יִלּוֹד (*yillôd*) ***born.*** An adjective equivalent to the passive participle of *yālad*.

867e †יָלִיד (*yālîd*) ***born.*** Used only in the construct state.

867f †מוֹלֶדֶת (*môledet*) ***kindred, relatives.*** Sometimes wrongly translated as "nativity" or "birth."

867g †תּוֹלְדוֹת (*tôlēdôt*) ***descendants, results, proceedings.*** Always used in the plural and in the construct state or with a pronominal suffix.

The root *wld* (*yld* in Northwest Semitic) is a common Semitic root (cf. Arabic *walada,* Akkadian *(w)aladu,* Ugaritic *yld* and Phoenician inscriptions *yld.*

In its narrowest sense *yālad* describes the act of a woman in giving birth to a child (e.g. Ex 1:19; I Kgs 3:17–18), but it is sometimes used of the father's part in becoming a parent (e.g. Gen 4:18; 10:8, 24, 26; 22:23, 25:3; I Chr 1:10–20, Prov 23:22). It may be used with reference to the whole procedure involved in producing a child (e.g. Gen 38:27–28) or it may even be specifically applied to the pains of a woman prior to the actual birth (e.g. Gen 35:16; Mic 5:33). Although predominantly used of human beings it is occasionally used of animals (e.g. Gen 30:39; 31:8; Job 39:1–2, Jer 14:5; Ezk 31:6). A man's part in the production of a child is generally represented by the Hiphil, but sometimes the Qal is used. [Critics sometimes explain this usage as due to documentary division. It is claimed that the Hiphil usage as in Gen 11 is characteristic of P and the Qal as in Gen 10 betokens J. It is more likely that the different forms mean different things. In most every instance actual paternity is represented by the Hiphil and a more general relationship like relationship of peoples (the Table of Nations, Gen 10) uses the Qal. Thus Ps 2:7 is not causative, but refers to a relation of love. The Qal is used. R.L.H.] In the Piel the verb means "to do the office of midwife." Except for Ex 1:16 this usage is confined to the Piel participle. Both Niphal and Pual are commonly used for the passive of the Qal. Hophal is used occasionally with the same meaning (Gen 40:20, Ezk 16:4–5). Hithpael is used once to mean "declare their pedigrees" or "register by ancestry" (Num 1:18).

The word is often used in a figurative sense. Thus it may refer to a city or nation as having given birth to its inhabitants (e.g. Isa 23:4; 51:18; Ezk 16:20). It may refer to the wicked as having brought forth evil, lies or stubble (e.g. Job 15:35; Ps 7:15; Isa 33:11). "Bringing forth wind" is used as a vivid figure of frusration (Isa 26:18). Often *yālad* is used as a simile for distress (e.g. Isa 42:14; Jer 30:6; Mic 4:10). Once it speaks of the day as bringing forth the events that will occur in it (Prov 27:1). God is spoken of as having given birth to Israel (Deut 32:18). The word may be followed by an accusative, but is often used without an object. When used in the passive the effective agent is generally introduced by lamed.

The word does not necessarily point to the generation immediately following. In Hebrew thought, an individual by the act of giving birth to a child becomes a parent or ancestor of all who will be descended from this child. Just as Christ is called a son of David and a son of Abraham, *yālad* may show the beginning of an individual's relationship to any descendant.

The various derivatives indicate special aspects or relationships that are in some way connected with birth, though sometimes this relation is rather distant.

The word is used in several important theological connections.

A constant threat to the Lord's promise that the patriarchs' seed would be innumerable and a blessing to all the families of the earth was the barrenness of their wives (Gen 16:1; 17:17; 18:13; 25:21). But God fulfilled his promise by causing their barren wombs to bear. Then too, during such times of crisis in the life of his people, the Lord demonstrated his sovereign saving control of their destiny by promising that elect women would give birth to sons who would save their people (Jud 13:3, 5, 7; I Sam 1:2–10). This theme finds its consummation in the birth of Jesus Christ (Isa 7:14; 9:5; Mt 1).

Great joy accompanied the birth of a son. But some found the trials of life so severe that they wished they had never been born (Job 3:3; Jer 15:10; 20:14). More tragic, however, is the case of Judas Iscariot who, because of his betrayal of Jesus, would have been better off had he never been born (Lk 16:24).

The apostasy of Israel becomes more painful and tragic in the light of the reality that the Lord "begot" them, a metaphor denoting that he gave them life and cared for them during their tender years (Deut 32:18; cf. Ezk 17:20; 23:4, 37). See *'āb* "father" and *ben* "son".

yālad in Ps 2:7 (note that it is not Hiphil) refers to the relationship of love between the Father and the Son. The NT interprets it of Christ's resurrection and session at the Father's right hand (Acts 13:33; Heb 1:3–5; 5:5) (cf. Buswell, J. O., Systematic Theology of the Christian Religion [Zondervan, 1962] pp. I, 107–112; II, 18).

yeled. ***Child, young man, son, boy, fruit*** (RSV similar; adds youths). **yaldâ.** ***Girl, damsel*** (RSV "girl," "maiden").

These words are generally used for very young children but may refer to adolescents and sometimes even young adults (e.g. I Kgs 12:8–14; II Kgs 2:24; II Chr 10:8–14). Once *yeled* refers to a fetus (Ex 21:22). In Job 38:41; 39:3 and Isa 11:7 the plural is used for the young of animals. In one instance the word is used to mean descendants (Isa 29:23). It is used in a figurative sense to represent the Israelites as either "children of transgression" (Isa 57:4) or "a child of delights" (Jer 31:20).

yillôd. ***Born.*** An adjective equivalent to the passive participle of *yālad*.

yālîd. ***Born, children, sons*** (RSV "born," "descendants"). This noun found only in the construct state, has the same meaning as a passive participle of *yālad*. It is generally used to designate the children born to slaves already possessed by an Israelite (seven occurrences). It is also used three times of the children of Anak and twice of sons (or children) of "the giant(s)" (or Rephaim). Willesen tries to prove that the word must always refer to slaves, since he feels that it would be too much spread of meaning for the one word to be used for men of distinction and also for slaves. With such meager evidence, the argument is not well founded. Note the breadth of meaning in such words as *pᵉqūddâ* and *mipqād*.

môledet. ***Kindred, nativity, issue, born, begotten, native*** (RSV translates similarly, but adds "birth"). This noun should properly be interpreted as "relatives" or "kindred" (occasionally referring to one individual, but generally used as a collective). All its occurrences can be interpreted in line with this meaning, although in a few cases explanation may be necessary (see below).

It has been suggested that *môledet* must mean "birthplace" since the prefix *m-* is sometimes used to form nouns indicating place. However, this prefix also forms nouns of other types, having nothing to do with place. Frequently *môledet* has a general meaning (six times following the construct of "land" and five times being parallel to "land" or "country.") Often "kindred" or "birthplace" would fit equally well. But there are a few contexts where *môledet* could not possibly mean "birthplace." In Gen 48:6, where it points to Joseph's posterity, "relatives" would fit, but "birth" or "birthplace" would be quite meaningless. In Est 8:6, and probably also in Est 2:10 and 2:20, "kindred" fits the context and "birth" or "birthplace" does not. In Ezk 16:3–4 it seems to refer more to people than to place. In Ezk 16:4 the translation "birth" or "nativity" would merely repeat the idea expressed in the following words, while "kindred" would point to the indifference of the relatives. In Gen 43:7 "kindred" fits much better than "birth" or "birthplace."

If taken as "birthplace" in Gen 24:4, it would contradict the statement in Gen 11:28–31 that Abram came originally from Ur of the Chaldees. To assume such a contradiction is quite unnecessary since the meaning "kindred" would fit just as well in all cases, and many of Abram's kindred had moved to Haran.

A difficulty might be assumed in Lev 18:9, 11. Yet in these two verses it would seem that relationship rather than actual birth is of primary importance.

tôlēdôt. ***Generations, birth*** (RSV similar). The precise meaning of this derivative of *yālad* "to bring forth," will be discussed below. It occurs only in the plural, and only in the construct state or with a pronominal suffix. In the KJV it is always translated "generations" except for one case (two in the RSV) where it is rendered "birth." RSV generally translates it "generations" but occasionally uses "genealogy." In six occurrences it renders it as "descendants" and once as "history."

The common translation as "generations" does not convey the meaning of the word to modern readers. The English word "generation" is now limited almost entirely to two meanings: (1) the act of producing something or the way it is produced; (2) an entire group of people living at the same period of time, or the average length of time that such a group of people live. Neither of these meanings fits the usage of *tôlēdôt*.

As used in the OT, *tôlēdôt* refers to what is produced or brought into being by someone, or follows therefrom. In no case in Gen does the word include the birth of the individual whose *tôlēdôt* it introduces (except in Gen 25:19, where the story of Isaac's life is introduced by reference to the fact that he was the son of Abraham). After the conclusion of the account in which Jacob was the principal actor, Gen 37:2 says, "These are the *tôlēdôt* of Jacob" and proceeds to tell about his children and the events with which they were connected.

In line with these usages it is reasonable to interpret Gen 2:4, "These are the *tôlēdôt* of heaven and earth," as meaning, not the coming of heaven and earth into existence, but the events that followed the establishment of heaven and earth. Thus the verse is correctly placed as introducing the detailed account of the creation and fall of man. It is not a summary of the events preceding Gen 2:4.

The often repeated statement that the book of Gen is divided into natural sections by the word *tôlēdôt* does not work out on close examination. Sometimes, as in Gen 36:9, it merely introduces a genealogical table.

In Gen 10:32, 25:13, Ex 6:16, 19 and in eight of the nine occurrences in I Chr the word is introduced by the preposition *l* and in Ex 28:10 it is introduced by *k*. The significance of the prepositions is not clear, particularly since we have no other evidence relating to the history of the sons of Ishmael (Gen 25:13) or the arrangement of the stones on the breastplate (Ex 28:10). Therefore we do not know in accordance with what principle the arrangement was made. In both cases the word "birth" must be considered to be only a guess.

Bibliography: Willeson, Folker, "The Yālīd in Hebrew Society," *Studia Theologica* 12: 192–210. TDNT, I, pp. 665–675; V, pp. 636–54. THAT, I, pp. 733–35.

יַלְדוּת (*yaldût*). See no. 867c.
יִלּוֹד (*yillôd*). See no. 867d.
יָלִיד (*yālîd*). See no. 867e.

868 *יָלַל (*yālal*) ***howl, wail.***

Derivatives

868a יְלֵל (*ye lēl*) ***howling,*** only in Deut 32:10.
868b יְלָלָה (*ye lālâ*) ***howling, wailing.***
868c תּוֹלָל (*tôlāl*) ***tormentor.*** Occurs only in Ps 137:3. Derivation uncertain.

yālal is used twenty-nine times, only in the Hiphil. ASV sometimes uses "wail," but RSV uses "wail" consistently. Occurs only in the prophets.

The parallel of the verb with *zā'aq* "cry out, call" (q.v.) points to a relationship with anxiety, sorrow, and distress. But the parallel with *sāpad* "wail, lament" (q.v.) makes it clear that mourning for death and destruction is in view. The LXX uses *threneō* "mourn, lament." The emphasis is not on singing a dirge, although that is sometimes in view (cf. Amos 8:3), but rather on violent lamentation. Joel (1:5, 8, 11, 13) calls on priests and drunkards, city and land, farmers and ministers to "wail" because of the disaster which would come on the day of the Lord. Micah the prophet experiences this bewailing (1:8). However, not only the people of God are called to wail (which in essence is a call to repentance from sin), but the gentile nations are also called by a sovereign God to wail for the destruction awaiting them (e.g. Babylon, Isa 13:6; Moab, Isa 15:2; etc.).

For content of mourning and lamentation, see Lam, Jer 9:18–20, Amos 5, Isa 14. Also see article on *qînâ* "elegy, dirge." (An interesting article on the customs of mourning in the ancient near east is TDNT, III, Stahlin, in pp. 148ff).

P.R.G.

יָלַע (*yālaʻ*). See לוּע, no. 1098.

869 ילף (*ylp*). **Assumed root of the following.**
869a יַלֶּפֶת (*yallepet*) ***scab, scales, an eruptive disease.*** Occurs only in Lev 21:20; 22:22.

870 ילק (*ylq*). **Assumed root of the following.**
870a †יֶלֶק (*yeleq*) ***young locust.***

Perhaps from the verb *lāqaq* "to lick, to lap." The word occurs nine times. It is translated by the KJV as "caterpillar" or "cankerworm," i.e. a destructive caterpillar. The LXX renders the word as *brouchos* "unwinged locust."

In Joel 1:4 and 2:25 the *yeleq* may represent the young larval stage of the locust; the NEB and JB suggest "hopper." But in Jer 51:27 the *yeleq* is described as "rough," alluding to the hornlike sheath which covers the rudimentary wings of the nymph stage. In Nah 3:16 the last nymph stage is indicated, when the locust molts and then unfurls its wings.

See also *'arbeh.*

E.Y.

יַלְקוּט (*yalqûṭ*). See no. 1125b.
יָם (*yām*). See no. 871a.
יֵמִם (*yēmim*). See no. 871b.
יָמִין (*yāmîn*). See no. 872a.
יְמִינִי (*y^e^mînî*). See no. 872b.

871 ימם (*ymm*). **Assumed root of the following.**
871a †יָם (*yām*) ***sea, west, westward,*** (ASV and RSV similar, although RSV sometimes uses adjective "western").
871b יֵמִם (*yēmim*). ***Meaning dubious.*** Occurs only in Gen 36:24.

yām is used over three hundred times referring to "sea," and over seventy times referring to "west" or "westward." Once (Ps 107:3) it is translated "from the south" but this must be a manuscript error, although in Isa 49:12 also *yām* is opposite to north.

Specific seas are mentioned, namely, (1) the Mediterranean, called "the great sea" (Num 34:6), "the hinder sea," i.e. the western sea (Deut 11:24), "the sea of the Philistines" (Ex 23:31) and in Ezr 3:7 "the sea of Joppa"; (2) the Dead Sea, named "the salt sea" (Num 34:3), "the east sea" (Ezk 47:18) and "the sea of the Arabah" (Deut 3:17); (3) the Red Sea, *yām sûp,* lit. "sea of weeds" (Ex 10:19), "the sea of Egypt" (Isa 11:15), and in the NT "the red sea" (Acts 7:36); (4) the Sea of Galilee, known as *kinneret* (Num 34:11) with sometimes a slight modification in orthography, then in I Macc 11:67 "the water of *Gennesar*," and then in NT times known as the Sea of Gennesaret (Lk 5:1) or Galilee (Mt 4:18) or Tiberias (Jn 21:1). Also, *yām* is used of the Nile river (Nah 3:8) undoubtedly because of its vastness, as also the Euphrates (Jer 51:36; cf. Isa 21:1 where it may refer to the Persian Gulf). Often it is used in general, as contrasted to earth or sky. According to I Kgs 7:23ff., Solomon's temple court had an immense laver called "the bronze sea." Any symbolism to be connected with *yām,* however, would be purely conjectural. It was doubtless so called because of its size.

The location of the Mediterranean may well have given rise to the use of "west" in Hebrew particularly and semitic thought generally. Ugaritic has the same cognate for "sea." Israel was never noted for its maritime enterprises. Solomon indeed had a merchant fleet, but he may have hired Phoenician sailors to man it.

The OT speaks of the Lord as the creator of the sea (Gen 1:10), who also imposed a limit on its waters (Ps 104:6–9; Prov 8:29). The mighty power of God who controlled the Red Sea at the time of the Exodus, becomes the cause for celebration then (Ex 15) and later (Ps 78:13; 136:13). This in turn becomes a symbol for expected victory by the same omnipotent God, so that prayer and promises are made with full confidence (Isa 51:10; cf. Ps 107:23–32). Heathen nations are likened to the roaring sea (Isa 17:12) but they will be rebuked by the Lord and will flee away (17:13).

In Daniel, the satanic world powers take on the figure of beasts that rise up from the sea (7:3), but in keeping with the sovereign power of the creator, the most high overthrows these as he establishes his everlasting kingdom.

To the people of ancient Israel, the sea must generally have been perceived as a place of dread, fraught with dangers. Jonah 2:2f. gives expression to the close relation between Sheol and the seas from which Jonah was delivered. It may well be that this fear of the seas is what rives rise to John's eschatological vision "the sea shall be no more" (Rev 21:1).

Bibliography: TDNT, IX, pp. 585–91.

P.R.G.

872 ימן (*ymn*). **Assumed root of the following.**
872a †יָמִין (*yāmîn*) ***right hand, right side.***
872b יְמִינִי (*y^{e}mînî*) ***on the right.***
872c יָמַן (*yāman*) ***go to or choose the right, use the right hand.*** Denominative verb.
872d יְמָנִי (*y^{e}mānî*) ***right hand, right.***
872e †תֵּימָן (*têmān*) ***I, south, southward.***
872f †תֵּימָן (*têmān*) ***II, Teman.***

yāmîn. ***Right hand, right side.*** The word *yāmîn* is used literally of a man's right hand as opposed to *ś^{e}m'ōl* "the left" (which is also used for the "north"). An excellent illustration of this is in Gen 48:13–14 where Jacob blesses the two sons of Joseph stretching out "his right hand and laid it on the head of Ephraim, who was younger, and his left hand on Manasseh's head, crossing his hands, although Manasseh was the first born." Joseph was displeased and tried to exchange Jacob's hands, for there was already a significance attached to the right hand. As Jacob refuses to remove his right hand from the head of Ephraim, he explains, "He [i.e. Manasseh] also shall become a people and he also shall be great. However, his younger brother shall be greater than he, and his descendants shall become a multitude of nations" (v. 19). The idea of favor and strength being transmitted through the right hand of blessing begins to emerge. It should be noted that Benjamin "son of (my) right hand" clearly is a name showing special favor and position as the youngest son of Jacob. The name was also used earlier in the Mari tablets of a tribe of Semites. In that case it probably had the other meaning"Sons of the South." One other literal usage should be mentioned. Jonah 4:11 concludes with the Lord's expression of covenantal love and concern for those in Nineveh "who cannot distinguish between his right hand and his left hand."

The more important usage for theological consideration is the figurative expression "the right hand of the Lord" which exhibits the omnipotence of God especially on behalf of his people Israel. One of the earliest and most explicit statements is found in Moses' song of triumph after they had crossed the Red Sea and the Egyptian army had been destroyed. In Ex 15:6 he claims, "Thy right hand, O Lord, is majestic in power; Thy right hand, O Lord, shatters the enemy." The last phrase is even more explicit when coupled with 15:1*b*, "The horse and its rider he has hurled into the sea," and further on, "Thou didst stretch out Thy right hand, the earth swallowed them" (v. 12). Hence, the almighty power of God is pictured by his right hand as an instrument for delivering his people from their enemies. This in turn becomes the theme of many a psalm of praise, e.g. Ps 98:1, "His right hand and his holy arm have gained the victory for him." Cf. also Ps 20:7; 21:9. Furthermore, it is the Lord's right hand that becomes the hope and confidence of God's people in time of need. Isaiah 41:10*b* explicitly conjoins strength and help to the instrumental usage of right hand, "I will strengthen you, surely I will help you, surely, I will uphold you with my righteous right hand." See also Isa 41:13; Ps 18:35 [H 36]. In Isa 45:1 Cyrus of Persia is said to be "taken by the right hand." We understand this to mean that Cyrus's right hand was strengthened by the Lord.

The scriptures also acknowledge that the power of God's right hand strengthened the people to conquer Canaan and more specifically the holy hill of Zion (Ps 78:54). The location "at the right hand" of God is specifically noted in Ps 16:11 as a place where godly people taste eternal pleasures and delights. Also, it is used eschatologically of Messiah's throne "The Lord says to my Lord, 'Sit at my right hand until I make thine enemies a footstool for thy feet' " (Ps 110:1). This begins to be fulfilled at the ascension of Christ as noted by Peter in Acts 2:33–35, "Therefore having been exalted to the right hand of God." With reference to the second coming of Christ, it is said that he will separate the sheep from the goats, "and he will put the sheep on his right, and the goats on the left," declaring to those on the right, "Come, you blessed of my Father, inherit the kingdom prepared for you from the foundation of the world." This gives added significance to Ps 16:11, noted above. In response to the high priest on the night of his betrayal, Jesus said, "Hereafter you shall see 'the Son of Man sitting at the right hand of power' " (Mt 26:64). Quoting from Ps 110:1, he clearly demonstrates the divine omnipotence by the addition *tēs dunameōs* "of power" (cf. Stephen's vision of the exalted Christ in Acts 7:55).

yāmîn locative is used as a "wall on the right hand and on their left hand" in Ex 14:22, 29; or directional, as in Deut 2:27, "Let me pass through your land . . . I will not turn to the right or to the left." This directional usage may also express figuratively the potential for moral and spiritual deviation from the law of God (Deut 17:11,20; Josh 1:7; 23:6, etc.). *yāmîn* is also used of other parts of the body, e.g. shoulder, thigh.

Finally *yāmîn* is translated "south," since when facing east, the right hand is on the south. Note especially Ps 89:12 [H 13] *ṣāpôn w^{e}yāmîn* "the north and the south, thou hast created them." The kingdom of Yemen in southern Arabia still shows this meaning "South."

It is interesting to note that Ugaritic *ymn* is a precise cognate, the only exception being the eschatological notion regarding Messiah. It should be noted that Egyptian orientation "called for facing upstream (thus 'right = west'"; UT 19: no. 411).

têmān ***I. South, southward, south wind*** (lit. "what is on the right [hand, as one faces south]).

It is used most frequently (over one hundred times) with reference to the Negev, which is the most common word. *têmān* is often used poetically, as BDB observes. Job 39:26 speaks of the soaring hawk "stretching his wings toward the south." Job 9:9 refers to "Orion, and the Pleiades, and the chambers of the south." Zechariah 9:14 speaks of the "whirlwinds (or stormwinds) of the south." In this connection, Asaph refers to the sovereign control of God over the "east wind" and adds, "by his power he directed the south wind" as he brought the quail and manna to the Israelites who had been recently redeemed from Egypt (Ps 78:26). Cf. Song 4:16.

têmān ***II. Teman.*** The name of Esau's grandson, the son of Eliphaz, who was an Edomite chief (Gen 36:11, 15). Seven times it is used of a district northeast of Edom (Jer 49:20; Ezk 25:13) upon which fire will come as predicted by Amos (1:12), and which was known for its mighty wise men (Ob 8f.; Jer 49:7). Seemingly incongruous is Habakkuk's vision wherein he sees the holy God coming from Teman. The parallel perhaps explains it: God is viewed as coming from that general direction as in the exodus and wilderness experience. Nelson Glueck identifies Teman with Tawilan, in *The Other Side of Jordan,* pp. 25f.

P.R.G.

יְמָנִי (*ye mānî*). See no. 872d.

873 יָנָה (*yānâ*) ***oppress, vex, do wrong.***

Of its twenty usages, only six are in the Qal; the others are in the Hiphil. However, in Ezk 46:18 it is translated "to thrust them out of their inheritance." ASV and RSV are similar. The LXX uses *thlíbō* or *thlipsis* for *yānâ* as also for several Hebrew synonyms, the most common of which is *ṣārar* "to treat someone with hostility," Hiphil "to constrict someone." These words in Hebrew express a whole range of afflictions. *yānâ* seems to be used in the sense of "doing wrong" to someone as in the Mosaic legislation which protects the rights of the *gēr* "resident alien." Exodus 22:21 [H 20], "And you shall not wrong a stranger or oppress him" (*lāḥaṣ* "press, crush, oppress") appending the rationale, "For you were *gērîm* in the land of Egypt." See further Lev 19:33 where the opposite of *yānâ* is to "love him as yourself." Similarly Deut 23:16 [H 17] expresses the great king's concern for the refugee slave, seeking asylum from a foreign land, that he not be maltreated. The Levitical legislation further protects the economic rights of people who could easily be bilked by the abuse of the year of Jubilee (Lev 25:14, 17). In sum, covenantal stipulations forbad the maltreatment of the poor and infirm, particularly the alien, by the rich and powerful.

The prophets of the Babylonian crisis use the participle of *yānâ* in referring to Jerusalem the "oppressing city," because her civil rulers have turned from the Lord, behave as "roaring lions," profaning the sacred and doing violence to the law. Jeremiah 46:16 speaks of the oppressing sword (cf. 50:16).

The prophets considered these oppressive activities to be nothing less than sin against God. Hence political oppression and private affliction of slaves or aliens were denounced as contrary to God's will for the covenantal people of the Lord.

P.R.G.

יְנִיקָה (*ye nîqâ*). See no. 874c.

874 יָנַק (*yānaq*) ***suck, nurse.***

Derivatives

874a †יוֹנֵק (*yônēq*) ***suckling, sapling.***
874b †יוֹנֶקֶת (*yôneqet*) ***young shoot.***
874c יְנִיקָה (*ye nîqâ*) ***young shoot, twig,*** found only in Ezk 17:4.

Compare Ugaritic *ynq* "to suck," Akkadian *eniqu* "to suck," *mušeniqtu* "wet nurse," Egyptian *snq* "to suckle." The word appears approximately sixty-two times in the OT.

Properly, the verb belongs to the action of an infant suckling at its mother's breast (Job 3:12; Song 8:1; Joel 2:16). Often it occurs as a substantive, a suckling or a babe (Num 11:12; Deut 32:25).

It then broadens to become a metaphor of abundance and honor. In Deut 33:19, Issachar and Zebulun will suckle "the abundance of the seas and the treasures hid in the sands." Isaiah 60:16 uses the same figure to predict the great wealth and power that will come to Jerusalem from the converted gentiles, for they will give of their life energies just as a mother gives milk to an infant. Indeed she will "suck the breast of kings." This is similar to a subject frequently depicted in the art of he ancient near east. A young prince is portrayed as being suckled by the goddess who conferred royalty to the next ruler of the pagan nations. In Isa 66:11–12, it is a picture of satisfaction and comfort.

The Hiphil stem means "to give suck to,

nurse." It is used in the participial form of a nursing woman (Ex 2:7; Gen 24:59). This stem also is used of animals (Gen 32:15 [H 16]; Lam 4:3) and in a figurative expression, of causing one to suck honey (Deut 32:13). Another such metaphorical expression has both kings and queens of the gentile nations being Israel's foster fathers and nursing mothers.

yônēq. ***Suckling, sapling, young plant*** (RSV). This form appears only once, in a messianic reference (Isa 53:2). It is parallel to *shōresh* "root." To men, the servant appeared as a shoot growing from the main stalk, to be pruned off since it sapped or sucked strength from the main plant.

yôneqet. ***Young shoot, twig.*** Appears only six times. It refers in Job 14:7 to the "shoots" which come up around the stump of a felled tree. Job uses this as an argument for his hope of immortality, for just as trees sprout again, after they have been cut down, so a man must wait until his "change" or "release" or "second growth" comes (v. 14) (see *ḥālap*). Already, Bildad had referred to shoots spreading over the garden (8:16). Then Eliphaz echoed Bildad's type of argument (15:30). These two men both applied our word to the wicked.

In Ps 80:11 [H 12], the (cf. Ps 44:2 [H 3]) classic picture of Israel as a vine occurs. There it speaks of the vine's shoots going down to the river. But in Hos 14:6 [H 7] it is a shoot from a poplar tree, if *lib^{e}neh* "poplar" is read for the MT *l^{e}bānôn* as it is in Hos 4:13.

The most significant passage, which is similar to the abbreviated form in Isa 53:2, is Ezk 17:22. There the Lord will take a "sprig" (*ṣammeret*) which by interpretation is a descendant of David's house, from the top of the cedar tree. Then he will break off from the topmost of its young twigs, "a tender one" (*rak*), i.e. the Messiah himself. Note the corporate solidarity of the whole line of David, yet its final and ultimate representative in Jesus Christ.

W.C.K

יַנְשׁוּף (*yanshûp*). See no. 1434b.

875 יָסַד (*yāsad*) ***establish, found, lay foundation.*** (ASV, RSV similar.)

Derivatives

875a יְסֻד (*y^{e}sūd*) ***foundation, beginning,*** only in Ezra 7:9.
875b †יְסוֹד (*y^{e}sôd*) ***foundation, base.***
875c יְסוּדָה (*y^{e}sûdâ*) ***foundation,*** meaning city founded. Occurs only in Ps 87:1.
875d מוּסָד (*mûsād*) ***foundation laying, foundation.***
875e †מוּסָדָה (*mûsādâ*) ***foundation.***
875f מוֹסָד (*môsād*) ***foundation.***
875g מַסַּד (*massad*) ***foundation.***

The primary meaning of *yāsad* is "to found, to fix firmly," from which the major nominal meanings derive, i.e. "foundation" especially of a building. Hence the verb is translated "to establish" a city, etc. It is used in a literal sense just a few times, as in Ezr 3:12 "the old men... wept with a loud voice when the foundation of this house (i.e. the second temple) was laid before their eyes." The Piel and Pual are used more often in this sense (i.e. with reference to the temple, I Kgs 5:31; Ezr 3:6,10; Zech 4:9, etc.), but also of the foundation of a city. Both Josh 6:26 and I Kgs 16:34 both refer to the curse of rebuilding Jericho upon the pain of laying such foundation with the death of a son. Note also the foundation of Zion, Isa 14:32. *y^{e}sôd* is evidently used of the "foundation" for a city wall. Solomon's temple had large blocks of stone (12′ × 15′) upon which it was built. See I Kgs 5:17; 6:37. The NT uses *themelios* for this literal sense of foundations of houses, towers, and cities (cf. Lk 6:48f.; 14:29; Acts 16:26; Heb 11:10; Rev 21:14,19).

The metaphorical usage would signify something which cannot be moved. The NT *katabolē* "a casting or laying down" is often used of "the foundation of the world" (e.g. Mt 13:35; Eph 1:4). This cosmological usage reflects many passages from the OT, e.g. Ps 24:2, "For he has founded it [the world] upon the seas." See also Ps 78:69; 89:11 [H 12]; 104:5.

Several passages refer to the foundation of the earth and the heavens together, as Prov 3:19 "The Lord by wisdom founded the earth; by understanding He established (Heb *kônēn*) the heavens" (see also Ps 102:26; Isa 48:13; 51:13, 16). Some other cosmological references are to the foundations of mountains and lands as well as the heavens and the earth. And yet in a significant verse Job says that God "suspends the earth over nothing" (Job 26:7, NIV).

Isaiah 54:11 speaks of the future of Israel, "Behold, I will set your stones in antimony, and your foundations I will lay in sapphires." This eschatological note anticipates the New Jerusalem described with precious stones and metals in Rev 21–22.

Two verses in the Psalms have an unusual use of *yāsad* in the Niphal, "The kings of t e earth set themselves (*yityaṣṣ^{e}bû*), and the rulers take counsel together (*nôs^{e}dû*) against the Lord and his anointed" (Ps 2:2; cf. Ps 31:13 [H 14]). As BDB puts it, the meaning here is "fix or seat themselves close together, sit in conclave" which is closely parallel to the first verb, *yāṣab* (q.v.) in the Hithpael. The notion is of ieople firmly setting themselves against someone, here specifically against the Messiah.

This leads us to a further usage in messianic prophecy, namely that of Isa 28:16. The Lord speaks, "Behold I am laying in Zion for a foundation a stone, a tested stone, a precious cornerstone, of a sure foundation. He who believes will not be in haste" (RSV). The context is a message of judgment to "the drunkards of Ephraim" (28:1) and more specifically "the scoffers who rule this people who are in Jerusalem" (28:14) who now boast of having made "a covenant with death and with Sheol" and "made a lie our refuge and falsehood (or false gods) our hiding place" (NIV). They thus entertain the false hope that "the overwhelming scourge [i.e. Assyria] will not reach us." Isaiah, as often before, maintains that the only basis for real hope is faith in the covenant Lord. The apostle Peter gives the inspired interpretation of our passage when he refers to Jesus Christ as "the precious cornerstone," indeed "as to a living stone" upon whom believers, "you also, as living stones, are being built up as a spiritual house" (I Pet 2:4–8). Paul also confirms this in Rom 9:32f. where, however, he conflates Isa 28:16 with Isa 8:14 which speaks of a "stumbling stone" which Isaiah uses to refer to Immanuel who will be to both houses of Israel "a stone to strike and a rock to stumble over" (Isa 8:13–15). It is important to note that the NT references agreeing with some LXX manuscripts add *ep' autō* "in him" following the "he who believes." The MT does not make this explicit. The *yissad b^e ṣîyyôn* "I lay for a foundation in Zion" has reference to the holy city as the city of God, but extending the meaning to include the people of God, the church, and its foundations. It is this conception of a solid and firm foundation which is the backdrop for understanding the statement "upon this rock I aill build my church" (Mt 16:18). Also in Eph 2:20, the apostle speaks of the "household of God, having been built upon the foundation (*themelios*) of the apostles and prophets, Christ Jesus himself being the cornerstone." See also Rev 21:14, 19f. where there may well be a christological and ecclesiological significance.

y^esôd. ***Foundation, base.*** Seven of its eighteen usages refer to the "bottom" of the altar, (so KJV, but ASV and RSV translate "base"). Once it is used of "repairing" the temple (II Chr 24:27).

mûsādâ. ***Foundation.*** Used only twice, once in Isa 30:32 of a rod of "punishment" (KJV "appointment")

Bibliography: THAT, I, pp. 736–37.

P.R.G.

יְסוֹד (*ye sôd*). See no. 875b.
יְסוּדָה (*ye sûdâ*). See no. 875c.
יִסּוֹר (*yissôr*). See no. 877a.
יָסַךְ (*yāsak*). See סוּךְ, no. 1474.

876 יָסַף (*yāsap*) ***add, increase, do again*** (ASV, RSV similar.)

Derivative

876a †יוֹסֵף (*yôsēp*) ***Joseph.***

yāsap occurs almost two hundred times, mostly in the Qal and Hiphil (six times in the Niphal). The LXX translates usually with *prostithemi.* No cognate is found in Ugaritic.

A very common usage of *yāsap* is "to do again," as in Gen 4:2, "And again, she gave birth to his brother Abel" (cf. 38:5). In the case of Abraham taking Keturah as wife, Gen 25:1 states, "Now Abraham had taken another [lit. added or took again a] wife." Sometimes, especially with a negative particle, it is translated "no more" as in the moving scene where Judah quotes Joseph, "Unless your youngest brother comes down with you, you shall see my face no more" (lit. you shall not add to; see Gen 44:23).

The literal idea "to add" is clearly evident in Lev 27:13, 15, 19, 27 where repeatedly Moses writes about the person who makes a vow that "he shall add a fifth of the value" if he should wish to redeem an object or property. The case of Hezekiah also is to the point, where in response to his prayer, the Lord promises, "I will add fifteen years to your life" (Isa 38:5). Rachel, in naming her firstborn Joseph, prays, "May the Lord give me [lit. add to me] another son." Both Isaiah and Rachel acknowledge that longevity and progeny are at the sovereign discretion of God. In this connection observe Prov 10:27, "The fear of the Lord prolongeth days." See also Prov 9:11.

There is a negative note in connection with *yāsap.* This is the human ethical problem of sin. It is first encountered with Pharoah, "But when Pharoah saw that the rain and the hail and thunder had ceased, he sinned again (lit. he added to sin) and hardened his heart" (Ex 9:34). But this is the case even with the people of God, as the recurring phrase in Judges "and the children of Israel did evil again (lit. added to do evil) in the sight of the Lord" (3:12; 10:6, etc.). This heaping up of something need not be totally negative. Psalm 71:14 quotes the psalmist as saying, "I will increase thy praise" or as KJV "and will yet praise thee more and more."

Nevertheless, there are instances where a positive note is struck. The incorporation of men into a society occurs several times. A striking episode is the concern expressed by the Egyptians over the growth of the Israelite population: "Come, let us deal wisely with them, lest they multiply and in the event of war, they also join themselves to those who hate us and fight against us" (Ex 1:10). The Psalmist prays, "May the Lord give you increase, you and your children" (Ps 115:14). Cf. Is 14:1. One should note the similar NT usage in Acts 2:41,47; 5:14; 11:24, where "believers were continually added to the Lord," i.e. the Lord was adding them to the church (passive rather than middle, "they joined themselves"). There is in this connection, an eschatological hope in the OT related to the doctrine of the remnant, i.e. "and the surviving remnant of the house of Judah shall again take root downward and bear fruit upward, for out of Jerusalem shall go forth a remnant, and out of Mount Zion survivors" (II Kgs 19:30, 31). Admittedly this prophecy may have been fulfilled in part either after Sennacherib's army was decimated or following the Babylonian exile, nevertheless if the writer understands Rom 11 aright, the apostle Paul confidently hoped for an even greater and more glorious fulfillment. (Cf. Nah 1:15 [H 2:1].) In a similar vein, Jeremiah speaking of the regathered people of Israel, says, "And their life shall be like a watered garden, and they shall never languish again" (31:12). Note also Isa 52:1 where Jerusalem is called to awake, "For the uncircumcised and the unclean will no more come into you" (cf. Rev 22:14–15).

yāsap is frequently used as part of an oath, as for example, when Ruth entreats Naomi not to force her to leave, "For where you go I will go, and where you lodge I will lodge; your people shall be my people and your God my God. . . . May the Lord do so to me and more also (lit. so may he add) if even death parts me from you" (Ruth 1:17). Cf. also I Sam 3:17; II Sam 3:9, 19:13 [H 14].

The phrase "to do so to me and more also" seems to involve an ellipsis, which may be understood when the literal expression is completed, such as "so may he add curses upon me if." This is plausible when one reads in the treaties of nearby kings the list of blessings for obedience but a longer list of curses for disobedience or rebellion.

yôsēp, y^e^hôsēp. ***Joseph.*** *y^e^hôsēp* is found once, in Ps 81:5 [H 6]. The name appears over 200 times in the OT, referring primarily to the older son of Jacob and Rachel. It is used for the tribe, i.e. Ephraim and Manasseh (Deut 33:13; Josh 14:4; 17:1f.), for the northern kingdom (Amos 5:6, 15, Zech 10:6), and for the whole nation of Israel (Ps 80:1 [H 2], 81:5 [H 6]). Four other men in the OT have this name: 1) Num 13:7, a man from Issachar; 2) I Chr 25:2, 9 a son of Asaph; 3) Ezr 10:42 one who took a foreign wife; and 4) Neh 12:14 a priest.

The name is derived from *yāsap* "to add, increase, do again" (q.v.). Rachel specifically names her son Joseph, saying, "May the Lord give me (lit. add to me) another son" (Gen 30:24). Hence at the very beginning of Joseph's life, there is an acknowledgment of the sovereign grace of God which magnificently anticipates God's providence for his people as developed in the story of Joseph (Gen 37–50). Note that in v. 23 there is a play on the word. *'āsap* "take away, remove" which is in assonance with Joseph. In Gen Joseph must be considered a historical character. His name is not used in the patriarchal appellative for God, as in "the God of Abraham, Isaac, and Jacob," doubtless because there were twelve brothers in his generation. However, he becomes the important link from the creation and patriarchal revelation with the great revelation at the exodus from Egypt.

Joseph is not to be taken merely as an example for ethical conduct (Gen 39). His dealings with his brothers as a young man might betray him (Gen 37). However, Gen 39:9 clearly points to the theological basis for his ethics. "How then could I do this great evil, and sin against God?" Indeed, throughout the narrative, God's activity in the history of his people is the focus of attention. This is most clear in Joseph's insistence that "God sent me before you to preserve life" (45:5 is repeated in order that the message might not be lost, 45:6–9). After Jacob's death, he again emphasizes this "good" providence of God even when "evil" had been intended (50:20f.). Furthermore, on his deathbed he anchors his faith to the oath-bound covenantal promises made by God to his forefathers. Based on this assurance he demands that his remains be interred in the promised land (50:24f.; cf. Heb 11:22).

Joseph's explanation of Pharaoh's dreams that "God has shown Pharoah what he is about to do" (41:25, 27, 32, 39) must also apply to Joseph's own dreams (ch. 37). See also 40:8. Finally, his life bore clear testimony to a close walk with the Lord (39:3). Even in naming his two sons, he was conscious of God's gracious activity (41:51f.).

P.R.G.

877 יָסַר (*yāsar*) ***discipline, chasten, instruct.***

Derivatives

877a יִסּוֹר (*yissôr*) ***one who reproves.*** Only in Job 40:2.

877b †מוּסָר (*mûsār*) ***discipline.***

The LXX translates primarily as *paideuo,* which emphasizes the notion of education. The Ugaritic cognate *ysr* meaning "to chasten, instruct" (UT 19: no. 1120).

From the usage and parallels in the OT, one must conclude that *yāsar* and *mûsār* denote correction which results in education. The theological basis for discipline is grounded in the covenant relationship which Yahweh establishes with his people. The words are found almost ninety times, nine times in the Pentateuch, twenty-six times in the prophets, and fifty times in the Hagiographa, (thirty-six of these in Prov). In Lev 26:18, 28 *yāsar* is used in the formula "I will chastise (NASB punish) you seven times for your sins," with a clear parallel in v. 24, "I will punish you seven times" (*nākâ* "to beat, strike, hit"). God's corrective discipline seeks the reformation of the people (v. 23). The other six uses in the Pentateuch are found in Deut, the all important covenant renewal document. Key to an understanding of *mûsār* is Deut 11:2ff., "Consider the discipline of the Lord your God, his greatness, . . . his signs and his deeds which he did in Egypt to Pharaoh . . ., and what he did to the army of Egypt . . ., and what he did for you in the wilderness." In short, the *mûsār* of Yahweh is his mighty activity in covenant history by which he reveals himself (cf. v. 7 with 4:35f.).

The discipline of Yahweh is not to be taken negatively, for the hardships in the wilderness were balanced by his miraculous provisions both designed to test "what was in your heart, whether you would keep his commandments or not" (Deut 8:2). Hence, by their hunger, as well as by the manna which he provided, they were to "understand that man does not live by bread alone, but . . . by everything that proceeds from the mouth of Yahweh" (8:3). Thus, they were to know in their hearts that Yahweh was disciplining them (8:5). This discipline then might be considered education that is theocentric, indeed, theofugal. That Deut 8:5 uses the comparative expression "as a man disciplines his son" is not without covenantal and theological significance. The ancient treaties often refer to the suzerain king as a father and to the vassal as his son (cf. McCarthy, CBQ 27: 144–47). In Moses' covenant hymn we read that Yahweh is referred to as Father (Deut 32:6; cf. 1:31; Isa 1:2) of the covenant people (although Ex 4:22; Deut 1:31 teach the same concept). Hence, the theological basis for an earthly father's discipline over his son is in the covenant. He bears the image of his covenant Lord, and as such stands in parallel relationship over his children—chastening, correcting, instructing, providing—which are expressions of an interpersonal relationship of love. So also the thirty usages in Prov and elsewhere, e.g. Prov 3:11–12 where *mûsār* and *tōkaḥat* "reproof, correction" are said to come from Yahweh "for whom the Lord loves (*'āhab*) he reproves (*yākaḥ*), even as a father the son in whom he delights." Hence, discipline gives assurance of sonship, for *mûsār* primarily points to a God-centered way of life, and only secondarily to ethical behavior. Proverbs 1:7 couples it with the "fear of Yahweh," and 1:8 with *tôrâ* "instruction, teaching." Hence, also the pricelessness of *mûsār* (8:10) and the reason why fools despise it (15:5, 32). Proverbs and other wisdom literature speak of discipline with emphasis on instruction. It is tempting to see that the seemingly disparate notions of correction and instruction converge beautifully only in the covenant.

How was discipline administered? Proverbs 22:15 speaks of the "rod of correction." But most often, *mûsār* is oral instruction, hence the close association with the *tôrâ*. In Job 5:17 ff., when he urges Job not to "despise the discipline of the Almighty," Eliphaz shows insight concerning the means which God may use to discipline his children: pain and wounds, famine and war. Amos would add drought, mildew, locusts, epidemics, and earthquakes (4:6–11).

The prophets develop the theme of *mûsār* as in Deut 11:2, revealing God's discipline through his mighty acts in the history of the people of Israel and Judah in particular and the nations in general. God deals with his people from the standpoint of warning and correction. The severity of the exile must be thus understood (cf. Hos 5:2; 7:12; Isa 8:11). But all such discipline becomes futile through the resistance and stubbornness of those to whom it is given (cf. Jer 2:30; 5:3; 7:28; 17:23; 32:33). Isaiah 53:5 adds "the chastisement of our peace was upon him" (RSV "the chastisement that made us whole"). This is clearly a context of substitutionary atonement. Here the Servant of the Lord is seen as taking "the severe punishment" vicariously, more clearly revealing God's merciful ways of dealing with his rebellious (*pesha'*) people through redemptive judgment and suffering.

Bibliography: THAT, I, pp. 738–41.

P.R.G.

יָע (*yā'*). See no. 879a.

878 יָעַד (*yā'ad*) ***appoint, betrothe, assemble, meet, set.***

Derivatives

878a †עֵדָה (*'ēdâ*) ***congregation.***
878b †מוֹעֵד (*mô'ēd*) ***appointed place.***
878c מוֹעָד (*mô'ād*) ***place of assembly,*** only in Isa 14:31.
878d מוּעָדָה (*mû'ādâ*). Occurs only in phrase *'ārê hammû'ādâ* "cities appointed" (Josh 20:9).

The basic meaning of this root is "to appoint," in which sense it occurs in the Qumran War Scroll, the Thanksgiving Psalms, and the Messianic Rule. ASV and RSV similar, except ASV uses " espoused" and RSV, "designate" (Ex 21:8) and ASV, "agreed" (Amos 3:3).

The root is used in the Qal for the betrothal of a

woman (Ex 21:8), to designate a time (II Sam 20:5) and place of meeting, and to appoint a rod (RSV "tribe"; Mic 6:9).

The Niphal form is used for God's meeting Israel at the sanctuary (Ex 25:22; 29:43f.; 30:6, 36) and for the assembling of the congregation for worship in the sense of appearing (Num 10:3; I Kgs 8:5; II Chr 5:6) or for other purposes. It is of interest that God's meeting with Israel's representative at the "mercy seat" (*kappōret,* q.v.) is an appointed meeting (Ex 25:22). So also were the other times when God met with the people before the tabernacle. The people were expected to come and God promised to meet them there. God keeps his appointments.

The Niphal form may also be used with the preposition against (*ʿal*) for an assembling against the Lord (Num 14:35; 16:11; 27:3) in rebellion. It is used for kings joining their forces (Josh 11:5).

It may also designate making an appointment (Amos 3:3; Job 2:11; Ps 48:4 [H 5]). The Hiphil signifies to appoint (Jer 49:19) or in some cases to summons (Jer 50:44; Job 9:19).

The Hophal participle, *mûʿādim*, signifies that which is ordered or set (Jer 24:1; Ezk 21:16 [H 21]).

ʿēdâ. ***Assembly, congregation, multitude, people, swarm*** (ASV and RSV similar except ASV tends to render *ʿēdâ* uniformly by "congregation."). *ʿēdâ* occurs frequently, in Qumran materials as a self-designation of the community.

ʿēdâ is a feminine noun from *yāʿad* "to appoint," hence is an assembly by appointment and is rendered in the KJV most frequently as "congregation." First appearing in Ex 12:3, the noun occurs 145 times in the OT and is rendered *synagōgē* 127 times in the LXX. However the noun itself does not imply the purpose of the gathering; hence we have a swarm of bees (Jud 14:8) and a multitude of bulls (Ps 68:30 [H 31]). It may be a gathering of the righteous (Ps 1:5), but there is also the assembly of the wicked (Ps 22:16 [H 17]), violent men (Ps 86:14), and the godless (Job 15:34). The followers of Korah (Num 16:5) and Abiram (Ps 106:17–18) are frequently termed a company. Assembly is sometimes used in the KJV for *ʿēdâ* for variety when it occurs in proximity to some of the other terms rendered congregation (Num 16:2; 20:8; Prov 5:14). *ʿēdâ* designates the assembly of people gathered before the Lord in judgment (Ps 7:7 [H 8]). Similar is the designation of an assembly of the officers of God (Ps 82:1) which is nearly identical with a Ugaritic expression for an assembly of the subordinate gods of the pantheon (Text 128:II, 7, 11).

Despite the fact that we have "congregation and assembly" (*qāhāl wᵉʿēdâ,* Prov 5:14), *qāhāl* and *ʿēdâ* seem to be synonymous for all practical purposes. *ʿēdâ* is also used for groups of animals, but *qāhāl* is not. *ʿēdâ* occurs most frequently in Ex, Lev, and Num, and occurs only three times in the prophets (Jer 6:18; 30:20; Hos 7:12). *qāhāl,* on the other hand, is infrequent in those portions of the Pentateuch, but is frequent in Deut. The book of Chr uses *qāhāl* frequently, but *ʿēdâ* only once (II Chr 5:6= I Kgs 8:5). A man may be excluded from the *ʿēdâ* (Ex 12:19), but the same is true of the *qāhāl* (Num 19:20). Bastards, Ammonites, and Moabites are excluded to the tenth generation; but Edomites and Egyptians are barred only to the third.

Most characteristic of the OT is the use of *ʿēdâ* for the congregation of Israel. "The congregation" (*hāʿēdâ*) occurs seventy-seven times in Ex, Lev, Num, and Josh. We also have "the congregation of the Lord" (Num 27:17; 31:16; Josh 22:16–17); "the congregation of Israel" (Ex 12:3; Josh 22:20); and "all the congregation." There is the "assembly of the congregation of Israel" (*qᵉhal ʿădat yiśrāʾēl,* Ex 12:6) and the "assembly of the congregation of the children of Israel" (*qᵉhal ʿădat bᵉnê yiśrāʾēl,* Num 14:5).

Moses headed the *ʿēdâ* when it was in the wilderness, but there were other designated officials: princes (Ex 16:22; 34:31; Num 4:34, etc.), elders (Lev 4:15; Jud 21:16), heads of the fathers (Num 31:26), and renowned persons (Num 1:16; 26:9). The men of fighting age were "those numbered of the congregation" (Ex 38:25).

The *ʿēdâ* was signalled to assemble when two silver trumpets were blown (Num 10:2). It gathered for war (Jud 20:1), to deal with breach of the covenant with the Lord, for tribal affairs, for worship (I Kgs 8:5; Ps 111:1), and at times of national calamity. It gathered to crown a king (I Kgs 12:20) and for other political affairs. It acted as a unit in sending men to war (Jud 21:10, 13). The term *ʿēdâ* appears last in the historical literature (at I Kgs 12:20) at the division of the kingdom. Its absence in Chronicles and Ezra-Nehemiah would militate against the view that it was coined by the postexilic community.

môʿēd. ***Appointed sign, appointed time, appointed season, place of assembly, set feast.*** (ASV and RSV similar.)

This masculine noun occurs 223 times. It frequently designates a determined time or place without regard to the purpose of the designation. It may be the time for the birth of a child (Gen 17:21; 18:14; 21:2), the coming of a plague (Ex 9:5), the season of a bird's migration (Jer 8:7), an appointed time (I Sam 13:8; 20:35), the time for which a vision is intended (Hab 2:3), the times of the end (Dan 8:19), or the time for the festivals (Lev 23:2) and solemnities (Deut 31:10).

The heavenly bodies are for determining the seasons (Gen 1:14; Ps 104:19). Each festival is a *môʿēd,* but collectively they are the "feasts of the

Lord" (*mô'ădê* YHWH, Lev 23:2, etc.). Appearing at times (Hos 9:5) with *ḥag* (which designates the three great annual festivals), *mô'ēd* must be thought of in a wide usage for all religious assemblies. Jerusalem became the city of assemblies (Isa 33:20; cf. Ezk 36:38) which were characterized by great rejoicing and were deeply missed during times of exile (Zeph 3:18; Lam 1:4).

Once *mô'ēd* is an appointed sign (Jud 20:38) by which men should act.

The Lord met with Moses at the "tent of meeting" (*'ōhel mo'ēd*). He appeared in the cloud at the door of the tent and spoke to him as "a man speaks to his friend" (Ex 33:7, 11; Num 12:8). The purpose of Yahweh's meeting Moses and Israel is revelation (Ex 29:42; 33:11; Num 7:89). The LXX translates *'ōhel mô'ēd* over one hundred times as *skēnē marturiou* (tent of witness) which probably connects (incorrectly) *mô'ēd* with *'ēd* or *'ûd*. But the general idea conveyed of the place of revelation is sound. According to some passages, the tent was outside the camp (Ex 33:7–11; Num 11:24–30), but according to others it was located in the middle of the camp (Ex 25:8). Literary critics have traditionally explained these passages as coming from two sources, E and P, with P not reflecting a historical situation. It is, however, entirely possible that there were two successive tents called *'ōhel mô'ēd*. The first was Moses' tent, which was used before the completion of the tabernacle, which was also called *'ōhel mô'ēd*, as well as *mishkān*.

mô'ēd also designates an "assembly" in such a phrase as "picked men of the assembly" (Num 16:2). This usage has been paralleled by Wilson in the Wen Amun story (JNES 4: 245) for the city council of ZakarBa'al of Gebal. The King of Babylon dreams of a seat in the "mount of assembly" (*har mô'ēd*) in the north (Isa 14:13), a term similar to the Ugaritic expression for the council of the gods (see above). Scholars have seen a parallel between these terms and the words for the court surrounding the Lord or the gathering of the officers of God, which is described as the "assembly of El" (*'ădat 'ēl;* Ps 82:1) in which he stands and and judges.

mô'ēd is also the worshiping assembly of God's people, hence Yahweh's foes roar in the midst of his assemblies (Ps 74:4). It may possibly be an early designation for the synagogue ("appointed places of God *mô'ădê 'ēl;* Ps 74:8). However that this phrase actually refers to early synagogues is disputed.

Bibliography: Haran, Menahem, "The Nature of the *'Ohel Mo*ᶜ*edh* in Pentateuchal Sources," JSS 5: 50–55. Pope, M. H., "Congregation," in IDB, pp. 669–70. Scott, John A., "The Pattern of the Tabernacle," Unpublished Ph.D. Dissertation, University of Pennsylvania, 1965. Weinfeld, Moshe, "Congregation," in *Encyclopedia Judaica,* III, pp. 893–96. THAT, I, pp. 742–45.

J.P.L.

879 יָעָה (*yā'â*) ***sweep together.*** Occurs only in Isa 28:17.

Derivative

879a יָע (*yā'*) ***shovel.***

יָעוֹר (*yā'ôr*). See יָעַר, no. 888a.

880 *יָעַז (*yā'az*). Occurs only as a Niphal participle, in Isa 33:19, *'am nô'āz* "a barbarous (?) people."

881 יָעַט (*yā'aṭ*) ***cover.*** Occurs only in Isa 61:10, *m*ᵉ*'îl ṣ*ᵉ*dāqâ y*ᵉ*'āṭānî* "he has covered me with a robe of righteousness."

882 *יָעַל (*yā'al*) ***I, profit, gain, benefit.*** Hiphil only, used twenty-three times. LXX translates nineteen times with *ōphelō*, etc., meaning "to help, aid, benefit, be of use to."

There is a predominantly negative connotation in the use of *yā'al* as it appears in the OT. It seems not to be used in Ugaritic. Even the NT *ōphelō* has a negative note. Religiously, heathen idols are unprofitable, e.g. in Isaiah's famous satire on the manufacture of idols: "All who make idols are nothing, and the things they delight in can do nothing (lit. "are of no *profit*"). Who fashions a god has cast an image that is profitable for nothing" (Isa 44: 10, as rendered by C. Westermann). In Jer 2:8, 11, Israel is scathingly rebuked for exchanging the Lord for what were not gods, "But my people have changed their glory for that which does not profit." See also Jer 16:19; Hab 2:18; I Sam 12:21.

Politically, the prophets warn against the futility of trusting in foreign alliances, as Isa 30:5 speaking of an alliance with Egypt, "Everyone will be ashamed because of a people who cannot profit them, who are not for help or profit, but for shame and also for reproach."

Wealth carries no weight in terms of eternal destiny. Proverbs 11:4, "Riches do not profit in the day of wrath, but righteousness delivers from death," should be compared with Christ's words, "What shall it profit a man if he should gain the whole world and lose his own soul?" (Mt 16:26).

Even where there is a positive denotation to *yā'al* (only three times) there is a negative connotation as in Job 30:13 (of those who would profit from Job's destruction) and Isa 47:12 (of Babylon who might profit from her sorceries). Isaiah 48:17 is the only positive use, which magnifies the Lord as the one who brings benefits to his people: "I am the Lord your God, who teaches you to profit, who leads you in the way you should go." This clearly reflects the biblical concept of stewardship, that all that one has and possesses belongs to him only because of God's gracious provision (cf. II Cor 8:9; 9:8).

Bibliography: THAT, I, pp. 746–87.

P.R.G.

883 יעל (*y'l*) **II. Assumed root of the following.**
883a יָעֵל (*yā'ēl*) ***mountain goat.***
883b יַעֲלָה (*ya'ălâ*) ***female mountain goat.***

יַעַן (*ya'an*). See no. 1650e.

884 יען (*y'n*). **Assumed root of the following.**
884a יָעֵן (*yā'ēn*) ***ostrich*** (only in Lam 4:3).
884b יַעֲנָה (*ya'ănâ*) only in combination *bat ya'ănâ*. ***Ostrich*** BDB, GB. KJV, NIV ***owl.***

885 יָעֵף (*yā'ēp*) ***I, be weary, faint.***

Derivatives

885a יָעֵף (*yā'ēp*) ***weary, faint.***
885b יְעָף (*y^e'āp*) ***weariness, faintness.***

886 יעף (*y'p*) **II. Assumed root of the following.**
886a תּוֹעָפָה (*tô'āpâ*) ***eminence.***

887 יָעַץ (*yā'aṣ*) ***advise, counsel, purpose, devise, plan.*** (ASV, RSV similar.)

Derivatives

887a †עֵצָה (*'ēṣâ*) ***counsel, purpose.***
887b מוֹעֵצָה (*mô'ēṣâ*) ***counsel, plan.***

This verb is translated in LXX by *bouleuō* or a compound over seventy times, "to give counsel, deliberate, purpose, determine." The first occurrence of *yā'aṣ* is in Ex 18:19. Jethro, seeing the tremendous burden of Moses, says, "I shall give you 'counsel,' and God be with you." He then gives him an organizational plan and advises him how to carry out the administrative responsibilities for ruling and judging his people. Jethro gives counsel from wisdom attained by age and/or experience. One may remember Rehoboam's rejection of the counsel (*'ēṣâ*) of the old men (I Kgs 12:8, 13). Moses, as chief administrator of the people of God, is not obligated to accept such counsel. A case in point is Absolom's rejection of Ahithophel's good counsel which was countered by Hushai's evil counsel (II Sam 17). Jethro, as counsellor, presents a carefully thought out plan together with a procedure for its implementation. In II Kgs 18:20 Rabshakeh's taunt of Hezekiah's claim, "I have counsel and strength for the war" reflects the usual careful deliberation that goes into planning for battle, in this case for defense.

Psalm 33:10 speaks of nations and peoples devising counsels and plans (Heb *maḥăshābâ* "thought, device, plan, purpose") albeit not in accordance with God's "counsels (*'ēṣâ*) and plans" (cf. Isa 8:10; 30:1).

In contrast to the counsels of men and nations, the OT speaks of the "counsel of the Lord." Psalm 33:10f. presents this thought most clearly. "The Lord nullifies the counsel of the nations; he frustrates the plans of the peoples. The 'counsel' of the Lord stands forever, the plans of his heart from generation to generation." Noteworthy here is the overruling power of God as he nullifies and frustrates the plans of men. The case of Ahithophel's counsel is apropos. In II Sam 15:31 David prays to the Lord to "make the counsel of Ahithophel foolishness." He thereby acknowledges that God sovereignly disposes what man proposes. Further, in II Sam 17:14 after Absalom chooses the advice of Hushai over that of Ahithophel, the inspired author makes the theological comment, "For the Lord had ordained to thwart the good counsel of Ahithophel, in order that the Lord might bring calamity on Absalom." Cf. Neh 4:15 [H 9].

The counsel of the Lord is eternal, "It stands forever." The enduring character of God's counsel and plan is grounded in the unchangeableness of God himself. The "plans of his heart" may be equated with "the secret things" which belong to the Lord our God. It is God who guarantees the accomplishment of his eternal decrees. Isaiah beautifully integrates these thoughts, "Remember the former things long past, for I am God, and there is no other; declaring the end from the beginning and from ancient times things which have not been done, saying, 'My purpose will be established, and I will accomplish all my good pleasure'; Calling... the man of my purpose (lit. the man who executes my purpose, i.e. Cyrus) from a far country. Truly I have spoken; truly, I will bring it to pass. I have planned it, surely I will do it" (46:9–11). It is well to remember that *'ēṣâ* is translated in the LXX by *boulē*, a word replete with theological significance in the NT (see Acts 2:23; 4:28; 5:38–39; 20:27; Eph 1:11 where "the counsel of his will" expresses the immutable foreordination of God's will); cf. Heb 6:17, "the unchangeableness of his purpose").

Arising from the theological conceptualization are anthropological and ethical conclusions. Moses anticipates the waywardness of Israel as a "nation void of counsel," i.e. not following the plans and purposes of God (Deut 32:28). Job acknowledges that through lack of knowledge, he has darkened counsel (42:3; cf. 38:2). In Prov, counsel is rejected and spurned to one's own detriment (1:25, 30) but "he who listens to counsel" is a wise man (12:15). From Prov 19:20–21 we understand that the counsel the godly man is urged to listen to is the "counsel of the Lord" which will stand, in contrast to the many "plans in a man's heart." The blessed man of Ps 1:1 is one "who walks not in the counsel of the ungodly." Further, in Ps 32:8 the psalmist is encouraged by the Lord's instruction and teaching, together with the assurance "I 'will counsel' (*yā'aṣ*) you with my eye upon you" (cf. 73:24).

Two christological passages need to be studied in this connection. The only hope of Judah, Isaiah claims, is to be found in the person of the Messiah, who is characterized by four compound names, the first being "Wonderful Counsellor" (9:6). The child who is to come, on whose shoulders the government of the world shall rest, is one whose plans, purposes, designs and decrees for his people are marvellous. We further learn from 11:2 that "counsel" is a gift of God's own Holy Spirit. Consequently, Jesus Christ is revealed as the counsellor *par excellance*.

Bibliography: THAT, I, pp. 748–52.

P.R.G.

888 יער (*y'r*) **I. Assumed root of the following.**

888a †יַעַר (*ya'ar*) ***I, forest, woods, thicket.*** LXX translates *drumos*. The Ugaritic cognate *y'r* is quite common, used as a personal name, place name, and as gentilic. ASV and RSV use similar words.

Specific forests are identified in the OT, e.g. the forest of Lebanon (I Kgs 7:2), Ephraim (II Sam 18:6), Hareth (I Sam 22:5), the Negev (Ezk 20:47 [H 21:3]), Carmel (though this may be better translated "its choice cypresses," II Kgs 19:23; Isa 37:24 as in RSV and NASB). Joshua designates the forested area in the hill country of Ephraim as the possession of the sons of Joseph, encouraging them by saying, "If you are a numerous people, go up to the forest and clear a place for yourself" (Josh 17:15; cf. v. 18).

The forests apparently were dense enough in OT days that wild animals roamed at will, e.g. bears (II Kgs 2:24), a roaring lion (Amos 3:4; Mic 5:8 [H 7]; Jer 5:6; 12:8), boars (Ps 80:13 [H 14]), and beasts generally (Isa 56:9; Ezk 34:25).

Psalm 29:9 ascribes glory to God by claiming that "the voice of the Lord makes the deer to calve (or "twists the oaks" NIV) and strips the forests bare." Other metaphors or similes appear referring to the Lord's judgments, as for example, judgment on Assyria in Isa 10:18, "And he will destroy the glory of his forest and of his fruitful garden." Cf. Ps 83:14 [H 15]; Jer 21:14. Sometimes, the figure of judgment is turned around so that rather than being cut down, it is pictured as allowed to grow into a wilderness forest, as in Mic 3:12, "Zion will be plowed as a field, Jerusalem will become a heap of ruins, and the mountain of the temple will become high places of a forest," i.e. thick and overgrown.

The symbolism of a forest is not altogether negative, however. The Lord's mighty act of salvation and forgiveness calls for shouts of joy, as in Isa 44:23, "Break forth into a shout of joy, you mountains, O forest, and every tree in it, for the Lord has redeemed Jacob." In a slightly different context, the maiden in the canticle speaks of her lover "like an apple tree among the trees of the forest, so is my beloved among the young men. In his shade I took delight and sat down and his fruit was sweet to my taste" (Song 2:3).

P.R.G.

889 יער (*y'r*) **II. Assumed root of the following.**

889a יַעַר (*ya'ar*) ***II, honeycomb.***

889b יַעְרָה (*ya'râ*) ***honeycomb.***

890 יָפָה (*yāpâ*) ***be fair, beautiful, handsome.***

Derivatives

890a †יָפֶה (*yāpeh*) ***fair, beautiful.***

890b יְפֵה־פִיָּה (*ye pēh-pîyâ*) ***very beautiful,*** reduplication giving the force of diminutive, "pretty."

890c יְפִי (*ye pî*) ***beauty.***

yāpâ appears only eight times, including Ps 45:2 [H 3] *yopyāpîtâ* which many try to emend. But Dahood suggests it may be a genuine dialectical form as in Ugaritic *d' d'* "well known" from *yd'*, and *ysmsmt* "beauty" (in AB, *Psalms,* I, p. 271). The consonants may be taken as simply a reduplication of the adj *ye pî* which is then made into a stative verb. KJV, ASV, RSV consistently use "be fair" and "be beautiful" even of men, as in II Sam 14:25.

yāpeh. ***Fair, beautiful, excellent.*** Translated in LXX by *kalos* "beautiful, useful, good." Ugaritic has a word *yp (?)* probably a cognate (UT 19: no. 412).

Esthetically, *yāpeh* denotes "beauty as to outward appearance," e.g. Gen 12:14 regarding Sarah, "When Abraham came to Egypt, the Egyptians saw that the woman was very 'beautiful'." In the case of Rachel (29:17), "She was beautiful and lovely" (Heb *ye pat tō'ar wîpat mar'eh,* literally "beautiful in form and beautiful to look upon"). Cf. Song 7:6 [H 7]; II Sam 13:1 of Tamar; I Kgs 1:3, 4 of Abishag the Shunammite. Elsewhere these words describe young men, e.g. Gen 39:6, "Now Joseph was handsome and good looking" (RSV). Cf. II Sam 14:25 of Absalom; I Sam 17:42 of David; Song 1:16. Under the figure of a woman, Jerusalem is called "beautiful in elevation" (Ps 48:2 [H 3]). Cf. also Ezk 16:13, 14, 15, 25. Tyre (Ezk 27:3) and Egypt are also called beautiful, the latter as a metaphor with the reduplicated diminutive in Jer 46:20, "Egypt is a pretty heifer." However, it is used literally of cows in Gen 41:2, 4, 18 where "beautiful and fat" cows are contrasted with "ugly and gaunt" ones in Pharaoh's dream, Other objects of beauty mentioned in Scripture are olive trees and cedars (Jer 11:16; Ezk 31:3), feet (Song 7:2); eyes (I Sam 16:12). In Ezk 33:32, the prophet's ministry is described as being "like a sensual song by one who has a beautiful voice and plays well on an instrument." Ecclesiastes 3:11 describes everything in general as God's creation "beautiful in its time."

Several times these words are used in Ezk 28 to describe the king of Tyre and the wisdom for which Tyre was known. Her enemies will "draw their swords against the beauty of your wisdom and defile your splendor" (v. 7). The king himself is described as "full of wisdom and perfect in beauty" (v. 12). But this proved his downfall, as v. 17 declares that "your heart was lifted up because of your beauty; you corrupted wisdom by reason of your splendor." If the king of Tyre stands for Lucifer, one can appreciate the potential for the seduction of God's people. Jeremiah speaks of craftsmen beautifying their wooden idols, "They decorate it with silver and gold" (10:4).

There are two messianic passages which use our words. In Ps 45:2 [H 3], in a song celebrating the marriage of the king, the songwriter says, "You are fairer than the sons of men; grace is poured upon your lips; therefore God has blessed you forever." Prophesying the future hope of Israel as being in the person of Messiah, Isaiah says, "Your eyes will see the king in his beauty, they will behold a far distant land" (Isa 33:17). The LXX translates *doxa* (rather than *kalos*), thinking of his heavenly glory. But this translation for *ye pî* is unusual.

If these are messianic references, then what is the meaning of Isa 53:2, "He has no stately form or majesty that we should look upon him, nor appearance that we should be attracted to him"? There is no mention of "beauty" in Isa 53. Further, the servant is depicted as suffering, especially in the crucifixion scene. In view of 52:14, "His appearance was marred more than any man," coupled with the NT description of the brutal beatings (e.g. the crown of thorns pressed on his brow), we conclude that Christ in his suffering would not manifest the beauty described elsewhere. Some theologians have opposed the idea of an ugly Christ based on the Hellenistic notion that beauty is intrinsic to deity. If the church's interpretation of the Song of Solomon as being messianic is valid, then the many uses of *yāpeh*, etc. for the beloved, would tend to support our view of a handsome Christ. That beauty may be defined in the spiritual sense of inward beauty should not detract from the outward physical appearance of our Lord.

One final reference should be noted. Zechariah 9:16f. speaks of the ransomed people of God, "And the Lord their God will save them in that day as the flock of his people; for they are as stones of a crown, sparkling in his land. For what comeliness and beauty will be theirs!" May God's people even now reflect the beauty of the Lord our God (cf. Ps 90:17).

P.R.G.

יְפֵה-פִיָּה (*ye pēh-piyyâ*). See no. 890b.

891 *יָפַח (*yāpaḥ*) ***breathe, puff.*** This by-form of *pûaḥ* occurs only in the Hithpael stem, in Jer 4:31, *tityappēaḥ* "she gasps for breath."

Derivative

891a יָפֵחַ (*yāpēaḥ*) ***breathing or puffing out.*** Occurs only in Ps 27:12, *wîpēaḥ ḥāmās* "puffing out violence."

יְפִי (*ye pî*). See no. 890c.

892 *יָפַע (*yāpa'*) ***shine forth, cause to shine.*** Used eight times in the Hiphil only. ASV and RSV similar except in Job 10:3 where "favor" is used.

Derivatives

892a יִפְעָה (*yip'â*) ***brightness, splendor.*** In Ezk 28:7, 17 of the king of Tyre.

yāpa' is used of the Lord shining forth from Mount Paran (Deut 33:2), Zion (Ps 50:1), among the cherubim (Ps 80:1 [H 2]). Undoubtedly these are references to the majestic splendor of his holiness, as revealed by the theophanic brilliance of the Shekinah glory. But further the Lord's shining forth is made explicit by Jesus' claim to be the light of the world. In Job 37:15 the reference may be to literal light, possibly lightning, which God has created.

Job's plaint in 10:3 alludes to God's light shining with favor on the wicked, whereas he himself feels keenly the darkness of his plight. Similarly, his cursing the day of his birth is expressed by a desire that no "light shine on it," i.e. that it may not be looked upon with favor, joy, or celebration. Much later, the derivative *yip'â* "splendor" is used to describe the lofty and exalted position of the king of Tyre, from which he will have fallen because of pride.

It is interesting to note that Ugaritic *yp'* is the

semantic cognate, appearing both in texts as well as in many personal names (cf. *yp'b'l* "may Baal shine forth."). But the root in Ug does not clearly refer to a theophany in the OT sense. Aistleitner (AisWUS No. 1215) translates it "be sublime" (*hehr sein*).

Bibliography: THAT, I, ppl 753–54.

P.R.G.

893 יָצָא (*yāṣā'*) ***go out, come out, go forth.***

Derivatives

893a יָצִיא (*yāṣî'*) ***coming forth,*** only in II Chr 32:21.

893b †צֶאֱצָא (*ṣe'ĕṣā'*) ***offspring, produce.***

893c †מוֹצָא (*môṣā'*) ***act or place of going out.***

893d †מוֹצָאָה (*môṣā'â*) ***origin*** (Mic 5:1), places of going out to, i.e. privy (II Kgs 10:27). Occurs only in the plural.

893e †תּוֹצָאָה (*tôṣā'â*) ***outgoing, border.***

yāṣā' appears over a thousand times in Qal and Hiphil, but only five times in the Hophal. The Hiphil has the usual causative meaning "cause to go out, bring out, lead out." ASV and RSV similar.

The basic notion of *yāṣa'* is "to go out." It is used literally of going out from a particular locality or from the presence of a person. It is used of nature, i.e. water out of a rock, sun rising out of the east, etc. For our purposes we shall note the following uses. First, it is used frequently of the great exodus event which forms the major focus of theological attention in the OT. The Hiphil with its causative function is used extensively. Moses is the human element in bringing the people of God out of Egypt (e.g. Ex 3:10ff.; 14:11). Aaron is mentioned with Moses in Ex 6:13, 26f. But far greater emphasis is given to Yahweh, the Lord God who is involved in this great act of redemption from Egypt. Moses himself puts the emphasis on God's work in Ex 13:3 as he addresses the people of God on that memorable day, "Remember this day in which you went out from Egypt, from the house of slavery; for by a powerful hand the Lord brought you out from this place." The historical event was recorded in 12:50f. Moses reiterates four times the mighty power of God in the exodus redemption so as to underline the revelation which this great miracle proclaimed. (Cf. 13:3,9,14,16.) Both the consecration of the firstborn and the passover feast will serve as constant reminders. Further, in the inscripturation of the Sinaitic covenant, all that need be said by way of a historical prologue to identify the benevolent activity of the great King is to refer to this saving action: "I am the Lord your God, who brought you out of the land of Egypt, out of the house of slavery" (Ex 20:2). The record shows that history is theologically related, the great "going out" event was to symbolize the mighty redemption of God's people from the shackles of sin by his sovereign powerful grace. In Deut 4:37 a reason is given: "Because he loved your fathers, therefore he chose their descendants. . . . And he personally brought you from Egypt" (cf. Eph 1:4). Throughout Israel's history, the covenanted people of God are called to remember this God-initiated redemption and to live accordingly. (Cf. Deut 6:12; 26:8; Jud 2:12; I Sam 12:8; I Kgs 8:16; Jer 11:4; Dan 9:15 and numerous references in the psalter, particularly Ps 136:11, but note also 106:6–12.)

A second usage arises from the exodus motif. In a technical sense *yāṣa'* is used for the emancipation of a Hebrew slave, probably an indentured servant. Exodus 21:2 puts the maximum limit of service at six years, "But on the seventh he shall go out as a free man without payment." U. Cassuto points out that these laws aim to protect certain rights of the Hebrew slave, and in effect say to the Israelite, "You have been Hebrew slaves in Egypt, and, therefore, you must act with love and compassion towards the people who are Hebrew slaves, even as you were, irrespective of their racial origin." It seems significant that this section reads so much like the preamble to the Decalogue, reminding the people of God that as you went forth from Egyptian bondage, even so shall your identured servant go out free.

Somewhat related is a technical usage meaning "revert." Leviticus 25:8–55 records the regulations for the year of Jubilee. Property or dwellings which had been sold on account of poverty, no near of kin being able to redeem it, "at the jubilee [it] shall revert (lit. "go out"), that he may return to his property" (25:28, 30, 31, 33). It may well be that Isaiah had the above two ideas in mind when he uttered the evangelical message "to proclaim liberty to captives, and freedom to prisoners; to proclaim the favorable year of the Lord" (61:2–3).

Another theological usage of *yāṣa'* is an extension of the exodus theme. The prophets see the irremediable corruption of Israel and Judah which inevitably leads to exile but after that a return. Ezekiel, himself an innocent victim of such judgment, quotes the Lord's promise of a new exodus-like redemptive activity from the exile. "As a soothing aroma I shall accept you, when I bring you out from the peoples and gather you from the lands where you are scattered" (20:41; cf. v. 34). Its true fulfillment may only come after the good shepherd "will bring them out from the peoples and gather them from the countries and bring them to their own land" (34:13). Hence, an eschatological note of hope is introduced.

Sometimes *yāṣa'* is used with a special emphasis on source or origin, particularly when that source is the Lord himself, as of fire (Lev 9:24), providential guidance (Gen 24:50), or salvation (Isa 51:5). It is used of words going forth from the mouth of a speaker, as in Job 8:10; Prov 10:18; Neh 6:19. In Deut 8:3 Moses utters one of the cardinal principles of the spiritual life, "That he might make you understand that man does not live by bread alone, but man lives by everything that proceeds out (*môṣā'*) of the mouth of the Lord." (Cf. Christ's use of this in Mt 4:4.) Although both Ezekiel and Daniel use this expression once, only Isaiah emphasizes the notion of the word of God going out with effectual force. Following a universal invitation to be saved, the Lord guarantees its effectualness by an oath, "I have sworn by myself, the word has gone forth from my mouth in righteousness and will not turn back, that to me every knee will bow, every tongue will swear allegiance" (45:23). Similarly, on a context of Gospel invitation to seek the Lord and call upon him, Isaiah uses the analogy of life-producing rain coming down from heaven to illustrate the effectual working of his Word, "So shall my word be which goes forth from my mouth; it shall not return to me empty, without accomplishing what I desire, and without succeeding in the matter for which I sent it" (Isa 55:11). It is tempting to consider that these passages might have been the genesis of John's theology of Jesus as the Word of God. Consider the relation that Ps 33:6 might have to Jn 1:3. One should note also the christological interpretation of 45:23 as given by Paul in Phil 2:10f. If this is true, one wonders if Isaiah did not have in mind a person when he spoke of the "Word" going forth (cf. Jn 16:28), and not returning empty, but "succeeding in the matter for which I sent him" (cf. Jn 17:4).

ṣe'ĕṣā'. ***Offspring of men, produce of the earth.*** Used eleven times (all plural) in Isaiah and Job.

môṣā'. ***Act or place of going out; hence, issue, source,*** such as a spring of water or mine (for silver). Used twenty-seven times.

môṣā'â. Place from which one comes or to which one goes. Used only twice in very different connections. In II Kgs 10:27 it means "latrine." The meaning in Mic 5:2 [H 1] the plural is debated. The translation "origin" (RSV) is unsuitable for the messianic reference. The meaning of the KJV "going forth" is obscure. The NIV "whose origins are from of old, from ancient times" agrees with the idea that the ancestry of the expected ruler traces back to David's time as well as David's city. The NEB "roots" is similar.

tôṣā'â. ***Outgoings, borders.*** Used twenty-three times (all plural), mainly in geographical contexts.

Bibliography: THAT, I, pp. 755–60.

P.R.G.

894 יָצַב (*yāṣab*) ***stand, set or station oneself, present oneself*** (only in the Hithpael). The LXX uses *paristēmi, histēmi, anthistēmi* plus other compounds of *histēmi*. The more common Hebrew words are *'āmad* and *nāṣab* which KB calls a byform of *yāṣab*. It appears forty-five times in MT. ASV and RSV are similar.

The word appears in Ugaritic only as the name of the son of Keret.

The simple usage is found in Ex 2:4 where Miriam, Moses' sister, "stood at a distance to find out what would happen to him." Habakkuk also uses the word similarly, "I will stand on my guard post . . . and I will keep watch to see what he will speak to me" (2:1). Cf. II Sam 18:13 where it is translated "stood aloof." However, there is more to the idea than simply standing.

It is used of those who set themselves against others. Specifically, in the well-known messianic psalm, "the kings of the earth take their stand . . . against the Lord and against his anointed" (Ps 2:2). Hence, it means "to oppose" or possibly "to oppress" as the parallel phrase might also indicate. In a twist to the metaphor, Num 22:22 expresses God's anger against Balaam so that "the angel of the Lord took his stand in the way as an adversary against him." In a military sense, it is used in I Sam 17:16 where Goliath stood in defiance of the Lord and the army of Israel. Cf. Jer 46:4. However, several times we find the promise of God that the enemy will not be able to stand before the godly, i.e. to oppose him. The most familiar passage is Josh 1:5, "No man will be able to stand before you all the days of your life" (cf. Deut 7:24; 11:25). Sometimes the people of God are told to take their stand, passively and quietly awaiting the mighty deliverance of the Lord as in Ex 14:13f., "Do not fear! Stand by and see the salvation of the Lord which He will accomplish for youtoday . . . the Lord will fight for you while you keep silent" (cf. I Sam 12:7, 16 and II Chr 20:17).

Furthermore, God calls on the righteous believers to take their stand against evil: "Who will stand up (Heb *qûm*) for me against evildoers? Who will take his stand (*yāṣab*) for me against those who do wickedness?" (Ps 94:16; cf. II Chr 11:13 where the priests and Levites of the northern ten tribes stood firm with Rehoboam when Jeroboam divided the kingdom).

In another usage *yāṣab lipnê* means "to present oneself before." Moses is commanded, "Present yourself before Pharoah" (lit. "station yourself") in Ex 8:20 [H 16]; 9:13. Deuteronomy 31:14 is instructive because God tells Moses and Joshua to "present themselves" at the tent of meeting, that he might commission him" i.e. install him for service. Similarly, in Josh 24:1 the elders of Israel, heads, judges, and officers are to present themselves before God as they anticipate taking the oath of leadership. Cf. I Sam 10:19; Jud 20:2. This note of service is more clearly revealed in Zech 6:5, "These are the four spirits of heaven, going forth after standing before the Lord of all the earth." They are depicted as emissaries of God, accomplishing his work. This illuminates Job 1:6; 2:1 where "the sons of God came to present themselves before the Lord, and Satan also." Satan's malevolent "roaming about on the earth" need not detract from the high service which the sons of God rendered. Furthermore, we need not denigrate the service performed as being servile, but rather an honorable task. It is this idea which indubitably is behind the proverb, "Do you see a man skilled in his work? He will stand before kings; he will not stand before obscure men" (Prov 22:29). One who thus stands before kings implicitly makes himself available and ready for service. Cf. Milton's memorable words in his sonnet on his blindness, "They also serve who only stand and wait."

One further idea may be considered. If they who stand before kings are servants and couriers ready to serve, how much more should those who present themselves to the great king, the Lord of lords, be submissive to his will and command. This seems to be the thought in Ex 19:17 where "Moses brought the people out of the camp to meet God, and they stood at the foot of the mountain." The people gave a response of reverent obedience, "All the words which the Lord has spoken we will do, and we will be obedient" (24:3, 7).

P.R.G.

895 יָצַג (*yāṣag*) ***set, place, establish.***

Used sixteen times, in the Hiphil and Hophal only. It is a synonym of *śûm,* its primary meaning being to set or place. The notion of placing someone or something in such a position as to be exhibited to all may be seen in Job 17:6, "But he has made me a byword of the people, and I am one at whom men spit." Hosea 2:3 [H 5] likewise, "Lest I strip her naked and expose her as on the day when she was born" (NASB).

P.R.G.

יִצְהָר (*yiṣhār*). See no. 1883c.
יָצוּעַ (*yāṣûa'*). See no. 896a.
יִצְחָק (*yiṣḥāq*). See no. 1905b.
יָצִיא (*yāṣî'*). See no. 893a.
יָצִיעַ (*yāṣîa'*). See no. 896b.

896 *יָצַע (*yāṣa'*) ***lay, spread.*** Occurs only in the Hiphil and Hophal.

Derivatives

896a יָצוּעַ (*yāṣûa'*) ***couch, bed.***
896b יָצִיעַ (*yāṣîa'*) ***flat surface.***
896c מַצָּע (*maṣṣā'*) ***couch, bed.*** Occurs only in Isa 28:20.

897 יָצַק (*yāṣaq*) ***pour, pour out, cast*** (metal). (ASV, RSV similar.)

Derivatives

897a יְצֻקָה (*y^eṣūqâ*) ***a casting*** (of metal), only in I Kgs 7:24.
897b מוּצָק (*mûṣāq*) ***a casting,*** only in I Kgs 7:37; Job 38:38.
897c מוּצֶקֶת (*mûṣeqet*) ***pipe*** (Zech 4:2); a casting (II Chr 4:3).

yāṣaq is used about fifty times, about one fourth of them used of casting or pouring molten metal. ASV and RSV similar. The Ugaritic *yṣq* has the same range of meaning.

The basic meaning is to pour out a liquid, e.g. Elisha poured water on the hands of Elijah (II. Kgs 3:11), pouring oil, e.g. the widow filling containers with oil (II Kgs 4:4–5), or pouring soup or food from a pot (II Kgs 4:40–41).

Ceremonially, it is used of pouring oil in anointing, e.g. on the head of the priest (Ex 29:7, Lev 21:10) or the head of a king (II Kgs 9:3, 6; I Sam 10:1). The principle of inauguration or ordination to office is clearly involved. But perhaps another more subtle principle is implied, that of representation and solidarity. When Ps 133:2 speaks of the oil that ran down Aaron's head to the beard and onto the collars of the priests' robes, God's blessing on the people as well as on the priest was thereby symbolized. Hence, the significance of the "oil of gladness." The meal offering in Lev 2:1, 6 was to have oil poured upon it and mixed with frankincense as a sweet smelling offering symbolic of one's complete consecration to the Lord, to be pleasing before him. Further, in the sacrificial system, blood was poured out at the base of the altar, making atonement for Aaron and his sons (Lev 8:15).

Eschatologically, the Lord promises through Isaiah (44:3) to "pour out water on the thirsty land" (or "on him who is thirsty") and in the parallelism he alludes to Joel's prophecy (2:28), "I will pour out My Spirit on your offspring, and my blessing on your descendants." The implications for the doctrine of the Trinity in the OT are inescapable, but neither should one lose sight of the greater blessings to be realized following the fulfillment in Acts 2. The Holy Spirit is not to be conceived as a liquid poured out, but rather manifesting his activities among the people of God in "these latter days."

Interestingly, the word is never used for casting idol images. It is used frequently for casting the golden temple furniture and for the great bronze casting which Solomon accomplished in the Jordan valley—no small feat of engineering for his day (I Kgs 7:46).

P.R.G.

898 יָצַר (*yāṣar*) ***fashion, form, frame.*** (RSV and ASV generally similar except that RSV translates "planned" in II Kgs 19:25; Isa 37:26, and ASV has "ordained" in Ps 139:16.)

Derivatives

898a †יֵצֶר (*yēṣer*) ***form.***
898b יְצֻרִים (*y^eṣūrîm*) ***forms, members,*** only in Job 17:7, referring to parts of the body as having been fashioned.

The basic meaning of this root is "to form," "to fashion." While the word occurs in synonymous parallelism with *bārāʾ* "create" and *ʿaśâ* "make" in a number of passages, its primary emphasis is on the shaping or forming of the object involved.

As with many Hebrew words of theological significance, the root *yāṣar* may be used of human as well as divine agency. When used in its secular sense it occurs most frequently in the participial form meaning "potter," i.e. one who fashions (clay). The word is used in this form frequently in the prophets where "the potter" provides an apt vehicle for the communication of the prophetic message (Isa 29:16; Jer 18:2, 4, 6; Zech 11:13).

The concept of "fashioning" is particularly clear in Isa 44:9–10, 12 where an idol is pictured as being shaped (*yāṣar*) by hammers (v. 12). See also Hab 2:18. The same concept is evident in the use of the word in Ps 94:20 where wicked rulers use the law to devise or frame means of wrongdoing.

When used of divine agency, the root refers most frequently to God's creative activity. It describes the function of the divine Potter forming man and beasts from the dust of the earth (Gen 2:7–8, 19). It occurs in association with *bārāʾ* "create" and *ʿāśâ* "make" in passages that refer to the creation of the universe (Isa 45:18), the earth itself (Jer 33:2), and the natural phenomena (Amos 4:13; Ps 95:5). See also Ps 33:15; 74:17; 94:9; Jer 10:16; 51:19; Zech 12:1).

The word also occurs in the sense of God's framing or devising something in his mind. It is used of his preordained purposes (II Kgs 19:25; Isa 37:26; 46:11; Ps 139:16) as well as his current plans (Jer 18:11).

The root is used of God's forming the nation of Israel in the sense of bringing it into existence. It is used in this way only by Isaiah and always connotes God's activity in this regard (Isa 43:1, 7, 21; 44:2, 21, 24).

The participial form meaning "potter" is applied to God in Isa 64:7 where mankind is the work of his hand.

When applied to the objects of God's creative work, the emphasis of the word is on the forming or structuring of these phenomena. The word speaks to the mode of creation of these phenomena only insofar as the act of shaping or forming an object may also imply the initiation of that object. In this way the root *yāṣar* is an appropriate surrogate for *bārāʾ* but not an exact synonym.

yēṣer. *Form.* The noun *yēṣer,* which connotes the concept of "form," may refer either to the shape of an object or the object itself, i.e. that which has been formed. It refers to the external shape of an idol in Hab 2:18, but to pottery itself in Isa 29:16. Its most frequent usage in the latter sense refers to that which is formed in the mind, e.g. plans and purposes (Gen 6:5; 8:21; Deut 31:21) or even the state of mind (Isa 26:3).

Bibliography: TDNT, II, pp. 1005–28. THAT, I, pp. 761–64.

T.E.M.

יָצַר (*yāṣar*). See no. 1970, *ṣārar* I.

899 יָצַת (*yāṣat*) ***burn, kindle, set on fire.***

The most common word for burning is *bāʿar.* *yāṣat* is used largely by the prophets to depict the coming desolation. The word is always used to express destruction by fire. For ordinary burning as of wood on the altar *bāʿar* or *yāqad* would be used, although these words too are often destructive.

yāṣat is used in Josh 8:8, 19 where the city of Ai was destroyed by fire. This was done by express command from the Lord. Cf. Jud 9:49 where the tower of Shechem was set on fire. It is used of setting fields on fire (II Sam 14:30f.), forests (Jer 21:14), gates (Neh 1:3; 2:17), thorns (Isa 33:12), houses (Jer 51:30). Jeremiah uses this word 15 times, mostly to predict the fiery destruction of Jerusalem and Judah. But such destruction is not to come upon Jadah exclusively, but on foreign nations as well, e.g. Egypt (46:19), Ammon (49:2), Damascus (49:27), Babylon (50:32; 51:30). Jeremiah laments (Lam 4:11) most bitterly that Zion has been thoroughly destroyed by fire, "The Lord has accomplished his wrath, he has poured out his fierce anger; and he has kindled a fire in Zion which has consumed its foundations."

Jeremiah's use of *yāṣat* may have been impressed on him by the discovery of the scroll of the law during Josiah's reign. Josiah expressed his concern for what was read to him, by commanding Hilkiah the priest and others, "Go, inquire of the Lord for me . . . for great is the wrath of the Lord that burns against us, because our fathers have not listened to the words of this book, to do according to all that is written concerning us" (II Kgs 22:13).

For the metaphoric use of the burning anger of the Lord, see the article on *yāqad*.

P.R.G.

900 יקב (*yqb*). **Assumed root of the following.**
900a יֶקֶב (*yeqeb*) ***wine vat.***

901 יָקַד (*yāqad*) ***burn, kindle.*** (ASV, RSV similar.)

Derivatives

901a יְקוֹד (*y^eqôd*) ***a burning*** only in Isa 10:16.
901b מוֹקֵד (*môqēd*) ***burning, hearth,*** used only twice (Ps 102:4; Isa 33:14).
901c מוֹקְדָה (*môq^edâ*) ***hearth,*** used only once (Lev 6:2).

The more common words for burning are *bā'ar* and *yāṣat* for the literal expression, *qāṭar* "burn incense," *ḥārâ* for the figurative of "anger burning," plus several others of less significance.

yāqad and its derivatives are mostly used in connection with the brazen altar. It is used several times in Lev 6 where instructions are given for the burnt offerings, e.g. "the burnt offering itself shall remain on the hearth (*môq^edâ*) on the altar all night until the morning, and the fire on the altar is to be kept burning (*yāqad*, Hophal) on it" (Lev 6:9 [H 2]; cf. 6:12 [H 5]; 6:13 [H 6]).

By and large these words are used metaphorically for the wrath of God in judgment. Although *ḥārâ* is more commonly used, nevertheless *yāqad* is used in this sense, as in Deut 32:22, "For a fire is kindled (*qādaḥ*) in my anger, and burns (*yāqad*) to the lowest part of Sheol, and consumes the earth with its yield, and sets on fire (*lāhaṭ*) the foundations of the mountains." Isa 10:16 picks up this figure of fiery judgment. Jeremiah uses the same metaphor in 15:14, and in 17:4 accuses Judah of kindling the fire of God's anger. In a slight twist to the metaphor, Isaiah reveals God's frustration with the recalcitrant people of Judah, declaring of them, "These are smoke in my nostrils, a fire that burns all the day" (Isa 65:5).

The Aramaic cognate *y^eqad* is used eight times in Dan 3 as a participle "burning" modifying the fiery furnace. Also, in an eschatological passage, the fourth beast of Dan 7 is slain "and its body was destroyed and given to the burning fire" (v. 11) which anticipates "the lake of fire and brimstone" into which the devil, the beast, and the false prophet are thrown (Rev 20:10).

P.R.G.

902 יקה (*yqh*). **Assumed root of the following.**
902a †יְקָהָה (*yiqhâ*) ***obedience.*** (ASV and RSV similar.)

It is used only twice, in Gen 49:10 and Prov 30:17. It is presumably from *yāqah* (not used in Hebrew). The Gen passage is the familiar Shiloh prophecy concluding "and to him shall be the obedience of the peoples." However, LXX renders our word by *prosdokía* "expectation" (as if from *qāwâ*) expressing the hope of the peoples awaiting Shiloh's coming. Proverbs 30:17 "despiseth to obey a mother" is rendered "scorns a mother's old age" in NEB following LXX *gēras* "old age." The parallel with "mocking a father," the Arabic cognate *waqhat* "obedience" and the usage in Gen 49:10 would seem to suggest that obedience to both father and mother is in view. Such scorn by the eye (of a son) would be severely judged.

P.R.G.

יְקוֹד (*y^eqôd*). See no. 901a.
יְקוּם (*y^eqûm*). See no. 1999f.
יָקוֹשׁ (*yāqôsh*). See no. 906a.
יָקוּשׁ (*yāqûsh*). See no. 906b.
יַקִּיר (*yaqqîr*). See no. 905c.

903 יָקַע (*yāqa'*) ***be alienated, dislocate (Qal); hang (Hiphil).*** (ASV and RSV essentially the same.)

Of the eight usages of this word, half are causative. Genesis 32:25 [H 26], "So the socket of Jacob's thigh was dislocated while he wrestled," clearly establishes the basis for the metaphoric sense meaning "be alienated, separated." The Hiphil clearly brings out the causative, although it serves euphemistically for the idea of execution by hanging or, more likely at that time by impaling (as in Num 25:4 as NASB translates "and *execute* them in broad daylight . . . so that the fierce anger of the Lord may turn away from Israel"). Normally in ancient Israel execution was carried out by stoning (*sāqal* or *rāgam,* q.v.). For the curse associated with hanging, see Deut 21:23, see the synonym *tālâ* "hang." The several references to hanging bodies may refer not to death by hanging, but to the exhibition of the corpses of those killed some other way (cf. II Sam 21:12; Josh 10:26).

P.R.G.

904 יָקַץ (*yāqaṣ*) ***awake.*** (RSV, ASV similar.)

Derivative (?)

904a *†קִיץ (*qîṣ*) ***awake.*** Hiphil only.

It is difficult to determine the precise relation of *yāqaṣ* and *qîṣ*. BDB treats them in separate articles. It may be they go back to a common Semitic biradical root. KB takes *yāqaṣ* as a by-form of *qîṣ*. A Ugaritic tablet tells of El inviting gods to a banquet as *ṣḥ l qṣ* "he shouts to wake (them) up" (UT 19: no. 474).

Most of the uses are of a narrative nature relating the fact that a person "awoke" from his sleep, e.g. Noah (Gen 9:24), Jacob (Gen 28:16), Pharaoh (Gen 41:4), Samson (Jud 16:14), Solomon (I Kgs 3:15), etc.

Several times in the Psalms, it is associated with one's awaking and finding God's sustaining presence. Ps 139:18 exalts the omnipresence of God; "When I awake, I am still with thee" (Ps 17:15). In a slight metaphorical change, Prov . .:22 speaks of the law as guiding one and "when you sleep, they will watch over you and when you awake, they will talk to you." The thought is clear: God reveals himself through the inscripturated revelation, not through mystical experience. Ancient mythology expresses the limitation of the gods as needing to sleep, hence, having to shout to awaken them. (Cf. the Ugaritic example noted above and I Kgs 18:27). An allusion to this is made in several Psalms with reference to the Lord, e.g. Ps 78:65, "Then the Lord awoke as if from sleep, like a warrior overcome by wine." From the human viewpoint, one may so speak of the Lord who keeps silent when sin and rebellion goes on without repentance. However, our theology is rather built on Ps 121:3–4, "He who keeps you will not slumber. Behold he who keeps Israel will neither slumber nor sleep."

Finally, *qîṣ* is used four times with the meaning "to awaken from the dead," i.e. resurrection. Before Elisha brought the Shunammite widow's son to life, Gehazi reported, "The lad has not awakened" (II Kgs 4:31).

Job, in a pessimistic section, speaks of man lying down and not rising again, indeed, "He will not awake nor be aroused out of his sleep" (Job 14:12; see also v. 14). Job did, however, hope for the resurrection (19:25; 14:14*b* (NIV), see *ḥālap*). In Isaiah's apocalypse, the resurrection hope is explicitly stated with respect to Judah, "Their corpses will rise. You who lie in the dust, awake and shout for joy" (26:19).

But it is Daniel (12:2) who gives the clearest expression of the eschatological hope of resurrection: "And many of those who sleep in the dust of the ground will awake, these to everlasting life, but the others to disgrace and everlasting contempt." The NT follows LXX by using *egeirō* and *exegeirō* for the literal and figurative concepts of *yāqaṣ* and *qîṣ*.

P.R.G.

905 יָקַר (*yāqar*) ***be precious, valuable, costly, esteem.*** (ASV and RSV similar; cf. Zech 11:13, "the goodly (RSV "lordly") price that I was prized at (RSV "paid off") by them"; be (much) set by" ASV in I Sam 18:30.)

Derivatives

905a †יָקָר (*yāqār*) ***precious.***
905b יְקָר (*yᵉqar*) ***preciousness, honor, splendor, pomp.***
905c יַקִּיר (*yaqqîr*) ***very precious, honor.***

The root and its derivatives are employed 65 times. It comes from a Semitic root which conveys the idea of "heavy," "honor," "dignity." An object is considered precious or valuable either because of its intrinsic worth or its rarity.

Some things considered precious are wisdom, more precious than jewels (Prov 3:15; cf. Job 28:16); the steadfast love of God (Ps 36:7 [H 8]); the death of the saints in God's sight (Ps 116:15); the lips of knowledge (Prov 20:15). When one visits his neighbor infrequently, it has value in true friendship (Prov 25:17). Another precious object is God's thoughts, which are inexhaustible to the believer (Ps 139:17; cf. Jer 15:19). Here true value exists in quality, not quantity. Conversely, the phrase "the word of the LORD was precious in those days" means it was seldom heard (I Sam 3:1).

Honor also is associated with this root. One who performs an outstanding deed receives the king's honor (Est 6:3, 6). The daughters of a king are called "ladies of honor" (Ps 45:9 [H 10]). The citizens of Israel are also referred to as "the precious sons of Zion, worth their weight in fine gold" (Lam 4:2).

The root frequently appears with stone or alone to refer to jewels and other valuable objects. Solomon in building the temple hewed out huge, well dressed stones for the foundation of the temple (I Kgs 5:17 [H 31]; 7:9 f.). The fame and splendor of that temple are legendary. Also the objects within the temple were very valuable. When a foreign king conquered the land, he first sought out these treasures for his spoil (cf. Jer 20:5). Isaiah foresaw the construction of a new temple founded on "a stone, a tested stone, a precious cornerstone" (Isa 28:16). The content of this prophecy gains significance in the light of Solomon's temple and indicates the coming of a new temple for a new order of approach to God.

Life is valued very highly in the OT. David would not kill Saul even when he had the upper hand because he valued his life (I Sam 26:8–11, 21; II Kgs 1:13f.). An adulterous woman is most damaging because she claims the most precious aspect of a man, his life (Prov 6:26). God also protects and delivers his people from oppression and violence because he values their blood (Ps 72:14). Man's life exceeds the value of his ability to redeem himself. He does not have the money, nor can he offer himself, for he is a sinner (Ps 49:7f. [H 8f.]). Consequently God alone can redeem man, and out of love he will provide the redemption necessary, even at great cost (Isa 43:1–4).

yāqār. ***Precious, rare, splendid.*** In Job 31:26 in reference to the "moon moving in splendor" (ASV "brightness"). Used with "spirit" in Prov 17:27 to indicate a cool or controlled disposition.

J.E.H.

906 יָקֹשׁ (*yāqōsh*) ***lay a snare, set a trap, snare.*** (ASV, RSV similar.)

Derivatives

906a יָקוֹשׁ (*yāqôsh*) ***bait-layer, fowler,*** only in Hos 9:8.
906b יָקוּשׁ (*yāqûsh*) ***bait-layer, fowler.***
906c †מוֹקֵשׁ (*môqēsh*) ***snare.***

yāqōsh and its derivatives occur forty times. It refers to setting a trap to catch some prey, but more frequently in a metaphorical sense of entrapping people.

A snare metaphorically is something that allures one from his real purpose and then destroys him. In such a light Saul to ruin David gave his daughter Michal to him in marriage so that she might become a snare to David (I Sam 18:21). Pharoah's servants considered Moses a snare to Egypt (Ex 10:7). Similarly a godless ruler is a snare to the people (Job 34:30). Because of its inescapable hold, the power of death is referred to as the "snares of death" (Ps 18:5 [H 6]). Other snares include wickedness (Prov 29:6), fear of man (Prov 29:25), vowing rashly (Prov 20:25) and being friends with a man given to anger (Prov 22:24f.).

The wicked seek to ensnare the just (Jer 5:26). He who argues their defense or presents a just case at the court assembled in the gate also constantly confronts the attempts of the wicked to trip him up (Isa 29:21). So too does the prophet who seeks to turn the people to God (Hos 9:8). Therefore the righteous turn to God in prayer to be kept from being thus snared (Ps 141:9).

Those who follow idolatry become ensnared and can no longer serve Yahweh (Ex 23:33). Gideon made an ephod out of the spoils from battle. The ephod became a snare to himself and his family, for they fell to worshipping it (Jud 8:27). For this reason God charged the people to destroy utterly the inhabitants of Canaan, even their artifacts, so that they would never serve their gods and leave Yahweh (Deut 7:16, 25; Ex 23:32f.; but cf. Ps 106:34ff.).

God, on the other hand, prepares a trap for his opponents. They become so self-sufficient in their opposition to him that they are unaware of the snare (cf. Jer 50:24). Initially they become entrapped by their own sin (Prov 29:6). Although sin is destructive in itself, it remains for Yahweh's direct intervention to seal the trap and judge the victim (Ps 9:16 [H 17]). God's words and his deeds set the snare. Those who resist and belittle the proclaimed word are broken and ensnared (Isa 28:13). Immanuel too will be a stone of stumbling, a rock of offense, and a trap and a snare; people will stumble over him, fall and be snared (Isa 8:14f.). This imagery emphasizes the climactic finality of Israel's resistance to God's communication by word and by flesh.

môqēsh. ***Snare, gin*** (ASV.) G. R. Driver argues that it is the upper moveable part of a jaw-like trap (*paḥ*), "striker"; then it may stand for the whole trap, especially in metaphorical language.

Bibliography: Driver, G. R., "Reflections on Recent Articles, II Heber *Môqēsh* 'Striker,'" JBL 73: 131–36. Gilman, Henry S., "Notes on *môqsh*" JBL 58: 277–81. Heaton, Eric W., *Everyday Life in Old Testament Times,* London: B. T. Batsford, 1956. TDNT, VII, pp. 340–44.

J.E.H.

907 יָרֵא (*yārē'*) ***I, fear, be afraid, revere.***

Derivatives

907a †יָרֵא (*yārē'*) ***fearing, afraid.***
907b †יִרְאָה (*yir'â*) ***fearing, fear.***
907c †מוֹרָא (*môrā'*) ***fear.***
907d מוֹרָה (*môrâ*) ***terror*** (prob.). Occurs only in phrase *shîtâ môrâ lāhem* "appoint terror" i.e. an awe-inspiring exhibition of power (Ps 9:21).

In this discussion, biblical usages of *yārē'* are divided into five general categories: 1) the emotion of fear, 2) the intellectual anticipation of evil without emphasis upon the emotional reaction, 3) reverence or awe, 4) righteous behaviour or piety, and 5) formal religious worship. Major OT synonyms include *pāḥad, ḥātat,* and *ḥārad* as well as several words referring to shaking or quaking as a result of fear.

Typical examples of fearing as an emotional reaction are the Jews' fear of the fires on Mount Sinai (Deut 5:5) and the fear of the Jews at Mizpah when they heard of the Philistine mobilization (I Sam 7:7). Other examples give more emphasis to the anticipation of evil without necessarily pointing to the emotional reaction. David's recognition while in Achish's court that his reputation was a danger to him (I Sam 21:13) is an example along with Jacob's anticipation that his family might be taken from him (Gen 31:31).

These two usages are in mind in using the negative command not to fear as a comforting phrase or a greeting (e.g. Gen 50:19–20). In such cases *yārē'* is often used parallel to one or more synonyms (e.g. *ḥātat* "be demoralized"; *'āraṣ* "be terrified"). A similar motif is the defining of security as the lack of fear (e.g. Ps 56:4).

There are many examples of the third usage listed above. Such reverence is due to one's parents (Lev 19:3), holy places (Lev 26:2), God (Ps 112:1), and God's name (Ps 86:11). Habakkuk's "fearing" of God's work (Hab 3:2) and the fearing of Job's friends at seeing his misery are best considered as this kind of fear (Job 6:21).

In several passages, "fearing" and proper living are so closely related as to be virtually synonymous ideas (Lev 19:14; 25:17; II Kgs 17:34; Deut 17:19). It is plausible that this usage of "to fear" as a virtual synonym for righteous living or piety grew out of viewing "fear"—in any of the senses above—as the motivation which produced righteous living. This practical, active fear is the kind of fear for which God rewarded the Egyptian midwives (Ex 1:17, 21). This kind of fear was most appropriately learned by reading the Law (Deut 31:11–12). One righteous deed repeatedly and emphatically associated with "fearing" God is kindness to the stranger or resident alien (e.g. Deut 10:18–20; 25:18).

The clearest example of "fearing" as formal religious worship occurs in describing the religious syncretists of the northern kingdom who "feared" the Lord in respect to cultic worship (II Kgs 17:32–34), while not "fearing" the Lord in respect to righteous obedience to his law. The formal cultic elements mentioned in Deut 14:22–23 suggest that this is the kind of fear to be learned in that context. In light of the above discussion and of the context of Josh 22, the RSV is probably correct in translating "fear" as "worship" there (v. 25).

There are a few passages in which "fearing" seems to mean "being a devotee or follower." This usage could reflect either usages 4 or 5 above. Related substantival examples will be discussed below under *yārē'*, but possible verbal examples are found in Job 1:9 and II Chr 6:33.

Fear of various sorts may be caused by God's great deeds (Ex 14:31; Josh 4:23–24; I Sam 4:7–9), by judgment (Isa 59:18–19), and God's law (Deut 4:10) as well as by various human agencies (I Sam 7:7; 15:24).

In the Piel, *yārē'* means "to make to fear" (II Sam 14:15; Neh 6:9, 14, 19; II Chr 32:18). In the Niphal, the meaning is passive, "to be feared" (Ps 130:4). The Niphal participle is frequently used to describe things as "terrible," "awesome," or "terrifying." This is a good example of the gerundive character of the Niphal participle, "to be feared" (GKC, 116e). It may describe places (Gen 28:17), God (Ex 15:11), God's name (Deut 28:58), God's deeds (Ex 34:10), people (Isa 18:2), and the Day of the Lord (Joel 2:31 [H 3:4]).

The discussion of *yārē'* is complicated by the need to distinguish between those examples which are genuinely substantival—and therefore discussed in this section—and those examples which are involved in periphrastic verbal form and thus discussed above with the verb. This distinction is not always clearly made in translation; and often need not be made. The most frequent usage of the substantive is to refer to the "God-fearer" (different names or expressions for God may be used). Clearly substantival examples which show fear as an emotion (1 above) or as an anticipation of evil (2 above) are found (e.g. Ex 9:20; Deut 20:8; Jud 7:3). More frequently the emphasis is upon awe or reverence rather than terror (Ps 112:1; Eccl 8:12).

The "God-fearer" will implement his fear in practical righteousness or piety. Job, as a God fearer, avoids evil (Job 1:1). In Ps 128:1 the "fearer" of the Lord walks in his ways. The fearers of the Lord may be those whose particular piety is evidenced by a response to God's message. The "fearer" of God is contrasted with the wicked (Eccl 8:13). It is desired that office holders be fearers of God (Neh 7:2). Blessings are provided for fearers of God: happiness (i.e. "blessed"; Ps 112:1), goodness from God (Ps 31:19 [H 20]), provision of needs (Ps 34:9 [H 10]), protection (Ps 33:18–19 [H 19–20]), overshadowing mercy (i.e. *ḥesed;* Ps 103:11), and promise of fulfilled desires (Ps 145:19).

An interesting usage of this term is found in Ps 22. There the phrase "thou who fear God" parallels "sons of Jacob" and "sons of Israel" on the one hand (v. 23 [H 24]) and "the great congregation" on the other hand (v. 25 [H 26]). These parallels, especially the last, suggest that the term is used to refer to the worshiping congregation, gathered for worship. Two other possible examples of this usage are found (Ps 115:10, 11, 13; Ps 118:3–4).

môrā'. ***Fear, terror, terribleness.*** (RSV "terrible deeds," Deut 34:12.) It may refer to the emotion of fear as in the case of the fear of Noah placed in the animals (Gen 9:2) or reverence toward God (Mal 1:6). *môrā'* may refer to external objects of fear. In the clearest example, *môrā'* (Isa 8:12: RSV "fear") parallels an external "dread" (lit. "which makes to fear"). In other passages, it parallels God's great signs and wonders and thus can be taken as referring to external objects of fear (Deut 26:8; 34:12; Jer 32:21). The variant Hebrew spelling (*môrâ*) in Ps 9:20 [H 21] should be noted. It is easier simply to take this as an acceptable orthographic variant rather than to enter into textual emendations (e.g. KB).

yārē'. ***Fearing, afraid*** (often "who fear"). An adjectival form which serves both as a substantive and as a participle for the verb *yārē'*. It has almost the same range of meanings as the verb.

yir'â. ***Fearing, fear,*** etc. Used both as a noun and as the infinitive for *yārē'*. Found in all usages (above) of *yara'*, except 5.

The usages of this noun are similar to those of the verb. It may refer to the emotion of terror or fear (Ps 55:5 [H 6]; Ezk 30:13). This terror may be put into men's hearts by God (Ex 20:20; Deut 2:25). Isaiah 7:25 uses the term for an unemotional anticipation of evil. When God is the object of fear, the emphasis is again upon awe or reverence. This attitude of reverence is the basis for real wisdom (Job 28:28; Ps 110:10; Prov 9:10; 15:33). Indeed, the phrase sets the theme for the book of Proverbs. It is used in 1:7; recurs in 9:10 and twelve other verses. The fear of the Lord is to hate evil (8:13), is a fountain of life (14:27), it tendeth to life (19:23), and prolongeth days (10:27). Numerous passages relate this fear of God to piety and righteous living: it motivates faithful living (Jer 32:40). Fear of God results in caring for strangers (Gen 20:11). Just rule is rule in the fear of God (II Sam 23:3). Fear of the Almighty does not withhold kindness from friends (Job 6:14). Economic abuses against fellow Jews were contrary to the fear of God (Neh 5:9). The fear of the Lord turns men from evil (Prov 16:6).

Bibliography: TDOT, IX, pp. 197–208. THAT, I, pp. 765–77.

A.B.

908 יָרָא (*yārā'*) ***II, shoot, pour.*** Doubtless a by-form of יָרָה (q.v.). The single case of the Hophal, Prov 11:25, seems to come from *rāwâ*. There are variations among the Hebrew manuscripts.

909 יָרַד (*yārad*) Qal: ***go down, descend, decline, march down, sink down*** (of sun); Hiphil: ***bring down, take down, pour out (down), put off (ornaments).***

Derivatives

909a מוֹרָד (*môrād*) ***descent, slope, steep place, also hanging (work)*** (I Kgs 7:29, ***beveled [work],*** RSV); RSV also ascent, Josh 10:11.

909b †יַרְדֵּן (*yardēn*) ***Jordan.***

The hill country of Palestine is flanked on the west by the Mediterranean Sea and on the east by the deep rift Arabah, far below sea level. Therefore about any place traveled in Israel is either up or down. Since Jerusalem is the geographical focal point, a traveler either "goes up" (*'ālâ*) or "goes down" (modern Hebrew "immigrant" and "emigrant"). In a few places *yārad* is used when the destination is actually up hill; then it appears to mean a southward direction or down country, or else going up and down (cf. Isa 15:3 *yōrēd babbekî,* ASV "weeping abundantly," RSV "melts in tears," or possibly "going up and down while weeping"). There is also the feeling of moving from a place of prominence to one of lesser importance, i.e. from the temple or palace to a private house (e.g. II Sam 11:9f.). Further to come down is to leave one's place of prestige, to humble oneself (Isa 47:1; Jer 48:18). It often means a military maneuver to encounter the enemy in battle. In the defeat of battle, soldiers, cities and walls all come down (Hag 2:22; Deut 20:20; 28:52), and whoever is brought down is thus defeated (cf. Jer 51:40; Hos 7:12). Other uses include taking apart something, getting down from an animal or out of a chariot, throne or bed, lowering things to the ground, the coming down of rain or tears, and sailors going down to the sea (cf. Isa 42:10, RSV emends the text).

"To go down to Egypt" has the overtone of leaving the promised land to dwell among people outside the covenant. The first time the sons of Jacob went to Egypt to settle, God had to appear and instruct Jacob as to his purpose in directing them to Egypt (Gen 46:2ff.). Then after they gained control of Palestine, "to go down to Egypt" was to forsake God and to seek the help of man which would fail (Isa 30:2; 31:1).

Since Sheol (q.v.) is considered to be in the earth beneath, whoever dies goes down to Sheol (*e.g.* Num 16:30). Sheol's appetite is large and will swallow up all that go down (Isa 5:14). Prov emphasizes that whoever will follow the adulterous woman discovers her house is "the way to Sheol, going down to the chambers of death" (7:27).

A theophany is described as God coming down. He leaves his abode and comes to communicate with man either directly through the word or indirectly through some instrument. God descended on Mt. Sinai in fire (Ex 19:18; cf. II Chr 7:1ff.) and on the tent he appeared in a pillar of cloud (Ex 40:34f.; Num 12:5). To lighten Moses' load God came down among the elders and distributed some of his Spirit from Moses to the elders (Num 11:17). Further God comes down to bring salvation to his people; *e.g.*, he appeared to deliver his people from Egyptian bondage (Ex 3:8). On the other hand, God also descends to judge. But before God judges, he comes down to investigate the actuality of man's wickedness (e.g. at the tower of Babel, Gen 11:5, and at Sodom and Gomorrah [Gen 18:20f.]). Convinced of the sinfulness he descends and treads on the high places (Mic 1:3); i.e. he begins the judgment by destroying the centers of idol worship. Then he proceeds to bring down the rebellious nations to their defeat (cf. Ob 4).

J.E.H.

yardēn. ***Jordan.*** Most scholars would derive the name from the verb *yārad* "to descend," hence "the descender." The name occurs in Egyptian as *ya-ar-du-na*. Cyrus Gordon compares the name with the *Iardanos* rivers in Crete and Greece, and concludes that all of them derive from an East Mediterranean word for "river." The fact that almost all of the 183 occurrences of the word, with the exception of poetical passages (Job 40:23; Ps 42:6 [H 7]), are with the definite article, indicates that the word was originally a common noun. The LXX transliterates the word as *Iordanēs*.

The Jordan is formed by four sources. The *Nahr Banias* arises from Paneas (modern Banias, NT Caesarea Philippi) at the base of Mount Hermon. The Nahr el-Leddan springs from Dan (Jud 18:29), Israel's northernmost city. The Nahr Hasbani flows twenty-four miles through a valley west of Mount Hermon (possibly the "Valley of Mizpeh," Josh 11:8). The Nahr Bareighit, a small stream, west of the former, flows from Merj 'Ayun (cf. Ijon, I Kgs 15:20).

The Jordan flows seven miles hrough a once swampy area into what was a small lake, Lake Huleh, drained in 1955. Just south, at the Bridge of Jacob's Daughters, the ancient international highway to Damascus may have passed by a ford; the great site of Hazor lies four miles to the west. The Jordan then flows eight miles through a basalt gorge to the Sea of Galilee (the Sea of Chinnereth, Num 34:11). The river has descended from 230 feet above sea level N of the Huleh region to 690 feet below at the Sea of Galilee.

The river reforms at the south end of the Sea of Galilee and descends to the Dead Sea, 1290 feet below sea level, the lowest spot on earth. Thus it flows through a portion of the Great Rift Valley which extends from between the Lebanon and Anti-Lebanon mountains to the great lakes of Africa. The air distance between the two lakes is but sixty-five miles, but the Jordan in its meandering covers almost two hundred miles. Except at flood stage the river is only three to twelve feet deep, and ninety to one hundred feet broad.

The Jordan can be forded at about sixty sites. Jacob crossed the Jordan to get to Aram and then recrossed with the household he had acquired there (Gen 32:10 [H 11]). After Ehud killed Eglon, the king of Moab, the Israelites seized the fords and killed many of the Moabites who were trapped on the west side of the Jordan (Jud 3:28–29). After Gideon had defeated the Midianites at Moreh he called upon the Ephraimites to seize the fords (Jud 7:24–25).

The Israelites under Joshua were able to cross the Jordan near Jericho dry-shod as the Lord dammed up the waters (Ps 114:3, 5; Josh 3:16) at Adam (sixteen miles north) as far as Zarethan (Tell es-Sa'idiyeh, ten miles further upstream). Landslides have been known to dam up the Jordan: for ten hours in 1267 and for twenty-one hours in1927. The conquest (Josh 1–11) begins with the crossing of the Jordan and the capture of Jericho; the distribution of the land (Josh 13–21) terminates at this river. This procedure corresponds to Moses' directive (Num 34:12).

The width of the Jordan Valley broadens from four miles below the Sea of Galilee to fourteen miles above the Dead Sea. The *Ghor* "Rift" or upper valley can be cultivated north of Gilead. In the arid southern parts below the Ghor are the sterile chalk hills called Qattara. The green flood plain is known as the Zor, the Arabic word for "thicket."

The latter was known as the *gā'ôn* of the Jordan, translated by the KJV "swelling," by the RV "pride," by the NEB "dense thickets," by the NIV "thickets," and by the RSV "jungle." It was noted as the habitat of wild animals such as lions (Jer 49:19; Zech 11:3). Jeremiah is asked how, if he fell down in a safe land, he would do in a dangerous place like the "jungle of the Jordan" (Jer 12:5).

The uninhabitable nature of the Zor and the Qattara made the Jordan River an effective regional barrier. Moses was concerned that the tribes of Reuben, Gad, and half of Manasseh, who were assigned territories east of the Jordan, might not assist their brethren who had to conquer Cis-Jordan to the west (Num 32). In a relatively short time dialectal differences appeared. The Ephraimites from the west betrayed themselves at the fords by saying "Sibboleth" instead of "Shibboleth" like Jephthah's Gileadites from the east (Jud 12:6). The word "Shibboleth" means "river" and was a natural test.

The west side of the Jordan River is fed by the Nahr Jalud from Beth-shean and by the Wadi Farah from Tirzah. The key sites were Jericho, Gilgal, Beth-shean; Egyptian texts reveal Rehob south and Yenoam north of Beth-shean.

The east side receives ten perennial tributaries. The Yarmuq, which enters the Jordan five miles south of the Sea of Galilee, contributes as much water as the Jordan itself but is not named in the Bible. The Zerqa (biblical Jabbok) rises near Amman and feeds into the Jordan just above Adan.

Nelson Glueck identified thirty-five sites which were populated between the thirteenth and sixth centuries B.C. The OT mentions only nine sites in the Jordan Valley. The site of Penuel where Jacob wrestled with the angel was near the Jabbok (Gen 32:22–32). SKUCCOTH, WHERE Jacob built booths for his cattle (Gen 33:17) and a city which refused aid to Gideon (Jud 8:5–8), was located by the Jabbok.

When Abraham and Lot came to a parting of ways, Lot saw that the *kikkar* of the Jordan (KJV "plain"; RSV "valley"; Gen 13:10) was well watered. In this case the *kikkar*, literally "round shape," included the region souhh of the Dead Sea. Solomon cast copper works in the *kikkar*, perhaps the oval depression of the Jordan between Succoth and Zarethan (I Kgs 7:46). Cd. Gen 19:17, 25; Deut 34:3.

The expression *yardēn yᵉrēḥô* the "Jordan of Jericho" which occurs at Num 22:1; 33:50; 34:15; Josh 13:32; 16:1; 20:8; and I Chr 6:78 [H 63] is translated by the RSV "Jordan at Jericho" and "Jordan by Jericho." As the phrase can indicate not just the territory east of Jericho (Josh 16:1), but the entire eastern border of Ephraim and Manasseh, Elmer Smick has suggested that *yardēn* should be treated as a common noun so that the phrase would mean the "river of Jericho," i.e. the Jordan River in its entirety.

If the behemoth (Heb *bᵉhēmôt*) in Job 40:15ff. is the hippopotamus, the *yardēn* of 40:23 may simply refer to a "river," not the Jordan. Hippopotamuses were found in the Orontes in Syria c. 1500 B.C. and in the Lower Nile until the twelfth century A.D., but not in the Jordan.

Bibliography: Cohen, S., "Jordan," in IDB. Driver, G. R., "Mistranslations," *Palestinian Exploration Quarterly* 79: 1236–26. ______, "*'lh* 'Went Up Country' and *yrd* 'Went Down Country'," ZAW 69: 74–77. Glueck, Nelson, *The River Jordan*, Westminster, 1946. Leslau, Wolf, "An Ethiopian Parallel to Hebrew *'lh* 'Went Up Country' and *yrd* 'Went Down Country'," ZAW 74: 322f. Leslau demonstrates in Ethiopic *yrd* "down south" or "west"). Smick, Elmer B., *Archaeology of the Jordan Valley*, Baker, 1973. TDNT, VI, pp. 608–13.

E.Y.

יַרְדֵּן (*yardēn*). See no. 909b.

910 יָרָה (*yārâ*) ***throw, cast, shoot*** (Qal); ***teach*** (Hiphil). (ASV, RSV similar.)

Derivatives

910a †יוֹרֶה (*yôreh*) ***early*** (ASV "former," RSV "autumn") rain, in contrast to *malqôsh* "latter rain." The early rains fell from the end of October until the beginning of December.

910b מוֹרֶה (*môreh*) ***I, early rain,*** only in Josh 2:23; Ps 84:7.

910c מוֹרֶה (*môreh*) ***II, teacher.***

910d †תּוֹרָה (*tôrâ*) ***law.***

The basic idea of the root *yārâ* is "to throw" or "to cast" with the strong sense of control by the subject. Lots were cast in regards to dividing the land among the various tribes (Josh 18:6). God cast the Egyptian army into the Red Sea (Ex 15:4; cf. Job 30:19). With stones it has the idea of placing them in a certain place; God laid the cornerstone of the world (Job 38:6) and Laban set up a heap of stones and a pillar as a witness between Jacob and himself to their covenant of peace (Gen 31:51f.). The three most frequent uses of this root deal with shooting arrows, sending rain and teaching.

A most deadly weapon of the ancients was the bow and arrow. They could shoot from a distance and from behind protection. Some missiles were shot from specially designed engines (II Chr 26:15). Three of Israel's kings fell on the battlefield because of the archers' range, namely Saul (I Chr 10:3), Ahab (I Kgs 22:35), and Josiah (II Chr 35:23). Metaphorically the wicked from behind ambush shot suddenly at the blameless (Ps 64:4 [H 5]; cf. Ps 11:2). On the other hand, God too is pictured as shooting an arrow at the wicked and wounding them suddenly to protect the upright (Ps 64:7 [H 8]). In addition, shooting of arrows could be used as a sign (I Sam 20:20; cf. II Kgs 13:17).

yôreh. ***Early rain.*** God gives the early rain and the latter rain to assure abundance of harvest (Deut 11:14). Joel compares the future blessing to the coming of the early and latter rains (Joel 2:23; cf. Hos 6:3; Jas 5:7). God will restore to his people abundance of produce; this promise encompasses both material and spiritual blessings; e.g. Hos 10:12, "It is the time to seek the Lord, that he may come and rain salvation upon you."

tôrâ. ***Law, teaching.*** ASV always "law," RSV sometimes "teaching," "instruction" and "decisions." The word is used some 221 times.

Teaching is the special task of the wisdom school as seen especially through the book of Prov and of the priesthood. The latter accompanies a revealed religion. The priests are to teach the law given by Moses (Lev 10:11; Deut 33:10); e.g. King Jehoash acted uprightly because he was instructed by the high priest (II Kgs 12:2 [H 3]). Ezra the priest faithfully taught the Law of Moses in the fall Feast of Tabernacles in accordance with the Deuteronomic injunction (Deut 31:9–11; Ezr 8:1ff.). Unfortunately the priests were not always true to God; they taught for money and became teachers of lies (Isa 9:15 [H 14]; Mic 3:11). Similarly an idol is deemed "a teacher of lies" (Hab 2:18f.).

Teaching is associated with the anointing of the Holy Spirit. Bezalel and Oholiab were inspired to teach the skills of the artisan so that the tabernacle and its furnishing could be built (Ex 35:34). God himself is particularly described as a teacher. He taught Moses both what to do and say (Ex 4:15). He also teaches sinners the right way (Ps 25:8) and instructs those who fear him in the way they should choose (Ps 25:12). Therefore the Psalmist often beseeches God to teach him so that he may keep the statutes and walk in the way of truth (Ps 27:11; 86:11; 119:33; cf. Job 6:24; 34:32). In the last days God promises the people of Jerusalem a teacher whom they will behold (Isa 30:20). The nations also will come to Jerusalem so that God might teach them (Isa 2:3). No wonder Jesus, as God incarnate, assumed the title of teacher and performed much of his ministry as a teacher.

Scope of the Word

The word *tôrâ* means basically "teaching" whether it is the wise man instructing his son or God instructing Israel. The wise give insight into all aspects of life so that the young may know how to conduct themselves and to live a long blessed life (Prov 3:1f.). So too God, motivated by love, reveals to man basic insight into how to live with each other and how to approach God. Through the law God shows his interest in all aspects of man's life which is to be lived under his direction and care. Law of God stands parallel to word of the Lord to signify that law is the revelation of God's will (e.g. Isa 1:10). In this capacity it becomes the nation's wisdom and understanding so that others will marvel at the quality of Israel's distinctive life style (Deut 4:6). Thus there is a very similar understanding of the role of teaching with its results in the wisdom school, in the priestly instruction, and the role of the law with its results for all the people of the covenant.

Specifically law refers to any set of regulations; e.g., Ex 12 contains the law in regard to observing the Passover. Some other specific laws include those for the various offerings (Lev 7:37), for leprosy (Lev 14:57) and for jealousy (Num 5:29). In this light law is often considered to consist of statutes, ordinances, precepts, commandments, and testimonies.

The meaning of the word gains further perspective in the light of Deut. According to Deut 1:5 Moses sets about to explain the law; law here would encompass the moral law, both in its apodictic and casuistic formulation, and the ceremonial law. The genius of Deut is that it interprets the external law in the light of its desired effect on man's inner attitudes. In addition, the book of Deut itself shows that the law has a broad meaning to encompass history, regulations and their interpretation, and exhortations. It is not merely the listing of casuistic statements as is the case in Hammurabi's code. Later the word extended to include the first five books of the Bible in all their variety.

Law and Covenant

Covenant precedes law; and the law was given only to the nation which had entered into covenant with God [although in the sense of moral principle, law is as old as human sin and God's governance, Gen 3:7; 9:6; 26:5.—R.L.H.]. The law specifically is the stipulations of the covenant. But in the broad sense of law, namely God's teaching, covenant plays the central part. Law and covenant may parallel one another (e.g. Ps 78:10). Since they are so closely tied together, to break one is to break both. Their interconnection is further witnessed to in that the tables of the testimony were placed in the ark of the covenant and a copy of the book of the law placed beside it as a perpetual witness to the covenant between God and his people (Ex 40:20; Deut 31:26).

The law, as well as the covenant, brings with it blessings or curses. He who follows its precepts will be blessed (Deut 29:9 [H 8]), but whoever breaks them will be cursed (Deut 29:20–21 [H 19–20]). Following the law is the source of life; it makes life a joy and lengthens its days (Deut 6:1–2). On the other hand, as the standard it tests Israel to determine whether they follow God completely or not (Deut 8:2; Jud 3:4).

Frequently the OT says Moses wrote the law and refers to the book of the law (e.g. Deut 30:10; 31:9; Josh 24:26). These references give weight to the importance placed on a written code from the beginning of Israel's history. It became the objective standard from which interpretation was made (cf. Deut 17:8–11). In addition, it was to be read and meditated on so that its precepts should become an integral part of the lifestyle of the people (cf. Josh 1:7f.). It was their guidebook; more than that it was their constitution. Israel was a religious state; as such, the fundamental document that determined its character was the law given through Moses. E.g., the king was to have his own copy, and he was to read it all the days of his life so that he would learn to fear Yahweh by keeping all the words of the law (Deut 17:18–19). Since the written law was superior to the king in Israel, the king could never become a god or a religious innovator. His right to rule was subordinate to the law.

References to the written law or the law of Moses are numerous in the historical books. The most significant ones may be collected for convenient reference: Deut 17:18; 28:61; 29:21 [H 20]; 30:10; 31:9, 24; Jos 1:7,8; 8:31f.; 23:6; I

Kgs 2:3; II Kgs 14:6; 22:8; 23:25; II Chr 23:18; 30:16; Ezra 3:2; 7:6; Neb 8:1–2.

The Property of the Priests

The law was the special property of the priests. They were to teach its precepts and follow its regulations (Deut 17:8–11; 33:10). They were known as "those who handle the law" (Jer 2:8). But unfortunately the priesthood became blind and arrogant. They forgot God (Hos 4:6). They no doubt had the law memorized but failed to see its spiritual dimensions. Instead they turned it into a means of enhancing their own power and wealth (Ezk 22:26; cf. Zeph 3:4). Therefore God sent his prophets to call the people back to true observance of the law (II Kgs 17:13). The prophets' task was to apply the law to their own situation. Their message was founded on the law; they struck out at its misapplication.

The Law at the Time of Ezra and Nehemiah

In the postexilic community under the leadership of Ezra and Nehemiah, the law became central to the community's life. Both men struck out at the lax, selfish lives the people were living and sought to turn them back to the true worship of God through having the law taught. Ezra read the law before the assembly and interpreted it so that the people were sure to understand its application (Neh 8:2–8). Upon hearing the law the people wept (Neh 8:9). But Nehemiah and Ezra comforted the people and led them to celebrate the feast of booths according to the law (Neh 8:13–17) as Moses had ordered to be done (Deut 31:10–11). Each day of the feast the law was read (Neh 8:18). Afterwards they repented of their sins and made a covenant to follow the entire law (Neh 9:3; 10:29–31). The activities of these two men led the people back to God, and their use of the law became formative for the community's life with effects lasting even past the destruction of Jerusalem in 70 A.D.

Praise for the Law

Some psalms render praise to the law. The chief, of course, is Ps 119. The Psalmist yearns for understanding in order that he can keep the law, the object of his delight and love (vv. 1, 61, 92). Psalm 19 speaks about God communicating his glory through the heavens and through his spoken word. The latter communicates directly and specifically God's will. The law turns (RSV "reviving the soul") the whole person to God. Thereby it enlightens, makes wise and is a cause of rejoicing (vv. 7–8 [H 8–9]). It also warns against evil and prevents one from inadvertently turning from God (v. 11 [H 12]). No wonder its value is higher than the finest gold and its taste sweeter than honey (v. 10 [H 11]).

The Law in the Coming Age

Because of Israel's constant disobedience, the prophets looked for a time when once again the law, directly from God, would go forth from Jerusalem (Isa 2:3). Then God himself will both teach and judge according to the law. Such is a part of the suffering servant's task, namely to render judgment according to truth and to give forth a new teaching or law (Isa 42:3f.). It will surpass the Mosaic law because of its source through a new prophet-leader. It will not disagree with the old but build on it. Also its scope will be universal. Jeremiah sees the establishing of a new covenant in which the law will be written on the heart (Jer 31:33). Man will be able to obey God from his inner life outwards. Then the true purpose of the law, namely, to lead man into a fruitful, abundant life of fellowship with God, will be fully realized.

Bibliography: Cole, R. A., "Law in the OT," in ZPEB, III, pp. 883–94. Davies, W. D., *Torah in the Messianic Age and/or the Age to Come,* Society of Biblical Literature, 1952. Jacob, Edmond, *Theology of the Old Testament,* tr. Arthur W. Heathcote and Philip J. Allcock, Harper & Row, 1958. Manley, G. T., *The Book of the Law,* Inter-Varsity, 1957. Payne, J. Barton, *The Theology of the Older Testament,* Zondervan, 1962. Vriezen, Th. D., *An Outline of Old Testament Theology,* Branford, 1966. Zimmerli, W., *The Law and the Prophets,* tr. R. E. Clements, Oxford: Basil Blackwell, 1965. Zuck, Roy B., "Hebrew Words for 'Teach'," BS 121: 228–35.

J.E.H.

911 יָרָה (*yārah*). Used only once (Isa 44:8). Probably to be read as from *yārē'* "be afraid" (so DSS).

יָרוֹק (*yārôq*). See no. 918c.

912 יְרוּשָׁלַיִם (y^e*rûshālayim*), יְרוּשָׁלֵם (y^e*rûshālaim*) ***Jerusalem.***

An ancient city of southern Canaan, capital of the Davidic dynasty and religious center of Judaism until its rejection of Jesus and the resultant destruction by Titus in A.D. 70. It was taken also as a symbol of the Christian church, predicted seat of the future messianic kingdom, and prototype of the ultimate New Jerusalem that succeeds God's final judgment. Mentioned by name 669 times in the OT alone, Jerusalem is the world's most significant city (Ps 48:1–2 [H 2–3]). It was God's earthly dwelling place (I Kgs 8:13), the scene of Christ's resurrection (Lk 24:47) and will be the place of his return in glory (Zech 14:5).

Although Paleolithic tools have been recovered southeast of modern Jerusalem, urban settlement seems to have begun with the Early Bronze Age

Canaanites (3000–2000 B.C.). The choice of site appears to have been dictated by the presence of a road junction, the military strength of the hill Ophel, or Zion, and the perennial water of the Gihon spring in the Kidron Valley on the city's east. Its first mention comes at the close of this period, when Abraham honors its priest-king Melchizedek (Gen 14:20), a type of Christ (Ps 110:4; Heb 7) in his double office. On the adjoining hill of Moriah (II Chr 3:1) Abraham was willing to offer his son Isaac as a sacrifice to God (Gen 22:2, c. 2050 B.C.).

The city is first mentioned in the Ebla tablets according to preliminary reports (Kitchen, K. A., *The Bible in its World*, Paternoster, 1977, p. 53). Then it is mentioned in the Middle Bronze Age (2000–1600) Egyptian Execration Texts of the Twelfth Dynasty, as *Urusalimum?* foundation (?) of Shalem." This form is probably to be read in the Amarna letters (fourteenth century B.C.) as Ursalimmu. In early Hebrew it therefore was pronounced *yerushalem* probably meaning "Foundation of Shalem," shalem being a god known from a Ugaritic mythological text, but in Hebrew coming to mean peace or security.

Its initial biblical designation, in Moses' writing of Genesis (c. 1450 B.C.), is simply "Salem" (14:18; cf. Ps 76:2 [H 3]), *shālēm,* meaning complete, prosperous, peaceful. Its form in biblical Aramaic, *ye rûsh^e lem* (Dan 5:2) and in the LXX, *ierousalēm,* is therefore probably more correct than the medieval Masoretic Hebrew, *ye rûshālayim,* which may be modeled after *miṣrayim,* the dual noun for Egypt.

Although captured by Joshua in the Late Bronze Age (Josh 10:1) and occupied for a brief period after his death (Jud 1:8, c. 1390), Jerusalem remained in Canaanite (Jebusite) hands (1:21) until its capture by David in 1003 B.C. (II Sam 5:6–9). By bringing up the ark of the covenant into a special tent (6:17) David made Zion the throne of God's presence (Ps 132:13). In 959 Solomon completed the permanent temple, which, though destroyed by Nebuchadrezzar in 586, was rebuilt by Zerubbabel, 520–515, into which Jesus later entered with God's true peace (Hag 2:9). Jerusalem is thus "the city of the Great King" (Ps 48:2 [H 3]; Mt 5:35). To be "born in Zion" seems to be equated with participation in divine salvation (Ps 87:4–5), whatever one's actual nationality may be (v. 6; ICC, *Psalms,* II, p. 240; cf. Gal 4:26). The name of the city comes to designate heaven itself (Heb 12:22–23).

Bibliography: Kenyon, K., *Jerusalem: Excavating 3000 Years of History,* McGraw-Hill, 1967. Payne, J. B., "Jerusalem," in ZPEB. Simons, J., *Jerusalem in the OT,* Brill, 1952. Yadin, Yigael, ed., *Jerusalem Revealed,* Yale, 1976.

J.B.P.

913 ירח (*yrḥ*). **Assumed root of the following.**
913a †יָרֵחַ (*yārēaḥ*) ***moon.***
913b †יֶרַח (*yeraḥ*) ***month.***

yārēaḥ. ***Moon.*** (ASV and RSV the same.) The word occurs 27 times. "The moon," frequently paralleled by "the sun," was created by God to rule the night and to indicate the seasons, especially the occasions of feasts (Ps 104:19; 136:9). The moon gives off enough light in the Near East by which to perform many tasks, and during full moon journeys could be made at night. People with certain mental disorders were considered by some to be moon struck (Ps 121:6). [In Gr. the word for "epileptic" is from words meaning "moonstruck" (Mt 4:24 NIV). The etymology of the word need not argue that the concept was then current that the moon caused such illness. Cf. our word "lunatic" which in its etymology reflects much older notions. Obviously, the moon is harmless, but as Dahood observes ("Psalms," in AB, III, p. 202) many ancients believed otherwise. David asserts that it cannot harm the believer. It is also possible that David had in mind the pagan deities: the sun god and the moon god are nonentities.—R.L.H.] The moon was viewed as having a powerful effect on life.

Sin, the moon god, was the main god worshipped at Ur in southern Babylonia and at Haran in northwestern Mesopotamia. He was associated with order and wisdom. Both of these cities were deeply rooted in the life of Abraham before he left to follow God. The movements of the moon were carefully observed and various omens were given by its relationship to the sun, its son. An eclipse was an ill omen, and special rituals were performed to avert any disaster. Thus the moon-god had a profound effect on ancient Near Eastern life. Such worship, however, was strictly forbidden in Israel (Deut 4:19). Any who were so attracted were under the penalty of stoning (Deut 17:3ff.). Job, to proclaim his innocence, asserted that he had never been allured by any of these heavenly bodies, including the moon (Job 31:26ff.).

In Israel the moon was constantly affirmed as Yahweh's creation. It had no external power. Thus the pilgrim to Jerusalem did not have to fear being moon struck, for Yahweh would most assuredly protect them (Ps 121:6). As his creature, the moon is to praise Yahweh (Ps 148:3). Because the moon is subject to Yahweh, Joshua was able to command it and the sun to stand still while he completed the battle (Josh 10:12f.).

When the day of the Lord comes, all of the heavenly bodies will be affected. Joel speaks about the sun and the moon becoming darkened (Joel 2:10; 3:15 [H 4:15]) and the moon turning to blood (2:31 [H 3:4]; cf. Mk 13:24; Lk 21:25; Rev 6:12). Isaiah 13:10 confirms that the moon shall not give its light during the day of Yahweh. In the new age Isaiah sees that there will be no need of the moon's light or patterns of movement (Isa 60:19f.).

Interestingly the covenant with the house of David to rule Israel is pictured as firmly established like the moon (Ps 89:37 [H 38]). No doubt the certainty as well as the temporality of this covenant is indicated. As long as there is a moon, so the covenant stands, but in the new age when there is no longer any need for the moon so there will be no need for that covenant.

yeraḥ. ***Month.*** Aramaic, "new moon," also in Ugaritic (ASV and RSV same except former "moons" in Deut 33:14). This noun is used twelve times. The primary unit of time in the Semitic world is the month (more often called *ḥōdesh,* q.v.), especially for establishing festivals. Months named with *yeraḥ* include *ziw,* second month (I Kgs 6:37), *'etānîm*, seventh month (I Kgs 8:2), and *bûl,* eighth month (I Kgs 6:38). These three month names with a fourth, *'ābîb,* are probably the old Canaanite names. Two of them (*bûl* and *'ētānîm*) are also found in Phoenician. More often the OT gives the month by number—e.g. seventh month, etc. In exilic and postexilic books (Est, Neh, Zech), the Babylonian names Nisan, Sivan, Elul, Chislev, Tebeth, and Shebet (Sebet) are mentioned. The Hebrews reckoned time by the lunar month, but to keep in step with the solar calendar they put in an extra leap month about every three years. By this method the spring festival always came in the spring and the fall festivals in the fall. See also *ḥôdesh,* no. 613b.

A month of days means a full month; a girl taken captive was allowed to mourn the death of her parents a full month before becoming a wife (Deut 21:13). The number of months fulfilled may mean the time it takes an animal to come to birth (Job 3:6; 39:2). Similarly in regard to harvest it appears in the blessing given Joseph; namely he is to be blessed "with the choicest fruits of the sun, and the rich yield of the months" (Deut 33:14). Certain events are numbered by months. Moses was hid at home three months by his mother (Ex 2:2). Shallum reigned one month in Samaria (II Kgs 15:13; cf. Zech 11:8). Month in these instances indicates a short period of time, but when used to measure suffering or one's longings, it means a long time has passed. Job lamented, "So I am allotted months of emptiness, and nights of misery are apportioned to me" (Job 7:3); and "O that I were as in the months of old, as in the days when God watched over me" (Job 29:2).

Bibliography: Conteneau, George, *Everyday Life in Babylon and Assyria,* Norton, 1966. Hooke, S. H., *Babylonian and Assyrian Religion,* London: Hutchinson House, 1953. Lilley, J., "Calendar," in ZPEB.

J.E.H.

914 יָרַט (*yāraṭ*) ***be precipitate, precipitate*** (Num 22:32).

יָרִיב (*yārîb*). See no. 2159b.

915 יְרִיחוֹ (*y^erîḥô*), יְרִיחֹה (*y^erîḥōh*), יְרֵחוֹ (*y^erēḥô*) ***Jericho.*** (ASV, RSV the same.)

The names appear 38 times. Jericho is located approximately 900 feet below sea level and 10 miles north of the Dead Sea. Its plain is made green by a plentiful spring, known as the Fountain of Elisha. Its weather is almost always warm and dry, pleasant in winter, hot in summer. Here it controlled the less used roads along the Arabah and a permanent ford of the Jordan River. The mound known as Tell es-Sultan is OT Jericho, and is one of the oldest walled cities of man, going back to at least the eighth millennium B.C.

After the long wilderness journey the Israelites under Joshua crossed the Jordan and encamped at Gilgal. To gain a foothold on the west bank they had to capture Jericho, then a city covering five to eight acres enclosed by forbidding walls. The Israelites marched around the city for six consecutive days. On the seventh day, they marched around the city seven times; then on the seventh time, through the miraculous intervention of God amidst the sounding of trumpets and the shouting of the people, the walls collapsed causing the utter discomfiture and defeat of the inhabitants of Jericho (Josh 6). Rahab's family only escaped due to her faith and to her siding with Israel (Josh 6:22f.; Jas 2: 25). Afterward the city was burned, but the valuable vessels became a part of the treasury of the Lord's house (Josh 6:24). The fall of Jericho became a symbol of God's power and intent to give the land to the Israelites and firmly established the leadership of Joshua as Moses' successor. The conclusive manner in which it was taken provided the standard for future attacks. Ai was to be captured in the same fashion (Josh 8:2). These mighty deeds also bore witness to the inhabitants of Canaan that Israel was a force to be reckoned with, because God was on their side. The men of Gibeon realized this, feigned their habitation and entered into covenant with Joshua (chapter 9). After Adonizedek, king of Jerusalem, learned what had happened to Jericho and Ai, he summoned a coalition of kings to Jerusalem to plan a concerted effort against Israel. With God's help that coalition was soundly defeated and the kings slain (Josh 10:1–28).

Excavations at Jericho by Garstang and K. Kenyon have uncovered significant artifacts and aroused a tremendous debate over its fall into Israelite hands. Garstang argues for a late fifteenth century date and Kenyon a late fourteenth century date. Kenyon claims, however, there is very little evidence left of the city which was taken by Joshua; therefore the archaeologist will not be able to shed much light on that city or the exact date of its fall.

The defeat of Jericho brought Joshua's curse on anyone who dared to rebuild it (Josh 6:26). In the days of King Ahab, Hiel of Bethel dared and it cost the death of his two sons (I Kgs 16:34). The city is mentioned as the boundary between Benjamin and Joseph, and as belonging to Benjamin (Josh 16:1, 7; 18:12). In this area there was a settlement at the time of David, for David's servants recovered here from their humiliation at the hand of Hanun the Ammonite (II Sam 10:1–5). Further, a school of the prophets resided here during the days of Elijah and Elisha, and Elisha miraculously healed the spring that had turned brackish (II Kgs 2:5; 19–22).

Bibliography: Garstang, John, and J. B. D., *The Story of Jericho*, London: Marshall, Morgan and Scott, 1948. Garstang, John, "The Walls of Jericho," *Palestinian Exploration Quarterly* 63: 186–96. Kenyon, Kathleen, M., *Digging Up Jericho*, London: Ernest Benn, 1957. Smick, E. B., *Archaeology of the Jordan Valley*, Baker, 1972, pp. 63–66. Vincent, L. H., "The Chronology of Jericho," *Palestinian Exploration Quarterly* 63: 104f.

J.E.H.

יְרִיעָה (*y*ᵉ*rî'â*). See no. 917a.

916 ירך (*yrk*). **Assumed root of the following.**
916a †יָרֵךְ (*yārēk*) ***thigh, loin.***
916b †יַרְכָה (*yar*ᵉ*kâ*), יְרֵכָה (*y*ᵉ*rēkâ*) ***flank, side.***

yārēk. ***Thigh, loin, side, base.*** ASV and RSV similar; "that comes out of his loins" = "offspring" RSV (e.g. Gen 46:26), but "of his body begotten" (Jud 8:30 ASV). The thigh stands for man's foundation (e.g. "the place of girding on the sword" (cf. Jud 3:16, 21)) and for the source of life. Thus a hand placed under the thigh affirmed the strongest oath, especially during the patriarchal age (cf. Gen 24:9). And smiting the thigh was a sign of intense repentance (Ezk 21:12 [H 21]; Jer 31:19). The Hebrews recognized the beauty of the female thigh (Song 7:1 [H 2]). However, a woman jealously accused of adultery had to drink water of bitterness and utter a curse. If she was guilty, her body swelled and her thigh fell away (Num 5:21f.); perhaps a miscarriage of an illegitimate child is hereby indicated. Also the word refers to the "side" of the tabernacle (Ex 40:22) and of the altar (Lev 1:11) and the "base" of the lampstand (Ex 25:31).

No wonder the angel in his wrestling match with Jacob at Peniel smote Jacob's thigh. He showed his superior strength, and he indicated that the very basis of Jacob's life was altered, further signified by the change of his name. A perpetual reminder was given to Jacob in his constant limping and to the nation in its being forbidden to eat the sinew of the thigh (Gen 32:25, 31f. [H 26, 32f.]).

yarkâ. ***Flank, side, rear, extreme or uttermost parts, innermost parts, depths, recesses.*** (RSV more varied than ASV, often using "far(thest)," but for "rear" ASV reads "hinder part.") It appears twenty-eight times. The word refers to the backside or farthest part of anything. It is employed to indicate the rear of a building, the extent of a border (Gen 49:13), the back country (Jud 19:1), the deepest part of a cave and the inner parts of a ship (Jon 1:5). "The far recesses of Lebanon" indicates where the great cedars grew (II Kgs 19:23). Also Sheol is called the depths of the pit (Isa 14:15; cf. Ezk 32:23).

The remotest parts, particularly the distant north, are conceived of as those away from God. All countries, except Egypt, had to approach Jerusalem from the north, because of desert and sea. Consequently in those remotest parts the enemies of God are viewed as assembling and planning their attack on Jerusalem. Jeremiah saw the source of the coming destruction against Jerusalem as "a great nation . . . stirring from the farthest parts of the earth" (Jer 6:22; *cf.* 25:32; 50:41; Ezk 38:6, 15; 39:2). The recesses can extend even beyond the globe. Babylon, intending to rule all the world, affirmed, "I will sit on the mount of assembly in the far north" (Isa 14:13).

Although the recesses are a refuge for God's opponents, they are never beyond his control. From the farthest parts of the earth, God will bring back his people (Jer 31:8). Mount Zion is placed figuratively in the far north to show that the city of God rules the entire world (Ps 48:2 [H 3]). [The word is also used with less emphasis to mean merely "end" of anything (Ex 26:22–23 etc.; I Kgs 6:16; Ezk 46:19). It is possible that Ps 48:2 [H 3] only means to say that the temple was on the north end of Jerusalem, although a common view is the one expressed that Zion is placed figuratively in the far north. A variant of this view is that Zion is figuratively like the northern mountain, Zaphon, sacred to the Phoenicians. R.L.H.]

J.E.H.

917 יָרַע (*yāra'*) ***quiver,*** only in phrase *napshô yār'â lô* "his soul quivers to him," i.e. is in terror and distress.

Derivative

917a †יְרִיעָה (*y^erî'â*) ***curtain.*** (ASV and RSV the same, except sometimes RSV "tent.")

It occurs fifty-one times. Since tents were made out of curtains, these two words are paralleled frequently in the OT. The color of the tents was quite dark (Song 1:5), and children helped set them up (Jer 10:20). In times of war they, along with all the flocks and goods, were taken as spoils (Jer 49:29; 4:20). The tabernacle was composed of ten curtains woven from fine twined linen and blue, purple and scarlet stuff (Ex 26:1). The curtains were held together by a series of loops. A covering over the tabernacle consisted of eleven curtains made from goats' hair; a half curtain hung over the back. The ark of the covenant was viewed as dwelling within curtains (II Sam 7:2; I Chr 17:1; RSV "tent"). In symbolic language God is pictured as spreading out the heavens like a tent (or curtain, Ps 104:2). Little effort on his part and yet his complete control is thus emphasized.

It is of some interest that all the tabernacle curtains were 4 cubits (6 ft) wide, which was the standard width of an Egyptian horizontal loom—all except the court hangings which were five cubits wide. The extra cubit may have come from a section woven on the low hand loom, which was about one cubit wide.

After God's great saving act through the suffering servant, the effect is anticipated in the command to Israel to "enlarge the place of [his] tent and [to] let the curtains of [his] habitations be stretched out" (Isa 54:2). This exhortation means that the number of people reached by God's revelation becomes increasingly larger.

Bibliography: Dickson, H. R. P., "The Tent and Its Furnishings," in *People and Cultures of the Middle East,* ed. Ailon Shiloh, Random House, 1969.

J.E.H.

918 ירק (*yrq*) **I. Assumed root of the following.**

918a יֶרֶק (*yereq*) ***green, greenness.***

918b יָרָק (*yārāq*) ***herbs, herbage.***

918c יָרוֹק (*yārôq*) ***green thing*** (only in Job 39:8).

918d יֵרָקוֹן (*yērāqôn*) ***mildew, paleness, lividness.***

918e יְרַקְרַק (*y^eraqraq*) ***greenish, pale green.***

919 יָרַק (*yāraq*) ***II, spit.***

יֵרָקוֹן (*yērāqôn*). See no. 918d.

יְרַקְרַק (*y^eraqraq*). See no. 918e.

920 יָרַשׁ (*yārash*) ***take possession off, dispossess, inherit, disinherit, occupy, seize, be an heir, impoverish*** (Qal); ***come to poverty, impoverish, be poor*** (Niphal); ***devour*** (Piel; Deut 28:42, the cricket devours the trees and the fruit of the ground); ***inherit, drive out, cast out, dispossess, destroy, make poor*** (Hiphil).

Derivatives

920a יְרֵשָׁה (*y^erēshâ*) ***a possession,*** only in Num 24:18.

920b יְרֻשָּׁה (*y^erūshshâ*) ***possession, inheritance.***

920c †רֶשֶׁת (*reshet*) ***net.***

920d †מוֹרָשׁ (*môrāsh*) ***possession.***

920e †מוֹרָשָׁה (*môrāshâ*) ***a possession.***

It is used with its derivatives (except *reshet*) 260 times. In civil matters the verb means to become an heir (cf. Jer 32:8). In military matters it means to gain control over a certain area by conquering and expelling the current inhabitants of that area. In such a light the word came to take on the meaning of "dispossess," "drive out," "cast out," and "seize."

Possession and Covenant

In Israel's history the root takes on its double force, to inherit and to dispossess, in relationship to the covenant. God made a covenant with Israel that they would become his own special people (e.g. Ex 19:5f.). A major benefit on Israel's side was the promise of an inheritance, namely a land where they could develop into a holy nation (Gen 15:8; Ex 6:8). Israel, however, became a people in Egypt before they occupied a land. Therefore to become a nation they had to gain possession of a land. They left Egypt, agreed to the covenant at Sinai and then proceeded to take Palestine as their possession. However, forty years passed between Sinai and the first successful attempt at conquest.

View of Taking Possession of the Land Found in Deuteronomy

The book of Deut was composed in the light that the people after the long years in the wilderness were about to begin their conquest. Consequently the highest number of occurrences of *yārash* appear in Deut. The program of conquest described in Deut emphasizes that the people had to live according to the law given at Sinai in order to have God's help in conquest (Deut 6:17ff.). Above all they had to be sure to live justly (Deut 16:20). Thereby God obligated himself to help them defeat the nations and to possess the land (Deut 12:29). However, before God could act it was imperative that the people come to the land.

I.e. they had to respond in faith expecting God to overcome their enemies by placing their lives in jeopardy on the battlefield. In other words, they had to present themselves to receive the promise. As long as they were obedient, God would go before them to dispel the inhabitants even though they were greater and mightier than Israel (Deut 7:1; 11:23; 31:3; Ps 44:2f. [H 3f.]). Deuteronomy anticipated that God would drive out the inhabitants in spectacular ways if needed, such as sending "hornets" among the nations (Deut 7:20). Here there was the crucial balance between the act of God and the responsive participation of the people, both of which were necessary to accomplish God's purpose (Deut 9:3). There was no doubt that it was God who gave them the land and the victory to possess it; yet they had to respond by actively participating in the taking possession for the plan of God to be realized. Further God acted through his people, but also through nature and circumstances so that the outcome accomplished was the best.

There was a fully moral basis to the conquest. Gen says Abraham could not possess the land because the sin of the Amorites was not yet complete (Gen 15:16). Leviticus 18:24–30 teaches that the morality of a people either allows them to occupy a land or else causes the land to expel them. The reason Israel possessed Canaan by dispossessing the Amorites was that the sin of its inhabitants abounded to the point that God no longer allowed them to occupy that land. In such a light Israel became the means of God's judgment on these nations (Deut 9:1–5; 18:12). Just as later Assyria was God's rod to punish Judah (Isa 10:5f.) Israel was not allowed to dispel the Amorites because Israel was larger, or more noble than they, but rather solely under the sovereignty of God did Israel serve as his instrument of judgment and solely under his love did they become the recipients of the inheritance (Deut 4:37f.). There is a definite theological pattern established here. Covenant results in inheritance, but one must come to the inheritance to obtain it. And he must be willing to face all opponents in obtaining the inheritance. Yet in reality it is God who defeats the opponents and allows the inheritance to be gained.

[An additional justification may be found here even on the secular plane, in that Canaan in the 15th–14th centuries was nominally a part of the Egyptian empire just then losing its grip. The Israelites had paid in bitter service in Egypt for every cubit of land the Lord gave them in Canaan! R.L.H.]

After possessing the land by expelling and destroying its inhabitants, the Israelites were to settle in it and establish a way of life based on obedience to the love of God (Deut 11:31f.). For this way of life to be realized the law was given to them for a possession (Deut 33:4). As long as this lifestyle would be maintained the land would be theirs forever (I Chr 28:8). Their ownership of the land was eternal, but their right to occupy it depended on their obedience to God. If they turned from God and followed abominable pagan practices, they lost the right to live there. Yet as long as they were obedient to God, he allowed them to continue their occupation of the land by helping them to overcome their enemies (e.g. II Chr 20:5–17).

Israel's Response

Under Joshua, Israel drove out many nations and occupied large portions of the land (Josh 12). However, there was much land left to be possessed (Josh 13:1–6; Jud 1). God used the nations which remained to test Israel in order to determine how complete was Israel's obedience to the law (Josh 23:12f.; Jud 2:3, 21ff.). When Israel fell to false worship, they became weak and encountered the wrath of God which caused these nations to oppress Israel. But when they turned back to God, he brought them deliverance. This pattern continued until Israel fell captive to Babylon (Neh 9:26–31). Prior to that day they suffered all kinds of misfortune which was intended to lead them to repentance. But the majority stubbornly continued to act disobediently; therefore God allowed other nations to possess them as their just punishment (Ezk 7:24; 33:23–24). Under the Persians a remnant returned to settle the land, but their continued occupation was dependent upon the same obedient response to God's law (cf. Ezr 9:10–15).

The Concept of Possession Generalized in the Psalms

The Psalms build on this pattern of living in the land by emphasizing that possession of the land belongs to those who fear the Lord (25:12f.), those who wait on the Lord (37:9), the meek (37:11), those blessed by the Lord (37:22) and the righteous (37:29). Those who enter into covenant with God receive an inheritance, but they must act to take possession of it and must live uprightly to maintain their inheritance. This idea is no doubt the background for the beatitude - "blessed are the meek, for they shall inherit the earth" (Mt 5:5).

Its Eschatological Use

The prophets pick up the themes around *yārash* as they foresee God's establishing his reign at the end of the age. The people will experience a "new Exodus," and they will again possess the land (Jer 30:3). Isaiah looks for the time when their descendants will possess the nations; i.e. instead of defeating them in battle the nations will also become God's people (Isa 54:3;

cf. Amos 9:12). Since the people will be transformed to follow righteousness, they will always hold the land (Isa 60:21). The idea carries over to the New Covenant in that the people of faith have the promise of an inheritance and yet before it is fully enjoyed the final conquest of their greatest opponent Satan must be accomplished.

môrāsh. ***A possession.*** In Job 17:11 *môrāshê lᵉbābî* (lit. "the possessions of my heart") is rendered "the desires of my heart" (RSV; ASV "thoughts"; BDB gives "my cherished thoughts").

môrāshâ. ***A possession, inheritance*** (ASV; cf. Ezk 33:24, RSV "to possess"), heritage (ASV; Ex 6:8).

reshet. ***Net.*** (ASV and RSV the same.) It appears twenty-two times. Net is an instrument used to catch game, as birds (Prov 1:17); it was made out of cords woven together. Sometimes a net was spread over a pit; the animal became entrapped in the net as he fell into the hole. It also indicates the bronze grate placed under the altar which extended (or set in the middle (?)) halfway to the ground and had four bronze rings at its corners (Ex 27:4f.; 38:4f.). It is translated "network" when used with *ma'ăśeh* "work."

This word is employed metaphorically to describe people being trapped by their enemies. The wicked spread nets to overcome the righteous (Ps 140:5 [H 6]), and the arrogant lay a net by flattery (Prov 29:5). However, they often become trapped in their own deeds (Job 18:8). Priests and rulers too lay a net for the people by entangling them in sin (Hos 5:1). On the other hand, God spreads a net for disobedient Israel (Hos 7:12; Ezk 12:13; 17:20; cf. 19:8) and for Pharoah (Ezk 32:3). It means they shall be taken into captivity. This image draws from real life, for a picture in ANEP 288 shows a Mesopotamian king containing his enemies in a net (cf. Lam 1:13). The righteous, however, escape the net of the wicked by confidently calling on God, their refuge (Ps 25:15; 31:4 [H 5]).

Bibliography: Miller, Patrick D., "The Gift of God: The Deuteronomic Theology of the Land," *Interp* 23: 451–65. Richardson, TWB, p. 112. Weinfeld, Moshe, *Deuteronomy and the Deuteronomic School,* Oxford: Clarendon, 1972.

J.E.H.

יִשְׂחָק (*yiśḥāq*). See no. 1905b.

921 יֵשׁ (*yēsh*) ***existence, there is, are.*** (RSV and ASV similar.)

As a noun only in Prov 8:21 where RSV reads "wealth" and ASV "substance." Elsewhere it appears as a particle which draws attention to the existence or presence of an object or a quality, the opposite of the negative *'ayin*. Generally a noun follows it; e.g. "there was grain in Egypt" (Gen 42:1). It is so employed to draw attention to the dynamic presence of God with his people in this world (cf. I Sam 17:46; Gen 28:16). Occasionally a noun precedes *yēsh* for additional emphasis (e.g. I Sam 21:4 [H 5]). With a participle it emphasizes that there is a person who exhibits the action or quality denoted by the verb, e.g. "One man pretends to be rich, yet has nothing" (*yēsh mit'ashshēr,* Prov 13:7). It can also take a pronominal suffix before the verb to indicate that the action denoted by that verb is actually being performed by that person (e.g. Gen 24:42, 49). After questions it may stand alone to indicate an affirmative answer (cf. I Sam 9:11f.). However, placed in a question it may express a doubt about the thing questioned; e.g., "are there any among the false gods of the nations that can bring rain?" (Jer 14:22).

Often it is accompanied by the preposition *l* to indicate possession; e.g. "I have enough" (Gen 33:11). With the infinitive preceded by *l* it suggests the possibility of the verb (e.g. II Chr 25:9). It appears also with other prepositions and adverbs of place (e.g. Jon 4:11; Jud 4:20). Used with *'et* or *'im* (with) it indicates accompaniment. *yēsh 'ăsher* in Num 9:20f. is translated "sometimes." Of interest is *yēsh 'et-napshᵉkem:* "(if) it be your mind" (ASV) or "(if) you are willing" (RSV, Gen 23:8).

J.E.H.

922 יָשַׁב (*yāshab*) ***sit, remain, dwell.***

Derivatives

922a †שֶׁבֶת (*shebet*) ***seat, dwelling.***
922b †שִׁיבָה (*shîbâ*) ***sojourn,*** only in II Sam 19:33.
922c †מוֹשָׁב (*môshāb*) ***seat, assembly.***
922d †תּוֹשָׁב (*tôshāb*) ***sojourner.***

This verb is used 1090 times. The root *yshb* appears in most Semitic languages, and now in Ugaritic *yṯb* "to sit." One new development is that when *yṯb* or Akkadian *wašābu* appear with *kussi* "throne," the verb yields the sense of "ascending the throne" (e.g. I Kgs 1:46).

Some have argued that this verb *yāshab* is never used of Yahweh "dwelling" on the earth or any appearance of Yahweh to Israel. According to this view, the verb *shākan* and its derivatives are reserved for any concepts of the immanence of God or of his "tabernacling with the men" of the OT. Usually the Lord is said to dwell in heaven (Ps 2:4; 9:7 [H 8]; 29:10; 55:20; 102:13; Lam 5:19) or is "enthroned with the cherubim" (I Sam 4:4; II Sam 6:2 = I Chr 13:6; II Kgs 19:15; Ps 99:1). In places where the Lord is said to dwell in heaven or in Zion, the thought is that he is enthroned. He is also "enthroned on the praises of Israel" (Ps 22:4), perhaps as a metonymy for the sanctuary where the Lord was praised. The idea of the cherubim must not be associated too closely with the ark of the tabernacle, since the verb does not mean "indwelling" and the cherubim elsewhere in Scripture are used in various self-manifestations of Yahweh (e.g. Ps 18:11, Ezk 1,10). According to M. Woudstra, this expression "served rather to direct the attention of the worshiper to the heavenly sanctuary with its heavenly Occupant, of which the earthly counterpart meant to be a faithful image" (M. Woudstra, *The Ark of the Covenant*, 1965, p. 70). *shākan* then would be a temporary indwelling on the earth, but as Solomon asks, "Will God indeed 'dwell' (*yēshēb*, permanently) on the earth?" (I Kgs 8:27). The answer is clear. On the other hand, it may be argued that some verses refer to the Lord's dwelling above the ark on earth, e.g. Ps 9:11 [H 12] reads: "Sing praises to the Lord who dwells in Zion." Also the statements about his being enthroned with the cherubim may refer to the ark.

The verb *yāshab* is also used of men. The Qal stem can be divided into four categories: 1. to sit on anything; 2. to remain, stay, linger; 3. to dwell in a house, city, territory; and 4. of a place, city, or country being inhabited.

The first category includes some special situations such as the sitting of judges in judgment (Ps 9:4 [H 5]; Isa 10:13; Ex 18:14) and of kings on their thrones (I Kgs 1:35,46). The second is usually followed by an accusative of place, or a dative of person. Even inanimate objects such as a bow can "remain" strong (Gen 49:24). In the third semantic range, one of the key verses theologically is Isa 45:18. God formed the earth for dwelling, i.e. for men to inhabit it. It was not meant to be a desolation or a chaos. One of the most frequent forms here is the Qal active participle, dweller, inhabitant (215 times according to BDB). Therefore when the prophets predict the desolation and depopulation of an invader's land they speak of it as being "without inhabitant" (Isa 6:11; Jer 4:7; Zeph 2:8). The opposite of this depopulation is category four, a land, city, or country "abiding in its place" (Isa 13:20; Jer 17:6; Ezk 26:20; Zech 2:8).

The verb is used in the Piel stem once (Ezk 25:4), Niphal stem fifteen times, Hiphil stem about forty times, and three times in the Hophal stem.

shebet. *Seat, dwelling, place.* There are only six instances of this word used as a substantive (rather than as an infinitive of *yāshab*) in the OT. Its basic meaning is expressed in its use as the seat on Solomon's throne (I Kgs 10:19; II Chr 9:18). Literally the text is "the place of sitting."

In Amos 6:3, it refers to the "seat or throne of violence." This abstract sense uses "seat" as a technical term for a judicial seat or throne. Cf. the Ugaritic evidence for this new meaning.

Obadiah 3 uses it to refer to Edom's dwelling place. Numbers 21:15 and II Sam 23:7 illustrate its use as site, location, or spot. The former relates to the "location (or site) of Ar" while the latter says "they are burned on the spot." These usages are similar to those of *môshāb* in II Kgs 2:19 and Ezk 8:3 (see below).

shîbâ. *Sojourn* (RSV "stay"). This form of the noun is found only in II Sam 19:32 [H 33]. It is most unusual since there is an anomalous aphaeresis of the initial yod and the introduction of a medial yod as if it were influenced by the root *shûb* "to return." The meaning of the corrected reading *b^{e}shibtô* "during his sojourn" or "while he stayed" is clear.

môshāb. *Seat, assembly, dwelling place, dwellers.* This masculine noun appears forty-five times. Basic to its other meanings is the seat of David or Saul at the banquet table (I Sam 29:18, 25; cf. Job 29:7) or even the imagined seat among the gods which the king of Tyre had conjured up in his mind (Ezk 28:2). Collectively, many seats taken together refer to a sitting or even an assembly of officials (I Kgs 10:5), the wicked (Ps 1:1), or elders (Ps 107:32).

Then the dwelling place of a city, tribe, or people was so designated (Gen 10:30; 27:39; Num 15:2; 31:10). Zion is called the dwelling place of Yahweh (Ps 132:13). Even houses could be called dwellings (Lev 25:29; Ex 12:20 etc.). Then the people in them were called inhabitants, or dwellers (II Sam 9:12).

Several unusual applications appear: the site or setting for a city (II Kgs 2:19), the location of an idol (Ezk 8:3) and by metonymy, the time of dwelling in Egypt (Ex 12:40).

Many commentators wish to change "their dwelling places" in Ezk 37:23 to "their apostasies," from *meshûb*. The textual evidence is limited to Syriac with the Greek reading "their abominations."

tôshāb. *Sojourner.* Occurring fourteen times, seven times in Lev 25, this noun refers to the temporary, landless wage earner. The term is used with *gēr* (permanent resident, alien) to describe Abraham in Canaan (Gen 23:4), and the Israelites in God's eyes (Lev 25:23, 35; Ps 39:12 [H 13]; I Chr 29:15). It is also used as a synonym for a hired servant (Ex 12:45; Lev 22:10; 25:40). The *tôshāb* could not eat the Passover, and his children were not exempt from being sold as slaves (Lev 25:45). But he could seek the protection of the cities of refuge (Num 35:15).

So his freedom was not as great as that of the *gēr* even though he shared some of his privileges.

Bibliography: Cross, Frank, "The Priestly Tabernacle," in *Biblical Archaeologist Reader,* G. Ernest Wright, David N. Freedman, eds., vol. I, Doubleday, 1961, pp. 225–27. DeVaux, R., *Ancient Israel,* McGraw-Hill, 1961, pp. 75–76. Woudstra, Martin, *The Ark of the Covenant from Conquest to Kingship,* Presbyterian and Reformed, 1965, pp. 68–77.

W.C.K.

923 ישה (yshh). **Assumed root of the following.**
923a †תּוּשִׁיָּה (*tûshîyâ*) ***wisdom, sound knowledge.*** Delitzsch (*Proverbs,* p. 77) suggests "an advancement of that which profits," particularly true wisdom. (For synonyms see *ḥokmâ.*)

Among the usages of this technical word is sound efficient wisdom, i.e. sound judgment, wisdom that leads to practical success. Thus the son will find life and honor if he follows his father's sound judgment (Prov 3:21f.). Because personified wisdom gives this quality to kings, they rule effectively. On the other hand, God frustrates the shrewd so that their hands cannot attain success (Job 5:12). Sound judgment is based on the righteous character of God's rule. The upright have sound wisdom hidden in them (Prov 2:7). But Job questioned whether his wisdom, his ability to succeed, was driven from him in his adversity (Job 6:13).

L.G.

יְשׁוּעָה (*yeshû'â*). See no. 929b.

924 ישח (yshḥ). **Assumed root of the following.**
924a יֶשַׁח (*yeshaḥ*) ***emptiness (of hunger).*** Meaning conjectured from context. Occurs only in Mic 6:14.

925 *יָשַׁט (*yāshaṭ*) ***extend, hold out.*** Occurs only in the Hiphil (Est 4:11; 5:2; 8:4).

926 יִשַׁי (*yīshay*) ***Jesse.*** (ASV and RSV the same.) Derivation uncertain.

The name appears seventeen times. Jesse, an inhabitant of Bethlehem in Judah, had eight sons, including David the king. Jesse was a pious man and a strong supporter of the state. David is often called the son of Jesse, and the Messiah is referred to as the root or stump of Jesse (Isa 11:1, 10), in line with the tendency to use alternative expressions to indicate the promise to David's line. Cf. the "Branch of David" (Jer 23:5), the "tabernacle of David" (Amos 9:11) and, probably, the city of David, "Bethlehem" (Mic 5:2 [H 1]).

Bibliography: Bauer, H., "Die hebräischen Eigennamen als sprachliche Erkenntnisquelle," ZAW 48: 77. Clines, D. J. A., "X, X Ben Y, Ben Y: Personal Names," VT 22: 266–87. He argues persuasively that the references to David as son of Jesse are not derogatory. Driver, G. R., "New Aramaeo Jewish Names in Egypt," JEA 25: 175f.

יְשִׁימָה (*yeshîmâ*). See no. 927a.
יְשִׁימוֹן (*yeeshîmôn*). See no. 927b.
יָשִׁישׁ (*yāshîsh*). See no. 931b.

927 יָשַׁם (*yāsham*) ***be desolate, ruin.*** (ASV "desolate"; RSV also "ruin," "strip" and "appall."

Derivatives

927a †יְשִׁימָה (*yeshîmâ*) ***desolation.***
927b †יְשִׁימוֹן (*yeshîmôn*) ***waste, desert.***

yāsham and its derivatives occur eighteen times. The root is primarily concerned with the desolate condition of arid land, most often the desert land around the Dead Sea, the Negeb, and the Sinai.

During the years of famine in Egypt at the time of Joseph, the Egyptians sold their land and themselves for food and bought seed so that they could sow the land that it might not become desolate (Gen 47:19). Three of the four occurrences of the verb appear in Ezk to describe the coming judgment on Judah. Armies were about to march through, destroying crops, polluting fertile fields, often burning and devastating fortresses and cities. As a result the land would become desolate (Ezk 12:19; 19:7). Particular destruction was directed at the high places, the quiet groves which were lush and refreshing and where altars to fertility gods were erected (Ezk 6:6). The desolation of these shrines demonstrated to the people that those gods were false, unable to help in time of distress.

After the Exodus from Egypt, God led the people through the desert. He encircled them and protected them from their enemies (Deut 32:10). According to Ps 107:4ff., God found Israel wandering in the desert and became their guide and protection. It was here that God appeared through many natural phenomena and spoke to the people directly and through Moses (cf. Ps 68:7f. [H 8f.]). However, before and after Mt. Sinai the people tested God by complaining about their condition and by craving food and water (Ps 106:14). Each time God was able to meet their complaints and supply their needs; however, some type of judgment against the unbelief generally accompanied the granting of the request. Isa in the latter part of his prophecy picks up the theme of God's new saving events, which will be a new Exodus. Once again the people in leaving the land of their captivity and returning to Jerusalem will have to pass through the desolate wilderness. As in the former Exodus, God will make a way through the desert and will provide rivers of water to meet the parched thirst of his people (Isa 43:19).

y^e^shîmâ. ***Desolation*** (Ps 55:15 [H 6]). ASV and RSV accept Qere (*yashshîmāwet*): "Let death come upon them"; *i.e.* when they go down to Sheol. Of course, the Kethib, "desolation be upon them," makes sense, for there is no place more desolate than Sheol.

y^e^shîmôn. ***Waste, desert, wilderness.*** Frequently *y^e^shîmôn* is paralleled with "wilderness" (*midbār*) and translated "desert." RSV takes it as a toponym in I Sam 23:19, 24; 26:1, 3; possibly it is a proper name in Num 21:20; 23:28; it is most likely located in the Arabah, near the north side of the Dead Sea and to the north and west of the hill of Hachilah and to the north of Maon. In this vicinity David hid from Saul.

J.E.H.

928 יָשֵׁן (*yāshēn*) Qal, ***sleep, be asleep;*** Piel, ***make (one) go to sleep*** (Jud 16:19). (ASV and RSV similar; but RSV "dream" in Ps 90:5; in Hos 7:6 ASV "their baker sleepeth," while RSV [with different vocalization] "their anger smolders.")

Derivatives

928a יָשֵׁן (*yāshēn*) ***sleeping.***
928b יָשָׁן (*yāshān*) ***old.***
928c שֵׁנָה (*shēnâ*), שֵׁנָא (*shēnā'*), שְׁנָת (*sh^e^nāt*) ***sleep.***

Sleep is a blessing; it provides rest and refreshment. One who works hard, though poor, has sweet sleep; but the rich in their surfeit are denied this refreshment (Eccl 5: 12 [H 11]; cf. Ps 3:5 [H 6]; 4:8 [H 9]). One is not to love sleep, for that will lead to poverty (Prov 6:10f.; 20:13). Neither is one to rob himself of rest to increase his wealth (Ps 127:2). Sleep, however, can afford the opportunity for an opponent to gain the advantage; e.g. Delilah robbed Samson of his strength during his sleep (Jud 16:20).

In the new age Yahweh will make a new covenant of peace restoring harmony between man and nature once again. Then man may lie down to sleep in the woods unafraid of nature (Ezk 34:25).

God may communicate a message during one's sleep; e.g. God caused Pharoah to dream about the approaching famine (Gen 41:1–7). While Adam slept very deeply, the Lord took part of his side and created Eve (Gen 2:21f.).

Sleep was a quality ascribed to pagan gods, e.g. Elijah's taunt concerning Baal's being asleep (I Kgs 18:27). In contrast, the Psalmist says concerning Yahweh, "He who keeps Israel will neither slumber nor sleep" (Ps 121:4). Amidst a polytheistic environment this confession possessed dramatic content. Yet figuratively sleep is attributed to Yahweh for his apparent inactivity by one who has heard about but not experienced his great deeds (Ps 44:23 [H 24]). Similarly Yahweh's bursting into action is described as his awaking from sleep (Ps 78: 65f.).

Sleep may stand as a euphemism for death (Ps 13:3 [H 4]). In the last days Yahweh will raise up "those who sleep in the dust of the earth" (Dan 12:2). Their new life will be one of either everlasting life or everlasting contempt.

J.E.H.

929 *יָשַׁע (*yāsha'*) ***be saved, be delivered*** (Niphal); ***save, deliver, give victory, help; be safe; take vengeance, preserve*** (Hiphil); ASV, "rescue" "defend cause"; RSV, substantive "savior." (ASV and RSV similar, but interchange synonyms.)

Derivatives

929a יֵשַׁע (*yēsha'*) ***salvation, deliverance.***
929b יְשׁוּעָה (*y^e^shû'â*) ***salvation.***
929c †שׁוֹעַ (*shôa'*) ***independent, noble.***
929d מוֹשָׁעָה (*môshā'â*) only as *môshā'ôt,* saving acts (Ps 68:21).
929e תְּשׁוּעָה (*t^e^shû'â*) ***salvation, deliverance.***

yāsha' and its derivatives are used 353 times. The root meaning in Arabic is "make wide" or "make sufficient"; this root is in contrast to *ṣārar* "narrow," which means "be restricted" or "cause distress." That which is wide connotes freedom from distress and the ability to pursue one's own objectives. To move from distress to safety requires deliverance. Generally the deliverance must come from somewhere outside the party oppressed. In the OT the kinds of distress, both national and individual, include enemies, natural catastrophies, such as plague or famine, and sickness. The one who brings deliverance is known as the "savior." The word may be used, however, in everyday life free of theological overtones; e.g., at a well Moses saved the daughters of Reuel from being driven off by the shepherds (Ex 2:17). But generally in the OT the word has strong religious meaning, for it was Yahweh who wrought the deliverance. Thus he is known as the "God of our salvation" (Ps 68:19f. [H 20f.]). Although salvation could come through a human agent, it was only because God empowered the agent. In the NT the idea of salvation primarily means forgiveness of sin, deliverance from its power and defeat of Satan. Although the OT begins to pointin this direction, the majority of references to salvation speak of Yahweh granting deliverance from real enemies and out of real catastrophies.

Kinds of Salvation

At various times Israel, oppressed by other nations, had to go to war to win and to maintain its freedom. In these battles the nation turned to God for help. They believed that the outcome of the battle belonged to Yahweh (I Sam 17:47). Thus they ventured out in the assurance of a victorious outcome. The focal point of God's saving deeds in the OT was the deliverance of Israel from Egyptian bondage (Ex 14:30). Thereby they became known as a people saved by Yahweh (Deut 33:29). Such deeds of salvation became a witness of the lordship of Yahweh not only to future generations, but also to the surrounding nations (cf. Ps 106:8; I Sam 4:6ff.). Later as the Israelites anticipated entering the promised land, Moses said, "the Lord your God is he that goes with you, to fight for you against your enemies, to give you the victory" (Deut 20:4). God fulfilled this promise through Joshua, who led the people to take possession of Canaan. Afterwards when Israel was oppressed by one of the surrounding nations, God delivered them through a judge (Jud 2:16). The general pattern was to endow the judge with his Spirit in order that he could defeat Israel's enemies. Later under the kingdom Israel defeated their enemies by a righteous king who was anointed and aided by Yahweh (I Sam 9:16; Ps 20:6 [H 7]). The truly believing leader ventured forth in the spirit of the words of Jonathan, "nothing can hinder the Lord from saving by many or by few" (I Sam 14:6). The salvation from God was the king's glory and firmly established his authority over the people (Ps 21:5 [H 6]). It became imperative as the nation grew in power and prestige for the king and the people to realize that salvation does not come by a mighty army, but solely from the power of God (Ps 44:1–8 [H 2–9]). Although God generally used human agents to bring salvation, the obstacles surmounted were so spectacular that there unquestionably had to be special help from God himself (cf. Prov 21:31). Here is the creative tension between divine action and human response which establishes God's purpose on earth and yet builds the character of his people. Sometimes God may do the work totally, and all man has to do is wait and see the mighty deeds of the Lord (II Chr 20:17; cf. Hos 1:7). Building on this historical pattern of God's saving deeds through a charismatic leader arose the concept of a future savior who would fulfill the role of a king anointed with God's Spirit (cf. Jer 23:5f.).

Salvation may be not only offensive, but also defensive. When opposition comes, one may retreat to a refuge for safety. God is frequently viewed as this refuge for his people; "On God rests my deliverance and my honor; my mighty rock, my refuge is God" (Ps 62:7 [H 8]). One who experiences salvation does not need to be tormented by internal anxiety. It is true that he will have to endure opposition, but God will ensure that his opponents do not destroy him. The protective nature of salvation is seen in other concepts, namely "the shield of salvation" (Ps 18:35 [H 36]), "a helmet of salvation" (Isa 59:17; Eph 6:17), "the garments of salvation" (Isa 61:10). Thus salvation is not merely a momentary victory on the battlefield; it is also the safety and security necessary to maintain life unafraid of numerous dangers. As the OT looks for the city of God at the end of the age, it sees that its walls will be called "Salvation" (Isa 60:18). This city is only for the righteous, and it provides all the security attending salvation (Isa 26:1).

Spiritual Meaning

The word "save" developed a theological meaning in that God saves by forgiving sin and by changing the character of an individual; e.g. "I will save them from all the backslidings in which they have sinned" (Ezk 37:23). David realized this and prayed, "Deliver me from bloodguiltiness, O God, thou God of my salvation" (Ps 51:14 [H 16]; cf. Ps 79:9). In Jer 17:14 "save" parallels "heal"; i.e. salvation becomes a dynamic force bringing emotional and physical well-being.

Salvation and Righteousness

All of Yahweh's saving deeds are built on righteousness, reflected by the fact that "righteousness" and "salvation" are often found in parallelism (e.g. Isa 51:8). Although every act of deliverance contains judgment, those who are judged are guilty and therefore deserve this justice (cf. Ps 76:8f. [H 9f.]). On the other side, God is true to the covenant and to the creation of man in his own image by acting to provide man a means of deliverance from his original disobedience. In this regard God fulfills his responsibility as Redeemer through being a Savior. Yahweh is thus known as "a righteous God and a Savior" (Isa 45:21).

Character of God Revealed

The salvation which God accomplishes reveals his universal reign (cf. Isa 33:22). His kingdom over the entire world allows him to work salvation for whomever he wills. Further deeds of salvation destroy the purposes of the forces of evil, often personified as the sea and the sea monster (Ps 74:12ff.). Thus every victory moves toward the final salvation for all of his people. God's ability to give salvation provides the basis for man to worship him; i.e. only a god who can save is worthy of worship. Therefore a frequent polemic against idolatry is to challenge the other gods to bring deliverance to their oppressed followers (Isa 46:7; Jud 6:31). Their failure to respond demonstrates that those gods are vain and leads to the confession that besides Yahweh there is no savior (Isa 43:11; Hos 13:4). To ensure that the deeds of salvation are not viewed as a mere accident of history, Yahweh reveals what he is going to do before he does it (Isa 43:12). Then he is faithful to his word by performing it. Afterwards the act is interpreted and proclaimed. The saving deed then is determinative for the nature of each generation's relationship with Yahweh, and its proclamation inspires the faith to establish and to maintain the relationship (*cf.* Isa 52:7).

Further salvation witnesses to the fact that God cares about his people. Salvation flows from his love (cf. Deut 7:7f.). Because the faithful comprehend God's steadfast love, they turn to him for deliverance in times of distress (Ps 6:4 [H 5]; 109:26). Salvation is thus God's love in action.

Salvation also witnesses to the active presence of God among his people and with his leaders. Many commissioned with a task were promised his presence in a special way. God promised Jeremiah, "I am with you to deliver you" (Jer 1:8, 19; cf. Mt 28:20). Jeremiah was later imprisoned, and at various times his life was endangered, but his opponents were never able to destroy him. Moses too succeeded by this promise (Ex 3:12). Thus the presence of God among his people accomplishes their deliverance from adversaries and out of troubles.

Preparation and Response of the People

A. Repentance and Trust. Man must prepare himself to receive God's salvation. When in distress, he must seek God in prayer (e.g., Jud 3:9; Ps 69:1 [H 2]). I. e., he must recognize his need and humble himself before God with a contrite heart (cf. Job 22:29; Ps 34:18 [H 19]). Turning to God involves forsaking sin, for sin hinders God from helping those in distress (Isa 59:1f.).

Once man has sincerely turned to God, he must express his confidence in God by waiting for salvation (Isa 30:15). God chooses the time to act; man must wait in hope. God expects his people to endure difficult circumstances in faith as he chooses the most opportune time to bring salvation. While one awaits salvation, he is actively involved in pursuing righteousness and in expressing love (Isa 56:1; Hos 10:12; 12:6).

B. Hymns of Praise. Man's immediate response to God's saving deeds, actual or anticipated, is in hymns of praise. The Song of the Sea was composed and sung immediately following the deliverance at the Red Sea (Ex 15:1–18). Isaiah's description of salvation through the coming Messiah is followed by song in chapter 12, and three of the servant songs end with singing: 42:10ff.; 49:13; 54:1ff. Singing gives expression to the joy attending God's salvation. Joy is frequently mentioned as man's inner response to God's victory (e.g., Ps 13:5 [H 6]). Further those who have received Yahweh's help feel compelled to share it with others; "I have not hid thy saving help within my heart, I have spoken of thy faithfulness and thy salvation" (Ps 40:10 [H 11]). Thus God's salvation fills life with meaning and joy.

Future Salvation

The return of Israel from captivity is anticipated in the language of salvation. Yahweh says, "I will save you from afar" (Jer 30:10; Zech 8:7). Since God considers the people his flock, he declares, "I will save my flock, they shall no longer be a prey" (Ezk 34:22).

Since there is no salvation outside of Yahweh, he extends the invitation, "Turn to me and be saved, all the ends of the earth! For I am God, and there is no other" (Isa 45:22; cf. Ps 67:2 [H 3]). The prophets look to the time when salvation will affect all nations and be everlasting. Isaiah foresees this salvation coming through the suffering servant. Because of the servant's obedient endurance of suffering, God promises, "I will give you as a light to the nations, that my salvation may reach to the end of the earth" (Isa 49:6). In other words, the acts of salvation in the OT build toward the final act of salvation which will include all people under its possible blessing (Isa 52:10).

shôʻa. ***Noble, honorable, rich*** (RSV and ASV), bountiful (ASV). Whether its root is *y-sh-ʻ* (BDB) or *sh-w-ʻ* (KB) is debated. In Isa 32:5 it parallels "the noble" (*nādîb*) and in Job 34:19 it stands in contrast to "the poor" (*dal*). It probably indicates those who receive recognition due to their wealth in property. But God does not grant special favor to the noble over the poor, for both are his work. And during the reign of the righteous king, the world's false values will be altered in that the knave will no longer be considered noble.

Bibliography: Foerster and Fohrer, "Sōzō," in TDNT, VII, pp. 965–1024. Pedersen, Johs, *Israel, Its Life and Culture,* vols. 1–2, London: Geoffrey Cumberlege, 1964. Barr, James, "An Aspect of Salvation in the OT," *Man and His Salvation,* ed. E. J. Sharp and J. R. Hinnels, Manchester Univ Press, 1973, pp. 39–52. Richardson, TWB, pp. 219–20. TDNT, VII, pp. 970–89; 1012–15; III, pp. 284–93. THAT, I, pp. 785–89.

J.E.H.

929.1 יָשְׁפֵה (*yāshpeh*) ***jasper.***

930 יָשַׁר (*yāshar*) ***be level, straight, (up) right, just, lawful.*** (ASV, RSV, NEB similar except that they vary translations with "honest," "righteous.")

Derivatives

930a †יָשָׁר (*yāshār*) ***(up-) right.***
930b יֹשֶׁר (*yōsher*) ***uprightness, straightness.***
930c יְשָׁרָה (*y^e^shārâ*) ***uprightness.***
930d †יְשֻׁרוּן (*y^e^shūrûn*) ***upright, law keeping, Jeshurun.***
930e †מֵישָׁר (*mêshār*) ***uprightness, straightness.***
930f †מִישׁוֹר (*mîshôr*) ***level place, uprightness.***

The root *y-sh-r* is employed in at least three ways.

1. Literally. "To go straight or direct in the way" (I Sam 6:12), but more frequently in the intensive (Piel) "to make (a way) straight," i.e. direct and level and free from obstacles, as when preparing to receive a royal visitor. This is the work of God for man (Prov 3:6 KJV "direct"), but also of man for God (Isa 40:3). It is "to look straight ahead of you" (Prov 4:25), to do something evenly (I Kgs 6:35, KJV) as Solomon's overlaying the cherubs with gold or Hezekiah's designing the aqueduct bringing it straight (II Chr 32:30, KJV) to the west of Jerusalem.

2. Ethically. Uprightness as the manner of life is a characteristic of the blameless (Prov 11:5) and of the man of discernment (Ps 119:128, "I have lived uprightly"). Thus the fact that God has made man upright (Eccl 7:29) is probably to be interpreted as granting him the ability to recognize the divine law, rather than some inborn character as honest or straightforward (so NEB). It is said of the reckless that his soul is not upright within him (Hab 2:4) and this leads to pride and failure.

yāshār. ***Upright.*** The attributive adjective is used to emphasize an attribute of: a. God, describing his reign over his people (Deut 32:4), his ways (Hos 14:10), words (Ps 111:8), and judgments (Ps 119:137); b. especially qualified persons, as a parallel to the righteous (Ps 33:1) or the perfect (Job 1:1, 8). It is a quality of heart and mind (Ps 7:11; 11:2, et al.) which enables the upright man to keep loyally to any legally binding agreement (II Kgs 10:15). It is not always possible to be sure whether the "level" path (Jer 31:9) or "straight" foot is to be understood as an ethical appraisal of the way of life or literally. Certainly the nouns meaning "uprightness" are used of a moral quality of heart (*yōsher*, Deut 9:5; I Kgs 9:4), as often in Prov (2:13; 4:11) which results in "right paths," i.e. right both morally and practically (Job 33:23). This was a characteristic of David's life (I Kgs 3:6, *y^e^shārâ*, only here). It is used both of words spoken (Job 6:25) and written (Eccl 12:10).

3. As an idiomatic expression with "eyes." "To be right in the eyes (of a person)" is to have his approval by keeping his commands. It is used of God (Num 23:27; Jer 27:5) perhaps also under the figure of the Potter (Jer 18:4). When marriage was so considered by Samson (Jud 14:3, 7), Saul, and David (I Sam 18:26), it can be rendered "lawful" as in Ugaritic (*yšr;* Van Zijl, *Alter Orient und Altes Testament* 10:83). Similarly when a treaty (II Sam 17:4) or religious action (II Chr 30:4) was ratified by an assembly.

A fuller phrase "to do what is right (*hay yāshār*, the right) in the eyes of the Lord" is linked with obedience to his commands (Ex 15:26; Deut 6:17–18) and covenant (Deut 12:28; 13:19). It is commonly used by the so-called Deuteronomist historian in his summary evaluation of the reigns of the kings of Israel and Judah. Thus David is said to have followed the Lord's commands (I Kgs 15:5–7) and the laws of Moses (I Kgs 14:8) as did Solomon when he followed his father's statutes, which were the same as those of the Lord (I Kgs 3:3, 14). Asa (I Kgs 15:11; II Chr 14:1) and Josiah (II Kgs 22:2) were similarly described as having done the right. So Jehoshaphat did the same as had Asa (II Chr 10:32), Azariah as did Amaziah (II Kgs 15:3; cf. II Chr 25:2) and Amaziah as did Joash (II Kgs 14:3). Hezekiah did the right in that he kept the commandments which the Lord had commanded Moses (II Kgs 18:6). Note that this phrase implies the existence and knowledge of the law of God, and that individual kings were thought to have kept it. This was shown by the king taking action (the so-called reforms) to ensure that the people also kept the Law. Such action was marked by public decrees which might include remission of dues, deliverance from oppressive legislation (Josh 9:23ff.), and the observance of religious festivals (Passover). Even when a king was said to have done the right, any major omission in his endorsement of the whole law is carefully noted ("except in the case of") Hezekiah's public act was initiated in the first full regnal year. It has been pointed out that there is a somewhat similar practice among Mesopotamian kings who effected the continuity of law and order by issuing *mēsharum*, decrees (Wiseman, D. J., "The Laws of Hammurabi Again," JSS 7: 167–68). In this phrase the OT uses *yshr* with the force of law-keeping, doing justice according to the law, which was the norm (as the Akkadian *išartu* is used of what is normal in writing).

mîshôr. ***Level place, uprightness.*** **mêshār.** ***Uprightness, straightness (in government), justice.*** *mêshārîm* and *mîshôr* could well be translated "justly" (with justice) or "lawfully" (as in Ug 'Anat 3.3) and describe the way judgment is given (Ps 58:1 [H 2]; 75:2 [H 3], RSV "with equity"). With the verb "to judge" it means "decide in favour" (KB). It is the way a people should be judged (Ps 67:4 [H 5]; KJV righteously; RSV with equity; NEB with justice). To do this is holding to the covenant (Mal 2:6). It is the Lord who declares "justice" (Isa 4 :19) and this sense of the word persists (Dan 11:6, *la'ăśôt mēshārîm* "to make an equitable arrangement"). Occasionally these nouns are clearly used in a legal context (Prov 2:9; cf. Ps 17:2). They are not really synonymous with righteousness (*ṣedeq*) although often used in parallel with it, with good (*ṭôb*) and with judgment (*mishpāṭ*). Cf. also Ugaritic *ṣdq*. In Akkadian documents "justice" also appears as a deity (^{d}Mišarum; *Ugaritica* 5: 220, line 166), namely the son of the sun-god Shamash, who was in Mesopotamia the primary god of justice.

y^{e}shûrûn. *Jeshurun.* Jeshurun is a proper name used only of Israel, in four passages. The parallelism of Jacob and Israel with Jacob and Jeshurun (Deut 32:15; Isa 44:2, Jeshurun) makes it clear that the reference must be to Jacob under his name Israel (so Deut 33:5). The Lord is "God of Jeshurun" (Deut 33:26).

While it might designate Israel as an ideal, upright one (so Gr, Vulg *rectissimus, dilectus*) it is more probable that the sense of law-keeping or upholding justice is appropriate here; they are a *Rechtsfolk* who possess the law. The old etymology as a diminutive of *yāshûr* "good little people" cannot be supported since there is no evidence of such a diminutive formation in Hebrew; nor would the title be apposite. Personal names in *-ûn* do occur (possibly as hypocoristica) and the possibly contemporary name of Jesher, the son of Caleb (I Chr 2:18) the Ras Shamra name of Mišara (*Ugaritica* 5, RS 17.325), and Ugaritic *bn mšrm* "son of uprightness" (UT 19: no. 1566) may be compared, even though they lack the termination.

The "book of Jashar" (Josh 10:13) is given as a source or record of Israel's defeat of the Amorites. It also recorded the defeat and death of Saul and Jonathan at the hands of the Philistines and David's lament for them (II Sam 1:18). It contained information which could be quoted or taught. While most scholars consider it a collection of ancient national poetry, it may well have been part of the pre-monarchy state records which would have included written agreements or other publicly issued statements similar to the *mšrm* decrees.

The noun *mîshôr*, derived from *yāshār*, means primarily "a level place," and is used for geographical descriptions as well as to connote "justice" discussed above in connection with *mêshārîm*.

Thus it marks the "plain" in contrast to the hills (I Kgs 20:23–25; it is so rendered by KJV, RSV, JB, NEB, or as opposed to the valleys (Isa 40:11). In Isa 42:16 it may be translated "level tracks" (JB) or "(straighten) twisted roads" (NEB). As used in David's prayers (Ps 26:12; 27:11; 143:10), the word could mean a level place or be figurative for a place of safety, comfort, and prosperity (BDB). It may denote justice or the blessing which follows from lawkeeping in view of the invocation of the Lord as judge (Ps 26:1f.). In Jer 21:13, "the rock of theplain" seems to refer to a precise topographical location in Jerusalem (KB), perhaps the palace on Ophel (JB).

In a number of verses *mîshôr* marks a specific region of Jordan, north of the Arnon River, which was captured by the Hebrews. It lay in the desert wilderness (Deut 4:43) where there was grazing (II Chr 26:10). Within the area were villages (Deut 3:10) as well as one of the cities of refuge (Josh 20:8).

Bibliography: Finkelstein, J. J., "Some new *misharum* material with its implications," in *Studies in Honor of B. Landsberger*, ed. Hans G. Güterbock and Thorkild Jacobsen, Chicago: University Press, 1965. Richardson, TWB, p. 273. THAT, I, pp. 790–93.

D.J.W.

יְשֻׁרוּן (*y^{e}shūrûn*). See no. 930d.

931 ישׁשׁ (*yshsh*). **Assumed root of the following.**

931a יָשֵׁשׁ (*yāshēsh*) ***aged, decrepit.*** Occurs only in II Chr 36:17.

931b יָשִׁישׁ (*yāshîsh*) ***aged.*** Occurs exclusively in Job (12:12; 15:10; 29:8; 32:6).

932 יתד (*ytd*). **Assumed root of the following.**

932a †יָתֵד (*yātēd*) ***peg, stake, pin.*** (ASV prefers "pin" and "nail"; RSV "peg.")

It appears twenty-four times. Pegs were used to secure tents and bronze pegs held the tabernacle together (Ex 27:19). They were also fastened into the wall to hang utensils on and used in conjunction with a loom (Jud 16:14). In his parable Ezekiel points out that when a vine ceases to bear fruit, its only value, it can not be used even for a peg (Ezk 15:3). One was to carry a peg (ASV "paddle," RSV "stick") with him in order to dig a hole in case of an emergency (Deut 23:13 [H 14]). Jael, while entertaining Sisera in her tent, performed a heroic deed by hammering a peg through his skull (Jud 4:21f.; 5:26).

Interestingly peg is used in a positive manner in regard to the blessing of God. Ezra speaks about the blessing God has bestowed in terms of giving a nail (RSV "secure hold") within his holy place

(Ezr 9:8). To emphasize the extending importance of the servant's ministry Isaiah exhorts to enlarge the tent, to lengthen the cords and to strengthen the stakes (Isa 54:2). Similarly Jerusalem will become "an immovable tent, whose stakes will never be plucked up" (Isa 33:20). The certainty and stability of David's throne is pictured as a nail fastened in a sure place (Isa 22:23, cf. Zech 10:4). However, before God establishes the true kingdom, the false rulership, as a securely fastened peg, and all that relies on it will give way (Isa 22:25).

J.E.H.

יָתוֹם (*yātôm*). See no. 934a.
יָתוּר (*yātûr*). See no. 936, passive participle.

933 יתח (*ytḥ*). **Assumed root of the following.**
933a תּוֹתָח (*tôtāḥ*) ***name of a weapon, perhaps a club or mace (Job 41:21).***

934 יתם (*ytm*). **Assumed root of the following.**
934a †יָתוֹם (*yātôm*) ***orphan, fatherless.*** (ASV and RSV similar.)

It occurs forty-one times. The orphan, generally associated with the sojourner and the widow, is the object of special concern. The quality of one's devotion is measured by how one treats the widow and the orphan. Justice is especially due them (Deut 24:17); if not, the curse of God comes on the congregation (Deut 24:19). Although they have occasion to mourn, they are not excluded from the pilgrim festivals. They are invited to join and rejoice as are all the sons of Israel (Deut 16:11–14). A corrupt society extorts the sojourner, wrongs the orphan and the widow, and expresses contempt for father and mother (Ezk 22:7; cf. Isa 10:2). E.g., they drive away the orphan's donkey and take the widow's ox in pledge (Job 24:3). Those who mistreat the orphan and the widow are paralleled with adulterers, sorcerers and perjurers in Mal 3:5. But God himself provides for the basic needs of these unfortunates (Deut 10:18) and is known as the "Father of the fatherless" (Ps 68:5 [H 6]). This fact is reflected in the laws that forbid picking up fallen sheaves, or regleaning the vine or the olive tree (Deut 24:19ff.). Also they along with the Levites receive a portion of the tithes of the produce given every third year (Deut 14:28f.). The word occurs also in Ugaritic (UT 19: no. 1168) where the chief god El also is said to be beneficent to the orphan and the widow. This common consciousness of mercy is not surprising. The specific laws of Ugaritic on such matters have not been preserved.

J.E.H.

935 יתן (*ytn*). **Assumed root of the following.**
935a †אֵיתָן (*'êtān*) ***I, perennial, everflowing.***
935b †אֵיתָן (*'êtān*) ***II, Ethan.***

'êtān, ***I. Perennial, everflowing, permanent, enduring.*** (ASV and RSV differ frequently, ASV prefers words related to "strong.")

It is used thirteen times. It refers to the continual existence of a phenomenon of nature as the perennial running water in a stream (Deut 21:4); such a stream is especially valuable in Palestine, where the majority of the wadies are dry much of the year. The seventh month bears the name Ethanim, "the month of steady flow," perhaps in relationship to the time when these are the only streams with water (I Kgs 8:2). It means also the eternal movement of the sea which God stopped only long enough to allow Israel to pass through safely (Ex 14:27, "wonted flow" RSV; "strength" ASV). Psalm 74:15 describes this feat as the drying up of everflowing streams ("mighty" ASV). Thus Amos 5:24 bears a powerful image, "But let justice roll down like waters, and righteousness like an ever-flowing stream." Justice is truly the permanent, enduring quality that every believer seeks and which will become the foundation of the kingdom of God. The mountains are considered the enduring foundations of the earth. Therefore, because of their continual presence, they are in a position to witness in favor of the Lord and against Israel at the great judgment (Mic 6:2).

This word is applied also to the human sphere. For instance, man is faced with the continual problem of strife in his body (Job 33:19); this reflects the enduring nature of the curse on man for his original sin. In Job 12:19, translated "the mighty," it probably indicates the nobles whose status is continuous by heredity, yet who can be overthrown by God. Further, some nations are considered enduring ("mighty" ASV, Jer 5:15; cf. Num 24:21). The nation intended here is Babylon, which was a nemesis to Israel throughout her history. Although the dwelling place of man may appear ever enduring (ASV and RSV "strong") like the sheepfolds near the Jordan, God is able to destroy them, even by a ravaging lion (Jer 49:19; 50:44; KB understands the phrase as "pastureground on the everflowing river"). The concept here is not so much of strength, but the fact that they have been around so long they appear permanent.

Jacob's blessing describes Joseph as amidst intense battle, holding his bow *steady* and discharging arrows in rapid succession (Gen 49:23f., Skinner). Another difficult text is Prov 13:15, "the way of the faithless is *enduring*" ("hard" ASV; "ruin" RSV emends text). The MT makes good sense, for lack of faith forms its own rut from which there is no escape.

'êtān, ***II. Ethan*** (ASV and RSV the same.) The name occurs eight times. At least three different men bore this name.

1. Ethan was known as a wise man and heads the list consisting of himself, Heman, Calcol and Darda. Solomon's wisdom is compared to Ethan's as surpassing it (I Kgs 4:31 [H 5:11]). Ethan must have been a legendary man, indeed. He is listed as one of the sons of Zerah (I Chr 2:6), who was of the tribe of Judah, and his son was Azariah (I Chr 2:8). He is called the Ezrahite (the son of Zerah). Psalm 89 bears the inscription "A Maskil of Ethan the Ezrahite." Maskil (q.v.) might mean a wisdom song composed for instruction. This Psalm concerns the eternal covenant with David to rule Israel.

2. Another Ethan, son of Kushaiah of the Levitical family Merari, is listed as a Levitical singer, along with Heman and Asaph (I Chr 15:17, 19; 6:29). They shared a large part of the responsibility of the temple music and sounded the cymbals as they sang. Perhaps he also bore the name Jeduthun, which occurs in the same capacity along with Asaph and Heman in I Chr 25:1, 6; II Chr 5:12; 35:15.

3. A third Ethan is mentioned as the son of Zimmah, of the Levitical family Gershom (I Chr 6:42 [H 27]).

Bibliography: Driver, S. R., *Deuteronomy,* in ICC, V, pp. 241f. Pope, Marvin H., *Job,* in AB, XV. Skinner, John, *Genesis,* in ICC, I. Smend, Rudolf, *Die Weisheit des Jesus Sirach,* Berlin: Georg Reime, 1906, pp. 373f.

J.E.H.

936 יָתַר (*yātar*) ***remain over, leave;*** Hiphil, leave in excess, preserve, let escape (Ezk 12:16, RSV), have preeminence. (ASV, RSV translate similarly.)

Derivatives

936a יֶתֶר (*yeter*) ***I, rest, remnant.***
936b †יֶתֶר (*yeter*) ***II, cord, bowstring.***
936c יִתְרָה (*yitrâ*) ***abundance, riches.***
936d יוֹתֵר (*yôtēr*), יֹתֵר (*yōtēr*) ***more, better, advantage.***
936e יֹתֶרֶת (*yōteret*) ***appendage.***
936f יִתְרוֹן (*yitrôn*) ***advantage, excellency.***
936g מוֹתָר (*môtār*) ***profit, abundance.***
936h †מֵיתָר (*mêtār*) ***cord, string.***

yātar and its derivatives are used some 227 times. It refers to one portion of a quantity which has been divided. Generally it is the smaller part and sometimes it is the part of less quality. It may refer to the portion less in quality but more in quantity (Jud 7:6); e.g., in Neh it includes the people besides the priest, nobles and officials (Neh 2:16; 4:14 [H 8], 19, [H 13]). It may also be used in the sense of "advantage" or "more than."

The concept of remain occurs in a wide variety of contexts with many connotations. Food left over is an indication that one's need has been abundantly met (Ruth 2:14; II Chr 31:10). The people gave liberally for the building of the tabernacle so that items were left over (Ex 36:7). Most of the sacrifices were to be eaten on the day offered; any leftovers were to be consumed (Ex 12:10; Lev 8:32). But a votive or freewill offering was allowed to remain three days before being consumed (Lev 7:16f.).

The future of a person's life is referred to as the remaining years (Isa 38:10). The unrecorded events of a king's reign are called "the rest of [his] acts." In Gen 49:3f. the word carries the idea of pre-eminence; there Jacob declared to Reuben, "you are... pre-eminent in pride and preminent in power; unstable as water you shall not have pre-eminence." In Prov 17:7 *ś^{e}pat yeter* "a lip of excess" is taken as "arrogant speech" by BDB, "fine speech" by RSV and "excellent speech" by ASV.

The wisdom school, especially Eccl, often employs this root in search of the real advantage or the true excellence in life. Prov emphasizes that abundance can be gained by toil and diligent effort (Prov 14:23; 21:5). But abundance must not become the goal of life, for after necessities have been met that which is left then becomes the inheritance of one's family (Ps 17:14).

Kohelet uses this word family to get across many of his ideas. One is not to be too wise or too righteous; i.e. one cannot authenticate himself by putting his wisdom and righteousness on display so that they appear greater than they really are (Eccl 7:16). Truly the best advantage belongs to one with wisdom (Eccl 7:11). He uses *yitrôn* in the manner of "advantage," "gain" or "profit." There is advantage for an agricultural community to have a king, no doubt so that its production can be fully realized (Eccl 5:9 [H 8]). He also finds advantage or benefit in wisdom over folly (Eccl 2:13). Wisdom shows man how to overcome a difficult problem and knowledge allows wisdom to preserve the life of its owner (Eccl 7:12; 10:10). Prov points out there is advantage in toil over laziness (Prov 14:23). But Eccl probes deeper by continually asking what profit does one gain from his toil (Eccl 1:3; 3:9). The answer is nothing, especially if it is to accumulate goods which cannot be taken at death (Eccl 2:11; 5:15). Eccl here feels the full force of the curse on man's work which makes it toil and he clearly sees that ultimate value can not reside in man's labor or its results.

In military contexts this root frequently indicates the survivors of the people who have been defeated (Josh 12:4; 23:12). Also it may refer to those who have survived a conspiracy (e.g. Jud 9:5). A truly devastating event is when no one is left (Josh 11:11, 22). Sometimes one is left and feels quite alone; e.g. Elijah complained, "I, even I only, am left a prophet of the Lord" (I Kgs

18:22). In regard to Israel it refers to those who escaped the destruction of Jerusalem by Babylon (Ezk 6:8; 12:16; cf. Isa 1:9; but most often the idea of "remnant" comes from the root *sh'r*). The survivors will become God's weapon of punishment against other nations (Zeph 2:9). But at the end of time the survivors in Jerusalem will never be wiped out again (Zeh 14:2).

yeter. ***Cord, bowstring, tentcord.*** (ASV and RSV similar; but in Jud ASV "withes.") It is used six times. In the series of attempts by Delilah to discover the source of Samson's strength, Samson told her to bind him with seven new, not even dried, bowstrings; certainly they would tighten intensely as they dried. While he was asleep, they so tied him; but on awaking he was able to snap the bowstrings (Jud 16:7ff.). The attempt of the wicked to destroy the righteous is pictured as their fitting an "arrow to the string to shoot in the dark at the upright in heart" (Ps 11:2). In regard to life the cord being loosed means that one's health has been broken so that one is near death (Job 4:21; 30:11).

mêtār. ***Cord, string, tentcords.*** (ASV and RSV similar.) This word occurs nine times. Most frequently it appears in conjunction with the pegs and bases of the tabernacle (Ex 35:18). The cords of the new tent will have to be lengthened (Isa 54:2). Conversely broken cords indicate a people about to succumb to their enemies (Jer 10:20). In Ps 21:12 [H 13] the word stands for the bow as the instrument the righteous use to overcome the aggressive, deceitful plans of their enemies.

Bibliography. TDNT, IV, pp. 196–208.

J.E.H.

יִתְרוֹן (*yitrôn*). See no. 936f.
יֹתֶרֶת (*yōteret*). See no. 936e.

כ

כ

937 כְּ (k^e) ***as, like, the like of.***

Basically a substantive, it is often used as a preposition of comparison attached to its noun. Quantitatively, especially with numbers and time it can mean "about." Qualitatively, it can mean "according to" (Gen 1:26). In a correlative expression the preposition appears twice "my people are like your people" (like my people so your people, I Kgs 22:4). Before an infinitive it expresses the time at which action occurs, therefore "when, as, or while." It may express contemporaneity "while" more than b^e with an infinitive which is more conveniently rendered "when."

938 כְּמוֹ (k^e*mô*) ***like, as, when.***

The word k^e stands by itself fifty-six times and when it does it always uses the expanded form k^e*mô*. This is the form used in combination with the light suffixes, e.g. *kāmônî* "like me," *kāmôkā* "like you," and it is sometimes used with the heavy suffixes, e.g. either k^e*môhem* or *kāhēm* "like them." The usage in Ugaritic is similar. The prepositions b^e and l^e also use the form with the enclitic mem, but less commonly than does k^e.

939 כַּאֲשֶׁר (*ka'ăsher*) ***as, when, according as.***

Combined with *'ăsher*, k^e still means "as, when, according as," perhaps with some emphasis, but in addition may show causal force, "since, because."

940 כָּאַב (*kā'ab*) ***be sore, have pain, be sorrowful.*** ASV, RSV similar.

Derivatives

940a †כְּאֵב (k^e*'ēb*) ***sorrow.***
940b †מַכְאוֹב (*mak'ôb*) ***sorrow.***

kā'ab occurs with its derivatives thirty times, all but four of which are found in poetry. Although the root does not appear in Ugaritic, it is found in Aramaic, Akkadian, and Arabic. The former two emphasize the pain aspect while the Arabic usage stresses sadness and sorrow. Although the root can be used to express physical suffering, it much more commonly has to do with mental anguish.

Only four usages of *kā'ab* refer to physical pain. Genesis 34:25 refers to the pain of circumcision; Job 14:22 and 33:19 to the bodily pain which is said to be the lot of humanity; and Ezk 28:24 to thorns which cause pain (although used figuratively of Israel's enemies).

For the most part, however, it is impossible to separate the mental and physical anguish as far as this word is concerned. A case in point would be Ex 3:7 where God's compassion for his people's affliction is expressed. Surely they were suffering physical pain, but their total situation was cause for anguish, as well.

Because of Israel's inability to serve God faithfully she was plunged back into such anguish during the Exile (Lam 1:12, 18). But the word of hope is that Jesus has borne all of this suffering, this "heartbreak" (Isa 65:14) that we might be healed (Isa 53:3–4)

k^e'ēb. ***Sorrow, grief, pain.*** (ASV similar. RSV uses "pain" in place of "sorrow.") Six occurrences.

mak'ôb. ***Sorrow, grief, affliction, pain.*** (ASV similar. RSV almost always translates with "pain," where KJV has "sorrow.") Sixteen occurrences, of which at least eleven have to do with mental suffering.

J.N.O.

941 *כָּאָה (*kā'â*) ***be disheartened, cowed.*** Occurs only in the Niphal and Hiphil stems (e.g. Dan 11:30; Ezk 13:22).

Derivative

941a כָּאֶה (*kā'eh*) ***cowed*** (Ps 10:10).

942 כבב (*kbb*). **Assumed root of the following.**
942a †כּוֹכָב (*kôkāb*) ***star.*** (ASV and RSV the same.)

The nations around Israel worshiped the stars, both individually and in constellations. Astrologers and wise men carefully studied their movements to determine the will and the messages of these gods but to no avail (Isa 47:13). Such was their lot from Yahweh (Deut 4:19; *cf.* Amos 5:26), but Israel was strictly forbidden to worship them. In Israel's thought the stars influenced life, but only as agents of Yahweh. God made the stars to give light and to rule the night (Gen 1:16 f.; Ps 136:9). He "determines the number of the stars, he gives to all of them their names" (Ps 147:4). No star exists outside of Yahweh and their destiny is determined by him. Also the vast number of stars was a symbol for God's promise of abundant descendants to Abraham (Gen 22:17; 26:4).

The stars are sometimes personalized. They may be identified with the sons of God, who sang forth praise at the creation (Job 38:7; cf. Ps 148:3). God, however, is unquestionably superior even to the highest stars (Job 22:12). God used the stars to fight on Israel's side to defeat Sisera (Jud 5:20). In climax, the individual who will bring salvation to Israel is foreseen as "a star [which] shall come forth out of Jacob" (Num 24:17). Jesus, in Rev, says, "I am . . . the bright morning star" (Rev 22:16; cf. II Pet 1:19). Then too the faithful who diligently labor to turn people to God shall shine like the stars forever (Dan 12:3; cf. I Cor 15:41f.).

J.E.H.

943 כָּבֵד (*kābēd*) ***be heavy, grievous, hard, rich, honorable, glorious.*** (ASV, RSV similar.)

Derivatives

943a †כָּבֵד (*kābēd*) ***I, great.***
943b †כָּבֵד (*kābēd*) ***II, liver.***
943c כֹּבֶד (*kōbed*) ***great.***
943d כָּבוֹד (*kābôd*) ***I, glorious,*** occurs only as the feminine singular *k^{e}bûddâ* (Ezk 23:41; Ps 45:14).
943e †כָּבוֹד (*kābôd*) ***II, glory.***
943f †כְּבוּדָּה (*k^{e}bûddâ*) ***abundance, riches.*** Only in Jud 18:21.
943g כְּבֵדֻת (*k^{e}bēdūt*) ***heaviness,*** only in Ex 14:25.

This root with its derivatives occurs 376 times in the Hebrew Bible. It is especially prominent in Ps (sixty-four occurrences) and Isa (sixty-three), as well as Ex (thirty-three), Ezk (twenty-five) and Prov (twenty-four). Of the total number of occurrences, 114 are verbal. The root is a common Semitic one, occurring in all except Aramaic where *yāqār* seems to take its place. The basic meaning is "to be heavy, weighty," a meaning which is only rarely used literally, the figurative (e.g. "heavy with sin") being more common. From this figurative usage it is an easy step to the concept of a "weighty" person in society, someone who is honorable, impressive, worthy of respect. This latter usage is prevalent in more than half the occurrences.

The literal use of the term occurs only in I Sam 4:18, "Eli was heavy" (*kābēd,* adjective), and II Sam 14:26 "Absalom's hair was heavy" (*kābēd,* noun).

kābēd usually carries a negative connotation. The Qal and Hiphil stems comprise the most of these occurrences in the verbal form, while *kābēd* and *kōbed* are the nouns whose meanings fit the category. Generally speaking, there are three groupings of figurative uses. The first would relate to parts of the body, expressing slowness, dullness or implacability. The second relates to events or experiences, describing their severity in terms of heaviness. The third would express size or number in such terms.

The first usage is found most often in relation to Pharaoh, in seven places (Ex 7:14; 8:15 [H 11], 28 [H 32]; 9:7, 34; 10:1; I Sam 6:6). Pharaoh's refusal to be sensitive to the situation or to the pleas of the Hebrew people is spoken of as a heaviness or hardening of the heart (cf. the discussion by Girdlestone, SOT, pp. 66–67.) Similarly the ears (Isa 6:10; 59:1; Zech 7:11), the tongue (Ex 4:10), and the eyes (Gen 48:10) may become dull and insensitive, while the hands may grow weary (Ex 17:12). In the latter three cases physical infirmity is involved, but the former express spiritual problems.

Heaviness as a figure for severity relates to work (Ex 5:9, etc.), servitude (I Kgs 12:10 etc.), warfare (Jud 20:34, etc.) and pestilence (Gen 41:31 etc.). Three times the severity of such misfortunes is expressed as the hand of the Lord being heavy upon them (cf. I Sam 5:6, 11; Ps 32:4). In the same way a person's hand can be heavy on someone else (Jud 1:35, Job 33:7). Also, a person, without necessarily intending to, can become burdensome to another (II Sam 13:25, II Chr 10:10, 14; 25:19; Neh 5:15). The fact that the severity of bondage is often expressed by means of the figure "a heavy yoke" (I Kgs 12:4; II Chr 10:4, 11) makes Jesus' declaration, "My yoke is easy" (Mt 11:28), all the more significant.

From severity to magnitude is a simple step and in several cases it is not easy to be perfectly clear which connotation is in view. For instance, the statement that the sin of Sodom and Gomorrah was very heavy (Gen 18:20). Is this to say that the sin was great or that it was severe? So also Isa 24:20; Ps 38:4 [H 5]; Job 6:3, etc. At any rate it is plain that sin is a burden which weighs down the one who carries it, making the person himself heavy and dull (Isa 1:4; Prov 27:3). Other usages are quite clear however. Cf. e.g. Num 20:20 "Edom came out with a heavy people," or II Kgs 6:14 "a heavy host." Similar references would be Ex 12:38; II Chr 9:1; Isa 36:2. Habakkuk 2:6 uses the word in this way when it attacks those who *increase* pledges (cf. Nah 3:15). In one case, Abraham is said to be very heavy (Gen 13:2), and the context makes it plain that the magnitude of his wealth is being spoken of. This has significance for the succeeding usages.

The second major group of connotations is a further extension of the figurative use of the term. In this case the idea is of that which is weighty in the sense of being noteworthy or impressive. Common translations are "honorable, honored, glorious, glorified." The Niphal and Piel stems normally have these connotations.

The reputation of an individual is of central importance in these usages. Thus the person of high social position and accompanying wealth was automatically an honored, or weighty, person in the society (Num 22:15, etc.). Such a position, its riches, and long life were commonly assumed to be the just rewards of a righteous life (I Chr 29:28, etc.). While one would be honored automatically if one attained this stature, it is also clear that one was expected to merit the honor and the glory. The book of Prov makes it clear that the trappings of glory without an accompanying weightiness of character was an offense to life (21:21; 22:4; 26:1; etc.).

Likewise persons in positions of responsibility and authority were deserving of honor (Ex 20:12; Mal 1:6). It is significant to remind oneself that giving honor or glory is to say that someone is deserving of respect, attention and obedience. A life which does not back up one's honorable words is hypocrisy of a high form. Israel was again and again guilty of honoring God with her lips, while by her actions making him appear worthless (Isa 29:13).

One could also become honored as a result of heroic feats of courage, fidelity, etc. David's mighty men are spoken of in this way (I Kgs 11:21 etc.) These were people who had made a name for themselves. In this vein God is also to be honored. God's name is glorious in righteousness, faithfulness, judgment, and salvation (Ps 66:2; 79:9; Isa 40:5). He is the king of glory (Ps 24:7–10), who has done gloriously. So he is not only to be honored because of his position as sovereign head of the universe, but because of his surpassing character in all realms.

The accoutrements of glory were commonly impressive in their beauty. Thus the garments of the priests were expressly designed to be unusually beautiful, in order to convey some of the great dignity and importance of the office (Ex 28:2, 40). The glory of the great kingdoms is commonly compared to the splendors and beauties of the great forest of Lebanon (Isa 8:7; 10:18). It appears that the particular beauty of man is his capacity for rational and moral response (Gen 49:6; Ps 108:1 [H 2]; Jer 2:11).

Yet it is at the point of these beauties that the Bible speaks most devastatingly of the transience of all glory except God's. Isaiah is especially pointed. How quickly beauty fades. How suddenly a great cedar forest can be reduced to a sickening field of stumps (Isa 10:18). How easily man can exchange his true glories for that which really cheapens and destroys him (Ps 106:20). Any impressiveness or noteworthiness which man has created for himself in his own pride and arrogance is doomed to destruction (Isa 16:14; 17:4; 21:16).

[A few references to "glory" (*kābôd*) may better be taken as misvocalized references to the "liver" (*kābēd* II) spoken of as we do the heart. Thus Ps 16:9 "my glory rejoices" may mean "my liver rejoices." Note the mention of bodily parts in the context. Of course, it is not the liver literally, but the person that rejoices. Properly, therefore, the LXX and NT translate "my tongue rejoices." R.L.H.]

Over against the transience of human and earthly glory stands the unchanging beauty of the manifest God (Ps 145:5). In this sense the noun *kābôd* takes on its most unusual and distinctive meaning. Forty-five times this form of the root relates to a visible manifestation of God and whenever "the glory of God" is mentioned this usage must be taken account of. Its force is so compelling that it remolds the meaning of *doxa* from an opinion of men in the Greek classics to something absolutely objective in the LXX and NT.

The bulk of occurrences where God's glory is a visible manifestation have to do with the tabernacle (Ex 16:10; 40:34; etc.) and with the temple in Ezekiel's vision of the exile and restoration (9:3, etc.). These manifestations are directly related to God's self-disclosure and his intent to dwell among men. As such they are commonly associated with his holiness. God wishes to dwell with men, to have his reality and his splendor known to them. But this is only possible when they take account of the stunning quality of his holiness and set out in faith and obedience to let that character be manifested in them (Num 14:10; Isa 6:3; Ezr 10, 11).

The several references which speak of God's glory filling the earth and/or becoming evident are instructive. On the one hand they quite legitimately refer to that reputation for greatness which God alone deserves, not only because of his natural position as king, but because of his unsurpassed activity as deliverer and saviour. However, as the preceding discussion indicates, something more is intended here. It is not merely God's reputation which fills the earth, but it is the very reality of his presence. And his desire is that all persons may gladly recognize and own this. His first step toward the achievement of these goals was o fill the tabernacle with his presence and then the temple.

But nowhere is the reality and the splendor of his presence and his character seen as in his son (Isa 4:2). Here the nearblinding quality of his glory is fully portrayed, "We beheld his glory, the glory as of the only son of the Father, full of grace and truth" (Jn 1:14; cf. 17:1–5). Through him and through his presence in the church, God's glory is indeed filling the earth.

kābēd ***I. Great, grievous, hard, heavy.*** An adjective, this word does not occur with the meaning "honored," or "honorable." Moreover, it and the following are distinct from other forms of the root in the fact that they sometimes carry the connotation of number or volume (eleven out of forty for *kābēd,* one out of four for *kōbed*), whereas other forms rarely do so.

kābēd ***II. Liver.*** The heavy organ. Fourteen occurrences, of which nine are found in Lev 3–9.

kābôd. ***Glory, glorious, honor, honorable.*** A noun, often in construct with a preceding word, thus taking on an adjectival aspect ("King of Glory" equals "Glorious King"). Occurs two hundred times, never with the idea of weight or heaviness directly in view.

k^e^bûddâ. ***An adjective only used in the feminine, glorious, stately, carriage.*** In Ps 45:13 [H 14] where KJV reads "glorious," RSV reads "wealth." In Jud 18:21 KJV translates "carriage," evidently meaning "things to be carried" (RSV "good").

Bibliography: Caspari, Wilhelm, *Die Bedeutung der Wortsippe* כבד *in Hebräischen,* Leipzig, 1908. Caird, G. B., "The Glory of God in the Fourth Gospel," *New Testament Studies* 15:265–77. Forster, A. H., "The Meaning of δὸξα in the Greek Bible," *The Angelican Theological Review* 12:311–16. Kittel, Gerhard, "δὸξα in the LXX and Hellenistic Apocrypha," in TDNT, II, pp. 242–45. Morgenstern, Julian, "Biblical Theophanies," *Zeitschrift für Assyriologie,* 25:139–193; 28:15–60. Richardson, TWB, p. 175. Von Rad, Gerhard, "כָּבוֹד in the Old Testament," in TDNT, II, pp. 238–42. TDNT, II, pp. 238–47. THAT, I, pp. 794–811.

J.N.O.

כְּבֵדוּת (*k^e^bēdût*). See no. 943g.

944 כָּבָה (*kābâ*) ***quench, put out, be quenched, be put out.*** (ASV and RSV similar.)

kābâ occurs twenty-four times, thirteen in the prophets. The root also appears in Arabic with the same meaning. It always relates to fire and to the act of putting a fire out. It is to be distinguished from *dā'ak* (q.v.), which has a similar meaning, by the fact that *dā'ak* commonly refers to a lamp which has gone out while *kābâ* in more than half of its occurrences refers to a fire which cannot be quenched by anyone other than God (the fire referring to his wrath).

Out of the six references to literal fire, five are fires which do not go out. Of these, four refer to lamps and fires in the temple (Lev 6:12–13 [H 5–6]; I Sam 3:3; II Chr 29:7). This concern that something not be quenched is reflected also in the figurative usages where life (II Sam 14:7; 21:17) and love (Song 8:7) are figured as fire.

The majority of the figurative usages relate to God's anger which no one but he can quench. In particular, the prophets speak in this way calling for repentance, lest this "fire" break out (Jer 4:4, etc.). Similar language is picked up by Jesus concerning hell in Mark 9:48. But, at the same time, when the Messiah comes his gentleness will be such that he will not even quench smoking flax (Isa 42:3), i.e. he will not extinguish the weak and poor—even dull—of society; rather he will save them.

J.N.O.

כָּבוֹד (*kābôd*). See nos. 943d,e.
כְּבוּדָּה (*k^e^bûddâ*). See no. 943f.
כַּבִּיר (*kabbîr*). See no. 947a.
כָּבִיר (*kābîr*). See no. 948a.

945 כבל (*kbl*). **Assumed root of the following.**
945a כֶּבֶל (*kebel*) ***fetters*** (Ps 105:18; 149:8).

946 כָּבַס (*kābas*) ***wash, be washed, perform the work of a fuller.*** (ASV and RSV similar.)

This root occurs fifty-one times, all in verbal forms. Of these, all but nine appear in the Pentateuch, thirty-one in Lev alone, and twenty-one in Lev 13–15. It also appears in Arabic ("to knead, stamp") and Akkadian ("tread down"). In Hebrew it means "to full," that is "to make stuffs clean and soft by treading, kneading and beating them in cold water" (KB, p. 422). Thus it is always used of clothing, "to launder" and never of "washing" the body, where *raḥaṣ* (*rāḥaṣ* which see) is used or of "rinsing" which is denoted by *shāṭap*.

In all but one case (II Sam 19:24), washing is associated with ceremonial cleanness. Both the priests and the people were to be in clean clothes when they appeared before God (Ex 19:10, 14; Num 8:7; 19:7). Involvement in the rituals which dealt specifically with atonement and death resulted in ceremonial uncleanness and necessitated washing the clothes (Lev 16:26, 28; Num 19:7, 8, 10, 19, 21).

The bulk of the references have to do with washing of clothes which have become contaminated in one way or another (28 times). Particularly important contaminants would be leprosy and related maladies for, aside from the hygienic factor, these were evidently types of sin. This imagery is picked up in Ps 51 (2 [H 4], 7 [H 9]) and Jer 2:22 and 4:14. That David depicts his sin as a contagious leprosy in need of cleansing is further validated by his petition that God use hyssop, the instrument employed in cleansing a leper (Lev 14:6–7). Jeremiah 2:22 and 4:14 are significant because while speaking of the impossibility of washing out the stain, they proclaim the necessity of such cleansing. The answer to this dilemma is found in Mal 3:2 in the one who would appear as refiner's fire and fuller's soap to deal with the sins of his people.

J.N.O.

947 *כָּבַר (*kābar*) **I, *multiply, be in abundance.*** (ASV, RSV similar.)

Derivatives

947a †כַּבִּיר (*kabbîr*) ***many, mighty.***
947b †כִּבְרָה (*kibrâ*) ***distance.***
947c כְּבָר (*kᵉbār*) ***I, already.*** Occurs nine times, only in Eccl.
947d †כְּבָר (*kᵉbār*) ***II,Chebar.***

This root and its derivatives occur twenty-four times, only two of which are verbal. Both of these verbal uses occur in the Hiphil in Job (35:16; 36:31). It seems likely that they are denominative. The root meaning is "to be much." It is perhaps to be distinguished from *rāb* (q.v.) on the basis of its stress upon volume ("mighty waters," Isa 17:12; 28:2) rather than number, but this should not be overdrawn. The meanings are similar in Akkadian, Aramaic, and Arabic; cf. the Arabic expression *Allah akbar,* "Allah is great."

The word is used in both negative and positive ways. From the negative point of view its usages stress the vanity of greatness apart from God. Job's comforters feel that Job's abundance of words is vain (8:2; 35:16). Similarly the mighty men who stand up against God will be broken (Job 34:24) until they see their smallness (Isa 16:14).

Only God is the source of true might (Job 36:5). In his hand is abundance of power (Isa 17:12), justice (Job 34:17), and provision (Job 36:31).

kabbîr. ***Many, mighty, much, strong, most.*** Nine occurrences, six of which are in Job. Commonly used adjectivally stressing the greatness of the noun modified.

kibrâ. ***A little way.*** This meaning is that derived from the construction *kibrat-'ereṣ*, lit. "much of land," which is the way this word is found in its three occurrences. The rendering "a great way" which one would expect from the etymology seems contradicted by the contexts as well as the LXX.

kᵉbār. ***Chebar.*** (ASV and RSV similar; NIV "Kebar.") A channel of the Euphrates which leaves it near Babylon and returns near Warka (60 miles south). The group of Judean captives among whom was Ezekiel were settled along the Chebar (Ezk 1:1; 3:15). It was here that Ezekiel had the vision which shaped the rest of his ministry (1:1, 3; cf. 3:23; 43:3, etc.).

J.N.O.

948 כבר (*kbr*) **II. Assumed root of the following.**
948a כָּבִיר (*kābîr*) ***something netted, either a quilt or a fly net spread over the face of a sleeping person*** (I Sam 19:13, 16).
948b כְּבָרָה (*kᵉbārâ*) ***sieve*** (a net-like instrument), only in Amos 9:9.
948c מַכְבֵּר (*makbēr*) ***netted cloth or coverlet,*** only in II Kgs 8:15.
948d †מִכְבָּר (*mikbār*) ***grate.*** ASV, RSV "grating."

The root of this noun does not occur in verbal form, but evidently it meant something like "to intertwine." *mikbār* appears six times, all in Ex, and all with reference to a grating, or grillwork, which extended around the altar of burnt offering at its midpoint. Its function is unknown. On its four corners were rings through which poles were inserted for carrying the portable altar of the tabernacle.

J.N.O.

949 כֶּבֶשׂ (*kebeś*), כֶּשֶׂב (*keśeb*) ***lamb, sheep.*** (ASV and RSV similar.)

This root and its derivatives occur 128 times in the Old Testament. Of these, only 17 do not occur in the context of sacrifice. *kebeś* itself occurs 106 times with only 6 of these being nonsacrificial. As might be expected, 105 of the total occurrences are in the Pentateuch, but Num has a high proportion of these: 60, with 26 in chap. 7, 14 in chap. 28 and 23 in chap. 29.

This root is attested in Akkadian, where it also means "lamb," and in Arabic (*kabšun*) where it means "young ram." It is interesting to note that *kbś* is not attested in Ugaritic and that the common Ugaritic term for sacrificial lamb, *'imr,* if it appears at all in Hebrew, only does so in a few priestly names. This may reflect a conscious repudiation on the part of the Hebrews of certain Canaanite technical religious terms.

950 כִּבְשָׂה (*kibśâ*), כִּשְׂבָּה (*kiśbâ*) ***ewe lamb, lamb.*** Feminine form of *kebeś*. In the sin offering a female kid or lamb was required (Lev 4:32; 5:6; 14:10; Num 6:14).

keśeb seems to be a metathesized form of *kebeś* (cf. Ges 19n). However, it appears to be used slightly differently in that it normally occurs in circumstances where a distinction is being drawn between the two kinds of animals of the flock: sheep and goats. In only two cases (out of a total of thirteen) is this not the case.

Although the initial instructions for the sacrifice (Lev 1–8) do not, for the most part, specify that lambs must be offered as opposed to full-grown sheep, it is clear from both preceding and following materials that lambs (sheep less than one year old) were important elements in the sacrificial system.

In four circumstances lambs were required: the Passover observance (Ex 12:5; Lev 23:12); the sin offering (Lev 4:32, etc.); certain purification ceremonies (childbirth, Lev 12:6; leprosy, 14:10; Nazirites, Num 6:12) and the morning and evening sacrifice. The number of lambs offered in the daily sacrifice was increased at the new moon (Num 28:11) and during the great festivals (Num 28, 29). It was perhaps because the daily offering was a burnt offering that lambs came to be included along with rams and bulls as the burnt offering on special occasions. Whatever the reason, this was in practice as early as the dedication of the tabernacle in Num 7 and continued in force as late as Ezra's return (Ezr 8:35).

As with all the sacrificial animals, the elements of perfection, costliness and substitution were primary elements in the sacrifice of every lamb.

It was undoubtedly the association of lambs with Passover, the sin offering and the daily sacrifice which led John the Baptist to proclaim that Jesus Christ was "the Lamb of God, which takes away the sin of the world" (Jn 1:29,36: cf. also Rev 5:9). Then too, Isaiah had already used this imagery for the Suffering Servant who would passively accept God's judgment for the sin of the people as a lamb (Heb *śeh*) is led to slaughter (Isa 53:7).

J.N.O.

951 כָּבַשׁ (*kābash*) ***subdue, bring into bondage, keep under, force.*** (ASV, RSV similar.)

Derivative

951a כֶּבֶשׁ (*kebesh*) ***footstool.*** Refers to the footrest of Solomon's throne (II Chr 9:18; cf. *hădôm*).

This verb and its derivative occur fifteen times in the OT. It is evidently related to Akkadian *kabāsu* "to tread down," and Arabic *kabasa* "to knead, stamp, press" (cf. also Arabic *kabaša* "to seize with the hand"). In the OT it means "to make to serve, by force if necessary."

Despite recent interpretations of Gen 1:28 which have tried to make "subdue" mean a responsibility for building up, it is obvious from an overall study of the word's usage that this is not so. *kābash* assumes that the party being subdued is hostile to the subduer, necessitating some sort of coercion if the subduing is to take place. Thus the word connotes "rape" in Est 7:8, or the conquest of the Canaanites in Num 32:22, 29; Josh 18:1; I Chr 22:18. In II Chr 28:10; Neh 5:5; Jer 34:11, 16 it refers to forced servitude.

Therefore "subdue" in Gen 1:28 implies that creation will not do man's bidding gladly or easily and that man must now bring creation into submission by main strength. It is not to rule man. However, there is a twistedness in humanity which causes us to perform such a task with fierce and destructive delight. Try as we might, we cannot subdue this. But it can be subdued and this is the promise of Mic 7:10, "He will subdue our iniquities."

J.N.O.

952 כִּבְשָׁן (*kibshān*) ***kiln, for lime or pottery*** (e.g. Gen 19:28; Ex 19:18). Derivation uncertain.

כַּד (*kad*). See no. 953a.

953 כדד (*kdd*). **Assumed root of the following.**

953a כַּד (*kad*) ***jar*** (e.g. I Kgs 17:12; Eccl 12:6).

953b כִּידוֹד (*kîdôd*) ***spark*** (Job 41:11).

953c כַּדְכֹּד (*kadkōd*) ***a precious stone, perhaps a ruby*** (Ezk 27:16; Isa 54:12).

כַּדּוּר (*kaddûr*). See no. 954b.
כַּדְכֹּד (*kadkōd*). See no. 953c.

954 כדר (*kdr*). **Assumed root of the following.**

954a כִּידוֹר (*kîdôr*) ***onset, attack*** (Job 15:24).

954b כַּדּוּר (*kaddûr*) ***ball*** (Isa 22:18).

955 כֹּה (*kōh*) ***thus, here.*** Demonstrative adverb of manner, place, or time.

956 כָּכָה (*kākā*) ***thus, perhaps a more emphatic form than*** *kōh*. Probably derived from 955.

957 כָּהָה (*kāhâ*) ***I, be dim, darkened, restrained, faint, fail.*** (ASV and RSV similar, except that RSV reads "blinded" instead of "darkened.")

Derivatives

957a †כֵּהֶה (*kēheh*) ***be dark.***

957b †כֵּהָה (*kēhâ*) ***healing.***

The root and its derivatives occur seventeen times with the general idea of being weak, ineffective, or colorless. The idea of the eyes becoming weak in old age is prominent. The cognate in Akkadian means "to be weak" and in Arabic "to grow disheartened."

kēheh. ***Be dark, wax dim, smoke, heavy.*** An adjective occurring chiefly in Lev 13 ("if the plague be somewhat dark," six times). Cognate evidence seems to suggest "colorless" as a better translation (RSV "dim," NEB "faded").

kēhâ. ***Healing*** (ASV and RSV "assuaging.") According to Nahum 3:19, Nineveh's destruction cannot be done away with.

J.N.O.

958 *כָּהָה (*kāhâ*) ***II, rebuke.*** Occurs only in the Piel, in I Sam 3:13, "he did not rebuke them."

959 כָּהַן (*kāhan*) ***minister in a priest's office, act as priest.*** Denominative verb.

Parent Noun

959a †כֹּהֵן (*kōhen*) ***principal officer or chief ruler, priest.***

959b כְּהֻנָּה (*k^e hūnnâ*) ***priesthood.***

The verb *kāhan* occurs twenty-three times, only in the Piel. It is translated "minister in a priest's office," "be priest," or "serve as priest" (RSV).

kōhen. *Chief ruler, priest.* The underlying verbal root of *kōhēn* does not appear in the OT and is of unknown etymology (KB, p. 424). In light of its early secular usage, the idea of *khn* might be of "serving as a minister" (cf. S. R. Driver, *Notes on the Hebrew Text of the Books of Samuel,* pp. 284–85). Four summaries, pertaining to the time of the United Kingdom, mention both Levitical high priests and, simultaneously, others who occupy a similarly designated office of *kōhēn* (I Kgs 4:5; II Sam 8:18; 20:26; I Chr 18:16, 17). Zabud son of Nathan was "principal officer" under Solomon (I Kgs 4:5, KJV). During the lapse between the earlier and later lists under David, the occupancy of this second type of *kōhēn* office shifts from David's own sons (II Sam 8:18) to Ira the Jairite (20:26). This is doubly significant, for the former were necessarily non-levitical, and their replacement by the latter suggests responsibilities adversely affected by the intervening failures of the king's sons. *kōhēn* seems therefore to connote "confidential advisor" (KD, *Samuel* p. 369); cf. the further description of Zabud as "king's friend" and of David's sons as, literally, "the first ones at the king's hand" in the parallel passage (I Chr 18:17; n.b., liberal criticism here dismisses Chr as a later attempt to disguise an originally non-levitical priesthood, ICC, *Samuel,* p. 310).

Another possibility may be considered in view of the overwhelming usage and the fact that in Ugaritic also *khn* means "priest." All of these four verses may be differently interpreted.

Not only does I Chr 18:17 lack the designation *kōhēn* for David's sons, the LXX of the parallel passage II Sam 8:18 itself lacks it. The Hebrew of II Sam 8:18 may be in error. As it stands it has the impossible reading, "And Benaiah son of Jehoiada and the Cherethites and the Pelethites and the sons of David were priests."

Ira the Jairite (II Sam 20:26) who is mentioned nowhere else may indeed have been a priest who served David especially and personally as Abiathar had done (cf. I Sam 30:7).

Finally, Zabud (I Kgs 4:5) is also not mentioned elsewhere. He may have been a priest who served Solomon personally. Or the word "priest" here could even refer to Nathan, Zabud's father. Actually most MSS of the LXX omit the word "priest" here and they could be correct. At least it is of interest that only these four verses suggest that *kōhēn* may refer to a different kind of office.

Elsewhere in the OT, *kōhēn* reflects the more restricted concept of a minister for sacred things, especially sacrifice; cf. the functioning of Melchizedek and of Jethro, the first priests named in Scripture (Gen 14:18; Ex 18:12; negative criticism, by contrast, usually associates priestly origins with the delivery of oracles, TDNT, III, p. 260). In the beginning men served at sacrifice as their own priests (Gen 4:3; Job 1:5), but already in Noah's time priestly ministration had become the responsibility of the patriarchal family head (Gen 8:20; cf. Gen 12:8; Job 1:5; Ex 19:22, 24 in subsequent periods).

In a sense, all Israel were the Lord's priests (Ex 19:6; cf. Hos 4,6 on their rejection from *kihēn* "being a priest" to God). But at Sinai he restricted legitimate priesthood to the family of Moses' brother Aaron, of the tribe of Levi (Ex 28:1; 40:12–15; Num 16:17; 17:8; Cf. the evolutionary views of supposedly Canaanitish serpent-worshiping Levites and bull-worshiping Aaronites, T. J. Meek, *Hebrew Origins,* pp. 119–47). Indeed, efficacious priesthood can exist only when it is established by the Lord (Num 18:7, *k^e hūnnâ*), for according to Scripture only God or his official representative can accomplish the atonement by which satisfaction is made for sin (Ps 65:3 [H 4]; Ex 29:36; A. B. Davidson, *The Theology of the OT,* p. 321). Aaron wore the names of the twelve tribes inscribed on his vestments (Ex 28:12, 21, 29) so as to bring them before God when he appeared to minister divine propitiation and reconciliation (v. 38). He continued to occupy his post, despite failure at the incident of the golden calf (32:4, 21).

Shortly after the completion of the tabernacle (Ex 35–38, 40), including the elaborate priestly regalia (Ex 39; cf. Isa 61:10, as a bridegroom "decketh himself," *kihēn,* marg., "deck as a priest") and the revelation of God's laws of sacrifice (Lev 1–7), Aaron was consecrated as Israel's high priest and his four sons as priests (Lev 8–9). Their primary function was to officiate at the new sanctuary (Deut 18:5) and pray on behalf of the people (Joel 2:17). They were also to set a personal example of holiness (Deut 33:9), to "enquire of God" for oracles (see *'ûrîm*), and to teach the law (Lev 10:11; Mic 3:11; Mal 2:7; even traveling, II Chr 17:9). The latter two responsibilities made it appropriate for the priests to serve also as judges (Deut 17:9). Soon after their appointment, Aaron's two older sons were slain by God for violating their office (Lev 10:2). But descent from Eleazar and Ithamar, who remained, continued to be the basis upon which

Israel henceforth distinguished their divinely authorized priests (Ezr 2:62; I Chr 24).

The OT priests were types of Christ (Heb 8:1), who accomplished the ultimate propitiation for the sins of the people (2:17). Prophecy suggests a future reappearance of Levites (Jer 33:18; Zech 12:13; Ezk 41:46ff); but the NT church exhibits a universal priesthood of believers (I Pet 2:5; Rev 5:10; Jer 31:34).

Bibliography: AI, pp. 345–405. Payne, J. B., *Theology of the Older Testament,* Zondervan, 1971, pp. 372–80. Richardson, TWB, pp. 210–11. TDNT, III, pp. 260–63.

J.B.P.

960 כּוֹבַע (*kôba'*) ***helmet.*** (ASV and RSV similar.)

Although T. H. Gaster has suggested that this is a loan word from Hittite (*kupahi*), (JAOS, 57, 73ff., followed by KB[2]); more recently J. L. Palache (*Semantic Notes on the Hebrew Lexicon,* pp. 17, 40) has claimed that it is part of a bi-consonantal family, kb, qb, gb which denotes an upward or downward convexity. If this claim were correct it would help to explain the alternate spelling of this word: *qôba'* (q.v.) which appears in I Sam 17:38 (note *kôba'* in 17:5) and Ezk 23:24 (*kôba'* in 27:10 and 38:5; cf. also Ugaritic *gb't* "goblets.")

kôba' appears six times in the Old Testament (*qôba'* twice); two of these are in historical literature, the others in the prophets. In II Chr 26:14 Uzziah is said to have gathered a considerable armory, including helmets, while I Sam 17:5, in describing Goliath's armor, mentions his bronze helmet.

In the prophets, shields and helmets are mentioned with respect to the great armies (often of mercenaries, Ezk 27:10) which surged across the near east in the Iron Age. The prophets envisioned such armies on the move again in the end times (Ezk 38:5). Against the mighty of the earth, and eaten away by sin inside, it would seem that God's people would be helpless. Yet God himself has entered the battle against oppression and sin and stands forth victorious (Isa 59:17).

J.N.O.

961 *כָּוָה (*kāwâ*) ***burn, scorch, brand.*** Occurs only in the Niphal (Isa 43:2; Prov 6:28).

Derivatives

961a כִּי (*kî*) ***burning, branding.*** Occurs only in Isa 3:24.

961b כְּוִיָּה (*k^ewîyâ*) ***burning, branding*** (Ex 21:25).

961c מִכְוָה (*mikwâ*) ***burned spot; burn scar*** (Lev 13:24, 25, 28).

כֹּחַ (*kôaḥ*). See no. 973a.
כְּוִיָּה (*k^ewîyâ*). See no. 961b.
כּוֹכָב (*kôkāb*). See no. 942a.

962 כּוּל (*kûl*) ***contain, hold, abide, bear, nourish, provide.*** (ASV, RSV similar, except that RSV translates "endure" instead of "abide" or "bear.")

The primary meaning of this root is "to contain as does a vessel." It occurs thirty-eight times. The Qal stem occurs but once, with the remainder in either the Hiphil or the intensive. In six cases, it is not possible to distinguish the meanings of the Pilpel from the Hiphil. The other nineteen occurrences, however, show the particularized meaning "to provide with food." Evidently this reflects the causative function of the Pilpel stem: "to cause to contain, supply."

Examples of the primary meaning are found in passages such as I Kgs 7:26, 38; 8:64; II Chr 4:5; 7:7 where the sizes of the molten sea and the bronze lavers in Solomon's temple are described in terms of the number of *baths* of water they contain.

Jeremiah then uses the word in a figurative sense when he expresses the impossibility of containing within himself the Lord's fury which is like a burning fire (Jer 6:11; 20:9). In a somewhat similar vein. Solomon remarks in his prayer at the dedication of the temple that it is silly to think of that house as containing God since the heaven of heavens cannot contain him (I Kgs 8:27; II Chr 2:6 [H 5]; 6:18).

As a logical extension of the above meanings are those which express the possibility or impossibility of enduring (or containing) something (Prov 18:14; Joel 2:11; Amos 7:10; Mal 3:2). Two of these (Joel and Mal) express the impossibility of enduring God's wrath when he comes and are reminiscent of Rev (6:15, 16, etc.).

J.N.O.

963 כום (*kwm*). **Assumed root of the following.**

963a †כִּימָה (*kîmâ*) ***Pleiades.*** (ASV and RSV similar.)

Group of seven stars in the constellation Taurus. The word appears in Amos 5:8 and Job 9:9 and 38:31. In each of these places it is used in connection with the creative power of God. In view of his capacity to put the stars in place, both ungodly living (Amos), and the questioning of God's wisdom (Job) are inappropriate. (See also *mazzal(r)ot, 'āyish,* and *k^esîl,* which are used in the same contexts to refer to stars or constellations).

J.N.O.

כּוּמָז (*kûmāz*). See no. 990a.

964 *כּוּן (*kûn*) ***established, prepared, made ready, fixed, certain, right.*** (ASV, RSV similar.)

Derivatives

964a †כֵּן (*kēn*) ***I, right, true.***
964b †כֵּן (*kēn*) ***II, thus, so.***
964c †מָכוֹן (*mākôn*) ***place.***
964d †מְכוֹנָה (*m^e kônâ*) ***base.***
964e †תְּכוּנָה (*t^e kûnâ*) ***fashion.***
964f †כַּוָּן (*kawwān*) ***cake.***

This root occurs with its derivatives more than 288 times. Two hundred seventeen of these occurrences are verbal, appearing in all stems but the Qal. The Niphal and the Hiphil occur most often. The root meaning is to bring something into being with the consequence that its existence is a certainty. This latter is not so much in view in the cognate languages which seem to stress existence, or the bringing into existence, of a thing. With this meaning the root appears in Ugaritic, Akkadian, and Arabic.

Five somewhat different connotations can be discovered in the usages of this root, all having basic theological significance. These connotations move from provision through preparation and establishment to fixity and rightness.

1) As noted above, the word as used in Hebrew, rarely means simply to bring into being. So rare is it, in fact, that BDB and KB suggest that the root meaning is "to be firm" (KB also adding "straight"). However, evidence of the original etymology may be found in those occurrences where something is said simply to have been formed or fashioned (brought into existence) (Jud 12:6; Job 31:15; Ps 119:73; Ezk 16:7). In none of these is the idea of fixity or firmness in view, but rather of basic formation. Particularly in the second and third of these, God's role in forming the human body is significant.

Probably this same basic idea is involved where the word is translated "to provide for" (cf. II Chr 1:4; Job 38:41; Ps 65:9 [H 10]; 78:20; Prov 6:8). Especially in question here is God's ability to provide food for his people and creation. At numerous points it is difficult to know whether certain usages should be translated "provide" or "prepare." It seems likely that the several references in Chr to David's "preparing" materials for the temple could just as appropriately be understood as referring to his "providing" such materials.

2) At any rate, however, it is clear that a very significant group of occurrences must be translated with "prepare." In view of something in the future, certain things are set in order. Meal preparation (Gen 43:16; Josh 1:11; Neh 8:10) and military preparation (Josh 8:4; Ezk 7:14; 38:7; Amos 4:12) are two circumstances in which the word is used in this way. In the latter case many of the references indicate it is God who will war on the ungodly and they should prepare themselves as best they can (cf. Job 15:23; Jer 46:14; 51:12, etc.). On the other hand, God has made preparations as well. These would include his creative functions (Ps 147:8; Job 28:27; Prov 8:27) as well as his judicial ones (Ps 7:11, 13 [H 12,14]; 9:7 [H 8]; Prov 19:29; Zeph 1:7).

The meaning of a group of references which speak of persons "preparing" their hearts to seek the Lord (cf. I Chr 29:18; II Chr 12:14, etc.) is somewhat unclear. It seems likely that the RSV rendering "set," in keeping with the several passages in Ps (cf. 57:7 [H 8] "my heart is fixed [RSV "steadfast"], O God") is more appropriate.

3) As with the previous connotation, there is some ambiguity at the border between "prepare" and "establish." This is especially true in God's creative acts. While Prov 8:27 says that God "prepared" the heavens, Prov 3:19 has him "establishing" the heavens. Here come the special overtones of certitude. They are implicit in the very character of the biblical deity, a God who does not change (Ps 119:90). Because God has brought heaven and earth into existence they are fixed forever (Jer 33:2). So the use of "establish" is especially appropriate. The references where this translation is appropriate may be divided into three groups. All three of these have royal overtones. God, as the divine king has established the heavens as his throne (Ps 103:19) and the earth as his dominion (I Chr 16:30; Ps 93:1; Isa 45:18). As the divine king, his work is accomplished through wisdom and understanding (Prov 3:19; Jer 10:12; 51:15). This in itself leads to the fixity of what he has done.

4) It is the divine king who then guarantees or refuses to guarantee human kingship. Some twenty-five times the word is used with reference to the establishment of a dynasty. It is made plain that, in and of itself, no human line can be established. Only by relation to the One in whom kingship abides is this possible (Ps 89:37 [H 38], etc.). The culmination of this thought is found in Isa 9:6 [H 7] where the kingdom of the Messiah is established by God.

On a somewhat more human level, the book of Prov shows that establishment, on the throne or elsewhere, is not possible apart from adherence to the divine standards of righteousness (16:12, etc.).

But the great test of God's kingship is the problem of sin. This problem is dealt with through the establishment of a people (Deut 32:6). The particular creation language of this verse is significant. Redemption is a part of the total work of creation. Furthermore, God overcomes sin by establishing his sanctuary in the midst of his people (Ex 15:17; Isa 2:2).

5) The sense of well-being which results from

being under God's hand is best expressed in the final connotation. If our heart is fixed on God (Ps 112:7, etc.) then we may be sure that he will establish (also direct, order) our ways (Ps 37:23; 90:17; Prov 16:9). Apart from this kind of confidence, a person's ways are temporary and shaky. But with it there comes a certainty, a rightness (Jer 23:10, etc.), which imparts some of the glory of the infinite to the finite.

kēn ***I. Right, true.*** An adjective, occurring at least twelve times, perhaps more often since its usage is often difficult to distinguish from the following. Used in modern Hebrew for "yes."

kēn ***II. Thus, so.*** A widely used adverb expressing the realization of something previously spoken. Often coupled with prepositions such as *'aḥărê, 'ad, 'al* and *lᵉ*.

mākôn. ***Place.*** Occurs seventeen times, all but one (Ps 104:5) referring to God's dwelling place, either in heaven or the temple.

mᵉkônâ. ***Base.*** Occurs almost entirely in I Kgs 7, and always with reference to the ornate bases designed to support the ten brass lavers in the Solomonic temple.

tᵉkûnâ. ***Fashion, store, seat.*** Occurs three times, each translated differently: the "fashion" of the temple (Ezk 43:11); the "store" of Nineveh's pleasant furniture (Nah 2:9 [H 10]); the "seat" of God (Job 23:3).

kawwān. ***Cakes.*** Occurs twice, both referring to an element used in the worship of the Queen of Heaven (Jer 7:18; 44:19).

Bibliography: THAT, I, pp. 812–16.

J.N.O.

965 כּוֹס (*kôs*) ***I, cup.*** (ASV and RSV similar.)

Of the four words usually translated "cup" (*gābîa', 'aggān, sāp), kôs* is the most common, occurring thirty-three times. *gābîa'* occurs next most frequently with thirteen occurrences. *kôs* seems to denote a drinking goblet, whereas *gābîa'* may (Jer 35:5) or may not (Ex 25:31) be associated with drinking. An *'aggān* is more of a bowl, a larger vessel; a *sāp* also is larger, like a bowl, but it was used for drinking (Zech 12:2). Both Ugaritic and Arabic have cognate nouns for drinking cup from this root.

Of the thirty-one occurrences, about ten speak of literal cups. Of these, five occur in Gen 40 where Joseph interprets the dream of Pharaoh's cupbearer. It is interesting to note that Joseph's cup discussed in Gen 44 is *gābîa'*.

Sixteen of the figurative usages present the cup in a negative light. Primarily these relate to God's judgment upon sinful nations (Jer 25:15). They now drink to the bitter dregs (Isa 51:17, 22) the folly which they have chosen. The result is as drunkenness; staggering (Isa 51:22) and shame (Hab 2:16). It is the cup of the Lord's fury (Jer 25:15). It was this cup which stood before Christ's eyes in Gethsemane (Mt 26:39).

Because of God's forgiveness through Christ the cup offered to us may be one filled with blessing and not curse (Ps 16:5; Ps 23:5). Human beings must choose the cup they will drink: fury or salvation (Ps 116:13).

J.N.O.

966 כּוֹס (*kôs*) ***II, a kind of owl*** (Lev 11:17; Deut 14:16; Ps 102:7).

967 כּור (*kwr*) **I. Assumed root of the following.**

967a כַּר (*kār*) ***basket-saddle,*** only in Gen 31:34, *bᵉkar-haggāmāl* "in the camel-basket," a sort of palankeen bound on the saddle itself.

967b †כּוּר (*kûr*) ***furnace.***

967c †כִּיר (*kîr*) ***range*** (for cooking).

967d †כִּיּוֹר (*kîyôr*) ***laver, pan.***

kûr. ***Furnace.*** (ASV and RSV similar.) A smelter's furnace for the refining of metal. It is only used figuratively in the Old Testament, appearing nine times. Three times it is used of Egypt, from which Israel was delivered (Deut 4:20; I Kgs 8:51; Jer 11:4). In these references there seems to be no stress upon refinement, but merely on the heat symbolizing affliction. On the other hand, the furnace of the exile is definitely depicted as one of refinement (Ezk 22:18, 20, 22) from which Israel will once more emerge as God's chosen (Isa 48:10).

kîr. ***Range*** (for pots). (ASV similar; RSV "stove.") Evidently a platform which held pots over the cooking fire. Occurs in Lev 11:35 where it is said to be unclean if an unclean animal dies on it.

kîyôr. ***Laver, pan, hearth, scaffold.*** (ASV and RSV similar.) Apparently a pan-like construction, having low sides (thus II Chr 6:13, Solomon stood on a bronze scaffold [RSV "platform"]). Apart from the preceding, all other references have to do with a pan as such. The word appears twenty-three times, of which twenty have to do with the laver of the tabernacle or those of the temple. Whereas that in the tabernacle was for the washing of the priests' hands and feet (Ex 30:18), the ten lavers in the temple were for the washing of sacrifices (II Chr 4:6). The molten sea (II Chr 4:2, 6) filled the function of the earlier laver. [It is probable that the great sea also served as a reservoir from which the basins were filled. The basins were on wheeled stands so they could be moved to the sea for filling then taken to various places for use. The priests doubtless did not wash *in* the sea which was a high structure. They washed their hands and feet *with* the water of the sea (cf. Ex 30:18–21). R.L.H.]

J.N.O.

968 כּוּר (*kûr*) ***II, bore, dig, hew*** (meaning dubious). Occurs only in Ps 22:16 [H 17], and there with a medial aleph, *kā'ărû* in some few MSS. The LXX also has a verb *orussō* dig, for the MT *ka'ărî*. The verb in Ps 22:10 [H 17] may be an hapax *kā'ar*. The meaning "dig, wound, pierce" would derive from the context and LXX.

Derivatives

968a מְכֹרָה (*mᵉkōrâ*), מְכוּרָה (*mᵉkûrâ*) ***origin (place of digging out?)*** (e.g. Ezk 29:14; 21:35).

968b מְכֵרָה (*mᵉkērâ*) ***the name of a weapon*** (Gen 49:5).

R.L.H.

969 כּוּשׁ (*kûsh*) ***Ethiopia, Cush, Ethiopians.*** (ASV, RSV similar.)

Derivative

969a †כּוּשִׁי (*kûshî*) ***Ethiopian.***

kûsh refers to the region immediately south and east of Egypt, including modern Nubia, the Sudan, and the Ethiopia of classical writers (not modern Abyssinia). It would begin at about the First cataract, where the Aswan dam now stands. A satellite, and sometimes ruler, of Egypt. The name derives from Egyptian *ksh*. Along with its gentilic (see below) it appears fifty-seven times in the Old Testament.

As indicated in the table of nations (Gen 10:6–8), Cush was associated with the southernmost parts of the known world, falling in Egypt's sphere of influence. Other indications of this view of Cush's extremity are found in the statement of extent of the Persian empire (from India to Ethiopia, Est 1:1; 8:9) and in the promise that exiles would return from beyond Cush (Isa 11:1; Zeph 3:10; cf. Isa 18:1). To the Israelites who in pride saw themselves located at the center of the world and also at the center of God's favor, the Lord (Amos 9:7) said that the distant Ethiopians were just as much his children.

The conjunction of Cush with Sheba (in southern Arabia, Isa 43:3; 45:14, etc.), statements of her mercantile wealth (Job 28:19; Isa 45:14) and the fact that Moses' wife is called a Cushite (Num 12:1; but cf. Ex 2:21 where Zipporah is clearly Midianite) have all combined to lead some students to believe that there was a Cush in Arabia. However, a glance at a map will show that southern Arabia is only separated from Ethiopia by a small expanse of water. Furthermore the fact that the Ethiopian language is Semitic is a further indication of the connection. A number of other possible solutions make it unnecessary to identify Zipporah and the Cushite woman.

Although a number of suggestions as to the location of Cush in Gen 2:13 have been put forward, none has yet proven conclusive. The view of Speiser may be mentioned, however, that *kûsh* sometimes equals Akkadian *kashshu* Cassites, and refers to the mountain country east of Mesopotamia. In this view, the river Gihon of Gen 2:13 ran into the Tigris-Euphrates valley from the east (Speiser, E. A., "The Rivers of Paradise" in *Oriental and Biblical Studies*, Univ. of Penna., 1967, 23–30. Also Harris, R. L., "The Mist, The Canopy, and the Rivers of Eden," JETS 11: 177–79).

In several cases, especially in the prophets, Ethiopia is used in parallel construction as a synonym of Egypt (Isa 20:3–5; Ezk 30:4; Nah 3:9). This probably represents the dominance of Ethiopia (or, more precisely, Nubia) over Egypt between 750 and 663 B.C. Terhakah was a notable Nubian pharaoh who tried, unsuccessfully, to block Sennacherib's westward expansion (II Kgs 19:9; Isa 37:9). After 663 B.C. Egypt was independent of Nubia (Jer 46:9; Ezk 25:4, 5, 9). The Ethiopian army of Zerah referred to in II Chr 14:9 [H 8] ff. is somewhat puzzling in that no extra-Biblical evidence as yet supports the idea of this large an Ethiopian force (one million) operating that far north in the time of Asa (*c.* 900 B.C.).

kûshî. ***Ethiopian, Ethiopians, Cushi.*** Usually a gentilic of the above (Cushite), it also appears three times as a Hebrew proper name: 1) II Sam 18:21–32, a soldier appointed to run to David with news of Absalom's death. RSV translates "Cushite." His apparent ignorance of the nuances of the situation may indicate that he was a foreigner and that RSV is correct; 2) Jer 36:14 great grandfather of Jehudi, a Judean prince; 3) Zeph 1:1, father of Zephaniah.

J.N.O.

כּוֹשָׁרָה (*kôshārâ*). See no. 1052a.

970 כָּזַב (*kāzab*) ***lie, be found a liar, be in vain, fail.*** (ASV, RSV similar.)

Derivatives

970a †כָּזָב (*kāzāb*) ***lie.***

970b אַכְזָב (*'akzāb*) ***lie,*** a noun occurring twice (Jer 15:18; Mic 1:14).

This root and its derivatives occur forty-nine times in the Old Testament. The basic meaning is to speak that which is untrue and therefore false to reality. It is often used in connection with *shāw'* "vanity, emptiness." In distinction from words translated "deceive, lie," etc., *kāzab* stresses the actual act of lying. The cognate is found in Aramaic, Arabic, and Akkadian.

Fundamental to the concepts of truth and falsehood in the Old Testament is the understanding that the God of Israel does not lie (Num 23:19; Ps 89:35 [H 36]). He is faithful to all that he has said and expects his followers to do the same. This is why false witness was such a serious offense (Prov 6:19; 19:5, etc.). Not only was a person denying the truth, but he was calling the God of Truth to be a witness to his crime.

An equally serious offense was false prophecy in God's name (Ezk 13:6–9, 19; Mic 2:11, etc.). Such prophecy was vanity because it was empty of any reality.

Because of man's alienation from God the Truth, lying has become endemic to us (Ps 4:2 [H 3]). Having lied to ourselves about the true nature of our relation to God and thus lost the security of trusting him, we are forced into greater lies about life (Isa 57:11). The essence of wickedness then is a denial of faithfulness and commitment, either to people or to facts (Ps 62:4 [H 5]). Indeed, it becomes a commitment to lies (Isa 28:17). By contrast, a faithful person will not lie (Prov 14:5).

But trust in anything or anyone other than God is vain—a lie (Job 41:9 [H 1]; Prov 30:6). Indeed *kāzāb* "a lie" is probably used in Isa as a derogatory substitute for "idol" (Isa 28:15, 17, cf. also Am 2:4; Ps 40:4 [H 5]). Lies can only deceive and fail one (Prov 23:3). It is this which God was trying to demonstrate to Israel through the prophets. Israel's hope that she could get her temporal needs supplied without commitment to God was a lie (Amos 2:4) and the longer she followed that road the more barren she became (Hos 12:2). Her only hope was to accept God's redemption and return to reality (Isa 28:17; Hos 7:13). Then she would discover freedom (Zeph 3:13) and fruitfulness (Isa 58:11) in life as it was meant to be (Ps 40:4 [H 5]; 25:10–13).

kāzāb. ***Lie, deceitful, false, lying, leasing.*** (ASV and RSV similar, but use one of the other words instead of "leasing.") A noun occurring thirty-one times, all but two (Jud 16:10, 13) in Ps, Prov, and the prophets.

Bibliography: THAT, I, pp. 817–22.

J.N.O.

971 כזר (*kzr*). **Assumed root of the following.**
971a †אַכְזָר (*'akzār*) ***cruel, fierce.***
971b †אַכְזָרִי (*'akzārî*) ***cruel.***
971c †אַכְזְרִיּוּת (*'akzerîyût*) ***cruel.***

'akzār. ***Cruel, fierce.*** (ASV and RSV similar.) Occurs four times, all in poetic passages. Connotes insensitivity and lack of compassion.

'akzārî. ***Cruel.*** (ASV and RSV similar.) Occurs eight times in Prov, Isa, and Jer. Twice in Jer (6:23; 50:42) cruelty is defined as being merciless and in Prov 12:10 even the mercies of the wicked are said to be cruel. The Day of the Lord, for the wicked, will be one of cruelty (Isa 13:9).

'akzerîyût. ***Cruel.*** Occurs in Prov 27:4 where wrath is said to be cruel.

J.N.O.

971.1 כֹּחַ (*kōaḥ*) ***a small reptile, lizard(?)*** Occurs only in Lev 11:30.

972 *כָּחַד (*kāḥad*) ***kick, conceal, cut off, cut down, make desolate.*** (ASV and RSV similar.)

This verb, which appears in the Nilhal, Piel, and Hiphil, occurs thirty-two imes in the Old Testament. It means to keep something back, to refuse to make it known. Since something which is unknown has no independent existence, the verb also denotes non-existence or effacement. There are no known cognates in the other Semitic languages.

In distinction from the other Hebrew words rendered "hide" or "conceal" (*ḥābā', ṭāman, sātar,* and *'ālam,* which see), *kāḥad* has to do with refusing to declare something. When someone was asked to report something, he was charged "not to hide anything" (Gen 47:18; Josh 7:19; I Sam 3:17; II Sam 14:18, etc.). Similarly, if a person was possessed of some special knowledge, he ought not to keep it to himself (Job 15:18). Particularly was this so about the faithful character of God (Job 6:10; 27:11; Ps 40:10 [H 11]; 78:4).

The Hebrews were convinced that in the last analysis nothing could be hidden, or kept from God's knowledge: neither one's nature (Ps 139:15), nor one's character (Ps 69:5 [H 6]; Hos 5:3).

The word in the sense of cutting off or annihilating is used by Israel's enemies (Ps 83:4 [H 5]) by the Lord against those enemies (Ex 9:15; Ex 23:23; II Chr 32:21; Zech 11:8) and against sinful Israel (I Kgs 13:34; Zech 11:9).

J.N.O.

973 כחח (*kḥḥ*). **Assumed root of the following.**
973a †כּוֹחַ (*kôaḥ*) ***strength, power, ability, might, force, substance.*** (ASV and RSV similar.)

Capacity to act, understood both in physical and figurative terms. The word, a noun, appears 126 times in the OT. It is relatively evenly distributed in its occurrences, the most in any one book being twenty in Job. It also occurs twelve times in Isa and Dan, and eleven times in Ps. The only cognate language in which this root appears is

Arabic where it has the verbal idea "to batter down."

In a static sense *kôaḥ* suggests the capacity to endure, as of a stone (Job 6:12), but more commonly it expresses potency, capacity to produce. This may be expressed in sexual terms (Job 40:16; Gen 49:3), or it may express the product of the earth's potency (Gen 4:12; Job 31:39; etc.), but usually physical strength is intended, as in the references to Samson (Jud 16:5; etc.). By extension the word comes to connote general ability to cope with situations (Deut 8:17–18; I Chr 29:14; Ezr 10:13; etc.).

When applied to God, this term suggests that he is indeed omnipotent. His power is seen in creation (Jer 10:12; 32:17; etc.), in the Exodus events (Ex 9:16; 15:6; etc.), in his capacity to subdue his enemies (Job 36:19) and deliver his people (Isa 63:1). As compared to his power, human strength is nothing (II Chr 20:6; Job 37:23; Ps 33:16; Amos 2:14; etc.). The folly of relying upon human strength alone is seen both in Job and in the story of Samson. He is strongest who has discovered the finite limitations of his own capacities in the light of the limitless resources of God through his Spirit (Job 36:22; Isa 40:31; Mic 3:8; Zech 4:6).

Bibliography: THAT, I, pp. 823–24.

J.N.O.

974 כָּחַל (*kāḥal*) ***paint (eyes).*** Occurs only in Ezk 23:40.

975 כָּחַשׁ (*kāḥash*) ***fail, be found liars, belie, deceive, deny, dissemble, deal falsely, lie.*** (ASV, RSV similar, except that RSV has "come fawning," or "come cringing" in place of "submit to.")

Derivatives

975a †כַּחַשׁ (*kaḥash*) ***leanness.***
975b †כֶּחָשׁ (*keḥash*) ***lying.***

The word *kāḥash* which, with its derivatives, occurs twenty-nine times in the Old Testament, has an unusually large range of meanings. This might suggest two, or even three separate, but homophonous roots. However both KB and BDB see only one root involved. BDB suggests the unifying idea to be "to disappoint" and thus, "to deceive, fail, grow lean." KB has no overarching meaning to suggest. The Hebrew usage seems to stress the relational aspect of the word, emphasizing the undependable nature of a person or thing in a given relationship. The root is not attested in any other Semitic language unless Albright's suggestion (BASOR 83:40, n. 7) is correct that Ugaritic *ṯkḥ* (Gordon UT "shine") is a metathesized form of *kḥsh.*

In thirteen other places the prominent idea is that of dealing falsely with someone to that person's detriment. In such cases it is associated with treachery and robbery. In Lev 6:2 [H 5:21] deceiving a person in a matter of deposit or security is a trespass, as is lying about something one has found (6:3 [H 5:22]). The prophets (especially Hos [4:2; 7:3; 10:13; 12:1]) forecast a grim harvest from the climate of deception and unfaithfulness in which Judah and Israel lived.

It may be the idea of deception which lies behind those usages which KJV translates "submit" and RSV "cringe" (Deut 33:29; II Sam 22:45= Ps 18:44 [H 5]; 66:3; 81:15 [H 16]). Both BDB and KB suggest that feigned obedience or fawning are involved here., The remainder of the occurrences are translated by "deny." Here the idea is to fly in the face of the facts (Gen 18:15; Job 8:18). Five of these references have to do with denying God. To deny God is to live a lie. One may deny him by forgetting what he has done (Josh 24:27), by despairing of his goodness, or forgetting one's own need and living without dependence on him (Prov 30:9). One may deny him without ever intending to do so by leading a crooked and corrupt life (Job 31:28; Isa 59:13). And if one doubts his ultimate justice as applied to oneself, God is denied (Jer 5:12).

kaḥash. ***Leanness, lies, lying.*** (ASV and RSV similar.) A noun translated "lies" or "lying" five times, "leanness" once.

In four cases the idea of failing is involved. In Ps 109:24 the Psalmist complains that his body "fails from fatness" (RSV has "become gaunt"). In Job 16:8, Job sees his leanness as a sign of God's judgment, and in Hab 3:17 the writer says he will trust God even if the olive crop fails (cf. also Hos 4:2). One may not depend on either body or crops in place of God.

keḥash. ***Lying.*** Occurs once in Isa 30:9 where Israel, because of her refusal to trust God, is said to be a "rebellious people, lying (or false) sons."

Bibliography: THAT, I, pp. 825–27.

J.N.O.

976 כִּי (*kî*) ***as though, as, because that, but, certainly, except, for, surely, since, that, then, when,*** etc. (ASV and RSV similar.)

A particle expressing a temporal, causal, or objective relationship among clauses expressed or unexpressed. It is perhaps related to the inseparable preposition k^e "like, as." The same particle used in similar ways is found in Ugaritic (*k*), Phoenician, Moabite, Akkadian (*kī*), and Arabic. It occurs about 4250 times in the Old Testament.

In Hebrew *kî* is used in four ways: to introduce an objective clause especially after verbs of seeing, saying, etc. and translated "that"; to introduce a temporal clause and translated "when" (some of these are almost conditional clauses, thus making "if" appropriate); to introduce a causal clause, "because, for, since"; and with *'im* to express the reason why some case might not occur "except, but rather." In all four usages *kî* introduces a given which is the result of some other fact or action or will influence some other fact or action. Some would add an asseverative usage giving emphasis to what follows.

Examples are as follows: (objective) "believe *that* the Lord . . . has appeared to you" (Ex 4:5); (temporal) "*when* you buy a Hebrew servant . . ." (Ex 21:2); (causal) "The earth is the Lord's . . . for he has founded it . . ." (Ps 24:1, 2); (with *'îm*) "I will not lct you go, except you bless me" (Gen 32:27).

J.N.O.

כִּי (*kî*). See no. 961a.

977 כיד (*kyd*). **Assumed root of the following.**
977a כִּיד (*kîd*) ***destruction.*** Derivation and meaning uncertain. Used only in Job 21:20.
977b כִּידוֹן (*kîdôn*) ***dart, javelin*** (e.g. Josh 8:18; Jer 50:42).

כִּידוֹד (*kîdôd*). See no. 953b.
כִּידוֹן (*kîdôn*). See no. 977b.
כִּידוֹר (*kîdôr*). See no. 954a.

978 כִּיּוּן (*kîyûn*) ***kiyyun.*** (ASV similar, RSV "kaiwan.")

This word occurs once in the Old Testament, in Amos 5:26, along with *sikkût* (q.v.). It is evidently an Assyrian loan word, being the name of one of the Mesopotamian star gods. *skt* and *kyn* both seem to denote the star god Saturn in the mythic literature of that region.

Both *sikkut* and *kiyyun* have apparently been revocalized with the vowels from *shiqquṣ* "abomination." This was one of several means by which Biblical writers expressed their contempt for paganism (replacing Baal in names with *bōshet* "shame" [II Sam 9:6], calling Bethel "house of God," Bethaven "house of iniquity," after the golden calves had been established there [Hos 5:8], speaking of the "dung" of the pagans instead of the "idols" of the pagans [Ezk 20:7, etc., *gillulîm*, q.v.]), etc.

As noted in the article on *skt,* becoming subject to the Assyrians involved worship of their gods. Amos here says that such action will result in the destruction of Israel.

J.N.O.

כִּיּוֹר (*kîyôr*). See no. 967d.
כִּילַי (*kîlay*). See no. 1366b.
כִּימָה (*kîmâ*). See no. 963a.

978.1 כֵּילַפּוֹת (*kîlappôt*) ***axe.***

979 כִּיס (*kîs*) ***bag, purse*** (e.g. Deut 25:13; Mic 6:11).

כִּיר (*kîr*). See no. 967c.
כִּישׁוֹר (*kîshôr*). See no. 1052c.
כָּכָה (*kākâ*). See no. 956.
כֹּל (*kōl*). See no. 985a.

980 כָּלָא (*kālā'*) ***withhold, shut up, keep back, refrain, forbid.*** (ASV, RSV similar.)

Derivatives

980a †כֶּלֶא (*kele'*) ***imprisonment.***
980b כלוא (*klw'*) ***Kethib,*** כְּלִיא (*k^e^lî*) ***Qere, imprisonment*** (Jer 37:4; 52:31). See *kele'.*
980c מִכְלָה (*miklâ*) ***enclosure, fold.***
980d כִּלְאַיִם (*kil'ayim*) ***two kinds.***

The basic meaning of this root is to restrict the flow or movement of a thing or person. The root appears in Ugaritic, Akkadian, Aramaic, and Ethiopic with similar meanings. In Arabic it means "to protect." It is somewhat similar to *kālâ* (q.v.) but distinct in meaning and apparently unrelated.

kāla' seems to indicate the interruption of what is in progress or would naturally be in progress. Thus, the windows of heaven were stopped up after pouring out the Flood (Gen 8:2). Similarly, the calves of the cattle pulling the cart with the ark were shut up from following them (I Sam 6:10). The only thing which can prevent the great natural processes is disobedience (Hag 1:10). Given the fallen nature of humanity, such disobedience itself must be restrained (I Sam 25:33; Ps 119:101).

The speaking of truth and praise to God ought not to be stopped (Num 11:28, Ps 40:9 [H 10]). If they are not, then neither will God's mercies be stopped (Ps 40:11 [H 12]). If such intercourse with men and God is stopped, a nearly intolerable pressure will build up (Ps 88:8 [H 9]).

kele'. ***Imprisonment.*** Always used in construct with another word, chiefly *bayit* "house," in which case the construct is translated "prison" (I Kgs 22:27, etc.). It is one of several words translated by "prison" (e.g. *maṭṭarâ, masgār, 'ēsûr* [all of which see]). While there may be slight differences in the connotations of these according to the different root meanings, they seem to be used interchangeably.

It is of interest that imprisonment is not a penalty under the Mosaic code. But it was well-known in Egypt, as Joseph found out, and it was used by the Kings of Israel.

J.N.O.

כִּלְאַיִם (*kil'ayim*). See no. 980d.

981 כלב (*klb*). **Assumed root of the following.**
981a †כֶּלֶב (*keleb*) ***dog.***
981b כְּלוּב (k^e*lûb*) ***basket, cage*** (Jer 5:27; Amos 8:1).

keleb. Dog. The thirty-two occurrences of *keleb* are divided among four emphases, none of them positive. In eleven instances outright contempt is involved. To treat someone like a dog was to treat them as worthless (I Sam 17:43, etc.). Furthermore dogs were to be feared because they were rapacious (Jer 15:3). As an extension of these nuances, for one's body to be eaten by dogs was the ultimate in tragic ends to a life. Finally, the barking of a dog is compared to the sniping of an enemy (Ps 59:6 [H 7]).

The expression, "the hire of a dog" (Deut 23:18 [H 19]) is commonly interpreted to refer figuratively to wages from male prostitution; but some think that *klb* designates a type of Canaanite cultic personnel, and not a dog (See J. Gray, *The KRT Text in the Literature of Ras Shamra*, Brill, 1964, p. 64).

J.N.O.

982 כָּלָה (*kālâ*) ***I, accomplish, cease, consume, determine, end, fail, finish.***

Derivatives

982a †כָּלָה (*kālâ*) ***full end.***
982b כָּלֶה (*kāleh*) ***failing with desire, longing.*** Occurs only in Deut 28:32, w^e*'ênekā rō'ōt* w^e*kālôt 'ălêhem* "while your eyes look and fail longingly for them."
982c כִּלָּיוֹן (*killāyôn*) ***failing, pining*** (of eyes, Deut 28:65); ***annihilation*** (Isa 10:22).
982d †מִכְלָה (*miklâ*) ***completeness, perfection,*** only in II Chr 4:21 in the phrase *miklôt zāhāb* "perfections of gold," i.e. purest gold.
982e †תִּכְלָה (*tiklâ*) ***perfection.***
982f †תַּכְלִית (*taklît*) ***end, perfection.***
982g †כְּלִי (k^e*lî*) ***vessel, utensil.***

The basic idea of this root is "to bring a process to completion." The root occurs in all its forms 237 times. Of these 206 are verbal. As a verb it occurs with an intransitive meaning in the Qal stem 64 times. Transitively it appears in the Piel 140 times. The two remaining occurrences as a verb are in the Pual. The root also appears in Ugaritic and Akkadian. The fact that the Akkadian root is *kālû* which would reflect an original *kl'* and that *kālû* has both the meanings "cease, end, finish" and "delay, hold back" has suggested to some that *kālâ* "cease" is a derivative of *kalā'* "hold back" (q.v.). While this is possible the usages of the two roots in the Hebrew Bible show little connection.

The processes which are brought to an end may be either positive or negative. That is, something may be continually added to until it is full or complete, or something may be taken away from until there is nothing left. The English word "finish" coincides very nicely with *kālâ* in that it too can have either positive or negative connotations.

Processes which are brought to completion include the building of the temple (II Chr 8:16, etc.), speaking (Gen 17:22, etc.), eating (I Kgs 1:41, etc.), drinking (Gen 24:19, etc.), offering (I Sam 13:10, etc.), harvesting (Ruth 2:21, etc.) and numerous others. There seems to be an emphasis upon totality in these references. It is not that a person simply came to a certain point in the process and stopped, but that he or she carried it out in full. An example is found in Ruth 3:18 where Naomi tells Ruth that Boaz will not rest "until he has *finished* the thing." The noun *kālâ* demonstrates the same point in that it must often be translated "full end" to differentiate it from some other end which may be merely a stopping place. On the other hand, to say that *kālâ* means "to bring to perfection" is somewhat misleading in modern English idiom. "Perfect" implies "without flaw" whereas "complete" does not address the question of flaws.

On the negative side something which is "used up, vanished, spent, consumed" is also finished. The first three connotations occur chiefly in the Qal, while the fourth occurs often in the Piel. So one's days can be spent (Job 7:6) as can one's strength (Isa 49:4). Grass can dry up and fail (Isa 15:6; 32:10) and, through weeping, the eyes can also (Jer 14:6; Ps 69:3 [H 4]; 119:82, etc.). The spirit and the soul, because of separation from God, can pine away to the point of fainting (Ps 84:2 [H 3] 119:81; 143:7). Finally, the body itself must be consumed (Job 33:21; Prov 5:11).

The idea of being consumed is most commonly applied to violent destruction, often by war (Deut 7:22; I Sam 15:18; Jer 16:4). In the biblical context such destruction is directly connected to one's relation with God. Those who forsake the Lord will be consumed (Isa 1:28) as will the terrible ones and the scorners (Isa 29:20), the wicked (Ps 37:20), and all his enemies (Ps 18:37 [H 38]). In such destruction God's wrath is *accomplished* (RSV "completed," Ezk 5:13; 7:8, etc.). So Israel was commanded to consume the Canaanites (Deut 7:22), Amalekites (I Sam 15:18), and Syrians (II Kgs 13:17). As a corrective to any temptation to say that such commands are merely projections upon God of the Israelite lust for battle, are the many more numerous references to God's consuming an apostate Israel (Josh 24:20; Jer 5:3; Ezk 22:31, etc., etc.). God's holiness could no more be at peace with pagan Israelites than with pagan Canaanites.

However, the consuming fire of God's anger is not the last word. The truly faithful Israelites were conscious of the fact that God would have been totally justified in destroying Israel long before he did, and that utterly (Ex 32:10; 33½3; Num 16:21; Lam 3:22). That they were not consumed was only because of his mercy (Lev 26:44; Num 25:11; Ezk 20:17). Even in the exile, when destruction did come, a merciful God would not make a "full end" of his own (Neh 9:31; Jer 4:27; 5:10; 5:18; 30:11, 46:28). If Boaz could not rest until he had finished the task of redeeming Ruth, neither will God rest until he has accomplished his purpose of redeeming all who will let him (Job 36:11; Dan 12:7; Jn 19:28).

kālâ. ***Altogether, consume, consumption.*** This noun form must be translated as an English verb in several instances in order to make the sense plain. It expresses the limits of a thing or an idea. Occurs twenty-two times.

miklâ. ***Perfect*** (RSV "pure"). Occurs in II Chr 4:21 with reference to gold. Here the meaning evidently is "unblemished."

tiklâ. ***Perfection.*** Occurs once in Ps 119:96 where the author makes a- pun saying that he has seen the end (*qēṣ*) of all completeness (*tiklâ*).

taklît. ***End, perfection, perfect.*** The sense here is of totality rather- than of being unblemished. A noun occurring five times, three of which are in Job.

k^eli. ***Armor, bag, carriage, furniture, instrument, jewels, sacks, stuff, thing, tools, vessel, weapons.*** (ASV and RSV similar.) A noun denoting the equipment, containers, tools, etc., appropriate to a given service or occupation. KB takes *k^elî* to be from the otherwise unattested root *kālâ* III, "to contain." The word occurs 319 times.

As is evident from the variety of words used to translate *k^elî*, the translators have used English words appropriate for the situations involved. Thus a soldier's equipment will be armor or weapons (Jud 18:16) or even baggage (I Sam 17:22). A musician's equipment will be an instrument (I Chr 15:16), whereas a builder's will be a tool (I Kgs 6:7). Finely worked items of gold and silver are called jewels (Gen 24:53; Num 31:50–51) or vessels (II Kgs 12:13 [H 14]), depending on the context.

One hundred seven of the occurrences have to do with the equipment of the tabernacle and the temple. The KJV conmonly uses "vessels" or "furniture" as the translation in these instances (as does ASV) while RSV uses "utensils." The term does not refer to the main items in the sanctuary such as altar or lampstand, but to the equipment used in serving these. Nebuchadnezzar, finding no idol in the temple to take into captivity, could only take off this equipment as symbolic of its owner (II Chr 36:7). However, God was not controlled by the equipment, as Belshazzar was to discover (Dan 5:2).

Bibliography: TDNT, VII, pp. 359–62. THAT, I, pp. 831–32.

J.N.O.

983 כלה (*klh*) **II. Assumed root of the following.**

983a †כִּלְיָה (*kilyâ*) ***kidneys, reins.*** (ASV similar. RSV translates with "heart," "mind," or "soul" whenever KJV and ASV use "reins" as a figurative term.)

Occurs thirty-one times in Hebrew as well as in Akkadian, Aramaic, Arabic, Ethiopic, and Ugaritic. In all of these languages, the term refers to the twin organs located in the lower back, the function of which is to filter impurities from the blood. With the fat they were of special significance in certain Hebrew sacrifices. When used figuratively, the term refers to the innermost aspects of personality.

Sixteen of the occurrences relate to sacrificial practices: twelve occurring in God's instructions and four in statements of the fulfillment of the commands. Animals given for the peace, sin, and trespass offerings, as well as those offered for consecration of the priests, were to have the internal fat, the kidneys, and the caul above the liver removed and burned on the altar (Ex 29:13, 22; Lev 3:4, 10, 15; 4:9; 7:4; 8:16, 25; 9:10, 19).

No clear reason for the removal is specified in the Scripture, nor has any been forthcoming as yet from cognate studies. Suggestions have included: fat was a special delicacy reserved for God and since the kidneys are usually encased in fat they belonged to him (ISBE, III, p. 1797); perhaps because of their density and color they were associated with the blood (IDB, III, p. 9f.). Furthermore it might be suggested that there was an understanding of the vital connection of the kidneys with the purity of the blood. On the whole, the first suggestion probably has the fewest difficulties. The idea of the special delicacy of the fat and kidneys is apparently born out by Deut 32:14 where the choicest wheat is called "the fat of the kidneys of wheat" (RSV "with the finest of the wheat"). (Cf. also Isa 34j;6.)

Twice (Job 16:13; Lam 3:13) death and destruction are spoken of as arrows slashing into the kidneys. If a near eastern warrior could be fired on from the rear, he was very vulnerable. Here both writers are claiming that God has surrounded them and overcome them with his superior strength.

In two other places the kidneys are used as a

figure for the entire body. The psalmist (139:13) says that God has possessed his "body" from the beginning, having clothed it in the womb. On the other hand, Job (19:27) testifies that when his "body" is no more, he will still have eyes to see God. (NEB contests this rendering, rather connecting the phrase to the next line and reading, "My 'heart' failed me when you said.")

The remaining nine references all use kidneys as a symbol of the innermost being. This is probably so since in dismembering an animal the kidneys are the last organ to be reached. In this usage it is frequently paralleled with heart (as it is at least once in Ugaritic). Jeremiah seems to be emphasizing this innermost idea when he says that the religion of the wicked is superficial, on their lips, but far from their kidneys (12:2). The idea that the wicked would prosper grieves the heart and kidneys of the psalmist (73:21), but they rejoice in the writer of Proverbs when his son speaks right (23:16). Five times in Jer and Ps the importance of inner religion is stressed when it is said that God tries the heart and the kidneys (Jer 11:20, etc.).

J.N.O.

כַּלָּה (*kallâ*). See no. 986a.
כְּלוֹא (*kᵉlôʾ*). See no. 980b.
כְּלוּב (*kᵉlûb*). See no. 981b.
כְּלוּלָה (*kᵉlûlâ*). See no. 986b.

984 כלח (*klḥ*). **Assumed root of the following.**
984a כֶּלַח (*kelaḥ*) ***firm or rugged strength*** (Job 5:26; 30:2).

כְּלִי (*kᵉlî*), כֵּלַי (*kēlay*). See nos. 982g, 1366b.
כִּלְיָה (*kilyâ*). See no. 983a.
כִּלָּיוֹן (*killāyôn*). See no. 982e.
כְּלִיל (*kᵉlîl*). See no. 985b.

985 כָּלַל (*kālal*) ***I, perfect, make perfect.*** (ASV, RSV similar.)

Derivatives

985a †כֹּל (*kōl*) ***all.***
985b †כָּלִיל (*kālîl*) ***perfect.***
985c †מִכְלוֹל (*miklôl*) ***most gorgeously.***
985d †מַכְלֻל (*maklūl*) ***all sorts of things.***
985e †מִכְלָל (*miklāl*) ***perfection.***

Except for the particle *kōl* "all," which occurs upwards of 5000 times, this verb and its derivatives occur 21 times, 8 of which are in Ezekiel. The root meaning is "to be complete, whole." The verb is perhaps denominative since it appears but twice, both in Ezk 27 (v. 4, 11). Both of these verbal usages are associated with "beauty." The translation "perfect" only appears when the root is so associated (5t. in Ezekiel [4t. with ref. to Tyre], once in Lam 2:15 and Ps 50:2, both of which refer to Jerusalem as the "perfection of beauty."

kōl. ***All, every, any, whole, none.*** A very common particle, occurring about 5400 times. Of these all but about 800 are in a genitive relation with the following word, signifying thus, "the whole of something." It is commonly translated "all" if the following word is plural, and "every" if the word is singular and without the article. It can also have a suffix attached to it: "the whole of it, all of it." This particular formation may then follow a given noun, stressing the aspect of totality (II Sam 2:9). It can also be used in this way with the noun understood, as does Isaiah when he expressed the corruption of the entire people by saying, "All of it loves a bribe" (1:23; cf. also 9:17 [H 16]). In some contexts it denotes "all kinds of," "of all sorts." Thus Eliezer took with him "all of the good thing of his master" i.e. "a great variety of good things" (Gen 24:10; cf. Lev 19:23).

kōl can also stand by itself, or absolutely, to express "everything." The sense in which "all" is to be taken must be gathered from the context (cf. Jer 9:3). When used with the article it refers to something just mentioned (Lev 1:9; etc.), or, in a wider sense, to the whole of creation. Such passages as Ps 103:19; 145:9 and Jer 51:19 use this construction when expressing the idea of God's lordship over all things.

kālîl. ***Perfect, whole, wholly, all.*** A noun used both adjectivally and verbally. It occurs fifteen times expressing totality, both of accomplishment and of destruction.

kālîl the substantive is used in three ways, all closely related and having to do with wholeness, or completeness. Four occurrences relate to beauty, and, as noticed above, are translated with "perfect." That which is wholly beautiful is said to be perfectly beautiful. Israel is spoken of in this sense (Ezk 16:14). Her beauty is that of the chosen bride of the Lord, but she has prostituted that beauty with other lovers so that the final result is destruction and the mocking question recorded in Lam 2:15 "is this the city men call the perfection of beauty?" So also the term is used of Tyre and her king (Ezk 27:3 and 28:12; cf. also verbal usages in 27:4, 11). All of these usages remind the reader that perfection of beauty apart from submission to the Lord may finally be more of a curse than a blessing.

Three occurrences have to do with making an entire object of one color, namely blue. Two times one of the high priest's garments, the robe of the ephod, is referred to (Ex 28:31; 39:22), and the third reference (Num 4:6) is to the cloth which was to cover the ark when it was being moved.

The remaining occurrences of *kālîl* (eight) refer to total consumption. Of these, six refer to the whole burnt offering, while of the remaining two, one (Isa 2:18) speaks of God's utter destruction of idols, and the other (Jud 20:40), of a whole city going up in smoke (ASV and RSV; KJV "the flame of the city ascended").

The usual word for the burnt offering (Lev 1) is *'ôlâ* (q.v.). This offering was the chief sacrifice, being offered both daily and at every great festival. It dealt not so much with specific sins as it did with the general alienation of man from God and the need for continual sacrificial atonement if holy God and fallen man were to live together in fellowship. From the Gospels (Jn 1:29) to the Revelation (21:9, 14, 22, 27) Christ is seen to be the fulfillment of this sacrifice, in particular, and all the sacrifices in general.

When *kālîl* is joined with *'ôlâ* (I Sam 7:9; Ps 51:19 [H 21]) it is emphasized that unlike the other offerings, where certain portions belonged to the offerer or to the priest, the burnt offering belonged wholly to God. At least once (Deut 33:10; 13:16 [H 17], RSV) *kālîl* is used by itself as "whole burnt offering." This emphasis upon totality seems to indicate that atonement can be achieved by God alone and that only through a total surrender and consumption of the sacrifice as seen finally in Christ.

miklôl. ***Most gorgeously, all sorts of armor.*** There is little agreement over the correct translation of this word. The fact that it occurs but twice (Ezk 23:12; 38:4), does not ease the problem. In both cases it is used in contexts describing the splendid appearance of military men. A literal translation would seem to be "clothed fully." But clothed in what? RSV has "in full armor" in both cases, while NEB gives "in full dress" for 23:12 and "all fully equipped" for 38:4. ASV duplicates the KJV.

maklûl. ***All sorts of things.*** Occurs once in Ezk 27:24 describing the wares of Tyre's clients. ASV translates "choice wares," RSV "choice garments," NEB "gorgeous stuffs." BDB suggests "thing made perfect."

miklāl. ***Perfection.*** Occurs once in Ps 50:2 "Zion, the perfection of beauty" (cf. Lam 2:15).

Bibliography: THAT, I, pp. 828–30.

J.N.O.

986 כלל (*kll*) **II. Assumed root of the following.**
986a †כַּלָּה (*kallâ*) ***daughter-in-law.***
986b †כְּלוּלָה (*kᵉlûlâ*) ***espousal.***

kallâ. ***Daughter-in-law, spouse, bride.*** (ASV and RSV similar, except that RSV does not use "spouse.") Denotes the circumscribed relationship of a woman who is sworn to one's self or one's son. It may refer to a bride or to a woman long married, like Tamar (Gen 38:11) or Ruth (Ruth 1:6). The root is presumed to be *kll,* but this is not certain. In Akkadian *kallatu* is a "reserved one" and in Ugaritic *klt* refers to goddesses (51:1.16; 4.54) or human beings (1175.2) who are reserved to the gods. Joel 2:16 refers to the fact that the bride was "closeted."

In this sense nine of the references have to do with sexual irregularity involving the daughter-in-law or bride. Anything which breaks the sanctity of the created order of relationships is sternly forbidden (Lev 18:15, etc.). Though Judah and Tamar out of deception on the part of both entered into an incestuous relationship, a crime worthy of death according to the Law of Moses (Lev 20:12), God's grace overruled their sin so that Perez, the offspring of that union, became part of Israel's royal lineage (Gen 38).

Seven occurrences are in Ruth where the stress seems to be upon the fact that the relationship can become something much more than simply official as God's providence works through it (e.g. 4:15).

The Song of Solomon six times in ten verses (4:8–5:1) refers to the beloved as the bride (and sister). In the context the point seems to be that she is a lovely enclosed garden reserved for her husband alone.

The joy of the consummation of the marriage agreement is dwelt on in Jer and Isa. Jeremiah says three times that because of judgment such festal scenes as marriages will be stopped (7:34; 16:9; 25:10). But that is not the final word. The prophet foretells the day when such joys will be restored (33:11).

Isaiah sees redeemed Israel as God's chosen bride, responsive to him alone, decking herself with jewels and a robe of righteousness in preparation for his coming (49:18; 61:10). In that day, says Isaiah, God will delight over her as a bridegroom over a bride (62:5). It is evident that this imagery provides the prototype for the figure of the Church as the Bride of Christ in the New Testament (Rev 21:2).

kᵉlûlâ. ***Espousal.*** Occurs once in Jer 2:2 where God remembers the love which Israel professed to him in the early days of the covenant in the wilderness. Israel's agreement to serve God only is compared to a young girl's oath to know no other man as her husband (cf. *kallâ* "daughter-in-law, bride").

J.N.O.

987 כָּלַם (*kālam*) ***be ashamed, confounded, reproached, hurt, be put to shame, be put to confusion, blush.***

Derivatives

987a כְּלִמָּה (*k^e limmâ*) ***confusion, dishonor, reproach, shame.***

987b כְּלִמּוּת (*k^e limmût*) ***shame.*** Occurs only in Jer 23:40.

kālam denotes the sense of disgrace which attends public humiliation. In thirty cases the root is used in parallel with *bôsh* "to be ashamed" (q.v.). Any distinction between the meanings of the two roots is therefore small. However, when *kālam* appears by itself it does not often have the idea of disgrace which comes through a failed trust (a prominent element in *bôsh*). Rather it is a more general disgrace resulting from any kind of humiliation. The fact that the Arabic cognate means "to wound" suggests the idea of a "wounded" pride.

kālam seems to refer to 1) wounding of the body, 2) wounding of the spirit through public humiliation, and 3) wounding of the spirit because of defeat and captivity.

The first usage is supported by two references, both in I Sam 25 (7, 15) where Nabal's men are said not to have been "hurt" by David.

An example of the second kind of usage is found in I Sam 20:34 where Saul is said to have done shame (or hurt) to David by maligning his character to Jonathan. Other examples of such undeserved humiliation are: "I hid not my face from shame and spitting" (Isa 50:6; cf. also Num 12:14; II Sam 10:5). To be charged with wrongdoing brought its own shame (Jud 18:7), whether the charge was correct or not. So Boaz told his workers not to shame (or reproach) Ruth for gleaning among them (Ruth 2:15), and Job's "comforters" felt it necessary to shame Job for mocking God (Job 11:3; 19:3).

There were some kinds of activity by which a person ought to be humiliated even without being reproached for them. Prostitution was one of these and the prophets charged the Hebrew people with religious prostitution. (Even the Philistines were embarrassed by the Hebrews' actions according to Ezk 16:27.) However, the people had not even the grace to blush (Jer 3:3; 6:15; 8:12). Therefore, the prophets promised that shame would come from another quarter: defeat and captivity. If they would not be embarrassed and ashamed because of their sins, they would be so because of their helplessness (Isa 30:3; Ezk 32:30).

However, Israel will not finally be ashamed through God's punishment, but rather through his goodness. According to Ezekiel (16:54, 61, 63; 43:10–11) it is when God, in undeserved grace, restores Israel and defends her (cf. Isa 54:4) that Israel will become truly ashamed of the way she has treated him.

J.N.O.

כִּכָּר (*kikkār*). See no. 1046c.

כְּלִמּוּת (*k^e limmût*). See no. 987b.

988 כָּמַהּ (*kāmah*) ***faint*** (Ps 62:3).

כְּמוֹ (*k^e mô*). See no. 938.

989 כְּמוֹשׁ (*k^e môsh*) ***Chemosh.*** (ASV and RSV similar.)

God of Moab, referred to eight times in the Old Testament and known from contemporary Assyrian inscriptions, as well as the Moabite Mesha Inscription. [*Chemosh* in the form *kamīshu* is now reported to be attested in the Ebla tablets (R. Youngblood)].

Little is known about the character or worship of Chemosh. It is striking that the Moabite king, Mesha, in his inscription on the famous Moabite stone thanking Chemosh for deliverance from Israel, uses language which is very reminiscent of that used in the Bible to praise Yahweh (cf. also Jud 11:24). It is possible that Moab, long under the domination of Israel, had appropriated some of her conceptions about God or that such honorific expressions were common in the ancient near east.

It is clear from the Bible that the influence of the worship of Chemosh also went in the other direction. Along with Ashtoreth (Astarte) of Sidon and Milcom of Ammon, Chemosh had been given a worship center on the outskirts of Jerusalem by Solomon (I Kgs 11:7, 33). These were probably part of Solomon's system of alliances with these countries. The worship centers remained influential for some 300 years until defiled by Josiah (II Kgs 23:13).

In two aspects, the separation between Yahweh and Chemosh is clear. One is the idolatry of Chemosh. So long as he was represented by an image he was subject to this world. He could go into captivity (Jer 48:7) and Yahweh could not. As an embodiment of this world he could only fail Moab as Israel's bulls had failed her (Jer 48:13).

Furthermore, Yahweh, as the giver of life, forbad human sacrifice. It is clear that Chemosh, like the other ancient near eastern deities, accepted, and may have demanded, such sacrifice. Milcom (or Molech) with whom Chemosh seems to be identified in Jud 11:24 was clearly such a blood-thirsty deity and is condemned as such by the writers of Scripture.

Bibliography. Cross, F., and Freedman, D., *Early Hebrew Orthography*, American Oriental Society, 1952, p. 39, n. 13.

J.N.O.

990 כמז (*kmz*). **Assumed root of the following.**

990a †כּוּמָז (*kûmāz*) ***tablets.*** (ASV "armlets," marg. "necklaces"; RSV "armlets," "beads," NEB "pendants.)

It is clear from the context in which this word occurs that it is some kind of ornament (Ex 35:22; Num 31:50). Further precision is not possible. In both cases they are part of freewill offerings to God.

J.N.O.

991 כמן (*kmn*). **Assumed root of the following.**
991a מִכְמָן (*mikmān*) ***hidden stores*** (Dan 11:43).
991b כַּמֹּן (*kammōn*) ***cumin.***

992 כָּמַס (*kāmas*) ***store up*** (Deut 32:34).

993 *כָּמַר (*kāmar*) ***I, yearn, be kindled, be black*** (ASV similar, RSV instead of "be black" has "be hot.")

The root meaning is to be warm, hot. Three of the four occurrences (Gen 43:30; I Kgs 3:26; Hos 11:8) all of which are Niphal express the emotions of filial attachments, in the latter case those of God for his people.

J.N.O.

994 כמר (*kmr*) **II. Assumed root of the following.**
994a כִּמְרִיר (*kimrîr*) ***darkness, gloominess*** (Job 3:5).

995 כמר (*kmr*) **III. Assumed root of the following.**
995a מִכְמָר (*mikmār*) ***net, snare*** (Isa 51:20).
995b מַכְמֹר (*makmōr*) ***net, snare*** (Ps 141:10, 11).
995c מִכְמֶרֶת (*mikmeret*) ***net, fishing net*** (Hab 1:15).
995d מִכְמֹרֶת (*mikmōret*) ***net, fishing net*** (Isa 19:8).

996 כֹּמֶר (*kōmer*) ***priest, idolatrous priest.*** (ASV and RSV similar. RSV always translates "idolatrous priests.")

This word occurs three times in the Old Testament: II Kgs 23:5; Hos 10:5; Zeph 1:4. All of these refer to priests who had led Israel in idolatrous worship. The references cover the broad spectrum of pagan influences in Hebrew religion: bull worship in North Israel, Baalism in Judah and fertility rites on the "high places."

The root meaning of the word is not known. Mowinckel, in an article which appeared in ZAW 38:238f. suggested that it was drawn from the root *kmr* I "to be warm, hot." If this were so *kōmer* would mean "the excited one" and would refer to the dervish aspect of pagan worship. However, the word may be related to an Egyptian root (cf. KB p. 442). This would be very appropriate in view of the interrelations between Canaanite and Egyptian religions. The word is used in old Aramaic but does not appear in Ugaritic which uses the root *khn*. Albright argues that the word refers to eunuch priests—which, of course, were forbidden in Israel (Deut 23:1 [H 2]; Albright, FSAC, p. 234).

J.N.O.

כִּמְרִיר (*kimrîr*). See no. 994a.
כֵּן (*kēn*). See nos. 998a, 999a, 964a,b.

997 *כָּנָה (*kānâ*) ***give flattering titles to, surname, be surnamed*** (ASV and RSV similar.)

Occurs four times, only in Piel and Pual (Job 32:21–22; Isa 44:5; 45:4). Twice Eliphaz says he does not know how to give false titles. In Isa God promises that in the Restoration, Israel's title will be a truth, not a misnomer.

כַּנָּה (*kannâ*). See no. 999b.
כִּנּוֹר (*kinnôr*). See no. 1004a.

998 כנן (*knn*) **I. Assumed root of the following.**
998a †כֵּן (*kēn*) ***foot, base, place, office, estate.*** (ASV and RSV similar.)

A noun from a theoretical root *knn* "to be firm, substantial." It denotes the physical base or foundation of something (especially the bronze laver). The remainder of the occurrences refer to a person's position or office.

J.N.O.

999 כנן (*knn*) **II. Assumed root of the following.**
999a כֵּן (*kēn*), כִּנִּם (*kinnim*), כִּנָּם (*kinnām*) ***gnat, gnats, gnat swarm.*** Meaning dubious.
999b כַּנָּה (*kannâ*) ***support (of tree),*** i.e. root, stock (Ps 80:16).

1000 כָּנַס (*kānas*) ***gather, collect, wrap*** (in a cover, Hithpael).

Derivative

1000a †מִכְנָס (*miknās*) always plural *miknāsayim*, ***trousers.***

kānas occurs eleven times in the OT, seven times in the Qal, three in the Piel, and once in the Hithpael.

One usage of *kānas* refers to David's gathering people in order to prepare for Solomon's construction of the temple (I Chr 22:2). In a similar vein Esther sent word to Mordecai to gather together all the Jews who were in Shushan (Est 4:16). The power of God is extolled (Ps 33:7) in gathering the waters of the sea as though in a heap.

Nehemiah 12:44 records the appointment of men to collect offerings, tithes, and portions of the harvest for priests and Levites. Israel is warned that God intends to gather them to undergo the fire of his anger (Ezk 22:21). Isaiah likens Israel's untenable international position to a man whose bed covering is so narrow that he cannot wrap himself in it (Isa 28:20).

miknās. ***Trousers or drawers*** (for priests) (KJV, ASV, RSV render similarly, breeches). This noun occurs only in the dual (*miknāsayim*). It is found five times in Ex and Lev and once in Ezk 44:18. Trousers were ordered by God in the interests of decorum, and were made of linen to absorb perspiration.

C.L.F.

1001 כָּנַע (*kānaʿ*) ***be humbled, subdued, brought down, low, under, brought into subjection.*** (ASV, RSV similar.)

Derivative

1001a כִּנְעָה (*kinʿâ*) ***bundle, pack.*** Occurs only in Jer 10:17, "pack your bundle (and take it) out of the land."

This verb occurs thirty-six times. It denotes bringing a proud and recalcitrant people or spirit into subjection. The only cognate is found in Arabic where the root means "to fold (the wings of a bird)."

No thoroughgoing distinction is possible between *kānaʿ* and the two other words *ʿānâ* and *shāpēl* which are most commonly translated "be humble." However, slight distinctions may be drawn: *ʿānâ* seems to stress the aspects of forcible humiliation (including rape), whereas *shāpēl* contrasts height and lowness. *kānaʿ* compares dominion and subjection (Ps 106:42).

Eighteen of the occurrences refer to military subjection, most of these being nations which had oppressed Israel or at least threatened to do so. But Israel's God has made them subject to her (Neh 9:24, etc.).

Of the eighteen references to a spiritual submission, fifteen relate the actions of a king in submitting himself and his nation to God (I Kgs 21:29, etc.). The emphasis is upon a proud and independent spirit abasing itself.

Two key references are Lev 26:41 and II Chr 7:14 which indicate that so long as a person, or nation, is arrogant and self-sufficient, God can do nothing for them.

J.N.O.

1002 כְּנַעַן (*kᵉnaʿăn*) ***I, Canaan.***

Derivatives

1002a †כְּנַעֲנִי (*kᵉnaʿănî*) ***Canaanite.***
1002b †כְּנַעַן (*kᵉnaʿan*) ***II, merchant.***

kᵉnaʿan is the name of either a person or a territory. Most of its ninety occurrences are in the Pentateuch (thirty-nine in Gen). The expression "land of Canaan" occurs sixty-two times.

Canaan, one of the sons of Ham, is first mentioned in Gen 9:18. He is listed as the father of Sidon, Heth, and nine other peoples including Jebusites and Amorites (I Chr 1:13). The curse upon Canaan which destined him to be a servant to his brothers (Gen 9:25, 27) likely pointed forward to the later subjugation of the inhabitants of Canaan at the hands of the Israelites in the times of Joshua and the Davidic monarchy. The name of the land may derive from this forbear, or there may be in Gen 10:15–18 a play on the word "Canaan" which is identical in sound with the name of Noah's grandson. Speiser derived the word "Canaan" from a word for purple dye found in Nuzi. (The Greek word for Phoenicia, *phoinix*, means purple.) Later study makes this unlikely. Maisler and Albright argued for an original meaning "purple merchant." Millard, following Landsberger, claims that derivation from a purple color is impossible, but is not able to offer a fully defensible origin. See the bibliography for references.

In such expressions as "inhabitants of Canaan" (Ex 15:15) or "kings of Canaan" (Jud 5:19) the population of a territory is in view. The "language of Canaan" in Isa 19:18 is the Hebrew language though there were also other dialects.

Canaan, as an Egyptian administrative district in the second millennium, comprised Palestine and southern Syria. Biblically, Canaan consists of the land west of the Jordan and is distinguished from the area east of Jordan (Num 32:29–33; 35:14; Josh 22:32). Though its extent is variously described in the Bible, the land of Canaan broadly includes the area from the wilderness of Zin in the south to Rehob at Lebo-hamath in the north, a distance of approximately three hundred miles, yet as the excavations at Ras Shamra have shown, Canaanite culture actually extended along the Syrian coastline as far north as Hamath itself. Its western border was the Mediterranean Sea and its eastern border the Jordan river (Num 13:2; 17–33; 34:2–12; cf. Gen 10:19). More narrowly considered, Canaan referred to the coastal strip, especially the northern section which was known also as Phoenicia (Num 13:29; Josh 5:1). In Israel's early history, the Canaanites inhabited the coastlands and plains, and the Amorites the hills (Num 13:19; Josh 5:1; 11:3; Jud 1:27ff.).

Canaan was an inhabited land (Ex 16:35; cf. Josh 5:12). The patriarchs lived there (Gen 31:18; 37:1). The territory when referred to as the "land of the Canaanites" is described as a "land flowing with milk and honey" (Ex 3:8; 13:5), an expression which signifies the fertility and abundance of the land. Located in Canaan were the cities of Hebron (Gen 23:2, 19), Shechem (Gen 33:18), Luz (or Bethel, Gen 35:6), Mamre (Gen 49:30), and Shiloh (Josh 21:2). Once Canaan is referred to as the "land of the Philistines" (Zeph 2:5).

A few Scriptures give a negative evaluation to Canaan. Isaac admonished Jacob not to take a wife from the daughters of Canaan (Gen 28:1, 6; cf. 36:15). Israel was also instructed, "You shall not do what is done in the land of Canaan" (Lev 18:3). A later author complained, however, that Israel disobeyed and "sacrificed to the idols of Canaan" (Ps 106:38).

The land of Canaan takes on a theological character not only as "the land in which they (the patriarchs) dwelt as sojourners" but as the land which is God's gift (Ex 6:4). Canaan is the land which the Lord gives to Israel (Num 13:2). God said to Abraham, "I will give to you and to your descendents after you . . . all the land of Canaan for an everlasting possession" (Gen 17:8). This covenant with Abraham is referred to in Ex 5:22–6:8, a significant passage which summarizes God's intentions with Israel in response to Moses' inquiry. It is part of God's intention that Israel dwell in Canaan, the place of abundance, and to this place she returns following the Exile. God desires good for his people. Canaan is given Israel for a possession (Lev 14:34; Deut 32:49) and for an inheritance (I Chr 16:18=Ps 105:11). Many interpret Isa 11:10–12 to say that all the dispersed Jewish remnant is to be regathered to their ancestral land under the lordship of the messianic Root of Jesse.

k^e^na'ănî. ***Canaanite(s)*** refers either to the descendants of Canaan or to the inhabitants of Canaan and sometimes to merchants (see *k^e^na'an* II).

One of Simeon's descendants had a Canaanite mother (cf. Gen 46:10=Ex 6:15)—an example of intermarriage that kept Israel from remaining an ethnically "pure" race.

Those who inhabited Palestine before the conquest were known as Canaanites (Gen 12:6). Their destruction had been ordered by God and they were listed as dispossessed by Israel (Josh 5:1; 11:3; 13:4). Israel's failure to obey fully meant that Canaanites continued to live among the Israelites (Josh 16:10; Jud 1:27–33). The Canaanites were immoral in their practices, as is clear both from Scripture (Ex 23:23–24) and from literature found since 1929 at ancient Ugarit. Negative evaluations of them were already expressed in the time of the patriarchs (Gen 24:3; 28:8). Israel was therefore directed to demolish their idols, refrain from covenant with them (Ex 34:11–16) and destroy them lest they pervert Israel's pure religion (Deut 7:1–5ff.; 20:17–18). Actually the Israelites did not destroy the Canaanites through weakness or misplaced mercy or some other reason. They reaped a bitter harvest in the sacrificing of their own innocent children (Ps 106:35–38). Albright says that archaeological evidence fully supports the claim of the moral degradation of the Canaanites before the Hebrew conquest (FSAC, pp. 231–5, 281). The Canaanites who lived on the plain are to be distinguished from the Amorites who were hill people (Num 13:29; Josh 5:1). One view holds that Canaanites were urbanized Amorites (Kenyon).

The term *k^e^na'ănî* is generally used collectively but may occasionally refer to an individual (cf. king of Arad, Num 21:1). The term can also mean "merchant" (q.v. Canaan, II). In Zech 14:21 ASV renders "Canaanite" and RSV "trader," in a context where the ancient versions favor the meaning "trader" since the sanctity of bowls and pots in the coming age will make exchange at the temple unnecessary.

k^e^na'an ***II. Trader, merchant.*** (ASV renders "traffic"; RSV "trading," "trade.") Since the Canaanites were known for their trading expertise, it is not always clear whether the term refers to a race or to the trading profession (cf. various translations of Zeph 1:11; Ezk 16:29; 17:4 where considerations of poetic parallelism make "trade" the preferable reading). The trade, originally in red-purple wool, led to the use of "trader" as a general term, quite without stigma (cf. Prov 31:24).

A stele of Amenophis II (c. 1440 B.C.) demonstrates the antiquity of this usage. From this Maisler concludes that the term denoted the "merchant plutocracy" of the coastal and trading centers of Syria and Palestine (see bibliography).

Bibliography: Albright, W. F., "The Role of the Canaanites in the History of Civilization," in *The Bible and the Ancient Near East,* ed. G. E. Wright, Doubleday, 1965, pp. 427–28. Kenyon, Kathleen, *Amorites and Canaanites,* London: Oxford University, 1966. Maisler, B., "Canaan and the Canaanites," BASOR 102:7–12. Millard, A. R., "The Canaanites," in *Peoples of Old Testament Times,* ed. D. J. Wiseman, Oxford: Clarendon, 1973, pp. 29–52.

כְּנַעֲנִי (*k^e^na'ănî*). See no. 1002a.

1003 כנף (*knp*). **Assumed root of the following.**
1003a †כָּנָף (*kānāp*) ***wing, winged, border, corner, shirt.*** (ASV, RSV similar.)

Occurs 107 times: Ezk 26; Ps, 12; I Kgs, 10; II Chr, 10. Appendage of a bird with which it flies, denoting speed as well as protection. The word occurs in Arabic, Akkadian, Aramaic, and Ugaritic with the same meaning. No verbal prototype for the noun is known; the verbal usage which exists (only once, *yikkānēp,* Isa 30:20) has denominative meanings (hide, enclose, assemble) based on the uses of the noun.

Only ten of the occurrences of this noun literally refer to a bird. Of these ten references, in at least eight "wing" is used to qualify "bird" (cf. Gen 1:21 "every fowl of a wing").

Many more references use the term figuratively, most of these referring to God and most having a positive connotation. The deliverance from Egypt is twice described in terms of God bearing his people upon eagle's wings (Ex 19:4; Deut 32:11). But mostly he is seen as sheltering his own beneath his wings as a hen does her chicks (Ps 17:8; Ruth 2:12). Commonly some statement of God's proven trustworthiness is related to the statement of an intent to seek shelter under his wings (Ps 36:7 [H 8], "How excellent is thy loving-kindness, O God, therefore the children of men put their trust under the shelter of thy wings"). Malachi 3:20 speaks of the Sun of righteousness rising with healing in his wings. Evidently this is an appropriation of the winged sun disc symbol which is used throughout the ancient near east as a manifestation of the deity's protection. The appropriation of this ancient theme in a prediction of Christ is very significant. He alone is the true manifestation of God's benevolence and he comes to heal (not merely protect) those who cast away their pride through fear of God.

However those wings which offer deliverance and security to those who fear him, can bring terror to those who defy him. Jer 48:40; 49:22 tell that God will spread his eagle's wings over Moab and destroy them, just as an eagle may swoop upon a hapless rabbit. In Isa 8:8 Assyria is the eagle overshadowing Judah (cf. also Ezk 17:3, 7).

The remaining figurative usages speak of the speed of wings. The wind is said to have wings (II Sam 22:11, etc.). Three of the six occurrences deal with God's riding on the wind. Money is said to have wings (Prov 23:5), as does gossip (Eccl 10:20). The lovely passage in Ps 139:9 speaks of the wings of the morning being unable to outstrip God's care.

The exact origin of a separate set of figurative usages is difficult to determine. Here the word either means the flowing hem of a robe or the ends of the earth. Perhaps the similarity of the robe to wings, and then the "end" of the robe to the ends of the earth accurately describes the transference.

The remainder of the references to *kānāp* have to do with either the cherubim over the ark, or Ezekiel's visions. It is tempting to see in these numerous occurrences some theological statements concerning Yahweh, especially in the light of the winged seraphim in Isa 6:2. It may be that the wings of his messengers speak of his ability to transcend his creation and yet be at any moment immanent in it. The fact that he is elsewhere said to ride on the wings of the wind may support such conjectures. However, apart from more explicit biblical statements they must remain in the realm of conjecture.

Bibliography: THAT, I, pp. 833–35.

J.N.O.

1004 כנר (*knr*). **Assumed root of the following.**
1004a †כִּנּוֹר (*kinnôr*) ***harp.***
1004b †כִּנֶּרֶת (*kinneret*), כִּנֲרוֹת (*kinărôt*) ***Chinneret.***

kinnôr. ***Harp.*** (ASV and RSV similar.) A musical instrument having strings and a wooden frame. Commonly associated with joy and gladness. The word seems to be of Indian derivation, there being an Indian stringed instrument called a *kinnāra*. The word itself, if not the entire instrument, seems to have come into the Hebrew vocabulary via Hittite (cf. KB, *in loc*). Probably the *kinnôr* was a lyre rather than a true harp. Lyres are pictured in a number of ancient paintings and sculptures.

Although most of the references to harps depict them in a cultic context, about six references indicate that it was a general accompaniment for recreation and relaxation. Its accompaniment was common in feasts (Gen 31:27), presumably played by dancing girls (Isa 23:16).The *kinnôr* is the first musical instrument mentioned in the Bible.

Both Job (21:12) and Isa (5:12) declare that it is the wicked who have times of rejoicing and gladness, and both contemplate the injustice of this.

Most of the references show the harp in a religious setting. It and other instruments characterized the sons of the prophets (I Sam 10:5; Ps 49:4 [H 5]; cf. I Sam 16:23). After the prevalence of the harp and other instruments in the rejoicing over the ark's return (II Sam 6:5; I Chr 13:8), instrumental music seems to have come into its own in Israel's worship (I Chr 25:1, 3, 6). Study of the joyous psalms associated with harps shows that the steadfast love, faithfulness and justice of the Creator-Redeemer were central to Israel's rejoicing.

Bibliography: Best, H. M., Huttar, D., "Music, Musical Instruments," in ZPBD. Sellers, O. R., "Musical Instruments of Israel," BA 3:33–48.

kinneret, kinărôt. ***Chinnereth, Chinneroth.*** Lake in northern Palestine significant as a boundary point for the land of Israel. The NIV spells it with a "k" to avoid a common mispronunciation. It is known as the Sea of Galilee or Gennesaret in the New Testament. Occurs four times with the ending—*eth* and three times with—*oth*. The name appears in Egyptian topographical lists. No Semitic etymology has been agreed upon. Albright suggests a connection with the goddess of the lyre, Kinnâr in Ugaritic (YGC, p. 144).

In Num 34:11 Chinnereth is given as one element in the eastern border of the land of Canaan. In Josh 12:3 the westernmost border of Sihon's territory was designated as the Jordan Valley from the Salt Sea to Chinneroth. In Deut 3:17 this same designation is given for the western side of the territory which was given to the half tribe of Mannaseh, and the tribes of Gad and Reuben (cf. also Josh 13:27).

As in New Testament times the region just west and north of the lake (roughly the same as the territory of Naphtali) was called by the same name as the lake. So Ben-Hadad of Syria is said at one time to have captured all Chinneroth (I Kgs 15:20). There was also a city in Naphtali of the same name, provisionally identified with tell el-ʿoreimeh (Josh 19:35).

J.N.O.

כִּנֶּרֶת (*kinneret*). See no. 1004b.

1005 כְּנָת (*kᵉnāt*) ***associate, colleague*** (Ezr 4:7).

1006 כֶּסֶא (*kese'*) ***full moon*** (Prov 7:20; Ps 81:4).

1007 כִּסֵּא (*kissē'*) ***seat, stool, throne.*** (ASV, RSV similar.)

Occurs 136 times, of which 34 are in I Kings, 17 in Jeremiah and 15 in Chronicles. Of these occurrences, all but 7 refer to royal or divine thrones. In all cases it is a seat of honor. The identical root appears in Ugaritic (*ks'*) and Akkadian (*kussû* < Sumerian GU. ZA), while both Aramaic and Arabic show an additional r: *karsa'* (Aramaic), *kursīyu* (Arabic). Perhaps a loan word.

As mentioned above, the basic idea of the root seems to be "seat of honor" (Ehud, Jud 3:20; Eli, I Sam 1:9; 4:13; 18, etc.). The one possible exception to this is found in the description of the prophet's chamber (II Kgs 4:10) where KJV simply translates "table and stool" (RSV "chair").

In the usages translated by "throne" the minority have to do with literal thrones. These are either descriptions of thrones (I Kgs 10:18; Ezk 1:26, etc.) or statements concerning kings sitting on specific thrones for matters of judgment (Est 5:1; Jer 1:15; etc.), affairs of state (I Kgs 22:10), or royal honor (II Kgs 25:28).

The great bulk of the references to throne take the term figuratively. Thus to sit on the throne of the kingdom was to rule the kingdom, or in some cases, to begin to rule the kingdom (cf. I Kgs 16:11, etc.). Of the eighty-seven figurative usages, at least forty-seven indicate that it was God who either placed a person on, or removed him from, the throne. Many of these are related to the establishment of the Davidic line, and of these the vast majority relate to Solomon's accession (I Kgs 1–2). The frequent statement that God has "established" (*kûn,* q.v.) someone's throne further indicates that royal stability, wherever it is found, is a function of God's sovereignty.

The book of Prov on several occasions emphasizes that no throne is established by force, but rather through mercy, justice, and righteousness (Prov 16:12; 20:8, 28; 25:5; 29:14). But, of course, the immediate question is: according to whose standard? For the Hebrew this was not a difficult question. It is plain that the true King by whom all humans, even kings, are judged is the Heavenly One. Study of *kissē'* as it relates to God bears this out. His throne is established forever (Ps 93:2; 103:19; Lam 5:19). It is fixed in the heavens (Isa 66:1; Jer 3:17) as well as in his chosen place, Jerusalem. The pronouncements from his throne of judgment are altogether true and right (Ps 74:8 [H 9]; 89:14 [H 15]). Nowhere is the dichotomy between the fallible human king and the infallible divine king more clearly brought out than in I Kings 22. Here Jehoshaphat and Ahab sit on their splendid royal thrones to receive Micaiah's prophecy (v. 10). But Micaiah reports that he has seen God sitting on his throne and that he has given a word of doom concerning their royal enterprises against Syria (v. 10). God is the king of Israel and Judah (cf. also Isa 6:1).

This dichotomy is forever resolved in the Messiah. As the Israelites looked at the long string of sorry kings visited on them, and as they compared these with God's perfect standard they came to long for that Son of David who would rule them, and the world, out of love and not selfishness, with equity and not partiality (Isa 9:7 [H 6]; 16:5; Jer 22:11–23:6; Zech 6:13). The testimony of the NT is that he has come and that all creation waits breathlessly for his coronation day when he will assume his throne forevermore.

J.N.O.

1008 כָּסָה (*kāsâ*) ***I, cover, conceal, hide.*** In a few places used in the sense of "forgive." (RSV, NASB and NIV similar.)

Derivatives

1008a כָּסוּי (*kāsûy*) ***outer covering*** of the tabernacle. Used only in Num 4:6, 14.

1008b †כְּסוּת (*kᵉsût*) ***covering.***

1008c †מִכְסֶה (*mikseh*) ***a covering.***

1008d מְכַסֶּה (*mᵉkasseh*). In form, this word is a Piel participle and in its four usages can be handled as an active noun, "that which covers."

The usual usage of the verb *kāsâ* I is the literal meaning "to cover." Frogs covered Egypt (Ex 8:6 [H 2]). The pillar of cloud covered the tabernacle (Num 9:16).

It is also used more generally to mean "conceal" (Gen 37:26; Prov 10:18, KJV "hide") or "overwhelm" (Prov 10:6, 11, NIV "overwhelm"). In Gen 7:19–20 the hills were "covered;" the Hebrew does not specify with what. The NIV specification of water goes beyond the Hebrew. The Hebrew may merely mean that the mountains were hidden from view by the storm.

It is probably the meaning "hide" that leads to the sense, forgive. In the well-known verse, Ps 32:1, "cover," *kāsa* (Qal) is paralleled by "forgive" (*nāśā'*). The word is used in v. 5 in the sense of "hide." Psalm 85:2 [H 3] is very similar and has the same parallel (*nāśā'*). This sense also occurs in Neh 4:5 [H 3:37] where the parallel is "blot out" (*māḥâ*). In Prov 17:9 and 28:13 the meaning is likely "conceal" (so NIV in the latter verse). The contrast is to confess or to make known. It is probably too much to found an OT theology of forgiveness on these verses in Ps and Nehemiah. It has been argued, more on the basis of *kāpar* "atone" (q.v.), which some translate "cover," that the OT sacrifices merely covered sin until it was dealt with *de facto* on the cross. This view of course has the truth that the blood of bulls and goats could not pay the price of sin in the OT. But it seems that we should say that the OT sin was indeed forgiven by God on the basis of the final sacrifice to come. The OT sacrifices were symbolic and typical but the forgiveness was real. At least, the other words *nāśā'* (take away), *māhâ* (blot out), *sālaḥ* (forgive), etc. imply a real forgiveness so that sins were removed to an immeasurable distance (Ps 103:3, 11–12).

kᵉsût. *Covering.* Used only eight times, most of these referring to clothing. But note Gen 20:16 where "covering of the eyes" (*'ēnayim*) is taken by the NIV as "to cover the offense" (probably reading *'ĕwōnîm*).

mikseh. *A covering.* This noun refers mostly to the leather (KJV badgers' skins, NASB porpoise skins, NIV hides of sea cows) covering of the tabernacle. Once it refers to the covering of Noah's ark. Does this mean that the ark had a protective roof of animal hides?

Bibliography: Girdlestone, SOT, pp. 135–38.

R.L.H.

1009 כסה (*ksh*) **II. Assumed root of the following.**

1009a כֶּסֶת (*keset*) ***band, fillet.***

1010 כָּסַח (*kāsaḥ*) ***cut off or away, a plant*** (Ps 80:17; Isa 33:12).

כְּסִיל (*kᵉsîl*). See no. 1011c,e.

כְּסִילוּת (*kᵉsîlût*). See no. 1011d.

1011 כָּסַל (*kāsal*) ***be foolish.***

Derivatives

1011a †כֶּסֶל (*kesel*) ***confidence, hope.***

1011b †כִּסְלָה (*kislâ*) ***confidence, folly.***

1011c †כְּסִיל (*kᵉsîl*) ***I, fool, dullard.***

1011d †כְּסִילוּת (*kᵉsîlût*) ***stupidity.***

1011e †כְּסִיל (*kᵉsîl*) ***II, constellations, Orion.***

kāsal the verb occurs once, in Jer 10:8, where idol worshipers are called foolish. The Arabic cognate seems to have an original meaning "to be sluggish," referring to that which is thick, plump, or fat (BDB). From *kāsal* come a number of derivatives.

kᵉsîl ***I. Fool, dullard.*** This noun, except for three occurrences in Ps, is found only in Prov and Eccl. In Prov three words are rendered fool, *kᵉsîl* referring to the dull or obstinate one, referring not to mental deficiency, but to a propensity to make wrong choices. *'ewîl* refers to moral insolence, and *nābāl* to the boorish man of mean disposition.

Folly and fool are opposite to wisdom and wise. *kᵉsîl* refers to a way of life that is enticing to the immature, but can lead to destruction and ruin. Qohelet sums up the argumentation for either wisdom or folly by stating that wisdom excels folly as light excels darkness(Eccl 2:1–13). Involved in this conclusion is that wisdom leads a person on the right path to the brightness of the full day while folly entices one to the way that leads into darkness (Prov 4:18–19).

We note the kind of choices which the *kᵉsîl* makes. His eyes are unable to see any proper way or conduct. He may roam the earth seeking it, but miss it completely. Apparently he does not concentrate on what is right (Prov 17:24). The fool imagines that he can buy wisdom when actually he has no inclination for it (Prov 17:16). He takes no delight in understanding (Prov 18:2), hates knowledge (Prov 1:22), and therefore does not choose the fear of the Lord (Prov 1:29). The end of the fool's complacency is destruction (Prov 1:32).

The fool is a serious menace to the community. Associating with a fool, who has a twisted sense of values deprives one of knowledge (Prov 14:7). He can cause serious problems to his fellow man, for he actually enjoys doing wickedness (or lewdness; Lev 18:17; Prov 10:23). A fool's utterances bring strife and involve him in blows with his adversaries (Prov 18:6). Anyone who befriends him will be destroyed (Prov 13:20). Parents of the fool suffer greatly. His mother is grieved with him (Prov 10:1) and his father can never have any joy over him (Prov 10:1; see also

Prov 17:25; 19:13*a*). Yet for his part, thc fool despises his mother (Prov 15:20).

kesel. ***Confidence, hope.*** Confidence and hope relate to trust (or lack of it) in God (Prov 3:26; Job 8:14). As folly, it is identified as evil (Eccl 7:25) and applied to the person whose way of life is to live for this world only (Ps 49:13 [H 14]). In five other usages, *kesel* is rendered "flanks" (Lev 3:4, 10, 15; Ps 38:7 [H 8]).

kislâ. ***Confidence, folly.*** The fear of God was Job's confidence (Job 4:6) while at the same time a people who have experienced the peace of God are not to turn back to folly (Ps 85:8 [H 9]).

k^esîlût. ***Foolish.*** Describes Folly, in opposition to Wisdom (*ḥokmâ*), personified as a woman. Sexual immorality, characterized as *k^esîlût,* is contrasted to Wisdom who calls the immature to a life of rectitude.

k^esîl ***II. Constellations*** (Isa 13:10), ***Orion*** (Job 9:9; 38:31; Amos 5:8). (ASV and RSV same.) The relation to *k^esîl* is uncertain, since in the Job and Amos passages, *k^esîl* refers to a specific star, while in Isa the plural *k^esîlêhem* "their constellations" is used more generally.

In Job 9:9 the LXX translates *k^esîl* as "Hesperus" (related to the mythological Evening Star, therefore, the West). The Vulgate does the same. In Job 38:31, "loose the bands of Orion" (KJV), the LXX is similar, "opened the barrier of Orion." The Vulgate here reads Arcturus for Orion.

There are differences of opinion concerning the astral groups. Arcturus is used differently in the versions: in Job 9:9 Arcturus is used to render the group *'āsh* but the LXX translate "Pleiades," and the RSV and NASB "the Bear." Arcturus is used in the LXX for the astral *kîmâ* (Job 9:9), but in 38:31, Pleiades is used for *kîmâ.* The Vulgate uses Arcturus for *k^esîl.* In Isa 13:10, "the stars of heaven and the constellations thereof," the plural *k^esîlêhem,* is rendered by the LXX, "for the stars of heaven and Orion."

There are other possibilities. Targum Jonathan renders *k^esîl* as "giant" in Job 9:9 and 38:31. For Isa 13:10 the Targum reads, "the stars of the heavens and their titans." In modern usage the Arabic designation for the constellation Orion is *al gibbar,* modern Hebrew *gîbbôr* "the strong one."

Bibliography: Blanck, S. H., "Folly," in IB, II, pp. 303–304. Fraenkel, J., "Astronomy," in *Encyclopedia Judaica,* I, p. 795. Greenstone, Julius, *Proverbs,* Jewish Publication Society, 1950. Harris, R. Laird, "Proverbs," in WBC. "Hesperus," in *Oxford Classical Dictionary.* Kidner, Derek, *Proverbs,* Inter-Varsity, 1964. "Orion," in *Oxford Classical Dictionary.* "Orion, the Pleiades, the Hyades," in *Larousse Encyclopedia of Mythology,* Prometheus, 1959, pp. 164–65. Toy, C. H., *Proverbs,* in ICC. Walker, W. L., "Fool, Folly," in ISBE, II, pp. 1124–25. THAT, I, pp. 836–37.

L.G.

1012 כִּסְלֵו (*kislēw*) **Chislev.** The ninth month of the Babylonian calendar. Used only in the post-Exilic books Zech 7:1; Neh 1:1. For other months see *ḥodesh,* no. 613b.

1013 כָּסַם (*kāsam*) ***shear, clip*** (Ezk 44:20).

Derivatives

1013a כֻּסֶּמֶת (*kūssemet*) ***spelt.***

1013b *כִּרְסֵם (*kirsēm*) ***tear off.*** Occurs only in the Piel, in Ps 80:14 "boars from the forest tear it off."

כֻּסֶּמֶת (*kūssemet*). See no. 1013a.

1014 כָּסַס (*kāsas*) ***compute*** (Ex 12:4).

Derivatives

1014a מֶכֶס (*mekes*) ***computation, proportion to be paid, tax*** (Num 31:28).

1014b מִכְסָה (*miksâ*) ***computation*** (= number, Ex 12:4; = valuation, worth, Lev 27:23).

1015 כָּסַף (*kāsap*) ***yearn for, long after*** (with *l^e*, Ps 17:12; Job 14:15).

Derivative

1015a †כֶּסֶף (*kesep*) ***silver, money.***

In the Niphal stem it means yearn for (Gen 31:30); be ashamed (Zeph 2:1, so KB, BDB, GB, ZOR.). With *lō',* it means be shameless. (Some trace connection with *kesep* "silver" as the pale metal; hence Middle Hebrew *hiksîp,* become pale with yearning.)

kesep. ***Silver; (silver) money.*** *Kesep* refers to silver as freshly mined and smelted (Prov 25:4; 26:23; Ezk 22:18); as material for vessels, trumpets, idols (Gen 44:2; 24:53; Num 10:2; Ex 20:23; Isa 2:20). It is often used with numbers to indicate shekels of silver (with *sheqel* or *sh^eqālîm* omitted; Gen 20:16; 45:22). It is also used with minas (Ezr 2:69) or talents (Ex 38:27; I Kgs 20:29; I Chr 19:6). It may be used for price (of sale, Lev 25:50).

Silver is found as native metal in some mines in Greece. It was also extracted from its ores by smelting with lead. The lead-silver alloy was purified by heating and burning off the lead as oxide. The impurities are skimmed off. There are frequent OT references to the refiner's fire and the dross of silver (Ezk 22:18–22).

Silver was the usual standard of trade. Two shekels was the price of a ram in Moses' day (Lev 5:15). Silver coins were used in Greece as early as 670 B.C. There are no clear references to silver coins in the OT, but the Persian gold daric may be mentioned in Ezra 8:27.

Bibliography: Bowes, D. R., "Metallurgy," in ZPEB, IV, p. 210. Archer, G. L., "Coins," in ZPEB, I, p. 903.

G.L.A.

כֶּסֶת (*keset*). See no. 1009a.

1016 כָּעַס (*kā'as*) ***be vexed, indignant, angry, wroth, be grieved, provoke to anger and wrath.*** (ASV, RSV similar.)

Derivatives

1016a †כַּעַס (*ka'as*) ***vexation, grief.***
1016b כַּעַשׂ (*ka'aś*) ***vexation.*** Dialectical variation of *ka'as*.

The root meaning of *kā'as* is to vex, agitate, stir up, or provoke the heart to a heated condition which in turn leads to specific actions. This term, as well as the synonyms for anger and wrath (*'ap, ḥēmâ, qaṣap,* and *'ebrâ*; see discussion of synonyms at *qāṣap*) are used anthropomorphically and anthropopathically of God. They refer to God's inner self as vexed and provoked by rebellion or sin. The term when applied to God, implies that man can affect the very heart of God so as to cause him heat, pain, or grief to various degrees of intensity.

In the Qal stem the verb is used five times to indicate the state of vexation in men. Thus, king Asa was vexed or exasperated when he was rebuked by the prophet Hanani (II Chr 16:10); likewise Sanballat when he saw builders at work on the walls of Jerusalem (Neh 4:1 [H 3:33]). From these instances we may gather that the state of vexation is not normally proper for a true child of God. In fact, Eccl 7:9 teaches that the child of God should not be hasty in spirit to be vexed, because such vexation rests in the bosom of fools.

God is said not to continue in this state of vexation when his jealousy is quieted (Ezk 16:42). Indeed, vexation is not an abiding attribute of God. Yet, his people may provoke him to anger and wrath by their unfaithfulness. Because God is holy and loving he will only share himself with a people whom he has bound to himself in covenant love, and whom he has taken to himself for fellowship and service. He never shares himself with the profane and wicked. Hence when his covenant people become unfaithful to him, he, by virtue of his holiness and jealous love (Ex 34:14), is provoked to anger and wrath against them. Thus he may be deeply vexed, agitated, pained, or grieved by disobedient Israel. This is the general burden of the forty-five passages in the OT in which the Hiphil stem of the verb is used. E.g., Moses warned the Israelites that if their descendants, after having been in the promised land, corrupt themselves by making graven images in any form, the Lord will be deeply vexed at them. He calls heaven and earth to witness that God in his vexation will make them to utterly perish from off the earth (Deut 4:25). Moses speaks also of his fear of God when God has been aroused to a highly vexed state (Deut 9:1–8). And when God has been continuously and deeply provoked, vexed, grieved, much is required to quiet the heart of God. E.g. king Mannesseh provoked God so deeply by his pervasive involvement in idolatry (cf. II Kgs 21:1–26) that when Josiah attempted reforms, the Lord was not appeased. Judgment had to fall upon Judah (II Kgs 23:26), a judgment which destroyed many of the people and removed the nation from the promised land. This judgment, in keeping with God's justice is not contrary to divine love. Rather, it is an expression of divine love which has been offended, rejected and deeply grieved. Divine love suffers long; it also defends itself and removes the objects of its vexation and sorrow.

ka'as. ***Vexation, provocation, anger, wrath, spite, grief, sorrow*** (ASV and RSV have "provocation" in place of "wrath").

This noun is not used of God in quite the same way the verb is. Rather it speaks of what man does in relation to God.

Man vexes and provokes God to anger. This act of man is referred to a number of times: Jeroboam provoked God by his sinful provocations, i.e. calf worship (I Kgs 15:30) as Israel did later with her idolatries, which are called "provocations" (Ezk 20:28). This emphasizes the fact that man vexes God; man, created and called to please and glorify God, when he falls into sin, gives him a deep agitation of heart.

Man also is a source of vexation to his fellowmen. Peninnah provoked Hannah to vexation and caused her much grief (I Sam 1:7, 16). A foolish son produces vexation or grief for his father (Prov 17:25). Adversaries, physical and spiritual, are a source of vexation and tears for the righteous (Ps 6:7 [H 8]). Thus sinful man, by nature, tragically fails to live in peace and happiness with his fellow men as God commands him to do.

Bibliography: THAT, I, pp. 838–41.

G.V.G.

כַּעַשׂ (*ka'aś*). See no. 1016b.

1017 כֵּף (*kēp*) ***rock*** (Jer 4:29; Job 30:6).

כַּף (*kap*). See no. 1022a.

1018 כָּפָה (*kāpâ*) ***subdue*** (Prov 21:14).

כְּפוֹר (*k^e^pôr*). See nos. 1026a,b.
כְּפִים (*k^e^pîs*). See no. 1021a.
כְּפִיר (*k^e^pîr*). See no. 1025a.

1019 כָּפַל(*kāpal*) ***fold something double, double over*** (Ex 29:6; 28:16; 39:9). Niphal: be doubled (over, Ezk 21:19, of two ways at a crossroads). (Arabic *kiflun* "double"; Akkadian *kapālu* "to coil, twist.")

Derivatives

1019a כֶּפֶל (*kepel*), כִּפְלַיִם (*kiplayim*) ***a double*** (Job 41:13 [H 5]), i.e. the doubled thickness of the crocodile's hide). The dual *kiplayim* refers to a double portion (of chastisement, Isa 40:2).

1019b †מַכְפֵּלָה (*makpēlâ*) ***Machpelah*** (perhaps Double-cave?).

Name of the cave purchased by Abraham for Sarah's burial, and later for himself and for Jacob, in the northeastern field of Hebron belonging to Ephron son of Zohar, the Hittite (Gen 23). It was purchased for four hundred shekels of silver. The location faced Mamre (v. 19).

[The transaction has been much discussed. It has been treated as a typical oriental bargaining match with Abraham as a semi-foreigner ending up having to pay a large figure. M. Lehmann (see bibliography) held that here we have an example of Hittite law. Abraham asked for only the cave. But Ephron insisted that he take the whole property and thus Ephron divested himself of feudal responsibilities to his overlord. Speiser (in AB, *Genesis,* pp. 171–73) doubts that Ephron was a member of the distant Hittite nation. He thinks rather that Ephron was a non-Semite who could more readily be persuaded to sell to an alien like Abraham. At least it is agreed that four hundred shekels was dear.

The tomb of Machpelah shown to tourists today was built in Herodian times, as its lower masonry testifies. Over that was built a church, now a mosque. The site therefore has been identified since before the dispersion. It may be the authentic place. See the article by H. G. Stigers (see bibliography) who assisted in the Hammond excavations at the tell of ancient Hebron. R.L.H.]

Bibliography: Lehmann, M., "Abraham's Purchase of Machpelah and Hittite Law," BASOR 129:15–18. Stigers, H. G. "Machpelah," in ZPEB, IV, pp. 26–28.

G.L.A.

1020 כָּפַן (*kāpan*) ***be hungry, hunger.*** Occurs only in Ezk 17:7, *kāpnâ 'al* "stretched hungrily."

Derivative

1020a כָּפָן (*kāpān*) ***hunger, famine*** (Job 5:22; 30:3).

1021 כפס (*kps*). **Assumed root of the following.**

1021a כָּפִיס (*kāpîs*) ***rafter, girder(?).*** Occurs only in Hab 2:11.

1022 כפף (*kpp*). **Assumed root of the following.**

1022a †כַּף (*kap*) ***the palm of the hand, hand*** (opened or turned upward so as to expose the hand, in contrast with *yad* "hand" in general, whether open or closed in a grasp or fist); flat of the hand, sole of the foot (Gen 40:11; II Kgs 4:34; Lev 14:16; Gen 8:9; Josh 3:13). Also "handful" (of meal, II Kgs 17:12).

1022b כִּפָּה (*kippâ*) ***branch, leaf.***

kap. ***Palm of the hand.*** *kap* is also used of hands spread out in prayer (Ex 19:29; Isa 1:15). It may also refer to a pan or concave vessel (Ex 25:29; Num 4:7); or the hollow of a sling (I Sam 25:29). Not used as extensively as *yad* nor so much in the various extended usages of that word (e.g., *yad* also means "strength, force"). In Ugaritic *kp* is used to refer to the amputated hands of the enemy apparently used in body count (UT 19: no. 1286). This gruesome usage is not clearly witnessed in the OT, but may be suggested in Jud 8:6, 15.

G.L.A.

1023 כָּפַר (*kāpar*) ***I, make an atonement, make reconciliation, purge.*** (Denominative verb.) This root should probably be distinguished from *kāpar* II "to smear with pitch."

Parent Noun

1023a †כֹּפֶר (*kōper*) ***I, ransom, gift to secure favor.***

1023b †כִּפֻּר (*kippūr*) (used in the plural *kippūrîm*) ***atonement,*** used especially in the expression "day of atonement."

1023c †כַּפֹּרֶת (*kappōret*) ***place of atonement;*** KJV, "mercy seat."

The root *kāpar* is used some 150 times. It has been much discussed. There is an equivalent Arabic root meaning "cover," or "conceal." On the strength of this connection it has been supposed that the Hebrew word means "to cover over sin" and thus pacify the deity, making an atonement (so BDB). It has been suggested that the OT ritual symbolized a covering over of sin until it was dealt with in fact by the atonement of Christ. There is, however, very little evidence for this view. The connection of the Arabic word is weak and the Hebrew root is not used to mean "cover." The Hebrew verb is never used in the simple or Qal stem, but only in the derived intensive stems. These intensive stems often indicate not emphasis, but merely that the verb is derived from a noun whose meaning is more basic to the root idea.

kōper. ***Ransom.*** Every Israelite was to give to the service of the sanctuary the "ransom" money of half a shekel (Ex 30:12). Egypt, in God's sight, was given as a "ransom" for the restoration of Israel (Isa 43:3). This word "ransom" is parallel to the word "redeem" (*pādâ,* which see) in Ps 49:7. There is a warning that a man guilty of murder must be killed—no "ransom" can be given in exchange for his life (Num 35:31). The word is also used in a bad sense as a "bribe" which wrongly purchases favor (I Sam 12:3).

From the meaning of *kōper* "ransom," the meaning of *kāpar* can be better understood. It means "to atone by offering a substitute." The great majority of the usages concern the priestly ritual of sprinkling of the sacrificial blood thus "making an atonement" for the worshipper. There are forty-nine instances of this usage in Leviticus alone and no other meaning is there witnessed. The verb is always used in connection with the removal of sin or defilement, except for Gen 32:20; Prov 16:14; and Isa 28:18 where the related meaning of "appease by a gift" may be observed. It seems clear that this word aptly illustrates the theology of reconciliation in the OT. The life of the sacrificial animal specifically symbolized by its blood was required in exchange for the life of the worshipper. Sacrifice of animals in OT theology was not merely an expression of thanks to the deity by a cattleraising people. It was the symbolic expression of innocent life given for guilty life. This symbolism is further clarified by the action of the worshipper in placing his hands on the head of the sacrifice and confessing his sins over the animal (cf. Lev 16:21; 1:4; 4:4, etc.) which was then killed or sent out as a scapegoat.

kippūr. ***Atonement.*** **kapporet.** ***Mercy seat.*** These two nouns are derived from the verb as used in the intensive stem: The first is used today in the name of the Jewish holiday *yom kippur* "day of atonement" (used only in the plural in the OT) which was the tenth day of the seventh month, Tishri. This solemn day was the only day of fasting prescribed for Israel. It was celebrated by a special sin offering for the whole nation. On that day only would the high priest enter within the inner veil bearing the blood of the sin offering (cf. Heb 9:7). A second goat was released as an escape goat to symbolize the total removal of sin (see *'ăzā'zēl* "scapegoat").

kappōret. ***Mercy seat.*** This noun is used twenty-seven times and always refers to the golden cover of the sacred chest in the inner shrine of the tabernacle or temple. It was from above the mercy seat that God promised to meet with men (Num 7:89). The word, however, is not related to mercy and of course was not a seat. The word is derived from the root "to atone." The Greek equivalent in the LXX is usually *hilastērion,* "place or object of propitiation," a word which is applied to Christ in Rom 3:25. The translation "mercy seat" does not sufficiently express the fact that the lid of the ark was the place where the blood was sprinkled on the day of atonement. "Place of atonement" would perhaps be more expressive.

R.L.H.

1024 כָּפַר (*kāpar*) ***II, cover over with pitch.*** This denominative verb is used only in Gen 6:14 in the waterproofing of the ark. The cognate word is used in the Babylonian flood story.

Parent Noun

1024a כֹּפֶר (*kōper*) ***II, pitch.*** A noun, from which the above verb was doubtless derived. Pitch, bitumen, asphalt was used in early antiquity as an adhesive to hold inlays into statues. It was a logical material for caulking the ark as specified both in the Bible and the Babylonian flood story.

R.L.H.

1025 כפר (*kpr*) **III. Assumed root of the following.**

1025a †כְּפִיר (*k^epîr*) ***young lion.***

1025b כֹּפֶר (*kōper*) ***III, name of a plant*** (henna?, Song 1:14; 4:13). Derivation uncertain.

1025c כָּפָר (*kāpār*) ***village.*** Derivation uncertain. An element in the NT name "Capernaum."

1025d כֹּפֶר (*kōper*) ***IV, village.*** A variant of *kāpār*. Possibly the same as the plural in Neh 6:2.

k^epîr. ***Young lion.*** That the word specifies the age of the lion is doubtful. To distinguish between the different words for lion is difficult. Cf. *lābî'*.

Often it is used in parallelism with *'aryeh* "lion" (the generic term, usually an adult). In Ezk 19:3, the *k^epîr* learns how to catch prey. Occurs frequently in narrative, prophetic books, and poetry. Other words for lion are *lābî', layish, shaḥal* and *shaḥaṣ*. It is difficult to distinguish between these words. Some may refer to age, some to prowess, etc.

G.L.A.

1026 כפר (*kpr*) **IV. Assumed root of the following.**

1026a כְּפוֹר (*k^epôr*) ***I, bowl*** (I Chr 28; Ezr 1:10; 8:27).

1026b כְּפוֹר (*k^epôr*) ***II, hoarfrost*** (Ps 147:16; Ex 16:14; Job 38:29).

כַּפֹּרֶת (*kappōret*). See no. 1023c.

1027 *כָּפַשׁ (*kāpash*) ***make bent, press or bend together.*** Occurs only in the Hiphil (Lam 3:16).

1028 כַּפְתּוֹר (*kaptôr*) ***I, the island of Crete.*** In Egyptian spelled *k-f-t-y(w)*; Akkadian *kaptara;* Ugaritic *k-p-t-r*. Homeland or at least a staging center of the Philistines (Amos 9:7; cf. Deut 2:23; Jer 47:4). The gentilic is *kaptōrî* "Cretan." (At Mari spelled *ka-ap-taru-u*.)

1029 כַּפְתּוֹר (*kaptôr*) ***II, a capital on top of a pillar*** (Amos 9:1; Zech 2:14). (2) A knob or bulb on the lampstand (Ex 25:31; 37:17). (Apparently derived from the name of Crete, as the place from which such ornamentations were first imported.)

G.L.A.

1030 כַּר (*kar*) ***pasture.*** Derivation uncertain.

1031 כֹּר (*kōr*) ***a measure, usually dry.*** Equal to a homer, therefore 10 ephahs (q.v.).

1032 *כרבל (*krbl*) ***be-mantle or bind around.*** Occurs only in the Pual, in I Chr 15:17, "bemantled with a robe of byssus."

1033 כָּרָה (*kārâ*) ***I, dig, excavate; dig through.***

Derivatives

1033a כָּרָה (*kārâ*) ***cistern or well.***

1033b מִכְרֶה (*mikreh*) ***pit—of salt(?)*** Only Zech 2:9.

1033c מְכֻרָה (*m^ekūrâ*), מְכוּרָה (*m^ekûrâ*) origin.

The object of this verb is usually a pit, trench, or cistern. It is used figuratively for entrapping a person with an evil plot or strategem (Prov 16:27). In the Niphal it means "be dug" (Ps 94:13). There is a different root, *kārâ,* meaning "to trade in" (a commodity), do business in; buy (Job 6:27 with *'al,* with dir. acc., Deut 2:6; Hos 3:2).

G.L.A.

1034 כָּרָה (*kārâ*) ***II, get by trade, trade.***

1035 כָּרָה (*kārâ*) ***III, give a feast.*** Occurs only in II Kgs 6:23, *wayyikreh lāhem kērâ g^edôlâ* "and he gave a great feast for them."

Derivative

1035a כֵּרָה (*kērâ*) ***a feast*** (II Kgs 6:23).

1036 כְּרוּב (*k^erûb*) ***Cherub.***

The name of various representations of angelic beings which are represented as part human, part animal. Usually used in the plural, cherubim. The English, cherubims, uses a superfluous plural ending.

The derivation of the word is dubious. The Akkadian cognate verb means, "to bless, praise, adore" (CAD). As one of the characteristics of the cherubim was adoration of God, this derivation would appear suitable.

Cherubim are mentioned first as angelic guardians of Paradise lost (Gen 3:24). Next they appear as winged figures of pure gold facing each other and overshadowing the atonement cover (NIV, the KJV is mercy seat, Ex 25:20). They were also a prominent figure in the decorations of the tabernacle curtains (Ex 26:1, 31). Nothing is said here of their shape except that they had faces, presumably human, and wings. Significantly, Ex 25:22 says that God will speak with men from above (*mē'al*) the atonement cover from between (*mibbin*) the cherubim (so also Num 7:89). It is assumed by Albright *et al.* that the iconography represented Yahweh standing on the cherubim as the storm god of Syria, Hadad, is represented as standing on a sacred bull (W. F. Albright, "What Were the Cherubim?" in *The Biblical Archaeologist Reader,* I, p. 95). Indeed, in most places the RSV translates the phrase "dwells (at) the cherubim" (no preposition is expressed) as "on" (II Sam 6:2; II Kgs 19:15: I Chr 13:6; Ps 80:1 [H 2]; 99:1; Isa 37:16). In these places the NASB supplied "above," the KJV and NIV "between" in line with the use of *bîn* in Ex 25:22.

In Solomon's temple, cherubim were widely used for decoration (I Kgs 6:29, 32; 7:29). In the most holy place he made two large cherubim of olive wood overlaid with gold. These cherubim faced forward with their two inner wings touching above the ark and their two outer wings touching the walls of the shrine. Thus the wingspread of each was fifteen feet. Presumably the original ark with its two solid gold cherubim was under these large touching wings.

In Ezekiel's symbolic or millennial temple, cherubim were used for decoration (Ezk 41:18–20, 25) but no ark with its cherubim are mentioned. The cherubim of the decorations each had two faces, of a man and of a lion, facing in opposite directions. The easiest way to understand this is to hold that the cherub was standing upright with faces turned right and left something like the

Hapsburg eagle, but certainty is not possible. There is no need to suppose with Albright and many that they were sphinxes.

More detail can be gleaned from the vision of Ezk 1 which is mentioned again in 9:3 and chapter 10 and in 11:22. There the cherubim stand as corner posts of the structure bearing the throne of God. They had a human body and hands (1:5; 10:7) but the feet went straight down like a calf—without the human ankle and toes. These cherubim had four wings. Two covered their bodies in modesty, two were extended upward so that their tips touched the wings of the cherubim at the other corners. The seraphs (fiery ones) of Isa 6 seem to be similar creatures. They had six wings using the extra two to fly on God's errands. The description of Rev 4:6–8 has features reminiscent of both Ezk and Isa. The cherubim of Ezk 1 had four faces—of a man, lion, ox and eagle. Why these four we do not know. It may be that they represented birds, tame animals, wild animals and men in attendance before God. Their four faces were so placed that the structure could travel east, west, north and south with lightning speed and always go face forward with no steering mechanism. The intersecting wheels (Ezk 1:16, NIV) looking something like a gyroscope had the same result. That these cherubim bore the throne of God is perhaps the reason that the temple cherubim are called a chariot in one verse (I Chr 28:18) though the reference is obscure. In the theophany of Ps 18:10 [H 11] parallel to II Sam 22:11, the imagery is that God "mounted the cherubim and flew, he soared on the wings of the wind" (NIV).

Evidently the representation of these high angelic beings varies from place to place, but they are regularly near the throne of God engaged in worship and service.

Bibliography: Albright, W. F., "What Were the Cherubim?" in *The Biblical Archaeologist Reader,* I, p. 95. Acomb, D. E., "Cherub," in ZPEB, I, pp. 788–90. Woudstra, M., *The Ark of the Covenant from Conquest to Kingship,* Presbyterian and Reformed, 1965, pp. 68–77.

R.L.H.

כְּרִיתוּת (*kᵉrîtût*). See no. 1048a.

1037 כרך (*krk*). **Assumed root of the following.**

1037a תַּכְרִיךְ (*takrîk*) ***robe.*** Occurs in the phrase *wᵉtakrîk bûṣ wᵉ'argāmān* "a purple robe of fine linen" (Est 8:15).

1038 כרכב (*krkb*). **Assumed root of the following.**

1038a כַּרְכֹּב (*karkōb*) ***a rim*** (Ex 27:5; 38:4) referring to the *ledge* of an altar. Middle Hebrew, a bowl.

1039 כַּרְכֹּם (*karkōs*) ***saffron*** (Song 4:14).

כַּרְכָּרָה (*karkārâ*). See no. 1046.

1040 כָּרַם (*kāram*) ***tend or dress vineyards or vines.*** A denominative verb.

Parent Noun

1040a †כֶּרֶם (*kerem*) ***vineyard.***

Vineyards are mentioned over ninety times in the OT, first in connection with Noah (Gen 9:20). Grape growing was and still is an important part of Palestinian farming. The "grain, new wine, and oil" were the three prominent products of the field (see *tîrôsh*). Grapes were trodden to make juice for wine and also were dried to make raisins which were widely used, to judge from Abigail's gift to David (I Sam 25:18; cf. II Sam 16:1). Treading the winepress became a forceful figure of divine judgment (Isa 63:3; Rev 14:19). The grapes of Palestine were part of the proof of the productivity of the land (Num 13:23), especially significant because Egypt did not specialize in grapes. Vineyards were not to be picked clean, but gleanings were to be left for the poor (Lev 19:10). Famous is Naboth's vineyard, his patrimony which he would not part with, but which Ahab secured to his own destruction.

Israel is God's vineyard (Isa 5:1ff.; Jer 12:10). God gave it special care, but it yielded bitter fruit. "He looked for justice, but saw bloodshed; for righteousness, but heard cries of distress" (Isa 5:7, NIV). Vineyards are part of the figures of plenty and peace in the millennial day (Isa 65:21; Amos 9:13). The vine is also used in the precious NT figure, "I am the vine, you are the branches" (John 15).

R.L.H.

1041 כַּרְמֶל (*karmel*) ***I, plantation, garden-land; garden-growth, fruit; orchard.***

Often a garden planted between rows of fruit-bearing trees (Isa 10:18; Jer 2:7; Jer 48:33; of a garden-like forest (Isa 37:24) or of a stand of stately cedars (II Kgs 19:23). Also of a kind of food, whether made from fruit or from mashed or compacted kernels forming a paste (Lev 23:14; 2:14).

1042 כַּרְמֶל (*karmel*) ***II, a promontory just below Haifa*** (fertile and fruitful, Josh 19:26; I Kgs 18:19); ***a mountain town on the west of the Dead Sea*** (Josh 15:55; I Sam 25:5).

The Carmel range is prominent and famous. It forms today the harbor of Haifa, which, however, was blocked by marshes in former times. The southern boundary of the fertile valley of Esdraelon, it stretches back about thirteen miles to the southeast attaining a height of 1742 feet. Megiddo, situated by a pass through the range, was the scene of crucial battles in the past. There Thutmosis III won a famous victory and Josiah met his death at the hands of Pharaoh Necho.

The Carmel area has been inhabited since very ancient times. The caves of Skhul and Tabun and others in the Wadi el-Mugharah have yielded the important skeletons of "Carmel Man." First dated about 130,000 years ago they are now dated by Carbon 14 at about 35,000. The presence of Neanderthal features mixed with modern features was a surprise and possibly suggested the restudy of Neanderthal man which has concluded that he was erect and modern in many ways (cf. Albright, W. F., *The Archaeology of Palestine,* rev. ed., Pelican, 1961, p. 55; for the dating, see *Time and Stratigraphy in the Evolution of Man,* publ. 1469, National Academy of Sciences, Washington, 1967, p. 20.).

Bibliography: Baly, D., *Geography of Palestine,* Harper, 1957, especially pp. 152–53. Mare, W. H., "Carmel," in ZPEB, I, pp. 754–55.

R.L.H.

1043 כַּרְמִיל (*karmîl*) ***crimson, carmine.***

כִּרְסֵם (*kirsēm*). See no. 1013b.

1044 כָּרַע (*kāra'*) ***bow down, kneel, sink down to one's knees, kneel down (to rest, of an animal), kneel in reverence, before God or a king*** (Ps 22:30; 72:9).

Derivative

1044a כֶּרַע (*kera'*) ***leg.*** Always used in the dual and always of legs of an animal. Once used of the hopping legs of locusts, etc (Lev 11:21).

The verb means to bow down, but is applicable both to bending in general and to bowing in worship or obeisance (thirteen times). It clearly refers sometimes to kneeling. At least in II Kgs 1:13 the captain went down on his knees. Also, in Jud 7:6 the majority of Gideon's army got down on their knees to drink. Job 4:4 refers to the knees, "you have strengthened the feeble (bowed) knees."

But the word can be used more generally. It refers to an animal's crouching to rest (Num 24:9). It also refers once to a woman bending in labor pains (I Sam 4:19). The Hiphil more often refers figuratively to bringing one low.

It is a natural picture that one who falls on his knees in obeisance also bends his back. This apparently is the connotation of the word as used for the posture of worship. It does not mean to fall prostrate on the ground; it means to fall on the knees and bow in worship.

The important thing, naturally, is not the position, but the attitude. The word may give a clue, however, to ancient positions used in prayer and worship. Other words are *qādad,* bow the head, *shāḥâ* (properly *ḥāwâ*) the most common word for bow in worship.

R.L.H.

1045 כַּרְפַּס (*karpas*) ***cotton or fine linen*** (Est 1:6).

1046 *כָּרַר (*kārar*). Occurs only in the Pilpel, *m^{e}karkar* "dancing" (literally whirling, only in II Sam 6:14, 16).

Derivatives

1046a †כַּר (*kar*) ***lamb.***
1046b †כִּרְכָּרָה (*kirkārâ*) ***beasts.***
1046c †כִּכָּר (*kikkār*) ***round disk.***

kar. ***Lamb, ram, captains.*** (ASV and RSV similar.) This word, which occurs thirteen times, has no clear verbal root in Hebrew. Similar nouns are found in both Akkadian and Ugaritic. It refers to lambs raised for slaughter but not necessarily in a cultic setting. Three times in Ezekiel it refers to battering rams.

kirkārâ. ***Swift beasts.*** (ASV and RSV "dromedaries," NIV "camels.") Appears only in Isa 66:20 relating the swift modes of travel by which their former captors will hurry the Jewish exiles back to the homeland.

G.V.G.

kikkār. ***Round disk; district; loaf of bread.*** This noun carries three different meanings. (1) A *round disk:* of a leaden lid (Zech 5:7); of a disk of gold or silver bullion, usually weighing one talent (II Sam 12:30; I Kgs 10:10); as a unit from which smaller objects are made (Ex 25:39; I Kgs 9:14; the talent weighed c. 75 pounds or 34.3 kilograms). (2) A (circular) *district, territory,* used especially of the Jordan Valley (Gen 13:10; I Kgs 7:46), or of the district of Jerusalem (Neh 3:22; 12:28). (3) A circular *loaf* of bread (I Sam 2:36; Prov 6:36). (The *kikkār* as a talent weighed 3000 shekels.)

G.L.A.

1047 כרשׂ (*krś*). **Assumed root of the following.**
1047a כָּרֵשׂ (*kārēś*) ***belly*** (Jer 51:34).

1048 כָּרַת (*kārat*) ***cut off a part of the body, e.g. head, hand, foreskin; cut down trees, idols; cut out, eliminate, kill; cut (make) a covenant.***

Derivatives

1048a †כְּרִיתוּת (*k^{e}rîtût*) ***dismissal.***
1048b †כְּרֻתוֹת (*k^{e}rūtôt*) ***beams.***

Cognates are found in the Akkadian verb *karātu* "to cut off" and verbal adjective *kartu* "cut up," as well as in Tigre where the verbal equivalent means "to bring to an end."

In addition to the literal meaning of this root, "to cut off" (Ex 4:25; I Sam 5:4) and "to cut down" (I Kgs 5:20; a "woodcutter" in Isa 14:8) there is the metaphorical meaning to root out, eliminate, remove, excommunicate or destroy by a violent act of man or nature. It is sometimes difficult in a given context to know whether the person(s) who is "cut off" is to be killed or only excommunicated. Verses like Gen 9:11, "Neither shall all flesh be cut off any more by the waters of a flood" clearly refer to destruction, but Ex 12:15 appears to refer to exclusion from the community. An interesting passage which illustrates the difficulty in deciding whether the word is literal or metaphorical in usage is Num 11:33. Did the Lord strike the Israelites with a plague before the meat of the quails was chewed (literally "cut off") or was it while they were still eating quails before the quails ceased to come or were removed?

The most important use of the root is "to cut" a covenant *b^e rît* (q.v.). The word here is pregnant with theological meaning. A covenant must be cut because the slaughter of animals was a part of the covenant ritual (Speiser, *Genesis*, in AB, p. 112; BA 34:18). Genesis 15 is a significant passage in this regard. The Lord made (cut) a covenant with Abram (v. 18) involving a mysterious ceremony. Animals were cut in half and the parts laid opposite each other. E. Kutsch (THAT, I, p. 859) says that this ritual does not mean (a) the union of the two contracting parties (Gen 15:18) designated by the flame's passing through between the two pieces (so C. F. Keil) because this meaning does not fit in Jer 34:18 (J. J. P. Valeton, ZAW 12:227): (b) the "mystical-sacramental unification" of the two partners (B. Duhm, *Das Buch Jeremia*, 1901, p. 284; J. Henninger, *Biblica* 3:344–53, esp. 352f.), because in Gen 15:18 and Jer 34:18 only the subject of the *b^e rît* goes through, not the partner; (c) neither "the purification" of the one who goes between the halves of the animal (cf. O. Masson, "A propos d'un rituel hittite pour la lustration d'une armee," *Revue de l'Histoire des Religions*, 137:5–25), nor (d) that to this one is communicated the living power released by the death of the animal in order to increase his capabilities (W. R. Smith, *Die Religion der Semiten*, 1899, p. 243; E. Bickerman, "Couper une allinace," *Archives d'histoire du droit oriental*, 5:133–56; F. Horst, *Gottes Recht*, 1961, p. 309) because neither of these interpretations finds support in the context (D. J. McCarthy, *Treaty and Covenant*, 1963, pp. 55ff.). Rather it depicts the self-destruction of the one making the contract in an analogous way: that the fate of the animal should befall him in the event that he does not keep the *b^e rît* (so already Rashi and today the majority of interpreters). This meaning is suggested by Jer 34:18 and is supported by parallels in classical antiquity (cf. R. Kraetzschmar, *Die Bundesvorstellung im AT*, 1896, pp. 44f; e.g. Livius I, 24), and in Israel's world (e.g. E. Kutsch, *kārat b^e rît* "eine Verpflichtung festsetzen," F. S. Elliger, 1971 [Rem. 26]). An eighth-century treaty reads, "As this calf is cut to pieces so may Mati'el be cut to pieces" (Sefireh, I,A). God's covenant with Abraham involved the redemptive history of the world. And so the Creator of the universe binds himself through this theophany-ritual to an unconditional promise ratified by blood. The binding is symbolized by the smoking furnace and flaming torch passing between the pieces of the slain victims. Perhaps it was a symbol that ultimate fulfillment would come only when the God-man as an innocent victim bore the curse of a broken body in behalf of those who have broken the Covenant.

k^erîtût. ***Dismissal, divorce.*** It seems very likely that this word is related to the root *kārat*. The word is used only a few times in the OT (Deut 24:1, 3; Isa 50:1; Jer 3:8).

k^erūtôt. ***Beams hewn and cut off*** (I Kgs 6:36; 7:2, 12).

Bibliography: THAT, I, pp. 857–60.

E.S.

כְּרֻתוֹת (*k^e rūtôt*). See no. 1048b.
כֶּשֶׂב (*keśeb*). See no. 949.

1049 כָּשָׂה (*kāśâ*) ***be sated, gorged with food.*** Occurs only in Deut 32:15, "you grew fat, became thick, were gorged."

כַּשִּׁיל (*kashshîl*). See no. 1050a.

1050 כָּשַׁל (*kāshal*) ***stumble, totter, stagger*** (usually from weakness or weariness, or in flight from attackers).

Derivatives

1050a כַּשִּׁיל (*kashshîl*) ***ax*** (perhaps as an instrument for felling trees) only Ps 74:6.
1050b כִּשָּׁלוֹן (*kishshālôn*) ***a stumbling, a calamity.***
1050c †מִכְשׁוֹל (*mikshôl*) ***a stumbling, a stumbling block.***
1050d מַכְשֵׁלָה (*makshēlâ*) ***decay, ruin.***

The verb is usually used of physical falling, but numbers of times the figurative use of failing or ruin occurs (Ps 64:8 [H 9]; II Chr 25:8). However, the root is rarely used in the sense of the NT *skandalidzō* "cause one to fall into sin." The nearest to this is Mal 2:8 where the priests by their teaching "have caused many to stumble" (NIV). In Jer 18:15 it says the idols made the people "stumble in their ways," but here the figure is the frequent one of a path representing the path of life. Proverbs 4:16 says the wicked cannot sleep "till they make someone fall" (NIV) which probably, like Jeremiah, refers to stumbling in the path of life. It is perhaps from this figure that the idea of causing someone to stumble into sin arose in the NT and in the Syriac usage of this root.

mikshôl. ***Stumbling-block,*** means or occasion of stumbling: Lev 19:14; Isa 57:14; obstacle, cause for guilt, occasion of stumbling (Job 7:19; 14:4; Ezk 7:19; 14:4). Or: defense of the heart (I Sam 25:31); *ṣûr mikshôl* "a rock of offence."

R.L.H.

כִּשָּׁלוֹן (*kishshālôn*). See no. 1050b.

1051 *כָּשַׁף (*kāshap*) ***use witchcraft.*** Denominative verb.

Related Nouns

1051a †כֶּשֶׁף (*keshep*) ***witchcraft.***
1051b †כַּשָּׁף (*kashshāp*) ***sorcerer.***

This verb and its related nouns mean the same as the Akkadian *kašapu* and the Ugaritic *kṭp* (sorcery). It occurs six times, in the Piel stem only. The participial form is used five times.

The pharaoh of the exodus had those who practiced this variety of the occult in his retinue of advisers (Ex 7:11). They are grouped with the *ḥăkāmîm* (wise men) and *ḥarṭummîm* (magicians, q.v.).

These sorcerers were outlawed in Israel. In Ex 22:17 the feminine form appears (*mᵉkashshēpâ*) and in the long list of Deut 18:10 the masculine (*mᵉkashshēp*). The penalty was death.

Among the sins of King Manasseh was witchcraft (II Chr 33:6). This is the only occurrence of the finite verb form.

Another occurrence of the participle is in Dan 2:2. Like the pharaoh, King Nebuchadnezzar summoned his "sorcerers" along with his "magicians" (*ḥarṭummîm*), enchanters (*'ashshāpîm,* q.v.), and Chaldeans (*kaśdîm*).

Malachi saw these sorcerers being judged in the end along with adulterers, liars, and oppressors of widows, orphans, and foreigners (3:5).

keshep. ***Witchcraft, sorcery, soothsayer, spell.*** This masculine noun occurs six times in the OT, always in the plural (II Kgs 9:22; Isa 47:9, 12; Mic 5:12 [H 11]; Nah 3:4 twice).

kashshāp. Occurs only once, Jer 27:9, "sorcerer."

Bibliography: Davies, T. W., *Magic, Divination, and Demonology,* 1898, reprint, KTAV, 1969.

R.L.A.

1052 כָּשֵׁר (*kāshēr*) ***be right and proper to*** (in the eyes of, Est 8:5); to prosper (Eccl 11:6). Cf. Akkadian *kašāru* "succeed"; *kishrôn* is: skill; success (Eccl 2:21; 4:4); advantage (Eccl 5:10). (Medieval Hebrew *kosher* = "right and proper," i.e. according to the rules of ritual purity.)

Derivatives

1052a כּוֹשָׁרָה (*kôshārâ*) ***singing.*** Cf. UT 19: no. 1335.
1052b כִּשְׁרוֹן (*kishrôn*) ***success.***
1052c כִּישׁוֹר (*kîshôr*) ***distaff.***

G.L.A.

1053 כָּתַב (*kātab*) ***write, record, enroll.***

Derivatives

1053a כְּתָב (*kᵉtāb*) ***writing, document, edict.*** Only used in exilic and postexilic books.
1053b כְּתֹבֶת (*kᵉtōbet*) ***a mark, perhaps a tattoo*** (Lev 19:28).
1053c מִכְתָּב (*miktāb*) ***writing, the thing written.***

kātab is the only general word for "write" and it is widely used. Curiously, it is not used in Genesis. Moses wrote on a scroll God's curse on the Amalekites (Ex 17:14). God himself wrote the Ten Commandments (Ex 31:18). Moses also is specifically said to have written the Book of the Covenant (Ex 24:4), the Sinai legislation (Ex 34:27), the names of the leaders of the tribes (Num 17:2–3 [17–18]), the wilderness itinerary (Num 33:2), the law "from beginning to end" (Deut 31:9, 24) and Moses' final song (Deut 31:22, 24). It is quite possible that the general references of Deut 31:9 and 24 refer to the whole of the Pentateuch (cf. Deut 28:58–61; 29:20–21) although critical scholars refer it only to Deut—and question even that.

References to writing abound in the rest of the OT. Joshua wrote (Josh 24:26), a young man wrote for Gideon (Jud 8:14, NASB, NIV), Samuel wrote the constitution of the kingdom—and others, prophets, kings, scribes and common people wrote as well. It appears from the many references in I and II Kgs that the court records of both Israel and Judah were written, preserved and available. The series of such notations begins with Solomon (I Kgs 11:41) and goes to the breakup of the kingdom under Jehoiakim (II Kgs 24:5). Similar records were kept by the Babylonian kings and some have been discovered (Wiseman, D. J., *Chronicles of the Chaldean Kings,* British Museum, 1956). Fortunately for Mordecai such records were also kept by the Persian kings. Like modern minutes and records, they apparently made dry reading (Est 6:1–2).

The enigmatic references to the Book of Jasher may possibly be explained as referring to similar records. The word Jasher (like Jeshurun, Deut 33:26) is probably a poetic name for all Israel. The Book of Jasher may thus have been a record book of the events of Israel in the pre-monarchy days as the annals of the kings of Judah and of Israel were in later days. It is mentioned only in Josh 10:13 and II Sam 1:18. It bears no relation to the apocryphal book of the same name.

According to R. K. Harrison, Wellhausen still in his day held that the Hebrews did not write before the times of the monarchy (HIOT, p. 201). Such a view seems odd today, but it reminds us how little archaeology was really known one hundred years ago. Writing began among the Sumerians shortly before 3000 B.C. and at about the same time in Egypt. There was a wealth of literature by Abraham's day and Moses, trained in the learning of the Egyptians, surely could write Egyptian, Akkadian and Hebrew, possibly also Hurrian and Hittite.

Some have argued that although writing was available it was little used among the Hebrews who have left us few examples of their writing in comparison to the nearly one million clay tablets found in Mesopotamia and the abundant inscriptions and papyri in Egypt. Actually, we do have sporadic Hebrew writing scattered from Solomon to Ezra. We have very little after Ezra until the Dead Sea Scrolls. One possible explanation for this is that the Hebrews who used alphabetic script wrote on papyrus and leather. These materials are well preserved in Egypt (and the Dead Sea caves), but soon deteriorate in the Palestinian rainy season.

F. F. Bruce rightly emphasizes that the Hebrews in Palestine had a great advantage over the Egyptians and over those in Mesopotamia who wrote on clay tablets. The Hebrews had an alphabet. Whereas one must know several hundred signs to read Akkadian and also a large number to read Egyptian, the Hebrews only had to learn twenty-two. Says Bruce, "It is worth noticing that it was the alphabet that made it possible for all classes to be literate; its invention is therefore a landmark of great importance in the history of civilization," and, we may add, in the spread of the knowledge of God's word (*The Books and the Parchments,* rev. ed., 1963, p. 30). Harrison draws a significant conclusion, "It is no longer necessary to assume that an extended period of oral transmission is a necessary prerequisite to the written form of many if not all of the OT documents as is common in liberal circles" (HIOT p. 209).

Bibliography: Bruce, F. F., *The Books and the Parchments,* 3d ed., Revell, 1962. Cerny, J., *Paper and Books in Ancient Egypt,* Ares, 1977. Driver, Godfrey R., *Semitic Writing: From Pictograph to Alphabet,* rev. ed., 1954. HIOT, pp. 201–207. White, W., in ZPEB, V, pp. 995–1015.

R.L.H.

כְּתֹבֶת (*k^e tōbet*). See no. 1053c.
כְּתִית (*k^e tît*). See no. 1062a.

1054 כתל (*ktl*). **Assumed root of the following.**
1054a כֹּתֶל (*kōtel*) ***wall of house.***

1055 *כָּתַם (*kātam*) ***I,*** only Niphal: ***be stained, be defiled.*** (Aramaic *k^e tam; kitmā,* a stain; Syriac *k^e tam* "be defiled." Akkadian *katāmu* "to cover.")

1056 כתם (*ktm*) **II. Assumed root of the following.**
1056a †מִכְתָּם (*miktām*) ***miktam.*** A technical term which appears in Psalm titles. Meaning unknown. For related terms, see *sela.*

This term is used in six Psalm titles, always linked with *l^e dāwîd* "of" or "belonging to David" (Ps 16, 56–59). All six are psalms of lament and four of the headings have historical references to David's struggles with the Philistines (56), Saul (57, 59) and the Arameans (60). If it comes from a root "to cover" (cf. Akkadian *katāmu*). *miktām* could mean a "song of covering" or "atonement." Another view understands the term to mean an "engraving," such as an inscription on a stone slab, perhaps with gold letters (*ketem* = gold). For other such terms see *selâ.*

H.W.

1057 כֶּתֶם (*ketem*) ***gold.***

Apparently this word is of Nubian origin. Egyptian spells *k-t-m.t* in syllabic writing, implying a loan word. But cf. Akkadian *kitimmu* "goldsmith". See Ps 45:10; Job 28:16, 19; Isa 13:12; Prov 25:12; Dan 10:5.

G.L.A.

1058 כתן (*ktn*). **Assumed root of the following.**
1058a †כְּתֹנֶת (*kuttōnet*) ***tunic, a long shirt-like garment, usually of linen*** (Gen 37:3; II Sam 15:32; Isa 22:21).

Adam's was made of fur (Gen 3:21). Also worn by women (II Sam 13:18; Song 5:3). Worn especially by priests (Ex 28:4; 29:5; 39:27; Lev 8:7; 10:5; Ezr 2:69; Neh 7:69). (Cf. Akkadian *kitinnu* or *kitintu,* a linen garment made from *kitū* linen; the Aramaic *kittûnā'* is the same as the Hebrew.) The word was borrowed by the Greek χιτών.

כֻּתֹּנֶת (*kūttōnet*). See no. 1058a.

1059 כָּתֵף (*kātēp*) ***shoulder, shoulder-blade, side or slope*** (of a hill).

(Distinct from שְׁכֶם *sh*[e]*kem* which includes neck and shoulders.) Of man: I Sam 17:6; Deut 33:12; of refractory beasts: Neh 9:29; of butchered meat: Ezk 24:4; shoulder-piece of ephod: Ex 28:7; mountain-slope: Num 34:11; supports of the bases for the lavers beside the temple: I Kgs 7:30.

G.L.A.

1060 *כָּתַר (*kātar*) ***surround*** (Piel); ***surround*** (with hostility, Hiphil).

Derivatives

1060a כֶּתֶר (*keter*) ***crown*** (Est only).
1060b *כָּתַר (*kātar*) ***to crown.*** Denominative verb.
1060c כֹּתֶרֶת (*kōteret*) ***capital of a pillar.***

כֹּתֶרֶת (*kōteret*). See no. 1060c.

1061 כָּתַשׁ (*kātash*) ***pound, pound fine, bray.*** Occurs only in Prov 27:22, *'im-tiktośh 'et-hā'ĕwîl bammaktēsh* "if you pound the fool in the mortar."

Derivative

1061a מַכְתֵּשׁ (*maktēsh*) ***mortar*** (Prov 27:22).

1062 כָּתַת (*kātat*) ***crush to pieces, crush fine.***

Derivatives

1062a כָּתִית (*kātît*) ***beaten, pounded fine, in a mortar, costly.***
1062b מְכִתָּה (*m*[e]*kittâ*) ***crushed fragments*** (Isa 30:14, only).

ל

ל

1063 לְ (l^e) ***to, at, in, in reference to, of, by etc.*** In recent translations, occasionally "from."

Even though Hebrew possessed, at least in its later stages, a large number of prepositions, many prepositional functions remained concentrated in the four prefixes; b^e, k^e, l^e, and *min*. Of these, l^e most nearly corresponded to the Indo-European dative case. (The present article relies very heavily on the BDB entry.)

l^e may indicate direction, either of physical movement ("that I may go 'to' my country" Gen 30:25) or of personal attention or attitudes. The Psalmist asked God to attend "to" him (Ps 55:2 [H 3]). The Psalmist also affirmed that his soul would not be deserted "to" Sheol (Ps 16:10). God mocked "at" rebels (Ps 2:4; RSV "have in derision.").

It may indicate the direction or result of a transformation or change. God's fashioning of Adam's rib "into" a woman (Gen 2:22) and the expressions, "who put bitter 'for' sweet and sweet 'for' bitter" (Isa 5:20) are clear examples. A process might endow a given object with a new character or role. Plant life was designated as being man's "for food" (Gen 1:29). The Levite took on service "for a priest for Micah" (Jud 17:13).

It expresses location both in space and in time. Spatial location is exemplified in such phrases as "at the door" (Gen 4:7) and "at Michmash" (Isa 10:28); temporal location by such phrases as "in times of trouble" (Ps 9:9 [H 10]) and "in the spring of the year" (II Sam 11:1).

A very numerous and vaguely defined body of usages is grouped under the heading, "reference." In these usages, the meaning of l^e is best regarded as something rather vague like "in reference to" with the exact meaning derived from the context. Abraham requested of Sarah, "Say, 'in reference to' me" (Gen 20:13). A census could be conducted "'in reference to' (i.e. "according to") fathers' houses" (Num 1:2).

It can indicate possession as in "the man 'of' you" (I Sam 2:33) and "your sons" (II Kgs 10:30; lit "sons 'to' you"). Such a construction, "my own possession" (Ex 19:5; lit. "possession 'to' me"), expresses God's special relation to his people within the requirements of the covenant.

l^e may express the construct relation in cases in which a construct chain would be grammatically awkward or impossible. It is especially useful if the writer wished to keep the possessed item indefinite (e.g. "two slaves 'to' Shimei" meaning two of Shimei's slaves, I Kgs 2:39).

The subject of passive verbal ideas may be thus introduced: "Blessed be Abram 'by' God" (Gen 14:19). From a purely descriptive perspective, the direct object of some verbs is marked by l^e "with which your enemies shall distress you" (Deut 28:53; i.e. "make distress 'for' you") and "save us" (Josh 10:6; i.e. "make deliverance 'for' us"). This is common in Aramaic.

Used with infinitives, it may indicate purpose ("for bearing," Eccl 3:2), result ("'so as to' walk . . . and 'to' fear," Deut 8:6), an infinitive of reference ("do not go far 'in reference to' going," Ex 8:28), or an objectival infinitive ("began 'to' multiply," Gen 6:1).

There is an additional meaning of l^e suggested from Ugaritic and now accepted by many in Hebrew, the meaning "from." Gordon says that the most interesting feature of Ugaritic prepositions is the meaning "from" for both *b* and *l* (UT 10:1). He alleges that Ps 84:11 [H 12], also Josh 2:4 where "from the tribes of Israel" with l^e is parallelled by 4:4, "from each tribe" with *min*. Dahood gives other examples from the Pss (*Psalms*, AB, III, p. 394). Holladay's Lexicon does not offer this usage, but does admit an emphatic and asseverative use in agreement with Dahood.

1064 לֹא (*lō'*) ***not, no.***

lō' was the primary Hebrew term for factual negation in contrast to *'al* which typically described potential negation. Other negatives functioned less frequently for factual negation (*e.g. 'ayin, bal* and *b^{e}lî*). This article will, first, examine the major syntactical functions of *lō'*, and, secondly, study some theologically significant negations expressed by this term.

Major syntactical functions. lō' negates factual statements in all time frameworks. It serves to negate omnitemporal, general statements. The happy man does not walk in the counsel of the ungodly (Ps 1:1). Further, he is likened to a tree whose foliage does not wither (vs. 3). It negates past statements ("I did not call," I Sam 3:6), present statements ("I am not a prophet," Amos 7:14 [many would take this as past time, but there are plenty of other possible illustrations. R.L.H.]), and future statements ("It will never be inhabited," Isa 13:20). It is used in emphatic future negations ("Surely, you shall not die," Gen 3:4). It negates adjectival attributes such as "a son, not wise" (Hos 13:13) and "a way, not good" (Ps 36:4).

It may be used in an emphatic negative command: "You shall not kill" (Ex 20:13). For a milder negative, *'al* with the jussive is used. The Hebrew imperative is never used with a negative.

lō' is used in negative final clauses as in Ex 28:43. "So that they not (i.e. "lest they") bring guilt." *lō'* followed by *l^e* with an infinitive states that something cannot or must not happen (e.g. "He could not drive out," Jud 1:19, and "We must not mention," Amos 6:10). As a negative adverb, it may indicate denial or refusal (Jud 12:5). Like English "not" it may indicate a question: "And should I not pity . . .?" (Jon 4:11). Double negation occurs (Zeph 2:2).

lō' is used in several negative compounds: *b^{e}lō'*, without; *hălō'*, not so?; *wālō'*, and/if not; *k^{e}lō'*, as though not; *l^{e}lō'*, without; and *'im lō'*, if not.

Some theologically significant negations. Philosophers have long referred to language of negation in describing the transcendent attributes of God. Biblical negations using *lō'* frequently describe God. God transcends humanistic models: "God is not a man" (Num 23:19). God so transcends human capacities, especially man's moral capacities, that men cannot see God and live (Ex 33:20). God is immutable; his character does not change (Mal 3:6). God's unchanging faithfulness is spoken of, most particularly in regard to his covenants (Ps 89:33–34). God's nearness ("not a God afar off," Jer 23:23) implies his omnipresence. God is not confined by finite (or infinite) space (I Kgs 8:27). Nor is God bound by time (Ps 102:27 [H 28]). God's holiness is shown in that evil cannot exist in his presence (Ps 5:4–5).

There are other negations worthy of notice. Several describe the powerlessness of idols: they are impotent (i.e. "They are not able") in the time of captivity (Isa 46:2); they cannot move from their place, do not answer, and cannot save (Isa 46:7). Finally, in the Davidic covenant, the Hebrews will someday be settled in the land not to be disturbed or afflicted again (II Sam 7:10). Neither shall God's covenant faithfulness turn from the Davidic dynasty (II Sam 7:15).

On occasion there is uncertainty as to whether *lō'*, not, or *lô*, to him, is intended in the Hebrew text (e.g. Job 13:15; KJV "Yet will I trust him," i.e. "to him," and RSV "I have no hope"). Context, versions, and general theology must be relied on in such cases.

1065 לאב (*l'b*). **Assumed root of the following.**
1065a תַּלְאֻבָה (*tal'ūbâ*) ***drought*** (Hos 13:5).

1066 לָאָה (*lā'â*) ***be weary, grieved, offended.***

Derivative

1066a †תְּלָאָה (*t^{e}lā'â*) ***toil, hardship.***

lā'â refers either to physical or psychological weariness and is used in poetic figures based upon both. The physical weariness of the runner is thus described (Jer 12:5). The Sodomites are described as physically wearied from searching for Lot's door (Gen 19:11). Physical weariness is sarcastically attributed to Moab from much activity in idolatry (Isa 16:12; cf. Prov 26:15).

Psychological weariness expresses several attitudes. On Job's part, discouragement (Job 4:5) and annoyance (Job 4:2) are thus described. Disgust is also indicated by *lā'â* when the Egyptians are said to be too "tired" to drink the corrupted waters of the Nile (Ex 7:18) and when God is depicted as "tired" of the Hebrews' insincere religious rituals (Isa 1:14). As a poetic figure weariness describes the land struck by drought conditions (Ps 68:9 [H 10]).

Often the idiom of "being weary" with something serves as a dramatic, poetic way of asserting that there is an objectionable excess of what causes weariness. The Hebrews were wearied by "too many" pagan, religious advisors (Isa 47:13). Attempting to hold in God's message of wrath was too much for Jeremiah to bear (Jer 6:11). God himself was weary from too much relenting (Jer 15:6).

t^{e}lā'â. ***Toil, hardship*** (RSV "hardship," "adversity"). The primary reference is to that which produces weariness. It refers to the wilderness hardships of the Hebrews (Ex 18:8; Num 20:14), the troubles of the restored Hebrew community (Neh 9:32), and the judgments which God brought upon his sinful people (Lam 3:5). Correspondingly, insincere religious services were called a source of weariness for God (Mal 1:13).

A.B.

1067 לָאַט (*lā'aṭ*) ***cover.*** Occurs only in II Sam 19:5, "the king covered his face."

לָאט (*lā'ṭ*). See no. 1092a.

1068 לאך (*l'k*). **Assumed root of the following.**
1068a †מַלְאָךְ (*mal'āk*) ***messenger, representative.***
1068b †מְלָאכָה (*m^{e}lā'kâ*) ***work, business.***
1068c †מַלְאֲכוּת (*mal'ākût*) ***message,*** only only in Hag 1:13.

mal'āk. ***Messenger, representative, courtier, angel.*** "Messenger" is an inadequate term for the range of tasks carried out by the OT *mal'āk*. These were 1) to carry a message, 2) to perform some other specific commission, and 3) to represent more or less officially the one sending him. There were both human and supernatural *m^{e}lā'kîm*, the latter including the Angel of Yahweh (i.e. the Angel of the Lord).

Human messengers. The human *mal'āk* could be a message bearer (Gen 32:2). The kinds of messages varied. They may have announced good news (I Sam 6:21), threats (I Kgs 19:2), or requests (Num 20:14; 22:5; Jud 7:24). However, the term was applied to courtiers or retainers sent for other purposes. They could spy (Josh 6:25) or kill (I Sam 19:11; II Kgs 6:32). David sent "messengers" to summon Bathsheba (II Sam 11:4). The *mᵉlā'kîm* could serve as diplomatic representatives (Jud 11:12–14; II Sam 5:11; I Kgs 20:2).

Men, particularly the prophets, could serve as God's messengers. For the prophets, the term implied official representation of God as well as message bearing (II Chr 36:15–16; Hag 1:13). David is called an "angel/messenger of God." A possible interpretation is that David represented God in that he represented some particular divine attribute: innocence (I Sam 29:9), wisdom (II Sam 14:17), or hoped-for graciousness (II Sam 19:27). In Isaiah, God's messenger is seen in weakness (Isa 42:19).

Supernatural messengers. (This section deals only with the term *mal'āk,* not with the broader area of angelology.) Supernatural messengers represented the same general range of functions as human messengers. Message-bearing might be central (Zech 1:9; 5:5). More often they performed some particular commission such as guarding a human effort like the search for Isaac's bride (Gen 24:40) or protecting the Hebrews in the wilderness (Ex 23:20). They executed judgment (II Sam 24:17; Ps 78:49), delivered (Gen 19:12–17), and protected (Ps 91:11).

A special function of supernatural messengers/angels is that they, by their very presence, present an aspect of God's glory (Gen 28:12–17; cf. angels in Isa 6, Ezk 1, Rev 4:6–8, and the cherubim in the Holy of Holies). In addition they join in active praise to God (Ps 148:2; cf. Isa 6:3).

The Messenger/Angel of Yahweh. This figure has the same general range of functions as other messengers. He brought messages, good (Gen 16:10–13) and threatening (Jud 5:23). He performed specific commissions of judgment (II Kgs 19:35; Ps 35:5–6) and deliverance (Gen 22:11; Ps 34:7 [H 8]). He could also be called the "angel of God" (Jud 13:6, 9, cf. v. 3), though this title is not exclusively his. He alone had the ministry of intercession with God in behalf of men (Zech 1:12; 3:1–5).

There has been extensive discussion of his identity. He seems to be God, since those who see him marvel that they have seen God (Jud 13:21–22) and he speaks for God in the first person (Gen 16:10; Ex 3:2, 6; Jud 2:1). He is identified with the pre-incarnate Christ on the grounds of similarity in functions, especially the intercessory function noted above.

mᵉlā'kâ. ***Work, business, craftsmanship, goods, property.*** Like the English "work," *mᵉlā'kâ* could refer either to the activity of working, the requisite skills of work, or to the results of work. In contrast to terms like *'āmal* and *yāga'* which emphasized the toilsome, laborious side of work, this term emphasized work as involving skill and benefits.

All work was banned both on the weekly Sabbath (Ex 20:9–10) and on the festal Sabbaths (Lev 16:29). God himself ceased from working on the Sabbath day (Gen 2:1–2).

Turning to specific usages of *mᵉlā'kâ*, it could refer to a particular task or project at hand (Neh 5:16) or it could refer to one's routine or habitual work, i.e. one's business (Gen 39:11; Prov 18:9). It referred to the king's business (I Sam 8:16) and that of the royal bureaucracy (I Kgs 9:23).

"Work" referred to skilled craftsmanship when God endowed men with supernatural skills for the skilled work of the tabernacle (Ex 31:3: RSV, "craftsmanship"), and Solomon imported Phoenician craftsmen for the skilled work of the temple (I Kgs 7:14).

The resulting products of work, both skilled and unskilled, were described by this term. Moses looked upon the skilled "work" of the tabernacle (Ex 39:43). Or it could refer to property in general without regard to special skills or value (e.g. I Sam 15:9, "all that was despised" for "every despised work"; cf. also Ex 22:8, 11).

Bibliography: Funderburk, G. B., "Angel," in ZPEB I, pp. 160–66.

A.B.

1069 **לאם** (*l'm*). **Assumed root of the following.**
1069a †לְאֹם (*lᵉ'ōm*), לְאוֹם (*lᵉ'ôm*) ***nation(s), people(s).*** (ASV and RSV agree.)

The Semitic root (as seen in Arabic *la'ama* "assemble") suggests that the meaning of the word is togetherness, i.e. the common people considered as a whole. The word is also found in Ugaritic, (UT 19:no 1346) Girdlestone (*Synonyms of the Old Testament,* Eerdmans, reprint, 1975, p. 257) translates *lᵉ'ōm* as "race." However, it is used to refer to peoples in their varied walks of life (Ps 44:14 [H 15]; Prov 11:26).

In Gen 25:23, Rebekah is told that two nations (*gôyîm*) are in her womb and two *lᵉ'ūmmîm* are to be separated from her. One *lᵉ'ôm* is to be stronger than the other. Isaac's progeny would consist of two distinct types of people, each identified by their unique quality. In Gen 27:29 *'ammîm* appears as a near-synonym for *lᵉ'ūmmîm*. The thought expressed is that people, in unified groups and reflecting varying characteristics, are to express homage to Abraham's grandson.

In Ps, *lᵉ'ôm* is used in synonymous parallelism with *gôyîm* (44:2 [H 3]) and *'ammîm* (Ps 7:7 [H 8]). In Ps 67 all three terms express the Psalmist's desire that all men, of whatever relationship or characteristic, praise the Lord. In Prov and Isa, parallel phrases indicate that the term is qualified by its synonyms, but the thrust of the term remains: all people in their definable groups. This clearly suggests the unity and the diversity of humanity.

G.V.G.

לֵב (*lēb*). See no. 1071a.

1070 לבא (*lb'*). **Assumed root of the following.**
1070a לְבִי (*l^e bî*) ***lion.*** Occurs only in Ps 57:5 in phrase *napshî b^e tôk l^e bā'im* and Nah 2:13, *lib'ōtāyw.*
1070b לְבִיָא (*l^e bîyā'*) ***lioness,*** only in Ezk 19:2.
1070c †לָבִיא (*lābî'*) ***lion*** (often "lioness" in RSV).

The Akkadian cognate is *labbu* (from an original *lab'u*?), Ugaritic *lbu,* Arabic *labu'at,* possibly the source of Greek *leon.*

lābî' often serves as a symbol of the violence of men (Gen 49:9; Num 23:24); the violence of God in judgment (Hos 13:8); desolation (Isa 30:6). God's great power overwhelms even the mighty lion (Job 4:11). Other words for lion include *k^e pîr, 'āryēh, layish* and *shaḥal.*

A.B.

1071 *לָבַב (*lābab*) ***ravish*** (Piel), ***become intelligent*** (Niphal). Denominative verb.

Parent Noun

1071a †לֵב (*lēb*), לֵבָב (*lēbāb*) ***heart, understanding.***
1071b †לִבָּה (*libbâ*) ***heart.***
1071c †לְבִבָה (*l^e bibâ*) ***bread.***
1071d †לִבֵּב (*libbēb*) ***cook bread.*** Denominative verb, occurring only in the Piel.

lābab occurs as a denominative verb from *lēb* (Song 4:9). Translated "ravished my heart" (KJV, RSV) and "made my heart to beat faster" (NASB). BDB suggests "encouraged."

"Become intelligent" suits the single Niphal usage (Job 11:12).

lēb, lēbāb. ***Heart, understanding, mind*** (also used in idioms such as "to set the heart upon" meaning "to think about" or "to want").

Concrete meanings of *lēb* referred to the internal organ and to analogous physical locations. However, in its abstract meanings, "heart" became the richest biblical term for the totality of man's inner or immaterial nature. In biblical literature it is the most frequently used term for man's immaterial personality functions as well as the most inclusive term for them since, in the Bible, virtually every immaterial function of man is attributed to the "heart."

Very few usages of *lēb* refer to concrete, physical meanings. The death accounts of Nabal (I Sam 25:37) and Joram (II Kgs 9:24) likely refer to the physical organ. The physical organ defined the location of Aaron's breastplate (Ex 28:29). Psalm 38:9 probably refers to the beating of the physical organ. Physical "innerness" is expressed by "heart." The deeps congealed "in the heart of" the sea (Ex 15:8) and the fires of Sinai rose "to the heart of" Heaven (Deut 4:11). The usage of "heart" for a divinely given vital principle may best fit Job 34:14–15 ("if he take back to himself the heart he gave," writer's paraphrase).

By far the majority of the usages of *lēb* refer either to the inner or immaterial nature in general or to one of the three traditional personality functions of man; emotion, thought, or will.

In referring to the inner nature, *lēb* may contrast some relatively obscure or less visible aspect of man's nature with the more public side of his being. It may be regarded as an inner reflection of the outer man (Prov 27:19; RSV "mind"). Dream consciousness may be meant when the heroine's "heart" was awake though her body slept in the Song of Songs (5:2). Statements such as "Why does your heart carry you away?" (Job 15:12) contrast the heart with the remainder of the person. However, in other contexts, "heart" expresses the totality of a man's nature and character, both inner and outer (I Kgs 8:23; Ps 9:1 [H 2]).

Closely related to the above is the usage of *lēb* as an emphatic personal term (cf. similar usage of *nepesh, 'eṣem,* etc.) The plagues are sent, not just upon Pharaoh, but upon Pharaoh's heart (Ex 9:14). Thus, Jacob's stealing of Laban's heart might emphasize Laban as the object of Jacob's actions rather than Jacob's subtlety (Gen 31:20; cf. RSV, "Jacob outwitted Laban"). Similarly, the breastplate of judgment on Aaron's heart may emphasize Aaron as the bearer of judgment as well as a bodily location (Ex 28:29). A variation of this usage is "heart" as reflexive: "Refresh your hearts" for "Refresh yourselves" (Gen 18:5) and "strengthen your heart" for "strengthen yourself (with food)" (Jud 19:5).

The whole spectrum of emotion is attributed to the heart. Examples of positive emotions are the following: Hannah's heart rejoiced (I Sam 2:1) as should the hearts of those who seek the Lord (I Chr 16:10). Love may be centered in the heart, as when Delilah complained that Samson's heart was not with her (Jud 16:15). Absalom gained for himself the loyalty of the Hebrew nation by stealing their hearts (II Sam 15:6). The joyful excitement from the news that Joseph was alive made Jacob's heart faint (Gen 45:26). Reception of comfort is seated in the heart as in the idiom "to speak to the heart" (Gen 34:3; Isa 40:2) for "to comfort."

As for negative emotions, grief is "evil of heart" (Neh 2:2; RSV "sadness of heart"). David's regret or bad conscience at cutting Saul's garment is expressed as "his heart struck him" (I Sam 24:6; cf. II Sam 24:10). God's regret at creating man is centered in God's heart (Gen 6:6). The broken heart accompanies being oppressed (Ps 34:18 [H 19]). Contempt (II Sam 6:16), envy (Prov 23:17), and anger (Prov 19:3) are all functions of the heart.

Idioms relating the heart to fear and bravery are so numerous as to deserve separate treatment. Fear is expressed as follows: The heart may "go out" or "leave" (Gen 42:28; KJV, RSV, "fail"); it may "fall" (I Sam 17:32; RSV, "fail"). To remove courage is to hinder the heart (Num 32:7, 9). Fear occurs when the heart "deserts" its owner (Ps 40:12 [H 13]; KJV, "fails") or "melts" (Josh 14:7). Trembling of heart may represent emotions ranging from the complete demoralization of God's people under judgment (Deut 28:65; cf. I Sam 28:5) to Eli's anxiety over the welfare of the ark of God (I Sam 4:13). On the other hand the "heart of a lion" speaks of courage (II Sam 17:10).

Thought functions may be attributed to the heart. In such cases it is likely to be translated as "mind" or "understanding." To "set the heart to" may mean to "pay attention to" (Ex 7:23) or to "consider important" (II Sam 18:32). Creative thought is a heart function. Wicked devices originate in the heart (Gen 6:5). The RSV translates "which came upon Solomon's heart" as "all that Solomon had planned" (II Chr 7:11).

Wisdom and understanding are seated in the heart. The "wise heart" (I Kgs 3:12; RSV, "wise mind") and "wise of heart" (Prov 16:23) are mentioned. This idiom can be so strongly felt that "heart" virtually becomes a synonym for such ideas as "mind" (II Chr 9:23; RSV) or "sense" (Prov 11:12; RSV). The heart functions in perception and awareness as when Elisha's heart (i.e. Elisha's perceptive nature; RSV "spirit") went with Gehazi (II Kgs 5:26). As the seat of thought and intellect, the heart can be deluded (Isa 44:20; RSV "mind").

The heart is the seat of the will. A decision may be described as "setting" the heart (II Chr 12:14). "Not of my heart" expresses "not of my will" (Num 16:28). The "hearts" of the Shechemites inclined to follow Abimelech (Jud 19:3). Removal of the decision-making capacity is described as hardening the heart (Ex 10:1; Josh 11:20). Closely connected to the preceding is the heart as the seat of moral responsibility. Righteousness is "integrity of heart" (Gen 20:5). Moral reformation is to "set one's heart aright" (Job 11:13). The heart is described as the seat of moral evil (Jer 17:9).

Personality dispositions may be considered as more or less permanent personality patterns. Some typical dispositions located in the heart are generosity ("generous heart"; Ex 35:5), pride ("his heart became high"; II Chr 26:16), and faith ("the heart made firm"; Ps 78:8).

libbâ. ***Heart*** (KJV, RSV), rage (KB). Unique form of unclear meaning (Ezk 16:30). Perhaps a variant of *lēb*.

l^{e}bibâ. ***A kind of bread.*** Perhaps pancakes (BDB) or heartshaped (KB) bread (II Sam 13:6, 8, 10).

libbēb. Piel denominative verb for cooking the *l^{e}bibâ* bread (II Sam 13:6, 8).

Bibliography: "Heart," *JewEnc*. Pedersen, Johs, *Israel, its Life and Culture*, vol. II, Oxford, 1959, pp. 102–8. TDOT, III, pp. 606–11; VII, pp. 908–13; IX, pp. 626–28. THAT, I, pp. 861–66.

A.B.

לְבִבָה (*l^{e}bibâ*). See no. 1071c.
לַבָּה (*labbâ*). See no. 1077b.
לְבוּשׁ (*l^{e}bûsh*). See no. 1075a.

1072 *לָבַט (*lābaṭ*) ***thrust down, out, or away.*** Occurs only in the Niphal (Hos 4:14; Prov 10:8, 10).

1073 לְבִי (*l^{e}bî*) ***lion.*** A form from *lb'* q.v.
לְבִיָּא (*l^{e}bîyā'*). See no. 1070b.
לָבִיא (*lābî'*). See no. 1070c.

1074 לבן (*lbn*). **Assumed root of the following.**
1074a †לָבָן (*lābān*) ***white.***
1074b *†לָבֵן (*lābēn*) ***be white.*** Occurs only in the Hiphil.
1074c †לְבָנָה (*l^{e}bānâ*) ***moon.***
1074d †לְבֹנָה (*l^{e}bōnâ*), לְבוֹנָה (*l^{e}bônâ*) ***frankincense.***
1074e †לְבָנוֹן (*l^{e}bānôn*) ***Lebanon.***
1074f לִבְנֶה (*libneh*) ***poplar.*** Occurs only in Gen 30:37; Hos 4:13.
1074g †לְבֵנָה (*l^{e}bēnâ*) ***brick.***
1074h לָבַן (*lāban*) ***make bricks.*** Denominative verb.
1074i מַלְבֵּן (*malbēn*) ***brick mold.***

The Semitic root *lbn* referred to a range of light colors including: the white of snow, the light brown or creamy color of fresh wood and manna, the grey of the moon, the white of yogurt (Lebanese Arabic), and, finally, either the white snow caps of the Lebanon mountains or their light colored limestone. The Hebrew derivatives vary in their individual theological overtones.

lābān. ***White.*** Describes goats (Gen 30:35), peeled wood (Gen 30:37), manna (Ex 16:31), horses (Zech 1:8; 6:3), milk (Gen 49:12), and the infection of leprosy (Lev 13). Its theological significance is relatively limited. As the color of leprous infection, it may represent corruption and death. Zechariah's white horses, particularly in comparison with the white horse of Revelation (6:2), may signify military conquest. In contrast, the white garments advocated by the Preacher accompany a restrained hedonism (Eccl 9:7–9). In Gen 49:12 the whiteness is probably descriptive and refers to prosperity and abundance.

lābēn. ***Be white.*** A denominative verb derived from *lābān*. Its major theological motif relates whiteness to moral purity. The cleansing which God brings to the sinner makes the sinner white as snow (Ps 51:7 [H 9]; Isa 1:18). The cleansing of martyrdom also makes white (Dan 11:35). A fourth (in the Hithpael) has been translated both reflexively (Dan 12:10; RSV "make themselves white"; and passively (KJV "made white"). While either translation is grammatically defensible, the latter translation avoids the misleading suggestion that such moral cleansing comes by self-reformation. The white tree branches of Joel 1:7 represent the judgment accomplished by voracious locusts.

lᵉbānâ. ***Moon.*** A poetic term for the moon (cf. *yārēaḥ*). It is used in poetic figures both for beauty and for glory. As a figure for beauty it describes a beautiful maiden (Song 6:10). The increased light of the moon symbolizes the miraculous glory of the coming golden age (Isa 30:26). On the other hand, the glory of the moon will be superseded by God's glory which is to be revealed in that same age (Isa 24:23).

lᵉbōnâ, lᵉbônâ. ***Frankincense.*** A resin from the bark of trees of the genus Boswellia. As the amber resin dries, white dust forms on the drops or tears of frankincense thus giving rise to its Semitic name. In biblical times most frankincense came either from or via Sheba in southern Arabia. It was a major item in the ancient luxury trade in spices.

In the OT it is significant as one of the ingredients of the holy incense (Ex 30:34) and as part of the cereal offering (Lev 2:1; KJV "meat offering"). The frankincense seems to have held a high degree of sanctity since all the frankincense was included in that portion of the cereal offering given as God's memorial portion (Lev 6:15). It was excluded from the cereal offering for jealousy (Num 5:15). It was also sprinkled on the shewbread (Lev 24:7). Frankincense seemed to be such a characteristic element in the sacrificial system that the term could be used to represent the entire system (Isa 43:23; Jer 6:20).

It could also symbolize luxury and sensuality (Song 3:6; 4:6, 14).

lᵉbānôn. ***Lebanon.*** Generally refers to the Lebanon mountain range more or less coinciding with the present Mount Lebanon. In OT ideology "Lebanon" was important both as a part of the promised land and as a literary symbol for such ideas as majesty, power, or grandeur.

Lebanon in Old Testament History. From early times Lebanon, or part of it, was included in the promised land (Deut 1:7; Jud 3:3). The Lebanese coast, Phoenicia, up to and including the land of the Gebalites (i.e. Byblos) is listed in the promised but unconquered lands (Josh 13:5). Hebrew military and commercial activities in the Lebanon (I Kgs 9:19; II Chr 8:6) were probably confined to the foothills of Mount Lebanon bordering the Beqaa Valley. The Lebanon range provided cedar wood for building the Old Testament temples (II Chr 2:8; Ezr 3:7).

Lebanon in Literary Symbolism. Lebanon and its cedars were symbols of greatness in popular proverbs (II Kgs 14:9), folk tales (Jud 9:15), and in the more literary imagery of the prophets. The Assyrian is said to have indicated the magnitude of his conquests by boasting that he had penetrated Mount Lebanon (II Kgs 19:23). God's greatness is shown in that God planted the cedars (Ps 104:16) and in the manner in which the Lebanon skips or leaps at the sound of his voice (Ps 29:5). Yet God's power is such that he can also destroy those cedars (Isa 10:34). The mighty cedars are used elsewhere as appropriate symbols for proud, arrogant men (Ezk 31:3). They may also symbolize flourishing prosperity (Ps 92:12).

The Lebanon region also served as a poetic image for the mysterious and romantic, as notably in the Song of Solomon. It is used in romantic entreaties (Song 4:8, 11, 15; cf. 3:9). Its connotations may have been a factor in naming one section of the Solomonic palace the House of the Forest of Lebanon" (I Kgs 7:2).

lᵉbēnâ. ***Brick.*** Most usages of this term occur in contexts showing the toil and futility of human effort. A sarcastic, poetic doublet emphasizes that the Tower of Babel, an archetype of futile, human effort, was built of brick (Gen 11:3). Futility is seen again when the apostate Ephraimites under judgment defiantly boast that they will rebuild the fallen bricks of Samaria (Isa 9:9). Brick-making characterized the Hebrew toil in Egypt (Ex 5:6–14). In light of the above, the brick used by Ezekiel for an object lesson (4:1; KJV "tile") may conceivably have emphasized the futile toil of the Jewish defense effort. A variant form of this word refers to the surface beneath God's feet in theophanies (Ex 24:10), a surface which elsewhere is referred to as the firmament (*rāqîa'*; Ezk 1:26).

Bibliography: "Lebanon," in ZPEB. Van Beek, Gus, W., "Frankincense and Myrrh," in *The Biblical Archaeologist Reader*, vol. II, pp. 99–126.

A.B.

לִבְנֶה (*libneh*). See no. 1074f.
לְבָנוֹן (*l^e bānôn*). See no. 1074e.

1075 לָבֵשׁ (*lābēsh*) ***dress, be clothed.***

Derivatives

1075a †לְבוּשׁ (*l^ebûsh*), לְבֻשׁ (*l^ebūsh*) ***garments, apparel.***
1075b †מַלְבּוּשׁ (*malbûsh*), מַלְבֻּשׁ (*malbūsh*) ***vestments.***
1075c †תִּלְבֹּשֶׁת (*tilbōshet*) ***garment.***

lābēsh and its derivatives show three levels of usage: 1) being clothed, 2) being clothed as a sign of rank, status, or character, and 3) poetic figures likening abstract qualities to clothing.

In addition to simply referring to clothes as something to be put on (Song 5:3), clothes may reveal something about the wearer. David's daughters showed both their royal status and their virginity by their clothing (II Sam 13:18). The purple of Ezk 23:6 was intended to show nobility or royalty. The king's favor, and resulting positions, were marked by special clothing for both Joseph (Gen 41:42) and Mordecai (Est 6:11). Clothing could reveal sensuous luxury (Jer 4:30) or prosperity (Prov 31:21). A change in garments will typify the holiness needed to enter the Holy of Holies of Ezekiel's future temple (Ezk 42:14). Professional offices could be revealed by garb such as the prophet (Zech 13:4) or the warrior (Ezk 38:4).

Occasions of grief were marked by the wearing of special clothing. Garments of widowhood may be the best known example (Gen 38:19). Mourning (II Sam 14:2; Est 4:1) and repentance (Jon 3:5) could be marked by wearing special clothing. In Zechariah's vision Joshua's sinful state is revealed by his filthy garments (Zech 3:3; see below). The poetic figure describing Job as "clothed with worms" (Job 7:5) showed Job's unhappy state.

When God clothed Adam and Eve in skins (Gen 3:21), he provided a rich symbol of their new status. These garments are generally interpreted as showing the need for sacrifice through the need to kill the animals to provide the skins. However, the conversation between the Mesopotamian hero, Gilgamesh, and Utnapishtim suggests that the wearing of skin clothing might also symbolize all the frailties of fallen human life.

The richest level of usage is using clothing as a poetic figure for abstract qualities. God wears majesty and strength as garments (Ps 93:1). God is challenged to put on strength, i.e. to use his power (Isa 51:9). God clothes himself in righteousness, salvation, vengeance, and fury in preparing for judgment (Isa 59:17).

Men may be "clothed" in various qualities. Job was clothed in righteousness (Job 29:14). Salvation (II Chr 6:41) and strength (Isa 52:1) may be worn. Men were clothed in the Spirit for specific purposes (Jud 6:34; I Chr 12:19; II Chr 24:20). Negative qualities like shame (Ps 35:26; cf. Job 8:22) and cursing (Ps 109:18) also were worn like clothing.

The most significant figure of this sort is the one likening God's imputed righteousness to clothing. The individual's own good deeds are filthy rags (Isa 64:6; cf. Joshua in Zech 3:3) which God removes and then clothes his own in salvation and righteousness (Isa 61:10). Then, like Joshua in Zechariah's vision, men clothed in God's righteousness can stand before God.

l^ebûsh. ***Garments, apparrel.*** This and other derivatives cover the same general range of meanings as the verb. *l^e bûsh* may refer to the formal vestments of an office (II Kgs 10:22). It could refer to literal clothing representing grief (Ps 35:13), luxury (II Sam 1:24), glory (Ps 45:13 [H 14]), and transitoriness (Ps 102:26). It was used as a poetic figure for abstract qualities like strength and dignity (Prov 31:25).

tilbōshet. ***Garment.*** Used once likening vengeance to a garment (Isa 59:17).

malbûsh. ***Vestment, garment.*** Used to refer to literal clothing such as royal livery (I Kgs 10:5) and priestly garments (II Kgs 10:22) and as a poetic figure for abstract qualities. Red-stained garments symbolized vengeance (Isa 63:3) and certain fine garments showed luxurious glory (Ezk 16:13).

Bibliography: Sandars, N. K., tr., *The Epic of Gilgamesh*, Penguin, 1964, pp. 97, 102–4. THAT, I, pp. 867–69.

A.B.

1076 לֹג (*lōg*) ***a liquid measure, about one-half liter*** (Lev 14). There were probably seventy-two logs in one bath (*bat*, q.v.).

1077 להב (*lhb*). **Assumed root of the following.**
1077a †לַהַב (*lahab*) ***flame, blade.***
1077b †לֶהָבָה (*lehābâ*) ***flame, tip of weapon.***
1077c †שַׁלְהֶבֶת (*shalhebet*) ***flame.***

lahab. ***Flame, blade, point.*** This term refers either to the flame of fire or to the tip or blade of a weapon probably due to the rough similarity in appearance between the two objects. The Arabic *lahiba* means "burn with thirst." The Akkadian *la'bn* means "fever." The Aramaic shaphel form *shalhēl* is "burn (up)."

lahab refers to the tips or blades of daggers (Jud 3:22), spears (Job 39:23; "point of spear" rather than "flashing spear" as in RSV), and swords (Nah 3:3).

It denotes the flames from Leviathan's mouth (Job 41:21) and the literal flames of an altar on which the angel ascended to Heaven (Jud 13:20). The "crackling of a flame" is one of the noises of invasion (Joel 2:5).

A supernatural "flame of fire" will be among God's great judgments at the end of history (Isa 29:6; cf. Isa 30:30; 66:15–16).

lehābâ. ***Tip (of weapon), flame.*** Once describes a weapon tip, that of Goliath's spear (I Sam 17:7).

In all other usages, it serves as a poetic figure for some human or divine act. The "flame" from Sihon symbolized military conquest (Num 21:28; cf. Jer 48:45). Anger was described as a "fire of flame" (Hos 7:6; RSV "flaming fire"). The "flame" represented dangers from which God would protect his people (Isa 43:2).

God's judgment was repeatedly likened to a flame. The "flame" is associated with God's judgment upon his own sinful people (Isa 5:24), on Egypt during the Exodus (Ps 105:32; RSV "lightning that flashed"; literally "fire of flame"), and the Negev (Ezk 20:47; RSV "blazing flame"; Hebrew *lahebet shalhebet,* see below). God's "holy one" will someday be a flame of judgment upon God's enemies (Isa 10:17) as will God's people also (Ob 18). God's very presence is symbolized by a "fire of flame" (Isa 4:5; RSV, KJV "flaming fire").

The overlap between the meanings "blade" and "flame" raises the possibility that at some point the image of the voice as a flame of fire (Ps 29:7) and the image of the tongue as a sword (Rev 19:15) were originally the same image.

shalhebet. ***Flame.*** Used as a poetic symbol, twice of judgment (Job 15:30; Ezk 20:47) and once as a symbol of jealousy (Song 8:6). Apparently this was derived from a shaphel form from the root *lāhab.* See the Aramaic form cited above.

A.B.

1078 להג (*lhg*). **Assumed root of the following.**

1078a לַהַג (*lahag*) ***study,*** i.e. devotion to books (Eccl 12:12).

1079 לָהָה (*lāhâ*) ***languish, faint*** (Gen 47:13).

1080 *לִהְלֵהַּ (*lihlēah*) ***amaze, startle.*** Occurs only in the Hithpalpel participle in Prov 26:18, "like a madman shooting firebrands" (NIV).

1081 לָהַט (*lāhaṭ*) ***kindle, burn.***

Derivative

1081a †לַהַט (*lahaṭ*) ***flame, blade(?).***

lāhaṭ may refer to literal burning, or it may be used as a poetic figure to describe God's judgment. The Akkadian *la'aṭu* means "consume with fire." The Aramaic *l*ᵉ*haṭ* means "consume," "burn up."

Some typical examples of *lāhaṭ* in the sense of literal burning are: the burning of Korah's followers (Ps 106:18; *cf.* Num 16), the burning of mountain forests (Ps 83:14 [H 15]), and of trees (Joel 1:19). The breath of Leviathan kindled coals (Job 41:21 [H 13]). It refers to the burning behind the invaders mentioned in Joel (2:3). Once it refers to the way in which lightning burns up God's enemies (Ps 97:3) and it describes as "flaming" the fires which serve God (Ps 104:4).

In purely figurative usages, it describes men as "burning" in their desire to destroy others (Ps 57:4 [H 5]; cf. RSV "greedily devour"). It describes divine attributes and acts such as God's anger in burning the foundations of the mountains (Deut 32:22). Evil-doers will burn as chaff in the great coming day of judgment (Mal 4:1 [H 3:19]). The verb may even describe God's own people as burning in God's judgment (Isa 42:25).

lahaṭ. ***Flame, (blade?).*** Used once (Gen 3:24) where it is usually translated as "flaming" (literally "flame of the sword"). However, the overlap in meaning between "flame" and "blade" (cf. *lahab*) suggests that "blade" (of a sword) deserves consideration as a possible interpretation.

A.B.

1082 *לָהַם (*lāham*) ***swallow greedily.*** Occurs only in the Hithpael, in Prov 18:8, *mitlahămîm* "bits greedily swallowed" (see also Prov 26:22).

1083 לָהֵן (*lāhēn*) ***on this account, therefore*** (Ruth 1:13).

1084 לַהֲקָה (*lahăqâ*) ***band, company*** (I Sam 19:20). Meaning and etymology dubious.

1085 לוּ (*lû*), לוּא (*lû'*)***would that, I wish, perhaps.*** A Hebrew particle used to mark several kinds of potential constructions.

1085a לוּלֵא (*lûlē'*) ***if not, unless*** (e.g., Jud 14:19; I Sam 25:34).

lû marks three degrees of personal desire or agreement: wishes, entreaties, and statements of assent. It also marks two types of potential clauses: "perhaps" clauses and conditional clauses.

When used to express a wish, it may be translated "would that" or "I wish." Abraham's desire that Ishmael might live before God (Gen 17:18) and Joshua's rhetorical wish that the Hebrews had remained beyond the Jordan (Josh 7:7) are both marked by this particle. Combined with other devices to indicate potentiality, it may express a very strong wish (I Sam 14:30). In Abraham's petition that the Hebronites would hear him (Gen 23:13), *lû* serves as a particle of entreaty. Finally, it marks Laban's agreement with Jacob's proposition on wages (Gen 30:34).

When introducing pure potential clauses, it may be translated as "perhaps" as when Joseph's brothers speculated that Joseph might hate them (Gen 50:15; RSV "it may be"). When accompanied by a statement of consequence, i.e. an apodosis, the *lû* clause becomes the protasis of an unreal conditional sentence. "If the Lord had meant to kill us" (Jud 13:23) and "if Absalom were alive" (II Sam 19:7) are good examples of this (cf. Job 16:4; Ezk 14:15).

A.B.

1086 לוֹא (*lô'*) ***not.*** Alternative form of לֹא (q.v.).

1087 לָוָה (*lāwâ*) ***I, join, be joined.***

Used once in the Qal (Eccl 8:15); the remaining usages are in the Niphal. *lāwâ* refers to the joining of an item or person to someone or something else. Most significant theologically is its usage to refer to foreigners who join themselves to God's people as converts.

In general usage it refers to the way in which hedonistic pleasures "stay with" a man (Eccl 8:15); also it is used for joining in a military alliance (Ps 83:8 [H 9]), the conjugal joining of husband to wife (Gen 29:34), and the joining of the Levites with Aaron for service at the tabernacle (Num 18:2–4).

As a term referring to conversion it describes those who, impressed by God's work in restoring his people, will join themselves to the Hebrews in the worship and service of God, i.e. will be spiritually converted (Isa 14:1). Others will join themselves to God as a result of some divine judgment (Zech 2:15; cf. Est 9:27). Such Gentile converts are assured that they will not be separated from God's Covenant (Isa 56:3–6). Someday God's repentant people will (re)join themselves to a true covenant relationship to God (Jer 50:5).

This usage of *lāwâ* to reflect religious dedication supports the notion that the name "Levi" expressed the religious dedication of the tribe of that name to the Lord's service.

Bibliography: "Levi," in ZPEB. Albright, W. F., *Archeology and the Religion of Israel,* 5th ed., pp. 106, 203.

A.B.

1088 לָוָה (*lāwâ*) ***II,*** ***borrow*** (Qal), ***lend*** (Hiphil).

This may be a specialized usage of *lāwâ* (*supra*). In contrast to the purely economic significance of borrowing and lending in modern life, these acts were endowed with a special theological significance in the OT. Only once is borrowing referred to as a primarily economic act in the borrowing of the restored Hebrew community to raise money for paying taxes (Neh 5:4). Also, the borrower and the lender are once referred to as one of several pairs expressing all classes of society (Isa 24:2).

Remaining usages reflect the special theological and moral perspectives of the OT. The Hebrew was not permitted to receive interest for loaning to another Hebrew (Ex 22:24–25). [Another view (reflected in KJV) is that interest on loans was allowed but not excessive interest (usury). In defense of this position, E. A. Speiser shows that in the surrounding cultures a loan was discounted with interest paid in advance. The thing prohibited in Akkadian sources and in the biblical laws was additional interest after a defaulting debtor was enslaved. See the fuller discussion and refs. under *neshek.* R.L.H.] Willingness to lend was a sign of righteous graciousness (Ps 112:5). Sometimes, the expectation or obligation of concrete repayment may be so remote or inappropriate that "lending" becomes almost synonymous with "giving" (Prov 19:17; note also "loan" and "give" as parallel in Ps 37:26).

The want or poverty which leads to borrowing is said to indicate the absence of God's blessing (Deut 28:44), while the ability to grant a loan characterizes a God-given prosperity (Deut 28:12). Inability to repay debts shows the futility of the wicked (Ps 37:21). Finally, Scripture observes that the borrower is a slave to the lender (Prov 22:7).

Bibliography: "Loans" in *JewEnc.*

A.B.

1089 לוה (*lwh*) **III. Assumed root of the following.**

1089a לִוְיָה (*liwyâ*), לֹיָה (*lōyâ*) ***wreath.*** Occurs in the phrase *liwyat ḥēn,* referring to the instruction of parents (Prov 1:9), and to the work of Wisdom (Prov 4:9).

1089b לִוְיָתָן (*liwyātān*) ***large aquatic animals,*** may be crocodile (Job 41:1 ASV marg.), serpent (Isa 27:1), or whale (Ps 104:26), usually rendered

"Leviathan" (consistently in KJV, ASV, and RSV).

liwyātān appears six times in the OT, as a literal animal, a figure for Egypt (Ps 74:14), and a figure for sinful mankind in general (Isa 27:1).

Derived from a root attested in Arabic, *lwy* "to twist" (*liwyâ* "wreath," Prov 1:9), *liwyātān* is reflected in Ugaritic *ltn,* a monster called Lotan. Biblically, however, it appears only with other beasts: *nāḥāsh* "snake" (Isa 27:1), or *tannîn* "large reptile" (Ps 74:13–14).

Yahweh overawed Job by confronting him with his invincible creature *liwyātān* (Job 41 [H 40:25ff.]). Clearly the Nile crocodile, with scaly hide (vv. 7, 15–17 [H 40:31; 41:7–9]), terrible teeth (v. 14 [H 6]), and swift swimming (v. 32 [H 24]), it is described poetically, i.e. "his sneezes flash forth light . . . out of his nostrils smoke goes forth" (vv. 18–21 [H 10–13]), but not mythological. Other hyperbolical comparisons follow: "he spreads out like a threshing sledge on the mire; he makes the depths boil like a pot" (vv. 30–31 [H 22–23], NASB)]. In the Psalter (cf. *rahab* [q.v.] in Isa 51:9–10) the power of the crocodile becomes a natural symbol for the troops of Egypt, overthrown by the Lord at the Red Sea:

Thou didst divide the sea . . .
Thou breakest the heads of Leviathan
Thou gavest him to be food to the people inhabiting the wilderness (Ps 74:13–14).

Perhaps here *liwyātān* refers to the corpses of Egyptian soldiers that were washed up on the shore before Israel (Ex 14:31).

Elsewhere *liwyātān* swims in God's "sea, great and wide," a creature "whom Thou hast formed to play therein" (Ps 104:25–26), presumably a Mediterranean whale or dolphin (NBD, p. 729). Yet unlike the hostile beasts in the somewhat parallel "Hymn to the Sun," composed by the reform pharaoh Akhenaten, Leviathan et al. wait humbly upon God (v. 27) as mankind's "fellow pensioners" (C. S. Lewis, *Reflections on the Psalms*). The noun *liwyātān* may also designate serpents, such as might be roused by snake-charming magicians, who were also reputed to impose curses (Job 3:8; cf. Num 22:5–6). "Leviathan" thus comes to denote a swift sea serpent, slain of God, to symbolize his eschatological "punishing the inhabitants of the earth for their iniquity" (Isa 26:21–27:1).

Many scholars identify the OT leviathan with such mythological monsters of chaos as Lotan of Ugarit or Tiamat and Kingu of Babylon. Its crushed heads in Ps 74:13 (assumed to be seven) are equated with those of seven-headed dragons (illustrated in IDB, III, p. 116) slain by Baal (Scripture substituting the name Yahweh), and its aroused coils in Job 3:8 with those which were supposed to cause eclipses when wrapped about the sun.

Negative criticism holds that the writers of the Old Testament had a real faith in these creatures. But that the OT authors actually believed in such mythology should be roundly denied. However, some have held that the references to Leviathan as many-headed in Ps 74:14 and to its serpent character in Job 3:8 may be allusions to the current mythological themes (cf. Smick, bibliog.). Albright calls this a proper demythologizing by the biblical authors (YGC, pp. 183–93).

Bibliography: Kissling, N. K., "Antecedents of the Medieval Dragon in Sacred History," JBL 89: 166–77. Payne, J. B., *Theology of the Older Testament,* Zondervan, 1971. Pfeiffer, C. F., "Lotan and Leviathan," EQ 32: 208ff. Smick, E. B., "Mythology and the Book of Job," JETS 13: 106.

J.B.P.

1090 לוּז (*lûz*) ***turn aside, depart.***

Derivatives

1090a †לָזוּת (*lāzût*) ***deviation, crookedness.***
1090b לוּז (*lûz*) ***almond tree, almond wood.*** Occurs only in Gen 30:37, referring to the rods which Jacob stripped.

The verb *lûz* occurs in the Qal, Niphal, and Hiphil stems. The Qal imperfect is used in Prov 3:21, as Wisdom instructs her son not to let sound wisdom and discretion "slip from sight" (NEB). Maintaining such a focus assures him of life and grace.

In Prov 4:21 Wisdom encourages her listeners to heed her words and not let them slip out of mind (NEB; literally, do not let them depart from your eyes). In this passage *lûz* occurs in the Hiphil imperfect.

In the four following examples, *lûz* occurs in the Niphal participial form. Two passages use it figuratively of crooked or devious ways (Prov 2:15; Prov 14:2). (Note NEB "double-dealer" in 14:2.) Isaiah 30:12 also denounces those who rather than trusting in the Word of God, trust in oppressive and devious practices of their own scheming. In so doing, however, they draw the judgment of God.

Finally, Prov 3:32 uses the word figuratively of a crooked, perverse person who is detested by the Lord.

lāzût. ***Deviation, crookedness.*** Proverbs 4:24, the only passage that uses the word figuratively urges men to put away *lᵉzût śᵉpātayim* the "deviation of the lips," i.e. perverted talk.

W.C.K.

1091 לוח (*lwḥ*). **Assumed root of the following.**
1091a †לוּחַ (*lûaḥ*) ***tablet, plank, board.***

A cognate of the Akkadian *lî'u*^{m} or Sumerian ^{GIŠ}*LI.U* $_{5}$*UM, lûaḥ* appears over forty times in the OT. Since Sumerian uses the determinative for wood (*GIŠ*), we may suppose that originally tablets were made from wood. Any such wooden tablets have long since perished. The first known tablets consist of pictographs on clay, found in layer IV B of Uruk (cf. D. J. Wiseman, *Illustrations from Biblical Archaeology,* Eerdmans, 1958, pp. 10–11). *lûaḥ,* however, can refer to writing surfaces of stone (the tablets of the Ten Commandments in Ex 24.12, 34:28), the wooden planks of the tabernacle (Ex 27:8; 38:7) or of a ship (Ezk 27:5), and the metal plates on the base of the lavers in Solomon's temple (I Kgs 7:36).

lûaḥ is also used figuratively. Men are told to write God's commandments on the "tablet of [their] heart" (Prov 3:3; 7:3). The sin of Judah, ironically, is engraven on the "tablet of their hearts" (Jer 17:1). The prophet Habakkuk is instructed to write the vision on a billboard(?) so that it will be plain for a messenger to read and run (Hab 2:2).

The stone tablets handed to Moses were the work of God and the writing of God (Ex 31:18; 32:16; 34:1); yet God employed Moses, as a secondary agency, to write the words he wanted on the tablets (Ex 34:27, 28). This is in keeping with other biblical statements which attribute to God directly what is accomplished through the agency of men. Ultimately, all must and does originate and end with God (e.g., the crucifixion, Acts 2:23).

Just as Moses is commanded to record the battle with the Amalekites as a memorial for young Joshua (Ex 17:14), so Isaiah is told to write the prophecy against dependence on Egypt "on a tablet and note it in a book" (Isa 30:8). These texts with such others as Jer 36 document the process of inspiration.

Bibliography: Driver, G. R., *Semitic Writing,* rev. ed., London: 1954, pp. 16, 79–80.

W.C.K.

1092 לוּט (*lûṭ*) ***wrap closely, envelop.***

Derivatives

1092a †לָט (*lāṭ*), לָאט (*lā'ṭ*) ***secrecy.***
1092b לוֹט (*lôṭ*) ***envelope, covering.*** Occurs only in Isa 25:7.

lāṭ. ***Secrecy, mystery.*** Used in Ex 7:11, 22; 8:7 [H 3], 18 [H 14] in the plural with the preposition *b*^{e} to refer to the enchantments or secret arts (RSV) practiced by Pharaoh's magicians (*ḥarṭūmmîm,* a name borrowed from an Egyptian word *hry-tp* "chief lector-priest") in their attempt to keep up with Moses' and Aaron's plagues of God. In four other nontheological contexts it is used as an adverb, secretly, softly (Ruth 3:7; Jud 4:21; I Sam 18:22; 24:5).

Bibliography: Vergote, J., *Joseph en Egypte,* 1959, pp. 66–73.

W.C.K.

1093 לֵוִי (*lēwî*) ***Levi.***

Derivative

1093a †לֵוִי (*lēwî*) ***Levite, denoting a member of the tribe of Levi.***

Levi was the third son born to Jacob by Leah, his less-favored wife (Gen 29:34).

Levi, progenitor of the tribe of Levi, took part in a distinctly odious incident (Gen 34). His sister Dinah had been raped by Shechem, son of the Canaanite Hamor. He would be permitted to marry her if he and his whole city would consent to be circumcised. This they did, but while they were still recovering from the operation, Simeon and Levi went and slew all the males of the city (Gen 34:25–26).

Jacob was so indignant over this deed that he still remembered it on his deathbed. Instead of blessing Levi, he predicted that both it and Simeon would be scattered in Israel (Gen 49:7). While this curse turned out to be the eventual end of Simeon's identity in the land of Canaan, Levi's descendants by faith turned it into a blessing. Their scattering became the occasion for ministering on behalf of the Lord to all Israel. God adopted this tribe as his own inheritance in lieu of the firstborn male of every household (Num 3:11–13).

No other information is given about the man Levi or his tribe until the family went down to Egypt. The historicity of their sojourn in Egypt may be attested in part by the number of Egyptian names among the Levites: Merari, Moses, Phinehas, and Hophni (*mrry* "beloved"; *mss* "born of," according to some; *3p-nḥsy* "the bronze-colored one, and *ḥfnr* "Nubian").

An unnamed descendant of Levi married an unnamed Levite woman who bore Moses, Aaron, and Miriam (Ex 2:1ff.). The reference to Amram and Jochebed in Ex 6:20 "giving birth" to Moses and Aaron is typical of biblical genealogies. The immortalized ancestors are frequently credited with bearing the children of subsequent generations. (Note the language of Gen 46: 15, 18, 25.) There were 8,600 descendants of four brothers or cousins, of whom 2,750 were between the ages of 30 and 50 years (Num 3:17–20, 27–28; 4:35–37). Obviously, the record implies that there are more than four generations connecting Levi and Moses; this Amram was not Moses' actual father, who remains unnamed (Ex 2:1).

Aaron becomes the high priest in the line of the

Levites who showed their fidelity in Ex 32:26–29. Aaron in turn hands the office to his son Eleazar (Deut 10:6) and he hands it to his son Phinehas (Jud 20:27, 28). Then the high priesthood is transferred from the line of Eleazar to the Aaronic line of Ithamar in Eli (I Chr 24:3; I Sam 2:22, 28). Eli's sons are too wicked to deserve this pre-eminence (I Sam 2:27–36), so in Solomon's day Abiathar is deposed and the Aaronic Zadok takes over as predicted by the "man of God" in I Sam 2:27–28, 35; I Kgs 2:26–27, 35).

lēwî. ***Levite.*** Despite strong disclaimers to the contrary, it is evident that the tribe of Levites was descended from the ancient Levi. Levi was Jacob's third son by his wife Leah (Gen 29:34). Since Leah was competing with her prettier sister Rachel for Jacob's attentions and affection, she named her son Levi, adding the wordplay, "My husband and I shall surely be united [or joined]."

The Lord alluded to this remark when he instructed Aaron that he and his sons would bear the responsibility for the sanctuary and the priesthood, while the tribe of Levi was joined to him to assist him in carrying out these duties (Num 18:1–2). Note how the NEB translation of these verses distorts the Hebrew distinctions in the text so as to favor a critical interpretation!

The Wellhausen theory insists that division of the priesthood into priests and Levites derives from the reform of Josiah (621 B.C.) at the earliest. Wellhausen claimed that the high priest was still unknown even to Ezekiel, for the first actual reference to such a division is Ezk 44:6ff. where the services of the temple and altar are assigned to the sons of Zadok.

Why then is the high priest expressly mentioned in II Kgs 12:10; 22:4, 8; 23:4 and possibly in II Sam 15:27? Why does Deut 18:1–8 make such an obvious distinction between the "priest" ministering at the sanctuary (vv. 3–5) and the "Levite" otherwise occupied (vv. 6–8)? Even the phrase "the priests the Levites" (Deut 17:9, 18; 18:1; 24:8; 27:9; Josh 3:3; 8:33; Jer 33:18, 21 [note reverse order in v. 21]; Ezk 43:19; 44:15; II Chr 23:18; 30:27) only implies that all priests are Levites, not the reverse. In Hebrew the limiting word is always placed after the word it limits, hence the phrase means "the Levitical priests." (Note the RSV wrongly inserts "that is" between the phrases "the Levitical priests" and "all the tribe of Levi" (Deut 18:1). The Levites are not to be equated with the priests on the basis that the terms used to describe the Levites' duties in Deut 18:7 are the same as those used of priestly duties, i.e. "to minister in the name" (cf. 18:5 of priest, 17:12; 21:5) "to stand before" (cf. I Kgs 10:8, etc.). These terms are used of priestly duties, but so are they used of subordinates like young Samuel (I Sam 2:11, 18; 3:1).

In the hierarchical order of the cultures, the Levites take second place after the Aaronite priests as compared with other Israelites. According to the Mosaic legislation, some of the Levites' duties included bearing the ark (I Sam 6:15; II Sam 15:24), performing various services in the tabernacle (Ex 38:21; Num 1:50–53), and ministering to Aaron and his sons (Num 3:9; 8:19). David placed them in charge of the liturgical music (I Chr 15:16, 17, 22) and of policing the temple (I Chr 9:26; 26:17). In the time of Ezra, they taught the people the Law (Neh 8:7–8; cf. Deut 31:25).

But most important of all, the tribe of Levi was to serve as a substitute for the firstborn of all Israelite males (Num 3:11–13). Scripture thereby resists the analogical deduction (hence a warning in other areas such as double predestination) that would demand human sacrifice, since all the firstborn of the earth belong to the Lord. Instead of human sacrifice, God once again accepted a substitute; this time one Levite for each firstborn male in Israel.

Bibliography: Cody, Aelred, *A History of Old Testament Priesthood,* Pontifical Biblical Institute, 1969. MacRae, A. A., "Numbers," in NBC, pp. 166–67. Orr, James, *The Problem of the Old Testament,* London: Nisbet & Nisbet, 1909, pp. 180–92. TDNT, IV, pp. 239–41.

W.C.K.

לִוְיָה (*liwyâ*). See no. 1089a.
לִוְיָתָן (*liwyātān*). See no. 1089b.

1094 לוּל (*lûl*) ***shaft or enclosed space with steps or ladder.*** Occurs only in I Kgs 6:8, *ûbeᵉlûlîm ya'ălû.*

1095 לולו (*lwlw*). **Assumed root of the following.**

1095a לוּלַי (*lûlay*) ***loop.***

לוּלֵא (*lûlē'*). See no. 1085a.
לוּלַי (*lûlay*). See no. 1095a.

1096 לוּן (*lûn*), לִין (*lîn*) ***lodge, spend the night.***

Derivatives

1096a †מָלוֹן (*mālôn*) ***lodging place, inn.***

1096b מְלוּנָה (*mᵉlûnâ*) ***lodge, hut.*** Occurs only in Isa 1:8; 24:20.

Usually *lûn* is used of men lodging for the night in some place. Thus Lot graciously invited the two angels, who had come to destroy Sodom (Gen 19:2), to lodge with him. Jacob spent the night at Bethel (Gen 28:11). But more interesting illustrations of the use of the word are figurative: Ps 30:5 [H 6] says, "Weeping may endure for a night, but joy comes in the morning." The theological usage emphasizes the brevity of God's anger as opposed to the life-giving power of his abundant favor.

Righteousness lodges in a faithful city (Isa 1:21), while the man who fears the Lord dwells at ease (Ps 25:13). Indeed, he who listens to life-giving reproof will abide among the wise (Prov 15:31). Proverbs 19:23 says it succinctly: "The fear of the Lord is life indeed [emphatic lamed], and he who has it shall abide satisfied." The converse is likewise briefly stated: "Man being in honor does not endure; he is like the beasts that perish" (Ps 49:12 [H 13]).

The best verse of all is Ps 91:1. "He who dwells in the secret place of the most High shall abide in the shadow of the Almighty."

mālôn. ***Lodging place, inn.*** There are eight references to lodging places such as the one chosen by Joseph's brothers as they returned from Egypt (Gen 42:27; 43:21). The most famous is the one where Moses and Zipporah stopped for the night on their way back to Egypt. There God sought to kill Moses (afflict him with a fever or disease?) because he had failed to circumcise his son (apparently because of Zipporah's protestations, Ex 4:24).

In other cases, it is the prophet who longs for some sort of camp in the wilderness so that he can leave his people, because their sins are loathsome (Jer 9:2 [H 1]). In Isa 10:29 the approach of the Assyrian king and his nightly stopovers are noted with fear. Indeed, a proud Sennacherib boasted that he would enter Lebanon's remotest campground (II Kgs 19:23; cf. Isa 37:24).

The feminine form *m*^e*lûnâ* also occurs. It refers to a hut or cottage in a vineyard (Isa 1:8) built for the watchman of the crop. An eschatological passage states that the earth will reel to and fro and totter like a cottage (Isa 24:20). Notice then, both its proverbial fragility and isolation.

W.C.K.

1097 לוּן (*lûn*) ***murmur, rebel (against).***

Derivative

1097a †תְּלֻנָּה (*t*^e*lūnnâ*) ***murmuring.***

Except for Josh 9:18, a reference to Israel's displeasure with Joshua's handling of the Gibeonite lie, all occurrences of the verb *lûn* are to be found in six chapters in the Pentateuch: Ex 15, 16, 17; Num 14, 16, 17, each with the preposition *'al* "against." In each case the subject of the murmuring is all of the congregation of Israel. Numbers 16:11, however, may refer only to Korah (cf. 16:19). The object of their verbal assaults is usually Moses and Aaron (Ex 16:2; Num 14:2); occasionally, Moses is singled out (Ex 15:24; 17:3; Num 14:36) or Aaron (Num 16:11); at other times the Lord himself is the object of their abuse (Ex 16:7–8; Num 14:27, 29). In the final analysis their murmuring was always against God who commissioned the leaders of the people. The murmuring, of course was not without reason, namely, hunger or thirst in the desert, or an apparently unattainable goal. But they sinned because they doubted God and cast aspersion on his justice, goodness, and power.

Noeldeke suggests that a double *'ayin* root, *lnn,* or (on the basis of an interchange between *lamed* and *resh,*) *rnn* "to cry aloud." But no evidence exists to support either idea. Even KB's connection with Arabic *l(y)m* "to blame" likewise fails. Whether in the Niphal or Hiphil form, the verb means to express resentment, dissatisfaction, anger, and complaint by grumbling in half-muted tones of hostile opposition to God's leaders and the authority which he has invested in them.

The true nature of this murmuring is seen in the fact that it is an open act of rebellion against the Lord (Num 14:9) and a stubborn refusal to believe God's word and God's miraculous works (Num 14:11, 22, 23). Thus the right attitude in real difficulty is unconditional acceptance and obedience. God's own must never stand in judgment upon him.

t^{**e**}**lūnnâ.** ***Murmuring.*** Always used of Israel's murmurings (pl. const. noun) against the Lord; an act of rebellion, disbelief, and disobedience to duly constituted authority (Ex 16:7, 9, 12; Num 14:27; 17:5, 10 [H 20, 25]).

Bibliography: Coats, George W., *Rebellion in the Wilderness,* Abingdon, 1968, pp. 21–28. THAT, I, pp. 870–71.

1098 לוּעַ (*lûa'*), לָעַע (*lā'a'*) ***I, swallow, swallow down.***

Derivative

1098a לֹעַ (*lō'a*) ***throat.*** Occurs only in Prov 23:2, "and you will put a knife to your throat" (to restrain oneself from overindulgence in food).

1099 לוּעַ (*lû'a*), לָעַע (*lā'a'*) ***II, talk wildly.***

לוּץ (*lûṣ*). See no. 1113.

1100 לוּשׁ (*lûsh*) ***knead.***

לָזוּת (*lāzût*). See no. 1090a.
לַח (*laḥ*). See no. 1102a.
לֵחַ (*lēaḥ*). See no. 1102b.

1101 לחה (*lḥh*). **Assumed root of the following.**
1101a †לְחִי (*l*^e*ḥî*) ***jaw, cheek.***

This noun occurs twenty-one times in the OT and is attested in the Ugaritic *lḥy* (e.g. UT, 16:II

Aqht:1:29–30 *ṭbq lḥt niṣh* "who will shut the jaws of his detractors").

The most famous jawbone appears in Jud 15: 15–17, 19. Samson uses it to slay or vanquish (see *nākâ*) one thousand men, and thereby names the place Ramath-leḥi, "hill of the jawbone."

In Job 41:2 [H 40:26], God reduces Job to thoughtful silence while asking him if he is capable of taming Leviathan (poetic name for a crocodile) by putting a hook through its jaw. But God is able to put the hook in its jaw and in the jaw of *tannim,* an aquatic figure for the Egyptian Pharaoh (Ezk 29:4) and in the jaw of Gog (Ezk 38:4). He will put a bridle in the jaws of the people of the nations (Isa 30:28) but take it from the jaws of his own so that they may eat (Hos 11:4).

While men like Micaiah, the true prophet of the Lord, may be smitten on the cheek by false prophets like Zedekiah (I Kgs 22:24; II Chr 18:23) and Job may be verbally smitten on his cheeks by his miserable comforters (Job 16:10), God will deliver the last blow to the enemies' cheeks (Ps 3:7 [H 8]). Men will even smite with a rod the leader of Israel on the cheek (Mic 5:1 [H 4:14]). The Servant of the Lord, the Messiah, will voluntarily submit his "back to the smiters and [his] cheeks to those that pluck out the beard" (Isa 50:6), but he too will emerge triumphant.

W.C.K.

לְחוּם (*leḥûm*). See no. 1104b.

1102 לחח (*lḥḥ*). **Assumed root of the following.**
1102a לַח (*laḥ*) ***moist, fresh, new.***
1102b לֵחַ (*lēaḥ*) ***moisture, freshness.***

לְחִי (*leḥî*). See no. 1101a.

1103 לָחַךְ (*lāḥak*) ***lick*** (e.g. Num 22:4; I Kgs 18:38).

1104 לָחַם (*lāḥam*) ***I, fight, do battle.***

Derivatives

1104a †לָחֶם (*lāḥem*) ***war (?).*** Only in Jud 5:8.
1104b לְחוּם (*leḥûm*) ***intestine, bowels (?).***
1104c †מִלְחָמָה (*milḥāmâ*) ***battle, war.***

The most significant usages of the verb *lāḥam,* which occurs 171 times, pertain to God's role in Israel's wars. When God calls Israel to arms against an enemy, it is because of the enemy's moral degradation (Deut 7:4, 16, 25; 20:18, etc.). In such conflicts, it is the Lord who does battle on Israel's behalf (Ex 14:14, 25; Deut 1:30; 3:22; Josh 10:14, 42; Jer 21:5; Neh 4:14; II Chr 20:29). In doing so, Yahweh often calls into his service not only Israel, but also the elements of nature (Josh 10:11; 24:7; Jud 5:20). Nevertheless, the Israelites must also join the battle and fight with the Lord. Even though their land has been deeded to them as an inheritance, they must conquer it in battle (Ex 23:27–33). Bauernfeind comments: "Nevertheless, neither their equipment (Jud 7:2ff; I Sam 14:6; 17:45, 47) nor their numbers (Jud 7; II Sam 24:1ff; Ex 30:12) turned the scale. It was Yahweh who went before them (Jud 4:14; Deut 20:4; II Sam 5:24), gave them courage (I Sam 30:6) and took it from their foes (Ex 15:15–16; 23:27f) by miracles (Josh 10:11; 24:7; Jud 5:20; by terror, I Sam 14:15). To him and him alone belonged the praise (Ex 14:4, 18; Zech 4:6)" (TDNT, VI, p. 508).

Israel constituted the "armies of the Yahweh" (Ex 12:41) whose troops had to be holy (Isa 13:3). Even the Israelites' weapons and campgrounds had to be holy if the Yahweh was to camp with them (Deut 23:10–15; II Sam 1:21; Isa 21:5). Thus "if it had not been the Lord who was on our side, when men rose up against us, then they would have swallowed us up alive" (Ps 124:1–3 [H 4]; 118:10–14). "Fight against those who fight against me, O Lord" (Ps 35:1). But Israel's trust must be in the Lord, warn the prophets, not in horses, chariots, weapons, or men (cf. Deut 17:16–17; I Sam 17:47; Isa 31:1–3; Hos 8:14).

Israel itself was subject to attack from God if they flaunted his laws and indulged in sin. Amos 2:14–16 comes very close to describing all-out warfare against Israel. Isaiah 63:10 states explicitly that when the Israelites rebelled against the Holy Spirit, God became their enemy and fought against them.

There is yet coming a time when God will fight once more; this time against all the nations which have attacked Israel (Zech 14:3). Yahweh has decreed the death of the beast and the end of his power (Dan 7:11, 26; 8:25; 11:45). God will personally put on the breastplate of righteousness, helmet of salvation, suit of vengeance, and coat of zeal as he judges the enemies from the nations, until the fear of him is spread from east to west (Isa 59:17–19).

lāḥem. ***War (?).*** This word appears only in Jud 5:8 and is usually translated "then was there war [at] the gates." Others read it as "then was there barley bread" or "the barley bread was exhausted." The first is probably to be preferred.

milḥāmâ. ***Battle, war.*** Of the 319 occurrences of this noun, our interest centers on the battles in which Yahweh was involved. While much has been made of the concept of "holy war" popularized by von Rad, the demure of men like A. Weiser must be raised. There is greater breadth to the concept than simply the fulfillment of an ancient sacral ordinance.

True, Yahweh is a "man of war" (Ex 15:3) and his name Yahweh *ṣᵉbā'ôt*, "LORD of hosts" does on occasion reflect the fact that he is commander-in-chief of Israel's armies (I Sam 17:26, 45). David acknowledged that "the Lord saves not with the sword and spear: for the battle is the Lord's" (I Sam 17:47). And there was a book containing "the wars of the LORD" (Num 21:14). However, not every battle was a war of *ḥerem* wherein everything in the captured city was devoted to destruction.

Further, many of Israel's wars were fratricidal wars between the tribes (Jud 19–21) and even selfish wars of aggression (II Sam 24; I Kgs 22; Jud 17). Israel also fought defensive wars (Num 31; I Sam 11–17; 28–30; II Sam 5, 8) and offensive wars (Num 21:21–35; Deut 2:26—3:17; Josh 6–12).

Just before Yahweh makes "wars to cease" (Ps 46:9*a* [H 10]) and forever destroys the implements of war (Ps 46:9*b* [H 10]; Isa 2:1–5; Mic 4:1–5) the nations shall raise their arms against Israel and their Messiah, but to no avail (Ps 2; Ps 45:3ff. [H 4]; Zech 14).

Bibliography: AI, pp. 247–67. Gross, H., "War," in Sacramentum Verbi, III, pp. 958–61. Pederson, J., *Israel: Its Life and Culture,* vols. III–IV, Copenhagen, 1940, pp. 1–32. von Rad, G., *Studies in Deuteronomy,* Regnery, 1953, pp. 45–49. TDNT, VI, pp. 507–11.

W.C.K.

1105 לָחַם (*lāḥam*) ***II, use as food, eat.***

Derivative

1105a †לֶחֶם (*leḥem*) ***food, bread, grain.***

This noun occurs 296 times in the OT. But "man does not live by bread alone, but by every word that proceeds from the mouth of the LORD" (Deut 8:3). Man is not what he eats!

Yet all food is the gift of God. He planted the garden of Eden and caused all the trees to grow which were good for food (*ma'ăkāl*, Gen 2:9). Likewise the Psalmist asserts that God "caused the grass to grow for the cattle and vegetables for the service of man: that he may bring food from the ground . . . and bread which strengthens man's heart" (Ps 104:14–15). Yes, he "gives food to all flesh" (Ps 136:25); to the hungry (Ps 146:7) and to the beasts and young ravens (Ps 147:9). God himself even instructs man the art and principles of agriculture: how to prepare the ground, how to sow the seed in rows or to broadcast others, and how to harvest each after patiently waiting the appointed number of days (Isa 28:24–29, note grain in v. 28).

Man must never presume that this "staff" on which he leans will always be available, regardless of how he acts. God can and did "break the whole staff of bread" (Ps 105:16; Isa 3:1; Ezk 4:16; 5:16; 14:13; Amos 4:6). This was the principle announced by Moses in Lev 26:26: God would send increasingly severe judgments on any nation that refused to walk in righteousness before he brought the ultimate calamity. Even worse than a famine of bread was famine of the Word of God (Amos 8:11) both of which resulted from the same cause: compounded sin.

Sadly enough, even though God was richly supplying Israel with her grain, fine flour, oil, and honey (Ezk 16:19), she, like the adulterous Gomer, insisted on running after her lovers, not realizing that God had been the source of those gifts (Hos 2:5, 7–8 [H 7, 9–10]).

What could the few righteous like Habakkuk do when they saw their nation headed for such disaster as a result of hardened and entrenched sinfulness? He would "rejoice in the Lord" and "joy in the God of [his] salvation" even though outwardly he was shaking with fear and the fields yielded no food (*'ōkel*), (Hab 3:17–18).

There is another kind of bread, wine, and milk that can be bought without money or labor. Men may have it if they repent and seek the Lord (Isa 55:1–7). Jesus later calls himself the true bread from heaven just as the manna in the wilderness was "bread from heaven" (Ex 16:4ff.). Even Elijah was fed food by God's ravens when there was none to be had (I Kgs 17:6). At other times, God provided grain by sending visions and leadership in Joseph (Gen 41:54, 55; 43:25, 31, 32; 45:23; 47:12, 13, 15, 17, 19, 20). Both spiritual and physical bread come from the Father of all good gifts.

The dough which the Israelites took with them from Egypt was unleavened, because they had to leave in haste (Ex 12:34, 39). Note, however, Lev 23:17. The Pentecost wave loaves were to be baked with leaven! So leaven cannot always be a principle of evil. The "bread of wickedness" (Prov 4:17) or the "bread of deceit" (Prov 20:17) is always obtained by wrong and results in bitterness of life. No better is the "bread of adversity" (Isa 30:20), which spells times of persecution, or the "bread eaten in secret" (Prov 9:17) with the seductress, for the act of adultery will poison a man's whole life.

There is a better day coming when God will restore the bread and grain to its creation—state. The heavens and the earth will flow with abundance as man enters into that "Rest" of which Canaan with its promised fruitfulness ("a land of wheat and barley, vine and fig trees and pomegranates, a land in which you will eat bread without scarcity, in which you will lack nothing, (Deut 8:7–9) was an earnest or down payment. Nature will erupt in uninterruptible, delicious productivity (Joel 3:18 [H 4:18]; Amos 9:13–14; Isa 55:10–13; Ezk 47:6–12).

Bibliography: Heaton, E. W., *Everyday Life in O.T. Times,* Scribner's, 1956, pp. 81–87; 97–115. Richardson, TWB, pp. 37–38. Ross, J. F., IDB, II, pp. 307–308.

W.C.K.

1106 לָחַץ (*lāḥaṣ*) ***squeeze, oppress.***

Derivative

1106a †לַחַץ (*laḥaṣ*) ***oppression, distress.***

No more graphic word picture of the meaning of *lāḥaṣ* in its nineteen examples can be given than that of Balaam's donkey squeezing up against the wall and thereby crushing Balaam's foot (Num 22:25*a,* 25*b*; II Kgs 6:32).

The word finds its most important usage in the realm of ethical theology. Israelites were not to oppress foreigners or strangers (Ex 22:21 [H 20]; 23:9), for they once had been strangers in Egypt, that great oppressor. Oppressive treatment was strictly forbidden to all and to Israel in particular.

Israel experienced a whole wave of oppressors during the period of the judges (Jud 1:34; 2:18; 4:3; 6:9; 10:12; I Sam 10:18). But the Lord sent deliverers in each situation. Later he sent oppressors, (the king of Syria and others; II Kgs 13:4, 22) against Israel on account of sin (Amos 6:14).

Other nations will face their oppressors (Isa 19:20), too. But God always hears the cry for mercy and deliverance, and he will then fight daily against those oppressors (Ps 56:1 [H 2]).

laḥaṣ. ***Oppression, distress.*** Almost all of the eleven instances of this word deal with the oppression of Israel by her enemies. One exception is the expression for a prisoner's rations, "the bread of oppression and the water of oppression" (I Kgs 22:27; II Chr 18:26). Isaiah 30:20 says that the Lord sends physical privations (in a seige here?) but there will still be left a Teacher, and ears to hear the exhortation, "This is the way, walk in it" (Isa 30:21). The word is usually translated in the LXX by *thlipsis* "tribulation."

W.C.K.

1107 לָחַשׁ (*lāḥash*) ***whisper, charm.***

Derivative

1107a †לַחַשׁ (*laḥash*) ***a whispering, charming.***

lāḥash is found in Aramaic and rabbinical Hebrew with the sense of "to hiss as a serpent." Thus the word may be a dialectal variant of *nāḥash,* since nun and lamed are of similar sound (cf. the verb *lāqaḥ* where the *l* acts like an *n;* the verb "to oppress," *lāḥaṣ* or *nāḥaṣ;* and the noun "room," *lishkâ* and *nishkâ*).

God will not listen to the prayers of serpent-charmers (note Ps 58:5 [H 6]). Their mouths are usually full of reptile-like poison.

Just as bad are those who whisper together (Hithpael) to devise evil (Ps 41:7 [H 8]; see also David's whispering serpents, II Sam 12:19).

laḥash. ***Whisper, charm.*** In Isa 3:20, the garishly attired women wear amulets or charms, perhaps as protection against snakes or demons. Professional enchanters (Isa 3:3) attempted to charm serpents (Jer 8:17; Eccl 10:11) as part of Israel's decline into magic and divination. Some have conjectured that these charms may have been serpent-shaped earrings (why not leg-bands?) since the words *ṭabbā'ôt* and *nizmê-hā'āp* in Isa 3:21 are words for finger-rings and nose-rings.

When God's chastening came upon Israel, they cried out to God with whispers of prayer (Isa 26:16); Ugaritic *lḫšt* "whispers" (UT 19:no. 1373). This does not appear to be an incantation.

Bibliography: Davies, T. Witton, *Magic, Divination and Demonology Among the Hebrews and their Neighbors,* KTAV, 1969, pp. 50–53.

W.C.K.

1108 לֹט (*lōṭ*) ***myrrh.***

לָט (*lāṭ*). See no. 1092a.

1109 לטא (*lṭ'*). **Assumed root of the following.**

1109a לְטָאָה (*leṭā'â*) ***a kind of lizard*** (Lev 11:30).

1110 לָטַשׁ (*lāṭash*) ***hammer, sharpen, whet.***

1111 לַיְלָה (*layelâ*), לַיִל (*layil*) ***night.***

Unlike the Egyptian *Hymn to the Aton* in which the night is dreaded because the sun (Aton) has gone home, the OT insists that the darkness and night were created by God (Gen 1:4, 5; Ps 74:16). During the night God is awake, providing for the beasts of the forest (Ps 104:20–22) and protecting men from pestilence (Ps 91:5–6). Indeed the very alteration and regularity of day and night is the result of God's covenant with each (Gen 8:22; Jer 33:20, 25) and thus each succeeding day and night is a reminder of God's faithfulness to his other covenant with Abraham and David (Jer 33:21–26). To God, the night is as bright as the day (Ps 139:11–12).

Of all the 242 occurrences of this word, the most memorable night was the one in which God delivered his peoole from slavery (Ex 11:4; 12:12, 29). It is annually recalled in the passover. Instructive, in this connection, are the three days and three nights of I Sam 30:12. Verse 13 plainly says, "Today is the third [day]." Therefore it may be concluded that the expression is a stereotyped formula which applies when any part of three days is involved, not an affirmation that seventy-two hours have expired (cf. our Lord's three days and three nights.)

Elsewhere the night appears as a time of trial, weeping, suffering, and communion with God (Isa 30:29; Job 7:3; Ps 6:6 [H 7]; 77:2 [H 3]; Isa 26:9; Ps 1:2; 42:8 [H 9]; 77:6 [H 7]; 88:1 [H 2]; 92:2 [H 3]; 119:55).

W.C.K.

1112 לִילִית (*lîlît*) ***Lilith.***

A female goddess known as a night demon who haunts the desolate places of Edom (Isa 34:14) The ruin of Edom is so complete that only wildcats, satyrs, and Lilith will stay there.

In late rabbinic literature, she is depicted as a creature with wings and long, flowing hair. No doubt she personifies the night or sunset.

In Ugaritic literature she receives sacrifices (UT 23:7) and is invoked in a hymn (UT 104) which calls her "the veiled bride" (*klt.mk[ktmt]*) and "our lady" (*bltn*). The former epithet she shares with the Babylonian goddess Ishtar.

Actually, these night spirits are to be correlated with the male *Lilis*. This masculine form covers both male and female genders, as explicitly stated in one of the many references contained in the Aramaic Magical Bowls (see Cyrus H. Gordon, *Archiv Orientální,* 6:322). She appears as *La-le* in Linear A and as *lly* in a Phoenician incantation from Arslan Tash. Isaiah in his reference does not encourage worship or respect for this demonic deity. The name may be used symbolically to depict a desolation. (Cf. KJV "screech owl.")

Is it not possible also that what was a night demon in the pagan culture was just a night creature (so NIV), perhaps a bat or owl, in Israel? The pagan with his animism fills realities with spirits. Cf. Hebrew *reshep* "pestilence" with Ugaritic *rshp* the "god of pestilence" and Hebrew *yām* "sea" with Ugaritic the "god who is Prince Sea." So *lîlît* might have been a real creature demonized in the surrounding culture.

Bibliography: Leuillet, René and Xavier Léon-Dufour, "Night," in DBT, pp. 346–47. For a picture of Lilith, see Henry Frankfort, *Art and Architecture of the Ancient Orient,* 1958, pl. 56, p. 56.

W.C.K.

1113 לִיץ (*lîṣ*) ***scorn.***

Derivatives

1113a לָצוֹן (*lāṣôn*) ***scorning*** (Prov 1:22). Occurs in phrase *'anshê lāṣôn* "men of scorning," i.e. scorners in Isa 29:8; 28:14.

1113b מְלִיצָה (*m^e^lîṣâ*) ***satire, mocking poem*** (Hab 2:6), ***figure, enigma*** (Prov 1:6).

Fools scorn and mock at sin (Prov 14:9) and judgment (Prov 19:28). The scorner (Qal participial form) himself may be described as proud and haughty (Prov 21:24), incorrigible (Prov 9:7), resistant to all reproof (Prov 9:8; 15:12), and hating any rebuke (Prov 13:1). Wisdom and knowledge easily elude him (Prov 14:6).

So despicable is the scorner that he may be labelled as odious to all men (Prov 24:9). Therefore he must be avoided (Ps 1:1) by all who would live godly lives. Further, he should be punished by hitting so that the easily pursuaded naive fool may benefit from the lesson (Prov 19:25; 21:11). One good way to remove contention from a group is to eject the scorner, and then "strife and reproach will cease" (Prov 22:10). A prepared judgment awaits all such scorners (Prov 19:29), for their trademark of life has been "to delight" in their scorning (Prov 1:22). They shall be brought to nothing and consumed (Isa 29:20).

That the particular type of wickedness of the scorner is pride is suggested by Prov 3:34. Here the scorner is contrasted with the humble. In this verse the LXX renders "scorner" by "proud" which is followed in the NT Jas 4:6 and I Pet 5:5. Cf. Prov 21:24. Dahood points out a parallel of this word with "evil" in the Karatepe I inscription (*Psalms,* I, in AB, p. 2).

Among the various mockers and scorners are wine (Prov 20:1), the proud (Ps 119:51), the king of Samaria's henchmen (Hos 7:5), and Job's friends (16:20).

As a Hiphil participle, the word means an interpreter, such as Joseph used to fool his brothers (Gen 42:23). The interpreters in Isa 43:27 are the teachers of Israel, God's priests and prophets who have sinned by refusing to give out God's word as he first gave it. In II Chr 32:31, the word represents ambassadors or representatives of Babylon.

The most interesting text is Job 33:23. Elihu speaks of God graciously teaching men through the discipline of suffering the more perfect path of the Lord. Then God sends an angel, i.e. a messenger otherwise known as an interpreter, ambassador, or even a mediator to show man what is right.

Bibliography: Harris, R. L., "Proverbs," in WBC, p. 560.

W.C.K.

1114 ליש (*lysh*). **Assumed root of the following.**

1114a לַיִשׁ (*layish*) ***lion.*** See *labî'* for other words for "lion."

1115 לָכַד (*lākad*) ***capture, seize, take.***

Derivatives

1115a לֶכֶד (*leked*) ***a taking, capture.*** Occurs only in Prov 3:26, in phrase *wᵉshāmar raglᵉkā millaked.*

1115b מַלְכֹּדֶת (*malkōdet*) ***a catching instrument, i.e. a snare, trap.*** Occurs only in Job 18:10, in phrase *malkūdtô ʿālê nātîb.*

Most of the 121 uses of *lākad* deal with men capturing or seizing towns, men, spoils, and even a kingdom (I Sam 14:47). It is used figuratively of the entrapment of men who are caught in snares of all sorts laid by their enemies (Jer 5:26; 18:22; Ps 35:8). In Prov 5:22 the wicked is captured with the cords of his own sins. Likewise, in Ps 9:15 [H 16] the heathen are seized in the very net which they hid to capture others. They are captured by their pride, haughtiness, and the words of their lips (Ps 59:12 [H 13]; Prov 6:2; 11:6).

This word also serves as a figure of divine judgment. The Stone of Stumbling will cause many to stumble, fall, be broken, be ensnared, and be captured (Isa 8:15). When God shakes the foundations of the earth, just prior to the Millennium ("many days" of Isa 24:22), the ungodly shall be seized in the trap (Isa 24:18) as were those who drunkenly mocked the prophet's message (Isa 28:13). When God moves in judgment, husband and wives (Jer 6:11), scribes and wise men (Jer 8:9) along with Moab (Jer 48:7, 44) will be included.

Others are ensnared by a woman (Eccl 7:26) or are caught in the "cords of affliction" (Job 36:8).

W.C.K.

1116 לָמַד (*lāmad*) ***learn*** (Qal), ***teach*** (Piel).

Derivatives

1116a †לִמּוּד (*limmûd*) ***taught.***

1116b †מַלְמָד (*malmād*), מַלְמֵד (*malmēd*) ***oxgoad.***

1116c †תַּלְמִיד (*talmîd*) ***scholar.***

As one of the twelve words for teaching in the OT, *lāmad* has the idea of training as well as educating. The training aspect can be seen in the derived term for "oxgoad," *malmēd*. In Hos 10:11 Ephraim is taught like a heifer by a yoke and goad. The Ugaritic *lmd* means "learn/teach" and *lamādu* means "learn" in Akkadian.

The principle use of this verb is illustrated in Ps 119. Here is repeated the refrain, "Teach me thy statutes" or "thy judgments" (vv. 12, 26, 64, 66, 68, 108, 124, 135, 171). At the request of king Jehoshaphat, a group of men went out and taught the book of the Law in the cities of Judah (II Chr 17:7, 9).

While Greek uses two different words for "to learn" (*manthanō*) and "to teach" (*didaskō*), each having its own content, goal, and methods, Hebrew uses the same root for both words because all learning and teaching is ultimately to be found in the fear of the Lord (Deut 4:10; 14:23; 17:19; 31:12, 13). To learn this is to come to terms with the will and law of God.

In other instances, men are trained in ways of war (I Chr 5:18) sometimes by the use of song (Ps 60: English heading [H 1]; Jud 3:2; Song 3:8). Micah envisions a time when men will no longer learn warfare (4:3; Isa 2:4).

No one, however, has taught the Lord or acted as his counselor (Isa 40:14). Rather, anyone who knows anything has learned it from him, the source of all truth.

limmûd. ***Taught.*** The taught ones in Isa 8:16 are the Lord's disciples who know his law. The Servant of the Lord, however, has the tongue and ear of the learned (Isa 50:4). Therefore all Israel's children await the messianic era with joy, for all will be taught by the Lord (Isa 54:13).

talmîd. ***Scholar.*** Only one OT passage, I Chr 25:8, uses this word. There "the small and the great, the teacher and the scholar" are included in the selection of the twenty-four divisions of priests. In rabbinical times, the teacher of the law was called the *talmîd* Rabbi and his pupils were known as *talmîdîm,* i.e. apprentices. Yet in another sense, all Israel were *talmîdîm,* apprenticed to the *torah* of God. The Jewish Talmud gets its name from this root.

malmēd. ***Oxgoad.*** Judges 3:31 is the only passage which notes that Shamgar slew (or vanquished? cf. *nākâ*) six hundred Philistines with this iron-tipped instrument attached to a long shaft used to goad the ox as it plows. Metal weapons were scarce because the Philistines held a corner on the market (I Sam 13:19–22), hence the amazing deliverance which God granted by the hand of this otherwise unknown judge.

Bibliography: Rengstorf, K. H., "*Manthanō,*" in TDNT, IV, pp. 400–405; pp. 426–41. THAT, I, pp. 872–74.

W.C.K.

לְמוֹ (*lᵉmô*). See לְ, no. 1063.
לְמוּד (*lᵉmûd*). See no. 1116a.
לֹעַ (*lōaʿ*). See no. 1098a.

1117 *לָעַב (*lāʿab*) ***jest.*** Occurs only in the Hiphil, in II Chr 36:16, "they mocked God's messengers" (NIV).

1118 לָעַג (*lāʿag*) ***mock, deride.***

Derivatives

1118a †לַעַג (*laʿag*) ***mocking, derision.***

1118b לָעֵג (*lāʿēg*) ***mocking,*** adjective. Occurs only in Ps 35:16, and possibly Isa 28:11.

Among the seven Hebrew terms for blasphemy (see below) and slander is this one, occurring eighteen times. Various subjects of this verb indicate its range of meaning.

The wicked mock the poor and thereby insult their divine Maker (Prov 17:6). Their wicked eyes mock their fathers (Prov 30:17). They delight in laughing at such servants of God as Job (Job 21:3), Jeremiah (Jer 20:7), Asaph (Ps 80:6 [H 7]), Nehemiah (Neh 2:19), the Jews (Neh 3:33), and Hezekiah's mailmen (II Chr 30:10).

Men who mock God's servants and message will ultimately be mocked in turn: delivered into the captivity of people who speak with what seems to be a stammering or mocking tongue (Isa 33:10).

The source of this kind of judgment is God. The classic text is Ps 2:4. The Lord will mock those rebels who say of God the Father and his Messiah, "Let us break off their bands and cast off their cords." God will laugh at the heathen; he will have all of them in derision (Ps 59:8 [H 9]). Likewise, Wisdom joins God in laughing at the calamities of the coarse and hardened fool; she mocks when their fear comes (Prov 1:26) just as "the virgin, the daughter of Zion" mocked the proud, boastful Sennacherib (II Kgs 19:21; Isa 37:22), when God delivered her.

la'ag. ***Mocking, derision.*** The Psalmist complains that God has made Israel a reproach (*ḥerpâ*), a scorn (*qeles*), and a derision to everyone around them (Ps 44:13 [H 14]; see also Ps 79:4). The same is said of the two sisters Samaria and Jerusalem: "Thou shalt be laughed to scorn and had in derision" (Ezk 23:32). This derision which is directed at Jerusalem in particular will come from the nations that surround her (Ezk 36:4).

Compare *lāshan* "to speak against," *rāgal* "spy out," "slander" (going about as a busybody), *rāgan* "to murmur," to backbite," *dibbâ* "defamation," *ṣāḥaq* "to laugh at," "deride," *qālas* "to scoff at."

The phrase *halla'ag hashsha'ănannîm* "the scorn of the nonchalant" (Ps 123:4) is not as "impossible" grammatically as Briggs thought it was; as Dahood has reminded us, it needs no emendation. The article is often present on the construct state in Phoenician and Hebrew construct chains. These mockers are either the heathen opposition or Israelite rogues whose air of independence makes them despicable to God and men.

The most controversial passage (at least in its application in the NT, I Cor 14:21) is Isa 28:11. God will speak to Israel with "stammering lips," i.e. in captivity the language of the foreign captors will appear to be unintelligible gibberish. Since Israel had regarded the prophetic word as so much nonsensical talk, God would pay them back in their own currency in Assyria. Such is the import of Hos 7:16. In return for the "rage," i.e. the defiant speeches of Israel's princes who openly disavowed the Lord, God would let the same Egyptians to whom they appealed for help turn on them in derision. One turncoat deserved another!

W.C.K.

1119 לָעַז (*lā'az*) ***speak indistinctly, unintelligibly.*** Occurs only in Ps 114:1, *'am lō'ēz* "a people speaking unintelligibly."

1120 *לָעַט (*lā'aṭ*) ***swallow (greedily).*** Occurs only in the Hiphil, in Gen 25:30, *hal'îṭēnî* "let me swallow."

1121 לַעֲנָה (*la'ănâ*) ***wormwood.***

לָעַע (*lā'a'*). See no. 1099.

1122 לפד (*lpd*). **Assumed root of the following.**
1122a †לַפִּיד (*lappîd*) ***torch.***

The flaming torch, like the pillar of fire, the lamp in the tabernacle, and the glory of God, signified the holy, awesome presence of the Lord moving among his people. Thus God moved as a flaming torch between the divided pieces to confirm his covenant with Abraham (Gen 15:17) and appeared in flashes of lightning on Sinai (Ex 20:18; cf. Ezk 1:13). When Zion is finally delivered, her salvation will be like a burning lamp (Isa 62:1) and her governors like a torch of fire (Zech 12:6).

W.C.K.

לַפִּיד (*lappîd*) See no. 1122a.
לִפְנֵי (*lipnê*). See no. 1780b.

1123 לָפַת (*lāpat*) ***twist, turn, grasp with a twisting motion.***

לָצוֹן (*lāṣôn*). See no. 1113a.

1124 לָקַח (*lāqaḥ*) ***take (get, fetch), lay hold of (seize), receive, acquire (buy), bring, marry (take a wife), snatch (take away).***

Derivatives

1124a †לֶקַח (*leqaḥ*) ***learning.***
1124b מַלְקוֹחַ (*malqôaḥ*) ***I, booty, prey.***
1124c מַלְקוֹחַ (*malqôaḥ*) ***II, jaw.*** Occurs only in Ps 22:16 in phrase *ûl^{e}shônî mūdbāq malqôḥāy* "my tongue is made to cleave to my jaws (i.e. gums)."
1124d מֶלְקָחַיִם (*melqāḥayim*) ***tongs, snuffers.***

1124e מִקָּח (*miqqāḥ*) ***a taking, receiving.*** Occurs only in II Chr 19:7, *miqqaḥ-shōḥad* "a taking of a bribe."

1124f מַקָּחָה (*maqqāḥâ*) ***ware.*** Only in Neh 10:32, *hammaqqāḥôt* "(their) wares."

This root is used over a thousand times in the OT, often taking its nuance from the words with which it is used. As in English one can take vengeance (Isa 47:3) or receive disgrace (Ezk 36:30), and God receives (accepts) prayer in Ps 6:10 where it is used in parallel with *shāmaʿ* "to hear" (cf. Job 4:12). A similar parallel exists between *lāqaḥ* "snatch" and *gānab* "steal" (cf. Job 4:12; Jer 23:30–31; Jud 17:2). In the passive stems (Pual and Niphal) the usage "be taken, carried away" (I Sam 4:11) or "be brought" (Gen 2:15) suggests that such "taking" is against the will of those taken. These basic meanings are also found in postbiblical Hebrew, Aramaic, Moabite, Phoenician, Arabic, Ugaritic, and Akkadian.

In addition to the common meanings of *lāqaḥ* there are a number of extended uses, some of which have theological significance. The "take" aspect of the word may extend, in some contexts, into the meaning "select" and/or "summon." According to Deut 4:34, God "took" (selected) Israel from among the nations (cf. also 4:30; I Kgs 11:37; Josh 3:12; 4:2). In Job 41:4 [H 40:28] the leviathan is "taken" (selected) as God's permanent vassal who has a binding covenant with him. "Summon" would fit equally well in some of these contexts. BDB (pp. 543, 546) finds "summon" for *lāqaḥ* in Num 23:11, Jud 11:5, and I Sam 16:11. One should be careful with the semantics here because "take or fetch" also makes sense, but this is true of many of the nuances of this word. An interesting but vexing usage of this type occurs in Ps 75:2 [H 3]. The translations differ considerably. The KJV renders it, "When I shall receive the congregation," RV "When I shall find the set time," RSV "I appoint," NASB "I select." M.Dahood's "summon" makes good sense here, "I will summon the assembly, I will judge with equity" (*Psalms,* II, in AB, p. 209).

Twice Jeremiah uses *lāqaḥ* for the "taking up" or "use" of words. In 23:31 he speaks against the false prophets who "use" (RSV, NASB) their tongues as if the Lord had inspired them. In 29:22 the exiles "use" a curse formula based on the demise of certain false prophets.

Fire from God is described with a reflexive use of the root *lāqaḥ* in Ex 9:24 and Ezk 1:4. The explanation that the fire seizes, enfolds upon itself is not entirely satisfactory.

Perhaps the most theologically interesting usage of *lāqaḥ* centers around the two clear contexts where the word describes bodily assumption into heaven. We refer to Enoch's disappearance when God "took" him (Gen 5:24) and Elijah's assumption in a whirlwind (II Kgs 2:3, 10–11). In the light of such physical assumption, it is not unreasonable to question whether there may be other similar uses. Elijah, whose body was assumed, used *lāqaḥ* to refer to death at the hands of his enemies "they seek my life, to take it" (I Kgs 19:10, 14; cf. also Prov 24:11). Just the opposite meaning appears in other places where God is the subject and a rescue from dying or distress is in mind. So Ps 18:16 [H 17] says, "He sent from on high, he took me; he drew me out of the deep waters." But there are at least three contexts where more than merely saving a person's life appears to be in the mind of the Psalmist. Psalm 49 presents a stark contrast between the end of the wicked and the end of the righteous. The wicked "die like beasts" (vv. 12 [H 13], 20 [H 21]) without any hope of immortality, "that he should live forever" (v. 9 [H 10]). The Psalmist, however, has a triumphant faith that "God will redeem him from the power of Sheol, for he will receive (*lāqaḥ* take, snatch) me" (v. 15 [H 16]). If the Psalmist is talking about being rescued from death for a few years when he knows he too must die like the beasts, then the Psalm has no point. Psalm 73: 23–25 [H 24–26] also contrasts the wicked with the righteous and once again a faith that reaches beyond this life is centered around the word *lāqaḥ*. "You will guide me with your counsel and afterwards receive (take) me to glory" (v. 24 [H 25]).

leqaḥ. ***Teaching, learning, persuasiveness.*** This word occurs nine times, in four of which it is the object of *yāsap* "to add more, increase" (Prov 1:5; 9:9; 16:21, 23). As with the root meaning "take, seize," the "grasping" is with the mind and hence "perceiving" is the nuance prominent in this derivative. Note some of the words with which it is paired: *bînâ* "understanding" (Isa 29:24), *ḥākām* "wisdom" (Prov 1:5; 9:9) and *tôrâ* "instruction, law" (Prov 4:2). In Prov 7:21 *leqaḥ* means "the persuasiveness" of a harlot. But in Prov 16:21 the word is used in a good sense of a teacher's persuasiveness.

Bibliography: THAT, I, pp. 875–78.

W.C.K.

1125 לָקַט (*lāqaṭ*) ***glean, pick, gather up.***

Derivatives

1125a †לֶקֶט (*leqeṭ*) ***gleaning.***
1125b †יַלְקוּט (*yalqûṭ*) ***wallet, bag.***

The objects of this verb vary as much as the subjects, e.g. they gather stones (Gen 31:46), manna (Ex 16:4–5, 26), money (Gen 47:14), grain (Ruth 2:3, 7; Isa 17:5), fallen grapes (Lev 19:10), arrows (I Sam 20:38), firewood (Jer 7:18), food off the ground (Jud 1:7), or a bunch of ruffians (Jud 11:3). Not only men, but also occasionally animals gathered (food, Ps 104:28).

A theologically important verse is Lev 19:9 (see also 23:22) in which Israel is warned not to reap the corners of their fields or gather the gleanings of [the] harvest. The gleanings were to be left for the poor and the resident alien, as illustrated in Ruth 2:15–18; cf. Lev 19:10; 23:22*b*.

Israel's final restoration to her land is depicted by Isaiah under the figure of grains picked up after being threshed by the Lord's judgment: "And you shall be gathered one by one, O you sons of Israel" in that day (Isa 27:12).

leqeṭ. ***Gleaning.*** Only found twice (Lev 19:9; 23:22), as discussed above.

yalqûṭ. ***Wallet, bag.*** This hapax legomenon is found in I Sam 17:40. It is the word for David's shepherd's bag into which he had placed five smooth stones. So far the word is unattested elsewhere.

W.C.K.

1126 לָקַק (*lāqaq*) ***lap, lick.***

1127 לקשׁ (*lqsh*). **Assumed root of the following.**
1127a לֶקֶשׁ (*leqesh*) ***after growth, i.e. spring crop.*** Occurs only in Amos 7:1.
1127b †מַלְקוֹשׁ (*malqôsh*) ***latter rain.***
1127c לָקַשׁ (*lāqash*) ***take the aftermath, i.e. take everything*** (Job 24:6). Probably denominative from *leqesh*.

malkôsh. ***Latter rain, spring rain.*** The latter rains occur during March and April, while the former rains (q.v.) begin the season of rain, usually including severe thunderstorms, in the second half of October to November (or even as late as January in a bad year). The latter rains of March and April are desperately needed for the coming harvest, hence Job's description of his miserable comforters in a marvelous simile (Job 29:23). If this rain fails, it is obvious that God is displeased with his people: "I also withheld the rain from you when there were only three months to harvest" (Amos 4:7; Jer 3:3).

But if all is well between God and his people, then "he will give the rain for [their] land in its season, the early rain and the latter rain so that [they] might gather in [their] grain and wine and oil" (Deut 11:14; Jer 5:24). When God returns to his people, it is like the coming of the latter and former rains upon the earth, proclaims Hosea (6:3). God invites men to ask him for rain at the time of the latter rain and he will send it copiously (Zech 10:1). In fact, when men repent, one of God's signs of immediate blessing is the rain (Joel 2:23).

Proverbs uses the appearance of the spring clouds preceeding the latter rains as a simile of the king's favor (Prov 16:15).

Bibliography: Baly, Dennis, *Geography of the Bible,* Harper, 1957, pp. 51–52, 99.

W.C.K.

1128 לשׁד (*lshd*). **Assumed root of the following.**
1128a לְשַׁד (*lāshād*) ***juice, juicy or dainty bit*** (Num 11:8; Ps 32:4).

לָשׁוֹן (*lāshôn*). See no. 1131a.

1129 לשׁך (*lshk*). **Assumed root of the following.**
1129a †לִשְׁכָּה (*lishkâ*) ***room, chamber.***

Most frequently this word designates the three tiers of rooms or cells allocated to priests, singers, and keepers of the temple (Ezk 40:17, 38, 44–46; 41:10; 42:1, 4, 5, 7, 8, 11, 12). During the time of Ezra and Nehemiah, the term was used of storerooms (Ezr 8:29; Neh 10:38–40) and personal chambers (Ezr 10:6; Neh 13:4, 5, 8, 9.) In Jer 36:12, 20, 21 it refers to the scribe's room in the palace.

One of the most theologically important passages is Jer 35:2, 4. Jeremiah was commanded to take the Rechabites to a room connected with Solomon's temple and offer some wine to them. They went but refused the wine out of deference and obedience to an old command given by one of their forefathers. Jeremiah learned that obedience to God was indeed possible if men could steadfastly obey merely human laws.

In Samuel's day there was another room connected with the high place (*bāmâ*) where he partook of a sacrificial meal with Saul, king-elect (I Sam 9:22; cf. v. 19).

nishkâ. ***Chamber.*** A late word, doubtless a by-form, with a similar-sounding letter interchange (l and n). It was used also of rooms for individuals (Neh 3:30; 13:7) and storerooms (Neh 12:44).

W.C.K.

1130 לֶשֶׁם (*leshem*) ***a precious stone in the high priest's breastplate*** (Ex 28:19; 39:12). NIV, RSV, NASB translate "jacinth."

1131 לָשַׁן (*lāshan*) ***slander.*** Denominative verb.

Parent Noun

1131a †לָשׁוֹן (*lāshôn*) ***tongue.***

Only two examples of the denominative verb appear. Psalm 101:5 warns that God will silence all who privately slander their neighbors and

Prov 30:10 cautions against disparaging a slave to his master lest the speaker be ill-spoken of in turn.

lāshôn. ***Tongue.*** This word occurs 117 times in the OT. The God-given organ of communication with one's fellowman and God, the tongue is shown to be at once the source of much good and evil. A few passages refer to the physical tongue, e.g. of men lapping (Jud 7:5), thirsting (Lam 4:4), and dumb (Job 29:10; Ps 137:6; Ezk 3:26) or of animals such as dogs (Ex 11:7), crocodiles (Job 40:25), and adders (Job 20:16). By extension, it carries geographical meaning such as the "tongue" of land which protrudes into the Dead Sea (Josh 15:2, 5; 18:19; Isa 11:15) or a tongue-shaped wedge of gold (Josh 7:21, 24).

However, most attention is focused on the misuse of the tongue, Ps 52 (especially vv. 2, 4 [H 4, 6]) being the classical teaching passage. Here Doeg, the Edomite, used his tongue deceitfully to lead Saul to destroy the priestly house of Ahimelech (I Sam 22:7ff.). But Ps 51 stands as an example of the proper use of the tongue, singing of God's righteousness after experiencing cleansing from sin (v. 14 [H 16]; see also Ps 126:2).

The tongue is the agent of many evils: subversion (Prov 10:31), slander (Prov 17:4), flattery (Ps 5:9 [H 10]), mischief and trouble (Ps 10:7), arrogance (Ps 12:4 [H 5]), hurt to others (Ps 52:2 [H 4]), and falsehood (Prov 17:4; 6:17; 12:19; 21:6; 26:28; Ps 78:36; 120:2–3; Mic 6:12). It can be like the tongue of a viper (Ps 140:3 [H 4]), a bow or arrow (Jer 9:3 [H 2], 8 [H 7]), a sharp sword (Ps 57:4 [H 5]; 64:3 [H 4]; Hos 7:16), a razor (Ps 52:2 [H 4]). The tongue can be used as a weapon (Jer 18:18) because "life and death are in the power of the tongue" (Prov 18:21). All such use of the tongue is ultimately directed against God, for while it violates mostly the ninth commandment, it is accompanied by an arrogance and boasting that usurps the place of God (Hos 7:16). God will teach all who mock his message and in drunken stupor complain about the prophets' wearisome "watch your *p*'s and watch your *q*'s," with "another tongue": foreign exile (Isa 28:11; cf. Jer 5:15, "a nation whose language you do not know").

Most presumptuous of all are the false prophets (Jer 23:31). They cry "peace, peace" in a move to seek popularity (23:16ff.). But they fail to distinguish their own dreams from real prophecy (23:28ff.), and they plagiarize and pervert the burden of the Lord (23:36ff.). Contrariwise was the reluctance of Moses who complained that he had a heavy tongue (Ex 4:10) even though Stephen testified that he was mighty in words and deeds (Acts 7:22). Moses' words did not, then, refer to a speech impediment, but rather to a certain type of quickness in debate. God's solution was a promise to be with his tongue and to send him another tongue, Aaron.

The tongue of a righteous man, however, is valued as highly as choice silver (Prov 10:20). When wise men speak they bring health to their listeners (Prov 12:18); they use knowledge in a proper manner (Prov 15:2). Wisdom and kindness characterize the tongue of the virtuous woman (Prov 31:26). Not a thought, answer, or word on the tongue is unknown to the Lord (Ps 139:4; Prov 16:1–2; II Sam 23:2).

In the future day of the Lord, the deceitful tongue will not be found among the remnant (Zeph 3:13); even the tongue of the dumb will shout for joy (Isa 35:6).

Bibliography: Surgy, Paul de, "Tongue," in DBT, p. 533. Behm, J., "*glōssa,*" in TDNT, I, p. 721.

W.C.K.

1132 לתח (*lth*). **Assumed root of the following.**

1132a מֶלְתָּחָה (*meltāḥâ*) ***wardrobe, wearing apparel.*** Occurs only in II Kgs 10:22.

1133 לתך (*ltk*). **Assumed root of the following.**

1133a לֶתֶךְ (*letek*) ***barley measure of uncertain size thought to be half an homer—five ephahs.*** Occurs only in Hos 3:2. (ZPEB V, p. 917.)

מ

מ

מַאֲבוּס (*ma'ăbûs*). See no. 10b.

1134 מאד (*m'd*). **Assumed root of the following.**
1134a †מְאֹד (m^{e}*'ōd*) ***exceedingly, much, force, abundance.***

This term is used three hundred times in the OT, mainly as an adverb. Infrequently, it is used as a substantive, e.g. Deut 6:5, "You shall love the Lord your God with your whole heart, with your whole soul, and with your whole strength." Thus it was said of King Josiah, the likes of whom Israel had never seen before, that he turned to the Lord with his whole heart, soul, and strength, according to the whole law of Moses (II Kgs 23:25).

It is found in many combinations, all expressing the idea of exceeding (e.g. Gen 1:31, in which the Creator calls his creation exceeding good) or very greatly (e.g. Ex 1:7, where this term is used twice in describing the prolificacy of the Israelites under the hand of God).

McBride observed: "The three parts of Deut 6:5: *lēbāb* (heart), *nepesh* (soul or life), and *me'ōd* (muchness) rather than signifying different spheres of Biblical psychology seem to be semantically concentric. They were chosen to reinforce the absolute singularity of personal devotion to God. Thus *lēbāb* denotes the intention or will of the whole man; *nepesh* means the whole self, a unity of flesh, will, and vitality; and m^{e}*'ōd* accents the superlative degree of total commitment to Yahweh." (See bibliography.)

The NT struggles to express the depth of the word m^{e}*'od* at this spot. In the quotation in Mk 12:30 it is rendered "mind and strength," in Lk 10:27 it is "strength and mind," in Mt 22:37 simply "mind."

Bibliography: TDOT, IX, pp. 617–37.

W.C.K.

1135 מֵאָה (*mē'â*) ***hundred.***

This noun occurs 583 times, usually in statements reporting ages of persons, census results, or the measurements of various objects.

The longevity of the antediluvian and postdiluvian fathers (Gen 5 and 11) has caused much comment. However, it is clear that these hundreds of years (the maximum being 969 years, reached by Methuselah) were real years, for God intended to show to all that mankind was built for immortality. Nevertheless, the effects of sin began to take their toll on man's physical being. Thus his life span grew shorter and, consequently, the period of procreation. By Abraham's time it was thought to be impossible for a one hundred-year-old man to father a child (Gen 17:17). But God miraculously provided Isaac, the child of promise.

A significant prophecy was given in Gen 15:13. Israel was to be in bondage for four hundred years and indeed they were. According to Ex 12:40, the exact time was four hundred and thirty years. If there is a round number here, it is in Gen 15:13.

In one place it appears probable that the word "hundred" (with consonants *m'h*) is a mistake for "cubit" (with consonants *'mh*). The porch of Solomon's temple is said to be 120 (supposedly cubits, so RSV). But this would be 180 feet, an impossible height. Some MSS of the LXX here read 20 cubits, the same height as the holy of holies. It seems probable that there has been a metathesis of the letters, and some LXX witnesses have preserved the original reading. The same metathesis occurs in a Qere/Kethib variation in Ezk 42:16.

An eschatological passage, Isa 65:20, says that in the new heavens and new earth "the child shall die an hundred years old, but the sinner being an hundred years old shall be accursed." Whether verses 20–25 are a part of the description of the new heavens and new earth, or are a subparagraph as Buswell claims (*Systematic Theology,* II, p. 517), is debatable. E. J. Young, however, argues that death will not deprive either the young child or old man of his days (Isa 65:20*a*). Neither will longevity be unusual, for a person who dies at the age of one hundred years will be considered just a baby or a sinner who has been cut down very early. Cf. NIV: "He who dies at a hundred will be thought a mere youth; he who fails to reach a hundred will be considered accursed."

Bibliography: Green, William Henry, "Primeval Chronology," in *Classical Evangelical Essays in O.T. Interpretation,* Baker, 1972, pp. 13–28. Young, E. J., *The Book of Isaiah,* III, Eerdmans, 1972, p. 515.

W.C.K.

מַאֲוַי (*ma'ăway*). See no. 40c.
מְאוּם (m^{e}*'ûm*). See no. 1137a.

1136 מְאוּמָה (m^{e}*'ûmâ*) ***anything.***

Used thirty-two times, usually in negative sentences. Ecclesiastes 7:14 has God setting prosperity alongside aversity so that men can find nothing apart from himself (cf. 3:11). Balaam protests in Num 22:38 that he has no power to do anything apart from the word of God. Often *m*^e*'ûmâ* is a euphemism for something bad, such as the thing Abraham was about to do to Isaac (Gen 22:12, "Do not do anything to the lad,") or the thing Ammon waited to do to Tamar (II Sam 13:2, "He thought it difficult to do anything to her").

W.C.K.

מָאוֹס (*mā'ôs*). See no. 1139a.

מָאוֹר (*mā'ôr*). See no. 52f.

מֹאזֶן (*mō'zen*). See no. 58a.

מַאֲכָל (*ma'ăkāl*). See no. 85d.

מַאֲכֶלֶת (*ma'ăkelet*). See no. 85e.

מַאֲכֹלֶת (*ma'ăkōlet*). See no. 85f.

מַאֲמָצָה (*ma'ămāṣâ*). See no. 117e.

מַאֲמָר (*ma'ămār*). See no. 118e.

1137 מאם (*m'm*). **Assumed root of the following.**

1137a †מְאוּם (*m'ûm*), מוּם (*mûm*) ***defect, blemish.***

This word denotes any physical defect, such as was not found in Daniel and his three friends (Dan 1:4ff.) and in the man who would be God's priest (Lev 21:17ff.), or any moral defect (Job 31:7; 11:15; Deut 32:5). The epitome of unblemished men was Absalom (II Sam 14:25); of women the Shulamite maiden (Song 4:7).

Animals offered as sacrifices to God had to be without spot or blemish (Lev 22:20, 21, 25; Num 19:2; Deut 15:21; 17:1). To offer anything less would be to disobey God and disregard the obvious teaching that man's substitute for his sins had itself to be totally blameless.

W.C.K.

1138 *מָאֵן (*mā'ēn*) ***refuse.*** Used only in the Piel.

Derivatives

1138a †מָאֵן (*mā'ēn*) ***refusing.***
1138b †מֵאֵן (*mē'ēn*) ***refusing.***

Especially significant are those occasions when Pharaoh (Ex 4:23; 7:14; 10:3) or Israel refused to obey God's commands. They simply "refused to walk in [God's] law" (Ps 78:10). Israel also refused to repent (Hos 11:5; Jer 3:3; 8:5) or to receive instruction (Jer 5:3; 9:6 [H 5]; 11:10; Zech 7:11). Only once is God ever said to have refused: he refused to give Balaam permission to curse Israel (Num 22:13).

mā'ēn. ***Refusing.*** This verbal adjective appears four times in the OT, three times in the phrase *'im-mā'ēn 'attâ l*^e*shallēaḥ*, of Pharaoh's refusal to release Israel from bondage (Ex 8:2 [H 7:27]; 9:2; 10:4). It is also used of Zedekiah's refusal to surrender to the Babylonians (Jer 38:21).

mē'ēn. ***Refusing.*** Only found in Jer 13:10, of rebellious Israel who kept on refusing to listen to God's word and worshiping other gods.

W.C.K.

1139 מָאַס (*mā'as*) ***I, reject, despise.***

Derivative

1139a מָאוֹס (*mā'ôs*) ***refuse.*** Occurs only in Lam 3:45, "offscouring and refuse you make us."

Examination of some seventy-three uses of this verb reveals that men despise the Lord who is among them (Num 11:20) and thus merit God's rejecting them (Hos 4:6). When Israel requested Samuel to appoint a king over them, they rejected the Lord (I Sam 8:7; 10:19).

Wicked men do not despise evil (Ps 36:4 [H 5]); they just reject the knowledge of God (Hos 4:6), the law of the Lord (Amos 2:4; Isa 5:24; Jer 6:19) the word of the Lord (I Sam 15:23, 26; Isa 30:12; Jer 8:9), the righteous decisions of God (Ezk 5:6; 20:13, 16), the covenant made with Abraham (II Kgs 17:15), the statutes of God (Lev 26:15; Ezk 20:24), and the disciplinary chastening of the Lord (Prov 3:11). In fact, they have totally rejected the "Stone" which has now become the "capstone of the building" (Ps 118:22).

Especially reprehensible in God's eyes is Israel's externalized religious practice. God hates and despises their feast days and offerings since they come to him without any genuine affection (Amos 5:21).

God rejects men who do not listen to him (Hos 9:17). However, he will never reject them totally, for that would break his covenant (Lev 26:44). God has chosen the seed of Abraham, his servant, and he will never cast them away (Isa 41:9). In fact, as long as God keeps his covenant with day and night (Jer 33:25) so long will he refrain from rejecting his covenant made with David and Levi (Jer 33:24). He will not despise the seed of Abraham, Isaac, Jacob, and David (Jer 31:37; 33:26). True, Ps 89:38 [H 39] does seem to contradict this strong affirmation by saying God has indeed rejected his anointed (cf. II Kgs 17:20; Jer 6:30; Ps 78:59, 67). This statement, however, refers only to individual participation and not to the abiding promise which remains open to all who will believe.

Bibliography: THAT, I, pp. 879–92.

W.C.K.

1140 *מָאַס (*mā'as*) ***II, flow, run.*** Occurs only in the Niphal (Job 5:7; Ps 58:8).

מַאֲפֶה (*ma'ăpeh*). See no. 143a.
מַאֲפֵל (*ma'ăpēl*). See no. 145e.
מַאֲפֵלְיָה (*ma'ăpēlyâ*). See no. 145f.
מַאֲפֵת (*ma'ăpēt*). See no. 152a.

1141 *מָאַר (*mā'ar*) ***pain, prick.***

This word appears four times, in the Hiphil stem. Once it is used figuratively of Israel's oppression by their neighbors (Ezk 28:24), who are likened to "pricking briars and scratching thorns." In the other three passages, it refers to a malignant (?) or rotten (?) mold associated with leprosy (q.v.) (Lev 13:51–52; 14:44).

W.C.K.

מַאֲרָב (*ma'ărāb*). See no. 156e.
מְאֵרָה (*me'ērâ*). See no. 168a.
מִבְדָּלָה (*mābdālâ*). See no. 203b.
מָבוֹא (*mābô'*). See no. 212b.
מְבוּכָה (*mebûkâ*). See no. 214a.

1142 מַבּוּל (*mabbûl*) ***flood.***

A technical term reserved for the watery catastrophe which God brought on the earth during the days of Noah. That event was so well known that *mabbûl* usually occurs with the definite article (except in Gen 9:11, 15). *mabbûl* is used only once outside Gen 7–11. Psalm 29:10 says that "the LORD sits upon the flood, indeed, the LORD is enthroned king forever." Instead of Baal, the god of storm and thunder who according to the Ugaritic myths defeated *yam* the sea god, the Lord's voice is heard in the thunder, and it is he who reigns over the destructive forces of nature, in this case the storm so beautifully described in Ps 29.

All attempted etymologies for this word have failed because of linguistic difficulties. A few of the suggestions have been: the Akkadian root *nbl* "to destroy," Akkadian *abūbu* from the alleged *wabūbu* "cyclone," Akkadian *bubbulu, biblu, bibbulu* "inundation," which is the best suggestion yet. But it also fails since the term is not used in any of the Akkadian flood stories. Hebrew *ybl* "to flow, stream" or *nbl* "waterskin" have also been suggested. But these suggestions are not linguistically supported and appear to be parents to the unwarranted thought that *mabbûl* refers to a "heavenly ocean" or a "heavenly store of water in jars."

While God himself brought the waters of the flood on the earth because of man's sin (Gen 6:17; 7:6), afterward he covenanted never again to destroy the earth with water (Gen 9:11, 15). Thus God's own can be certain that the earth will endure until the desired eschaton comes.

W.C.K.

מְבוּסָה (*mebûsâ*). See no. 216b.
מַבּוּעַ (*mabbûa'*). See no. 1287a.
מִבְחָר (*mibḥār*). See no. 231d.
מִבְחוֹר (*mibḥôr*). See no. 231e.
מַבָּט (*mabbāṭ*). See no. 1282a.
מִבְטָא (*mibṭā'*). See no. 232a.
מִבְטָח (*mibṭaḥ*). See no. 233e.
מַבְלִיגִית (*mablîgît*). See no. 245a.
מִבְנֶה (*mibneh*). See no. 255c.
מִבְצָר (*mibṣār*). See no. 270g.
מִבְרָח (*mibraḥ*). See no. 284c.
מְבַשְּׁלוֹת (*mebashelôt*). See no. 292b.

1143 מָג (*māg*) ***soothsayer, magician.***

This loan word from Akkadian *maḫḫu* "soothsayer" occurs only twice, and that in one chapter, Jer 39:3, 13. One of Nebuchadnezzar's princes was "Nergal-Sharezer the Rab-mag" (RSV). This was Neriglissar, the husband of Amel-Marduk's sister (the one Jeremiah called Evil Merodach, son and successor to Nebuchadnezzar). Neriglissar killed Evil Merodach and became king in his place.

Nergalsharezer's position was one of high military rank. He was chief soothsayer (*rab māg*) in the operations against Zedekiah during the seige of Jerusalem.

Bibliography: Thomson, R. C., in *Cambridge Ancient History*, II, Cambridge, 1960, p. 217.

W.C.K.

מִגְבָּלוֹת (*migbālôt*). See no. 307d.
מִגְבָּעוֹת (*migbā'ôt*). See no. 309c.

1144 מגד (*mgd*). **Assumed root of the following.**
1144a †מֶגֶד (*meged*) ***excellence.***
1144b מִגְדָּנָה (*migdānâ*) ***choice or excellent thing.***

meged. ***Excellence.*** Only eight passages in three chapters illustrate the usage of *meged*. It is always an evaluation of the gifts of nature as being choice, excellent or beautiful, and precious. Song 4:13, 15, 16 lauds the excellent fruit; only Song 7:13 [H 14] uses the word *meged* by itself. Deuteronomy 33:13, 14, 15, 16 bless the Lord for the choice things from the heavens, moon, hills, and earth. It appears to be a eulogistic word which sees the beauty of all things as God's gifts to lovers (Song) and to the tribes of Joseph (Deut).

W.C.K.

מִגְדּוֹל (*migdôl*). See no. 315g.
מִגְדָּל (*migdāl*). See no. 315f.
מִגְדָּנָה (*migdānâ*). See no. 1144b.
מְגוּרָה (*megûrâ*). See no. 330d.
מָגוֹר (*māgôr*). See no. 332a, 330c.
מַגְזֵרָה (*magzērâ*). See no. 340d.
מַגָּל (*maggāl*). See no. 1292a.

מְגִלָּה (*m^e gillâ*). See no. 353m.
מְגַמָּה (*m^e gammâ*). See no. 361b.
מָגֵן (*māgēn*). See no. 367c.
מָגַן (*māgan*). See no. 367e.
מְגִנָּה (*m^e ginnâ*). See no. 367d.
מִגְעֶרֶת (*mig'eret*). See no. 370b.
מַגֵּפָה (*maggēpâ*). See no. 1294b.

1145 מָגַר (*māgar*) ***cast, throw, toss*** (Ezk 21:17; Ps 89:45).

מְגֵרָה (*m^e gērâ*). See no. 386e.
מִגְרָעָה (*migrā'â*). See no. 384a.
מֶגְרָפָה (*megrāpâ*). See no. 385b.
מִגְרָשׁ (*migrāsh*). See no. 388c.
מַד (*mad*). See no. 1146a.
מִדְבָּר (*midbār*) I, II. See nos. 399k, l.

1146 מָדַד (*mādad*) ***measure.***

Derivatives

1146a †מַד (*mad*) ***measure.***
1146b †מִדָּה (*middâ*) ***measure, measurement.***
1146c מֵמַד (*mēmad*) ***measurement.*** Occurs only in Job 38:5.
1146d מָדוֹן (*mādôn*) ***stature.*** Occurs only in II Sam 20:21.

Usually *mādad,* which occurs fifty-three times, refers to measuring lengths or distances. It is used heavily in Ezk 40–47, which supplies measurements for the millennial temple which, according to many, is to be built during the messianic era (see also Zech 2:6).

But there are imponderables which are beyond the capacities of man's measurements—like the oceans of the earth. But God can measure these easily (Isa 40:12). He can also count the multitudes of future Israelites, although their number would appear to be as the sand of the sea (Hos 1:10 [H 2:1]). The innumerable stars of heaven and the sands of the sea indeed become models of the increase of Jacob and the security they enjoy under God (Jer 33:22; 31:27).

As God will increase the people, so he has measured out to them certain territories (Ps 60:6 [H 8]; see also 108:7 [H 8]). As he prepares his judgment, he stands and measures the nations with his discerning eye (Hab 3:6).

mad. ***Measure,*** and then ***what is measured, a cloth garment.*** The portion of Judah's measure (used figuratively) from the Lord is to be scattered because they have forgotten their Lord (Jer 13:25). This word usually denotes a priest's garment (Lev 6:3), a soldier's fighting garb (I Sam 17:38; 18:4; II Sam 20:8), or just an outer garment (I Sam 4:12; Jud 3:16). It is also used figuratively, as in Ps 109:18, which says that some men use cursing for their outer clothes. The simile is reflected in Ugaritic UT 16:Text 75:II:47–48 "like clothing was the abuse of his brothers, like vesture the abuse of his kinsmen" (after M. Dahood).

middâ. ***Measure, measurement.*** The measuringline used to measure God's future dwelling place (Zech 2:5; Ezk 40:3, 5; 42:16–19), it was also used to take the measurement of the walls of Jerusalem (Neh 3:11, 19ff.), a house of size or a man of size (Jer 22:14; I Chr 11:23; 20:6), and the size of the tabernacle curtains (Ex 26:2, 8 etc.). It is of some interest to note that the tabernacle curtains were four cubits (six feet) wide—just the width of a standard Egyptian loom. The word is used of time in Ps 39:4 [H 5]: "Lord make me to know mine end and the measure of my days, what it is; that I might know how frail I am." Note also its use of God's wisdom, the measure of which is longer than the earth and broader than the sea (Job 11:9).

W.C.K.

1147 מִדָּה (*middâ*) ***tribute.*** A loan word from the Akkadian *mandattu, middâ* occurs only in Neh 5:4.

מִדָּה (*middâ*). See no. 1146b.

1148 מדה (*mdh*). **Assumed root of the following, doubtless a by-form of *mādad*.**
1148a מָדוּ (*mādû*) מַדְוֶה (*madweh*) ***garment.*** Occurs in II Sam 10:4; I Chr 19:4.

מָדוּ (*mādû*). See no. 1148a.
מַדְוֶה (*madweh*). See nos. 411c, 1148a.
מַדּוּחַ (*maddûaḥ*). See no. 1304a.
מָדוֹן (*mādôn*). See nos. 426c, 1146d.
מַדּוּעַ (*maddûa'*). See no. 848h.
מְדוּרָה (*m^e dûrâ*). See no. 418c.
מִדְחֶה (*midḥeh*). See no. 420b.
מְדִינָה (*m^e dînâ*). See no. 426d.
מַדְמֵנָה (*madmēnâ*). See no. 441b.
מַדָּע (*maddā'*). See no. 848g.
מֹדַעַת (*mōda'at*). See no. 848f.
מַדְקָרָה (*madqārâ*). See no. 449a.
מַדְרֵגָה (*madrēgâ*). See no. 452a.
מִדְרָךְ (*madrāk*). See no. 453b.
מִדְרָשׁ (*midrāsh*). See no. 455a.

1149 מָה (*mâ*) ***what?***

This frequently-occurring interrogative pronoun is most significant when associated with the word "name." "What is your name?" is not a question which inquires after a person's family or personal name; it endeavors to find what character or quality lies within or behind the person. To ask for simple identification, one would say in Hebrew, "Who (*mî*) are you?"

Thus, the "man" who wrestled with Jacob asked him in Gen 32:27 [H 28], "What is your name?" When he responds, "Jacob" (supplanter), the "man" (called an angel in Hos 12:4 [H 5]) says that it is now "Israel" (Prince of God).

In Prov 30:4, Agur asks who has ascended to heaven and then descended? Who has gathered the wind in his fists? Who has bound the waters in a garment? Who has established the ends of the earth? What is his name? What is his son's name? The speaker is not asking for God's name. Rather, he seeks to know its character and meaning.

Accordingly, the question which Moses anticipates from his enslaved brethren, "What is his name?" (Ex 3:13), corresponds to our discussion above. The Israelites will wish to know Yahweh's character and qualities which will enable him to prevail over the difficulties they face. So Moses reveals just what the name Yahweh (YHWH) means: He is the God who will dynamically and effectively meet their need.

Finally, notice that God brings the animals to Adam to see "what" he will call them (Gen 2:19). As Motyer says, "Verse 20b indicates that qualitative issues are present" (p. 18, fn. 46). Other significant passages in which *mâ* is associated with persons include Ex 16:7–8; Num 16:11; II Sam 9:8; II Kgs 8:13; Job 7:17; 15:14; 21:15; Ps 8:4 [H 5]; 144:3; Song 5:9; Isa 45:10; Lam 2:13; Ezk 19:2. It is associated with impersonal items in ten passages: I Kgs 9:13; Zech 1:9, 19 [H 2:4]; 4:4, 11; 5:6; 6:4; Est 9:26.

Bibliography: Buber, Martin, *The Revelation and the Covenant,* Harper & Row, 1958, pp. 48–55. Motyer, J. A., *The Revelation of the Divine Name,* London: Tyndale, 1959, pp. 17–24.

W.C.K.

1150 *מָהַהּ (*māhah*) ***linger, delay.***

This word, in the Hithpalpel stem, occurs nine times. But only in two passages does it carry theological significance. In Ps 119:60 the Psalmist affirms that he has not delayed, but rather hastened to observe God's commandments. Habakkuk 2:3 encourages the prophet to wait for the vision, since it has an appointed time. It may seem to delay, nevertheless it will not tarry, it will come.

W.C.K.

מְהוּמָה (*m^e hûmâ*). See no. 486a
מָהִיר (*māhîr*). See no. 1152c.

1151 מָהַל (*māhal*) ***circumcise, weaken.***

The Aramaic "cognate," *m^e hal,* means to circumcise, but in Hebrew the word appears only once and that in a figuarative sense, "to cut wine" (Isa 1:22). Keil and E. J. Young point out that this semantic development is paralleled in other sources, e.g. Latin, *castrare vinum* and French, *couper du vin.* So much water has been added to the wine that its character has been weakened. The Aramaic word and the Hebrew (if that also means "circumcise") is doubtless a byform of the root *mûl* "to circumcise" (q.v.).

W.C.K.

מַהֲלָךְ (*mahălak*). See no. 498a.
מַהֲלָל (*mahălāl*). See no. 500b.
מַהֲלֻמוֹת (*mahălūmôt*). See no. 502c.
מַהֲמֹרָה (*mahămōrâ*). See no. 509a.
מַהְפֵּכָה (*mahăpēkâ*). See no. 512d.
מַהְפֶּכֶת (*mahpeket*). See no. 512d.

1152 *מָהַר (*māhar*) ***I, hasten,*** used only in the Niphal and Piel.

Derivatives

1152a †מַהֵר (*mahēr*) ***I, speedy, swift*** (adjective).
1152b †מַהֵר (*mahēr*) ***II, quickly*** (adverb).
1152c †מָהִיר (*māhîr*) ***quick.***
1152d †מְהֵרָה (*m^e hērâ*) ***haste.***

The feet of wicked men hasten (*māhar*) to shed blood and practice evil (Prov 1:16; 6:18; Isa 59:7). But God will come and bear prompt or swift witness against their sorcery, adultery, false swearing, poor wages to employees, and poor treatment of the widow, orphan, and stranger (Mal 3:5). To emphasize the swiftness of destruction, Isaiah symbolically names his second child "hasten prey, hurry spoil" (*mahēr-shālālhāshbaz,* Isa 8:1, 3), for God is now prodding on the Assyrians, the ax in his hand, to accomplish his punishment on Israel. In a later day he would bring that bitter and impetuous nation, Babylonia, to do the same thing (Hab 1:6).

Eliphaz lectured Job that God takes the wise in their own craftiness and that the plans of schemers are dissipated (?) (Job 5:13) only to have God heave the first part of his words back on him in Job 42:8 (hence the quotation formula in I Cor 3:19).

This verb usually has an adverbial meaning when it is linked with another verb, e.g. "they quickly forgot his works; they did not wait for his counsel" (Ps 196:13). Distress, however, prompts the prayer, "I am in trouble, hear me speedily" (Ps 69:17 [H 18]; 102:2 [H 3]; 143:7; cf. 79:8).

mahēr ***I. Hastening, swift, speed.*** One of the two occurrences of the adjective is important theologically. Zephaniah 1:14 warns that the day of the Lord is very near and it comes with great speed especially for those who are unprepared or who sigh for it as a panacea for all their troubles (cf. Amos 5:18–20).

mahēr ***II. Quickly, speedily.*** God expresses surprise at how quickly men have turned away from him to build the golden calf (Ex 32:8; Deut 9:16; cf. Jud 2:17). If Israel continued to do evil, they would quickly perish altogether from the land (Deut 4:26) and God's anger would destroy them suddenly (Deut 7:4). But if Israel would faithfully follow the Lord, they would quickly destroy the Canaanites in a major sweep through the land (Deut 9:3). Some of the nations, however, would be put out by God little by little so that the land would not be overrun with wild beasts (Deut 7:22; cf. Jud 2:23).

One proverb warns, "Do not go hastily to a debate, you may not know what to do in the end" (Prov 25:8).

māhîr. ***Quick, prompt.*** "Do you see a man diligent in his business? He shall stand before kings" says Prov 22:29. In its description of the Davidic throne, Isa 16:5 includes prompt justice as one of its characteristics.

m^e^hērâ. ***Haste, speed.*** In Ps 147:15 the word *m^e^ hērâ* is used to show that the Lord's word runs swiftly on the earth, while Isa 58:8 promises that in return for acts of mercy to others, one's health will spring forth speedily. Meanwhile, do not fret over evildoers, for they shall quickly be cut down like grass (Ps 37:2).

W.C.K.

1153 מָהַר (*māhar*) ***II, acquire by paying a purchase price.*** Denominative verb.

1153a †מֹהַר (*mōhar*) ***wedding money.***

The verbal form occurs only twice, in Ps 16:4 and Ex 22:16 [H 15]. The text of Ps 16:4 is difficult. It may mean that "sorrows shall be multiplied [for all] who hasten after another god" or who exchange (by paying a price, BDB).

The fiancé who gives wedding money is not thereby presenting gifts to the family or the girl. These are to be clearly distinguished as in Gen 34:12. The gifts were presents and rewards for accepting the proposal of marriage, but the wedding money was given in addition to these (cf. Rebekah's case in Gen 24:53; also Gen 29:24, 29; Josh 15:18–19; I Kgs 9:16).

mōhar. ***Wedding money, bride price.*** There are only three instances of this word in the Scriptures: Gen 34:12; Ex 22:16; I Sam 18:25. The *mōhar* was a sum of money or its equivalent, which the fiancé paid to the girl's father as a compensation to the family. It was not, strictly speaking, the purchase price, but the customary wedding money. Exodus 21:7–11 illustrates the outright purchase of a maidservant to be a concubine. Note also the penalty for violating a girl's virginity (Deut 22:29). (See the contrast between wedding money and marriage, and refusal of marriage and penalty to a seducer in Ex 22:16–17 [H 15–16]).

Jacob paid in services for his marriages to Leah and Rachel (Gen 29:15–30). David performed a valiant deed in battle for Saul's daughter, Michal (I Sam 18:25–27), just as Othniel did for Caleb's daughter (Josh 15:16). Hamor's son, Shechem, was willing to pay any sum to Jacob for his daughter Dinah (Gen 34:11).

Apparently the father was allowed to enjoy the use of the wedding money, but it would revert to the bride at her father's death or if the death of her husband reduced her to poverty. What else could have prompted the complaint of Rachel and Leah that their father Laban had "devoured their money" after having "sold" them (Gen 31:15)?

The Babylonian law called for the fiancé to pay to the girl's father or sometimes to the girl herself the *tirḫatu,* a sum varying from one to fifty shekels of silver. According to Assyrian law, the *tirḫatu* was given to the girl either as a compensation for her loss of virginity or as insurance in the event that her husband died. Even today among Palestinian Arabs the fiancé pays a *mahr* to the girl's parents.

Bibliography: AI, pp. 26–29. Gaspar, Joseph W., *Social Ideas in the Wisdom Literature of the Old Testament,* Catholic University of America Press, 1947, pp. 7–15.

W.C.K.

מַהֲתַלָּה (*mahătallâ*). See no. 2511a.

1154 מוֹ (*mw*). A paragogic syllable, attached to בְּ, כְּ, לְ, so as to form independent words, בְּמוֹ, כְּמוֹ, לְמוֹ.

מוֹאל (*mô'l*). See no. 1160.

1155 מוֹאָב (*mô'āb*) ***Moab.***

Derivative

1155a †מוֹאָבִי (*mô'ābî*) ***Moabite.***

Lot's son by his elder daughter (Gen 19:37). He became the father of a nation which settled east of the Dead Sea after God dispossessed the previous inhabitants (Emim) because of their unrighteousness (Deut 2:10–11). Moab attempted to hire Baalam to curse Israel (Num 22:3, 4, 7, 8, 10, 14, 21, 36; 23:6, 7, 17; 24:17) and practiced rites of religious prostitution connected with sacrifices to the dead (Num 25:1ff.; cf. Ps 106:28). The prophets directed these messages against Moab: Amos 2:1–3; Isa 15–16; Jer 48; and Ezk 25:8–11. Their god was Chemosh.

mô'ābî. ***Moabite.*** Although the deuteronomic code prohibited a Moabite from entering the congregation of the Lord even to the tenth generation (Deut 23:3 [H 4]), Ruth, a Moabitess, believed in the Lord and became the wife of Boaz and thus a forebear of King David and the Messiah (Ruth 1:22; 2:6; 4:10). David conquered the Moabites. They rebelled after Ahab's death finally gaining independence (II Sam 8:2; II Kgs 3:4–27).

[The Moabite Stone gives Moab's side of this campaign. It says that Moab served Israel "all the days of Omri and half the days of his son, forty years." This has recently been interpreted to mean "half the days of his grandson," i.e. Joram as given in II Kgs 3. The servitude would then include the reign of Omri (twelve years), Ahab (twenty-two years), Ahaziah (two years) and part of Joram (six years). Overlapping years would make the total forty (see D. Cross and N. Freedman, *Early Hebrew Orthography* (American Oriental Society, 1952, p. 39). R.L.H.]

Bibliography: Bartlett, J. R., "The Moabites and Edomites," in *Peoples of OT Times,* Oxford: Clarendon, 1973, pp. 229–58. Van Zyl, A. H., *The Moabites,* Brill, 1960. Wiseman, D. J., "The Moabite Stone," in ZPEB, IV, pp. 267–68.

W.C.K.

1156 מוּג (*mûg*) ***melt.***

So great in power is the Lord, that the earth melts when he touches the land (Amos 9:5). The mountains and hills totter, tremble, and shake at the sound of his voice (Nah 1:5; Ps 46:6 [H 7]; Ps 75:3 [H 4]). As all the forces of heaven and earth fought on the Lord's side in the past, so in the day of the Lord's future, final triumph even nature must tremble at his approach.

If Arabic *māǧa* "surge, be in tumult, totter" is to be connected with our Hebrew root, then "tremble" might be a better meaning especially since it is paralleled by *r'sh* "shake" in Nah 1:5. It serves as a figure of helpless, disorganized terror in the OT. Cathcart points to Jer 4:24 to support this rendering: "I saw the mountains, and lo they were quaking, and all the hills rocked to and fro." But in Mic 1:4 and Ps 97:5 the hills melt like wax. Therefore there must be a combination of ideas: trembling and melting.

God also can soften the earth with showers (Ps 65:10 [H 11] and cause a man's possessions to dissolve (Job 30:22).

Regularly this melting is a figure for the panic-stricken condition which God's judicial acts cause in the heathen: Canaan (Ex 15:15; Josh 2:9, 24), Philistia (I Sam 14:16; Isa 14:31), the earth and its population (Ps 75:3 [H 4]).

However, there is a final day coming when the mountains shall flow with new wine and the hills melt, shake, or wave with corn (Amos 9:13, NEB).

See *môṭ* "totter" for synonyms.

Bibliography: Cathcart, Kevin J., *Nahum in the Light of Northwest Semitic,* Pontifical Biblical Institute, 1973, pp. 52, 96, 104. McCarthy, D. J. "Some Holy War Vocabulary in Joshua 2," CBQ 33: 228–30.

W.C.K.

1157 מוד (*mwd*). **Assumed root of the following.**

1157a †תָּמִיד (*tāmîd*) ***continuity.***

Most frequently this word is used in an adjectival genitive construction with *'ōlâ* for the continual whole burnt offering made to God every morning and evening (Ex 29:42; Num 28:6, 10, 15, 23; Ezr 3:5; Neh 10:34; cf. Ezk 46:15, every morning; and the continual *minḥâ,* Num 4:16; Neh 10:34; Lev 6:13. The word is used alone to designate the daily burnt offering in Dan 8:11–13; 11:31; 12:11. Numbers 4:7 refers to the "bread of continuity" meaning the bread that was always there.

The word is also used adverbially in connection with the cult to denote constancy in cultic duties (e.g., Aaron's breastplate, Ex 28:29–30). Some passages, however, stress constancy of personal devotion, e.g., Hos 12:6 [H 7], "Turn to your God; keep mercy and justice and wait on your God continually." The Psalms likewise urge, let his praises continually be in your mouth (34:1 [H 2]; 71:6), hope continually in the Lord (71:14); let God's truth continually preserve you (40:11 [H 12]); let prayer be made to him continually (72:15), and keep his law continually (119:44). Isaiah promises that the Lord will continually guide those who respond to the social needs about them as evidence of true spirituality. Indeed, "Seek the Lord and his strength, seek his face continually" (I Chr 16:11).

W.C.K.

מוֹדַע (*môda'*). See no. 848e.

1158 מוֹט (*môṭ*) ***totter, shake, slip.***

Derivatives

1158a †מוֹט (*môṭ*) ***shaking, pole, bar of yoke.***

1158b †מוֹטָה (*môṭâ*) ***pole, bar of yoke.***

This verb, which occurs as a figure of speech referring to great insecurity, can also denote dependability and certainty when used of God and prefixed with a negative.

When *môṭ* is used with *regel* "foot," it speaks of the foot slipping or sliding in a time of calamity (Deut 32:35; Ps 38:16 [H 17]; 94:18). In Ps 82:5 this verb depicts general disorder on the earth: "all the foundations of the earth are slipping." It also is used to refer to the instability of dead idols mounted on platforms that are liable to topple over or be picked up and carted off by a conqueror. Isaiah has much sport urging idolatrous Israel to make sure their gods will not be moved (Isa 40:20; 41:7).

Two millennial psalms affirm that "the LORD reigns," therefore the inhabited world (*tēbēl*) cannot be moved (Ps 93:1, I Chr 16:30; Ps 96:10). Since the Lord also laid the foundations of the earth, it will not totter forever and ever (Ps 104:5).

Not as much can be said for the kingdoms of this world; they were moved when the Lord said so (Ps 46:6; note parallel verb *mûg* "to melt"). In a dramatic passage, Isaiah pictures the earth reeling to and fro like a drunkard or a little vineyard hut, (*m*^{e}*lûnâ*, see *mālôn*) in a violent storm. It convulses, reels and shakes violently (Isa 24:19–20) as God's hand moves in judgment just prior to the "many days" (millennium?) of Isa 24:22. David spoke poetically of the earth being split and trembling in need of God's healing when it was shaking (Ps 60:2 [H 4]), but this is probably to be classified with Ps 46:2 [H 3] which allows that even if the earth heaves (*mûr*) and the mountains slip into the heart of the seas, God will still be our refuge and strength. As these passages and Ps 82:5 show, the verb refers to the sudden, unexpected and disastrous shaking of the solid earth. Since this inconstancy is against the order of creation, it is associated with God's wrath. The power of his wrath is evident in such cosmic disorder.

Righteous men are unmoveable and secure, for they have the Lord as their Rock and Salvation (Ps 62:2 [H 3], 6 [H 7]; 112: 6; 15:5; 16:8; 21:7 [H 8]; 30:6 [H 7]). God gives them a hand on the pathway of life so that their footing does not slip (Ps 17:5). The enemy of the righteous will have no cause to rejoice in his being moved (Ps 13:4 [H 5]), for he trusts in the salvation of God.

Such assurance is strengthened even more by the everlastingly secure covenant which God made with Abraham and David. The promise is unconditionally maintained in perpetuity for all who will participate by faith. While the mountains may move (*mûsh*) and the hills shake, God's loyal love will never move (*mûsh*) and his covenant of peace (the new covenant, the Abrahamic and Davidic covenant) will never shake (Isa 54:10). See also *mûsh* "depart, remove" and *mûg* "melt, shake."

môt. ***Pole, bar*** (of the yoke), ***shaking.*** The word *môṭ* is used of shaking and therefore of a carrying pole that shakes as the bearer walks.

In three passages, it is used of a carrying pole such as the one used to carry the tabernacle furnishings (Num 4:10, 12) or the one used by the spies to carry back the grapes, pomegranates, and figs from Canaan (Num 13:23). Concerning the meaning of *môṭ* in Ps 55:22 [H 23], M. Dahood suggests that the word connotes stumbling into the netherworld (i.e. into the jaws of death). In Ps 66:9 it may even be a poetic name for the underworld, "Who has kept us among the living and has not put our foot in the quagmire." While the idea of the netherworld may be overdrawn, the idea of stumbling is not. Nahum 1:13 says, "I will break his yoke" (*shābar* and *môṭâ*); cf. also Jer 28:10–12; Lev 26:13; Ezk 30:18. Probably the *môṭ* is strictly speaking the bar across the animals' necks which becomes a name for the whole yoke.

môṭâ. ***Pole, bar.*** This feminine noun also is used for bars or staves to carry the ark (I Chr 15:15) or figuratively the yoke of oppression (Lev 26:13; Jer 27:2; 28:10, 12, 13; Isa 58:6, 9; Ezk 30:18; 34:27). The most colorful and theologically significant passage is in Jeremiah. The false prophet Hananiah dared to break Jeremiah's real yoke (a symbol of impending Babylonian bondage) only to find himself confronted with another real yoke of iron and a sentence of imminent death which occurred two months later.

It is probable that here belongs Prov 24:11: "Rescue captives from (preposition *lamed*) death, and do not restrain the rods from (preposition *lamed*) killing."

Bibliography: Dahood, M., *Proverbs and Northwest Semitic Philology,* Rome: Pontifical Biblical Institute, 1963, p. 51. *Psalms I,* in AB, pp. 78–79. ______, *Psalms II,* in AB, pp. 38–39.

W.C.K.

1159 מוּךְ (*mûk*) ***be low, depressed, grow poor*** (e.g. Lev 27:8; 25:47).

1160 מוּל (*mûl*) ***I,*** מוֹל (*môl*), מוֹאל (*mô'l*) ***front, in front of.***

1161 מוּל (*mûl*) ***II, circumcise, let oneself be circumcised, be cut off*** (a few forms may be taken as from מָלַל).

Derivative

1161a †מוּלָה (*mûlâ*) ***circumcision.***

The use of the verb in the OT begins in Gen 17. Here the Lord confirms his covenant with Abraham recorded in Gen 12:1–3. The practice of cutting off of the prepuce of the penis was a practice used even before the time of Abraham (Old Kingdom Egyptian tomb art and hieroglyphs *Egyptian Grammar,* A. H. Gardiner, p. 448). It was probably used as it is to this day as a puberty rite marking the passage of a son to the privileges of manhood, a rite sometimes accompanied by licentious overtones. The operation was performed on a boy about thirteen years old. God revealed to Abraham that he was to use this shedding of blood as a sign of the covenant with Abraham. In the OT God ordered the child to be circumcised on the eighth day of his life, removing it from a puberty rite to a sign with strictly religious significance. This infant circumcision seems to have been unique in antiquity. Moderns have proved the practice has hygienic value but there is no place in the OT where this point is made.

Since the practice symbolized God's covenant with Abraham and his descendants, it is from the various aspects of this covenant that circumcision derives its spiritual significance. To those in the OT who took its meaning seriously, it was the mark of submission to the sovereign will of God. As so often happens with religious symbolism, the Hebrews eventually used this sign of a deep spiritual reality as an end in itself and wrongly made of it an automatic entry into the kingdom of God.

The prophets became aware of this perversion and preached against mere circumcision of the flesh, that is, circumcision not accompanied by living faith. Jeremiah spoke of the circumcision of the heart. He said, "Circumcise yourselves to the Lord, and take away the foreskins of your heart, you men of Judah"(Jer 4:4). But long before Jeremiah the people had been warned of this danger. Indeed, Jeremiah was quoting Deut 10:16. The use of the verb in Deut 30:6 proves the statement above, that circumcision symbolized the deepest spiritual reality of the Hebrew religion. The verse says, "The LORD your God will circumcise your heart and the heart of your offspring, so that you will love the LORD your God with all your heart and with all your soul, that you may live." In Mt 22:36–40 our Lord instructed the Pharisees that this was indeed the greatest commandment and the sum and substance of all the law and prophets. The verse in Deut clearly teaches that true circumcision was a work of God in the human heart—the spiritual life God creates in his people. This is precisely the teaching of the apostle Paul in Col 2:11 where speaking of the full deity of Christ he says, "In whom also ye are circumcised with the circumcision made without hands, in putting off the body of the sins of the flesh by the circumcision of Christ." (Cf. also Rom 2:28–29 and 4:9–12.) Because baptism and circumcision both symbolize the regenerative work of God which always included cleansing from sin and love for God, some segments of the church baptize their infants just as God instructed the OT saints to circumcise them. Others in church do not stress this analogy and so baptize only those who profess faith in Christ after reaching the age of discretion.

mûlâ. ***Circumcision.*** This noun is used only once, in Ex 4:26, where Zipporah accused Moses of being a bloody husband because of circumcision. The context makes very clear the importance God placed on circumcision as a sign of God's covenant with his people. Even Moses the lawgiver was not free to neglect circumcising his son. To do so was tantamount to a denial of the covenant.

Bibliography: TDNT, VI, pp. 73–81.

E.B.S.

מוֹלֶדֶת (*môledet*). See no. 867f.
מוּסָב (*mûsāb*). See no. 1455b.
מוּסָד (*mûsād*), מוֹסָד (*môsād*). See nos. 875d,f.
מוּסָךְ (*mûsāk*). See no. 1492b.
מוֹסֵר (*môsēr*). See no. 141f.
מוּסָר (*mûsār*). See no. 877b.
מוֹעֵד (*mô'ēd*), מוֹעָד (*mô'ād*). See nos. 878b,e.
מוּעָדָה (*mû'ādâ*). See no. 878d.
מוּעָף (*mû'āp*). See no. 1581a.
מוֹעֵצָה (*mô'ēṣâ*). See no. 887b.
מוּעָקָה (*mû'āqâ*). See no. 1585b.
מוֹפֵת (*môpēt*). See no. 152a.

1162 מוץ (*mwṣ*). **Assumed root of the following.**
1162a מוֹץ (*môṣ*) ***chaff.***

מוֹצָא (*môṣā'*). See no. 893c.
מוּצָב (*mûṣāb*). See no. 1398d.
מוּצָק (*mûṣāq*). See nos. 897b, 1895c.
מוּצֶקֶת (*mûṣeqet*). See no. 897c.

1163 *מוּק (*mûq*), מִיק (*mîq*) ***mock, deride.*** Occurs only in Ps 73:8, probably in the Hiphil.

מוֹקֵד (*môqēd*). See no. 901b.
מוֹקֵשׁ (*môqēsh*). See no. 906c.

1164 *מוּר (*mûr*) ***change, exchange.*** Used in the Niphal, Hiphil and Hophal only.

Derivative

1164a †תְּמוּרָה (*t^emûrâ*) ***exchange.***

This verb appears in thirteen passages of scripture which deal with various topics. In Mic 2:4, Gog will spoil and change the portion of his people because of their sinfulness. Psalm 46:3 affirms in a hyperbolic phrase, "though the earth be altered," that God is still our refuge and strength. In Ps 15:4, the man who abides by his sworn word and does not change is the kind of man whom God will establish, but as for those who sin against him increasingly, he will change their glory into shame (Hos 4:7). When Israel worshiped the golden calf, they thereby changed their glory (i.e. their glorious God) into a bull that eats grass (Ps 106:20). Israel did what no other nation ever had done. The nations never changed their gods (which were not, after all, gods at all). But Israel changed their glory for that which did not profit at all (Jer 2:11).

A group of texts deals with vowed offerings. Once they have been dedicated to the Lord, they may not be changed good for bad or vice versa. If there is an exchange however, it and the exchange shall be holy to the Lord (Lev 27:10 [four times]; 27:33 [three times]).

t^e^mûrâ. ***Exchange, recompense.*** Two passages merit attention. Job 28:17 says that wisdom cannot be attained in exchange for jewels of fine gold. Ruth 4:7 records the ceremony of land redemption and exchange when Boaz married Ruth on the quitting of all claims by a closer relative.

W.C.K.

1165 מוֹרָג (*môrāg*) ***thresher.***

A piece of farm equipment made of a plank platform. Holes were bored in the bottom of it, through which protruded sharp stones or metal points. It was drawn by one or two animals and weighted down by stones or by the driver as he drove it over stalks of grain. Araunah gave such a piece of equipment to David to use as the wood for his sacrifice on the future holy site (II Sam 24:22; I Chr 21:23).

According to Isa 41:15, however, God will make Israel his threshing sledge to harvest his judgment in the eschaton.

hārûṣ was another type of thresher or disc harrow made of iron. It occurs in a parable (Isa 28:27). Amos mentions it as an instrument of destruction and uses it as a figure of brutality which incited the wrath of God (Amos 1:3).

Bibliography: Corswant, W., *Dictionary of Life in Bible Times,* Oxford University Press, 1960, pp. 279–80. (See the figures in IDB, IV, p. 391, fig. 67; p. 636, fig. 60.)

W.C.K.

מוֹרָד (*môrād*). See no. 909a.

1166 מוֹרָה (*môrâ*) ***razor*** (Jud 13:5; 16:17; I Sam 1:11).

מוֹרָה (*môrâ*). See nos. 907c,d.
מוֹרֶה (*môreh*). See nos. 910b,c.
מוֹרָשׁ (*môrāsh*). See no. 920d.

1167 מוּשׁ (*mûsh*) ***I, depart, remove.***

This term appears twenty times in the OT. It is first used to describe the pillar of cloud and the pillar of fire (the sign of the presence of God in the Israelite camp) which never left its place in front of the people day or night (Ex 13:22). Joshua did not depart from the tabernacle while Moses went into the camp (Ex 33:11). Later, the Lord instructed Joshua that the book of the law was never to depart from his mouth; he was to meditate on it day and night (Josh 1:8).

When Israel attempted to enter Canaan presumptuously, after having accepted the unbelieving majority report of the spies, the ark of the covenant of the Lord did not depart from the camp (Num 14:44).

Isaiah's use of the term is theologically significant. While the mountains will depart (Isa 54:10*a*), God's covenant of peace made with Abraham and David, and the new covenant of Jeremiah will not be removed (Isa 54:10*b*; 59:21). It is permanent! If God's ordinances with the sun, moon, and stars depart, then his promise with Israel will do likewise (Jer 31:36). As of this writing, however, the sun, moon, and stars continue to shine and therefore his covenant promise to Israel continues.

In the final day when the Lord appears a second time, he will remove the iniquity of the land (of Israel) in one day (Zech 3:9). So magnificent will be his appearing that the Mount of Olives will split and one half will remove itself to the north and the other half to the south (Zech 14:4).

Men who trust in the Lord will be like trees planted by a river; they will not cease yielding fruit (Jer 17:8).

W.C.K.

1168 מוּשׁ (*mûsh*) ***II, feel*** (e.g. Gen 27:21; Ps 115:7; Jud 16:26).

מוֹשָׁב (*môshāb*). See no. 922c.
מוֹשָׁעָה (*môshā'â*). See no. 929d.

1169 מוּת (*mût*) ***die, kill, have one executed.***

Derivatives

1169a מָוֶת (*māwet*) ***death, dying, Death (personified), the realm of the dead.***
1169b מָמוֹת (*māmôt*) ***death.***
1169c תְּמוּתָה (*t^e^mûtâ*) ***death.*** Occurs only in phrase *b^e^nê t^e^mûtâ* "children of death," i.e. those worthy of death and appointed to death (Ps 79:11; 102:21).

mût may refer to death by natural causes or to violent death. The latter may be as a penalty or otherwise. The root is not limited to the death of humans although it is used predominantly that way.

This is a universally used Semitic root for dying and death. The Canaanites employed it as the name of the god of death and the netherworld, Mot (cf. ANET, pp. 138–42). In Hebrew it is occasionally used metaphorically as when Job speaks of the death of wisdom (12:2). But the literal demise of the body in death is usually in view. Ezekiel reminds us that God has no pleasure in the death of men, for his purpose was and is that they live (18:32). The normative OT teaching about death is presented in Gen 3:3, where God warns Adam and Eve that death is the result of rebellion against his commands. Since God's purpose for our first parents was never ending life, the introduction of death was an undesirable but a necessary result of disobedience. The physical corruption of the human body and the consequent suffering and pain brought about by the Fall were only the obvious symptoms of death. Death is the consequence and the punishment of sin. It originated with sin. A grand theme of the OT is God's holiness, which separates him from all that is not in harmony with his character. Death, then, in the OT means ultimate separation from God due to sin. And sin is any rebellion or lack of conformity to his holy will. All men then, in a sense, are what the Hebrews would call *bᵉnê māwet* "sons of death"; that is, they deserve to die because they are sinners. This and a related term (*'îsh māwet* "man of death") are used (Ps 79:11; 102:20 [H 21]) of the people of God in captivity who must look to him for deliverance from impending doom.

In Ugaritic (ANET, above) the god Mot was a well-defined figure who ruled the netherworld, a land of slime and filth. He fought with Baal, the god of fertility for which he suffered the displeasure of El, head of the pantheon. Baal, as the provider of fertility, rain, etc., was a hero god to the Canaanites and as such his cult became a distinct snare to the Israelites. The same is not true of Mot, so he was not mentioned in the OT, although some claim to find occasional references to him. M. Dahood (*Psalms,* in AB, XVI, XVII, XVIIa) attempts to read Mot into the Psalmist's references to the foe, but he is not convincing. Jeremiah in one case personifies death, describing it as one who comes in through the windows (9:20). What may be clearer is the use of *māwet* "death" as referring more broadly to the realm of the dead. In Isa 38:18 we read:

> "For Sheol cannot praise you,
> death cannot celebrate you;
> they that go down into the pit cannot hope
> for your truth."

There is certainly room for difference of opinion here, for the place Isaiah has in mind could be either the grave or the realm of the dead. It would appear that Job 38:17 which says, "Have the gates of death been revealed to you?" is a clearer reference to "death" as the realm of the dead. Other passages that may be taken this way are: Isa 28:15, 18; Hos 13:14; Hab 2:5; Ps 6:5; 49:14 [H 15]; and article *lāqaḥ*; Prov 7:27; Job 28:22, etc.

But see *shᵉ'ôl* and R. L. Harris, "The Meaning of Sheol as Shown by Its Parallels," JETS 4:129–35.

This passage in Isa 38:18 leads us to the OT statement that "The earth the Lord hath given to the children of men, but the dead praise not the Lord" (Ps 115:16*b*f.; Isa 38:11; Ps 6:5; 30:10; 88:11ff.). Bultmann notes "After death, then, the righteous are outside the infinitely important sphere of life in which cultic relationship with God is maintained" (TDNT, II, p. 847). However, he is mistaken when he extends this line of thinking to conclude: "Death and its kingdom are outside the stream of power which has subjected all the kingdoms of life to itself" (ibid.). We have shown elsewhere (see *ḥayyim*) that God is the Lord of life and death and that he will conquer death.

In the Mosaic ceremonial law corpses were considered unclean—another indication of the OT attitude toward death as an intruder and the result of sin. The Canaanites on the other hand "normalized" death through the myths of the "godly Mot" who like other gods was subject to appeasement. The Canaanites had rituals which included bodily mutilation and sacrifices for the dead. The Israelites were forbidden to practice such rituals (Deut 14:1). The law of Moses was also designed to protect Israel from one of the vilest effects which the "normalization" of death had on the Canaanites, and that was child sacrifice.

> For everything that is detestable to the LORD
> they have done for their gods,
> even to burning their sons and daughters
> in fire for their gods" (Deut 12:31).

Because of its view of death OT revelation places a high premium on life. A long life is considered a great blessing (Prov 3:2) and an immortal life the ultimate in blessing (Ps 16:11; 21:4 [H 5]; 73:23–26). The Canaanites felt the latter belonged only to the gods (ANET, p. 151, vi).

Contrary to the opinion of many moderns, the OT teaching that requires capital punishment for premeditated murder arose out of a high view of life, not a low view. The same is true of God's order to destroy those people who were committed to the detestable practices mentioned above. Psalm 106:34–38 explains why this is so: Because Israel did not destroy these peoples they learned their practices and sacrificed their own sons and daughters to demons.

Bibliography: Heidel, Alexander, "Death and the Afterlife in the OT," in *The Gilgamesh Epic,* University of Chicago. Richardson, TWB, p. 60. THAT, I, pp. 893–96.

E.B.S.

מוֹתָר (*môtār*). See no. 936g.
מִזְבֵּחַ (*mizbēaḥ*). See no. 522b.

1170 מזג (*mzg*). **Assumed root of the following.**
1170a מֶזֶג (*mezeg*) ***mixture,*** i.e. ***mixed wine.*** Occurs only in Song 7:3, in phrase *'al-yeḥsar hammazeg* "(that) never lacks blended wine."

1171 מזה (*mzh*). **Assumed root of the following.**
1171a מָזֶה (*māzeh*) ***sucked out, empty*** (Deut 32:24; Isa 5:13).

מָזוּ (*māzû*). See no. 534b.
מְזוּזָה (*mᵉzûzâ*). See no. 535b.
מָזוֹן (*māzôn*). See no. 539a.
מָזוֹר (*māzôr*). See nos. 75a, 543c.

1172 מֵזַח (*mēzaḥ*) ***girdle.*** Probably a loan word.
1172a מְזִיחַ (*mᵉzîaḥ*) ***girdle.*** Occurs only in Job 12:21, "loosen the girdle of might," i.e. weaken them, make them defenseless by ungirding.

מַזְלֵג (*mazlēg*). See no. 552a.

1173 מַזָּלוֹת (*mazzālôt*) ***constellations.*** (ASV "planets," RSV similar.)

Appears in II Kgs 23:5 and Job 38:32. The Akkadian cognate refers to the phases of the moon, but the usage of the term in Judaic writings indicates that zodiac constellations are being referred to in Hebrew. In Kings the word is used with reference to the pagan worship of the stars with all such worship's astrological significance. In Job it is used with *kîmâ kᵉsîl* and *'āyish* (the Pleiades, Orion and the Bear, all of which see), to indicate God's creative power and the folly of questioning his wisdom.

G.L.C.

מְזִמָּה (*mᵉzimmâ*). See no. 556c.
מִזְמוֹר (*mizmôr*). See no. 558c.
מַזְמֵרָה (*mazmērâ*). See no. 559c.
מְזַמֶּרֶת (*mᵉzammeret*). See no. 559d.
מִזְעָר (*miz'ār*). See no. 571b.

1174 מזר (*mzr*) **I. Assumed root of the following.**
1174a †מַמְזֵר (*mamzēr*) ***bastard, child of incest.***

Only found in Deut 23:2 [H 3], it is used of an illegitimate child who is refused entrance to the congregation of the Lord until the tenth generation. Zechariah 9:6 may refer to an individual, but more likely it figuratively depicts the mixed population of Ashdod. It is possible that the Deut reference also refers to a child of mixed parentage—Hebrew and pagan.

W.C.K.

1175 מזר (*mzr*) **II. Assumed root of the following.**
1175a מָזוֹר (*māzôr*) ***net.*** Meaning dubious.

מִזְרֶה (*mizreh*). See no. 579a.

1176 מַזָּרוֹת (*mazzārôt*). Occurs only in Job 38:32. Meaning dubious. Perhaps it refers to a particular star or constellation. See *mazzālôt*.

מִזְרָח (*mizrāḥ*). See no. 580c.
מִזְרָע (*mizrā'*). See no. 582f.
מִזְרָק (*mizrāq*). See no. 585f.
מֵחַ (*mēaḥ*), מֹחַ (*mōaḥ*). See nos. 1181a,b.

1177 מָחָא (*māḥā'*) ***strike (=clap the hand,*** e.g. Isa 55:12; Ezk 25:6).

מַחְבֵּא (*maḥbē'*). See no. 588a.
מַחְבֹא (*maḥbō'*). See no. 589a.
מְחַבְּרָה (*mᵉḥabbᵉrâ*). See no. 598k.
מַחְבֶּרֶת (*maḥberet*). See no. 598j.
מַחֲבַת (*maḥăbat*). See no. 600b.
מַחֲגֹרֶת (*maḥăgōret*). See no. 604d.

1178 מָחָה (*māḥâ*) ***I, wipe, wipe out.***

Almost all of the thirty-three occurrences of this verb are theologically significant. It is first found in the flood narrative. Every living thing on the face of the earth that breathed was blotted out (Gen 7:22–23) including all human beings, except eight. *māḥâ* figures prominently in the prayer in which Moses begged God to forgive the sin Israel incurred when they worshiped the golden calf. "If not, blot me out of your book," prays Moses (Ex 32:32–33). It had been God's intention to blot out Israel's name from under heaven (Deut 9:14), as repeated in Deut 29:20 [H 19] (see also Ps 69:28 [H 29]). Whether he regards it thus as a stain (as in Ps 51:3, 11) or a debt in a ledger (as in Col 2:14) is not known with certainty. But he was willing, as was the apostle Paul, to be accursed for the sake of his brethren.

Note that erasures in ancient leather scrolls were made by washing or sponging off the ink rather than blotting. "Wipe out" is therefore more accurate for the idea of expunge.

When God did move in judgment, he wiped Jerusalem as one wipes a dish, wiping it and turning it upside down (II Kgs 21:13). During the time of the judges, the entire tribe of Benjamin was almost blotted out (Jud 21:17).

The sinner prays as David did that God will blot out, i.e. erase his transgressions and iniquities (Ps 51:1 [H 3], 9 [H 11]). God does so for his own sake and remembers those sins no longer (Isa 43:25). Thus sins which loomed as a thick cloud were blotted out (Isa 44:22). While God is omniscient, these sins he deliberately remembers against us no longer. The reverse action can be seen in Ps 109:14, and Neh 4:5 [H 3:37].

māḥâ is also used to describe the lifestyle of an adulterous woman who eats, wipes her mouth, and protestingly claims that she has done no wrong (Prov 30:20).

Then there is the case of the jealous husband who suspected his wife of adultery. As part of the psychological ordeal to which she was subjected in the presence of the Lord, the woman had to drink bitter water into which curses written on a scroll had been wiped in order to determine her innocence or guilt. (Num 5:23).

Finally, Isa 25:8 proclaims that God will wipe away tears from all faces.

W.C.K.

1179 מָחָה (*māḥâ*) ***II, strike.*** Occurs only in Num 34:11, *ûmāḥâ 'al-ketep yam-kinneret* "and (the border) will strike upon (i.e. reach to) the shoulder of the Sea of Kinneret."

Derivative

1179a מְחִי (*m*^e^*ḥî*) ***stroke.*** Occurs only in Ezk 26:9.

מְהוּגָה (*m*^e^*hûgâ*). See no. 615b.

1180 מָחוֹז (*māḥôz*) ***city.*** Loan word from the Akkadian *maḫāzu* "city." Occurs only in Ps 107:30.

מָחוֹל (*māḥôl*). See no. 623g.
מַחֲזֶה (*maḥăzeh*), מֶחֱזָה (*meḥĕzâ*). See nos. 633f,g.

1181 מחח (*mḥḥ*). **Assumed root of the following.**

1181a מֵחַ (*mēaḥ*) ***fatling.***

1181b מֹחַ (*mōaḥ*) ***marrow.*** Occurs only in Job 21:24, where it symbolizes prosperity.

1181c *מָחָה (*māḥâ*). Verb derived from *mōaḥ*. Occurs only in the Pual, in Isa 25:6, *sh*^e^*mānîm m*^e^*mūḥāyim* "fat pieces full of marrow."

מְחִי (*m*^e^*ḥî*). See no. 1179a.
מִחְיָה (*miḥyâ*). See no. 644b.
מְחִיר (*m*^e^*ḥîr*). See no. 1185c.
מַחֲלָה (*maḥălâ*), מַחֲלֶה (*maḥăleh*). See nos. 655c,b.
מְחִלָּה (*m*^e^*ḥillâ*). See no. 660f.
מַחֲלוּיי (*maḥălûy*). See no. 655d.
מַחֲלָף (*maḥălāp*). See no. 666d.
מַחֲלָצָה (*maḥălāṣâ*). See no. 667b.
מַחֲלֹקֶת (*maḥălōqet*). See no. 669d.
מַחְלְקוֹת (*maḥl*^e^*qōt*). See no. 670g.
מַחֲלַת (*maḥlat*). See no. 655 or no. 623h.

1182 מַחֲמָאֹת (*maḥămā'ōt*) ***curd-like.*** Occurs only in Ps 55:21 [H 22]. Perhaps *min* comparative plus *ḥem'â* "curd" (q.v.).

מַחְמַד (*maḥmad*), מַחְמֹד (*maḥmōd*). See nos. 673d,e.
מַחְמָל (*maḥmal*). See no. 676b.
מַחְמֶצֶת (*maḥmeṣet*). See no. 679d.
מַחֲנֶה (*maḥăneh*). See no. 690e.
מַחֲנָק (*maḥănaq*). See no. 697a.
מַחְסֶה (*maḥseh*). See no. 700b.
מַחְסוֹם (*maḥsom*). See no. 702a.
מַחְסוֹר (*maḥsôr*). See no. 705e.

1183 מָחַץ (*māḥaṣ*) ***strike, wound severely.***

Derivative

1183a †מַחַץ (*maḥaṣ*) ***severe wound.***

This word is well attested in Ugaritic poetry. It is found in the OT in parallel pairs with itself (Ps 110:5–6), with *ṣmḥ* "to annihilate" (Ps 18:39–41; note that the two verbs *māḥaṣ* and *sāmaḥ*, both in the first person singular, form an inclusion as in Ugaritic poetry), and with *kly* "to annihilate" (II Sam 22:39; Ps 18:38–39). The blow denoted by *māḥaṣ* is generally lethal and decisive, as Jael's was to Sisera (Jud 5:26).

The Lord will smite kings of many countries in the day of his great wrath (Ps 110:5–6). In fact, he does so even now to all who continue to walk in their sins (Deut 33:11; Ps 68:21 [H 22]). Hence, the kingdom of the ungodly can expect increasing hostilities until the final deliverance of God comes in the end (Hab 3:13). God smites and he heals; "neither is there any that can deliver out of his hand" (Deut 32:39). Even Eliphaz recognized this (Job 5:18). No picture of God moving in his vengeful justice is more vivid than Ps 68:23 [H 24], which portrays God smiting his foot in the blood of his enemies (who have come against a revived nation of Israel in the eschaton). There is a possibility that this verse may be explained by Ps 58:10 [H 11] where the verb is wash (*rāḥaṣ*) the feet in blood. The ancient versions read "wash" also in Ps 68:23 [H 24].

maḥaṣ. ***Severe wound.*** Only Isa 30:26 uses this word. The Lord will heal the blow of the wound that came to his people. This will take place in "that day" when the moon shall be as bright as the sun and the sun shall be seven times more luminous than it is now.

Bibliography: Fisher, Loren, *Ras Shamra Parallels*, I, Pontifical Biblical Institute, 1972, pp. 80, 227, 257–58.

W.C.K.

מַחְצֵב (*maḥṣēb*). See no. 718a.
מֶחֱצָה (*meḥĕṣâ*). See no. 719d.
מַחֲצִית (*maḥăṣît*). See no. 719e.

1184 מָחַק (*māḥaq*) ***annihilate.*** Occurs only in Jud 5:26.

מֶחְקָר (*meḥqār*). See no. 729b.

1185 מחר (*mḥr*). **Assumed root of the following.**
1185a †מָחָר (*māḥār*) ***tomorrow.***
1185b †מָחֳרָת (*moḥŏrāt*) ***the morrow.***
1185c †מְחִיר (*m*ᵉ*ḥîr*) ***hire, price.***

māḥār. ***Tomorrow.*** Occurring fifty-two times, *māḥār* is seldom used substantively, e.g. "tomorrow is the new moon" (I Sam 20:5). In other passages it is used adverbially: "Let us eat and drink, for tomorrow we die" (Isa 22:13) or "Tomorrow the Lord shall do this thing."

Of theological interest is the use of *māḥār* to mean in future time, e.g. Ex 13:14 and Deut 6:20, "When in time to come your sons ask you" (NEB). In Josh 4:6, 21 memorial stones were set so that in future days when the children asked what they meant, the answer could be given. Similarly, the transjordanian tribes feared that the time would come when they would be cut off from the heritage of Israel, so they also erected a memorial (Josh 22:24, 28). Laban and Jacob looked forward not just to the morrow in the sense of the following day, but to time that would come (Gen 30:33). Significantly enough, none of the prophets used this phrase to designate the eschatological era.

Proverbs warns against boasting about what one will do on the morrow (Prov 27:1). Neither should one promise to give tomorrow to a neighbor when he has it to give right then and there (Prov 3:28). God is in charge of our tomorrows, therefore we must be hesitant to plan as if the future were entirely in our hands.

mohŏrāt. ***Tomorrow.*** The most interesting feature about this feminine noun is that "on the morrow of" means after (Lev 23:11, 15, 16; Num 33:3; Josh 5:11). Twice the preposition *l*ᵉ is used before *māhŏrāt* to mean "on the morrow" (Jon 4:7; I Sam 30:17).

mᵉ**ḥîr.** ***Hire, price.*** Relation to above root unclear. This word is used only fifteen times in the OT. Deuteronomy 23:19 prohibits bringing the price of a "dog" (male prostitute) into the house of God. Isaiah 55:1 describes the free offer of God's salvation as being without money and without price. Wisdom cannot be purchased with gold, not at any price (Job 28:15). In a similar vein, Prov 17:16 asks why put a price (tuition?) into the hand of a fool to get wisdom (an education) when you know he has no heart (motivation) in it?

One of the great tragedies in Israel was that the rulers judged for reward, the priests taught for a price or reward and the prophets divined for money (Mic 3:11). Contrariwise, the pagan Cyrus, whom God raised up, released the captives of Israel for no price or reward (Isa 45:13). This is the opposite of Antichrist who will divide the land for personal gain (Dan 11:39).

W.C.K.

מַחֲרָאָה (*maḥărā'â*). See no. 730b.
מַחֲרֵשָׁה (*maḥărēshâ*). See no. 760d.
מָחֳרָת (*mohŏrāt*). See no. 1185b.
מַחְשֹׂף (*maḥśōp*). See no. 766b.
מַחֲשָׁבָה (*maḥăshābâ*). See no. 767d.
מַחְשָׁךְ (*maḥshāk*). See no. 769d.
מַחְתָּה (*maḥtâ*). See no. 777a.
מְחִתָּה (*m*ᵉ*ḥittâ*). See no. 784g.
מַחְתֶּרֶת (*maḥteret*). See no. 783a.
מַטְבֵּחַ (*maṭbēaḥ*). See no. 786e.
מַטֶּה (*maṭṭeh*), מִטָּה (*miṭṭâ*), מֻטֶּה (*mūṭṭeh*). See nos. 1352b,c,e.
מַטְוֶה (*maṭweh*). See no. 794a.
מְטִיל (*m*ᵉ*ṭîl*). See no. 1186a.

1186 מטל (*mṭl*). **Assumed root of the following.**
1186a מְטִיל (*m*ᵉ*ṭîl*) ***wrought metal rod.*** Occurs only in Job 40:18, *m*ᵉ*ṭîl bārzel*. This phrase refers figuratively to the bones of the hippopotamus.

מַטְמוֹן (*maṭmôn*). See no. 811a.
מַטָּע (*maṭṭā'*). See no. 1354c.
מַטְעָם (*maṭ'ām*). See no. 815b.
מִטְפַּחַת (*miṭpaḥat*). See no. 818d.

1187 מָטַר (*māṭar*) ***rain.*** Denominative verb.

Parent Noun

1187a †מָטָר (*māṭār*) ***rain.***

Genesis 2:5 states that the Lord "had not caused it to rain on the ground." The garden was watered by a "mist" or, better, a "river" (Harris, R. L., "The Mist, the Canopy and the Rivers of Eden," JETS 11:177–80). These statements explain why there were no "plants of the cultivated land" (perhaps thorns arising from rain action) or "herbs of the cultivated land" (perhaps cereal grains? cf. Gen 3:18).

Destructive rain from God fell on the earth in the flood of Noah's day (Gen 7:4). God rained down hail on the unbelieving Pharaoh (Ex 9:23), and fire and brimstone on Sodom and Gomorrah (Gen 19:24). He will yet rain down great hailstones, fire, and brimstone on Gog and his hordes in that great concluding battle of history

(Ezk 38:22). Such a prospect is in view for all the wicked (Ps 11:6).

The connection between man's spiritual condition and the amount and timing of the rainfall is seen in passages like Amos 4:7. When man's heart is right with God, he graciously gives the command to the clouds and they refresh the earth (Isa 5:6), just as he graciously rained manna on Israel in the wilderness (Ex 16:4; Ps 78:24).

māṭār. ***Rain.*** The rain (in some thirty-eight references) is never to be taken for granted by mankind; it comes from the hand of God (Ps 147:8; Job 5:10; 28:26; 36:27) in amounts proportionate to the spiritual condition of the inhabitants of that land (Deut 11:11, 15 [H 14]. When men love the Lord their God and serve him with all their heart and soul (Deut 11:13), he sends rain on their land in its regular season (Deut 11:14; 28:12). But when they turn and go after other gods, the rain is shut off in heaven. Men and beasts languish (Deut 11:17) and the land is turned into powder and dust (Deut 28:24). Thus the condition of the promised land was itself a witness to the spiritual life of the people.

It may be noted that the Bible does not support the fanciful cosmology often attributed to it. The "windows of heaven" (Gen 7:11) are more accurately translated "sluice gates" (cf. *ḥallôn* and the reference there to *'ărubbâ*). The Hebrews knew from observation that rain comes from clouds (Isa 5:6; I Kgs 18:44).

The prophets pointed to the rain as a sign for the people of God's anger or favor (Isa 5:6; 30:23; Amos 4:7; Zech 10:1). Rain that fell during the wheat harvest was a sign of God's judgment, for it came out of season and at the worst moment possible (I Sam 12:17–18). Solomon prayed that God would open the heavens, closed by the people's sin, after they had called upon him in prayer (I Kgs 8:36; see also II Chr 6:27). Elijah had just such a prayer ministry (I Kgs 18:1). Indeed at the very juncture in history when Israel chose to worship Baal the storm god (I Kgs 16-:31–32), Elijah appeared with the warning, "There will be neither dew nor rain these years except by my words" (I Kgs 17:1).

Waiting for the rain became proverbial: like a man waiting for the rain with his mouth held open wide (Job 29:23). It is also used in similes: the Messiah will come down like rain on the mown grass (Ps 72:6). He will dawn on them as the tender grass shining after the rain (II Sam 23:4). In that day a tabernacle will provide shelter from the storm and rain (Isa 4:6).

Rain accompanied by thunder was sent on the Egyptians as a sign of supernatural power during the plagues (Ex 9:33–34; cf. Deut 11:10). There are three occurrences of the statement, "He causes the vapors to ascend from the ends of the earth; he makes lightnings with rain, and brings the wind out of his treasures" (Ps 135:7; Jer 10:13; 51:16).

Bibliography: Baly, Denis, *The Geography of the Bible,* Harper, 1957, pp. 41–52.

W.C.K.

מַטָּרָה (*maṭṭārâ*). See no. 1356a.

1188 מַי (*may*) ***water,*** מַיִם (*mayim*) ***waters.***

Found only in the plural form, it occurs some 580 times. The theological importance of water may be discussed in terms of its historical, ritual, metaphorical, and eschatological aspects. The scarcity of water in Palestine explains the numerous references in the OT to man's quest for water.

Historical Aspects

The waters of heaven and earth were created by God. In an all-embracing summary, Ps 104 relates that God created the waters in the clouds (v. 3) and on the earth (v. 6). He controls their boundaries (vv. 7–9), appoints springs to break out on the earth (v. 10), and rain to fall at his bidding (v. 13), thereby fructifying the earth and gladdening the heart of man (vv. 11–18).

Many liberal critics draw a crude picture of biblical cosmology in which the "waters on high" are held back by a solid firmament, being permitted to fall to the earth through "windows" (see the drawing after S. H. Hooke in ZPEB, I, p. 395). Actually, this is a strange mixture of mistranslation and misuse of poetic imagery. The biblical account depicts Elohim creating the upper waters, the watery clouds of heaven, and the lower waters by the word of his mouth (Gen 1:7, 9). An "expanse" (rather than the Greek and Latin derivative "firmament") was created between the two bodies (Gen 1:6). No idea of hardness, dome-like effect or solidity is attached here. Rather, as in Ezk 1 and 10, it is merely a separating expanse. Neither are the lower waters, especially the "deep" of Gen 1:2 (*t^ehôm*) to be connected with any primeval deep or mythological monster of chaos. *t^ehôm* is a good Canaanite word for the sea, cf. Ugaritic (UT 19: no. 2537) just as the "waters under the earth" (Ex 20:4; Deut 4:18; 5:8) are not necessarily infernal, but simply water below the shoreline in which men can fish. Likewise the "windows of heaven" (Gen 7:11; 8:2) are metaphorical representations, for on other occasions these same "windows" pour forth grain (II Kgs 7:2), blessings, perhaps shekels (Mal 3:10), and trouble (Isa 24:18). (See *'ărubbâ* in article on *ḥallôn.*)

God is also the regulator and dispenser of all the waters: he causes the rains to fall "in time" (Lev 26:4; Deut 28:12). He opens the floodgates in judgment (Gen 7:17–20) and closes them (Gen

8:2–3). But even the normal flow of rivers (Num 24:6) and the presence of wells and springs (Gen 16:14; Ex 15:23, 27) continue to be his concern. His ability to provide water was proved by the provision of water in the wilderness.

One of the factors controlling the dispersement and availability of water is the conduct of man. Water is withheld from covenant breakers, lawless and disobedient peoples (Lev 26:19; Deut 28:23; Amos 4:7; I Kgs 18:18), but given graciously as a sign of the blessing of God to that nation or city which obeys the voice of God.

This divine mastery and ownership is demonstrated in the flood of Noah's day (Gen 7), the Red Sea deliverance (Ex 15:1–18), the Jordan River crossing (Josh 3:16; 4:18), and Elijah's crossing of the Jordan (II Kgs 2:8). Thus the waters of the Red Sea distinguish between the people of God and hardened idolaters, while the waters of the Jordan recognize the authoritative command of its ruler's messengers. Likewise water sprang from the rock for a thirsty nation at the word of God's servant Moses (Ex 17:1–7; Num 20:1–13; Ps 78:16, 20; Isa 48:21).

Ritual Aspects

Various ritual ablutions were performed to symbolize inner moral purity, preparation for meeting or worshiping God, and innocence. Ritual washing was required in the case of ordination (Ex 29:4; Lev 8:6), the high priest's preparation for the Day of Atonement (Lev 16:4, 24), leprosy (Lev 14:5–7, 50–52), sexual emissions (Lev 15:13), and contact with a corpse. While the rites in theselelves were powerless to bring about inner moral purity, they signified one's prior inner state of purity and his sense of God's holiness.

There is one use of water in a kind of psychological ordeal (Num 5:11–31) which has no known parallels in the ancient near east. That is the trial of jealousy. (A true ordeal in the near east involved physical danger from which an innocent person was supposed to be delivered, e.g. being thrown into a river. In the Middle Ages, handling hot iron or walking through fire was supposed to be a test of innocence. The Bible contains no examples of this kind of ordeal.)

If a jealous husband suspected his wife of adultery (there being no witnesses), he could bring her before the priest. He (the priest) then sprinkled dust from the sanctuary floor over a vessel of water, thereby making it "bitter water." The woman was required to repeat a formula of curses which the priest wrote on a scroll and then washed into the bitter water. No doubt the resulting effect on the woman's body, after she drank the water, was psychosomatic, God using the mind and emotions to produce the signs that indicated guilt or innocence. Jeremiah refers to this ordeal when he announces (8:14; 9:15 [H 14]; 23:15) that all Israel is due to drink "bitter" or "poisoned" water.

Water also plays an important role in the ritual performed in the case of an unsolved murder. Those living closest to the scene of the crime were required to wash their hands over a sacrificed heifer (Deut 21:1–9) in order to cleanse the area, which probably gave rise to the custom of washing one's hands in innocence (Ps 26:6; 73:13; cf. Mt 27:24).

The OT never encouraged "refreshment" (or "pouring out water") for the dead as some would argue from Deut 26:14; I Sam 7:6; Jer 16:7. Neither did it connect water with magic, for Deut 18:9–14 is clearly against all such practices. Joseph's cup of divination (Gen 44:5) is a case of deception to fool his brothers based on the idolatrous practice of hydromancy.

Metaphorical Aspects

Water is an element in many metaphors. The desire for God, he who is the source of "living water" (Jer 2:13), is like a deer's thirst for water (Ps 42:1 [H 2]). Consequently, all who drink of him (Isa 55:1–2) are "like a watered garden and like a spring of water, whose waters fail not" (Isa 58:11) or like trees by the river of waters (Ps 1:3; Jer 17:8). Apart from God, man is like a dry, waterless land doomed to die (Ps 143:6).

In the realm of marriage, sexual enjoyment with one's own wife is likened to drinking "living water" from one's own well (Prov 5:15; Song 4:15), while harlotry involves drinking "stolen waters" (Prov 9:17).

Other figures depict a fearful heart as melting and becoming water (Josh 7:5), the knowledge of God as wide and broad as the waters of the seas (Hab 2:14; Isa 11:9), and death as the spilling of water (II Sam 14:14; Ps 22:14 [H 15]). Distress is likened to much water (II Sam 22:17) or deep waters (Ps 69:3, 15).

Great rivers symbolize imperial powers that can swamp other nations; thus the Euphrates (Isa 8:7) and the Nile (Jer 46:7–8). God used these "rivers" to punish his people.

Eschatological Aspects

When Israel is restored to their land in a new exodus, God will again miraculously refresh his people by watering the old desert (Isa 35:6–7; 43:20) and by changing the land into a garden showplace (Isa 41:17–20), although some hold that this passage refers metaphorically to the spiritual refreshment of his people. Paradise will be restored when a river from the temple in Jerusalem will flow down toward the Dead Sea. The trees lining its banks will be a source of life and healing (Ezk 47:1–12; Zech 14:8).

In the coming messianic era, God will grant rain in its season (Ezk 34:26) so that thirst and want are forgotten (Isa 49:10; Jer 31:9). The Lord will "sprinkle clean water" on the restored tribes and they will be purified of all their filthiness (Ezk 36:24–25).

Bibliography: Harris, R. L., "The Bible and Cosmology," JETS 5:11–17. Reymond, Philippe, "L'eau, sa vie, et sa signification dans l'Ancien Testament," Supp VT, 1958. Richardson, TWB, pp. 279–80. TDNT, VIII, pp. 317–22.

W.C.K.

1189 מִי (*mî*) ***who.***

Whereas *mâ* "what?" inquires after the character or quality of things and sometimes persons, *mî* "who?" usually refers to persons and seeks only the identity, ancestry, or some external fact.

mî is used with personal association in thirty-six passages, e.g. Gen 24:65 in which Rebekah asks Eliezer, "Who is this man walking toward us?" He answers, "It is my master." Pharaoh asks Moses and Aaron, "Who precisely is to go?" (Ex 10:8). The reply is, "All" (Ex 10:9). David, astounded by the announcement of God's grace to him, cried out, "Who am I, O Lord Yahweh and what (*mî*) is my house (dynasty)?" (II Sam 7:18). Other passages demonstrating the same idea are: Ex 15:11; 32:26; Deut 3:24; 4:7–8; 5:26; 20:5–8; Jud 9:28, 38; 10:18; 21:5, 8; I Sam 18:18; 25:10; II Sam 7:23; 22:32; II Kgs 6:11; 9:5; I Chr 17:21; Job 5:1; 34:7; Ps 24:8, 10; 25:13; 34:12 [H 13]; 89:48 [H 49]; Isa 48:14; 50:1; Ezk 27:32.

Some believe that Ex 3:11; II Chr 2:6 [H 5] and Gen 33:8 are exceptions to the rule just announced. However, Moses asks in Ex 3:11, "Who am I to go to Pharaoh?" Apparently he is just claiming to be a nobody. He is not referring to his character, but rather to his ancestry. Likewise Solomon asks in II Chr 2:6 [H 5], "Who is able to build [God] a house?" and "Who am I then?" His ancestry in light of the greatness of the task is nothing. He assumes a stance of humility, as did his father David (II Sam 7:18). When Esau asks Jacob, "What (*mî*) was all that company of yours that I met?", he refers only to its size, not its potential or character. When Mic 1:5 asks, "What (*mî*) is the transgression of Jacob?" and "What (*mî*) are the high places of Judah?" it is calling only for an identity or list of sins and high places; their character and meaning is transparently evil.

Bibliography: Motyer, J. A., *The Revelation of the Divine Name,* London: Tyndale, 1959, pp. 19–20.

W.C.K.

מֵיטָב (*mêṭāb*). See no. 863a.

1190 מִיכָל (*mîkāl*) **brook** (meaning dubious). Occurs only in phrase *mîkal hammāyim* (II Sam 17:20).

1191 מִין (*myn*), מוּן (*mwn*). **Assumed root of the following.**

1191a †מִין (*mîn*) ***kind.***

1191b †תְּמוּנָה (*tᵉmûnâ*) ***likeness, form.***

mîn. ***Kind.*** The word *mîn* occurs in thirty-one passages (chiefly Gen 1, 6, 7; Lev 11; Deut 14), thirty of which belong to Moses' Pentateuch. The other one is Ezk 47:10.

The etymology of *mîn* cannot be established with certainty. Ludwig Koehler would have it come from the noun *tᵉmûnâ* "form" with some such meaning as "to think out" or "to invent." Skinner's *International Critical Commentary* on Genesis rejects this line of reasoning and selects rather an Arabic root meaning "to split (the earth in plowing)," with the resulting idea of dividing.

Three significant grammatical points are noted by Barton Payne: 1. *mîn* is always used with the preposition *lᵉ* "to" or "in respect to, according to" and thereby provides specification or, in Driver's phrase, "technical enumeration." 2. *mîn* always occurs in the singular form even though English translations sometimes render it as plural (Ezk 47:10, KJV). But it is in fact a collective noun giving the generic form in each case. 3. *mîn* always is followed by one of five suffixal pronominal endings. Affixation of these endings strongly suggests that each form has his, her, or its own generic group to which it belongs by order of the creator.

Some have argued that when God created *mîn,* he thereby fixed the "species." This is a gratuitous assumption because a link between the word *mîn* with the biologist's descriptive term species cannot be substantiated, and because there are as many definitions of species as there are biologists.

In light of the distinctions made in Gen 1, such as the distinction between herbs and grasses which are, however, members of the same class (Angiosperms), it is possible that in some cases the biblical term *mîn* may indicate a broader group, such as an order. Elsewhere, in Lev 11:14, 15, 16, 19, 22 (four times), 29, *mîn* appears consistently as equivalent to nothing broader than genus. However, Lev 11:4 "the falcon after its kind," and 11:16 "the hawk after its kind," refer to divisions within the order Falconiformes, yet both have subdivisions called *mîn.* Likewise, as Payne points out, the locust, bald locust, cricket, and grasshopper all belong to the order Orthoptera and the locust, bald locust, and grasshopper belong to the family Acridiidae, but again each has its subdivisions called *mîn* (genus?).

God created the basic forms of life called *mîn*

which can be classified according to modern biologists and zoologists as sometimes species, sometimes genus, sometimes family or order. This gives no support to the classical evolutionist view which requires developments across kingdom, phyla, and classes.

t^e^mûnâ. ***Likeness, form.*** A nocturnal apparition of a spirit with an undiscernible form (Job 4:16). In Num 12:8, Moses witnesses the similitude of the Lord, i..e., his passing-by glory (see Ex 33:22; also Ps 17:15 of the Psalmist's wish to see God when he awakes). Elsewhere men are warned against making images in the likeness of anything which God created (Ex 20:4; Deut 5:8; 4:16, 23, 25).

Bibliography: Payne, J. Barton, "The Concept of 'Kinds' in Scripture," JASA 10:17–19. TDNT, I, pp. 181–82.

W.C.K.

1192 מִיץ (*myṣ*). **Assumed root of the following.**

1192a מֵץ (*mēṣ*) ***squeezer, i.e. oppressor*** (Isa 16:4).

1192b מִיץ (*mîṣ*) ***squeezing, pressing, wringing*** (Prov 30:33).

מִיק (*mîq*). See no. 1163.
מִישָׁר (*mîshār*), מִישׁוֹר (*mîshôr*). See nos. 930e,f.
מֵיתָר (*mîtār*). See no. 936h.
מַכְאוֹב (*mak'ôb*). See no. 940b.
מַכְבֵּר (*makbēr*), מִכְבָּר (*makbār*). See nos. 948c,d.
מַכָּה (*makkâ*). See no. 1364d.
מִכְוָה (*mikwâ*). See no. 961c.
מָכוֹן (*mākôn*). See no. 964c.

1193 מָכַךְ (*mākak*) ***be low, humiliated*** (Ps 106:43; Eccl 10:18; Job 24:24).

מִכְלָה (*miklâ*). See nos. 980c, 982d.
מִכְלוֹל (*miklôl*), מַכְלֻל (*maklūl*), מִכְלָל (*miklāl*). See nos. 985c,d,e.
מַכֹּלֶת (*makkōlet*). See no. 85g.
מִכְמָן (*mikmān*). See no. 991a.
מִכְמֶרֶת (*mikmeret*), מִכְמֹרֶת (*mikmōret*). See nos. 995c,d.
מִכְנָס (*miknās*). See no. 1000a.
מֶכֶס (*mekes*). See no. 1014a.
מִכְסֶה (*mikseh*), מְכַסֶּה (*m^e^kasseh*). See nos. 1008c,d.
מַכְפֵּלָה (*makpēlâ*). See no. 1019b.

1194 מָכַר (*mākar*) ***sell.***

Derivatives

1194a †מֶכֶר (*meker*) ***merchandise.***
1194b †מִמְכָּר (*mimkār*) ***sale, ware.***
1194c מִמְכֶּרֶת (*mimkeret*) ***sale.*** Occurs only in Lev 25:42.
1194d מְכֵרָה (*m^e^kērâ*) ***swords.***

One of the central teachings of the OT is that God, his people, and the real estate which he gave to them belonged together. Since God remained the sole owner of the land, he attached certain conditions to the Israelites' occupation of it. One condition was that the land was not to be sold permanently (Lev 25:23). If someone became so poor that he had to sell his property, his nearest kinsman was to redeem it (Lev 25:25). If he had no kinsman, and never recovered sufficient means to buy it back himself, it remained in the hands of the purchaser until the year of Jubilee. In that year, the seventh seven, every family was to return to its ancestral possession. The law of Jubilee was the first land reform in history.

Selling fellow Israelites into slavery was prohibited (Ex 21:16; Deut 24:7; Joel 3:3 [H 4:3]; Amos 2:6; Neh 5:8; Zech 11:5). They could, however, sell themselves, i.e. their services and work, but their servitude was terminated in the seventh year (Deut 15:12) and in the year of Jubilee, when all servants went free (Lev 25:39, 40, 47, 48, 50; Deut 15:12; Jer 34:14). Also in the sabbatical year debts were cancelled (Deut 15:1–3).

The Lord sold his people into the power of their enemies when he became displeased with them (Deut 32:30; 28:68; Ps 44:12 [H 13]; Isa 50:1; Ezk 30:12). Actually, the Israelites sold themselves: for nothing! But God would yet redeem them without money (Isa 52:3). I Sam 12:9 spells it out, "When they forgot the Lord their God, then he sold them...," which happened repeatedly during the time of the judges (Jud 2:14; 3:8; 4:2; 10:7).

Joseph was sold by his brothers to the Ishmaelites who in turn sold him into Egyptian slavery (Gen 37:27, 28, 36; 45:4). But when Joseph revealed his identity to his astonished brothers he said, "Be not grieved, not angry, with yourselves that you sold me here, for God sent me ahead of you to preserve life" (Gen 45:5) and more pointedly in Gen 50:20, "You devised it for evil but God planned it for my good."

Esau sold his birthright (Gen 25:31, 33). Thus he forfeited his right to be the chief heir for a little soup. The Nuzu tablets (*c.* 1500 B.C.) witness two other cases of men yielding inheritance rights to a younger brother for some immediate temporal consideration.

One passage uses the verb figuratively, "buying the truth and selling it not" (Prov 23:23). Perhaps the Israelite king, Ahab, illustrates that passage, since "he sold himself to work wickedness" under the instigation of his pagan wife,

Jezebel (I Kgs 21:20, 25). Unfortunately, the same could be said for all Israel (II Kgs 17:17): completely committed and sold out to accomplish wickedness!

meker. ***Value.*** Used in four passages, only one of which is significant here. Proverbs 31:10 mentions the "virtuous woman," who has a value far above rubies. The reason is apparent from the description given of her in the context.

mimkār. ***Sale, ware.*** Most of the passages using *mimkār* deal with the sale or things sold as collateral and how one goes about redeeming them in the year of Jubilee (Lev 25:14, 27, 29, 33, 50; see also Neh 13:20).

Bibliography: Vaux, R. de, AI, pp. 164–66; 175–77. Harris, R. L. *Man: God's Eternal Creation,* Moody, 1973, pp. 137–38.

W.C.K.

מַכָּר (*makkār*). See no. 1368f.
מִכְרֶה (*mikreh*), מְכֻרָה (*mᵉkūrâ*). See nos. 1033b,c.
מִכְשׁוֹל (*mikshôl*), מַכְשֵׁלָה (*makshēlâ*). See nos.1050c,d.
מִכְתָּב (*miktāb*). See no. 1053c.
מְכִתָּה (*mᵉkittâ*). See no. 1062b.
מִכְתָּם (*miktām*). See no. 1056a.
מַכְתֵּשׁ (*maktēsh*). See no. 1061a.

1195 מָלֵא (*mālē'*) ***be full, to fill.***

Derivatives

1195a מְלֹא (*mālē'*) ***fullness, that which fills.***
1195b †מְלֹא (*mᵉlō'*) ***fullness.***
1195c מְלֵאָה (*mᵉlē'â*) ***fullness, full produce.***
1195d מִלֻּאָה (*millū'â*) ***setting of jewel.***
1195e מִלּוּא (*millû'*), מִלֻּא (*millū'*) ***setting, installation.***
1195f מִלֵּאת (*millē't*) ***setting, border, rim.*** Meaning dubious.

Examination of 249 occurrences of this verb (in the Qal and Niphal) reveals that it can have either a spatial signification or by extension the important theological concept of temporal signification.

The spatial signification is found in Ex 10:6, the locusts filling the houses, Joel 3:13 [H 4:13], the winepress full of juice, and II Kgs 4:6, the widow pouring oil into empty vessels until they are full.

The temporal signification is seen in the completion of a fixed time, e.g. the days of Rebekah's pregnancy, which were fulfilled when she gave birth (Gen 25:25), the seven days that had elapsed, i.e., ended, were full after the Lord struck the Nile (Ex 7:25), and the three weeks which were completed while Daniel fasted (Dan 10:3).

Even more significant is the use of this term to represent the omnipresence of God: "Do not I fill heaven and earth? says the Lord" (Jer 23:24). He is not only universally present and fills the whole earth with his glory (Num 14:21; Ps 72:19; Isa 6:3), but he is also locally visible by his glory (*kābôd*) in the cloud which fills the tabernacle (Ex 40:34–35; I Kgs 8:10–11; Isa 6:1; Ezk 10:3; 43:5; 44:4).

This term is also used of God's ability to finish a work begun or accomplish a word promised. The Piel form of *ml'* seems to emphasize the fulfillment of utterances.

Men fulfill their words when they practice idolatry as they said they would (Jer 44:25). When Solomon expelled Abiathar from his priesthood, Eli's words were fulfilled (I Kgs 2:27) just as Jeremiah's words were fulfilled by the seventy-year exile (II Chr 36:21). God acted to fulfill his word spoken to David when he built the temple (I Kgs 8:15, 24; II Chr 6:4, 15). God will also act to fulfill the counsel and petition of his Messiah (Ps 20:4, 5 [H 5, 6]).

Von Rad lists other theological terms that show how the Lord's prophetic word functioned in history: "does not fail" (*lō'-nāpal* Josh 24:45 [H 43]; 23:14; I Kgs 8:56; II Kgs 10:10); "it will be established" (*qûm,* I Sam 1:23; 15:11, 13; II Sam 7:25; I Kgs 2:4; 6:12); "it comes to pass" (*bô',* Josh 23:15); cf. also Ezk 12:25, 28, "Thus has the Lord Yahweh spoken: None of my words will be delayed any longer; the word which I speak is performed, says the Lord, Yahweh" (*Theology of the Old Testament,* II, p. 94).

The Piel form of *mālē'* is also used to denote a period of time, i.e. number of days (Gen 29:27–28), years (II Chr 36:21) or length of gestation (Job 39:2) which must be completed. Consequently, the emphasis is not to be placed solely on the predicted word, but also on the faithful God who will achieve, perfect, and do what was said: The time between the prediction and its fulfillment contains significant happenings which evidence this same powerful and faithful God who continues to fill chronological time (*chronos*) with opportune moments (*kairoi*). This belongs generically to that final achievement of all that the word promised (cf. NT *pleroun,* Heb. *kālâ,* Gr. *teleō,* Heb. *tāman,* Gr. *teleō*). Interestingly enough, Moule, citing J. A. Fitzmyer, says that "Qumran literature lacks both the fulfillment formula found in Matthew and also the 'pattern' in the use of the Old Testament . . . [found] in the New Testament . . . [and] scarcely any examples of the use of *ml'* in a phrase referring to the confirmation or completion of God's promises or plan" ("Fulfillment-Words in the New Testament," p. 309).

In figurative expressions, the earth is often portrayed as full of violence (Gen 6:13; Mic 6:12;

Jer 23:10; 51:5; Ezk 7:22) and sometimes as full of the glory, mercy, goodness, and knowledge of the Lord (Ps 33:5; 119:64; Isa 11:9; Hab 3:3). The land can be filled with sin (Jer 16:18; Ezk 8:17). "To fill one's hand" (with sacrifices) is "to consecrate" one's service (I Chr 29:5; Ex 32:29) or a priest (Jud 17:5). Likewise to fulfill the desire of a man is "to satisfy" him (Ex 15:9).

m^e^lō'. ***Fullness.*** It means "what fills up" a large number. Gen 48:19 has Jacob predict that Joseph's son Ephraim would become a multitude of nations or as the NEB has it, "a whole nation in themselves" just as Isa 31:4 speaks of a mass or multitude of shepherds.

Most frequently this word is used with land and speaks of the fullness or the entire contents belonging to the Lord (Deut 33:16; Ps 24:1) or to the threatening invader (Mic 1:2; Amos 6:8 [i.e. of the city]; Jer 8:16; 47:2; Ezk 12:19; 19:7). But when Isaiah witnessed the vision of his call, the whole earth was full of his glory (Isa 6:3).

The Lord claims all the inhabited world (*tēbēl*) as his own along with all of its contents (Ps 50:12; 89:11 [H 12]; 98:7; Isa 42:10; I Chr 16:32). Indeed, even the sea is invited to sing and roar in praise to the Lord with all of its contents (Ps 96:11).

The other significant theological usage occurs in the reference to the homer-full of manna stored in the presence of the Lord, in the ark (Ex 16:33).

Bibliography: Childs, Brevard S., "Prophecy and Fulfillment," *Interpretation* 12:259–71. Moule, C. F. D., "Fulfillment-Words in the New Testament—Use and Abuse," NTS 14:308ff. Fitzmyer, J. A., "The Use of Explicit O.T. Quotations in Qumran Literature and in the NT," NTS 7:297ff. Richardson, TWB, pp. 87–88. THAT, I, pp. 897–99.

W.C.K.

מַלְאָךְ (*mal'āk*), מַלְאָכוּת (*mal'ākût*). See nos. 1068a,c.
מִלֵּאת (*millē't*). See no. 1195f.
מַלְבֵּן (*malbēn*). See no. 1074i.
מַלְבּוּשׁ (*malbûsh*). See no. 1075b.
מִלָּה (*millâ*). See no. 1201a.
מִלּוּא (*millû'*). See no. 1195e.
מַלּוּחַ (*mallûaḥ*). See no. 1197c.
מְלוּכָה (*m^e^lûkâ*). See no. 1199d.
מָלוֹן (*mālôn*). See no. 1096a.

1196 *מָלַח (*mālaḥ*) ***I, tear away, dissipate.*** Occurs only in the Niphal, in Isa 51:6, *shāmayim ke'āshān nimlāḥû* "the heavens will vanish like smoke" (NIV).

Derivative

1196a מֶלַח (*melaḥ*) ***rag*** (Jer 38:11–12).

1197 מָלַח (*mālaḥ*) ***II, salt, season.*** Denominative verb.

Parent Noun

1197a †מֶלַח (*melaḥ*) ***salt.***
1197b מְלֵחָה (*m^e^lēḥâ*) ***saltiness, barrenness.***
1197c מַלּוּחַ (*mallûaḥ*) ***mallow, a plant which grows in salt marshes*** (Job 30:4).
1197d מַלָּח (*mallāḥ*) ***mariner.***

Only three passages use this denominative verb. According to Lev 2:13, the meal offering is to be seasoned with salt. In Ex 30:35 the ingredients used in compounding incense were to be salted (KJV, "tempered together").

Nowhere does there occur the aspect of entering into friendly relations by eating bread and salt together. Arab society to this day retains such expressions as "there is salt between us" or "I love you as I love salt."

The third passage is Ezk 16:4, which uses a Hophal perfect and infinitive absolute to describe a newborn baby being rubbed or washed with salt. Probably this is merely to cleanse and heal the child rather than to establish any covenant [of salt] between the newborn and God. We may hope the salt solution was dilute!

melaḥ. ***Salt.*** Various uses of salt are mentioned in twenty-eight passages of the OT. It was obtained from large quarries located on the southwest side of the Dead Sea (Gen 19:26; Ezk 47:11; Zeph 2:9). In Job 6:6 it is mentioned as a condiment. Salt and oil were always mixed with the meal offering (Lev 2:13). Ezekiel 43:24 notes that the priest will cast salt on the burnt offerings of the millennial age. The incense offering, the symbol of public worship to God, must also be "seasoned with salt" (Ex 30:35). Some hold that salt in these offerings represents that which prevents putrefaction, while honey and leaven do not prevent it and were excluded for that reason. Others point out that the use of salt as a preservative is not clear in the Bible. The burnt offerings, at least, were not to be kept and incense does not putrefy. Therefore the use of salt in these offerings may be a matter of seasoning or of dedication, for salt was an item of value. Honey, on the other hand, does not easily putrefy.

The term "covenant of salt" is applied to the perpetual statute by which revenue was to be given to the priests (Num 18:19), and to the covenant established with David whereby he was accorded an everlasting reign over Israel (II Chr 13:5). These relationships are thereby designated as irrevocable and binding (see also Lev 2:13).

The preservative qualities of salt are perhaps seen in the prophet Elisha's using it to purify the spring at Jericho (II Kgs 2:20–21), though the efficacy here was miraculous. On the other hand, salt was scattered over the site of a city devoted to God for destruction (Jud 9:45) which thus became the symbol of barrenness and desolation (see also Deut 29:23 [H 22]; Job 39:6; Zeph 2:9).

Bibliography: Corswant, W., *A Dictionary of Life in Bible Times*, Oxford University Press, 1960, pp. 233–34. Ross, J. F., "Salt," in IDB, IV, p. 167.

W.C.K.

מִלְחָמָה (*milḥāmâ*). See no. 1104c.

1198 *מָלַט (*mālaṭ*) ***be delivered, escape (Niphal), deliver, save (Piel).*** ASV and RSV similar. BDB "slip away."

Derivative

1198a מֶלֶט (*meleṭ*) ***clay (flooring).*** RSV mortar. Occurs only in Jer 43:9, an object lesson of the coming destruction of Egypt.

mlṭ is one word of the cluster that includes *gā'al, yāsha', nāṣal, pālaṭ* and *shālôm*. These words are translated in the LXX by several Greek words: *sōzō* (including *diasōzō* and *anasōzō*) about seventy times, *hryomai* eight times, and *exaireō* five times. This distribution suggests that they have similar meanings with somewhat different emphases.

Although *mālaṭ* may denote escape from court services to see one's relatives (I Sam 20:29) or deliverance of the needy from affliction (Job 29:12), the most prominent facet of meaning is of deliverance or escape from the threat of death, either at the hands of a personal enemy (I Sam 19:11; 23:13) or a national enemy (II Sam 19:10), or by sickness (Ps 107:20).

The usual emphasis is on the role of Yahweh in deliverance (particularly parallelling the LXX *hryomai*; Ps 116:4; 107:20; 22:5 [H 6]). His salvation is for the righteous (Prov 28:26; Job 22:30) but his judgment on sin cannot be escaped (I Kgs 19:17; Amos 2:14–15). Deliverance is possible only for those who call on him (Joel 2:32 [H 3:5]). He is the protecting, delivering God. By contrast, escape is not found in the strength of a horse (Ps 33:17), the might of another nation (Isa 21:6), riches (Job 20:20), or in one's own understanding.

Bibliography: TDNT, VII, pp. 971–73, 978–80; VI, pp. 998–1003.

G.L.C.

מְלִילָה (*m^e lîlâ*). See no. 1202.
מְלִיצָה (*m^e lîṣâ*). See no. 1113b.

1199 מָלַךְ (*mālak*) ***I, be, become king or queen, reign.*** Denominative verb.

Parent Noun

1199a †מֶלֶךְ (*melek*) ***king.***
1199b †מַלְכָּה (*malkâ*) ***queen.***
1199c †מְלֶכֶת (*m^e leket*) ***queen.***
1199d מְלוּכָה (*m^e lûkâ*) ***kingship, royalty.***
1199e מַלְכוּת (*malkût*) ***sovereign power.***
1199f מַמְלָכָה (*mamlākâ*) ***sovereignty.***
1199g מַמְלָכוּת (*mamlākût*) ***sovereignty.***
1199h †מֹלֶךְ (*mōlek*) ***Molech, a pagan god.***
1199i †מַלְכִּי-צֶדֶק (*malkî-ṣedeq*) ***Melchizedek.***

Since Semitic nouns are usually derived from verbs, the reverse is always a signal to look to the noun for the essential meaning. *mālak*, though employed over three hundred times, appears only in Qal and Hiphil stems (except for one Hophal, Dan 9:1). The meaning of the Qal (over two hundred times) is always "to reign," i.e. to be and exercise functions of a monarch, whether male (king) or female (queen).

The normal sense of the Hiphil of *mālak* would be to cause to be king (or queen) and such is the case—"make king, cause to reign." This can be the act of inauguration by anointing (II Sam 2:9; 5:17) or anointing *and* crowning (II Chr 23:11). It can also be the act of God or men in exalting a man to such an office, the ceremony not being considered (I Sam 15:35; I Kgs 12:20). The Hophal, employed only once, at Dan 9:1, seems specifically to indicate that Darius was not regarded by the author, Daniel, as supreme monarch of the Medo-Persian empire but rather was made (passive voice) sub-*melek* at Babylon, an important but secondary, city and area of the realm.

melek. ***King.*** Since the Bible was written when sovereignty (seat of authority) in civil government was viewed somewhat differently than it is today, officials and functionaries whom men today would designate by other titles (commandant, governor, chieftain, etc.) are regularly designated *melek*. That thirty-one columns, averaging about eighty-five entries per column, are devoted in *Englishman's Hebrew and Chaldee Concordance* to this word is an indication of its prevalence in the OT.

melek is simply the most common word for chief magistrate and is similar in meaning to several other words usually translated lord, captain, ruler, prince, chief and such like: *nāgîd, nādîb, nāsîk, nāsî', qāṣîn, rōzēn* (always pl.), *śar* (very frequent). As nearly as can be determined, none of these terms is consistently employed in the Hebrew Scriptures to designate a well-defined office. Conclusions based on the use of one or another of them are precarious, as for example that *nāgîd* always designates Gentile rather than Israelite magistrates or the other way around.

The essential theology of the OT with reference

to *melek* (king) is not to be obtained merely by examining the over 2500 occurrences of the word. Rather we must examine the OT idea of magistracy, i.e., of civil authority. Underlying all civil society was *consuetudinary,* i.e. common or customary law. No state then (including the Mosaic) or now could operate by statutory laws alone. Furthermore, civil government was the rule of magistrates. They were rulers (*śarîm*) in a greater sense than are rulers in the West today. For though responsible to statutory law and to custom, part of the custom was to rely simply on decisions of the magistrate—for whom there are many designations (see above)—to supply whatever leadership, control, and support people expected from their government. Government, therefore, in a degree much greater than in any Western land, was rule by just (hopefully) men rather than by laws that were just.

Proverbs 8:15–16 supplies a locus of materials for our search for a theology of the king or supreme magistrate: "By me [wisdom] kings reign, And princes decree justice. By me rulers rule, And nobles, even all the judges of the earth." The least definite is king, the first. Let the four others amplify the idea of kingship. "Princes" (singular *rōzēn*) occurs only six times, always in poetry. By reference to a cognate Arabic word it is understood to mean one who is "weighty, grave, firm of judgment"— incapable of being shaken, of majestic repose, dignified in speech and action as befits one invested with great power. "Rulers" (*śārîm*), a common word means head man, one of recognized authority in whatever realm he operates ("powers that be," Rom 12:1). There is no metaphor when leading merchants are denominated princes (*śārîm,* Isa 22:8). Certain angels are called *śārîm* (Dan 10:13, 21). "Nobles" (sing. *nādîb*) is one inclined toward liberality, of noble character, hence also of position. "Judges" (sing. *shōpēt* < *shāpat* q.v.) is perhaps the most comprehensive term for one who exercises civil authority, whether executive, judicial, or legislative. A sixth word, *nāgîd* is a favorite name for Hebrew kings, twice occurring in Prov (8:6; 28:16), means one who stands in front.

These are the main OT ideas about kings and other rulers. Though rulers were to be benign, the idea of democracy, that authority moves from people to rulers, is difficult to find in the Bible. Rulers were thought to be constituted by divine authority rather than human. To come before the judge was to come before God (Ex 22:8, 9 [H 7–8]). It is to be observed that in Ex 22:9 [H 8], *'ĕlōhîm* must be rendered magistrates (pl.) rather than God (sing.), for the verb *yarshî'ūn* is Hiphil third person masculine plural of *rāsha'* "to condemn."

The term *melek* appears in modified form in almost every Semitic language with approximately the same meaning (BDB in loc.). The Hebrew idea was shared everywhere in oriental antiquity.

We must guard against assigning consistent technical meaning to *melek,* even when clearly literally intended. It can mean emperor (of an empire) as in the case of Nebuchadrezzar king of Babylon (Jer 46:2), or one of an emperor's vassals as in the case of Jehoiakim, king of Judah (Jer 46:2) or the chieftain of a tiny city-state such as the Canaanite and Philistine towns (e.g., Gen 14:2–8; 20:2; 26:1, 8; many times in Josh). One of a joint-rulership or, possibly, triumvirate such as we now know Belshazzar to have been (Dan 5:11, Aram. equivalent to Heb. here) or a subordinate governor of a province as Darius ruler over Babylon under Cyrus emperor of Persia (Dan 5:30) might likewise be called *melek.*

Two important related matters must be noted.

1. *The place of kingship in Israel.* There was no magistrate called King in Israel in earliest times. Civil authority was wielded in patriarchal times by tribal elders, in early years of the settlement, by village and tribal elders. During the time of the *shōphᵉṭîm* (usually, but misleadingly, rendered "judges") there were temporary charismatic (in the proper sense: by divine gift) heads of tribal alliances. But ancient ideas of monarchy usually (but not invariably) associated dynasty with kingship. The books of Samuel tell the story of the first effort, against the express will of God, to establish a permanent national monarchy. Though dynasty was desired by the house of Saul, Providence prevented it. But kingship had been anticipated in Mosaic Law (Deut 17:14–20; 28:36) and God established David and his dynasty forever over Israel. As Bright says, "The theology of Davidic kingship is best seen in the royal psalms [Royal psalms include: Ps 2; 18 (II Sam, ch. 22); 20; 21; 45; 72; 89; 101; 110; 132; 144:1–11], which, though they cannot be dated precisely, are all preexilic and for the most part relatively early. Its classical expression, however, is in the oracle of Nathan (II Sam 7:4–17), a piece undoubtedly developing an ancient nucleus (cf. also II Sam 6; I Kgs 8). It is also found in the old poem of II Sam 23:1–7, ascribed to David himself. The tradition is by no means incredible: cf. O. Procksh, "Die letzten Worte Davids" (BWANT, 13 [1913], pp. 112–125); A. R. Johnson, *Sacral Kingship in Ancient Israel* (Cardiff, University of Wales Press, 1955, p. 15)—where there is further bibliography. The substance of this theology is that Yahweh's choice of Zion and the Davidic house is eternal (Ps 89:3 [H 4]; 132:11–14): though kings might for their sins be chastened, the dynasty would never be cut off (II Sam 7:14–16; Ps 89:19–37 [H 20–38]). The king ruled as Yahweh's "son" (Ps 2:7; II Sam 7:14), his "first-born" (Ps 89:27 [H 28]), his "anointed"

(Ps 2:2; 18:50 [H 51] [H 7]; 20:6). Because he was established by Yahweh in Zion, no foe would prevail against him (Ps 2:1–6; 18:31–45 [H 32–46] [H 8–13]; 21:7–12; 132: 17 f.; 144:10 f.); on the contrary, foreign nations would submit to his rule (Ps 2:7–12; 18:44 [H 45]f.; 72:8–11). The Davidic covenant developed the pattern of the patriarchal covenant, in that it was based in Yahweh's unconditional promises for the future [See G. E. Mendenhall, *Law and Covenant in Israel and the Ancient Near East* (The Biblical Colloquium, 1955)]" (John Bright, *A History of Israel*, Westminster, 1959, p. 204).

2. *The relation of king and the national religion and ritual (cult).* As seen above, the king was a sacred person—he ruled in a divinely appointed estate and by divine authority (see also R. D. Culver, *Toward a Biblical View of Civil Government*, Moody, 1975, pp. 41–55, 74–76, 87, 88, 123, 129, 169, 170, 251). But he had no place in the priesthood. To intrude into that holy office was regarded as grossest sin (cf. the case of Saul's invasion of the priest's office, I Sam 13:1–14).

There is a school of radical biblical-historical thought which asserts that Israel's practice of kingship, being borrowed from the pagan neighbors (II Sam 8, esp. v. 20), involved also a pagan theory and a ritual pattern to express it, supposed to be common in the ancient near east. According to this view the king, being in theory a divine king, became the central figure in an annual new year festival, dramatically enacting the dying and rising again (as the seasons) of the fertility deity. Therein the king ritually (as a sort of *pontifex maximus*, high priest) re-enacted the struggle of creation, subsequent victory over the powers of chaos, and a sacred marriage and then re-assumed his actual throne. All this, it is said, was to ensure the spring revival of nature and the fruitfulness of field and flock for another annual cycle of the seasons, as well as stable government for the year. This theory is stoutly maintained with variations by a large number of scholars (A. Bentzen, *King and Messiah* [Eng. tr., London: Lutterworth Press, 1955]; I. Engnell, *Studies in Divine Kingship in the Ancient Near East* [Uppsala: Almqvist and Wiksells, 1943]; S. H. Hooke, ed., *Myth and Ritual* [London: Oxford Univ. Press, 1933]; *The Labyrinth* [London: S.P.C.K., 1935]; G. Widengren, *Sacrales Koenigtum im Alten Testament und im Judentum* [Stuttgart: W. Kohlhammer, 1955]). But though many of the psalms are alleged by these writers to reflect the annual ritual described above, the theory is really without a shred of biblical evidence and there are scholars who throw much doubt on the whole idea (See bibliography, especially Frankfort who points out that although the king was deified in Egypt he was not in Mesopotamia, with rare exceptions.)

malkâ. ***Queen,*** except for twice in plural at Song 6:8–9 always of foreigners, sometimes apparently head of state (I Kgs 10:1), more frequently a king's consort (Est 1:9; 2:22). In the case of females: Athaliah, (II Kgs 11:3; II Chr 22:12), Esther (Est 2:4), Vashti (Est 1:9), and Nebuchadnezzar's consort (Dan 5:10), the circumstances vary the meaning. In the former the usurping, murderous grandmother employs power illegitimately. The latter exercised no civil power at all, being only the favored consort of the *melek*. As a *malkâ*, Esther had no monarchial power but only such as her social position as king's consort supplied. Of the thirty-three (thirty-five with Aramaic of Dan 5:10) appearances of *malkâ*, all save two (Song 6:8–9) refer to queens of foreign lands. The "queen" in oriental antiquity was not usually the king's wife and she was not usually a reigning person, so the name for her position was not normally the feminine form of *melek* but rather *g*ᵉ*bîrâ*, meaning great lady (I Kgs 11:19; 15:13; II Chr 15:16; Jer 13:18; 29:2). The "queen (*m*ᵉ*leket*) of heaven" (Jer 7:18; 44:17, 18, 19, 25) was a pagan female deity worshiped at Jerusalem. The word may be a proper name. (Also, rarely, *sârâ*, and *shēgāl*, are used of kings' consorts).

mᵉleket. Infrequent difficult form indicating a certain pagan queen of heaven (Jer 7:18).

mōlek. ***Molech*** (KJV, followed by most modern versions) or ***molek.*** The name found in the Hebrew Bible for the pagan male deity, presumably borrowed from Israel's neighbors, to whom apostate Israelites sacrificed infants in the valley of Hinnom immediately south of Jerusalem. The consonants, *mlk*, are the word *melek* "(divine) king," while the vowels are those which the Masoretes, following immemorial custom, supplied from the Hebrew word *boshet* "shame." Just what the synagogue reader, say in Jesus' time, may have read—*bosheth*, *melek* or *molek*—is hard to say. It is even rendered *moloch* (μολοχ) in the LXX, which also renders it "their king" (I Kgs 11:7 [H 5]) and "the king Moloch" (Jer 32:35 [H 39:25]).

Molech (= *Milcam*) was a favorite of the Ammonites, worshiped by human sacrifice (I Kgs 11:5; II Kgs 23:10; Jer 32:35) but the god and the dreadful practice of infant sacrifice in his honor were carried by northern Canaanite (Phoenician, Punic) people throughout the Mediterranean area. Waltke (ZPEB, V, pp. 269–70) gives an excellent discussion and bibliography as also Helmbold (WBE, II, pp. 705–6). *National Geographic* provides a popular description of the Phoenicians and their worship of Baal-Maloch (August 1974, pp. 166–67).

In biblical thought Moloch is connected forever with the ultimate in apostate worship of a false *melek* by the people who should have worshipped only Jehovah "their king" [*Milcam*]. The two worst apostates among the kings of Israel and Judah, Ahab and Manasseh, promoted it in the ravine later called *Gehenna* (NT) which became the name thereby of eternal hellfire. See II Kgs 16:3; II Chr 28:3; II Kgs 26:6; II Chr 33:68, *vid.* also Jer 7:31; 32:15). Pious horror of the practice, with lurid—perhaps accurate description—is to be found in Jewish sources. David Kimchi says the image of Moloch was of brass and was hollow. A fire was kindled within the idol. When the extended hands became hot, Moloch's priest taking the babe from its father's hand, placed it in Moloch's hands to the accompaniment of drums to prevent the father from hearing the screams of his dying offspring (comments on II Kgs 23:10).

For further study cf. YGC pp. 234–244. Albright's view is that the *mōlech* sacrifice was not to a god *molech,* but was the royal sacrifice, i.e. the extreme sacrifice of infants. It was common in Carthage. Albright gives credit to Israel's higher standards for the diminishing of the practice in her neighbor Phoenicia.

malkî-ṣedeq. ***Melchizedek.*** This name occurs only in Gen 14:18 and Ps 110:4. Formed from *melek* "king" and *ṣedeq* "righteous," with the transitional hireq yod. Whether it indicates a construct (possessive) relation or the first personal singular pronominal suffix is a matter of dispute. If the former were true, the name would mean "king of righteous [one?]"; if the latter, "my king is righteous." "Salem" almost certainly refers to Jerusalem. The geography of the campaign in Gen 14 allows it. The similarity of "Adonizedek," king of Jerusalem (Josh 10:1) supports it. Comparison with David, king of Jerusalem (Ps 110:4), cements the connection with Jerusalem. The appearance of Melchizedek in the Bible is important theologically. It lends strong support for the notion that knowledge of the true God possessed by Noah and his sons did not die out. Monotheist Abraham (Gen 18:25) forthrightly acknowledged Melchizedek as priest of the same *'ēl 'elyôn* "God Most High," whom Abraham worshipped (Gen 14:18–20). We simply do not know how many Melchizedek-like persons, under more stress than Lot (II Pet 2:6–8), survived the pervasive idolatry of the ancient world. We inevitably think of Job. There were the monotheistic-like views of the fourth century B.C. philosophers of Athens and of Akhenaton, youthful pharaoh of Egypt who lived a millennium earlier. Similar sentiments were expressed in Vedic literature. In the person of Melchizedek we find evidence of an ancient near eastern tradition of true worship at Jerusalem long before Ornan the Jebusite transferred title of the rocky "Mount Moriah" to the crown (II Sam 24:18–25; I Chr 21:18–30). Perhaps Moses knew already something of "the place which the LORD your God shall choose" for the central sanctuary (Deut 12:5). The book of Hebrews, building on the announcement of Messiah's non-Aaronic priesthood in Psalm 110 elaborates the doctrine of our Lord's completely successful priesthood on this textual basis (Heb 6:20; 7:1–8:13).

Bibliography: Bright, J., *A History of Israel,* Westminster, pp. 204–207. Frankfort, H., *Kingship and the Gods,* University of Chicago, 1948, pp. 317ff. ———, *The Problem of Similarity in Ancient Near Eastern Religions,* Oxford: Clarendon, 1951. TDNT, I, pp. 565–74; IV, pp. 568–69. THAT, I, pp. 908–19.

R.D.C.

1200 *מָלַךְ (*mālak*) ***II, counsel, advise.*** Occurs only in the Niphal, in Neh 5:7, "I consulted with myself."

מַלְכֹּדֶת (*mal^{e}kōdet*). See no. 1115b.
מַלְכִּי־צֶדֶק (*malkî-ṣedeq*) See no. 1199i.
מְלֶכֶת (*m^{e}leket*), מַלְכוּת (*malkût*). See nos. 1199c,e.

1201 *מָלַל (*mālal*) ***I, say, utter, speak.***

Derivative

1201a †מִלָּה (*millâ*) ***word, speech.***

mālal occurs only on the lips of Sarah, Bildad, Elihu, and a psalmist (Gen 21:7; Job 33:3; 8:2; Ps 106:2) and only in the Piel. Its major synonym is *dābar*(q.v.).

millâ. ***Word, speaking, speech, talking, by word, what to say, anything to say, answer, matter;*** in the Aramaic of Daniel: thing, words, matter, commandment.

millâ occurs thirty-four times in Job, once in II Sam, twice in Ps, once in Prov, and twenty-four times in Daniel. There seems to be no discernible difference in usage between *millâ* and *dābār* through *millâ* might relate more to word as expression and *dābār* as meaning.

In the first three verses of II Sam 23 four words for speech occur including *millâ* (v. 2), "his word was in my tongue." In Prov 23:9 "the wisdom of thy words," *millâ* is parallel with *dābār* (v. 8). For the revelation of God (Ps 19) among the terms used is *millâ* (v. 4), "words to the end of the world." The Psalmist in 139:4 says God's knowledge extends to every word on the Psalmist's tongue.

In Job (KJV) *millâ* is "words" nineteen times, "speech" or "speeches" six times, "speaking" twice, while "talking, byword, matter, anything to say, answer, to speak, what to say" each once—all speaking of the arguments advanced by Job and his friends.

In Daniel *millâ* refers to the substance of dreams, the interpretation of dreams, or to various official statements, decrees or verdicts. Of the twenty-four references only seven are translated by "word" or "words," while "thing" or "things" occur eleven times, "matter" five and "commandment" once.

E.S.K.

1202 מָלַל (*mālal*) ***II, rub, scrape*** (Prov 6:13).

Derivative

1202a מְלִילָה (*m*ᵉ*lîlâ*) ***ear of wheat.*** Occurs only in Deut 23:26.

1203 מָלַל (*mālal*) ***III, languish, wither, fade*** (e.g. Job 18:16; 24:24).

1204 מָלַל (*mālal*) ***IV, circumcise,*** a by-form of *mûl* (Josh 5:2; Gen 17:11, Ps 58:8).

מַלְמָד (*milmād*). See no. 1116b.
מַלְקוֹחַ (*malkôaḥ*). See no. 1124b.
מַלְקוֹשׁ (*malqôsh*). See no. 1127b.
מֶלְקָחַיִם (*melqāḥîm*). See no. 1124d.
מֶלְתָּחָה (*meltāḥâ*). See no. 1132a.
מַלְתָּעָה (*maltā'â*). See no. 2513d.

1205 *מָלַץ (*mālaṣ*) ***be smooth, slippery.*** Occurs only in the Niphal, in Ps 119:103, *māh-niml*ᵉ*ṣû 'imrāteḵâ* "how smooth (i.e. pleasant) are your words to my palate."

1206 מֶלְצַר (*melṣār*) ***guardian*** (Dan 1:11, 16). A Babylonian title, meaning dubious.

1207 מָלַק (*mālaq*) ***nip, nip off*** (Lev 1:15; 5:8).

מַמְגֻּרוֹת (*mamgūrôt*). See no. 330e.
מֵמַד (*mēmad*). See no. 1146c.
מָמוֹת (*māmôt*). See no. 1169b.
מַמְזֵר (*mamzēr*). See no. 1174a.
מִמְכָּר (*mimkār*). See no. 1194b.
מִמְכֶּרֶת (*mimkeret*). See no. 1194c.
מַמְלָכָה (*mamlākâ*), מַמְלָכוּת (*mamlākût*). See nos. 1199f,g.
מִמְסָךְ (*mimsāk*). See no. 1220b.
מֶמֶר (*memer*). See no. 1248j.

1208 מַמְרֵא (*mamrē'*) ***Mamre,*** LXX Mambrē.

This name first appears in Gen 13:18 as the site where Abraham settled after his separation from Lot. Genesis 14:13, 24, make it evident that at this time the area was not a town, but the personal property of an Amorite named Mamre. He and his two brothers Eshcol and Aner had entered an alliance with Abraham against the confederacy that had captured Lot. The relationship seems to have been mutually beneficial—use of the land in exchange for military support (Gen 14:13).

The site is usually identified with Râmat el-Khalîl (Ḥalul) about two miles north of Hebron, just east of the main road, although the traditional location of the Cave of Machpelah "east of Mamre" which became the patriarchal tomb (Gen 23:19–20; 25:9; 35:27; 49:30; 50:13), is in the city of Hebron itself.

Mamre was the place where Abraham received the promise of Isaac's birth (Gen 18:1–15) and the destruction of Sodom and Gomorrah (cf. Heb 13:2). It was not this event, however, that made the site a holy place. Abraham had already built an altar to Yahweh at his campground (Gen 13:18).

Bibliography: Mader, E., *Mambre* (Ḥaram Râmat el-Halîl), 2 vols., 1957. Vaux, Roland de, *Supplement au Dictionnaire de la Bible,* 1957, cols. 753–758, figs. 542–43. Masterman, E. W. G., "Mamre," in ISBE, III, pp. 1973–74.

G.L.C.

מַמְרוֹר (*mamrôr*). See no. 1248k.
מִמְשַׁח (*mimshaḥ*). See no. 1255d.
מִמְשָׁל (*mimshāl*). See no. 1259b.
מִמְשָׁק (*mimshāq*). See no. 1261b.
מַמְתַקִּים (*mamtaqqîm*). See no. 1268d.

1209 מָן (*mān*) ***I, manna.***

Manna was the basic food of the Israelites during their wilderness wanderings. It occurred along with the miraculous provision of water and quail. The English spelling "manna" is derived from the LXX. In Ex 16:14 the LXX reads "man" but elsewhere "manna."

Although manna played a crucial role in the life of the Israelites, the word appears only fourteen times in the OT, all but four of them occurring in Ex 16, Num 11, and Deut 8. Manna is called the "bread" from God (*leḥem,* Ex 16:15), "food" from heaven (*d*ᵉ *gan,* Ps 78:24, ASV), and "angel's food" (*leḥem 'abbîrîm,* Ps 78:25). The translation "angel's food," while picturesque, is not accurate. The ASV "bread of the mighty" is preferable. There is no other instance of "angel" being used to translate *'abbîrîm.* "Mighty" or "strong" is more usual, and fits the parallel structure of the Psalm better. Possibly it could be "bread of God" using the word *'ābîr* (q.v.) as a surrogate for deity (cf. Jn 6:33).

The Israelites ate manna from the middle of the second month after the Exodus (Ex 16) until the day of their arrival in Canaan (Josh 5:12; Ex 16:35). Only the portion preserved by Aaron in the tabernacle remained after that time. According to Deut 8:3, 16, the purpose of the giving of the manna was to teach God's people to depend upon him and his words for their lives and their needs. If the Word of God is his creative instrument in bringing the cosmos into existence (Gen 1:3ff; Ps 33:6, 9), then here too what God utters from his mouth is concretely realized. Man can only survive by depending on his saving creative Word. (Note the use of Deut 8:3 by Jesus in his response to Satan's temptation to turn stones to bread in Mt 4:4 and Lk 4:4. John 6 develops at length the role of Jesus as the true manna.)

There have been many attempts to identify manna with some natural edible substance found in western Sinai. The most widely held theory identifies the manna with a secretion from the tamarisk tree (*Tamarix gallica*). Certain types of insects puncture the bark and small, sticky, light-colored drops of sap crystallize on the twigs or drop to the ground. In the cool of the morning, before the hot sun melts them, these sweet particles can be gathered and eaten. There are obvious resemblances between this natural phenomenon and the biblical manna: both appear in the morning "with the dew" (Num 11:9); the material looks like small white globules or flakes (Ex 16:14, 31; Num 11:7; the description "appearance of bdellium" was interpreted by the rabbi's as "like pearls," LXX *krystallos*); the taste is sweet, "like wafers made with honey and oil" (Ex 16:31; Num 11:8); and both substances melt in the sun (Ex 16:21).

However, there are also differences between these two substances. Manna could be ground or milled, baked or boiled (Ex 16:23; Num 11:8); the tamarisk secretion cannot be processed this way. Only on the sabbath could the manna be kept for more than a day without becoming wormy. The tamarisk secretion occurs only for a few weeks in the summer, while manna was a daily provision for forty years in the Negeb as well as western Sinai, suddenly ceasing when Israel entered Canaan. This suggests that in fact the manna was a miraculous provision for the nation.

G.L.C.

1210 מָן (*mān*) ***II, what, who, whomsoever.***

Exodus 16:15 contains the only use in the Hebrew OT of the interrogative pronoun *mān*. The KJV, ASV (marg), and RSV (marg) translate *mān-hû'* as "it is manna," while KJV (marg) and the texts of ASV and RSV translate "what is it?" The comment "they did not know what it was" indicates that the ASV and RSV translation is to be preferred over the KJV. Most contemporary scholars follow BDB in identifying *mān* as a late popular etmology of *mān* "manna" based on the late Aramaic usage. *mān* is not the common OT word for "what," but this usage is not unknown in the second millenium B.C. UT 19: no. 1504 lists several occurrences of *mn(m)*, both personal "who" and impersonal "what." It appears that *mān* "what" is a common Semitic word—not a "popular etymology. (See also Huffmon, Herbert B., *Amorite Personal Names in the Mari Texts*, Johns Hopkins, 1965, pp. 103, 231.)

Bibliography: TDNT, IV, pp. 462–65.

G.L.C.

1211 מֵן (*mēn*) ***string of harp*** (Ps 150:4).

1212 מִן (*min*) ***from, out of, more than.***

This ubiquitous preposition has cognates in Aramaic and Arabic, but is not found in Ugaritic. There the meaning "from" is found in the prepositions *b* and *l*. In form, the preposition is often attached to its noun with the nun assimilated and the next letter doubled (if it is not a laryngeal). When used with light pronoun endings it is usually reduplicated (e.g. *mimmennî* "from me").

The many usages may be briefly classified, but various nuances will be adopted in translation.

First "from." With verbs of motion or separation; to go from, or to be away from, i.e. without; or away from in relation to some other spot or direction, therefore: on the east or beside a city.

Second, with other verbs, it means out of, e.g. out of Egypt. It is used for material out of which something is made. Allied with this is the causal force: to shake from the noise, or on account of our transgressions.

Third is the partitive *min:* He took some of, or even, one of. This last becomes anyone, a single hair, etc.

Fourth, used of time it usually means time from when, e.g. from antiquity. From of old can be used to mean in olden time.

Fifth, *min* is often used in comparisons to mean more than, above, beyond, etc., sometimes too much for, too great for.

Sixth, it may be prefixed to an infinitive in which case its causal force or consequential meaning comes out: because he knew, so as not to give. If the verb "to be" is understood: from being king, i.e. not to be king.

Like other Hebrew prepositions it is used in many combinations. *min* plus *'ad* means literally from . . . to, or inclusively, both this and that. *min* combines with *'et* "with," with *l* "to." Sometimes when the *l* precedes it practically loses its own force and just means "when," i.e. time from when.

b and *l* include the meaning "from" in Hebrew as well as in Ugaritic. An interesting case of the interchange is II Sam 22:14, "He thundered from the heavens," which has *min* but *b* in the parallel in Ps 18:13 [H 14] but two verses later the situation is reversed. N. Sarna has remarked that this usage of *b* for *min* was held by medieval Jewish grammarians before Ugaritic was discovered ("The Interchangeability of the Prepositions Beth and Min in Biblical Hebrew," JBL 78:310–16). It is not so clear that *min* can mean "in," though Dahood argues that it does (AB, *Psalms III,* pp. 395–96).

R.L.H.

מֵן (*mēn*). See no. 1215a.
מַנְגִּינָה (*mangînâ*). See no. 1291.1b.

1213 מָנָה (*mānâ*) ***count, number, tell, appoint, prepare.***

Derivatives

1213a †מָנָה (*mānâ*) ***portion, part.***
1213b †מָנֶה (*māneh*) ***pound, maneh, mina.***
1213c מֹנֶה (*mōneh*) ***counted number, time.***
1213d †מְנָת (*mᵉnāt*) ***portion.***
1213e †מְנִי (*mᵉnî*) ***number.***
1213f מָנוֹן (*mānôn*) ***grief.***

The primary meaning in the Qal and Niphal is "to count or number." The intensive stems place heavier stress on the idea of appointing or assigning. *mānâ* occurs in parallel with *sāpar* (q.v.). The root plus its derivatives occurs some fifty-five times, not counting six uses of the Aramaic cognate *mᵉnā'* or *mᵉnâ*.

The normal use of the root in the Qal and Niphal is in the context of arithmetical computations of various sorts. People (II Sam 24:1), money (II Kgs 12:11), animals (Jer 33:13), stars (Ps 147:4), days (Ps 90:12), dust (Gen 13:16), are all reckoned this way. *mānâ* can be used negatively also, in the sense of an infinite number that cannot be computed (e.g. Gen 13:16; Eccl 1:15).

Twice the intensive use "reckon" or "assign a place" is apparent in the simple stems. In Isa 53:12, the Servant is assigned a place with sinners. In Isa 65:12 the prophet puns on the name *Meni,* the god of fate (q.v.), "Destiny," with the promise that God will "destine" idolaters to the sword.

The idea appoint or ordain is usual in the intensive stems. Twice in Dan (1:5, 10) and four times in Jon (1:17 [H 2:1]; 4:6–8), inanimate things—Daniel's food, Jonah's fish, the gourd, worm, and hot wind—are under the control of God. In Dan 1:11 and I Chr 9:29, a hierarchy of authority is identified by *mānâ* as men or other creatures are given specific responsibilities.

Dahood (in *Psalms,* AB, XVII), following the Ugaritic example, identifies the *mn* of Ps 61:7 [H 8] and *mnw* of Job 7:3 as Qal forms rather than as Piels. However he retains the sense of appoint rather than the more usual Qal idea of computation. Similarly, although in Ps 68:23 [H 24], KJV translates *minēhû* "in the same" (i.e. "in the blood of thine enemies"), ASV and RSV "their portion" take the word as from this root.

There may be some suggestion in this use of *mānâ* that the power to number, count, or ordain is a somewhat mysterious power, particularly where large numbers are concerned, and is of divine origin. The role of God in ordering the universe and its creatures is evident in the reference to the stars (Ps 147:4) and the numbering of the descendants of Abraham (Gen 13:16). The specific idea conveyed by (e.g.) the Jonah passages reflects this divine activity.

This perspective illuminates the statement in I Chr 21:1 that Satan provoked David to "number" Israel. If "numbering" is, in fact, a divine activity, Satan's incursion into this field is another of his attempts to usurp the divine prerogatives.

On the other hand, according to the superscription of Ps 30, this lament psalm may be associated with the dedication of the temple site, an event that took place in connection with the sin of numbering the people (cf. I Chr 21:1). Here David confesses that he sinned in thinking and acting as though he had no need of the Lord: "I said in my prosperity, I will never be moved" (Ps 30:6 [H 7]). There is also the possibility that David's sin was not merely counting the people, but mustering them (*pāqad*) for war (R. L. Harris, *Man—God's Eternal Creation,* Moody, 1971, p. 150–51).

All of the derivatives seem to reflect the concept of numbering, i.e. reckoning up the constituent parts.

mānâ. ***Portion, part.*** This feminine noun identifies the choice parts of the sacrificial animals that were to be given to the priests and Levites. In other instances (e.g. Hannah, Esther, Nehemiah), the distribution of "portions" indicates the unity of the family or community, and emphasizes the high regard the giver had for the recipient.

māneh. ***Pound.*** A unit of weight. BDB suggests that the original meaning may have been a "specific part" of another known weight. The Hebrew unit was the equivalent of fifty shekels (cf. Ex 38:25–26) or about one and a quarter pounds. Ezekiel 45:12 defines the value following the old Mesopotamian usage at sixty shekels to the *māneh,* i.e. about one and a half pounds. Except for those in Ezk, all uses of the term are of weights of gold or silver.

[The famous handwriting on the wall was the enigmatic *mene, mene, tekel, uparsin.* It is probable that Belshazzar was puzzled not because he could not read it, but because the writing could be taken various ways. It could be simply denominations of weight (i.e. money). A mina, a tekel (Aramaic of shekel), and (the conj. "u") smaller pieces (Aramaic pl. for *peres,* half). But what would this mean? It could be taken verbally, one who counts, weighs, and those who divide. The last word could be a play on the Persians then attacking. Belshazzar was mystified and terrified until Daniel told him the full and fateful interpretation. See article Mene, mene, tekel uparsin by D. J. Wiseman in ZPEB with Bibliography, IV, 184–5. R.L.H.]

m^e^nāt. ***Portion.*** Identified by BDB as a late Aramaism, but *mnth* has been identified in the Ugaritic texts in the sense of a "portion" of the sacrifice. RSV in II Chr 31:3 translates the king's *m^e nāt* as his "contribution" to the sacrifice. Psalm 63:10 [H 11] is paraphrased by RSV as "be prey for jackals." The prayer here is not just for a violent death and no burial, but rather for the wicked to be as a sacrifice for the wild beasts.

m^e^nî. ***Number.*** This is a hapax legomenon which occurs only in Isa 65:11. The KJV derives *m^e ni* from *mānah,* "count, number," etc., translating the text, "But ye are they that forsake the Lord, that forget my holy mountain, that prepare a table for that troop, that furnish the drink offering unto that number." (marg. "a table for Gad... drink offering to Meni"). The ASV and RSV translate the two words as proper names "Fortune" and "Destiny." Jerusalem Bible simply transliterates "Gad" and "Meni."

While the general thrust of the text is clear—that Israel has turned from Yahweh to idolatry and is in table fellowship with idols, there is considerable diversity in the identification of the deities in question. Some relate them to the sun and moon (LXX *Daimoni* and *Tychê*), two of the four Egyptian gods who presided over the birth of men. Others suggest two of the planets, usually Jupiter and Venus, worshiped in Babylon as Marduk, the god of the fate of the city, and Ishtar, the fertility goddess.

Both names appear in the Mari texts where *mn* appears to be related to a root meaning "to love." In Ugaritic the personal name *bn mnyy* from the root "to be weakened" or "to lower," is found.

These themes fit either with Venus or the moon, both inconstant heavenly bodies.

Bibliography: Alexander, Joseph Addison, *Commentary on the Prophecies of Isaiah,* Zondervan, 1953, pp. 445–47. Delitzsch, Franz, *Isaiah,* II, Eerdmans, 1950, pp. 482–85. Muilenberg, James, "Exegesis: Isaiah 40–66" in IB. Gordon, C. H., UT 19:nos. 1496, 1502, 561, 571. Huffmon, Herbert B., *Amorite Personal Names in the Mari Texts,* Johns Hopkins, 1965, pp. 179, 231.

G.L.C.

מִנְהָג (*minhāg*). See no. 1309a.
מִנְהָרָה (*minhārâ*). See no. 1316b.
מָנוֹד (*mānôd*). See no. 1319c.
מָנוֹחַ (*mānôaḥ*). See no. 1323e.
מָנוֹן (*mānôn*). See no. 1213f.
מָנוֹס (*mānôs*). See no. 1327a.
מָנוֹר (*mānôr*). See no. 1361a.
מְנוֹרָה (*m^e nôrâ*). See no. 1333c.
מִנְזָר (*minzār*). See no. 1340d.

1214 מנח (*mnḥ*). **Assumed root of the following.**
1214a †מִנְחָה (*minḥâ*) ***meat offering, offering, present, gifts, oblation, sacrifice.*** (ASV uses "meal-offering." RSV uses "cereal-offering." Both use "tribute.")

Scholarly opinion is divided as to the root of *minḥâ*. Some trace this feminine noun to a verbal root *nḥh* "to lead or guide." Most, however, posit a Hebrew root *mnḥ* "to give." Arabic *manaḥa* has the technical meaning "to lend someone something" (e.g. a she-camel, goat, sheep, or a parcel of land) for a limited period of time so that the borrower can have free use of the produce of the loan (e.g. the offspring, milk, crops, etc.), and then return the original property. The fruit then becomes a free gift. Snaith sees no occurrence of the word in Ugaritic, but UT 19: no. 1500 tentatively identifies at least one occurrences of *mnḥ* in a tribute list (Text 137:38, not 137:28, as cited in UT) and another in the Anat/Baal Cycle in a parallel construction with "tribute" (AisWUS no. 1597 "gift," "tribute").

The word is used in secular contexts of gifts to superior persons, particularly kings, to convey the attitude of homage and submission to that person. In I Sam 10:27, the Israelites who despised Saul "brought him no present" (*minḥâ*), i.e. did not acknowledge the new king. Then, in I Kgs 4:21 [H 5:1], Solomon received tribute (*minḥâ*) from the kings of the nations he ruled. (LXX uses *dōron* about thirty times for *minḥâ*.) There are several other instances of this meaning, e.g. II Kgs 10:25; II Kgs 8:8–9; 17:4; 20:12; Isa 39:1.

The religious use of the term derives from the secular. Specifically, a *minḥâ* is a gift of grain, although Snaith seems to be correct in saying that since *minḥâ* originally meant gift or tribute, it could loosely be used in this sense even when it took on specific cultic meaning. Of particular interest in this connection is the distinction between *zebaḥ* (q.v.) and *minḥâ* in I Sam 2:29; 3:14; and Isa 19:21; between *'ôlâ* (q.v.) and *minḥâ* in Jer 14:12 and Ps 20:3 [H 4]; and between *shelem* (q.v.) and *minḥâ* in Amos 5:22. Cf. also Gen 4:3–4. Both Abel and Cain offered a *minḥâ* to the Lord (Gen 4:4–5). But whereas it is said of Abel that he offered the choicest portions of the animals to the Lord, an act reflecting his heartfelt commitment to him, it is merely said of Cain that he offered a *minḥâ* from the fruit of the ground. The Lord rejected this formality. Cain's lack of true submission (note also his bloodless sacrifice) issued finally in sinful behavior (Gen 4:7f.). These uses of *minḥâ* indicate that the term does not mean an animal sacrifice in the specific sense.

The cereal offering is defined in Lev 2:1–16 and 6:14–23 [H 7–16]. It could be in the form of raw grain in the sheaves, dry roasted grains coarsely crushed, ground into flour (wheat only; barley flour seems to have been reserved for the "jealousy offering" of Num 5:15, 25), or made into loaves or cakes and baked in an oven or panfried in oil. Frankincense and salt were also part of the prepared *minḥâ,* but no leaven or honey was to be added.

The *minḥâ,* offered every morning and evening, was a holy offering, eaten only by the priests, not shared with the worshipers. The idea of atonement is not specifically present in *minḥâ,* although that of propitiation certainly is. The offering of the new produce of the land along with ordinary leavened bread (Lev 23:16) indicates submission of the totality of the life of God's people to the Great Suzerain.

Bibliography: Driver, G. R., "Three Technical Terms in the Pentateuch," JSS 1:97–105. Pedersen, Johannes, *Israel: Its Life and Culture, vols. III and IV,* 2d ed. Oxford: University Press, 1959, pp. 330, 354, 368, 417f. Gray, George Buchanan, *Sacrifice in the Old Testament,* Oxford: Clarendon Press, 1925, pp. 13–17, 47, 398–402. Kaufman, Yehezkel, *The Religion of Israel,* University of Chicago Press, 1960, pp. 110–115. Kraus, Hans-Joachim, *Worship in Israel,* John Knox, 1966, pp. 112–118. Richardson, TWB, pp. 206–208. Snaith, Norman H., "Sacrifices in the Old Testament," *VT* 7:308–17. deVaux, Roland, AI, McGraw, pp. 225, 416–22.

G.L.C.

מְנֻחָה (*m^enūḥâ*). See no. 1323f.
מְנִי (*m^enî*). See no. 1213.
מִנְלֶה (*minleh*). See no. 1370a.

1215 מנן (*mnn*). **Assumed root of the following.**
1215a מֵן (*mēn*) ***portion*** (Ps 45:9).

1216 מָנַע (*māna'*) ***withhold, keep back, refrain, deny, keep restrain, hinder.*** (ASV and RSV similar, but RSV adds hold, hold back, refuse.)

Found only in the simple tenses where most references imply that the right or power to withhold something belongs ultimately to God or his representative.

Thus it is said that God withholds the fruit of the womb (Gen 30:2) and the rain (Amos 4:7). Man's sins cause God to withhold these good things from man (Jer 5:25), but he withholds no good thing from those who walk uprightly (Ps 84:11 [H 12]). Thus he does not withhold the request of his righteous king (Ps 21:2 [H 3]).

A wise man withholds neither food nor any good thing from the poor or those to whom it is due (Prov 11:20; 3:27; Job 22:7; 31:16), nor correction from the child (Prov 23:13).

G.L.C.

מַנְעוּל (*man'ûl*). See no. 1383c.
מִנְעָל (*min'āl*) See no. 1383d.
מִנְעַמִּים (*min'ammîm*). See no. 1384d.
מְנַעֲנֵעַ (*m^ena'ănēa'*). See no. 1328a.
מְנַקִּיָּה (*m^enaqqîyâ*). See no. 1412d.

1217 מְנַשֶּׁה (*m^enashsheh*) ***Manasseh.***

In Gen 41:51, popularly derived as a Piel from *nāshâ* (q.v.) and equal to "cause to forget." This is the name of four people and a territory. (The fifth person is obviously "Moses" and the scribal emendation of a supralinear "n" in Jud 18:30–31 is an obvious attempt to dissociate such a good name from the idolatrous priesthood at Dan).

Manasseh was the elder son of Joseph, and with his brother Ephraim substituted for Joseph and Levi in the twelve tribe territorial allocation in the Promised Land. Nothing of Manasseh's personal life is recorded in the OT, except the birth of his son Machir. [Note that in the ritual of Gen 48:5–20, Manasseh and Ephraim, Jacob's grandsons, were adopted so as to be legally his own sons. Therefore their descendants became two tribes in Israel. The adoption is reminiscent of Nuzi Law. R.L.H.]

The large tribe descended from Manasseh occupied two sections of the land, one in the Transjordanian territory of Gilead between the Jabbok and Yarmuk rivers, and the other in the territory north of Shechem to Mount Carmel and Mount Tabor, including the strategic center of Megiddo and much of the fertile Esdraelon Valley.

One of the kings of Judah, son of Hezekiah, and father of Amon, Manasseh reigned fifty-five years (696–642 B.C.). For the first ten years he was co-regent with his father. A loyal vassal of Assyria (he is named as a tributary in "prism B" of Essarhaddon's list [ANET, p. 291]; cf. II Chr 33:11), he introduced pagan worship practices into Judah (II Kgs 21). He became a legend for evil, and the cause of judgment on the land, although II Chr 33:12–13 indicates that he repented after a period of exile in Assyria. To date, there is no extant extrabiblical evidence on this latter point.

The two other men named Manasseh are Israelites listed in Ezr 10:30, 33 as having taken foreign wives.

G.L.C.

מְנָת (*m^enāt*). See no. 1213d.

1218 מַס (*mas*) ***tribute, tributary, levy, taskmasters, discomfited.*** (ASV "taskwork." RSV "forced labor," "vassal.")

The root of this word is unknown, although some attempt has been made to derive it from *māsâ* "to melt, grow faint." There is a possible link in Isa 31:8 (KJV "discomfited;" marg. "be for melting," or "tribute") or in the general concept that those under tribute are "weak." KB cites Egyptian *ms* "bearer."

Of the twenty-three uses of this term, all but three (Isa 31:8; Lam 1:1; Est 10:1) occur early in the literature.

The institution of tribute or corvee involves involuntary, unpaid labour or other service for a superior power—a feudal lord, a king, or a foreign ruler (Ex 1:11; Est 10:1; Lam 1:1). In Gen 49:15, Jacob's blessing on Issachar identifies him as bowing to "tribute." In Egypt, the Israelites find themselves in that position (Ex 1:11).

The subjugation of the Canaanites by Israel after the Conquest was by means of *mas* (e.g. Deut 20:11; Josh 16:10; 17:13). Under David there was an organized government department charged with keeping the *mas* functioning (II Sam 20:24).

During Solomon's reign, *mas* was extended to include Israelites as well as foreigners and war prisoners (I Kgs 5:13–14 [H 27–28] and the parallels in Chr; but cf. I Kgs 9:22) in the labor force necessary to carry out Solomon's extensive building programs (I Kgs 9:15). This unpopular measure, and Rehoboam's refusal to moderate it, was the immediate cause of the secession of the ten tribes and the establishment of the northern kingdom.

Bibliography: Mendelsohn, I., "On Corvee Labor in Ancient Canaan and Israel," BASOR 167:31–35. ———, "State Slavery in Ancient Palestine," BASOR 85:14–17.

G.L.C.

מַס (*mas*). See no. 1223a.
מֵסַב (*mēsab*). See no. 1456c.
מַסְגֵּר (*masgēr*). See no. 1462c.
מִסְגֶּרֶת (*misgeret*). See no. 1462d.
מַסַּד (*massad*). See no. 875g.
מִסְדְּרוֹן (*misd^erôn*). See no. 1467c.

1219 *מָסָה (*māsâ*) ***melt, dissolve.*** Occurs only in the Hiphil. *māsâ* may be a by-form of *māsas*.

מַסָּה (*massâ*). See no. 1223b.
מַסְוֶה (*masweh*). See no. 1472b.
מְסוּכָה (*m^esûkâ*). See no. 1475a.
מַסָּח (*massāḥ*). See no. 1374a.

1220 מָסַךְ (*māsak*) ***mingle, mix.*** (ASV and RSV similar.)

Derivatives

1220a †מֶסֶךְ (*mesek*) ***mixture.*** RSV well-mixed.

1220b †מִמְסָךְ (*mimsāk*) ***drink-offering, mixed wine.***

This verb occurs only five times and its derivatives once and twice respectively. The root has been identified in Ugaritic (UT, 19: no. 1509). As is frequently the case with seldom used words, the general meaning is obvious from the context, but there is considerable diversity in the understanding of the precise inflection intended by the author. Two broad categories have been proposed for this word group.

Four of the five uses of *māsak* are associated with drinking (*yayin* "wine," Prov 9:2, 5; *shēkār* "strong drink" or "beer," Isa 5:22; *shiqquy* "drink," "refreshment," Ps 102:9 [H 10]). According to Isa 19:14, God has mixed within Egypt a "spirit of confusion," and thus it staggers as a drunken man.

mesek. ***Mixture.*** (Ps 75:8 [H 9], RSV "well-mixed wine.")

mimsāk. ***Drink offering, mixed wine, spiced wine*** (NEB), ***libation*** (Prov 13:30; Isa 65:11). Traditionally, these nouns have been understood to mean some kind of mixed drink, usually wine with spices or honey (e.g. "cocktails," William McKane, *Proverbs,* p. 393. This, of course, is an anachronism. Cocktails are mixtures of distilled liquors with other liquids. Before the Arabs discovered distillation in the Middle Ages, there were no highly alcoholic drinks). Dilution with water is mentioned late in II Macc 15:39. (Cf. Mt 27:34; Mk 15:23.) In Isa 65:11, an "oblation" for Meni (q.v.) is paralleled with setting a sacrificial table for Gad. This juxtaposition of sacrificial terms is also found in Prov 9:2, 5 where Wisdom invites participation in her banquet.

Apart from these two uses in Prov, all three of these words are negative—the folly of the drunkard, the unavoidable wrath of God's bitter judgment poured out on evil.

Delitzsch (F. Delitzsch, *Isaiah,* I, p. 361) translated *māsak* as "poured out." Dahood (*Psalms in loc.*) and Scott (R.B.Y. Scott, *Proverbs,* AB, XVIII, p. 24) have followed this concept. To "pour out" or "drain to the bottom" makes excellent sense in all eight uses of these words.

G.L.C.

מָסָךְ (māsāk). See no. 1492a.
מַסֵּכָה (massēkâ). See nos. 1375c, 1376a.

1221 מִסְכֵּן (miskēn) **poor, poor man.**

This word occurs only in Eccl 4:13; 9:15–16. Some scholars argue that *m^e sūkkān* in Isa 40:20 and *miskanūt* in Deut 8:9 are incorrectly pointed in the MT and ought to be considered with *miskēn*. Similarly some argue that *misk^e nôt* (q.v.) is also the same word. Probably a loan word, cf. Akkadian *muŝkēnu*. The Arabic word *miskin* "peasant" has been borrowed into Italian and French.

The paucity of uses of *miskēn* makes it difficult to draw precise conclusions on the meaning of the word, although the general meaning is obvious in the contrast between the poor man and the king in Eccl 4:13. The LXX helps some. The Greek *penēs* is used of the man who does not have extensive possessions, and must work for his living. The "rich" man (*ploytos*) can live on his income without working. This is the disctinction drawn in the Eccl passages. Often the line between these two classes of people is indistinct. On the other hand, however, the *ptōchos* is the destitute mendicant—the man who is so poor he cannot work. There is a clearcut line between this class of people and the Greek *penēs*. In Mt 5:3, the "poor in spirit" are the spiritual beggars—so poor they cannot work for spiritual gain. In Isa 66:2, however, *'ānî* is used for "poor in spirit" and refers to one who trembles at God's word. See also *'ebyôn, 'ānî, dal,* and *rāsh*.

Bibliography: AI, pp. 68–79. Gordis, Robert, *Koheleth: The Man and His World,* 3d ed., 1968, p. 243. TDNT, VI, pp. 885–915, 37–40, 318–32, esp. 319–25.

G.L.C.

מִסְכְּנוֹת (misk^enôt). See no. 1494a.

1222 מִסְכֵּנֻת (miskēnūt) **poverty, scarcity** (Deut 8:19).

מַסֶּכֶת (masseket). See no. 1376b.
מְסִלָּה (m^e sillâ). See no. 1506d.
מַסְלוּל (maslûl). See no. 1506e.
מַסְמֵר (masmēr). See no. 1518b.

1223 מָסַס (māsas) **dissolve, melt.**

Derivatives

1223a מַס (mas) **despairing** (Job 6:14).
1223b מַסָּה (massâ) **despair.**
1223c תֶּמֶס (temes) **melting (away).**

The scarcity of uses of *māsa* and *māsâ* makes it difficult to distinguish clearly between the two verbal forms, since both are used in similar contexts, combining the concepts of physical and emotional distress. They are doubtless by-forms. In most cases, there is some outside force that causes the "melting" e.g., fear of a ruler (II Sam 17:10), of a more powerful army (Josh 2:11; 5:1), at bad news (Deut 1:28; Ezk 21:7 [H 12]), at sorrow and fear of death (Ps 22:14 [H 15]).

A couple of times *māsas* is used of garbage: the uncollected manna that "melted" in the heat of the sun, and the "refuse" left after the destruction of Amalek by Saul (I Sam 15:9), these, too, under the power of outside forces.

The predominant feature in several cases is the presence of Yahweh as the God of power. In his presence the mountains themselves dissolve (Ps 97:5; Isa 34:3; Mic 1:4) and the nations are powerless before him (Nah 2:11; cf. Jud 15:14)

Physical sickness causes "melting" of the flesh (Isa 10:18) but some commentators posit a root *nāsas* "to be sick" for this form.

Similarly, *temes* in Ps 58:8 [H 9] seems to fit this interpretation, particularly if the textual variant *shklwl* (*kālāh* "be consumed" for *shabb^e lûl* is correct. (Cf. Isa 10:18 where this combination appears in parallel.)

Bibliography: McCarthy, D. J., "Some Holy War Vocabulary in Joshua 2," CBQ 33:228–30.

G.L.C.

מַסַּע (massa'). See no. 1380a.
מִסְעָד (mis'ād). See no. 1525a.
מִסְפֵּד (mispēd). See no. 1530a.
מִסְפּוֹא (mispô'). See no. 1529a.
מִסְפָּח (mispāḥ). See no. 1534d.
מִסְפָּר (mispār). See no. 1540f.

1224 מָסַר (māsar) **deliver up, offer.**

The verb is used only two times in the OT, both of them in the account of the holy war against Midian (Num 31). The first one, v. 5, says "there were 'delivered' (RSV, "provided") out of the thousands of Israel, a thousand of every tribe." The meaning here is obviously, "to assign, apportion, count." Some have suggested an emendation of the Hebrew text from *wayyimmās^e rû* to *wayyisāp^e rû* on the basis of the LXX's *exērithmēsan*. The suggested change is quite unnecessary. The second use is in Numbers 31:16, "Behold, these caused the children of Israel 'to commit' treachery against the Lord."

Of special interest is the possible connection of this root with the "Masorah" which is the apparatus built around the Hebrew text of the OT to fix its traditional divisions, pronunciation, and mode of public recitation. This work was done by the Masoretes, who were Aramaic speaking Jews of Babylonia and Palestine, between A.D. 700 and the end of the tenth century.

If "Masorah," then, is to be derived from *māsar* "to deliver," it is that which is handed down from generation to generation: the text of the Bible. Others have suggested that *Masorah* is from the root *'āsar* "to bind," i.e. something which is bound and gathered: the detailed instructions for reading affixed to the text. Still a third suggestion is that *Masorah* is built off the verb *māsar* but with the primary meaning of "to count" (Ben-Ḥayyim).

Bibliography: Ben-Ḥayyim, Z., "*māsôrâ ûmāsōret,*" *Lešonēnū* 21:283–92. Wildeboer, G. *msr,* ZAW 29:73–74 and "Das Verbum msr, ZAW 29:219–20 vs. Bacher, W., "A Contribution to the History of the Term 'Massorah'," JQR 3:785–90 and "Das Verbum *msr*'" ZAW 29:218–19.

V.P.H.

מֹסָר (*mōsār*). See no. 877b.
מָסֹרֶת (*māsōret*). See no. 141e.

1225 מִסַּת (*missat*) ***sufficient, sufficiency.***

This translation is based primarily on the common Aramaic word. It is found but once in the OT, Deut 16:10, "Thou shalt keep the feast of weeks unto the Lord thy God with a 'tribute' of a free will offering of thine hand" (KJV). The worshiper is to bring whatever offering his means allow (cf. v. 17 in the same chapter). The etymology of the word is uncertain.

V.P.H.

מִסְתּוֹר (*mistôr*). See no. 1551c.
מִסְתָּר (*mistār*), מִסְתֵּר (*mistēr*). See nos. 1551d,e.
מַעְבָּד (*ma'bād*). See no. 1553f.
מַעֲבֶה (*ma'ăbeh*). See no. 1554b.
מַעֲבָר (*ma'ăbār*). See no. 1556h.
מַעְגָּל (*ma'gāl*). See no. 1560.

1226 מָעַד (*mā'ad*) ***slip, slide, give away.***

The root is found nine times in the OT if we include in Ezk 29:7 the reading *w^e ha'ămadtâ* as a metathesis for *w^e him'adtâ* and thus read "and make all their loins/thighs 'shake'" instead of "stand." Four of the nine uses of this verb are in Psalms (18:36 [H 37]= II Sam 22:37; Ps 26:1; 27:31; 69:23 [H 24]). The first three of these are used in a context suggesting security ("my feet did not give away") as a result of confidence in God. Proverbs 25:19 speaks of a "broken tooth and a 'palsied' foot." I Samuel 15:32 says that Agag came to David "totteringly."

Bibliography: Talmon, S., "I Sam. xv:32b: A Case of Conflated Readings," VT 11: 456–57.

V.P.H.

מַעֲדָן (*ma'ădān*). See no. 1567d.
מַעֲדַנּוֹת (*ma'ădannût*). See no. 1649a.
מַעְדֵּר (*ma'dēr*). See no. 1571a.

1227 מעה (*m'h*). **Assumed root of the following.**
1227a †מֵעֶה (*mē'eh*) ***inward parts, bowels.***
1227b מָעָה (*mā'â*) ***grain (of sand).***

The noun *mē'eh* is used thirty-two times in the OT, always in the plural, *mē'îm*. The KJV most often retains the translation "bowels" but the RSV opts for a more euphemistic translation unless the word is used in a passage with the literal sense of the intestines.

With three or four exceptions the noun is associated with persons, both male and female. Twice it is used in connection with the great sea-monster, the "belly" of which was the temporary underground abode of Jonah, and the place from which he prayed (Jonah 2:1–2). Twice the noun is found in phrases connected with God's emotions: Isa 63:15, "Where is your zeal (*qin'â*), your strength (*g^ebûrâ*), your compassion (*hămôn mē'ēkâ*) and your mercies (*raḥămîm*) toward me?" (cf. also Jer 31:20 [H 19] with the phrase *hamû mē'ay* parallel to *reḥēm 'ăraḥămennû*).

Most often, as we have indicated, the word is used of persons and crosses genders. It may be used of man: Job 30:27 (Job); II Sam 16:11; 17:12 (David); II Chr 21:19 (Jehoram); II Chr 32:21 (Sennacherib); Gen 15:4 (Abraham). In the following passages it refers to women: Ps 71:6; Isa 49:1 (my mother); Ruth 1:11 (Naomi); Gen 25:23 (Rebekah). Frequently when referring to a woman *mē'eh* is paralleled with *beṭen* "womb."

There are three major ways in which the word is used. First, the word may be used literally, to refer to one's internal organs, the bowels, the stomach. Thus, Ezekiel (Ezk 3:3) is told to eat and digest the roll which God has shown him (and *mē'eh* is parallel to *beṭen*), in his "belly" and "bowels." Cf. also Ezk 7:19 (parallel to *nepesh*). In II Chr 21:15 (twice), 18–19 there is a reference to the horrible disease with which the Lord afflicted Jehoram, the Judean king, in his "bowels." This must be some kind of an abdominal disease, perhaps a violent case of dysentery with or without prolapsus of the bowel.

The second way in which *mē'eh* is used is to refer to the reproductive organs, both male and female. Hence, more than simply digestive organs are involved. We are now thinking in terms of the reproductive system, the male and female sexual apparatus (Gen 15:4; 25:23; Ruth 1:11; II Sam 16:11; 17:12; II Chr 32:21; Isa 48:19).

The third way in which *mē'eh* is used is in a figurative, metaphorical sense to denote the seat of emotions. We have already noted this above in connection with God's compassion (Isa 63:15 and Jer 31:20). Thus, Isaiah in his lament over Moab quivers with his whole being (*mē'eh*), and his inmost self (*qirbî,* Isa 16:11). Jeremiah cries out, "My anguish, my anguish" (Jer 4:19). The author of Lam expresses similar emotion (Lam 1:20;

2:11). David hides God's law within his "heart" (Ps 40:9). The term is used to express the affection felt by the bride for her lover (Song 5:4).

Incidentally, this figure of speech extends into the NT. "Put on ... bowels (*splagchna*) of mercy" (Col 3:12). "If there be any consolation in Christ... if any bowels and mercies" (Phil 2:1).

The metaphorical use of organs of the body was more common in antiquity. Hebrew uses the liver (*kābēd,* sometimes mispointed *kābōd* "glory") in expressions of joy, the kidneys (*kᵉlayôt*) for affections, the heart (*lēb*) for both affections and mind and the abdominal organs (*mē'îm*) for compassion (see the various terms). In English the word "heart" is used for most of these expressions, and "heart" is a fair translation of most of these words. There is, of course, no problem in the Hebrew use of an organ to express a feeling. The Bible no more teaches that compassion resides in the abdomen than moderns think it resides in the chest. The Hebrew simply reflects the common linguistic usage (not invented by the Jews) whereby mental and emotional states are designated by organs the emotions affect in some way.

V.P.H.

מָעוֹג (*mā'ôg*). See no. 1575b.
מָעוֹז (*mā'ôz*). See no. 1578a.
מָעוֹן (*mā'ôn*). See no. 1581a.
מָעוּף (*mā'ûp*). See no. 1583b.
מָעוֹר (*mā'ôr*). See no. 1588a.

1228 מָעַט (*mā'aṭ*) ***be small, diminished.***

Derivative

1228a †מְעַט (*mᵉ'aṭ*) ***little.***

The verb is used twenty-two times in the OT, eight times in the Qal, once in the Piel (Eccl 12:3), and thirteen times in the Hiphil ("to bring to nothing, decrease, diminish"). Its meaning is fairly well established by the number of times it is used in juxtaposition to its antonym *rābâ* "be(come) much/many/great" (Ex 16:17–18; 30:15; Num 26:54; 33:54; Jer 29:6).

mᵉ'aṭ. ***Little, few, small,*** appears one hundred and one times in the OT. The basic meaning of *mᵉ'at* is seen in the following passages: Gen 30:30, "It was little you (Laban) had before I (Jacob) came"; 47:9, "The days of my pilgrimage have been few and evil"; I Sam 14:6, "There is no restraint to the Lord to save by many (*rab*) or by few"; Deut 7:7, "You were the fewest of all the people"; Ps 8:5 [H 6], "You have made him a little less than God," and so forth.

mᵉ'aṭ is joined with the word *'ôd* to form the expression *'ôd mᵉ'aṭ* "a little while." It occurs seven times, six of these indicating the cessation of God's patience with the wicked and the beginning of judgment: Ps 37:10; Isa 10:25; 29:17; Jer 51:33; Hag 2:6. In the seventh passage (Ex 17:4) Moses remonstrates with God that the people "are almost ready" to stone him. We may also note the frequency (nine times) with which the interrogative particle is prefixed to *mᵉ'aṭ* to form questions, most of which are rhetorical in nature. For example, "Is it a small matter that you have taken my husband?" (Gen 30:15; cf. Num 13:18; 16:9, 13; Josh 22:17, etc.).

A frequent phrase with this word is *kim'aṭ,* literally, "like a little" (eighteen times). In most cases the translation will be derived from the context. Thus, (1) "a little longer, almost, all but": Gen 26:10; Ps 73:2; 119:87; Prov 5:14; (2) "soon, shortly, straightway": Ps 81:14 [H 15]; Job 32:22; II Chr 12:7 ("in a little while"); Ps 2:12 ("quickly"); (3) "very few, a handful": Ps 105:12; Ezk 16:47; Isa 1:9.

V.P.H.

מַעֲטָפָה (*ma'ăṭāpâ*). See no. 1606a.
מְעִי (*mᵉ'î*). See no. 1577e.
מְעִיל (*mᵉ'îl*). See no. 1230b.
מַעְיָן (*ma'yān*). See no. 1613a.

1229 מָעַךְ (*mā'ak*) ***press, squeeze.***

The verb appears three times in the OT, possibly four (see discussion of Ezk 23:21 below): (1) Lev 22:24, "You shall not offer unto the Lord (an animal whose testicles) are "bruised" (*mā'ûk*), crushed (*kātût*), broken (*nātûq*), or cut (*kārût*)"; probably all referring to methods of castration; (2) I Sam 26:7, "Saul's spear was 'stuck/pressed' in(to) the ground"; (3) Ezk 23:3, "there their nipples were 'handled' (*mō'ăkû*), there their virgin breasts were fondled." This is an allegory of Jerusalem and Samaria depicting their intercourse with Egypt, involving idolatry.

Ezekiel 23:21*b,* the expression "for your young breasts" might better read "to fondle your young breasts" by changing the preposition *lᵉma'an* to read "*lim'ōk*" (Qal infinitive construct) or *lima'ēk* (Piel infinitive construct).

V.P.H.

1230 מָעַל (*mā'al*) ***transgress, commit a trespass, act unfaithfully.***

Derivatives

1230a †מַעַל (*ma'al*) ***trespass.***
1230b †מְעִיל (*mᵉ'îl*) ***robe.***

mā'al occurs thirty-five times, always in the Qal stem. It occurs most frequently in II Chr and in Ezk. Among the prophets, only Ezekiel uses this word (excluding Dan 9:7).

In almost all the biblical references *mā'al* is used to designate the breaking or violation of religious law as a conscious act of treachery. The victim against whom the breach is perpetrated is God. As we shall see, an almost formulaic phrase is *mā'al ma'al b^e yhwh* "to commit a tresspass against the LORD" (Lev 6:2 [H 5:21]; Num 5:6; Josh 22:31; I Chr 10:13; II Chr 12:2; 26:16; 28:19, 22; 30:7). A variant, in the first person, is *mā'al ma'al bî* "to commit a trespass against me" (Lev 26:40; Ezk 14:13; 20:27; 39:23, 26).

There are a few instances where the root is used in contexts in which God is not the object. There are three of these. (1) Prov 16:10: the mouth of a king transgresses (*yim'al*) not in judgment; (2) Job 21:34 (Job to the three comforters): how can you comfort me since in your answers there is falsehood? (Pope, in AB, *Job*, "sheer fraud"; JB, "nonsense"); (3) Num 5:12, 27. It is these last verses from Num that furnish the best clues as to the nuance behind the word *mā'al*. Numbers 5:12 says, "if a man's wife go aside (*śāṭâ*), and commit a trespass (*mā'al*) against him." Verse 13 continues, "and a man lie with her carnally" It is obvious, then, that to "commit a trespass" means to act unfaithfully, to break a contract. The general idea is defection or unfaithfulness. Our English word "perfidy" would come perhaps closest of all.

Occasionally the root is applied to the faithless acts of individuals, private citizens as in the case of Achan (Josh 7:1; 22:20; I Chr 2:7), but mostly royal figures (Saul: I Chr 10:13; Ahaz: II Chr 28:19; 29:19; Uzziah: II Chr 26:16, 18; Manasseh: II Chr 33:19; Zedekiah: Ezk 18:24). Most often it is an indictment against the nation of Israel from wilderness times (Num 31:16; Deut 32:51) down to the postexilic ministries of Ezra and Nehemiah (Ezra 10:2, 10; Neh 1:8). It is the cause of Judah's exile (Ezk 39:23; Dan 9:7). In one instance a foreign ruler (Shishak) enters Jerusalem because of Israel's "transgressions" (II Chr 12:2). This word does not describe the sins of unbelievers but of believers, covenant peoples, those who "break faith" with their suzerain. Thus, Ezk 18:24 pronounces the principle, "When a righteous man turns away from his righteousness and commits iniquity (*'āwel*)... in his trespass that he has committed (*mā'al*) and in the sin he has sinned (*ḥāṭā'*) he shall die."

Of the many words for sin in the OT, *mā'al* is used most frequently in a parallel phrase with *ḥāṭā'* (q.v.) "to sin, miss the mark": Lev 5:15, 21; Num 5:6; II Chr 33:19; Ezk 14:13; 18:24. There are a number of words used in the LXX for *mā'al*. Interestingly, in Ezk the word used most prominently is *parapiptō* "to trespass" while in Ezra and Nehemiah the word is *asunthetō* "to default, deflect." There is no equivalent pattern in translation in Chronicles.

ma'al. ***Trespass.*** The noun is used twenty-nine times, of which twenty instances are as a cognate accusative to the verb *mā'al*. Thus, we meet a phrase, "If a man commit (*mā'al*) a trespass (*ma'al*)."

m^e'îl. ***Robe, cloke, mantle.*** This type of clothing may refer to part of the priestly vestments worn by the high priest to cover the ephod. Like a shawl there was a hole in the middle, hence to be pulled over the head. It was also worn by men of repute: Samuel, I Sam 28:14 (in Sheol at that!); Saul, I Sam 24:5; David, I Chr 15:27; Ezra, Ezr 9:3; Job, Job 1:20 (and David's daughters, II Sam 13:18). For figurative usages cf. Isa 59:17; 61:10; Job 29:14; Ps 109:29. The relationship of *m^e'îl* to *mā'al* is uncertain. One suggestion is to relate the ideas of "covering" and "acting unfaithfully" i.e., sinning in secret or under cover, on the analogy of Hebrew *bāgad* "to act treacherously" and *beged* "garment" (Palache; see bibliography).

Bibliography: Palache, J. L., *Semantic Notes on the Hebrew Lexicon*, Leiden: Brill, 1959, esp. p. 10. Porúbčan, S., *Sin in the Old Testament:* Aloisana, Herder, 1963, esp. pp. 30–31. THAT, I, pp. 920–21.

V.P.H.

מֹעַל (*mō'al*), מַעַל (*ma'al*), מַעֲלֶה (*ma'ăleh*). See nos. 1624i,j,k.
מַעֲלָל (*ma'ălāl*). See no. 1627e.
מֵעִם (*mē'im*). See no. 1640c.
מַעֲמָד (*ma'ămād*), מָעֳמָד (*mo'ŏmād*). See nos. 1637d,e.
מַעֲמָסָה (*ma'ămāsâ*). See no. 1643a.
מַעֲמַקִּים (*ma'ămaqqîm*). See no. 1644e.
מַעֲנֶה (*ma'ăneh*), מַעֲנָה (*ma'ănâ*). See nos. 1650f, 1651b.
מַעֲצֵבָה (*ma'ăṣēbâ*). See no. 1666f.
מַעֲצָד (*ma'ăṣād*). See no. 1668a.
מַעֲצוֹר (*ma'ăṣôr*). See no. 1675d.
מַעְצָר (*ma'ăṣār*). See no. 1675e.
מַעֲקֶה (*ma'ăqeh*). See no. 1679a.
מַעֲקָשׁ (*ma'ăqāsh*). See no. 1684c.
מַעַר (*ma'ar*). See no. 1692d.
מַעֲרָב (*ma'ărāb*). See nos. 1686c, 1689b.
מְעָרָה (*m^e'ārâ*). See no. 1704a.
מַעֲרָךְ (*ma'ărāk*). See no. 1694c.
מַעֲרֶכֶת (*ma'ăreket*). See no. 1694e.
מַעֲרָם (*ma'ărām*). See no. 1588d.
מַעֲרָצָה (*ma'ărāṣâ*). See no. 1702c.
מַעֲשֶׂה (*ma'ăśeh*). See no. 1708a.
מַעֲשֵׂר (*ma'ăśēr*). See no. 1711h.
מַעֲשַׁקָּה (*ma'ăshaqqâ*). See no. 1713e.
מִפְגָּע (*mipgā'*). See no. 1731b.
מַפָּח (*mappāḥ*), מַפֻּחַ (*mappūaḥ*). See nos. 1390a,b.
מֵפִיץ (*mēpîṣ*). See no. 1745a.
מַפָּל (*mappāl*). See no. 1392b.
מִפְלָאָה (*miplā'â*). See no. 1768c.
מִפְלַגָּה (*miplaggâ*). See no. 1769d.
מַפֵּלָה (*mappēlâ*). See no. 1392d.
מִפְלָט (*miplāṭ*). See no. 1774e.

מִפְלֶצֶת (*mipleṣet*). See no. 1778b.
מִפְלָשׂ (*miplāś*). See no. 1777b.
מַפֶּלֶת (*mappelet*). See no. 1392e.
מִפְעָל (*mip'āl*). See no. 1792c,b.
מַפֵּץ (*mappēṣ*), מַפָּץ (*mappāṣ*). See no. 1394c, b.
מִפְקָד (*mipqād*). See no. 1802g.
מִפְרָץ (*miprāṣ*). See no. 1827a.
מִפְרֶקֶת (*mipreqet*). See no. 1828.
מִפְרָשׂ (*miprāś*). See no. 1831a.
מִפְשָׂעָה (*mipśā'â*). See no. 1841b.
מִפְתָּח (*miptāḥ*), מַפְתֵּחַ (*maptēaḥ*). See nos. 1854c,f.
מִפְתָּן (*miptān*). See no. 1858b.
מֵץ (*mēṣ*). See no. 1192a.

1231 מָצָא (*māṣā'*) ***find.***

There are approximately 450 usages of this root in the OT. Most of these are in the Qal stem (Gerleman, 306 times; but according to Koehler Baumgartner, KB, p. 553*b,* 310 times.) As we shall see, although its basic meaning is "to find" (in the LXX, mostly *euriskein*), *māṣā'* also assumes other shades of meaning. The Niphal stem of this verb appears 141 times (Gerleman) or 135 times (KB). Once again, the expected translation would be the passive of the Qal, "to be found." But such translations as "overpowered," "captured," and "apprehended" are also discoverable. Note that in the LXX the translation of *māṣā'* is often not *euriskō* but something like *haliskomai* "be caught. held."

The evidence of related languages is helpful. Hebrew *māṣā'* is to be related to Aramaic *m^{e}ṭā'* "to reach, attain" (the word in BA for "find" is *s^{e}kaḥ*); to Ethiopic *maṣ'a* "to come, arrive"; and to Ugaritic *mẓa/mṣa* "to reach" (UT 19: no. 1524).

There seems to be, then, sufficient grounds to establish for *māṣā'* in the Qal stem not only the meaning "to find" but also "to come upon, meet, reach." As a generalization, we may say that whenever *māṣā'* is used to describe a result following a time of "seeking" the translation is "to find." Thus, Deut 4:29, "if you seek (*bāqash*) the Lord, you shall find (*māṣā'*) him." Cf. Jer 29:13; Song 5:6. "Seek (*dārash*) the Lord, while he may be found (*māṣā'*) (Isa 55:6); cf. I Chr 28:9; II Chr 15:2; "they shall seek (*śāḥar*) me early, but shall not find (*māṣā'*) me" (Prov 1:28).

We may add to this list the copious references to finding favor (*ḥēn*) in the eyes of another (God or one's fellow man): Gen 6:8; 18:3; 19:19; 32:5 (H 6); 33:8, 10, 15; 34:11; 39:4; 47:25, 29; 50:4. The idea obviously is to gain acceptance or to win approbation. The phrase occurs approximately forty times in the OT.

There are twelve instances in which the subject of *māṣā'* is God: Gen 18:26, 28, 30; 44:16; Deut 32:10; Jer 23:11; Ezk 22:30; Hos 9:10; Ps 17:3; 89:20 [H 21]; Job 33:10; Neh 9:8.

For additional meanings of *māṣā'* in the Qal stem we might note the following: (1) "reach," "can you reach the perfections of the Almighty?" (Job 7:11); "they were unable to reach the door" (Gen 19:11); (2) "overtake," "your hand overtook your foes" (Ps 21:8 [H 9]); "the pangs of death overtook me" (Ps 116:3); "trouble and anguish have taken hold on me" (Ps 119:143); (3) "to happen to/to befall," "why has all this happened to us?" (Jud 6:13).

The Niphal stem also produces in certain cases the translations, "overpowered," "caught," "captured." Thus, Jer 50:24: O Babylon ... you are caught and seized (*tāpaś*); "a thief ... if he be caught" (Prov 6:30–31); "if a thief be caught breaking in" (Ex 22:1). This is also seen in cases where the Niphal participle (*han-nimṣā'*) is used. So, Jud 20:48 the phrases "all that they found" and "which they found" mean preferably "until the last 'captive'" and "all the 'captured' cities." In addition to these technical uses, *māṣā'* in the Niphal is often simply a synonym for *hāyâ* "to be": I Sam 9:8, "I have here at hand," literally, "there is found in my hand" (BDB 594b: 2a-f).

Bibliography: Dahood, M., "Northwest Semitic Philology and Job," in *The Bible in Current Catholic Thought,* ed. J. L. McKenzie, New York: Herder and Herder, 1962, pp. 55–74, esp. p. 57. Iwry, S., *whnmṣ'*: "A Striking Variant in IQIs^a" in *Textus* 5:34–43. THAT, I, pp. 922–24.

V.P.H.

מַצָּב (*maṣṣāb*), מֻצָּב (*mūṣṣāb*). See nos. 1398c,d.
מִצָּבָה (*miṣṣābâ*), מַצֵּבָה (*maṣṣēbâ*). See nos. 1398f,g.
מְצָד (*m^{e}ṣād*). See no. 1885c.

1232 מָצָה (*māṣâ*) ***drain (out).***

The verb is used seven times in the OT, four times in the Qal and three times in the Niphal. Sometimes the verb describes the literal draining of blood from a bird offered in sacrifice (Lev 1:15; 5:9) or the draining/squeezing of water from a fleece (Jud 6:38).

Three times the verb is used figuratively to describe the enemies of God who have drunk from the cup of his wrath down "to the last drop": Isa 51:17; Ezk 23:34; Ps 75:8 [H 9], "Oh, how they will drain it to the dregs." Dahood renders this verse, "Oh, how its dregs (i.e. of God's cup) will be drained, the wicked of the earth will drink the last drop." This rendering changes the MT *yimṣû* (Qal active) into *yumṣû* (Qal passive). The last part of Ezk 23:34, cited above, indicates what consequence befalls the wicked who drain this cup. In remorse and revulsion they smash the cup as the cause of their downfall and tear off their breasts as the peccant members through which they have sinned. A graphic picture!

The final use of this verb is in Ps 73:10 again to describe the wicked, "waters of abundance are 'drained' by them." The meaning is obvious enough. The wicked are so voracious that they swallow the ocean, leaving nothing for others (an effective hyperbole). It is unnecessary to connect the verb here with Ugaritic *mṣṣ,* "to suck" as Dahood has done (*Psalms,* in AB, *in loc.*).

V.P.H.

מַצָּה (*maṣṣâ*). See nos. 1234a, 1400a.
מִצְהָלָה (*miṣhālâ*). See no. 1881a.
מָצוֹד (*māṣôd*) I, II. See nos. 1885d,e.
מְצוּדָה (*m^eṣûdâ*) I, II. See nos. 1885g,i.
מִצְוָה (*miṣwâ*). See no. 1887b.
מְצוֹלָה (*m^eṣôlâ*). See no. 1889b.
מָצוֹק (*māṣôq*), מְצוּקָה (*m^eṣûqâ*). See nos. 1895d,e.
מָצוּק (*māṣûq*). See no. 1896a.
מָצוֹר (*māṣôr*). See no. 1898a.
מַצּוֹת (*maṣṣôt*). See no. 1400b.

1233 מצח (*mṣḥ*). **Assumed root of the following.**
1233a †מֵצַח (*mēṣaḥ*) ***brow, forehead.***
1233b †מִצְחָה (*miṣḥâ*) ***greaves.***

mēṣaḥ. ***Brow, forehead.*** The substantive appears thirteen times in the OT, five of which are in Ezk (3:7, 8 [twice], 9; 9:4). The etymology of the word is uncertain. One suggestion is to relate it to the verb *ṣāḥaḥ* "to be bright, dazzling," on the analogy of Arabic *ṣabaḥa* "to shine," *ṣabāḥ* "morning," and *ṣabāḥ* "forehead" (Blau; see bibliography).

The most interesting uses of *mēṣaḥ* are in the Ezk passages, plus one from Jeremiah. God says to Ezekiel (3:7) that all Israel is stiff of forehead (*ḥizqē mēṣaḥ*) and hardhearted (*q^eshê lēb*). The phrase "stiff/strong of forehead" suggests, perhaps, the picture of an animal, an ox or ram, butting its head. But in the next verse (3:8) God says that he has made the prophet's forehead stronger than the foreheads of his foes. That is to say, God will not only give him hardness equal to that of his foes, but that he promises Ezekiel to make him harder for the truth than the people are against it. There may be here an intentional play on the prophet's name which means "may God harden/strengthen" from the verb *ḥāzaq.* Cf. also 3:9.

In Ezk 9:4 God orders a divine agent to go through Jerusalem and put a mark on the forehead of the men who deplored and disapproved of the filth practised in the city. The word for "mark" is *taw,* the last letter of the Hebrew alphabet, which in the old Canaanite script was written X. Cf. also Gen 4:15 (*'ôt*); I Sam 21:14; Job 31:35; Rev 7:3, 4; 13:16; 14:1; 22:4. This might shed some light on Jer 3:3 when Jeremiah says of his audience, "You have a whore's forehead," rendered by JB as "you have maintained a prostitute's bold front." Could Jeremiah's accusation, however, be a reference to some trademark on the head of a prostitute, as is used today to mark the castes of India?

miṣḥâ. ***Greaves,*** found only once in the OT, I Sam 17:6, "And Goliath had 'greaves' of brass upon his legs." Greaves are the armor which protected the front of the leg below the knee.

Bibliography: Blau, J., "Etymologische Untersuchungen auf Grund des palästinischen Arabisch," VT 5:337–44, esp. p. 342. On *miṣḥâ*: Galling, K., *Biblisches Reallexicon,* Tübingen: J. C. B. Mohr, 1937, pp. 89–90. *idem.,* "Goliath und seine Rüstung," Supp VT 15:150–69, esp. pp. 163–65.

V.P.H.

מְצִיחַ (*m^eṣîaḥ*). See no. 1172a.
מְצֻלָה (*m^eṣūlâ*). See no. 1889c.
מְצִלָּה (*m^eṣillâ*). See no. 1919e.
מְצִלְתַּיִם (*m^eṣiltayim*). See no. 1919f.
מִצְנֶפֶת (*miṣnepet*). See no. 1940c.
מַצָּע (*maṣṣā'*). See no. 896e.
מִצְעָד (*miṣ'ād*). See no. 1943d.
מִצְעָר (*miṣ'ār*). See no. 1948c.
מִצְפֶּה (*miṣpeh*). See no. 1950b.
מַצְפּוֹן (*maṣpôn*). See no. 1953d.

1234 מָצַץ (*māṣaṣ*) ***drain out.*** Occurs only in Isa 66:11, *tāmoṣṣû w^ehit'annagtem* "(that) you may drain out and delight yourselves."

Derivative

1234a †מַצָּה (*maṣṣâ*) ***unleavened bread, unleavened cakes.***

A feminine singular noun from the root *māṣaṣ,* which occurs frequently as the plural *maṣṣôt* (forty-four times). In the LXX and NT, it is *azuma.* This quickly prepared bread was offered at ordinary meals to unexpected guests (Gen 19:3; Jud 6:19–21; I Sam 28:24). The Israelites, departing hastily from Egypt, did not have time to wait for bread to rise (Ex 12:39).

Unleavened cakes were offered in sacrifice when Aaron and his sons were consecrated to the priesthood (Ex 29:2), with the cereal offering (Lev 2:4–5), with the peace offering (Lev 7:12), and upon completion of the Nazirite vow (Num 6:15, 17, 19). The bread was carried in a basket (Ex 29:23; Lev 8:2, 26; Num 6:15, 17). The Levites assisted with the offering (I Chr 23:27–29). After the sacrifice, the remainder of the cereal offering was eaten by the priests (Lev 6:16; 10:12). At the time of Josiah's reform, priests of the high places ate unleavened bread among their brethren (II Kgs 23:9).

Because Israel had eaten unleavened bread on the night when they left Egypt (Ex 12:8) and during the first stages of their travels (Ex 12:39), annually thereafter they ate unleavened bread with bitter herbs at the Passover season whether the first or second Passover (Ex 12:14–20; Num 9:10). Eaten with bitter herbs, it is called the bread of affliction (Deut 16:3). Originally Passover, a one-night celebration, was distinct from the feast of unleavened bread, being the following seven days. But both days may be referred to as Passover or "the days of unleavened bread." The eating of unleavened bread began on the evening of the fourteenth of the month of Nisan (Ex 12:15, 18; 13:6; 34:18; Lev 23:6; Num 28:17; Deut 16:3; Ezk 45:21) and continued for seven days (Deut 16:8 gives six days with the seventh as a day of solemn assembly). Hence this season was called the feast of unleavened bread (*ḥag hammaṣṣôt*, Ex 23:15; 34:18; Lev 23:6; Deut 16:16; Ezr 6:22; II Chr 8:13; 30:13, 21; 35:17). Israel observed this custom at Gilgal when entering Palestine (Josh 5:11).

J.P.L.

מֵצַר (*mēṣar*). See no. 1973f.

1235 מִצְרַיִם (*miṣrayim*) ***Egypt.***

The Hebrew word is of uncertain derivation but is related to the Akkadian name *Miṣr* (*Muṣur*) and the Arabic name *Miṣr* for Egypt. In form, the Hebrew name for Egypt is in the dual, indicating her two basic constituent divisions: Upper Egypt (Southern Egypt) and Lower Egypt (the Delta area). The reason for the equation of upper with south and lower with north is because of the northward flow of the Nile. The Egyptians themselves referred to their land as *t3wy* "two lands" or *Kemi* "Black Land," this latter being a reference to the lush, irrigated soil that ran along the sides of the Nile. The name "Egypt," from Greek, possibly goes back to the Egyptian phrase *Hi-ku-Ptah,* the "House of the Spirit of (the god) Ptah," an ancient designation for Memphis (biblical Noph).

Briefly, Egyptian history may be conveniently divided into and highlighted by the following important periods: (1) The Old Kingdom/Pyramid Age/third-sixth Dynasties (2700–2200 B.C.); (2) The Middle Kingdom, especially the twelfth Dynasty (2000–1800 B.C.); (3) The New Kingdom or Empire Age, eighteenth-twentieth Dynasties (1570–1090 B.C.); (4) The Ethiopian period, especially the twenty-fifth Dynasty (715–663 B.C.); (5) Saitic/twenty-sixth Dynasty (633–525 B.C.); (7) Dynasty of the Ptolemies (306–30 B.C.). Generally speaking, ancient Egypt's history follows an undulating line of development. Times of innovation, greatness, expansion are followed by times of regression, retrenchment, the rise of centrifugal movements and the cycle repeats.

It is difficult, almost impossible, to pinpoint common denominators in Egyptian religion throughout almost three millennia of development. The gamut runs from a rampant polytheism to a solar "monotheism." Their religion never earmarked to everybody's satisfaction a supreme God. Was it Atum or Re or Horus or Amon-Re? No one would deny, however, that one characteristic of Egypt's religion was the emphasis on life after death. And yet this preoccupation with death was not a morbid one. Mortuary texts are inevitably gay and optimistic. The Egyptian concept of the afterlife is also an intensely materialistic one. The next life simply continues this one. This is why, for example, the body was mummified because corporeal existence was the only existence acceptable to the Egyptian.

In the OT it is the patriarchs who first have relationships with Egypt (Abraham, Gen 12). This would correspond roughly with the twelfth Dynasty of the Middle Kingdom. The Joseph story is obviously set in an Egyptian background, even to the extent of the cycle itself being in the form of a short story in simple prose (an Egyptian creation). However, from the time of Moses on, the Bible generally casts the land of Egypt in a very negative position. It is the oppressor of God's people, refusing to give Israel her liberation. It is the prophets particularly who inveigh against Israel leaning upon Egypt. "Leave her alone; she is under judgment and will topple" is their council.

And yet for all this denunciation of Egypt two passages in the OT about her are extremely interesting. One, the saintly Judean king Josiah died because he did not listen to the word of God from the Pharaoh Necho (II Chr 35:20ff.). Two, Isa 19:16ff. anticipates the conversion of Egypt (and Assyria) to the Lord, "blessed be my people Egypt" (v. 25). Traditional foes will be reconciled under God's blessings.

Bibliography: Gardiner, A., *Egypt of the Pharaohs,* New York: Oxford University, 1966. Wilson, J., The Culture of Ancient Egypt, University of Chicago, 1956. Steindorff, G. and Seele, K. C., *When Egypt Ruled the East,* University of Chicago, 1942.

V.P.H.

מַצְרֵף (*maṣrēp*). See no. 1972b.
מַק (*maq*). See no. 1237a.
מַקֶּבֶת (*maqqebet*). See nos. 1409c,d.
מִקְדָּשׁ (*miqdāsh*). See no. 1990f.
מַקְהֵל (*maqhēl*). See no. 1991d.
מִקְוֶה (*miqweh*), מִקְוָה (*miqwâ*). See nos. 1994c, 1995a.

מָקוֹם (*māqôm*). See no. 1999b.
מָקוֹר (*māqôr*). See no. 2004a.
מִקָּח (*miqqāḥ*). See no. 1124e.
מִקְטָר (*miqṭār*), מֻקְטָר (*mūqṭār*). See nos. 2011d,e.
מִקְטֶרֶת (*miqṭeret*). See no. 2011f.

1236 מַקֵּל (*maqqēl*) ***rod, staff*** (e.g. Gen 30:37; Jer 1:11). Derivation uncertain.

מִקְלָט (*miqlāṭ*). See no. 2026a.
מִקְלַעַת (*miqla'at*). See no. 2031a.
מִקְנֶה (*miqneh*), מִקְנָה (*miqnâ*). See nos. 2039b,c.
מִקְסָם (*miqsām*). See no. 2044b.
מִקְצֹעַ (*miqṣōa'*), מַקְצֻעָה (*maqṣū'â*). See nos. 2057a, 2056b.

1237 *מָקַק (*māqaq*) ***decay, rot, fester, pine away.***

Derivative

1237a מַק (*maq*) ***decay, rottenness*** (Isa 3:24; 5:24).

māqaq occurs nine times in the OT, eight times in the Niphal, once in the Hiphil. The verb is used most often to describe those who "perish" or "waste away" because of their sins, which dehumanize them: Lev 26:39, Ezk 4:17; 24:23; 33:10. Sin sows its own seeds of decay. Similar to this is the judgment of God meted out to those who attack Jerusalem in history's great eschatological struggle (Zech 14:12, three times), "Their flesh will 'molder'... their eyes will 'rot' in their sockets; their tongues will 'rot' in their mouth." Cf. also Isa 34:4.

The basic meaning of the verb is discoverable in Ps 38:5 (H 6), "My wounds stink and are 'festering' because of my foolishness."

V.P.H.

מִקְרָא (*miqrā'*). See no. 2063d.
מִקְרֶה (*miqreh*), מְקָרֶה (*m^e qāreh*). See nos. 2068c,f.
מְקֵרָה (*m^e qērâ*). See no. 2077d.
מִקְשֶׁה (*miqsheh*), מִקְשָׁה (*miqshâ*) I, II. See nos. 2086b,a; 2083b.
מַר (*mar*), מֹר (*mōr*). See nos. 1249a, 1248a,b.

1238 *מָרָא (*mārā'*) ***I, flap (?).*** Occurs only in the Hiphil, in Job 39:18, "she (the ostrich) flaps away, she laughs at the horse and his rider."

1239 מרא (*mr'*) **II. Assumed root of the following.**

1239a †מְרִיא (*m^e rî'*) ***fatling.***
1239b מֻרְאָה (*mūr'â*) ***crop or alimentary canal, of bird.*** Occurs only in Lev 1:16, "he is to remove the crop with its contents" (NIV).

m^e rî'. *Fatling.* *m^e rî'* occurs eight times in the OT. BDB (p. 597) lists this word under *mārā'* II, "to be fat, well-fed" but does not document the verb in the OT. Some have suggested that *m^e rî'* in Isa 11:6 read *yimr^e'û;* hence the translation of this verse in JB, "The calf and lion cub feed together."

In all but one of the eight passages, *m^e rî'* is used of cattle who were intentionally raised and fed for meat for the purpose of sacrifice to God. The Hebrew word is not concerned with the species but rather with the quality of the animal. The significance is that when one offers a sacrifice to his Lord, he offers his best and most valuable.

Both David (II Sam 6:13) and Adonijah (I Kgs 1:9, 19, 25) on festive occasions offered "fatlings" to the Lord. And yet the Lord rejects the offerings of these same animals whenever sacrifice and external religious performance become a substitute for personal morality and integrity (Isa 1:11; Amos 5:22). Ezekiel says that in addition to human flesh and the meat of other animals, the birds shall feast on fatlings in the day of God's judgment upon Israel's enemies (Ezk 39:18; cf. Rev 19:17–18, 21).

The only passage in which *m^e rî'* occurs in a non-sacrificial context is Isa 11:6.

Bibliography: Aharoni, I., "On Some Animals Mentioned in the Bible," *Osiris* 5:461–78. Bodenheimer, F. S., *Animal and Man in Bible Lands,* Leiden: Brill, 1960. Brueggemann, W. "Fatling," in IDB, II, p. 246.

V.P.H.

מַרְאָה (*mar'â*), מַרְאֶה (*mar'eh*). See nos. 2095h,i.
מְרַאֲשׁוֹת (*m^e ra'ăshôt*). See no. 2097f.
מַרְבָד (*marbād*). See no. 2102a.
מַרְבֶּה (*marbeh*). See no. 2103b.
מַרְבִּית (*marbît*). See no. 2103d.
מַרְבֵּץ (*marbēṣ*). See no. 2109b.
מַרְבֵּק (*marbēq*). See no. 2110a.
מַרְגּוֹעַ (*margôa'*). See no. 2117b.
מַרְגְּלוֹת (*marg^e lôt*). See no. 2113c.
מַרְגֵּמָה (*margēmâ*). See no. 2114b.
מַרְגֵּעָה (*margē'â*). See no. 2117c.

1240 מָרַד (*mārad*) ***be rebellious, rebel, revolt.***

Derivatives

1240a †מֶרֶד (*mered*) ***rebellion.***
1240b †מַרְדּוּת (*mardût*) ***rebellion.***

The verb is used twenty-five times in the OT, all in the Qal stem. It appears in Josh more often than in any other book (five times, 22:16, 18, 19 [twice], 29).

The verb *mārad* may indicate either rebellion against man (twelve times) or rebellion against God (twelve times). The one passage open to question in translation is Josh 22:19 (KJV): "Rebel not against the Lord, nor rebel against us (*timrōdû*). The RSV reads this: "Rebel not against the Lord, nor make us rebels" (reading *timridû* for *timrōdû*). This is certainly possible in light of the following verse, v. 20, which is a reminder, from the Achan incident, that the sin of one implicates many more than just the individual who is the immediate culprit. Hence, the translation of JB: "Do not rebel . . . or make us accomplices in rebellion."

In those instances where *mārad* signifies man rebelling against man it is always in reference to a Judean king or the people of Israel trying to resist the heavy yoke or the unwelcomed presence of a royal power. The one exception is Jeroboam I who is condemned by his contemporary monarch in southern Judea, Abijah, for "rebelling" against Solomon (II Chr 13:6). In some instances the Bible describes this rebellion with approbation and sometimes with disapproval. Thus, the Bible warmly endorses Hezekiah's actions against the Assyrians: II Kgs 18:7, 20 (=Isa 36:5). On the other hand, the actions of Jehoiakim against the Babylonians (II Kgs 24:1) and those of Zedekiah against the same foe (II Kgs 24:20 =Jer 52:3; Ezk 17:15; II Chr 36:13) are seen as being in violation of God's will. Whether the rebellion is being spoken of positively or negatively, it is, obvious that what is meant by the term is rebellion in the sense of an attempt to nullify or abrogate a covenant, on the part of the vassal. For similar uses of the term cf. Gen 14:4 and Neh 2:19; 6:6.

If *mārad* in an international political context refers to disloyalty and disunity among nations in covenant then it is only natural to assume that it is in this context, i.e., the context of a broken covenant, that the term refers to man's rebellion against God (the five passages in Josh 22 for example).

For synonyms we may note the use of *mārad* with: (1) *shûb*: Josh 22:16, 18, 29; II Kgs 24:1; (2) *pāsha'*: Ezk 2:3; 20:38; (3) *mā'al*: Josh 22:16, 22: (4) *mārâ*: Neh 9:26; (5) *qûm*: II Chr 13:6; (6) Dan 9:5, parallel to *ḥāṭā', 'āwâ, rāsa'* (all of which, see).

mered. ***Rebellion.*** Found only once once in the OT, Josh 22:22, parallel to *ma'al* "transgression, breach of faith."

mardût. ***Rebellion.*** Used only in I Sam 20:30. Saul, charging his son Jonathan with subversive activity in aiding David, hurls this approbrium at him: "Thou son of perverse rebellion." The phrase has in most cases been emended. As it stands, it is written *ben-na'ăwat hammardût.* The second word, *na'ăwat,* is a Niphal feminine participle of *'āwâ* "bend, twist." On the basis of the LXX, which for this word has *korasiōn,* most scholars have emended *na'ăwat* to *na'ărat* "girl." Hence, the translation, "son of a rebellious woman," or "son of a wanton" (JB).

Bibliography: Driver, S. R., *Notes on the Hebrew Text of the Books of Samuel,* Oxford: Clarendon, 1890, pp. 134–35. THAT, I, pp. 925–27.

V.P.H.

מִרְדָּה (*mirdâ*). See no. 2121a.
מַרְדּוּת (*mardût*). See no. 1240b.

1241 מְרֹדָךְ ($m^e r\bar{o}d\bar{a}k$) ***Marduk,*** the patron deity of the city of Babylon.

Marduk is mentioned in the Bible only in Jer 50:2, "Babylon is captured, Bel (*bēl*) is disgraced, Merodach (Marduk) is shattered." Note that here the name Marduk is paralleled by the word *bēl*, a transliteration of the Akkadian attribute of Marduk, *belum* "lord." Apart from its appearance in Jer 50:2, the name of Marduk appears only in the Bible in personal names such as Merodach-baladan Mardukapal-iddina, Evil-merodach (Awel-Marduk), and Mordecai.

The origin of Marduk's name is unknown, though several etymologies have been offered. The form of his name in Sumerian is ^{d}*AMAR-UD* and in the earliest syllabic renderings (Old Babylonian) it is *marutuk* (*ma-ru-tu-uk*). The translation would be, "The young bull/son of Utu (the sun-god)." Another possibility is that his name means "son of the storm," the picture given of Marduk in texts being more akin to a god of storm, rain, lightning, and thunder, rather than to a solar figure (Jacobsen).

The vocalization of his name in Hebrew, $m^e r\bar{o}d\bar{a}k$ is interesting (in the LXX it is *marodak*). Some have suggested a deliberate likeness to *'ădōnay* "my lord." More likely, it could be a euphemistic vocalization, akin to $m^e b\bar{o}r\bar{a}k$ "accursed."

It is commonly asserted that Marduk was exalted to his position of supremacy in the Babylonian pantheon when Hammurabi made Babylon the political capital of southern Mesopotamia (eighteenth century B.C.), although he was known as a minor god as early as the third millenium B.C. A case can be made, however, for the view that it was not until the reign of Nebuchadnezzar I (*c.* 1100 B.C.) that Marduk actually became "king of the gods" (Lambert; see bibliography). Marduk was the son of Enki (Ea) of Eridu, the god of wisdom and the patron of the arts of magic. Marduk himself fathered Nabu, who, toward the end of the neo-Babylonian period (sixth century B.C.), supplanted his father in popularity.

Marduk was the city god of Babylon. His temple there was called *É-sag-ila* "the house that raises high its head." Adjacent to it was the famous step-tower (ziggurat) *É-Temen-an-ki,* "the house of the foundation of heaven and earth," approximately ninety-one metres high. The temple's great eastern portal, the holy door, bricked up the whole year, was opened on Marduk's principal feast, the *Akitu* (New Year's) festival. On this day Marduk's wedding with his bride, Šarpanitu, was celebrated by bringing their two statues together outside the city walls. By means of simulated sexual intercourse between the two, the land's fertility would be ensured for the coming year. Also at this feast the *Enuma Elish* (the Babylonian creation epic) was recited. Marduk, the hero of this story, is appointed by the gods to lead the fight against Tiamat, and after victory fashions the universe from her body.

Though mentioned specifically by name only in Jer 50:2, Marduk's helplessness as god of Babylon under the name of Bel is ridiculed in Isa 46:1; Jer 51:44; and especially Dan 14:1–22.

Bibliography: Jacobsen, T., "The Battle Between Marduk and Tiamat," JAOS 88:104–108. Lambert, W. G., "The Reign of Nebuchadnezzar I: A Turning Point in the History of Ancient Mesopotamian Religion," in *The Seed of Wisdom,* ed. W. S. McCullough, University of Toronto, 1964, pp. 3–13. Schott, A., "Die Anfänge Marduks als eines assyrischen Gottes," ZAW 43: 318–21.

V.P.H.

מֻרְדָּף (*murdāp*). See no. 2124a.

1242 מָרָה (*mārâ*) ***be rebellious against, disobedient towards.***

Derivative

1242a †מְרִי (*merî*) ***rebellion.***

The verb occurs forty-five times in the OT most frequently in the (historical) Psalms (ten times) and eight times in Deut. Twenty-two times the verb is used in the Qal stem and twenty-three times in the Hiphil stem. In this latter case the meaning or translation is something like "to provoke (by defiance)."

With but five exceptions all uses of *mārâ/merî* refer to rebellion against God. These five exceptions are: (1, 2) Deut 21:18, 20, dealing with disciplinary procedures to be pursued by parents with a stubborn (*sôrēr*) and "rebellious" son; (3) Job 17:2, "Are there not mockers with me and my eye continues in their 'provocation/spitefulness'?" (4) Job 23:2, "My lament is still rebellious"; (5) Prov 17:11, "The wicked man thinks of nothing but rebellion."

The rebellion to which *mārâ* refers is specifically the rebellion of Israel/Judah against God. Only on a few occasions is the nation not involved. These would be the five verses noted in the above paragraph plus the reference to the anonymous "man of God" who disobeyed God's orders not to linger or eat at Bethel but to continue immediately on his way, and as a result was mauled and killed by a lion (I Kgs 13:21, 26); also, in the third "suffering-servant" song (Isa 50:5), "I was not rebellious/made no resistance." In Lam 1:18, 20 the confession of the "I" is personified Jerusalem speaking.

Not only does *mārâ/merî* refer to the rebellion of Israel, but primarily it refers to the rebellion of Israel in the wilderness as God led her toward Canaan. Some concurrent references which document such aberrant behavior are: Num 20:10, 24; 27:14 plus numerous passages in Deut such as 1:26, 43; 9:7, 24 *inter alia.* Elsewhere, there are a number of later books which at points are recapitulations of early Israelite history and this sin is cited: Ps 78:8, 17, 40, 56; 106:7, 33, 43; Isa 63:10; Neh 9:26 (upon entry into the promised land).

This sin of rebellion may be in word: Num 17:10 [H 25]; 27:14, complaining; Ps 78:17ff., challenging and defying God to do the abnormal, to cater to their tastes and delicacies. Or, it may be a rebellion in deed: I Sam 12:15, obedience to man over God; I Kgs 13:21, 26, actions contrary to God's clearly expressed will by a "clergyman"; Jer 4:17, "your own behavior and actions"; Isa 3:8, "their words and their deeds." What is most often rebelled against is "the commandment/the word of the Lord," (*'et*) *pî* (literally, "the mouth"). This is the most frequent direct object of the verb *mārâ*: I Kgs 13:21, 26; Lam 1:18; Ps 105:28; Num 20:24; 27:14, *inter alia.*

mārâ is found in series or parallel with the following Hebrew words: (1) *sôrēr* "stubborn": Deut 21:18, 20; Jer 5:23; Ps 78:8; (2) *'āṣab* "to hurt, grieve": Isa 63:10; Ps 78:40; (3) *mā'an* "to refuse": Isa 1:20; Neh 9:17; (4) *pāsha'* "to transgress": Lam 3:42; (5) *nā'aṣ* "to scorn": Ps 107:11; (6) *ḥāṭā'* "to sin": Ps 78:17; (7) *nāsâ* "to test": Ps 78:56; (8) *mārad* "to rebel": Neh 9:26; (9) *mā'as* "to reject" and *ḥālal* "to profane": Ezk 20:13; (10) *merî* parallel to *hapṣar,* a Hiphil infinitive absolute of *pāṣar* "to press," perhaps here "arrogance, presumption": I Sam 15:23.

merî. ***Rebellion.*** Of the twenty-three usages of this noun in the OT, sixteen are in Ezk, and preponderantly these are in the phrase, "house of rebellion" (in reference to Judah): 2:5, 6, 8; 3:9, 26, 27; 12:2 (twice), 3, 9, 25; 17:12; 24:3; also 2:7 and 44:6 for variations of this phrase.

Bibliography: THAT, I, pp. 928–30.

V.P.H.

מַרְהֵבָה (*marhēbâ*). See no. 2125d.
מָרוֹד (*mārôd*). See no. 2129a.
מָרוֹם (*mārôm*). See no. 2133h.
מֵרוֹץ (*mērôṣ*). See no. 2137a.
מְרוּצָה (*m^erûṣâ*). See no. 2212b.
מָרוּק (*mārûq*). See no. 1246a.
מָרוֹר (*mārôr*). See no. 1248e.
מַרְזֵחַ (*marzēaḥ*). See no. 2140a.

1243 מָרַח (*māraḥ*) **rub.** Occurs in Isa 38:21, "let them take a cake of figs and rub it on the eruption."

מֶרְחָב (*merḥāb*). See no. 2143c.
מֶרְחָק (*merḥāq*). See no. 2151c.
מַרְחֶשֶׁת (*marḥeshet*). See no. 2152a.

1244 מָרַט (*māraṭ*) ***make smooth/bald, polish.***

The verb is used fourteen times in the OT in a variety of contexts. Three times it refers to the tearing out of one's hair, either the hair on the crown of the head or the beard. Once, this action is indicative of the grief which Ezra felt upon his discovery that his fellow Israelites had intermarried with foreigners (Ezr 9:3). Two other times this same action describes not grief but rather an act of violence (Neh 13:25), something Nehemiah did to those who intermarried; and Isa 50:6, "I (i.e., the suffering servant) gave my back to the smiters and my cheeks to them that 'tore' at my beard." In connection with these passages we may note the use of the same verb to describe the condition of baldness (Lev 13, 40–41) in the context of leprosy diagnosis. Ezekiel 29:18 says that the heads of the people of Tyre were "made bald" by Nebuchadnezzar. This does not mean he tore out their hair; rather, the baldness was the result of carrying loads on their heads as corvée labor gangs.

Besides the passage in Ezk 29:18, the verb is used five times more in that book: 21:9 [H 14]; 21:10 [H 15]; 21:11 [H 16]; 21:28 [H 33]. Each case refers to the Lord's sword which is "furbished/polished," ready to be given into the hands of the slaughterer, the Babylonians, to execute judgment upon God's people.

Finally, this verb is used to describe the vessels of 'burnished' brass put into the Jerusalem temple of Solomon (I Kgs 7:45). It is employed in Isaiah's oracle against Cush, the name of ancient Ethiopia, whose people are pictured (Isa 18:2, 7) as "tall and bronzed," not "scattered and peeled" as in KJV.

V.P.H.

מְרִי (*merî*). See no. 1242a.
מְרִיא (*m^erî'*). See no. 1239a.
מְרִיבָה (*m^erîbâ*). See no. 2159c.
מְרִירִי (*m^erîrî*). See no. 1248h.
מְרִירוּת (*m^erîrût*). See no. 1248i.
מֹרֶךְ (*mōrek*). See no. 2164c.
מֶרְכָּב (*merkāb*). See no. 2163e.
מַרְכֹּלֶת (*markōlet*). See no. 2165c.
מִרְמָה (*mirmâ*). See no. 2169b.
מִרְמָס (*mirmās*). See no. 2176a.
מֵרֵעַ (*mērēa'*). See no. 2186f.
מִרְעֶה (*mir'eh*). See no. 2185b.
מַרְעִית (*mar'ît*). See no. 2185c.
מַרְפֵּא (*marpē'*). See no. 2196c.
מַרְפֵּשׂ (*marpēś*). See no. 2199a.

1245 *מָרַץ (*māraṣ*) ***be/make sick.***

The verb occurs four times in the OT. Three of these (I Kgs 2:8; Mic 2:10; Job 6:25) are in the Niphal, and mean "to make sick," i.e. "sore" or "grievous." So, "a grievous curse" *q^elālâ nimreṣet,* in I Kgs 2:8 and "grievous pain" *ḥebel nimrāṣ,* in Mic 2:10.

The third passage, Job 6:25, is open to question as to its translation: "how 'forcible' are right words" (KJV). This rendering gives to *māraṣ* an otherwise unknown meaning. Pope (in AB, *Job,* pp. 49, 55) translates, "how 'pleasant' are honest words," perhaps on the suggested relation of *nimr^eṣû* to *niml^eṣû* (Ps 119:103), "smooth, pleasant." A third possibility is to read the phrase as a question, "what is there sick in righteous words?" (Tur-Sinai) or "how are honest words bitter?" (Driver). The advantage of these last two suggestions is that they both retain the basic idea of *māraṣ* as something undesirable.

The fourth use of this root is Job 16:3 (Hiphil): "what 'emboldeneth' thee that you answer?" or better JB, "what a plague—you need to have the last word."

Bibliography: Driver, G. R., "Some Hebrew Words," JTS 29:390–96, esp. pp. 394–95.

V.P.H.

מַרְצֵעַ (*marṣēa'*). See no. 2209a.
מַרְצֶפֶת (*marṣepet*). See no. 2210b.

1246 מָרַק (*māraq*) ***I, scour, polish.***

Derivatives

1246a מָרוּק (*mārûq*) ***a scraping, rubbing*** (Est 2:12).
1246b תַּמְרוּק (*tamrûq*) ***a scraping, rubbing*** (Prov 20:30).

1247 מרק (*mrq*) **II. Assumed root of the following.**

1247a מָרָק (*mārāq*) ***juice stewed out of meat, broth*** (Jud 6:19; Isa 65:4).

מֶרְקָח (*merqāḥ*). See no. 2215f.
מִרְקַחַת (*mirqaḥat*). See no. 2215h.

1248 מָרַר (*mārar*) ***I, be bitter, strengthen, be strong.***

Derivatives

1248a †מַר (*mar*) ***bitter.***
1248b מֹר (*mōr*) ***myrrh.***
1248c †מָרָּה (*morrâ*) ***bitterness.***
1248d †מֹרָה (*mōrâ*) ***grief.***
1248e †מָרוֹר (*mārôr*) ***bitterness.***
1248f †מְרוֹרָה (*m^{e}rôrâ*) ***bitter thing.***
1248g מְרֵרָה (*m^{e}rērâ*) ***gall*** (only Job 16:13)
1248h †מְרִירִי (*m^{e}rîrî*) ***bitter.***
1248i †מְרִירוּת (*m^{e}rîrût*) ***bitterness.***
1248j †מֶמֶר (*memer*) ***bitterness.***
1248k †מַמְרוֹר (*mamrôr*) ***bitterness.***
1248l †תַּמְרוּר (*tamrûr*) ***bitterness.***

The verb *mārar* is used fifteen times, always with man as subject, never God, unless the verb describes an interpretation given by man to God's actions and will. For example, Job (and this root plus its various derivatives appear more frequently in Job than in any other OT book [ten times]) complains: The Almighty has vexed my soul (27:2), Hiphil of *mārar*. Similarly, Naomi says, "Do not call me Naomi, call me 'Mara' for the Almighty has dealt very bitterly with me" (Ruth 1:20).

It is interesting to note that the Hebrews expressed tragic, unpleasant experiences in terms of the sense of taste, the bitter. Actually, we employ the same figure of speech in our English language: It was a galling experience; his actions were not in very good taste, I thought; your wife is always so tastefully dressed.

For the root *mārar* we suggest not only the traditional translation "to be bitter/embitter" but also the translation "to be strong/strengthen." The reason for this is that in Ugaritic/Arabic/Aramaic the root *mrr* may mean one of "to strengthen, bless, commend." In at least four OT passages this seems the preferable translation. Thus, Ex 1:14 might better read not "they made their lives bitter," but "they strengthened their lives," i.e. the Egyptians, by imposing hard labor, only toughened the Hebrews. The context suggests this. Judges 18:25 refers not to "embittered men" but "tough men." Ecclesiastes 7:26 traditionally reads: "I found more bitter than death the woman whose heart is snares and nets." It will be observed, however, that the author is not stressing a woman's bitterness but her strength; hence, "I found stronger than death" (cf. Song 8:6). Finally, Ezk 3:14 reads, "I went in bitterness, in the heat of my spirit." But why should the prophet be "bitter" especially in light of what he saw and heard in vv. 12–13? We suggest the translation, "I went forth strengthened by the fervor of my spirit."

mar. ***Bitter, strong.*** Thirty-seven times in the OT. Most frequently the adjective is used in a figurative sense, as is the verb, to describe an emotion, though a few examples of *mar* in a literal sense may be found. The Scriptures speak of bitter grape clusters (Deut 32:32); bitter water (Ex 15:23); food in general (Prov 27:7), which, though bitter, is palatable to the hungry (cf. Isa 5:20).

Of special interest in the literal category is the phrase "water of bitterness" in Num 5:18–19, 23–24, 27. Combined with dust and ink, and hence decidedly unhygienic, it was used in an instance of investigation to determine whether a husband's jealous suspicions of his wife's unfaithfulness were correct or not. The idea is, of course, that often consciousness of guilt will produce somatic symptoms, the principle behind our modern lie detector testing of suspected criminals. This investigation is sometimes called trial by ordeal, but that is not quite accurate. The trial by ordeal, used in antiquity and up to the Middle Ages, required the accused to undergo obvious physical danger like walking through fire or being thrown bound into the river. The person who was unharmed was presumed innocent. Trial by ordeal was common in Assyria, but the OT used rather the more sensible rules of evidence we are accustomed to. The "water of bitterness" is indeed more like a lie detector test as suggested above. Only a woman who was innocent could normally undergo this solemn ceremony without breaking down. The further effect, apart from the unhygienic water, was caused by the providence of God punishing the guilty.

As we have indicated, the more frequent use of *mar* is a figurative one, to express the emotional response to a destructive, heart-crushing situation. Some of these situations are: (1) in the case of a woman, barrenness and sterility, I Sam 1:10; (2) an unfulfilled death-wish, Job 3:20; (3) family turmoil, Gen 27:34; (4) the exploitation and deprivation of minority peoples, Est 4:1; (5) personal suffering and hardship, Job 7:11; 10: 1; Isa 38:15; (6) a hostile and precarious situation, Ps 64:3 [H 4]; grief over the apostasy of believers, Jer 2:19; (7) the Lord's judgment on unbelievers, Zeph 1:14; (8) discontentment with lacklustre leadership, I Sam 22:2; (9) the thought of death, I Sam 15:32; (10) the crumbling of dreams and aspiration, Ezk 27:30, 31.

morrâ. ***Bitterness, grief.*** Used only in Prov 14:10. "Only the heart knows its own grief." The form of the word in Hebrew is unusual, with a *dagesh forte* in the *resh*.

mōrâ. ***Grief*** (in the sense of disappointment). Only in Gen 26:35, expressing Isaac's chagrin at Esau's decision to marry Hittite women.

mārôr. ***Bitterness, bitter herb.*** According to Ex 12:8 and Num 9:11 the bitter herb was to be eaten on Passover with the passover meal. At first the bitter herbs signified the haste with which the meal was prepared (Ex 12:8) and later Jewish tradition saw in the bitter herb a reminder of the bitter treatment to which the Jews were subjected in Egypt. Cf. Lam 3:15.

m^e^rôrâ. ***Bitter thing, herb, poison(ous).*** In Job 20:14 the word pictorally describes the viper's venom. Cf. also Deut 32:32; Job 13:26; 20:25.

m^e^rîrî. ***Bitter, bitterness.*** Deuteronomy 32:24. The reading in Job 3:5 is problematical. Instead of kaph plus the root *mārar* what we most likely have is the root *kāmar* II, "to be dark," and hence the translation, "O 'Eclipse' terrify it (i.e., the day of my birth)."

m^e^rîrût. ***Bitterness.*** Only in Ezk 21:6 [H 11].

memer. ***Bitterness, grief.*** Only Prov 17:25, parallel to *ka'as* "sorrow."

mamrôr. ***Bitterness.*** Only in Job 9:18.

tamrûr. ***Bitterness.*** The best known verse in which this word appears is Jer 31:15 (=Mt 2:18). Cf. also Jer 6:26 and Hos 12:14 [H 15].

Bibliography: Dahood, M., "Qoheleth and Recent Discoveries," *Bib* 39:302–18, esp. pp. 308–10. Gordon, C. H., UT 19: no. 1556. Michaelis, W., "Pikros," in TDNT, VI, pp. 122–25. On *mōr* "myrrh": Van Beek, G. W., "Frankincense and Myrrh," BA 23:70–95. ______, "Frankincense and Myrrh in Ancient South Arabia," JAOS 78:141–52.

V.P.H.

1249 מרר (*mrr*) **II. Assumed root of the following.**

1249a מַר (*mar*) ***drop.*** Occurs only in Isa 40:15, *goyim k^e^mar midd^e^lî* "nations (are) like a drop (hanging) from a bucket."

מְרֵרָה (*m^e^rērâ*). See no. 1248g.
מִרְשַׁעַת (*mirsha'at*). See no. 2222l.
מַשָּׂא (*maśśā'*). See nos. 1421d,e.
מַשֹּׂא (*maśśō'*). See no. 1421f.
מַשְׂאֵת (*maśś^e^'ēt*). See no. 1421h.
מִשְׂגָּב (*miśgāb*). See no. 2234a.
מַשּׂוֹר (*maśśôr*). See no. 1423a.

1250 מְשׂוּרָה (*m^e^śûrâ*) ***measure.*** Derivation uncertain.

מָשׂוֹשׂ (*māśôś*). See no. 2246b.
מִשְׂחָק (*miśḥāq*). See no. 1905f.
מַשְׂטֵמָה (*maśṭēmâ*). See no. 2251a.
מְשׂוּכָה (*m^e^śūkâ*). See no. 2241a.
מַשְׂכִּיל (*maśkîl*). See no. 2263b.
מַשְׂכִּית (*maśkît*). See no. 2257c.
מַשְׂכֹּרֶת (*maśkōret*). See no. 2264.1.
מִשְׂרָה (*miśrâ*). See no. 2288a.
מַשְׂרֵפָה (*maśrēpâ*). See no. 2292d.

1251 מַשְׂרֵת (*maśrēt*) ***pan, dish*** (II Sam 13:9).

מַשָּׁה (*mashshâ*). See no. 1424a.
מַשָּׁאוֹן (*mashshā'ôn*). See no. 1425a.
מַשָּׁאוֹת (*mashshā'ôt*). See no. 1425b.
מִשְׁאָלָה (*mish'ālâ*). See no. 2303b.

1252 מִשְׁאֶרֶת (*mish'eret*) ***kneading trough/bowl.***

Flour would be mixed with water in this household vessel, *mish'eret,* which already contained fermenting dough. They were small enough that they could be wrapped in one's clothing and transported on the shoulders (Ex 12:34) with even the warmth of the body helping the process of fermentation. The frogs filled these vessels in one of the plagues in Egypt, Ex 8:3 [H 7:28]. Cf. also Deut 28:5, 17. The word may be related to *ś^e^'ōr* "leaven."

V.P.H.

מִשְׁבְּצוֹת (*mishb^e^ṣôt*). See no. 2320b.
מַשְׁבֵּר (*mashbēr*), מִשְׁבָּר (*mashbār*). See nos. 2321c,d.
מִשְׁבָּת (*mishbāt*). See no. 2323c.
מִשְׁגֶּה (*mishgeh*). See no. 2325b.

1253 מָשָׁה (*māshâ*) ***draw.***

This verb appears only three times in the OT. One is in the passage dealing with the giving of the name Moses, Ex 2:10. The other reference is II Sam 22:17 (and its parallel in Ps 18:16 [H 17]): "(the Lord) draws me from deep waters."

1254 מֹשֶׁה (*mōsheh*) ***Moses.***

The important verse surrounding the naming of Moses is Ex 2:10. It reads: "She called his name Moses (*mōsheh*): and she said, because I drew him (*m^e^shîtihû*) out of the water." In Hebrew the proper name "Moses" is a Qal active participle (masculine/singular) of the verb *māshâ* "to draw (out)," and hence is to be translated as "drawer out" or "he who draws out." Morphologically, the form of the name is what one would expect from a type of verb such as *māshâ,* variously described by Hebrew grammarians as "final weak," "*tertia infirma,*" "*lamed he*" and so forth. Thus, one encounters the verb *bānâ* "to build" and *bōneh* "builder" in the same pattern.

It should be clear that the etymology given in Ex 2:10 is not intended to be a precise philological explanation, as is the case with most of the onomastica of the Old Testament. If such were the case, we would expect the name given to the infant by the daughter of Pharaoh to be, not *mosheh* "he who draws out," but *māshūy* "He who is drawn out," i.e., a participle that is passive in form.

This does not mean then that the explanation of the name given in Ex is misleading. Nor should we go to the extreme of denying the historicity of the event by suggesting that such a story rose as an etiology of the name, i.e., that the story was fabricated to answer someone's query, "why was our great ancestor called *mosheh*?" The answer is that the name "Moses" is like many others a pun, a word play based on assonance. The name is explained not because Moses is derived from *māshâ* but because it resembles it in sound.

For further clues some have looked to the spelling of Moses in the Septuagint. There the Greek form is *mōysēs*. Ancient writers explained this as either "saved (*ysēs*) from the water (*mō*)" or "taken (*sēs*) from the water (*mōy*)."

The consensus today is that "Moses" goes back to an Egyptian root *ms* "child," *mss* "to be born." *ms* appears as a personal name in Egyptian but is better recognized as the second part of theophoric names: Ahmose: Ah is born; Ptahmose: Ptah is born, taking *mose* as the Egyptian old perfective of the verb *mss*. This Egyptian root definitely appears in the Bible in the names "Rameses" (*ra'amsēs*, Ex 1:11) and "Ramses" (*ra'm^e sēs*, Gen 47:11; Ex 12:37; Num 33:3, 5). In Egyptian the form is *R'-ms-sw*, "Re is he that hath borne him," the active participle *mas* followed by the pronoun *se* "him."

Linguistically, the problem is to account for the relationship between the sibilants *s* in Egyptian and *sh* in Hebrew. The problem is removed by the demonstration that Egyptian writings of Semitic names show mostly *s* for Semitic *sh* (Griffiths, pp. 229–30).

Bibliography: Cassuto, U., *A Commentary on the Book of Exodus*, Jerusalem: Magnes Press, 1967, pp. 20–21. Cole, R., "Exodus," in *Tyndale O.T. Commentaries*, Inter-Varsity, 1973, pp. 58–59. Gardiner, A., "The Egyptian Origin of Some English Personal Names," JAOS 56:189–97 ,esp. pp. 192–94. Griffiths, J. G., "The Egyptian Derivation of the Name Moses," JNES 12: 225–31. TDNT, IV, pp. 848–64.

V.P.H.

מַשֶּׁה (*mashsheh*). See no. 1427b.
מְשׁוֹאָה (*m^e shô'â*). See no. 2339b.
מְשׁוּבָה (*m^e shûbâ*). See no. 2340e.
מְשׁוּגָה (*m^e shûgâ*). See no. 2341a.
מָשׁוֹט (*māshôṭ*). See no. 2344e.

1255 מָשַׁח (*māshaḥ*) ***anoint, spread a liquid.***

Derivatives

1255a †מִשְׁחָה (*mishḥâ*) ***anointing oil.***
1255b †מָשְׁחָה (*moshḥâ*) ***portion.***
1255c †מָשִׁיחַ (*māshîaḥ*) ***anointed one.***
1255d מִמְשַׁח (*mimshaḥ*) ***expansion*** (Ezk 28:14). Meaning uncertain.

The verb *māshaḥ* with its derivatives occurs about 140 times. It is most frequent in the Pentateuch and historical books; in the prophets it is found as a verb only twice with its religious connotation of sacred anointing (Isa 61:1; Dan 9:24).

māshaḥ could refer in everyday usage to such acts as rubbing (*māshaḥ*) a shield with oil (Isa 21:5), painting (*māshaḥ*) a house (Jer 22:14), or applying (*māshaḥ*) oil to the body (Amos 6:6).

Used in connection with religious ritual, *māshaḥ* involved a ceremonial application of oil to items such as the tabernacle, altar or laver (Ex 40:9–11), or even the sin offering (Ex 29:36). More frequently *māshaḥ* is used for the ceremonial induction into leadership offices, an action which involved the pouring of oil from a horn upon the head of an individual. Easily the most frequent mention of *māshaḥ* is with kings such as Saul and David of Israel (II Sam 12:7; but note Hazael, an Aramaean, I Kgs 19:15). The high priest was anointed (Ex 29:7; Num 35:25) and so were other priests (Ex 30:30). Twice there is mention of anointing a prophet (I Kgs 19:16; Isa 61:1).

There is a fourfold theological significance of *māshaḥ*. First, to anoint an individual or an object indicated an authorized separation for God's service. Moses anointed Aaron "to sanctify him" (*l^e qadd^e shô*, Lev 8:12; cf. Ex 29:36 for the altar). Note the expression "anointed to the Lord" (I Chr 29:22). *māshaḥ*, while representing a position of honor, also represents increased responsibility. Both Saul and David are called to account for their sin with the reminder, "I (the Lord) anointed (*māshaḥ*) you king" (I Sam 15:17; II Sam 12:7). Secondly, though the agent might be the priest or prophet, writers speak of anointed ones as those whom the Lord anointed (e.g. I Sam 10:1; II Sam 12:7). Such language underscores that it is God who is the authorizing agent; that the anointed is inviolable (I Sam 24:8ff.); and that the anointed one is to be held in special regard (cf. I Sam 26:9ff.). Thirdly, one may infer that divine enablement was understood as accompanying *māshaḥ*. Of both Saul and David it is said in connection with their anointing that "the Spirit of God came mightily upon him" (I Sam 10:6ff; I Sam 16:13ff.). Finally, in the form *māshîaḥ*, *māshaḥ* was associated with the coming promised deliverer, Jesus. Though this association with the term *māshaḥ* is not as prevalent in the OT as often supposed, the prospect of a righteous, Spirit-filled ruler is increasingly discernible in the OT (cf. Isa 9:1–7; 11:1–5; 61:1).

māshîaḥ. ***Anointed, anointed one*** (ASV and RSV similar). This word used as adjective and noun occurs about forty times in the OT, primarily in I–II Sam and Ps. While it may designate an office such as the high priest (Lev 4:3), *māshîaḥ* is almost exclusively reserved as a synonym for "king" (*melek,* q.v.) as in poetry where it is in parallel position with king (I Sam 2:10; II Sam 22:51; cf. Ps 2:2; 18:50 [H 51]; but cf. Ps 28:8 where "people" is a counterpart term). Striking are the phrases "the Lord's anointed" (*māshîaḥ* YHWH) or equivalents such as "his anointed" referring to kings. Certainly a title of honor, the expressions also emphasize the special relationship between God and the anointed.

A much discussed point is the mention of Cyrus, a non-Israelite, as the Lord's anointed (*limshîḥô,* Isa 45:1). If *māshîaḥ* is envisioned as an ideal king, godly and upright, then the designation of "anointed" causes difficulty, for Cyrus was a worshiper of Marduk and other pagan deities. Yet Cyrus was the Lord's appointee for a definite task. The Isaiah passage suggests that *māshîaḥ* be understood as one singled out or "chosen" (*bāḥar* q.v.) for a task, characteristically one of deliverance—a deliverance of Israel from their Babylonian captors returning them to their homeland.

As for the king, that task centered on a righteous rule in the context of grace included in which was deliverance from oppression. Saul, the first king, in his first major encounter exemplified the qualities of a *māshîaḥ* (I Sam 11).

He was Spirit-endowed, brought victory over the enemy Amalekites, and extended life to a group who, because of their action, deserved death (I Sam 11). Because of Saul's sin and general stance before God, it is David who becomes the archetype of the *māshîaḥ*.

The Psalm literature especially regards *māshîaḥ* as God's agent or vice-regent (as in Ps 2:2). In this much discussed passage the first level of meaning may be that of an immediate Israelite king, as the *māshîaḥ* against whom, since he is aligned with God, enemies strike in vain. Even the promise that the ends of the earth be the possession of the *māshîaḥ* fit the anticipations of Israel for their national king (Ps 72:8ff; Ps 18:44–48). But from the NT we learn that the meaning of *māshîaḥ* in Ps 2 cannot be limited to a king about to be enthroned, but is a reference to the unique vice-regent, Jesus Christ (Acts 13:32ff; cf. Heb 1:5; 5:5). The so-called royal psalms, including Ps 2 therefore, may be regarded legitimately as messianic, even though some may refer initially to Israel's monarch. The Psalm statements underline the just administration, the saving function and the universal rule of Jesus Christ.

[This view of double reference or a typical fulfilment is doubtless applicable in some OT passages. It is widely held, however, that there are some psalms and other prophetic passages which can not refer to Israel's king or some contemporary situation, but must refer to Christ directly.

Thus the royal psalm 45:6 [H 7] by natural and strict translation speaks of the king as divine and Ps 110:1–5 [H 2–6] refers to David's son as David's Lord—and also says that this king is a priest, a thing not allowed in Israel. (True, II Sam 8:18 seems to call David's sons priests in the Hebrew, but there probably is a textual problem here. The Hebrew strictly seems to call Benaiah and the Cherethites priests. Actually, the LXX of this verse and the Hebrew and LXX of the parallel in I Chr 18:17 do not use the word "priest.") There is warrant, therefore, for a direct messianic reference on Ps 2. Indeed, v. 12 as normally taken would imply that men are exhorted to put their faith in this anointed son—surely not David.

It is true, however, that the coming Son of David is seldom called Messiah in the OT, but see below. Many other designations are used (Branch, Shoot, Son of David, etc.). Even in the DSS the use of the word "Messiah" is ambiguous. There is mention of a Messiah of Aaron and a Messiah of Israel, apparently two figures, a king and a priest, perhaps neither one *the* Messiah. But also in the DSS there is expressed in the Testimonia and the Florilegium the hope of a coming great Figure not identified with their leader, the teacher of righteousness, nor called Messiah (except once in the quotation of Ps 2:2), but called the Scion of David, etc. (T. H. Gaster, *The Dead Sea Scriptures,* rev. ed., Doubleday, 1964, pp. 297, 329, 334–39). The extensive use of the term Messiah (Christ) as a title of the coming great Son of David is primarily a NT phenomenon. R.L.H.]

Not all who agree that the *māshîaḥ* is a reference to Christ in Dan 9:26, also interpret *māshîaḥ* in the same manner in Dan 9:25, where the description is of a prince. It should be stressed, however, that the OT did employ the term *māshîaḥ* to designate the coming Savior, Jesus.

The repeated claim that *māshîaḥ* in the OT never refers to an eschatological figure, the Messiah, hinges also for its validity on the interpretation of Dan 9:26. While some hold that the anointed one (*māshîaḥ*) "who is to be cut off" was Onias III (deposed as high priest 175 B.C.), there is strong warrant on the basis of the context (v. 24) to regard the *māshîaḥ* as none other than Jesus Christ.

mishḥâ. ***Anointing oil; anointment.*** (ASV and RSV similar.)

Found only in Ex, Lev, and Num, *mishḥâ* refers to the oil used in ritual anointing. The oil, prepared according to prescription (Ex 30:22ff.), was sprinkled (*nāzâ*) on officials and their garments (Ex 29:21) but poured, *yāṣaq,* on the head of the high priest (Ex 29:7; cf. Lev 8:10–12).

Described as holy, its application to tabernacle and its furnishings sanctified (*qiddēsh*) these. Priests who were anointed were restricted in activity (Lev 21:12; cf. Lev 10:7). The setting apart of men and things to God's service is better understood and appreciated through the tangible symbol in this instance, a fragrant oil.

moshḥâ. ***Portion.*** A part of some offerings (i.e. peace offering, Lev 7:28–35) was reserved as a consecrated portion (*moshḥâ*) to the priest. ASV, focusing on the priest renders *l*ᵉ*moshḥâ* "by reason of the anointing" (Num 18:8).

Bibliography: Ellison, H. L., *The Centrality of the Messianic Idea* for the OT, 1953. Harris, R. L. "Psalms" in *The Biblical Expositor* ed. C. F. H. Henry, Holman, 1973, pp. 435–452. J. Jocz, "Messiah" ZPEB IV pp. 198–207. Payne, J. B., *The Theology of The Older Testament,* Zondervan, 1962, pp. 257–84. Richardson, TWB, pp. 44–45. TDNT, IX, pp. 496–527.

V.P.H.

מִשְׁחָר (*mishḥār*). See no. 2369b.
מַשְׁחִית (*mashḥît*). See no. 2370a.
מַשְׁחֵת (*mashḥēt*), מִשְׁחַת (*mishḥat*). See nos. 2370b,c.
מִשְׁטוֹחַ (*mishṭôaḥ*). See no. 2372b.
מִשְׁטָח (*mishṭāḥ*). See no. 2372a.
מִשְׁטָר (*mishṭār*). See no. 2374b.

1256 מְשִׁי (*meshî*) ***a costly material for garment, perhaps silk*** (Ezk 16:13).

מָשִׁיחַ (*māshîaḥ*). See no. 1255c.

1257 מָשַׁךְ (*māshak*) ***draw, drag, seize.***

Derivatives

1257a †מֶשֶׁךְ (*meshek*) ***a drawing.***
1257b מֹשֶׁכֶת (*mōsheket*) ***cord.*** Occurs only in Job 38:31, *mōshkôt k*ᵉ*sîl* "the cords of Orion."

The verb appears thirty-six times in the OT with a variety of nuances attached to it.

All but six instances of the verb are in the Qal stem. Three times the Niphal is used (Isa 13:22; Ezk 12:25, 28) all with the meaning "prolonged." This is not, however, a distinctive use in the Niphal. Thus, Ps 85:5 [H 6], "Will you prolong your anger to all generations?" and Ps 36:10 [H 11], "Continue your loving kindness unto them that know you" (both in the Qal stem). Cf. Neh 9:30. Also, there are three uses of the Pual (Isa 18:2, 7, "scattered" (KJV) and parallel to *māraṭ,* in KJV "peeled," but better "tall and bronzed"); also, Prov 13:12, "Hope 'deferred' makes the heart sick."

The following meanings are attached to the verb *māshak* in the Qal: (1) To draw in the sense of "to raise" (Gen 37:28, "They drew, and lifted (*'ālâ*) up Joseph from the pit." Jeremiah 38:13, "So, they hauled up Jeremiah with ropes," again parallel to *'ālâ.* (2) To draw in the sense of "to extend," Ps 36:10 [H 11]; 85:5 [H 6] have already been noted. Cf. also Ps 109:12 and Jer 31:3, "For you have I prolonged kindness." (3) To draw in the sense of "to draw in, associate with"; Ps 28:3, "Do not rank me with the wicked"; Hos 7:5, "He stretched out his hand (*māshak yādô*) with scorners" possibly means, "He associated with scoffers." (See Gordon, UT 19: no. 1582 for the phrase *yd mṯkt.*) (4) To draw in the sense of "to entice, allure, woo"; Job 24:22, "He lures the mighty with his power"; perhaps also Job 21:33, "After him (the deceased) all men will follow," if the phrase means that the surviving will seek consciously to imitate the deceased's life style, rather than simply a reference to a funeral procession. Into this category we could also place Hos 11:4, "I drew them with cords of a man"; Jud 4:7, and at the level of human love, Song 1:4. (5) To draw in the sense of to draw on a weapon, a bow especially, I Kgs 22:34; II Chr 18:33; Isa 66:19; or blow extensively on a musical instrument, a trumpet: Ex 19:13; Josh 6:5. (6) To draw in the sense of "seize" or "drag away": Ps 10:9 (possibly); Job 41:1 [H 40:25]. Tur-Sinai in his commentary on Job, in a footnote on p. 335 says that "nowhere in the Bible does *māshak* ='draw' but always like Arabic *maska* "to take hold of, to snatch." The statement is highly debatable. (7) To draw, simply as a synonym for "go/march" Jud 4:6, or "take" (Ex 12:21). (8) Finally we may note the phrase in Eccl 2:3, "I sought in my heart 'to draw' (*limshôk*) my flesh with wine." The usual interpretation of this is seen in the rendering of this by the JB, "I resolved to have my body cheered with wine." Appeal, however, for this translation can only be made to a passage in the Babylonian Talmud, Hagigah 14a, *b'ly 'gdh mwškyn lbw šl 'dm kmym,* "masters of the Aggada (homiletic discourse) refresh the heart of men like water."

meshek. ***A drawing, bag, pouch, price.*** This segholate noun occurs only twice. (1) Job 28:18: "The 'price' (or 'acquisition' according to Tur-Sinai) of wisdom surpasses rubies." (2) Ps 126:6: "He that goeth forth and beareth 'precious' seed" (KJV). Though this is a time honored and traditional translation, a more preferable and exact one is, "though he went forth weeping, bearing/carrying a 'bag' of seed (*nōśē' meshek hazzāra'*)." This Hebrew phrase can be connected with Amos 9:13, "... the treader of grapes shall overtake the strewer of seed (*mōshēk hazzāra'*)." *meshek,* then, would be the seed container carried by the sower. In several related languages the word *mshk* means "skin, leather," perhaps the substance from which such a pouch would be made. Gordis (see Bibliography) translates the phrase in Ps 10:9 *bmshkw,* not "he catches the poor 'when he draws him' into his net" but, "he catches the poor in his bag (*b*ᵉ*mashkô*)" parallel to *reshet* "net, trap."

Bibliography: Gordis, R., "Psalm 9–10: A Textual and Exegetical Study," JQR 48: 104–22, esp. pp. 116–117. On *māshak* in Eccl 2:3, Corré, A. D., "A Reference to Epispasm in Koheleth," VT 4:416–18, vs. Driver, G. R., "Problems and Solutions," VT 4:225–45, esp. pp. 225–26. On *mešek,* Köhler, L., "Hebräische Vokabeln II," ZAW 55:161–74, esp. pp. 161–62.

V.P.H.

מִשְׁכָּב (*mishkāb*). See no. 2381c.
מְשַׁכֶּלֶת (*m*ᵉ*shakkelet*). See no. 2385e.
מִשְׁכָּן (*mishkān*). See no. 2387c.
מֹשֶׁכֶת (*mōsheket*). See no. 1257b.

1258 *מָשַׁל (*māshal*) ***I, represent, be like.***

Derivatives

1258a †מָשָׁל (*māshāl*) ***proverb.***
1258b †מָשַׁל (*māshal*) ***II, speak in a proverb.***
1258c †מֹשֶׁל (*mōshel*) ***I, like(ness).***
1258d †מְשֹׁל (*m*ᵉ*shōl*) ***byword.***

The verb occurs seven times, five times in the Niphal (Ps 28:1; 49:12, 20 [H 13, 21]; 143:7; Isa 14:10). Inevitably the meaning is "to become like, to be comparable to." The root appears once in the Hiphil (Isa 46:5 parallel to *dāmâ*) again with the meaning "to compare," and once in the Hithpael (Job 30:19) with similar force in the translation.

In all of the above passages the two objects compared assume a contrast that is in its nuance derogatory and belittling. Thus, "I have become like those who go down to the pit" (Ps 28:1). "To whom will you liken me and make me equal?" (Isa 46:5). "I have become like dust and ashes" (Job 30:19).

Exactly what the relationship, if any, of *māshal* "to be like" to *māshal* "to rule" is not clear. As for cognate evidence it is sufficient to note that the translation "to rule" is unique to Hebrew, but the translation "to be like" is common in most Semitic languages. It has been suggested that the Hebrew translation "to rule" evolved from the mentality involved in the idea of sympathetic magic; that is, that symbolic action (here, ruling action) resembles the effects it hopes to reproduce (Godbey). This association has generally been discredited.

māshāl. ***Proverb, parable, allegory, byword, taunt, discourse.*** Of great interest is the wide number of translations for this word in most English translations of the Old Testament. The substantive appears thirty-nine times (eight times in Ezk).

To translate *māshāl* simply as "proverb" misses the wide sweep of the word, suggested by the many suggested translations. We are accustomed to think of a proverb as a short, pithy, epigrammatic saying which assumes the status of gnomic truth. In the Old Testament, however, the word *māshāl* may be synonymous with an extended parable (and hence the frequent LXX translation *parabolē*) (Ezk 17:2 and vv. 2–24; 20:49 [H 21:5] and vv. 45–49 [H 21:1–5]; 24:3 and vv. 3–14). It may refer to an extended didactic discourse (Prov 1:8–19 for example). A person (Saul, I Sam 10:12; Job, Job 17:6) or a group of persons (Israel, Ps 44:14 [H 15], may function as a *māshāl.*

In this last connection notice the verse in I Sam 10:12, "So the saying, 'Is Saul also among the prophets?' became a proverb." What is involved here is the creation of a public example, in this case the example of one, a royal figure, whose public antics were questionable. The "proverb" would then be applicable to anyone charged with unorthodox behavior.

In a similar vein, note passages which translate *māshāl* as "byword": Ps 44:14 [H 15]; 69:11 [H 12]; Jer 24:9; Ezk 14:8; Deut 28:37; I Kgs 9:7; II Chr 7:20; Job 17:6. In each of these verses some kind of doom has, or will, come upon Israel or an individual. The result? God has made Israel a *māshāl* among the nations. Job has become a *māshāl* to his counselors and acquaintances. What can this mean? Much more is involved than simply scorn or derision. The point is that God has made Israel/Job a public example, an object lesson to their respective contemporaries. "Look, observe, and see your own life under my judgment," the Lord says.

Analogous to these are the three times prophets are told to lift a *māshāl,* Isaiah against the king of Babylon (Isa 14:4f.); Micah against his own people (Mic 2:4) and similarly Habakkuk (Hab 2:6). One might also add the passages in the Balaam narratives, "And Balaam took up his *māshāl* (KJV discourse)" (Num 23:7, 18; 24:3, 15, 20, 21, 23). In each of these instances there is an object lesson painted. The haughty are humbled. Those to be cursed are blessed and vice versa. The first are last.

A. S. Herbert has well stated that in the Old Testament the "proverb"/*māshāl* had "a clearly recognizable purpose: that of quickening an apprehension of the real as distinct from the wished for . . . of compelling the hearer or reader to form a judgment on himself, his situation or his conduct . . . This usage . . . comes to its finest expression in the Parables of Jesus" (Herbert, p. 196).

māshal II. To speak in a proverb, proverbialize. All of the examples of this verb are in the Qal stem (nine times) except for one use of the root in the Piel, Ezk 21:5, "Is he not a maker of parables?" (*m^e mashshēl m^e shālîm*). Or, in modern idiom, "He's always preaching."

mōshel. ***Like(ness).*** The noun occurs one time in the Old Testament, Job 41:33 [H 25], "Upon earth there is not his like (the crocodile)."

m^eshōl. ***Byword.*** This is used only once, Job 17:6 and, in form, is the infinitive construct of the verb *mshal* II.

Bibliography: Godbey, A. H., "The Hebrew *Māšāl,*" AJSL 34:89–108. Herbert, A. S., "The 'Parable' (MĀŠĀL) In the Old Testament," SJT 7:180–96. Johnson, A. R., "מָשָׁל" VTS 3:162–69. McKane, W., *Proverbs,* Westminster, 1970, pp. 22–33.

V.P.H.

1259 מָשַׁל (*māshal*) ***III, rule, have dominion, reign.***

Derivatives

1259a †מֹשֶׁל (*mōshel*) ***II, dominion.***
1259b מִמְשָׁל (*mimshāl*) ***dominion.***
1259c †מֶמְשָׁלָה (*memshālâ*) ***rule, realm, dominion.***

māshal occurs about eighty times in Qal, three times in Hiphil.

māshal usually receives the translation "to rule," but the precise nature of the rule is as various as the real situations in which the action or state so designated occur. It seems to be the situation in all languages and cultures that words for oversight, rule, government must be defined in relation to the situation out of which the function arises.

This will be illustrated by examining in order the first several appearances of *māshal* in the Bible. The sun and moon are said "to rule over the day and over the night" (Gen 1:18). They are merely the most prominent luminaries over day and night. Eve, standing for all wives, was given to understand that in the home the husband "shall rule over thee" (Gen 3:16). Such leadership as is appropriate—and it varies greatly—for a man to give his family is meant. Cain was told by God that he ought to master sin in his life, "Do thou rule over him" (Gen 4:7). Management over all the material goods of a master, as his steward, and management of all the personnel of the enterprise is indicated in the case of Abraham's "servant" (Eliezer of Damascus? Gen 15:2): "his eldest servant of his house, that ruled over all that he had" (Gen 24:2). Direction of affairs of a large family as "firstborn-designate" is indicated by Joseph's version of the sheaves—at least so his angry brothers interpreted the vision: "Shalt thou indeed reign over us" (Gen 37:8). *māshal* is used of Joseph's administration of Egypt as Pharaoh's prime minister. So Joseph claimed he had been made "a ruler throughout all the land of Egypt" (Gen 45:8); and his brothers agreed, "he is governor over all the land of Egypt" (Gen 45:26). The word occurs only once in Ex and there of the rule of law [very significant] over citizens of the Mosaic, Israelite civil commonwealth "to sell her he shall have no power" (Ex 21:8). The word is not in Lev or Num, but in Deut 15:6 Moses asserts that the nation Israel shall reign over other nations, under certain conditions—some sort of national subservience to a superior nation—and twice he uses *māshal,* once *Qal* perfect and once *Qal* imperfect. Context seems to mean that the rulership is in being the lending nation rather than the borrowing one.

Other instances, chosen somewhat at random, show that the supremacy of rich people over poor ones (Prov 22:7), of a fierce king over oppressed people (Isa 19:4), oppressive rule of one people over another (Jud 14:4; 15:11), leadership of a league or alliance of nations (I Kgs 4:4–21), the rule of God in providence (Ps 89:10 [H 9]), and even the power of self-control (Prov 16:32) are covered by the meaning of this word.

There is no specific theology to be drawn from the meaning of the word. Yet the passages cited and the seventy or so others not cited demonstrate the importance of the principle of authority, the absolute moral necessity of respect for proper authority, the value of it for orderly society and happy living and the origin of all authority in God, himself. Authority is of many degrees and kinds. It has various theoretical bases. It originates in God. Man has no authority at all as man but simply as God's viceregent.

mōshel. ***Dominion.*** Derived from *māshal,* like that word it is not always clear when sphere, geographical area of rule, is indicated and when the bare fact of authority, sovereignty. It appears only twice, viz., Zech 9:10, apparently in the sense of geographical area ("sea to sea . . . River to the ends of the earth") and Dan 11:4 apparently in the sense of sovereignty ("dominion wherewith he ruled"). Controversies about Messiah's predicted reign, whether referring to bare fact of rule (sovereignty) or geographical area (sphere) will not be settled by the bare meaning of this and cognate nouns and verbs.

memshālâ. ***Rule, realm, dominion.*** Though used of God's rule (sovereignty, Ps 145:13) and realm of rule (Ps 103:22), also of man's rule (might, II Chr 32:9; sovereignty, government, Isa

22:21; Mic 4:8), there is no case where it is outrightly used of Messiah's *memshālâ*. Four of the seventeen occurrences relate to the prevalence of the sun's light by day and of the moon's by night (Gen 1:16; Ps 136:8, 9). A theology of the kingdom of God," so earnestly sought from this word and others like it in form and meaning, apparently cannot be derived from this quarter.

Bibliography: THAT, I, pp. 930–32.

R.D.C.

מִשְׁלַח (*mishlaḥ*). See no. 2394d.
מִשְׁלוֹחַ (*mishlôaḥ*). See no. 2394e.
מִשְׁלַחַת (*mishlaḥat*). See no. 2394f.
מְשַׁמָּה (*m^eshammâ*). See no. 2409f.
מִשְׁמָן (*mishmān*), מַשְׁמָן (*mashmān*). See nos. 2410e,f.
מִשְׁמָע (*mishmāʿ*). See no. 2412f.
מִשְׁמַעַת (*mishmaʿat*). See no. 2412g.
מִשְׁמָר (*mishmār*). See no. 2414f.
מִשְׁמֶרֶת (*mishmeret*). See no. 2414g.
מִשְׁנֶה (*mishneh*). See no. 2421c.
מְשִׁסָּה (*m^eshissâ*). See no. 2426a.

1260 משע (*mshʿ*). **Assumed root of the following.**

1260a מִשְׁעִי (*mishʿî*) ***cleansing.*** Occurs only in Ezk 16:4, "you were not washed for cleansing."

מִשְׁעוֹל (*mishʿôl*). See no. 2432b.
מִשְׁעִי (*mishʿî*). See no. 1260a.
מִשְׁעָן (*mishʿān*), מַשְׁעֵן (*mashʿēn*). See nos. 2434a,b.
מִשְׁעֶנֶת (*mishʿenet*). See no. 2434d.
מִשְׁפָּחָה (*mishpāḥâ*). See no. 2442b.
מִשְׁפָּט (*mishpāṭ*). See no. 2443c.
מִשְׁפְּתַיִם (*mishp^etayim*). See no. 2441c.

1261 משק (*mshq*). **Assumed root of the following.**

1261a †מֶשֶׁק (*mesheq*) ***acquisition.***

1261b מִמְשָׁק (*mimshāq*) ***possession.*** Occurs only in Zeph 2:9, *mimshaq ḥārûl* "a place possessed by weeds."

mesheq. ***Acquisition, possession.*** (Both translations are conjectural.) The word appears only in the difficult verse 15:2, "and the 'heir' is Eliezer of Damascus" (KJV). The translation "heir" is based on the hypothesis that the phrase *ben-mesheq* is "the son of acquisition," i.e. heir together, with the reference in v. 3 to the "son of my house" (likely Eliezer) as his heir. Another possibility is to connect *mesheq* with the verb *shāqaq* "to rush," and translate "the attacker of my house" (Snijders). Still a third possibility is to relate *mesheq* to the verb *shāqâ* "to drink" and translate "the possessor of the goblet of my house" (Gordon).

Bibliography: Eissfeldt, "The Alphabetic Cuneiform Texts from Ras Shamra Published in 'Le Palais Royal D'Ugarit' Vol. II, 1957," JSS 5:1–49, esp. pp. 48–40. Gordon, C. H., "Damascus in Assyrian Sources," IEQ 2:174–75. Snijders, L. A., "Genesis xv—The Covenant with Abraham," OTS 12:261–79.

מַשָּׁק (*mashshāq*). See no. 2460a.
מַשְׁקֶה (*mashqeh*). See no. 2452c.
מִשְׁקוֹל (*mishqôl*). See no. 2454b.
מַשְׁקוֹף (*mashqôp*). See no. 2458c.
מִשְׁקָל (*mishqāl*). See no. 2454c.
מִשְׁקֶלֶת (*mishqelet*). See no. 2454d.
מִשְׁקָע (*mishqāʿ*). See no. 2456a.
מִשְׁרָה (*mishrâ*). See no. 2464a.

1262 מָשַׁשׁ (*māshash*) ***feel.***

The verb is used twelve times in the OT, three times in the Qal (Gen 27:12, 21, 22), Isaac's "feeling" of Jacob for purposes of identification. In the Piel it appears six times with either the meaning "to grope" (Deut 28:29 [2 times]; Job 5:14; 12:25) or "to search" (Gen 31:34, 37). Three times the verb is used in the Hiphil with the basic meaning of "to feel" (Ex 10:21; Jud 16:26).

Bibliography: Rüger, H. P., "Zum Text von Sir 40, 10 und Ex 10, 21," ZAW 82:102–9.

מִשְׁתֶּה (*mishteh*). See no. 2477c.

1263 מַת (*mat*) ***man.***

One of the five words in Biblical Hebrew for "man," the other four being *'ādām, 'îsh, 'ĕnôsh,* and *geber*. There seems to be no particular nuance attached to this word as there is to some of its synonyms, for example, *'ādām* "earthling"; *geber* "hero." Isaiah 3:25 uses *mat* parallel with *geber*. Deuteronomy 2:34 and 3:6 distinguish *mat* from the *nāshîm* "women" and *tap* "children" all of whom were placed under the ban by the Israelites in the latter's conquest of Sihon's and Og's kingdoms.

The substantive appears twenty-three times in the OT, most often in Deut and Job (six times each). The root is known both from Ugaritic and Phoenician where the root *mt* means "lord, master." The translation "lord, master" is not found in Biblical Hebrew, but may possibly be documented in non-Biblical Hebrew (Yadin). Of the twenty-three occurrences of the root in the Bible it is not impossible that some of them may be, in fact, derived from the verb *mût* "to die." So Pope (*Job* in AB) reads Job 24:12 "from the city the dying groan" instead of the traditional "from out of the city men groan." The emendation is from *m^e tîm* to *mētîm*. The second half of the verse would seem to support this, "the gasp of wounded cry out."

In the Bible the most interesting uses of *mat* are those in which it is fossilized in expressions like *m^e tê mispār* "few" and in personal names such as "Methushael" (Gen 4:18) and "Methuselah" (Gen 5:21–22, 25–27).

The use of *m^e tê mispār* "few," is the most prevalent use of *mat*. It describes the minimal fighting force available to Jacob (Gen 34:30) and to Reuben his firstborn (Deut 33:6). The phrase may also refer to the sparse number of Hebrews in Egypt before the Exodus (Deut 26:5; Ps 105:12=I Chr 16:19). Or, it describes a remnant of Jews that escape catastrophe (Deut 4:27; 28:62; Jer 44:28). How the phrase *m^e tê mispār* comes to mean "few" is obvious. It means literally, "men of number," i.e. numerable, as opposed to innumerable, and therefore "few."

The translation of the name of the Bible's elder statesman, Methuselah, seems straightforward, "man of the spear/weapon" composed of the two Hebrew words, *mat* "man" and *shelaḥ*, "weapon" (and comparing the second element with the Hebrew name Shelah in Gen 19:24; 11:14; I Chr 1:18). It has been suggested (Tsevat) that *shelaḥ* has nothing to do with "spear" or any other weapon but that this represents a divine name *shalaḥ*, the god of the infernal river of the Canaanite population of Palestine and Phoenicia. Thus Methuselah means "man of Shalaḥ." Nothing, however, militates against the traditional translation.

Finally, we may note that the Hebrew *mat* describes disreputable or disadvantaged men. Thus, Isa 41:14 says, "Fear not you worm Jacob and you men of Israel." The latter part of this verse is rendered by JB, "Israel, puny mite." In Ps 26:4 the Psalmist expresses his dissociation from *m^e tê-shāw^e'* "vain persons" KJV, (also Job 11:11). Similarly, Job 22:15 refers to *m^e tê-'āwen* "wicked men." On the other hand, Job 19:19 refers to "the men of my secret" who have forsaken Job. The phrase "men of my secret" means something like "bosom friends." Job (31:31) refers to the "men of my tent" whom he had befriended.

Bibliography: Gordon, C. H., "The Authenticity of the Phoenician Text from Parahyba," *Orientalia* 37:75–80, esp. p. 76. *idem.*, UT 19: no. 1569. Tsevat, M., "The Canaanite God Šālaḥ," VT 4:41–49. Yadin, Y., "A Hebrew Seal from Tell Jemneh," *Eretz-Israel* 6:53–55.

V.P.H.

מַתְבֵּן (*matbēn*). See no. 2493a.

1264 מתג (*mtg*). **Assumed root of the following.**
1264a מֶתֶג (*meteg*) ***bridle.***

מָתוֹק (*mātôq*). See no. 1268c.

1265 מָתַח (*mātaḥ*) ***spread out.*** Occurs only in Isa 40:22, *wayyimtāḥēm* "and he spread them out."

Derivative

1265a אַמְתַּחַת (*'amtaḥat*) ***sack*** (Gen 42–44).

1266 מָתַי (*mātay*) ***when.***

This interrogative particle appears forty-three times in the OT, most frequently in Ps (thirteen times) and Jer (seven times). Twenty-one times it follows the preposition *'ad* to form the expression *'ad mātay* "until when" or "how long?" Such a construction is similar to the Hebrew *'ad 'ān(â)* also meaning "how long?" In a few instances *mātay* appears in a simple question asking for an answer with information: Ex 8:5; Neh 2:6; Dan 8:13; 12:6. Preponderantly, however, the word (or phrase) is used in a rhetorical question urging appropriate action by the addressee: (1) by God himself, I Sam 16:1; Ps 82:2; (2) by man addressed to God, Ps 6:3 [H 4]; 42:2 [H 3]; 74:10; 82:2; 90:13; 94:3; 101:2; 119:82, 84; (3) by man to his fellow man, Gen 30:30; I Kgs 18:21, inter alia. Comparable in the NT is the phrase *heōs pote* (Mt 17:17; Jn 10:24; Rev 6:10).

Bibliography: Jenni, E., "mātay" in THAT, I, 933–36.

מַתְכֹּנֶת (*matkōnet*). See no. 2511c.
מְתַלְּעוֹת (*m^e tall^e'ôt*). See no. 2516d.
מְתֹם (*m^e tōm*). See no. 2522e.

1267 מתן (*mtn*). **Assumed root of the following.**
1267a †מָתְנַיִם (*motnayim*) ***loins, hips.***

The word appears forty-seven times in the Bible with perhaps one instance of its use in question (see the discussion below on Prov 30:31). Dahood (in AB, *Psalms* I, p. 267) changes the word division (and the vocalization) of the phrase in Ps 44:19 [H 20]), *bim^e qôm tannîm* "in the place of the monsters/dragons" to *b^e môq motnayim*, and translates the verse, "tho' you crushed us with festering of the loins and covered us with total darkness." Like other words in Hebrew for parts of the body *motnayim* is dual in form. Compare similarly, *'oznayim* "ears," *yādayim* "hands," *raglayim* "feet," *ḥălāṣayim* "loins" (parallel to *motnayim* in Isa 11:5).

Generally speaking, we may say that *motnayim*, used in a purely physical or anatomical sense, refers to the hips or lower part of the back, i.e. the middle of the body. Some (see Held in Bibliography) have objected to the translation "loins." Held argues for something like "tendons" or "sinews" and says that Hebrew *motnayim* "refers to the strong musculature linking the upper part of the body with the lower part and not 'Loins' as such." For support of this note that in Job 40:16 *b^emotnāw* "in his loins" is parallel to *bishrîrê biṭnô* "in the muscles of his stomach" (not "in the navel of his belly" as in KJV). We also know that Akkadian *matnu* means "bowstring" and in Ugaritic *mtn* was used in making composite bows, and thus a very strong material. So then, the Ugaritic phrase *mtnm b'qbt ṯr* means "tendons of the hoofs of a bull."

In a very few, if any, places is *motnayim* a symbol of the generative organs of mankind, and hence a description of one's descendants. (But possibly so in Job 40:16.) Thus, in the phrase in Gen 35:11, "And kings shall come out of thy loins" the word used is *ḥālāṣ* (also I Kgs 8:10; II Chr 6:9). Another word used to refer to the "loins" as a seat of procreative power is *yārēk*, "Which came out of the loins (*yārēk*) of Jacob" (Gen 46:26; also Ex 1:5; Jud 8:30). But to repeat, *motnayim* is not employed in such a context.

Primarily *motnayim* is used simply to indicate the middle of the body. Ezkiel (47:4) saw the stream flowing from the temple rise, first of all, as high as his knees, then as high as *motnayim* "his waist." (Cf. also Ezk 1:27; 8:2.) Here is where a belt/linen cloth was fastened: I Kgs 2:5 (Joab and David); II Kgs 1:8 (Elijah); Isa 11:5 (used figuratively and messianically); Jer 13:1, 11—Jeremiah is told (in a symbolic vision) to take the linen loincloth he is wearing around his waist and bury it in the hole of a rock by the Euphrates. The intent of this is to show that Israel, whom the Lord had fastened as close to himself as a belt, had now broken away from her Lord and would decay. From this part of the body a soldier's sword was hung: II Sam 20:8; Neh 4:18 [H 12]. When the Lord says (Isa 45:1) that before Cyrus he will subdue nations "and strip the loins of kings" the latter phrase probably means to render the kings powerless by taking away their weapons from their belt. Here is where a scribe hung his ink horn (Ezk 9:2–3, 11; "side" in KJV).

Several times people are told to "gird up their loins" that is, tie up the long lower garments around the middle of the body in preparation for running (I Kgs 18:46 with the verb *shānas*); or quick traveling (Ex 12:11; II Kgs 9:1; 4:29 with the verb *ḥāgar*); and in a figurative sense (Jer 1:17 with the verb *'āzar*. Here "to gird up your loins" means "brace yourself for action." Compare in the New Testament the identical phrase in Lk 12:35; Eph 6:14; I Peter 1:13 (*osphys*).

The loins are the seat of strength (Job 40:16; Nah 2:1 [H 2]), especially of male as connected with virility, but also of the female (Prov 31:17). To damage the loins is to weaken or render helpless (Deut 33:11; Ps 69:23 [H 24]).

Proverbs 30:30–31 mentions in order (according to KJV) the lion, greyhound, he-goat, a king. The second one, greyhound, in Hebrew is *zarzîr motnayim*, literally "girt at the loins." Most modern commentators prefer the identification "cock."

Bibliography: Held, M., "Studies in Comparative Semitic Lexicography," in *Studies in Honor of Benno Landsberger On His Seventy-fifth Birthday*, University of Chicago, 1965, pp. 395–06, esp. p. 405. On Prov 30:31, Bewer, J. A., "Two Suggestions on Prov. 30:31 and Zech. 9:16," JBL 67:61–62. McKane, W., Proverbs, Westminster, 1970, pp. 260, 663–64.

V.P.H.

מַתָּן (*mattān*). See no. 1443b.

מָתְנַיִם (*motnayim*). See no. 1267a.

1268 מָתֹק (*mātōq*) ***be sweet.***

Derivatives

1268a מֶתֶק (*meteq*) ***sweetness*** (Prov 16:21; 27:9).

1268b מֹתֶק (*mōteq*) ***sweetness*** (Jud 9:11).

1268c מָתוֹק (*mātôq*) ***sweet, sweetness.***

1268d מַמְתַקִּים (*mamtaqqîm*) ***sweetness*** (Neh 8:10; Song 5:16).

A stative verb (on the pattern of *qāṭōn* "be small") appearing eight times in the OT, all in the Qal stem except for Job 20:12, "If evil gives a sweet taste in his mouth" and Ps 55:14 [H 15], "We used to take sweet counsel together." Both are Hiphil.

The precise definition of this root is seen in its frequent juxtaposition, for purposes of contrast, to one of the Hebrew words for honey or honeycomb, something quite palatable. Thus Ps 19:19 [H 11] asserts God's judgments are "sweeter than honey (*d^ebash*) and the honey that drips from the comb (*nōpet ṣûpîm*)." A similar idea is expressed in Ps 119:103, although the word there for "sweet" is the verb *mālaṣ* "be smooth, agreeable." In response to Samson's riddle the people say, "What is sweeter than honey?" Ezekiel (3:3) says God's word was to him "as honey for sweetness" (cf. Rev 10:10). Kindred ideas are found in Prov 16:24; 24:13.

It should be recalled that honey (*d^ebash*) in the OT not only refers to bee's honey but also to date syrup. There are at least two references, however, to bee's honey: (1) Samson in Jud 14:8ff.; (2) Jonathan in I Sam 14:24–30. Along with leaven it was banned in the burnt offering (Lev 2:11). Naturally, its quality of sweetness caused it to be used figuratively for gracious and pleasant things including God's Word (Ps 19:10 [H 11]), the wisdom of the Torah (Prov 24:13), and the speech of a friend (Prov 16:24).

Waters also might be sweet (Ex 15:25; Prov 9:17); the lack of insomnia (Eccl 5:12 [H 11]); the fruit of an apple tree (Song 2:3); the light of day (Eccl 7:11).

V.P.H.

מַתַּת (*mattat*). See no. 1443d.